Rod Machado's Private Pilot Handbook

Written and illustrated by
Rod Machado

Published by The Aviation Speakers Bureau

© Mark Rasmussen - Fotolia

Copyright Information

Third Edition
Reprinted February 2021

Please visit (and *bookmark*) our
web site for any additional book updates:
www.rodmachado.com

Published by: The Aviation Speakers Bureau,
P.O. Box 6030, San Clemente, CA 92674-6030

Nothing in this text supersedes any operational documents or procedures issued by the Federal Aviation Administration (FAA), the aircraft and avionics manufacturers, any aircraft's Pilot Operating Handbook (POH), flight schools or the operators of the aircraft. The opinions in this book are solely those of the author and not the publisher.

The author has made every effort in the preparation of this book to ensure the accuracy of the information. However, the information is sold without warranty either expressed or implied. Neither the author nor the publisher will be liable for any damages caused or alleged to be caused directly, indirectly, incidentally or consequentially by the information in this book.

Don't even think about using any performance chart in this book for performance computations in your airplane. Go get a performance chart appropriate for your airplane and use it. Also, don't even think about using this book for navigation. In other words, there are aeronautical chart excerpts in this book, but none of them should in any way be used in lieu of current charts for any type of information. All of the charts, graphs and tables in this book are for training purposes only.

Cover layout by Diane Titterington
Front cover artwork by Sam Lyons
All material created, written and produced by Rod Machado
All illustrations in this book designed and drawn by Rod Machado (QuarkXPress, Corel, Photoshop)
Photographs (unless marked otherwise or in the public domain) by Rod Machado

Table of Contents

Acknowledgments

The author wishes to acknowledge the help and or support of the following individuals, companies or groups:

Brian Weiss of WORD'SWORTH, Santa Monica, CA.

Diane Titterington of The Aviation Speakers Bureau, San Clemente, CA.

Diamond Aircraft Corporation. Diamond was instrumental in helping with graphs, charts, pictures and much, much, more. Thanks for all the help!

The New Piper Aircraft Corporation. Charts and graphs provided by Piper are to be used for information purposes only. The Pilot's Operating Handbook is the only true source of information.

The Cessna Aircraft Corporation. Cessna authorized the use of their materials with the understanding that they are to be used for training purposes only, not the actual operation of an aircraft.

Air Time Aviation of Palomar airport, CA.

Robert Crystal of Simulator & Instrument Training Center in Van Nuys, CA.

Bill Johnson of Instrument Service Inc. of Van Nuys, CA.

John & Joanne Italiano of Windsock pilot supplies in Newport Beach, CA.

Jeannie and Fernando Molina at the Pilot Supply Shop at Long Beach Airport

Danny Mortensen, President of Airline Ground Schools

Skip Forster, President of Results Pilot Training, San Jose, CA.

Captain James P. Johnson of James Johnson Associates

Christopher W. Tompkins

John A. Ryan

Grahame K. Gates

Douglas L. Mather

Dave Gwinn

Al Chelini

Sarah Cochrane

Douglas Fairbairn

Ken Dravis

Captain Ralph Butcher

Tim Peterson

Captain John Dill

Captain Al Englehardt

Captain Ed Shaffer

Gwen Ledbetter

Ed Helmick

Don Eick

Sherry Knight

Ron Marks

Chad Gregory Holcomb

C.J. Logue

Jackie Spanitz

Aviation Supplies and Academics (ASA)

Pat O'Brien of Mag Time, John Wayne Airport, CA

Iceman Aviation Supplies, Ontario, Canada

Simon Wheaton Smith

All the folks at ASRS, Moffett Field, CA

Paul & Linda Neumann

Phil Hewitt

Paul Stebelton

Dave Franson

Kim Wheeler

Barry Wallis

Gene Croxton

Rich and Ron Lovick

Fred L Gibbs

Joe Castrey of Southern Aviation Maintenance

Flight Training Magazine

Fotolia Photo source

Clipart from the following companies:
3G Graphics, Archive Arts, BBL Typographic, Cartesia Software, Image Club Graphics Inc., Management Graphics Ltd., One Mile Up Inc., Studio Piazza Xilo Inc., Techpool Studios Inc., Totem Graphics Inc., TNT Designs, SmartPics.

The instructor at American Flyers responsible for the "F111, C152, 1 Coke memory aid" (your name here when identified).

Foreword

There are many exhilarating activities you can try, but few offer challenges and rewards comparable to learning to fly. It is an activity that requires the unique combination of physical skills needed to fly the airplane while engaged in the mental activities of analysis and problem solving. Learning to fly gives you the satisfaction of seeing yourself make great strides in learning, and at the same time it challenges you to learn more. You acquire the ability needed to take the airplane up solo rather quickly, but you will spend the rest of your flying career improving your skills and judgment.

There are a variety of courses, video programs and books available to help you acquire the knowledge and attitudes needed to become a pilot. Which resources you use will depend on your individual preferences, but *Rod Machado's Private Pilot Handbook* should certainly be one of the learning tools you use. Educators know that people learn more readily if written material is supported with pictures; if examples are used to support ideas; if analogies are used to tie the unknown to the known and if ideas are linked together in a memorable manner. Rod does an amazing job of building this book around these concepts. In addition, he focuses on just the information that is of great practical importance to pilots, which helps keep the task of learning the material reasonable. He also does a magnificent job of using humor to get you through the tough material and keep you alert regardless of the topic. Books only provide value if people will read them, and Rod makes it very easy to get value from this book.

Dr. Gerry Fairbairn

Rod Machado's Private Pilot Handbook is an essential resource for anyone who is learning to fly. The material can be easily understood by those with no previous aviation experience. For those who already have their certificates, it is an excellent way to update your knowledge, get a refresher on material you once knew, and learn material you were never able to understand because it was too boring or presented in a manner that was incomprehensible. The book is also an excellent resource for flight instructors who want to expand their "toolkit" of explanations, examples, and visual aids to help their students gain insights into the wonderful world of flight.

Dr. Gerry Fairbairn is a professor of aviation at Daniel Webster College and lives in New Boston, New Hampshire. He has been a flight instructor since 1965 and is an aviation lecturer for the AOPA Air Safety Foundation.

DEDICATION

This book is dedicated to three very important people whose contributions had a considerable influence on my aviation career.

Amelia Reid gave me my first job in aviation as a teenager. I fueled and taxied airplanes at Amelia Reid Aviation at Reid-Hillview airport in Northern California. I was in heaven and will always be grateful for that opportunity.

Jan Sakert is perhaps the most charismatic, clever and humorous speaker I've ever heard. He gave me the opportunity to teach aviation ground school and learn the business of speaking and teaching. He was always wise, infinitely supportive and a very patient man. His podium demeanor still influences my behavior to this day.

Mr. Paul Stebelton is one of the most understanding, friendly and sincere men I've ever met. As an Accident Prevention Specialist in the Long Beach FSDO, he allowed me to do aviation safety programs to my heart's content. There were times when my antics got Paul in hot water with the higher-ups, but his support never wavered. He was one of the few educators I've met who realized the value of humor in education.

About the Author

Rod Machado traded his motorcycle for flying lessons at the age of 16. His parents were delighted he gave up riding with the vegetarian motorcycle gang known as the *Sprouts*. Captured by the romance and adventure of flight in a Taylorcraft L-2 at Amelia Reid Aviation in San Jose, California, Rod has remained hooked ever since. In fact, he is one of the few airline-transport-rated pilots who still gets excited by a Cessna 150 fly-by.

Rod is a professional speaker who travels across the United States and Europe delighting his listeners with upbeat and lively presentations. Machado truly loves mixing it up with the audience. His unusual talent for simplifying the difficult and adding humor to make the lessons stick has made him a popular lecturer both in and out of aviation. Rod speaks on both aviation and non-aviation topics, including risk assessment, IFR charts, aviation weather, in-flight emergencies, and safety awareness. He is also known for his rapid fire, humorous banquet presentations.

Rod Machado

A pilot since 1970 and an active flight instructor since 1973, Rod is also a National Aviation Safety Counselor. He has over 10,000 hours of flight experience earned the hard way—one CFI hour at a time. Since 1978, Rod has taught hundreds and hundreds of flight instructor revalidation clinics and safety seminars across the United States and Europe. He was named the 1991 Western Region Flight Instructor of the Year. You might have read his monthly column, "License to Learn," in *AOPA Pilot* magazine as well as his monthly columns in *Flight Training Magazine*.

Rod's eclectic interests are reflected by his equally varied academic credentials. He holds degrees in aviation science and psychology.

Rod believes you must take time to exercise or you'll have to take time to be sick. Holding black belts in the Korean disciplines of Tae Kwon Do and Hapkido and ranking in Gracie Jujitsu, he gets his exercise from practicing and teaching martial arts. He also runs 20 miles a week and claims it's uphill both ways.

Visit Rod's web site at www.rodmachado.com.

Flying & Flapjacks

The Book Cover

Sam Lyons

About the Artist

Since childhood, Sam's love of aviation has led him down the road to his present career as a world renowned aviation artist. Sam has flown aircraft from J-3 Cubs to F-15, 16 and 18's, which gives him a unique perspective for painting award winning aviation paintings from the classics to modern jets.

For more information on

Aviation Art by Sam Lyons

contact:

(863) 644-5010

or

https://lyonsstudio.com/

"This book is an aviation bible. Obey these commandments and your rewards are endless."

Cliff Robertson

Introduction

Basic aviation knowledge is to the pilot what the fish is to the angler—an indispensable part of the union. One cannot exist without the other. Yet, learning the basics of aviation is sometimes considered the least enjoyable part of the process. In some small way I hope this book changes that perception.

I wrote this book to make the process of basic aviation education a pleasant one. A little humor was an important ingredient, along with a reasonable amount of simplification. I've always believed that new ideas are easier to learn if you can compare them to things you already know. Throughout this book I try to make these connections. That's why I speak of aerodynamics in terms of how automobiles climb hills.

You do not need to be a physicist, aerodynamicist, scientist or engineer to become a pilot. In fact, the only math you'll need in this book is grocery-store math. That's basic *adds*, *takeaways*, *times* and *goes-intos*. If you need a cash chaperone at a grocery store, or think that doing addition in an airplane at 10,000 feet is higher math, then you might want to consider taking up sailing instead of flying. This is the extent of the technical knowledge required for the book. The rest of the information can be understood using your common, everyday experience. (Believe me when I say that you know a lot more about the science of flying than you think you do. Honest!)

You've probably noticed this book contains quite a few pictures to supplement the text. These are not just for the learning impaired. In some cases the pictures and their accompanying text offer a slightly different subject explanation than that contained in the body text. This isn't unintentional redundancy—it's quite intentional. It's often nice to see something presented in more than one way. Pictures also allow you to review major concepts without having to reread entire sections of material. Most important, it's my book and I like pictures.

Rod Machado

When asked, "How do you eat an elephant?" I hope you say, "Give me another menu" instead of, "one bite at a time." That's why I've included something known as *Postflight Briefings* at the end of most chapters. These are alternate menus. Some topics can be frustrating if consumed as a whole. It simply makes good sense to put them at the end of the chapter where they can be absorbed at your convenience once the necessary groundwork of knowledge has been laid.

If you're like me (and I know I am), you enjoy hearing about the experiences of others. Therefore, I've included excerpts from the Aviation Safety Reporting System (ASRS) files. These are reports sent to NASA by pilots describing their experiences, ideas and *faux pas*. They're the closest thing you get to real experience without being there.

Airplanes. Airplanes. Airplanes. Few words in the English language seem to embody as much adventure, reward and pleasure. That's what flying is all about, isn't it? I hope your experience learning to fly is filled with wonder and excitement. I hope this book makes the process of flight training more enjoyable for you.

Rod Machado

Updating Your Book

Because the world of aviation changes quickly, you should make it a regular practice to update your book by visiting my web site located at:

http://www.rodmachado.com

Visit the book/slide update page for any changes that may affect this text or changes in the FAA knowledge exam.

Author's Note

Any errors found in this book are solely the responsibility of the author, Rod Machado.

Chapter One

Airplane Components:

Getting to Know Your Airplane

Let me take you on a short tour of a few typical general aviation airplanes. (*General aviation* is the term often used for "private" flying.) I want you to become familiar with the basic parts of these airplanes, and the common terminology you're likely to encounter at the airport and in the cockpit.

Before starting the tour, let me say that while almost everything I'll point out can be found on almost every airplane you're likely to fly, there are always exceptions. Be flexible (the wings are).

Airplanes are like people (sort of). They come in all sizes, shapes, and colors. But looks really can be deceiving. Airplanes are more similar than they are different (Figure 1). We'll examine several varieties in this chapter.

Think of an airplane as a cigar with two Hershey bars on the sides, a propeller beanie cap on the front, and a tail at the back and you'll have the general picture. The rest of this is just details.

In the Beginning

Let's begin at the beginning, with the *propeller*. Most general aviation airplanes have propellers of some shape or form (Figure 2). When spun by the engine, the propeller produces thrust, which propels (as in propeller) the airplane forward. Atop the prop sits the spinner, a generally cone-shaped piece of metal which deflects air slightly, encouraging it to enter the engine cowling where it helps cool the engine. Engines are by nature hotheads, and most airplane

AIRPLANES ARE MORE ALIKE THAN DIFFERENT.

AIRPLANE PROPELLERS

Airplanes have propellers of some shape or form, and some, such as the Adam A500 on the right, have a pusher and a puller propeller configuration.

engines typically depend on air (rather than water, as in your car) to keep their cool. Some airplanes do use water for engine cooling. The Katana is a good example (Figure 3).

Look down at the feet. Not yours, the airplane's. If it's like most modern general aviation airplanes, your aircraft has three rubber feet attached to sort of spindly legs. This is referred to as a *tricycle gear,* and has nothing to do with your need for trainer wheels. The front foot is the *nose gear.* Figure 4 shows a typical nose gear and nose gear strut assembly. The long, leggy thing above the nose gear rubber tire is the *strut* (or oleo), a piston within a cylinder. It acts to absorb the abrupt bounces you encounter while shuttling to and from the runway, as well as the shock of being dropped to the ground after landing.

The nose strut's major function is to help steer the airplane on the ground, which you accomplish by applying pressure on the bottom part of a *rudder pedal* inside the cockpit (the top part of the rudder pedal is generally the brake). That's right, you steer an airplane that's on the ground with your feet. We instructors get a nostalgic kick out of watching first time students taxi an airplane (maneuver it on the ground). Who doesn't remember frantically whipping the control wheel back and forth in utter amazement as nothing happens? During my first taxi attempt I remember looking at my instructor like I looked at the DMV lady when she asked if I wanted to donate any of my organs (not realizing she meant *after the accident*). This demonstration, more than anything else, disabuses the pilot novitiate of the idea that learning to fly is just like learning to drive a car (it isn't).

Please note that you do not (intentionally, at least) ever land on the nose gear. When your instructor asks how many landing gear an airplane has, he or she doesn't mean to imply that you land on all three at the same time. You land on the two main gear, then (gently, we hope) lower the nose gear.

ENGINE COOLING SYSTEMS

Unlike most airplanes, the Katana has a water cooled rather than an air cooled engine.

THE AIRPLANE'S NOSE STRUT ASSEMBLY

The nose gear and nose strut assembly allows it to turn as well as acting like a shock absorber. Pushing the right or left rudder pedal turns the nose wheel via a mechanical linkage.

AN AIRPLANE WITH A CASTERING NOSE WHEEL

Some airplanes have a castering type nose wheel. Applying brakes on either the right or left main gear allows the airplane to turn.

A RETRACTABLE GEAR AIRPLANE

Retractable gear mean less drag (when retracted) and allows the airplane to attain higher speeds for a given amount of power.

Though it may do a good turn for you on the ground, once airborne the airplane's nose gear extends fully and locks in a centered position, something like an army private standing at attention during inspection. Step on the rudder pedal in flight (top or bottom) and you will move the rudder, at the rear of the plane. The nose gear knows it's not needed now. The strut compresses on landing, and the nose gear is once again free to turn, turn, turn.

Some airplanes don't have a rudder-controlled nose gear assembly (see, I told you there were exceptions). Instead, they have a castering (swiveling type) nose gear as shown in Figure 5. Applying either the right or left main gear brake (gently, please) sets the plane to pivoting about one of its main wheels, turning it the way Nureyev would turn a ballerina. Once airborne, aerodynamic pressure centers the castering nose gear.

The other two feet on an airplane are the *main gear*. These are either fixed ("down and welded" in pilotspeak), or retractable. A fixed gear causes drag in flight, which slows an airplane, but it's simple, reliable, inexpensive to maintain, and is always there when you need it. A retractable gear plane (Figure 6) is more efficient because the gear is tucked up, reducing drag and allowing it to fly faster for a given amount of power. The pilot, however, is responsible for remembering to put the gear back down again before landing. Forget to put it down and the gear will *not* be there when you need it. This is very hard on the underside of the airplane, the runway, the passengers, and your pocketbook. Retractable gear also need more maintenance. This can be expensive over the long haul.

Wing a Ding

While you're crawling around down there, look up. The large things casting a big shadow are the *wings*. These are generally considered important because they make the airplane fly. We'll talk a lot more about wings in the next chapter; for now, it's enough to know that there should be two of them (one on each side of the plane, preferably).

Under each wing on most airplanes is a *fuel tank sump drain* (Figure 7). Water and gunk of various sorts can invade the fuel system, and it must be drained before flight. (Water and gunk are put in the fuel by fuel fairies, trolls, and other things mere mortals can't see.) Using a fuel strainer (Figure 8), you drain a little fuel from each sump or drain site and examine what comes out for the presence of anything that shouldn't be there.

THE UNDER-WING FUEL TANK SUMP DRAIN

Under the wing is a fuel tank sump drain. Since airplane engines don't seem to run very well on impurities, the sumps should be drained before every flight and after every fueling.

FUEL CONTAMINATED WITH WATER

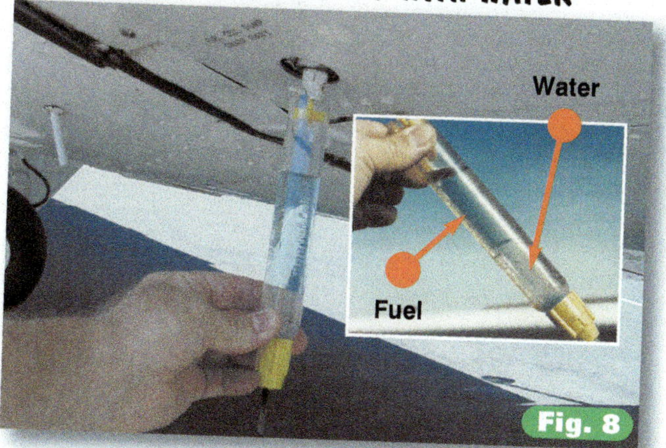

Clear plastic fuel strainers are common equipment in a pilot's flight bag. These allow you to sample the fuel and look for contaminants.

Under the left wing of most airplanes, where it can poke a tall pilot in the nose, is the *pitot tube* (Figure 9). That's *pee-toe,* not *pilot.* Now you know one word of French, and speak it like a native. The pitot tube takes in moving air, which is mechanically converted into an airspeed reading and displayed on a dial in the cockpit. I'll tell you how that happens later. Pitot tubes are usually encased in electric heating elements, which help prevent ice formation. As you will see, the opening on a pitot tube isn't very large; even a little bit of ice or a kamikaze fly would shut down operations, and without the pitot source, you wouldn't have an airspeed indication on your airspeed indicator. Pitot heat is turned on and off via a switch (one of many) in the cockpit.

Not satisfied just to sample moving air, we also have a *static source* (Figure 10). This is not where you get static electricity when you want to make your instructor's hair stand on end (you'll learn lots of other ways to do that). The static source provides information about the outside air pressure. This information is used by several instruments, including the altimeter, vertical speed indicator and the airspeed indicator (which computes airspeed by mechanically subtracting static pressure from pitot pressure). Sometimes the static source is a dual port configuration that's located directly behind and below the opening on a different variety of pitot tube (Figure 11). No matter where they are, the openings for the pitot and static sources must be free of any foreign matter (bugs, dirt, bubble gum, etc.).

THE PITOT TUBE

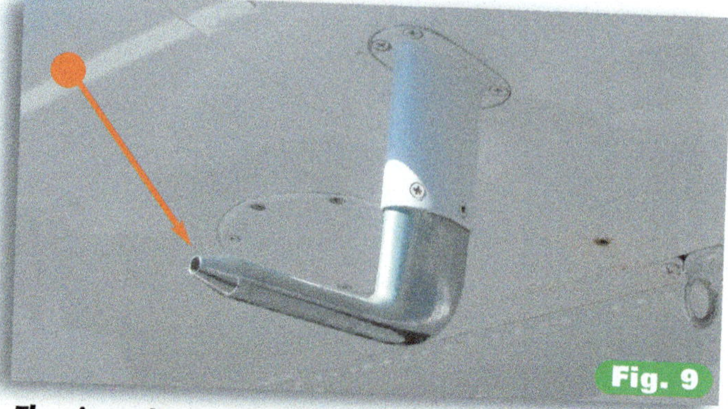

The pitot tube (usually located under the wing) collects moving air and ports it to the airspeed indicator where it's mechanically converted into an airspeed reading.

THE STATIC SOURCE

The airplane's static source is the mouth through which several of the flight instruments breathe. Non moving air pressure is sampled through this source (that's why this source is often flush with the flow of air).

THE COMBINED PITOT/STATIC MAST

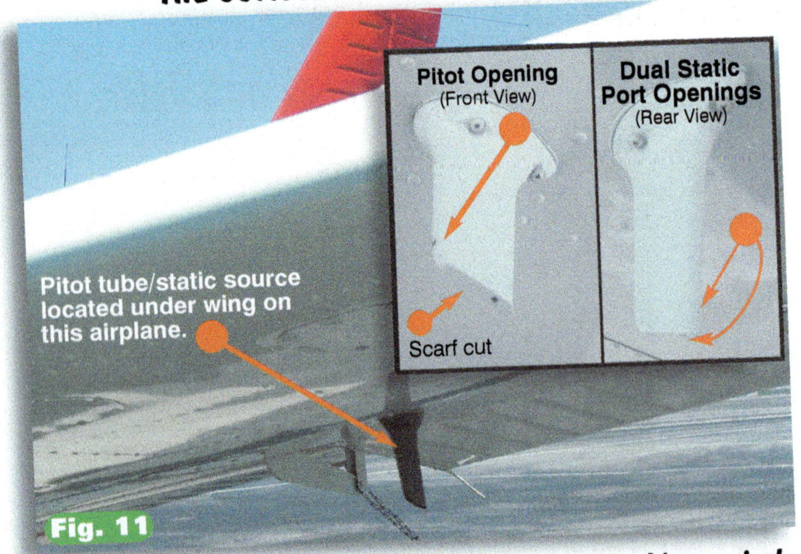

Sometimes the pitot tube and static source are combined into a single unit. The static source is a combination of two small holes, one on the bottom (the scarf cut) and one at the rear of this device. A slightly larger hole in the front acts as the pitot source.

Stop Stalling

Most airplanes have a device to warn of an impending stall. (In aviation, the word stall means the wings have stopped flying, as opposed to an engine that won't start. I'll explain how and why this happens in the next chapter. Stay tuned.) The first type of *stall warning device* is the suction type (Figure 12A), and the second is the electric type (Figure 12B). Get the plane headed for a stall, and the warning horn will bawl.

The suction type works because a slight vacuum forms as air flows over it in an approaching stall. This sets off the horn. The electric version works because two metal contacts come into contact as the plane gets into an unhappy configuration. This closes a circuit, sounding a horn in the cockpit. Either way, you'll hear about it if a stall is imminent.

Figure 13 shows *fuel tank caps* in action—well, actually, in inaction. They don't jump around a lot, but they do keep the fuel in the tank, which is useful. Inside the tank you

A SUCTION-TYPE STALL WARNING DEVICE

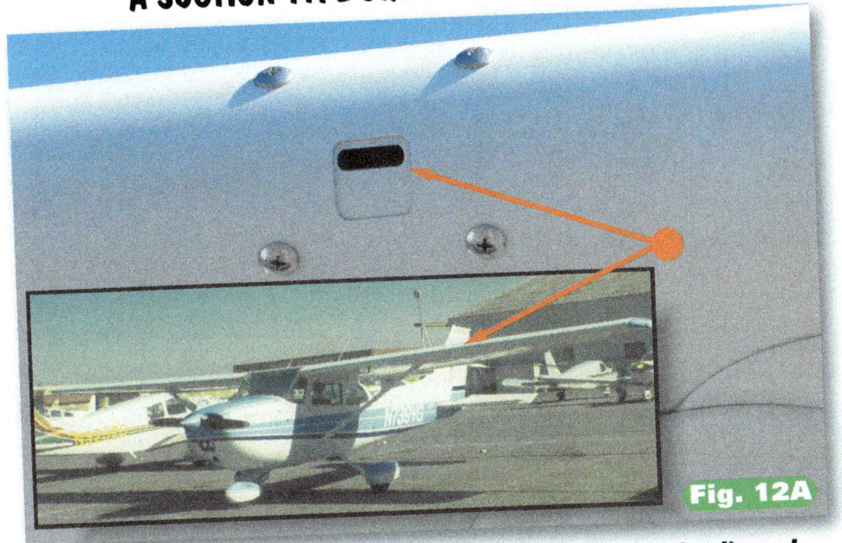

A suction-type stall warning device located on the wing's leading edge provides an audible warning to the pilot when a stall is near.

AN ELECTRIC STALL WARNING DEVICE

An electric stall warning device provides the pilot with a similar stall warning by connecting two small metal tabs and activating a cockpit buzzer.

VENTED FUEL TANK CAPS & TANK TABS

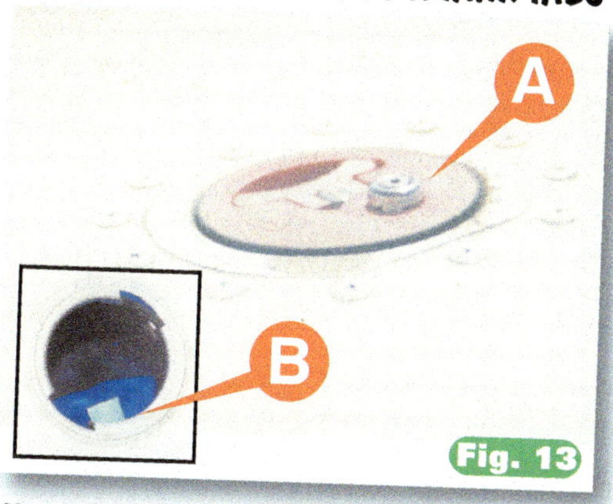

Vented fuel caps (position A) allow air to enter the tank and replace the fuel consumed by the engine. A marking tab (position B) inside the tank used to visually indicate the fuel level.

FUEL TANK VENT LINE

Some airplanes have tank vent lines which also allows airflow into the fuel tanks. A tank filled to the brim may need to purge some of its fuel through this line as the air in the tank expands.

will sometimes see a marking tab, used to visually calibrate the tank's fuel quantity. Some caps are vented—they have an opening for air to enter and exit. If the tank were tightly sealed, as fuel was used in flight a vacuum would form in the tank, and eventually fuel flow would be restricted or might even stop. Not good. Instead of vented caps, some airplanes allow air into or out of the tank via tank vent lines (Figure 14A). Crankcases also need to breathe through the crankcase breather tube (Figure 14B).

> *"Instead of our drab slogging forth and back to the fishing boats, there's a reason to life! We can lift ourselves out of ignorance, we can find ourselves as creatures of excellence and intelligence and skill. We can be free! We can learn to fly!"*
>
> *Richard Bach, Jonathan Livingston Seagull*

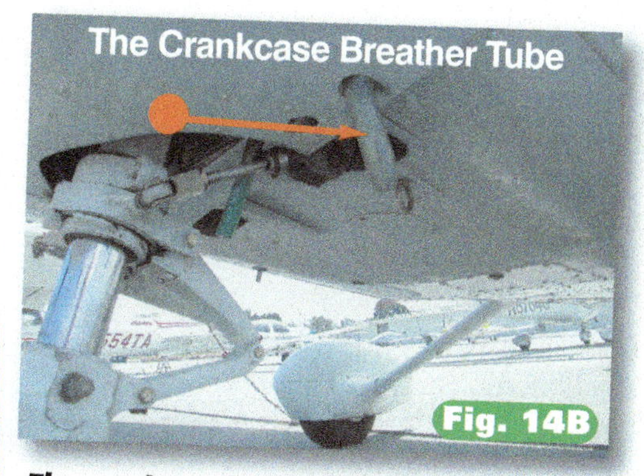

The crankcase breather tube allows air to flow in and out of the crankcase. Check to ensure it's not plugged, which can happen in very cold conditions where outside moisture might freeze over the vent.

THE POSITION AND ANTI-COLLISION LIGHTING SYSTEM

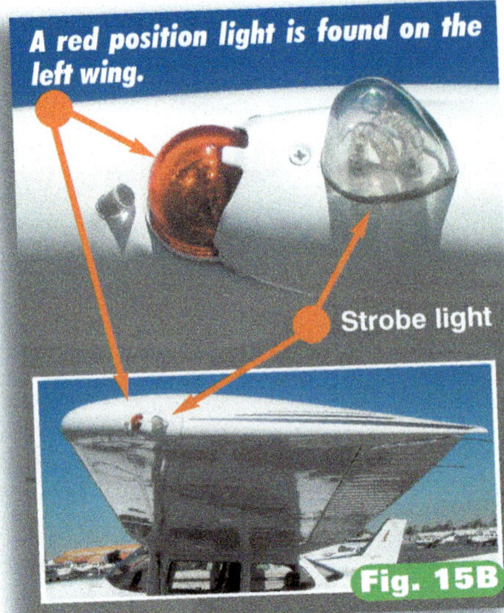

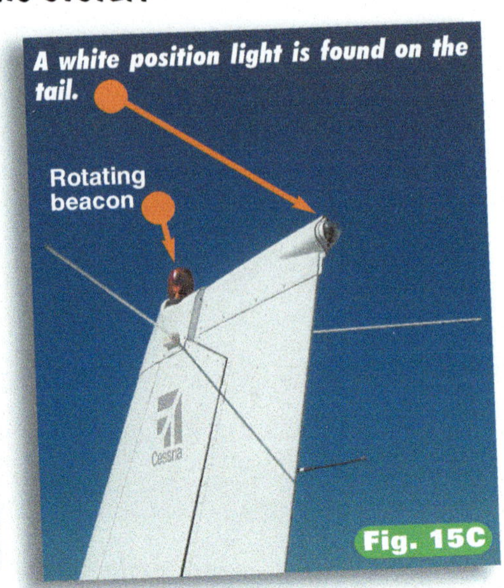

An airplane's lighted position lights and an anti-collision light system help other airplanes better identify your airplane when it's in operation on the surface or in the air between the period from sunset to sunrise.

There are three *position lights* (also referred to as *navigation lights)* on the airplane, as shown in Figure 15 (A, B & C). Just as prairie dogs aren't really dogs, navigation lights don't actually help the pilot navigate. Each is a different color, and each has its assigned place. The one on the left wingtip is always red, the one on the right wingtip is always green, and the one atop the tail is always white. At night, this enables other pilots to know whether you're coming or going, since the plane itself is not visible. (There is, unfortunately, no device to tell the pilot whether he or she is coming or going. You have to figure it out for yourself.) An optical light sensor is sometimes placed on the wingtip, to let the pilot know if the navigation light is working. The rules require a plane's navigation lights to be illuminated any time the plane is moving between sunset and sunrise.

There are usually *strobe lights* on the wingtips (and sometimes the tail, as well). These powerful, flashing lights can be seen from a great distance, especially at night, and help alert others to your presence. This is necessary because screaming out the window does not work.

Moving Parts

The *ailerons* are the moveable, flap-like appendages found along the outer part of the wing's trailing edge (Figure 16). Notice that as one aileron moves up, the other moves down. Yin and yang, cosmic balance, and the ability to turn the airplane all stem from this. Ailerons make slight changes in the lift developed by each wing, causing the airplane to bank and turn. A downward-moving aileron increases the wing's lift, and an upward-moving aileron decreases the wing's lift. Turning the control wheel (so that's what it does!) right or left deflects the ailerons in the appropriate direction for a turn. We'll be talking a lot more about the ups and downs of ailerons in the next chapter.

Flaps (Figure 17) allow the airplane to develop the lift needed for flight at slow speeds, such as when landing. When deflected, flaps change the wing's curvature, and in some instances increase its surface area. An increase in curvature and surface area means the wing produces more lift, as well as more drag. The reason you care about all this will become evident in the next chapter.

THE AILERONS

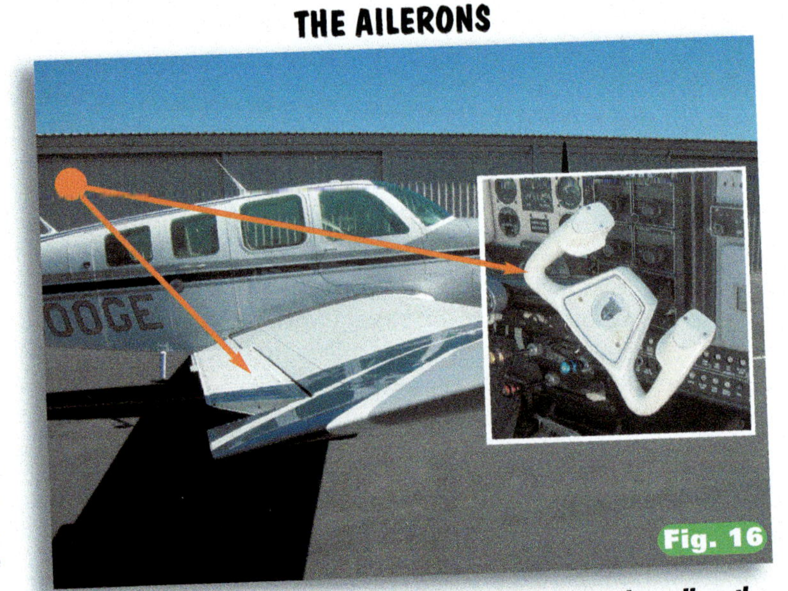

Ailerons are the moveable appendages on the wing that allow the airplane to bank and turn. Turning the control wheel (or deflecting the control stick) deflects the aileron and banks the airplane.

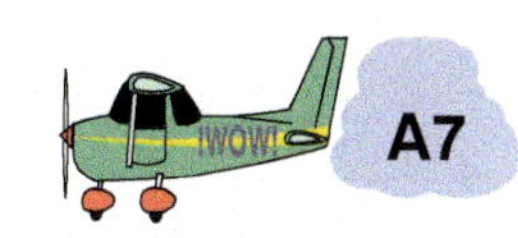

THE FLAPS

Flaps increase the wing's curvature and its surface area. Pilots frequently use them during landing to produce the required lift at slower airspeeds.

THE FUSELAGE

The fuselage is the long, cigar shaped portion of the airplane onto which everything else is bolted, riveted or glued.

The *fuselage* is the big piece in the middle (the cigar) to which everything else (wings, engine, etc.) is bolted (Figure 18). The *empennage* is the tail feathers, the aft part of the airplane (Figure 19).

Staying Stable

The empennage is home to the *vertical and horizontal stabilizers*. The horizontal version has a moveable surface *(the elevator)* connected to it (Figure 19). Forward or aft movement of the control wheel (or control stick) in the cockpit deflects the elevator. This changes the lift produced by the horizontal portion of the tail and points the airplane's nose up or down. It's the elevator control that allows you to select the attitudes (the plane's attitude, not yours) needed for takeoff, climb, cruising flight, and descents.

Moving onward and upward, we see the *vertical stabilizer* (Figure 19). It, too, has a moveable appendage—the *rudder,* which you may recall is controlled by the rudder pedals beneath the pilot's feet. Application of right or left rudder changes the lift produced by the vertical portion of the tail and swings the nose to the right or left. This allows the pilot to point the nose of the airplane in the appropriate direction of turn (As you will soon learn, the airplane's nose doesn't always want to point in the direction the pilot wants to go.)

Instead of a horizontal stabilizer and elevator, some planes are designed so that the entire tail surface moves. Such structures are called *stabilators,* or flying tails (Figure 20).

THE HORIZONTAL AND VERTICAL STABILIZER

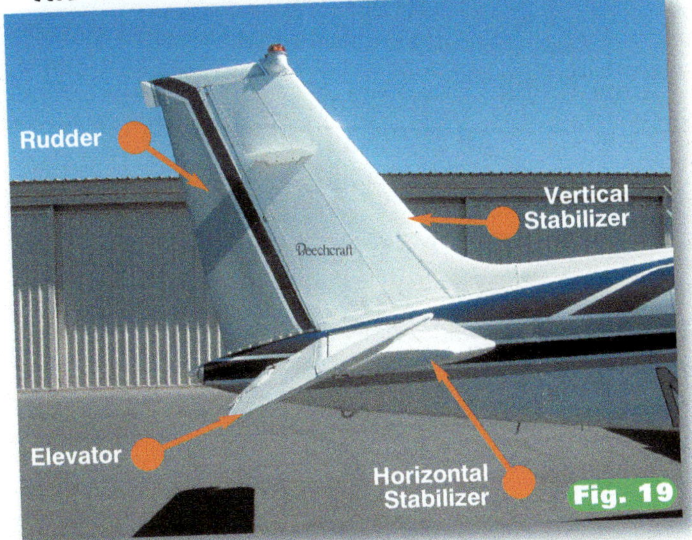

The horizontal and vertical stabilizers are the stationary portions of the tail surface. They contain moveable appendages called the elevator and rudder respectively.

THE STABILATOR

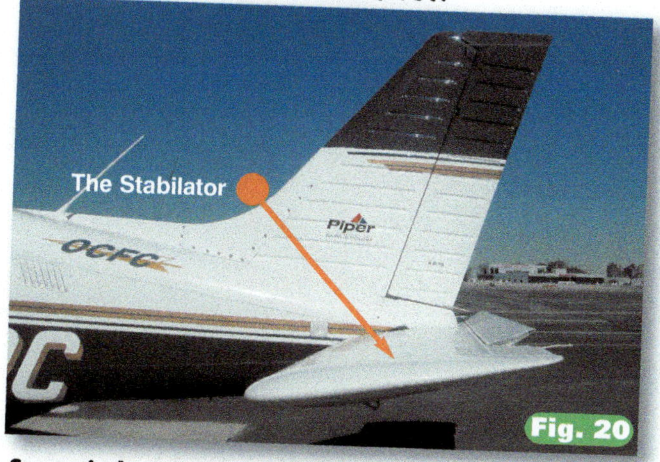

Some airplanes have a combination of horizontal stabilizer and elevator rolled into one. This is called a "stabilator" and the entire horizontal surface moves as a single unit.

THE TRIM TAB

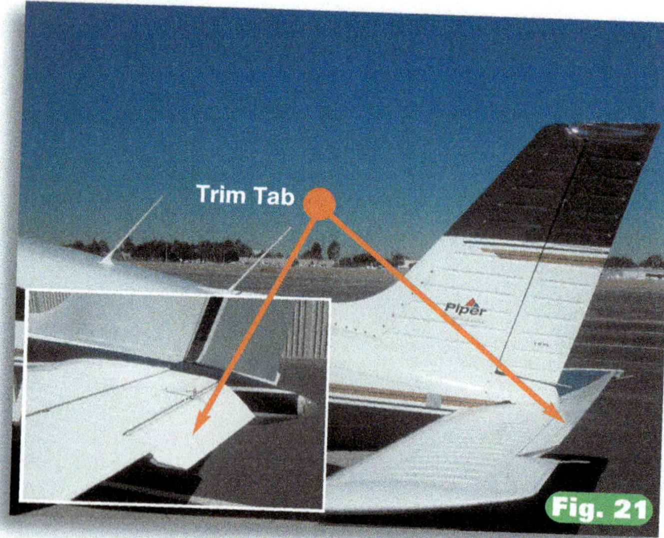

A trim tab on the tip of the stabilator or elevator is a small moveable surface that holds the elevator in the position desired by the pilot. This prevents the pilot's arms from becoming tired on long (or short) flights.

THE FUSELAGE

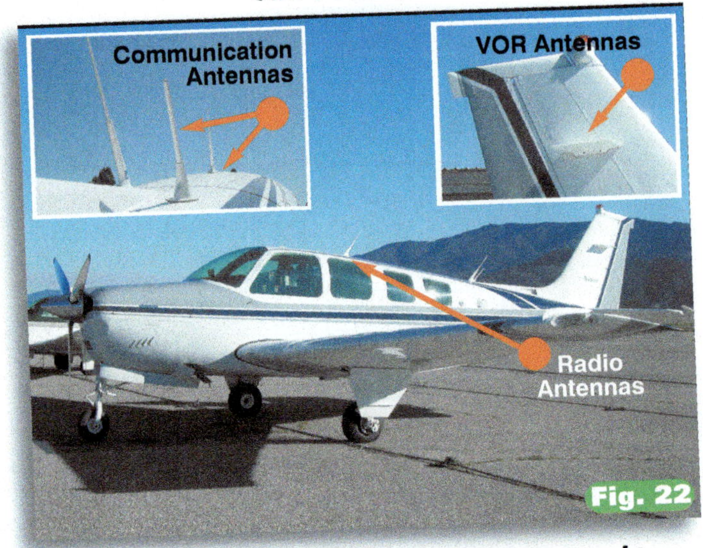

Airplanes are home to many antennas. It's not unusual to see five, six, seven or more antennas sprouting from some portion of an airplane.

Most elevator surfaces have a small, moveable appendage called the *trim tab* (Figure 21). Turning the trim wheel in the cockpit moves the trim tab, which accomplishes aerodynamically what the pilot would otherwise have to do through brute force in order to maintain a desired pitch attitude.

OPENABLE ENGINE COWLING

Some airplanes have cowlings that are easily opened for inspection.

THE COWLING

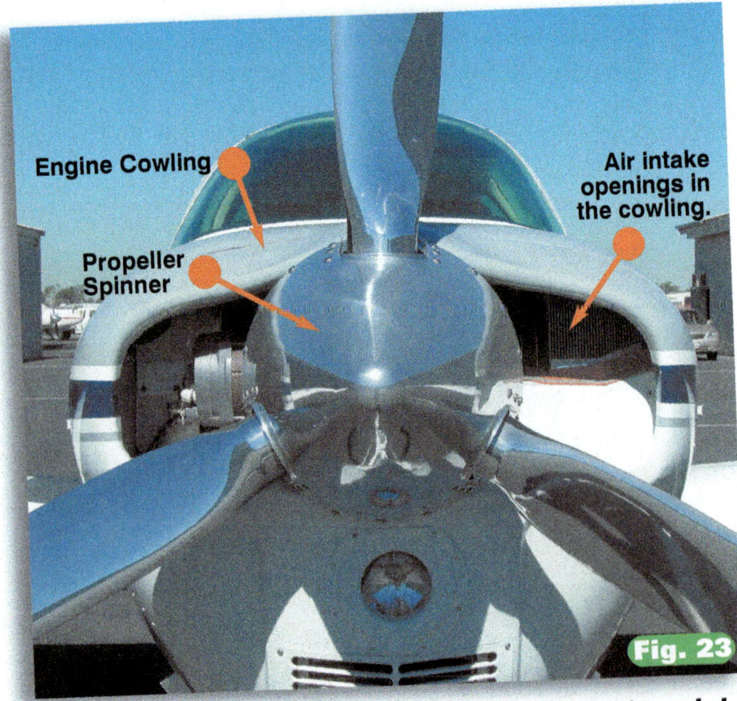

The engine cowling modifies the flow of air into the engine to help keep it cool. The propeller spinner helps deflect air into the air intake sections of the cowling.

AN ENGINE ACCESS DOOR

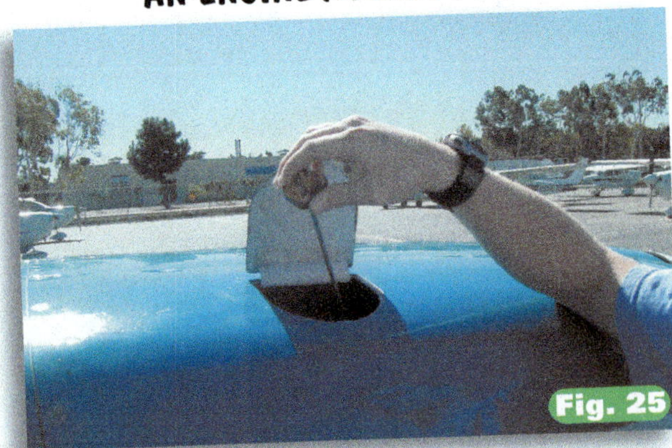

A small pop-open door is often your only immediate access to the engine.

ENGINE ACCESS

Fig. 26

We often check the engine's oil quantity just like we do in a car—with a dipstick.

Fig. 27

On some airplanes, you pull on the quick drain lever for a fuel sample (watch your shoes!).

Fig. 28

Some airplanes have a different version of the fuel strainer located on the side of the cowling.

Antenna Farm Deluxe

Airplanes, like police cruisers, are virtual antenna farms. Atop the tail you will probably see two *VOR antennas* (Figure 22). VOR stands for very high frequency omnidirectional range, a navigation system that depends on receiving signals from ground stations. A variety of other antennas, usually mounted on top of the fuselage, permit communication with controllers on the ground and with other aircraft. More on antennas later.

Back Up Front

Let's get back to where we began—the front of the airplane, where you will find (I hope) the *engine cowling* (Figure 23). Some airplanes have engine cowlings that can be easily opened for inspection before every flight (Figure 24). Unfortunately, many modern general aviation airplanes have only a small pop-open door (Figure 25) through which you try to peer to see if everything under the hood is good. The experience is something like looking inside a Coke can through the pop top in the dark. It's through this door that you generally check for adequate engine oil (using a dipstick much like that of a car, as shown in Figure 26), and drain a sample of fuel from the lowest engine point to check for contamination before taking to the air (Figure 27).

Checking the fuel is a simple procedure. You pull on the lever in Figure 27 which activates a *quick drain valve*. Fuel drains onto the asphalt although you should try to capture it in a sampling container. This makes it easier to detect the presence of water. Some airplanes have a different version of a fuel strainer, as shown in Figure 28. These airplanes allow the sampling of the fuel strainer's contents by a valve located on the outside of the cowling. Most small general aviation airplanes have three drain valves (one for each of the two fuel tanks, and one for the fuel strainer) while more complex craft have five or more drains.

Entering the cockpit (a.k.a. "the front office") you will see a wide (actually, bewildering) array of instrumentation as shown in Figure 29. These instruments are often known as *analog* flight instruments

THE TRADITIONAL INSTRUMENT PANEL

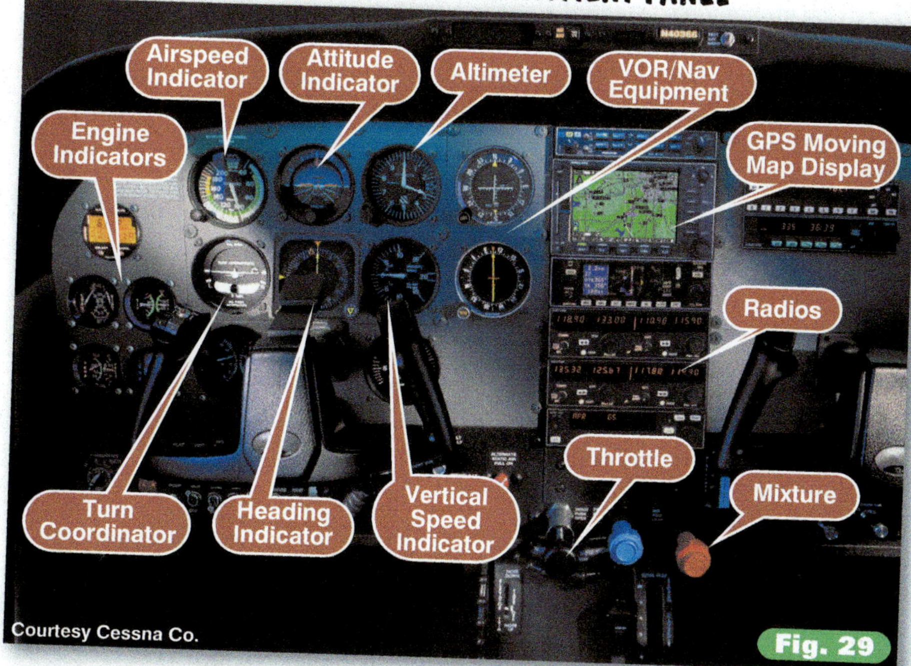

Fig. 29

No, it isn't the Space Shuttle, even though it seems to have as many dials, switches, knobs and lights. Soon they'll all become very familiar to you.

THE LATEST GLASS COCKPIT PANEL

The primary flight display uses solid state technology to generate its flight instruments. These instruments are similar to those found in the traditional analog-instrument equipped airplane. Nevertheless, the essential analog instruments (airspeed indicator, attitude indicator, magnetic compass and altimeter) are still found in many glass cockpit airplanes. The multi-function display provides computer generated engine instruments, checklists, weather information as well as GPS-generated information in the form of a moving map, terrain information, essential airspace information and much more.

because they are mechanical in nature. On the other hand, glass cockpit technology is often found in the newest technically advanced general aviation airplane cockpit as shown in Figure 30 and 31. (Read more about primary flight displays in Postflight Briefing #5-2 on page E36.) Each instrument or item has a specific name and serves an important purpose (this includes the plastic cup holders, if your airplane is so equipped). Before long you will become intimately familiar with each item. It may look overwhelming at first, but within a few hours of starting to fly you will be right at home with all these tools of the trade. Then you can bring your friends out and dazzle them with your knowledge. This is part of the thrill of aviation.

Now that we've become somewhat familiar with the airplane and its components, it's time to take a look at what makes an airplane fly. The science of aerodynamics is fundamental to the safe operation of any airplane. Since safe operation is really the only kind that makes a whole lot of sense when you're talking about airplanes, let's find out what's keeping you up in the air.

PRIMARY FLIGHT DISPLAY INSTRUMENTS

The newest primary flight displays (PFDs) provide the same instrumentation as analog instruments. The main difference is in how these instruments are interpreted.

We often use mechanical equipment without completely understanding how it works. Don't take my word for that. Go stand at a hardware store some Saturday morning, and listen to people talk about *thingamajigs, doohickies,* and *gizmos* while waving their hands, hyperventilating, and attempting to describe for the clerk what isn't working. Do you think Aunt Maude understands why her toaster toasts? Do you think your boss understands why his or her personal computer can do what it does?

As a young bachelor my parents gave me a vacuum cleaner for my birthday. Several months later mom called and asked, "Are you having trouble finding bags for your vacuum cleaner?" I said, "Bags? What bags?"

How was I to know the thing needed bags?

Technological ignorance has its advantages, but not when you're up in the air. You don't need a Ph.D. in aerodynamics to be a pilot, but moderate-to-decent understanding of why an airplane stays airborne will prove very helpful and life sustaining.

As one aviator elegantly put it, "The wing is the thing." It's the thing that performs the magic; the pilot simply manages the show.

May the Four Forces Be With You

Yoda, the transcendental handheld philosopher from the Star Wars movie trilogy, frequently dispatched Luke Skywalker with the benediction, "May The Force be with you." In aviation, there are Four Forces and they are *always* with us, whether Yoda or your flight instructor intervenes or not.

Under Yoda's tutelage, Luke extracted from Mother Nature the mightiest of her secret powers. Aeronautical engineers—taller, without green complexions, blanketed with pocket protectors—do the same, designing airplanes to create a compromise among The Four Forces. This results in the ability of your trusty airplane to fly. Compared to crafting this compromise, settling the Middle East conflict is novice-level work.

The Four Forces—*lift, weight, thrust* and *drag*—are present any and every time a plane is airborne. Look at Figure 1, which shows the action of The Four Forces. Of course, enormous arrows don't really protrude from the airplane. I know this will disappoint those of you who still

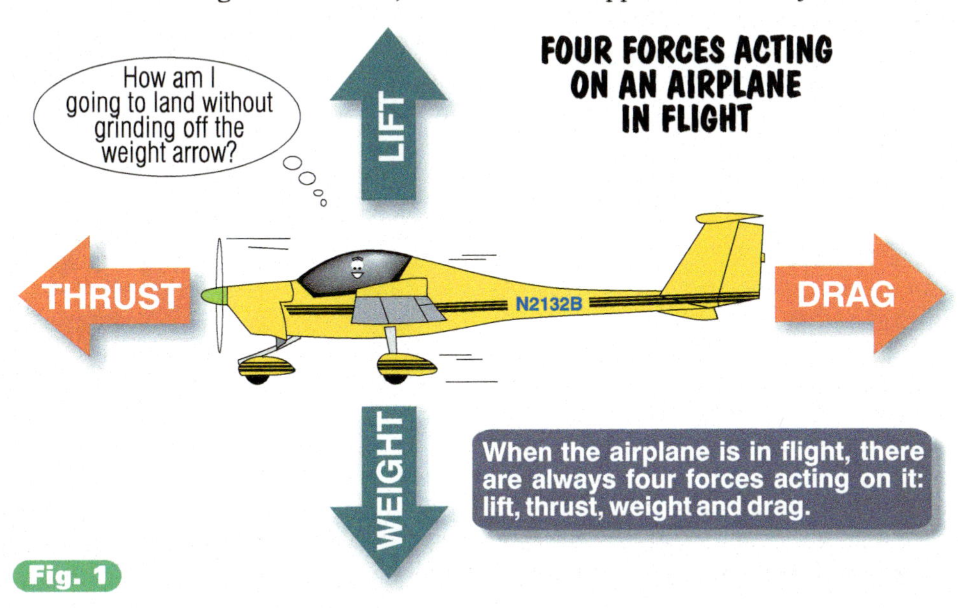

Fig. 1

Professor Bob:

While hiking on Mount Pinitubo during the last eruption, Professor Bob had an aerodynamic brainstorm when he fell into a lava pit. He reasoned that if you turned the airplane upside down and backwards, the drag vector would pull it forward as you reduced thrust. Reducing lift would allow the weight vector to pull the airplane skyward. Once again, we see the perils of skipping one's medication, even for a day.

expect the states to be colored blue and red and have lines drawn around their borders as you fly over them, but you'll get used to it. The arrows do serve to show that what we've got here is a highly competitive new game—four-way tug-of-war. Your job, as pilot, is to manage the resources available in order to balance The Four Forces. Learning to fly is really learning to manage The Four Forces. Almost everything you do in the cockpit will result in making a change to one or more of these forces. Let's see what they're all about.

Lift is the upward-acting force created when an airplane's wings move through the air. Forward movement produces a slight difference in pressure between the wings' upper and lower surfaces. This difference becomes lift. It's lift that keeps an airplane airborne.

I discovered how lift works at four years of age, during my very first visit to church. The collection plate passed in front of me and I picked out a few shiny items. My grandfather chased me around the pew and I thought, "Wow, church is fun!" Picking me up by my sweater, grandpa held me suspended four feet off the ground and toted me outside. It was the lift from grandpa's arm, precisely equaling my weight, which kept me airborne. Wings do for the airplane what grandpa's arm did for me—provide the lift to remain aloft.

Weight is the downward-acting force. It's the one force pilots control to some extent by choosing how they load the airplane. With the exception of fuel burn, the airplane's actual weight is difficult to change in flight. Once airborne, you should not be burning cargo or acquiring extra passengers (or losing them). Unexpected discharge of passengers while in flight is a violation of some FAA rule, so please don't do it.

In unaccelerated flight (when the airplane's speed and direction are constant), the opposing forces of lift and weight are in balance.

Thrust is a forward acting force produced by an engine-spun propeller. For the most part, the bigger the engine (meaning more horsepower) the greater the thrust produced and the faster the airplane can fly—up to a point. Forward movement always generates an aerodynamic penalty, called *drag*. Drag pulls rearward on the airplane and is simply the atmosphere's molecular resistance to motion through it. In plain English (which pilots and engineers rarely use), it's wind resistance. Few things are free with Mother Nature. As Confucius might say, "Man who get something for nothing not using his own credit card."

Thrust causes the airplane to accelerate, but drag determines its final speed. As the airplane's velocity increases, its drag also increases. Due to the perversity of nature, doubling the airplane's speed actually quadruples the drag. Eventually, the rearward pull of drag equals the engine's thrust, and a constant speed is attained.

My high school VW Bug knew these limits well (it's called a Bug because that's the largest thing you can hit without totaling the car). The Bug's forward speed is limited by its engine size. With four little cylinders (three of which worked at any one time), this VW simply wouldn't go faster than 65 mph. Figure 2 shows the results of maximum thrust meeting the equal and rearward pull of drag at this speed. Maintaining a slower speed requires less power, since less drag exists. At any speed less than the maximum forward speed of the car, excess thrust (horse-

Fig. 2

A constant velocity is attained when the automobile's engine thrust equals the drag produced by wind resistance. At full throttle, the car's top speed is limited by the maximum thrust the engine can produce (same for airplanes too).

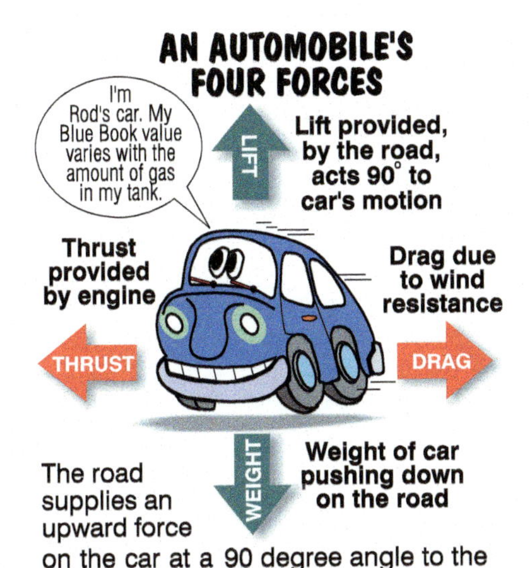

The road supplies an upward force on the car at a 90 degree angle to the direction of travel. Lift (developed by the wings) supplies a similar force on the airplane at a 90 degree angle to the direction of travel.

Fig. 3

power) is available for other uses, such as accelerating around other cars or perhaps powering a portable calliope if you are so inclined.

The same is true of airplanes. At less than maximum speed in level flight, there's power (thrust) to spare. Excess thrust can be applied to perform one of aviation's most important maneuvers—the climb.

Climbs

One of aviation's biggest misconceptions is that airplanes climb because of excess lift. This is similar to believing that putting hand lotion in your airplane's fuel tank will make your landings smoother, softer and younger looking.

Airplanes climb because of excess thrust, not excess lift. Let's use my car as an example to see how thrust, not lift, is responsible for the climbing action of an airplane.

Figure 3 shows my car sprouting more arrows than the hat Custer wore at the Little Big Horn. Notice that the car's weight is offset by the upward push of the road on the tires. In effect, the road simulates the lift of an airplane's wings. In other words, if the road were quicksand, there would be little upward push (lift) and the car would slowly be absorbed by this evil liquid.

Figure 3 also shows the lifting force acting at a 90 degree angle to the car's motion (it's the only way this lift can possibly act since the road pushes directly against the car's tires). Weight, on the other hand, always acts downward toward the center of the earth (pointing toward a Kung-Fu school in China somewhere). Now let's allow the car to move up a hill (climb).

Figure 4 shows the forces on the climbing car. Notice that the lifting force is still perpendicular to the road, thus 90 degrees to the car's motion (arrow A). Lift appears tilted rearward slightly, because the road is inclined upward. The total weight of the car, however, still acts directly downward, toward that Kung Fu school (arrow B). No matter how steeply the road tilts, weight will always point toward the center of the earth (and the author's decision is final on that!).

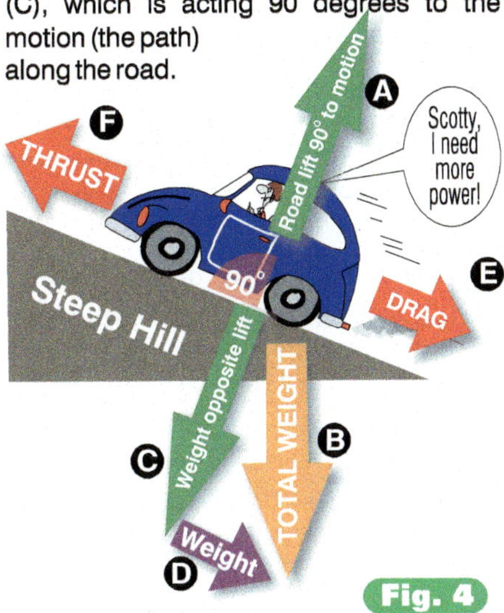

Fig. 4

We can think of weight as two separate forces. Part of the car's weight pushes on the road in a perpendicular direction (arrow C). A smaller part acts rearward (arrow D). Do you see what's happening here? In a climb, some of the car's weight starts acting rearward, in the direction of drag. Anything that pulls aft and impedes acceleration—even if it's the car's weight—acts like drag. The steeper the hill, the larger the rear-

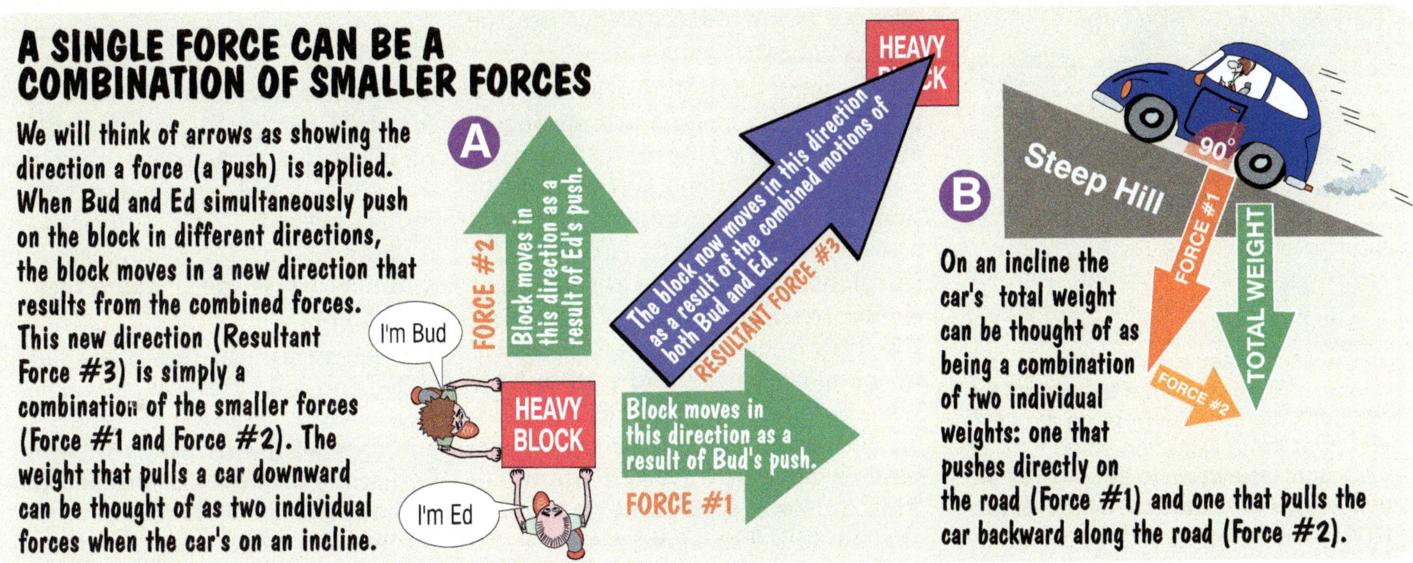

ward acting forces. (If you're having trouble with vectors, see the accompanying sidebar at the bottom of page B3.)

Here's what you've been waiting for: The upward push of the road on the car (arrow A) is equal to the car's weight on the road (arrow C). In other words, lift still equals weight, even in a climb. Part of the weight, however, now acts like drag (arrow D), which really *is* a drag, because it gets added to the wind resistance. As we've already learned, thrust is the force that overcomes drag.

The forces acting on an airplane during a climb are similar to those of the car (Figure 5), the only major difference being that you (the pilot) choose the slope of the hill you climb. This is done using the elevator control in the cockpit (more on the elevator control later).

As you can see, it's excess thrust, not lift, that allows an airplane to climb. Given this very important bit of knowledge, you'll now understand why smaller airplanes with limited power can't climb at steep angles like the Blue Angels do at airshows.

AN AIRPLANE'S FOUR FORCES IN A CLIMB

Similar to the automobile, it is engine thrust (F), not extra lift (A) from the wings, that pulls an airplane up its "pilot-made" hill. The steeper the angle of climb (the hill) the more the force of weight (B) acts aft (D). That portion of the weight (D), acting in the direction of drag (E), pulls the airplane aft and acts just like drag. Lift (A) still acts opposite the portion of weight (C) that acts 90 degrees to the flight path (which is also the relative wind).

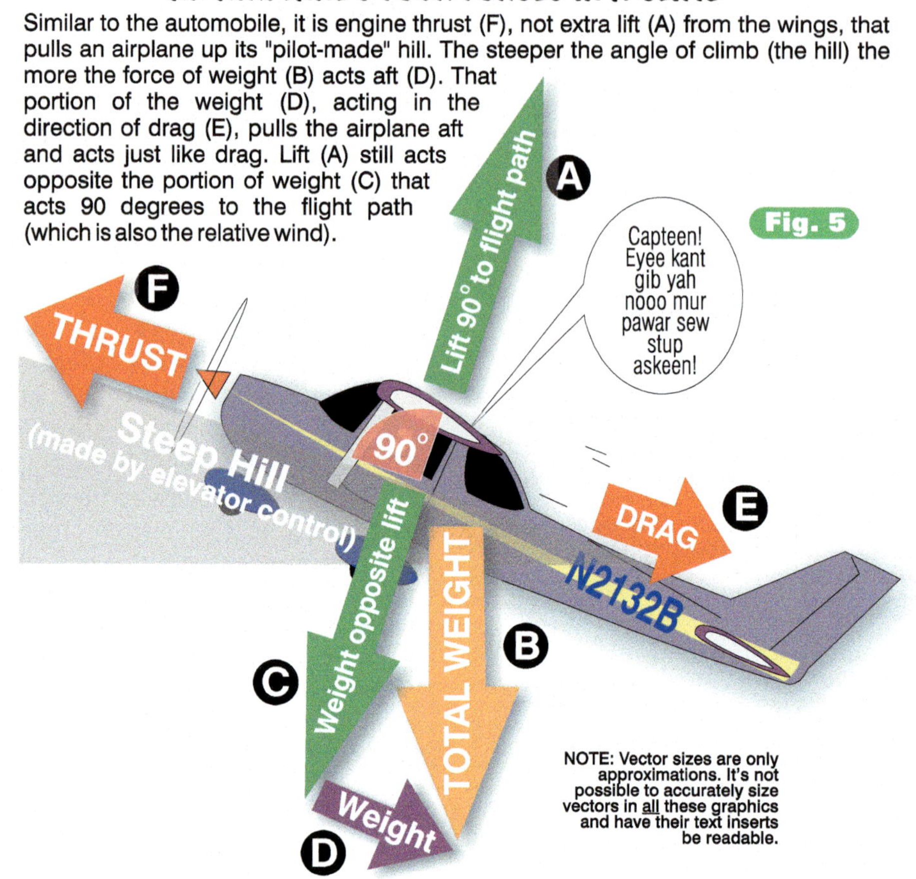

Let's go back to the automobile and climb a steep hill (Figure 6). The maximum forward speed of our car on a level road with full power is 65 mph (Car A). As we move up a hill (Car B) our speed drops to 50 mph. An even steeper hill slows the car to 40 mph (Car C). The limited horsepower of the car's engine simply can't match the drag caused by wind resistance plus rearward-acting weight as the hill steepens, so the car slows. A bigger engine or redesign of the car to produce less wind resistance are the only options that will help.

POWER AND CLIMB ANGLE

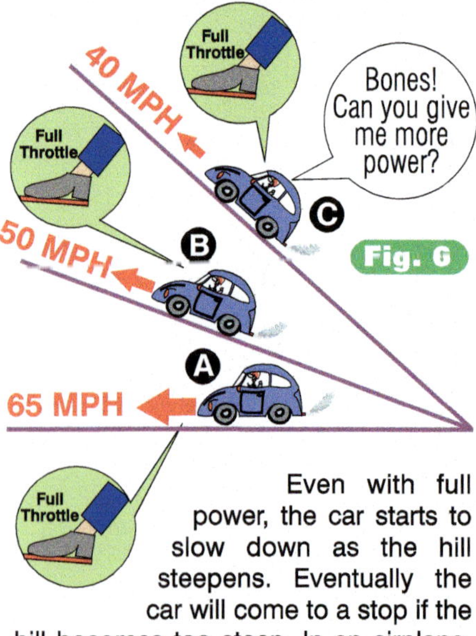

Even with full power, the car starts to slow down as the hill steepens. Eventually the car will come to a stop if the hill becomes too steep. In an airplane, you don't try to climb too steep a hill or you might slow down to the point where your wings can't develop the necessary lift to remain in flight.

The same analysis works, up to a point, for an airplane attempting to climb a hill in the air (Figure 7). Let's say your airplane has a maximum speed of 120 knots in straight and level flight with full throttle (Airplane A). (Airplane throttles are similar to automobile throttles except that they're hand operated. You push in for more power and pull out for less.) Applying slight back pressure on the elevator control points the airplane's nose upward (Airplane B). This causes the airplane to climb a shallow hill. The speed decreases to 80 knots just as it did in the car. Attempting to climb a steeper hill (Airplane C) slows our speed down to 70 knots. We can't climb the hill we just selected faster than 70 knots because we don't have the extra horsepower (thrust) to do so.

As we continue to steepen the angle of climb, our airspeed decreases further, just like the car's speed did. Here, however, is where the airplane goes its own way. Airplanes need to maintain a minimum forward speed for their wings to produce the lift required to stay airborne. Ever wonder why airplanes need runways? Same reason long jumpers do. Airplanes (and long jumpers) must attain a certain speed before they can take flight.

This minimum forward speed is called the *stall speed* of the airplane. It's a very important speed that changes with variations in weight, flap setting, power setting and angle of bank. It also varies among airplanes (no need to worry because

later I'll show you how to recognize when you're near a stall). As long as the airplane stays above its stall speed, enough lift is produced to counter the airplane's weight and the airplane will fly.

If the stall speed of Airplane C (Figure 7) is 60 knots, then climbing at a slightly steeper angle will result in insufficient lift for flight. We call this condition a *stall*. Done unintentionally, it leads to such primitive linguistic sounds as "Uh-oh," "yipes," "ahhhhh," as well as "I think I need to have my chakras balanced." Needless to say, these sounds make passengers reluctant to ever fly with you again. This is why some of your time as a student pilot will be spent finding out about stalls, and doing them (intentionally, that is). Instructors have special biological filters installed that keep them from making these sounds on those rare occasions when you unintentionally stall the airplane. That's why they are sometimes referred to as *certified* flight instructors.

What you need to know is that airplanes with a lot of power (like jet fighters) can climb at steep angles; those with limited power, however, must climb at less steep angles.

Knowing it's extra thrust and not extra lift from the wings that is responsible for the climb allows you to draw some interesting conclusions. For instance, anything that causes the engine to produce less power prevents you from achieving your maximum rate of climb. Among the things resulting in less power production are high altitudes and high temperatures. More on these factors a bit later.

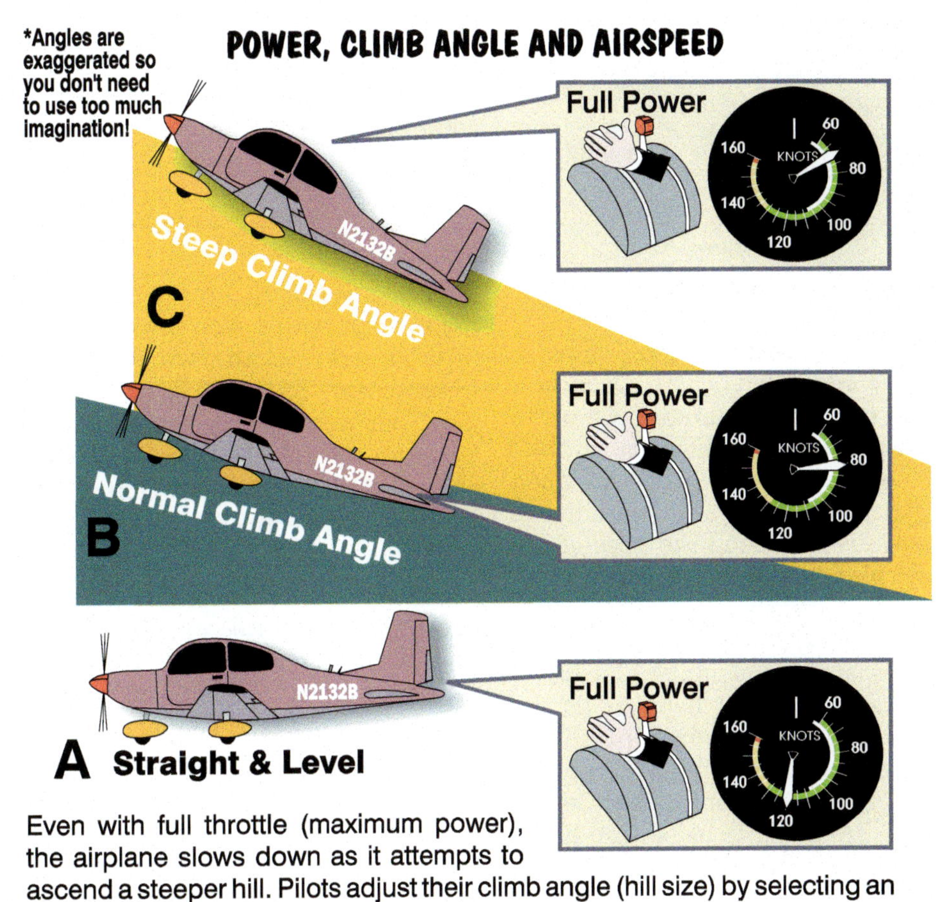

Even with full throttle (maximum power), the airplane slows down as it attempts to ascend a steeper hill. Pilots adjust their climb angle (hill size) by selecting an attitude that gives them a specific climb airspeed. Fig. 7

At this point you should be asking an important question. I certainly don't mean questions of the "Zen-Koan" type, such as "What is the sound of one cylinder firing?" or "If an airplane lands hard in the forest and nobody is there to hear it, does it really make a sound?" A good question for you to ask is, "How can I determine the proper size hill for my airplane to climb?" Let's find out.

Airplanes have a specific climb attitude (steepness of hill) that offers the best of all worlds—optimum climb performance while keeping the airplane safely above its stall speed. You can determine the proper climb attitude for your airplane by referring to its airspeed indicator.

With climb power applied (usually full throttle in smaller airplanes) the pitch attitude is adjusted until the airspeed indicates one of two commonly used climb speeds. These speeds are known as the *best angle of climb* and the *best rate of climb* airspeed. The best *angle* of climb provides the greatest vertical gain in height per unit of forward travel; the best *rate* of climb provides the greatest vertical travel per unit of time. You select best angle when you need to get up in the shortest possible distance, usually to clear an obstacle. You choose best rate of climb to gain the most altitude per minute. Let's put this in concrete terms. Say there's a concrete tower 750 feet high half a mile off the end of the runway. You definitely want to be above 750 feet at one-half mile out, and you

What happens if the engine quits? The airplane becomes a glider, not a rock.

do not really care how long it takes you to get there. Your choice is best angle of climb.

Under normal circumstances you will climb at the best rate of climb speed, or a bit faster. Sometimes pilots climb at airspeeds slightly faster than the two reference airspeeds when better over-the-nose visibility is required. Raising the nose of the airplane results in a slower airspeed; lowering it picks up the pace. Where you place the nose—how steep you make the hill—determines what happens on the airspeed indicator. Unlike the ground-bound world, pilots decide how steep the hills in the air are going to be (within limits of course!). With just a little experience, you'll be able to determine the correct size hill (nose-up attitude) by simply looking out the front window instead of having to rely solely on the airspeed indicator.

When I was a student, any specific airspeed was the one place on the dial where the pointer never went. I was not gifted with much coordination as a youngster. My reflexes were so slow I was almost run over by two guys pushing a car with a flat tire. I'm a living exhibit that one can be a competent pilot even without the coordination and reflexes of a 13-year-old Olympic gymnast.

During a climb with full power, where you place the nose—how steep you make the hill—determines what happens on the airspeed indicator.

Descents

While engine power moves a car uphill, gravity pulls it down. Without your foot on the throttle, the car's downward speed is determined by the steepness of the hill it's descending (Figure 8). The steeper the hill, the faster it goes. If the hill shallows out, then the speed decreases. If the hill becomes too shallow, then some power is necessary to maintain sufficient forward speed.

Airplanes can also move downhill without power. Just lower the nose (Figure 9) and you'll get what appears to be a free ride (it isn't, but let's not get into *that*). You can adjust the nose-down angle with the elevator control and descend at any (reasonable) airspeed you desire.

You now have the answer to a question I guarantee every first-time passenger will either ask or want to ask you: "What happens if the engine quits?" The airplane becomes a glider, not a rock.

Unlike climbing, you may elect to descend within a wide range of airspeeds. There are, however, many factors to be considered such as forward visibility, engine cooling and the structural effects of turbulence on the airframe (all of these items will be discussed in this book).

However, during the last portion of the landing approach (known as *final approach*), you should maintain a specific airspeed. Usually this speed is at least 30% above the airplane's stall speed. When preparing to touch down, excess airspeed or erratic control forces often lead to difficulty in making a smooth landing (it's also the reason pilots make good humored fun of one another).

Now that The Four Forces are no longer a mystery, let's examine the most important force—lift. Without this force, airplanes are nothing more than very expensive ground bound vehicles that are impossible to parallel park.

AN AUTOMOBILE'S FOUR FORCES IN A DESCENT

The steeper the angle of descent, the more the car's total weight (B), acts forward (D), in the direction of thrust (E). Drag (F) primarily results from air resistance. Lift from the road (A) still acts perpendicular to the car's motion and is still equal and opposite to the car's weight on the road (C).

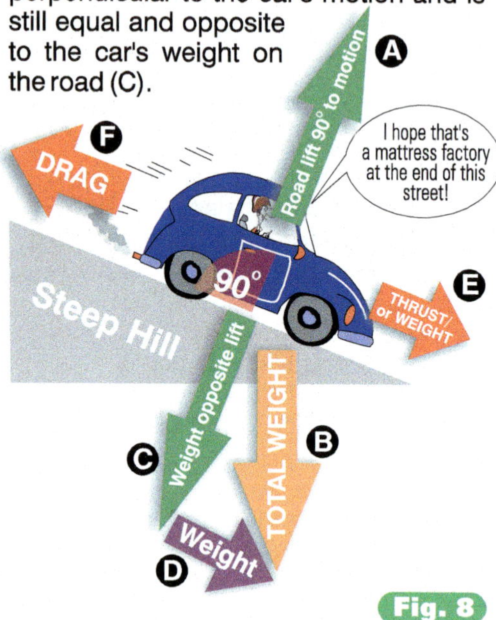

Fig. 8

AN AIRPLANE'S FOUR FORCES IN A DESCENT

The steeper the angle of descent, the more the airplane's total weight (B), acts forward (D), in the direction of thrust (E). Drag (F) is aerodynamic drag. Lift (A) still acts perpendicular to the flight path (the relative wind). Lift (A), is still equal and opposite to that part of the weight (C) which acts 90 degrees to the flight path.

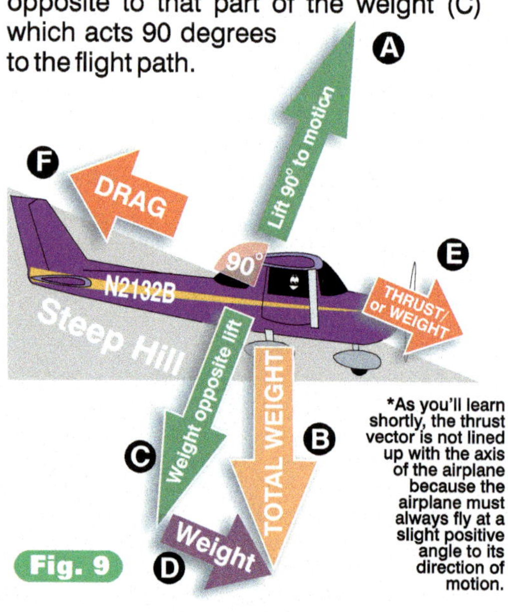

*As you'll learn shortly, the thrust vector is not lined up with the axis of the airplane because the airplane must always fly at a slight positive angle to its direction of motion.

Fig. 9

The Wing and Its Things

Defining the Wing

In ground school many years ago, my instructor asked me about the origin and definition of the word *wing*. I replied, "Ma'am, I think it's Chinese and means 'the arm of a bird'." She mumbled something about why many animals eat their young at birth, then went to the dictionary to look up the definition. *Wing* was defined as "a moveable, paired appendage for flying." She looked at me and said, "Well, what does that sound like to you?" I said, "Well ma'am, that sounds like the arm of a bird to me." We agreed to disagree, even though I was right.

The wing has several distinct parts. These are the *upper cambered surface, lowered cambered surface, leading edge, trailing edge* and *chord line* (Figure 10).

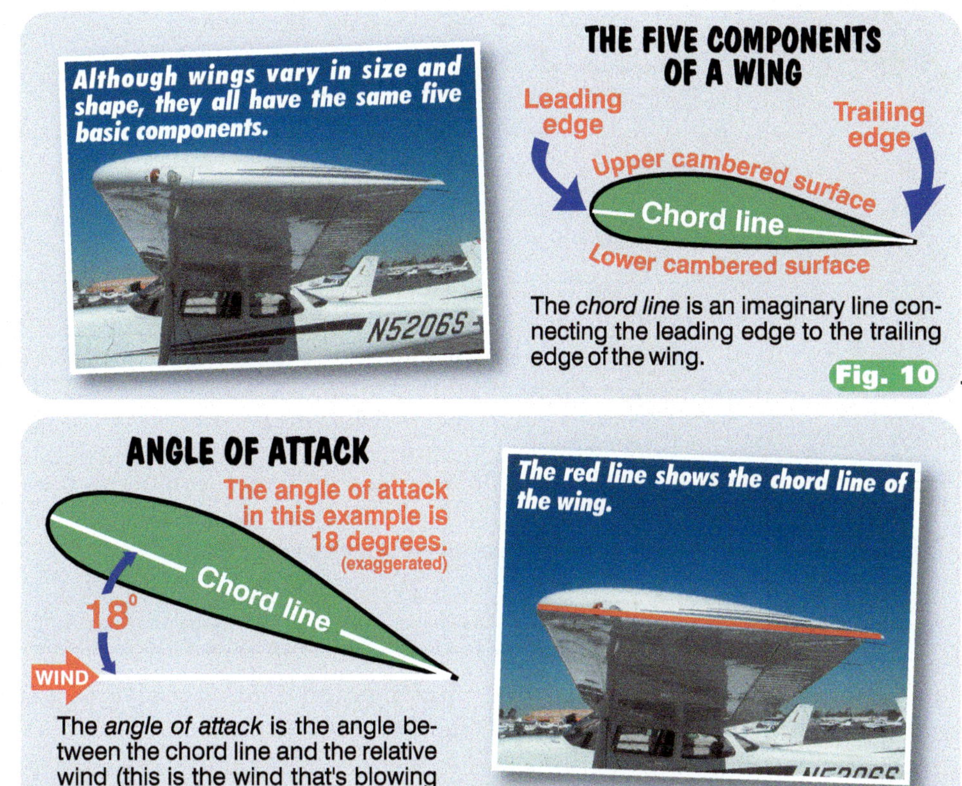

The *chord line* is an imaginary line connecting the leading edge to the trailing edge of the wing. Fig. 10

The *angle of attack* is the angle between the chord line and the relative wind (this is the wind that's blowing on the airplane's wing). Fig. 11

Notice that the upper cambered (meaning *curved*) surface seems to have a greater curve to it than the lower cambered surface. This isn't accidental. In fact, this is so important that we'll talk about it in detail shortly.

Perhaps the only term whose definition isn't intuitively obvious is the *chord line*. The chord line is an imaginary line connecting the leading edge with the trailing edge. Believe me, there is no line inside the wing that looks like this. It's only imaginary, just like the arrows showing The Four Forces. When the shoe salesman points to your foot and says, "Your toe is here," you want to respond by saying, "Thanks, I've been looking for that." In reality he or she is pointing out the position of something not visually obvious. The chord line does something similar. Given the wing's curved surfaces, it's difficult to tell which way the wing points. Since engineers don't like uncertainty, they agreed that the chord line will represent the general shape of a wing.

Your author is especially proud of his Cessna "lifting body" airplane. He believes it has a glide ratio similar to a meteorite. Take special notice of the canvas cooling system!

How the Wing Works

To understand lift, you must visualize how the wing attacks the air. Aeronautical engineers talk about the wing *contacting* or *attacking* the air at a specific angle. This occurs in much the same way a pitbull attacks a mailman—mouth first. What part of the wing does the attacking? Is it the leading edge? Is it the trailing edge? Or, is it the bottom of the wing? This is where the definition of chord line becomes useful.

Because wings come in variable sizes and shapes (just like airline pilots), it is sometimes difficult to determine exactly how and where the wind strikes the wing. Fortunately, the chord line substitutes as a general reference for the shape of the wing. If I say that the wind blows onto the wing at an 18 degree angle, I'm saying that the angle between the wind and the chord line is 18 degrees (Figure 11). This distinction, although seemingly trite, is as important to an engineer as tightly-stitched pant seams are to a matador. Only one more definition need be absorbed before the secrets of lift

The *relative wind* is wind resulting from an object's motion. Despite the actual wind blowing from behind him at 3 mph (position 1), the jogger (running at 6 mph, position 2) feels a 3 mph "relative wind" on his face (position 3) as a result of his running motion. Relative wind is *relative* (opposite and equal) to the movement of an object.

are revealed. That term is called the *relative wind* (which is not a reference to an uncle who's like a Kamikaze pilot—the type of person who does all his bragging ahead of time).

Relative Wind

Movement of an airplane generates wind over the wing. This wind is called the *relative wind* because it is relative to (or results from) motion. For instance, in Figure 12, no matter which way the jogger runs, he feels wind in his face that's relative (opposite and equal) to his motion.

Relative wind is movement-generated wind. To illustrate this point, stick your hand out the window of a moving automobile (keep all other body parts inside, please). You'll feel wind blowing opposite the motion of the car. Drive a car backwards on the freeway and you will feel wind, and hear a lot of horns, blowing from directly behind you (you'll also attract the police, so have those doughnuts ready). Relative wind is movement-generated wind that's equal and opposite to the motion of the airplane.

Relative wind is independent of which way the airplane's nose is pointed.

Move the airplane forward as shown by Airplane A in Figure 13 and wind blows on its nose. Move the airplane up or down a hill and wind still blows on its nose (Airplanes B and C). Drop an airplane and the wind blows on its belly (Airplane D). As far as Airplane D is concerned, the wind is blowing on its belly despite the level attitude (as for the passengers, they're probably underneath the front seat in the fetal position, making spiritual transmissions that don't require a radio—do not scare your passengers. It isn't nice, and they don't like it).

Relative wind blows from a direction that's opposite the direction of airplane motion, irrespective of what direction the airplane's pointed. The following point is so important I want you to put one finger in your ear. Go ahead, do it before reading any further! I want you to do this because I don't want this information to go in one ear and out the other. *The important principle to remember is that relative wind is independent of which way the airplane's nose is pointed.* Relative wind is opposite in direction and equal to the airplane's velocity. Let's see how the wing actually attacks the wind to develop lift.

Attacking the Air

Hunting is a sport to some people. It's also a sport where your opponent doesn't know it's a participant. Attacking a mammal means that the hunter must point his weapon precisely at the prey. The hunter looks though the gunsight and sees the path of the bullet. An airplane is unlike a gun (and a car) in that its vertical climb path is different from its

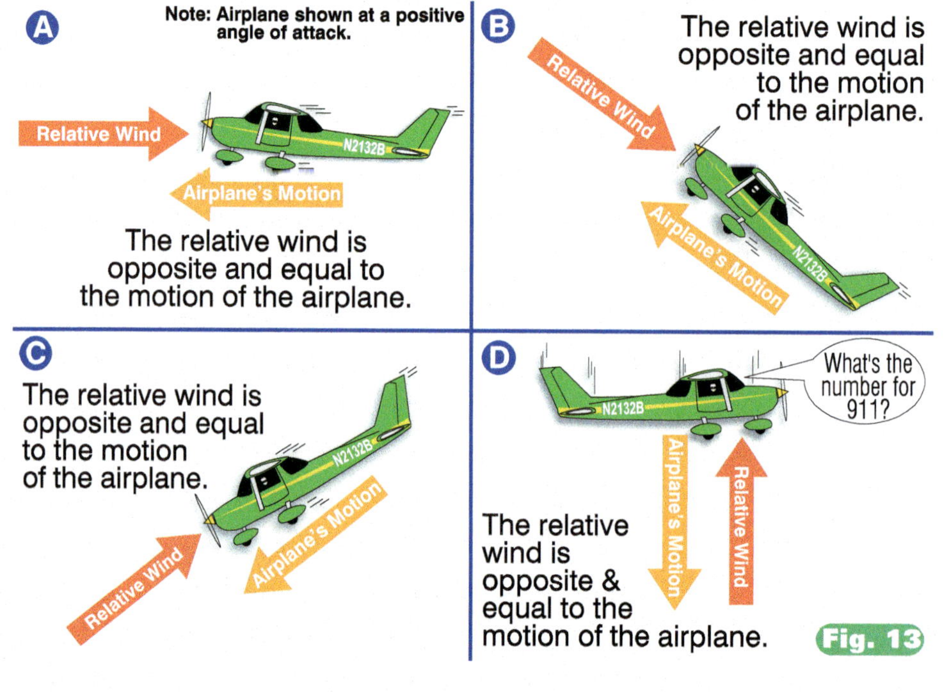

Fig. 14

incline (the direction it points upward). Remember that 750 foot tower off the end of the runway? On takeoff, if you point your airplane slightly above the top of that obstacle (like a rifle sight), it's unlikely that you're going to clear it. In fact, the only thing being cleared is the area—as the firemen try to talk you down from the side of that tower. Remember, airplanes with limited thrust have shallower climb paths—unlike some fighter jets.

The most important principle to understand here (put that finger back in the ear) is that the nose (therefore the wing) can be pointed on an incline that's different from the actual climb path. An angle exists between the amount the wing is inclined and its climb path (you'll soon see why). Remembering that the relative wind is always equal and opposite to the flight path, it's more precise to say that an angle exists between the chord line and the relative wind. This angle is known as the *angle of attack* (Figure 14).

Figure 15 shows the wing (chord line) of Airplane A making a 5 degree angle to the relative wind. A more common way of saying this is that the wing's angle of attack is 5 degrees. Airplanes B, C and D show increasing angles of attack of 10 degrees, 30 degrees and 45 degrees, respectively. The greater the difference between the wing and the relative wind, the greater the angle of attack. And, as you're about to see, the wing's lift is directly associated with its angle of attack.

How Lift Develops

The wing is the ultimate air slicer. As powerful as any Ginzu knife, Samurai sword or karate chop, it's a precision device for slicing air in a very specific way. Wings are expressly built to plow through air molecules separating them either above or below while offering little resistance in the horizontal direction. Any horizontal resistance slows the wing down. This horizontal resistance is drag, and it's definitely a case of less being better.

ANGLE OF ATTACK

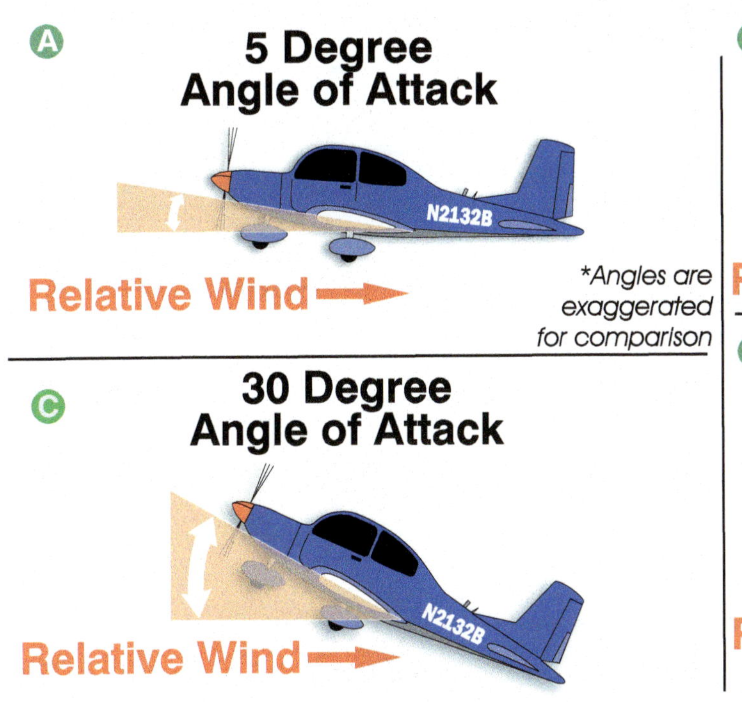

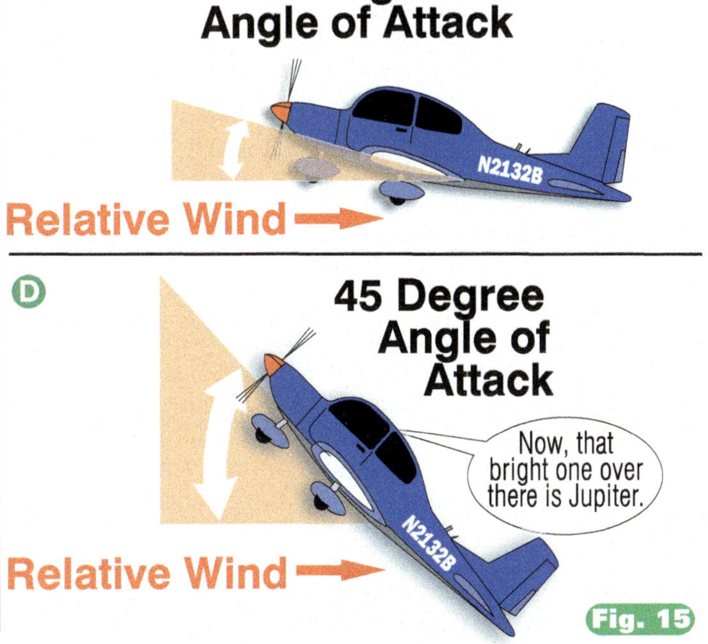

Fig. 15

Figure 16 shows how the airfoil splits the wind when it's at a 10 degree angle of attack. Airflow strikes the leading edge of the wing forcing some air over and some under the *airfoil* (a fancy name for a wing). Both the air flowing over and the air flowing under the wing are responsible for generating lift. Let's first examine how the airflow striking the bottom of the wing produces some of the total lift that is developed.

Impact Versus Pressure Lift

Sticking your hand out the window of a moving automobile does two things: it demonstrates how a relatively flat surface develops lift and it signals a left turn. Figure 17 shows that wind is deflected downward when it strikes your hand.

According to Sir Isaac Newton, who knew about such things, for every action there is an equal and opposite reaction. Wind deflected downward by the airfoil creates an upward (opposite) movement of the wing. This upward movement is caused by the impact energy of billions of tiny air molecules striking the underside of the wing. Also, higher pressure on the bottom surface of the wing results from this molecular impact. The wing moves upward as if it were pushed from below.

This type of lift is known as *barn door* or *impact* lift. It generally contributes only a small portion of the total lift produced by the wings, which means that man and woman do not fly by barn door lift alone. If we could, it would mean people in the Midwest would report flying barn doors instead of UFOs.

A more subtle and powerful form of lift occurs from curved airflow over the top of the wing.

Wind deflected downward by the airfoil creates an upward (opposite) movement of the wing.

Bending the Wind With the Wing

The Japanese invented the art of paper bending and called it origami. They then experimented with people bending and called it judo. This art was not perfected, however, until the airlines adopted the practice, which is referred to as "flying coach."

Airliners (indeed all airplanes) bend something else—they use their wings to bend the wind. *Wind bending* did not sound sophisticated enough to explain why airplanes fly, so it was given a fancy Greek title. We call wind bending *aerodynamics*. Simply stated, the wing is a precision device for bending or curving the wind downward.

But how does bending the wind over the wing create lift? Let's see.

Figure 18 shows a cross section of an airfoil. Examine its shape carefully. At small angles of attack, air flowing above the wing is bent or curved with great precision as it follows the upper cambered surface. The air below the wing isn't curved quite as much but is deflected downward both by the bottom of the wing and by the air flowing over, around and down behind the wing. Bending or curving the wind above the wing forces air to speed up compared to the less curved air below the wing. Curve the air more and it speeds up more. Nice, eh? Since the air above the wing has increased its velocity, it always reaches the trailing edge before the air traveling below the wing.

For example, assume you are walking your pitbull (named *Bob*) on a leash. You are on the sidewalk and Bob is walking in the gutter (Figure 19). Bob encounters a parked VW and decides to walk over the car rather than around it (remember, it's a pitbull). Obviously, the distance over the car is greater than the distance you will travel on the sidewalk. In order for Bob to avoid being choked by the leash he will have to speed up slightly as he covers this greater distance.

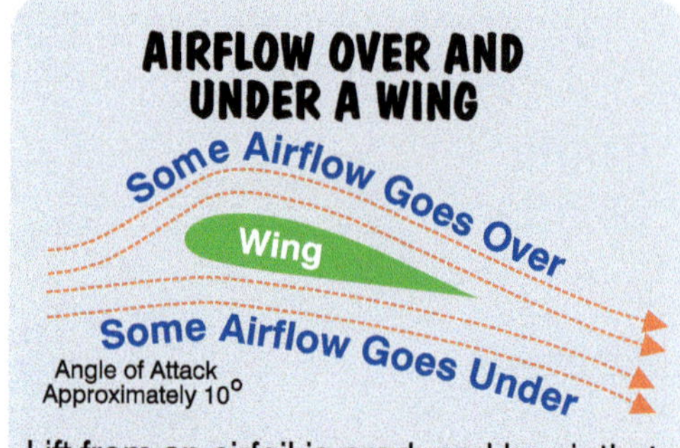

Lift from an airfoil is produced by air that flows both over and under the wing.

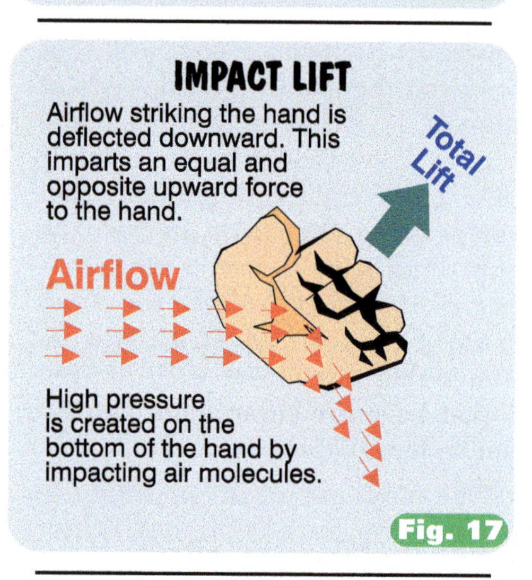

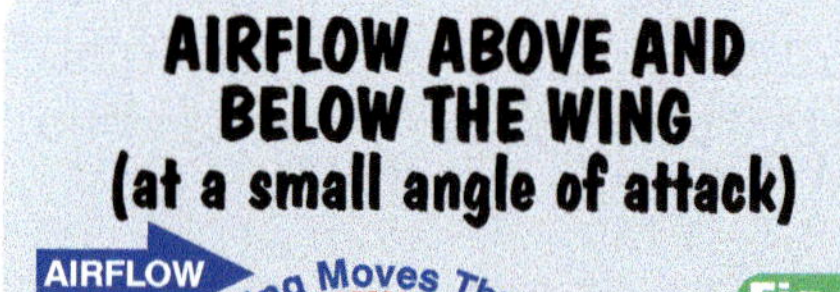

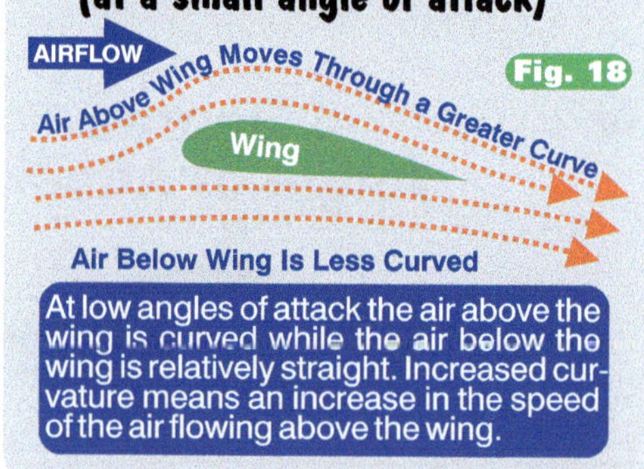

At low angles of attack the air above the wing is curved while the air below the wing is relatively straight. Increased curvature means an increase in the speed of the air flowing above the wing.

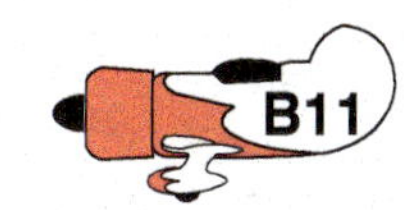

DIFFERENCE IN SPEEDS THAT RESULT FROM MOVING ALONG A CURVE AND MOVING ALONG A PATH THAT'S LESS CURVED.

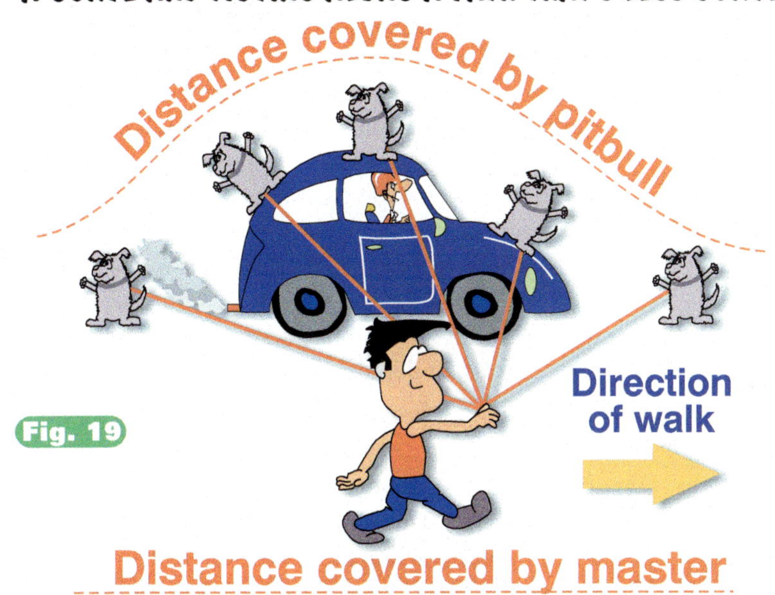

As Bob (the pit bull) walks over the car (shaped like a wing) he must travel faster (because of the curved path) to keep up with his master and to keep from being choked by his master's leash (and, you never want to choke a pit bull without getting its permission first).

Hey! What Are You Doing Up There?

This pilot was caught checking for those mysterious little Bernoullis that are responsible for the creation of lift. He didn't find any.

Do you notice the resemblance of the VW's profile to a wing? It's curved on top and rather straight on the bottom. As air flows over the wing, it curves and speeds up.

Something remarkable happens when air, flowing over a surface, increases its speed. A physicist named Bernoulli (pronounced BRR-*NEW*-LEE) figured out that lower pressure is a consequence of air that flows faster over a curved surface. Thus, high velocity airflow results in a slight decrease in pressure on the wing's upper surface. In other words, the pressure on top of the wing is now less than the pressure on the bottom of the wing. (Don't ask why. It has to do with conservation of mass, momentum and and energy, and explaining it will give you something that feels like a two scoop lobotomy.) Known as *Bernoulli's principle,* this wonderful trick is what keeps airplanes from being large and expensive doorstops.

Try an experiment. Take a piece of writing paper and hold it in such a way that the top surface is curved downward (Figure 20). With a little imagination, you can see how the bent paper is similar in appearance to the wing's upper cambered surface. Blow over the top of the paper. What happens? The paper should rise upward (a hundred years ago the Indians would

Did You Know...

Did you know that the reduction in air pressure above the wing caused by higher velocity airflow is actually less than that of a young child sucking on a bottle?

When you take into account the total wing area, even a small amount of pressure reduction per square inch of wing adds up to a significant total pressure difference. Each square foot of wing area on a Cessna 172 provides 13.2 pounds of lift. Since there are 144 square inches in a square foot, you can see that each square inch of wing provides less than .1 pound of lift.

Idea Source:
Barry Schiff, *The Proficient Pilot*

BERNOULLI'S PRINCIPLE

Blowing over the top of the paper creates higher velocity airflow which reduces pressure causing the paper to lift upward similar to a wing's lift.

have made you chief of the tribe for this magic demonstration!). Yes, the high velocity of air over a curved surface results in lower pressure on that surface. This means you have low pressure above the wing and high pressure underneath. Since high pressure always moves toward low pressure, the wing (which just happens to be in the way) is pushed upward in the process. Bernoulli's principle offers a simple explanation for the lift developed by an airplane. Impact or barn door lift is a sibling component to the generation of lift. Ultimately, however, it's Newton's laws that explain why Bernoulli's principle works, but this is beyond the scope of this book to cover.

Most wings are designed with their upper surface curved and their lower surface relatively straight. Because of the wing's shape, even at a very small angle of attack, a cambered wing still adds a slight curve and acceleration to the wind. This produces the lift you learn to love, particularly if you think an airplane should fly.

There are more wing shapes than there are body shapes at a Weight Watchers convention. Each shape has its own lift and drag characteristics (bodies too!). Figure 21 shows a variety of these different airfoils. Big ones, thick ones, small ones, skinny ones. They all serve one purpose—generating lift. Sometimes, however, the engineered shape of the wing all by itself can't produce the necessary lift for flight. In these instances the angle of attack becomes the major player in lift production.

Angle of Attack And the Generation of Lift

During takeoff on a commercial airliner, have you ever noticed that the pilot always raises the nose slightly to begin the climb after attaining a minimum forward speed? This is called *rotation* and it isn't something done to the airplane's tires.

As the airplane accelerates for takeoff, it eventually reaches a sufficient speed to begin flying. At this relatively slow speed, however, the wing's engineered curve isn't capable of curving or deflecting enough air downward to produce the necessary lift for flight. This is why the airplane doesn't hop off the ground like a grasshopper that just landed on a hot barbecue. The pilot must do something extra to add an additional curve to the wind. Raising the nose slightly increases the angle of attack. This forces the air to undergo an additional curve greater than what the engineered shape of the airfoil can produce. Figure 22 depicts this process.

An intimate and sizzling relationship exists between angle of attack and lift.

With this additional curvature, air travels a greater distance, its speed increases, pressure lowers on top of the airfoil, and sufficient lift to begin flying is produced at a slower airspeed (thanks for the lift, Bernoulli!). Greater impact lift results from increased exposure of the wing's lower surface to the relative wind. The result is that an increasing angle of attack permits the airplane to produce the necessary lift for flight at a slower airspeed.

Fig. 21

Now you know how airfoils generate the required lift at slower airspeeds. You also know why airplanes, taking off or landing at slower speeds, seem to have a rather nose-high attitude. But what happens at higher airspeeds? Have you noticed that in cruise flight, at cruise airspeeds, airplanes fly at near-level flight attitudes?

Figure 23 shows an airplane at several different angles of attack. At higher speeds airplanes can fly at lower angles of attack because the wing's shape generates sufficient lift. Slow the airplane and the wing must artificially bend the wind by increasing its angle of attack.

An intimate and sizzling relationship exists between angle of attack and lift. If lift and angle of attack were Rhett and Scarlet, Atlanta wouldn't be the only thing on fire. At small angles of attack (such as during cruise flight), the engineered shape of the airfoil generates sufficient lift for flight as long the airspeed is high. The impact of air underneath the wing doesn't play as big a role in lift development at higher (cruise) speeds because less of the wing's underside is exposed to the wind.

In summary, the slower an airplane moves, the greater the angle of attack needed for flight. There is, however, such a thing as too much of a good thing. Bend the air too much and instead of flowing smoothly over the wing and creating lift, it bubbles and burbles and pretty much fails to be very uplifting. We call this condition a *stall*.

What kind of instructor would I be if I didn't say, "Let's find out how and why a wing stalls"?

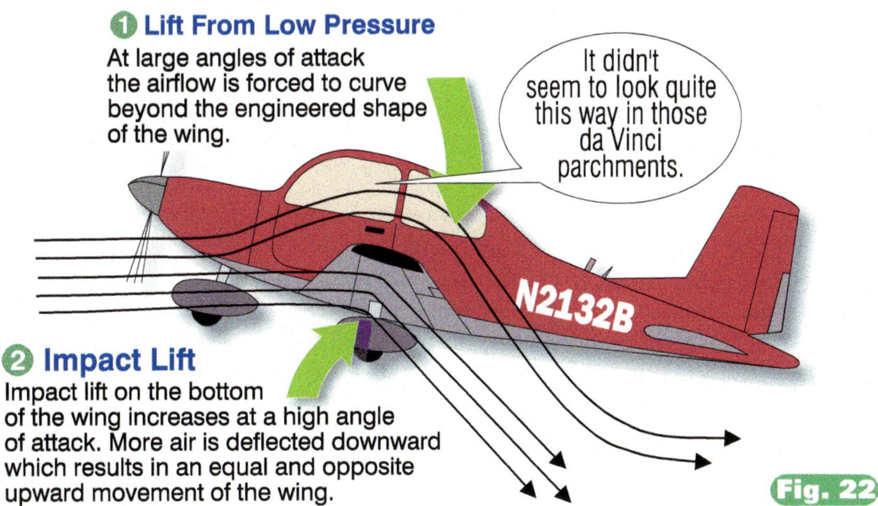

Fig. 22

Different Designs

CANARDS

Two lifting surfaces are apparent on airplanes having the *canard* design. Think of the forward surface as a miniature wing ahead of the main wing. Unlike the tail of a traditional airplane, the canard produces lift (an upward force) while the tail produces a downward force to prevent the nose from rotating forward. While both wings on an airplane equipped with a canard produce lift, the forward wing (the canard) stalls at a lower angle of attack than the main wings. When this happens the canard's angle of attack immediately decreases and the nose lowers. This prevents the main wings from stalling, thus making airplanes with the canard configuration stall resistant. Canards are also faster and more fuel efficient since there is no drag from a horizontal stabilizer and elevator. The canard design, however, is limited in its total lifting capability. Center of gravity travel is usually limited as well.

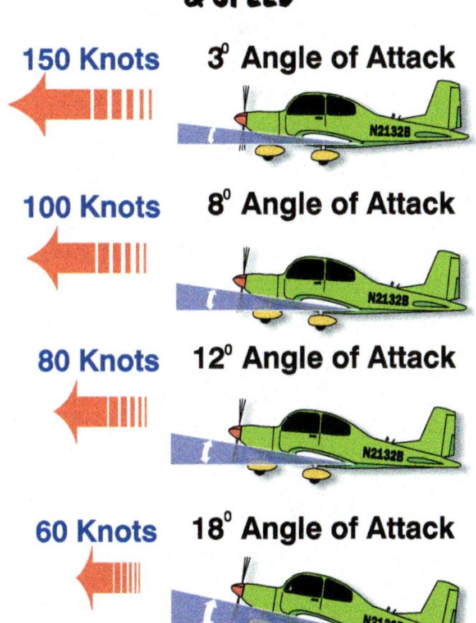

With speed variations in level flight, the relationship between the angle of attack and airspeed is clearly shown. With increasing airspeed, the airplane requires a smaller angle of attack to remain airborne. As the airplane's airspeed decreases, a larger angle of attack is necessary.

Fig. 23

STALLS

Stall, Angle of Attack, And How the Nose Knows

A pilot's job is to work The Four Forces, maintain lift, and avoid the burbling air condition that results in a stall.

Think of air molecules as little race cars moving over the wing (Figure 24). Each car and air molecule has one objective: follow the curve over the wing's upper cambered surface. Of course, if the wing is at a low angle of attack, the curve is not very sharp and it's a pretty easy trip (Figure 24A).

But look at the curve made by these cars and air molecules when the wing is attacking the wind at a very large angle. As the angle of attack exceeds *approximately* 18 degrees (known as the *critical angle of attack* for reasons you will soon see), these speed-racer air molecules don't negotiate the turn (Figure 24B). When this happens, they spin off or burble into the free air, no longer providing a uniform, high velocity, laminar airflow over the wing (Figure 25). The wing stalls.

(See "Seeing the Stall" in Postflight Briefing #2-6, page B46 for a view of how the wing stalls.)

Remember, according to Bernoulli, lower velocity airflow over the wing produces less lift. There is still impact lift provided by air molecules striking the underside of the wing, but we've already learned that this doesn't provide nearly enough lift to sustain the airplane. When there's less lift than weight, bad things happen to good airplanes. The wing goes on strike and stalls. Abandoned by Bernoulli, gravity summons the airplane to earth on its own terms.

All wings have a *critical angle of attack* (the angle varies slightly among airplanes). Beyond this angle the wing and the wind don't work and play well together. All the whispered theory in your heart won't overcome the laws of physics and aerodynamics. The wing police are always watching. Exceed the critical angle of attack and the air

THE RADICAL INSTRUCTOR

Some instructors dream of letting their students experience a stall from a very unusual vantage point. (Just kidding!)

THE CRITICAL ANGLE OF ATTACK

Air molecules, like race cars, can easily curve around a wing at a small angle of attack.

LOW ANGLE OF ATTACK

When forced to undergo too large a curve, air molecules, like race cars, may skid off the top of the wing resulting in a stall.

CRITICAL ANGLE OF ATTACK

STALLED VS. UNSTALLED WINGS

When the wings exceed their critical angle of attack, airflow over their upper surface, becomes chaotic and starts to burble. It is no longer smooth, high velocity airflow. Consequently, lift decreases.

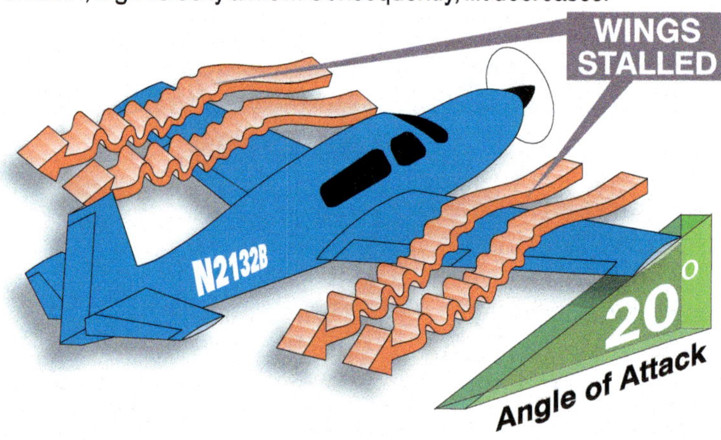

Wings operating below their critical angle of attack allow smooth, high velocity airflow to move over their upper surface. This keeps the pressure on the wing's upper surface low and maintains the required lift.

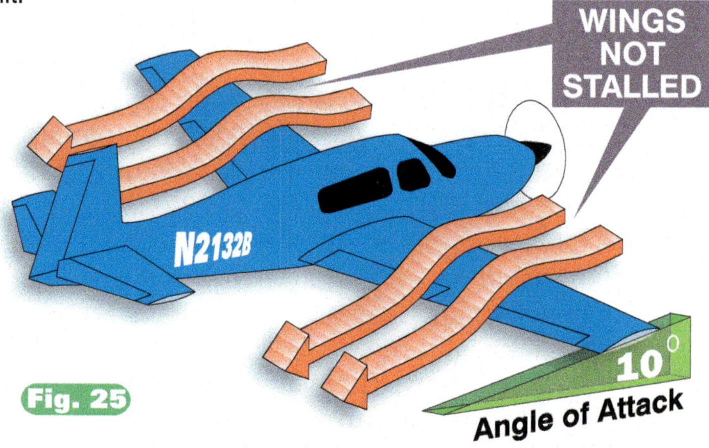

STALLING AND EXCEEDING THE CRITICAL ANGLE OF ATTACK

Pilot raises the nose too steep during a climb.

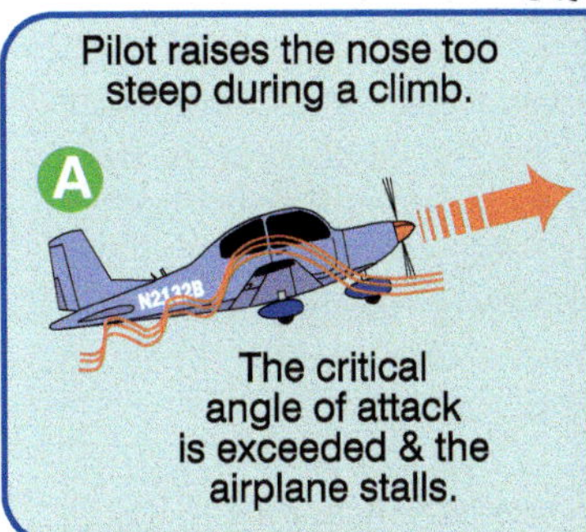

The critical angle of attack is exceeded & the airplane stalls.

The pilot lowers the nose (adds full power if not already so) and reduces the angle of attack (to less than the critical value).

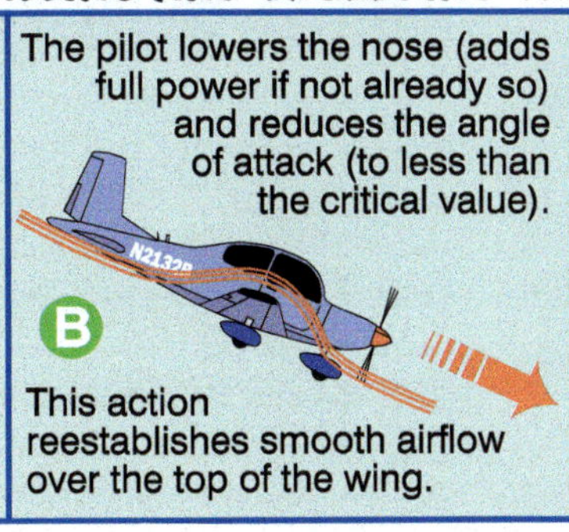

This action reestablishes smooth airflow over the top of the wing.

Once the airplane is no longer stalled, the pilot raises the nose slowly.

Fig. 26

Pilot now resumes climb without exceeding the critical angle of attack.

molecules won't give you a lift. Sounds serious, and it can be. Fortunately, there's a readily available solution, and it is *not* screaming, "Here, you take it" to the instructor. Put your finger back in your ear; here comes the important stuff again. *You can unstall a wing by reducing the angle of attack.* You do this by *gently* lowering the nose of the airplane with the elevator control (Figure 26, sequence A, B, C and D). Easy does it here, Power Ranger. Once the angle of attack is less than its critical angle, the air molecules flow smoothly over the top of the wing and production of lift resumes. It's as simple as that. Please don't ever forget this.

STALL RECOVERY

This airplane is stalled with its nose pointed downward while doing 150 knots.

Fig. 27

The only way to recover is for the pilot to move the elevator control forward. As contrary as this may seem, lowering the nose slightly by moving the elevator control forward (or releasing the back pressure on the elevator control) reduces the angle of attack to less than its critical value. The wing will once again start flying and the airplane will no longer be stalled. At this point the pilot should pull back slowly without (hopefully!) exceeding the critical angle of attack.

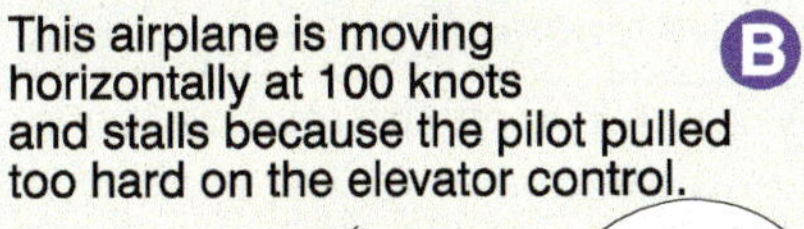

This airplane is moving horizontally at 100 knots and stalls because the pilot pulled too hard on the elevator control.

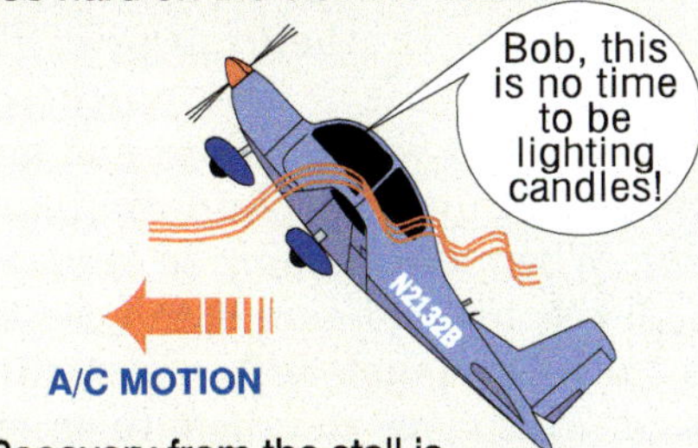

Recovery from the stall is accomplished by moving the elevator control forward (or releasing back pressure) and decreasing the angle of attack to less than its critical value.

These are illustrations for demonstration only. It's unlikely you'll ever find your airplane in these attitudes at these airspeeds.

Why am I making such a big deal out of this? Why did I make you put your finger back in your ear? Because in a moment of stress (having the wing stop flying creates stress for many pilots) you will be inclined to do exactly the opposite of what will help. It's a natural pilot response to pull or push on the elevator control to change the airplane's pitch attitude. During a stall, as the airplane pitches downward, your untrained instinct is to pull back on the elevator control. You may yank that critter back into your lap, and the result will not be good. The wing will remain stalled and you, my friend, will have the look of a just gelded bull.

If the wing stalls, you need to do one very important thing: reduce the angle of attack to less than its critical value. Only then does the wing begin flying again. Adding full power also helps in the recovery process by accelerating the airplane. The increase in forward speed provided by power also helps reduce the angle of attack.

Don't just sit there with stalled wings. There's a reason why you are called the pilot-in-*command*. Do something. But do the right thing.

Stall at Any Attitude Or Airspeed

You should realize that airplanes can be stalled at any attitude or at any airspeed. Put your finger back in your ear. *It makes no difference whether the nose is pointed up or down or whether you are traveling at 60 or 160 knots. Whether an airplane exceeds its critical angle of attack is independent of attitude or airspeed.*

Figure 27 depicts two instances showing how this might happen. Airplanes have inertia, meaning they want to keep on moving in the direction they are traveling. Airplane A is pointed nose down, diving at 150 knots (don't try this at home!). The pilot pulled back too aggressively, forcing the wings to exceed their critical angle of attack. The airplane stalls. Wow! Imagine that. It stalls nose down at 150 knots!

What must the pilot do to recover? The first step is to decrease the angle of attack by moving the elevator control forward or releasing back pressure on the control wheel/stick (remember, pulling back on the elevator control was probably responsible for the large angle of attack inducing the stall in the first place.) This re-establishes the smooth, high velocity flow or air over the wings. The airplane is once again flying.

*The airplane will always stall when the wings exceed their **critical angle of attack**. It's the law!*

The second step requires applying all available power (if necessary) to accelerate the airplane and help reduce the angle of attack

Once the airplane is no longer stalled, it should be put back in the desired attitude while making sure you don't stall again. Stalling after you've just recovered from a previous stall is known as a secondary stall. Unlike secondary school, it is not considered a step up, especially by the participating flight instructor. (You'll know your instructor is unhappy when you hear her make subtle statements like, "Hmm, come to think of it, childbirth wasn't all that painful.")

Stalling an airplane intentionally, at a safe altitude, is actually fun, or at least educational. Stalls are relatively gentle maneuvers in most airplanes. Stalling an airplane close to the ground, however, is serious business because it is usually not an intentional act. During flight training you'll have ample practice in stall recovery.

Managing a stalled airplane is one thing; managing your natural instincts, another. For example, a typical stall trap you could (literally) fall into involves a high sink rate during landing. While on approach, you might apply back pressure on the elevator, attempting to shallow the descent. If you exceed the critical angle of attack the airplane will stall. The runway now expands in your windshield like a low orbit view of a supernova.

If you follow your untrained instincts and continue to pull backward on the elevator, the stall deepens. Trained pilots know better. They are aware of the possibility of stalling and apply the appropriate combination of elevator back pressure and power during landing to change the airplane's glide path without exceeding the critical angle of attack (your instructor will show you the appropriate use of elevator and power during landing). How do pilots know the proper amount of rearward movement to apply to the elevator? How do they know they won't stall the airplane?

Managing a stalled airplane is one thing; managing your natural instincts, another.

Bad Thing

I recall a student who was a quick study and was a real pleasure to teach. During his first introduction to stalls he elected to pull all the way back on the elevator control and hold it there. He couldn't talk. He just looked at me, pointed to the elevator control with his right hand and said, "BAD THING." Because of this, the airplane remained in a stalled condition.

When stalled, the flight controls are relatively ineffective. As one wing dipped, he turned the wheel, attempting to raise the paralyzed half of the plane. Discovering that his controls were ineffective, he reached over and grabbed mine (I just love it when that happens!). He was thinking I might have played a dirty trick by somehow disabling his set of flight controls.

Upon discovering that my controls didn't work either, he grabbed my arm and made a sound somewhat similar to the stall horn but higher in pitch (probably causing bats to fly into walls). Once he let go of the controls, the airplane nosed forward on its own (as it's designed to do), decreased its angle of attack and recovered from the stall all by itself. Had he intentionally lowered the nose in the first place, I wouldn't have had an enormous bruise on my arm.

If there was an angle of attack indicator in your airplane, stall recognition would be easy. You'd simply keep the angle of attack less than what's critical for that wing. Angle of attack indicators, although valuable, are very rare in small airplanes. Fortunately, there are several ways to recognize a stall's warning signs.

Five Stall Warning Signs

There are five good early warning clues to indicate the onset of a stall. Good pilots know and watch for all of them.

First, an unmistakable buffet or shaking is usually felt in the airplane and on the flight controls. You might think your instructor is shaking the other set of controls trying to get you to let go of them. Not true. As airflow begins to separate from the top of the wing, it buffets (burbles). For those with only food on their mind, this is *BUFF*-ETTES, *not* BOO-*FAYS*. One means getting lunch, the other can mean losing it. Inside the cockpit, this buffet is felt as vibration and is one of the best early warning clues to an impending stall. If you feel this buffet, simply release some of the backward pressure on the elevator until the buffeting stops.

Second, flight control response usually diminishes when the airplane approaches a stall. If you feel the controls becoming mushy or less effective, this is your cue that things aren't going well. Think stall. Think lower angle of attack. Think quickly.

Third, when the airspeed indicator is nearing the beginning of the white or green arc, you're approaching stall territory. Airplanes must have airspeed to fly. Slow the airplane down too much and it will eventually stall.

Keep an eye on the airspeed indicator and make sure it's a healthy distance above the beginning of the green arc. This is the power-off stalling speed without flaps and gear extended (called the *clean configuration*). When approaching to land, the usual recommendation is to keep the airspeed at least 30% above stall speed. This gives you room to accommodate slight, unexpected variations in airspeed caused by poor technique or wind shear. A good visual clue indicating slow speed is when cars on the road below are moving faster than you are. . . at rush hour.

Fourth, a distinct difference in sound occurs when approaching a stall. When I was taking lessons this sound usually came from my instructor yelling, "Lower the nose, goofball, lower the nose!" When airflow strikes the airplane at higher angles of attack, it often makes a different, but recognizable sound.

Fifth, all modern airplanes have stall warning horns or lights. These tattletale devices activate a few knots above stall speed and provide an excellent pre-stall warning—when they're working and when the pilot's listening. On some airplanes it's difficult to test the stall warning horn during the preflight walkaround. That means you won't know it's not working until you need it. You will also be surprised what you can ignore while concentrating on the radio, your instructor, or the pretty colors on all the gauges. That's why you must use *all the clues*, not just one or two.

Aside from these five basic stall warning signs, the seat of your pants provides an additional clue. Let me explain.

Stalling Speed, Gee Whiz And G-Force

Ever watched somebody use a personal computer when something goes wrong? What's the first thing they do? They repeat what they just did, as if the electrons might go with a different flow the second or third time around.

Computers are highly predictable, and so are airplanes. For instance, when the weight of an airplane increases, the aircraft will stall at higher speeds. That's right, every time. Son of a gun.

Let's assume that a lightly loaded airplane begins flying at 42 knots when the angle of attack is slightly less than its critical value (Figure 28, Airplane A). At 42 knots, just enough lift is developed to equal the airplane's weight (although the airplane is on the verge of a stall). An increase in weight means the wings must develop more lift to remain airborne. Certainly the airplane won't fly at or beyond its critical angle of attack (18 degrees for *this* airplane) since this is the built-in design limit of the wing.

Under these conditions, the only way a heavier airplane can develop more lift is to move forward at a slightly faster speed. A heavier airplane in our example might need a minimum forward speed of 48 knots before the wings develop enough lift to equal the increase in weight as shown by Airplane B.

The critical angle of attack at which the wing stalls never changes, but the minimum speed at which the airplane begins flying does change. If the airplane is heavier, it stalls at a higher speed. The converse is also true; lighter weights mean slower stall speeds. (I don't want to give you the impression that we start climbing during the takeoff once we're at or slightly above the airplane stall speed. That's not true! We normally

HOW WEIGHT AFFECTS STALL SPEED Fig. 28

Airplane A, weighing only 1300 pounds, starts flying at when it's slightly above 42 knots and the wing is just a little below its critical angle of attack. Another way of saying this is the airplane's stalling speed is 42 knots at this weight.

A heavier Airplane B needs to develop more lift than its lighter cousin before it can fly. At a little less than its critical angle of attack, Airplane B needs a little more than 48 knots of airflow over its wings before lift equals weight. In other words, the stalling speed of the heavier Airplane B is 48 knots. Despite weight differences between Airplanes A and B, both airplanes stall at the same critical angle of attack.

HOW CENTRIFUGAL FORCE CAUSES YOU AND THE AIRPLANE TO FEEL HEAVIER IN A TURN

A During a sharp turn on a level road, you feel a newly generated force known as "centrifugal force." This force pushes you out the door while gravity pulls you downward. If the door pops open, you'll move in the direction of the resultant force.

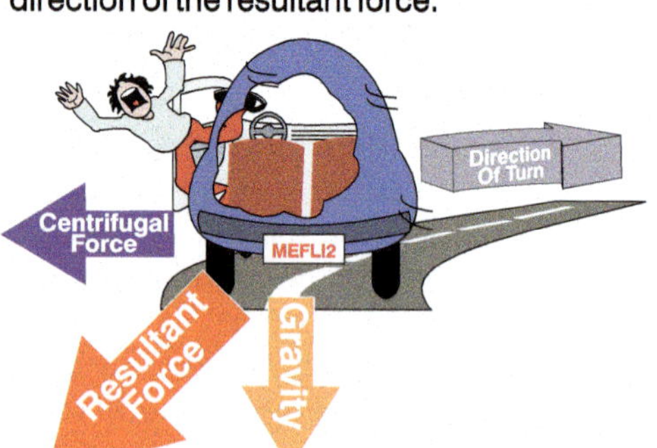

B Turning on a banked road causes the resultant force to pull you straight down in your seat. The sharper the turn in the car, the greater the resultant force or G-force you feel in your seat (i.e., the heavier you feel).

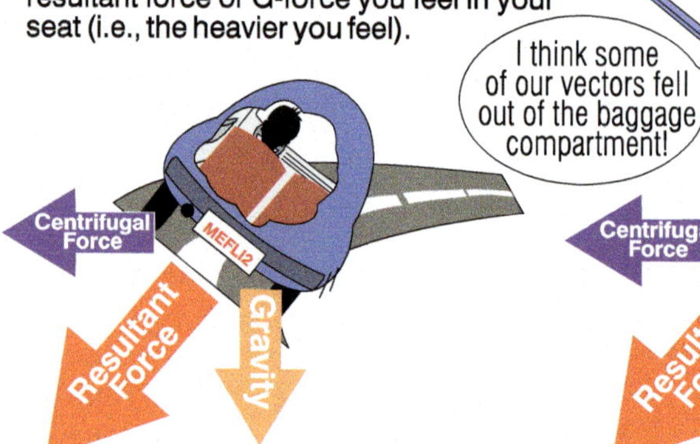

C Airplanes in a bank feel this same increase in G-force (load factor). Remember, if you feel heavier in a turn, then the airplane also feels heavier. Therefore the airplane must increase its lift to remain aloft in a turn.

Fig. 29

accelerate to a safe margin above stall speed—30% or more depending on what your flight instructor recommends—then climb.)

Here's the question that wins a free pizza: Is it possible to make the airplane think it weighs more without adding any weight to it? May I have the envelope, please? The answer is *yes*. (Mushroom, no anchovies, thank you.) "Gee whiz," you're probably saying. No, not gee whiz, or Cheese Whiz, but simply G.

Think back to the last time you were on a rollercoaster. On the straightaway all you felt was speed. Turns, however, forced you down in the seat. You experienced an increase in your apparent weight when turning because of something known as centrifugal force. This is the same force that makes you feel you might fall out of the car while turning if your seat belt isn't fastened (Figure 29).

Because airplanes bank (like cars on a banked road), centrifugal force and gravity pull you down in your seat. You and the airplane can expect to feel this apparent increase in weight during a turn. The wings don't know what's causing the airplane to feel heavier, and frankly, my dear, they don't give a darn. They only know that it's getting heavier.

The steeper the turn, the greater the centrifugal force and the more you and the airplane appear to become heavier. This force is often called *G-force*. Perhaps it was so named because students often say, "Geeeeeeeeeee" whenever they feel their apparent weight increase. The term the pocket protector set (or engineers) use for G-force is *load factor* (we'll use both terms synonymously).

Figure 30 shows a load factor vs. bank chart. Using this chart we can assess the exact amount of G-force you'll experience in any given bank while maintaining altitude. According to this chart, a 60 degree bank produces 2Gs. This means you and the airplane feel twice as heavy as you actually are. If the airplane weighed 2,300 pounds, its structure is required to support 4,600 pounds in a 60 degree bank at a constant altitude.

Here is the most important point about increasing the G-force (finger in the ear again!). *If the airplane feels twice as heavy as it actually is, then the lift must double if the airplane is to maintain altitude.* How can you increase lift? Creating a larger angle of attack by applying elevator back pressure, going faster by increasing the power, or a combination of both will increase the airplane's lift production.

During steep turns you typically apply back pressure on the elevator control while attempting to maintain your altitude. This increases your angle of attack and increases lift to compensate for the increasing G force (Figure 31). Prior to entering a slight bank at an airspeed of 100

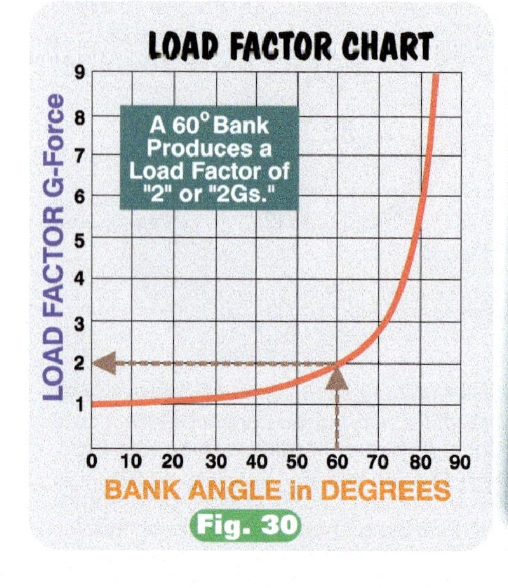

Fig. 30

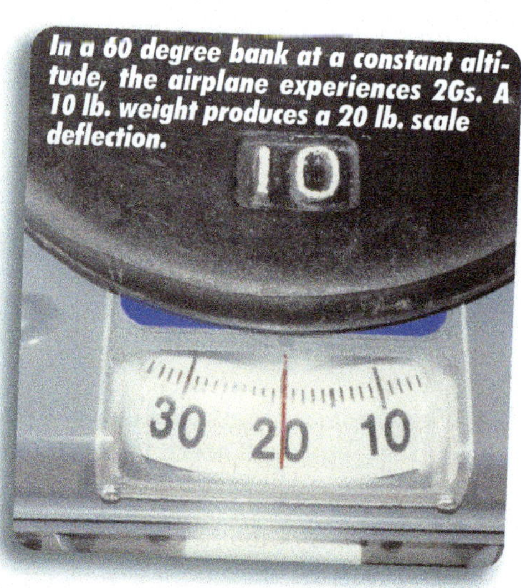

In a 60 degree bank at a constant altitude, the airplane experiences 2Gs. A 10 lb. weight produces a 20 lb. scale deflection.

knots, this airplane's angle of attack was 4 degrees. With a slight bank, back pressure is required and the angle of attack increases to 6 degrees as shown by Airplane A. The increased angle of attack provides an increase in lift but it also exposes more of the wing's underside to the airflow and increases drag. Now the airspeed drops to 93 knots.

As the angle of bank steepens the angle of attack must be increased to maintain altitude. The airspeed continues to decrease because of the increased drag. Airplanes B, C and D depict this sequence. If you were paying attention back in the stall department, you can see where this flight is going. When the bank is very steep, the airplane reaches its critical angle of attack as shown by Airplane D. Having slowed to 84 knots, Airplane D is now at its critical angle of attack. Any further attempt to increase the bank while holding altitude stalls the airplane.

ANGLE OF BANK AND ANGLE OF ATTACK RELATIONSHIP

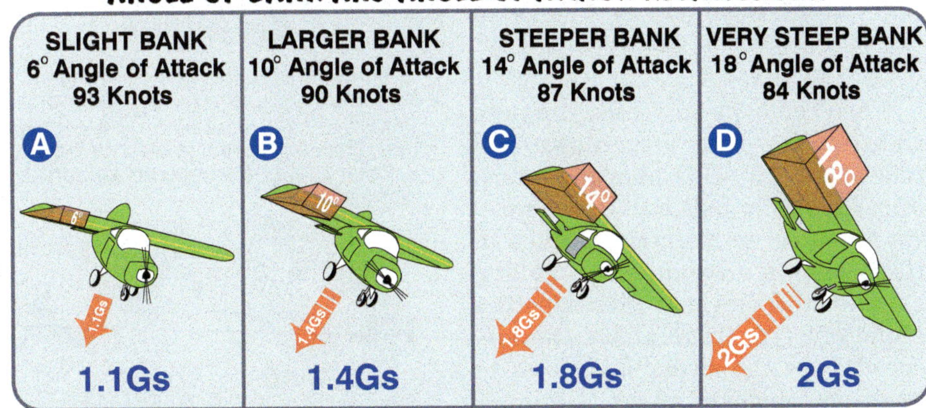

As the angle of bank is increased in level flight, the angle of attack must increase to maintain the necessary lift. As the angle of attack increases so does the lift and the drag which causes the airspeed to decrease. Eventually the angle of attack required for level flight reaches its critical value (Airplane D). A further increase in angle of attack will cause the airplane to stall at a very high speed (also known as an *accelerated stall*).

Fig. 31

There are five good early warning clues to indicate the onset of a stall. Good pilots know and watch for all of them.

While this particular airplane stalled at 60 knots in level flight, it now stalls at 84 knots in a very steep bank. The moral of this story is that an increase in weight (apparent or real) causes the speed at which the airplane stalls to increase. In other words, when you feel an increase in G-force (load factor), the airplane's stalling speed is also increasing.

Normally you would increase your power in a steep turn to prevent the airspeed from getting too slow. Giving this particular airplane full throttle in a very steep turn might keep the airspeed at 90 knots. This gives you a 6 knot buffer above the steep turn stalling speed in this example. Of course, this assumes that your engine is capable of producing this extra power in the first place. This simply isn't an option in our smaller, horsepower anemic airplanes, is it?

The increase in stall speed with bank angle is as predictable as a politician's addiction to podiums. Figure 32 shows that a 60 degree bank increases stall speed by 40%. This is certainly nice information to know, but are you expected to carry a Cray supercomputer and punch in percentages prior to any turn? Of course not. What you need to have is a high index of suspicion. If the seat of your pants says you're weighing in at a level that qualifies you for the main event on a heavyweight boxing card, you should think (quickly) about how the stall speed increases in a turn. For those of you frightened by higher math (adds, takeaways, times and goes-intos) there is an easier way to calculate this.

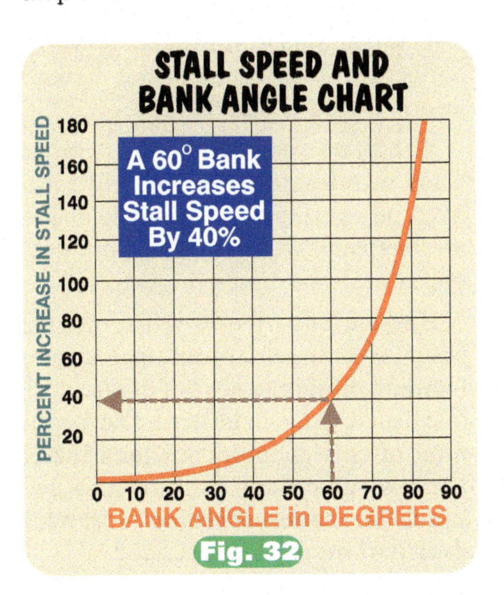

Fig. 32

Figure 33 is typical of the stall charts found in most owners' manuals. It provides you with the stall speeds for specific angles-of-bank under variable flap conditions (we'll discuss flaps in a bit).

Avoiding stalls while in a steep bank with smaller, power-limited airplanes means you must be prepared to do two things. At the first sign of a stall, you must unload the wings by releasing back pressure on the elevator and simultaneously reducing the angle of bank. This decreases the load factor and reduces the stall speed.

For example, assume that you're in the traffic pattern and are making a turn onto final approach. Because of poor planning (it happens to everyone once in a while), you find yourself

STALL SPEED CHART

Power Off **Stalling Speeds** Knots =IAS

Gross Weight 2,550 lbs. / Condition	Angle Of Bank 0°	30°	45°	60°
Flaps Up	50	54	59	71
Flaps 10°	42	45	50	59
Flaps 30°	40	43	48	57

Fig. 33

overshooting the runway centerline. Increasing the bank is a natural response to prevent overshooting—but it's also a risky one.

When the bank increases, the nose wants to lower or pitch down (I'll talk about why this happens later). Pilots typically pull back on the elevator control to maintain altitude in response to a dropping nose. Pulling back on the elevator increases the angle of attack and slows the airspeed. Now the airplane is closer to its critical angle of attack at a lower airspeed. If the airplane was flying slow to begin with, the airplane may stall. What's the solution?

Whenever you are making a turn, especially when close to the ground, be especially sensitive to the amount of bank you use. *Be sensitive to the G-force you experience.* If you feel your apparent weight increasing, you now know your stall speed is also increasing. Your derriere becomes the ultimate stall sensing device (and to think you've been packing that thing around all these years and didn't realize its usefulness). This is what is called, "flying by the seat of your pants." If anyone accuses you of sitting down on the job, you just tell them you're testing your stall detector.

By the way, there is a time when we want our wings to stall before they experience too many Gs. The speed at which this occurs is called the "design maneuvering speed." (See Postflight Briefing #2-5).

DEFLECTING AN ADVERSARY

The martial arts master gently deflects his opponent's energy in the vertical (up or down) direction. The master feels little horizontal resistance but his assailant feels an unusual amount of discomfort.

Fig. 34

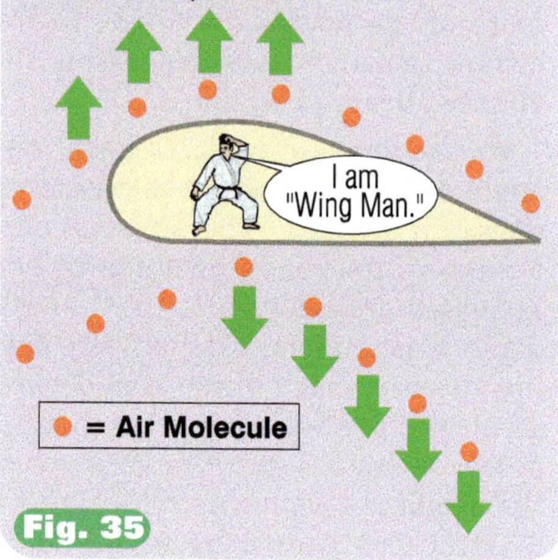

THE WING & THE MASTER

Think of the wing doing the same thing as the martial arts master. The wing deflects the air molecules vertically (up or down), attempting to produce as little horizontal resistance as possible.

Fig. 35

DRAG

What a Drag

You can't get something for nothing in aviation. Although Burt Rutan (a famed airplane designer) comes close, there is no free lunch when it comes time for an airfoil to pay for the lift it develops. Drag is that price.

Drag is the natural response to an object's movement through the air. Try an experiment. Stick your head out a moving automobile (amazing what you can learn about flying while sticking parts of you out a car window). At 60 MPH your mouth puffs open, your eyes bug out, your head is thrown back and your hair looks like it was blow dried with a Pratt & Whitney jet engine. You look like a rock star! This is all the result of the wind resistance known as drag.

Horizontal and Vertical Movement of Air

An Aikido martial arts master is trained to deflect his adversary vertically without offering any resistance in the horizontal direction. Upon encountering a head-on adversary, the Aikido master makes the Bruce Lee karate call sound and gently deflects the assailant either upward or downward (Figure 34).

Wings do something very similar. They are designed, as you will recall from our earlier discussion, to deflect air vertically while offering very little horizontal resistance (Figure 35).

Regardless of how efficient the wing is, some horizontal resistance to forward motion is always present. We discussed drag briefly at the beginning of this chapter, but let's take a somewhat closer look at the two kinds of speed retardant—*parasite drag* and *induced drag*.

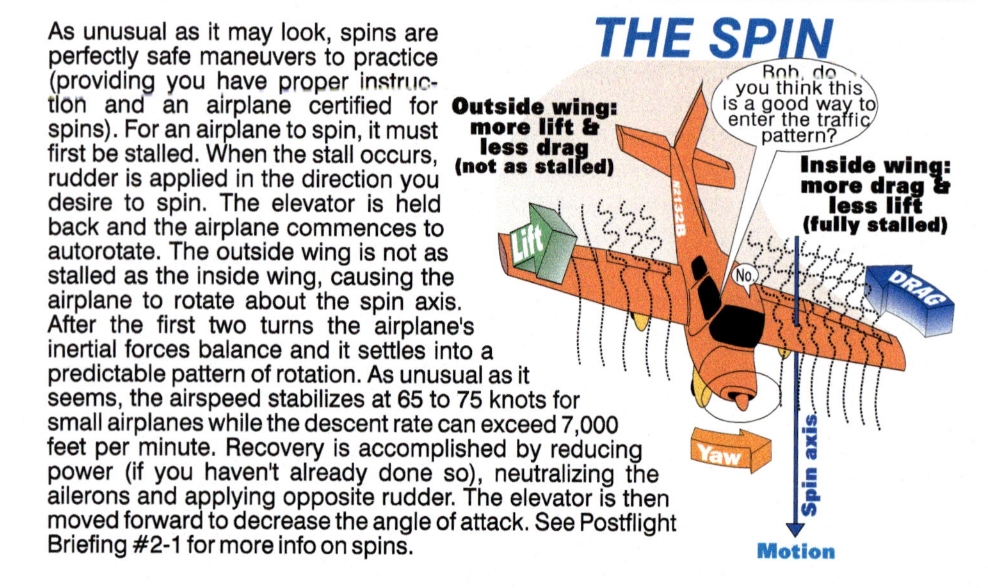

As unusual as it may look, spins are perfectly safe maneuvers to practice (providing you have proper instruction and an airplane certified for spins). For an airplane to spin, it must first be stalled. When the stall occurs, rudder is applied in the direction you desire to spin. The elevator is held back and the airplane commences to autorotate. The outside wing is not as stalled as the inside wing, causing the airplane to rotate about the spin axis. After the first two turns the airplane's inertial forces balance and it settles into a predictable pattern of rotation. As unusual as it seems, the airspeed stabilizes at 65 to 75 knots for small airplanes while the descent rate can exceed 7,000 feet per minute. Recovery is accomplished by reducing power (if you haven't already done so), neutralizing the ailerons and applying opposite rudder. The elevator is then moved forward to decrease the angle of attack. See Postflight Briefing #2-1 for more info on spins.

Drag is a very complicated subject. I've seen both blood and entire pots of coffee spilled over the lurid details of a subject so arcane that even engineers with multiple degrees disagree. If you want some ammunition for the next session of hangar flying or want more indepth information, see Postflight Briefing #2-2 at the end of the chapter.

For the moment, what you need to know is that there are two kinds of drag. Parasite drag is the result of friction. Trying to move something through the air results in friction with air molecules. This resistance isn't useful and that's why it's called parasite drag. It's there because it's there. Hang on to the idea that as airspeed doubles, parasite drag quadruples, and there's very little you can do about it. Rats!

Induced drag is resistance to motion *induced* by the wing turning some of its lift into drag. (See Postflight Briefing #2-2 if you want a more detailed understanding of induced drag.) What you need to know here is that induced drag does the complete opposite of parasite drag—it increases as the airplane slows down.

Total Drag and Your Go Far Speed

What does all this talk about parasite and induced drag mean to you as a pilot? It could mean as little as knowing how to save a few bucks on fuel, or it could mean as much as knowing how to protect your remarkably fragile hide in the event of an emergency.

I gather I now have your full attention again?

As the airplane speeds up, induced drag decreases while parasite drag increases. Hmm. Is there a specific speed, a number better than all other numbers, where the total drag on the airplane is at a minimum? Yea verily, there is.

Figure 36 shows the airplane's *total drag curve,* affirming that—unlike Bigfoot, the Loch Ness Squid and Elvis—a minimum drag speed actually exists. When the induced and parasite drag curves are added together to produce a total drag curve, there is always a point where the sum of both curves is at a minimum. The lowest spot in the total drag curve is your magic number, a specific airspeed known as the *best L/D speed* (pronounced "best L over D speed," which stands for "lift over drag"). Put your finger back in your ear again, this is important! *Since minimum drag occurs at this speed, minimum thrust for forward flight must also occur at this speed.* So it is written. Verily, so it will be! Wow, this is good stuff!

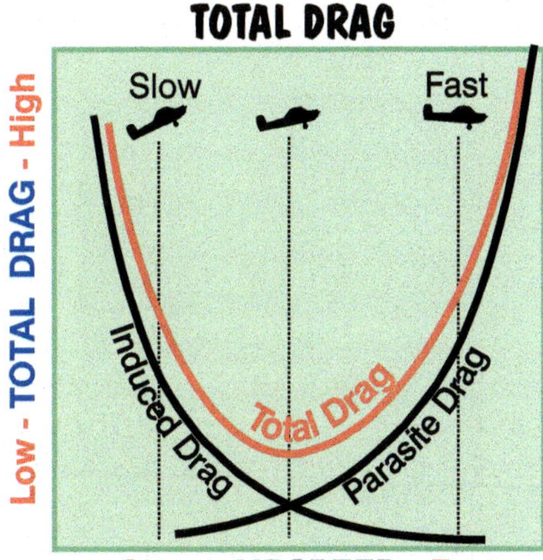

Parasite drag increases with increasing airspeed while induced drag decreases with increasing airspeed. The total drag curve is a summation of both types of drag. The lowest point on the total drag curve is the point where the airplane experiences the least amount of drag.

Fig. 36

Minimum thrust means we obtain maximum forward distance for a given amount of fuel consumption. The best L/D speed yields the maximum range for a tank (or a gallon or a thimbleful) of fuel in a no-wind condition. If L's and D's and minimum thrust don't stick well, try thinking of this magic number as your "maximum range" or "go far" speed. (See Postflight Briefing #2-3 for a more detailed discussion of the airplane's maximum endurance and maximum range capabilities.)

This speed also yields the airplane's maximum power-off glide range, which is where the saving your hide part comes in. "Power-off glide" is a nice way of saying the engine isn't working at the moment and you are now the pilot of a glider, looking for a landing spot. So immediately establish the proper gliding attitude and airspeed. This is a time when you will want the ability to go as far as is necessary to find that spot.

Figure 37 shows an excerpt from the Cessna 210's Pilot Operating Handbook (POH). This is the maximum distance power-off glide speed for this airplane. This speed should be as familiar to you as sandpaper is to a safecracker. Know the number for your airplane.

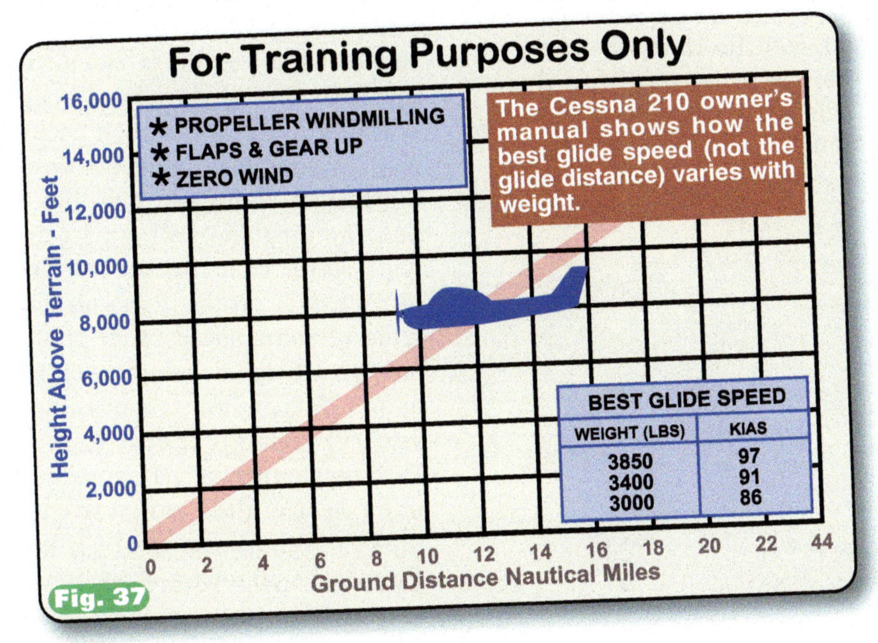

BEST GLIDE SPEED	
WEIGHT (LBS)	KIAS
3850	97
3400	91
3000	86

Fig. 37

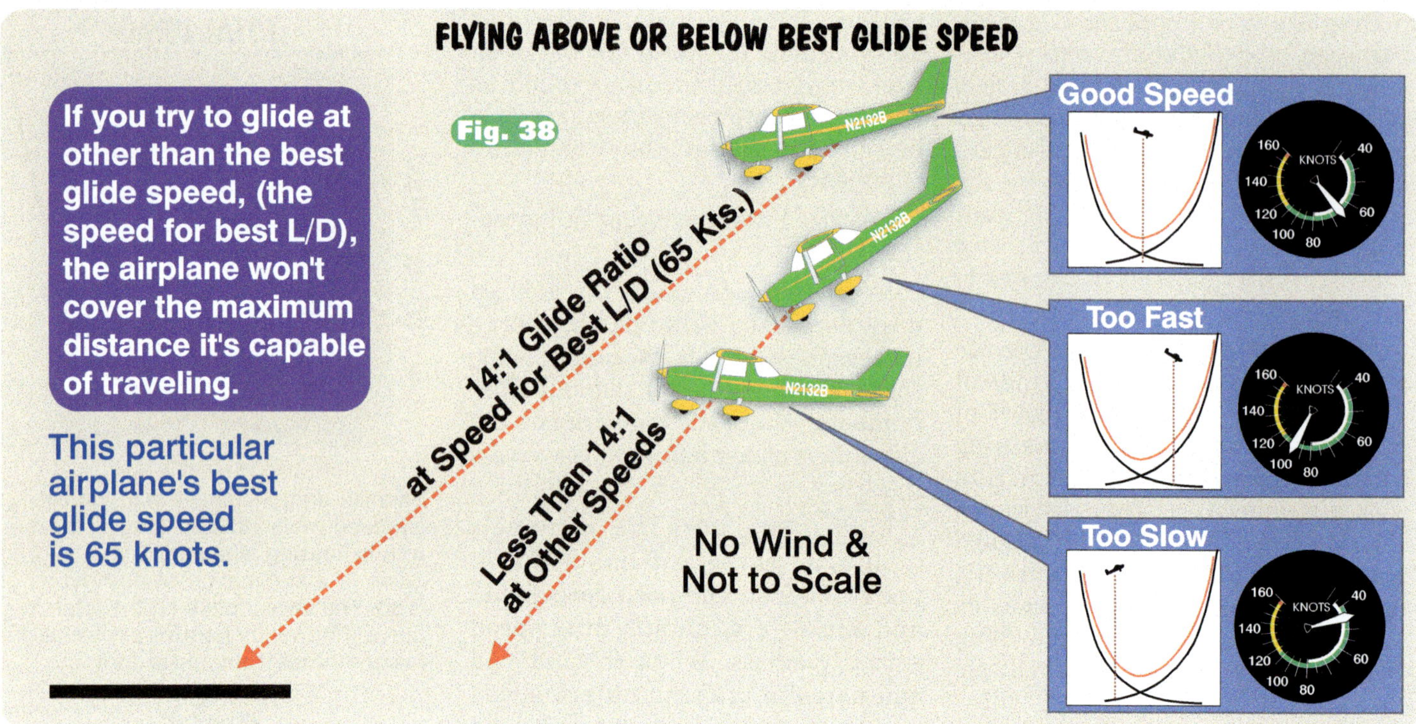

Stretching the Glide, Saving the Hide

A friend of mine was reading the newspaper *USA Today* (he's into primary colors). He said, "Hey Rod, it says here on page 13 that 52% of the American public is mathematically illiterate." I said, "That's not a good sign." He replied, "Yeah, imagine that, nearly one-third of the population can't do math!"

As a precaution, I have avoided, to the extent possible, using mathematics in this book. However, I want you to think of L/D as a ratio of lift to drag. Don't think about a ratio as a "goes-into" or division problem. Think of it as comparing one value (lift) placed on top of another (drag), separated by a line.

A "power-off glide" happens under one of two conditions. One is instructor-induced. It comes accompanied by some ominous-sounding incantation such as "You've just had an engine failure," and the instructor pulling the throttle back to idle. This is a not-really-power-off glide. You may, at this awkward time, be asked what the plane's best L/D speed is, or what the glide ratio is.

The other occasion is a real power-off glide, caused by a real engine failure. This is the time when you wish you were wearing your Kevlar power suit and accompanying roll bar. At moments like that, you really do want to know the best L/D speed and have some idea of what the plane's glide ratio is.

In a power-off glide, the best L/D speed allows the airplane to glide a maximum forward distance with a minimum amount of altitude loss. For example, the DA20 Katana has a lift-over-drag ratio of approximately 14 to 1 (also written as 14:1) at its best L/D speed (65 kts.). At this speed the airplane experiences minimum drag (at the bottom of the total drag curve) and moves 14 feet forward for every foot it descends. No matter what you do to the airplane, this is the best glide ratio it's capable of attaining. You can rock back-and-forth in your seat and yell, "Come on big fellow, come on, yee-hawww!" and the airplane still isn't going to glide better than 14 feet forward for every foot it drops. If you attempt to glide at some speed other than this one, your airplane simply won't glide as far (Figure 38). It's possible that you're sitting there munching Doritos wondering, "Hey, what happens to the glide range if the airplane's weight changes?" If so, see Postflight Briefing #2-4 for more details on this interesting subject.

Fig. 39A Drooped wingtips help create a more efficient wing.

Winglets are another method used to increase wing efficiency. Fig. 39B

WINGTIP VORTEX

Air sneaks from underneath the wing where the pressure is high, to the top of the wing, where the pressure is lower. As the wing moves forward, it creates a spiral of air trailing off the wingtips. This spiral moves outward, upward, and inward, trailing behind the wing.

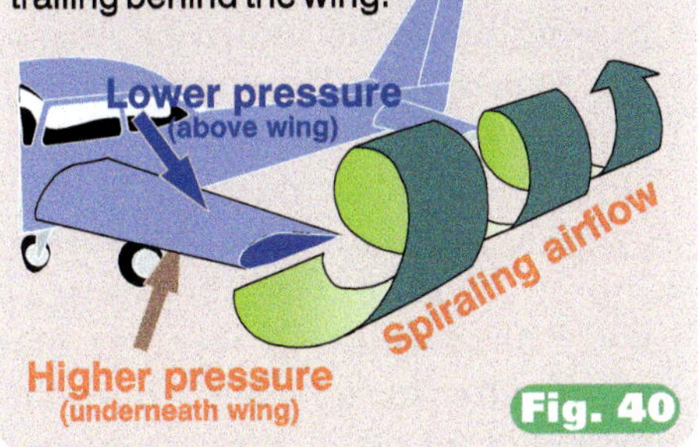

Fig. 40

Now you have a basic idea of how parasite and induced drag affect an airplane and you're ready to take a closer look at how induced drag can fool you into believing your airplane is ready to fly when it isn't.

Ground Effect

The object of golf is to hit the ball the least number of times. Do this and you win. Recently, I was asked to play at a professional tournament. I used a new strategy. I stayed home, never hit the ball, and claimed victory. If wings can bend air, why can't I bend the rules of golf?

Here's one of those nifty pilot nuggets (or nougats) with which you can win a hamburger some day. Is it possible to unbend the air which is bent by the wing at a large angle of attack? Yes, using the wizardry of something called *ground effect.*

Ground effect allows an airplane flying close to the runway to remain airborne at a slightly lower-than-normal speed. During landing, this means the airplane might have a tendency to float (continue to glide just above the runway). During takeoff, the airplane can become airborne before it has sufficient speed to climb. Either event is like buying new glasses, taking them back because you can't read, then finding out you're illiterate. Both cause a lot of chagrin, but a takeoff like this can be dangerous. To understand how ground effect affects an airplane, you need to know something about how wind tries to escape around a wing.

Attempting to climb out of ground effect at too slow a speed can cause the airplane to sink back onto the runway (if there is any runway left to sink back to at this point!).

Remember that a wing generates lift because of increased pressure on its lower surface and decreased pressure over its upper surface. At high angles of attack, this pressure differential is quite large. Large pressure differences cause air molecules to act like lots of little prison inmates, with each molecule waiting for the slightest chance to break out of jail. Given that chance, air molecules underneath the wing would gladly sneak over the top, where lower pressure resides. This reduces the wing's lifting efficiency. Unfortunately, it's difficult to design wings that preclude this escape.

Figures 39A and 39B show several attachments added onto wingtips to thwart escaping air. Drooped wingtips are a common sight on many airplanes. They create a barrier to help contain escaping high pressure air from under the wing. Winglets are another common sight on larger airplanes. They also create a barrier that minimizes the escape of under-the-wing, high pressure air. Since they bend upward, they also give the impression that the airplane attempted to taxi between two closely parked gas trucks.

The perils of ground effect become obvious when you're too fast on the approach!

Air sneaking from under the wing spirals upward and over the wingtip (Figure 40). Couple this spiral with air moving backward over the wing and you get a vortex similar to a horizontal tornado. Called a *wingtip vortex,* this tornado spirals outward, then upward, then inward behind each wing. You can expect this vortex action to increase at large angles of attack, where the pressure differential between the top and bottom of the wing is greater.

If these vortices only affected the air at the wingtips, aerodynamicists would have many fewer design problems. Unfortunately, not only does this vortex spiral around the wingtips, it also adds a downwash or downward flow to the air behind and along the wing's span as shown by Airplane A in Figure 41. The wing itself also thrusts air downward. At higher angles of attack this results in the downward bending of the relative wind in the vicinity of the wing. This newly bent relative wind is often called the *local relative wind*. Recalling that lift is always perpendicular to the relative wind, the total lift now tilts rearward slightly. It does so to remain perpendicular to the newly bent relative wind. Part of the total lift is now acting in a rearward direction. This results in an increase in induced drag at high angles of attack.

When the wing moves close to the ground (usually within one wingspan's length or less), its vortices, thus its downwash, diminish. In other words, the downwash can't shove the air into the ground. Voila, the local relative wind in the vicinity of the wing unbends as shown by Airplane B.

This has the effect of allowing the wing's total lifting force to tilt upward slightly, despite the wing's large angle of attack. An upward tilting of the total lifting force means the airplane experiences less induced drag (less rearward pull of lift). This becomes quite evident when you compare Airplanes A and B in Figure 41. The net result is that it takes less power to produce the necessary lift for flight while in ground effect.

You win the hamburger.

Where to Use Caution

Attempting to emerge from ground effect before the plane is really ready to fly is like a newly hatched butterfly taking off before its wings are dry. It's not going to work. Trying to climb out of ground effect at this slower speed can cause the airplane to sink back onto the runway (if there's any runway left to sink back to at this point!).

WING PERFORMANCE OUT OF GROUND EFFECT

At large angles of attack, wingtip vortices result in a downwash behind the wing. This acts to bend the relative wind and tilt the total lifting force aft (the total lift force tilts so as to remain perpendicular to the bent relative wind). A component of the total lift force, called "effective lift," acts vertically, opposite weight. This is the component responsible for keeping the airplane in the air. Induced drag is part of the total lifting force which pulls the airplane aft. This makes the airplane slow down quicker and prevents faster acceleration.

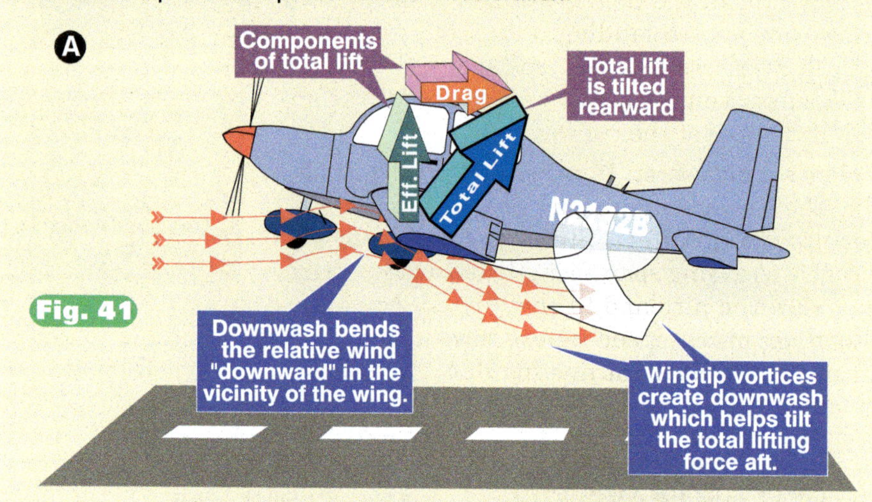

Fig. 41

WING PERFORMANCE IN GROUND EFFECT

At the same large angle of attack within ground effect, the previously bent relative wind (in the vicinity of the wing) is straightened. Downwash can't blow into the ground. Therefore the total lifting force is tilted upward slightly to remain perpendicular to the relative wind. This acts to reduce the rearward pull of induced drag on the airplane, allowing the airplane to become airborne earlier and remain airborne longer (float) with less drag. Therefore, it's possible to float on landing or liftoff at too slow a speed for a safe climb.

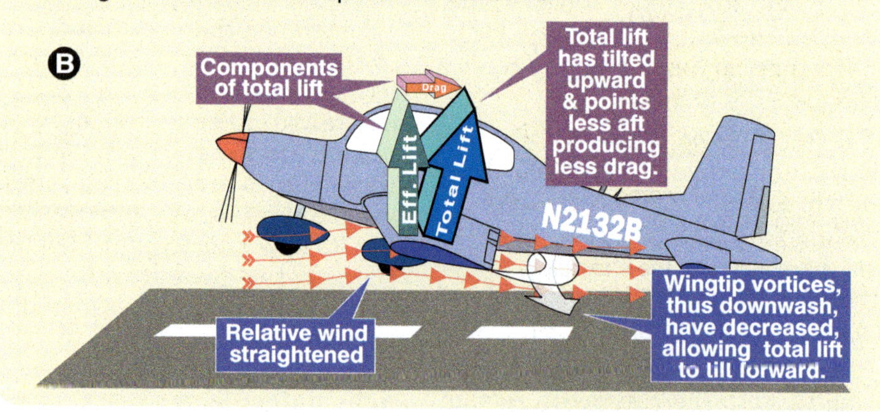

GROUND EFFECT AND PITCH CHANGES

Wing Performance Out of Ground Effect

A — Nose held up

Downwash blows downward on tail which pushes the nose up.

Wing Performance in Ground Effect

B — Nose wants to drop

Downwash diminishes in ground effect and no longer blows down on tail. This causes the nose to pitch down.

Fig. 42

You must reach the airplane's minimum climb speed before charging out of ground effect.

Because of the rather large reduction in induced drag, ground effect can also cause the airplane to float during landing. Higher approach speeds make this particularly noticeable. Certainly this isn't much of a problem if you're landing at the Bonneville Salt Flats (don't try it). If, however, you're landing on a 1,000 foot strip and approach at excessive speed, you might need a contractor's license (you'll need it to rebuild all the houses, fences and sheds at the runway's end).

Here's a big secret. If you're approaching at a speed above the normal approach speed, slow down before entering ground effect. Since ground effect becomes noticeable at a wing span's length and exists until touchdown, slow the airplane to the manufacturer's recommended approach speed before reaching this height. Continue your descent at this speed.

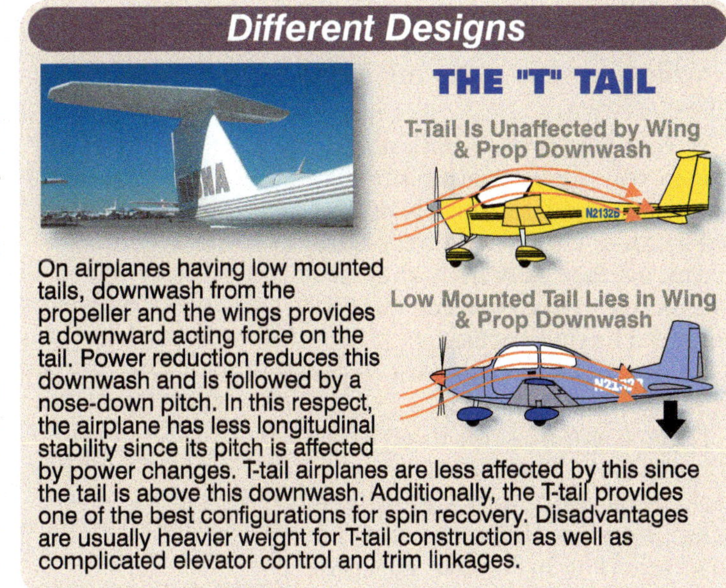

On airplanes having low mounted tails, downwash from the propeller and the wings provides a downward acting force on the tail. Power reduction reduces this downwash and is followed by a nose-down pitch. In this respect, the airplane has less longitudinal stability since its pitch is affected by power changes. T-tail airplanes are less affected by this since the tail is above this downwash. Additionally, the T-tail provides one of the best configurations for spin recovery. Disadvantages are usually heavier weight for T-tail construction as well as complicated elevator control and trim linkages.

Pitch Changes In and Out of Ground Effect

As if floating on landing and an inability to climb after takeoff aren't enough of a problem, expect to experience subtle pitch changes when entering or leaving ground effect. As the airplane becomes airborne and flies out of ground effect, the wing's downwash increases. This blows air downward on the tail as shown by Airplane A in Figure 42. It's possible to become airborne without sufficient speed, then attempt to climb and have the nose pitch up slightly. This is the last thing you want to happen when the speed is low. If you're not prepared for this, it will be an unhappy surprise (and pilots don't like surprises!).

During landing, as the airplane enters ground effect and the downwash diminishes, the nose tends to pitch forward. If you are not prepared for this you might land suddenly or sooner than expected. The secret to managing ground effect is to anticipate it. Expect ground effect to increase when the airplane is within a wing span's height above the runway. Low wing airplanes experience more ground effect than their high wing cousins. Be prepared for a slight nose-up pitch during takeoff and a slight nose-down pitch when landing.

HOW FLAPS CHANGE THE WING'S CURVATURE

Wing Slightly Curved

FLAPS UP

Chord Line

Wing Curved More

FLAPS DOWN

Chord Line

When flaps are lowered, the wing's curvature increases (surface area can increase too) and the chord line moves to increase the wing's angle of attack. This allows the wing to produce more lift for a given airspeed.

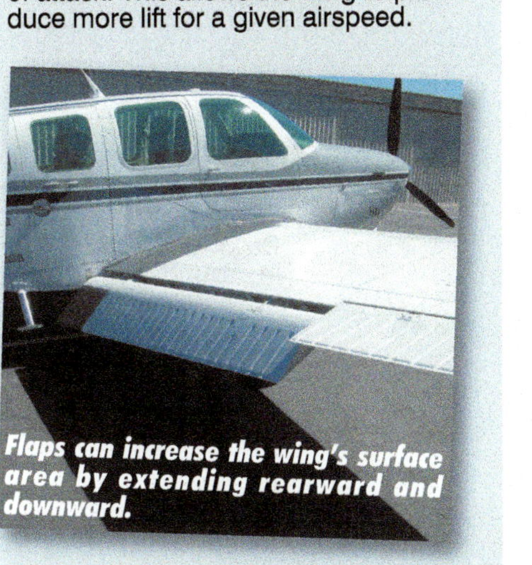

Flaps can increase the wing's surface area by extending rearward and downward.

Fig. 43

Flap Over Flaps

Ever wondered why the wings of large commercial airplanes sprout aluminum prior to takeoff and landing? Fast airplanes require small, thin wings to achieve the eye-popping velocity needed to satisfy today's speed-hungry air traveler. The problem with thin, small wings is that they stall at a very high speed. Most jet airliners would have to take off and land at close to 200 MPH to achieve a safe margin above stall if they couldn't enlarge their wing's surface area and change their camber to create a temporary low speed wing. Engineers, however, design wings to do just that by supplying them with flaps. Extending or retracting flaps changes the wing's lift and drag characteristics.

Lowering flaps lowers the trailing edge of the wing as shown in Figure 43. The wing's lift is increased in two ways. First, the lowered trailing edge increases the angle the chord line makes with the relative wind. Greater lift results from this increased angle of attack. Second, the lowered trailing edge increases the curvature on part of the wing resulting in increased air velocity over the wing's upper surface (many flaps even increase the wing's surface area by extending downward and outward).

Because of the larger angle of attack and greater curvature, flaps provide you with more lift for a given airspeed.

In case you haven't noticed, this is also why flight control surfaces (ailerons, rudders and elevators) work. They change the curvature of the surface to which they are connected. This changes the lift produced by that surface.

Flap Varieties

Flaps come in several varieties (Figure 44). They all serve two basic purposes: to increase lift and drag. Fowler flaps (A) extend downward and backward. This provides a nice addition to wing curvature as well as increasing the surface area of the wing. Fowler flaps are common on smaller single engine Cessnas like the C-150, C-152, C-172 and C-182.

Other varieties of flaps, like the plain type (B), offer an increased wing curvature without an increase in the wing's surface area. Plain flaps are found on airplanes like the Grumman American Yankee trainer. Slotted flaps (C), increase curvature of the wing and add fast moving air to the trailing edge of the wing (fast moving air helps prevent burbling and airflow separation which results in a stall). This type of flap is typical on airplanes like the Piper Warrior and Piper Archer. Split flaps (D), found on airplanes like the Cessna 310, increase the impact energy under the wing, thereby adding to the wing's lift (this impact energy results from the barn door lift we previously discussed). These flaps also add a great deal of drag to the wing.

Why Use Flaps?

What's the reason for putting flaps on small airplanes? First and foremost, they create the lift necessary to maintain flight at slower airspeeds. When landing, your goal is to approach and touch down at a reasonably slow speed. You certainly don't want to touch down at cruise speed. Such a high speed landing might just turn your tires into three little puffs of smoke. Flaps allow you to approach and land at a slower speed while maintaining a safe margin above the stall speed.

A slower speed on touchdown means less runway is used to stop. This is an important consideration if the runway is short. Alternatively, if the wind is gusty, you might consider approaching with little or no flap extension. At the slower speeds allowed by flaps, the airplane becomes more difficult to control (the controls are not as responsive). Let's see how effectively the flaps increase lift by referring to the airspeed indicator (Figure 45).

Since many flaps are painted white (we'll assume they are for this discussion), the airspeed indicator's white arc represents the flap operating range. The beginning of the white arc (B) is known as the power-off, full-flap stalling speed (in nonaccelerated flight at the airplane's maximum allowable weight). It's the speed at which the airplane stalls with flaps fully extended, power off and the gear extended. In Figure 45, the airplane will fly when 53 knots of wind blows over the wings if they are below their critical angle of attack.

The high speed end of the white arc is the maximum speed you may fly with flaps fully extended. Flying beyond this speed can damage the flaps. In this example, you wouldn't want the airspeed indicator to indicate more than 107 knots with flaps extended (some airplanes, however, allow you to fly at a higher speed with partial flaps extended). Bringing broken or bent airplanes back from a flight isn't a good idea, even if they are rentals (you'll find out how bad an idea it is when you get the bill for unbending the metal).

Notice that the white arc (B) begins at a speed seven knots slow-

TYPES OF FLAPS

A Fowler flaps move rearward and downward thereby increasing wing area and wing curvature. High velocity airflow from underneath the wing, flowing up and over the flap, helps delay the onset of a stall.

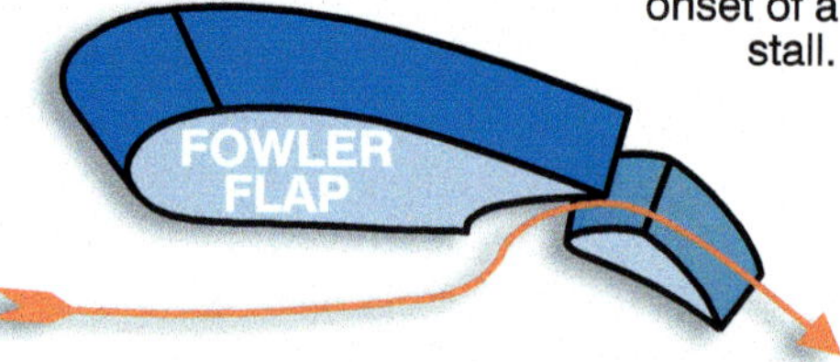

B Plain flaps lower the trailing edge of the wing, increasing its curvature. This acts to increase the wing's lift.

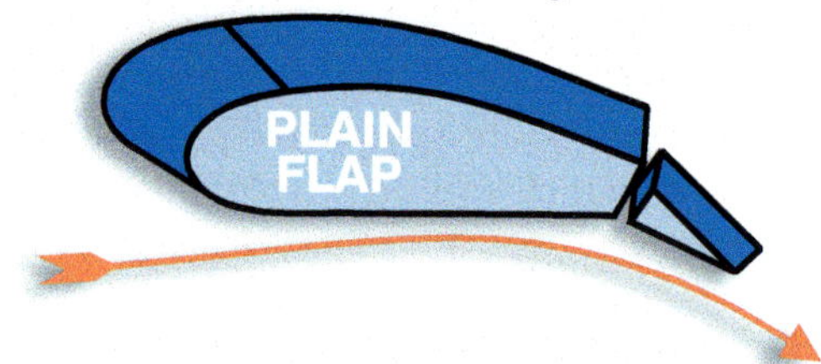

C Slotted flaps allow high velocity airflow from underneath the wing to flow up and over the flap. This helps prevent airflow separation and delays the onset of a stall.

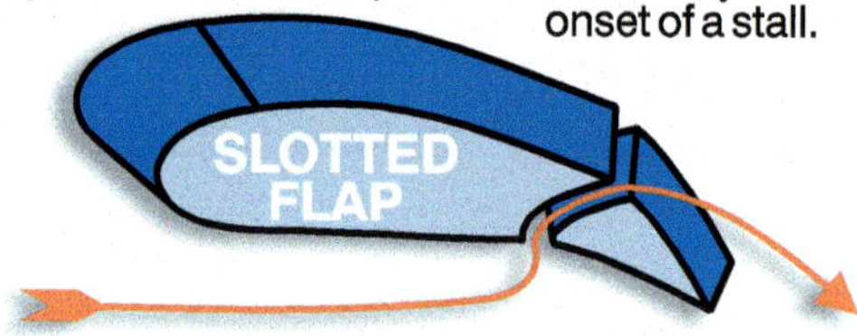

D Split flaps generate some lift and a lot of drag since they disrupt airflow on the underside of the wing.

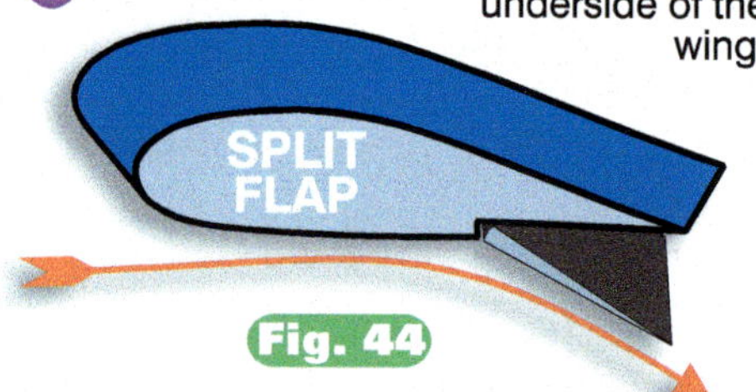

Fig. 44

FLAP SPEED RANGE

Flaps extended - 53 kts. (beginning of white arc)

No flaps - 60 kts. (beginning of green arc)

B A KNOTS 60 80 100 120 140 160 Green Arc White Arc

Fig. 45

er than the green arc (A). From an earlier discussion, we learned that the green arc is the power-off stalling speed with flaps retracted (gear retracted too). This airplane must have 60 knots or more of wind flowing over the wings to fly with flaps retracted. With flaps fully extended, you can touch down at a slower speed—seven knots slower, to be exact (the full flap stall speed on the airspeed indicator assumes the airplane is at its maximum allowable weight).

Application of flaps in the traffic pattern allows you to have better visibility over the airplane's nose, making it easier to observe traffic and see the runway.

But, as Confucius might say, "Man who sow 'wild oats' . . . eventually have crop failure." In other words, you don't get something for nothing. Flaps provide you with lift but they also produce drag. Full flaps create a very low speed wing. Try to accelerate it and at some point, drag defeats your efforts. Fortunately, the first half of flap travel usually provides more lift than drag. The last half usually provides more drag than lift. This is why some aircraft manuals recommend only 10 to 25 degrees of flaps for takeoffs on short fields (usually one or two notches on a three to four notch, manual flap system).

If you're high while on approach to land, you can select full flaps to increase the airplane's drag. It's considered normal to use flaps only when descending within the traffic pattern and not when descending from cruise flight. After all, cruise flight descents are efficient and fast at higher speeds where the parasite drag is greater. If you wanted to descend with flaps from cruise flight, you'd have to slow the airplane down below maximum flap extension speed (the top of the white arc) before applying flaps. This would be cumbersome. The airplane can descend faster at cruise speed with reduced power while getting you to your destination sooner.

Since flaps provide more lift at slower speeds, think carefully about how and when they are retracted while airborne. If you're making a full flap approach and it's necessary to go around (i.e., give up this approach, climb, and return for another landing attempt), don't retract the flaps all at once! This would be like having someone remove a part of your wing at a slow speed. The sudden and often dramatic increase in stall speed could place you near a stall before you can accelerate to a safer speed. Apply full power first, then retract the flaps in increments. In airplanes with 30 to 40 degrees of flap extension, retract the flaps to their least-drag/maximum-lift position. Usually, this position is found at one-half flap travel (depending on the airplane). In airplanes with three notches of manually applied flaps, retract one notch first, followed by the other two once the airplane begins to accelerate.

Do be careful in low wing airplanes when the flaps are up and someone is standing on the inboard section of the wing (be especially careful if you're airborne at the time—you're in a Twilight Zone movie). A friend was on the checkride for his private pilot's license when he damaged the FAA checkpilot. Before takeoff, the check pilot boarded the airplane, realized he forgot something and decided to return to the flight school. He opened the door, stepped out on the wing over an "approved step" as labeled on the inboard flap section. My friend, realizing that he hadn't checked the flaps during the preflight, decided to lower the hand-lever-activated flaps. An "ahhhhhhh," then "thud," were heard. The checkpilot went aerobatic and fell straight down. My friend, trying to break the tension with a little humor, looked over and said, "Hey, while you're down there, how about checking those tires for me?" On his second checkride . . .

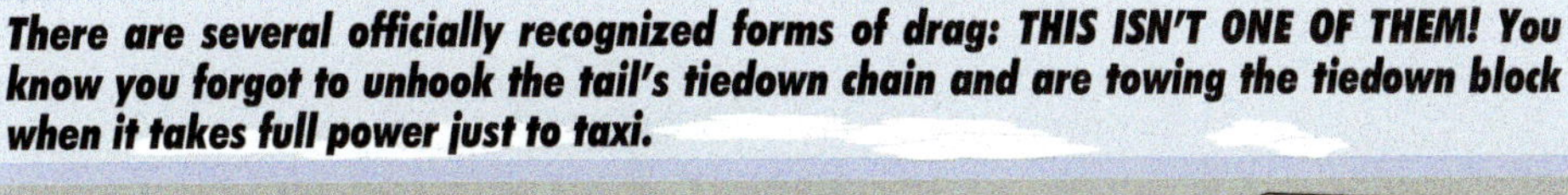

There are several officially recognized forms of drag: THIS ISN'T ONE OF THEM! You know you forgot to unhook the tail's tiedown chain and are towing the tiedown block when it takes full power just to taxi.

How Airplanes Turn

There are many misconceptions in aviation. For instance, there are pilots who think prop-wash is a highly specialized detergent. And a select few think that carburetor ice comes in three flavors. Sometimes pilots even have misconceptions about how airplanes turn. Let's examine what causes an airplane to turn, then look at how to perform this nifty little maneuver.

As a young student pilot, an FAA inspector asked me how an airplane turns. I looked at him and said, "With the wheel, sir." He clutched his chest and shook his head in disbelief. I admit that my answer was a little off and that he was a tad upset (the foam from around his mouth and his eyebrows merging with his hairline were good clues). Nevertheless, shouldn't I get partial credit? I guess Mother Nature doesn't grade on a curve.

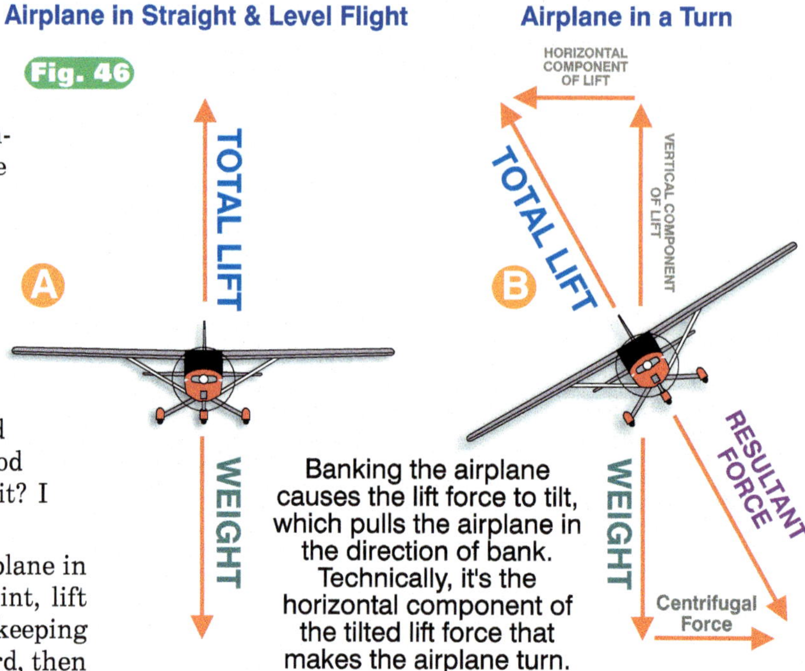

Airplane A in Figure 46 shows a view of an airplane in straight, wings-level flight. From this vantage point, lift acts vertically. Lift pulls upward on the airplane, keeping it suspended in flight. Surely, if lift can pull upward, then it can pull a little to the left or right. When it does this, the airplane turns. (To be precise about it, lift actually pushes upward on the wing but I'll use the term *pull* instead. It makes the concept of forces a little easier to visualize.)

OK, so how do you make an airplane turn? If you said, "With the wheel," I am deeply indebted and promise not to have a heart attack. In fact, turning the wheel or deflecting the control stick (i.e., banking the airplane with ailerons), is exactly how we tilt the total lifting force and start a turn (I'll explain control usage shortly).

Airplane B shows the total lift force in a banked airplane. Part of the lift force pulls the airplane up (the vertical component of lift) and part pulls the airplane in the direction of the turn (the horizontal component of lift). You can use your imagination and visualize two separate and smaller forces making up the total lifting force. (There are those arrows again. You will not see these on a real airplane, so enjoy them while you can.) The arrows simply represent the forces of lift.

If you're asked why an airplane turns, respond by saying that it's the horizontal component of lift that's responsible. The horizontal component of lift pulls the airplane in an arc. The larger the angle of bank, the greater the horizontal component and the quicker the airplane can turn.

The horizontal component of lift is responsible for turning the airplane.

Remember, you never get something for nothing. Tilting the total lift force while in a turn means less lift is available to act vertically against the airplane's weight, as shown by Airplane B in Figure 46. The airplane responds by moving in the direction of the momentarily larger force—downward, in the direction of weight. We compensate for this by increasing our lift slightly whenever we enter a turn. By now, diligent student that you are, you know that applying back pressure on the elevator will increase the angle of attack which increases the airplane's total lift. Unfortunately, the increase in angle of attack also increases the drag which slows the airplane down. In a shallow banked turn (somewhere around 30 degrees or less) this decrease in speed isn't a concern. Steeper turns (45 degrees or more) may require the addition of power to prevent the airspeed from decreasing too much.

Your job as a pilot is to keep The Four Forces acting on an airplane under control and in balance. To do so you need to know something about the airplane's flight control system.

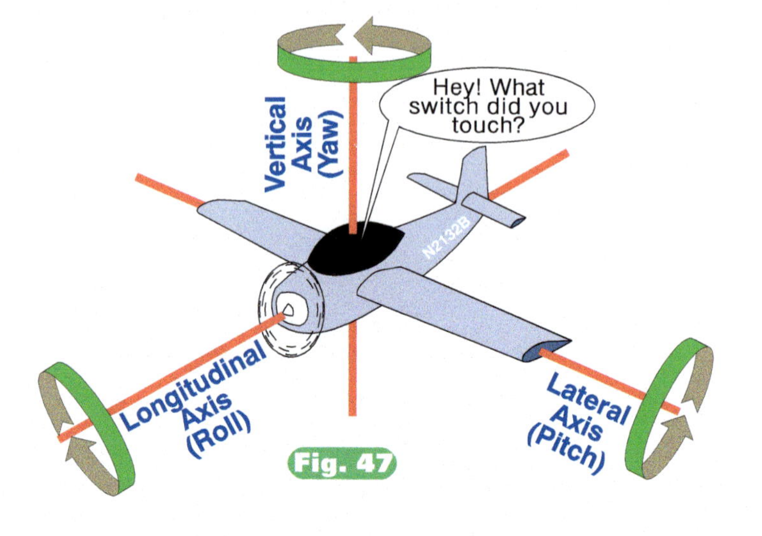

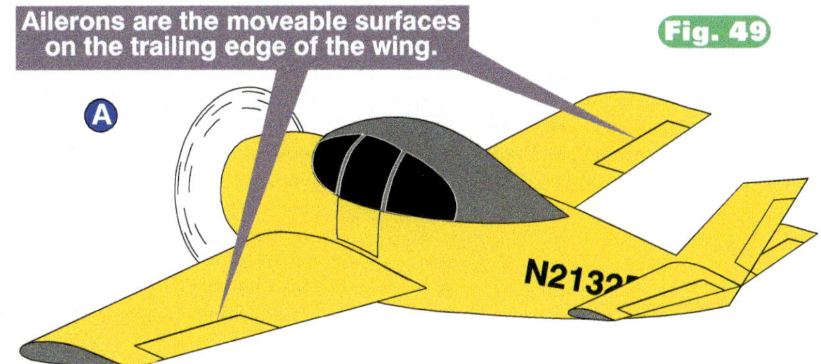

Flight Controls

If you're ready-made pilot material you've been patiently licking your chops waiting for the discussion on flight controls. Gandhi would applaud your patience (but Gandhi isn't here, so I will). Figure 47 shows the three imaginary axes of the airplane. By use of the flight controls, the airplane can be made to rotate about one or more of these axes.

The longitudinal or long axis runs through the centerline of the airplane from nose to tail. Airplanes *roll* or *bank* about their longitudinal axis.

A sideways pass in football is called a lateral pass. Similarly, the lateral axis runs sideways through the airplane from wingtip to wingtip. Airplanes *pitch* about their lateral axis.

The vertical axis of the airplane runs up and down from the cockpit to the belly. Airplanes *yaw* about their vertical axis. Think of yawing motion as *yawning* motion. In the morning you yawn by standing and stretching vertically, rotating right and left, waiting for those vertebra to kick in. Let's examine each of the three main flight controls that cause an airplane to move about its axes.

Ailerons

Ailerons are the moveable surfaces on the outer trailing edges of the wings (Figure 48). Their purpose is to bank the airplane in the direction you want to turn (Figure 49). When the control wheel is turned to the right or the left, the ailerons simultaneously move in opposite directions. One raises and one lowers as shown by Airplanes B & C in Figure 49 (this doesn't mean they're broken either). Ailerons work this way on purpose, allowing one wing to develop more lift and the other to develop less. Differential lift banks the airplane, which tilts the total lifting force in the direction you want to turn.

A lowered aileron increases the curvature, angle of attack and lift on a portion of the wing as shown by Figure 49D. Conversely, an upward moving aileron reduces the angle of attack, decreases the curvature and decreases the lift on a portion of the wing as shown by Figure 49E. (Any reference to control wheel also applies to airplanes with a control stick.)

While ailerons change the wing's lift, they also change its drag, and the change in drag is different for each wing. This results in the airplane's nose yawing in a direction opposite the direction of turn. Right turn, left yaw. This is referred to as *adverse yaw,* since it tries to turn the airplane opposite the direction the pilot intended to turn.

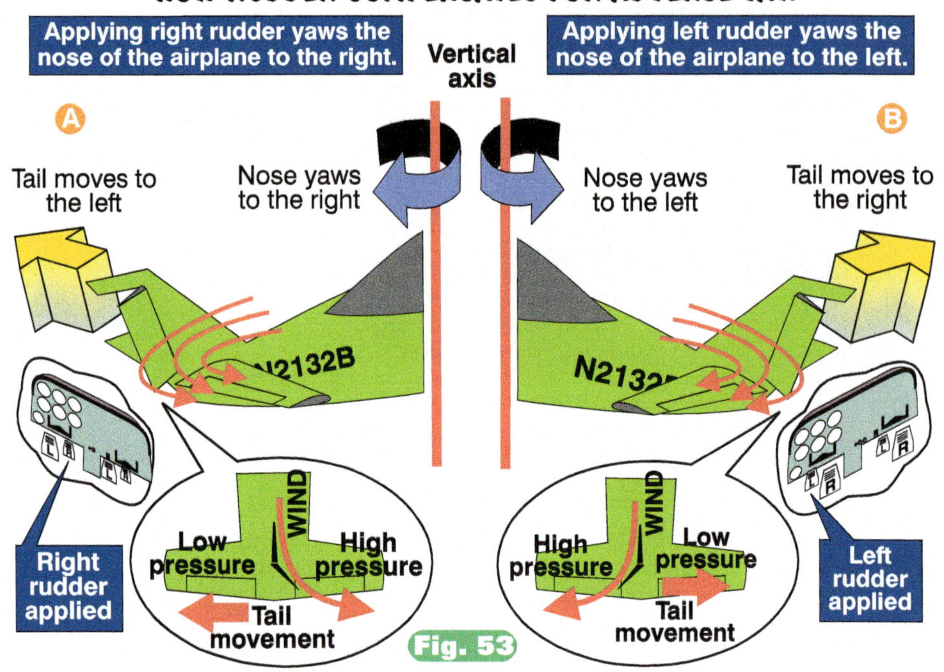

Adverse Yaw

A few old sayings are still floating around that I'd like to revise. For instance, "The pen is mightier than the sword." This is true unless you're one-on-one with a modern incarnation of Zorro. A wonderful saying I wouldn't care to upend is, "You can't get something for nothing." It sure works that way in aviation. When an airfoil develops lift, it's always paid for by an increase in drag. The lift produced by the aileron is no different.

Downward moving ailerons create more lift and thus more drag (Figure 50). This results in *adverse yaw.* For instance, in a right turn, the downward moving aileron on the left wing creates more drag than the upward moving aileron on the right wing as shown in Figure 53A, and the airplane yaws (turns) to the left. A similar and opposite effect occurs with a left control wheel deflection (Figure 53B).

Adverse yaw presents a problem. You can't have the nose yawing or pointing in a different direction than you bank. Fortunately, airplanes have a control surface designed to correct for adverse yaw. It's called a rudder and is shown in Figure 51.

Rudders

The rudder's purpose is to keep the airplane's nose pointed in the direction of turn—not to turn the airplane! Remember, airplanes turn by banking. Rudder simply corrects for adverse yaw and keeps the nose pointing in the direction of turn. Think of a rudder as a vertical aileron located on the tail of the airplane. A right or left deflection of the rudder foot pedals located on the cockpit floor (Figure 52) changes the vertical stabilizer's angle of attack and yaws the airplane about its vertical axis. This yawing motion keeps the airplane's nose pointed in the direction of turn.

Applying right rudder pedal, as shown by Airplane A in Figure 53, forces the tail assembly to swing in the direction of lower pressure. As the tail moves, the airplane rotates

ADVERSE YAW

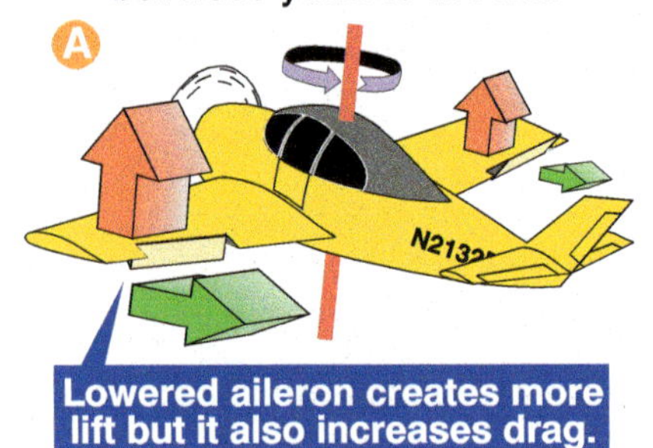

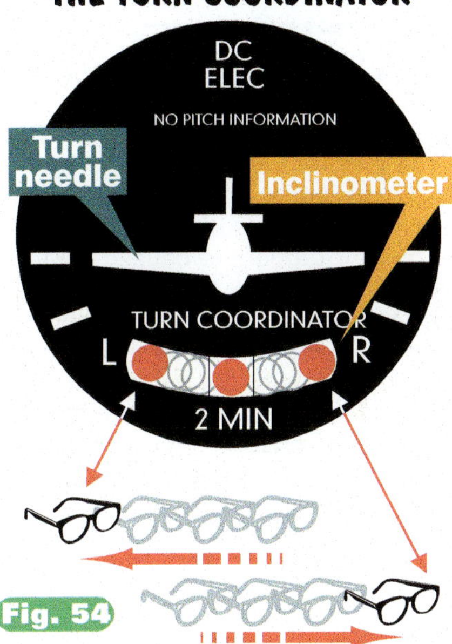

The movement of the ball corresponds to the movement of the sunglasses on your car's dashboard. The same force that moves the glasses also moves the ball. The ball, however, slides more easily than the glasses. The ball's deflection from center identifies when the airplane's nose is pointed other than in the direction of turn. Rudder is used to move the ball back to the centered position.

about its vertical axis. Application of right rudder pedal yaws the nose to the right. Applying left rudder pedal (I'll just say *rudder* from now on), shown by Airplane B, yaws the nose to the left (surprising, huh?).

When should you use the rudder? Any time you turn the airplane. If you don't use rudder while trying to turn, part of the airplane is going one way, and another part points in the opposite direction. This is not a pretty sight, and your instructor's eyebrows will raise so high that they will scratch his or her back. Right turn, right rudder. Left turn, left rudder. Feet and hands move together.

Now the question foremost in your upper brain is "How much rudder is enough?" Good question. Figure 54 shows an inclinometer, also known as *the ball,* as a part of another instrument called the *turn coordinator* (located on the instrument panel).

The little white airplane in the turn coordinator shows the direction of turn, while the ball tells you if the proper amount of rudder is applied. The ball is free to roll right or left within the glass tube. Any inappropriate rudder use (or lack of use) applies an unnecessary side force to the airplane. This deflects the ball in much the same way sunglasses scoot across your car's dash when rounding a sharp corner. Your job is to keep the ball centered by using the rudder.

Figure 55 shows an airplane in a turn. Airplane A's nose is pointed outside the turn (probably because of insufficient right rudder or too much

SLIPS & SKIDS MADE EASY

An easy way to understand slips or skids is to think of the ball as the tail and the glass tube at the wings of the airplane. (Right turn shown.)

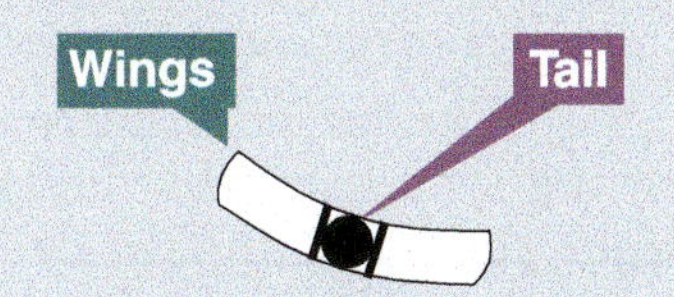

In a right turn, if the ball (tail) is to the left of center, this implies the tail is skidding to the outside of the turn.

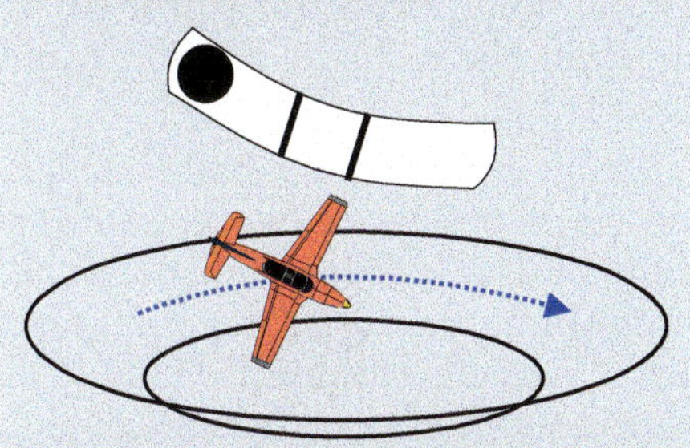

In a right turn, if the ball (tail) is to the right of center, this implies the tail is slipping to the inside of the turn.

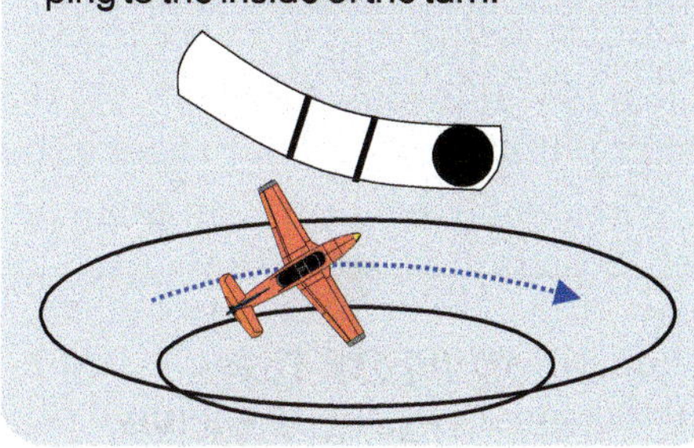

AN EASY WAY TO UNDERSTAND SLIPPING & SKIDDING IN AN AIRPLANE

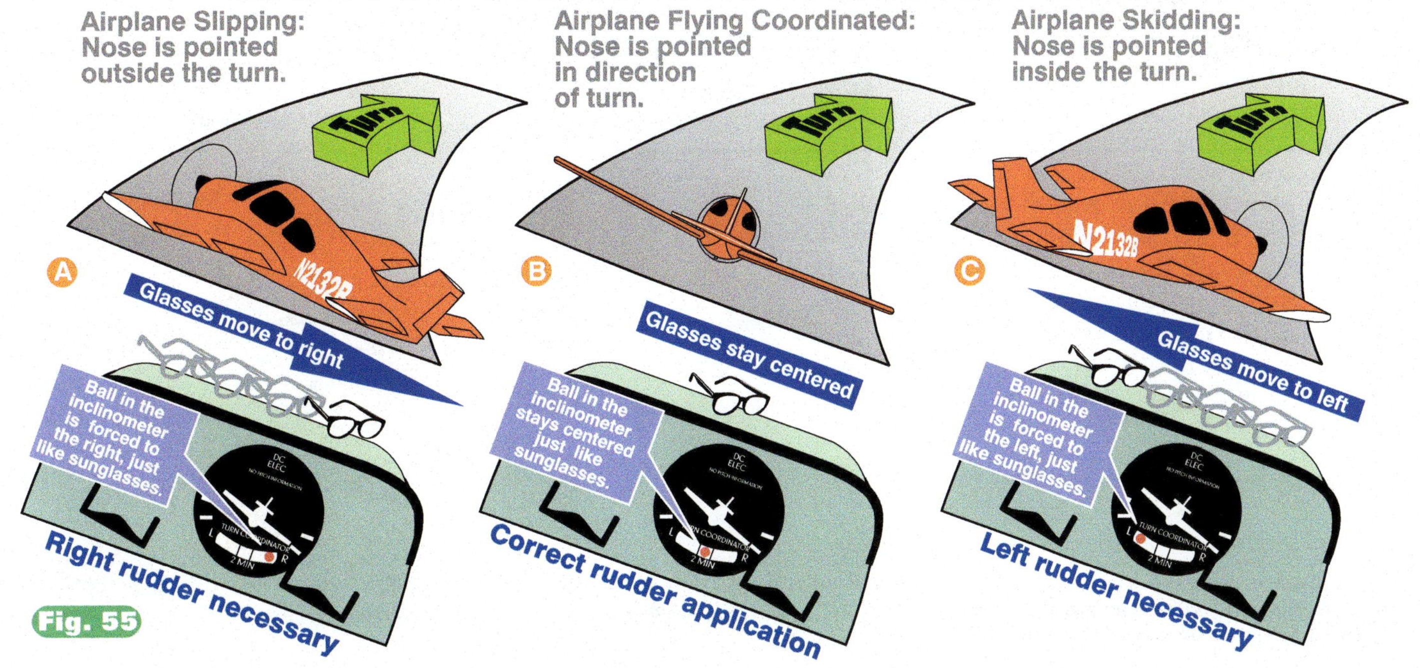

right aileron is applied). The ball and the airplane slip to the right, toward the inside of the turn. In other words, you need to point the nose slightly to the right for a precisely aligned turn. By adding enough right rudder to align the airplane in the direction it's turning, the ball returns to the center as shown by Airplane B.

Airplane C's nose points toward the inside of the turn (probably because too much right rudder is applied or insufficient right aileron is used.) The ball and the airplane skid to the left, toward the outside of the turn. Adding a little left rudder keeps the nose pointed in the direction the airplane's turning and centers the ball.

Simply stated, if the ball is deflected to the right or left of center, add enough right or left rudder to center the ball. Sometimes you'll hear your instructor say, "Step on the ball!" This is simply your instructor's way of telling you to add right rudder for a right-deflected ball and left rudder for a left-deflected ball. Don't even think about placing your foot on the turn coordinator, or your instructor will question you about your SAT scores. Don't put marbles in your shoes either.

When entering a turn, aileron and rudder are applied simultaneously, in the same direction. This is what pilots mean when they refer to flying coordinated. Aileron establishes the degree of bank and rudder keeps the nose pointed in the direction of turn. If the ball is centered during this process, we say that the controls are properly coordinated.

One last point about the rudder. It is the last control forfeited in a stall. Even when the airplane is stalled, it continues to move forward with airflow over its surface. This allows some degree of rudder authority even at very slow speeds. During a stall you'll find that the rudder is very effective for maintaining directional control. In a spin, the rudder is very important for spin recovery. More on spins in Postflight Briefing #2-1.

Coordination Lube

Devious Instructor Device

Hey! What about two boxing gloves suspended by string that act like the ball in the inclinometer?

It won't take long before you won't need to look at the ball in the inclinometer to know whether or not you're flying coordinated. With a little practice you'll be able to fly by the seat of your pants (assuming you wear pants while flying). Pressure on the right or left side of your derriere is caused by the same force that moves the ball to the right or the left. It doesn't matter how big the airplane is; a 747 or a Cessna 150 Land-o-matic can be flown by the seat of the pants. Use the inclinometer as sort of a biofeedback device cuing you to sense pressure on your derriere when the ball is deflected. And don't feel bad if it takes a little practice to get used to coordinating rudder and ailerons. My first instructor told me that even if they put cold Vaseline in the inclinometer (instead of mineral oil), I would still get the ball to bang back and forth against the ends of the glass.

HOW THE ELEVATOR CONTROL CHANGES THE AIRPLANE'S PITCH

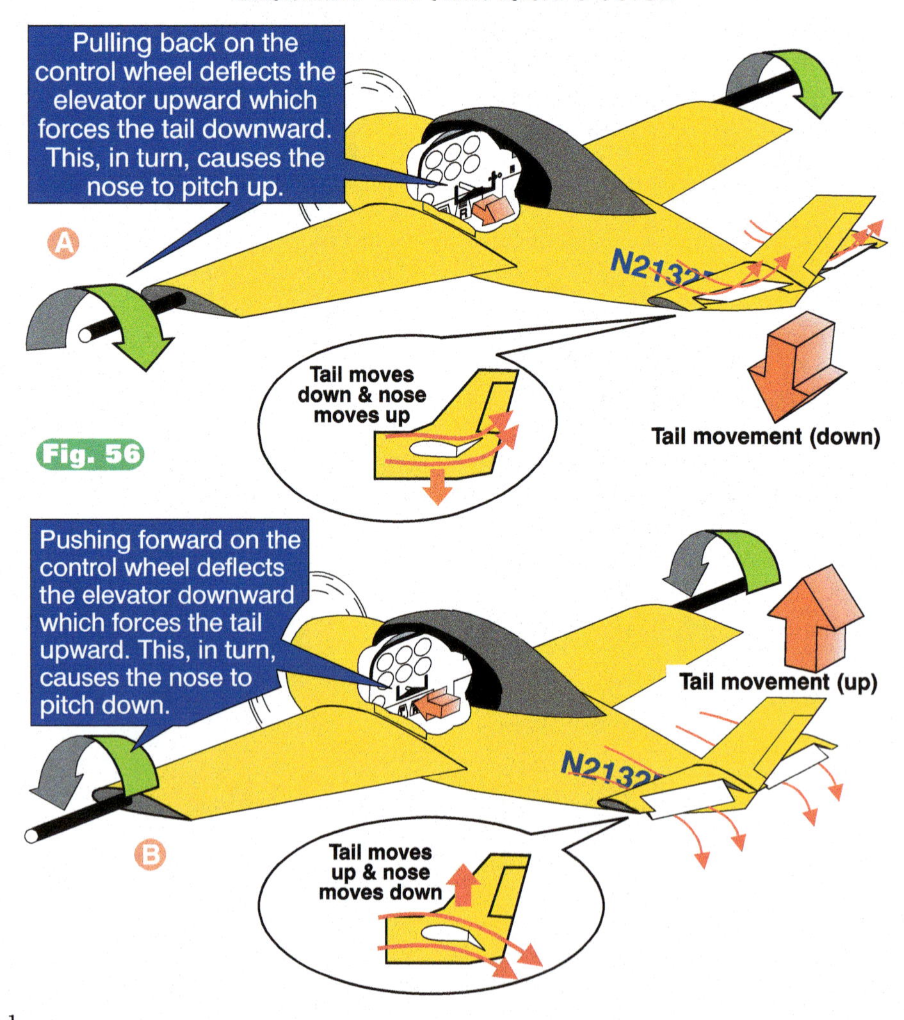

Fig. 56

Elevator

The elevator is the moveable horizontal surface at the rear of the airplane. Its purpose is to pitch the airplane's nose up or down.

The elevator control works on the same aerodynamic principle as the rudder and aileron. Applying back pressure on the control wheel of Airplane A in Figure 56 deflects the elevator surface upward. Lower pressure is created on the underside of the tail which moves it downward, and the nose of the airplane pitches up.

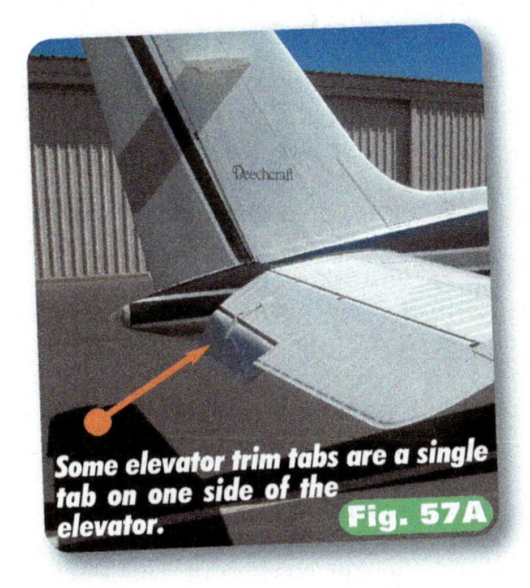

Some elevator trim tabs are a single tab on one side of the elevator. Fig. 57A

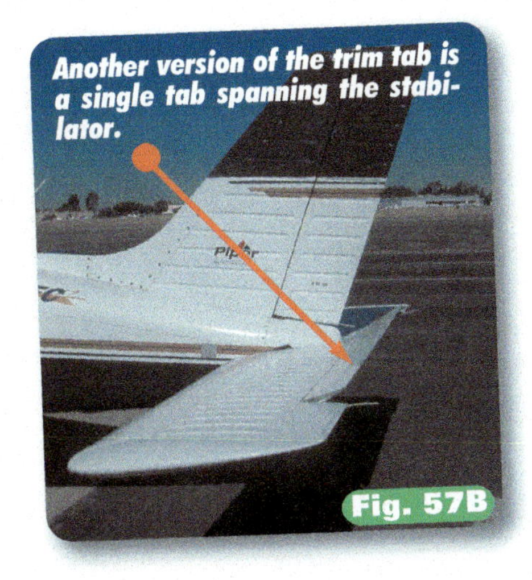

Another version of the trim tab is a single tab spanning the stabilator. Fig. 57B

The Elevator Trim Wheel Fig. 57C

Airplane B shows what happens when the control wheel is moved forward. The elevator surface moves down creating lower pressure on the top side of the tail.

This causes the tail to rise. The nose rotates about the lateral axis in a downward direction. Simply stated, to pitch up, pull the control wheel back; to pitch down, move the control wheel forward.

Trim Tabs

If you had to apply continuous pressure on the control wheel to maintain pitch attitude, your arms would tire quickly (Schwarzenegger would be proud of you but I wouldn't). Fortunately, airplanes have something known as a *trim tab* to take the pressure off the control wheel (and off the pilot!).

A trim tab is a small, moveable surface attached to the main surface you want to control (in this case, it's the elevator. Ailerons and rudder can have trim tabs too). Figures 57A, 57B and 57C show two different types of trim tabs and the trim wheel used to change the trim tab's position (the wheel is usually located between the two front seats or the lower portion of the instrument panel).

Moving the trim tab creates a slight pressure difference on the very end of the control surface to which it's attached (Figure 58). Just enough pressure is created to keep the primary control surface in the desired position without having to hold the control wheel in place. Notice that the trim tab moves in a direction opposite to the primary control surface it affects. If you want the elevator to deflect upward (as if you're pulling back on the wheel in a climb), the trim tab must move down as shown by Elevator A. To maintain a downward deflection of the elevator (as if you're in a descent), the trim tab must move upward as shown by Elevator B.

Using elevator trim is quite simple. Select the attitude desired with the elevator, then rotate the trim wheel (up or down) to take the pressure off the control wheel. How do you know which way to twist the trim wheel? Most trim wheels say *nose down* or *nose up* above or below the wheel. Simply twist the wheel in the direction you want the nose to stay. Aileron and rudder trim are equally simple to use.

When flying with other pilots, accept the fact that they won't like the way you trimmed the airplane. You might have flown the last 200 miles without touching the plane. Hand it over to the other person and the first thing he or she does is start fiddling with the trim. I can only conclude that this action is a form of primitive territorial claim. It's annoying, but it's better than how wild animals claim their territory isn't it?

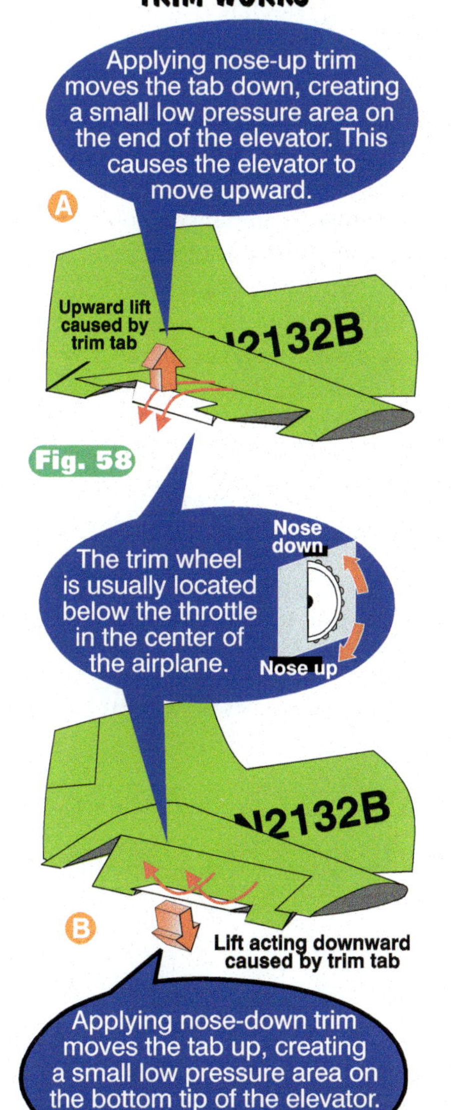

Fig. 58

Left Turning Tendencies (not political)

Having mastered The Four Forces, you now need to know there *are* others. Not many others, and not as significant, yet they are forces to be reckoned with.

Torque—Newton (Isaac, not Wayne) once said that for every action there is an equal and opposite reaction. Crankshafts rotate to the right in most single engine airplanes (as seen from the cockpit). An equal and opposite reaction is for the airplane to rotate to the left. That's exactly what the airplane does when the engine is developing power. This is known as *engine torque* or just *torque,* as shown in Figure 59 (I've often wondered if Spanish instructors call this *Torquemada?)*

Expect the effect of torque to be greatest when power is at a maximum and the airspeed is slow. During the takeoff run, with maximum power, torque makes the airplane want to roll to the left, creating slightly greater pressure on the left tire. This creates a little more friction on the left tire and causes the airplane to turn to the left as it accelerates for takeoff (as you'll soon see, there are other forces that aid in this left-turning tendency). Once airborne, the airplane still wants to roll to the left because of torque.

Pilots can compensate for torque by the applying the appropriate rudder and aileron control inputs. This is one reason why you need a lot of right rudder on takeoff (there are other reasons as you'll see shortly). Use of rudder and aileron trim also helps when the airplane wants to go somewhere other than straight during a climb. Torque is only one reason most airplanes like to turn left as they accelerate for takeoff. There are other forces that yaw an airplane to the left during slow speed, high angle of attack

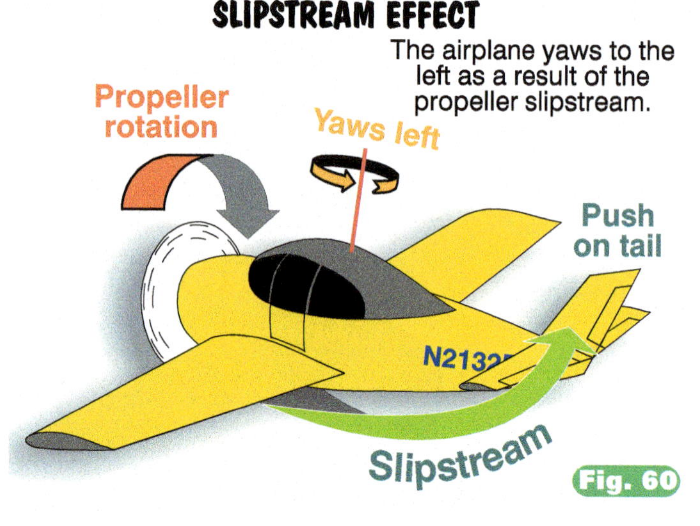

Fig. 60

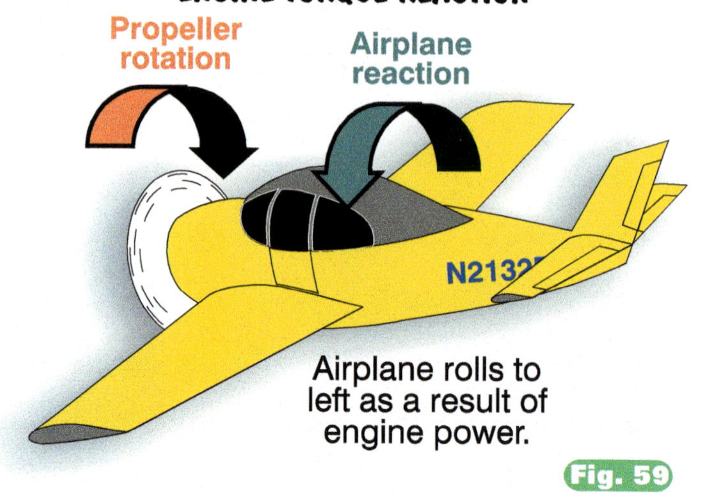

Fig. 59

flight. The effect of the propeller slipstream is one of these.

Slipstream Effect—A clockwise rotating propeller (as seen from the cockpit) imparts a curve or spiral motion to air flowing past the fuselage. This is known as the *propeller slipstream.* Figure 60 shows how this swirling air affects the airplane. Under high power conditions (such as during takeoff or climb), a curved spiral of air swirls around the airplane striking the vertical stabilizer and the rudder, yawing the airplane's nose to the left. Airplane design, power usage and airspeed all determine how the slipstream affects the airplane.

Before we proceed further, you should understand that the propeller is nothing more than a wing moving around a crankshaft.

We now have two forces that separately roll and yaw our airplane to the left. This explains why flight instructors are always saying three things: "More right rudder," "Let go, I've got it," and "Do you want to pay me now?" Your instructor's admonition to use "more right rudder" to counteract the left-turning tendency is quite common during slow speeds and high power settings. Alas, there is still one more force that yaws an airplane to the left.

P-Factor—No, this is not something you experience on a long cross country flight. Often called *asymmetric disk loading,* P-factor (or "propeller factor") is one more thing that makes your airplane turn left. Think about the word "asymmetric." It means "not symmetrical," or "not spread out evenly." Asymmetric disk loading occurs when lift, produced by the propeller (which is a rotating disk), isn't evenly distributed.

Before we proceed further, you should understand that the propeller is nothing more than a wing moving around a crankshaft. While airplane wings develop lift when pulled through the air, propellers develop their lift when spun around a crankshaft. Each half of the propeller is

like a wing, and it follows all the laws that a wing must follow (i.e., the greater the angle of attack, the greater the lift and drag for a given speed, etc.).

If one side of the propeller develops more lift than the other, the airplane experiences a twisting or yawing motion. This causes one side to pull more than the other, inducing a yaw about the vertical axis.

P-factor is noticeable at *high angles of attack* for one very important reason: the downward moving half of the propeller develops more lift than the upward moving half. Figure 61 shows an example of this. At a low angle of attack (A), both the upward and the downward moving propeller blade strike the air at similar angles. At higher angles of attack (B), the downward moving blade has a larger angle of attack than the upward moving blade. This means the downward moving blade creates more lift than its upward moving companion (Figure 62). Therefore, the downward moving blade imparts a yaw to the left about the vertical axis.

Figure 63 is your last and final way of visualizing P-factor (honest!). Airplane A is at a *high angle of attack* and is moving toward you. Its downward

ASYMMETRICAL DISK LOADING (P-FACTOR)

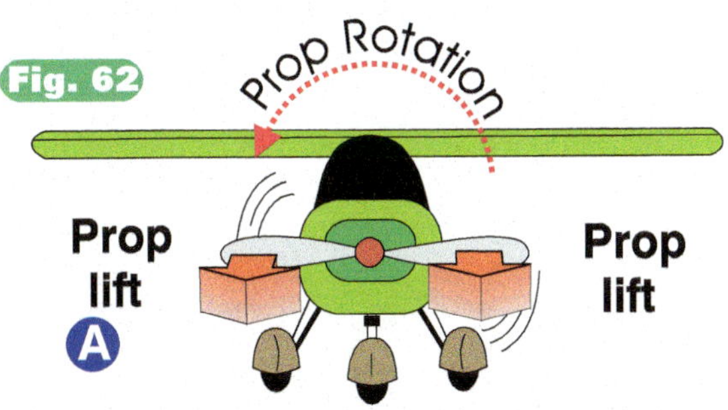

At a low angle of attack, lift is evenly distributed on both the upward and downward rotating side of the propeller.

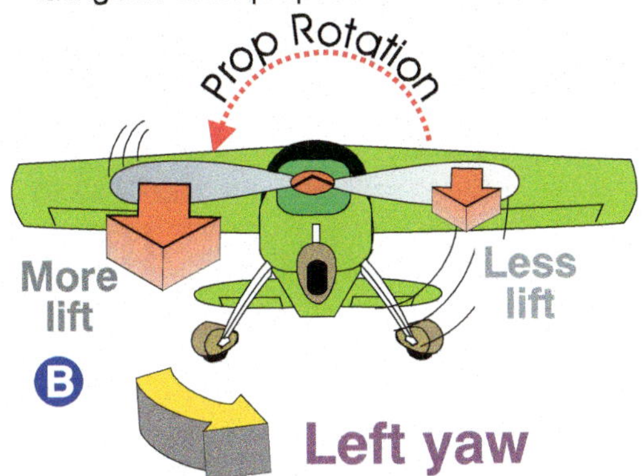

At higher angles of attack, lift increases on the downward rotating side of the propeller and decreases on the upward rotating side. This causes the airplane to yaw to the left.

ANOTHER LOOK AT P-FACTOR

When the airplane is at a low angle of attack, the rising and falling blades of the propeller have almost the same angle of attack. In other words, each half of the propeller produces an equal amount of lift and there is little or no P-factor.

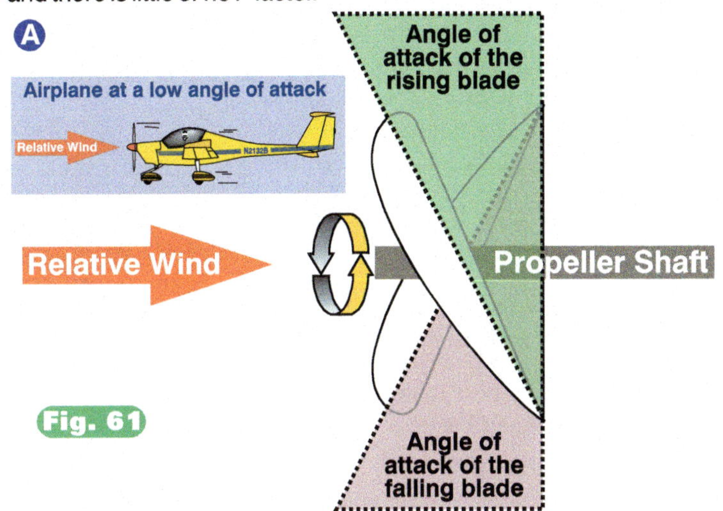

B When the airplane is at a higher angle of attack, the falling blade has a larger angle of attack than the rising blade. This difference in angle of attack between blades results in the falling blade producing more lift than the rising blade. Thus, P-factor increases and the airplane yaws to the left.

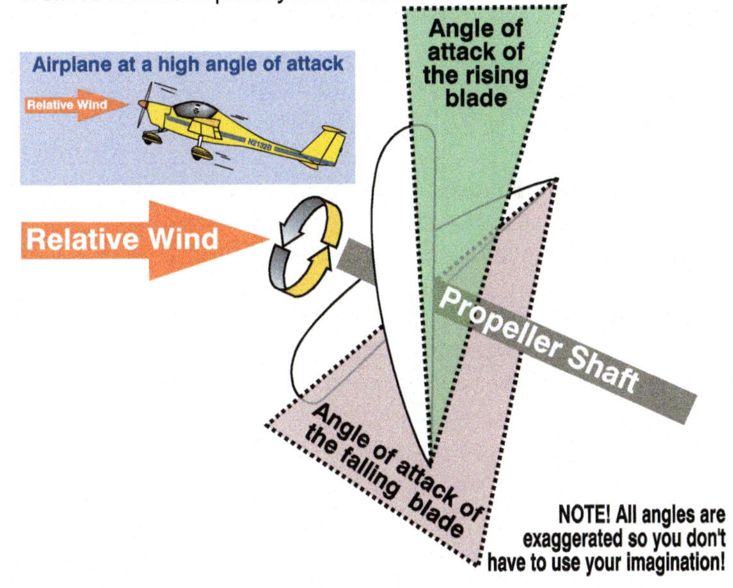

moving blade swings forward into the wind. The upward retreating blade rotates with the wind. The downward moving blade feels more wind blowing on it than the upward moving blade. It is reasonable to conclude that the blade moving downward develops more lift than its rising counterpart. This is exactly what happens. Airplane B shows the net result of this lift differential as a left yawing tendency. Higher angles of attack increase this difference in lift, while lower angles of attack decrease it.

Expect to notice P-factor at higher angles of attack, such as during takeoff and climb. Couple this with the slipstream effect and torque, and it certainly seems like a left-wing conspiracy.

At slow speeds and high power settings, a healthy amount of right rudder is necessary to keep the airplane from yawing to the left in this condition. I fully expect that genetic engineers will, one day, create an entirely new breed of pilot known as Homo torquedown man. This hybrid species will have an enormous muscular right leg useful in correcting for torque, slipstream and P-factor when climbing airplanes without rudder trim.

Hopefully, this chapter has helped you understand how to make the wing of your airplane work better for you. Don't worry if you don't feel like you quite understand these concepts yet. Seeing is believing, and it almost always takes a few flight lessons before the practical realities of aerodynamics sink in.

Learning aerodynamics is like eating vegetables—they're good for you, even if you're not sure why. It's like my little nephew's first introduction to broccoli. My sister used guilt as a motivator to get him to eat the stuff. She'd always say, "Brad, eat your broccoli. Why? Because there are children in China who are starving." Little did he know that the parents of children in China were saying, "Chan, eat your rice. Why? Because there are children in America who have to eat broccoli." Hopefully this chapter was a little more pleasant than eating broccoli. The more you fly, the more you'll appreciate how important these concepts are.

ASYMMETRICAL DISK LOADING (P-FACTOR)

At a positive angle of attack, the downward moving blade develops more lift than the upward moving blade. This causes the airplane to yaw to its left.

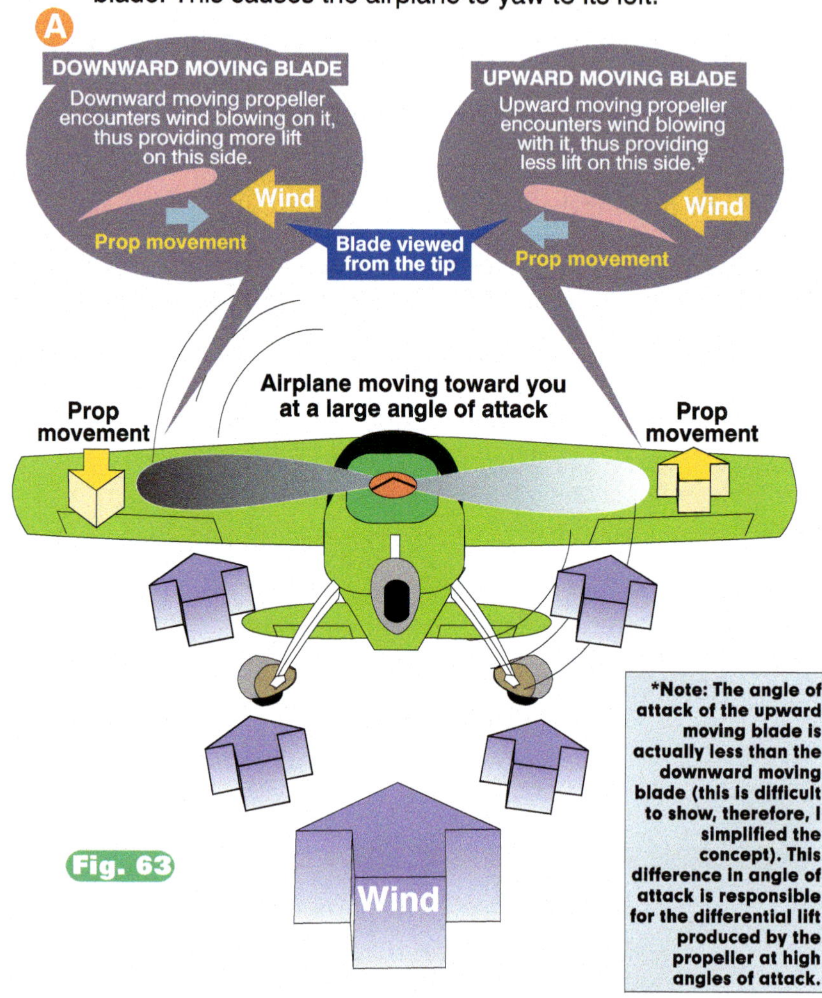

Fig. 63

Now that you know how an airplane flies, we'll turn our attention to the item that pulls an aircraft through the air in the first place—the engine.

Postflight Briefing #2-1

HOW A SPIN OCCURS

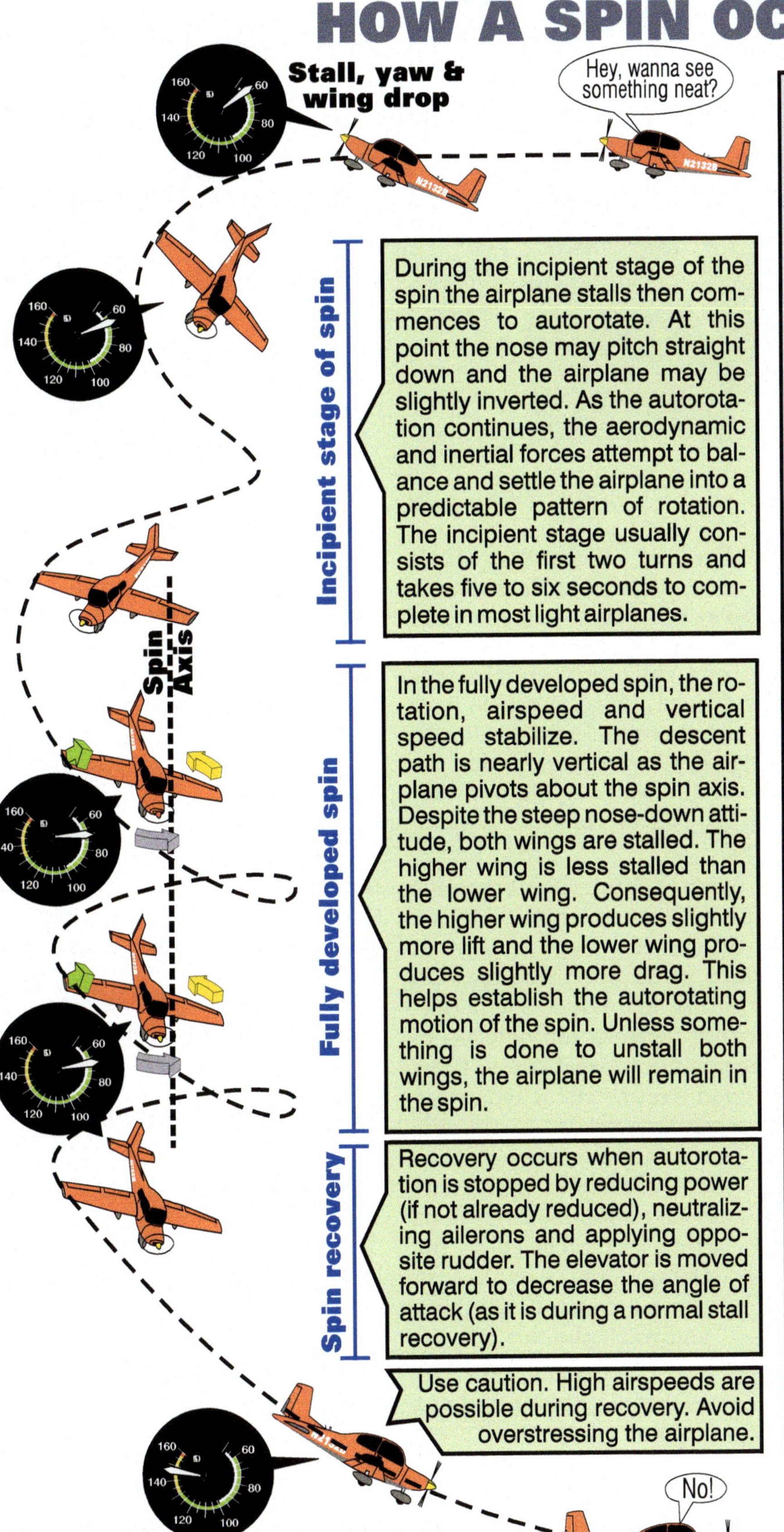

During the incipient stage of the spin the airplane stalls then commences to autorotate. At this point the nose may pitch straight down and the airplane may be slightly inverted. As the autorotation continues, the aerodynamic and inertial forces attempt to balance and settle the airplane into a predictable pattern of rotation. The incipient stage usually consists of the first two turns and takes five to six seconds to complete in most light airplanes.

In the fully developed spin, the rotation, airspeed and vertical speed stabilize. The descent path is nearly vertical as the airplane pivots about the spin axis. Despite the steep nose-down attitude, both wings are stalled. The higher wing is less stalled than the lower wing. Consequently, the higher wing produces slightly more lift and the lower wing produces slightly more drag. This helps establish the autorotating motion of the spin. Unless something is done to unstall both wings, the airplane will remain in the spin.

Recovery occurs when autorotation is stopped by reducing power (if not already reduced), neutralizing ailerons and applying opposite rudder. The elevator is moved forward to decrease the angle of attack (as it is during a normal stall recovery).

Use caution. High airspeeds are possible during recovery. Avoid overstressing the airplane.

THE FULLY DEVELOPED SPIN

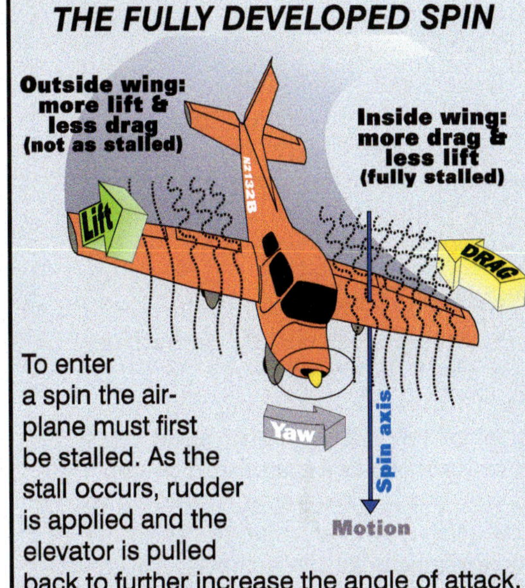

To enter a spin the airplane must first be stalled. As the stall occurs, rudder is applied and the elevator is pulled back to further increase the angle of attack. Applying rudder (to the left in the above example) causes the left wing to simultaneously move downward and rearward. This causes a left roll that increases the left wing's angle of attack and slows its speed relative to the right wing. The right wing, on the other hand, moves upward and forward. This decreases its angle of attack and increases its speed. Despite the fact that both wings are stalled in the fully developed spin, the outside (higher) wing is less stalled than the inside (lower) wing.

Pilots making skidding turns to final put themselves in a critical position that's conducive to spin entry. If the pilot sees he will overshoot the turn to final, he might apply rudder to align the nose with the runway while holding the bank constant with aileron. All the while, he's pulling back on the elevator control in an attempt to keep the nose up. This is the precise condition described above for entering a spin. Unfortunately, when a spin occurs in the traffic pattern, there is often insufficient altitude available for recovery.

In a fully developed spin, the airspeed remains constant (for smaller airplanes it's about 65 to 75 knots). The descent rate can exceed 7,000 feet per minute.

Postflight Briefing #2-2

Your Airplane-What a Drag

Drag is a passenger that doesn't chip in for lunch. It's also a constant companion on every flight.

Drag is not something a pilot has a great deal of control over, but understanding what the two types of drag are, and how they accumulate and affect flight, is important in certain situations.

Parasite Drag

A parasite is usually something you don't like that seems to attach itself to you or something you value. A large leech that bolts itself onto your forehead is a parasite. You don't like it, but it likes being connected to you (it is, however, good for sparking conversations at the airport). An airplane's struts, landing gear, wires and antennas (Figure 64) are all parasites as far as an aerodynamicist is concerned, and the drag they create is referred to as *parasitic drag*.

These protruding parts grab air molecules and slow airplanes down like flies doing touch-and-goes on No-Pest strips. These and other parts of the airplane are, however, necessary aerodynamic evils. Fortunately, clever engineers work remarkable magic in reducing the effect these parasitic items have on airplane performance.

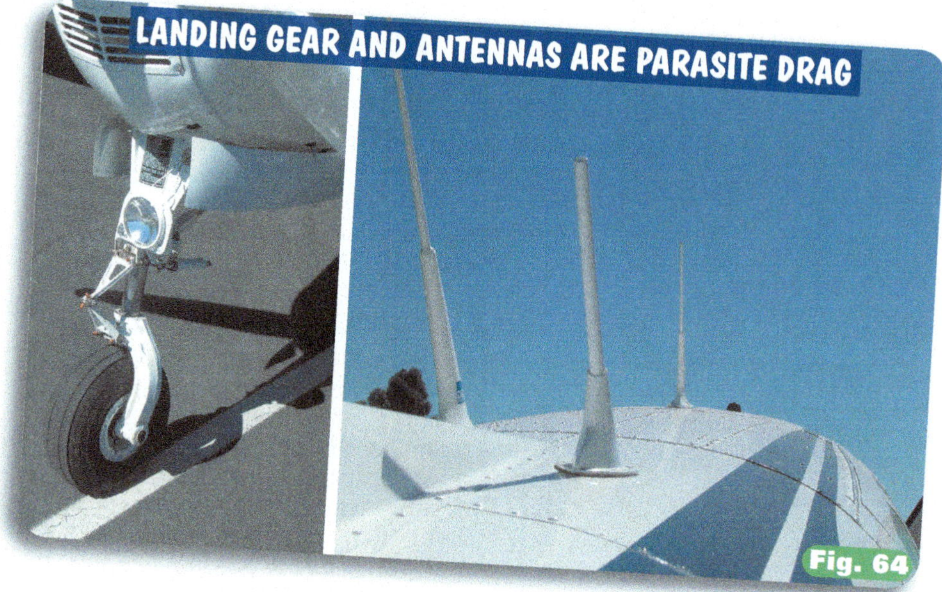

Fig. 64

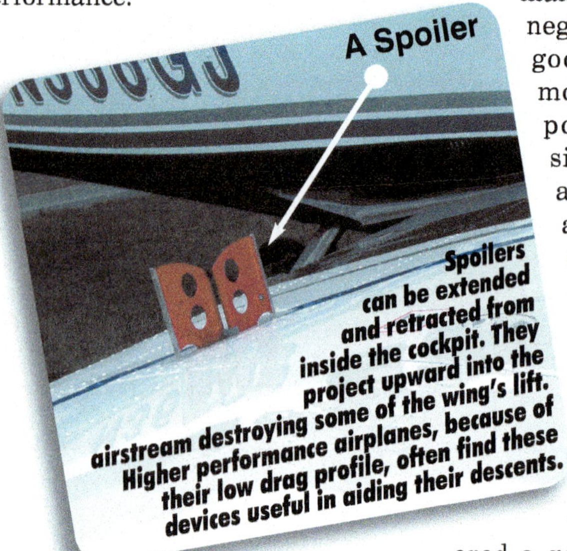

You might wonder, "Why talk about drag if the pilot can't do anything about it?" Well, first off, it gives you something to debate with other pilots on a day when you can't go flying. Second, not many people understand this stuff, so it makes you sound cool. Third, pilots do have some control over an airplane's parasite drag. For instance, polishing the surface of the wings minimizes skin friction (one of several forms of parasite drag).

On certain high performance sailplanes, a good shine job can be good for several miles of increased glide performance. On training airplanes, the performance increase can be close to negligible. Nevertheless, it's a good excuse for a Saturday morning's escape to the airport. Curious spouses are simply told that important aerodynamic modifications are to be performed on the airframe (don't blink, look serious, control breathing and you'll pull this off).

Nothing can (or should!) be done about the struts on an airplane having them. They're holding the wings on, which is generally considered a good thing. Remember, no wings, no lift. No lift, no fly. No fly, no fun. Unfortunately, struts clobber air molecules and increase parasite drag. Flying airplanes with struts and fixed gear has its advantages and disadvantages, and parasite drag is definitely one of the disadvantages.

Remember, parasite drag rises dramatically with increasing speed. In fact, doubling the speed of the airplane *quadruples* the parasite drag. Figure 65 shows how parasite drag increases with speed. You might get the impression that at slower speeds the airplane experiences very little total drag. While some parasite drag is always present at slower speeds, a different form of drag actually increases with a reduction in speed. This is called *induced drag*.

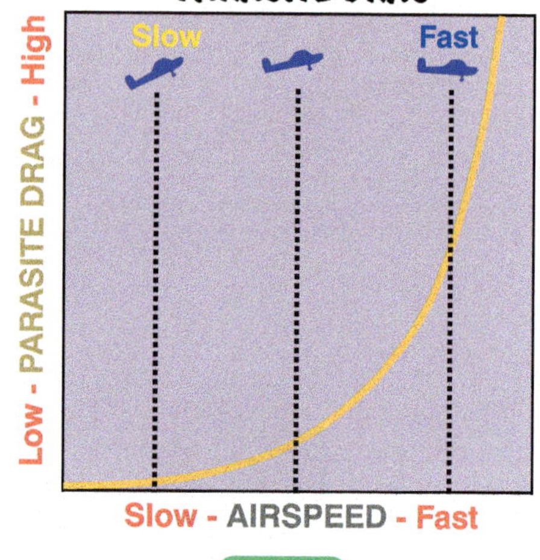

Fig. 65

When your hand (think "wing")has a "zero" degree angle of attack with the relative wind, no lift and very little drag is produced.

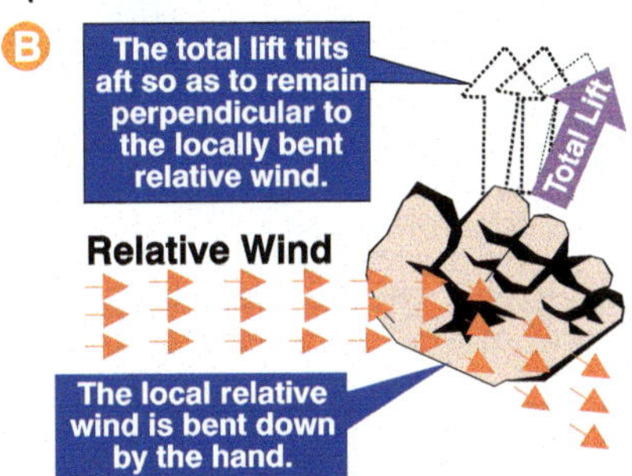

As the hand's angle of attack increases, the relative wind in the local vicinity of the hand (underneath it) is bent slightly. The total lift the hand produces is now tilted slightly rearward so as to remain perpendicular (90 degrees) to this newly-bent relative wind.

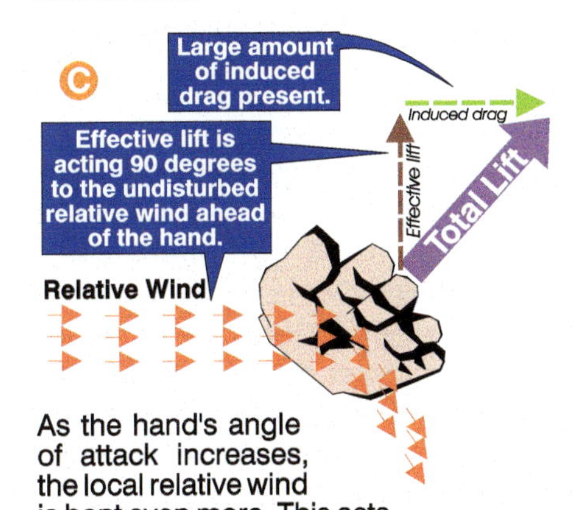

As the hand's angle of attack increases, the local relative wind is bent even more. This acts to further tilt the total lifting force aft. The component or portion of the total lift acting vertically is called "effective lift." The portion acting rearward is called "induced drag." It's very important to notice that the larger the angle of attack, the more rearward the total lift acts, thus the greater the induced drag becomes. Yet, the effective lift still acts 90 degrees to the undisturbed relative wind ahead of the wing.

Induced Drag

People can sometimes be induced to act in an unfortunate way. This occurs when a TV commercial recommends that you purchase a do-it-yourself acupuncture kit. After a little experimentation, you discover that you don't feel any better but your body is capable of picking up cable TV. Wings aren't people, but sometimes they induce the lift they produce to act in unfavorable ways. In particular, wings can induce their total lifting force to act rearward instead of in an upward direction. Remember, any force acting rearward on the airplane acts like drag. (At this point I'll offer you a choice. You can either believe me when I say that induced drag increases when the airplane slows down or you can plow through the following few paragraphs and I'll prove it to you. Most pilots can and do fly safely without knowing the nuances of drag formation.)

Time for another experiment (yes, back to the car again). Stick your hand (and *only* your hand) out the window as you're moving. Hold your hand parallel to the relative wind so that it has little or no angle of attack as shown by Figure 66A. You should feel little or no lift and relatively little rearward drag. Now, increase the hand's angle of attack as shown by Figure 66B. Notice how your hand wants to rise (we call this *lift*) but it also wants to move rearward slightly (we call this *drag*). As the hand's angle of attack increases, the local relative wind in the vicinity of the hand is bent downward slightly. Earlier we learned that lift acts perpendicular to the relative wind. Therefore, the total lifting force is tilted rearward as the hand's angle of attack increases. A further increase in the hand's angle of attack, as shown by Figure 66C, increases the upward and rearward pull of the total lifting force.

Here's the point (finger in the ear again!). *The total lifting force acting on the hand pulls it upward and backward as the angle of attack increases.* The upward, or vertical portion of the total lift force works against the airplane's weight to keep it aloft. The rearward pull of the total lifting force acts in the direction of drag; we call it *induced drag*.

Although hands are much less sophisticated in generating lift than

TOTAL LIFT, EFFECTIVE LIFT AND INDUCED DRAG

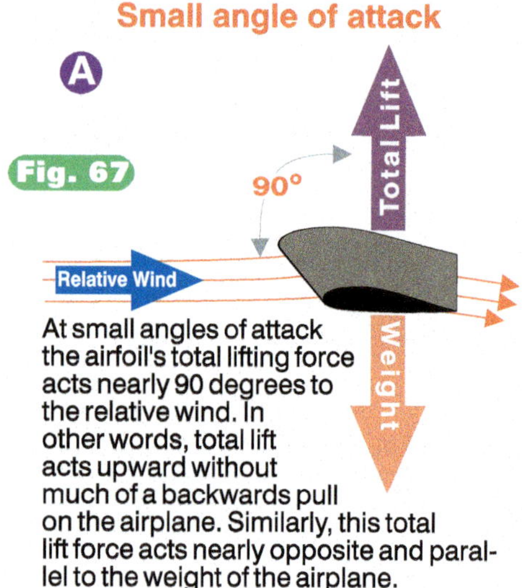

At small angles of attack the airfoil's total lifting force acts nearly 90 degrees to the relative wind. In other words, total lift acts upward without much of a backwards pull on the airplane. Similarly, this total lift force acts nearly opposite and parallel to the weight of the airplane.

Increasing angle of attack

Local relative wind bent downward by the wing's downwash.

B

Relative Wind

Local Relative Wind

As the angle of attack increases, the wing actually bends the relative wind (in its local vicinity) downward slightly. The downwash created by the wing at this high angle of attack is responsible for bending the local wind underneath and slightly ahead of the wing downward. The bent relative wind is called the *local relative wind*.

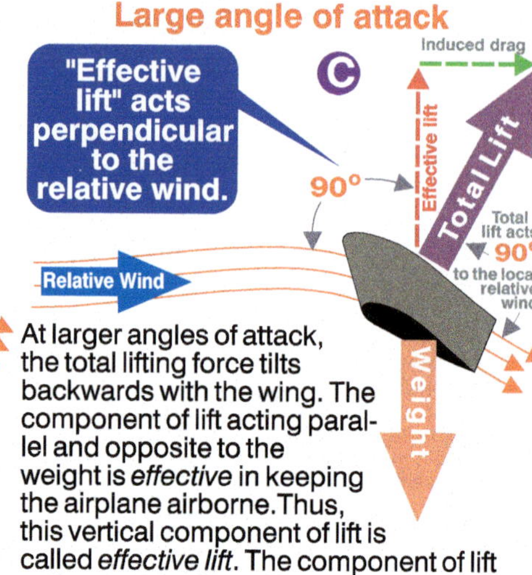

At larger angles of attack, the total lifting force tilts backwards with the wing. The component of lift acting parallel and opposite to the weight is *effective* in keeping the airplane airborne. Thus, this vertical component of lift is called *effective lift*. The component of lift acting rearward is called *induced drag*.

are wings, there are similarities between them. In Figure 67, Wing A is at a low angle of attack. Its total lifting force is nearly perpendicular to the relative wind and acts nearly opposite the airplane's weight.

As Wing B's angle of attack increases, downwash from the wing bends the relative wind slightly in advance of the moving wing. The total lifting force tilts aft so as to remain perpendicular to the newly-bent, *local relative wind* as shown by Wing C. We can take the portion of the tilted lift force acting straight up, opposite the airplane's weight, and call that component the *effective lift*. It's the part that's effective in keeping us airborne since it acts opposite the airplane's weight. This effective lift also acts at a 90 degree angle to the undisturbed relative wind ahead of the airplane.

INDUCED DRAG

Slow | Fast

Low - INDUCED DRAG - High

Slow - AIRSPEED - Fast

Fig. 68

The horizontal portion of the tilted lift force acts rearward, in the direction of drag. We call this rearward pull *induced drag*. Obviously, when the angle of attack is small, the total

Professor Bob carefully points out that max. endurance also applies to the human bladder since it's smaller than most fuel tanks.

lifting force acts in more of an upward or vertical direction with little rearward pull on the airplane. As the angle of attack increases the drag induced by the rearward component of total lift increases. Consequently, when the airplane slows, the angle of attack increases and induced drag increases. As the airplane's speed increases, the angle of attack decreases and the induced drag decreases. This relationship between induced drag and airspeed is shown in Figure 68.

Sort of wish you'd just taken my word for it, don't you?

Postflight Briefing #2-3

Maximum Endurance And Range

Maximum Range

If you are ever over water with limited fuel, trying to make the shoreline, you'll gain a fuller understanding of just *how* important it is to know the speed for attaining maximum range. Most new pilots believe that they can simply add more power and try to get to the shoreline quicker. You will soon discover that in aviation, the first thing that makes sense is often the last thing that's likely to work.

Faster speeds mean greater parasite drag. You end up going faster, at the tremendous cost of an increase in fuel consumption because drag has increased. The end result is that you land short of the maximum distance you would have traveled at the best L/D speed.

Some pilots think they can slow the airplane way down close to the stall speed to conserve fuel. This doesn't work either. Remember, when the airplane slows below the best L/D speed, induced drag increases. You'll simply run out of fuel without having traveled the maximum distance possible at the best L/D speed.

If you're ever trying to make a destination on limited fuel, use the airplane's maximum range speed. Unfortunately, this is often not published in your airplane's Pilot's Operating Handbook (POH). If you can't find the maximum range speed, use the airplane's best L/D speed (Figure 69). (Once again, aerodynamics has its catches and qualifications. In theory, best range should be precisely the speed for minimum total drag—the best L/D speed. However, based on propeller efficiency considerations, the maximum range speed can sometimes be a little higher than the posted best L/D speed for that airplane. Practically speaking, this doesn't amount to all that much of a difference.)

POWER REQUIRED VS. AIRSPEED GRAPH

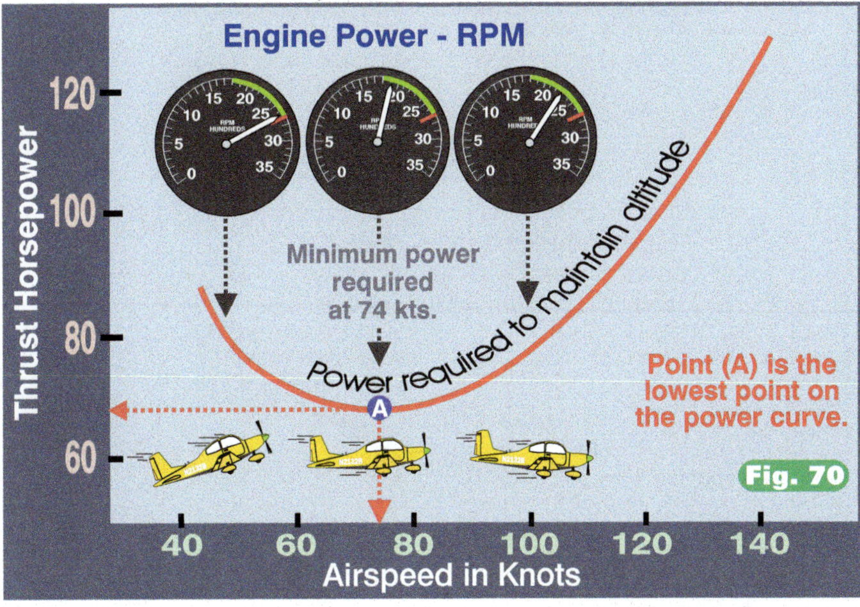

Fig. 70

Maximum Endurance

Maximum endurance occurs at a speed where minimum power (thus minimum fuel consumption) is required to remain airborne. This is the speed that allows you to remain aloft for the longest possible time.

The maximum endurance speed becomes an important consideration when you're circling above the only airport within range while waiting for the weather to clear. The last thing you ever want to be is low on fuel (Oops! Excuse me. To be politically correct we now say "fuel challenged"). I hope you'll never find yourself in this situation. Not knowing anything about your airplane's maximum endurance (minimum fuel consumption) speed is like using a cast iron commode on the dark side of an iceberg—a very uncomfortable experience.

At first glance, it might appear that the speed for maximum endurance is the best L/D speed. After all, minimum drag at the best L/D speed should require minimum thrust, thus minimum power. This might be true if it weren't for the fact that parasite drag and induced drag affect the power requirements for level flight differently. Simply stated, the engine must work harder in overcoming parasite drag (as you speed up) than in overcoming induced drag (as you slow down). Therefore, flying a little below the best L/D speed, even at the expense of increasing induced drag, lowers the power required to sustain level flight (up to a point of course).

That's why you'll find the speed for maximum endurance (minimum power) below the minimum drag (best L/D) speed. The speed for maximum endurance (minimum power) is generally less than the best L/D speed (it's *approximately* 75% of the best L/D speed for most propeller driven airplanes, although this percentage can vary considerably from air plane to airplane). Think of this as you would the difference between gross and take home pay—one of them (maximum endurance speed) is smaller than the other (best L/D speed). Figure 69 shows these two speeds.

In some cases airplanes with long thin (high aspect ratio) wings have maximum endurance speeds that are very close to their stall speeds. This makes maximum endurance speed in these airplanes impractical to use.

The maximum endurance speed can be seen more clearly on the power vs. airspeed graph (Figure 70). This chart compares the power required to maintain altitude at different airspeeds. At the lowest portion of the power curve (A), the airplane maintains its altitude with minimum power, thus minimum fuel consumption. A speed of 74 knots establishes the minimum power point (maximum endurance speed) for this airplane. Airspeeds above or below this speed require that you increase power to maintain altitude.

Figure 71 shows maximum endurance speed occurring below the minimum drag speed as shown by the drag curve inserts in the top of the figure.

The power-required curve also provides a valuable clue as to how the airplane responds in a descent. Let's say you're descending at 74 knots

RANGE AND ENDURANCE SPEED FOR A TYPICAL HIGH PERFORMANCE AIRPLANE

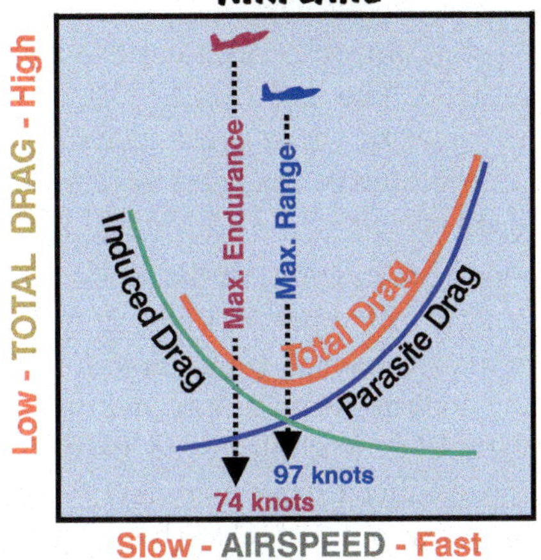

Fig. 69

POWER REQUIRED VS. TOTAL DRAG

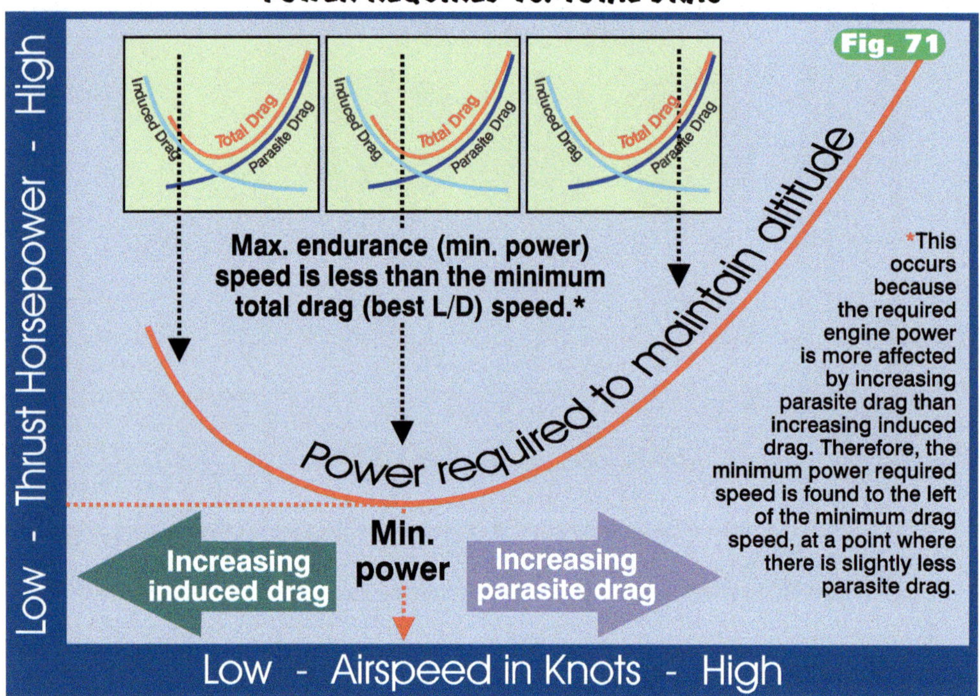

(the bottom of the power curve) at a slightly lower power setting than required to maintain altitude. Let's also say that this lower power setting produces a 500 foot per minute descent rate in this particular airplane. This is the minimum rate of descent you can expect in this airplane at this power setting. Any decrease in airspeed will increase the rate of descent. Why? The power required to maintain the descent rate *increases* as the airspeed *decreases*. This is a very important point!

If you haven't heard about it yet, you will eventually hear about an airplane operating "behind the power curve" or operating in the "region of reversed command." Either of these statements means the pilot is flying at a speed less than the minimum power-required speed. A decrease in airspeed requires more power to hold altitude or maintain a desired rate of descent (this is "reversed" from what you normally expect and explains why it's called the "region of reversed command"). Without this addition of power the airplane starts to descend or descend more quickly, as shown in Figure 72.

There comes a point where an airplane flying behind the power curve is unable to hold altitude, even with full power applied. It's conceivable that a pilot flying a real slow approach might apply full power to go around and raise the nose too quickly before the airplane has a chance to accelerate to climb airspeed. The pilot notices that the airplane is still descending, even with full power. He raised the nose further to arrest the descent and actually increases the descent rate. The pilot's only option in this instance is to lower the nose and allow the airplane to accelerate. Once the airplane is in a region requiring less power to maintain altitude, it can use its excess power to climb.

Suppose you're on an approach to landing and your airspeed is deep within the region of reversed command (close to stall speed). In this condition, you must not attempt to stretch a glide by raising the nose without adding power. Doing so will only increase your rate of descent. Many pilots have fallen victim to the region of reversed command. Think of it as licking honey off a thorn—you could get stuck if you're not careful. Operating in this region is perfectly safe as long as you're aware of these principles. But what happens if your engine quits and you have no power? What's the best way to obtain the airplane's maximum glide distance? To find out, we need to look a little closer at the best L/D speed (see Postflight Briefing #2-4).

THE REGION OF REVERSED COMMAND

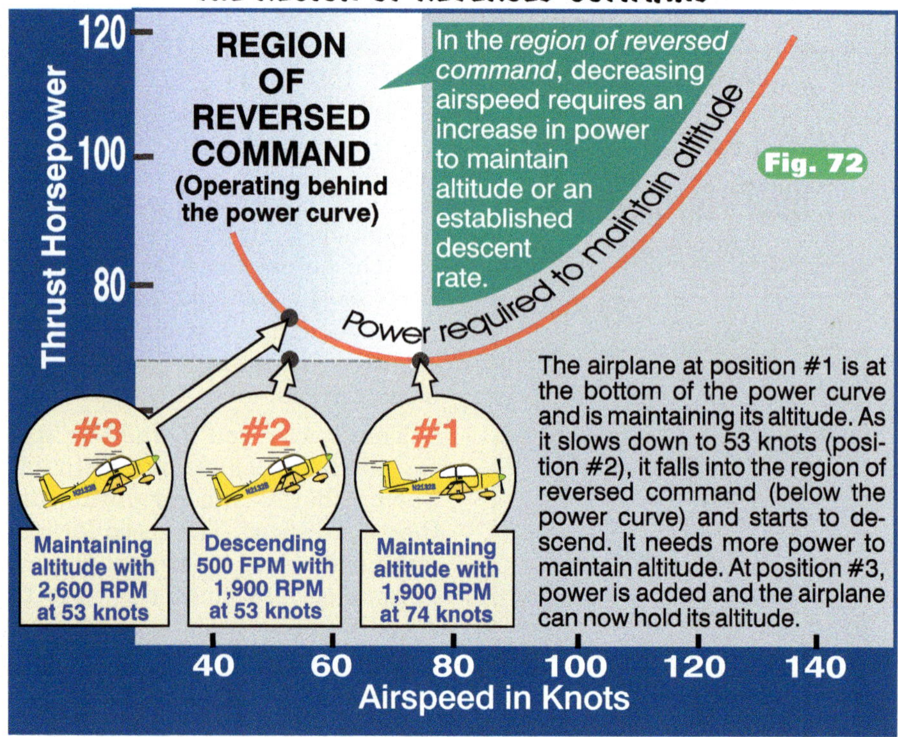

Postflight Briefing #2-4

Weight, Glide & the Ride

The Best Glide Speed And Weight Changes

What happens to our glide distance as the weight of the aircraft changes? Strangely enough, a change in weight doesn't affect the glide ratio as long as you make a change in glide speed. To obtain the best L/D of which the airplane is capable, a decrease in weight requires a decrease in airspeed. Let's see why.

The best glide speed of a particular Cessna Cardinal 177 is 74 knots at its maximum gross weight of 2,500 pounds. This speed gives the airplane a maximum glide ratio of 10:1. The L/D ratio can also be interpreted to mean that for every 10 pounds of lift developed by the wings, the entire airplane produces one pound of drag. At the airplane's maximum gross weight of 2,500 pounds (thus developing 2,500 pounds of lift), it produces 250 pounds of drag at its best glide speed of 74 knots.

Assume the Cardinal weighed 2,500 pounds before you took your flight bag out. Now it weighs 2,000 pounds (that's one heavy flight bag!). Only 2,000 pounds of lift are necessary to equal the airplane's weight in a descent. At 2,000 pounds of lift, an L/D ratio of 10:1 results in the airplane producing only 200 pounds of drag (remember, the L/D ratio is the best that specific airplane is capable of doing). Therefore, if 74 knots of airspeed produces 250 pounds of drag, it stands to reason that a slower airspeed would produce less drag (up to a point, of course). As the airplane's weight decreases, its airspeed must also decrease to maintain the best L/D.

Engineers tell us that an airspeed of 66 knots produces 200 pounds of drag in the Cardinal. At this slower speed, our L/D ratio is still 10:1 (2,000/200 = 10/1). At this lower weight, any speed other than 66 knots produces more than 200 pounds of drag which would decrease our 10:1 glide ratio (a shift of the total drag curve resulting from a change in weight). As the airplane's weight decreases, the speed to maintain the best L/D also decreases.

As long as the pilot keeps the airplane at the airspeed corresponding to the lowest part of the total drag curve, the L/D ratio remains constant. But how do you know what the best glide speed is if it varies with weight? Refer to the POH or to the owner's manual. Remember, in the event of a power failure, immediately establish the proper attitude to obtain the best glide speed.

Figure 73 provides information from a typical pilot handbook depicting several glide speeds for different weights. Remember, regardless of weight change, if the airplane is flown at the best glide speed for that weight, it will always glide the same maximum distance it's capable of. Keep in mind that most of the glide charts in your POH stipulate conditions like prop windmilling, no wind, flaps up. Any deviation from these conditions changes your glide distance.

LIFT/DRAG SPEEDS & VARIABLE WEIGHTS

Weight lbs.	Airspeed for Best L/D Knots - IAS
2,550	68 Knots
2,150	62 Knots
1,750	56 Knots

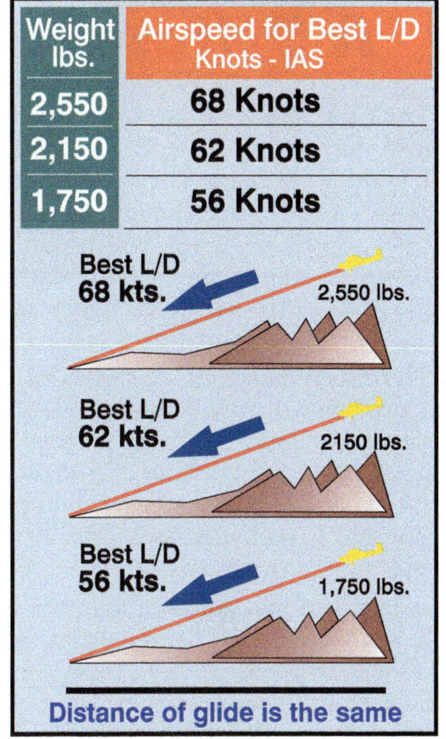

Fig. 73

Most small general aviation airplanes have L/D's somewhere around 10:1. In other words, you can glide approximately 10 times the distance of your height above terrain (assuming flat terrain). This is a typical glide ratio for most smaller airplanes. Gliders, on the other hand, have L/Ds upward of 40:1 or 50:1. (That's why they call them "gliders." Some aircraft, like the space shuttle, should be called "sinkers" for obvious reasons.)

Postflight Briefing #2-5

A Different Look at Maneuvering Speed

The first time you encounter turbulence I know what you're going to do. You'll peek out the right then the left window to make sure the wings are OK (as if you wouldn't know). Fair enough. Even though the wings are subject to lots of stress, you needn't worry about them breaking as long as you do one thing. Simply keep the airplane at or below its design maneuvering speed in turbulence. Here's how this works.

The design maneuvering speed (Va) is the speed at which the airplane will stall before exceeding its design limit-load factor in turbulent conditions or when the flight controls are suddenly and fully deflected in flight. Under these conditions the airframe experiences an increase in "G-force" or "load factor" (we'll use these terms synonymously).

The limit-load factor of U.S. certificated airplanes is based on the maximum amount of G-force the airframe can withstand before becoming damaged. Airplanes stressed up to but not beyond their limit-load factor should experience no structural damage. (This assumes the airplane is like new and not previously overstressed.)

For the purposes of *airplane* certification, airplanes are certified in one of three categories: *normal, utility, aerobatic.* The stress limits for these three categories are: +3.8Gs and -1.52Gs for normal category airplanes; +4.4Gs and -1.76Gs for the utility category airplane; +6Gs and -3Gs for the aerobatic category airplane. Let's examine how maneuvering speed prevents us from exceeding these limits.

Standing anywhere on planet Earth, you'll experience "one" time the force of gravity or 1G. It's gravity that pulls you toward Earth's center, providing the feeling of weight. On the surface, gravity exerts a constant 1G pull. In an airplane, however, you and the airplane can feel like you weigh more than your actual weight. This occurs when the airplane turns or the angle of attack suddenly increases (as it does in turbulence). This increase in apparent weight is called an increase in "G-force" or "load factor."

Let's suppose our airplane is cruising in straight and level flight at a constant airspeed. In this condition, lift is equal to weight and we experience a G-force of 1. We can represent G-force by the formula

Lift/Weight = G-force.

In straight and level unaccelerated flight the lift developed by the wings is equal to the airplane's weight. Thus, the G-force is 1G.

If the angle of attack suddenly increased (by pulling back on the elevator or encountering a vertical gust of wind for example), the wings would produce an instantaneous increase in lift. The airplane accelerates upward and you're forced downward in your seat. In other words, there is more upward pull by lift compared to the downward pull by weight. The G-force increases proportionally to the sudden increase in lift. Instantaneously doubling, tripling or quadrupling the lift doubles, triples or quadruples the G-force.

A direct (or nearly so), one-to-one relationship exists between lift and angle of attack. For instance, at a constant airspeed, in a 1G condition, a sudden doubling of the angle of attack doubles the wing's lift and doubles the G-force. Tripling or quadrupling the angle of attack triples or quadruples the G-force.

For instance, assume the airplane is flying at a fast cruise speed of 140 knots as shown in Figure 74. The airplane and its contents experience 1G at an angle of attack of 3 degrees for level flight. Suppose a *sudden* gust increases the angle of attack by an additional 3 degrees. The wing's original angle of attack has now doubled to 6 degrees (3+3=6). Consequently, lift *suddenly* doubles, producing 2Gs. A *sudden* increase in angle of attack to 9 degrees triples the lift and the G-force. An increase to 12, 15 and 18 degrees increases the lift and G-force to four, five and six times its original value.

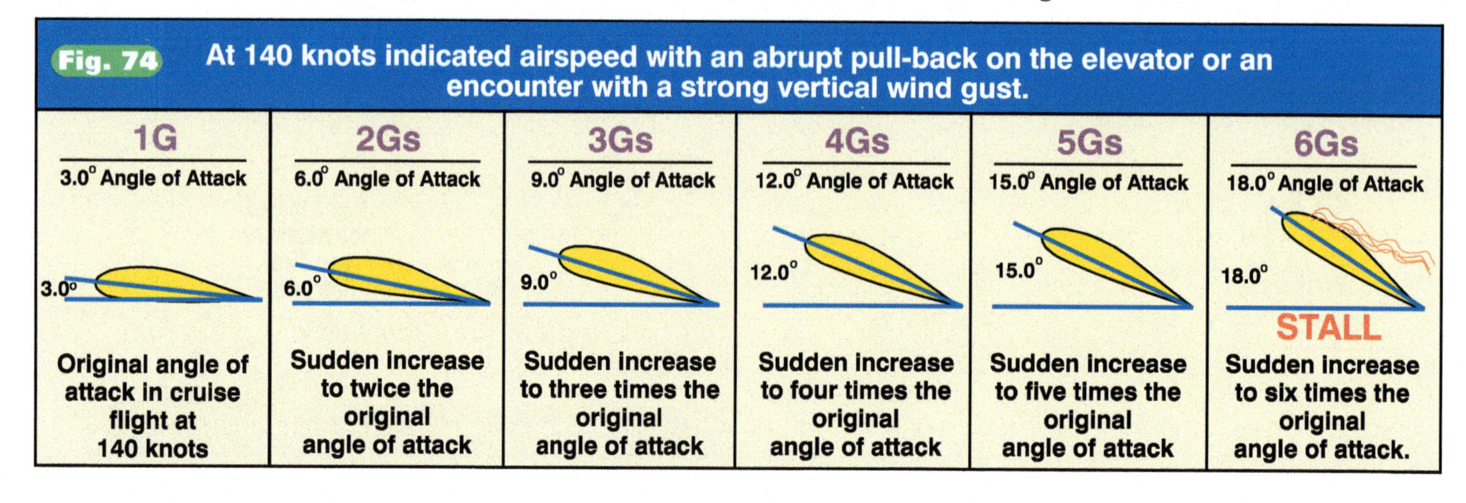

Since the wing stalls (and lift production decreases) at an angle of approximately 18 degrees, any further increase in angle of attack beyond six times the original value of 3 degrees won't increase the G-force. There-fore, at 140 knots this airplane is capable of experiencing 6Gs before the wings stall. If the airplane in this example had a limit load factor of 4Gs, the structure might experience some damage at this speed in strong turbulence. (I chose 4Gs instead of the actual limit loads of +3.8, +4.4 or +6Gs for this example to simplify the math.)

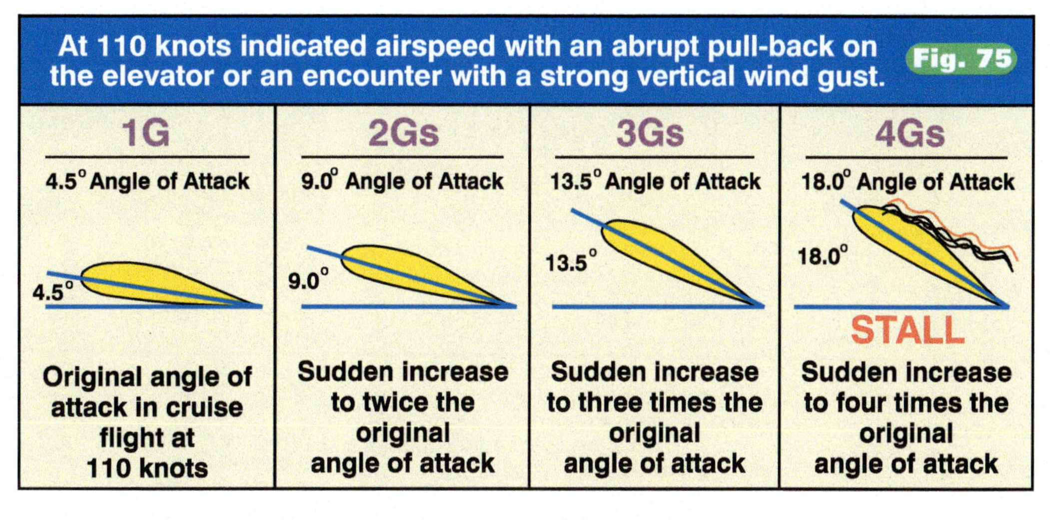

If we slow our airplane down to 110 knots (Figure 75), then let's assume a 4.5 degree angle of attack is necessary for a 1G, level-flight condition. If, at 110 knots, we suddenly double the original angle of attack to 9 degrees, the lift doubles. We now feel 2Gs. A sudden tripling of the original angle of attack to 13.5 degrees, triples the lift and we experience 3Gs. And finally, quadrupling the original angle of attack to 18 degrees produces four times as much lift. Therefore, we experience 4Gs. It's not possible to pull more than 4Gs in this example since the airplane will stall at 18 degrees. Consequently, 110 knots is the maneuvering speed for our airplane having a limit-load factor of 4Gs. At 110 knots, the airplane will stall before it exceeds this limit load factor in turbulent air or with full deflection of the flight controls. (Personally, in turbulence, I prefer to fly 10 to 15 knots below Va to prevent a gust from temporarily raising my indicated airspeed above Va.)

Whether a specific gust doubles, triples or quadruples the angle of attack, depends on the angle of attack of the airplane in its 1G condition. As is clearly evident from these examples, it's easier for a gust to double, triple or quadruple the angle of attack over its starting value when the airplane is flying faster (because it's at a lower angle of attack to begin with). Consequently, it's easier to experience more Gs for a given amount of turbulence at higher airspeeds.

Weight Change and Va

The airplane's posted maneuvering speed (Va) is based on the airplane being at gross weight. What happens when the airplane's weight decreases? The answer is, the maneuvering speed decreases. Let me explain.

Airplanes flown at weights below their gross weight require less lift for straight and level flight. Less lift means the airplane can be flown at a smaller angle of attack. In other words, an airplane at 2,500 pounds may require a 4.5 degree angle of attack at 110 knots to remain in level flight. Decreasing the weight to 1,800 pounds may require only a 3 degree angle of attack to remain in level flight at this speed. Does this angle of attack sound familiar to you?

With a speed of 110 knots, at this lower weight, a sudden and very strong gust could increase the angle of attack from 3 to 18 degrees. From our previous example, this produces six times the original lift for a force of 6Gs. This is way beyond the limit of a normal category airplane. At lighter weights, what can we do to keep from exceeding our example limit of 4Gs when in turbulence?

The answer is to slow the airplane down. At a slower speed (95 knots for example) a larger angle of attack (let's say 4.5 degrees) is necessary for level cruise flight at this lower weight.

At this speed, we can increase the angle of attack four times before the airplane stalls. Ninety-five knots becomes our new maneuvering speed if we want to limit ourselves to 4Gs. Thus, decreasing weight requires a decrease in the airplane's maneuvering speed.

Most of the newer pilot's operating handbooks publish two or three different maneuvering speeds for variable weight conditions (these are now called Vo's or *operating maneuvering speeds*, while the term Va refers to the maneuvering speed for max weight). If yours doesn't, try doing the following to compute a new one. For every 2% reduction in weight, reduce the max-weight maneuvering speed by 1%. In other words, if the gross weight decreases by 20%, reduce the max-gross weight maneuvering speed by 10%. This is simple math. (Besides, don't feel too bad if you are confused about math. For many years, I thought the logarithms was a singing group at MIT.)

A few final words. If you encounter turbulence in flight, fly a level flight attitude. Attempting to hold altitude at the expense of maintaining the proper airspeed might overstress the airplane.

For those engineers reading this, the airspeed-angle of attack values are approximations only. I also assumed that the zero-lift angle of attack is zero degrees. A linear-lift curve is also assumed with a lift coefficient that increases 0.1 for each degree angle of attack increase (this is close enough to the real world for our purposes).

Postflight Briefing #2-6 Aerodynamic Ideas for Your Consumption

STALL PATTERN PROGRESSION

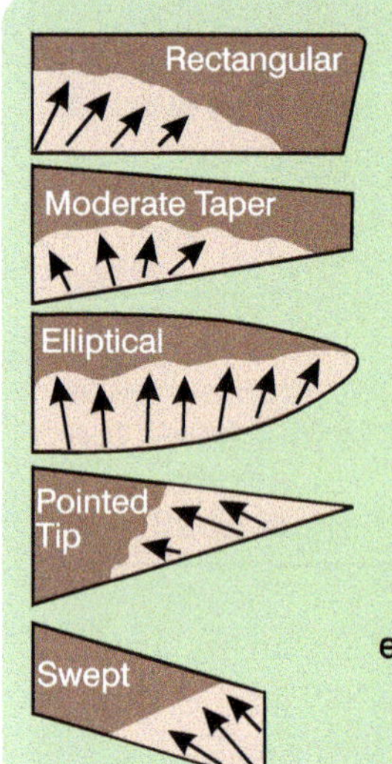

Wing design has an effect on how the airflow separates from the wing during a stall. The rectangular wing has the advantage of stalling at the root first. This keeps the ailerons effective at high angles of attack and provides you with a good stall warning buffet. A moderate taper on the wing allows more of the wing to reach a stall at the same time. This tends to reduce aileron effectiveness during a stall. All sections of the elliptical wing reach the stall at the same time. Ailerons may lack effectiveness during the stall on this wing. Pointed and swept wings stall at the tips first, then progress inward, rendering the ailerons ineffective during the stall.

STALL STRIPS

Some airplane manufacturers place "stall strips" on the wing's leading edge to ensure a specific part of the wing stalls first. Usually this is the inboard section of the wing. This keeps the ailerons effective during the stall. This means that the pilot still has roll control when experiencing the prestall (buffet) warning signs.

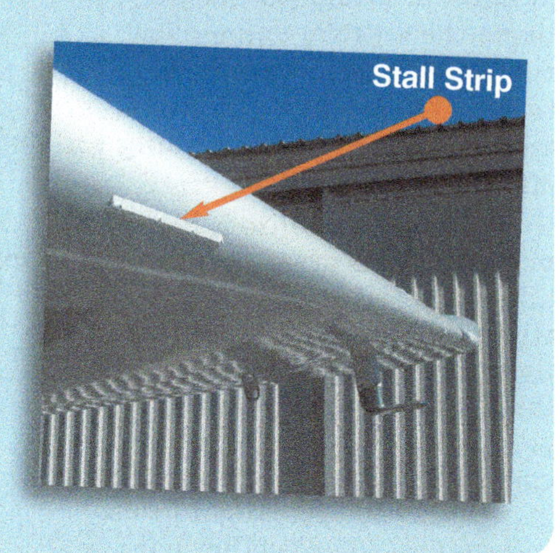

Courtesy *NASA*

Don't Even Think About It!

Frost on the airfoil disrupts the smooth flow of air over the wing. This causes earlier airflow separation resulting in decreased lift and increased drag. While the airplane may accelerate with frost on the wings, it may be impossible to achieve enough lift to become airborne. Frost also increases the stalling speed of the airplane. If a pilot does manage to become airborne, the airplane is now more likely to stall with any increase in load factor or decrease in airspeed.

Always remove all frost and ice from the airplane before takeoff. Usually it must be brushed off. Squirting down the airplane with a hose isn't a good idea either! Remember, frost forms when the temperature of the collecting surface is at or below the dewpoint of the adjacent air and the dewpoint is below freezing. Shooting water on the wings may simply increase the amount of frost and ice already present.

Photos courtesy of Captain Barry Schiff

Photos courtesy of Captain Barry Schiff

Photos courtesy of Captain Barry Schiff

Seeing the Stall

Stall progression is clearly seen with the placement of small strands of yarn taped along the wing. In picture A, air flows smoothly over the top of an unstalled wing. Picture B shows the progression of a stall from the wing root outward as the wing approaches its critical angle of attack. This is usually felt as a slight buffet which pilots know to be one of the early warning signs of the beginning of a stall. Picture C shows the wing in a complete stall. Notice how the yarn on the inboard section of the wing has actually reversed direction. This shows how the airflow over the wing becomes turbulent, no longer producing lift efficiently. Most general aviation airplanes have some variant of a rectangular-tapered wing. This allows the stall to progress from the wing root outward, allowing the ailerons to have some effectiveness for roll control as the stall is approached. This can be seen in C, above.

Postflight Briefing #2-7 Your Airplane's Stress Envelope: The V-g Diagram

Mention the phrase *V-g diagram* to most pilots and they immediately think of a map used by militant vegetarians to scout the location of edible but forbidden plants, or a 1970's vintage British singing group. In reality, the V-g diagram (sometimes called *V-n diagram* since technology usually refers to G-force as "n" values) is a useful tool in understanding an airplane's operating stress envelope.

Whether you realize it or not, your airplane is designed to withstand a great deal of stress. Unfortunately, many pilots are unfamiliar with these limits, which explains why there are quite a few misconceptions about how to fly airplanes in such a way that they aren't damaged or inadvertently recycled as scrap metal. For instance, some pilots believe that an airplane flown at the top of the airspeed indicator's green arc is incapable of exceeding its maximum allowable flight loads. Not true, as you will see in a minute. On the other hand, some aviators know that they should be in smooth air when flying in the airspeed's yellow arc, but they don't know why. So let's explore the airplane's stress envelope by actually constructing one.

The Positive-G Limit

Figure 76 shows the grid on which we'll build the V-g diagram. We'll label the horizontal axis as the airplane's *velocity* and the vertical axis as the *load factor* (also known as *G-force*, which has nothing to do with the number of FBI men it takes to knock down a door). Let's draw red dashed lines to represent our airplane's structural stress limits—the limits by which our airplane may be squeezed, pulled or blown upon by wind before the parts start refusing to fly in formation.

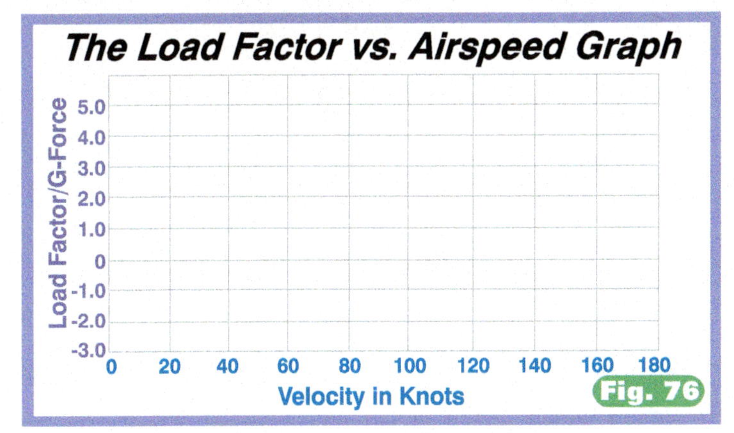

Fig. 76

Let's assume that the engineers who designed our airplane built it to withstand 3.8 positive Gs before the airplane's wings begin to deform (which is never a good thing). Place a horizontal line at the 3.8G limit, as shown in Figure 77. This line represents the upper or positive G-force stress limit for normal category airplanes, otherwise known as the *limit load factor*. (Light sport airplanes vary in their stress limits, but many have limits similar to the ones described in this postflight briefing.)

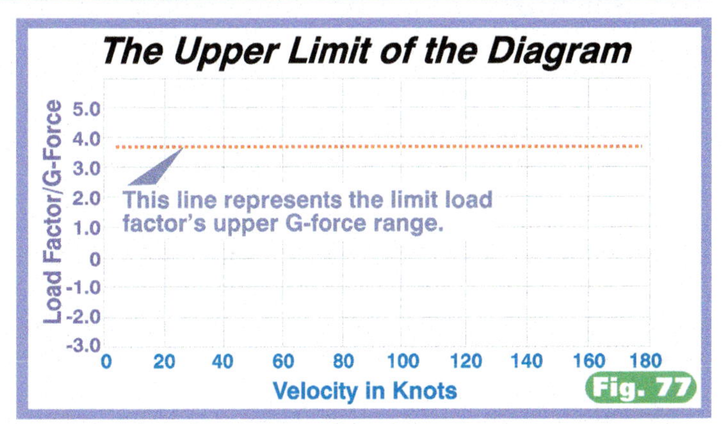

Fig. 77

We don't want to exceed +3.8Gs, for good reason. Initially, we'd begin losing secondary structures (flaps, gear doors, etc.). Then, given enough excess G-force, we'd lose primary structures (wings, engines, etc.). The fact that you could lose anything on an airplane in flight is disconcerting, even if it's a rental. Furthermore, you're not supposed to bring an airplane back from a flight missing any of its major components, but that assumes you'd even make it back to the airport.

Keep in mind that positive Gs are experienced when lift (via the wings) acts upward on an airplane. That's why positive Gs flex the wings upward and force you downward, into your seat. Negative Gs, on the other hand, flex the wings downward and force you upward, out of your seat. You might have experienced negative Gs when you placed a Wrestlemania-like grip on the flight controls and briskly moved the yoke or elevator control forward quickly during stall recovery. Were there any unlucky and unbelted passengers on board, you'd find them floating around the cockpit at the time—a sure sign of negative Gs.

The Negative-G Limit

Now let's draw the airplane's negative-G limit. For standard airworthy airplanes (and some light sport airplanes, too), the FARs require that they be capable of withstanding negative Gs not less than 40% of the airplane's positive-G load limit. This equates to 1.52Gs (or .4x3.8=1.52). Let's draw a horizontal line at the -1.52G level, as shown in Figure 78. (Many light sport airplanes

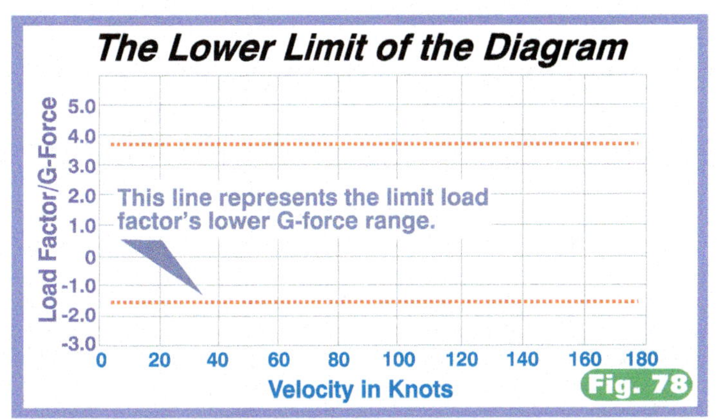

Fig. 78

are designed according to *consensus standards*, not the FARs. Therefore, their stress limits will vary between manufacturers).

Before we proceed further, consider the pressure you're under right now. In other words, how many Gs are you pulling right now as you sit in your chair? That's right. Your derrière is experiencing +1G (if we were discussing the FARs, your derrière might feel like it's experiencing 3Gs or even 4G's right now). Looking at the graph in Figure 76, the normal position for straight and level, unaccelerated flight is the 1G line, not the zero G line. Remember, you don't operate at zero Gs; if you did, you'd be weightless. Please keep this "1G" reference point in mind.

At this point it should be clear that our airplane isn't quite as strong structurally in the negative-G direction as it is in the positive-G direction. Why? Because the engineers don't figure that you will fly in the negative-G condition for any extended length of time. In other words, you don't fly inverted as a normal rule, because it's not normal. Normal airplane engineers found that negative-G limits aren't likely to be exceeded under typical flight conditions.

Think about it this way. If an upward gust were to increase the G-force by one positive G, then the same gust applied in a downward direction decreases the G-force by one positive G. If you start at 1G and subtract the downward gust effect of 1G, you're now at zero G's, not negative 1G. In other words, to experience negative Gs, the airplane must first move through the zero G (weightless) position.

Maximum Speed Limit

Now that we have the upper and lower G limits established, let's take a look at the upper speed limit of our V-g diagram. Airplane speed limits are typically determined by something known as *flutter*. Flutter is the violent and often destructive vibration of an airfoil, control surface or flight control. These are *not* good vibrations. The condition is usually associated with excessive airspeeds. Flutter can lead to airfoil disintegration. This may be what they meant in old time movies when the villain would say, "Curses, foiled again." At excessive speeds, the elastic and inertial dampening qualities of the airfoil and control surfaces are often unable to dampen vibration.

Many years ago, before oscilloscopes and sensitive vibration measuring devices were commonly available, aerodynamicists had a very straightforward means of identifying an airplane's flutter speed. This was called a *test pilot*. Engineers would find a skilled test pilot, show him a wheelbarrow full of money (in his dreams), then send him aloft with a Valium patch (maybe more than one) to dive the airplane at high airspeeds. The test pilot would pulse the flight controls at each increasing intervals of airspeed and observe the results. When flutter was experienced, the test pilot would note the indicated airspeed, pull back the power, slow the airplane down and return to the airport (usually). Upon landing, and after he stopped hyperventilating and regained his ability to speak, he'd tell his tale about the speed beyond which the airplane experienced flutter (then he'd go play with his wheelbarrow of well-earned money—in his dreams). This

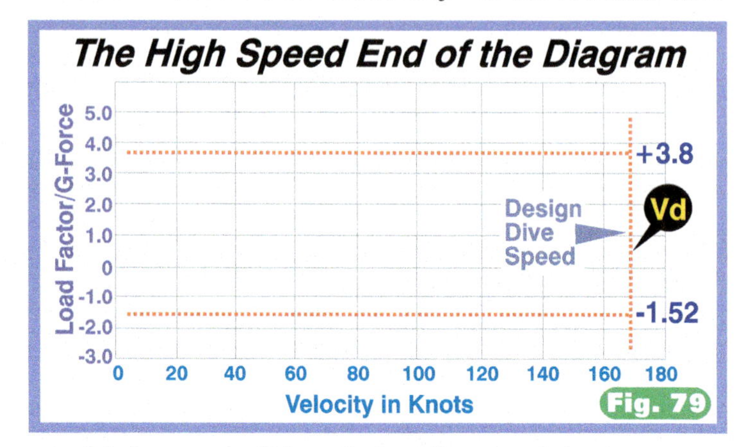

Fig. 79

speed is known as *Vd* or *design dive speed*. Let's use 169 knots indicated airspeed (IAS) as the design dive speed in our diagram and place a vertical line representing *Vd* at this value (Figure 79).

Of course, airplane manufacturers aren't going to let you fly the airplane right up to Vd like the test pilot did (they don't have your address, and thus wouldn't know where to deliver your wheelbarrow full of money and your Valium patches). That's why, in the spirit of safety, the FARs require that the airspeed indicator's red line or

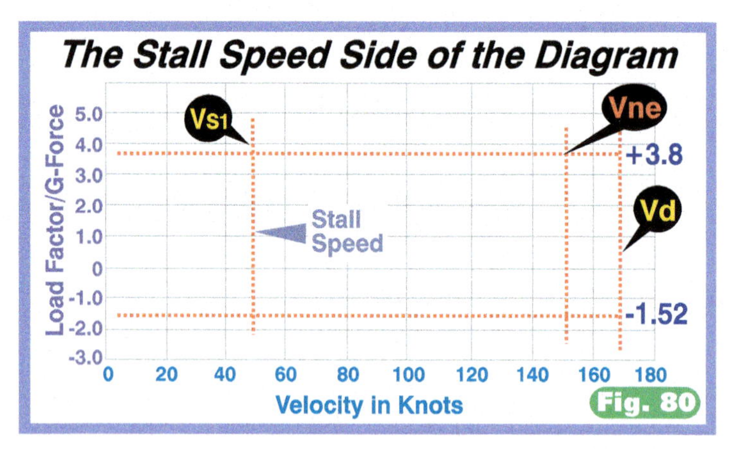

Fig. 80

Vne (velocity to never exceed) be marked at a value that's 90% of Vd. In our example, Vne is (.9x169) 152 knots (IAS). Let's make a vertical line at this location on our diagram in Figure 80.

The Stall Side

To complete the picture, we need to work on the left side—the slow speed side—of the V-g diagram. This side must represent a relationship between stall airspeed and G-force. Let's begin by creating a vertical line that represents the stall speed in a +1G condition, otherwise known as *Vs1*. This speed is 50 knots (IAS) for our airplane and it represents the airspeed at which the airplane stalls with

the power off and the gear and flaps retracted (Figure 80). Now ask yourself what happens to stall speed when the G-force changes. Yes, the stall speed must change, too.

Now we need to construct a chart showing the relationship between stall speed and G-force. These values are easy to determine for our airplane with just a little mathematics (wait, come back here! I mean only a teeny-weeny bit of math). To find the stall speed for a given load factor, we'll simply multiply the power-off stall speed in the clean configuration (i.e., gear and flaps retracted) times the square root of the load factor for a specified bank angle (refer to Figure 30 on Page B18). If our airplane stalls at 50 knots in the clean configuration at 1G, then it will stall at about 71 knots in a 2G condition (50 knots times the square root of 2 [or 1.414]=71 knots). When I calculate the accelerated stall speeds for 3Gs and 4Gs, I obtain the upward curving "stall speed" line in Figure 81A.

Notice that the positive-G stall line in Figure 81A doesn't continue below 1G. As an academic exercise, I'll continue the stall line to the left of the graph until reaching the zero-G point, as shown in Figure 81B, line A. In this area we don't speak of stall speed, since the airplane and its contents approach weightlessness. After all, if you're weightless, stall speed is meaningless. Now let's draw the stall speed line for negative-G flight, which involves inverted flight or outside maneuvers (we'll skip the calculations here). The negative-G stall line is roughly the mirror image of the positive-G stall line, as shown by line B.

Now we're ready to superimpose the positive and negative-G stall lines on the left side of our V-g diagram, as shown in Figure 82. As you can see, the V-g diagram is nearly complete in the sense that it has four basic sides: a low speed side, a high speed side, an upper positive-G limit and a lower negative-G limit. To complete the construction, let's shade the area with a green color to represent where normal operations are permitted, as shown in Figure 83 (I'll explain the yellow area soon; it's not the operating region reserved for sunset flights). What you now have is a completed V-g diagram.

Figure 84 shows the four basic regions of the V-g diagram. Region 1A is the stall region, sometimes referred to

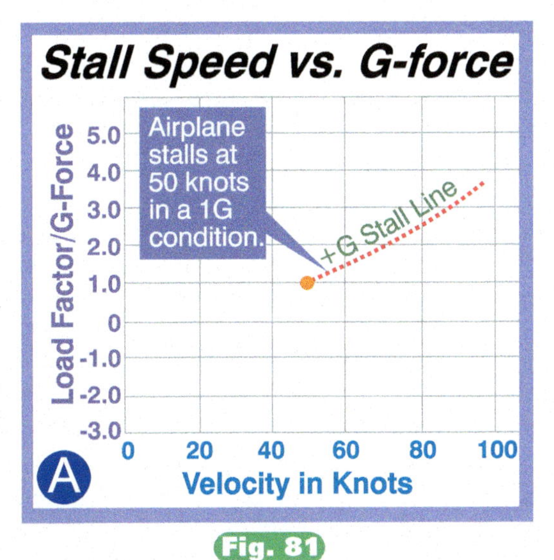

Fig. 81

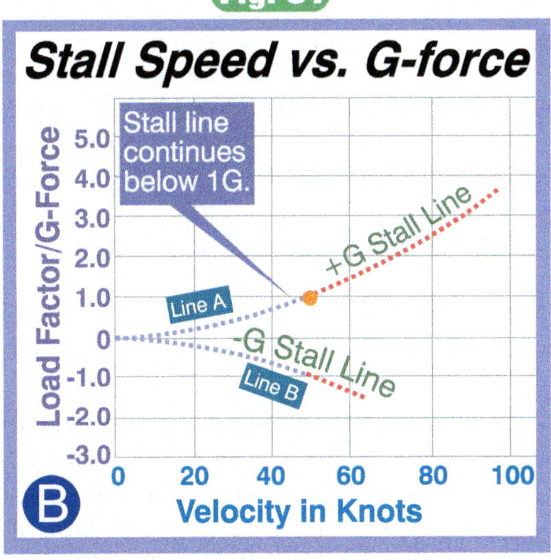

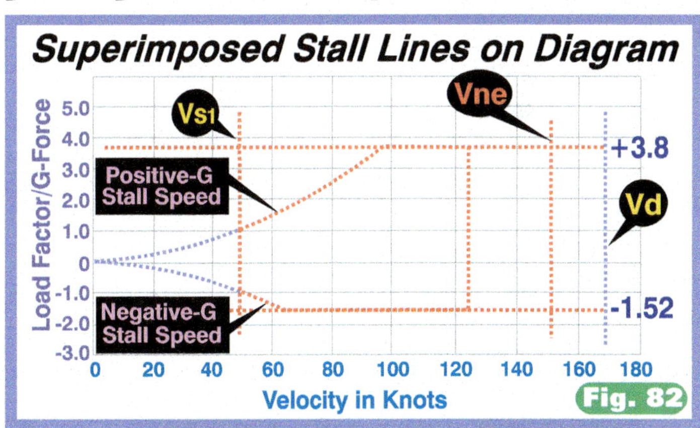

Fig. 82

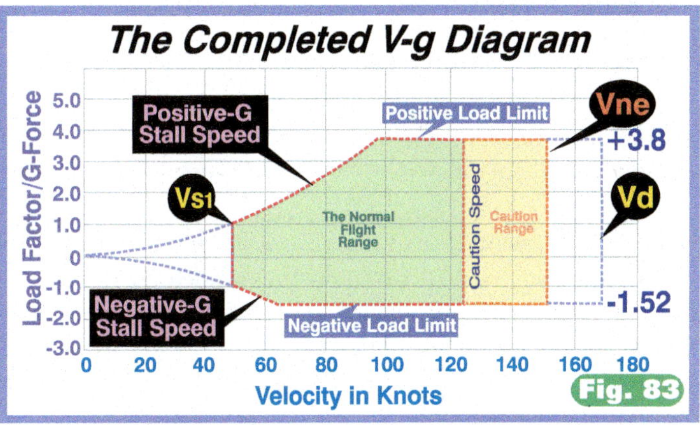

Fig. 83

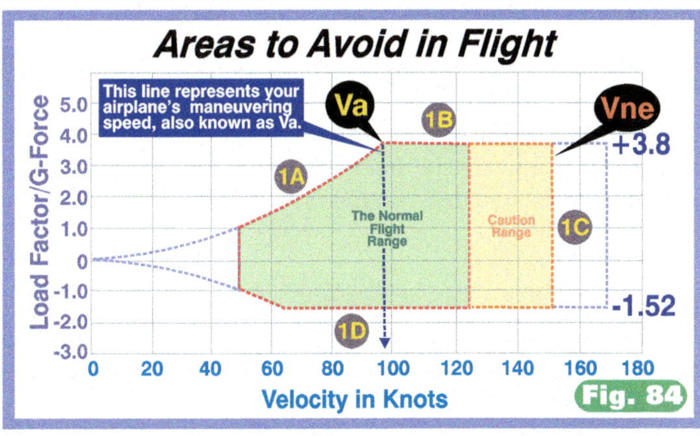

Fig. 84

by engineers as the *region of unavailable lift*. Those engineers have a great sense of humor. When operating at speeds between Vs1 and the top right portion of the positive-G stall speed line (97 knots), any accelerated stall results in a G-force that's won't exceed the upward limit established by that line. No matter now abruptly you pulled the elevator control at 80 knots, the airplane will stall before exceeding +2.5Gs. Said another way, there's no way to exceed +2.5Gs at 80 knots no matter how hard you pull aft on the elevator (the assumption here is that the airplane is at its max gross weight, too).

Let's focus a little more on the point where the curved positive-G stall line intersects the stress envelope's upper G-limit line. Draw a line downward vertically from this intersection. This line represents a speed of approximately 97 knots (IAS). At this speed, the airplane will stall before it can exceed more than +3.8 Gs. This is an important speed to know. After all, if we fly at or below this speed, the airplane will stall before exceeding the airplane's design limit load factor of +3.8 Gs. In case you haven't guessed, this vertical line represents the airplane's maneuvering speed or *Va* (*velocity of acceleration*) at its maximum gross weight (remember, maneuvering speed decreases with a decrease in weight. See Postflight Briefing #2-5).

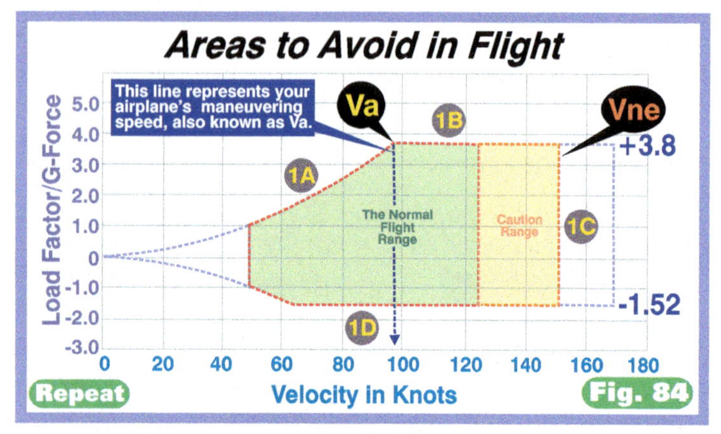

Suppose we were in extreme turbulence at 110 knots. Look at the positive-G stall line in Figure 84 and mentally project its curve upward and to the right. If our airplane stalled at 110 knots, it's obvious that the airplane can experience enough positive-Gs (region 1B) to put it outside the upper limits of its stress envelope. This is one reason we want to be at or below maneuvering speed when encountering turbulence.

It should also be clear that region 1C should be avoided because of the potential for destructive flutter. Region 1D should also be avoided because it's beyond the airplane's negative-G limits.

Gust Loading

Now let's look at how *gust loads* affect the airplane by constructing a *gust envelope* (which isn't the package the *gust lock* came in either!)

Here's what we know so far. Flight at or below maneuvering speed prevents the airplane from exceeding its design limit load factor in the event a flight control is suddenly and completely deflected (such as if you had to pull back immediately on the elevator control to avoid hitting a bird or a plane or even Superman). Regardless of how the elevator control is manipulated, an airplane certificated in the normal category will stall before exceeding its positive or negative limit load factors when flown at or below 97 knots (IAS). But pilot-induced wing loads aren't the only loads to which an airplane is exposed. It is possible, with no action by the pilot, that atmospheric gusts could increase the load applied to an airplane's wings. Fortunately, airplanes are designed to withstand these specific loads, too.

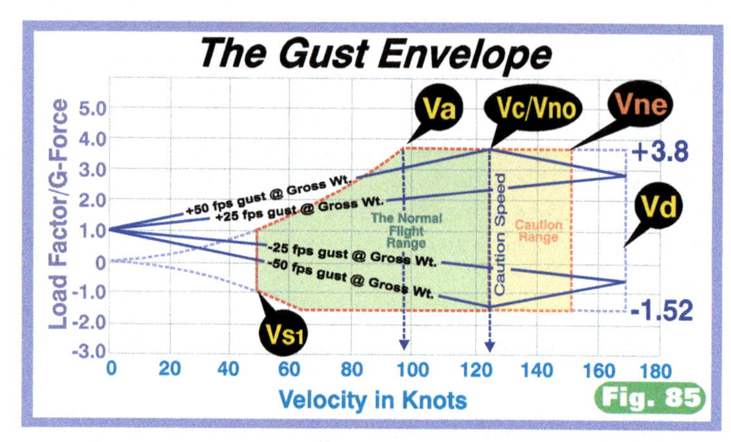

In straight and level flight, when the airplane encounters a vertical gust of air, it experiences an increase in lift because its angle of attack is increased. The airplane accelerates upward as a result. This occurs in much the same way you would experience an increase in lift by pulling back on the yoke (elevator) control and increasing the angle of attack, except that there is no actual force applied to the yoke. The question is, "How do these gusts affect the airplane?" Let's examine Figure 85 to find out.

Figure 85 shows the typical *gust envelope* for an airplane at full gross weight. The blue diagonal lines represent the effect of a mathematically determined *sharp edged* gust on the airplane. These are called *sharp edged gusts* because, as far as the engineers are concerned, there is no transition gradient between the smooth and rough air of a gust. Of course, Mother Nature may not work exactly this way, but this assumption makes the equations easier to solve (it works to your advantage too). Notice that the gust lines have their roots at the extreme left side of the diagram, starting at the 1G position (your normal, unaccelerated flight condition). Two gust lines are angled upward and to the right (the positive-G gust lines), and two are angled downward and to the right (the negative-G gust lines).

The upward angled gust lines represent the effect of a +25 fps (foot per second) gust and a +50 fps gust on the airplane. If you locate the intersection between the airplane's speed (horizontal axis) and the gust line, then

move to the left of the graph, you can determine the G-force imposed on the airplane as a result of that 50 or 25 fps gust. It should be immediately apparent that the higher the airplane's indicated airspeed, the greater the G-force imposed on the airframe by a gust. This is one reason you want to slow the airplane down in turbulent air, thus not exceeding the limits of its stress envelope. This is a very important point to keep in mind.

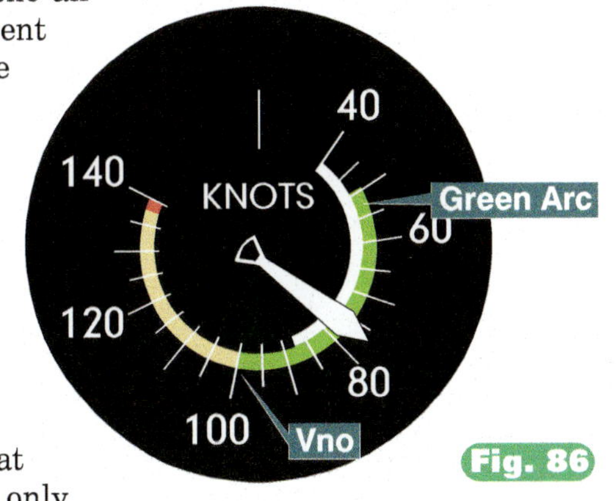

Fig. 86

Standard airworthy airplanes certificated after September 1969 are required to withstand a +/– 50 fps sharp edged gust at *Vc* or the *velocity of cruise* and a +/– 25 fps gust at *Vd* or *design dive speed*. As additional information, airplanes certificated prior to 1969 have lower gust load requirements. These are +/– 30 fps and +/– 15 fps, respectively. And just to be clear about this, I'm speaking of airplanes that are *certificated* after September 1969, not airplanes that were built or manufactured after that time. Airplanes certificated in the 1950s but being manufactured today are only required to meet the gust requirements in effect on or before September 1969. The date of certification is the date the airworthiness certificate was originally issued for that specific airplane by the FAA. Light sport airplanes, on the other hand, only have to meet the consensus standards for that particular machine. Fortunately, many light sport airplanes meet or even exceed these standards.

At 124 knots IAS (Figure 85), the airplane can withstand a +/– 50 fps gust and not exceed its design limit load factor. This is right at the limit of the stress envelope, but the maximum stress limit hasn't been exceeded. The FAA defines this specific speed at *Vc* or the *velocity of cruise*. While the FAA's equations provide several values for Vc, the value that's usually lowest is used to reference the high speed end of the green arc on your airspeed indicator (Figure 86). This is also known as *Vno* or *maximum structural cruising speed*. Beyond Vno is the yellow speed, or *caution* range.

Now you know why the green arc eventually becomes the yellow arc. It has to do with the gusts the airplane's capable of withstanding. Remember, the faster the airplane flies, the greater the load imposed on the airframe by a gust. In the yellow or caution range, the airplane should only be flown in smooth air.

But what if the air is extremely bumpy? Can we fly in turbulence at speeds up to Vno? Once again, since you don't know if there are sharp edged gusts exceeding +/– 50 fps, you don't fly near the top of the green arc in *heavy* turbulence. Instead, you fly at or slightly below the airplane's maneuvering speed (Va). This is the only speed that offers a reasonable guarantee that you won't exceed your airplane design limit load factor no matter how hard or to what extent the elevator control is displaced nor how strong (within reason) the gusts are.

Postflight Briefing #2-8 Incidentally, Here's Something About Your Wing

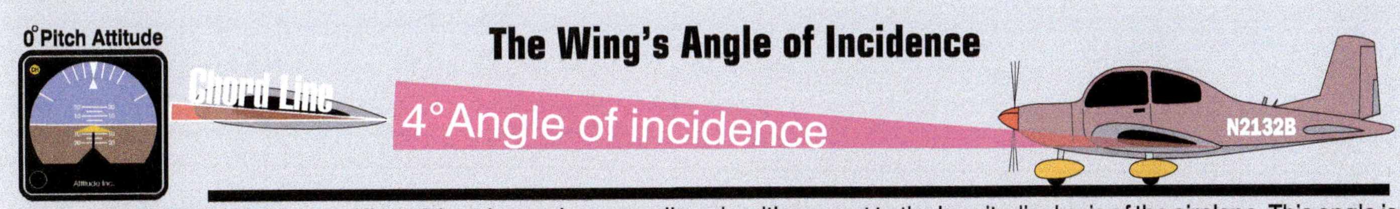

In a level flight attitude, the chord line of the wing makes a small angle with respect to the longitudinal axis of the airplane. This angle is known as the *angle of incidence*. The angle of incidence is somewhere around 4 degrees for many airplanes. This allows the fuselage to remain level at cruise speeds (where the airplane typically spends most of its time). The result is that the pilot and passengers sit perpendicular to the earth's surface (a comfortable position) during cruise flight. With the elevator in the neutral position during the takeoff roll, the airplane will naturally want to lift off on its own, but often do so at a higher than normal speed.

B52

Chapter Three

Engines

Knowledge of Engines Is Power

Introduction

"Ning, ning, ning, ning, ning," clanked the starter, but my 1963 high school Rambler refused to start. The light turned green. I turned red. A police officer walked up, gazed down over his lowered sunglasses and said, "What's the matter, don't we have a color that pleases you?"

I continued cranking. Suddenly, white smoke poured from beneath the engine. I thought this had to be the granddaddy of all fires, or perhaps a new Pope had just been elected. My car died.

Airplane engines have been far better to me than car engines. Good thing, given the difficulty of pulling over in the air to take a look under the hood.

The modern airplane engine is a thing of beauty. Not Meryl Streep or Margaux Hemingway beauty, you understand. More like Tom Hanks or Robert Redford beauty. Rugged, dependable. You, too, will learn to see the beauty in the bag of bolts up front as it churns away, hour after hour, turning the prop and helping to create lift so you can fly the friendly skies.

Due to the lack of backups for the engine after departing the ground, you will want to do everything possible to take care of the one you have on board (if you're lucky enough to have *two* engines on board, it still makes pretty good sense to take care of them). The reliability of modern aircraft engines is admirable, given the tremendous stresses and strains to which they're subjected. But don't get overconfident. The loudest sound in the world is an airplane engine that quits. At that precise instant, your body releases a jolt of adrenaline sufficient to keep all of New York City awake for a month and you suddenly remember all the words to *Ave Maria*—in Latin.

A little bit of care goes a long way toward making certain your engine goes a long way. Just as you didn't need a degree in aerodynamics to survive the last chapter, you won't need to demonstrate wrench-twirling skills in order to master this chapter and become a pilot. However, there are things you can and will do in the cockpit that have an effect on engine longevity and reliability. Besides, if you're going to order the correct maintenance for the workhorse under the cowling, you need to understand some of the basic principles of the internal combustion engine. That's what this chapter is about.

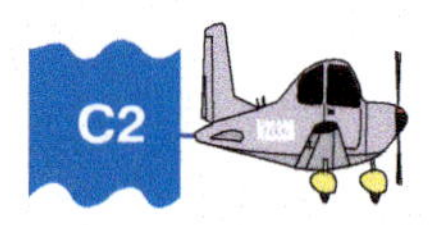

The Airplane Engine

Those two brothers who made it possible for man to fly (and I don't mean Ernest and Julio Gallo) made history by wedding a relatively lightweight and powerful engine to the Wright Flyer. Modern airplane engines are even more impressive in their ability to generate a tremendous amount of power for a given engine weight, as well as for their outstanding reliability.

Most general aviation airplane engines are of the *horizontally opposed* variety (Figure 1). Please try and get the term correct. I had a student who spent six months laboring under the illusion it was *horizontally upholstered*. Things went along OK until he called the couch cleaners to do a routine inspection on the engine.

In a horizontally opposed engine, the cylinders are placed opposite each other (that's the *opposed* part), and they work lying down. What a deal. Horizontally opposed cylinder arrangements pack a lot of engine into a small amount of space. Less space used by the engine means less overall drag.

Within the engine there are a variety of metallic organs, each of which is vital to the engine's life (and thus your life). Every engine contains *pistons, cylinders, valves, connecting rods, camshafts,* and *crankshafts,* in varying proportions and arrangements (Figure 2). If you skipped Hot Rod 101 in school and don't know what any of these parts are, don't worry about it. Remember the people in the hardware store still understand terms such as—*thingamajigs, doohickies,* and *gizmos.*

Because of the reliability of airplane engines, you'll probably never witness any of these components, individually or collectively, departing your airplane (the last phrase a pilot wants to hear from a passenger is, "Hey look, there goes one of our pistons!"). Treated properly, it's unlikely that you'll ever have any serious trouble with your airplane's engine.

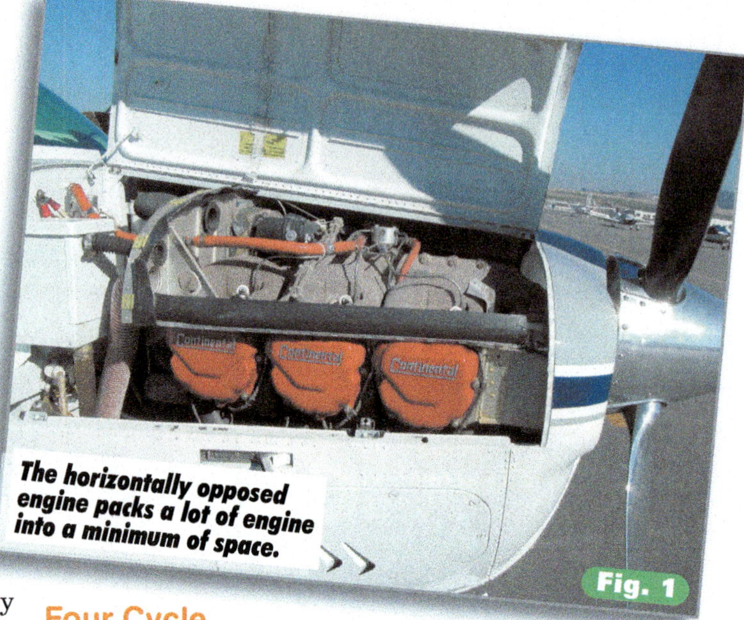

The horizontally opposed engine packs a lot of engine into a minimum of space.

Fig. 1

INSIDE THE ENGINE

Inside are such things as pistons, valves, a crankshaft, and much more.

Fig. 2

Four Cycle Engine

Airplane engines and humans are similar in how they process their fuel (food). Engines process fuel in a four-step or four-cycle process. Humans do likewise. Humans take in fuel by placing it in their mouths, compress it by chewing, digest it for power, and exhaust the remains (except that we don't have mufflers—now that would be a Kodak moment!).

Airplane engines also have four cycles: intake, compression, power, and exhaust.

The intake cycle occurs as the piston moves downward. Since the cylinder was filled with the piston as the cycle started, removing it creates a vacuum. Think of it as the presence of nothing, or the absence of everything (your choice). Nature abhors a vacuum. You've heard that fools rush in where angels fear to tread? While the piston is in its downward journey, the *intake valve* opens, and a mixture of fuel and air rushes in (Figure 3A). As you'll soon see, this sucking action is responsible for the term *manifold pressure,* which is used on higher performance airplanes.

The *compression cycle* occurs when the intake valve closes and the piston rises. The stuff that rushed in probably wouldn't have been in such a rush if it knew that the next thing to happen was The Big Squeeze (Figure 3B). With all the outlets closed, the fuel-air mixture gets compressed.

Now comes The Big Bang. A short chorus of "C'mon Baby, Light My Fire" would be appropriate here.

Just before the cylinder hits the top of its return journey, the *spark plugs* fire. (There are two plugs in each cylinder for increased safety and efficiency.) This sets off a wave of fire which spreads throughout the compressed mixture.

The burning mixture pushes the piston downward. This is the *power stroke* (Figure 3C). Once the expanding fuel's energy is absorbed by the piston, the piston

Efficient New Ignition Systems

FADEC or *Full Authority Digital Engine Controls* is the wave of the future. This system eliminates the use of carburetors and magnetos and provides precise automatic control of the fuel-air mixture entering the airplane engine. Manual control of the fuel-air mixture is no longer required by the pilot, thus simplifying pilot workload.

FADEC consists of three major components. First, specially designed fuel injector nozzles precisely match fuel flow to the actual airflow entering the engine. Second, a FADEC computer captures the exact state of the engine and its operating environment. The third component of FADEC is a collection of small computers that manage each cylinder by reading engine and environmental conditions then computing the fuel and spark timing necessary to precisely control the combustion process in each cylinder.

FADEC provides for improved fuel consumption, reduced pilot workload, ease of engine starting, smoother engine operation, less vibration and high tech service and maintenance with downloadable data provided to mechanics by FADEC computers.

ascends, expelling exhaust gases from the cylinders through the exhaust valve (Figure 3D).

This hot act is playing simultaneously on all four (six, or eight, depending on the engine) cylinders, though each cylinder is in a different phase of the production at any instant. It all adds up to a horizontal tower of power.

THE FOUR STROKE ENGINE

A Intake Stroke

B Compression Stroke

C Power Stroke

D Exhaust Stroke

Fig. 3

The Ignition System

I casually mentioned *spark plugs* a moment ago. We're going to zero in for a closer look at what sparks your engine's fire, because managing that system is crucial to getting the most (or sometimes to getting anything) from the powerplant.

Once the fuel-air charge is in the cylinders, it must be lit to do any useful work. That's why all powered aircraft have some form of ignition system. Even the space shuttle has one (and I don't think it's some guy with a Bic lighter).

In an internal combustion engine, the ignition system is a one-trick pony. All it does, hour after hour, is send a jolt of electrical energy to the spark plugs so they can spark. Like many specialists, the ignition system is very good at what it does. That's fortunate, because getting the job done right depends on precise timing that makes trapeze artists look klutzy.

In order to create a sheet of fire that spreads smoothly across the cylinder, the spark has to light the fuel-air mixture at a precise instant. The cylinder will not sit around waiting. The precise time of this auspicious moment has been worked out by the pocket protector people, and is not your immediate concern. Let's just agree there is A Right Time. (It's not a secret; the correct timing is stated in the engine's service manual, and is often marked on the engine, as well). Too early a spark and the charge starts expanding down while the cylinder is still headed up. Bad. Too late and some of the energy never gets used. Also bad.

Dual Ignition Systems

A moment ago I said there are two spark plugs in each cylinder. This is not solely for the enrichment of the spark plug manufacturers. It's actually for your protection.

Modern airplanes have dual ignition systems (Figure 4). When dual anythings are put on an airplane, it's an engineer's way of saying "This is really, really important and I want you to have at least one of these that works at all times, no matter what." That's Reason 1 why you have two spark plugs in each barrel. The other reason is that lighting the fire from a couple of spots creates a smoother, more even-spreading flame sphere, which is the goal of the controlled burn we refer to as *combustion*.

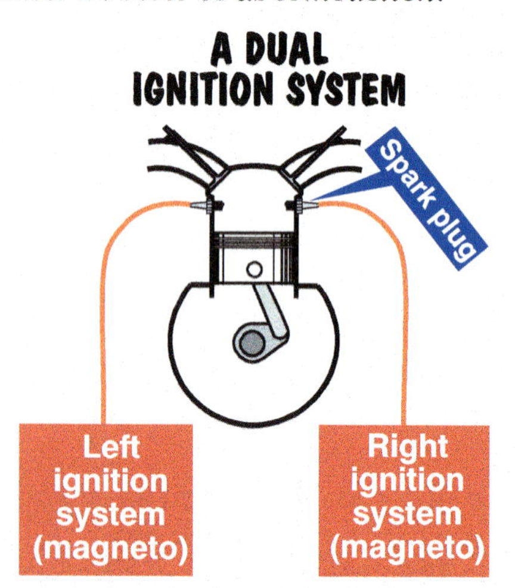

Dual ignition systems are installed in modern airplanes for increased safety. If the event one system fails, the other keeps the engine running. **Fig. 4**

Meet Mister Magneto

Having two spark plugs doesn't do an immense amount of good if you hook them up to *one* source of spark. It's the old thing about the chain and the weakest link. That's why I want you to meet Mr. Magneto (*mag* for short).

Magnetos contain spinnable magnets, housed in metal cases (Figure 5A). They are usually located on the rear of the engine as shown in Figure 5B. When their internal magnets are spun, they generate electricity for the spark plug. The magneto's electrical output forces electrons to rush to a tiny point on the spark plug. With millions more electrons pushing from behind like so many kids at a water fountain, each electron is forced to leap from the safety of that point to another spot located across a gap. In leaping the gap, a spark is created. That's why it's called a *spark plug*.

What's particularly interesting about magnetos is that they are self-contained spark generators. They require no outside source of electrical energy to work other than the turning motion of the airplane engine. That was a very important sentence, in case you were just scanning. It's important because it tells you the mags will work even if the alternator or battery is kaput.

From time to time I will let you in on some really fun instructor things—stuff we do that would be banned under the Geneva Conventions if it applied to flight instructors. One of those fun things to do is reach across in front of a student pilot, in flight, and turn off the big red switch that he or she has just learned is the electricity on/off gizmo. Whoa. That gets their full attention, because they are convinced the lights will go out (they will) and the engine will go off (it won't).

If you have an in-flight problem with your electrical system (alternator or battery failure for example), you won't need to worry about your engine being affected. In fact, your electrical system could be completely inoperative and the engine would continue to run. (A failed electrical system is an annoyance for a VFR pilot; on the other hand, a failed *engine* is like a dolphin hanging out with tuna—a more risky event).

Impulse Coupling

The next time a mechanic is hand-pulling a propeller through a couple of revolutions, listen for a clicking sound coming from the engine. The click results from something called an *impulse coupling* (Figure 5C). I know, you thought all couplings were impulse. Well, on some airplanes they are.

Fig. 5

An impulse coupling does limited duty. It's there to help get the engine all fired up about starting. Then it steps back and waits quietly to be summoned on another flight.

When you turn the key in the cockpit, you put the engine's *starter* to work. The starter is a small, electrically-driven motor that sets the engine spinning. You could do the same thing by spinning the propeller

(which is the way airplanes were started before starters were invented). However, *hand propping* an airplane is dangerous work, and almost impossible on a large engine.

The starter is the little motor that could. Except sometimes it can't. It often won't spin the engine quite fast enough to generate sufficient spark from the magnetos to set the fireworks show going. Enter the impulse coupling, stage left. The impulse coupling works somewhat like getting a boost over a fence. It's an extra shove that makes the climb easier. Impulse couplings are mechanical devices inside the magneto that save up a slight amount of spin energy on a spring. At a certain point, these springs release their energy causing the internal magnets to spin at a faster speed. This creates the electrical charge necessary to start the engine without having to equip airplanes with more powerful (and heavier) starters.

Once the engine starts, the impulse coupling stops, because the engine now generates sufficient speed and spark on its own.

Selecting Magnetos

From inside the cockpit, you have direct control over the magnetos using the switch shown in Figure 6A. Either the *left*, the *right* or *both* magnetos can be selected. Normally we operate with the magnetos in the *both* position, for maximum security and best spark distribution. You wouldn't want to select *off* in flight because it would kill the engine (and attract stares and gasps from your passengers) until you turned the mags back on.

Is there ever a time in flight when you might want to operate on only one magneto? Yes.

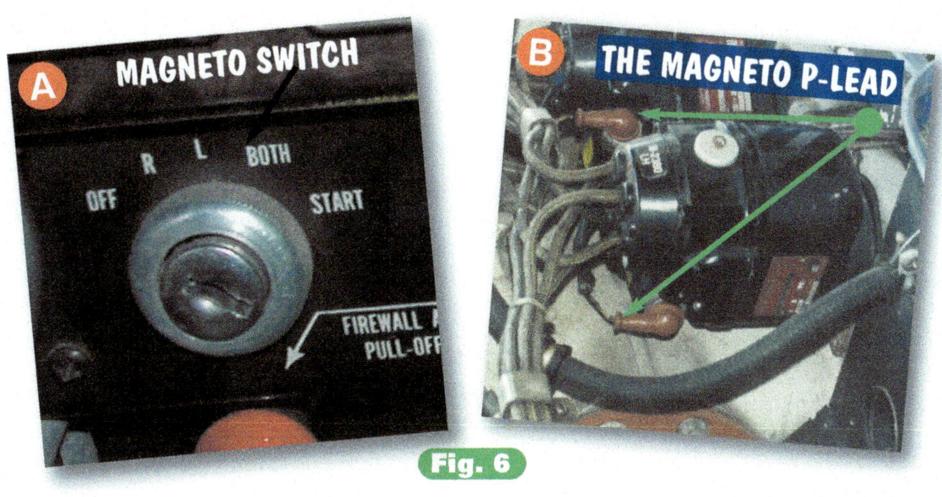

Fig. 6

Let's assume one magneto went bad in flight. It could randomly misfire, causing a very rough running engine despite the other magneto working properly. It could also stop working—the mechanical equivalent of a heart attack. You might try a single magneto and see what happens. Simply switch the mag switch from *both* to the *left* mag then to the *right* mag. How will you know which is the good or the bad mag? Don't worry, you'll know. You can tell by engine sound and vibration. If the engine sounds like it has lost power and/or runs rough, immediately switch to the other mag position.

Operating on one magneto is like operating on one lung. It can be done, but you're bound to experience a decrease in performance. In an airplane engine, this reveals itself as reduced engine RPM. Less spark within the cylinders means the combustion process takes longer. Therefore, the engine's speed typically drops around 100 to 150 RPMs (revolutions per minute). We refer to this as a *mag-drop* (no, this isn't where the mag falls off the airplane and rolls around on the runway).

In many cases we're concerned not only with the RPM drop on each magneto, but with the difference in RPM between each mag-drop (mag checks are done prior to takeoff in a special place called the *runup area*). This difference indicates the degree of timing error between each mag (since each mag is separately timed to the engine). For instance, the Pilot's Operating Handbook for a Cessna 172, Q-model, indicates that the drop for each mag shouldn't exceed 125 RPM, nor should the difference between the drops be greater than 50 RPM. A larger differential is symptomatic of an ignition system problem. Check your Pilot's Operating Handbook for acceptable drop limits.

Many pilots think that the lower the individual mag drop, the better. This isn't necessarily true. Little or no mag drop can mean improper engine timing or a broken P-lead.

The P-Lead

Selecting the right or left magneto deactivates the other mag by grounding it to the airframe (this neutralizes the magneto's ability to generate a spark). The absence of a mag drop can indicate that a mag that is supposed to be grounded (i.e., made inoperative) isn't.

Where that turns into trouble, appropriately enough, is on the ground. The mag is grounded to the airframe via a wire called the *P-lead* (Figure 6B). If the P-lead from a mag is broken or disconnected, it won't be grounded when it should be, including when the airplane is shut down. In that state, it is possible for the airplane

GOURMET NOTES

Aircraft struck a pheasant just before landing. The bird was delivered by the airport people to the crew, who arranged with their hotel to cook it for them for dinner. Another time, an air carrier, landing at a far North airport, whacked into a "2000" pound bull moose who had mounted his last charge.... Free moose steaks were offered to the delayed passengers, while a replacement aircraft was flown in....

ASRS Report

to start (or the engine to at least turn over a bit) if the propeller is turned by hand or accidentally bumped.

You will soon learn that the way to properly shut down an engine is *not* by simply turning the ignition switch to off, but rather by pulling out the mixture control knob. The reason for that, which many pilots don't really know, is it leaves the cylinders without fuel in them and thus minimizes the risk of an inadvertent startup in the event of a bad P-lead.

Several years ago I saw one of our school's less illustrious rental pilots sitting in the flight lounge with a bright, new arm cast. I said, "Skiing accident Bob?" He yelled, "No, just got my hand caught on the prop." He was moving the propeller by hand attempting to hook up the airplane's towbar. The propeller kicked, whirled a half turn, struck and broke his arm (of course, he was one of those "brag-it-up" type of pilots who told everyone else that an old Vietnam War injury was acting up. I happen to know he met his wife during the Vietnam War—she's Canadian).

No matter how the plane is shut down, the prop should always be treated with the utmost respect. Just like the family pitbull, it's generally quite tame, but on occasion it *can* bite. Rod's Rule: Don't touch the thing if you don't have to.

Mechanics (and flight instructors) sometimes recommend doing a P-lead security check just before shutting down. With the engine idling, quickly turn the mag switch from *both* to *off,* then immediately back to *both* again. If the magnetos are grounding properly, the engine should hesitate as you flick through the *off* part of the sequence. Engines that keep running as though nothing had happened probably have a magneto that isn't grounding. Then it's time for *you* to run—to the mechanic. Don't touch the propeller. Just put the airplane away, walk over to the flight school and use the proper incantation to summon a mechanic from his dark, tool-infested chambers. Let the mechanic handle the problem . . . and the prop.

CAPACITOR DISCHARGE IGNITION

Would you believe there's an ignition system that doesn't use magnetos, is completely free of maintenance and doesn't require any adjustment? It's true. It's a CDI or Capacitor Discharge Ignition system like the one found on the Katana DA-20. Unlike airplanes with magnetos, the CDI system uses solid state electronics to provide spark for the engine. This dual ignition system has two independent charging coils located on the generator stator that supply one ignition circuit each. CDI systems are very efficient in that there are no moving parts to wear and create errors in engine timing.

The Exhaust System

During the final cycle of a four-stroke engine, a rising piston forces hot gases out an opened exhaust valve and into the exhaust manifold (Figure 7). Most of the time these gases are released to the atmosphere, but in some instances they are put to productive use by the engine or the airplane.

When people say they're exhausted, it usually means that they are feeling useless, tired and worn out (perhaps from using exercise equipment like the StairMaster. That's why I prefer the ElevatorMaster). Exhaust gases, though, sometimes have an afterlife. They can be put to use spinning a *turbocharger* or indirectly heating the carburetor or cabin.

Air flowing over the outer shell of the exhaust manifold can be used to

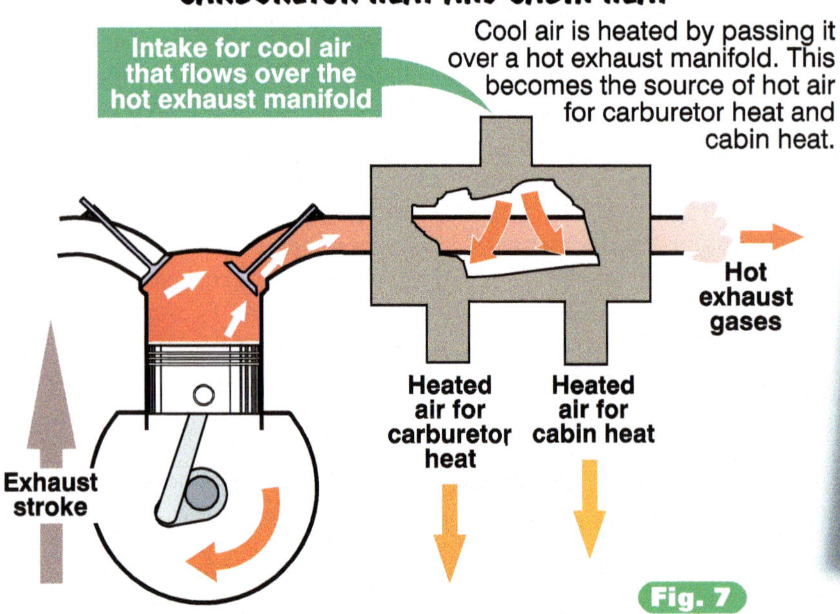

Fig. 7

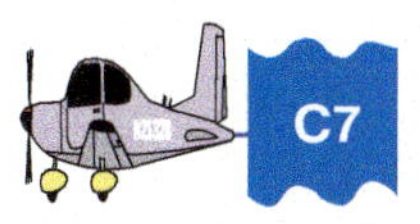

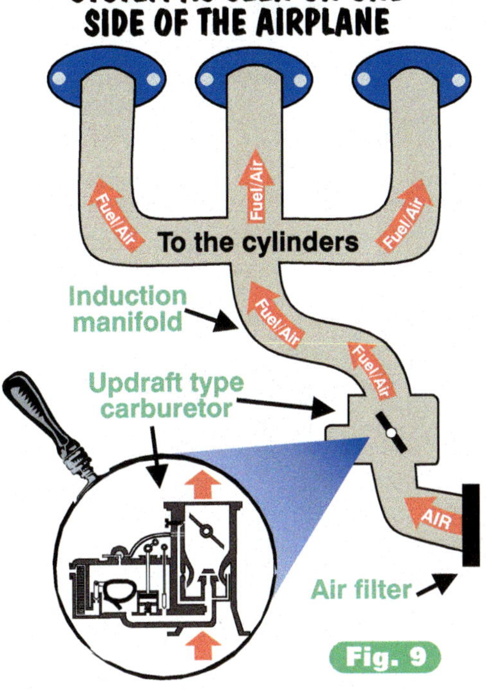

Fig. 9

raise the temperature of air entering the cabin or carburetor, as shown in Figure 7. Buildups of ice within the airplane's carburetor are prevented this way (we'll discuss carburetor ice later in this chapter). You simply pull the carburetor-heat lever to let heated air into the induction system which melts ice within the carburetor. Air used to heat the cabin results from the same process. Like carburetor heat, cabin heat is generated by bringing cooler air in contact with the hotter surface of the exhaust manifold.

Sometimes exhaust air is used to spin a small turbine, as shown in Figure 8. This, in turn, spins a compressor which sends compressed air to the cylinders. This device is a *turbocharger,* and it allows flight at higher altitudes by compressing air. Fed compressed air, the engine (which isn't all that smart) thinks it's at or near sea level, and puts out full power. This occurs because the presence of more air permits a larger fuel-air charge to be burned.

Think of it this way. If you go to the mountains, you will notice very quickly that you can't run, jump and play without huffing and puffing. The air is less dense. You simply don't have enough oxygen to perform at full capacity.

The same is true for a non-turbocharged engine. Less dense air at higher altitudes means decreased performance. Adding a turbocharger is like putting on an oxygen mask when you're in the mountains.

Airplanes with nonturbocharged engines typically fly at altitudes below 15,000 feet MSL (mean sea level, or above sea level). On the other hand, airplanes with turbochargers can fly at altitudes up to 25,000 feet MSL. Higher altitudes have other advantages—it's often possible to catch stronger winds, and if they're blowing your way, this cuts travel time and fuel consumption.

The Induction System

I had a student who'd apparently forgotten to register for the military draft. When I mentioned *the induction system,* he shot out the door leaving only a plume of smoking shoe tread.

To avoid problems, let me be specific. We're talking here about the airplane's induction system, which is the route by which fuel and air are absorbed for engine operations. The *air filter, carburetor* and *intake manifold* (pipes connected to each cylinder) make up the induction system on carburetor-equipped airplanes (Figure 9). Later on in this chapter we'll examine the induction system of airplanes with fuel injection. Let's start by examining an important part of the induction system known as the *carburetor.*

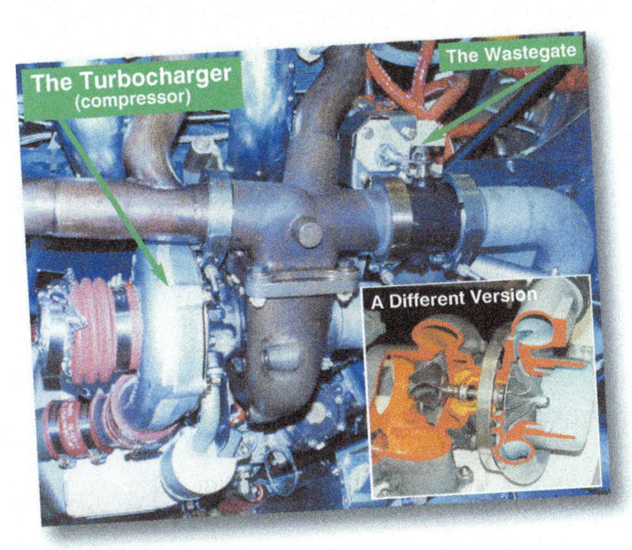

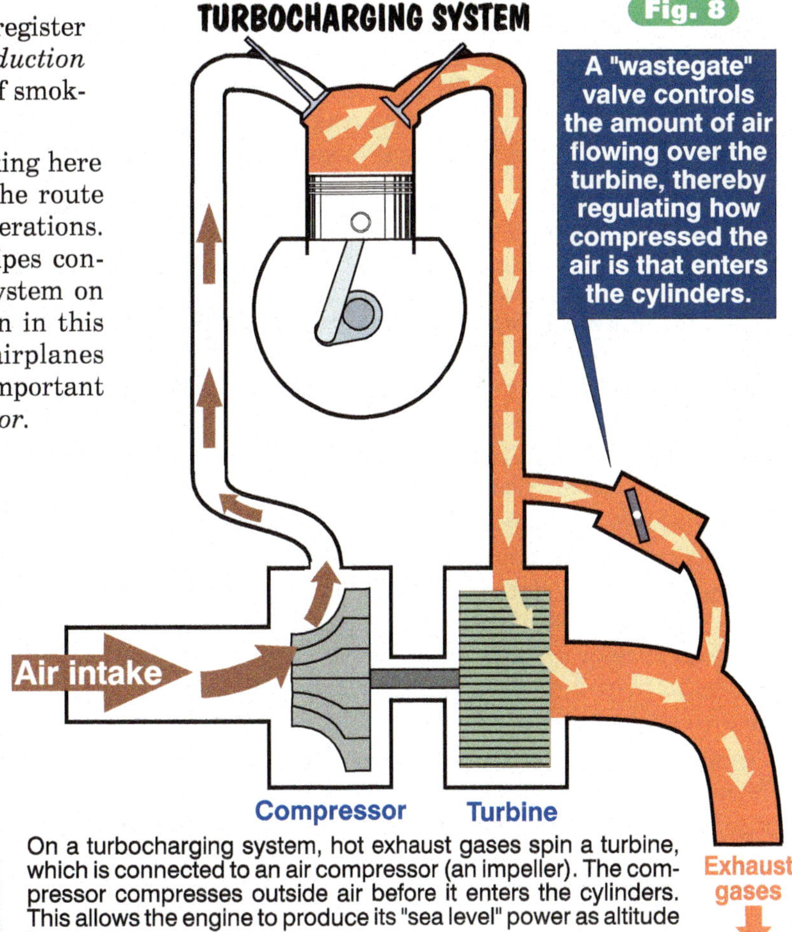

Fig. 8

On a turbocharging system, hot exhaust gases spin a turbine, which is connected to an air compressor (an impeller). The compressor compresses outside air before it enters the cylinders. This allows the engine to produce its "sea level" power as altitude increases.

The Carburetor

At a fancy party I once asked the bartender if he knew how to mix up a Grasshopper (the name of a drink). He said, "Well, you put a little blindfold on him and spin him around five or six times...." It seems that the bartender was as good at mixing-up answers as the carburetor is at mixing fuel and air. In fact, that's exactly what the carburetor is designed to do.

A carburetor is the ultimate mixmaster. Its job is to mix fuel and air in the right proportion for ideal combustion. Too much fuel, or too little air, and things won't go boom in the cylinder as they should. Since the fuel-air charge goes from carburetor to cylinder, you can think of this as the Shake 'n Bake system. The carburetor is one of the airplane's most important devices. You must understand its strengths and weaknesses, lest you become totally useless (kind of like a cabin attendant for a cargo airline) in the face of an engine problem.

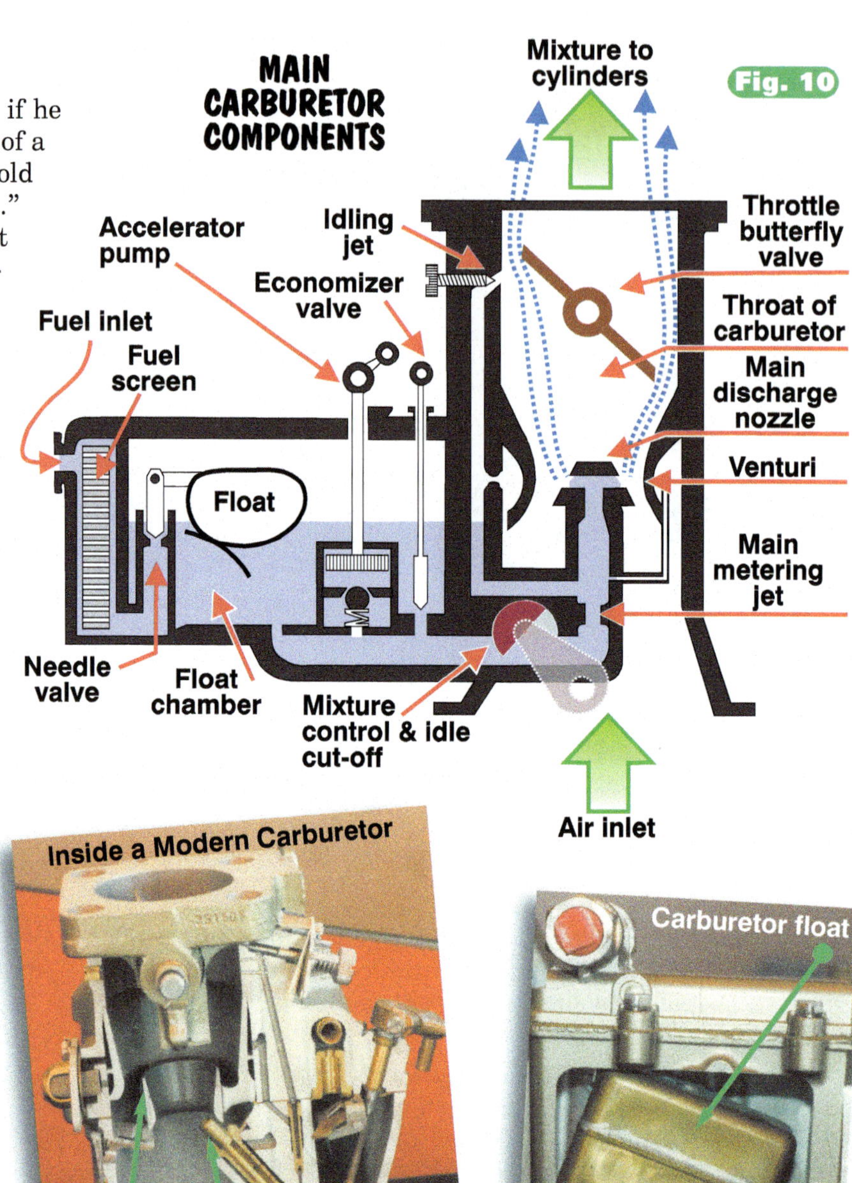

Float-Type Carburetor – Have you ever looked in the tank of a toilet? It's the place where you're supposed to keep the brick if you want to conserve water (not in the bowl!). Perhaps you've noticed a float on a lever that was capable of upward and downward movement within the tank. A similar float arm (not as big of course) is found in the float chamber of the carburetor, as shown in Figure 10.

As the toilet's tank loses water, the float lowers and opens a valve, which lets water in to replenish the loss. As the tank fills, the float rises, shutting off the valve, which restricts incoming water. In this way the water level is maintained at some desired level. Carburetors have similar mechanisms. A rising or lowering float in the float chamber regulates fuel entering from the intake line.

Of course, float systems, like toilets, only work when they're right side up, not inverted. While I doubt you'll ever be piloting an inverted toilet, it's possible to pilot an inverted airplane. Fortunately, some aircraft have an inverted carburetor system, which allows them to operate in an aerobatic mode. These aircraft can sustain inverted flight without having the engine quit.

Workings of the Float Type Carburetor – Carburetors are often located in-line directly behind the air filter at the front of the airplane (Figure 11). Air flows through the air filter, into the carburetor, then upward into the individual cylinders via the induction manifold. Airplane carburetors located underneath the engine are called *updraft* type carburetors because air and fuel must be drawn upward toward each cylinder. You'll find out in a moment why it's important to know what type of carburetion system you have on your airplane.

Air is drawn upward into the carburetor's throat and passes over a restriction—otherwise known as a *venturi* (see Figure 10). Notice that the cross section of the venturi is very similar in shape to the cross section of an airplane's wing. Air velocity increases over the venturi as it does when it flows over a wing.

Like an airplane's wing with high velocity air over the top, pressure decreases according to Bernoulli's principle. A reduction in pressure occurs near the outlet of the main discharge nozzle located in the middle of the venturi. Fuel in the float chamber is under normal atmospheric

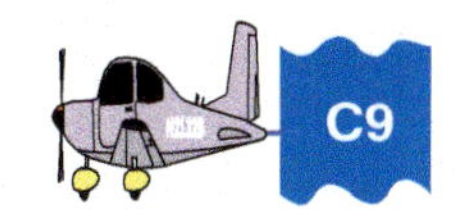

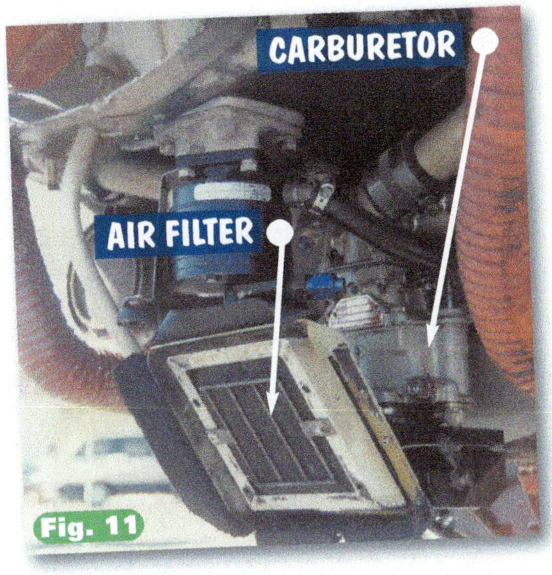

Fig. 11

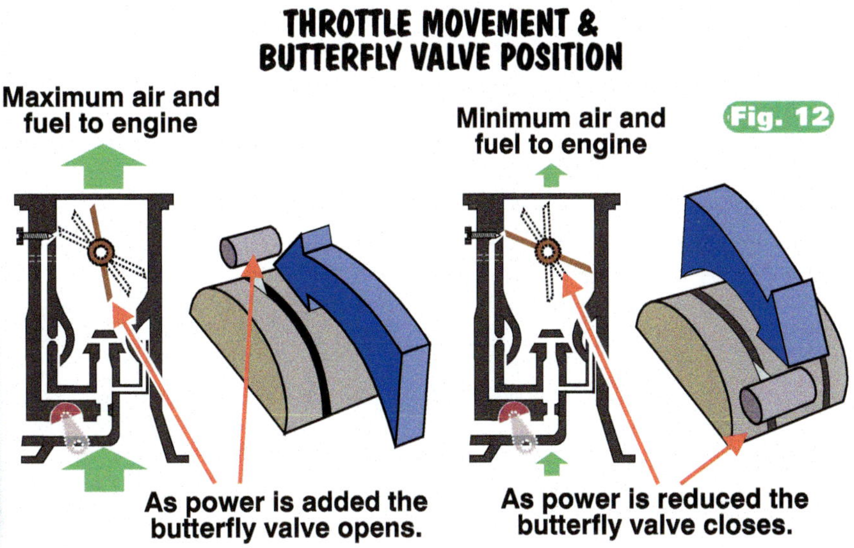

THROTTLE MOVEMENT & BUTTERFLY VALVE POSITION

Fig. 12

Maximum air and fuel to engine

As power is added the butterfly valve opens.

Minimum air and fuel to engine

As power is reduced the butterfly valve closes.

pressure, while the tip (outlet) of the main discharge nozzle is at lower pressure. Fuel flows from high pressure to low pressure as it's drawn upward into the carburetor's throat toward the cylinders.

As I mentioned earlier, air is drawn into the induction system by the sucking action of downward-moving pistons. This is similar to how air is drawn into our lungs. Our chest muscles expand, expanding the lungs, creating suction which pulls in air. If something is caught in our breathing passages, we're unable to inhale. We choke. Fortunately, we have the Heimlich maneuver to clear obstructions from blocked breathing passages (that's not the "Heineken" maneuver, so don't leave for a beer when someone's choking). Were it not for some restriction placed in the carburetor's throat, the engine would draw in maximum fuel and air and run at full power when started. Wouldn't that be interesting? You'd turn the key, crank the starter, pop a wheelie and take off! Air traffic controllers would love you.

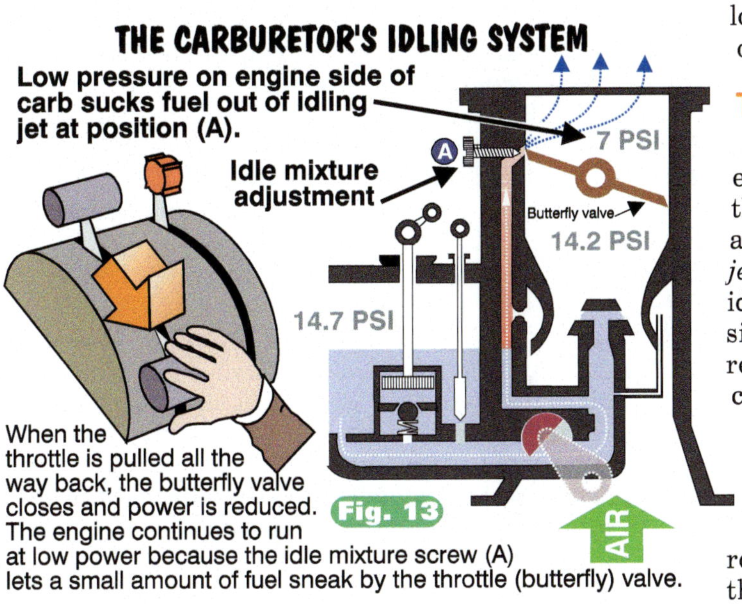

THE CARBURETOR'S IDLING SYSTEM

Low pressure on engine side of carb sucks fuel out of idling jet at position (A).

Idle mixture adjustment

A

7 PSI

Butterfly valve

14.2 PSI

14.7 PSI

AIR

Fig. 13

When the throttle is pulled all the way back, the butterfly valve closes and power is reduced. The engine continues to run at low power because the idle mixture screw (A) lets a small amount of fuel sneak by the throttle (butterfly) valve.

Fortunately, there is a device that restricts airflow in the throat of the carburetor. It's called the *throttle valve* or *throttle butterfly valve* and it's shown in Figure 12. The throttle valve is connected directly to the throttle lever located in the cockpit. Moving the throttle forward or aft opens or closes the throttle valve, controlling the amount of air entering the carburetor.

When the throttle is fully opened, the throttle valve is parallel to the intake airflow. In other words, the valve offers no restriction to the engine's suction. The engine draws in enormous amounts of fuel and air and runs at full power. A closed throttle moves the throttle valve perpendicular to the carburetor's airflow. Downward-moving pistons are causing tremendous suction but only a small amount of air and fuel gets past the closed throttle valve (just enough to let the engine idle). That's why the engine doesn't quit when you pull the throttle all the way back. A fellow pilot had his mom in the airplane and pulled the throttle to its idle position. The engine sound decreased as expected, but the engine still idled. She looked over at him and said, "Hey, turn that thing back on right now mister." Moms! Don't you love them?

The Idling System

If the throttle valve completely restricted air from entering the carburetor, the engine would quit when the throttle was closed. Fortunately, a small amount of fuel and air flows past the closed throttle valve. It's the *idling jet* that allows this to happen (Figure 13, position A). An idling jet is *not* a 747 sitting around waiting for permission to take off. It's more like a deliberate leak. The reduction in pressure downstream of the throttle valve continues to draw a small amount of fuel into the cylinders through the idling jet.

Since there is a rather inefficient mixing of air and fuel when the engine is idling for long periods, it's not unusual for spark plugs to foul and the engine to run rough rather than purr. If you're going to be operating the engine at the idle position for long periods of time, you might want to occasionally clear the engine with short applications of power (How often? Often enough to keep the engine from *loading up*. Experience will tell you how often to do this with your airplane).

The Accelerator Pump

Surely you've had the experience of being so thirsty that you gulped down a soda pop and proceeded to choke yourself in the process. Engines aren't much different. They can choke themselves if they try to gulp air too quickly. When the throttle is opened quickly, the vacuum created by the pistons could gulp large amounts of air—too much air for a given amount of fuel. The initial rush of air over the venturi is so quick that fuel can't be sucked through the nozzle of the metering jet fast enough, and the result would be a sudden hesitation in the development of engine power with rapid throttle application. That's something that will test your triple bypass.

Fortunately, carburetor engineers solved this problem with something known as an *accelerator pump*. Figure 14 depicts a small plunger-type mechanism linked to the throttle within the carburetor. When the throttle is opened quickly, it pushes the plunger downward, forcing an extra shot of fuel from the metering jet into the carburetor's throat. This compensates for the sudden in-rush of air that accompanies quick throttle application and provides for a smooth, continuous increase in RPM. Opening the throttle slowly allows fuel to slip around the sides of the small plunger, preventing an extra injection of fuel into the carburetor. (For your information, most but not all carburetors have some type of accelerator pump.)

THE CARBURETOR'S ACCELERATOR PUMP — Fig. 14

Extra shot of fuel to the cylinders to compensate for the sudden inrush of air.

PUSHES PLUNGER DOWN

When throttle is opened quickly, the accelerator pump squirts a small jet of fuel into the carburetor's throat to compensate for the sudden inrush of air into the engine. This pump prevents engine stammer and hesitation.

AIR

Initial rush of air into the carburetor when throttle rapidly opened.

Assuming the airplane has an updraft carburetor with an accelerator pump, what happens when the engine isn't running and the throttle is pumped? Yes, the accelerator pump squirts fuel into the carburetor. Without the engine running, there's no suction to inhale the fuel into the cylinders and fuel can fall to the bottom of the carburetor, soaking the air filter. Should the engine backfire during startup, your expensive airplane becomes a BBQ brazier. If you see people running toward you with hot dogs and buns, it may be a sign of the prime.

To avoid throwing an unscheduled BBQ event, it's best not to prime the engine by pumping the throttle on an engine with an updraft carburetor. If you insist on priming with the throttle, wait till the starter turns the engine, then pump the throttle. Any fuel squirted into the carburetor is more likely to be drawn upward into the cylinders. It's always safer, though, to use the engine primer. (See *Prime Time, page C23.*) That's what it's intended for. Besides, it gives you an extra thing to touch during engine start and this always impresses the passengers (especially if you mention phrases like, "Roger, Houston, we have T minus four and counting and are go for space dock....")

NO MIXTURE ADJUSTMENT?

It's true. Some airplanes have carburetors that don't require a mixture adjustment. They're generically called *altitude compensating carburetors*. On the advantage side, these carburetors reduce the pilot's workload because there's no mixture to manually adjust with changes in altitude. Increased economy often results because pilots are prevented from flying on the *overly rich* side of the mixture. Additionally, the potential damage from overleaning isn't a problem since airplanes with these type carburetors don't have mixture controls. Because the mixture is preset, the pilot can't make mixture adjustments for best economy or best power. The engine runs on the mixture setting provided by the manufacturer.

Altitude Compensating Carburetor

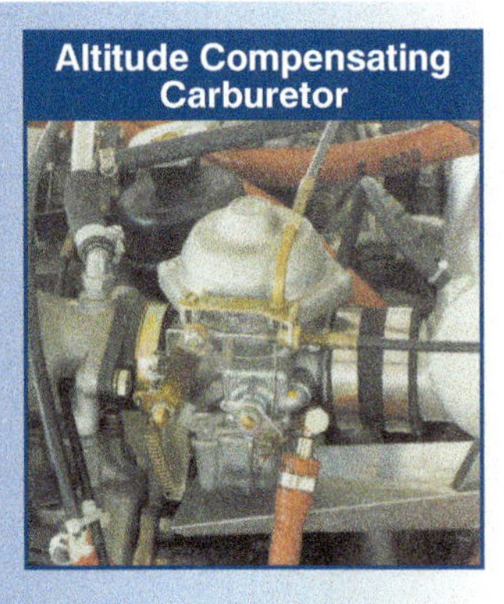

Atomization of Fuel

An atom is a very small particle of matter (about as small as the runway appeared during your first solo landing). Carburetors earn their keep by breaking up fuel into millions of tiny, atom-like droplets and mixing them with air. This process is called *atomization* and it makes the fuel-air mixture highly combustible—provided the fuel and air are mixed in the proper proportions.

The proportions or ratios of fuel to air must fall within certain limits for efficient combustion. The *fuel-air ratio*

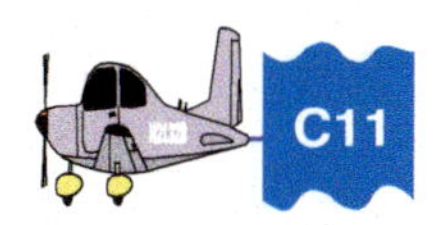

is simply the ratio of the weight of fuel to the weight of the air entering the engine. Fuel-air ratios of approximately one part fuel to 13 parts of air are the most efficient for combustion. This particular ratio produces a highly powerful mixture within the cylinders. Combustion can occur with fuel-air ratios of 1 to 8, all the way up to 1 to 20.

Too little fuel (1 to 20 fuel-air ratio) means there isn't enough fuel to cause a useful burn in the cylinders. Too much fuel (1 to 8 fuel-air ratio) means there is not enough air within the cylinders to efficiently burn the fuel that's available. (Most flight instructor cars operated at a 1:8 ratio. This allows students to keep an eye on their instructor's whereabouts by tracking the car's dark exhaust clouds on a satellite map.)

If airplanes operated at one altitude (where air density never changes), you wouldn't need to worry about manually changing your fuel-air ratio. Not many pilots fly at only one altitude, which means you need to know how to use the mixture control to maintain a specific fuel-air ratio.

Your Carburetor, The Ice Maker

Carburetors are great at atomizing fuel and mixing it with air. An interesting side effect of that process is that temperatures drop downstream of the main discharge nozzle. Temperature drops of as much as 70°F within the carburetor's throat are not uncommon (similar temperature drops are experienced in airline cabins when brand new flight engineers are manipulating the air conditioning controls).

Do you remember the last time you spilled a little fuel on your finger? It evaporated quickly didn't it? It also got a little chilly out there, didn't it? The process of evaporation requires heat. That's why you feel cooler when you sweat and the sweat evaporates, and why you feel miserable if you sweat and the humidity is high enough so there isn't much evaporation.

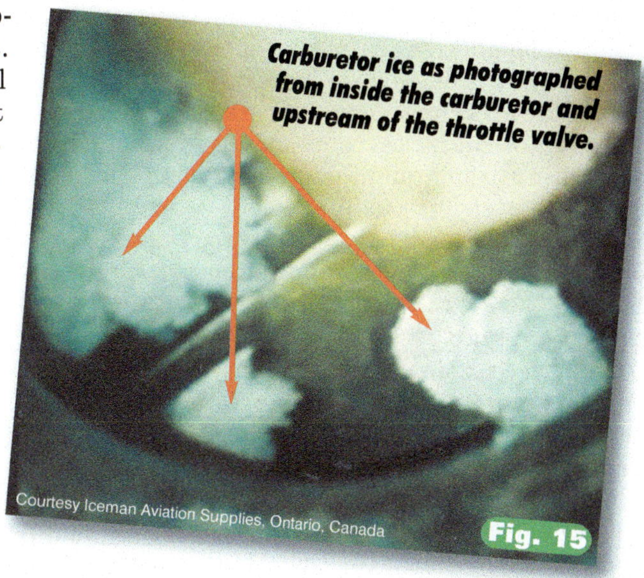
Carburetor ice as photographed from inside the carburetor and upstream of the throttle valve.

Courtesy Iceman Aviation Supplies, Ontario, Canada

Fig. 15

Your carburetor is a fine ice maker. Because of the considerable drop in temperature caused by the atomization and evaporation of fuel, any moisture present can and will freeze. Figure 15 is an actual shot of ice within the throat of a carburetor. With ice stuck in its throat, your carburetor (and thus your engine) can't breathe.

Impact ice seen on the airplane's nose area.

Courtesy NASA

Fig. 16

Carburetor Ice Can Occur At Any Temp – It's one of those gorgeous flying days. Bright, beautiful, maybe 80 degrees F outside. You're flying along without a care on your mind, and certainly no thought of ice.

Think again. A temperature drop of 70°F means that if the outside air temperature is 80°F, then the temperature in the throat of the carburetor can be 10°F! Wow, that's way below freezing. Be prepared for carburetor ice to form at almost any outside air temperature, though it's most likely to occur between outside temperatures of 20°F to 70°F. Soon you'll see how we can rid the carburetor of ice, should it form.

How to get maximum life out of your engine:

1. Let it warm up   2. Let it cool down   3. Never run it too hot

Ice: Just Your Type

Induction system ice comes in three varieties: impact ice, fuel ice, and throttle ice.

Impact Ice – *Impact ice* occurs when *visible moisture* is present (pilot term: *visible moisture* is water that can be seen, such as rain or a cloud) and the outside air temperature (OAT) is at or below freezing (Figure 16). Moisture can freeze over the induction system's air filter or inlet port and restrict incoming air. This deprives the engine of air and results in the engine taking a nap unless something is done to correct the problem.

Impact ice is usually the instrument pilot's dilemma because he or she is licensed to operate in the clouds (i.e., in visible moisture). It is possible, though, to have an air filter freeze over while nowhere near a cloud. If the air is moist and temperatures are low, water can accumulate on the air filter's membrane and freeze. This restricts the filter's ability to pass air in to the carburetor, resulting in a loss of power. While not one of the more extreme forms of impact ice, it is serious nevertheless.

Another occasion where impact ice is likely is during freezing rain (a very serious type of impact ice that I'll discuss in Chapter 12). For now, just know that if your air filter ever becomes clogged by impact ice, you have a remedy at hand. It's called the *carburetor heat* control. When you pull this lever, air that is *not* passed through the air filter goes to the heating shroud around the exhaust manifold, and then on to the carb and engine. It's like having an emergency nose through which your airplane can breathe. Airplanes having fuel injection (we'll discuss this shortly) have something known as an *alternate air lever* or an *automatic alternate air door* which provides the same breathing redundancy for the engine.

Fuel Ice – *Fuel ice* and *throttle ice* (unlike impact ice) are both types of carburetor icing. Fuel ice is an internal problem, rather than an external one, as shown in Figure 17. Fuel ice forms downstream of the main discharge nozzle. The expanding fuel-air mixture cools the air stream in much the same way underarm spray deodorant cools you. It's not unusual to apply a spray of deodorant and find yourself physically airborne, shocked by the large glacier that just formed under your arm. If the carburetor's internal temperature drops below 32°F, airborne moisture freezes, causing a restriction to incoming air. Once again, the engine can't breathe, which results in reduced engine power.

Fuel ice can occur at outside air temperatures as high as 85°F and at humidities as low as 50%. It is, however, more likely to form at temperatures between 20°F and 70°F under high-humidity conditions. Carburetor ice is unpredictable. From practical experience I will tell you that fuel ice as well as throttle ice can form at almost any outside air temperature and humidity.

Throttle Ice – *Throttle ice* forms on the rear side of the throttle valve (Figure 17). It is more likely to occur when the throttle is in a partially closed position. When the throttle is partially closed, air curves and bends around this valve in much the same way it bends across a wing. Bernoulli's principle is once again invoked. Air accelerates around this valve and pressure lowers. A reduction in pressure causes a decrease in air temperature, resulting in airborne moisture freezing on the back side of the throttle valve. Given enough airborne moisture and the proper conditions, throttle ice can also prevent an engine from breathing unless something is done to remove or prevent it.

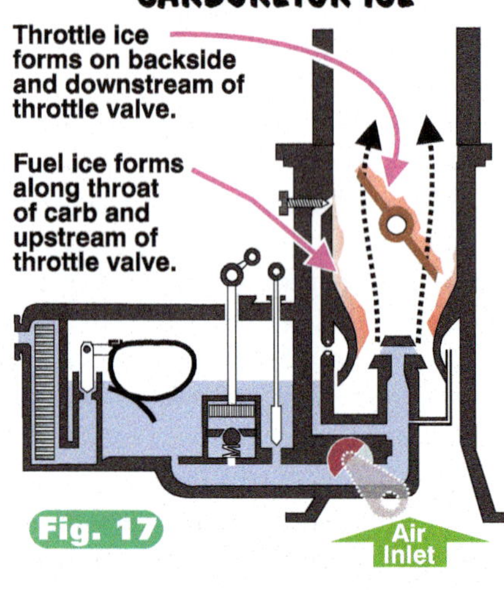

Fig. 17

Fig. 18

You should check your engine carefully, but this is going a bit too far!

It's been said that one day the cats and the birds will lie down together. I believe this is true if you have enough birds. Mixing cats and birds presents a significant hazard to the birds. Moisture and carburetors present a similar hazard to those not aware of icing problems. Smart pilots learn to anticipate carburetor ice during flight (we'll discuss the warning signs of carb ice in a moment). Regardless of your power setting or flight condition, you are not immune to carb ice. Remember (let's get that finger back in your ear), *visible moisture, in the form of clouds or rain, need not be present for fuel and throttle ice to occur.*

The Ice Eater: The Carburetor Heater

The antidote for carburetor ice is carburetor heat. Inside the airplane we have a carburetor heat lever (Figure 18). Pulling this lever allows heated air to enter the carburetor, raising the air temperature within its throat as much as 90°F. Provided you use it early enough, carburetor heat will quickly melt the ice and/or prevent further ice formation.

Heated air is obtained for the carburetor by passing air over the exhaust manifold, then piping it directly into the carburetor (Figure 19). This air is, as we've already mentioned, unfiltered. That's why you

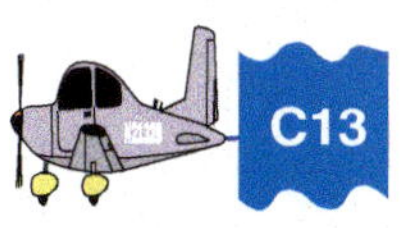

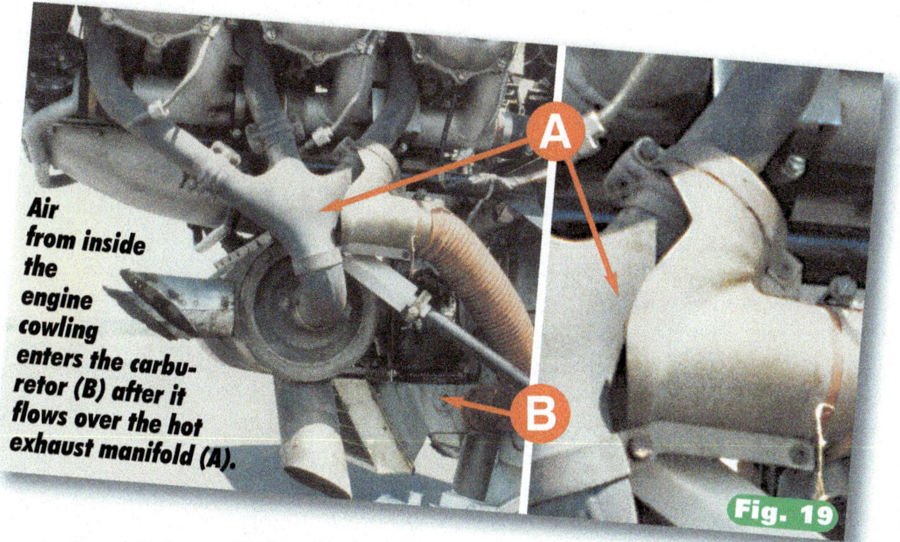

reach for this lever if the air filter is iced over. However, it's the reason you do *not* want to use carburetor heat for long periods of time while on the ground. Damaging dust and dirt particles can be drawn into the engine.

Carb Ice Symptoms

Carburetor heat should be used whenever you suspect ice formation. The best clue to the presence of carburetor ice on fixed-pitch propeller airplanes is an uncommanded decrease in engine RPM. Engine roughness is another sign of carburetor ice. Whenever engine power unexpectedly decreases, suspect the presence of carburetor ice and apply full carburetor heat.

Let's suppose you're cruising along in your little Cessna 172 and notice a slow but consistent RPM drop of 200 RPM over a period of 15 seconds. Suspecting carburetor ice, you immediately apply full carburetor heat. Some Pilot's Operating Handbooks (POHs) recommend that full throttle be applied first, then carburetor heat. There's a very good reason for this. First, for carburetor heat to be effective, the engine must be producing a certain amount of power. After all, heat comes from the hot exhaust system. Full throttle ensures adequate heat production is available to melt the ice. Second, applying full throttle lets more air into the carburetor. This is certainly a good thing, since it's restricted airflow that's causing the problem.

As you apply carb heat, the RPM decreases another 300 RPM (Figure 20 A and B), and you're looking around to see if the plane has parachutes available. Stay cool as a carb. You have not done the wrong thing, and in a few seconds things should get better. Honest! As we've previously seen, heated air is less dense than cooler air. Unleashing carb heat results in an RPM drop; in fact, that's how you test to make certain the carb heat is working before leaving the ground (more on this shortly).

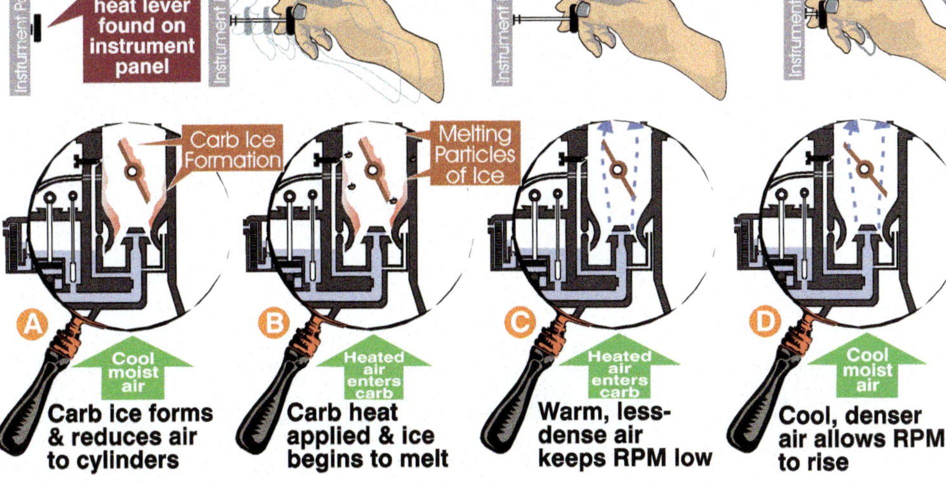

Fig. 20

If there is ice present, it will melt and RPM will rise, as shown in Figure 20C. In fact, the increase in RPM, after an initial drop, is a sure indication that you had carburetor ice. When the ice has melted, the rise in RPM ceases. As the carb heat is turned off, the RPM rises again to its previous (pre-ice) level as shown in Figure 20D.

When you apply carb heat, the engine may cough a couple of times as it digests chunks of melting ice from along the throttle valve or throat. Try not to worry (easy for me to say). The engine isn't going to quit because it ingested a little water and ice under these conditions. Nevertheless, a rough running engine always makes me feel on edge—like a dog wearing contact lenses with small cats painted on them.

Carburetor heat is actually a deicing device. You apply full

Don't Be a Jerker

Be careful about pulling too hard on the carburetor heat lever. I had one student pull the lever and its associated cable completely out of the panel. The knob, followed by a very long wire, just kept flowing out of the socket. After three feet of naked cable protruded out of the panel, he turned and looked at me, his mouth as wide open as a blimp hangar. Not wanting to miss an opportunity to have a little fun I said, "Hey, I didn't say to use that much carburetor heat did I?" Of course the engine continued to run with the carburetor heat in its full *on* position, but it ran about 100 RPM slower. Let me explain why this is.

One of the ways we check the operating condition of the carburetor heat mechanism is to apply full heat at a moderate engine RPM (approximately 1,700 to 2,000 RPM). You'll know it's working properly if there is about a 100 to 200 RPM drop (this varies among airplanes). Heated air entering the engine is less dense than cooler air. Since hot air is thinner, this means there is less air entering the engine. What does thinner air to do the engine's power output? It decreases it, resulting in a drop in RPM.

With the application of carburetor heat, you might notice a little engine roughness. Since hot air is less dense than cooler air, the mixture becomes richer when carburetor heat is applied. A richer mixture means less air is available for efficient combustion.

carburetor heat when you suspect ice is present. Once the ice melts, you turn the heat off. Seems simple. Should the iceman cometh again, just reach for that trusty lever. Using carb heat does not hurt the engine in any way. Lycoming (a major engine manufacturer) says, ". . . at cruise power, even with full heat, we have never experienced detonation or damage to the engine." To be on the safe side, always check the Pilot's Operating Handbook (or the engine manufacturer's handbook) for your airplane to make sure they offer similar advice.

After a few dozen cycles of yank out, push in, yank out, push in, you will get either tired or bored. Thoughts will enter your mind. One of them will be "Gee, I wonder what happens if I just leave the carb heat on?"

Be my guest. Keeping the heat on makes it too hot inside the carburetor for ice to form. Used this way, carburetor heat is an anti-icing device. Keep in mind that the mixture becomes richer when carburetor heat is applied. You'll need to re-lean the mixture with the application of continuous carburetor heat. Because of the reduced density of the air entering the engine, you should expect about a 10% to 15% reduction in power with application of full heat. That's the downside to using continuous carb heat.

Apply Carb Heat As A Precautionary Measure

Carburetor heat should be used as a precautionary measure when making descents at reduced power (reduced power means a closed throttle and a greater chance of throttle ice). I recommend that carb heat be applied fully when on final approach to land or when descending into the traffic pattern. Check your Pilot's Operating Handbook for specific recommendations on when to use carburetor heat.

If your airplane is equipped with a carburetor air temperature gauge (Figure 21), you'll have an even easier time anticipating the presence of carburetor ice. This gauge identifies those critical carburetor temperatures (identified by a yellow-colored arc) conducive to the formation of carburetor ice. Applying enough carburetor heat to keep the needle out of the critical range should keep ice from forming.

CARBURETOR AIR TEMP PROBE AND GAUGE

Fig. 21

Mixture to cylinders

Air Inlet

Carb-temp probe measures either air-temp before entering the carburetor or it measures the air-temp of the fuel-air mixture (depending on location of probe).

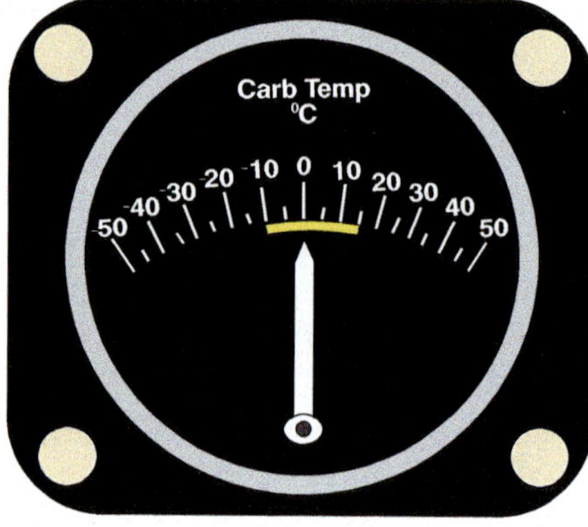

This Lycoming engine's induction system passes through the oil pan. This adds heat to the carburetor and air, which helps reduce the chance of carburetor icing.

Fig. 22

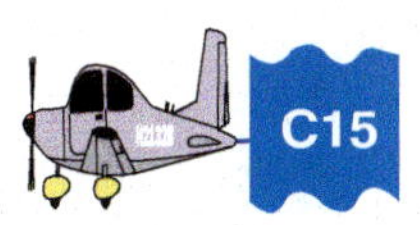

Hot Stick

On a hot summer day many years ago a student pilot, belonging to another instructor, showed up at the flight school to do an hour of pattern work. He planned to fly his high performance, fuel injected airplane, which was on lease to the school. The airplane was late returning from a previous flight, so this fellow decided to fly one of the school's trainers instead. He didn't realize that, as a student, he was required to be checked out in each individual make and model of aircraft he was to fly, though he was about to find out why that rule existed.

He grabbed a Cessna 150, preflighted it, and headed for the runup area. Somewhere in the back of his mind, he remembered he was supposed to use carburetor heat—something he wasn't familiar with, since his fuel injected airplane didn't have carburetor heat (you'll find out why later).

He spent about 30 minutes in the pattern before returning, drenched in sweat. I happened to be standing in the lounge when he walked in. I said, "Hey Marty, were you attacked by a garden hose?" He responded, "No, but I've got to tell you, that carburetor heat in the Cessna 150 works pretty darn good." I said, "How do you know that?" He replied, "Because every time I turned it on, it not only heated up the carburetor, it heated up the whole darn airplane."

It didn't take but a few seconds to make the connection. He was so unfamiliar with using carburetor heat that he mistakenly applied cabin heat, which has a look alike lever.

Carburetor Icing Potential In Different Engines

All engines are not created equal, at least when it comes to carb ice. Some engine makes and models are more susceptible to carburetor ice than others. This doesn't make them unsafe, any more than singing Gregorian chants makes you a Gregorian. You simply need to be aware of the icing potential of different engine models.

For example, the induction system on some airplane engines make them a little more resistant to carburetor ice. Figure 22 shows the reason for this. Lycoming engines with carburetors have their carburetor bolted to the bottom of the oil pan. An opening in the bottom of the oil pan is part of the induction system through which incoming air is warmed by the oil's radiant heat. The carburetor is also heated by conduction (touching) from the hot oil pan. This lessens the likelihood that the carburetor will develop ice as easily as carburetors on other makes of engines.

Frankly, it doesn't matter which engine your airplane has as long as you know what to do if carburetor ice appears. Don't be like those pilots who think they'll never get carburetor ice. You can tell who they are. They're the ones who drive through the hamburger stand and nod at the speakers—this doesn't bode well for humanity.

Fuel: Going With the Flow

The Mixture Control

The airplane's mixture control (the red knob with thorns along its side) allows you to keep the airplane operating at the proper fuel-air ratio as air density changes with altitude (Figure 23). Pulling out (toward you) on the mixture control decreases the amount of fuel for a given amount of air entering the engine. This process is called *leaning* (leaning is not where student pilots lean to the right or left during a turn). For now, just understand that leaning is accomplished by restricting the flow of fuel through the main metering jet (see Figure 10).

Pulling the mixture control out to its maximum rearward position of travel activates something known as *idle cutoff*. This kills the engine by restricting the fuel leaving the carburetor (Figure 24). Of course, we typically pull the mixture to the idle-cutoff position when stopping the engine on the ground at the end of the flight.

Be careful about mistaking the mixture control for the throttle. It happens. On some airplanes, especially older ones, the two knobs are not very distinct, and many a pilot has "throttled back" with the mixture control, producing the sounds of silence. At this point, your instructor starts making a lot of unusual noises. Any time the manufacturer paints something red and places symbolic thorns on its handle, I'd say they were trying to tell us something. Look or feel before you pull on a cockpit lever.

The Fuel/Air Mixture

With an increase in altitude the air becomes thinner and doesn't weigh as much for a given volume. The problem is that the amount of fuel flowing through the carburetor is regulated by the *volume*, not the *weight*, of

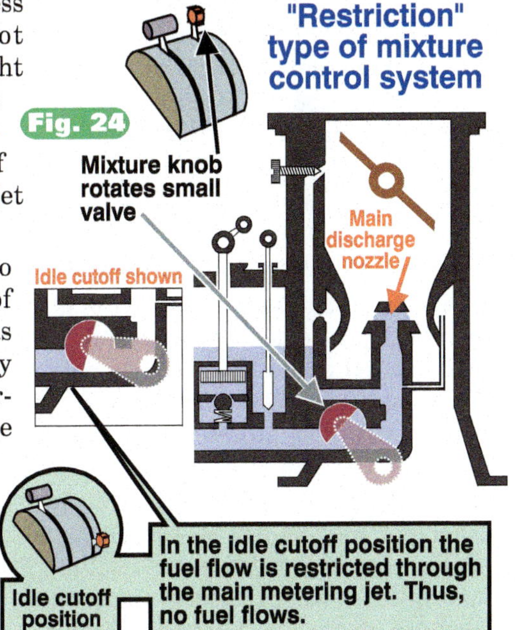

Carry On

Always Remember: If the engine runs, you pay!
Professor Bob Big Kahoona

A young pilot taxied into his tiedown spot, pulled the mixture control to idle cutoff, and waited for his engine to quit. It didn't.

He tried turning off the magnetos but the engine continued to idle—albeit a rough idle. He was nonplused. Apparently there was just enough fuel getting by the carburetor's idle cutoff valve to fuel the engine. This, coupled with a hot spot in the cylinders acting like a spark plug, kept his engine running. I was walking by the flight line when I heard, "Help, help, help." I ran toward the voice and found this young fellow in the airplane yelling, "Help, it won't shut off, it won't shut off." He was afraid to leave the airplane so he remained inside.

I opened the door and pushed the throttle in all the way. This caused such a lean mixture (lots of air for little fuel) that the engine immediately quit. He had been sitting there for 15 minutes yelling, "Help, help."

His first question for me was, "Hey, does the Hobbs meter (flying cost meter) still run when the airplane does this?" Unfortunately it does.

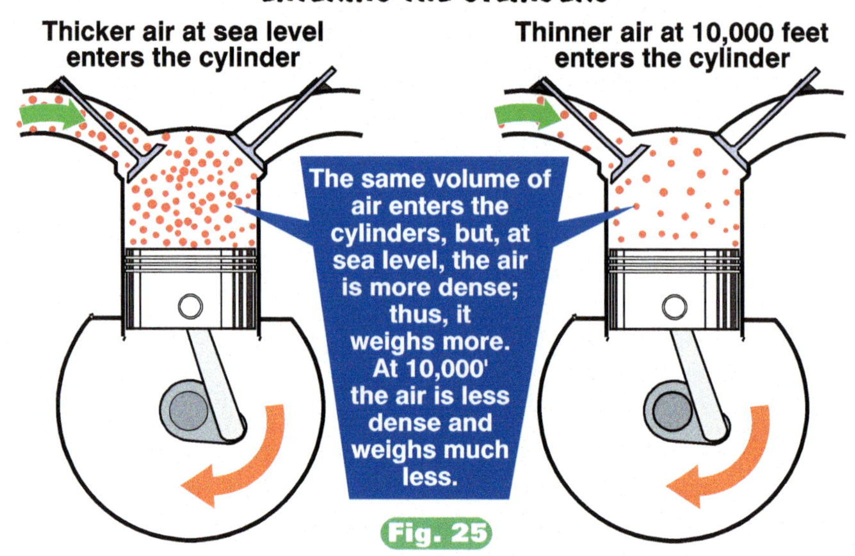

Fig. 25

the air passing over the venturi. Think about it this way: during the intake cycle, the pistons move downward, drawing air into the cylinders. The space within the cylinders is constant. The volume of air drawn into the cylinders is the same at sea level as it is at 10,000 feet MSL (Figure 25).

Since similar volumes flow through the venturi, the carburetor wants to send the cylinders the same amount of fuel at 10,000 feet MSL as it does at sea level. This presents a problem, since air has fewer molecules for a given volume at 10,000 feet MSL. In other words, the air at 10,000 feet MSL weighs less (fewer molecules) for a given volume than the air at sea level. To maintain the same fuel-air ratio at higher altitudes (or in less dense air), we must manually adjust the amount of fuel leaving the carburetor.

When to Lean

Most engine manufacturers recommend leaning the mixture whenever you're operating at or below 75% of the engine's maximum power output (check your POH to be sure).

The reason for this magic dividing line is that above 75% power, engines need all the cooling help they can get, and as we'll see in our discussion on exhaust gas temperature (EGT) gauges, adding fuel helps cool the engine. At power levels above 75%, the mixture should be in the full rich position (EGT starts on page C18).

But how do you know when you're operating at power levels greater than 75%? A few assumptions are necessary here. First, as the airplane ascends, the nonturbocharged engine produces less power, since there is less air to aid in the combustion process. If the airplane is operating with full throttle at less than 5,000 feet MSL, there's a good chance the engine is producing more than 75% of its maximum power output. Don't lean under these conditions. In other words, if you're climbing (with full throttle) at less than 5,000 feet MSL, the mixture should be full forward. Above 5,000 feet MSL, where the engine probably produces less than 75% of its maximum power (even with full throttle), you should lean the mixture for either best economy or best power. As a rule of thumb (aviation is all thumbs, and relies a lot on such rules), readjust the mixture every thousand feet of altitude change. (The 5,000 foot MSL recommendation is actually for a *density altitude* of 5,000 feet. We'll cover density altitude in Chapter 5. For now, 5,000 feet MSL is accurate enough).

Since most cruising is done at 55% to 65% power, you should always lean the engine regardless of your altitude at these power settings. Check the Pilot's Operating Handbook if you're not sure about the engine's power

OLE! TORO!

I was supposed to spray this field and I saw that two Black Angus bulls had strayed out of their pastures onto the field. On my second pass attempting to herd the bulls out of the field I reckon I got too low. This one bull made a lunge at me and my left gear hit him in the head. He knocked my left gear off but I killed him dayed (sic). I flew around to burn up some gas and then flew over to another airport and landed on the soft sod alongside the runway. Wiped off my left spray boom on the landing but otherwise no damage to me or the aircraft. I retrieved the gear, got some new parts, and was flying again in a couple of days. After talking with various people I am now in a heavy discussion with my insurance company.

ASRS Report

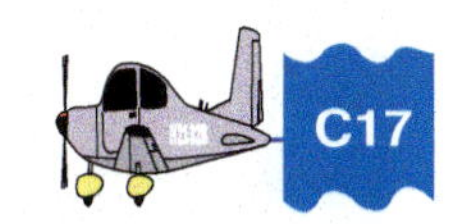

THE CARBURETOR'S ECONOMIZER SYSTEM

When throttle is opened to 60% or 70% of its travel, the economizer valve opens. Extra fuel flows into the carburetor's main metering jet, which helps cool the engine under high power conditions. It's called an economizer because the valve reduces the amount of extra engine-cooling fuel entering the cylinders at low power conditions (when it's not necessary).

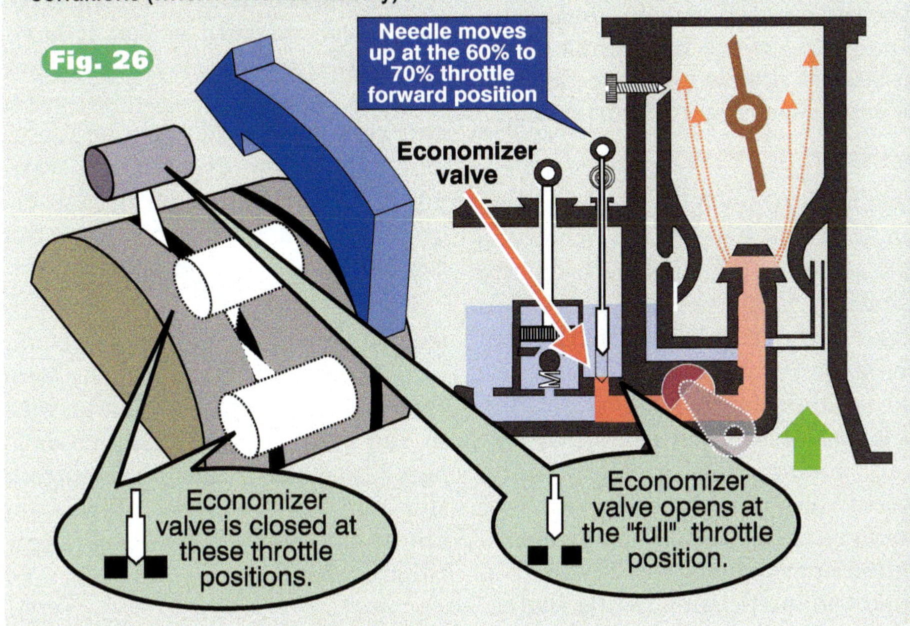

The Economizer Valve

Engineers were so concerned about the high heat production at power settings above 75% that they built a special device into the carburetor to aid in cylinder cooling. This device is known as the "economizer valve."

When the throttle is fully opened, the economizer valve is activated and an extra ration of fuel is fed to the engine (approximately 10% more). In other words, the mixture is purposely enriched at a full throttle setting. Dosing out extra fuel helps lower potentially higher cylinder temperatures at these power settings.

The economizer valve is activated by the throttle being in the full-forward position, as shown to the left. This is one reason you don't want to let the throttle creep backward during climb. In addition to a loss of power, you'll lose the additional cooling offered by the economizer.

output for a given altitude and power setting (I'll show you how to read and interpret that information in Chapter 15). Remember, failure to lean appropriately means you'll use up an extra portion of fuel unnecessarily. (It's important to note that some airplanes have *pressure type carburetors* or *altitude compensating carburetors* that automatically make mixture adjustments with changes in air density. This is why you don't see a mixture control in some airplanes. The bottom of page C10 has a quick review of one of these carburetors.)

USING THE TACHOMETER TO ADJUST THE MIXTURE

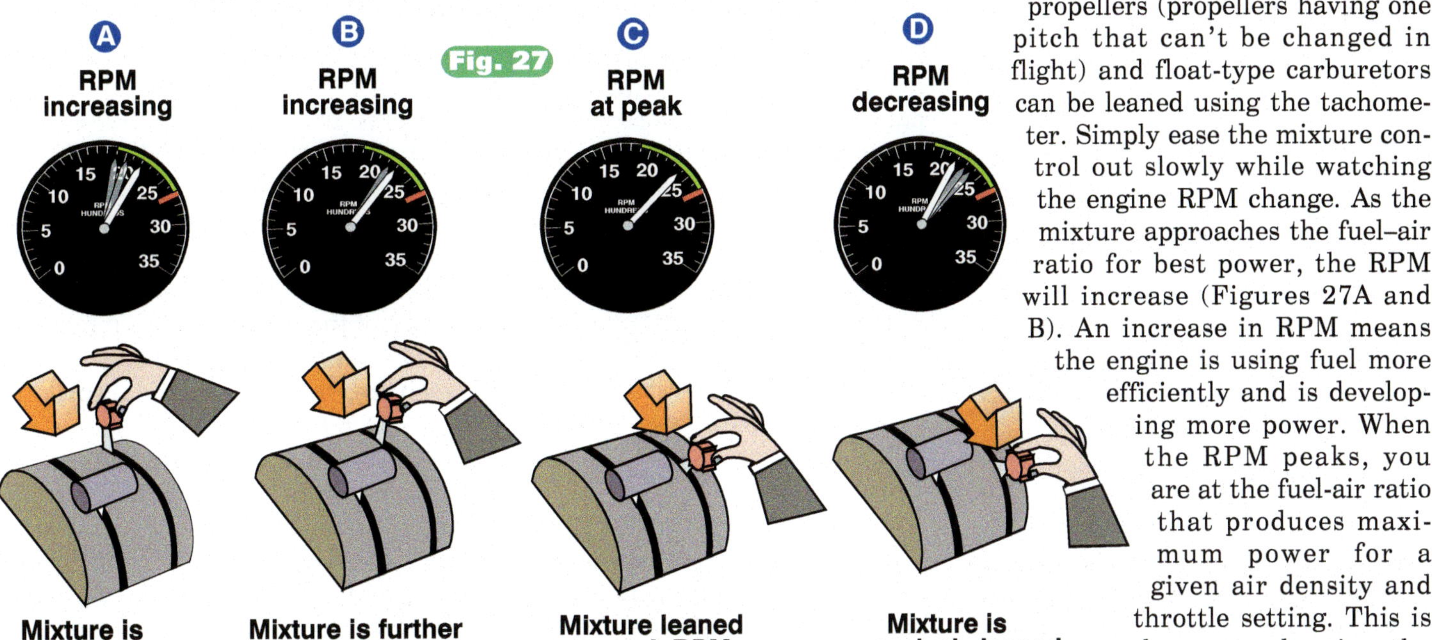

How to Lean

When someone asks you how you lean an airplane, don't say, "With the ailerons," or "Put it on a diet." You lean an airplane with the mixture control. There are a couple of ways to accomplish this, so let's take a look at them.

Airplanes with fixed pitch propellers (propellers having one pitch that can't be changed in flight) and float-type carburetors can be leaned using the tachometer. Simply ease the mixture control out slowly while watching the engine RPM change. As the mixture approaches the fuel–air ratio for best power, the RPM will increase (Figures 27A and B). An increase in RPM means the engine is using fuel more efficiently and is developing more power. When the RPM peaks, you are at the fuel-air ratio that produces maximum power for a given air density and throttle setting. This is known as leaning the mixture for *best power* (Figure 27C). Further pulling of the mixture will cause engine roughness and reduce RPM from over-leaning (Figure 27D). If you feel the engine running rough during the leaning process, enrich the mixture slightly until the engine smooths out.

Sometimes airplanes are equipped with fuel flow gauges (Figure 28) and/or exhaust gas temperature (EGT) gauges (Figure 29). With a fuel flow gauge you can set the manufacturer's recommended fuel flow rate for a given power condition. This is an approximate way of leaning the mixture for proper operation. Unfortunately, fuel flow gauges are often not accurate enough for precise leaning. Use of the EGT gauge offers a relatively precise means for leaning the engine (see Figure 30 for details).

Fig. 28

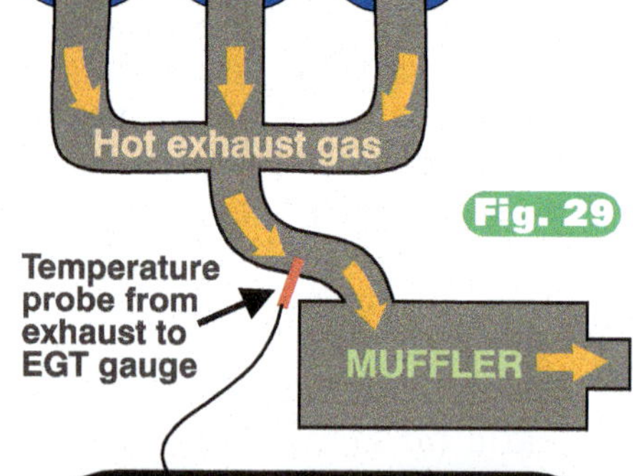

Fig. 29

Too Rich and Too Lean

Aside from inefficient fuel combustion, mixtures that are too rich or too lean cause difficulties with engine operation. A mixture that is too rich causes engine roughness. Spark plugs are carbon fouled when unburned fuel residue builds up between the plug gap, as shown in Figure 31. Lead, a component of high octane fuel, can also build up on spark plugs, exacerbating the fouling process. Fouled spark plugs can result in a rough and inefficient running engine.

It's interesting to note that a fouled spark plug in flight can be detected by an increase in EGT. Why? With only one flame source operating within the cylinder, it takes longer to reach the maximum combustion temperature of the cylinder's fuel-charge (it simply burns slower). As a result, the mixture is hotter as it exits the exhaust valve, resulting in a higher EGT.

Aside from a rough running engine, an excessively rich mixture contributes to high fuel consumption. This means you'll have less range, less endurance. and smaller fuel reserves. In fact, some estimates show operating at a full-rich mixture instead of a best economy setting can increase fuel consumption by as much as 70% (depending on the airplane, altitude and other variables). Even smaller percentages are significant. Do make it a point to lean properly.

A mixture that's too lean produces other problems. First, too lean a mixture means less power is produced. Small airplanes are anything but overpowered. We often need to use every one of those horses under the cowling. This is especially true when flying at high altitudes, where nonturbocharged piston engine airplanes don't perform very well in the first place.

The biggest danger with an excessively lean mixture is that it burns hot. It does so because it burns slower. This exposes the cylinder, piston and valves to higher temperatures, and high temperature is the worst enemy of metal, causing reduced cylinder life and other problems that can blow a hole in your pocketbook.

High cylinder temperatures also lead to something known as *detonation*. Instead of a smooth, even expansion of the fuel-air charge within the cylinder, the mixture detonates (explodes), causing damage to the engine. For more information about detonation, see Postflight Briefing #3–1.

Leaning & High Altitude Takeoffs For Nonturbocharged Airplanes

Takeoffs are normally made with a full-rich mixture. Aviation, of course, is comprised of exceptions to most rules.

One of those exceptions is high altitudes, which you can generally take to mean any airport above 5,000 feet MSL. It often puzzles students, but the fact is the airplane doesn't know it's on the ground. Honest. To an airplane, 5,000 feet is 5,000 feet, at least from an engine performance point of view. Remembering that the rule is to lean above 5,000 feet, you now know there's something that needs to be done before takeoff.

How should you lean the mixture? During the *runup* (that's a preflight check of the airplane engine) hold the brakes, apply full throttle, lean the mixture, then return the throttle to its idle position (make sure no one behind you will be affected by the propeller blast). This procedure can also be done while holding in position on the runway prior to taking off (this is the best way to do it as long as there are no other airplanes on final approach to land).

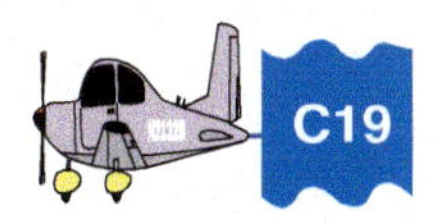

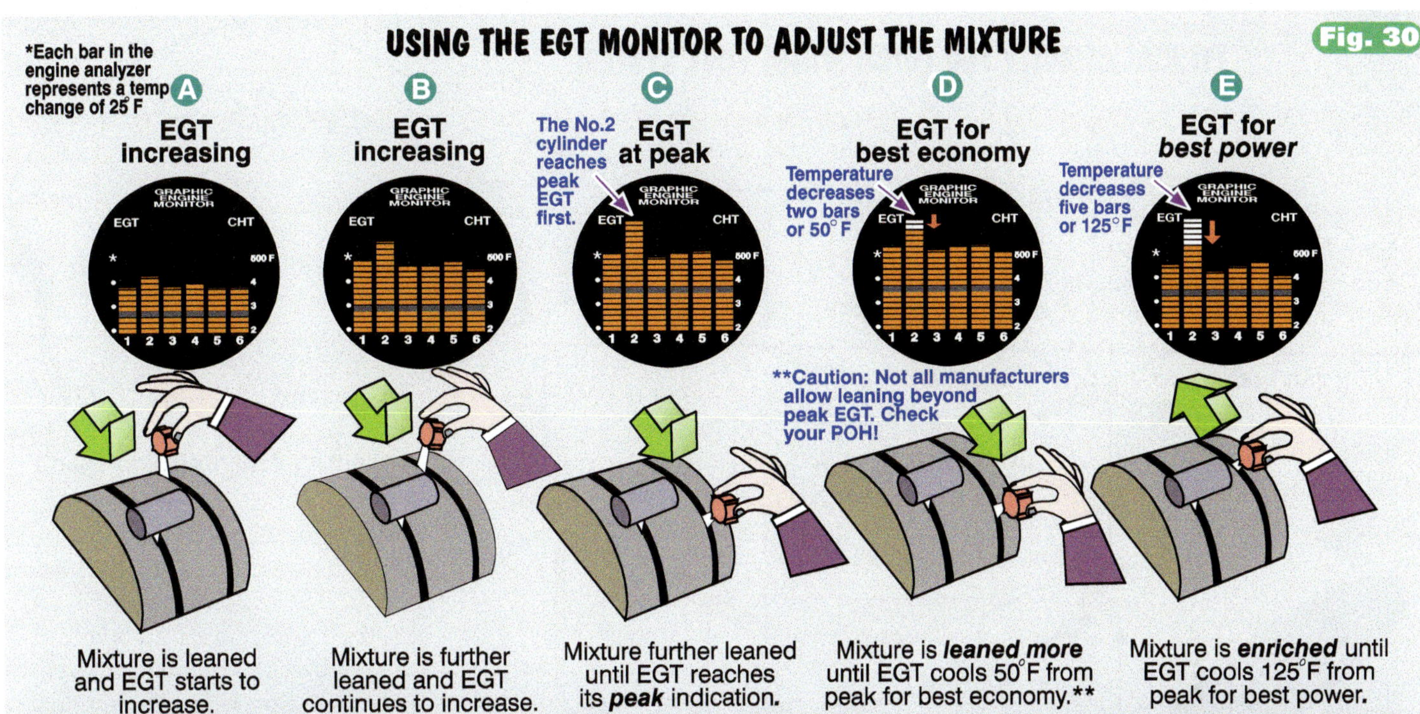

EGT Setting for Best Power or Best Economy

An EGT gauge is to a pilot what a drill is to a dentist—a fine, precision instrument with which to do good work. The EGT's precise measurement of exhaust gas temperatures allows you to select a mixture setting offering either best power or best economy of operation. Not every plane has a multi-probe EGT monitor, as shown above. Some have a simple gauge (Figure 29) that shows the EGT in only one of the engine's cylinders (typically the one that is known to operate the hottest). Here's how it works.

EGT monitors sense the temperature of the exhaust gas exiting one or more of the cylinders. This temperature is read on a calibrated vertical scale for each cylinder, as shown in Figure 30. Each vertical-bar increment on this six-cylinder engine analyzer represents a 25°F temperature change. As the mixture is adjusted, the EGT vertical bar responds rather quickly to changes in exhaust gas temperature.

The first step in leaning with an EGT analyzer is to find the peak exhaust gas temperature on the temperature scale. Pull the mixture back slowly until the one of the six vertical bar arrays peaks (as shown in Figure sequence 30 A through C). As you lean, not all cylinders will change their EGT at the same rate. Some become hotter than others. You want to reference the hottest cylinder.

The second step is to further lean or enrich the mixture (move the mixture control knob in slightly) to obtain either the *best economy* or the *best power* condition respectively.

For *best economy* (least fuel flow to develop a given amount of power), continue to ***lean*** the mixture until the temperature drops (cools) 50°F from peak EGT (Figure 30D). In real life, few engine manufacturers allow you to lean the mixture on the lean side of peak EGT (check your POH!). For *best power* (most usable power per unit of air), ***enrich*** the mixture until the temperature drops (cools) 125°F from peak EGT (Figure 30E). Cooling the exhaust gas from its peak value is also referred to as leaning X number of degrees *rich of peak*. It's a case of more is less; more fuel (a richer environment) produces less (cooler) temperature.

These numbers are general temperature values and vary between airplanes. You should refer to your airplane's Bible—the *Pilot's Operating Handbook*—for the specifics on the proper EGT values used for leaning your airplane.

Takeoff should be made at this mixture setting to ensure maximum climb performance. Leaning prior to departure is also a good idea when departing an airport (regardless of the elevation) where high temperature conditions decrease the air's density. Under certain conditions, if the outside air temperature is quite high, an airport at 2,000 feet MSL can have air with the same density as an airport at 6,000 feet MSL. Attempting to depart with a full rich mixture under these conditions produces the same decrease in performance as departing a high altitude airport.

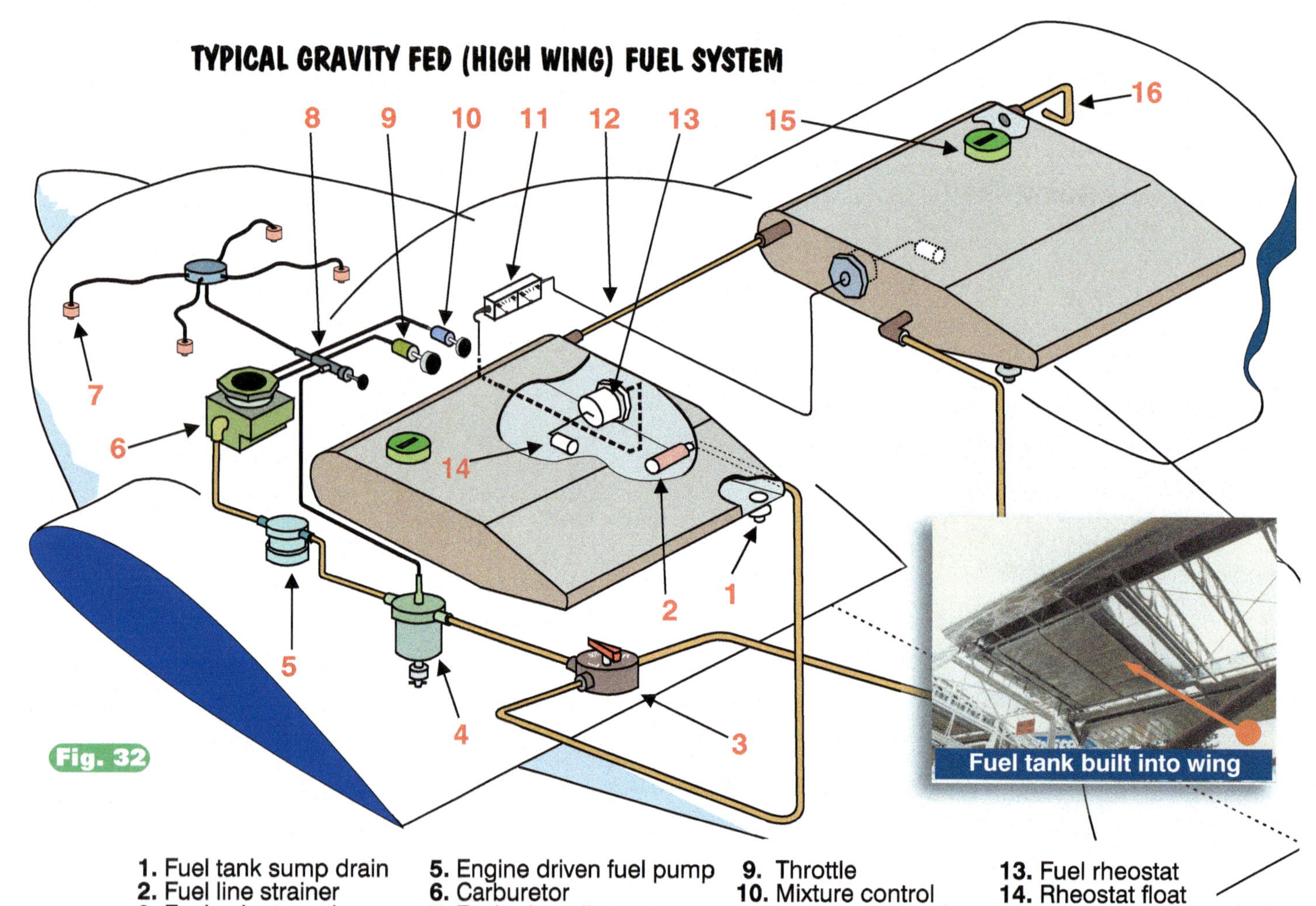

The Fuel System

Unlike solids, liquids present problems in three areas: selection, availability and contamination. Knowing how to select the proper fuel, ensuring its availability for use by the engine, and preventing contamination is part of every pilot's job. Figure 32 shows a typical high-wing fuel system.

Components

As pointed out in Chapter 1, airplane fuel is stored in fuel tanks that are normally located in the wings. Two of the most common types of fuel tanks are the *wet wing* and the *bladder-type.* A wet-wing tank is simply an internal portion of the wing that is sealed to hold fuel. Bladder tanks are sealed rubber containers resting inside the wings as separate units.

Fuel tanks serve the important purpose of transporting food for the engine. Unfortunately, engine food as well as human food can be contaminated. Neither you nor the engine should consume anything that's contaminated (I just read where they now have non-toxic Crayola crayons. Which makes me wonder just what I was eating as a kid).

Water is the most frequent contaminant found in fuel. Water, weighing approximately 8 pounds per gallon, is heavier than fuel, which

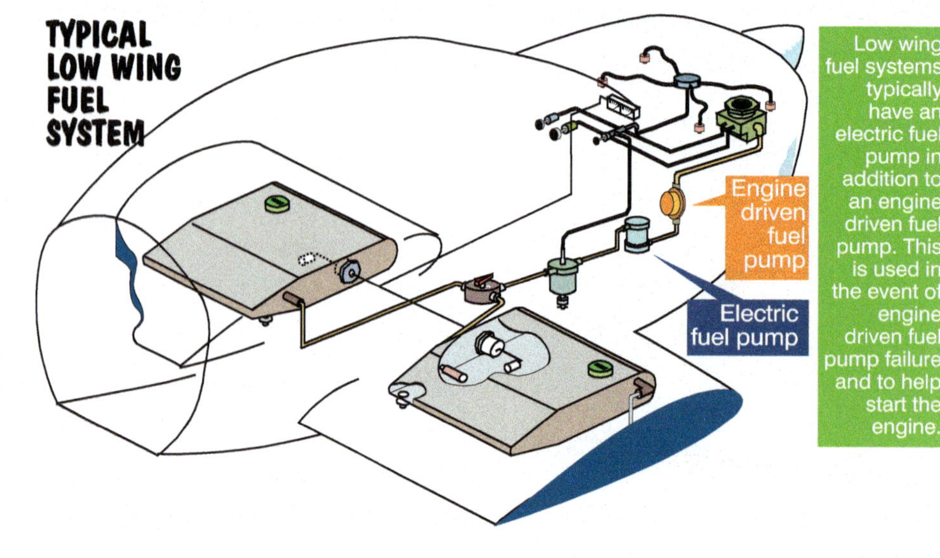

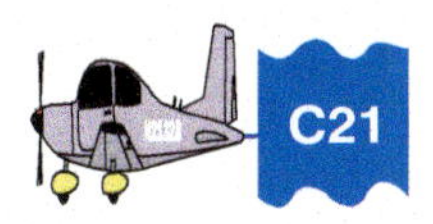

weighs approximately 6 pounds per gallon. If it's present, water rests on the bottom of fuel tanks, where it's the first thing to go to the engine. Since there are no engines that run on water (or walk on it, either), this presents a significant challenge.

Fig. 33

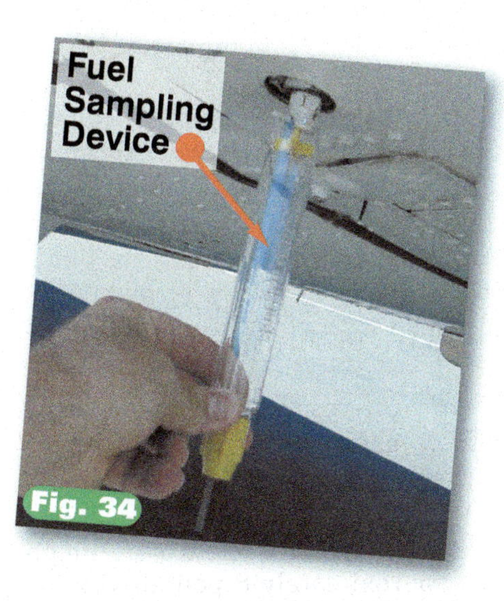

Fig. 34

Fig. 35

One of the ways pilots try to avoid water contamination is by filling their fuel tanks after the last flight of the day. Air usually contains moisture—sometimes, a *lot* of moisture. When cooled, that moisture condenses, just as it does on the outside of a cold glass on a warm summer's day. Once it's been wrung out of the air, that water waddles down to the bottom of the fuel tank. By filling the tanks, you force most of the air (and its moisture) out.

Fuel tanks have sump drains at the lowest part of the tank (Figure 33). These drains allow you to remove the impurities that have found their way into the fuel system. Make sure to drain the sumps (and fuel strainer, Figure 32, item #4) during each preflight. The sumps should also be drained after every refueling (you never know where that gas truck has been).

Sump draining isn't difficult at all. Simply take your draining device (usually a clear plastic container with a slim probe in the middle) and push it up inside the sump drain. This lets a small amount of fuel flow downward into the plastic drain (Figure 34), and sometimes onto your hand, down your arm, and onto your shirt, too.

Take a small sample, then remove the draining device. Make sure the drain is completely closed. Then inspect the sample. Check for water in the bottom of the container first. Then look for any impurities that may signal internal tank corrosion. Water is usually easy to identify since it visually contrasts with aviation fuel. Figure 35 shows a sample of fuel with water contamination.

If you do strike water, don't throw your arms up and shout "I found it!"People won't have the slightest idea what you're talking about. And you don't want them guessing about a statement like that. Just keep on draining until you get only fuel. If there's a lot of water, prudence dictates finding out why before setting forth into the sky.

Light My Fire

Be careful what you do with fuel samples after draining the sumps on the fuel tank. Most pilots simply throw the sample onto the ground. One of our flight school's chronologically challenged (old timer) flight instructors tossed a still-lit match on the flight line tarmac. A nearby student doing a preflight, casually tossed a rather large sample of 100 octane fuel near the burning match. Swooshhhhh, flames rose straight up like an earthly solar flare. The student, not aware a still-burning match had landed on that spot, looked over at his instructor and said, "Wow, that's some kind of powerful fuel eh?" I have no doubt this student's landings were a lot smoother that day.

On some airplanes, particularly high wing aircraft with bladder-type fuel cells, it's necessary to shake the wings and lower the tail in order to chase water from its hiding place among the folds of the rubber bladder.

What does it mean if you drain a sample from the fuel tank and it's perfectly clear? It probably means one of two things. You have either water or kerosene (jet fuel) in your tank. How would you know which one it is? The answer is to smell it. A little whiff of gas or kerosene isn't going to hurt you (unless you make it your job to whiff all the airplanes at the airport!). Kerosene has a distinctly oily smell to it. It's also oily to the touch, compared to aviation gasoline.

Fuel Colors

Your fuel is dyed. Not dead, dyed. And for a very good reason.

There was a time when aviation fuel (called AVGAS) came in several designer colors (red, green, blue). These fuels were dyed for easy identification. Today, there's only one color for aviation fuel and that's blue. Blue fuel is of the 100LL or *low lead* variety and is one of the most common

aviation fuels in use today. Jet fuel or kerosene is clear colored and must not be used in piston powered airplanes.

It's important to use only the proper grade of fuel for your airplane. Using a lower grade can cause serious problems such as detonation. Higher grades can foul plugs. However, if faced with the choice of using a lower or a higher grade of fuel, choose the higher grade for temporary operations. Under no circumstances, however, should you use jet fuel in your piston powered airplane. Believe me when I say it won't make you go as fast as a jet. In fact, it won't make you go at all! Jet fuel doesn't work in these engines.

One last word on fuel. Don't use automobile gasoline in your airplane unless specific approval, in the form of a *Supplemental Type Certificate (STC)* has been issued to you for your aircraft. An STC represents FAA permission for a modification to the original configuration or operating parameters of the airplane. It is granted after extensive testing and documentation, and frequently includes very specific instructions that must be followed. This is particularly true in the case of auto fuel. Unless your engine is specifically approved for automobile gasoline, it has *not* been tested and found safe for your specific engine. Using it would be both illegal and foolish, since you would be anointing yourself a test pilot.

Fig. 38

Fuel Vents

If you've ever tried to suck milk out of one side of a carton without poking a hole in the other, you'll understand why fuel tanks are vented. As the fuel pump sucks fuel from the tank, air must replace the departing fuel or a vacuum forms. If that happens, fuel starvation isn't far behind, since at some point the pump can't overcome the vacuum. Some gas caps are vented, allowing small amounts of air to replace consumed fuel (Figure 36).

Fuel tanks can also be vented by small tubes, as shown in Figure 37. It's always a good practice to make sure these vent lines are unobstructed. Sometimes you can see fuel overflowing from them on hot days, when the tanks are filled. This occurs because air in the tanks expands slightly as the plane sits in the sun and warms. This is a good sign the tubes are free of obstructions.

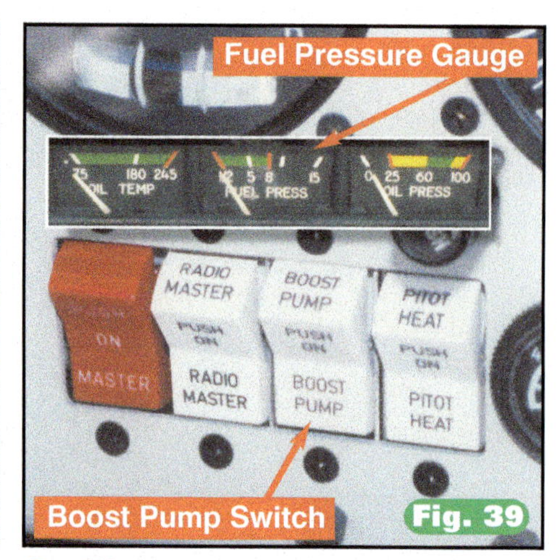

Fig. 39

Auxiliary Fuel Pumps

High wing airplanes have gravity-fed fuel systems. Nevertheless, these aircraft (like many modern airplanes) might still have mechanical fuel pumps to keep fuel within the system under pressure. Low wing airplanes, on the other hand, can't be gravity fed because the fuel tanks are located below engine level. These aircraft have auxiliary fuel pumps (sometimes called *boost pumps*) to maintain fuel pressure in the event of a mechanical fuel pump failure. Figure 38 shows a typical electric boost pump. While low wing airplanes are equipped with boost pumps as a matter of necessity, high wing airplanes can have them too. Airplanes like the Cessna 210, with fuel injection, have a boost pump to aid in starting as well as in emergencies.

Boost pumps are often used during engine start to pressurize the fuel system. This helps purge air trapped within the fuel lines. After the engine starts, the electric boost pump is turned off to see if the mechanical pump is operational and is pressurizing the system. Monitored by a fuel pressure gauge on the instrument panel (Figure 39), fuel pressure can be examined at any time by the pilot.

Most manufacturers of low wing airplanes recommend the boost pump be turned on for takeoff until the airplane is at least 1,000 feet above the ground. They similarly recommend it be turned on during descents when the airplane is within 1,000 feet of the surface (follow the specific recom-

Fig. 36

Fig. 37

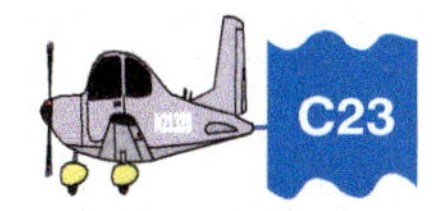

mendations in your Pilot's Operating Handbook). A failure of the engine's mechanical fuel pump at lower altitudes is especially critical in low wing airplanes, since gravity won't feed the system. It's also a good idea to activate the boost pump when switching fuel tanks. This helps pressurize the fuel system and purge any air that may have slipped into the fuel lines.

Some airplanes have both *high* and *low* boost pump settings. Normally, low boost pump settings are used for engine start and takeoff. High boost pump settings can be used to stabilize fluctuating fuel flow indications during a high altitude, hot day takeoff, where vapor lock is a threat. This setting may also be used to help purge air that has entered the fuel lines (this may result from running a fuel tank dry—not a good idea!). Be careful. Under some conditions you can easily flood an engine in flight with the high boost pump setting. This could cause a temporary or complete loss of engine power. Study the recommendations in your Pilot's Operating Handbook regarding the proper procedures for your particular airplane.

Prime Time

Do you remember how we shut the engine off by pulling back the mixture control, thus burning off the last of the fuel in the cylinders? Great. Now it comes time to crank the cranky thing over. Where is the fuel supposed to come from to get started? It's time to prime.

Priming is sort of like tipping the maitre d' a few bucks on a crowded night when you don't have reservations. It just sort of helps get things going in your favor. Most airplane engines can be primed through the use of a small plunger-like device called the *primer* (PRY-MER, not PRIM-ER,) which is located in the cockpit (Figure 40). The primer usually squirts fuel in the upper portions of the induction system, bypassing the carburetor completely. This is especially useful for startups on cold days when fuel and air are disinclined to mix. Once you're done with prime time, make sure the primer is locked back in place (this generally takes a slight turn of the lever after it's pushed all the way in). An unlocked primer can allow fuel leakage into the induction system, making for an extra rich fuel-air mixture.

Fig. 40

Fuel Injected Priming

Fuel injected airplanes have lots of advantages. Starting, particularly in warm weather, isn't one of them. As a first resort, try doing what the Pilot's Operating Handbook recommends. The procedure generally goes something like this:

1. Activate the boost pump
2. Move the mixture to its full rich position
3. Open the throttle slightly until a fuel flow indication is noticed on the fuel flow gauge
4. Retard the throttle
5. Turn the boost pump off

The engine is started and the boost pump is usually turned on again prior to takeoff. As a general rule, if the engine has been run within the last 15 minutes, it probably doesn't need priming. More priming is necessary on cold rather than warm days. Be cautious not to over-prime, since this can lead to engine fires while on the ground. Engine fires during startup are more common on cold days.

If this fails, try asking others with the same kind of engine. If nothing else, you will hear many new incantations.

Fuel Gauges

I want you to trust your airplane, your spouse, and your accountant. I want you to never, ever trust your fuel gauge.

For a variety of reasons, airplane fuel gauges are notoriously unreliable. They couple outmoded technology to demanding conditions. Electric float type fuel measuring systems, shown in Figure 41, use 1930's technology to measure fuel quantity. The result is somewhat less believable than a Tarot card reading.

Unfortunately, lulled by their experience with car gauges (which are generally pretty accurate) many pilots think that what they see is what they can get. Every year, there are dozens of fuel exhaustion accidents in which people are needlessly endangered. (*Fuel exhaustion* is the term generally applied to what normal people think of as *screwing up and running out of gas*. I always thought *fuel exhaustion* was an interesting term. It makes it sound as though the gas just sort of got tired and fell asleep.) Try and keep in mind that the regulations require fuel gauges to be accurate in only two conditions: when the tank is full and when it's empty (no useable fuel on board). There are more accurate measuring systems available, but they are also more expensive and thus confined for the most part to larger airplanes.

So, what's the solution? Finger in ear, please. *Never, ever leave the ground without looking for yourself to verify what's in the tanks, and always know how much fuel you will burn per hour of operation.*

Fuel level determination is absolutely, positively a do-it-yourself task. Don't take anyone's word for how full the tanks are. Find out for yourself. I recommend using a calibrated dipstick measuring device to plumb the fuel level, as shown in Figure 42. Make sure the dipstick is calibrated for your airplane (you can purchase specific dipsticks for individual makes and models of airplane).

Be careful about making your own dipstick. One of my students made his own and calibrated it by progressively filling the tank and marking measurements on the stick. The only thing he didn't do was put a big enough lip on the end of it. While plumbing the fuel, it escaped his grasp and fell into the tank. He stared into the tank for 10 minutes in total disbelief. Imagine that, dipsticks don't swim! Our local mechanic had to remove it before we could fly.

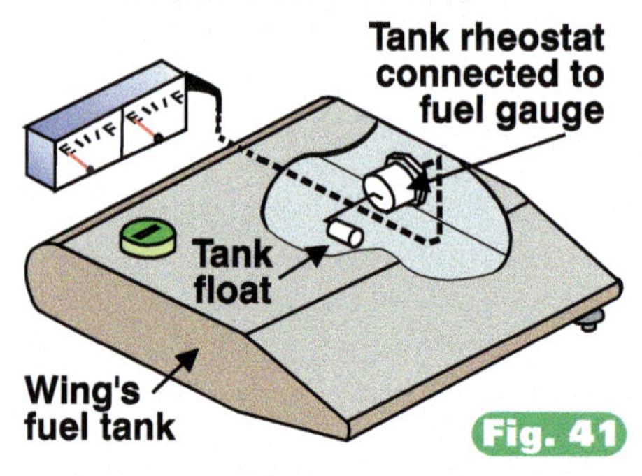

Fig. 41

FASTER THAN A SPEEDING BULLET

A flatlander flew her non-pilot husband across the beautiful but foreboding mountains of Alaska. Approaching a spectacularly high and jagged ridge, hubby climbed into the back seat to answer a calling. The pilot failed to inform her *nag-a-vator* of her decision to run the first tank dry before switching to the second tank. About midway through his task of a personal nature, the engine quit, leaving a tremendous auditory void. Quicker than Superman,her husband returned to the front seat, strapped in and sat wide-eyed alert. About that time, the aircraft responded to the pilot's flip of the fuel selector knob and the enormous silence was again interrupted with the sound of the purring engine. Today they both laugh about it.

Moral: Never run one tank dry before switching tanks. Foreign particles that settle harmlessly at the bottom of the tank could be forced into the engine causing damage. You could also damage your passenger's confidence in your piloting skills. D. T.

How Much Is Enough?

Everybody has their own idea on how much fuel is enough to carry. I'll share mine. Personally, I never operate an airplane with less than a quarter of its total fuel capacity. At the one-quarter mark, it's time to land and tanker up.

You will, until they invent midair refueling for small airplanes, have to land. This seems to be one of the reasons some pilots are reluctant to get fuel. Landing takes time and effort. It becomes easy to push on, because you know you've got enough fuel to make it to your destination, pretty much, sort of. Usually you will, too. Usually. But one time the weather gets bad, or the airport is closed because the person landing ahead of you neglected to unleash his retractable gear and the airplane has belly burns. That's how "accidents" happen. Fuel exhaustion accidents are one of general aviation's dark spots. They're needless, pointless, and dangerous.

One last word of caution. Be careful what you say to the gas person. Told to *top off* the tanks (which most pilots take to mean "fill 'er up,") the teenage boys who are usually gas wranglers have been known to take the tops off the tanks by removing the gas tank caps. With its cap off, a gas tank becomes a fuel dispersal device via the large opening on the top of the wing, where all that nice low pressure says "Gas, come to me." I've had it happen before. Of course, this should never happen because you will always, always check the gas quantity visually after refueling—won't you? Remember Rod Machado's fuel axiom No. 13: If you smell fuel on takeoff, go back and land. You probably left the cap off your tank. This is easy to identify on a low wing airplane. You can generally look out the window and watch a very spectacular plume of $4+ per gallon fuel going up and out from the wing. On high wing airplanes, the smell of gas is a good clue.

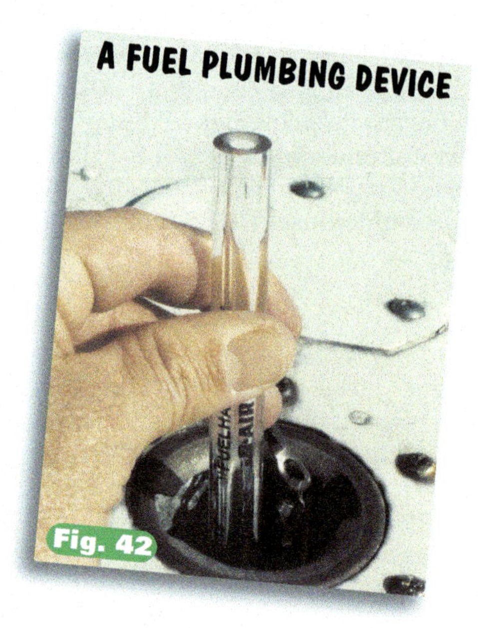

Fig. 42

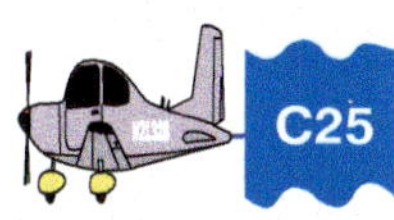

Sudden Loss of Oil

A student and I had firsthand experience with sudden oil loss. We departed in a Cessna 150 and suddenly, *swoosh,* a black cloud started forming on the windscreen. My 16-year-old student must have been raised at the beach, because his verbal assessment of the situation went, "Oh wow, man, that's awesome dude!" (This confirms my theory that the closer you get to the beach, the shorter the sentences become.) I found it more worrisome than awesome. Must have been a generation gap.

It took only a few seconds for most of the engine oil to stream up from where the oil cap should have been. I called the tower, told them what happened, and received clearance to land immediately, in the reverse direction of the departure runway.

I wanted to minimize my time in the air to prevent damaging the engine. Landing was interesting, given that there was no forward visibility through the newly-painted windshield. I tilted the plane to one side so I could peruse the runway out my side window. It looked good to me. We landed successfully. After touchdown, I looked over at my student and said, "Where did that oil come from?" "From Texas?" he replied (they don't get any closer to the beach than that!).

Moral of the story: make sure the oil cap is on and make sure the cap is tight!

Fer sure.

The Oil System

If it weren't for engine oil, your engine would run for no more than a few minutes before seizing in a blob of useless metal molecules. Oil creates a thin film that clings to metal surfaces, allowing them to slide over each other with minimal contact. It also acts as a liquid shock absorber, preventing metal parts from banging directly into one another as well as providing a seal between pistons and cylinders. If that weren't enough, oil also helps clean the internal workings of the crankcase, like a chimney sweep. Metal, carbon and other impurities are carried on a river of liquid lubricant to the oil filter and removed from circulation.

This wonderful fluid also acts as the engine's thermal equalizer. Oil is to an engine as water is to a radiator. Water carries heat away from the engine; so does oil. This helps keep engine temperatures within acceptable limits.

Change of Life

Oil is the airplane's lifeline. Renewing it regularly is inexpensive insurance. If you own an airplane, don't be stingy with oil changes. Oil is made up of complex molecules and, like anything that takes a beating, these molecules break down over time. Heat, friction, oxidation, as well as contamination with water all contribute to making oil a less effective lubricant. Some pilots change their airplane's oil once every 50 hours of flight time (as a young flight instructor with a beat up automobile, I was always tempted to drain the oil and change the car).

Malfunctions In The Oil System

I make it a point never to fly one of those super discount airlines. The last time I did, the flight attendant announced it was a no smoking flight, and the captain had to shut down the right engine. Don't be caught by surprise (by disreputable airlines or your airplane). Know how to detect malfunctions in the oil system.

Low or Fluctuating Oil Pressure– After engine start, adjust for the proper engine speed (usually about 1,000 RPM), then immediately check the oil pressure gauge. The oil pressure needle should point into the green arc within approximately 30 seconds (for most airplanes). If it doesn't, shut the engine down. You may have had an oil pump failure, a leak in a line, insufficient oil quantity, oil that's too cold, or even a stuck oil pressure relief valve.

A decrease in oil pressure during flight is serious business. The engine's internal cooling capability decreases dramatically with less oil circulating through the engine. What little oil is left in the crankcase must now disperse more of the engine's heat. Because of this, oil temperature should increase with falling oil pressure. If you notice a decrease in oil pressure and the oil temperature doesn't increase, you may have an oil pressure gauge that has failed.

If you experience a decrease in oil pressure, I'd recommend heading for the nearest airport. On the way, however, I'd attempt to confirm that oil pressure is actually falling by looking for an increase in oil temperature. If I didn't see it, I'd still find an airport, land and have the gauge examined (but I'd feel something more akin to urgency than emergency).

A Tribute to the Forgotten Mechanic

***Through the history of world aviation
Many names have come to the fore...
Great deeds of the past in our memory will last,
As they're joined more and more....***

***When man first started his labor in his quest to
Conquer the sky
He was designer, mechanic and pilot,
And he built a machine that would fly...
But somehow the order got twisted,
And then in the public's eye
The only man that could be seen
Was the man who knew how to fly...***

***The pilot was everyone's hero,
He was brave, he was bold, he was grand,
As he stood by his battered old airplane
With his goggles and helmet in hand...
To be sure, these pilots all earned it,
To fly you have to have guts...
And they blazed their names in the hall of fame
On wings with bailing wire struts...***

***But for each of these flying heroes
There were thousands of little renown,
and these were the men who worked on the planes
But kept their feet on the ground...
We all know the name of Lindbergh,
And we've read of his flight to fame...
But think, if you can, of his maintenance man,
can you remember his name?***

***And think of our wartime heroes, Gabreski,
Jabara, and Scott...
Can you tell me the names of their crew chiefs?
A thousand to one you cannot...***

***Now pilots are highly trained people
and wings are not easily won...
But without the work of the maintenance man
Our pilots would march with a gun...
So when you see mighty aircraft
As they mark their way through the air,
The grease stained man with the wrench in his
Hand is the man who put them there...***

Author Unknown

Low Oil Temperature – If it's very cold, expect the oil pressure to take a large majority of those 30 seconds to rise. Starts under very cold conditions wreak a lot of havoc. During the time it takes the oil to loosen up and circulate properly, the engine's delicate metal parts are merrily grinding themselves into pixie dust. That's why engines are generally preheated in extreme cold. Lycoming, for example, recommends the engine be preheated at temperatures below 10°F to prevent engine damage during startup. (Continental says 20°F.)

High Oil Temperature – High oil temperature can result from several causes, one of which is not enough oil within the engine. Excessive engine temperature can cause excessive oil consumption, loss of power and detonation. It can also damage the engine internally by scoring cylinder walls, damaging the pistons and rings as well as burning and warping valves. Attempt to cool the engine before the needle moves into the yellow arc of the oil temperature scale. Simply climb at a higher airspeed by lowering the airplane's nose, open the cowl flaps if the plane is equipped with them, or level off for awhile or even descend at lower power settings if engine temperatures don't diminish.

High Oil Pressure – High oil pressure is not without its problems either. Inside most airplane engines is something known as an *oil pressure relief valve*. This valve provides an alternate path for the flow of oil if the pressure within the system becomes dangerously high. This prevents oil from damaging engine seals with its hydraulic pressures. Once the engine has had a chance to heat up, oil pressure normally decreases. Nevertheless, keep an eye on the pressure. If it's too high, have a mechanic examine the system.

The Engine Cooling System

The powerplant (the engine) is also a heat plant. All that local motion results in the production of calories galore, and every bit of the heat is looking for a home.

Getting it out of the engine and into the air is one of the jobs that keeps engine and airframe engineers working late at night. Most modern airplane engines are air cooled. Water cooling may be more efficient, but it would mean carrying considerably more weight—the archenemy of lift.

Fig. 43

Fig. 44

It's Best Not to Be That Cool

When operating any engine, you want to avoid chopping the power to idle and leaving it there while the airspeed is increasing during a descent. This is one of the worst things you can do to your engine. If you're making a *cruise descent,* make small power changes. A good *rule of thumb* is to make no more than a 100 RPM per minute reduction in engine speed on small engines and no more than 1" of manifold pressure per minute on high performance airplanes. Always leave enough power on so as to not cool the cylinder head temperatures below allowable limits. Also, increase your mixture in increments on the way down. This helps cool the inside of the cylinder by preventing too lean a mixture. If you're not making a cruise descent, then try to reduce your airspeed as you reduce power. This helps keep engine temperatures higher by reducing the amount of cool air flowing over the engine.

Recommendation by: Tim Peterson, Aviation Consultant

Fortunately, there are several routes out of town for engine heat. It can be dissipated by oil coolers, from heated exhaust gas, and from air flowing over the cylinders. Even propeller spinners help cool the engine. Air hitting the spinner is split and efficiently channeled into the engine's cowling, where it flows over the cooling fins (Figure 43). Cylinder fins help cool engines by providing more surface area for heat dissipation.

Keep in mind that engine cooling is least effective at high power settings and low airspeeds, where a limited amount of air enters the engine cowling. Maintain a good watch of your engine instruments, especially during climbs on hot days.

While overheating is damaging, excessive cooling can also shorten engine life. Long or rapid descents under low power conditions might cause *shock cooling* of the engine, a condition in which the various metals of the cylinders cool suddenly and at different rates. This can lead to something getting bent out of shape. That can lead to buying expensive new engine parts, so pilots generally have a strong imperative to avoid doing it.

Properly planning your descents means you maintain some power to prevent the engine from overcooling—the more power, the better. You want to try keeping the cylinder head temperatures and exhaust gas temperatures from decreasing too quickly.

Keeping the cowl flaps (Figure 44) closed helps maintain engine temperatures during the descent. By adjusting these flaps with a lever from inside the cockpit, you can regulate engine temperatures (it's like driving your car with the heater on and regulating temperatures by opening or closing the window). Normally, cowl flaps are kept open for climbs to allow for maximum engine cooling. They are usually closed for descents to aid in keeping engine temperatures from dropping too rapidly (not all airplanes have cowl flaps. They're usually found on airplanes with larger engines, typically those having 200 or more horsepower).

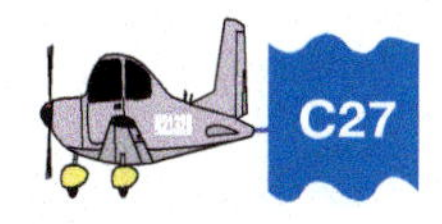

During a descent, your job is to maintain stable cylinder head temperatures (CHT) and oil temperatures (i.e., keep their temperature indications in the green). On some airplanes, gear extension or even partial flap extension at high speeds can be used in lieu of large power reductions to start a descent (check your POH). While momentary power reductions aren't as harmful if the power is immediately restored, large ones over long periods can be damaging. Try planning your descents so engine temperatures change slowly from their previous cruise values.

The Propeller

Propellers come in all sizes and colors, but they are of two basic types: *fixed pitch* and *constant speed.* In an airplane with a fixed pitch prop, one lever—the throttle—controls both power and propeller blade RPM (revolutions per minute). In a constant speed prop, there are separate controls for power and RPM.

When you start your flight training, you'll probably fly an airplane with a fixed pitch propeller. Fixed pitch propellers have their pitch (angle of attack) fixed during the forging process. The angle is set in stone (actually, aluminum). This pitch can't be changed except by replacing the propeller, which pretty much prevents you from changing the propeller's pitch in flight. Fixed pitch props are not ideal for any one thing, yet they're in many ways best for everything. They represent a compromise between the best angle of attack for climb and the best angle for cruise. They are simple to operate, and easier (thus less expensive) to maintain.

THE CONSTANT SPEED PROPELLER

A: Moving the propeller control forward allows the prop blades to take a smaller bite of air. Drag decreases and engine RPM speeds up.

B: Pulling the propeller control rearward forces the prop blades to take a bigger bite of air. Drag increases and the engine RPM slows.

Fig. 46

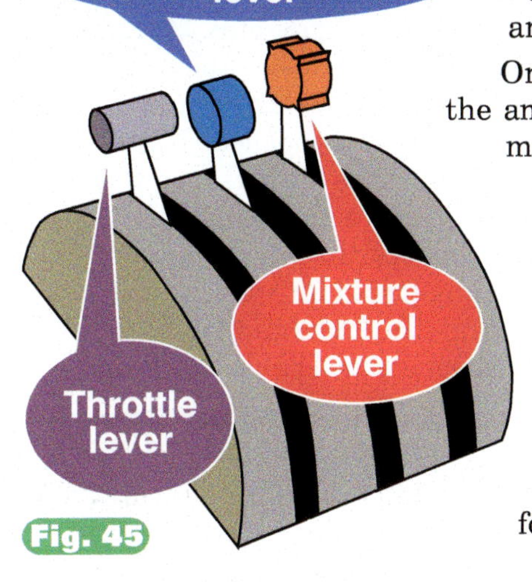

Fig. 45

On fixed pitch propeller airplanes, engine power and engine RPM are both controlled by the throttle. One lever does it all, power equals RPM, and that's the end.

As you move up into higher performance airplanes, you'll soon encounter *constant speed (controllable pitch)* propellers. Airplanes with these propellers usually have both a throttle and a propeller control, so you manage engine power and propeller RPM separately (Figure 45).

On airplanes with constant speed propellers, movement of the throttle determines the amount of fuel and air reaching the cylinders. Simply stated, the throttle determines how much power the engine *can* develop. Movement of the propeller control changes the propeller's pitch (its angle of attack). This directly controls how fast the propeller rotates (its speed or RPM) as shown in Figure 46. While throttle determines engine power, propeller pitch determines how efficiently that power is used. Let's examine how the controllable propeller works. Then we'll examine why changing the propeller's pitch is useful.

Forward movement of the propeller control causes both halves of the propeller to rotate about their axes and attack the wind at a smaller angle (i.e., take a smaller bite of air) as shown in Figure 46A. From aerodynamics, you know that a smaller angle of attack means less drag and less resistance to forward motion. Therefore, moving the propeller control forward increases propeller

Fig. 47

HOW ONE TYPE OF CONSTANT SPEED PROPELLER WORKS

Low pitch direction

High pitch direction

Propeller blade

Piston inside propeller dome

Propeller dome

Spring that pushes sliding arm forward as oil pressure decreases

High pressure oil from engine

Engine crankshaft

Sliding arm

Connecting link

Oil from engine enters propeller dome. Piston and sliding arm are moved aft causing prop to take bigger bite of air.

Keeping Up To (Constant) Speed

Figure 47 shows how the constant speed propeller system works on a typical single engine airplane. Oil pressure from the engine provides the hydraulic force used to increase the propeller's pitch. Moving the propeller control aft sends high pressure engine oil to a piston/cylinder arrangement within the propeller hub. This hydraulically pushes the propeller toward a high pitch position. Moving the propeller control forward reduces oil pressure within this piston/cylinder arrangement allowing centrifugal force to return the propeller blades to their low pitch (high RPM) position. We *cycle* the propeller during our runup (change the pitch from low to high and back again a few times) to make sure the system is working as well as to purge cold oil from the propeller's hydraulic system.

RPM. Pulling the propeller control rearward causes the propeller to attack the wind at a larger angle of attack (i.e., take a larger bite of air). Propeller drag increases and engine RPM slows, as shown in Figure 46B.

POWER LEVERS ON AIRPLANES WITH CONSTANT SPEED PROPELLERS

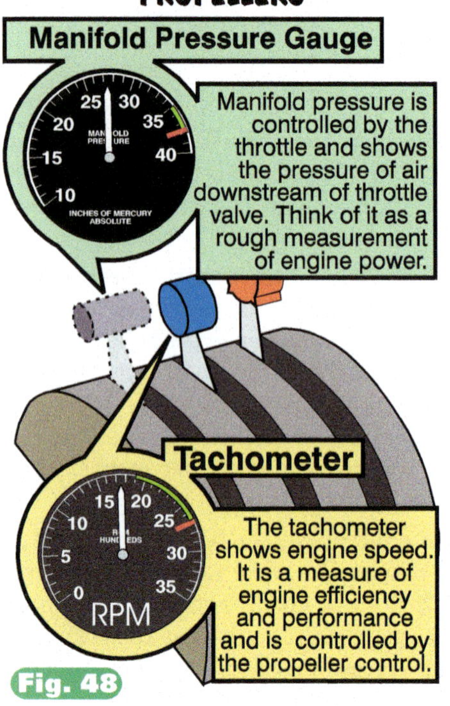

Fig. 48

Since the tachometer tells you how fast the propeller spins (its RPM), is there a gauge to tell you how much throttle is applied? Yes. It's called a *manifold pressure gauge* and it gives you an approximate measure of engine power (Figure 48).

At the beginning of this chapter, we said a vacuum is created in the induction system as a result of pistons descending on their intake strokes (Figure 49). With the throttle closed, the throttle valve in the induction system prevents air (thus fuel) from rushing into the cylinders and powering the engine. But what is it that forces air into the induction system in the first place? Yes, it's the pressure of the surrounding atmosphere. Because atmospheric pressure is higher than the pressure within the induction system, air flows into the cylinders. Simply stated, the atmosphere wants to push air into the induction system (toward the suction created by the downward moving pistons). The amount of this push is measured by the manifold pressure gauge (the gauge is nothing more than a barometric measuring device calibrated to read pressure in inches of mercury—just like altimeters that we'll discuss in Chapter 5).

Manifold pressure is measured downstream of the throttle valve, as shown in Figure 49. When the throttle is closed, air outside the engine (under higher atmospheric pressure) can't flow into the induction system, despite the vacuum on the engine side of the throttle valve. Figure 50A shows a manifold pressure of 14 inches of mercury with a closed throttle. The engine is sucking as hard as it can but the outside air can't get past the closed throttle valve.

Opening the throttle slightly causes an increase in manifold pressure as shown in Figure 50B. More air and fuel are drawn inside the engine, and power increases. Eventually, as the throttle is fully opened (Figure 50C), the pressure downstream of the throttle valve approaches that of the atmosphere. In other words, the air is being forced into the induction system at the maximum pressure the atmosphere is capable of pushing.

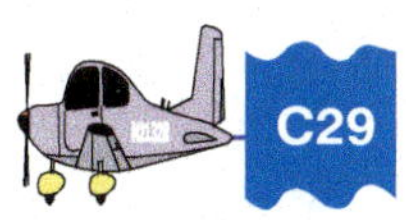

HOW THE ENGINE DRAWS IN AIR FOR COMBUSTION

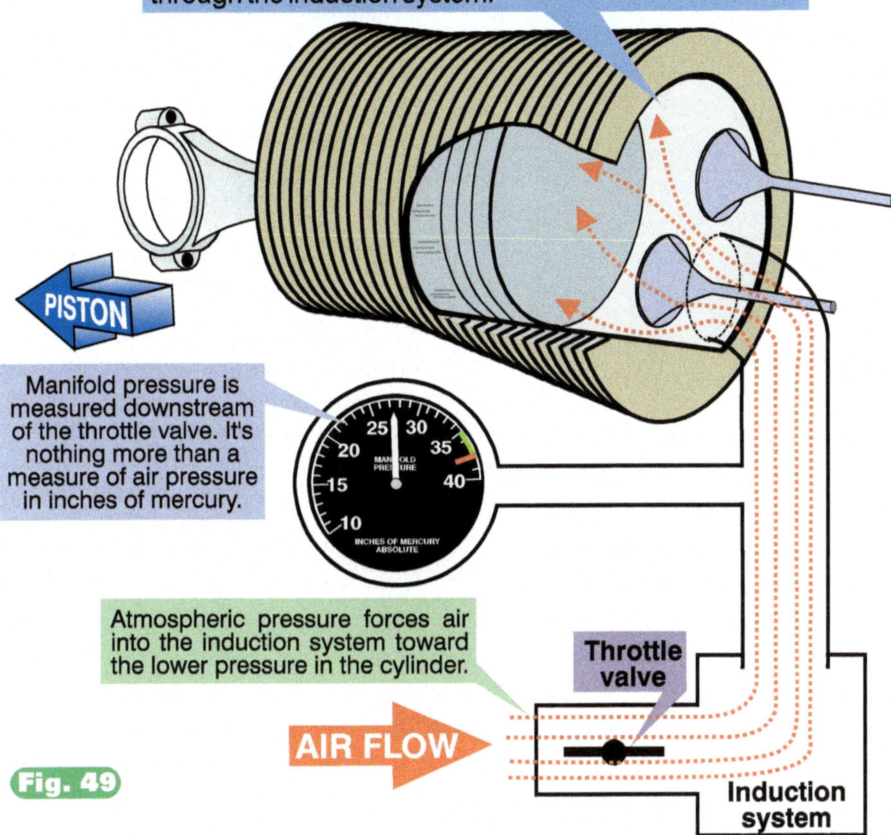

Fig. 49

Under normal conditions, the engine's manifold pressure can't rise above atmospheric pressure. Why? The atmosphere can only push an amount equal to how much it weighs. At sea level, atmospheric pressure weighs enough to push a column of mercury 30 inches into a glass tube containing a vacuum (see Chapter 5 for more details on barometric pressure). As a measurement of the atmosphere's weight, we say that the outside air pressure is 30 inches of mercury. Therefore, the engine's manifold pressure at full throttle is a little less than 30 inches (it's a little less because of air friction and intake restrictions within the induction system). Clearly, then, manifold pressures near 30 inches of mercury signifies more power is being developed by the engine. On the other hand, low manifold pressures (say 15 inches or so) indicate less fuel and air is entering the cylinders and less power is being produced.

As the airplane climbs, you'll notice the manifold pressure decreases even though the throttle is fully opened. Why? Atmospheric pressure decreases as you ascend. It decreases approximately one inch of mercury for every thousand feet of altitude gain (and increases approximately one inch of mercury for every thousand feet of altitude loss). At sea level you can develop approximately 30 inches of manifold pressure with full throttle. At 5,000 MSL, however, your manifold pressure will be approximately 25 inches with full

MANIFOLD PRESSURE

Fig. 50

Manifold pressure is measured downstream from the throttle valve and provides an approximate measure of engine power.

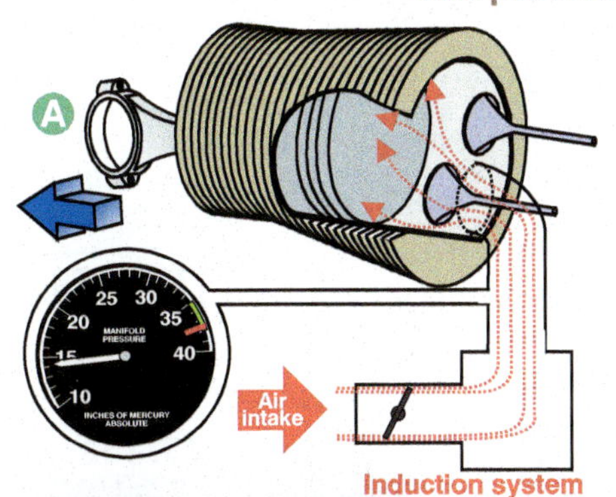

When the throttle is fully closed, airflow into the cylinders is restricted. Very little airflow gets past the throttle valve despite the piston's enormous suction (low manifold pressure).

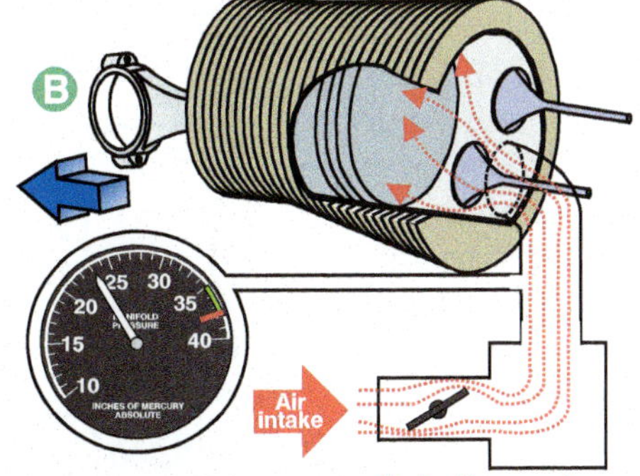

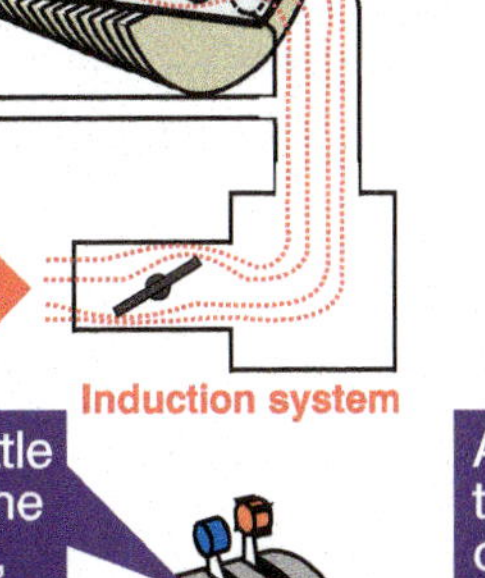

At partial power, a little more air flows into the cylinders. Therefore, the air pressure rises in the intake manifold resulting in a rise of manifold pressure.

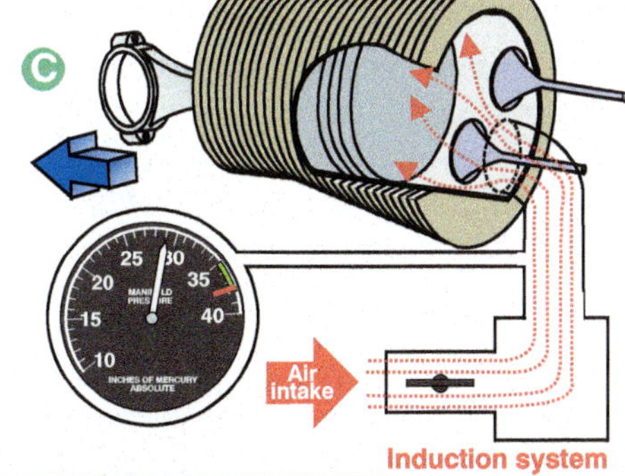

At full throttle in a non-turbocharged engine, air can't be forced into the engine at greater than atmospheric pressure (which is near 30 inches of mercury).

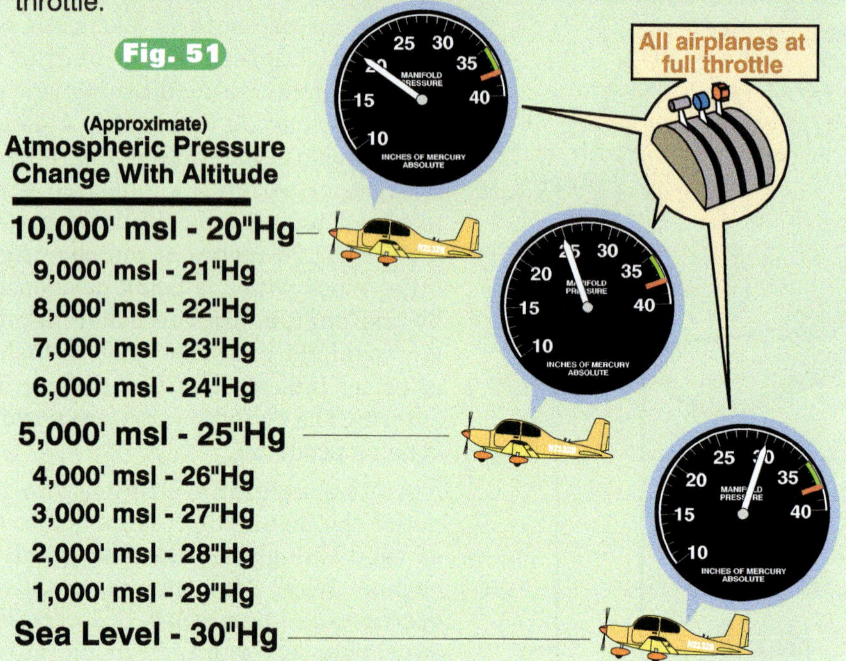

throttle (Figure 51). Remember, under normal conditions the atmosphere can't force air into the induction system at more than its own pressure (its own weight).

I mentioned that engine power is controlled by the throttle. That's basically true. But engine power can also be varied slightly by the RPM you've selected. In other words, the total power produced by the engine is really a combination of both manifold pressure and engine RPM. Think of it this way. You're on a 2000 calorie diet. You can eat 1500 calories for breakfast, 500 for lunch and skip dinner; 1000 for breakfast, and 500 each for lunch and dinner, etc. There are lots of combinations that will yield 2000 calories.

The same is true on a constant speed prop plane. Different combinations of manifold pressure and engine (prop blade) RPM can be used to attain a given power setting. Figure 52 shows how this works for one airplane. Any of the manifold pressure and engine RPM combinations listed can be selected to obtain the desired engine power output in cruise flight. The throttle selects the manifold pressure and the propeller control selects engine RPM.

Why would you want so many combinations of manifold pressure and RPM? The reason is that fuel consumption, airspeed and the percent of power produced all vary based on different combinations of manifold pressure and RPM. Noise levels and smoothness of engine operation also vary based on RPM. Even some of your airborne electronic equipment can be affected by engine speed. At least you have a choice among different combinations for power selection.

The big question is, "Why have a propeller that can change its pitch in flight in the first place?" After all, this is just another airplane knob you have to contend with, isn't it? Yes it is. But it's worth the trouble.

Airplanes having constant speed propellers are much more versatile in their operation. For instance, fixed pitch propeller airplanes have their propellers permanently configured (pitched) for either a fast cruise, a fast climb, or somewhere in between. You can't change their pitch in flight. Airplanes with controllable pitch propellers, however, can essentially reshape the prop, by changing its pitch, from within. The optimum angle of attack can be used for climb and cruise. Let's take a look at how a different pitch may result in increased performance.

Low Pitch And High RPMs – When climbing a very steep hill in a car, you want your automobile's engine to develop nearly 100% of its maximum power. That's why you start off in low gear. Low gear results in high engine RPM, thus more engine power being transferred to the wheels (Figure 53A). As a result, your car is less likely to bog down during the climb. Pay attention the next time you walk up a steep hill. You'll find yourself using lots of short steps (high RPM) instead of the long strides you'll use on the flatlands.

CRUISE POWER SETTINGS
65% MAXIMUM CONTINUOUS POWER (OR FULL THROTTLE)
2800 POUNDS

Fig. 52

PRESS ALT.	IOAT		ISA - 20 °C (-36 °F) ENGINE SPEED	MAN. PRESS	FUEL FLOW		TAS	
FEET	°F	°C	RPM	IN HG	PSI	GPH	KTS	MPH
S.L.	27	-3	2450	20.9	6.6	11.5	147	169
2000	19	-7	2450	20.4	6.6	11.5	149	171
4000	12	-11	2450	20.1	6.6	11.5	152	175
6000	5	-15	2450	19.8	6.6	11.5	155	178
8000	-2	-19	2450	19.5	6.6	11.5	157	181
10,000	-8	-22	2450	19.2				
12,000	-15	-26	2450	18.8				
14,000	-22	-30	2450	17.4				
16,000	-29	-34	2450	16.1				

Manifold pressure and RPM combinations that produce a specific brake horsepower under given temperature and altitude conditions.

NOTES: 1. Full throttle manifold pressure settings are approximate.
2. Shaded area represents operation with full throttle.

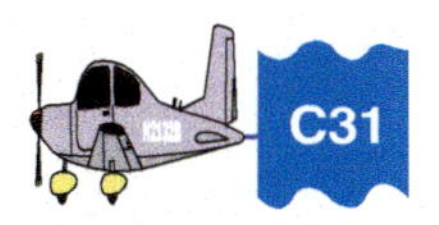

PROPELLER POSITION FOR TAKEOFF AND CLIMB

The car starts out in low gear when going uphill. The engine turns fast and more power is delivered to the wheels.

Fig. 53

Airplane also starts out in low gear when going up hill. In other words, when climbing, the prop is set to its full forward, high RPM position allowing the engine to develop maximum speed, thus maximum power. More power means more thrust.

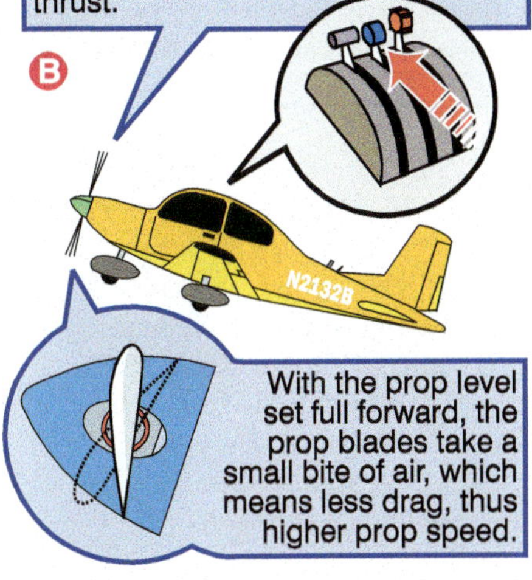

The same philosophy applies to airplanes. During a climb, we want the airplane's engine to develop maximum power. This allows maximum thrust to be produced (remember, it's excess thrust that allows an airplane to climb).

Engine power is dependent on its RPM. For an engine to develop its maximum power, it must be operated at its highest allowable RPM. At any lower RPM the engine develops only a fraction of its total horsepower. That's why on takeoff we want the propeller set to its lowest pitch (highest RPM) position (full forward on the prop lever). In this position the prop experiences less wind resistance, resulting in less drag and higher engine RPMs (Figure 53B). Under these conditions, the engine develops maximum power, thus maximum thrust for climbing and accelerating.

You may be thinking, "How can the propeller deliver maximum thrust if it doesn't take a big bite of air?" Think of it this way. If the propeller does take a big bite of air (a large angle of attack), it will surely develop more thrust—but only if the propeller continues to turn over at a high speed. That's the problem! Taking such a large bite of air increases the propeller's drag (just like a wing at a large angle of attack). This decreases the propeller's speed and prevents the engine from developing its maximum horsepower (it bogs it down, like the car). The final result is that the propeller produces less thrust than it's capable of producing.

One last way of conceptualizing this is to think about a blender (if you don't have one, simply send out a few wedding invitations). If hard vegetable fiber is dropped in before the blades have a chance to spin up, the machine bogs down (RPMs stay low). Nothing gets chopped because the motor has less spinning force or torque at slower speeds. However, once the blender's blades spin to a fast speed, nothing seems to resist the spinning force of the blades. High motor RPMs mean maximum power is developed and the blender's blades resist slowing when they encounter thick vegetable fiber. The net result of higher engine RPMs for the airplane is that maximum engine thrust is produced when the propeller spins faster, even though the blades are at a lower pitch.

High Pitch and Low RPMs – Are there times when you don't need to develop maximum engine power? Yes. For example, if you're on the freeway, your automobile only needs enough power to keep it moving at a reasonable speed—perhaps only 55% to 65% of its maximum power (if it's a VW Beetle). Anything more than that and it's red-light-in-the-back-window time. High gear (low engine RPM) is selected to maintain freeway speeds (Figure 54A). High gear means the engine turns over at a lower RPM, thus producing only the horsepower

PROPELLER POSITION FOR CRUISE FLIGHT

In cruise, the car doesn't need to develop maximum power. Therefore, higher gears allow the engine to turn slower while sufficient power is developed for freeway speeds.

Fig. 54

Airplanes also cruise in high gear. In other words, in cruise flight the prop is set to a higher pitch (big bite of air). This allows the engine to run slower, use less fuel and still develop the necessary thrust for a reasonably fast cruise speed.

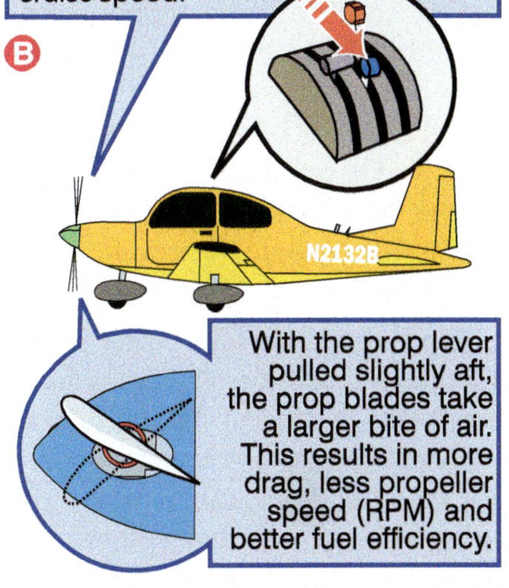

needed to keep the car moving along at an acceptable pace. This is achieved with less fuel consumption than if the car were running flat out.

Airplanes are operated in a similar manner during cruise flight (Figure 54B). There is no need to develop maximum horsepower during cruise flight. Our concern is to obtain a reasonably fast airspeed while keeping the fuel consumption low. After all, we could operate our airplane in cruise flight at full throttle—but why? The larger drag associated with higher speeds would consume enormous amounts of fuel and not allow us to move all that much faster anyway (remember, total drag increases dramatically at higher airspeeds). Therefore, cruise flight is a tradeoff between high airspeed and low fuel consumption.

With the proper combination of manifold pressure and engine RPM, you can obtain a reasonably fast airspeed for a given rate of fuel consumption. In cruise flight, we select the target manifold pressure with the throttle, and engine RPM with the propeller control. Now the propeller produces a specific amount of lift (thrust) for a given (lower) fuel consumption.

Why Constant Speed Propellers?

Controllable pitch propellers on general aviation airplanes are of the constant speed variety. Once the RPM is established, changes in manifold pressure (by moving the throttle) won't affect engine speed (Figure 55). In other words, opening or closing the throttle (or changing the airplane's attitude) doesn't vary the engine's RPM. This is why these controllable propellers are given the name constant-speed propellers. (Of course, if you pull the throttle all the way back, there's simply no power available to keep the propeller spinning. The engine's RPM has no choice but to drop.)

The reason constant speed propellers are put on an airplane is to reduce a pilot's workload. Instead of having to readjust the RPM with every change in power, you simply set the RPM and it stays where it's put—just like your home thermostat keeps the temperature constant.

What is the value of having a propeller that maintains a preset (constant) speed? It provides you with one less item to readjust while managing power. Let's suppose your Pilot's Operating Handbook suggests the most efficient use of engine power during climb occurs at 25 inches of manifold pressure and 2,500 RPM (pilots refer to this as *25 squared,* which proves how weak some of them are in math). As you climb, the manifold pressure decreases approximately one inch per thousand feet (because the outside air pressure decreases one inch for every thousand feet altitude gain). Since you have a constant speed propeller, the RPM automatically stays set at 2,500, despite variations in manifold pressure (or throttle positions). All you need to do is keep adding throttle to maintain the desired manifold pressure during the climb; the RPM needs no adjusting.

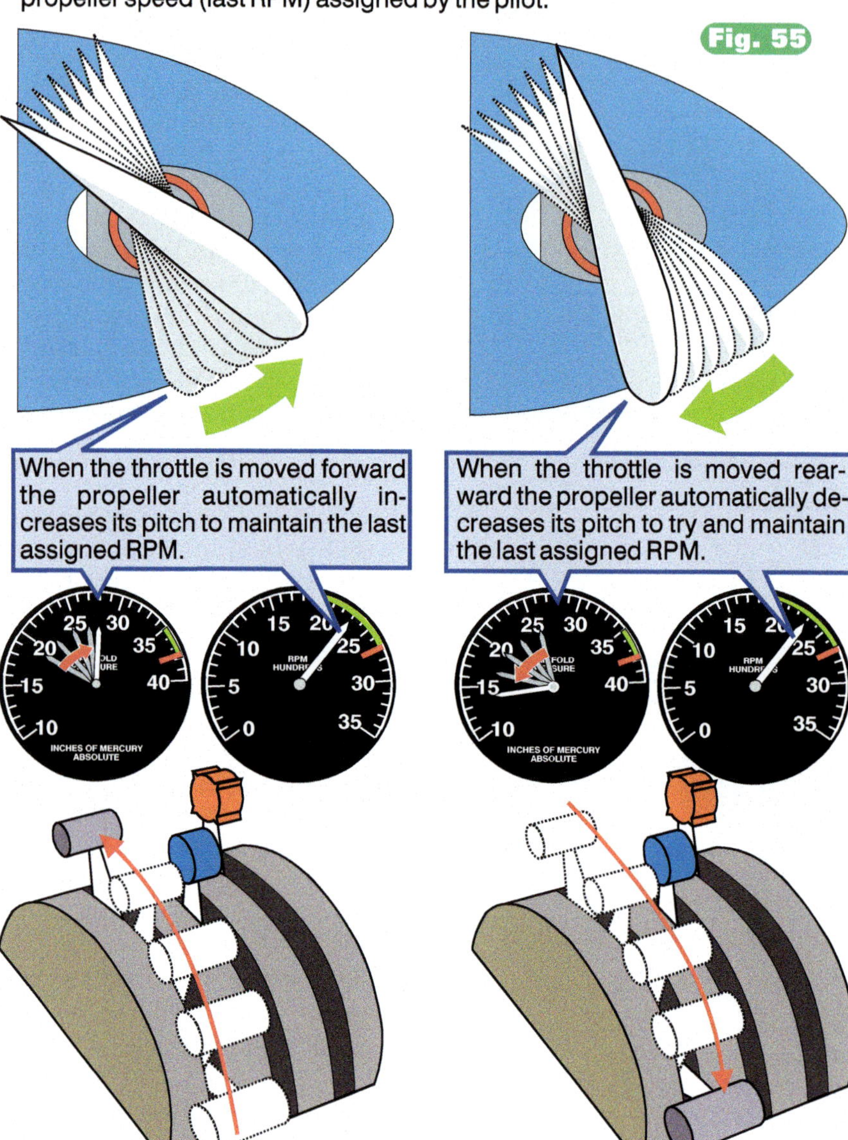

Keeping Up to Speed

You might be wondering how a constant speed propeller automatically maintains its assigned RPM. Here's how it's done.

As the throttle is moved forward, engine RPM wants to increase. The propeller governor senses this slight increase in speed and automatically changes the propeller's pitch to take a bigger bite of air. Engine power is absorbed by the change in pitch and the RPM remains unchanged. Likewise, when the throttle is pulled back, the propeller governor senses a slight decrease in speed. The governor automatically changes the propeller's pitch to take a smaller bite of air. This reduces the propeller's load, allowing it to maintain the last-established RPM. The engine now produces less thrust. Of course, pulling the throttle all the way back reduces the RPM despite the flattened pitch. There comes a point where, even with the lowest blade pitch possible, the propeller can't maintain the RPM selected by the propeller control.

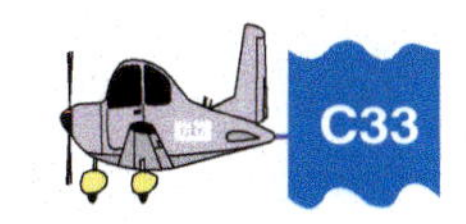

How to Make Power Changes

With the ability to vary propeller pitch, you need to understand a few very important principles about power management. It's relatively easy to overstress an engine if the throttle and propeller controls aren't used in the proper order during power changes.

For instance, suppose your manifold pressure and RPM are set at 23 inches and 2,300 RPM (Figure 56A). You want to increase the manifold pressure and RPM to 25 inches and 2,500 RPM. If you increase the manifold pressure to 25 inches first, it will increase the combustible mixture flowing to the cylinders. This would normally spin the propeller faster. Yet this doesn't happen, since the propeller takes a bigger bite of air to absorb the increase in power. Cylinder stress increases as the propeller keeps the RPM from increasing (i.e., the expanding gases push harder, yet are unable to move the pistons faster). Given enough cylinder stress, you could damage the engine.

When you want to increase both the manifold pressure and RPM, change the RPM first, then increase the manifold pressure. In other words, move the propeller control forward first, the throttle next, as shown in Figure 56B.

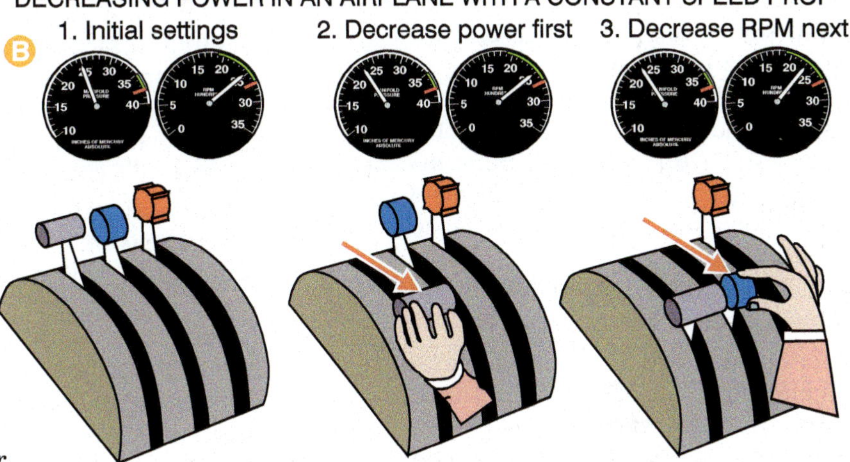

Fig. 56

Follow the same philosophy when decreasing manifold pressure and RPM. *Pull the throttle back first, followed by the propeller control.* Another way of thinking about this is to keep the propeller control lever physically ahead of the throttle during all manifold pressure and RPM changes. A memory aid for this is to *keep the prop on top* (or always in front of the throttle).

Propeller Tips and Ideas

Be aware that the propeller governor starts working only when the engine is operating above a specific RPM and not below. In other words, moving the throttle will change the RPM until the propeller reaches its minimum governing RPM. This is why the magneto check we discussed earlier is performed below this minimum governing RPM. Remember, we're interested in seeing how much of an RPM drop occurs on each mag as well as between the mags. Magneto checks done at higher RPMs wouldn't show any mag drops on the tachometer since the propeller would vary its pitch to maintain a specific RPM.

On complex, high performance airplanes (those with retractable landing gear and constant speed propellers) we use a verbal checklist while on final approach to land. It's the mnemonic GUMP. It stands for gas (fuel pump on), undercarriage (gear down), mixture (full in) and prop (propeller control full forward). Why is the propeller control put in the full-forward (low pitch—high RPM) position just before landing? We do so in the unlikely event there's a need to *go around*. A go around is an aborted landing; you apply full power, climb out, and go around for another attempt at landing. In this situation, it's important that the engine develop full power—just like on takeoff. That's why the propeller control is moved to the full-forward position—exactly where it is during takeoff.

Up, Up and Away

You now know the basics of what makes an airplane engine tick, kick, heat, and freeze. As I said at the beginning of this chapter, you don't have to be a wrench jockey to be a good pilot. But now you do have some vital information under your seatbelt—information that can help you fly safely and economically.

Enjoy it.

Postflight Briefing #3-1

Detonation and Preignition

Detonation

Heat is something a pilot should pay close attention to. This was apparent to me even before I started flying. My grandparents smoked like crazy when I was a kid. I would feel their bedroom door. If it was hot, I knew they were still up, puffing away (on their cigarettes, you understand). If you want to avoid engine-damaging problems from excess heat, you'll need to learn something about detonation.

The cylinder's fuel-air charge expands as it's ignited by the spark plugs. Properly done, this isn't an explosion so much as it is a smooth, progressive burning of the combustible gases within the cylinder. As these gases expand, they increase pressure, pushing the piston downward during its power stroke (Figure 57A).

Detonation occurs when the fuel-air charge explodes, burning in a short, fierce burst of energy rather than a controlled, even burn. Such an explosion (shown in Figure 57B) can be very damaging and sometimes fatal to the airplane engine.

Detonation occurs after the spark plug fires, when the unburned portion of the fuel-air charge, ahead of the burning charge, suddenly explodes. If you can imagine being kicked by a Kung-fu master from "Wong's Chinese Bulletproof Takeout" you might appreciate how damaging detonation can be to an engine. One kung-fu kick could damage the body as continued explosions damage the piston, cylinder and valves. Figure 58 shows detonation damage to an engine's components.

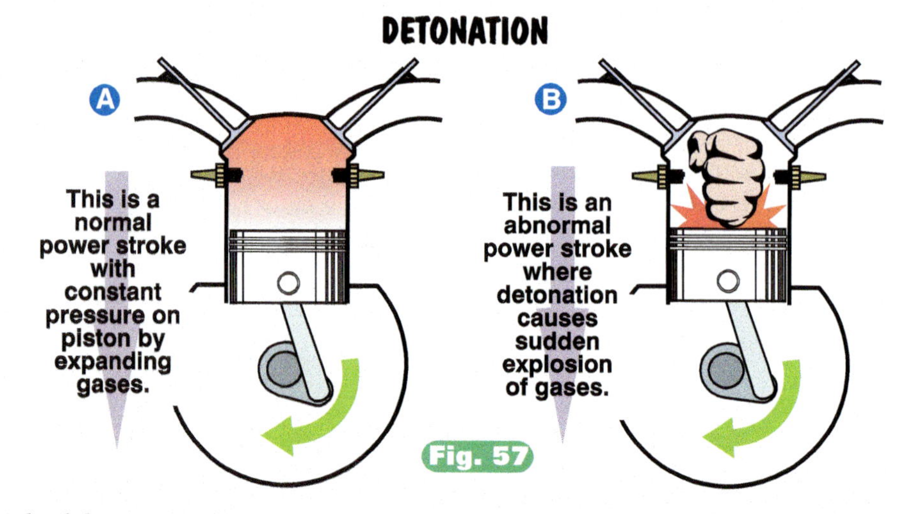

Fig. 57

High engine and cylinder head temperatures increase the likelihood of detonation. They may aid in the abnormal exploding vs. the normal burning of the ignitable gases within the cylinder. As an interesting note, the EGT reading actually decreases during detonation, while the cylinder head temperatures increase. Why? With the exploding of the cylinder's fuel-air charge, combustion takes place earlier. This suddenly and dramatically releases the heat from the combustion process to the cylinder, piston and valves (too much heat at one time—that's the problem). The exhaust gases that are released have already expended their heat. They're cooler, which is reflected in a lower EGT reading. If the throttle and mixture aren't moved and you see the EGT decrease while cylinder head temperatures increase, suspect detonation. Do whatever you need to do to cool the engine.

If you suspect detonation, there are several ways you can cool the engine's cylinders. First, enrich the mixture. Second, lower the climb angle, improving airflow over the cylinders. Third, if the airplane has cowl flaps, open them. Finally, reducing power is always a good practice if detonation is suspected. Do what you need to do to reduce those cylinder head temperatures.

The following are several known causes of detonation:

1. Using a lower grade of fuel than what is recommended by the manufacturer. Higher octane fuels have additives that help prevent detonation.

2. Using a time-expired fuel.

3. Over-leaning. Excessive leaning can raise cylinder head temperatures, increasing the likelihood of fuel exploding instead of burning within the cylinders.

4. Overheating an engine by climbing too steeply on hot days, as well as using excessive engine power (some engines have restrictions on the time maximum power can be used).

5. An abrupt opening of the throttle.

Fig. 58

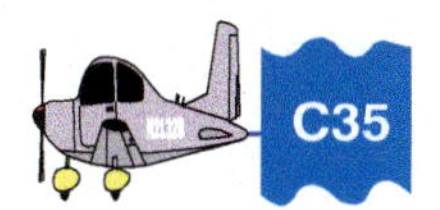

Preignition

Preignition isn't the ability to see sparks from the future. Preignition is ignition occurring before the spark plug ignites the cylinder's fuel-air charge. It's very different from detonation, which is an explosion within the cylinders. Preignition causes peak pressures within the cylinder to occur before the beginning of the power cycle. It is usually caused by a hot spot in the cylinders. This hot spot acts like a little spark plug, setting off the fuel-air charge prematurely. Glowing deposits of lead in the cylinders, overheated spark plugs, or using high power settings with lean mixtures can all lead to hot spot formation and preignition.

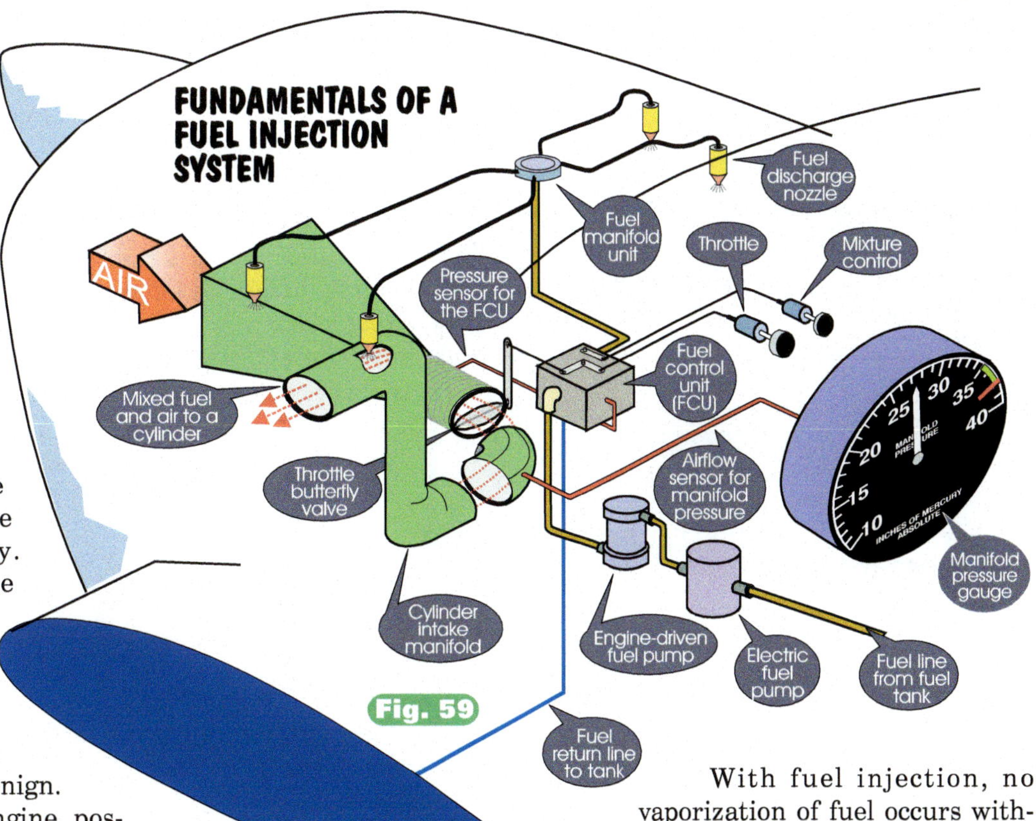

Fig. 59

Preignition is by no means benign. It can cause a rough running engine, possible backfiring, a sudden rise in engine temperatures, and possible engine damage (like piston or rod failure). Be alert for any of these signs and be prepared to reduce the temperature of the engine as recommended in the case of detonation.

Postflight Briefing #3-2

Fuel Injection Systems

Fuel injection is a process in which fuel is directly metered and distributed to each cylinder without the use of a carburetor (Figure 59). A carburetor provides fuel for *all* the cylinders. A fuel injection system allows a precise amount of fuel to be delivered to *each* cylinder individually, via the fuel discharge nozzles. These discharge nozzles squirt fuel, under pressure, into the cylinder's intake ports near the intake valves. Better fuel distribution (more accurate fuel-air mixture to each cylinder) results from fuel injection compared to a typical carburetion system.

The fuel control unit (FCU) regulates both the volume of airflow entering the engine and the quantity of fuel delivered to the FMU (fuel manifold unit), shown in Figure 60. Movement of the throttle varies the position of the throttle valve, which regulates the amount of air flowing over the venturi (much like that found in a typical carburetor). A small tube from the FCU samples the amount of airflow over the venturi and, based on the volume of incoming air, regulates the amount of fuel flowing to the FMU. This allows the FMU to maintain a specific fuel-air ratio for each cylinder.

With fuel injection, no vaporization of fuel occurs within the induction system. This means that a fuel injection system isn't subject to the refrigerator-like problems associated with moist air and vaporizing fuel. You can't get carburetor ice in a fuel injection system for one very important reason: there's no carburetor.

However, fuel injection isn't completely invulnerable to the effects of Mother Nature. Impact ice, mentioned earlier, is the Achilles heel of fuel injection. Anything that plugs the air intake port will suffocate the engine.

Fig. 60 THE FMU OR FUEL MANIFOLD UNIT

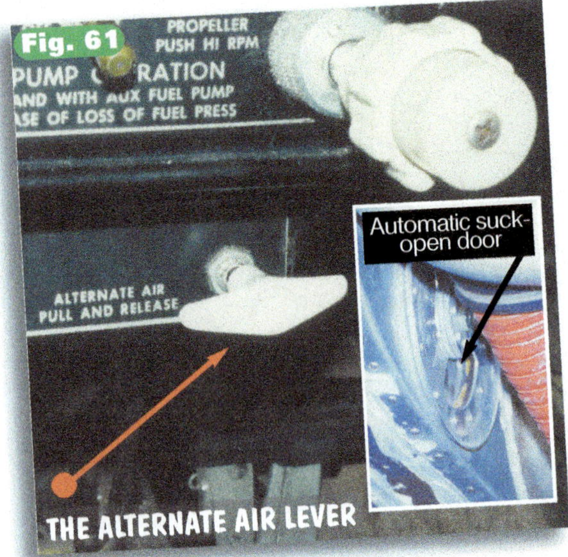

Fortunately, many fuel injected engines have something known as an alternate air lever located in the cockpit (Figure 61). Activating the alternate air lever allows the engine to draw air from an unobstructed source within the cowling. Some airplanes with fuel injection have a *suck-open alternate air door* in lieu of a manually activated lever. This is a spring- or magnet-held opening in the induction system. In the event the primary air source becomes plugged, the engine's sucking action automatically opens an alternate air door. Despite blockage of the primary air source, the engine still continues to run.

Most larger airplanes with bigger engines use fuel injection. The proper distribution of fuel becomes an important factor when larger, heat producing engines could be easily damaged from improper distribution of fuel within the cylinders.

Here are the advantages and disadvantages of fuel injection:

Advantages of fuel injection:

1. Improved control of fuel-air ratio.
2. More uniform delivery of the fuel-air mixture to each cylinder.
3. Increased engine efficiency.
4. Freedom from vaporization ice (fuel ice).
5. Instant acceleration of engine without tendency to hesitate.

Disadvantages of fuel injection:

1. Contamination by dirt and water can more easily affect fuel injected engines due to the small orifices of injector nozzles.
2. Difficulty starting engines on hot days due to vapor lock.
3. Any surplus fuel could be routed to one tank and cause a fuel imbalance if the pilot is not familiar with fuel system.

Postflight Briefing #3-3

Advanced Airplane Systems

Turbocharging

Humans, like airplanes, find their performance is best at sea level. Why? The air is more dense. It's as simple as that. Decrease the air density and performance decreases. On one occasion, I was flying at 17,500 feet MSL with four people aboard a Cessna 210. It wasn't a pressurized version so we were all wearing our oxygen masks. One of the passengers was fiddling with his mask and accidentally disconnected his tube without realizing it. As we conversed with one another he started to sound pretty weird. In fact, he started to sound like he was a few fries short of a Happy Meal. He was experiencing *hypoxia* or lack of oxygen. I hooked him back up and his mental performance (IQ) returned to a normal, high level. With sufficiently dense air, the engine's performance will also remain at higher levels.

At sea level, where atmospheric pressure is high, maximum manifold pressure is obtained for takeoff. As the airplane ascends, less atmospheric pressure is available to push air into the engine's cylinders. Airplanes with *turbochargers,* however, are able to produce sea level power at higher altitudes.

Turbocharging compresses air into the intake manifold by utilizing the normally unused exhaust gases exiting the engine. Figure 62 shows a typical turbocharging arrangement for general aviation airplanes. Exhaust gases are put to use in spinning a turbine which, in turn, is connected to the end of an air compressor. The speed of the compressor is controlled by automatically or manually adjusting the flow of exhaust gases over the turbine. This is done by something known as a *wastegate.*

When no turbocharging is needed, a wastegate valve is opened allowing hot, pressurized exhaust gases to escape and bypass the turbine. As

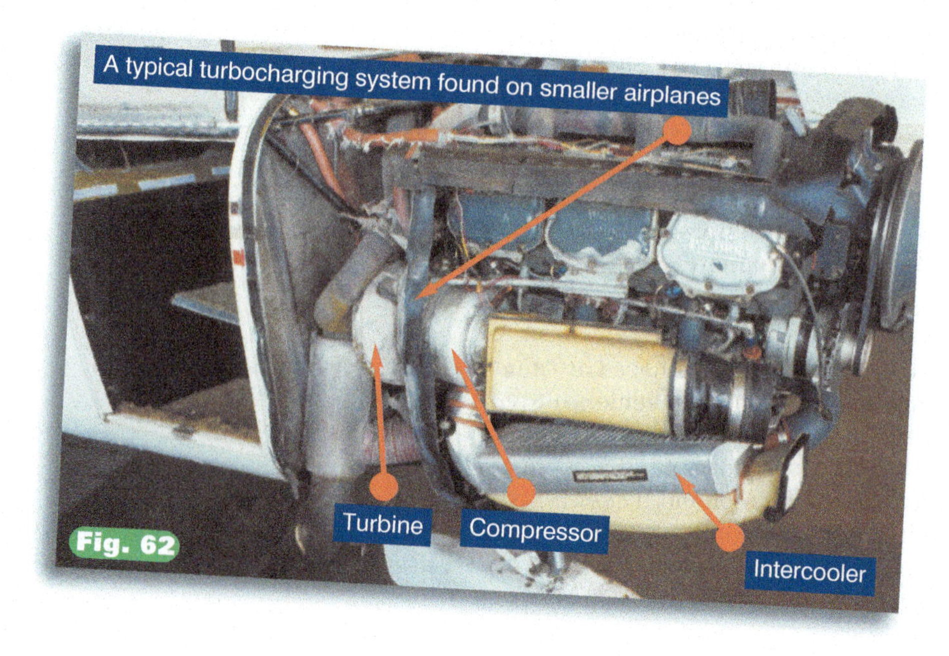

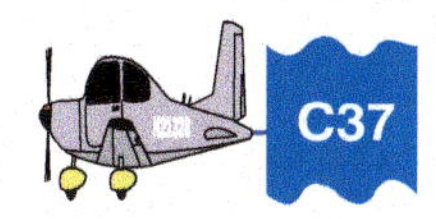

manifold pressures decrease with altitude gain, turbocharging becomes useful. The wastegate valve closes (either automatically or manually, depending on your airplane) allowing more exhaust to flow over the turbine. This spins the compressor, allowing compressed air to be pumped into the induction system. Greater manifold pressures are now possible at higher altitudes. More of the engine's maximum obtainable power is now available at these altitudes.

Most airplanes have automatic wastegate controllers that allow a specific manifold pressure, set by the pilot, to be maintained. These automatic systems can also prevent *overboosting* of the engine by automatically opening the wastegate valve in the event of excessive manifold pressures. (Overboosting the engine can cause excessive combustion pressures in cylinders and damage the engine.)

On some airplanes, the pilot must manually control the wastegate through a lever(s) in the cockpit. When flying an airplane with manual turbocharging, be careful to avoid taking off with the wastegate lever in the full turbocharged position. With application of full throttle, you could cause some pretty severe engine damage.

Without turbocharging, small airplanes typically have a *service ceiling* (an altitude above which they will not climb more than 100 feet per minute) of approximately 15,000 feet. Operational altitudes in excess of 25,000 feet are not uncommon in turbocharged, piston powered airplanes. But turbocharging is not without its price. Compressing air increases its temperature. Turbocharging adds heat to an already heated engine. Turbocharged engines are asked to operate at the outer limits of endurance, and there is little margin for pilot indiscretion or inattention.

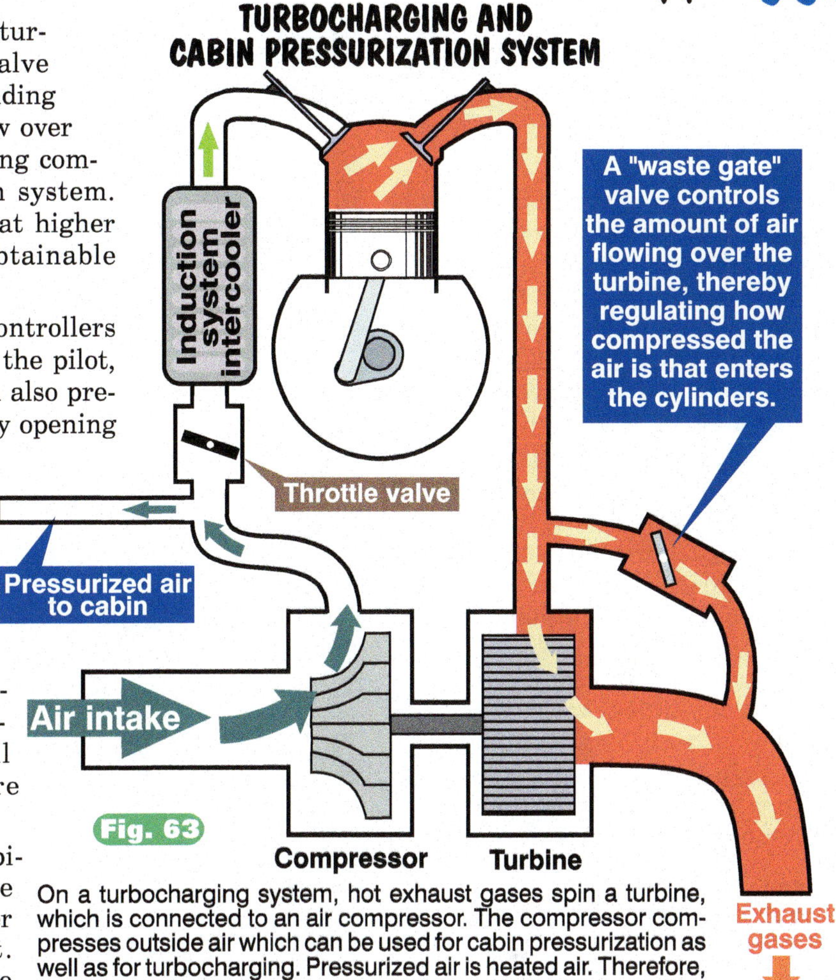

On a turbocharging system, hot exhaust gases spin a turbine, which is connected to an air compressor. The compressor compresses outside air which can be used for cabin pressurization as well as for turbocharging. Pressurized air is heated air. Therefore, an induction system intercooler is often installed to help cool the air before it enters the cylinders.

Pilots of turbocharged aircraft need to be especially cognizant of engine operating temperatures. In fact, some airplane manufacturers recommend their turbocharged airplanes be operated at extra-rich mixtures, to help keep the engine cooler. To help prevent heat–related problems, some airplanes with turbochargers have air cooling systems called intercoolers. Intercoolers cool the air that's leaving the air compressor before it enters the upper portions of the induction system.

Pressurization

I never cease to be amazed at the inventions of modern man. Some are an inconvenience; some are very practical. For instance, telephones once came with their own leash. It was almost impossible to misplace one. When I purchased a cellular phone, I lost it the first week. I had to call myself to find out where I left it. It's a great invention but it also produces a lot of frustration. Pressurization for airplanes, however, is an excellent idea.

Pressurizing an airplane allows you to fly at very high altitudes while remaining in a cabin environment with near-sea-level pressures (OK, pressures in the 4,000 to 8,000 foot range). This is accomplished by directing compressed air from the turbocharger (or from an auxiliary compressor) into the cabin as shown in Figure 63. Flight at higher altitudes is now possible while maintaining the cabin at pressures found at much lower elevations. For instance, one general aviation airplane model can fly at 25,000 feet while pressurizing the cabin to 8,000 feet. Essentially, you feel like you are breathing the air at an altitude of 8,000 feet as you're swooping along at 25,000 feet. It is a common misconception that pressurization places the cabin at "sea level" pressure. This is important to understand, because people with certain medical conditions can not stand higher elevations for long, if at all.

The fuselage of a pressurized aircraft is built stronger, allowing it to withstand the forces of pressurization. The next time you're walking around the airport, try and guess which aircraft are pressurized. Little, round windows are usually the telltale clue identifying pressurized airplanes. These windows are more capable of handling the differential in air pressure between the cockpit and the atmosphere. Pressurized airplanes also have airtight

seals on all doors and baggage compartments. Pressurization would be impossible if air could easily escape around and out doors, vents and windows.

Pilots control aircraft pressurization by means of a dial known as the *cabin altitude controller,* located in the cockpit. In the hands of an inept operator, this can become an instrument of torture, wreaking havoc on innocent eardrums. Easy does it is the operative thought here.

By rotating the dial, as shown in Figure 64, the pilot informs the pressurization system of the exact amount of pressure needed in the aircraft. Air from the compressor, also known as *bleed air*, is then pumped into the cockpit for pressurization. The cabin altitude controller also operates an outflow valve. When the outflow valve is nearly closed, the cabin becomes pressurized. An open outflow valve allows air to escape, depressurizing the cabin.

Pressurized airplanes have a limit on the amount of internal pressure they can withstand. There comes a point where the difference between low pressure air outside and high pressure air inside the cabin becomes too great. It's like overinflating a balloon. Too much pressure on the inside can cause it to pop. To prevent this, a limit known as the *maximum cabin differential pressure* is established. Fortunately a pressure release safety valve prevents excessive cabin pressures.

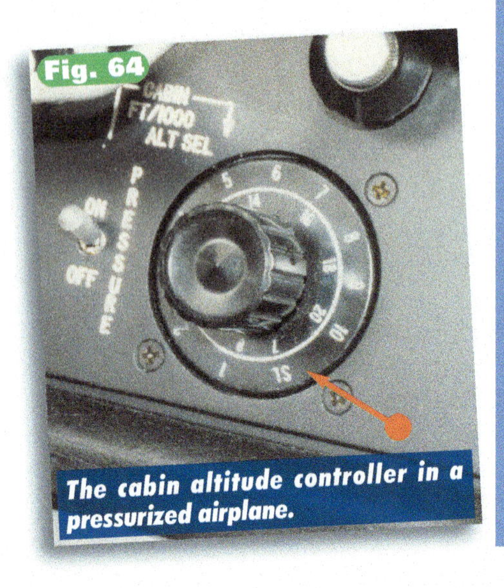

Fig. 64 The cabin altitude controller in a pressurized airplane.

Engine Operating Tips

Tim Peterson

Here are a few things to consider during your runup. First, when you check carburetor heat, make sure you apply the heat long enough to determine if ice is present. Many pilots pull the knob, look for a drop, then push the lever in without waiting to see if any ice actually melts. You must do a slow count to at least four with the heat on to determine if there is an increase in RPM which indicates the presence of ice.

While sitting in the runup area or waiting at the hold lines for departure, keep your RPMs around 1,000 to 1,200. This helps prevent spark plug fouling.

Always check your idle RPM before takeoff and make sure you know the RPM your airplane typically idles at. For instance, if your aircraft typically idles at 700 RPM and you get 800 RPM with the throttle fully retarded, you'll notice the effects during landing. Increased idle thrust will cause you to float during the landing flare.

During the magneto check, should you find an unacceptable drop or rough running engine, put the magneto switch back to the *both* position at once. Never just sit there looking at a drop thinking that it will improve. Switching back to *both* allows the fouled spark plugs to burn off the carbon matter that's usually responsible for causing the drop in the first place. Increase the power to a higher setting, lean for no more than 30 seconds then return the mixture and RPM to normal for another mag check. This is usually sufficient to burn off any foreign material responsible for fouling the spark plug. Remember, you are not only checking your magnetos during a mag check, you're also checking your spark plugs as well as your ignition harness.

If you have a *fast* mag drop that exceeds permissible limits, it's probably a plug or ignition harness problem. A *slow* and or *erratic* mag drop that exceeds the allowed limits usually results from magneto problems. Should you inadvertently turn the switch to *off* during a mag check causing a loud bang or loud noise, don't take off until you find a friendly mechanic to inspect the exhaust system. The *boom* sound was caused by unburnt air and fuel entering the exhaust system and exploding when the mag switch was turned back on. This little faux pas might have accidentally damaged your exhaust system.

Many instructors teach their students to do a magneto ground test at the end of each flight. This is done by reducing the RPM to idle and quickly turning the mag switch to *off* then back to *both.* If the magnetos are grounding properly, the engine should momentarily quit. If not, you have a live mag, indicating the potential for a cylinder firing if the propeller is turned by hand. Do this mag check only at idle or you might damage your exhaust system as described above. Just because you had a successful ground check you should still assume a hot prop exists. In other words, engine vibration may somehow be responsible for the grounding action taking place. ALWAYS TREAT THE PROP AS A GUN. The assumption is that it's loaded even though you just unloaded it in front of several witnesses on the flight line. If you must turn the prop, do so only after you make sure the throttle is in its idle position, the mixture is in the idle cutoff position and the fuel is turned off. This also assumes that you've been given instruction in how to physically handle a prop by a knowledgable flight instructor.

Tim Peterson
A&P mechanic, flight instructor and ATP rated pilot

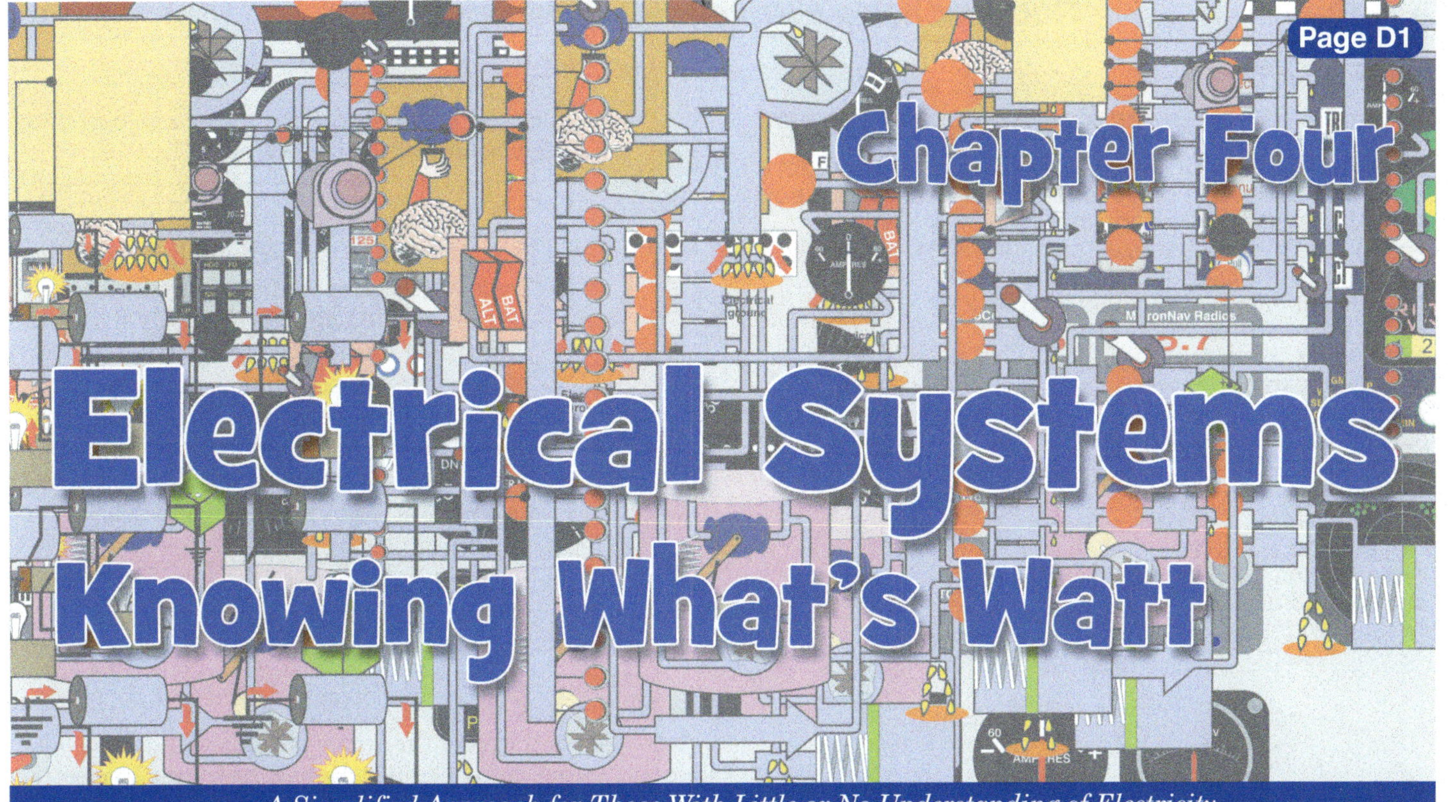

A Simplified Approach for Those With Little or No Understanding of Electricity

Welcome to Volts for Dolts, the Machado QuickCourse for those afraid of electricity.

Attention, class. This is going to be easy.

Watt? Easy? Yes, because we're going to learn what electricity does, rather than split atoms over what it is.

Let's be practical. You don't know, and don't much care, about the difference between jewels and joules. You do want and need to know how to detect and direct electrons in your airplane and put them to work for you. You also need to know when the electrical system is threatening to roll over and play dead, and what can be done about it.

Read on. Fear not. Think volt, not bolt.

Electricity and Water

Albert Einstein once said, "Make everything as simple as possible, but not simpler." For instance, Einstein's concept of time distortion is often discussed from a mathematical perspective. For most of us, this is like listening to a lecture delivered in Martian. Actually, Southern Martian. On the other hand, suppose someone said that the length of one minute depends on which side of the bathroom door you're on. Now we're communicating.

Unfortunately, the philosophy of simplicity has not been applied to understanding the airplane's electrical system—until now.

We're going to approach this like a plumber, by thinking about electricity as though it were water. This may be the only chance you will ever have to mix electricity and water safely, so pay attention.

A water model of electricity uses basic plumbing language to explain how electrons flow in a circuit. The only problem with the model is that you can't use it to build a computer. The model's language isn't precise enough to describe the intricate electrical nuances necessary to accurately convey the point (besides, what would you do if water suddenly shot out of your hard drive?). You can, however, use the water model to describe—accurately enough to suit any normal private pilot—how an airplane's electrical system works.

I caution you not to take this model literally, and if you actually are knowledgeable about things electrical, I also urge you not to take offense. The model is only used to help clarify certain cause and effect relationships.

WATER ANALOGY OF ELECTRICITY

The water analogy of electricity uses water to represent the flow of electricity in a circuit and pipes to represent wires. Water pressure represents the amount of voltage in a system. More voltage means greater water pressure. A 24 volt system (the bigger balloon) can push more water through the pipes than a 12 volt system. The amount of water actually flowing within the pipes represents the electrical current within the system. Therefore, a 24 volt system can provide more electric current (more water flow) than a 12 volt system.

12 Volts WATER UNDER PRESSURE

24 Volts WATER UNDER PRESSURE

5 Gal/Hr (Less Current)

10 Gal/Hr (More Current)

Fig. 1

One more disclaimer. This model uses *conventional* current flow, where things go from positive to negative. In reality, electrons flow from the negative to the positive side of a battery. The reason for the difference lies in physics theory, but that's not what this book is about. I use conventional flow because it makes much more sense to mere mortals when things flow from high to low, plus to minus, big to little, etc.

Electricity involves many terms that can be directly related to water or plumbing (Figure 1). Voltage is comparable to, and can be thought of as, the pressure that pushes water through pipes. Current is the amount of water actually flowing through the pipes at any given time. The greater the water pressure (voltage) in a line, the greater the amount of water (electric current) that flows (Figure 2). All the water analogy electrical definitions you'll need are listed in Figure 3.

For electrical equipment to work, something must provide voltage or electrical pressure. In most airplanes this device is called an *alternator,* as shown in Figure 4. Using the water analogy, the alternator can be thought of as the pump that provides water pressure to the *primary bus* and the *avionics bus* (Figure 5). (In the electrical world, a *bus* is a pathway for electricity, not a yellow conveyance for kids.)

A bus is essentially a drinking trough for hungry electrical equipment. Normally, it's a piece of conductive metal that thirsty electrical equipment taps into when drawing the electric current it needs to operate. (From now on I'll speak of electricity in terms of the water analogy as often as possible and, when possible, discuss how it relates to electrical theory.)

The Water Pump

Where might the water pump get the water it needs to pressurize the primary bus? Imagine a tray of water resting on the ground under the schematic of Figure 5. The water pump draws water up from the tray and pumps it into the primary bus. From here the water flows to the electrical equipment, where it does useful work. Then it flows back to the tray resting on the ground. This completes the circuit, allowing the water to return to its original source.

Electricity follows a similar circuit. A spinning alternator causes electric current to flow into the primary bus and through the electrical equipment, where it lights up lights, spins up motors, spins round gyros, and otherwise makes things go *bang, whang* and *clang* in the night (and day). After leaving the electrical equipment, electric current flows back to its original source in a manner similar to the tray in our water analogy. This tray is called the *electrical ground.*

WATER ANALOGY OF VOLTAGE AND CURRENT

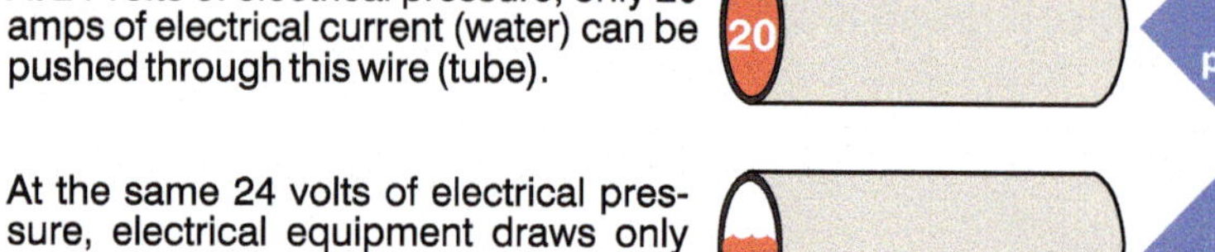

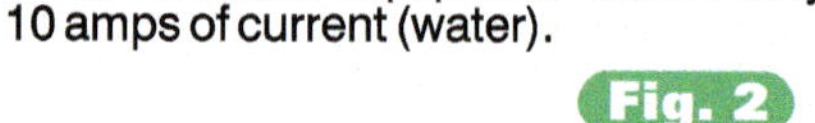

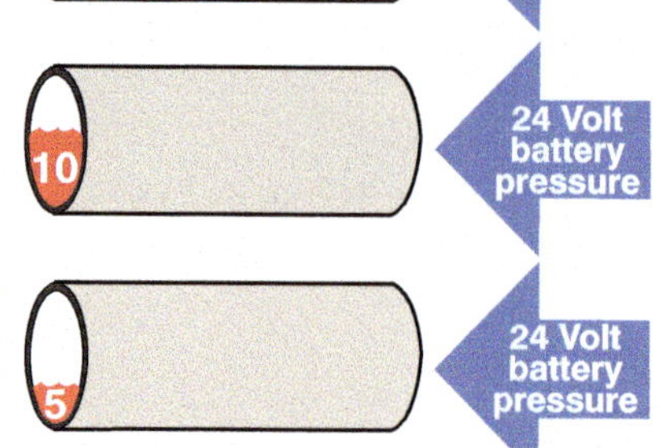

Fig. 2

Even though 24 volts can provide 20 amps of current (water), the electrical equipment here draws only 5 amps of current (water).

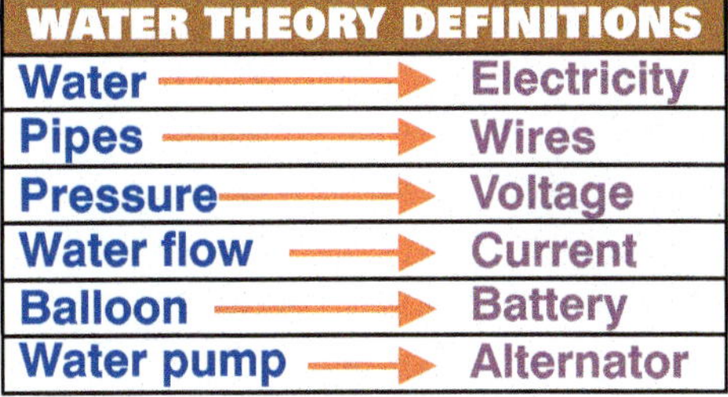

WATER THEORY DEFINITIONS	
Water	Electricity
Pipes	Wires
Pressure	Voltage
Water flow	Current
Balloon	Battery
Water pump	Alternator

Fig. 3

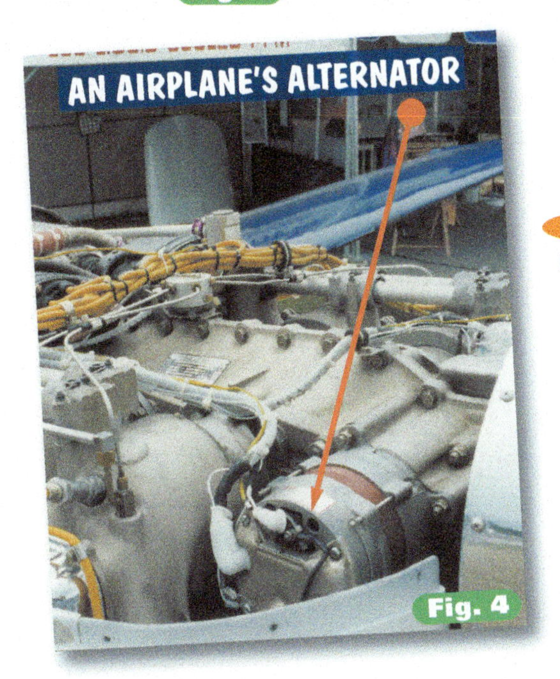

Fig. 4

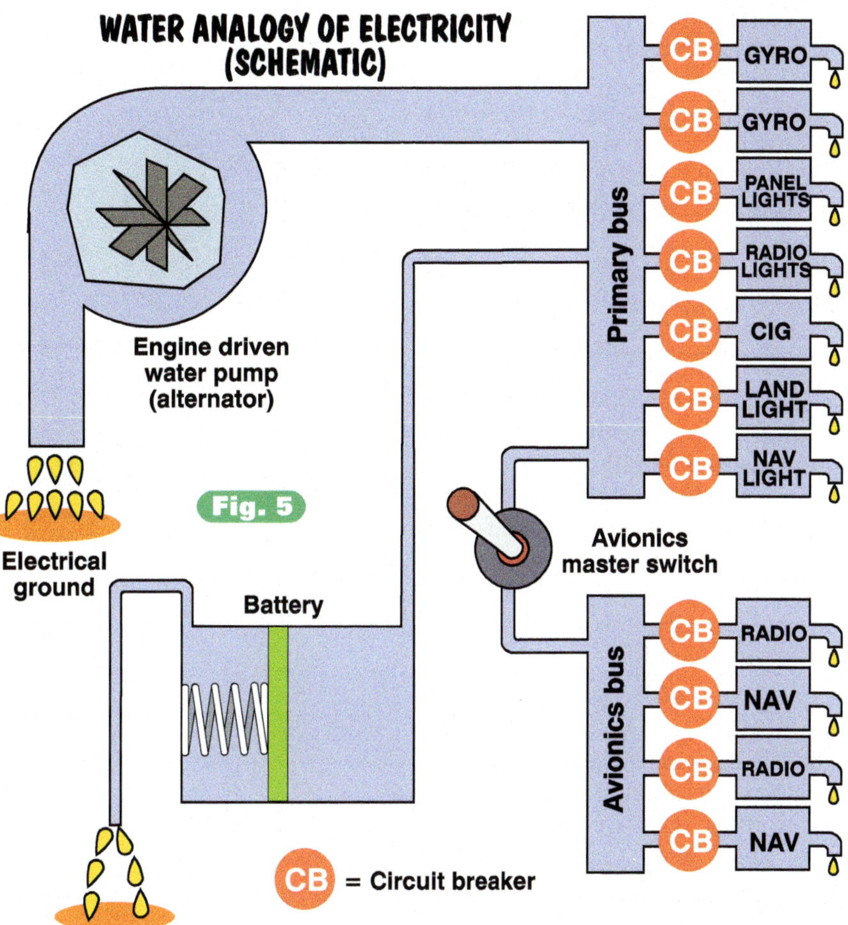

Fig. 5

For electrical circuits to work, electric current must have a way of returning to its original source, as shown in Figure 6A. Electric current flows from one side of the battery, through the light bulb (doing useful work), then back into the other side of the battery. If the return wire is broken, there is no way for the current to return to its source and the light doesn't shine (Figure 6B).

Even though the wires are not connected, as shown in Figure 6C, the light shines because the bulb and one side of the battery are connected to an electrical conductor, which allows electricity to flow between them. This conductor is the electrical ground, which is represented by small slashed triangles.

The Electrical Ground

The electrical ground is not the ground upon which you stand. It's usually the airplane's metal frame—which is a great conductor of electricity. This frame acts as one large wire,

Prior to my departure on a nighttime currency flight I placed my mini-flashlight in my pants pocket. The flight proceeded without incident and, after landing, I took out the flashlight to complete some postflight paperwork. A penny had become lodged in the lens and the light was completely blocked. It took a pocket knife to dislodge the coin. This would have been difficult had the necessity arisen in flight.

ASRS Report

Next time: no coins in pocket.

Flashlight Rules

Rule Number 1:
Always carry one flashlight (preferably two) on every flight.

Rule Number 2:
Always have your flashlight within easy reach in the event of complete electrical failure at night.

Rule Number 3:
In addition to spare batteries, carry a spare bulb!

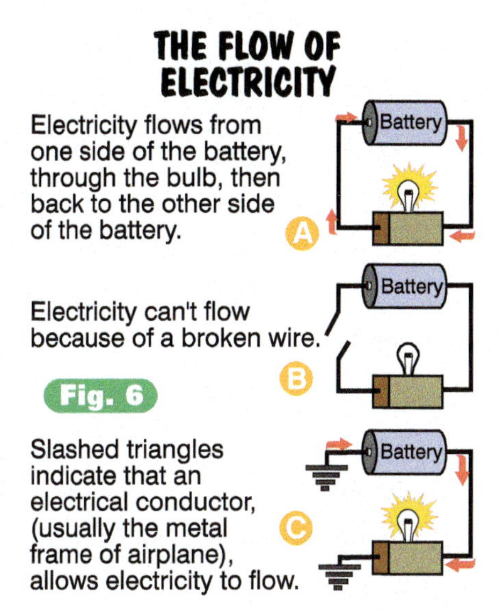

Fig. 6

returning current to the alternator (or any other piece of electrical equipment that's connected to the electrical ground). It is similar to the water tray in our water analogy which allows water to return to the pump. Since the alternator is connected to this electrical ground, the circuit is completed as electric current returns to its original source—the alternator.

Load Meter

A load meter is located between the pump and the primary bus of our plumbing system (Figure 7). It shows the water load placed on the pump by the airplane's water (electrical) system. In other words, it shows how much water is demanded from the pump by the airplane's water (electrical) equipment.

If the load meter reads zero (a full left deflection), either the pump isn't providing any pressure to the primary bus or the electrical (water) equipment simply isn't demanding any water. Load meter readings above zero represent the pump's water output. This output should equal the total water draw by equipment connected to both buses. An actual load meter is shown in Figure 8.

The load meter provides similar information about alternator output in an electrical system. A zero reading means the alternator isn't providing electricity to the primary bus or there is no electrical current drawn by the airplane's electrical equipment. This can happen because the alternator is disconnected from the bus, the alternator has failed, or all the airplane's electrical equipment is turned off.

Load meters are also known as *ammeters,* and their readings are calibrated in *amperes* (abbreviated as *amps*). Amps are a measure of current flow, equivalent to gallons per hour of water. If the airplane's electrical equipment demands 30 amps of current from the alternator, the load meter should indicate a 30 amp needle deflection.

The alternator circuit breaker (CB) is also located between the alternator and the primary bus, as shown in Figure 7. Circuit breakers protect electrical equipment (and wires) from receiving more current than they can safely handle. Figure 9 shows the airplane's alternator circuit breaker.

By now you should have a fair understanding of how the electrical system works when the alternator is turning. But since the alternator is driven by the engine, what source provides current for the airplane's equipment when the engine isn't running? The answer is simple. It's the thing missing from most children's Christmas presents—a battery. Figure 10A shows how the battery connects to the primary bus.

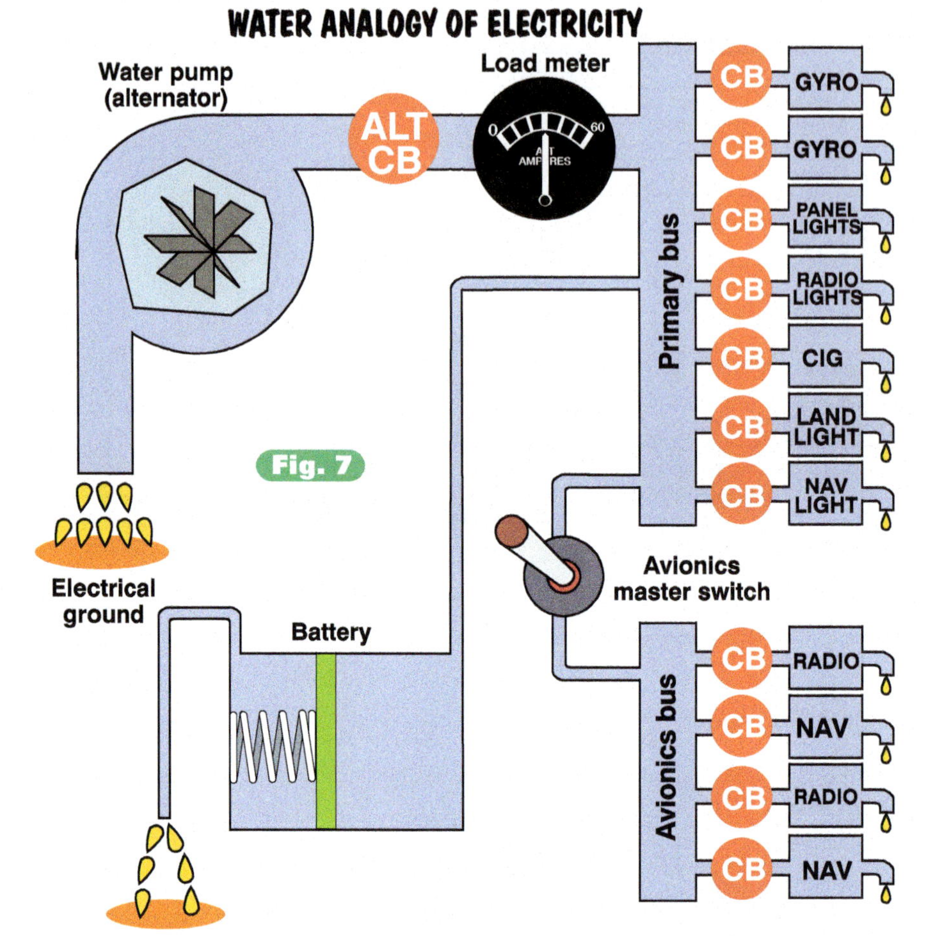

Fig. 7

Fig. 8

Fig. 9

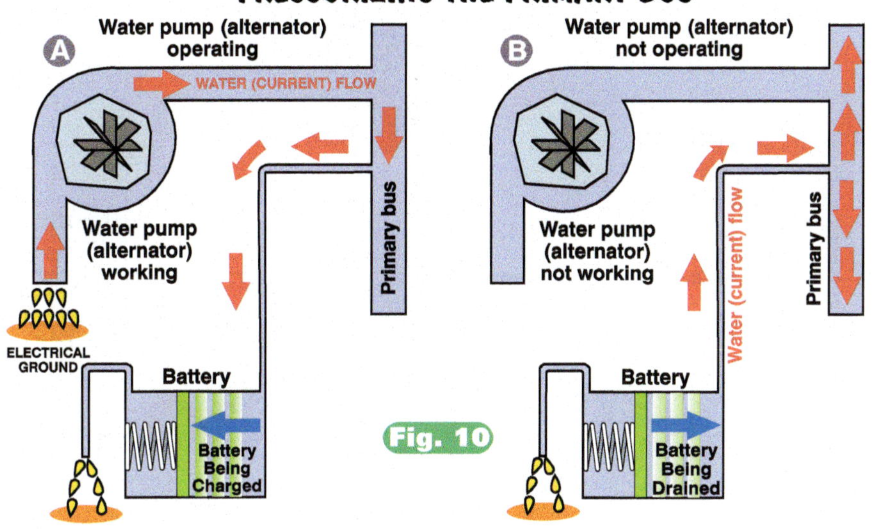

Fig. 10

The Battery

Using the water analogy, the battery can be thought of as a box containing a thin, square piston with a powerful spring on one side. The battery's square piston is capable of sliding toward or away from the spring depending on whether water flows into or out of the battery. Water flowing into the battery is said to *charge* it; water flowing out of the battery, *drains* or *discharges* it.

Since the primary bus is already pressurized by the spinning pump, water should easily flow into the battery. As it does, it pushes the sliding square piston to the left against the spring (Figure 10A). The battery has now stored water pressure and can be thought of as being fully charged. In the event the water pump stops working, the battery provides water under pressure (electrical current) to the primary bus (Figure 10B).

Have you ever used a pressure-type thermos to store your coffee? It's the kind where you put in the coffee, pump the handle on top, open a spigot, and out squirts coffee. The thermos stores coffee under pressure, so that caffeine-hungry pilots can quickly slake their thirst (on late night flights, pilots often lock their lips onto the spigot, push the handle and absorb just enough caffeine to vibrate through solid matter).

In an electrical system, the battery chemically stores the electrical charge provided by the alternator. The process is different, but the principle is the same as that of the coffee thermos. Most airplanes have either a 12 or 24 volt battery (think of a larger battery as one with a bigger spring that puts water under greater pressure). It's the battery that allows you to operate the airplane's electrical equipment when the engine isn't running or when the alternator fails in flight. Figure 11 shows an airplane battery.

Fig. 11

Battery Potential

You should know how much electricity your battery stores for one good reason: in-flight alternator failure. How much power the battery stores is indicated by its *amp-hour rating*. A 35 amp-hour battery should (in theory) provide 35 amps of continuous current to the electrical system for one hour. In other words, if the electrical equipment draws a total of 35 amps, the battery should run that equipment for one hour before it's depleted.

I say *theoretically* because this rating assumes many things: a new battery, a new electrical system, ideal conditions and perfect harmony with the universe. In reality, many battery engineers (people with two terminals protruding from their necks) say that you should only count on half of that rating. In other words, 35 amps for 30 minutes or 17.5 amps for one hour. You know those federal ratings of how many miles per gallon some shiny new car will give you? Keep in mind that there's always that little disclaimer, the one that says "Your mileage may vary." Very right, and it's not likely to vary on the high side.

While airplane batteries are rated at 12 or 24 volts, airplane electrical systems (their alternators) are rated for 14 or 28 volts. Why does the alternator have a higher voltage rating than the battery it charges? It's a lot easier and quicker to charge a battery to its full potential when the alternator pressure is stronger than the battery pressure. If we want the pump in our water system to store water in the battery, the pump must provide a little more pressure than the spring to push the piston back. The alternator's extra 2 or 4 volts is all it takes to keep the battery charged (to push against its chemical potential).

The Charge-Discharge Ammeter

Between the positive terminal of the battery and the primary bus is another version of an ammeter found on some airplanes (Figure 12). Ammeters of this variety are often called *charge-discharge* ammeters. Figure 13 shows a charge-discharge ammeter. As the name implies, the charge-discharge ammeter tells you if electrical current is flowing into or out of the battery. This directly informs you about your electrical system's state of health. Whether you have a load meter or a charge-discharge ammeter depends on the specific make and model of your airplane. Most airplanes have one or the other but seldom both.

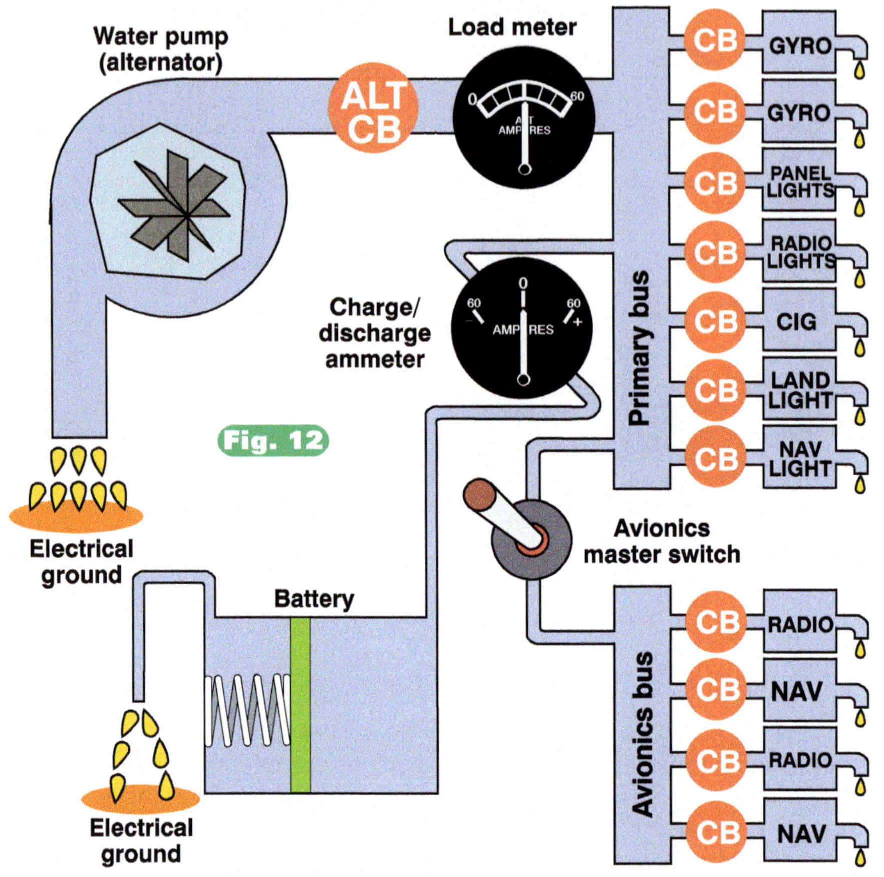

Fig. 12

Current flow from the primary bus into the battery is indicated by a positive needle deflection (Figure 14). Think of water (electrical current) pushing the needle toward the (+) or (-) side of the ammeter as it enters or leaves the battery. A positive deflection usually implies that the battery is being charged (water is moving into the battery). A negative needle deflection indicates that the battery is supplying the primary bus with electrical current (water is moving out of the battery).

Normally, the needle should be resting near the zero or center mark. This implies that the battery is neither being charged nor discharged (a good sign). Continuous needle deflections too far from center, however, are cause for concern. There are circumstances where the needle will indicate a large deflection from the center position for short periods.

Starter motors demand large amounts of electrical current for their operation. After startup, the battery is sure to be slightly drained. Expect to see a positive (+) needle deflection of five, maybe six or seven needle widths on the ammeter right after engine start. This means that the alternator is replenishing battery energy consumed by the current-hungry starter. Expect a similar ammeter indication if the radios were

Fig. 13

A wise man says, "Man who use tongue to test airplane battery find experience re-volting."

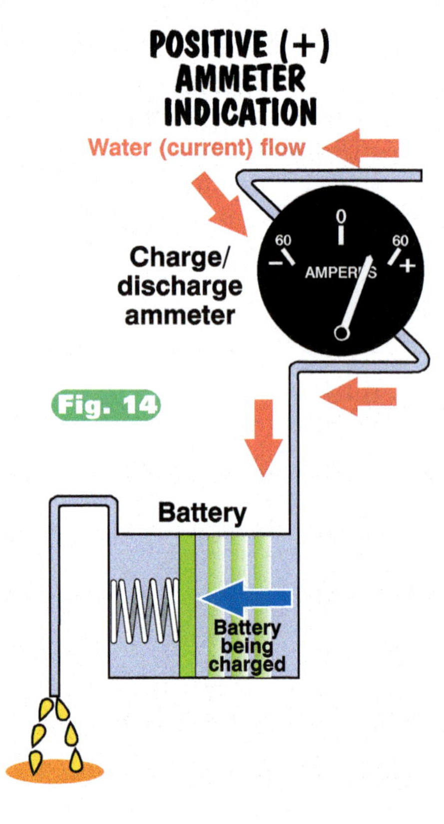

Fig. 14

used extensively prior to engine start. But beware! Too much charge is not a good thing—for batteries or credit cards!

Most airplane operation manuals suggest that after approximately 30 minutes of cruising flight, the ammeter needle should return to within a two-needle-width deflection from center on the positive (+) or charging side. A larger (positive) needle deflection suggests problems with the battery or the alternator. A runaway (unregulated) alternator can provide too much current and overcharge the battery. This is usually indicated by a large positive needle deflection (more than one or two needle widths).The excess voltage can boil off battery fluid (electrolyte), damaging the battery and possibly causing a battery fire.

A needle deflection on the negative (-) side means current is flowing out of the battery onto the primary bus (Figure 15). It also means the alternator isn't providing the necessary voltage to keep the battery charged. This situation is similar to a flight instructor's bank account, where more is going out than is coming in. Chances are the alternator has failed, has been automatically disconnected from the system, or is being improperly regulated. Any way you look at it, you have a problem. The battery will eventually lose its charge.

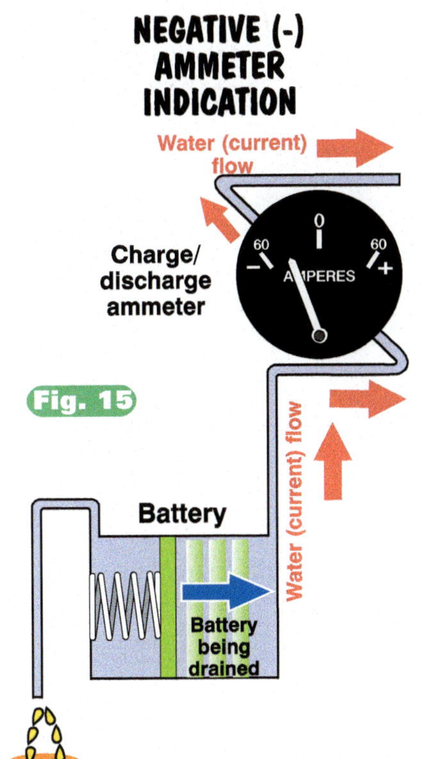

Fig. 15

Airplanes With Volt and Ammeters

The voltmeter gives you more direct information about the alternator's output or, if the alternator isn't on line, about the energy available in the battery. Unlike the ammeter, the voltmeter can tell you the condition of your battery before the engine is started.

An excessive system-voltage reading probably indicates voltage regulator trouble that can lead to battery overcharge and electrical equipment damage. Insufficient voltage indicates that the battery isn't being charged properly. Remember, system voltage must be higher than battery voltage for the battery to charge.

This situation is best handled by conserving battery energy (turning off everything you don't need) and, if necessary, landing at the nearest airport. Remember, you may need battery power to lower landing gear or flaps, or power the landing lights if flying at night. This is why good pilots carry flashlights (and bad pilots use flashlights to carry their dead batteries). A nearly centered charge-discharge ammeter needle usually means an electrical system that knows what's watt and is taking care of business.

In the early 1980's I had the pleasure of checking out an airline captain in a Cessna 152. We had a wonderful time learning the systems and flying the aircraft. He did quite well except for one thing. On every final approach he would call the tower and say, "Ahhh, John Wayne Tower, this is United heavy, we're on a long final approach for 1-9-Left." The controller thought this was really funny. The pilots of the little planes on short final for runway 19 Left didn't. The thought of an enormous metallic Pac Man gaining on them was downright scary! Attempting to understand the electrical system is somewhat like being the guy on short final for 19L. It's scary at first, but when you get a good, clear look at the threat, it's not so bad after all. Hopefully, you haven't been scared by the electrical system so far. Let's return to our discussion on load meters and discuss them in relation to the airplane's battery.

Load Meters

There are benefits and disadvantages to almost everything you do. For instance, whenever I travel to a location for a speech, I always get the most economical airfare for the client. However, economy is not without its disadvantages. On my last flight to Nome, Alaska I had four plane changes. Unfortunately, two were in flight. Load meters in lieu of charge-discharge ammeters have their benefits and disadvantages. Essentially, both kinds of meters provide pilots with the same type of information, but in a slightly different format.

Load meters provide important indications about the health of the airplane's electrical system. Unlike charge-discharge ammeters, they are calibrated to reflect the actual ampere load placed on the alternator. Both varieties of ammeter are shown in Figure 16. Remember, most airplanes will have either one variety of ammeter or the other.

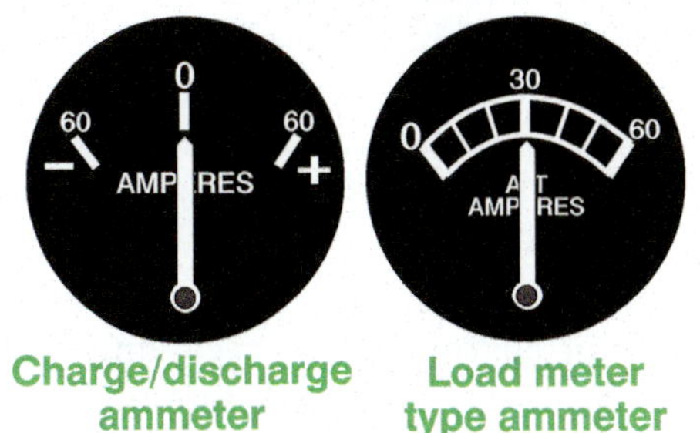

Fig. 16

Load meters with a zero or full-left deflection indicate the alternator isn't providing current to the primary bus. Any electrical equipment that's in use must be receiving its electrical energy from the battery. A full left deflection of a load meter needle is similar to a charge-discharge ammeter reading pointing to the negative (-) side of its scale.

Load meter needle deflections to the right of the zero index represent the electrical current drain on the alternator. Another way of saying this is that a right needle deflection represents the alternator's output. If you add all the electrical current used by the active electrical equipment, this sum should be equal to the amount the needle's deflected. After all, the alternator should be producing what the system demands, otherwise battery energy is being drained.

Electrical Drain

If you're piloting an airplane equipped with a load meter, you need to know how much electrical current each piece of electrical equipment consumes. Think of each piece of electrical equipment as having a minimum thirst level. Some equipment needs more water (current) to operate than others. *Amperes* are a measure of the amount of electrical current (gallons of water per hour) consumed by each of the airplane's electrical items. Understanding how thirsty each electrical item is, is the key to understanding if your alternator is working properly.

Radios typically consume one-half amp of current while receiving and about 5 amps while transmitting. Nav radios and gyros require about 1 amp, transponders about 2 amps, autopilots about 10 amps. Full deice equipment (this is special equipment for advanced airplanes) might gulp as much as 70 amps for continued operation.

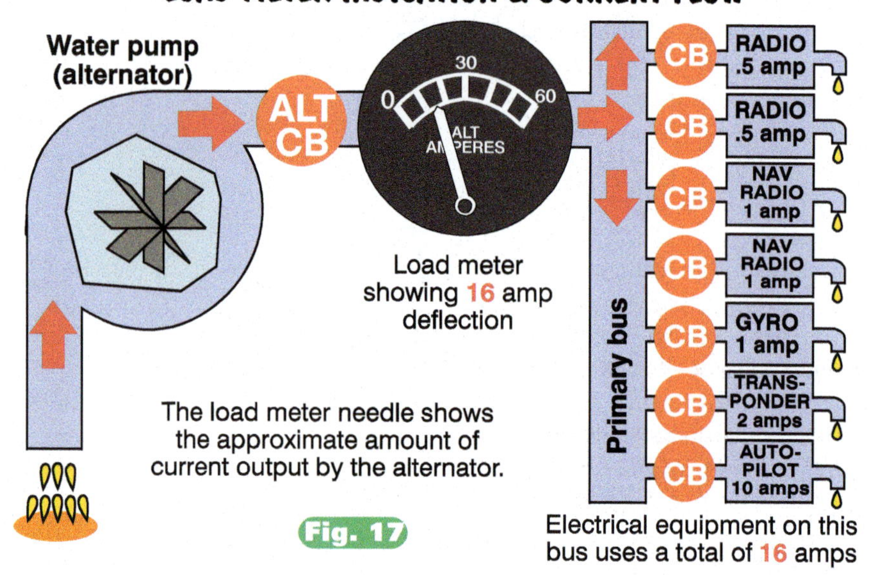

Fig. 17

With two receiving radios, two nav radios, one electric gyro, a transponder and an autopilot in use, a 16 amp deflection should be shown on the load meter (Figure 17). A needle deflection less than 16 amps implies that the alternator isn't providing enough current to run the equipment. Where is the extra electrical energy coming from? Need a hint? There's only one place: the battery. Needle deflections less than the summed amperage of active and properly working electrical equipment imply that the battery will eventually be drained. That's why it's absolutely necessary that you know how much current each piece of electrical equipment draws.

Suppose the load meter's needle deflection is greater than the needs of the electrical equipment, as shown in Figure 18. This is similar to a charge-discharge ammeter indicating a large, positive (+) needle deflection. In either case, such indications suggest that the alternator isn't working properly or that there is a leak in the electrical plumbing (otherwise known as a short). Soon, we'll discuss how the alternator is regulated and why it may develop problems.

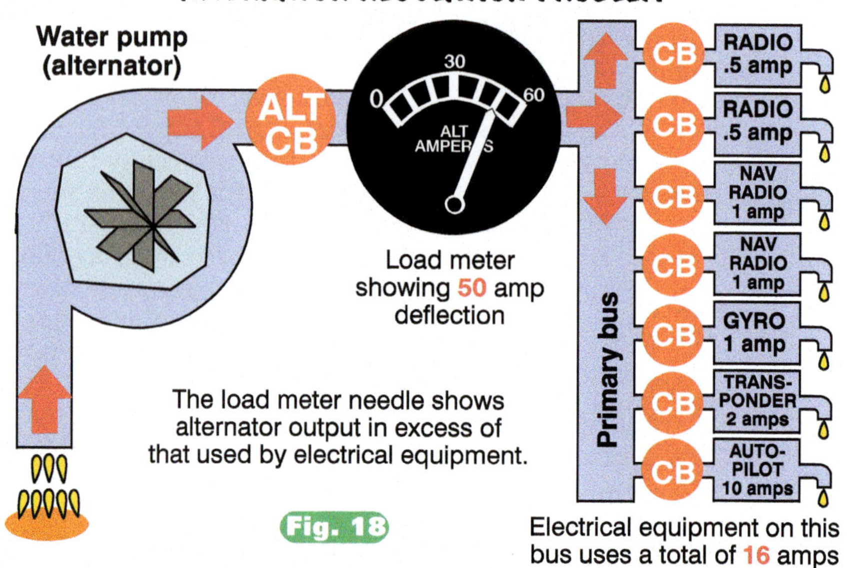

Fig. 18

What is Electricity?

Electricity is a form of energy that arises when electrons and positive ions become separated from each other. The atoms in the matter around us are made of a positively charged nucleus surrounded by negatively charged electrons. Sometimes an electron becomes separated from its atom. The part left behind (called a positive ion) has an electric charge equal to that of the electron but opposite in polarity.

How do electrons and ions become separated? One way is by a chemical reaction. In a battery, for example, a chemical reaction causes positive ions to collect at the positive terminal while electrons gather at the negative terminal. If a conductor is placed between the terminals, electrons will flow from the negative terminal to combine with the ions at the positive terminal. This flow of electrons is called electric current.

Another way to separate electrons and ions is by friction. In a thunderstorm, friction from turbulent air causes electrons and ions to separate, creating static electricity. Eventually, the electrons and ions dramatically recombine as lightning.

Electricity and magnetism are related. Movement of a conductor through a magnetic field will cause current to flow in the conductor. This principle is used in the magneto. Likewise, wherever current flows, a magnetic field is created. This is what makes the starter motor spin.

Skip Forster is president of Results Pilot Training, Inc. in San Jose, California and is a recovering electrical engineer.

Load meter indications in excess of the system's electrical demands are the system's cry for help. Ignored, this cry can lead to unhappy results such as evaporating battery fluid or battery and electrical fires. This is referred to as a battery losing its cool. You, in turn, will lose your juice. Remember, the alternator needs to replenish the battery energy drained by extended use of the starter or radio, so expect to see a slightly higher load meter reading immediately after engine start

I always make it a point to look at the ammeter right after engine start for two reasons. First, I get a sense of battery health by observing how fast the ammeter needle returns to its normal position after starter use. A failing battery will show up as an ammeter needle taking progressively longer to return to a normal position. Establishing a trend of needle response over a long period of time makes needle movement even more meaningful.

Second, starter motors have been known to stick and not disengage (actually it's the starter contactor that sticks but the results are the same). If this happens, the starter remains engaged, guzzling enormous amounts of battery current. You might not be able to hear the engaged starter once the engine is running, but you will see a very, very large negative (-) needle deflection on the charge-discharge ammeter right after start. On airplanes with load meters, a stuck starter contactor might be identified by an abnormally large reading, indicating an enormous drain on the alternator. Shut the engine down immediately if you see this type of unusual needle deflection right after starting the engine.

Don't be too concerned with ammeter needles that wiggle slightly. Ammeters have needle dampening mechanisms in them to steady wiggling needles. Sometimes these mechanisms just wear out. As a student, I thought it was my careless application of rudder that caused needle wiggling. I mentioned this to my instructor. He said that this wasn't possible since I never seemed to use the rudder.

Does an unusual ammeter or load meter indication in the air mean an immediate need to land? It depends. There are several things we can do about airborne electrical problems, but solving them requires an understanding of how alternator voltage is regulated.

The Voltage Regulator

Airplanes with complete electrical systems have voltage regulators or alternator control units (they're essentially the same thing). As the name implies, these devices regulate the alternator's output. If the engine is turning the water pump (alternator), it's logical to assume that higher RPMs produce greater water pressure. In an electrical system this results in alternators producing variable voltage. This would wreak havoc with electrical components that demand consistent voltage for accurate operation. Fortunately, voltage regulators—the brains of the electrical system—help alternators maintain a constant voltage output under variable RPM conditions.

Voltage regulators consist of transistors, diodes, capacitors and possibly relays and contact points. Describing the workings of these intricate components by use of the water analogy would get us into deep water, where we don't want to go. Therefore, let's use a human brain with a big hand connected to its cortex to represent these detailed electrical components (artist's license is such a wonderful thing)!

Figure 19 represents a water model of how a voltage regulator might work. Most turbine pumps (similar to that used as the model for our alternator) need to be primed before they will start pumping water. In other words, they need to have a little water running through them before they can create enough suction to pump more water. Alternators operate in a similar manner. They need a little bit of electricity running through them before they'll start producing more electricity. This small amount of electrical prime is called the *alternator field current.* Take away this alternator field current (prime) at any time, and the alternator stops producing electricity.

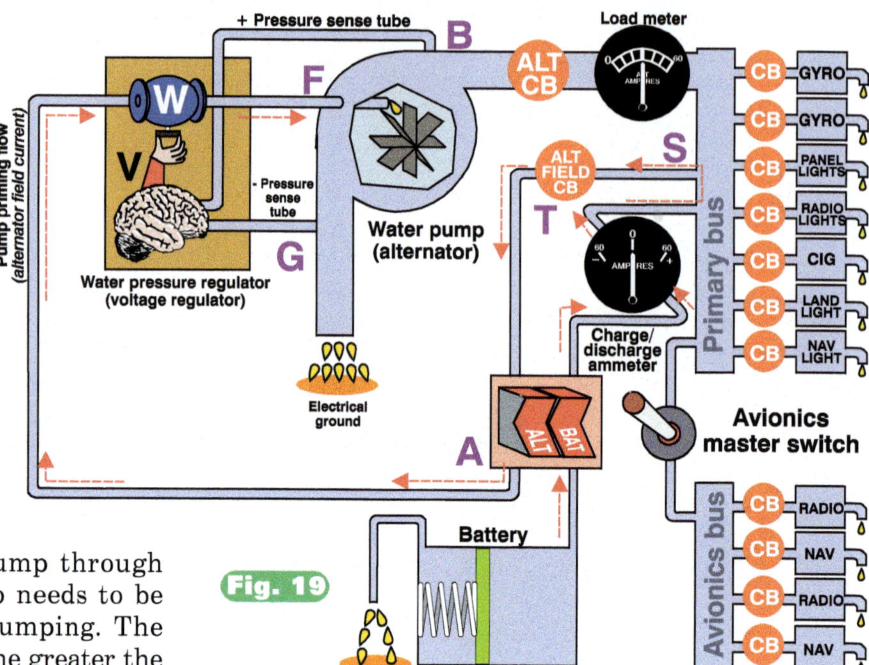

Fig. 19

Water prime flows directly into the pump through tube F. Like alternators, our water pump needs to be continuously primed if it is to keep on pumping. The greater the prime flowing through tube F, the greater the output of the pump. Alternator's operate similarly; varying the alternator field current varies the alternator's voltage output.

When the engine is not running, prime for the pump comes from the battery. In Figure 19, water flows from the battery to the primary bus. It then goes through line S and the alternator field circuit breaker T to the left hand side of a split-rocker master switch A. By turning on (pushing) the alternator side of the master switch (the left side), water flows into the voltage regulator V and through valve W which is inside the voltage regulator. Prime (alternator field current) must pass through valve W and through tube F, to get to the pump for priming.

Valve W is controlled by the hand attached to the voltage regulator's brain (those electronic components mentioned earlier). The brain tells the hand to open or close Valve W. This controls the amount of prime (alternator field current) reaching the pump.

How does the brain know whether to open or close the valve? It senses the pump's output water pressure, or in an alternator, its voltage. By comparing the pump's intake pressure at point G, with its output pressure at point B, the regulator's brain can compute the precise amount of prime needed to produce the required water pressure. In electrical terms, these sense lines allow the voltage regulator to restrict an alternator's output to 14 or 28 volts of electrical pressure.

When switch A is turned on during engine start, valve W starts in the full-open position, thus providing the initial prime. After engine start, the pump commences to produce water pressure (voltage) and brain V decides how much to close valve W to bring this output into regulation. It is in this initial startup period that the pump's output is momentarily unregulated and you DO NOT want your electrical equipment turned on. A sudden surge of pressure could damage this equipment—*despite* each piece of equipment having protective circuit breakers.

Sometimes brains in a voltage regulator, just like in humans, behave errantly. I recall a student pilot who was flying solo near the Southern California coast when he looked down and saw an aircraft carrier. A little devil on his left shoulder said, "Do it! Do it!!" A little angel on his right shoulder said, "Yeah, do it!" He did it—a carrier landing (actually, more like a touch-and-go). The captain of the ship was not amused. Neither was the FAA. It was a clearcut case of a brain gone astray, and it occasionally happens to voltage regulators as well. When the brain in a voltage regulator goes south, it usually presents definite symptoms. You can expect either an over or underproduction of voltage by the alternator.

Problems With Brains

Most airplanes have a warning light to alert pilots about electrical problems. This light is commonly known as either a high- or low-voltage warning light (Figure 20). When illuminated, it informs you that the alternator isn't supplying appropriate voltage to meet the system's electrical needs.

If your airplane has a low-voltage light, it can illuminate during low engine idle when there isn't enough RPM to develop even minimal voltage (pressure). Increasing the RPM raises the water pressure (voltage) and usually shuts off the light.

A low-voltage light can also illuminate if the alternator has been taken off line because of excessive voltage production. This usually follows a popped alternator *circuit breaker* or alternator field circuit breaker. As far as the electrical system is concerned, *no voltage* is interpreted as *low voltage.*

If your airplane has a high-voltage warning light, it can activate when an overvoltage condition occurs. The alternator field current (the prime) is automatically removed, which takes the alternator off line. This keeps the circuits from being damaged by excessive system voltage (pressure).

In either case, the activation of a high- or low-voltage warning light may follow a popped alternator or alternator field circuit breaker. When any circuit breaker pops, it is always worth paying attention. Personally, if I'm airborne and a circuit breaker pops, I don't reset it if the equipment it's protecting isn't essential. Resetting a circuit breaker is playing with fire—literally, and an in-flight fire is considerably less comforting than a campfire. If I need to use the equipment, I reset the circuit breaker once and only once, but only after letting it cool for several minutes. If it pops again, I leave it alone. In other words, it's not a good idea to reset a circuit breaker a second time.

If a popped circuit breaker (alternator CB or alternator field CB) takes the alternator off line, then if you manually pop either of these, it produces the same result. Manually taking the alternator off line becomes an important consideration if an overvoltage condition occurs and the circuitry doesn't *automatically* isolate the alternator. Figure 21 shows three ways of *manually* taking the alternator off line.

Occasionally, a benign overvoltage condition exists and the voltage regulator's brain automatically takes the alternator off line. This is sometimes called a nuisance tripout. Even human brains experience nuisance tripouts. It happened to a student pilot in a Cessna 150. This fellow taxied out to the runway and forgot his tail number (which is usually posted inside the airplane). Hoping to catch a glimpse of the number, he leaned out and slipped off his seat. He was hanging inverted, half outside, half inside the airplane, suspended by a loose shoulder harness. The funniest part was that he held onto the microphone and continued talking to the tower. I couldn't quite hear what he said, but I think it was, "Ahhh, tower... aghhh... I've fallen out and I can't get back in!" I ran over and helped this guy back into his airplane. I'm just glad he didn't forget

THE LOW- OR HIGH-VOLTAGE WARNING LIGHT

Illumination of the high- or low-voltage warning light indicates the alternator isn't supplying adequate system voltage. Most airplane electrical systems have self-protection circuitry that takes the alternator off line in the event it produces excessive voltage. This results in the illumination of the high- or low-voltage warning light. Follow your POH's recommended procedure for bringing the alternator back on line.

Fig. 20

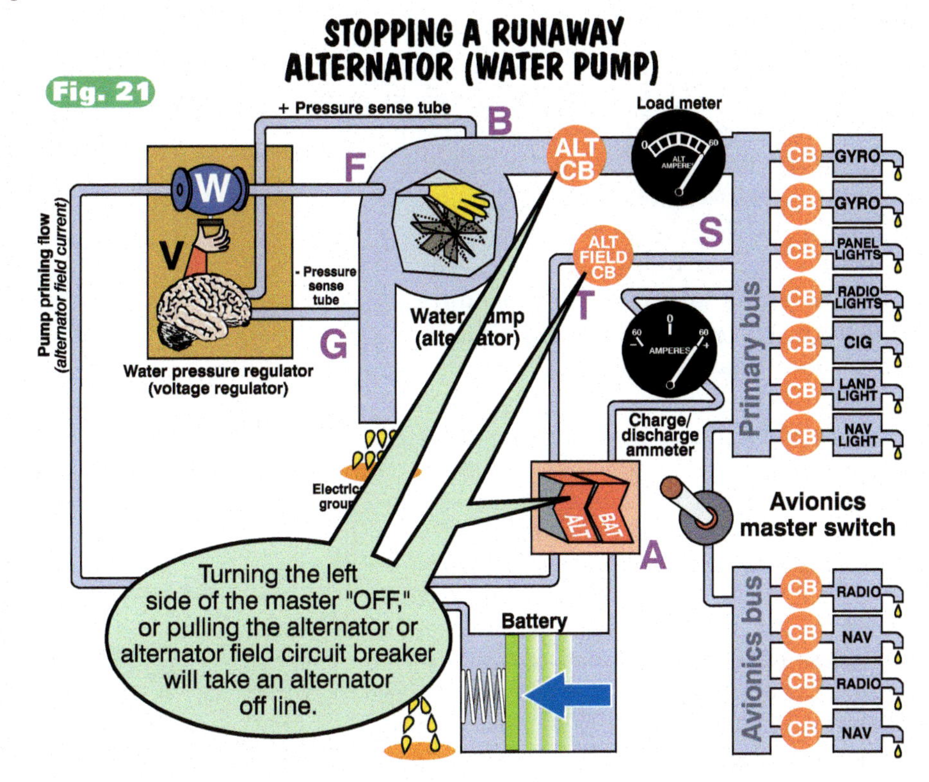

Fig. 21

his number while airborne! Mental nuisance tripouts are often amusing; in airplanes, they're simply annoying.

The brain in the airplane's voltage regulator is subject to similar perturbations. A nuisance tripout may be indicated by a low-voltage light or an overvoltage warning light, depending on how the airplane's electrical system is wired. We can attempt to reactivate the voltage regulator by turning the avionics master switch to the *off* position (to protect the avionics from a power surge), resetting the alternator or alternator-field circuit breaker (if popped), then turning both sides of the master switch *off* then *on* again (Figure 22). This signals the voltage regulator's brain to give the alternator another chance to produce normal voltage. Should the low-voltage or high-voltage light illuminate again, something is seriously wrong with the system. Conserve battery energy and land at the nearest airport.

HANDLING A HIGH OR LOW VOLTAGE WARNING LIGHT Fig. 22

Making Connections

Having gone downstream with our water analogy model this far, you now understand several important things about the limitations of alternators. First, if the battery is dead, the alternator isn't going to work. You can still start the engine by hand propping, but as explained earlier, this is a risky maneuver which is not recommended for those who enjoy being bilaterally symmetrical.

Since the magnetos are independent of the airplane's electrical system, they generate their own energy for ignition when spun. According to our water analogy, however, with a dead battery no prime is available through tube F in Figure 19 to coax the water pump into developing water pressure. The water pump will turn, but it will not pump. No priming, no pumping. It's as simple as that. In electrical terms, without enough battery energy for the alternator-field current, the alternator spins, but it doesn't produce any voltage. You will not have any electricity nor will the battery charge.

Second, if the brain in the voltage regulator goes bad and the alternator produces too much voltage, you can take the alternator off line. Pull the main alternator circuit breaker, located schematically between the alternator and the primary bus, as shown in Figure 23 (if the circuit breaker is the pullable type). Of course, this assumes that it hasn't already popped out on its own. You can turn off the alternator half of the master switch, which will shut off the alternator field current flow, thus deactivating the alternator. Pulling the alternator field circuit breaker eliminates the alternator-field current flow and shuts down the alternator.

Third, if you want to use the airplane's electrical equipment on the ground without starting the engine, you should activate only the battery half of the master switch. Leave the alternator half in the OFF position. This prevents alternator field current from flowing to the alternator, wasting precious battery power. It makes no sense to waste battery energy to prime the alternator if it won't be

WATER ANALOGY OF ELECTRICITY

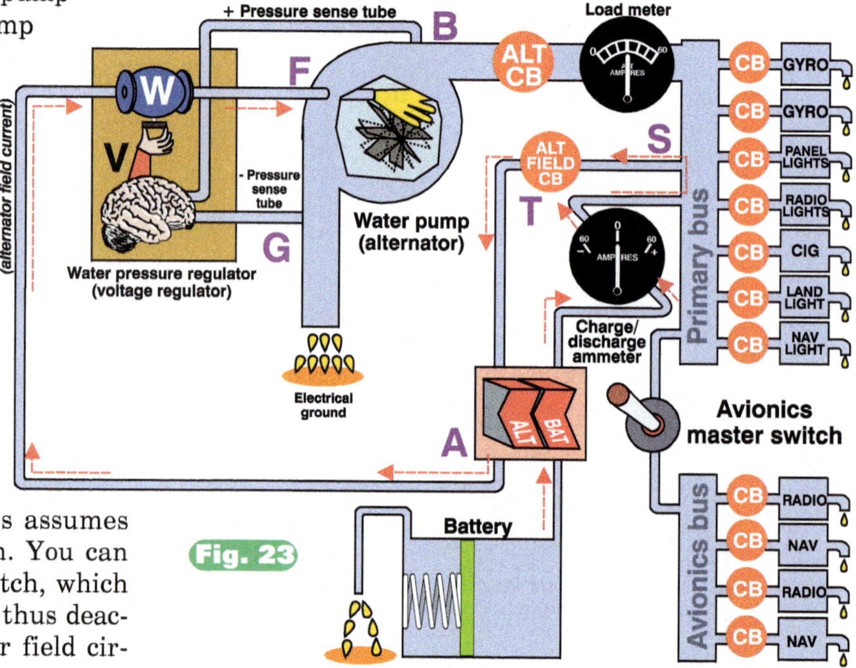

Fig. 23

in use. Airborne electrical emergencies caused by voltage regulator problems require conservation of battery energy. These situations should also be dealt with by turning the alternator half of the master switch to the *off* position.

If faced with an errant voltage regulator in flight, unload the system by turning off all nonessential equipment. This includes the waterbed heater and the disco strobe lights you installed in your Cessna 172. See if this returns the needle to a normal deflection. If not, then deactivate the alternator by turning the alternator half of the master switch to the *off* position. Let the battery provide the energy needs temporarily. This will allow an overheated voltage regulator to cool down (assuming that's the problem). After 5 to 10 minutes, reactivate the alternator by turning the alternator half of the master switch back on. See if the voltage regulator functions normally. If not, then deactivate the alternator by turning the alternator half of the master switch off and land as soon as practical.

I've had great success using this "cooling off period" approach. Most voltage regulators have moving parts (relays and contacts) that can stick when subjected to high heat loads. Cooling lets the components contract and return to their normal position. If this doesn't work, then it's best to leave the alternator off line, conserve electricity and head towards an airport for repairs.

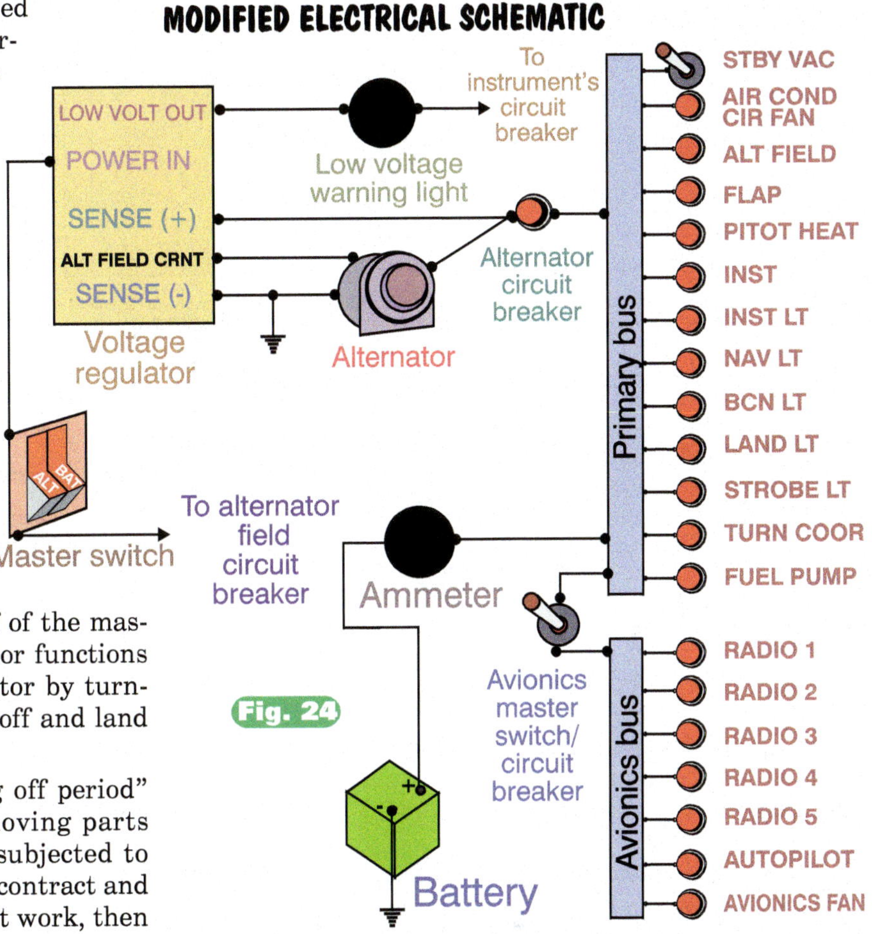

Fig. 24

Drawing It All Together

Figure 24 is an electrical schematic excerpted from a general aviation airplane's owner's manual. I have taken the liberty of leaving out a few items, such as the clock, starter, battery and starter contactor, Hobbs meter, etc. Of course, we would all like to see electrical schematics without a Hobbs meter, but I did this for the sake of simplicity. This figure should look familiar to you. It's the electrical version of the water analogy drawing in Figure 23.

The first introduction to the electrical system in ground school is traumatic for most students. After the first view of a schematic, many students sit limp, eyes bugged as if they've been hit by a megawatt stun gun. I hope the water analogy makes consumption of this technical subject more palatable. Take time to compare Figures 23 and 24. I think you'll be surprised at how much less frightening electrical schematics are.

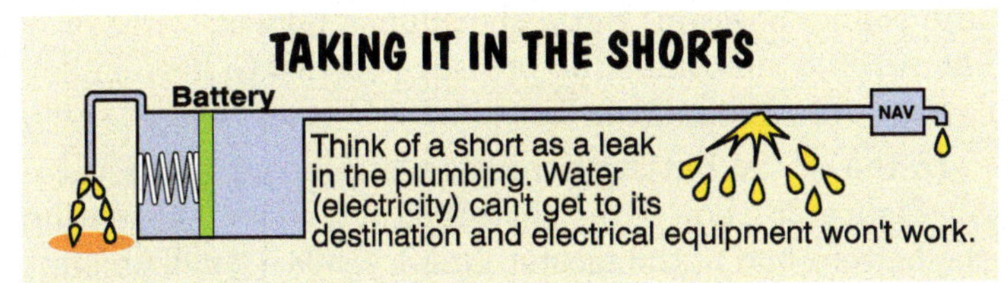

Have Rudder, Won't Travel

....This was the first flight after the annual inspection...I banked with the wind on takeoff and while moving the rudder to the right I noticed a restriction in rudder travel (I wasn't getting full rudder travel in both directions). So, I told the tower, "I have a problem...." The tower said I could have any runway.... I landed and taxied off the runway. After shutting down, I found my flashlight on the cabin floor near the rudder pedal on the passenger side. I usually keep it in the passenger seat before taxiing. It must have fallen to the floor on takeoff and gotten behind the rudder pedal....

ASRS Report

Proper stowage of cockpit equipment, including flashlights, will prevent hazardous incidents of this kind. Another preventive measure is to give special attention to the first preflight after annual inspection.

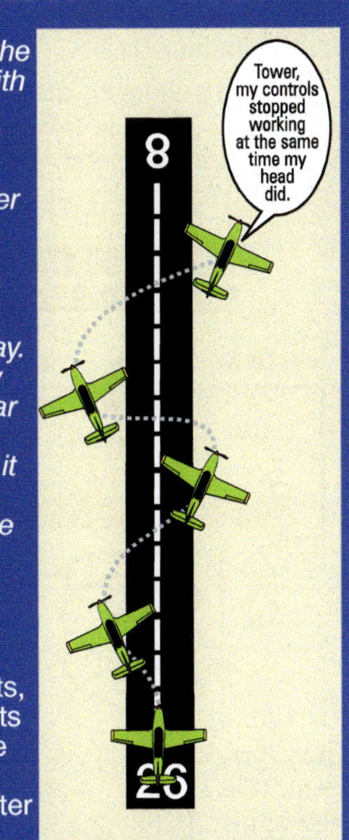

Postflight Briefing #4-1

Contact! How the Battery Contactor Works

An aircraft battery (very much like a car's battery) stores a tremendous amount of electrical energy. Anyone who's ever banged cables together while jump starting a car has seen the sparks fly. This is raw electrical energy on tap. Controlling this amount of current from the cockpit would require a rather large, well-insulated switch. In the cockpit, however, big switches mean increased weight, cramped space and a greater chance of sparks flying during a malfunction. Airplane engineers prefer a more indirect means of battery control—the battery contactor.

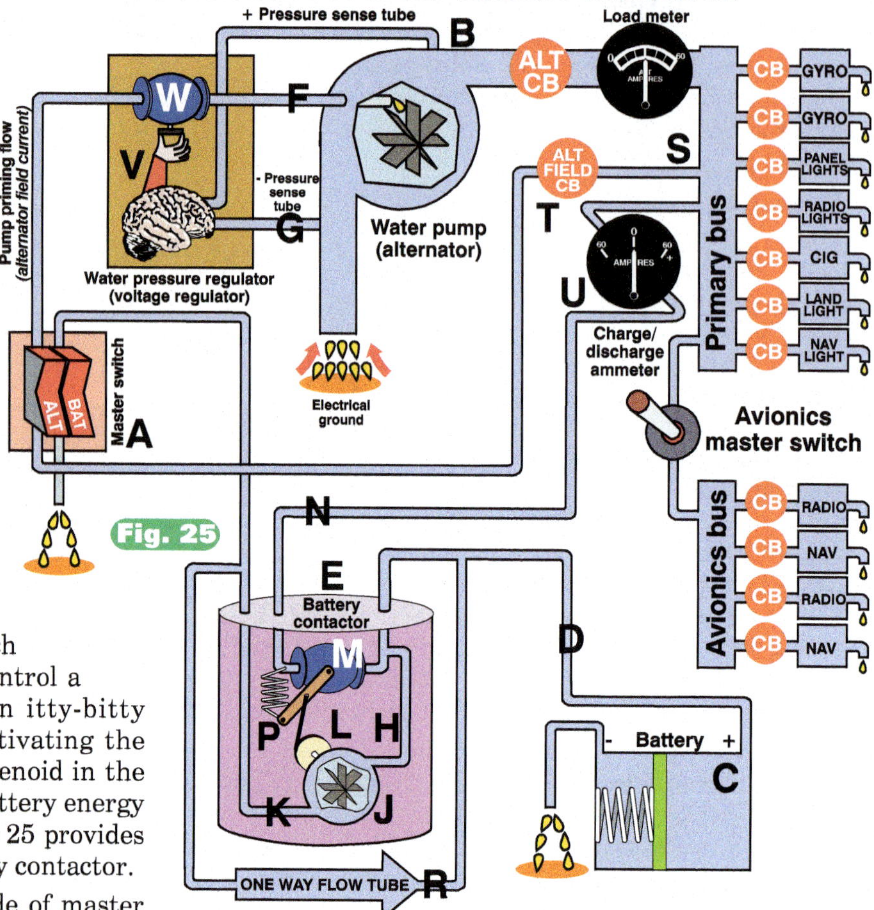

The battery contactor allows a small switch (the battery half of the master switch) to control a great deal of electrical energy. It gives an itty-bitty switch, galactic-power-switching ability. Activating the battery half of the master switch closes a solenoid in the battery contactor (the big switch) allowing battery energy to flow directly onto the primary bus. Figure 25 provides a working water analogy model for the battery contactor.

Activating the battery half or the right side of master switch (A) allows water to flow from the positive terminal (C) of the battery up through line D and into the battery contactor (E). As line D enters the contactor, a smaller line (H), splits off and flows to a small turbine/pulley arrangement (J).

Water flows over the turbine (J), spinning it counterclockwise. Then it flows out and up line K toward the battery half of master switch A. From here it flows to the ground (remember, we learned to think of the electrical ground as a thin pool of water underlying our plumbing circuitry). This completes the flow of water through the master switch.

BATTERY CONTACTOR SOLENOID & RELAY

Fig. 26

TO PRIMARY BUS

AMMETER

Z

Q

TO BATTERY HALF OF MASTER

TO (+) TERMINAL OF BATTERY

An interesting plumbing reaction occurs when turbine J spins counterclockwise. Pulley L is connected directly to turbine J and has a small rope wrapped around it that connects to the on/off lever of valve M. When pulley L spins counterclockwise, it pulls the lever down and opens valve M. This lets water from the battery flow through valve M and line N, pressurizing the primary bus.

In reality, a solenoid relay device in the battery contactor takes the place of turbine J, and valve M. Perhaps the most important item to be understood from this battery contactor model is that a small flow of water through line H and K allows a larger flow of water through line D and N. A small flow of electrical current, controlled from the cockpit via the master switch, allows the safe management of large amounts of battery energy.

Remember, the water model is for electrical cause and effect understanding only; don't take it literally. But do take the electrical results of our model's operation as fact. For instance, as water flows over turbine J it pulls the lever on valve M down opening the valve. For valve M's lever to remain open, water must continue to flow over turbine J. Turbine J will stop spinning once the pulley and rope have pulled the lever on valve M downward, into the *on* position. But a continuous flow of water over the turbine maintains the pressure needed to keep pulley L from unwinding. This keeps valve M open.

In the actual battery contactor, a solenoid opens valve M. Figure 26 shows this simplified schematic. Activating the battery half of the master switch sends a small amount

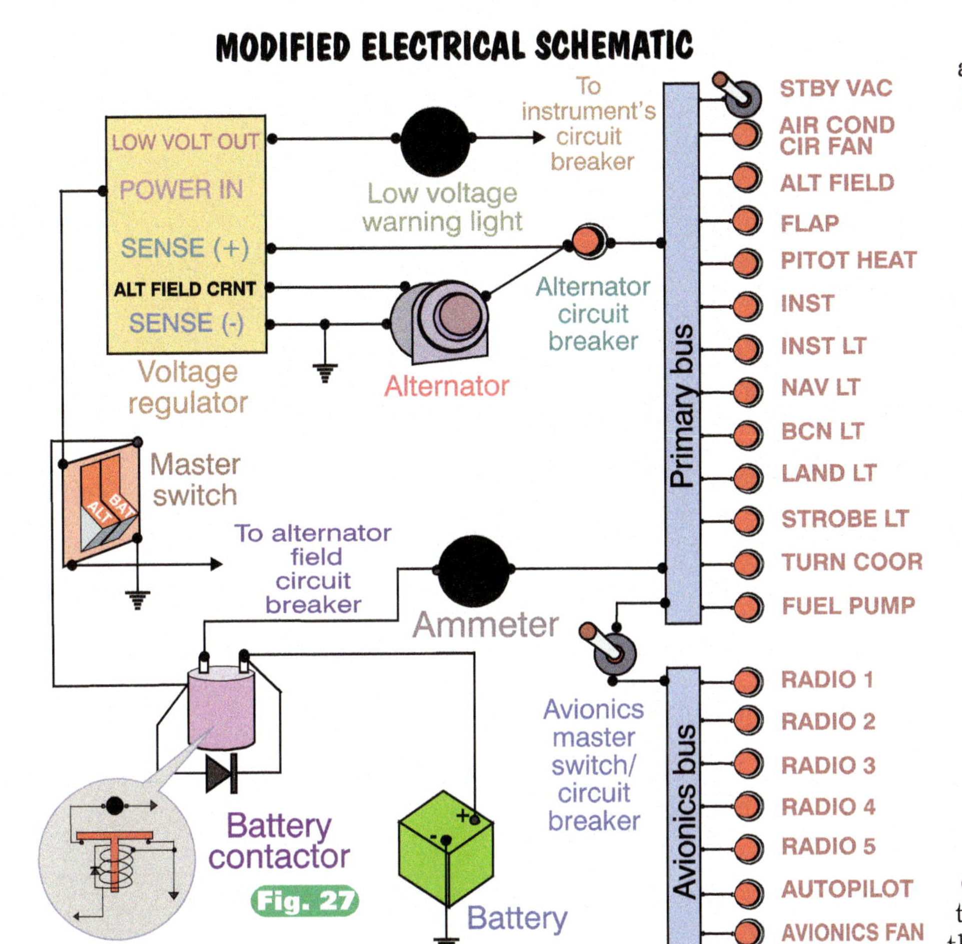

of current flowing through coil Q. This creates a magnetic field that pulls a heavy duty relay (Z) down onto two circuit points. Electricity now flows from the battery to the primary bus between these contact points.

Turning the battery half of the master switch off prevents water from flowing over turbine J in Figure 25. This allows spring P to pull valve M's lever upward into the *off* position which shuts off battery power to the primary bus. In a similar manner, placing the battery half of the master switch in the *off* position releases the pull on the solenoid in Figure 26. Relay Z pops up preventing electricity from flowing to the primary bus.

Notice there is a one-way flow valve R connecting line K with line D in Figure 25. This is known as a *clipping diode* in electrical parlance. It's designed to avoid voltage spikes across the coil relay, caused by a collapsing magnetic field, when turning off the master switch.

What was that??? A clipping what??? Here's another way of looking at what a clipping diode does. Turning off the battery half of the master switch causes turbine J to momentarily spin in a clockwise direction. This occurs because spring P pulls valve M's lever shut and unwinds the pulley. This might create a spike or surge of water flow into line K (or any other delicate elements of the circuitry). To prevent damage to line K the one-way valve (diode) allows the pressure in line K and D to equalize.

Having taken a reasonable amount of artist's license with this model, let's look at what it helps us understand. Unless a slight amount of battery energy exists, the battery contactor isn't going to work. Remember, it takes a slight amount of water pressure from the battery to pull valve M's lever open. Only the battery can provide the initial energy to activate the battery contactor. If the battery contactor doesn't work, water will not flow from the primary bus through line S to prime the water pump. In electrical terms, if the alternator field current isn't available, the alternator won't work. Inability to activate the battery contactor is another reason why an airplane with a dead or very low battery can't have its battery recharged by running the engine.

After engine start, assuming enough battery energy, the water pump will immediately provide water pressure to the primary bus. From the primary bus, water flows through the charge-discharge ammeter (U) (if your airplane has this type of ammeter) and down line N, through open valve M and into the battery. It does so until the battery is charged. Remember, the battery may have lost a little of its charge by operating a current-hungry starter or by operating the radios prior to engine start.

Because the pump is charging the battery, the ammeter has a deflection to the positive side. If your airplane has a load meter, it would indicate the water pump's output. If the battery's charge is low, expect an ammeter needle deflection to the positive side (+) until the battery regains its 12 or 24 volt charge. Similarly, expect the load meter needle to indicate an alternator output slightly greater than required by all the electrical equipment in use while the battery is being charged.

When the battery is charged, water no longer flows from the primary bus to the battery through line D. However, a slight amount of water continues to flow through valve M and down line H, over the turbine, thus keeping valve M open. This explains why the charge-discharge ammeter needle remains nearly centered in a healthy electrical system with a fully charged battery. Once the battery is charged, a load meter should show the approximate energy drain by the electrical equipment in operation. Readings higher than this should arouse a pilot's suspicion about the health of the electrical system.

Figure 27 shows a more complete electrical schematic with the battery contactor included.

D16

Chapter Five
Flight Instruments
Clocks, Tops & Toys

Not everyone remembers their first date, but just about every pilot remembers his or her first look inside the trainer plane. Eyes riveted on the instrument panel, prospective pilots tend to respond with one- or two-word expletives, followed by a swelling tide of self doubt.

That was my experience. Opening the door of an early model Cessna 150, I peeked inside the cozy, two-place trainer. I uttered the two-word initial response. My instructor, standing patiently nearby, was eager to offer encouragement on this demo flight. He said, "Well, what do you think?"

"Man, you sure can tell what time it is with all these clocks in here!," I said. "Clocks? Those aren't clocks, those are flight instruments," he barked, while rapidly recalculating the wisdom of trying to teach me to fly. "In a very short time, they'll become your best friend."

Uh huh. Those instruments and the IRS.

Well, it turned out to be true (about the instruments). If there is such a thing as pilot–instrument bonding, I experienced it. I learned to appreciate, respect and enjoy all those dials on the panel, except for one—the *Hobbs meter* (the meter that keeps track of how long the engine is running, and from which the flight school calculates how much you owe). Flight instruments provide you with valuable, essential information. Extracting and interpreting that information through our five sensory organs (OK, six, if you're into that theory) is the challenge we're about to address.

Figure 1 shows the basic instruments found on many traditional airplane panels. From the top left hand corner clockwise these instruments are: *airspeed indicator, attitude indicator, altimeter, vertical speed indicator, heading indicator* and *turn coordinator* Above the panel, near the top of the windscreen, you'll also find the *magnetic compass* (although not always part of the six basic instrument group, it's still as important as any other instrument). Figure 2 shows the basic fight instruments as they appear on a *primary flight display* (PFD). A PFD contains the same basic flight instruments but presents them using "glass panel" technology. You can learn more about PFDs in Postflight Briefing #5-2.

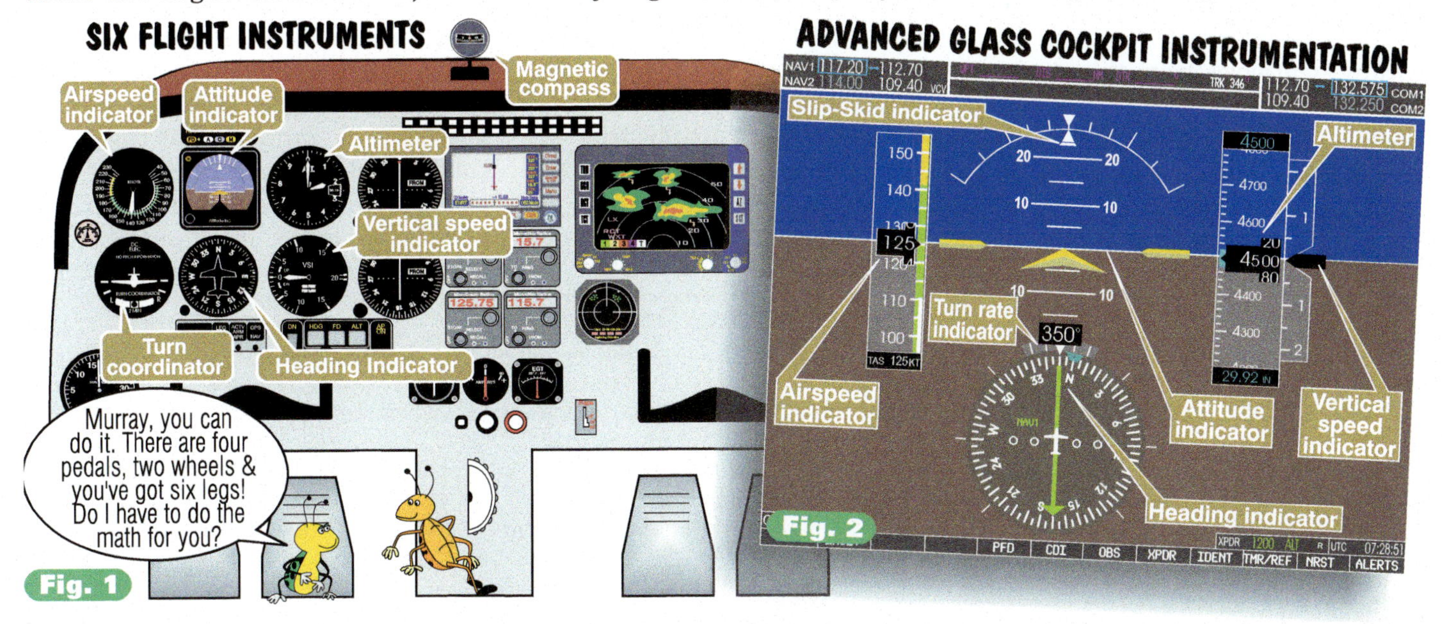

Fig. 1

Fig. 2

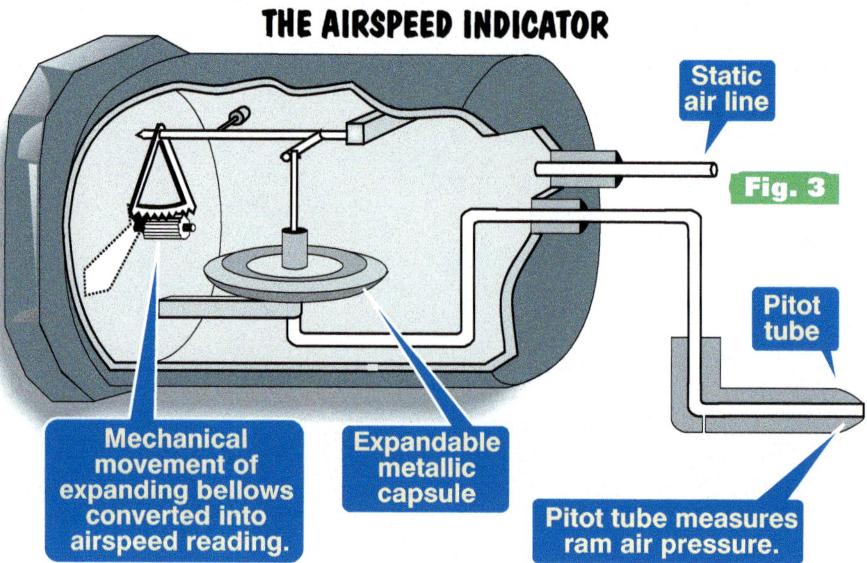

You're probably thinking, "Do you need all these instruments to pilot a plane safely?" It's certainly possible for a more experienced pilot to fly visually and by feel while looking out the window. This, of course, is done in *visual meteorological conditions* (VMC), when weather permits visibility above certain minimums specified in the rules. These instruments, however, make it much easier for you to maneuver the airplane precisely.

Where the flight instruments really earn their keep, though, is in *instrument meteorological conditions* (IMC), otherwise known as clouds. While you shouldn't be in the clouds without an instrument rating (an advanced license), these six instruments can help save your bacon should you accidentally fly into a cloud (all student pilots learn how to extricate themselves from this situation during their private pilot flight training).

All six flight instruments, each in its own way, provides you with information on three things: airspeed, height and attitude.

Airspeed is a measurement of the airplane's velocity through the air. The altimeter and vertical speed indicator provide information about your height above sea level as well as how fast your height is changing. The heading indicator, turn coordinator and attitude indicator provide information on the airplane's attitude (i.e., the degree of nose-up or down pitch, as well as the amount the airplane is banked).

Flight instruments will talk to you, if you let them. They speak a distinctive language, and the ability to hear and interpret it quickly and correctly is an important pilot skill. To fly without understanding your flight instruments is very uncomfortable, and potentially dangerous. It's like the proverb that says, "One day the lion and the lamb shall lie down together." Maybe, but you can be sure the lamb won't get much sleep.

It's time to learn to speak the language of the panel. Let's start our examination with the non-gyroscopic instruments.

Non-Gyro Instruments

Airspeed Indicator

The airspeed indicator is a wind indicator. It tells you the amount of wind blowing over the wings of your airplane as a result of the airplane's movement. Such information is useful for several reasons. First, with sufficient airspeed, the airplane will fly. The airspeed indicator, then, lets you know when it's safe to point the nose upward during the takeoff. Second, the airspeed indicator lets you know when you're above or below any of the airplane's critical speeds (i.e., the stall speed, maximum flap speed, maximum gear speed, never exceed speed, etc.).

Airspeed indicators work by sensing the impact pressure of air. Part of the airspeed indicator shown in Figure 3 is connected to the pitot tube, which I pointed out as we circled the airplane in Chapter 1. High velocity air rushes into the pitot tube and applies pressure within the

Hey? What Did You Do That For?

I require all my students to be able to land an airplane without looking at the airspeed indicator. While downwind, I'll usually distract the student by saying something like, "Oh look, it's Elvis in a UFO," or something like that. While the student is looking outside I stick a circular rubber soap-dish holder (the one with 50 little suction cups on each side) over the airspeed indicator. After an unsuccessful search, the student returns to the panel, sees the instrument covered and says, "Hey, what did you do?" I reply, "I simulated airspeed indicator failure, so fly the airplane using your sense of feel." Most students handle this experience quite well.

I did this to a smart young lady student of mine. When she returned to the panel she said, "Hey, what's going on here?" I replied, "I simulated airspeed instrument failure, Ha!" As I turned away I heard the sound of 50 little suction cups releasing their grip as the holder was pulled off the glass over the airspeed indicator. I looked at my student who was holding the soap dish holder in her hands and asked, "Hey what did you do that for?" She replied, "I simulated fixing it, ha!" **The Author**

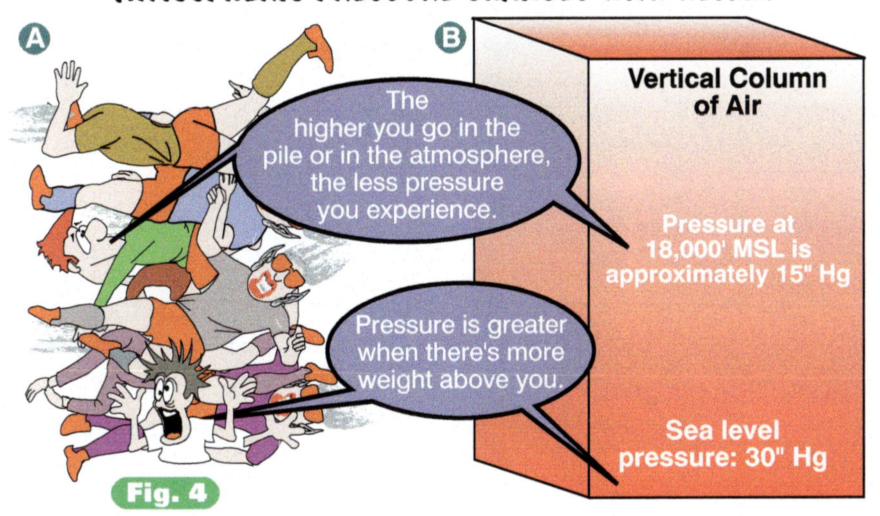

Fig. 4

metallic bellows located inside the body of the airspeed indicator. Expansion of the bellows is mechanically converted into movement of the airspeed needle via a gearing system (Figure 3 has been simplified slightly for ease of understanding and migraine prevention).

Notice that the container surrounding the bellows is connected to a static line which connects to a *static pressure* source. A static source allows non-moving (static) air to enter the airspeed container. This is simply the natural weight of the atmosphere, otherwise known as atmospheric pressure. A reading on the airspeed indicator is nothing more than the difference between impact air pressure entering through the pitot tube and static air pressure surrounding the metallic bellows. Let's take a closer look at air pressure and how it's measured.

Static Pressure

Imagine you are sandwiched between a bunch of leotard-covered professional wrestlers as in Figure 4A. You are halfway from the top. Your friend, Bob, is on the bottom. Who feels the greater weight or pressure? Why of course, it's Bob. He has more people above him than you do. Therefore, he experiences greater pressure. Atmospheric pressure behaves similarly.

Figure 4B shows a vertical slice of the atmosphere. Imagine air molecules piled on top of one another like professional wrestlers. At sea level, there is a great deal of static air pressure or weight because there are more air molecules at the top of the pile. As you ascend, there are fewer air molecules above you. *Atmospheric pressure or weight decreases with a gain in altitude.*

Since static pressure is the weight of non-moving air, how does an airplane measure something non-moving while it's in flight? The static port, shown in Figure 5, is the perfect device for such a task. Being flush against the side of the fuselage (out of the way of air striking it), the static port lets the natural weight of the air (atmospheric pressure) enter through its opening. Figure 6 shows an airplane's static port located on the side of the fuselage. Two additional instruments also require static air pressure to function: the vertical speed indicator and the altimeter. These instruments are also connected to the static port, as shown in Figure 5. We'll discuss these instruments later.

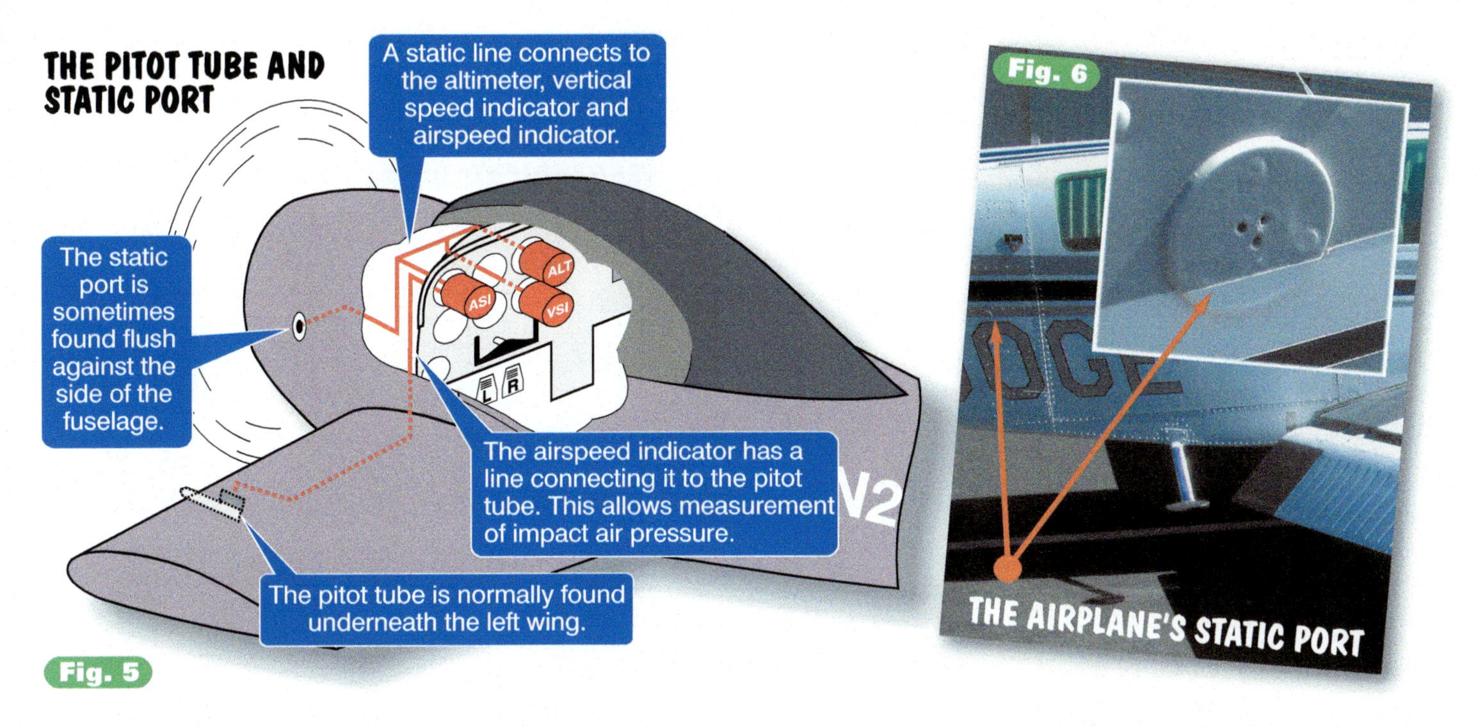

Fig. 5

Fig. 6

Pitot Tubes

Pitot tubes and *static ports* were discussed earlier. They can be found located in a variety of places on an aircraft. A common location for the static port is on the front left side of the fuselage. Pitot tubes are most often found under the left wing. Figures 7A and B shows two common pitot tube and static port arrangements. Figure 7A shows the pitot tube typically found on Cessnas. Figure 7B shows a combination pitot tube and static port common to Piper airplanes. In Figure 7B, impact pressure is sensed through the pitot opening on the front side, while static pressure is sensed through two holes, one on the bottom of the scarf cut and the other at the rear of the device. These two openings allow a balanced measure of static pressure.

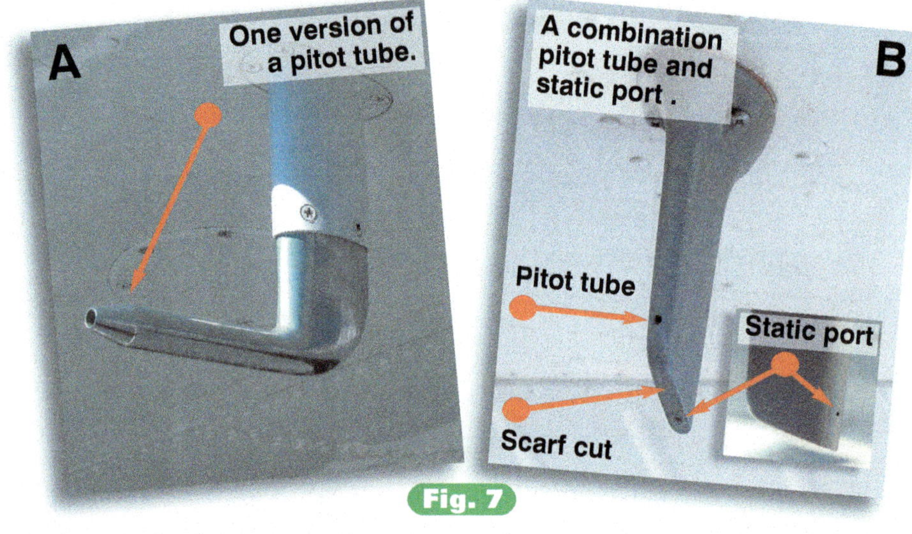

Fig. 7

Insects are a different matter. They don't drain as readily. On several occasions while giving flight instruction, I've had a small insect dive right into the pitot opening. Once, while approaching to land, a small bumblebee bumbled into the pitot tube opening. If the pitot opening is occluded by *anything*—animal, vegetable, or mineral—there is no impact air reading. This results, unfortunately, in an airspeed reading of zero. The student who was with me looked at the airspeed indicator and did what anyone would do to solve a similar problem—he hit it. In fact he was reaching for his airspeed indicator repair kit—his shoe—when I calmly reminded him that he should be able to land the airplane without having to look at the airspeed indicator. He did a fine job.

Soap Opera

These two incidents occurred several years ago in the traffic pattern:

Tower: *"Make a three-sixty for better separation."*
Pilot: *"You mean make another circle of the airport?"*
Tower: *"Negative. Make a three-sixty in place."*

Two weeks later, same pilot but now in the pattern at a different airport.

Tower: *"Make a three-sixty for better separation."*
Pilot *(showing off recently gained knowledge): "You mean in place?"*
Tower: *"Negative. Make another circuit of the field."*

ASRS Report

The Airspeed Indicator's Face

Modern airspeed indicators are color coded. This is not for your convenience in picking one that matches your airplane's carpet or curtains. Each of the colors is there to give you a piece of vital information about airspeed limitations (Figure 8). Four colors are used on single-engine airplanes: white, green, yellow and red.

The white arc of the airspeed indicator, as we learned earlier, represents the airplane's flap operating range. The beginning or low-speed end of the white arc is the power-off stall speed in the landing configuration (i.e., with flaps fully extended and gear down). This is called V_{so}. An easy way to remember this is to think of the velocity (V) of stall (s) with everything out (o) or V_{SO}. Of course, by *out* I mean flaps fully extended and gear fully extended (assuming, of course, it's a retractable gear airplane).

Our figure says that at V_{SO}, the airplane needs a minimum of 53 knots of wind flowing over the wings to become (or remain) airborne. The assumption here is that the airplane is always at its maximum allowable landing weight, since the airplane is configured for landing (i.e., gear and

AIRSPEED INDICATOR MARKINGS

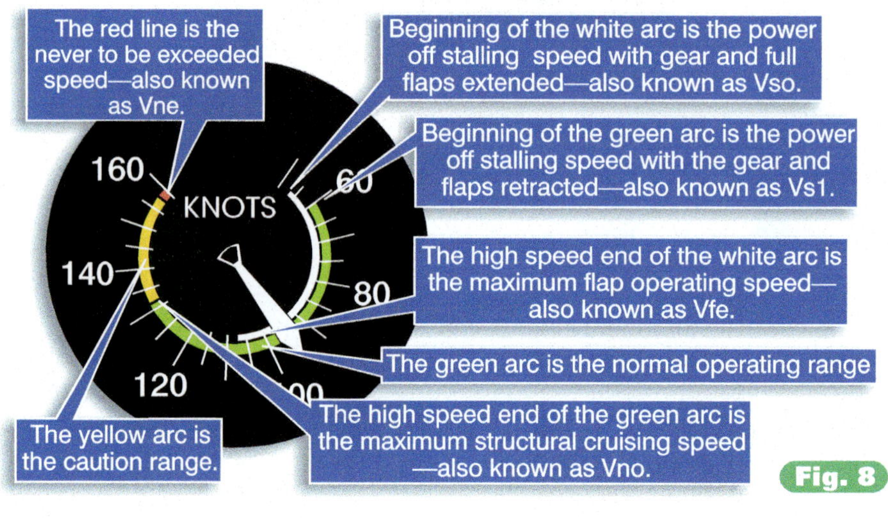

Fig. 8

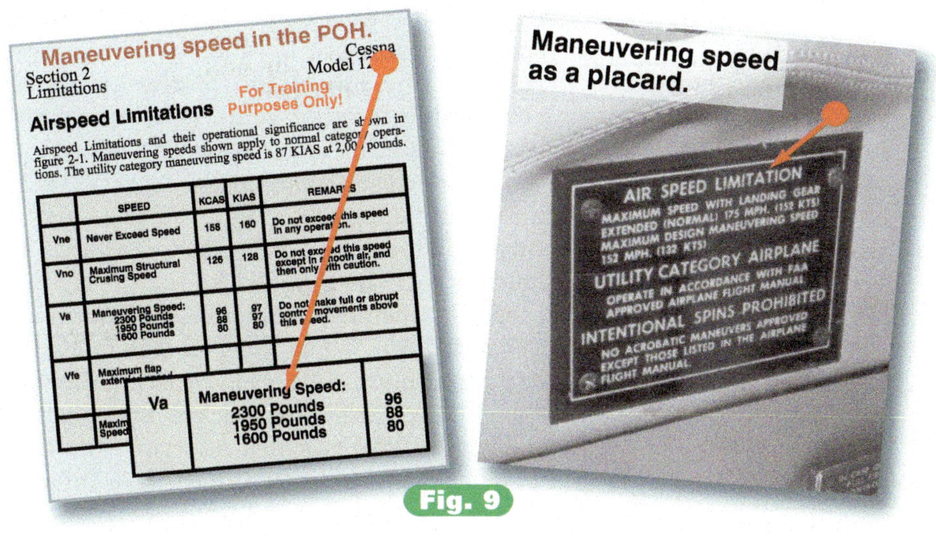

Fig. 9

flaps are down). Lighter weights reduce the stall speed below the colored minimum. (For your information, all color coded stall speeds can also be the minimum steady speed at which the airplane is controllable. Either definition is correct).

Following the white arc clockwise, we come to its high-speed end. This represents the maximum airspeed at which you may extend the flaps or fly with them extended. Called V_{fe} or velocity (V) of flaps (f) extended (e), flaps may not be used above this speed for fear of structural damage (and the prime directive of any pilot is to avoid breaking the airplane).

Most things green are good (money, guacamole, traffic lights). A green arc represents the normal operating range of the airplane. The beginning of the green arc represents the power-off stalling speed or minimum steady flight speed in a specified configuration. For the small airplanes we fly, this configuration occurs when the airplane is at its maximum takeoff weight and the flaps and gear (if retractable) are up. This is called V_{s1} or velocity (V) of stall (s) with everything inside (1)—think of the *1* as the letter *i* representing gear and flaps up or *inside*. With flaps up, gear up and power off, the beginning of the green arc in Figure 8 suggests this airplane needs a minimum of 60 knots of wind flowing over its wings before it starts flying.

The top end of the green arc is called V_{no} or the maximum structural cruising speed. Since the green arc is the airplane's normal operating range, think of the top of the green arc as the velocity (V) of normal (n) operation (o). At and below V_{no} airplanes have been certified to withstand substantial vertical gusts of air without experiencing structural damage (vertical gusts of 30 to 50 feet per second—depending on the date of airplane certification). Operations above V_{no} and within the yellow arc, are allowed only in smooth air.

Airplane wings are subject to a great deal of structural stress at higher airspeeds. Turbulence is a jolt of stress. If you add such a jolt to the stress of high speed, there are no promises about the wings remaining with you. Because the wings are very important, and because seeing them out there is such a comfort to most pilots, we'll talk more about handling turbulence in a bit.

There is one speed you should never exceed. Coincidentally, this speed is called V_{ne} or velocity (V) that you never (n) exceed (e). This is the red line on the airspeed indicator. It's also the maximum speed at which the airplane can be operated in smooth air. Things are painted red (by us or Mother Nature) when they are of critical importance (blood, chili peppers, traffic lights). Above redline, all bets are off (I hope you're getting test pilot pay if you fly beyond this speed). Exceeding V_{ne} can cause *flutter* (an uncontrollable and destructive vibration of certain airfoil surfaces), *dynamic divergence,* or *aileron reversal.* Take my word for it, these are bad things. On the other side of the red line lies territory no pilot should ever deliberately explore without packing a parachute. Consider this your Surgeon General's warning to avoid flying above the airspeed indicator's redline.

V_{ne} is 90% of the speed at which flutter occurs. Yes, there is a slight, built-in safety factor. But don't ever count on built-in safety factors. Besides, you aren't being paid as a test pilot. If you want thrills, go bungee jumping or bullfighting or bungee-bull fighting (that's where they dangle the bull from a crane—which suggests an entirely new line of velvet matador pictures).

There are three other important speeds, and they're *not* shown on the airspeed indicator. The first one is called *maneuvering speed* or V_a otherwise remembered as velocity (V) of acceleration (a). In turbulence, you should be at or below maneuvering speed, as we discussed in Chapter 2. I said the yellow arc is for smooth-air operations only. In strong turbulence, however, the only way to ensure that you won't exceed the airplane's structural limit is to fly at or below its maneuvering speed. Maneuvering speed is found well below V_{no}. Your Pilot's Operating Handbook or posted placards provide you with the airplane's maneuvering speed (Figure 9).

Don't forget to remove the pitot tube cover before flight. Pilots have taken off with the cover still on only to find their airspeed reading zero during the climbout.

Your POH shows the airspeeds for maximum gear operating speed (V_{lo}) and maximum gear extended speed (V_{le}).

AIRSPEED LIMITATIONS

Airspeed limitations and their operational significance are shown in figure 2-1.

V_{FE}	Maximum Flap Extended Speed: To 10° Flaps 10° - 20° Flaps 20° - 30° Flaps	 156 129 114	 160 130 115	Do not exceed these speeds with the given flap settings.
V_{LO}	Maximum Landing Gear Operating Speed	161	165	Do not extend or retract landing gear above this speed.
V_{LE}	Maximum Landing Gear Extended Speed	194	200	Do not exceed this speed with landing gear extended.

For Training Purposes Only!

Fig. 10

The last two speeds not shown on the airspeed indicator are V_{lo} and V_{le}. These speeds refer to the operation of the airplane's retractable landing gear (if equipped with retractable gear, of course). The velocity (V) of landing gear (l) operation (o) or V_{lo} is the maximum speed at which the gear may be raised or lowered. The velocity (V) with the landing gear (l) extended (e) is the maximum speed at which the airplane can be flown with the gear down. When the gear is in transition, it's often more vulnerable to the effects of speed. Once down and locked into position, the gear is able to resist a larger wind force. This is why V_{lo} is often much less than V_{le}. These two speeds are found either in your Pilot's Operating Handbook or on placards (Figure 10).

Air Error

Pitot tubes are not always installed in such a way that they can accurately sample impact-air pressure. Flying at variable angles of attack, the airplane's pitot tube sometimes simply can't scoop up a sample of air that accurately reflects the airplane's speed (Figure 11). Sometimes the pitot tube scoops up less air than is actually striking it. Other times it scoops up air which has been artificially accelerated by a curved surface, giving a slightly higher than normal indicated airspeed reading. The net result is that the pitot pressure, and thus the indicated airspeed, aren't always an accurate reflection of the windspeed blowing on the airplane.

Once again, the engineers come through with an answer. In this case it's a chart that allows you to correct for such errors (Figure 12). This chart allows you to calibrate your indicated airspeed readings for accuracy. When this is done you have the more precise airspeed reading known as calibrated airspeed.

Note: *The airspeed color arcs on newer "certificated" airplanes may be set to reflect "indicated" airspeeds, not "calibrated" airspeeds. For these airplanes, airspeed values above 30% of V_{S1} (the low end green arc), are required to have less than a 3% (or 5 knot) difference (which ever is higher) between the airspeed indicated and the actual calibrated speed of the airplane through the air. In these airplanes, you don't worry as much about the IAS-CAS difference when flying above V_{S1}. Please check your POH to see how your airspeed indicator is calibrated.*

KIAS = Knots Indicated AirSpeed/KCAS = Knots Calibrated AirSpeed

AIRSPEED CALIBRATION CHART

FLAPS UP											
KIAS	50	60	70	80	90	100	110	120	130	140	150
KCAS	50	64	72	81	89	98	107	116	126	135	153
FLAPS 10°											
KIAS	40	50	60	70	80	90	100				
KCAS	55	58	64	72	81	90	107				
FLAPS 30°											
KIAS	40	50	60	70	80	85					
KCAS	54	57	62	71	80	85					

Condition: Power required for level flight or maximum rated RPM dive

Fig. 12

CALIBRATED & INDICATED AIRSPEEDS

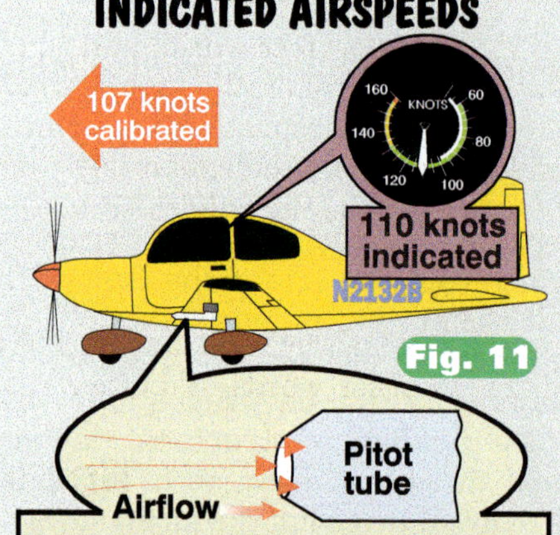

Sometimes the air striking the pitot tube is artificially accelerated which causes the indicated airspeed to read higher than the airplane's actual calibrated speed.

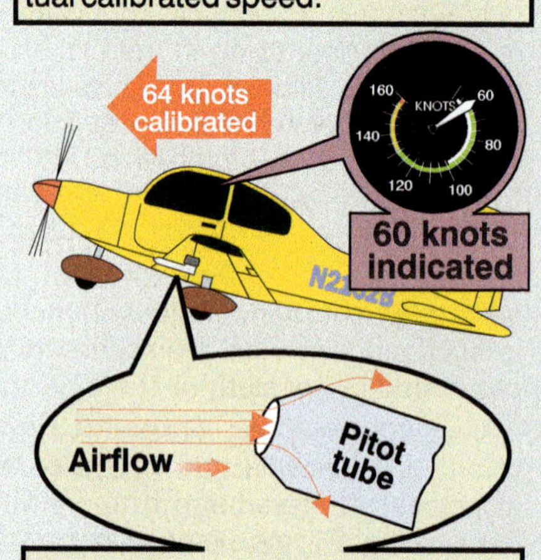

Sometimes the pitot tube's position or angle prevents it from capturing the moving molecules of air flowing over it. This results in the indicated airspeed being less than the calibrated airspeed.

Indicated Airspeeds

You will soon find that many things in aviation come in several styles and flavors. Altitude is one of those, and so is speed. Unlike being on the ground, where speed is speed (though it can be expressed in different units such as miles per hour or kilometers per hour), there are a variety of airplane speeds, each with its own significance to you, the pilot.

The number showing on the airspeed indicator is (sound of drum roll) the *indicated airspeed.* If the airspeed needle pointed to 80 knots, then 80 knots is the indicated airspeed (Sounds too simple doesn't it? It's somewhat like the question, "What time does the 11:00 a.m. flight leave?").

When a controller asks for your current airspeed, he or she expects to get back the indicated airspeed. (Controllers typically ask for this information by saying "Cessna 1234 Alpha, say airspeed." Those unable to resist the temptation to reply "airspeed" can expect to find a strange and inexplicable increase in their arrival and departure delays.)

Calibrated Airspeed

It's an imperfect world, and that's nowhere more evident than in aircraft instrumentation. The indicated airspeed is subject to (generally slight) errors due to a variety of factors including placement of the pitot and static sources, mechanical inaccuracies at various places in the range, etc. Like a trusty-though-cranky watch, if you know the amount of error, you can at any time correct the indicated time to get the actual time. The corrected, accurate reading is referred to as the *calibrated airspeed (CAS).*

Here's an Official Aviation Secret. While very important on FAA knowledge exams and to flight instructors who enjoy dabbling in such things, the differences between IAS and CAS are often (not always) much smaller than the inaccuracies caused by the small size of the dials you're attempting to read, and the differences in angle at which you read them. In other words, it's often a challenge to discern the difference between 56 and 58 knots on a small instrument with a fat pointer, which makes *parallax* a serious vocabulary word.

Differences between IAS and CAS are slightly larger at slower airspeeds and with flaps extended as well as at higher cruise speeds as shown in Figure 12, but overall these differences aren't worth worrying about. Besides, the errors at slower speeds usually work in your favor since your calibrated airspeed is usually higher than your indicated airspeed. Said another way, you're going slightly faster than what you think you are. Nevertheless, you should correct for these errors when appropriate, unless your POH recommends that your fly a specific indicated airspeed (IAS) on final approach. To facilitate this, we'll refer only to indicated airspeeds for the rest of this book.

While indicated airspeed represents the amount of wind blowing on the airplane, it doesn't reflect the airplane's true speed through the air. Welcome to aviation paradox #101.

Tips on Hot Lips

Here's one additional and important point about pitot tubes: Most of them are equipped with heating elements. Activating the pitot heat from inside the cockpit (Figure 13) heats electrical coils within the pitot tube. Pilots flying in the clouds can encounter ice. Pitot heat prevents ice from closing the opening, and thus sending the airspeed indication into oblivion.

Fig. 13

Why do I mention this? Because pitot tubes with their heaters heating become hot—uncomfortably hot. Several years ago, in ground school class, I encountered a student who'd discovered the pitot tube was hot stuff.

I was asking the class why they should never blow into the pitot tube. My intent was to determine if they knew how easy it is to damage the delicate airspeed instrument by doing so.

One young fellow raised his hand and said, "I know why, pick me, pick me!" "OK, why?" I replied. He blurted, "Because that sucker's hot!" He had the scars to prove it. Apparently he put his lips up against a hot pitot tube during a preflight. He claimed to have heard something that sounded like bacon frying. He walked around the flight school for days in a constant state of pucker, and bore a striking resemblance to Mick Jagger. Be cautious! Let the fryer beware!

True Airspeed

Indicated airspeed isn't the *true airspeed* (TAS).

While I promise to always tell you the truth, the airspeed indicator is incapable of such a promise. It's also incapable of such a performance, through no fault of its own.

It's the air's fault. Air at sea level is very dense. Drag is obviously quite high, since air molecules are packed closer together. As the airplane ascends, it experiences less-dense air. This means less drag since fewer air molecules are around to resist the airplane's forward motion. Airplanes flying at higher altitudes actually move faster through the air for a given power setting because of the decrease in density (Figure 14).

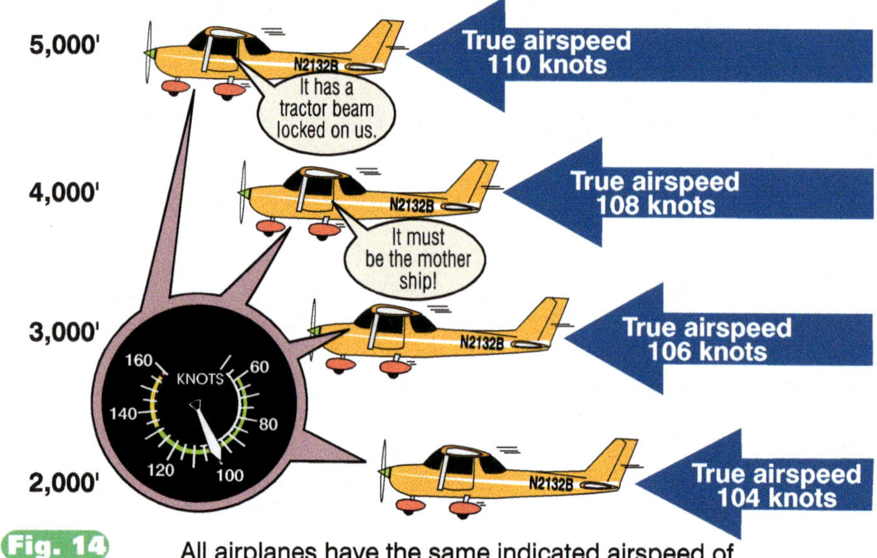

Fig. 14 All airplanes have the same indicated airspeed of 100 Knots, but their true airspeed varies with altitude.

No problem, plane goes faster, airspeed indicator goes up. Yes, but it doesn't go up as fast as the real airspeed. While the airplane goes faster through the thinner air, there are fewer air molecules striking the pitot tube and expanding the bellows of the airspeed indicator. The result is that at higher altitudes you are moving faster than your airspeed indicator shows.

Space shuttle astronauts are cruising around at approximately 17,500 miles per hour while in low earth orbit. They have a very high true airspeed. Would this true speed be shown on the shuttle airspeed indicator (we'll assume it has one)? Hardly. There are too few air molecules to even flicker an airspeed needle at that altitude. If you ever achieved low earth orbit in your little Cessna 152 "orbit-o-matic," you would also have a zero indicated airspeed (but wouldn't notice since your blood would be boiling—and that always puts a damper on my flights).

True airspeed is one of those concepts that seems to give you something for nothing. One time my dad came home and told me we were getting a new swimming pool. I was excited until he told me to go out to the car and bring it in. There's always a catch! Not so with true airspeed. You actually go faster and use less fuel (up to a point) as your altitude increases.

Air Density Lesson #1

Professor Bob
Chief Air Master

The air up there, at 10,000 feet,
Is thinner than my hair.
But if you want to go fast,
And spend less time in your seat,
Plan your LONG flights up there.

Touched by the New Age movement, professor Bob now believes the key to higher learning is based in making things rhyme. The professor's only problem is that he doesn't believe he's bald. He is convinced that he's simply taller than his hair.

Speed Math

Think of the airspeed indicator as a means of measuring molecule strikes per minute and you'll be on the road to understanding. It takes X number of molecules to push the dial to a given number. X pushes the dial to the right spot only (and only approximately) at sea level and a particular temperature. Everything else is an indicated airspeed that diverges from reality.

You'll find that for every thousand feet of altitude gain, true airspeed increases approximately 2% over indicated airspeed. Here's another way of saying the same thing: you go 2% faster than what is shown on your airspeed indicator for every thousand feet of altitude gain.

At 10,000 feet above sea level, with an indicated airspeed of 100 knots, your true speed through the air is approximately 120 knots. You simply take 2% and multiply it by 10 (which is your altitude in thousands of feet above sea level). This equals 20%. Take 20% of 100 knots which equals 20 knots and add this onto 100. This totals to a true airspeed of 120 knots.

Here's one more way of looking at the difference between true and indicated airspeed. At sea level, an indicated airspeed of 100 knots means that you have 100 knots of air moving over the wings. At 10,000 feet the airplane must move faster through the thinner air to grab the same number of molecule strikes per minute and indicate the same 100 knots of wind. Thus our true airspeed is greater (120 knots).

TAS and IAS While Approaching High Altitude Airports

The difference between true and indicated airspeed is very important for pilots making approaches to high altitude airports. Suppose you're on approach to an airport at 10,000 feet above sea level. Your indicated airspeed on approach is 80 knots. This means your true airspeed is 20% greater (or 96 knots). In other words, your wheels are going to touch down at 96 knots despite showing only 80 knots on the airspeed indicator (Figure 15). That runway is going to seem a lot shorter than it normally would. This is especially disconcerting if your mind was set for an 80 knot touchdown speed.

To lift off and accelerate for an 80 knot climb requires a longer-than-normal takeoff distance at high altitude airports. Your airplane must move along that runway a lot faster than 80 knots to generate an 80 knot indicated airspeed. In fact, at 10,000 feet, it must speed up to 96 knots to show only 80 knots on the airspeed indicator's face. What does that mean to you? It means high-altitude airports require longer takeoff runs and landing distances.

LANDING DISTANCE AND TRUE AIRSPEED

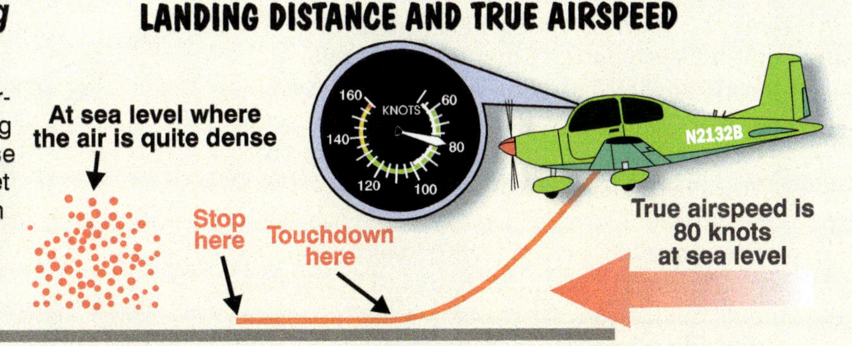

Landing distances at sea level are shorter for a given indicated airspeed.

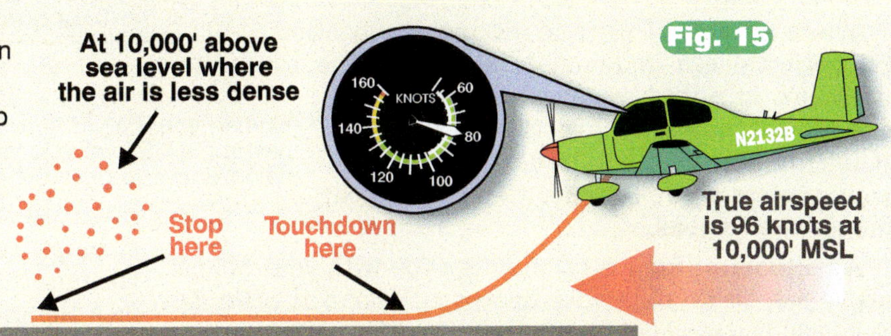

Landing distances at 10,000' MSL are longer for a given indicated airspeed.

Does this mean, while on approach to a high altitude airport, you should slow the airplane down? No! That wouldn't be good at all. Approach at the same airspeed you always use. Think about it for a second. The wings need a certain number of molecules per minute flowing over them to maintain lift. Your job is supplying those molecules. In thinner air, you will be moving faster (higher TAS) to achieve the same *indicated* airspeed, but indicated airspeed (total number of air molecules arriving at the leading edge) is all the wing (and the pilot) really cares about. *The airplane stalls at the same indicated airspeed whether you're at 1,000 feet or 10,000 feet.* If the airplane requires 60 knots of wind blowing over its wing to keep from stalling, you need to keep the indicated airspeed above 60 knots. (Remember, for most approaches, you want to be at least 30% above the stall speed.)

Dense Doings

You must be thinking, "Hey, if I go faster by flying higher, why not fly real high?" Nice try, but it won't fly! This logic doesn't hold water (or air), due to the perversity of nature and aviation. A little while ago I said TAS increases with altitude for a given power setting. Notice the *for a given power setting* part. It's the equivalent of the fine print in a contract from an aluminum siding sales rep.

As you climb, the ability of the engine to produce power decreases due to the reduced air density. So, the very thing that allows you to fly faster for a given amount of power (thinner air), limits the power you can produce! *That's* what I mean about the perversity of aviation. Turbocharging, as we discussed earlier, helps but it too eventually runs out of steam. Your Pilot's Operating Handbook identifies altitudes where you'll obtain the greatest gain in true airspeed for a given decrease in engine power.

Two factors affect air density: pressure and temperature. Is there some way to precisely predict your true airspeed? Yes, and you don't have to be psychic to do so (the other day I called the Psychic Hotline and they told me they saw a big phone bill in my future). Fortunately, true airspeed prediction is a little more precise.

Some airspeed indicators have a moveable ring on their outer scale to make determination of true airspeed easier (Figure 16). Just set the outside air temperature (OAT) on the outer ring directly over the pressure altitude (a value we'll discuss shortly) on the inner ring. The number to which your airspeed needle points on the outer ring is your true airspeed. Soon, I'll show you how to use a flight computer to determine your true airspeed based on the altitude and temperature conditions.

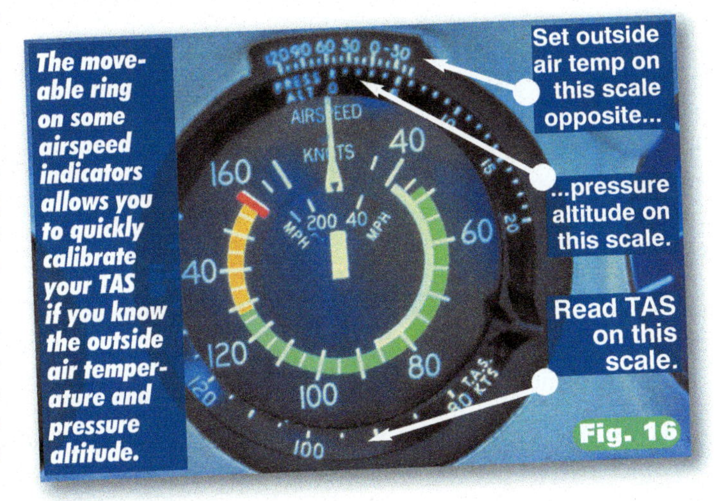

The moveable ring on some airspeed indicators allows you to quickly calibrate your TAS if you know the outside air temperature and pressure altitude.

The Altimeter

Welcome to the third dimension. One of the things that makes aviation unique is your ability to operate in 3D. No, you won't need any of those funny-colored glasses, but you will need some assistance figuring out where you are in the third dimension. This is why I would now like to introduce you to your *altimeter*.

Airplanes move left or right with great precision, flying specific headings and airways. This is two-dimensional navigation. Altimeters allow airplanes to fly at specific altitudes—a third dimension—with equal precision.

There are lots of ways to get high in aviation (all perfectly legal and honest, honest!). In the next few minutes, you will discover that there's altitude and then there's *altitude*. Knowing one from the other is crucial to your success as a pilot, not to mention your longevity as a person.

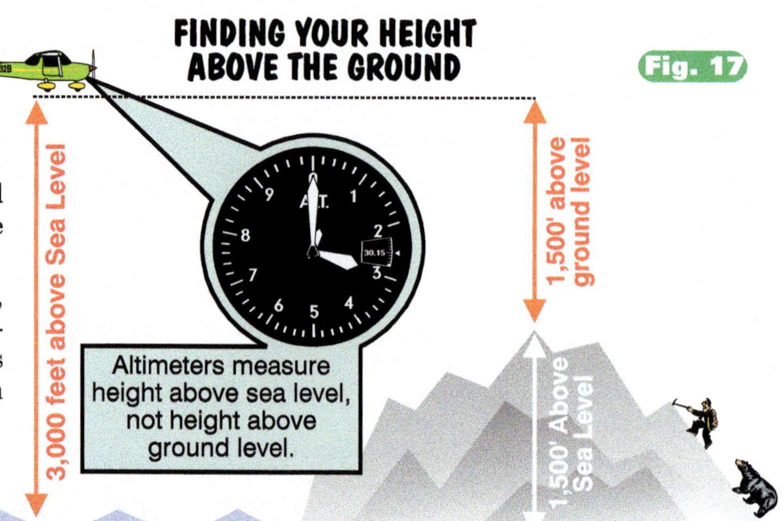

Finding your height above the ground requires that you subtract the ground's height (its MSL value is found on sectional charts—see Chapter 10) from your height above sea level (which is shown on your altimeter).

An altimeter (Figure 17) provides you with your height above sea level—otherwise known as your *true altitude*. Sea level is a worldwide standard; therefore, it's a consistent reference for altimeter measurement.

Altimeters do not directly tell you your height above the ground. Why? The ground isn't a consistent reference. Ground height varies dramatically. If, however, you know how high you are above sea level, and you also know the ground's height above sea level (this is found on navigational charts), then finding your height above the ground is simply a "take-away" math problem. Height above ground is technically known as your *absolute altitude*.

An altimeter works by measuring the difference between sea level pressure and pressure at the airplane's present altitude. Figure 18 shows how this is accomplished. Inside the altimeter is a small, expandable capsule somewhat similar to a metal-skinned balloon (they're actually called *aneroid wafers*). The expansion or contraction of the capsule is mechanically converted into a movement of altimeter hands, resulting in an altitude readout.

Notice that the altimeter's case is connected to the static port. This allows static air pressure to surround the capsule. Any change in static air pressure is then reflected by an expansion or contraction of the capsule, providing the altitude reading. To understand precisely how this process works, we need a clearer understanding of how atmospheric pressure changes with height.

Atmospheric pressure used to be measured by a mercury barometer. A tube of the heavy liquid metal mercury is filled and placed upside down in a vat of mercury (Figure 19A). The weight of the mercury inside the inverted tube creates a small vacuum as the column attempts to sink out of the tube and into the vat. It's the vacuum that prevents the mercury from entirely sinking into the reservoir. The column finally stabilizes at a certain height (Figure 19B). Let's say the height is 30 inches of mercury (sometimes abbreviated *Hg*, which is the chemists' symbol for the element mercury). Decreasing the atmosphere's pressure on the reservoir surrounding the tube allows the column to decrease in height. Increasing atmospheric pressure pushes on the reservoir, moving the column upward into the tube and increasing its height (Figure 19C).

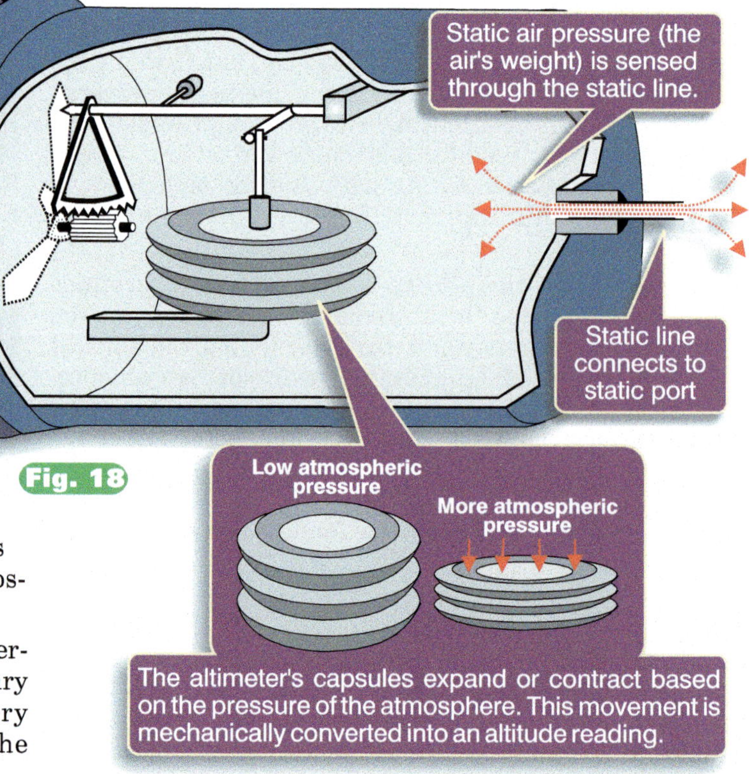

The altimeter's capsules expand or contract based on the pressure of the atmosphere. This movement is mechanically converted into an altitude reading.

HOW A MERCURY BAROMETER WORKS

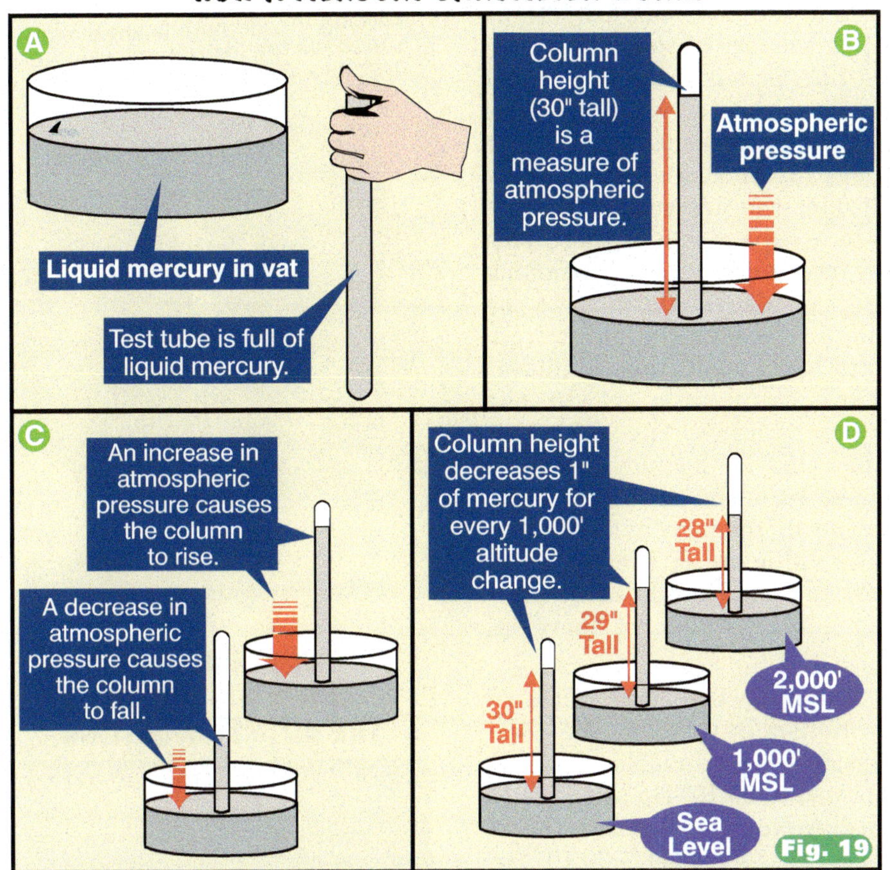

Fig. 19

The changing height of the mercury column represents atmospheric pressure in much the same way your tongue might represent the pressure of someone standing on your chest. A tongue sticking way out of your mouth would represent a lot of pressure on your chest. When the person stepped off your chest, your tongue would (we hope) recede into your mouth. One might be able to calculate the person's weight by measuring the exact amount of tongue protrusion. One might say that 200 pounds is worth 6 inches of tongue. Of course, I say this tongue in cheek since it's not all that accurate; after all, it's only a rule of tongue, and calibration would always be a challenge.

Even if we calculated tongue protrusion for a given amount of weight, this information is totally useless (but high in entertainment value, nevertheless). There is, however, great value in calculating the height, in inches, that a column of mercury will change if it's moved vertically. Since the weight of the atmosphere changes with height, this pressure change should be reflected by a lengthening or shortening of the mercury column. Indeed, this is exactly what happens. A column of mercury changes about one inch in height per thousand feet of altitude change, and this is the standard used to calibrate altimeters (Figure 19D).

Let's say that at sea level, under typical pressure conditions, our mercury column stands 30 inches tall. We say the atmospheric pressure is *30 inches of mercury*. At 1,000 feet MSL (mean sea level), the pressure decreases and the mercury column falls approximately one inch. It now stands 29 inches tall. The atmospheric pressure at 1,000 feet MSL is properly stated as *29 inches of mercury*. Altitude measurement is based on the consistency of this known pressure change.

Aircraft altimeters don't use mercury barometers. If they did, there would be a big, three-foot long tube protruding from the instrument panel (Not a pretty sight. Besides, it would keep poking you in the eye). Instead, the small expandable capsule's expansion or contraction is calibrated in inches of mercury. In other words, taken from sea level to 1,000 feet MSL, the capsule expands a small but predictable amount. Altimeter designers calibrate this change as equaling one inch on the mercury barometer.

Now you are ready to understand how altimeters can determine your airplane's height above sea level.

Figure 20A shows an altimeter resting at sea level, where the pressure is 30″ Hg. This is the pressure sensed through the airplane's static port; therefore, the pressure surrounding the expandable capsule is also 30″ Hg. Let's say the pressure inside the capsule is also at 30″ Hg. What's going to happen to the capsule? Will it expand? No. The pressure inside the capsule is the same as the pressure outside the capsule. Without any pressure difference, the capsule doesn't expand and the altimeter reads an altitude of zero feet.

HOW THE ALTIMETER CALCULATES YOUR ALTITUDE

3000' - 27"

The pressure inside the capsule is 3" greater than the outside static pressure. Therefore, the capsule expands an amount equivalent to three inches of mercury. This equates to an altitude reading of 3,000 feet above sea level.

2000' - 28"

The pressure inside the capsule is the same as the outside static pressure. Therefore, the capsule doesn't expand and the hands read "zero" altitude.

1000' - 29"

Sea level 30"

Fig. 20

Figure 20B shows an altimeter at 3,000 feet MSL. The static pressure at 3,000 MSL is 27″ Hg. If the pressure inside the capsule is still 30″ Hg, what will the capsule do? Yes, it will expand an amount equal to this difference in pressure. It will expand by an amount of pressure equal to three inches of mercury. This expansion equates to a 3,000 foot reading on the altimeter's face. (Remember, the capsule expands because its internal pressure is greater than the outside static pressure.)

Pressure Variations And The Altimeter

If the pressure at sea level always stayed at 30″ Hg, this would be the end of our altimeter story. Unfortunately, the pressure at sea level varies daily, hourly, and sometimes even minute-by-minute. The atmosphere actually changes weight slightly, causing air to push down harder on some parts of the earth than others. In the weather section you will have a chance to study these pressure differences more thoroughly. For now, let's agree that the pressure at sea level changes often.

The altimeter's job is to measure the difference between sea level pressure and the outside static pressure of the altitude at which you are flying. As we've already learned, the difference between these two pressures allows the altimeter to calculate your height above sea level. Since we've already agreed that sea level pressure changes at a fixed location, think about how quickly it can change when moving across the country in your airplane. You obviously need some way to keep your altimeter informed about the changing pressure at sea level. A small knob at the front of the altimeter (Figure 21) allows you to do just that.

Did you feel something?

I did!

Twisting this knob rotates the little numbers in the *Kollsman window,* as shown on the face of the altimeter in Figure 22A. This is the pilot's way of telling the altimeter what the pressure is at sea level. Changing the numbers in the Kollsman window recalibrates the pressure inside the altimeter's expandable capsule. This is done mechanically by repositioning an internal linkage, which gives the capsule a new starting point from which to begin measuring. Whatever pressure value you set in the Kollsman window, the altimeter assumes this is the new sea level pressure. Now the altimeter measures the difference between the pressure value set in the Kollsman window and the outside static pressure to obtain your height above sea level.

For instance, when 30.10″ Hg is set in the Kollsman window, the pressure inside the expandable capsule is recalibrated to 30.10″ Hg as shown in Figure 22A. Now the altimeter thinks the pressure at sea level is 30.10″ Hg. Setting 29.95″ Hg in the Kollsman window tells the altimeter the pressure at sea level is 29.95″ Hg (Figure 22B).

Figure 23 shows how this process works. Airplane A is over San Francisco (SFO) where the sea level pressure is 30.25″ Hg. This value is set in the Kollsman window. The difference between 30.25″ Hg and 27.25″ Hg is three inches of pressure or 3000 feet. The altimeter reads three thousand feet—the airplane's true altitude.* Airplane B is over Santa Barbara (SBA) where the sea level pressure has lowered to 29.25″ Hg. The static pressure at Airplane B's altitude of 3,000 feet is 26.25″ Hg. The difference between these two is three inches. Therefore, the altimeter reads 3000 feet.

**As you'll soon see, to obtain true altitude, you also need to correct the altimeter for non-standard temperature variations. For now, we'll just assume that true altitude is obtained by correcting the altimeter for pressure changes.*

Turning the altimeter's knob allows you to tell the instrument what the pressure at sea level is.

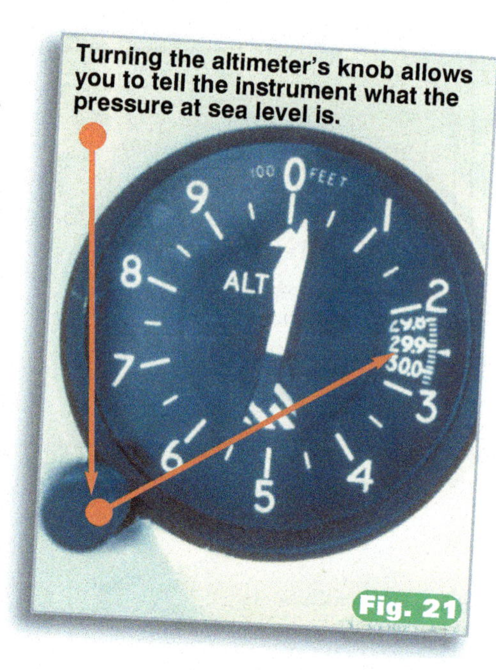

Fig. 21

WHAT HAPPENS WHEN YOU CHANGE THE ALTIMETER SETTING

Rotating the altimeter's knob, changes the numbers in the Kollsman window. This mechanically repositions an internal linkage that changes the starting point from which the altimeter begins its measurement. It is, however, much easier to think of the pressure inside the sealed capsule changing to equal the barometric pressure value set in the Kollsman window (trust me! Think about it this way and you'll never have difficulty understanding how the altimeter works).

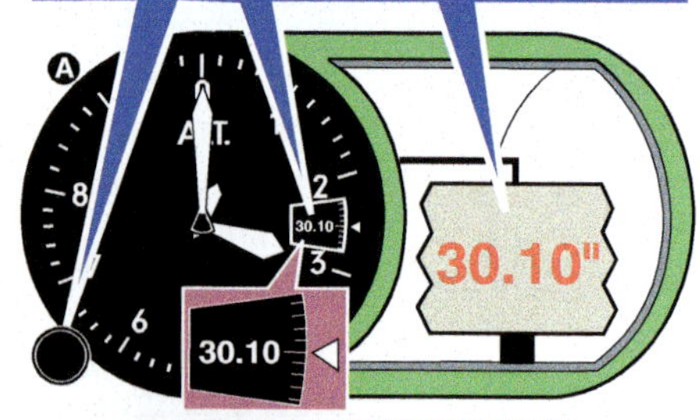

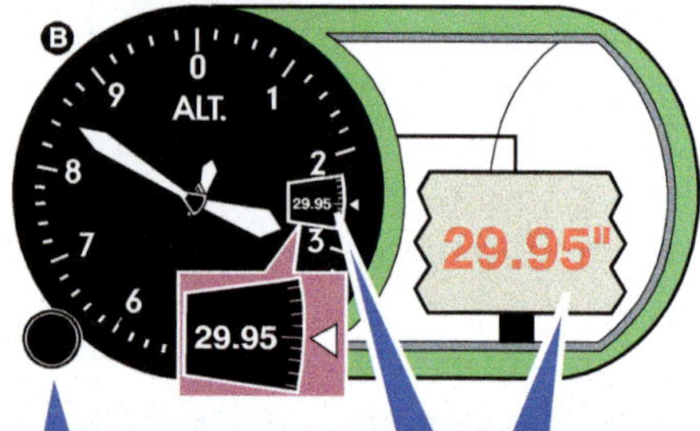

When the altimeter knob is rotated & 29.95" is set in the Kollsman window, the altimeter acts as if a pressure of 29.95" Hg has been set inside its sealed capsule.

Fig. 22

The point is that we should always set the sea level pressure in the Kollsman window so our altimeter can read true altitude. "OK," you wonder, "how do we get the sea level pressure to set in the Kollsman window in the first place?" This sea level pressure is called the *altimeter setting*. It's easily obtained from several sources, including air traffic control towers, flight service stations and automatic weather observation stations. A bit later in this chapter, I'll tell you about one more way you can get the right altimeter setting, even when nobody's home at the tower.

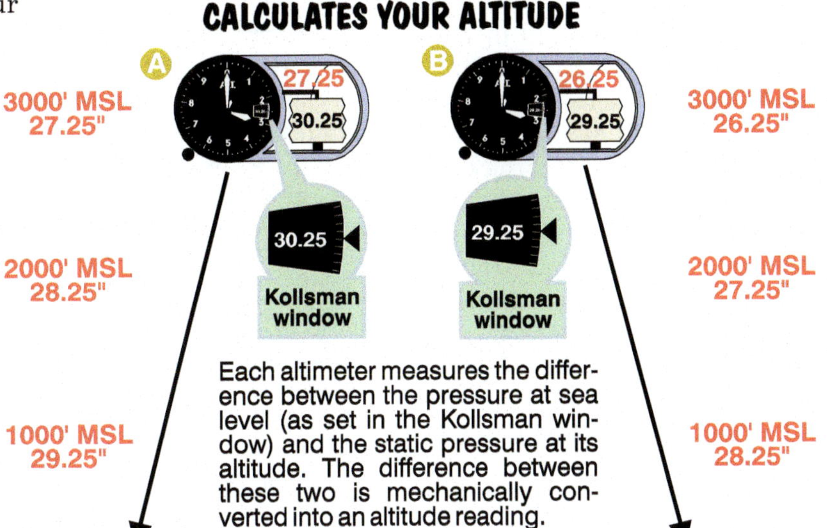

Fig. 23

What happens if you don't continue to update the altimeter setting during every 100 miles or so of flight? There's a good chance your altimeter will not be providing the correct information—you're not going to be at the altitude you think you're at. This can be a problem.

Think of the problem as being similar to driving across the country while listening to your car radio. If you're listening to a lecture about Jung and yang on that philosophical radio station KYMI, after a short distance you'll need to re-tune to another station carrying the same program. You'll be out of range of the first station. If you fly more than 100 miles from the source of your last altimeter setting, you're technically out of range from this source. An error in the altimeter's reading is possible unless you reset the Kollsman window to a closer source.

Figure 24 depicts this process. Notice that at 1,000 feet MSL above SFO, the pressure is 29.25" Hg (position A). This is the same as the sea level pressure at SBA (position B). Do you see how the 29.25" pressure level gradually sloped from 1,000 feet MSL down to the surface, between SFO and SBA? It can be said that pressure levels drop when flying towards an area of lower pressure.

At 3,000 feet above SFO, the static pressure is 27.25" Hg (position C). Approaching SBA, the 27.25" pressure level slopes downward to 2,000 feet above the surface (position D). With the SFO sea level pressure of 30.25" Hg set in the Kollsman window, the altimeter indicates 3,000 feet as long as you stay at the level where the outside pressure is 27.25" Hg as shown by position C. Can you see what's happening? The level where the pressure is 27.25" Hg actually slopes downward closer to the surface yet the altimeter is still reading 3,000 feet position D. If we don't continue to update the altimeter setting, the *indicated altitude* (what's shown on the altimeter's face) becomes different from our true altitude (our actual height above sea level).

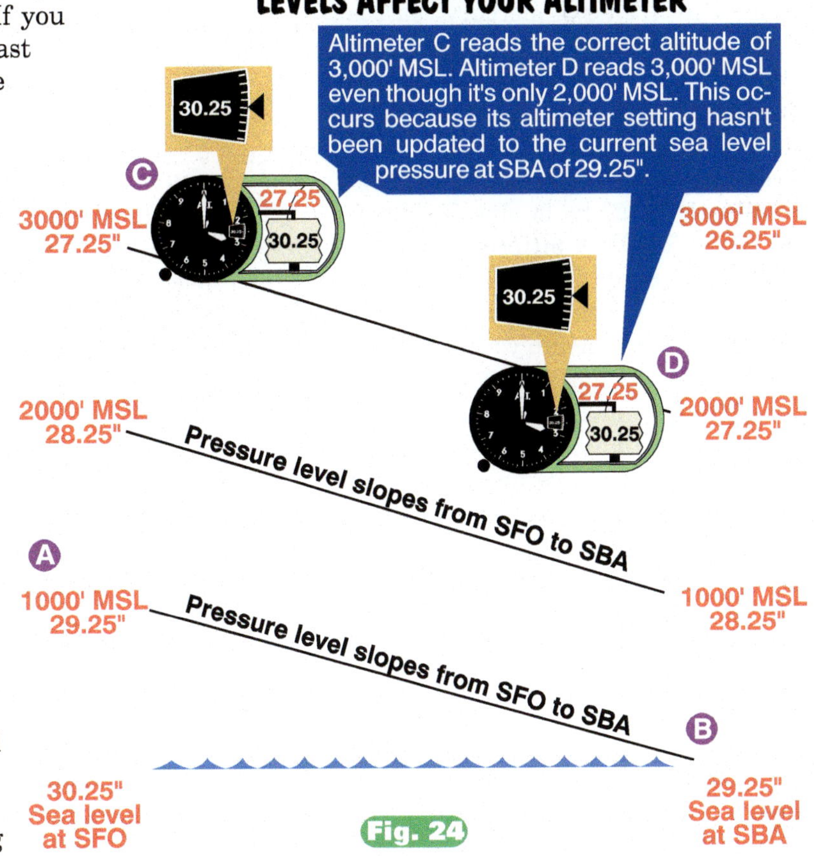

Fig. 24

Over SBA our indicated altitude is 3,000 feet but our true altitude is only 2,000 MSL as shown in Figure 24, position D. Is this a problem? Yes! What happens if there is a mountain at 2,500 feet MSL along your path? (Figure 25A). Looking at the face of the altimeter (its indicated altitude), it appears you'll clear the mountain by 500 feet. In reality, you're 500 feet below the top of the mountain. Under these conditions, there's a good chance that your airplane's landing gear might conk the head of some camper sitting around a campfire on top of that hill. What a shock it would be if it were night time and you thought you would clear that 2,500 foot mountain by 500 feet. You might end up with a Coleman stove, camping gear and raccoons stuck to your airplane.

Suppose you're over SBA and suddenly you realize your mistake of not updating the altimeter setting. You call the SBA tower and the controller tells you the altimeter setting is 29.25" Hg (He or she will actually say "Altimeter setting is two-niner-two-five." The "inches of mercury" part is understood and never spoken.) You set this in the Kollsman window. What will your altimeter read? The difference between the recalibrated pressure in the expandable capsule and static pressure is now two inches. Therefore, the altimeter reads a true altitude of 2,000 feet (Figure 25B), at which point you immediately begin climbing back to your previously selected altitude of 3,000 feet. By updating the altimeter setting, the indicated altitude (what the altimeter shows) is now the same as the true altitude (your height above sea level). Good pilots make it a point to update their altimeter setting at least every 100 miles (if not more often).

In Figure 25B, did you notice that twisting the knob and moving the numbers down from 30.25" Hg to 29.25" Hg caused the hands to unwind 1,000 feet worth? This progression is shown in Figure 26. From a strictly mechanical point of view,

When There's No Sea Beneath Thee

Whenever an ATC facility gives you the altimeter setting, that's the pressure at sea level underneath them. You are, I hope, wondering how an airport near Denver, Colorado, located at over 5,000 feet MSL, measures the pressure at sea level when there is no sea under the airport.

Sea level is a relative constant across the globe (excluding tides). ATC personnel can easily calculate what the pressure at sea level underneath them would be, if they could dig down to that level and if there were a sea there. This is often calculated by a mechanical device at the ATC facility (later I'll show you the device they use to calculate sea level pressure—you're not going to believe it.)

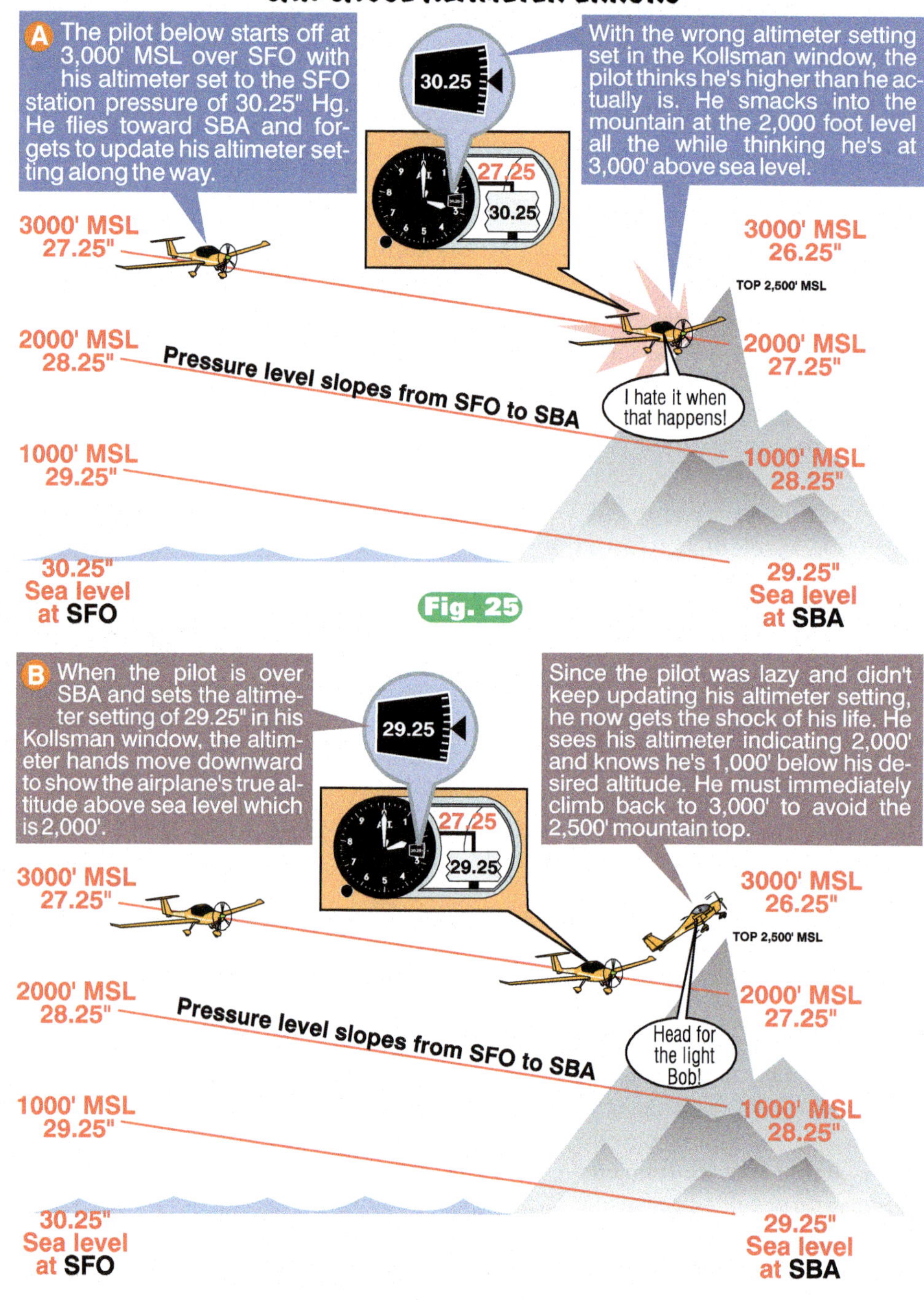

Fig. 25

HOW A CHANGING ALTIMETER SETTING MOVES THE ALTIMETER'S HANDS

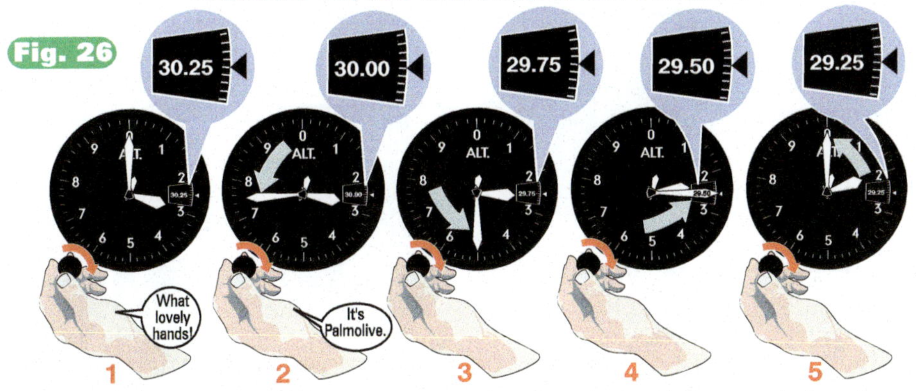

When you're over SBA and you rotate the numbers in the Kollsman window down from 30.25" to 29.25", (1" of Hg change) the indicated altitude moves down from 3,000 feet to 2,000 feet—which is now your true altitude over SBA. (Note: when the numbers go up or down, the hands also go up or down respectively. This is the way the mechanical linkage inside the altimeter works. Change the numbers 1" and the hands move 1,000', change them .5" and the hands move 500' or change them .1" and the hands move 100').

whenever the numbers in the Kollsman window move downward (get smaller), the hands also move downward (read less). Changing the numbers one inch in the Kollsman window is worth a one thousand foot altitude change on the altimeter's face. Figure 26 shows what the altimeter hands do when rotating the knob to the current altimeter setting over SBA.

A wise man says, "Pilot who refuse to get new altimeter setting feel let down—in more ways than one."

There's a very important point to be made here (move that finger to the preferred ear position). *When the altimeter is set too high, it reads too high in terms of altitude, and you will be **lower** than you think you are.* If the altimeter is set too low, it reads too low. Flying from SFO to SBA, toward an area of lower sea level pressure, and not updating the altimeter setting, meant the barometric pressure setting in the Kollsman window was too high. Therefore, the altimeter reads too high. In other words, the indicated altitude (3,000 feet) was higher than our true altitude (2,000 feet) as shown in Figure 25A.

Figure 27 shows an airplane flying from a low pressure area toward a high pressure area (in the opposite direction of our flight from SFO to SBA). The airplane maintains a constant indicated altitude of 3,000 feet without updating its altimeter setting. The airplane follows the 26.25" pressure level, which slopes upward as the high pressure area over SFO is approached. With the altimeter set too low, it will read too low and you will be ***higher*** than you intend to be. The indicated altitude will be 3,000 feet but you will actually be 4,000 feet above sea level when over SFO.

If you had to pick the most dangerous flight scenario, it would probably be flying from high pressure to low instead of low to high, and this is generally the example that shows up on FAA tests and instructor interrogations.

The point of all this is that you must keep the altimeter informed about the current altimeter setting. Regulations require you to adjust the altimeter to the current reported altimeter setting of a station along the route and within 100 nautical miles of your airplane. Keeping altimeters informed is similar to keeping your spouse informed. It produces a happy relationship.

FAILURE TO UPDATE YOUR ALTIMETER SETTING WHEN FLYING FROM A LOW TO HIGH PRESSURE AREA

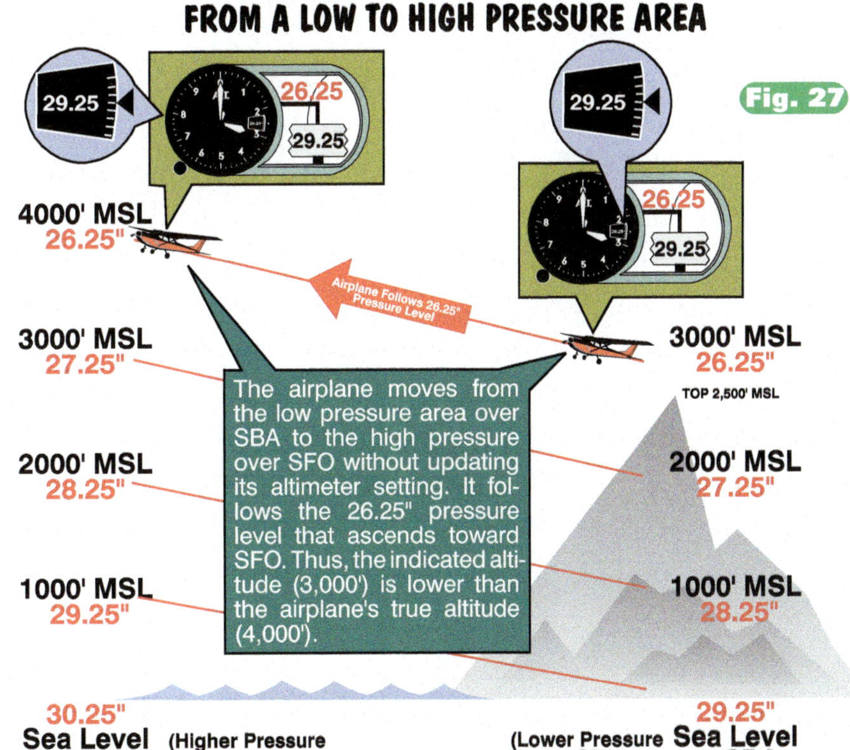

Temperature Variations and the Altimeter

Just when you think you've got all the exceptions down pat, another gem in need of consideration pops up. You just can't seem to win. It's like going to the one hour photo shop, only to find they have 30 minute parking. Don't fret. The altimeter's *temperature errors* are easy to understand.

Normal changes in temperature produce relatively small and negligible errors in altimeter readings. If, however, you're taking the family's Boeing 747 out for a little cross country flight, you could travel to exotic places having extreme temperatures (in particular, extreme cold). Under these conditions, it's possible to have altimeter errors of 500 feet or more. Practically speaking, most pilots never correct their altimeters for temperature variations. Nevertheless, it's important to know when these errors can affect you and how to correct for them.

Most of the time, pilots fly with plenty of terrain clearance and are not affected by small, temperature-induced altimeter errors. On the other hand, if you're planning a night flight over mountains and don't plan on crossing them by at least 2,000 feet or more, you should check and see if temperature errors will significantly affect your altimeter's reading. (You should also have a CAT scan to check for reduced blood flow to the judgment section of your cortex if you're crossing mountains at less than 2,000 feet above ground level at night.)

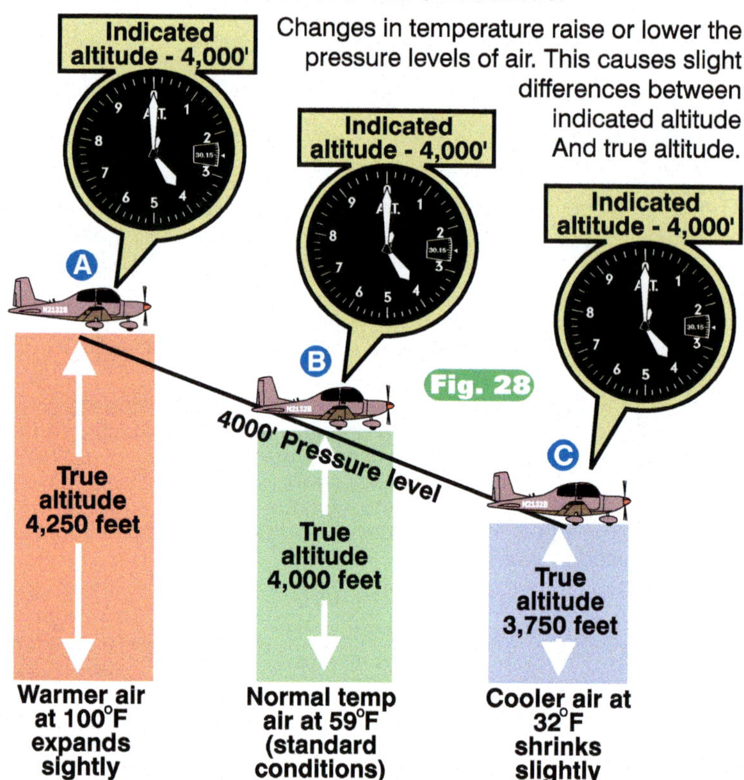

Figure 28 depicts the effect of temperature on columns of air. When air is at standard or normal temperature (59° F/15° C at sea level), the altimeter experiences no temperature error. Airplane B, sitting on top of a column of normal temperature air, has an indicated altitude (4,000 feet) which is equal to its true altitude (4,000 feet).

When temperatures are warmer, however, air expands. Airplane A rests atop an expanded layer of air. The air beneath Airplane A weighs the same as the air beneath Airplane B. The difference is that the warmer, expanded column of air is taller. This is similar to two guys both weighing 370 pounds, with one standing 6 feet tall and the other standing 4 feet tall. They both produce the same indication on a scale but their weight is distributed differently in the vertical direction. In a similar manner, a mass of air having temperatures that are different from standard distributes its weight differently in the vertical direction.

Because the pressure levels are taller or expanded in warmer air, Airplane A's indicated altitude is 4,000 feet and its true altitude is 4,250 feet. Colder air produces shorter or more closely spaced pressure levels. Airplane C's indicated altitude is 4,000 feet and its true altitude is 3,750 feet.

Think about it in the following way. Without correcting the altimeter for temperature variations, if the temperature is going down, then the airplane is going down; if the temperature is going up, then the airplane is going up.

On a flight from a warmer area to a colder area, without correcting for temperature, the indicated altitude is greater than the true altitude. In other words, the altimeter will indicate 4,000 feet but the true altitude will be 3,750 feet. *The temperature went down, so the airplane went down.* It went down 250 feet and you still think you're at 4,000 feet above sea level.

On a flight from a colder area to a warmer area, without correcting for temperature, the indicated altitude is lower than the true altitude. Imagine the airplane in Figure 28 flying from right to left. In the warmer area, the indicated altitude is 4,000 feet but the true altitude is 4,250 feet. Therefore, *if the temperature is going up, the airplane is going up.* It went up 250 feet and you still think you're at 4,000 feet above sea level.

YOU KNOW YOU'VE BEEN FLYING TOO MUCH WHEN...

1. You use the emergency brake to drop the flaps.
2. You yell "clear" before starting your car.
3. You get out of your car and look for tiedown ropes.
4. You brake on left turns and speed-up on right turns.
5. You tell the police officer that you're allowed to go 250 below 10,000 feet MSL.
6. You drive into a fog bank and immediately go on instruments.
7. You are entering the highway and hit *rotate speed* for the Cessna 150. You pull back on the wheel and don't become airborne. In a panic, you abort the takeoff and hit the brakes. (This drives the guy behind you crazy.)

WHEN THE ALTIMETER SETTING ISN'T AVAILABLE

If the altimeter setting is not available while on the ground at an airport, simply rotate the knob until the altimeter hands indicate field elevation. The numbers in the Kollsman window would be your altimeter setting if it were available from ATC.

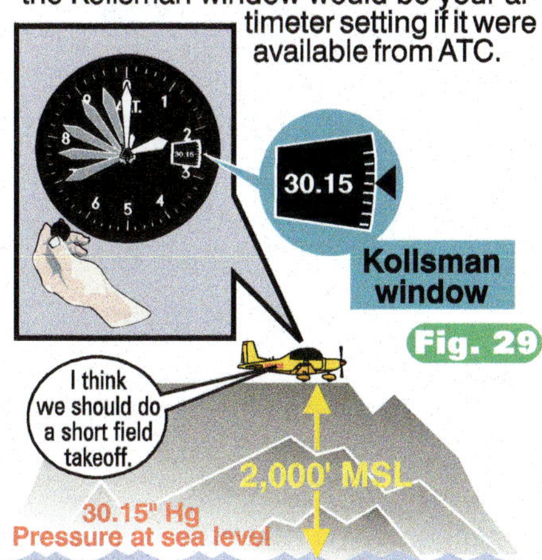

There's another excellent memory aid to help keep these altimeter errors straight: *When flying from high to low, look out below.* This rule assumes that you forgot to set in the nearest altimeter setting or correct your altimeter for temperature extremes. You must *look out below* because you are not as high as you think you are. The statement *look out below* should be an immediate cue of danger. Danger means that you are closer to sea level than your altimeter says you are.

Suppose you're arriving or departing an airport in extremely cold temperatures. You should think, "If the temperature is cold, then the thermometer has gone down. Therefore, the airplane is going down." In other words, your airplane's true altitude is lower than the indicated altitude.

You already know how to correct for pressure variations during flight. You simply adjust the altimeter setting to the nearest station within 100 nautical miles of the airplane. But how do you correct for variations in temperature? You can use your flight computer (mechanical or electronic) for these computations. Once again, we don't normally correct the altimeter for temperature variations unless the temperatures are extreme and we plan on crossing terrain at low altitudes.

Sensitive Altimeters

We call modern altimeters *sensitive altimeters*. This is not because they cry at movies. Sensitive altimeters are those with adjustable barometric scales and often have two or even three expandable capsules instead of one. This allows them greater precision or sensitivity in altitude measurement. It's possible to hold a sensitive altimeter in your hand, move it from the floor to the ceiling and record an altitude change (and poke a hole in your roof). Now that's sensitive!

Suppose you're departing an airport early in the morning before the tower opens and no altimeter setting is available. Remember, a couple of sections back I promised you one more way to get a stealth altimeter setting. It's remarkably easy. Simply rotate the altimeter knob until the hands point to field elevation, as shown in Figure 29 (field elevation is a number that's listed on almost all aviation charts, and in many other published sources). This is what the hands would read if you had the current altimeter setting isn't it? Now, in a backwards sort of way, the numbers in the Kollsman window give you an approximate altimeter setting for that area. At least this allows you to start your flight with a correct reading on the altimeter. However, as you progress along your route, keep updating the altimeter setting at least every 100 nautical miles. Remember, pressure at sea level can change quickly. The altimeter must be kept informed so it will provide accurate altitude information.

Cross checking the altimeter setting with the field elevation is always a good idea. You can sometimes catch a mistake in the altimeter setting you've heard (or thought you heard) by noticing that the resulting altitude is way off from what it should be for the airport.

Do you remember our discussion on how ATC personnel determine the altimeter setting? I said you wouldn't believe it when I told you how they did it. Well, many of them do it with a small altimeter of their very own. They simply turn the knob until the altimeter reads the field elevation or elevation of the tower cab, then look at the numbers in the Kollsman window! That's the altimeter setting they issue (and you thought it was done with smoke, mirrors and controlled substances).

Pressure Altitude

Every family has a cousin Ed. He's the typical cousin who's just one taco short of a combo plate. Our Ed would always tell us that he lived in a gated community. We interpreted this to mean prison. Uncle Ed would tell the type of jokes no one laughed at. He would always say, "Well, you had to be there!" I suppose if I was there I would understand his humor. The problem is, how do I get back there to understand?

A similar problem exists where airplane performance charts are concerned. When engineers create performance charts, they create them for specific altitude, temperature and pressure conditions. To use these charts, you must go back to the conditions the engineers used when the performance computations were made. We call the day on which these specific altitude, temperature and pressure conditions existed a *standard day*.

For an engineer, a standard day occurs when the temperature and pressure at sea level is 59°F (or 15°C) and 29.92" Hg, respectively. Most of the airplane's performance charts are based on these conditions. Here's the problem. What if the temperature and pressure at sea level isn't a standard 15°C and 29.92" Hg (and it rarely is)? Will these performance charts still provide you with reliable information? They will if you go back to standard day conditions. Let me show you how to do this with an actual performance chart.

Figure 30A is a climb performance chart. It requires two variables—pressure altitude and temperature—to

HOW TO FIND AND USE PRESSURE ALTITUDE

(A) Think of pressure altitude as the altitude the engineers were at when they created the airplane's performance charts. This is the altitude your altimeter reads when 29.92" of Hg is set in your Kollsman window.

WEIGHT LBS	PRESS ALT FT	CLIMB SPEED KIAS	RATE OF CLIMB - FPM			
			-20°C	0°C	20°C	40°C
2550	S.L.	73	795	730	665	600
	2000	73	705	645	585	525
	4000	73	625	565	510	450
	6000	72	540	485	430	370
	8000	72	460	405	350	295
	10,000	72	380	325	275	
	12,000	72	300	250		

(B) **How to obtain pressure altitude for the chart above** Fig. 30

To find your pressure altitude, simply set 29.92" in your Kollsman window. The altitude the hands point to is your pressure altitude. Once you know this, reset the numbers in the Kollsman window to the previous altimeter setting. Note that rotating the numbers from 30.42" down to 29.92" (a change of .5") moves the hands down 500'. Therefore, the hands move from 2,500' down to 2,000'.

1 — 30.42 — Ouch! I have tennis elbow.

2 — 30.17

3 — 29.92 — I wish I had an elbow!

determine climb rate. This thing called *pressure altitude* is the pressure condition the engineers experienced when they determined the airplane's performance. Since the pressure at sea level was 29.92" Hg when they tested the airplane, all you need to do in determining pressure altitude is set the altimeter's Kollsman window to 29.92" Hg and read the indicated altitude. This reading is your pressure altitude, as shown in Figure 30B. In this example, our pressure altitude is 2,000 feet. Using that value and the outside air temperature, we can determine our airplane's performance on the rate of climb chart provided.

Of course, once you've determined your pressure altitude you should immediately reset the altimeter back to the altimeter setting provided by Air Traffic Control (ATC). This keeps the altimeter reading the correct height above sea level (true altitude).

Remember, pressure altitude is used for performance computations. It's the height above a *standard datum plane,* which is nothing more than a fancy phrase for *an imaginary reference point.* This reference point is what the engineer's altimeter would have read if temperature and pressure at sea level was 59°F and 29.92" Hg.

Reading the Altimeter

Reading the altimeter is very similar to reading a watch. I say this with caution, knowing that some readers have been raised on digital watches and no longer know what it means when Mickey's little hand is on the 3 and his big hand is on the 12. Some may not even know which way Mickey's hands used to turn. I know this is a problem because the tower pointed out traffic for one of my students by saying, "32 Bravo, you have traffic at 2 o'clock." My student replied, "Well, it's only 1:30, so we've got a half hour before it gets here!"

Figure 31A shows a typical altimeter found in most airplanes. It has three hands, which is how many you'll wish *you* had sometimes when

Know the Code

Many airplanes now have *automatic pressure altitude reporting equipment* (either an *encoding altimeter* or a *blind encoder [most common]*). Also referred to as *Mode C capability,* this equipment is similar to an altimeter. It sends encoded pressure information to ATC radar via the airplane's onboard transponder. The transponder is a device that makes the airplane appear as an electronic blip on radar. Airplanes with altitude encoding equipment have their altitude information shown as well as their horizontal position depicted next to the radar blip.

Altitude encoding devices have their Kollsman windows permanently set to 29.92" Hg. They send pressure altitude pulses to ATC radar, where the computer automatically corrects this reading for local barometric pressure. This correction allows controllers to read the pilot's true altitude on the radar screen.

Some misinformed pilots, finding themselves several hundred feet off an assigned altitude while being radar tracked, reach up and turn the Kollsman window knob on their airplane's altimeter so that the altimeter hands read the proper height. They're hoping that ATC is seeing what the altimeter on the instrument panel is showing. Nice try, but no banana. ATC is getting its info elsewhere. The airplane's altitude encoder, which is typically hidden behind the instrument panel and totally invisible to the pilot, is telling tales on him. The visible altimeter talks only to you; the encoding altimeter device talks only to ATC.

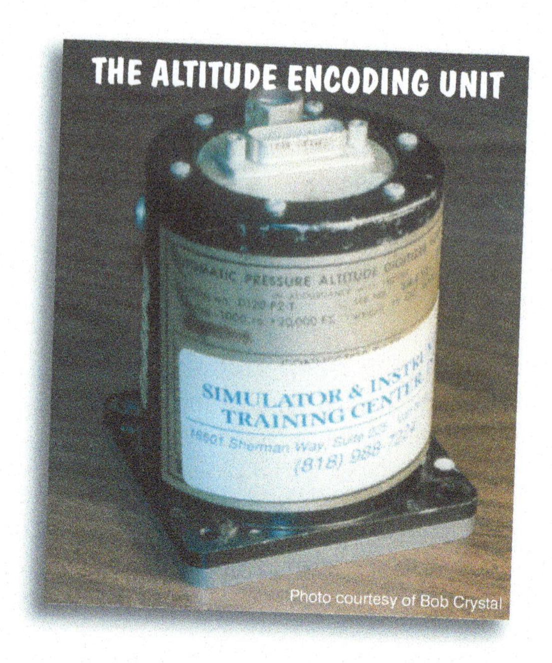

Photo courtesy of Bob Crystal

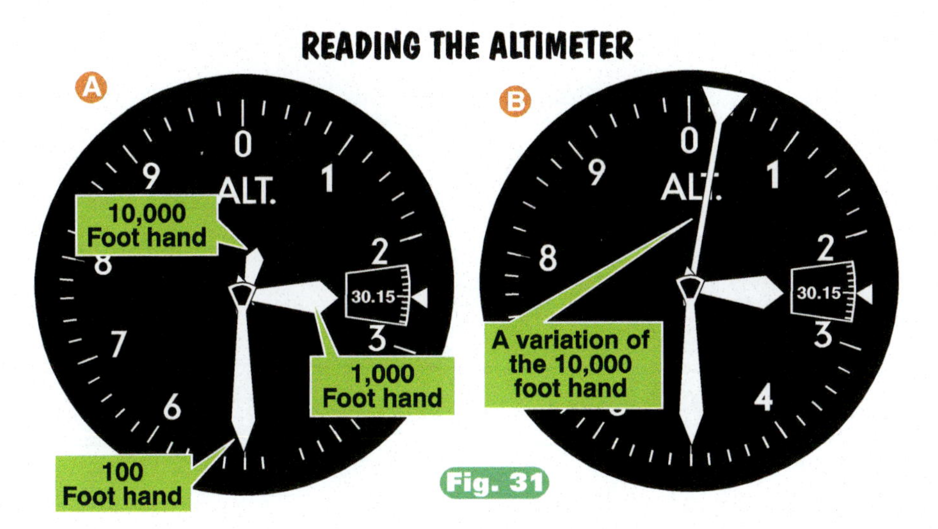

Fig. 31

things get busy in the cockpit. The shortest hand points to numbers representing the airplane's height in tens of thousands of feet. The medium, thicker hand represents altitude in thousands of feet. And the long, thin hand represents the airplane's altitude in hundreds of feet. On some altimeters a very long, thin hand with a triangle on the end is substituted for the 10,000 foot indicator as shown in Figure 31B.

The easiest way to read an altimeter is to read it just like you would read a clock. For instance, if Altimeter A in Figure 32 were a clock, what time would it read? Yes, it would read 3:00 o'clock. Since Altimeter A isn't a clock, it shows an altitude of 3,000 feet. The long (hundreds) hand points to zero hundred feet, and the medium (thousands) hand points to 3,000 feet. The altitude is 3,000 feet.

If Altimeter B were a clock, what time would it say? It would read 3:30, or half past 3:00 o'clock. As an altimeter it reads half past three thousand or 3,500 feet. The long (hundreds) hand points to 500 feet and the medium (thousands) hand points between 3,000 and 4,000 feet. The altitude is 500 feet past 3,000 feet or 3,500 feet.

What time would it be if Altimeter C were a clock? It looks like it would be somewhere around a quarter-to-seven. More precisely, the long (hundreds) hand shows 800 feet and the medium (thousands) hand points a little shy of 7,000 feet. Therefore, the altimeter reads 800 feet past 6,000 feet or 6,800 feet. Not too tough, is it?

Try reading Altimeter D like a clock. What time is it? Yes, it looks like it's 3:00, but take a closer look at the very short (ten thousands) hand. This hand points a little past a value of *1,* meaning you need to add 10,000 feet onto the value shown by the altimeter's medium and long hand. Altimeter D indicates an altitude of 13,000 feet. Keep an eye on the 10,000 foot hand, especially on FAA tests. It can be tricky if you aren't watching for it. A good general rule of aviation is to always check everything.

You're going to discover that the altimeter is a very handy little device (no pun intended). Not only is it useful for the obvious reason of maintaining a certain height above sea level, but it's also useful as a pitch instrument. Your first introduction to the altimeter will be during straight and level flight. I might warn you, these aren't two separate maneuvers; they're one. When my instructor first asked me for straight and level flight, I asked him, "Which one of those things do you want first, straight or level? I can't do them both at the same time."

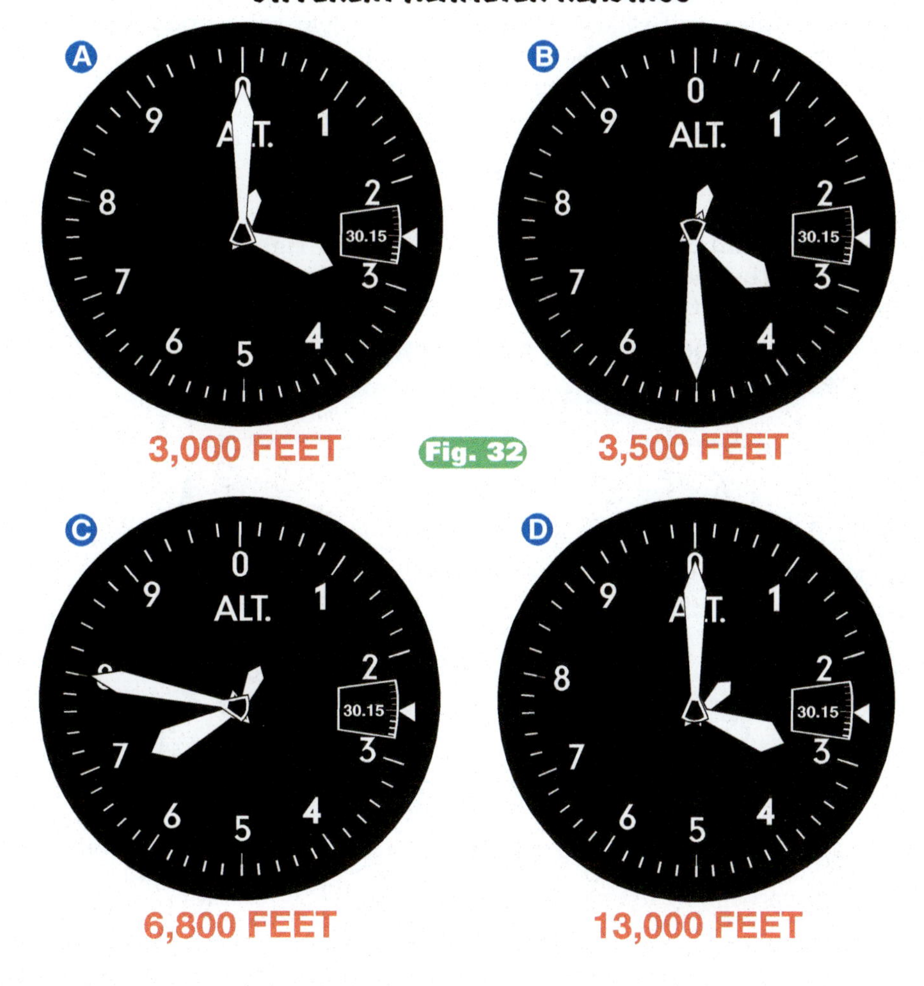

Fig. 32

The altimeter is relatively sensitive to pitch changes. Any deviation from level flight should be noticed as a slight movement of the altimeter's hundred-foot hand. You simply monitor the visual horizon to maintain a straight and level pitch while occasionally checking the altimeter for needle movement. When haze or other forms of obscuration make the horizon difficult to identify, the altimeter can be critical in confirming you're in a level-pitch attitude.

Referencing the altimeter also provides you with pitch-attitude feedback during steep turns. Since the horizon line changes quickly, glancing at the altimeter's hundred-foot hand is a good indication of any deviation from the desired altitude. Sharp pilots make it a point to constantly reference the altimeter during any maneuver requiring a constant altitude.

THE VERTICAL SPEED INDICATOR

Fig. 33

Learning to use your altimeter and other flight instruments properly should prevent the frustration I experienced as a student pilot many years ago. I was in the practice area with my flight instructor doing steep turns and having trouble maintaining altitude. During one turn my altitude dropped from 3,500 feet to 3,000 feet. In a humorous attempt to deal with the problem, I reached up, grabbed the altimeter knob and rotated it until the hands went back up to 3,500 feet. I looked over at my instructor and said, "Ahh, the altimeter setting has just changed." He looked back at me, smiled, and said, "So has the date you're going to solo!"

The Vertical Speed Indicator (VSI)

Also known as the vertical velocity indicator (VVI), the *vertical speed indicator* is located in the bottom right hand side of the instrument panel's six pack of instruments (Figure 33). Calibrated to read in feet per minute, the needle swings upward or downward, reflecting the airplane's rate of climb or descent.

THE VERTICAL SPEED INDICATOR

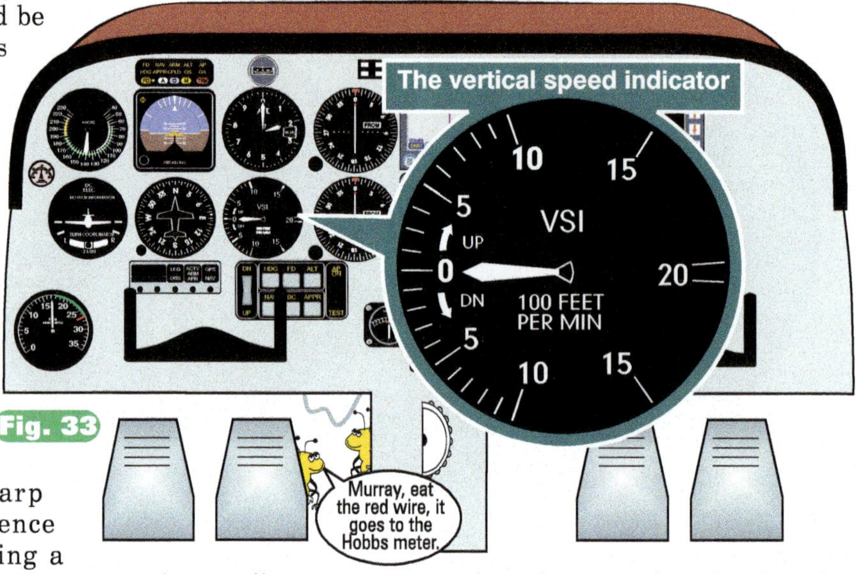

Fig. 34

Figure 34 shows the internal workings of the VSI. The case is vented to static pressure through an amazingly small opening called a *capillary tube* (also called an *airflow restrictor*). The expandable capsule connects to the static source via a normal size tube. At a constant altitude, the pressure in the case and the capsule are equal and no climb or descent rate is shown. During a climb, air pressure in the capsule decreases but air pressure in the case can't decrease as quickly because of the airflow restrictor. Therefore, pressure in the capsule is less than in the case, resulting in the capsule's *compression* which is mechanically converted into a *rate of climb* indication. Precisely the opposite happens during a descent, when the capsule is at a greater pressure than the case, resulting in the capsule's *expansion* which is mechanically converted into a *rate of descent* indication.

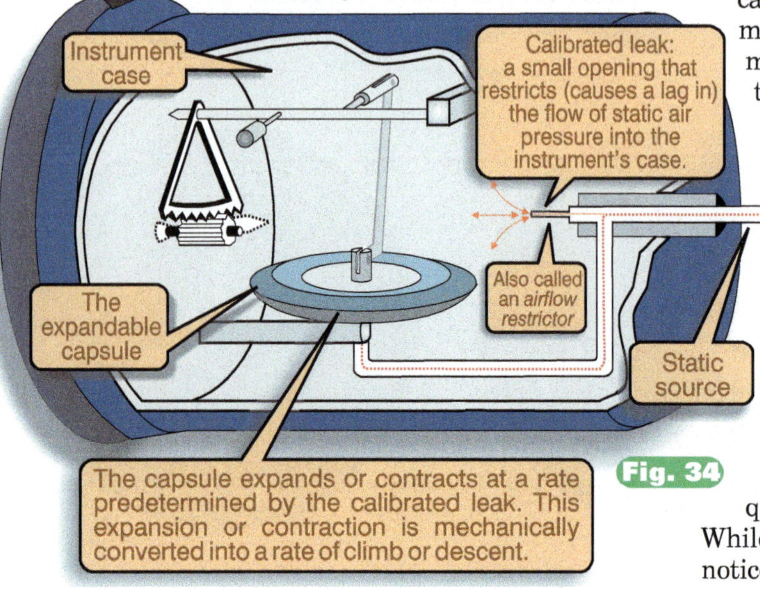

You'll find the vertical speed indicator very useful in helping you plan climbs and descents. Suppose you're 10 nautical miles from an airport and traveling at two nautical miles per minute (a 120 knot ground speed). It takes five minutes to cover those 10 miles. If the airplane's altitude is 3,000 feet above the airport elevation, a descent rate of 600 feet per minute is required to reach the airport. While this is only a rough estimate, it does aid you in planning your descents.

The VSI is also a useful instrument for detecting trends away from an established pitch attitude. We learned that the altimeter is very useful as a pitch instrument during straight and level flight, turns and steep turns. Frankly, I use the VSI more than I do the altimeter for determining changes in airplane pitch. During a steep turn I'll scan the VSI and watch for needle movement. Any deviation from a zero reading is quickly corrected by a change in elevator pressure. While the instrument does have a slight lag, it is hardly noticeable when small, non-abrupt pitch changes are made.

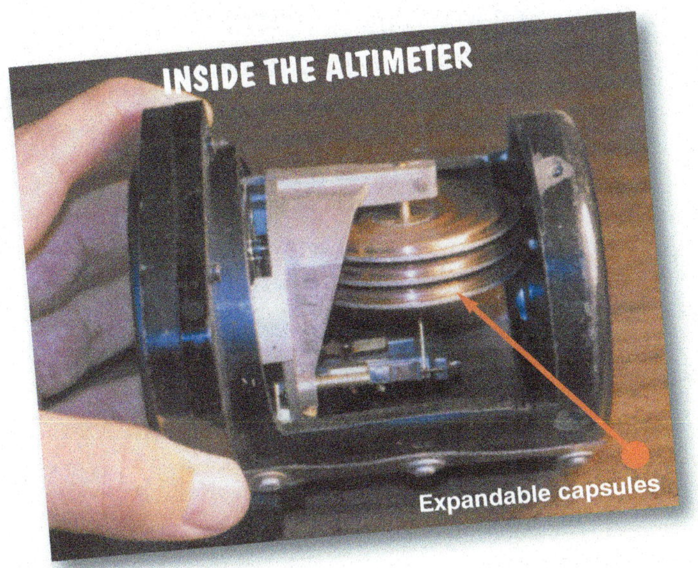

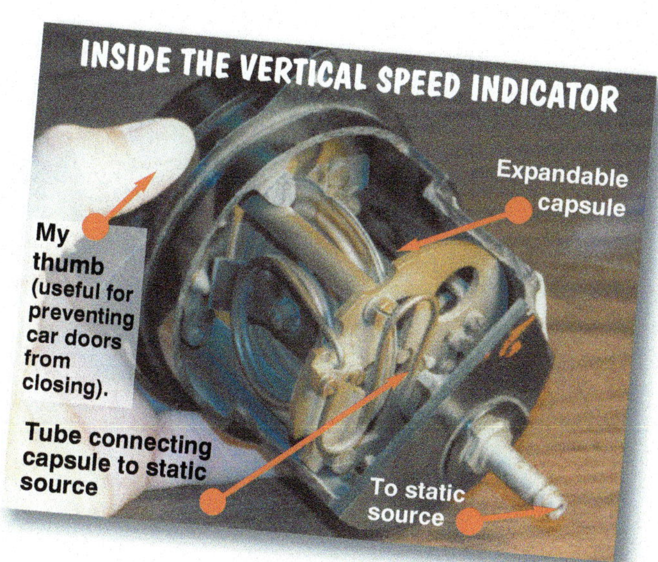

Alternate Static Source

A pilot reported downwind at one of our local airports on a quiet, calm morning. ATC said, "2132 Bravo, which runway would you like to land on this morning?" The pilot replied, "Ah, that one." To which the controller responded, "Ah, could you point a little louder?" Sometimes a pilot's brain is like an airplane's static source—it becomes clogged. Fortunately for airplanes, there's often an alternate source of static pressure in the event the primary source becomes plugged.

Since the airspeed indicator, altimeter, and vertical speed indicator all rely on static pressure, any clogging of the static source will affect these instruments. In fact, a plugged static port will prevent any static air pressure change, causing the altimeter to freeze at its last indication and the VSI to read zero, regardless of altitude change. It will also cause the airspeed to be in error if a climb or descent is made. Fortunately, some airplanes have *alternate static sources* that tap into another source of static air pressure.

Figure 35 depicts the alternate static source for the airplane's three pressure instruments. If the primary static source becomes plugged, a little valve, normally located under the instrument panel above the pilot's knee, can be opened (Figure 36). Cabin static air pressure now becomes the pressure source for the airspeed indicator, altimeter and VSI. Cabin static air pressure is slightly less than outside pressure, so selecting it will cause a slight, temporary jump in the VSI's indication and a small gain in altitude (usually less than 50 feet). This will generally be the least of your problems.

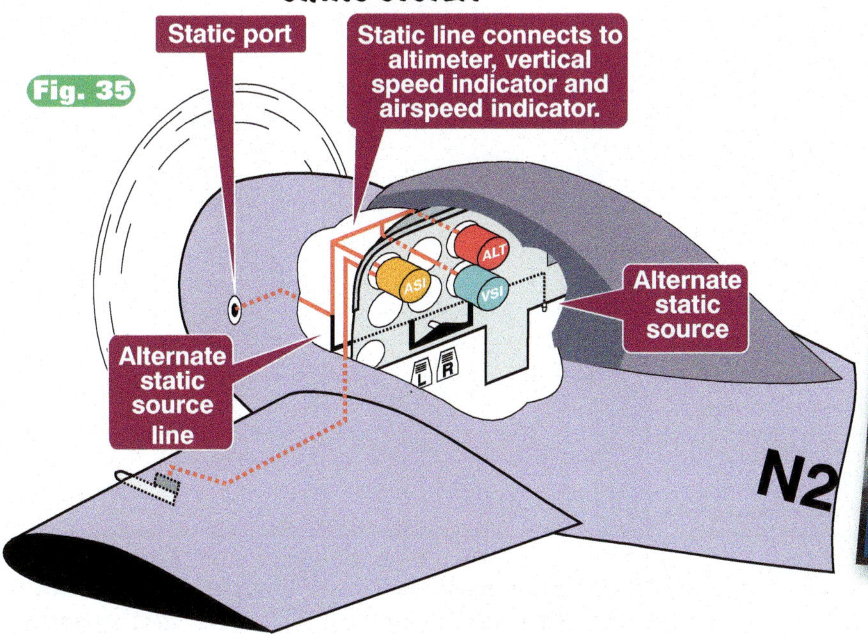

The alternate static source is activated by this valve in the cockpit (Note: Valve location and appearance will vary between airplanes.)

The Gyroscopic Instruments

The Attitude Indicator

The *attitude indicator* or *artificial horizon* is one of three gyroscopic instruments in the airplane. The other two are the heading indicator and the turn coordinator. The attitude indicator (Figure 37) is located in the top middle of the panel's six primary instruments. Consider this. If you acquired something important, like Leonardo da Vinci's "Mona Lisa" or its famed counterpart, the "Mona Larry," you'd put it on the wall for everyone would see. Well, that's why the attitude indicator is put smack in the middle of the instrument panel. You can safely assume it has considerable importance in order to merit such a position.

The attitude indicator provides you with attitude information in much the same way the outside, visible horizon does. Attitude indicators become especially valuable when the outside horizon is no longer visible. Accidentally flying into the clouds, flying in very hazy conditions toward the sun or night flight over the desert are all conditions where the attitude indicator helps you determine the airplane's pitch and bank condition (the only thing the attitude indicator can't help you with is when rear seat passengers put their hands over your eyes and say, "Guess where?" This is why you carry fire extinguishers in the airplane—one warning shot and they always let go).

Figure 38 shows how the attitude indicator presents its pitch and bank information. The basis of this presentation is a symbolic set of airplane wings resting over a moveable horizon card. Painted directly onto the horizon card is a white horizon line, a light colored area above the line representing the sky and a darker colored area below representing the ground (Even in smoggy Los Angeles, these two colors shouldn't be reversed). Bank and pitch markings are also shown on the card.

The symbolic wings are attached to the instrument's case, while the horizon card is free to rotate underneath them. Because the horizon card is mechanically attached to a stabilized gyro, it essentially remains fixed in space while the airplane rotates about it during flight. This gives the impression the symbolic airplane wings are the things that move (they don't move since they're attached to the instrument's case which is bolted to the instrument panel).

Figure 39 shows a sequence of variable attitude conditions on the face of the attitude indicator. (Remember, in each case the airplane has pitched or rolled around the horizon card that's remaining stationary in space.) A straight and level pitch attitude is shown on attitude indi-

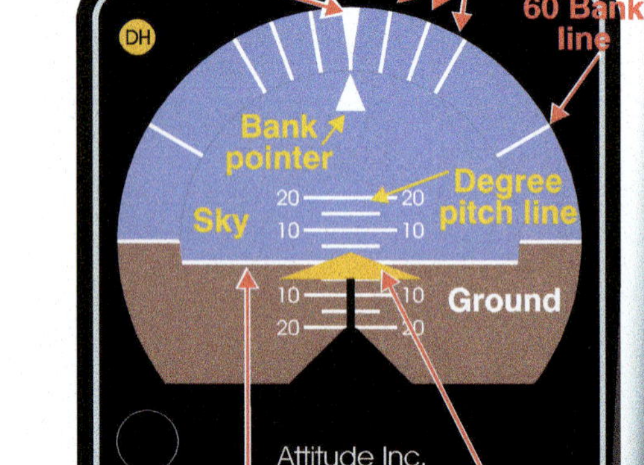

Fig. 38

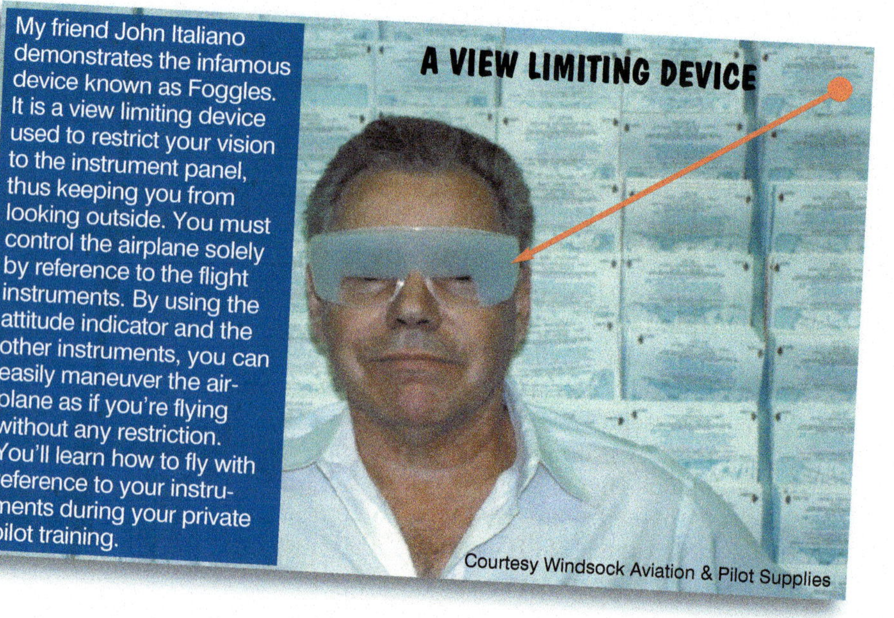

My friend John Italiano demonstrates the infamous device known as Foggles. It is a view limiting device used to restrict your vision to the instrument panel, thus keeping you from looking outside. You must control the airplane solely by reference to the flight instruments. By using the attitude indicator and the other instruments, you can easily maneuver the airplane as if you're flying without any restriction. You'll learn how to fly with reference to your instruments during your private pilot training.

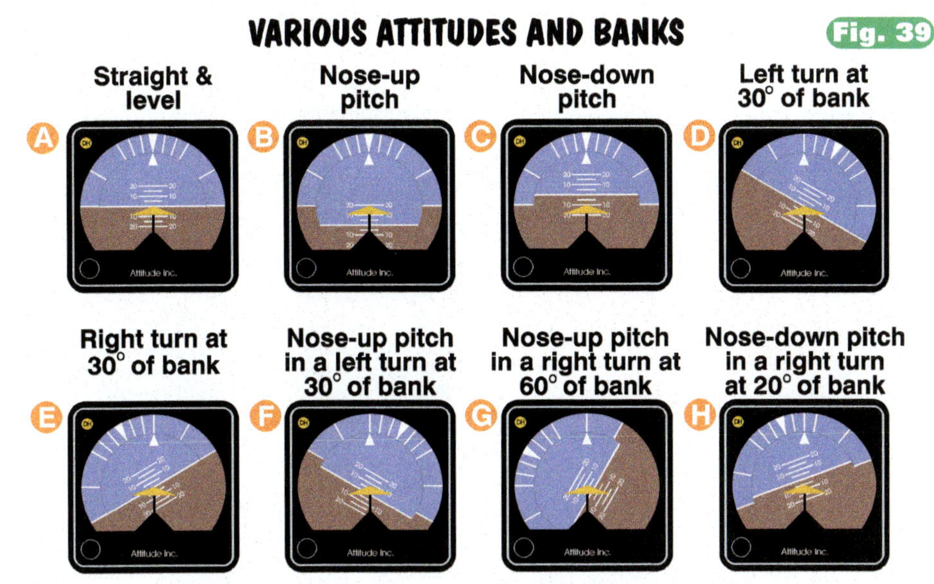

cator A. You know the airplane is flying straight because the symbolic airplane wings are not banked. The airplane's nose is level with the horizon, indicating it is probably holding its altitude (that's *probably* since we'd need to look at the altimeter to be sure). The picture made by the reference airplane is similar to the way reality looks out of your airplane's front windscreen during flight.

Attitude indicator B shows the airplane in straight flight with a nose-up pitch attitude. The little symbolic airplane's nose (the white ball—the head of a bald pilot) rests a little above the 10° pitch up index and the wings are level. Remember, the little airplane in the attitude indicator isn't moving, it's the horizon card behind the symbolic airplane that does all the moving (I'll explain how it does this in a moment).

Attitude indicator C depicts straight flight with a nose-down pitch attitude. The airplane's wings are level and the nose is pointed below the horizon.

Attitude indicator D depicts a left turn in a level pitch attitude. Sometimes it's a little difficult to determine which way the airplane is banked. Ask yourself, "Which wing is pointed toward the ground?" In this picture it's obvious that the left wing is pointed downward. The airplane must be in a left turn. I do hope this is as obvious as a chin strap on a toupee. After all, if the left wing is pointed to the ground, you should be making a left turn. The only time this wouldn't be true is if you're inverted. And if you're making inverted turns at this point in your career, then you either need more dual instruction or you have been anointed by Chuck Yeager or Neil Armstrong (in other words, you probably don't need to read this book).

Another important question to ask is, "If you wanted to return to straight flight in attitude indicator D, which wing would you raise?" (you've got a 50-50 chance on this one). Yes, the left wing. It's the one dipping toward the ground. If you ever lost sight of the horizon, you could maintain straight flight by simply asking which wing needs raising. Then you'd simply keep the small white ball on the white horizon line to maintain a level pitch attitude. Keep in mind that we refer to straight flight as both wings being parallel with the horizon and level flight as the airplane maintaining a constant altitude (when looking strictly at the attitude indicator we sometimes refer to *zero degrees* of nose up or down pitch as a "level pitch attitude"). Attitude indicator D shows the airplane in a level pitch attitude while in a bank.

What type of turn does attitude indicator E show? Ask yourself, "Which wing is pointed toward the ground?" The answer is, the right wing. The airplane is in a right turn. The vertical indicator at the top of the instrument points to the 30° bank increment (each of the first three indices represent 10° of bank). Therefore, the airplane is in a 30° right bank. If you wanted to return to straight and level flight, which way would you turn? You must turn the control wheel to the left to raise the right wing and return to straight flight.

Attitude indicator F depicts an airplane in a nose-up pitch attitude while in left 30° bank turn. Attitude indicator G shows an airplane in a nose-up pitch attitude while in a right turn at a very steep 60° of bank. Finally, attitude indicator H shows

GOOD GRIEF!

We were on a pleasure flight to an airport in the foothills of a mountain range...I flew over the airport at what I thought was 1000' above pattern altitude to check wind direction, then began a turn and descent to join the pattern. The hills seemed uncomfortably close as I turned to 45 degree entry, even though I still hadn't reached my target altitude. Ground features on downwind leg were closer than I remembered, even though I was still 1000' high. An uneasy feeling of things not being right was forming when Unicom called a warning to "aircraft on downwind at low altitude." By that time I had turned from base to final and saw that making a normal landing would be chancy, at best. I immediately initiated a go-around, still not understanding what had gone wrong. After getting things stabilized I glanced down at the airport information sheet clipped to the yoke and saw, to my horror, that the "pattern" altitude I had been descending to was, in reality, the altitude of the airport!

ASRS Report

When things don't look right, immediately start asking questions, mentally and verbally. On Unicom ask if they can verify the altimeter setting. If the altimeter setting checks out, verify the pattern altitude. Pilots like to help one another. Flying foolishly is a lot more hazardous to your health than swallowing some pride and requesting help.

D.T.

PITCH ATTITUDE AND FLIGHT CONDITIONS

All three airplanes have similar attitude indications on the attitude indicator.

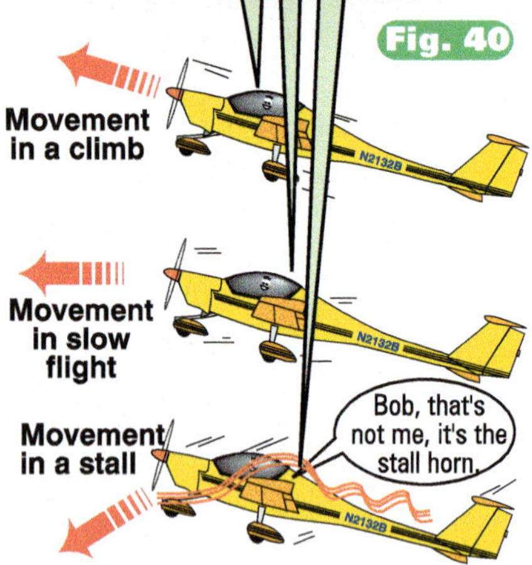

an airplane in a nose-down pitch attitude while in a right turn at 20° of bank.

Have you noticed that I have not mentioned climbing or descending in reference to pitch attitude? Even though a nose-up pitch attitude is normally associated with a climb, there are occasions where it's not. For instance, Figure 40 shows three different flight conditions associated with a nose-up pitch attitude. The airplane may either be climbing with full power, cruising with limited power, or stalling with no power. All these conditions are associated with a nose-up pitch attitude. When flying by reference to instruments, the only way you can tell what your airplane is doing is to consult some of the other flight instruments. You will learn about this a little later on.

How does the attitude indicator (as well as the other gyro-based instruments) accomplish the mysterious task of portraying attitude? It does this through a gyroscopic principle

GYROSCOPIC RIGIDITY IN SPACE

A child's toy top stays vertical or rigid in space when spun. When not spun, it easily falls to its side.

The same principle applies to modern day gyro instruments. A spinning gyro remains fixed in space allowing the airplane to rotate around it.

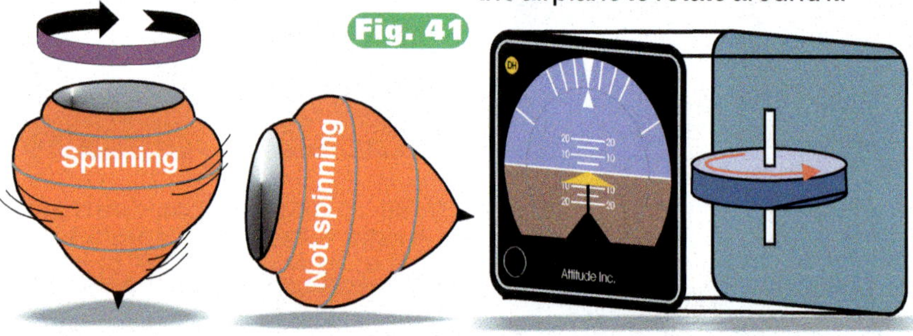

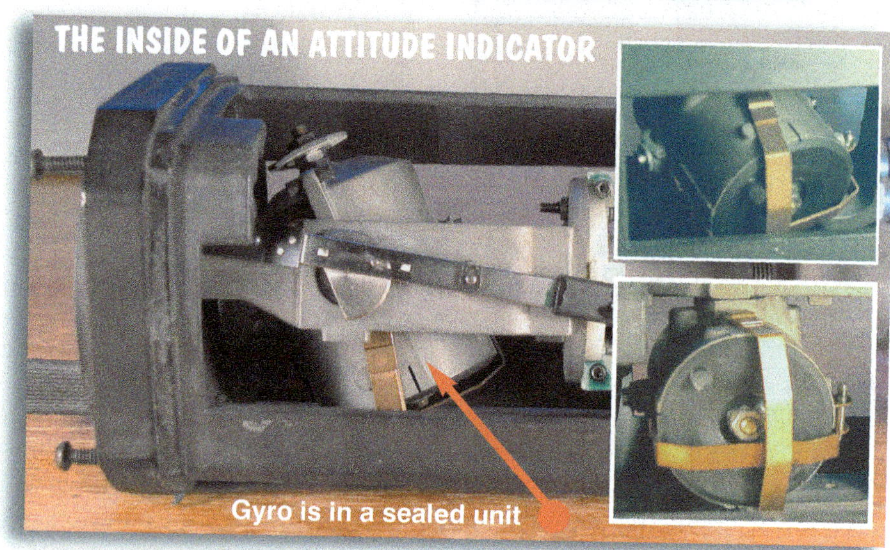

THE ATTITUDE INDICATOR

When the attitude indicator's gyro is spun by air, it remains rigid or fixed in space. The airplane rotates around the gyro and mechanically converts this movement into pitch and bank information on the face of the horizon card.

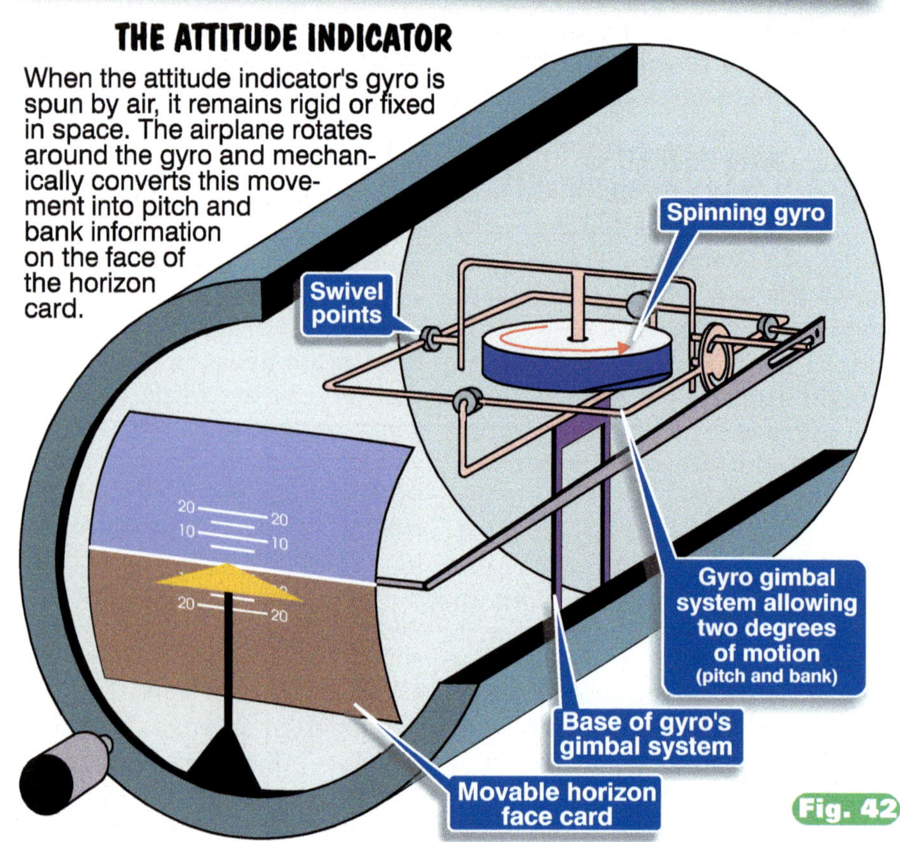

THE HORIZON LINE

The attitude indicator's horizon line remains parallel to the earth's surface at all times and the sky pointer always points upward toward the sky.

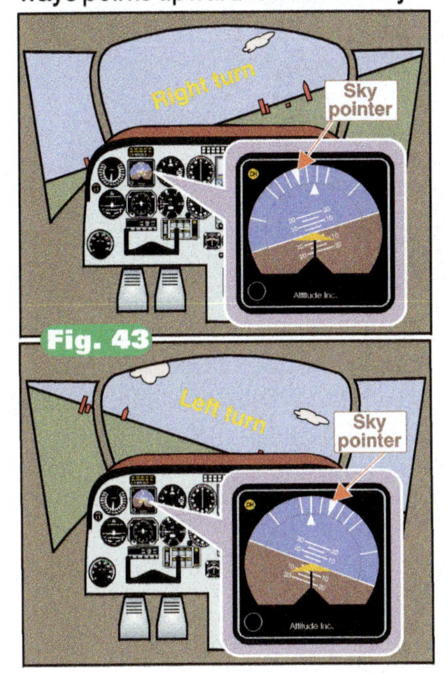

known as *rigidity in space*. Figure 41 shows a child's top in full spin. A spinning top, just like a spinning wheel inside the attitude indicator (Figure 41), acquires the unusual property known as rigidity in space. A small wheel (a gyro) spun at high speed tends to remain in a fixed or rigid position. That's why the child's top remains upright until is stops spinning. It's this property that allows the attitude indicator's horizon card to portray airplane attitude.

The internal workings of the attitude indicator are displayed in Figure 42. While this is a highly simplified drawing, it does allow you to understand the principles upon which the attitude indicator works. Notice the circular disk in the center of the instrument. This is the gyroscope. It is mechanically connected to the sky/ground horizon card on the face of the indicator. When spun, this disk takes on gyroscopic properties and maintains its position, fixed in space, relative to the earth. Thus, the horizon's face card, which is mechanically connected to the gyro, also remains fixed in space. From inside the airplane, the horizon face card accurately represents the real horizon in either a right or left hand turn as shown in Figure 43. As you can clearly see, the airplane rotates about the attitude indicator's gyro-stabilized (fixed) horizon card.

Most light airplane attitude gyros are spun by air pressure. A vacuum pump (Figure 44) sucks air through the instrument and over the gyro, spinning it at high velocity (Figure

THE SUCTION GAUGE

4"
5"
6"
Suction inches of Hg
Fig. 46

Operation within the green arc tells you that all your gyro instruments are getting enough vacuum pressure for proper operation.

45). This system is known as the *vacuum system* (and this isn't something you use to keep your airplane clean!).

Notice that the vacuum pump is connected to two instruments—the attitude indicator and the heading indicator. Both these instruments use gyroscopes that are typically spun by vacuum air pressure. You may also come across an airplane with a heading indicator whose gyros are electrically spun. Either way, the spinning of a gyro allows these instruments to work their magic.

Malfunctions of the airplane's air-spun gyro instruments are usually caused by the vacuum pump providing insufficient vacuum pressure. An airplane's vacuum gauge (Figure 46) keeps you informed about the

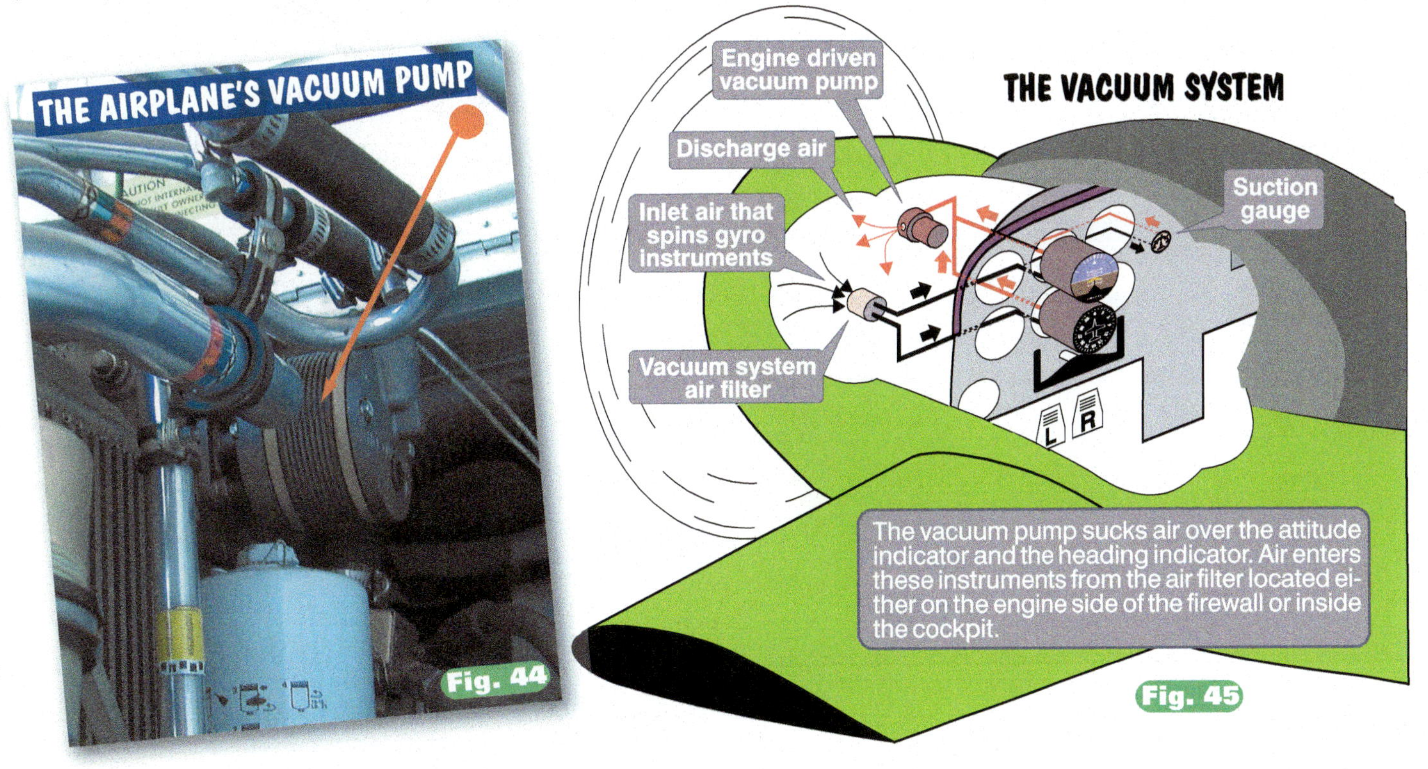

ATTITUDE INDICATOR ADJUSTMENT KNOB

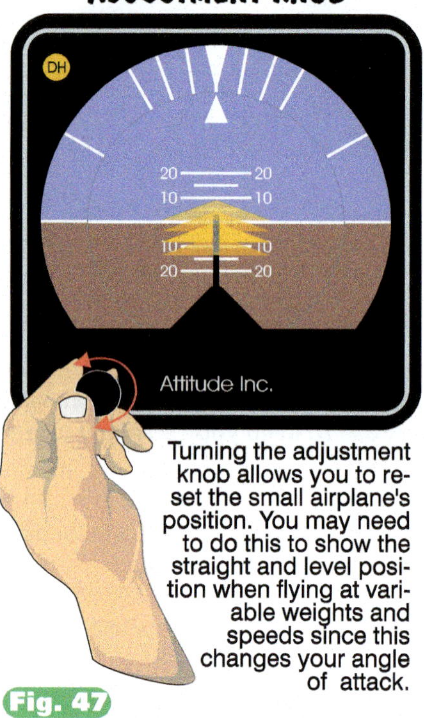

Turning the adjustment knob allows you to reset the small airplane's position. You may need to do this to show the straight and level position when flying at variable weights and speeds since this changes your angle of attack.

Fig. 47

amount of suction provided by the pump. Operations outside the normal range (green arc) on the gauge usually result in erroneous readings on your gyro instruments. On some airplanes, low power settings (such as a low engine idle before takeoff or long, low-power descents) produce insufficient vacuum for the instruments. Simply increasing power slightly usually takes care of the problem.

THE ATTITUDE INDICATOR'S DIAGONAL BANK LINES

Fig. 48

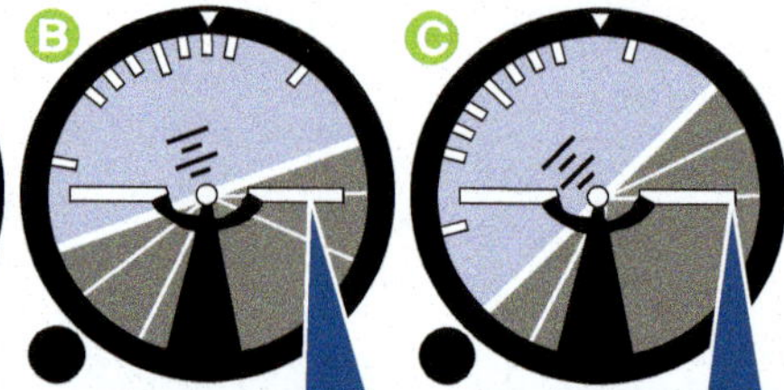
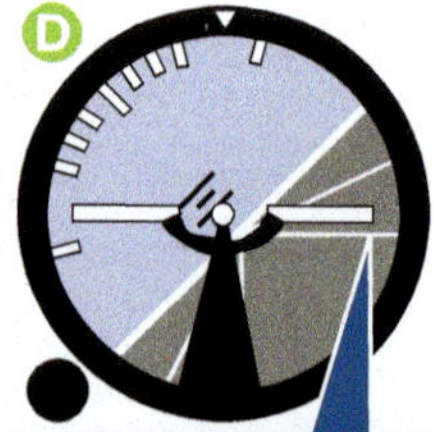
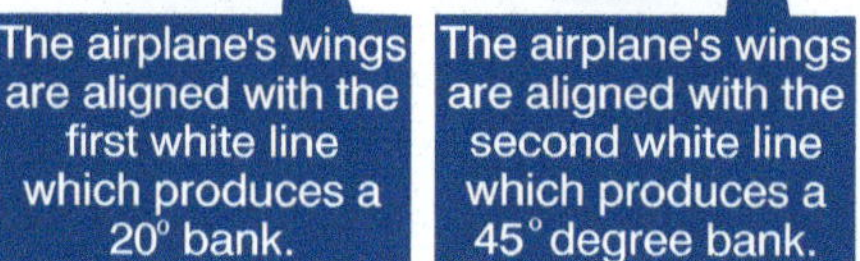

A: These are the attitude indicator's 20° & 45° bank lines (sometimes it's a 15° bank line vs. a 20° bank line).

B: The airplane's wings are aligned with the first white line which produces a 20° bank.

C: The airplane's wings are aligned with the second white line which produces a 45° degree bank.

D: The wings are above and parallel with the 45° bank line. The airplane is in a nose-up attitude at a 45° bank.

Here are a few more things about the attitude indicator you should know. First, observe the little knob on the bottom left of the instrument in Figure 47. Rotating this knob moves the reference airplane up or down in the attitude indicator's window. This allows you to set the symbolic wings precisely on the horizon line before takeoff and in flight. It's sometimes necessary to adjust the symbolic wings since there are several variables that can change the attitude required for level flight. These variables might be either the weight of the airplane or the speed at which it is flown.

The attitude indicator has bank markings calibrated at 10°, 20° and 30° increments with an additional calibration at 60° (there are no calibrations above 60° since no denture adhesive has been shown to work at these G-forces). But these bank indices don't help much if you're trying to do a 45° bank turn do they? Fortunately, some attitude indicators have diagonal bank lines that help identify additional bank angles. Figure 48 shows the 20° and 45° white bank marks on the bottom portions of these particular types of attitude indicators.

Banking the airplane so the symbolic wings are aligned with the first diagonal line, as shown in position B, produces a bank of 20° (on some instruments it produces a 15° bank). Further banking so the wings are aligned with the second diagonal line produces a 45° bank as shown in position C. What's informative about these bank lines is that they also provide you with pitch information as shown in position D. In other words, these bank lines also provide you with a horizon reference.

The next time you try a 45° bank turn, place the symbolic airplane's wings on or slightly above the second diagonal bank line and keep them there. You'll find the bank line acts like the horizon line in level flight. You can use the bank line as an attitude reference instead of keeping the little white ball on the horizon line. The diagonal bank line is easier to use as a pitch reference than the little white ball.

Fig. 49

THE HEADING INDICATOR

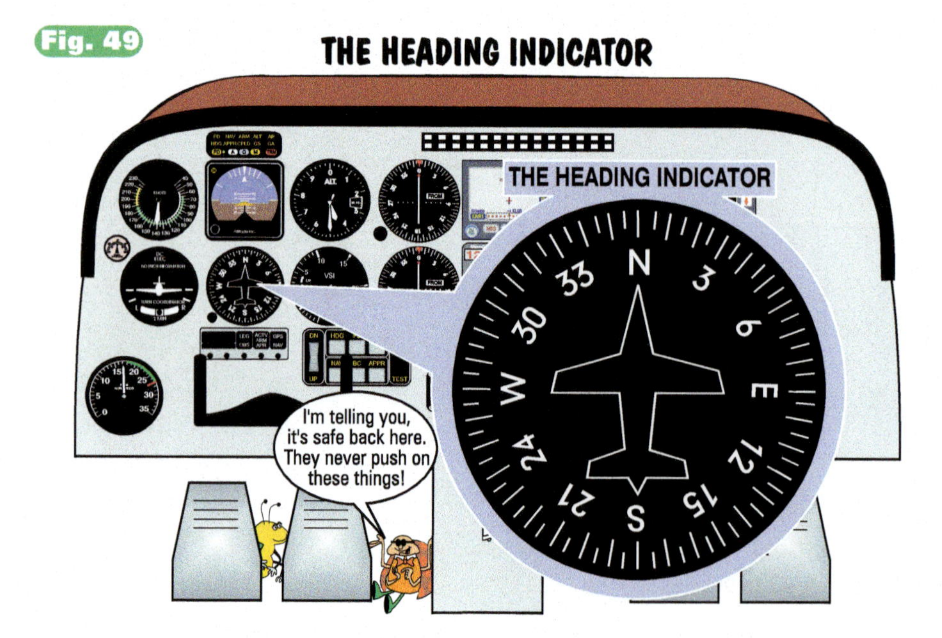

The Heading Indicator

The airplane's *heading indicator* is shown in Figure 49. Sometimes called the *directional gyro* or *DG*, the heading indicator is a gyro instrument that provides the same information

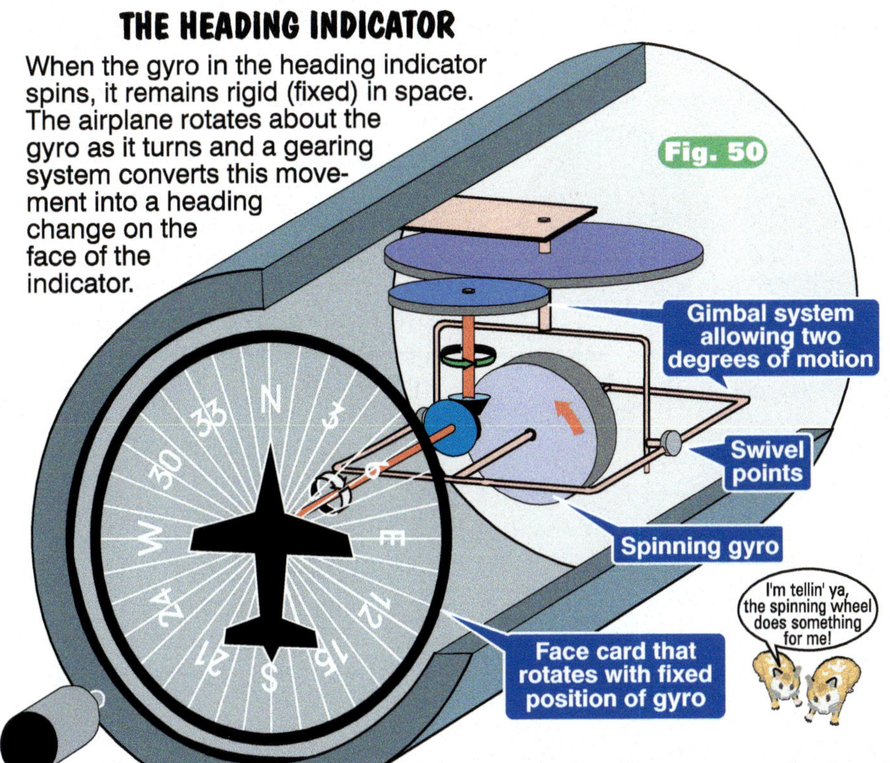

THE HEADING INDICATOR

When the gyro in the heading indicator spins, it remains rigid (fixed) in space. The airplane rotates about the gyro as it turns and a gearing system converts this movement into a heading change on the face of the indicator.

found on the magnetic compass—heading information. Why have two instruments to do one job? Because the magnetic compass is an instrument best read by one of those bobbing dolls you see in the back window shelf of cars. Like some passengers, the magnetic compass makes a poor candidate for air transport. The heading indicator is an attempt to remedy some of the ills of the magnetic compass, though the latter remains a key component in your pilot's instrument kit—without it, you wouldn't be able to set the heading indicator in the first place.

On the face of the heading indicator is a small outline of a stationary airplane superimposed over a compass card that's free to rotate. The nose of the small outline airplane always points straight up to a number that is your airplane's present heading. As the actual airplane turns, the compass card remains stabilized or fixed in space by an internal spinning gyro, as shown in Figure 50. The small outline airplane points to your airplane's magnetic heading.

Before takeoff, after the gyros have had sufficient time to spin up, set the heading indicator to the heading shown on the magnetic compass. Do this by pushing and rotating the heading indicator's adjustment knob, as shown in Figure 51. Once the heading indicator is set to the compass' magnetic heading, it should provide accurate directional information for a reasonable period of time. Like a cautious parent, you need to check up on this child occasionally, lest it wander. How much it wanders, and when, depends on how affected the heading indicator is by something known as *gyroscopic drift*.

Gyroscopic heading drift is caused by internal mechanical errors and/or the airplane's constantly changing position in space relative to the earth. The most important thing to remember is to keep checking or updating the reading on the heading indicator with the magnetic compass at least every 15 minutes. Do this more often if your airplane's heading indicator has a history of wandering, which is sometimes referred to as *precessing*. Despite gyroscopic drift, the heading indicator is much easier to use for navigation than the magnetic compass (as you'll soon see when we study the magnetic compass' errors).

Notice that the heading indicator in Figure 51 is calibrated in five degree increments. Every 30°, starting from north, is referenced by printed letters or numerals that are sometimes called *cardinal numbers* (which sounds much better than *archbishop numbers*). Between the letters and numerals are slashes, calibrated to five and ten degree increments. The slashes at 10° increments are slightly larger for easier identification (however, if the eye doctor tells you, based on your current eyeglass prescription, that you're only two lenses away from being a fly, you may need to move closer to the panel).

The heading indicator in Figure 51 shows that the airplane is currently heading north. This is called *360 degrees* or *zero* degrees, depending on who's talking. Either value is correct. The *E* represents east or 90°, *S* represents south or 180° and *W* represents west or 270°. If you want to sound like a pro, don't call them by the letters. I actually heard a pilot call a controller and say, "Ahhh, this is 2132 Bravo, ahhh, I'd like vectors to the airport." The controller said, "Roger 32 Bravo, what's your heading?" The pilot replied, "Ahhh,.. my heading is *Eeee!*" The controller came

HEADING INDICATOR

The outline airplane's nose in the heading indicator points to the actual airplane's magnetic heading. As the airplane turns, the numbered disk rotates under the outline airplane, allowing your new heading to appear on top.

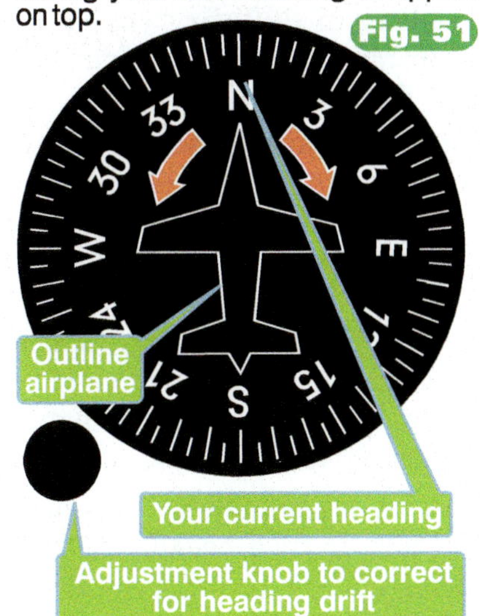

DIFFERENT HEADINGS

Heading
"zero-three-zero"

Fig. 52

back with, "Well, 32 Bravo, your heading is aiming you at another airplane, I suggest you do a *W* before you bump into it."

Heading indicator A in Figure 52 shows the airplane heading 30°. This is pronounced, "zero-three-zero degrees." Indicator B shows a heading of 140°. This is pronounced "one-four-zero degrees." Indicator C shows a heading of 300° or "three-zero-zero degrees." Indicator D depicts a heading of 305° or "three-zero-five degrees."

If you're instructed to turn to a particular heading, simply look for the number on the instrument and turn in the shortest direction toward it, unless instructed to "turn the long way" or "go the long way around." (This is similar to how we flight instructors find the exquisite dining facilities we're known to frequent. We simply turn in the direction of the nearest drive-through speaker).

Referring to Indicator B, which way would you turn to fly a heading of 60°? Yes, a left turn would be the shortest direction to get to a heading of 60°. If you were instructed to fly a heading of 240° in the same figure, which way would you turn? Of course, a turn to the right would be the shortest direction to the new heading.

One last word on heading indicators. If you accidentally fly into a cloud, you can fly back out by making a 180° turn (something General Custer should have done shortly after leaving the fort). One of the biggest mistakes pilots make when starting a 180° turn is in forgetting to look at the heading representing 180 degrees of turn. Simply look at the tail (the bottom) of the outline-airplane and turn to the number it points to. This is similar to looking for the nearest exit in a hotel. You need to know exactly where to go (what heading to turn to for 180° of turn) if you need a quick exit (especially true if the hotel has a name like "La Casa de Flash Fire").

For instance, if you accidentally flew into the clouds while on a heading of 030° as shown by heading indicator A, what heading would you turn to? The tail points to a heading of 210°. Simply establish a 15 or 20° bank on the attitude indicator while keeping the airplane's attitude level with the horizon. When 210° appears at the top of the heading indicator, you've completed the turn. Roll the wings level and wait for blue sky to appear.

The Turn Coordinator

The turn coordinator sounds like the guy who calls those commands at a square dance (square dance is the

THE TURN COORDINATOR

Fig. 53

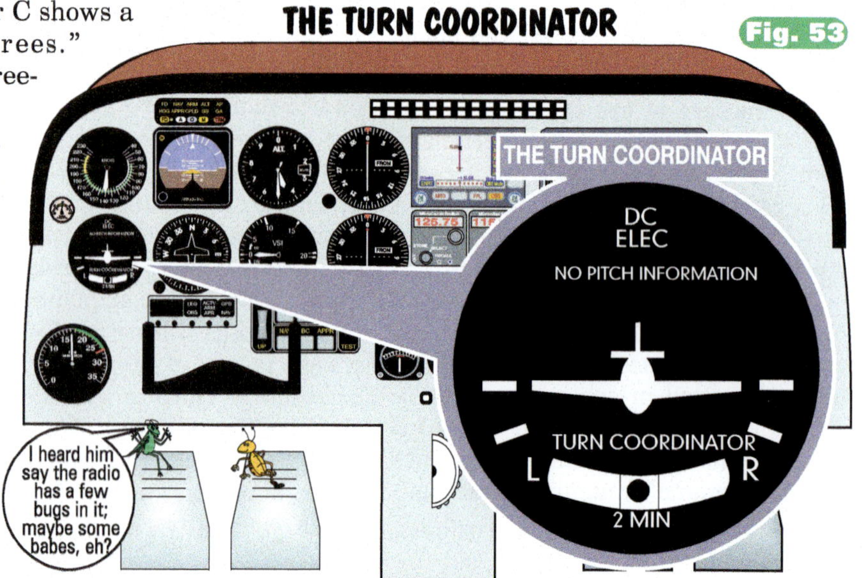

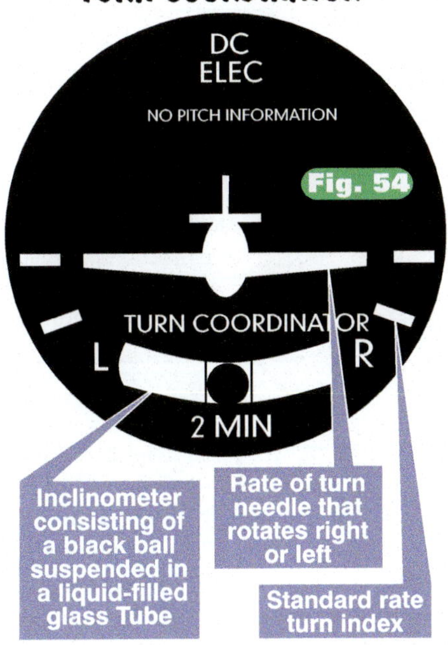

original source of rap music). The turn coordinator (Figure 53) is actually a gyro instrument that provides information on your airplane's direction of roll, rate of heading change and whether the airplane is slipping or skidding in the turns (i.e., movement about its yaw and roll axes).

Turn coordinators consist of two instruments: a needle and an inclinometer (Figure 54). We've already discussed the inclinometer in Chapter 2, so let's concentrate on the turn needle. The turn needle consists of a small symbolic airplane in the center of the instrument capable of rotating right or left.

Unlike the spinning gyros in the attitude indicator and heading indicator, the turn coordinator's gyro is usually spun by electricity. This is what causes the whining sound you hear when the airplane's master switch is first turned on during preflight (if you hear the whining and you aren't in the airplane, it could be coming from a sorrowful student whose airplane is down for maintenance). The turn coordinator's gyro is electrically powered, to keep at least one gyro instrument operating during a rare failure of the airplane's vacuum pump. For instrument pilots, this is a blessing. In the event the vacuum pump fails, the airplane's lateral control (not pitch control) can be maintained with the turn coordinator alone.

Figure 55 shows the internal workings of the turn coordinator. The turn coordinator's gyro is free to move in only one dimension, instead of three like that of the attitude indicator. During any rolling, turning, or yawing movement, the instrument's gyro feels a force applied to its side.

Say What?

"Ground Control told me to taxi to Runway 22. I taxied to an intersection at Runway 22, then I called the tower who told me to line up and wait (on the runway). I taxied onto the runway facing 220 degrees, ready for takeoff. I had about 600-700 feet behind me. The tower cleared me for takeoff then said, "Turn left 180 degrees immediately," while I was still on the runway. So I did a 180 degree turn on the runway and made a short field takeoff at the end of runway 04 and departed.... I was nervous and uptight about flying in Class C airspace for the first time. I was also worried about getting home before dark.... I should have thought about what the controller said before I acted...."

All things considered, not a bad carrier takeoff. **ASRS Report**

This causes the gyro to precess in a predictable manner.

To present turn information, the turn coordinator relies on a principle known as *gyroscopic precession*. Precession causes a force applied to a spinning body (the gyro), to be felt 90° in the direction of rotation. To most people, gyroscopic precession is as much a mystery as is a cargo airline that hires flight attendants. If you're interested in how precession

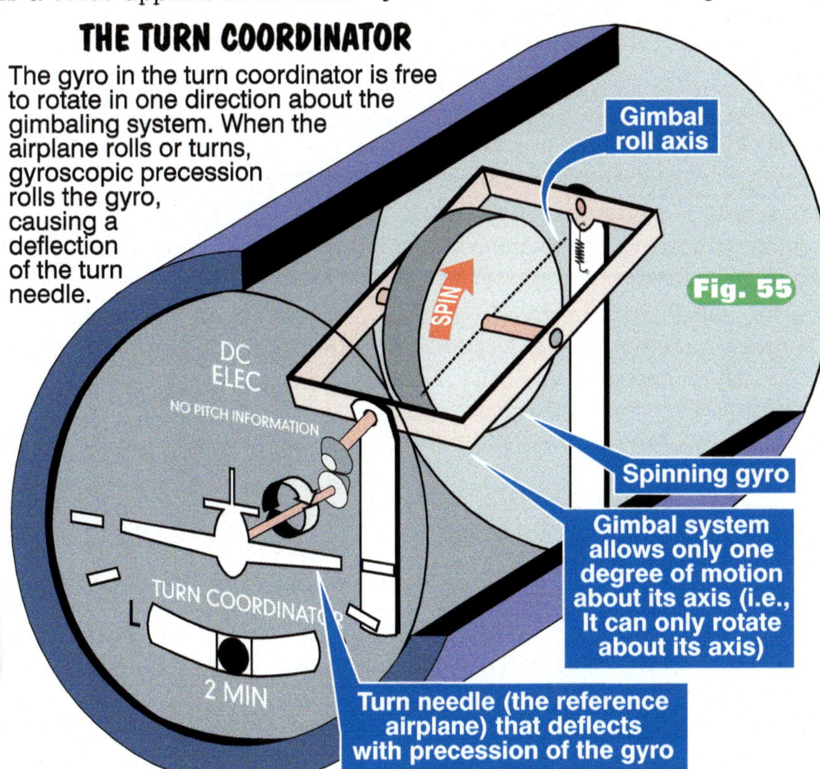

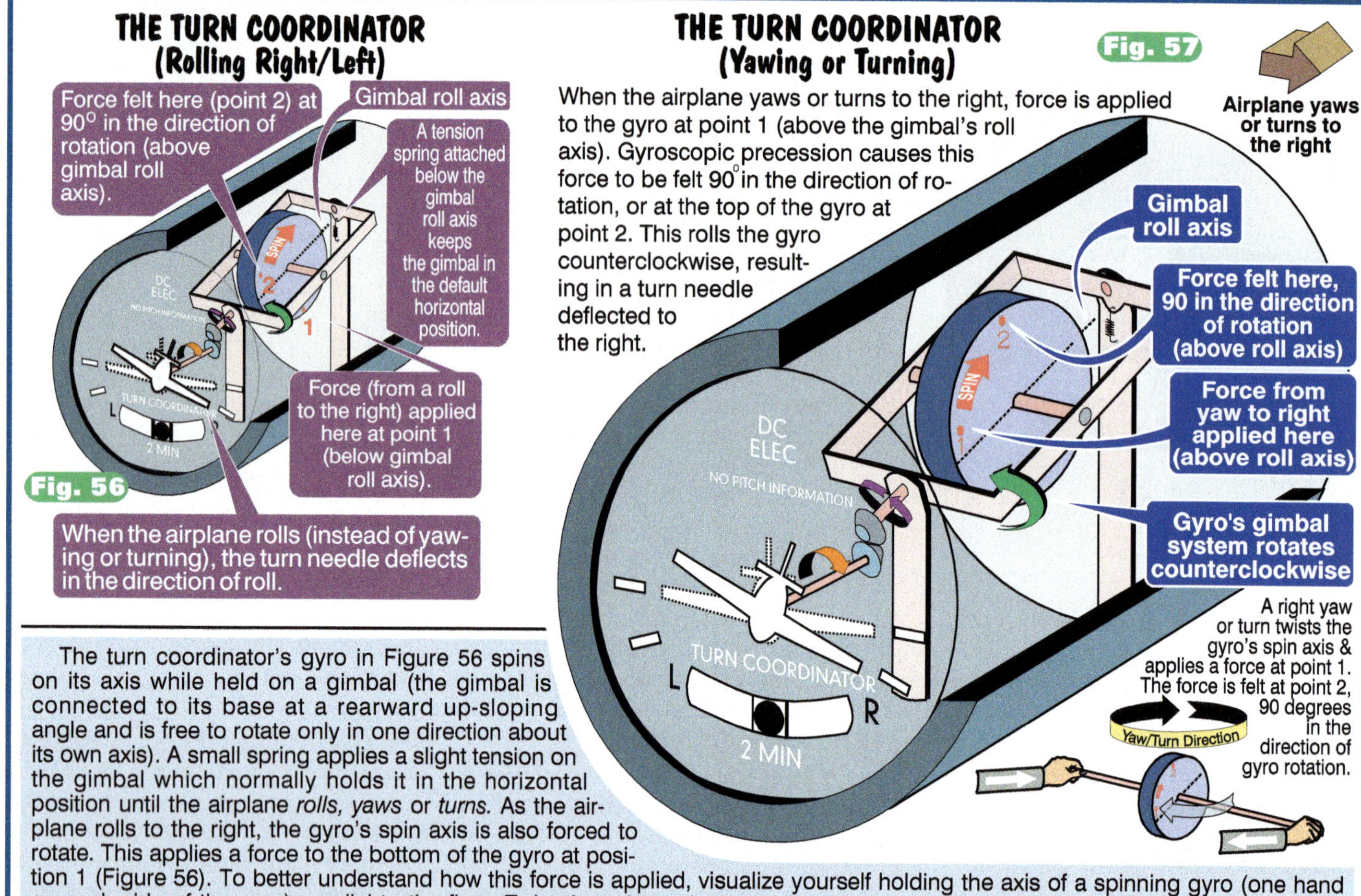

The turn coordinator's gyro in Figure 56 spins on its axis while held on a gimbal (the gimbal is connected to its base at a rearward up-sloping angle and is free to rotate only in one direction about its own axis). A small spring applies a slight tension on the gimbal which normally holds it in the horizontal position until the airplane *rolls, yaws* or *turns.* As the airplane rolls to the right, the gyro's spin axis is also forced to rotate. This applies a force to the bottom of the gyro at position 1 (Figure 56). To better understand how this force is applied, visualize yourself holding the axis of a spinning gyro (one hand on each side of the gyro) parallel to the floor. Twist the axis so that your right hand moves toward the ground and the left hand moves toward the ceiling. This simulates an airplane rolling to the right and results in a force applied to the gyro at position 1. Gyroscopic precession causes this force to be felt 90 degrees in the direction of gyro rotation at position 2. Since position 2 is above the gimbal's roll axis in Figure 56 (remember, the gimbal slopes at a rearward angle), the gimbal rotates counterclockwise. Mechanical gearing results in the *turn needle* (symbolic reference airplane) deflecting to the right, thus indicating a roll to the right.

In addition to the direction of roll, the turn coordinator also shows the direction of *yaw* and the *rate* at which the airplane changes *headings* (Figure 57). Yawing to the right applies a force to the gyro above the gimbal's roll axis at position 1. (See the small insert at the bottom right of Figure 57 to understand how the *yaw* or *turning* force is felt by the gyro.) Gyroscopic precession results in this force being felt 90 degrees in the direction of gyro rotation at position 2. This causes the gimbal system to rotate counterclockwise and, because of mechanical gearing, deflects the turn needle to the right. Once *established* in a right turn, this force is continually applied to position 1, resulting in a needle deflection which represents the airplane's rate of turn (how fast the nose moves across the horizon). The turn needle doesn't represent the angle of bank. It only shows direction of roll, yaw and the rate of turn. In fact, it's possible to bank the airplane to the right (or left) while adding opposite rudder to keep the nose from moving (heading is constant) and the turn needle shouldn't deflect. Try it with your instructor.

works, see Postflight Briefing #5-1, *Gyroscopic Precession Explained.* Other than personal curiosity, there is absolutely no need for you to understand how gyroscopic precession actually works. I provide the information for the intensely curious among you as well as for those who have taken up reading since your satellite dish was stolen.

Even though it may appear to, the turn coordinator doesn't show bank angle. Don't be fooled by this. Only *direction* of roll or yaw and *rate of turn* are derivable from the turn coordinator. Refer to the attitude indicator for bank angle.

Figure 58 shows two turn coordinators, each with a different amount of wing deflection on the symbolic airplane. Airplane A's wing is deflected to the white index mark indicating the airplane's heading is changing at 3° per second. In aviation parlance this is called a *standard rate turn.* Since there are 360 degrees in a full circle, it takes 120 seconds or two minutes to make a complete turn (360°/3° per second). This is why the instrument is labeled *2 min turn.*

Some students think this means we're going to cook in the cockpit and use the turn coordinator as an elegant means of knowing when to flip the waffles. You'll soon find that the only waffling in the cockpit will be by the pilot-in-training.

Miniature airplane B's wings are deflected halfway between the zero and three degree per second turn marks. The rate of turn is 1.5° per second. At this slower rate, the airplane takes twice as long to make a complete 360° turn.

Fig. 58

RATE OF TURN ON THE TURN COORDINATOR

Standard rate turn of 3 degrees per second

Half standard rate turn of 1.5 degrees per second

A

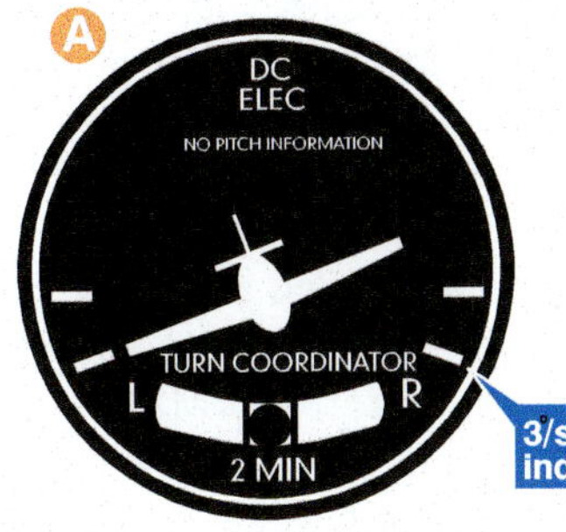

3/sec index

B

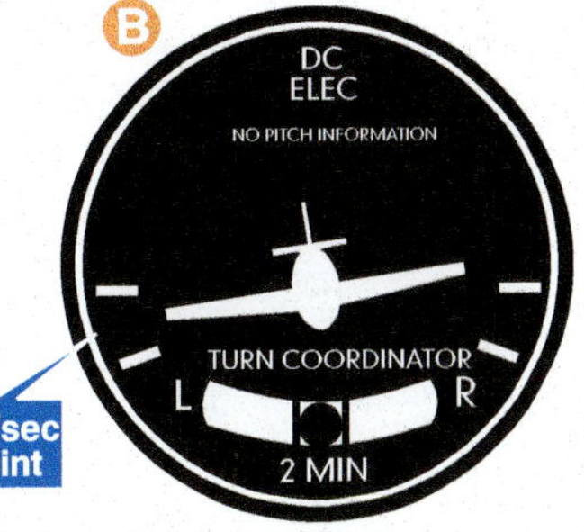

1.5/sec point

Both airplanes were previously established in a turn passing through a heading of 300 degrees.

297° 300°

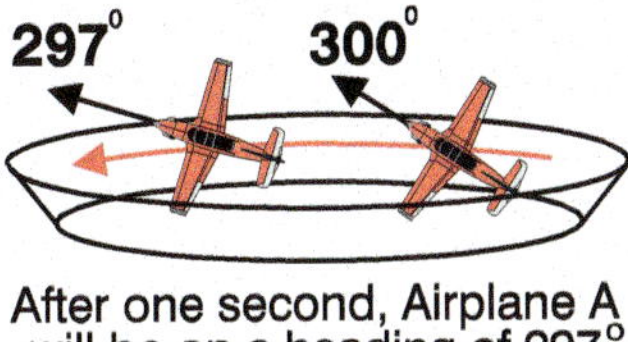

298.5° 300°

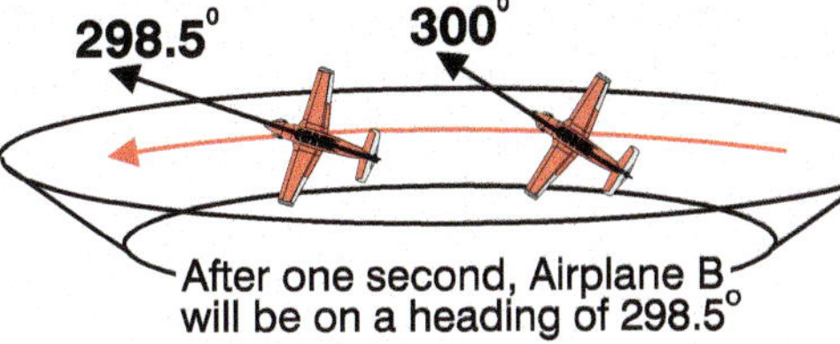

After one second, Airplane A will be on a heading of 297°

After one second, Airplane B will be on a heading of 298.5°

CHECKING THAT LIST...AND CHECKING IT TWICE

I did my runup but failed to set my heading indicator to coincide with my magnetic compass...was cleared for an immediate departure due to traffic on a short base (ready to turn final). I spotted that traffic, then proceeded on my takeoff roll without hesitation. I usually make another takeoff check of all my systems before starting my roll. I was handed off by the tower to Departure which instructed me to climb to 2,500 MSL on a heading of 320°. I had just settled on that heading when I was instructed to turn to 280°. My heading indicator was about 100° off so instead of 280° I was really flying 180° and climbing....

ASRS Report

Rushing to take the runway before you're really ready is taking a dangerous risk. Just say no and don't go until you're ready.

Why would you want to know the rate at which your airplane changes headings? Assume your heading indicator has failed and you accidentally fly into a cloud (it's obvious you're having an exceptionally bad day here). You could make a precise 180° exit from the cloud by making a standard rate turn for one minute (that's 3°/sec for 60 seconds=180°). This is one of several reasons why the turn coordinator is a very useful instrument. Instrument rated pilots find it useful for helping them anticipate the time it takes to make heading changes. When you venture forth and obtain an instrument rating (a license that allows you to fly in clouds), you'll find the turn coordinator a worthy and welcome ally in the event of attitude gyro failure.

Fig. 59

The Magnetic Compass

A friend of mine purchased a very nervous little puppy. Every time the phone rang, the puppy would wet the floor. My friend contemplated using radiator stop leak to solve the problem but decided on a better plan. He gave the puppy to his super mean mother-in-law. Every afternoon he would call her and ask, "Hey, ...how's your rug?" We call this *controlling an action at a distance.* The magnetic compass is similarly controlled (affected) by something a long distance away.

A *magnetic compass* (Figure 59) responds to the natural phenomena of the earth's magnetic pole, otherwise known as its *magnetic field.* This field is constantly pulling one end of the compass' needle, keeping it pointing north. Despite some peculiar errors in the compass, it is one of the oldest and most reliable navigational instruments known to man (next to moss, which supposedly grows on the north side of trees). In Chapter 11 we'll talk about navigational techniques. For now, let's discuss how the compass

THE MAGNETIC COMPASS NEEDLE

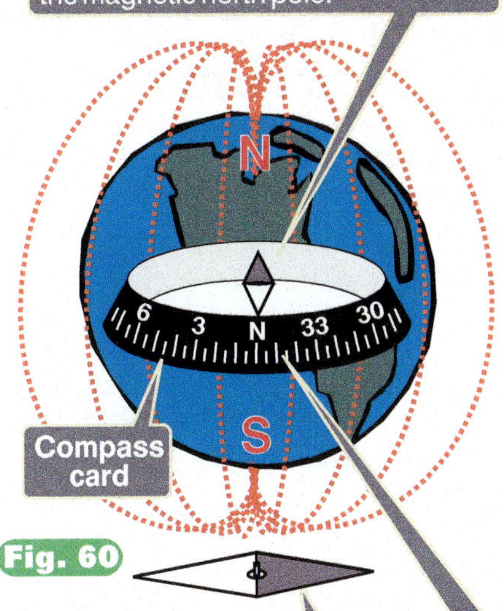

Fig. 60

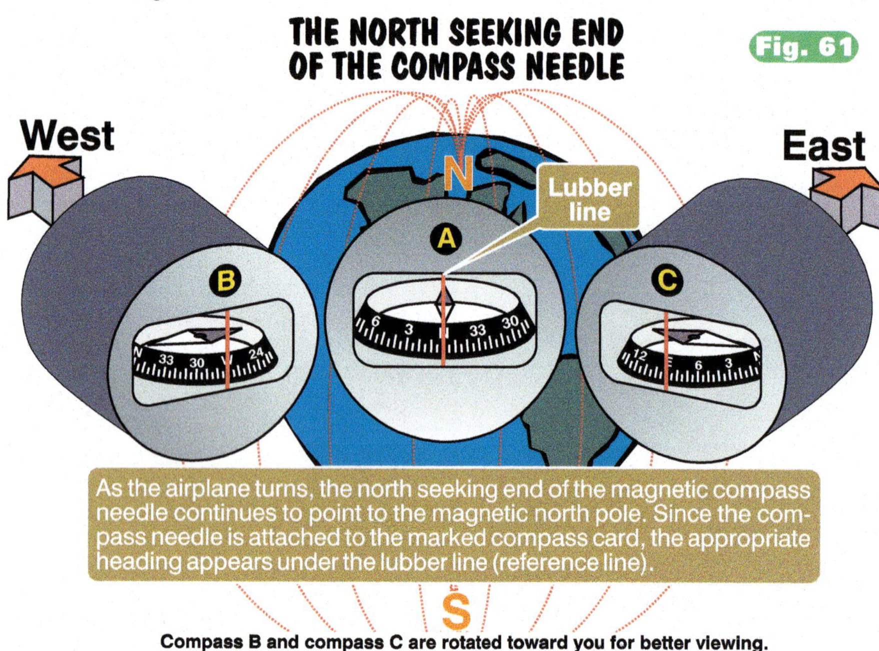

As the airplane turns, the north seeking end of the magnetic compass needle continues to point to the magnetic north pole. Since the compass needle is attached to the marked compass card, the appropriate heading appears under the lubber line (reference line).

Compass B and compass C are rotated toward you for better viewing.

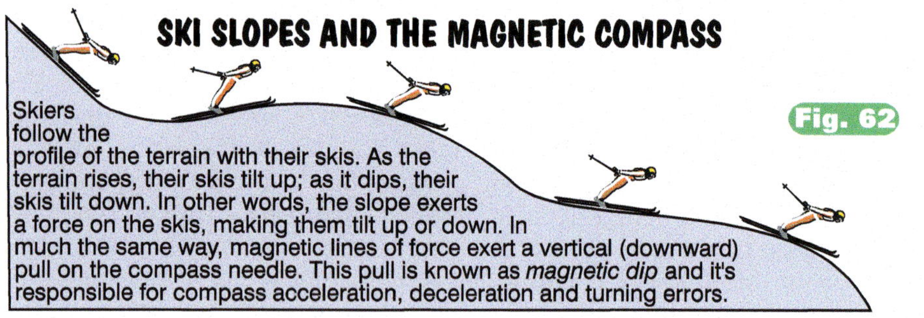

Skiers follow the profile of the terrain with their skis. As the terrain rises, their skis tilt up; as it dips, their skis tilt down. In other words, the slope exerts a force on the skis, making them tilt up or down. In much the same way, magnetic lines of force exert a vertical (downward) pull on the compass needle. This pull is known as *magnetic dip* and it's responsible for compass acceleration, deceleration and turning errors.

works and look at a few of its inherent errors (I don't trust moss as a navigational tool, since all four corners of my shower seem to point north).

Inside the magnetic compass is a small magnetic needle connected to a circular compass card (Figure 60). Both the card and the needle are free to rotate on a central pivot. One side of the needle is called the *north-seeking end* (dark-colored side in all my drawings) and it always points towards the earth's magnetic north pole. Thus, like a gyro fixed in space, the needle attempts to remain stationary. As the airplane changes direction, it rotates around the needle and its attached card, resulting in new headings appearing in the compass' window, as shown in Figure 61 (and all this time you've been thinking that the compass card actually does the rotating. That's OK. A lot of people still think that the Magna Carta is what you use when you're over the limit on your Visa card. The airplane's actual heading is read under a reference line or *lubber line* running down the center of the window.

Notice that the numbers printed on the compass card appear to be in the wrong place. In Figure 61, Compass A is heading north, yet westerly headings are shown on the right side of its card (i.e., 330°, 300° and *W* or 270° which is not visible yet). Easterly headings are shown on the left side of its card (i.e., 030°, 060° and *E* or 090° which is also not yet visible). This makes sense when you consider that as the airplane turns left, toward the west, it pivots about the stationary compass card as shown by Compass B. Eventually, westerly headings appear under the lubber line. A right 90° turn causes the airplane to pivot about the compass card with easterly headings

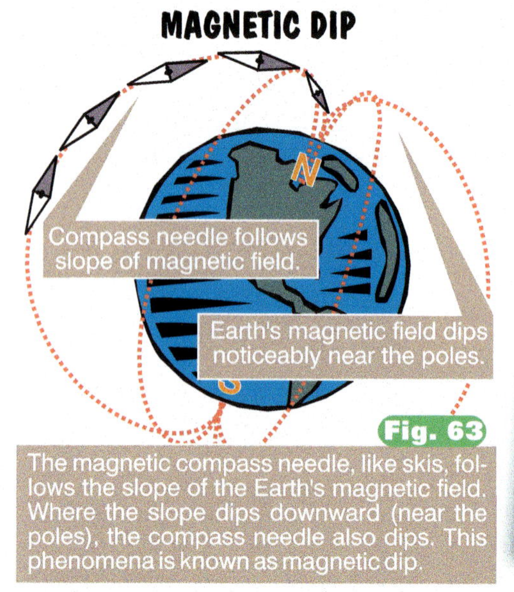

The magnetic compass needle, like skis, follows the slope of the Earth's magnetic field. Where the slope dips downward (near the poles), the compass needle also dips. This phenomena is known as magnetic dip.

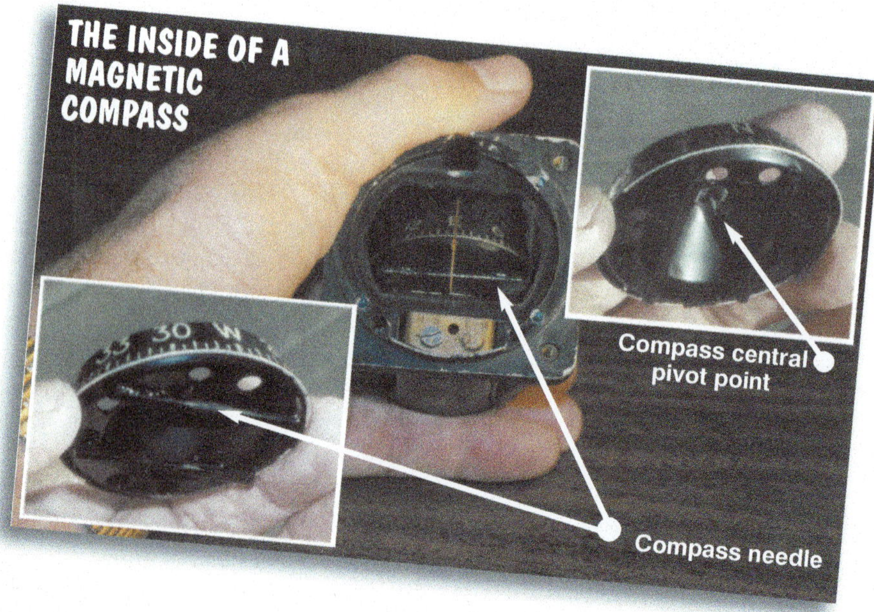

HANG THAT HEADSET ON YOUR HEAD

When making position reports I always used my headset, and upon completion I laid the headset on what seemed a very convenient place since the cockpit was crowded—the top of the instrument panel! During the few minutes it took to make the report I obviously never noticed that the compass read differently (I steered by the liquid compass because I had not found the operation of the slaved gyro satisfactory, and, of course I had swung the liquid compass)... Depending on how close to the compass I had laid the headset, the compass would show an erroneous reading of about 15 degrees to the left...

ASRS Report

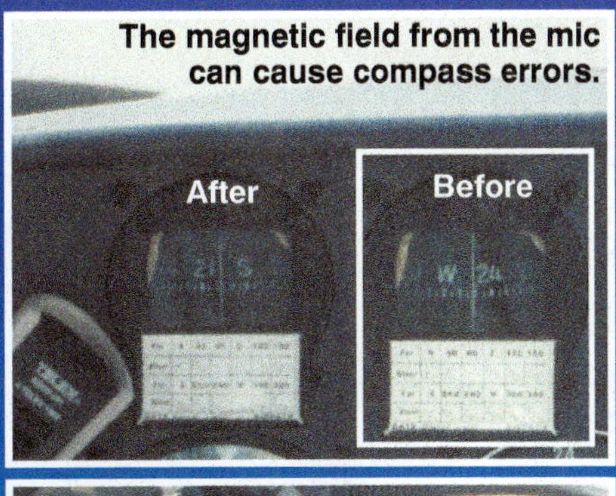

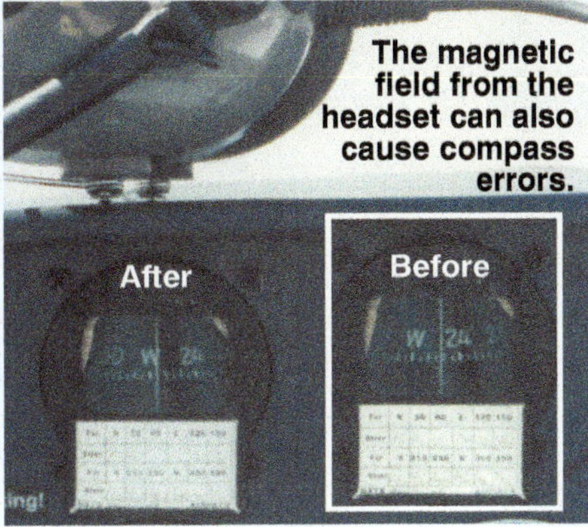

MAGNETIC DIP CORRECTION

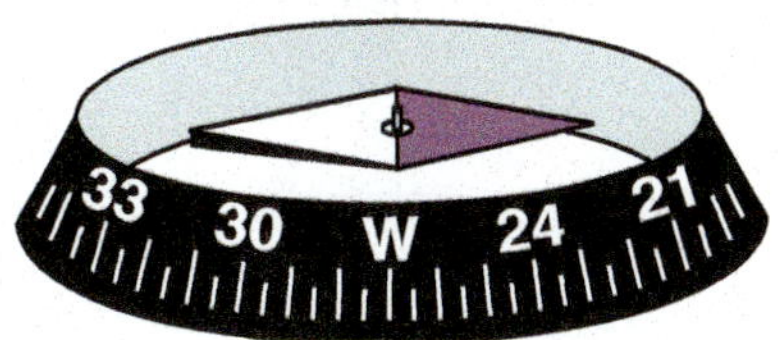

Instead of the simplified compass-needle drawing shown above, the compass actually has two needles, side-by-side with their north-seeking ends aligned. These needles are located on the bottom portion of the compass card and the entire card is suspended by a pivot. This gives the card a pendulous-type mounting (diagram below is also highly simplified for easy understanding).

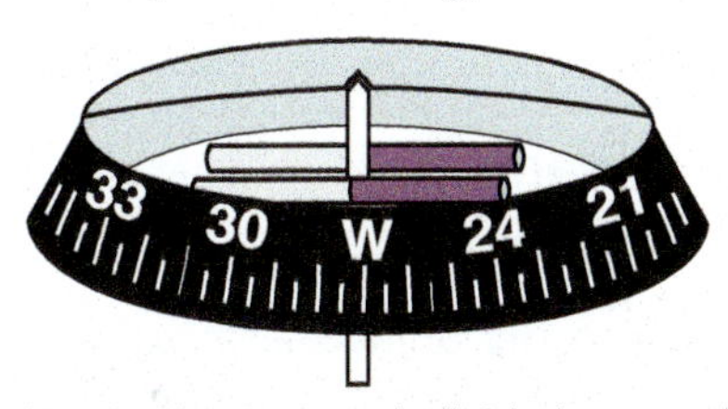

The earth's magnetic field tries to pull or "dip" the compass needles and the card downward as shown below. This would render the compass useless if it remained this way.

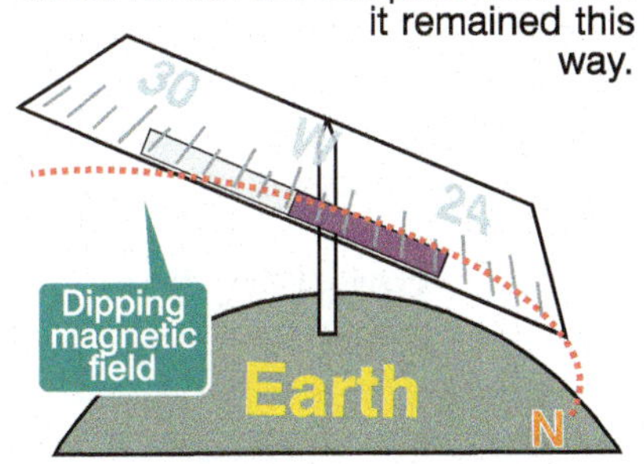

If the compass card is tilted as shown above, the card naturally tends to return to a near level position because of the "pendulum" effect. With the mass of the needles and additional items, the card remains nearly level despite magnetic dip, as shown below.

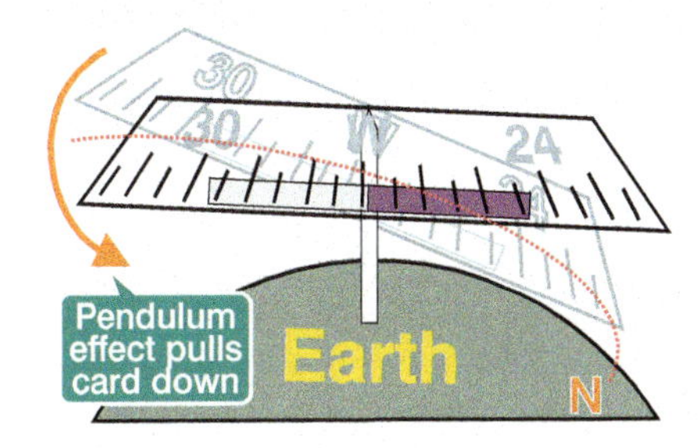

appearing under the lubber line, as shown by Compass C.

To fly any heading visible on the compass card, you must turn in the opposite direction to center it under the lubber line. For instance, if the heading you want to fly is visible to the right of the lubber line, turn to the left to center its value (now you know why the heading indicator is easier to use!).

To better understand how the compass works, we can compare its magnetic needle with skis. Skis are similar to compass needles in how they respond to changing terrain. In Figure 62, notice that as the terrain dips, so do the skis. If the terrain slopes upward, the skis, likewise slope upward. If the terrain dips downward, the skis dip downward. The point is, the magnetic compass needle is like a ski and the earth's magnetic field is like the terrain. The compass needle will always try to dip in the direction of the magnetic field.

Figure 63 depicts the earth's magnetic field. Notice that the field dips downward at nearly a 90° angle at the poles while there is very little dip in the equatorial regions. For most of the United States, the downward dip angle is around 70°. Just like skis following dipping terrain, the magnetic compass needle wants to tilt downward with the magnetic field. This is called *magnetic dip,* and is the only kind of dip pilots serve at parties.

It's also a serious problem for the magnetic compass. Unrestrained, this dip could render the compass unusable as a navigational device, since the card could get hung up on its pivot or in its container. Fortunately, the compass has been cleverly designed in such a way that the compass card's pendulous mounting counteracts this dip (Figure 64). As long as the compass card is allowed to hang parallel to the earth, it's not restricted by the dipping magnetic field. Therein lies the problem.

When the airplane accelerates or decelerates, the free-swinging compass card has inertia and tends to resist the speed change. This causes the compass card to tilt within its case. This results in what are known as *acceleration-deceleration errors* which are present on easterly and westerly headings only.

Whenever a turn is made, the compass card no longer hangs parallel to the earth's surface. Ordinarily, a turn won't affect the compass' reading unless the airplane is on a northerly or southerly heading at the time. Then the compass card temporarily leads or lags behind the airplane's actual heading. These are called the *northerly turning errors (even in a southerly direction).* Let's examine the acceleration and deceleration errors first.

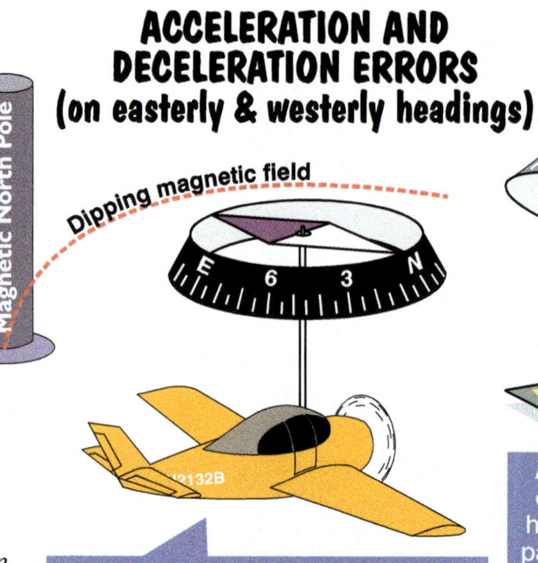

Fig. 65

ACCELERATE

DECELERATE

In level flight, on an easterly (or westerly heading), the compass reads the correct heading as long as the airplane doesn't accelerate or decelerate. Despite the dip in the earth's magnetic field, the compass card's pendulous mounting (and resultant center of gravity) keeps the compass needle from trying to bend downward with the dipping magnetic field.

As the airplane accelerates on an easterly (or westerly) heading, the rear of the compass card tilts upward as a result of the card's inertia. This allows the north-seeking end of the compass needle to dip downward as it tries to align itself with the earth's dipping magnetic field. This twists the compass card clockwise (as seen from above), resulting in the temporary appearance of a more northerly heading.

Deceleration on an easterly (or westerly) heading causes the rear of the compass card to swing downward. The north-seeking end of the compass needle dips downward, which causes the compass card to twist counterclockwise (as seen from above). This temporarily results in the compass indicating a more southerly heading.

Acceleration And Deceleration Error

Accelerating or decelerating on an easterly or westerly heading causes the compass to temporarily read in error. Accelerating causes the compass to give a more northerly heading than the one being flown. Decelerating causes the compass to read a more southerly heading than is actually being flown. An easy way to remember these errors is with the acronym: ANDS. This stands for Accelerate North, Decelerate South.

The acceleration-deceleration error occurs because a speed change forces the compass card to tilt within its case (Figure 65). As the card is forced to tilt, its pendulous properties are no longer as effective in correcting for the earth's dipping magnetic field. The compass needle's north-seeking end points downward in the direction of the dipped magnetic field. This results in a temporary heading error while the speed change is in progress.

Northerly Turning Errors

Turning errors are only experienced on northerly or southerly headings. These errors are also caused by the compass card being forced to tilt when the airplane is in a bank. Now the pendulous properties of the card can't prevent the compass needle's north-seeking end from pointing downward in the direction of the dipped magnetic field. This results in the appearance of a temporary heading error.

For instance, as the airplane turns from or through a northerly heading, the compass reading lags the airplane's heading (Figure 66). Airplane B is in a left turn and its heading is

The Whiskey Compass Made Easy to Remember

Here's an easy way to remember the northerly turning errors. A mechanic once told me that the magnetic compass used to be called the *whiskey compass* because it was filled with six ounces of clear whiskey. The liquid provides a dampening action for the compass card. (Don't rush to the plane. . .they don't use whiskey any more.)

Apparently, during World War II, Air Force mechanics would remove the top of the compass, insert a straw and suck out all the whiskey. Of course this didn't set well with compass manufacturers. A decision was made to put six ounces of kerosene into the compass. Then the Marine mechanics started drinking the liquid.

We flight instructors now inform our students that the compass is filled with molasses (not really, but read on). That's right! I said thick, gooey molasses. What happens when molasses gets cold? It thickens up. What happens when molasses gets hot? It thins out.

Therefore, if you're heading an airplane toward the cold north pole, think of the molasses thickening-up. As a result, the compass card lags within the thick fluid when turning.

Heading toward the hot, tropical south, the molasses heats up and thins out. The thin fluid causes the compass card to move more freely or lead the airplane's actual heading.

While the compass isn't actually filled with molasses, this little story does make it easier to understand which error is present on northerly or southerly headings.

approximately 360°. Yet its compass shows a heading of 030°—lagging behind its actual direction. Airplane C is in a right turn and its heading is also nearly 360°. Its compass shows a heading of 330°, which is lagging behind its actual direction. As the airplane turns away from a northerly heading, these turning errors disappear and the airplane's correct heading appears under the lubber line. Airplane A has no turning error because it's not in a turn. Its compass reads accurately.

NORTHERLY TURNING ERROR

Fig. 66

Magnetic north pole

Turning east (lagging actual heading)

Wings level

Turning west (lagging actual heading)

Heading north

As the airplane turns through or from a northerly heading, the compass needle (lying within the banked card) aligns itself with the earth's dipping magnetic field. This causes the card to twist, resulting in a heading that temporarily lags the airplane's actual heading.

Figure 67 depicts the turning error while on a southerly heading. Heading directly south with the wings level (the north pole is on the bottom of this figure) produces the correct reading in the compass window, as shown by Airplane A. As the airplane turns from or through a southerly heading, the compass reading leads the airplane's actual heading. As Airplane C turns from or through a southerly heading, its compass reading also leads the airplane's actual heading. As a heading of east or west is approached, the turning errors disappear.

SOUTHERLY TURNING ERROR

While on a southerly heading, the magnetic field rises upward from below the airplane. When the airplane turns from or through this southerly heading, the compass needle twists to align itself with the earth's dipping magnetic field. Thus, the compass card shows a heading that temporarily leads the airplane's actual heading.

Fig. 67

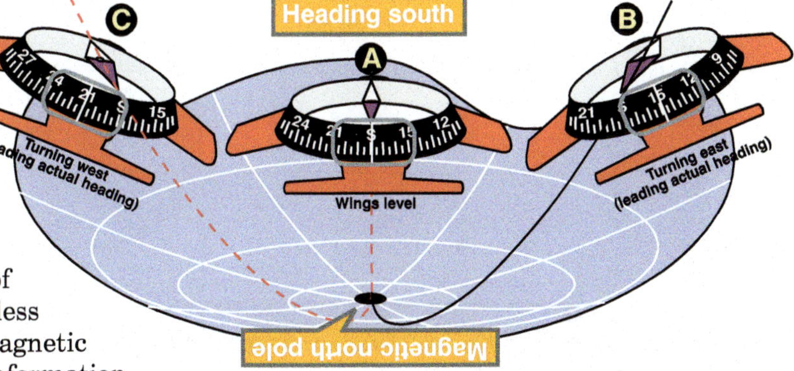

Remember, all compass errors are caused by the dip of the earth's magnetic field. If it weren't for this, these troublesome errors wouldn't exist. With all these errors, why do we have a compass in the airplane in the first place? Because it works. The compass has only one moving part, making it one of the most reliable pieces of equipment in the airplane next to the ashtray. Unless someone has sucked the kerosene out of it, the magnetic compass will provide the most accurate heading information during straight and level unaccelerated flight. If that's not convincing, just remember, that the compass has only one moving part, requires no external power, air source or input, which can't be said for *any* other instrument on the panel! Learn to use the compass and you'll never worry about getting lost.

With a heading indicator you don't need to worry about turning errors or acceleration/deceleration errors. The heading indicator is gyro-stabilized and its accuracy isn't affected by turning or a change in speed. There is, however, one thing you need to be aware of. When initially setting the heading indicator to the value in the magnetic compass, make sure the airplane is in wings-level, unaccelerated flight (this is the only time you can be sure the compass value is most accurate). This prevents setting an incorrect heading into the heading indicator.

You'll learn a lot about the capabilities and idiosyncrasies of the airplane's instruments as you fly with them. Like me, I think you will learn to appreciate the hard-working instruments and the vital flight information they provide.

Now it's time to move on and find out about the rules you'll fly by.

Postflight Briefing #5-1

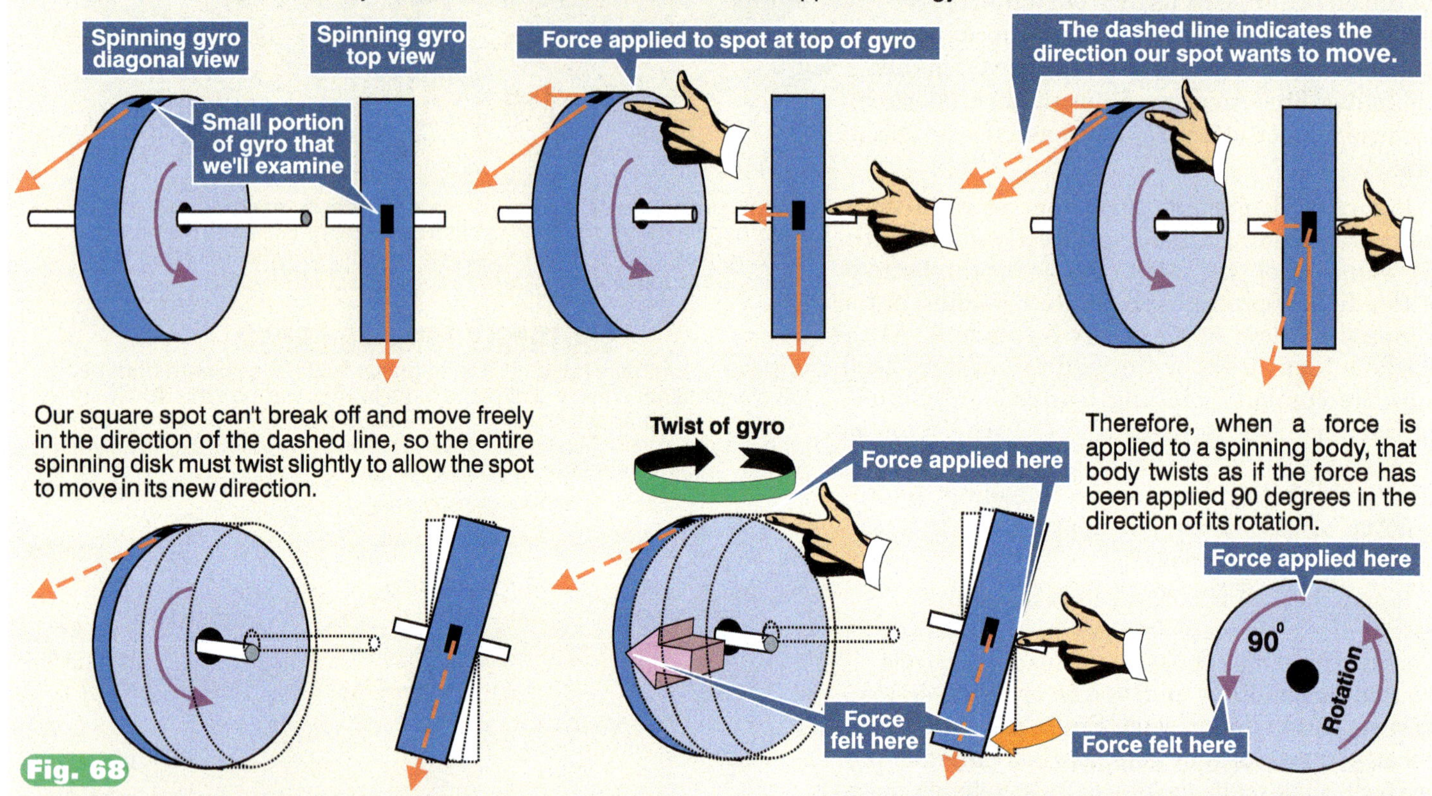

Postflight Briefing #5-2

Electronic Flight Displays (PFDs and MFDs)

If you've been observing the trends in aviation technology, you know that many of the newer airplanes on the market now have what is known as *electronic flight display* (EFD), consisting of either a *primary flight display* (PFD) and/or *multi-function display* (MFD). The EFD is also referred to as "glass cockpit" technology (Figure 69).

ELECTRONIC FLIGHT DISPLAY (EFD)

Avidyne's primary flight display and multi-function display are found in many technically advanced aircraft.

Despite looking like something found on the Starship Enterprise, this large electronic display provides the same information as the standard instrumentation found in other airplanes (and much additional information, too). The only difference is the way the information is presented. This is why you can transition from an airplane with mechanical-type gauges to one having a PFD with relative ease. However, mastery of all the bells and whistles on many PFDs will take hours of additional study time. Of course, you might be lucky enough to learn in an airplane having a PFD. Learning all the bells and whistles becomes part of your primary training, thus leading to mastery of all the instrument's gadgets *and* the ability to pilot the Starship Enterprise. (Note: the PFD integrates all the primary flight instruments into one screen. The MFD shows primary flight instruments and can show additional information on one screen.)

In Figure 70 (top left of next page) you can see that the airspeed is read from a tape-type airspeed indicator. The background of the entire display is an attitude indicator, with the white horizon line stretching from side-to-side on

INDIVIDUAL INSTRUMENTS OF THE PFD

Airspeed and altimeter information are presented as a moveable digital-tape strips while the entire background of the PFD presents attitude information.

DIGITAL-TAPE AIRSPEED READOUT ON THE PFD

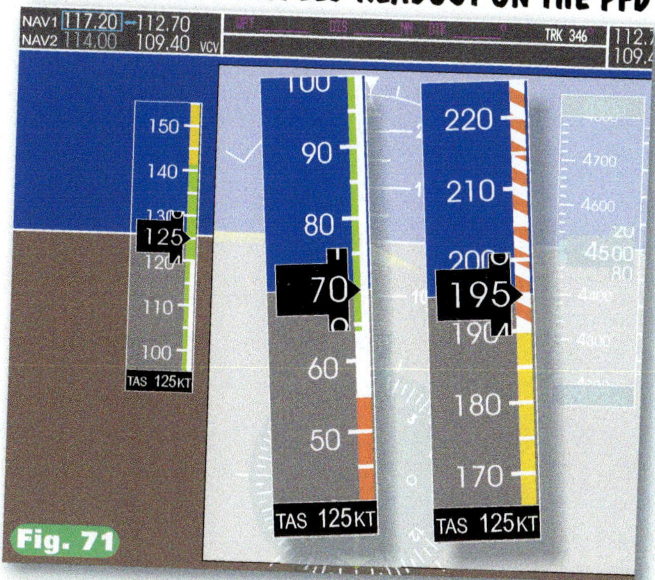

Airspeed information is presented in moveable tape format with the airplane's present airspeed shown digitally.

the instrument. At the top is the inclinometer-bank angle indicator. The altitude is also read from a tape-type indicator, and the vertical speed indicator is presented to the right of the altimeter tape. The heading indicator is similar in shape to an HSI.

Sure, it looks spooky, but it's only instrumentation. PFDs still use static and dynamic air pressure inputs to their air data computers to generate the airspeed, altitude and vertical speed information shown on their displays. We'll discuss this in detail, soon. First, let's examine each of the PFD's instruments in detail.

Digital Airspeed Readouts on PFDs

Primary flight displays provide digital airspeed readouts (Figure 71). The numerical airspeed tape moves vertically with airspeed change. The airplane's present airspeed is shown in the white-on-black box in the center of the tape. Notice that the yellow, green and white color codes correspond to the same color codes shown in Figure 8 of this chapter. On this primary flight display, the never-exceed speed region is indicated with a red striped line, and the stall speed region is marked with a solid red color. PFD manufacturers may vary the color coding used for these airspeed regions.

PRIMARY FLIGHT DISPLAY - PFD

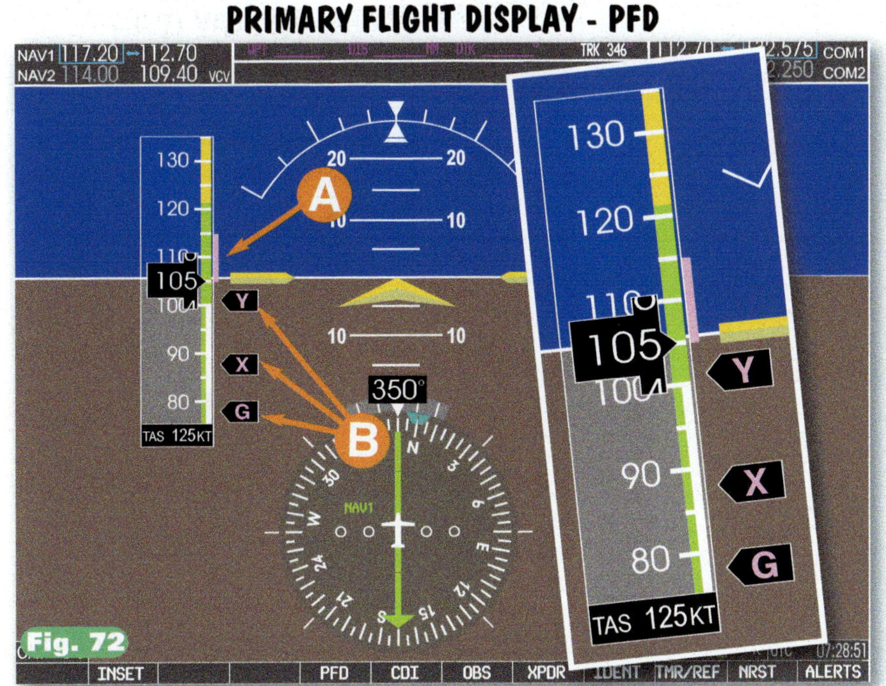

The magenta trend line (position A) tells you what your airspeed will be in six seconds at the airplane's present pitch and power setting. Best rate, best angle and best glide speed are identified by the Y, X and G tabs, respectively.

Some PFDs provide you with an automatic calculation of true airspeed, as seen at the bottom of the airspeed tape in Figure 71. The airplane's air data computer calculates the TAS based on the calibrated airspeed, pressure altitude, and outside air temperature (OAT). Isn't that nice? Now, if you could just use an English accent and say, "Earl Grey tea, hot" into the PFD and get your drink. Someday, perhaps. But not quit yet.

Some PFDs provide you with trend lines (the magenta line, Figure 72, position A) that show where your airspeed will be in six seconds (more on this in a minute). Best rate, angle and best glide speeds may also be shown by thumbnail identifiers (position B).

THE PRIMARY FLIGHT DISPLAY'S TREND LINES

One of the very unique features of the primary flight display is the trend line. This is the magenta line in positions A, B, C and D that show where a particular airspeed and altitude value will be in the next six seconds based on the airplane's present pitch and power condition. For instance, the nose up attitude on the left PFD shows a decreasing airspeed and increasing altitude. The airspeed trend line in position A indicates that the airspeed and altitude will be at 107 knots and 4,630 feet in six seconds. The pitch down attitude shown on the PFD to the right has trend lines indicating that the airspeed and vertical speed will be 182 knots (position C) and 3,710 feet (position D) in six seconds. The wonderful thing about trend lines is that they help you anticipate airspeed and altitude targets. Anticipating trends with round-dial instruments was more a matter of feel and it took some time to develop this skill.

Trend Lines

Trend lines aren't proof that the PFD is reading your mind. The projection is based on the airplane's present pitch and power condition. For instance, the nose up attitude on the left PFD (Figure 73) shows a decreasing airspeed and increasing altitude. The airspeed trend line in position A shows that the airspeed and altitude will be at 107 knots and 4,630 feet in six seconds. The pitch-down attitude shown on the PFD to the right has trend lines showing that the airspeed and vertical speed will be 182 knots (Figure 74, position C) and 3,710 feet (position D) in six seconds. The wonderful thing about trend lines is that they help you anticipate airspeed and altitude targets. Anticipating trends with traditional analog flight instruments is more a matter of feel and it takes some time to develop this skill.

Digital Altitude Readouts

Primary flight displays use a tape display of altitudes (Figure 75). As altitude changes, the numerical display tape of altitude moves up and down in the display window, while the number values in the white-on-black window in the center of the display (Figure 75, position A) change to reflect the airplane's current altitude. Figure 75, position B represents the target altitude you may (or may not) have previously selected in the PFD. Figure 75, position C represents the latest barometer setting you've dialed into the altimeter.

PRIMARY FLIGHT DISPLAY - PFD

On the PFD, altitude is read on a similar moving tape. The airplane's present altitude is shown digitally (position A), the target altitude (selected previously by the pilot) is read at position B and the current altimeter setting is read at position C.

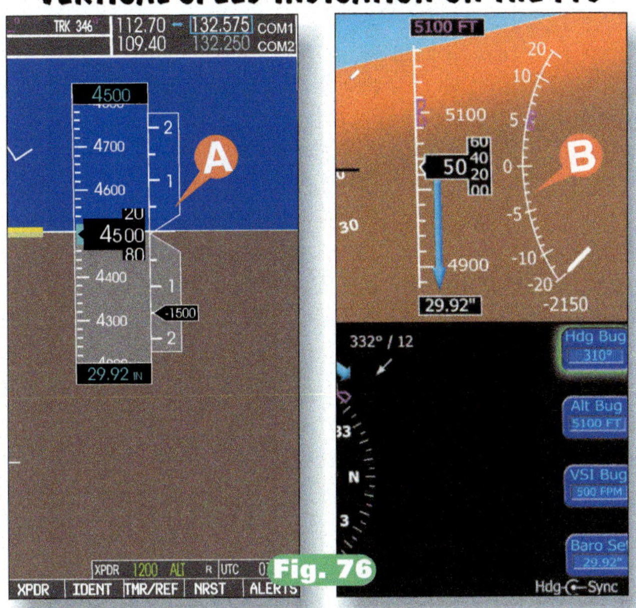

Vertical speed information is provided by a vertically moving pointer on the Garmin G1000 display (left) or a rotating needle on the Avidyne display (right).

Digital Vertical Speed Indicators

PFDs display vertical speed in similar but slightly different ways, as shown on the Garmin G1000 display (Figure 76, position A and the Avidyne display (Figure 76, position B). The G1000 PFD displays vertical speed with a vertically moving speed pointer. A numerical vertical speed value can also be read inside the moving needle when the vertical speed value exceeds 100 feet per minute. The Avidyne display creates a traditional swinging vertical speed needle to provide the vertical speed reading, along with a digital readout at the bottom (or top) of the vertical speed scale.

These display differences reflect, in part, the fact that we are still working to understand how pilots can most easily comprehend various graphical presentations of information. Should PFDs just try and look like digital versions of traditional instruments, or unleashed from the mechanics of dials and pointers, are there better ways to show various things? Everyone has an opinion (some people have several, one for each of their personalities), but so far not a lot of scientific data exist.

Attitude Indication On a PFD

Primary flight displays (Figures 77A and B) present a larger sky-ground horizon picture than traditional attitude indicators, making it much easier to identify the airplane's attitude even if you're sitting in the back seat (which I hope you aren't doing when you're the pilot in command). The pilot's attitude, fortunately, is not displayed.

On many PFDs, if the pitch exceeds 50 degrees above the horizon or 30 degrees below the horizon, you'll see the appearance of large red chevrons on the display (Figure 77C). This doesn't mean you're over a service station, either. It is a not-too-subtle suggestion that it's probably time to apply your unusual-attitude recovery techniques. Other than size, there really isn't much difference between the attitude picture shown on a traditional instrument and the picture painted by a PFD.

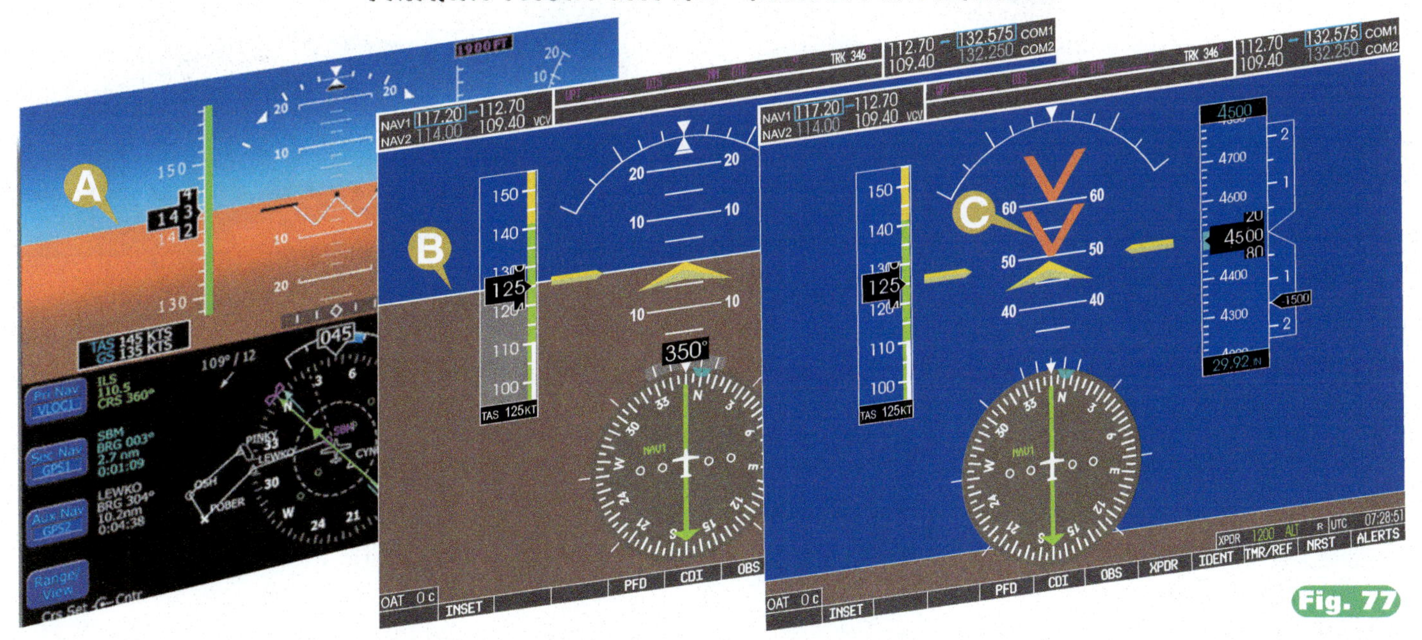

Attitude information on a PFD is a big deal, a really big deal, in that the background (so to speak) of the entire display fronts as the attitude indicator. The horizon line on two different PFDs in position A and B. When the attitude exceeds 50 degrees pitch above the horizon or 30 degrees below, large red chevrons appear (on Garmin's G1000 display, position C) pointing the direction toward a more normal flight attitude. Some PFDs use white chevrons to provide the same information.

HEADING INDICATION ON A PFD

In lieu of the traditional slip-skid indicator to show rate of turn, the PFD shows a trend line whose end indicates the airplane's heading six seconds in the future.

Heading Indication on a PFD

The heading indicator as part of the primary flight display is often in the form of the traditional horizontal situation indicator (Figure 78, position X). The main difference here is that the airplane's present heading is shown digitally (white on black) in the heading box, at the top of the instrument (Figure 78, position Y) .

Primary flight displays don't have the traditional turn coordinator commonly seen in non-technically advanced airplanes. Instead, the PFD often uses a trend line to identify turn rate, and a slip-skid trapezoid to indicate turn quality (Figure 78, position Y).

The right or left deflection of a magenta trend line shows what your heading will be in six seconds. The second hash mark (Figure 78, position Z) to the left of the airplane's present heading is 18 degrees off center. When the trend line touches this point, the airplane is turning at 3 degrees per second and is making a standard rate turn (18 degree offset/6 second trend= 3 degrees per second).

The inclinometer is represented by the bar under the trapezoid (Figure 78, position Y). Movement right or left

SLIPPING AND SKIDDING TRAPEZOID INDICATIONS ON THE PFD

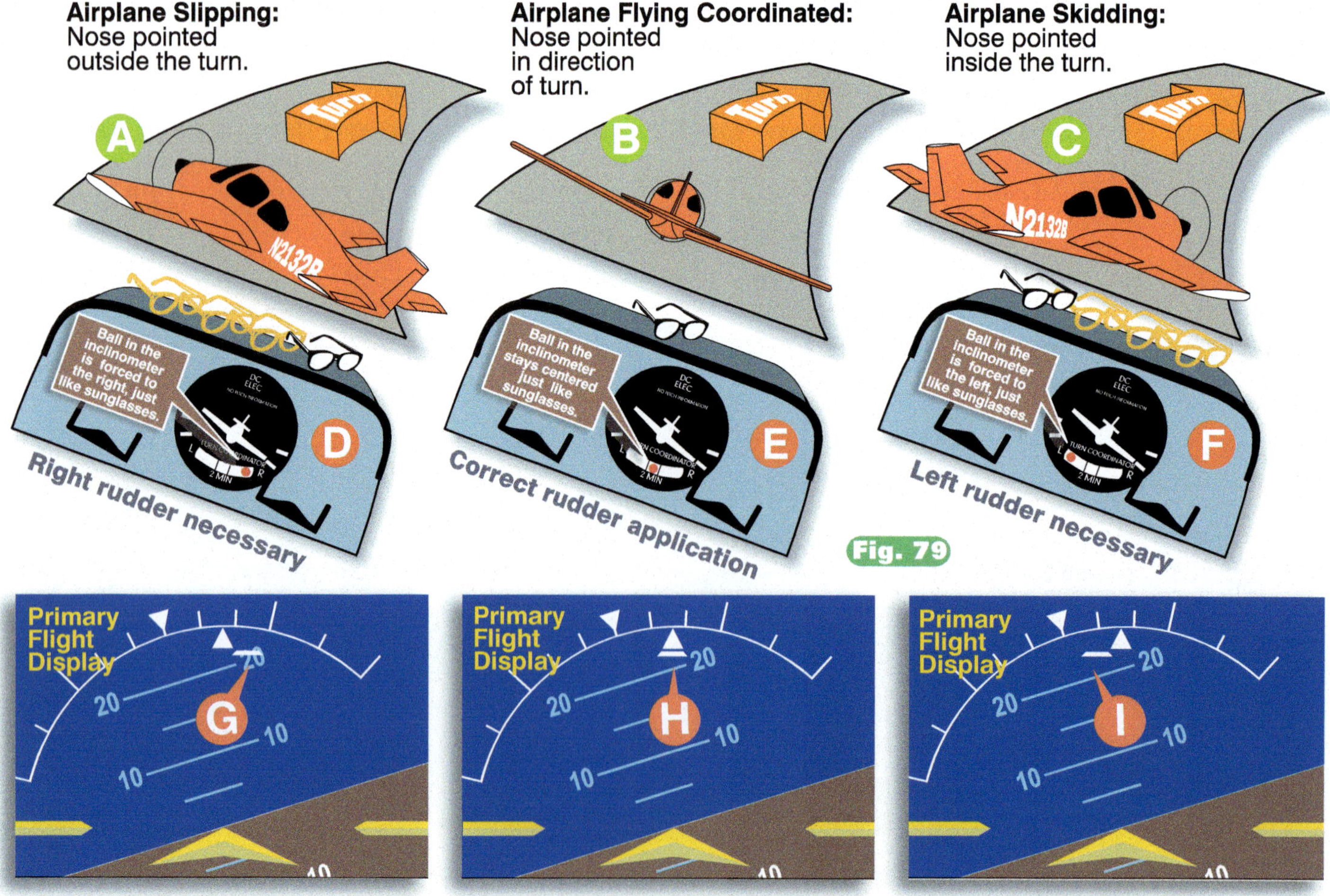

The primary flight display inserts above show how the moveable slip-skid (trapezoid) bar indicates a slipping turn (position G), a coordinated turn (position H) and a skidding turn (position I). These three indications correspond with the indications in the inclinometers (D, E and F) above.

THE INSIDE OF AN AHRS (ATTITUDE AND HEADING REFERENCE SYSTEM)

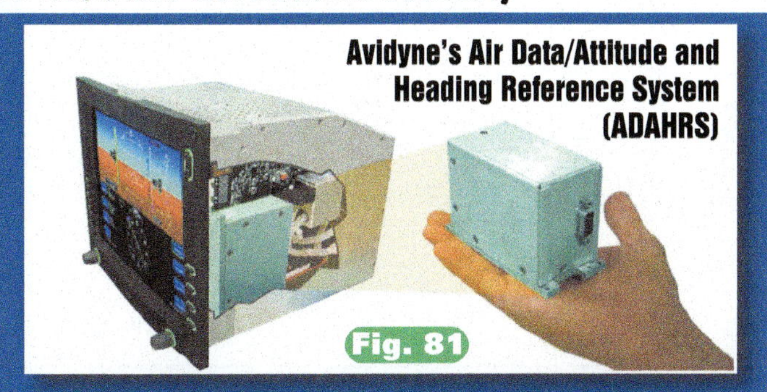

Avidyne's PFD uses an integrated air data computer and attitude and heading reference system (AHRS) in their single unit, otherwise known as the ADAHRS.

of the triangle indicates the degree of slipping or skidding (see Figure 79). The PFD in Figure 79 shows how the moveable slip-skid (trapezoid) bar indicates a slipping turn (Figure 79G), a coordinated turn (Figure 79H) and a skidding turn (Figure 79I). These three indications correspond with the indications in the inclinometers (D, E and F).

Now that you have a basic understanding of how PFDs present their information, let's take a look behind the curtain, so to speak. Modern PFDs don't use spinning gyros. Instead, attitude (pitch and bank) information is often provided by a unit called the *attitude heading reference system (AHRS)*, which is solid state and contains no moving parts (Figure 80). This unit contains solid state gyros that provide the attitude information used by the airplane's pitch and bank gyro instruments. You can read about how these solid state gyros work in Postflight Briefing #5-4 on page E42.

The air data computer that's part of the Avidyne display (Figure 81) takes information from the airplane's pitot and static lines and from the airplane's thermometer and processes this to provide the airspeed, altitude and vertical speed readouts. The air data computer, along with heading information, can also provide wind direction and speed as well as altitude information for use in Mode C transponder operations.

Airplane heading information for the PFD can be supplied by an external magnetic flux detector (sometimes called a *magnetometer*, Figure 83), which also provides heading information to the slaved gyro in a traditional horizontal situation indicator.

On the other hand, some PFDs, such as Avidyne's display, have an integrated air data computer and attitude and heading reference system (AHRS) within the unit, in which case it's known as an Air Data Attitude Heading Reference System (ADAHRS, Figure 81).

While there's a lot more to know about primary flight displays, at least you now know what type of information they provide and how they provide it.

Postflight Briefing #5-3

The Remote Indicating Compass (RIC)

The remote indicating compass is essentially a heading indicator that automatically aligns itself to the proper magnetic direction without the pilot getting involved in the process. The RIC consists of two panel mounted components and two remotely located components (thus the genesis of the word remote in RIC). One of the common panel mounted components is the horizontal situation indicator or HSI as shown in Figure 82.

One of the two remotely located components is the magnetic flux detector (flux valve) which is located somewhere on the airframe (usually a wing tip) away from sources of magnetic interference (Figure 83). The other component is an electrically powered directional gyro unit remotely located on the airframe, too. Here's how the device works.

A flux valve senses magnetic direction by detecting the earth's lines of magnetic force in its spokes as shown in Figure 84. Changing headings results in a change in the concentration of these lines of force throughout the individual spokes, which provides the means of sensing direction. Electrical signals from the flux valve are then sent to a small electric motor in the remotely located directional gyro.

The RIC's Flux Valve

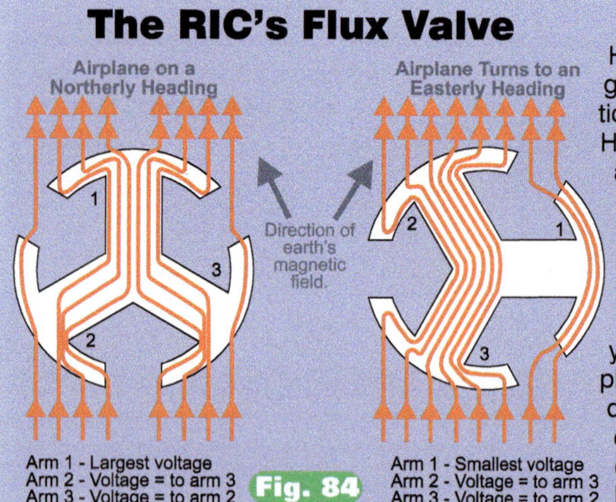

Fig. 84

which alters the position of (precesses) that gyro (no, there's no gyro in the HSIs found in most airplanes). As a result, the remotely located directional gyro is kept aligned to the airplane's current magnetic heading. The information from the remotely located directional gyro and flux valve is then sent to the HSI. Small motors in the HSI unit turn its vertical compass card to provide the airplane's correct magnetic heading. This process is called *slaving*, and it's what's being referred to when someone speaks of a *slaved gyro* (and no, you don't need to try and free all the world's slaved gyros, either).

The other component is a slaving meter-compensator unit (Figure 85). The slaving meter tells you when there's a difference between the airplane's actual magnetic heading and the heading displayed on the heading indicator. In the event an error between these two readings exist, the pilot could use the slaving meter to temporarily correct it before having the unit checked or repaired.

Fig. 85

Postflight Briefing #5-4

Three Ring Laser Gyro

To provide pitch and bank information, an attitude and heading reference system (AHRS) typically uses three laser gyros, one for each airplane axis (Figure 86). Computer assessment of all these three gyros (along with other components of the AHRS) provides the basic heading and attitude reference along with present position, groundspeed, drift angle and attitude rate information. The onboard computer begins assessing this information once it has been initialized by determining the initial vertical position and heading.

Courtesy of JAXA
Fig. 86

The ring laser gyro uses laser light to measure angular rotation. Each gyro (one for each airplane axis) is a triangular-shaped, helium-neon laser that produces two light beams, one traveling in the clockwise direction and one in the counterclockwise direction (Figure 87). Production of the light beams, or lasing, occurs in the gas discharge region by ionizing a low pressure mixture of helium-neon gas with high voltage to produce a glow discharge. Light produced from the lasing is reflected around the triangle by mirrors at each corner of the triangle to produce the clockwise and counterclockwise light beams.

Inside the 3-Ring Laser Gyro

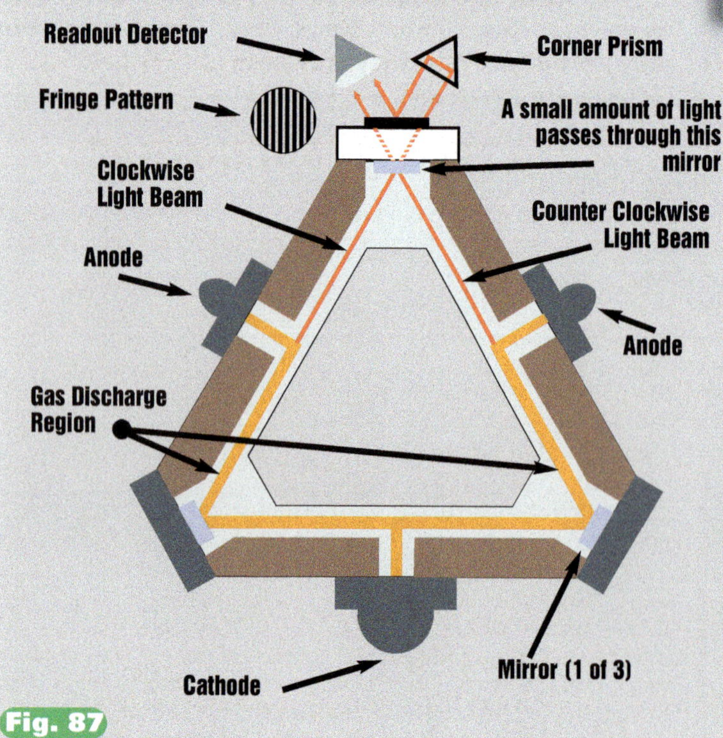

Fig. 87

When the laser gyro is at rest, the frequencies of the two opposite traveling laser beams are equal. When the laser gyro is rotated about an axis perpendicular to the gyro unit, a frequency difference between the two laser beams results. The frequency difference is created because the speed of light is constant. One laser beam will thus have a greater apparent distance to travel than the other laser

As a small amount of laser light from the two lasers passes through the mirror at the top of the diagram. Both light beams are now combined. If movement of the gyro has changed the frequency of the laser light, then the combined beams will produce a fringe or interference pattern. This is a pattern of alternate dark and light stripes. The onboard computer's analysis of this fringe pattern provides pitch and bank information to the airplane's instrument systems.

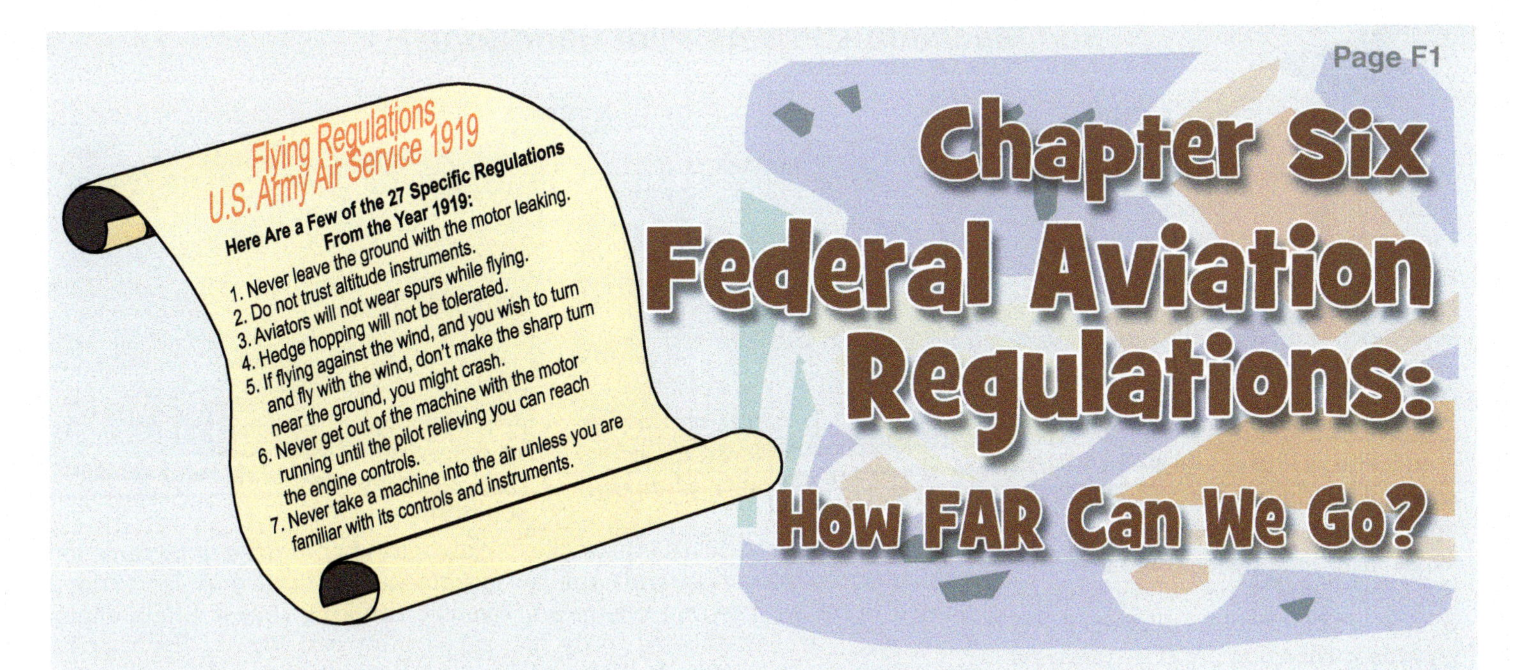

Chapter Six
Federal Aviation Regulations:
How FAR Can We Go?

Aviation, like lots of other things in life, has rules. In this case, the rules are written down, which should make them easier to understand. Unfortunately, they were written down by lawyers, which means they don't always say what they mean in language you or I might understand.

The collective rulebook, presided over by the Federal Aviation Administration (FAA), is called the Federal Aviation Regulations, and referred to by most pilots as the FAR's (legally referred to as CFR's or Code of Federal Regulations but we'll call them FAR's, OK?).

Not all regulations are complex and confusing. In fact, some are pleasingly simple. One FAR actually states that the airplane's takeoff run must not be longer than the length of the runway. That's a good rule. Why aren't all regulations as simple?

Explained properly, many of them can be.

Lawyers write for reasons other than lay understanding. If you don't believe this, simply look at the back of any car rental agreement. By the time you're finished reading, you could have walked to your destination. What the agreement should say is, "If you crash the car then you buy the car or you mow our lawns for eternity."

Knowing what the rules say and mean is vital to your pilot health. Part of getting a private pilot certificate is passing a test that shows you know the rules. Part of *keeping* your certificate once you get it is understanding the rules and how they're applied in the real world. (Sometimes people refer to a pilot *certificate* as a pilot *license.* Technically, it's called a certificate, not a license.)

Let's try to make sense of the regulations, despite their often complex and confusing nature. Because the by-the-book rules are long, complex, and boring many pilots never look at them and thus miss some vital information. What follows are the essentials, the information most often needed to safely and legally operate an aircraft.

Definitions

Understanding the regulations requires a working grasp of some basic definitions. For instance, some people in aviation are employed as fish spotters. At first glance, you might think this is someone who dabs a reluctant perch with oil based paint. Confusion is imminent when basic aviation definitions aren't understood. Here are some of the definitions you need to know in order to make some sense (as opposed to nonsense) of what goes on in aviation.

Aircraft – An aircraft is anything that flies. All airborne vehicles are divided into seven categories: *airplane, glider, rotorcraft, lighter-than-air, powered-lift, powered-parachute and weight-shift-control*. Anything airborne (except UFOs or what's inside Hangar 18) falls into one of these categories (Figure 1).

AIRCRAFT CATEGORIES HAVE SIMILARITIES

Powered parachute **vehicles have a semi-rigid wing connected to a fuselage.**

Gliders **have fixed wings and no powerplant.**

Rotorcraft **have powerplants and wings that rotate.**

Powered-lift **vehicles are capable of vertical takeoff, vertical landing & low speed flight that depends principally on engine-driven lift devices or engine thrust for lift during these flight regimes and on nonrotating airfoil(s) for lift during horizontal flight.**

Weight-shift-control **aircraft have a pivoting wing that allows a pilot to control pitch and roll by shifting his weight.**

Lighter-than-air **aircraft achieve lift by displacing air.**

Airplanes **have powerplants and fixed wings.**

Fig. 1

Fig. 2

Certificate shows the category of aircraft you're rated to fly.

Some pilots are rated to fly many categories of aircraft.

Category – For the purpose of *pilot certification* (unlike *airplane certification* on page B44) the term *category* of aircraft represents something flyable having *similar* operating characteristics. For instance, gliders are distinguished by their fixed wings and lack of an engine (*fixed wing* doesn't mean the wings have been repaired or rendered sterile; it means they don't rotate as do the wings of a helicopter). Helicopters, on the other hand, have rotary wings—wings that move. Powered-lift includes: tilt-rotor, VTOL (vertical takeoff & landing) and tilt-wing aircraft (see Figure 1 for definition of Powered-lift). The lighter-than-air category is unique in that lift for this type of aircraft is achieved by the displacement of air. Blimps, hot air balloons and gas balloons fit into this category. Finally, airplanes are distinguished by their fixed wings and powerplants.

A private pilot certificate allows you to operate one or more of these different categories of aircraft. It does not, however, automatically allow you to fly all categories of aircraft (I don't know how James Bond does it). Special training and a flight test by an FAA designated pilot examiner are required to pilot any new category of aircraft you fly. For instance, if you're certified to fly an airplane, you're not automatically certified to fly a helicopter (frankly, the first time I got into a helicopter I was afraid to touch the stick, fearing a wrong move would screw me and my instructor into the ground—not true!).

Your pilot's certificate states the particular category of aircraft you're allowed to fly, as shown in Figure 2A. Many pilots are certificated to fly in more than one category, and in some cases are certificated to fly all categories of aircraft as shown in Figure 2B.

Class – For the purposes of *pilot certification* (as opposed to *aircraft certification*) the term *class* represents a *subdivision* within a category. Airplanes, for instance, can have one, two, or more engines and be capable of landing on a runway (land), water or both. Because of these differences, the FAA decided to create another classification within each category of aircraft. Airplanes, for example, are made up of four classifications or classes: single-engine land (SEL), single-engine sea (SES), multi-engine land (MEL) and multi-engine sea (MES) as shown in Figure 3.

Because of the vastly different handling qualities of each vehicle, you need to be certificated in each class of aircraft you fly. Figure 4A shows a pilot certificate with an airplane class rating of *single-engine land*. Figure 4B shows a pilot certificate with an airplane class rating of *multi-engine land* and *single-engine land and sea* (and, if you're thinking that a single engine rated pilot can legally fly a multi-engine airplane by using only one of its engines—think again. Besides, these guys are easy to spot since they're always flying in circles).

Aircraft class designations also apply to other categories. For instance, within the category of lighter-than-air there are two classes: airship (blimp) and balloon. Finally, the term *class,* as used with respect to *aircraft certification,* means a broad grouping of aircraft having similar propulsion, flight or landing characteristics (e.g., airplane, rotocraft, glider, balloon, landplane and seaplane).

A pilot with an airplane single-engine land class rating.

Fig. 4

A pilot with a multi-engine land and single-engine land and sea class rating.

AIRPLANE CLASS VARIATIONS

Airplane single-engine land

Airplane multi-engine land

Fig. 3

Airplane single-engine sea

Airplane multi-engine sea

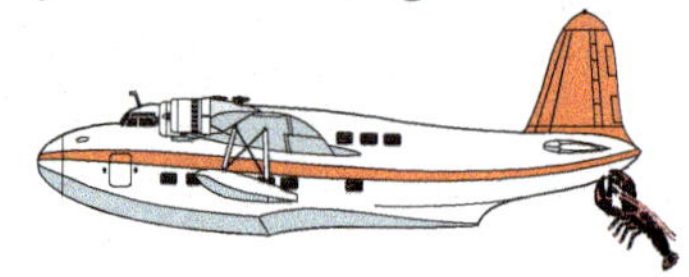

Fig. 5

Make and Model – Pilots are always asking each other what kind of airplane they fly. They aren't necessarily referring to the specific class as much as they are the particular *make and model* of airplane. This can be an A36 Beechcraft Bonanza, a Cessna 152 or a Piper Malibu. (I once asked a lady taking her first demonstration flight if she wanted to fly a Piper Cherokee—that's a specific make of airplane. She immediately stated that she didn't care who came along nor what instrument he played.)

According to the FAA, once you have your private pilot's certificate, you can legally fly any specific make and model of aircraft within the category and class for which you are rated (with a few exceptions to be noted later). In other words, if you are a private pilot with an airplane, single-engine land rating, you can legally fly a Katana DA-20, Cessna 150, Cessna 152, Cessna 172, Piper Warrior, etc., because all are single-engine land airplanes.

As a student pilot, things are a little different. You may only fly the specific make and model of aircraft endorsed in your pilot's logbook by your instructor as shown in Figure 5. If you are signed off to solo a Cessna 152, you may not solo a Cessna 150 unless your instructor endorses your pilot's logbook for that specific make and model. Individual makes and models, despite their similarity, might just be confusing enough to cause problems for a student pilot.

Type Ratings – Let's say you thought of purchasing a small general aviation airplane for your family, but decided you really wanted something a little bigger—say a slightly used Boeing 707, for those Sunday flights to the Holy Land. If you're thinking that a multi-engine rating is all you need to pilot this big beast, think again.

If an aircraft weighs over 12,500 pounds or is turbojet powered, a *type* rating is required to act as *pilot in command* (PIC) of that aircraft. A type rating is a specialized checkout in that specific airplane. Such checkouts usually entail extensive ground school on the aircraft's systems as well as substantial flight training. Personally, I'd recommend sticking with a smaller airplane before working yourself up to one of these aluminum overcasts.

Visual Flight Rules (VFR) – The basic premise of *VFR flight* is to see and avoid other aircraft. To do so, visual flight rules stipulate a minimum in-flight visibility as well as a minimum distance from any cloud formation. This ensures that a pilot can control his or her airplane by visual reference to the horizon or the surface.

If you can't maintain this visual reference, you'll be forced to fly by reference to your airplane's instruments. As you have probably guessed, this is a slightly more specialized skill, requiring an additional rating (an *instrument rating*) beyond the private pilot's certificate. Private pilots without an instrument rating are only allowed to fly under visual flight rules. Later in this chapter and in Chapter 9 (the chapter on airspace), you will learn the specific visibilities and distances from clouds that you're required to maintain for VFR flight.

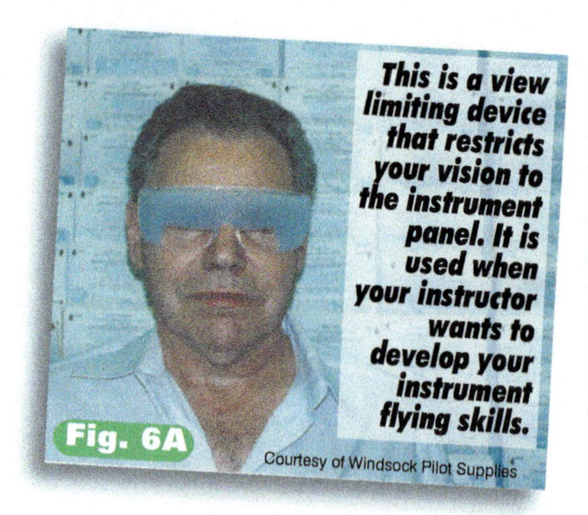

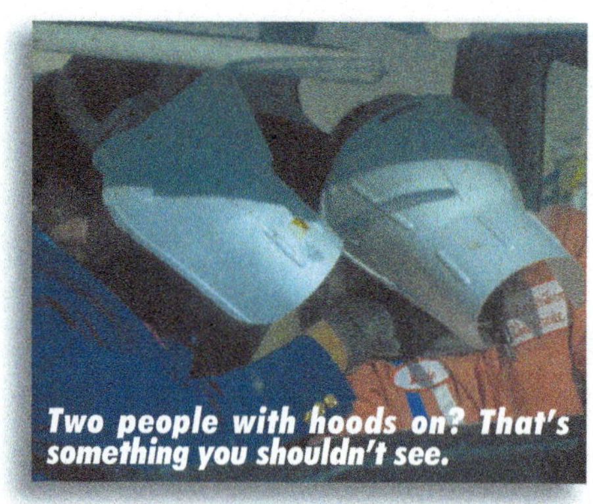

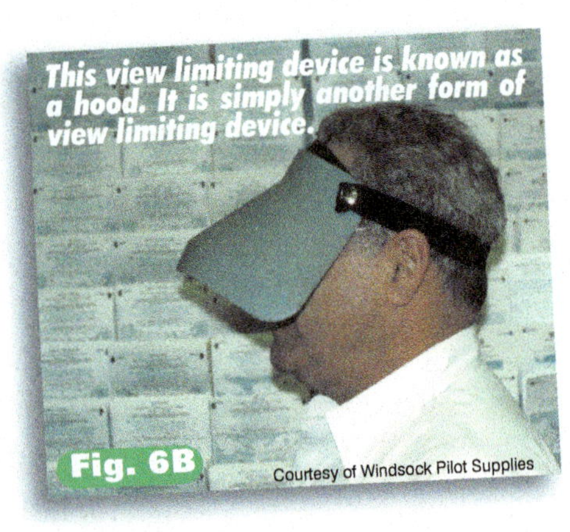

Instrument Flight Rules (IFR) – Once you obtain your private pilot's certificate, you can acquire the skills necessary to fly under *Instrument Flight Rules* (IFR). An instrument rating allows you to fly to your destination while in the clouds and land under low visibility conditions. *Air Traffic Control* (ATC), using sophisticated radar, provides separation between all airplanes operating under instrument flight rules. After all, if you're in the clouds, you can't see other airplanes; ATC acts as your eyes under these conditions. To obtain an instrument rating you need a private pilot certificate and the comprehensive flight and ground training listed in FAR 61.65 (not included in this book).

As part of your private pilot training you will receive a minimum of three hours of instrument flight training. This doesn't mean you'll necessarily be in the clouds for three hours. It does mean, however, that your instructor will find some means of simulating instrument conditions by limiting your vision to the instrument panel. The most common way of doing this is with view limiting devices known as Foggles (Figure 6A) or a *hood* (Figure 6B). A hood is sort of like a visor on steroids. It permits you to see directly in front of you—the instrument panel—but not outside unless you have eyes on stalks.

Many years ago, during my first lesson on instruments, my instructor slipped the hood over my head. He told me it was used to simulate flying in the clouds. I put it on and reluctantly began to scan my instruments. After a few minutes I lifted the hood up, looked around and put it back down. I did this three more times before my instructor said, "Hey, what are you doing?" I replied, "I'm practicing flying in and out of the clouds." At that point he said, "You owe me $5." "Why?," I replied. "It's a stupid-tax, that's why. You just did something stupid, so pay up." I paid him the money. He immediately looked over and said, "Well, that proves it, now you owe me another $5." (I guess I shouldn't have paid him that first $5. Pretty stupid, eh?)

Night – It would seem like the definition of *night* is pretty straightforward, right? Not quite. *Night* is officially defined as *the time between the end of evening civil twilight and the beginning of morning civil twilight*, as published in the American Air Almanac, converted to local time. I mention this because most regulations deal with the hours of darkness by referencing the time from sunset to sunrise. If the term *night* or *nighttime* is specifically used, you should refer to the definition listed above.

Pilot In Command (PIC) – The pilot in command is the captain of the ship and is responsible for the safe operation of the aircraft during flight. He or she is also the person the FAA will look to in the event of a violation, accident, or other unhappy event. No matter what the category or class of aircraft, there is always one (and only one) legal pilot in command at any particular instant during a flight. (PIC duties can change back and forth during a flight.)

There may be passengers who think they're in command, but the PIC is the legal decision maker (that's why some pilots make these back seat passengers or *nag-i-va-tors* wear oxygen masks—it muffles their constant complaints).

These are the definitions needed to get started. As we go along, we'll uncover more useful words and define them as necessary. You can also visit the Glossary (page R15-31) for more definitions. Let's jump directly into the regulations. We're concerned about two main groups of rules: *Part 61* and *Part 91* (the FARs are part of the Code of Federal Regulations, which is divided into numbered parts; thus *Part 61* and *Part 91*.)

Part 61 deals with the certification of pilots. It's the paperwork regulations concerned mostly with the administrative or record keeping duties of flying. Part 91 is the "how to" regulations concerned with the operational rules of flight. Let's start with Part 61.

PART 61

FAR 61.3 Requirement For Certificates, Ratings And Authorizations

To act as pilot in command or as a required flight crewmember (copilot or flight engineer for example) on an aircraft, you must have your pilot certificate and photo identification (a driver's license for example) in your personal possession or readily accessible in the aircraft. These can't be home in your dresser drawer or left in your disco-dance van. A private pilot certificate has no expiration date but, as you'll soon see, it can only be used if you meet a few other requirements. For instance, to act as PIC you need to have a current medical certificate with you (if required. We'll discuss the medical shortly). These documents need each other, and you need all of them to offer proof that you've acquired the skills needed to pilot the plane, are healthy enough to do so and that you are who you say you are.

You can be asked to present your pilot or medical certificate and photo ID for inspection by the Federal Aviation Administrator, a National Transportation Safety Board or Transportation Security Administration representative or any federal, state or local law enforcement officer. The U.S. Customs service is also authorized to act on behalf of the FAA and request these documents. I can almost guarantee that doing steep turns around the White House is sure to get your pilot certificate inspected by some official looking person (hopefully it won't be an ex-Green Beret pumped up on Maxwell House coffee).

Note that I said *present for inspection,* not *give the certificate up to this representative.* Don't let anyone take your pilot or medical certificate without due process. There are ways and means by which the FAA can suspend your flying privileges, but none of them involve physically turning over your license or medical certificate until an appropriate investigation is conducted.

Carrying these three items isn't much of a problem for most pilots. In fact, as a young aviator I was always trying to find a reason to show someone my private pilot certificate. Cashing a check at a supermarket was usually the best place. When the teller asked for ID, I'd proudly whip my license out for display. The teller would look at it, raise an eyebrow and ask, "What the heck is that?" Of course, this required an explanation that I was more than willing to give.

61.15 Offenses Involving Alcohol or Drugs

If you get high, it better be in an airplane. Don't even think of mixing airplanes with alcohol or drugs. If you're convicted for almost any illegal drug activity, there's a very good chance you'll have your pilot certificate suspended or revoked.

Any suspension, albeit temporary, is a blot on your record. Revocation is even more extreme. Once a certificate is revoked, it no longer exists. In some cases it's possible to reapply for that certificate after a minimum waiting period. A one year wait is not uncommon. Reapplying means a pilot must retake all applicable knowledge exams as well as the flight tests. On the other hand, your previous flight time is still applicable toward any rating you might wish to pursue.

Convictions for alcohol-related offenses are no less benign in the eyes of the FAA. Action taken against your driver's license because of a drug or alcohol problem is known as a *motor vehicle action.* After November 29, 1990, two or more motor vehicle actions within three years of each other is grounds for suspension or revocation of a pilot certificate or rating. This is also grounds for denial of an application for a certificate or rating up to a year after the date of the last motor vehicle action.

Unfortunately, those individuals who marinate their brains in drugs and alcohol may contemplate not informing the FAA about their alcohol or drug related offense. Well, FAA rule creators weren't born last night. These regulations require all drug and alcohol motor vehicle actions to be reported to the FAA within 60 days. Failure to do so is itself grounds for suspension or revocation of a certificate or rating as well as denial of any application for a certificate or rating for up to one year after the date of the motor vehicle action.

The Bottle to Throttle Rule

Regulations require you to avoid acting as pilot in command or as a required crewmember (copilot or flight engineer for instance) for 8 hours after consuming alcohol. In other words, you should have 8 hours from bottle to throttle. If you're a balloon pilot, think of it as 8 hours from bottle to bag!

The propeller tips on both sides of this prop are damaged. The pilot and his rear seat friend were on a flight to their favorite hunting grounds in a J-3 (Piper) Cub. The airplane has tandem seating (one seat in front and one behind) and fold down doors. The rear seater saw a coyote from a low altitude, got excited and took a shot at it through the open door and blew off one prop tip. The pilot had to land the airplane because of the prop imbalance. The rear seater, realizing what he had done, shot off the other side of the propeller to balance it. Take it from your author, the way to balance your propeller isn't with a shotgun! This was quite dangerous.

PEANUTS By Charles M. Schulz

Personally, I'd recommend at least 24 hours from bottle to throttle. Why? Another part of this rule states that you may not act as PIC if you have blood alcohol content of .04% or more (by weight). It takes about three hours to metabolize one ounce of alcohol, though individuals vary widely in their capacity to process booze. Age, sex, and genetic factors all enter into an equation over which you have no control and about which you may have little information. It's safe to say there is significant alcohol in your bloodstream long after you have ceased to feel any physical effects.

Depending on the amount of alcohol consumed, its effects can last up to 36 hours. Unfortunately, some people think they can drink on a full stomach and not be affected by alcohol. These are often the same folks who drink on an empty head. Besides, this regulation also states that you may not operate under the influence of alcohol or use any drug that can influence your faculties contrary to safety. Consider that some cold and cough medicines contain significant amounts of alcohol (I've often wondered why the cold medicine Nyquil doesn't have a worm in the bottom of the bottle). There are ample other reasons why you should not be flying when you have a cold. Be careful!

61.23 Duration of Medical Certificates

As mentioned in FAR 61.3, anyone acting as pilot in command must have a *medical certificate* in their personal possession or readily accessible in the aircraft. Medical certificates are usually just called *medicals* by pilots, and they come in three flavors: first, second, and third class, each with its own requirements and privileges (Figure 7A).

The medical certification process is there to weed out people who have physical or psychological problems which represent a compromise of safety. How well it does this is a matter of some controversy. The FAA tends to place great emphasis on some areas (such as cardiovascular problems) where the predictive value of a physical exam is not great, and where the ability of a physician to detect, during a brief exam, someone who should be wearing one of those neat jackets with arms that tie in the back is also limited. Whether it achieves its stated purpose or not, you must pass a medical to get the piece of paper needed to pilot an airplane.

To obtain a medical certificate, you'd visit an Aviation Medical Examiner (AME). These physicians are appointed by the FAA and are schooled in the requirements for administering an official aviation physical exam and doing the necessary paperwork. You can obtain the names of local AME's from your flight instructor.

Generally speaking, the greater the passenger carrying responsibility you have, the more stringent the medical exam, the shorter the duration of the medical certificate, and the more the exam will cost. For instance, if you are the captain of an airliner, you need a *first-class medical* (an exam having the most stringent health requirements). A first-class medical certificate is valid for 6 *calendar* months for operations requiring an airline transport pilot certificate (if you're under age 40, then it's good for 12 calendar months). For use with a private pilot certificate (that's you), it's good for 24 or 60 calendar months depending on whether you're 40 years of age or older or under 40 years of age, respectively.*

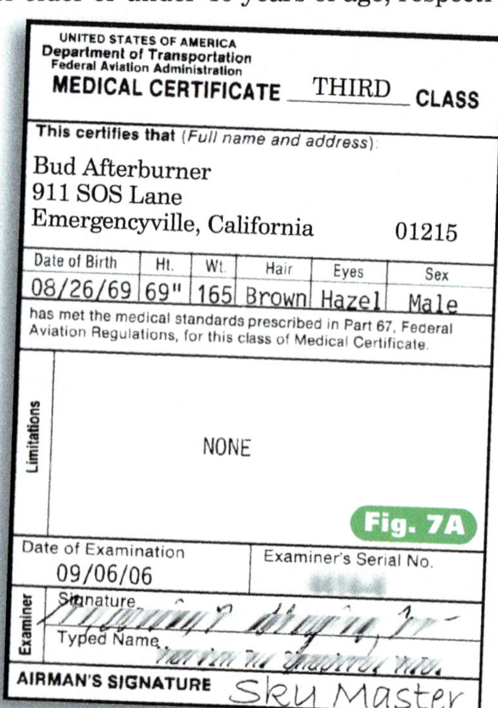

UNITED STATES OF AMERICA
Department of Transportation
Federal Aviation Administration
MEDICAL CERTIFICATE THIRD CLASS

This certifies that (Full name and address):
Bud Afterburner
911 SOS Lane
Emergencyville, California 01215

Date of Birth	Ht.	Wt.	Hair	Eyes	Sex
08/26/69	69"	165	Brown	Hazel	Male

has met the medical standards prescribed in Part 67, Federal Aviation Regulations, for this class of Medical Certificate.

Limitations: NONE

Date of Examination: 09/06/06
Examiner's Serial No.
Examiner: Signature
Typed Name
AIRMAN'S SIGNATURE Sky Master

A private pilot is required to have at least a third-class medical certificate to act as pilot in command.*

DURATION OF A THIRD-CLASS MEDICAL

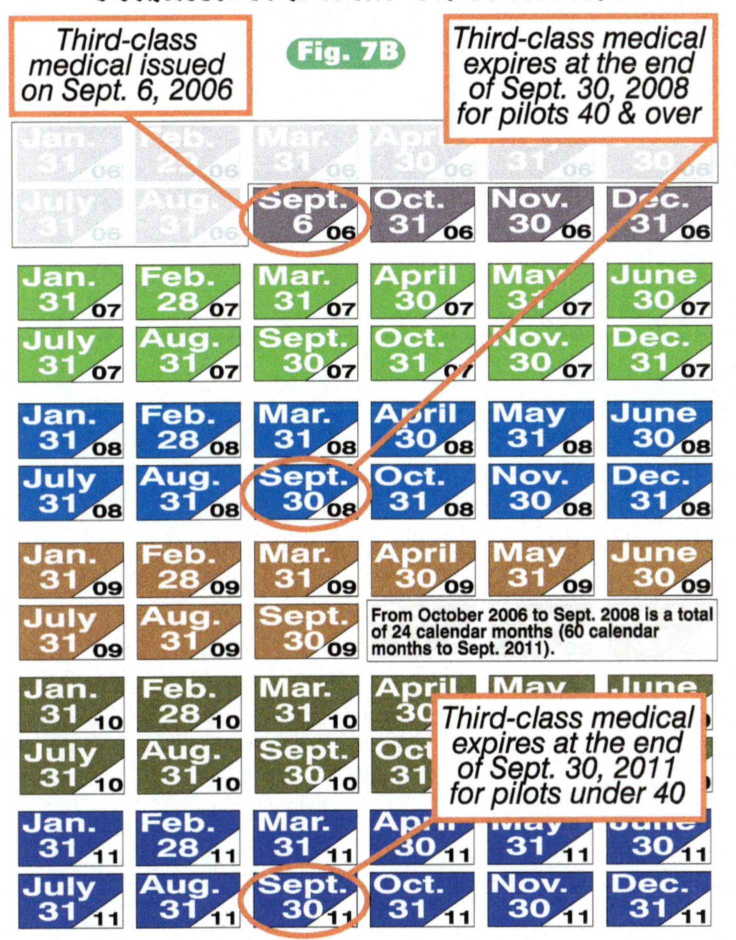

The terms of all medical certificates are calculated in *calendar months*. In other words, the clock starts ticking on the first day of the month *after* the month in which you obtain your exam. If you obtain your medical in January, the monthly count starts the following month (February). Think of the month in which you get your medical as free time. For instance, if you're an airline pilot (that's not you...yet) over 40 and take your first class medical on January 13, 2006 (or January 29th, or January 3rd), it is valid through July 30, 2006. This should make sense since February, March, April, May, June and July equal six calendar months of time.

If you have a commercial pilot certificate and are flying commercially (banner towing, pipeline patrol, sightseeing flights, etc.), you need a *second-class medical*. This medical is valid for 12 calendar months for commercial operations. For operations as a private pilot, the second-class medical is good for 24 calendar months if you're 40 or older and 60 calendar months if you're under 40. For commercial operations, if the medical is issued on July 13, 2006, the certificate is valid through July 31, 2007 for someone 40 or older. The monthly count starts in August (the month after it was issued) and goes 12 calendar months later to the end of July 31, 2007.

*As of May 1st, 2017, the FAA's new medical program called *BasicMed* allows pilots to act as PIC without having a third-class medical certificate. BasicMed subjects pilots to the following limitations: no flight for compensation or hire, aircraft has six seats or less, aircraft weighs up to 6,000 pounds, pilot flies no faster than 250 knots indicated airspeed and operates at or below 18,000 feet MSL. Pilots must also take a free online medical course every two years and visit a personal physician every four years. Read all about it in Postflight Briefing #6-7 starting on Page F58.

As a private pilot (or student pilot in solo operations), you are required to have a *third-class medical certificate* to act as pilot in command. A third-class medical is valid for 24 calendar months if you're 40 or over and 60 calendar months if you're under 40. For instance, if you're under 40 and obtain a third-class medical on September 6th, 2006, it's valid through September 30, 2011 (Figure 7B). If you're 40 or over and obtain a third-class medical on September 6, 2006, it's valid through September 30, 2008 (Figure 7B).

Someone once said that if you can see lightning and hear thunder, you can obtain a third-class medical. Well, the requirements are a little more stringent than that. Suffice it to say a third-class medical exam is a lot less stringent than the exam for a first-class medical.

Medical exams aren't too tough. Frankly, the only tough thing I remember about the third-class exam was when the doctor had me jump up and down on one foot for 20 seconds. I always thought this was some sort of standard in-flight maneuver used to dislodge a stuck gear. It's not. It's a heart stress test. In fact, as of this writing, no EKG (machine heart test) is required for the third or second-class exam.

A few conditions are outright disqualifying. Many others, however, fall in a gray area where the FAA *might* grant a medical, based on evidence you submit. If you don't meet the normal criteria, you must apply for a *waiver*. In some cases this means submitting to additional medical testing; in others, it involves demonstrating through a flight test that the condition does not limit your capability in the cockpit. It is possible to get a medical certificate if you only have vision in one eye, or have limited hearing, although restrictions may be imposed on when and where you may fly.

61.31 Additional Training Requirements

The part of this rather long regulation we're concerned with is the section dealing with the training and endorsements necessary to fly four different varieties of airplanes: high performance airplanes, complex airplanes, pressurized airplanes capable of operating at high altitudes and tailwheel airplanes. The rest of this regulation deals with matters either arcane or mundane, so I won't bother to use up your valuable storage capacity.

High Performance and Complex Endorsements – A *high performance airplane* is an airplane having more than 200 horsepower (Figure 8). A *complex airplane* is an airplane having retractable landing gear, flaps, and a controllable propeller (regardless of the horsepower). An airplane with retractable landing gear, flaps and an electronic engine control system that controls the engine and propeller (see FADEC sidebar on Page C3) is also considered a complex airplane. To act as pilot in command of a high performance airplane, you must have received and logged ground and flight training in such an airplane from an authorized instructor. Your instructor must also make a one-time endorsement in your certifying that you are proficient to operate a high performance airplane (Figure 9A).

To act as pilot in command of a complex airplane also requires ground and flight training from an authorized instructor and a one-time endorsement in your logbook, as shown in Figure 9B.

Training for the high performance or complex airplane endorsement can also be accomplished in a flight simulator or flight training device that represents either of these airplanes. It's doubtful that your Commodore 64 computer flight simulator—the one you shoot down Klingons with—is approved for such training.

Several years ago, a friend and I were standing at Fresno Chandler airport in California's San Joaquin Valley. We saw the pilot of a Comanche 250 (250 horsepower with retractable gear, flaps and controllable propeller) doing touch and goes. It seemed odd that after takeoff he never raised his gear and seemed to be using less than full power and no flaps. We walked over to him and asked if he was having engine or gear problems. He replied, "No, I just don't have my high performance signoff, so I ain't retracting my gear or using more than 200 of the 250 horses under the cowling of this puppy." Nice try, but that's not legal. (This is the result of some people having taken too many Fizzies in the 60's.)

Fig. 8 *The author standing next to an A36 Bonanza that has more than 200 horsepower as well as retractable gear, flaps and a controllable propeller. This makes it both a high performance and a complex airplane, thus requiring two endorsements in your logbook.*

The Cessna 182 (shown to the right) has more than 200 horsepower, but no retractable gear. Therefore it's considered a high performance airplane.

Photo courtesy of Cessna

This is what a high performance airplane endorsement (A) and a complex airplane endorsement (B) might look like in your logbook.

REMARKS, PROCEDURES, MANEUVERS	NO. INSTR APP.	NO. LDG.
(A) I certify that Mr. Al Timeter, private pilot, #7654321 has received the required training of § 61.31(f) in a Cessna 206. I have determined that he/she is proficient in the operation and systems of a high performance airplane.		
Rod Machado 10/13/08, Rod Machado 123456 CFI, Exp. 4/30/09		
(B) I certify that Mr. Al Timeter, private pilot, #7654321, has received the required training of § 61.31(e) in a Comanche 250. I have determined that he/she is proficient in the operation and systems of a complex airplane.		
Rod Machado 10/13/08, Rod Machado 123456 CFI, Exp. 4/30/09		

Fig. 9

Pressurized Airplanes Capable of Operating at High Altitudes – Airplanes are certainly a lot different than they were several years ago. We have general aviation airplanes that rival some airliners in their navigational equipment and even performance. Because of these advances, the *pressurized/high altitude airplane* rule was conceived.

The rule states that you may not act as PIC of a pressurized airplane capable of operating above 25,000 feet MSL unless you've received and logged ground training from an authorized instructor as well as flight training in a pressurized aircraft (Figure 10). Both the ground and flight training require separate logbook endorsements as shown in Figure 11.

Here is a pressurized airplane capable of operating above 25,000 feet MSL.

Fig. 10

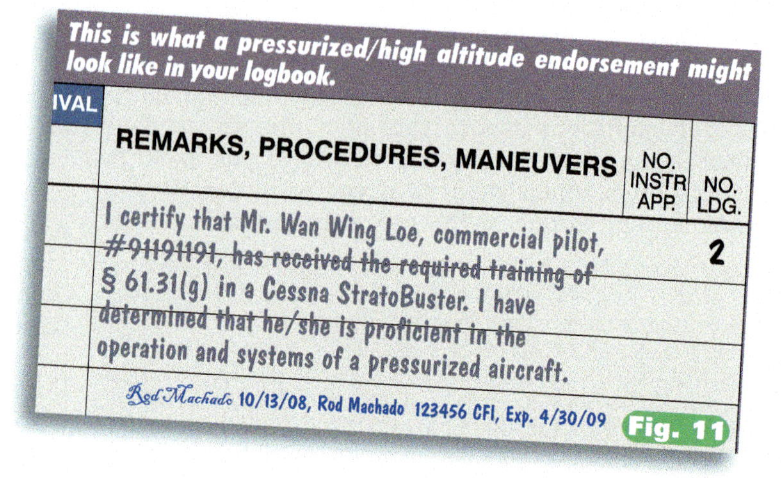
This is what a pressurized/high altitude endorsement might look like in your logbook.

IVAL	REMARKS, PROCEDURES, MANEUVERS	NO. INSTR APP.	NO. LDG.
	I certify that Mr. Wan Wing Loe, commercial pilot, #91191191, has received the required training of § 61.31(g) in a Cessna StratoBuster. I have determined that he/she is proficient in the operation and systems of a pressurized aircraft.		2
	Rod Machado 10/13/08, Rod Machado 123456 CFI, Exp. 4/30/09		

Fig. 11

Airplanes of this complexity require such training because of the unusual types of problems pilots might experience. Hypoxia or insufficient oxygen is perhaps the most serious of these. Airplane equipment is an additional problem. Pilots need to understand the intricacies of pressurization systems. Unfortunately, not all people understand the equipment they own and use. That's why many people have VCRs that are still flashing 12 midnight. A friend who's an engineer places black electrician's tape over the flashing numbers because he can't understand how to program the device. In an airplane, however, you can't just place tape over things you don't understand (student pilots would have to carry a lot of tape and some instructors would get really sore mouths).

Tailwheel Airplanes – *Tricycle gear airplanes* have the center wheel in front, as shown in Figure 12A. *Taildraggers* have the center wheel in back (Figure 12B). Why? Tail-draggers are better suited for off-airport work (dirt roads, fields, rough terrain) than tricycle gear airplanes. The tailwheel has less chance of being damaged in rough terrain, for several reasons. First, because it's located at the end of a long lever (the fuselage), the tailwheel has less physical force applied to it when supporting the airplane. Second, the wheel is smaller and usually spring suspended, which lessens the force of any impact. Tailwheel airplanes are often called *conventionally geared airplanes* because early manufactured airplanes commonly used this type of gear.

Tricycle gear airplanes have their center of gravity in front of the main wheels. This makes them quite stable on the ground. Tailwheel airplanes, on the other hand, have their center of gravity behind the main wheels, making them less stable on the ground. During landing, if the tailwheel airplane starts to swerve, the center of gravity often attempts to twist the airplane in a direction other than what the pilot intends. This is often referred to as a desire on the part of the airplane to *swap ends* (ground loop). Tailwheel airplanes need constant directional attention when they are in motion. Tricycle gear airplanes, on the other hand, are less sensitive to directional control problems.

That's why the FAA says that if you want to act as PIC of a tailwheel airplane, you must have received and logged flight training from an authorized instructor in a tailwheel airplane (*authorized* means the instructor is qualified in the plane in which he or she is providing instruction). The instructor must find you proficient in the operation of a tailwheel airplane including at least normal and crosswind takeoffs and landings, wheel landings (unless prohibited by the manufacturer) and go-around procedures. The instructor must place a one-time endorsement in your logbook as shown in Figure 13. This endorsement covers all the small general aviation tailwheel airplanes you're likely to fly.

If you are flying any of these airplanes as a student pilot, you may be wondering why you don't have these endorsements in your logbook. The reason is that this regulation doesn't apply to student pilots (it also doesn't apply in certain specific instances to *recreational pilots* acting under the supervision of a flight instructor but we don't discuss recreational pilots in this book). Simply stated, once you obtain your private pilot's certificate, you'll need endorsements for high performance, complex, high altitude or tailwheel airplanes.

A TRICYCLE GEAR AIRPLANE

Fig. 12A

A TAILWHEEL AIRPLANE

Fig. 12B

A TAILWHEEL ENDORSEMENT

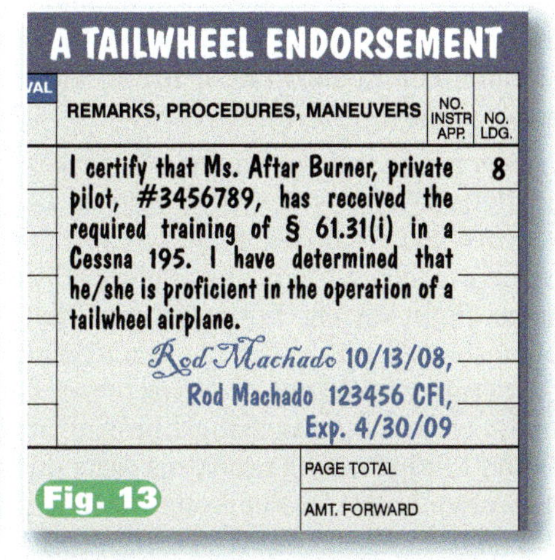

REMARKS, PROCEDURES, MANEUVERS	NO. INSTR APP.	NO. LDG.
I certify that Ms. After Burner, private pilot, #3456789, has received the required training of § 61.31(i) in a Cessna 195. I have determined that he/she is proficient in the operation of a tailwheel airplane. Rod Machado 10/13/08, Rod Machado 123456 CFI, Exp. 4/30/09		8
PAGE TOTAL		
AMT. FORWARD		

Fig. 13

61.56 Flight Reviews

Have you ever wondered just how long your *pilot* certificate (not your medical certificate) is valid? Well, it's technically valid forever. That's right, a private pilot certificate never expires. But having a certificate and being able to act as PIC of an airplane are two different things. In addition to having a pilot certificate, you need to meet a few additional requirements to act as PIC of an airplane.

To act as PIC, you must have had a *flight review* within the preceding 24 calendar months. Just as with the medical, the clock starts on the month following the month in which the review takes place. If you take a flight review on April 19, 2006, this review is valid through April 30, 2008 as shown Figure 14A (May 1, 2006 to April 30, 2008 is 24 calendar months). Of course, you can take as many flight reviews as you like, whenever you like. Each one resets the clock and gives you another 24 months of pilot life. Since it takes place every two years, this is sometimes referred to as a *biennial flight review* or *BFR*.

The purpose of the flight review is to ensure that you are still in possession of the basic piloting skills needed to fly safely. Flight reviews consist of a refresher on Part 91 of the regulations and the necessary flight maneuvers to convince the instructor giving you the review that you know what you're doing. A minimum of one hour of flight training and one hour of ground training is required for this review.

Since the purpose of the flight review is to determine your level of flight skill and ground knowledge, taking any checkride for a new certificate or rating automatically counts as a flight review. If you complete one or more phases of an FAA-sponsored pilot proficiency award program (sometimes called the *Wings Program*), this also counts as a flight review.

Keep one more thing in mind about the flight review. It's applicable for anything you're certified to fly. Suppose you are certificated to fly helicopters, airplanes, hot air balloons and gliders. You decide to take your flight review in a glider. Does this flight review apply to the other category and class of aircraft in which you're rated? Yes, it does. You don't have to take a flight review in each individual category and class of aircraft. This means you can pass a BFR in a balloon and be legal to fly an airplane, even if you haven't touched one in 18 years (Remember Rod's Rule of Rules. It doesn't have to make sense. Just follow it.)

Sorry, but you can't take a flight review in a *single-place* airplane. There was a time when a flight instructor could observe you from the ground as you flew a single-place airplane overhead. Flight instructors often considered this the safest flight review they could give. Many years ago a crusty pilot showed up in a four-place airplane with three of the four seats yanked out. He tried to convince me to give him a flight review by observing him from the ground. No dice. When I asked why he took his seats out, he replied, "Flight instructors make me nervous." I wonder if he ever had one?

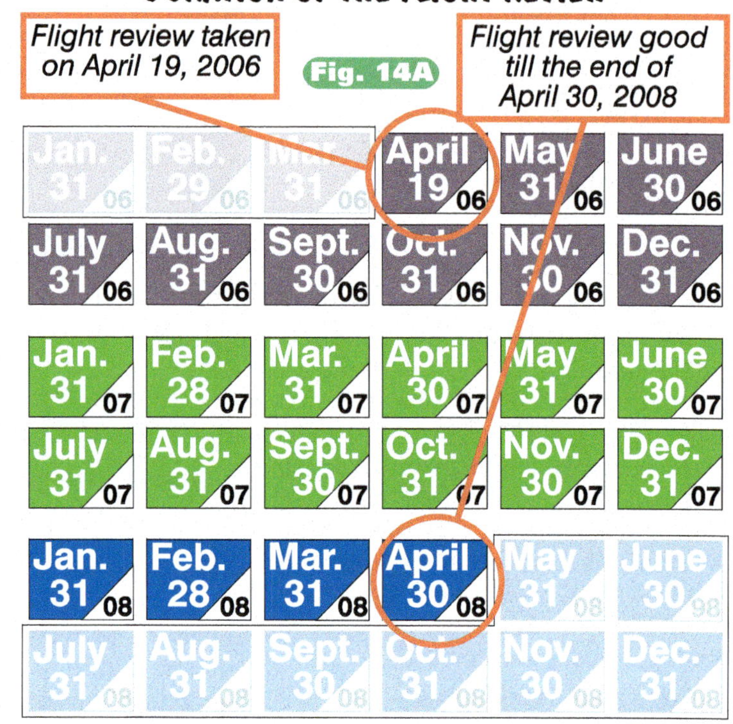

If you feel nervous about taking a flight review, find some comfort in this thought: You can't fail a flight review. You might not pass immediately, but you can't fail. There's no provision for marking a failure in your logbook. In other words, the instructor doesn't use an enormous red pen to indelibly write in a pilot's logbook "Bob has miserably failed his flight review, he's only half the man he should be." If at first you don't succeed, try, try again. The concept here is that the flight review is an educational experience, not a punitive one.

One time I gave a flight review to a fellow in a Citabria (a taildragger). He hadn't flown in quite a while, so his first landing was a thriller. We smacked the ground and started swerving down the runway. After swerving for a few hundred feet, the tower called and said, "32 Bravo, do you need some assistance, or perhaps you'd like a little music?" We continued practicing until he became proficient. Then, I signed him off for the flight review similar to the endorsement shown in Figure 14B.

This is what a flight review endorsement looks like in your pilot logbook.

REMARKS, PROCEDURES, MANEUVERS	NO. INSTR APP.	NO. LDG.
I certify that Ms. Martha Spinproof, private pilot, #212234521, has satisfactorily completed a flight review of § 61.56(a) on (10/13/2008).		6
Rod Machado 10/13/08, Rod Machado 123456 CFI, Exp. 4/30/09		

Fig. 14B

61.57 Recent Flight Experience: Pilot In Command

A flight review gets you PIC privileges, but the FAA thinks you ought to do a bit more to be entitled to carry passengers. The FAA assumes passengers are innocent and trusting souls, unschooled in the ways of aviation, and thus dependent on the pilot. More often than not, this is true.

If you want to take a passenger flying, you must have recent experience in the particular category and class of aircraft you intend to fly. Welcome to the *recency* rule.

The FAA states that, to act as PIC while carrying passengers, you must have made, within the preceding 90 days, at least three takeoffs and three landings as the sole manipulator of the flight controls in the same category, class and type (if a type rating is required) of aircraft you intend to fly. (Yes, it *is* possible to have more takeoffs than landings logged, or vice versa. Remember earlier that I said PIC designation can change at any time. If you go flying with a pilot friend, she could make a takeoff and you could make a landing. Each gets the appropriate credit.)

Figure 15 shows an example of a pilot's logbook. If today's date is March 15th, 90 days into the past would be December 16th. Does he meet the recency requirement? Yes, he has two landings in a Cessna 172 and one in a Katana—both single-engine land airplanes. He may act as PIC carrying passengers in a single-engine land airplane.

Suppose you only have two takeoffs and landings logged within the preceding 90 days? You aren't current to carry passengers until you log one more takeoff and landing. Simply go out, do one more takeoff and landing, log it, then invite your passengers into the airplane.

This is where tact becomes an asset. I do *not* recommend saying "Hey, you guys wait here, I'm going to go out and get current, then I'll come back and pick you up." That's one of those declarations that makes people suddenly remember they left the water running at their summer home 150 miles away, and they need to go deal with it immediately. Either get current before having friends join you at the airport, or be creative. "Let me go burn off some fuel, so there will be more room for your luggage" is usually a bestseller. They don't know that the luggage doesn't go in the fuel tank.

Touch-and-go landings in a *tricycle gear airplane* are acceptable for meeting the daytime recent experience requirements. If, however, you are planning on flying a *taildragger*, the landings must be made to a full stop. The reason is that the FAA doesn't consider a taildragger to

There was an airport here until your author, as a student pilot on a cross country flight, landed a little hard. Oh well.

RECENCY OF EXPERIENCE

December 2006 — 90 days into the past is December 16, 2006

January 2007

February 2007

March 2007 — Today's date: March 15, 2007

Fig. 15 *This pilot has had 3 takeoffs and 3 landings within the preceding 90 days in the same category and class of aircraft and is therefore legal to carry passengers.*

Date 06/07	AIRCRAFT MAKE & MODEL	...S, MANEUVERS	NO. INSTR APP.	NO. LDG.
12/22	Cessna 172 Skyhawk			1
12/30	Cessna 172 Skyhawk			1
3/1	Katana DA-20			1

have stopped flying until it has come to a complete rest. Of course, if you obtained your recent experience in a tailwheel airplane, this automatically applies to a tricycle gear airplane.

Recent Experience at Night – The recency rule has a dark side. Literally. There is a separate recency rule if you want to carry passengers on night flights.

Night time, for the purpose of passenger currency, begins one hour after sunset (when it's good and dark) and ends one hour before sunrise (while it's still dark). If you want to carry passengers during this time, you must have made three *night* takeoffs and three *night* landings within the preceding 90 days as sole manipulator of the flight controls (That's right! You shouldn't need someone else's hands on the controls to get this thing down). Once again, this must be done in the same category and class of aircraft in which you intend to carry passengers.

Suppose you're flying with passengers and are not night current. If official sunset is 1800 (that's 6 o'clock), what's the latest time you can legally carry these folks? You can carry them up to but not beyond 1900 (7 o'clock). You should be on the ground by 1900. Your only recourse is to land, deplane the passengers, do three takeoffs and landings, log it, and spend the rest of the time convincing your passengers why they should get back in the airplane with you. You might try the fuel-and-baggage explanation again, or suggest you were sweeping the airspace for aliens.

Figure 16 shows an example of a pilot's logbook meeting the recent experience requirements to carry passengers at night.

If today's date is December 15th, 2008, then this pilot has 3 takeoffs and 3 landings withing the preceding 90 days in a single-engine land airplane to a full stop at night time. He is, therefore, legal to carry passengers at night. **Fig. 16**

Date 2008	AIRCRAFT MAKE & MODEL	CONDITIONS OF DAY	CONDITIONS OF NIGHT	UVERS	NO. INSTR APP.	NO. LDG.
8/15	Katana DA-20	.9				1
9/25	Cessna 172 Skyhawk		1.2			1
11/5	Warrior PA-28-151	.8				1
11/7	Citabria		1.0			2
11/9	Mooney M-21		1.2			2

All landings for night currency must be done to a full stop. Touch-and-goes don't count. Perhaps to make up for the extra imposition, you'll be happy to know that if you're legal to carry night-flight passengers, you're also current for daylight flight with human company. It makes sense that if you can land at night, you most certainly can land during the day. This doesn't work the other way around, however. One of my students was having trouble landing smoothly at night. I said, "Hey Bob, how come you can't land smoothly at night?" He replied, "Because dark air has less lift in it than white air." I made $5 on that answer.

61.60 Change of Address

You've won the lottery and bought a big new house. You filed a change of address card to tell everyone from Aunt Mildred to the people who send you the mail order catalogs for rubber duckies. The one notification you're most likely to forget is the FAA. Unfortunately, your right to fly as PIC expires 30 days after the move unless you've told the FAA where you'll be headed.

Simply send a postcard (or anything else) with your new address to the: FAA, Airman Certification Branch ASF-760, P.O. Box 25082, Oklahoma City, OK, 73125-0082 (or notify them via email at www.faa.gov and follow the links). Whatever you do, don't send them your logbook, your pilot certificate, or a picture of you in a U-Haul moving van enroute to your new place.

FAR 61.87 Solo Requirements For Student Pilots

Nothing is more exciting than soloing (flying alone) an airplane. Your first command!

My flight instructor took me by complete surprise when I first soloed. I simply didn't expect it. He pulled out my logbook and signed it. Glancing over at me he gave his typical pre-solo speech, "Remember, it will be lighter with me out of the plane and it will want to climb faster." I was so nervous I thought he said, "Revenge her, it grills my ladder, it will help extinguish the pain and you'll turn to crime faster." I figured this was some sort of cryptic pre-solo benediction, and waited for the secret handshake that never came.

My instructor shut the door, saluted, mentioned something about insurance deductibles, and motioned me on. It would have been real quiet in there except for the loud pounding sound. I thought it was the flight guru trying to get back in. It was my heart, trying to get out. Smart heart.

Solo flight time was not created just to give your instructor a rest, though it accomplishes that worthwhile function. It's primarily a confidence building exercise. This is why regulations presently require a

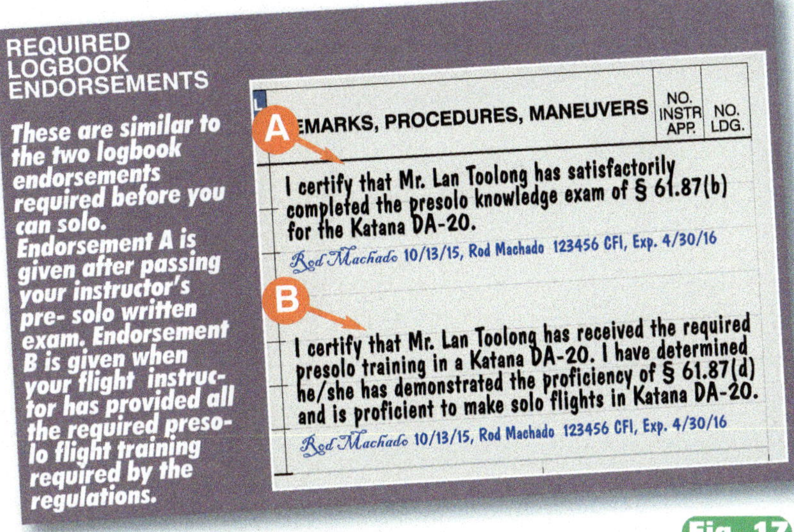

Fig. 17

THE STUDENT PILOT CERTIFICATE

As of April 1, 2016, traditional paper-type student pilot certificates (shown below) will no longer be issued by the FAA. Plastic student pilot certificates (see Fig. 5) will be issued and all solo endorsements will be entered in the student pilot's logbook.

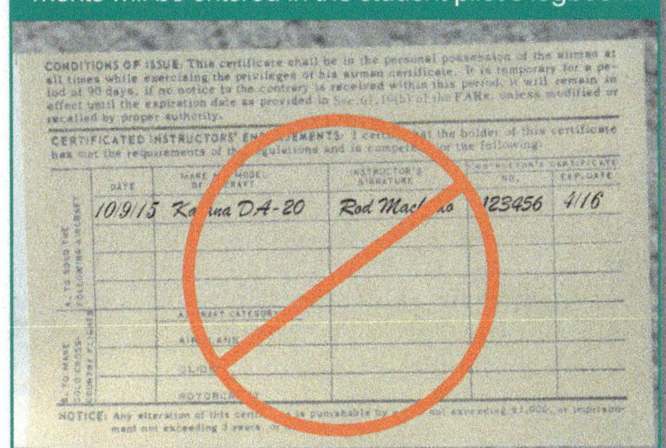

minimum of 40 hours total flight time with a minimum of 20 hours of flight training (sometimes called *dual instruction* with your flight instructor) and 10 hours of solo flight training (that's by yourself) in preparation for the private pilot certificate. Flying alone, dependent only upon yourself, builds tremendous self reliance.

Several things must be accomplished before you solo. First, your instructor must give you all the instruction required by the appropriate parts of FAR 61.87. This is the basic knowledge required to competently handle a single-engine airplane in solo flight. You must also take a pre-solo written test. Unlike the FAA knowledge exam, this is a rather informal exam consisting of approximately 20 questions designed by your instructor to test your understanding of the airplane and pertinent regulations.

Two administrative acts must be accomplished by your instructor before you take to the sky for solo flight. First, your logbook must be endorsed for the specific make and model of airplane you'll solo. Figure 17 displays a typical logbook endorsement for solo. Notice the logbook is endorsed for solo in a Katana DA-20. You couldn't fly a different make and model of Katana unless your instructor endorsed in your logbook for this airplane.

Once you've been soloed, can you continue to fly without being under the supervision of your instructor? No way. Instructors are required to endorse your logbook for solo every 90 days (Figure 18A). Being kicked out of the nest means you must return to the nest at least once every three months for an endorsement. Most instructors require that you keep them informed of all your solo flying activities. They seldom let you fly without some form of supervision.

If you desire to fly solo at night, your instructor must provide you with the flight training listed in FAR 61.87. He or she must also endorse your logbook as per the appropriate parts of FAR 61.87 (Figure 18B).

Keep in mind that student pilot certificates are issued by the FAA's Civil Aviation Registry. You can apply for this certificate through

90 DAY STUDENT ENDORSEMENTS

Student pilots need an endorsement in their logbook every 90 days from an instructor to continue their solo flights.

REMARKS, PROCEDURES, MANEUVERS	NO. INSTR APP.	NO. LDG.
I certify that Mr. James T. Kirk has received the required training to qualify for solo flying. I have determined he (or she) meets the applicable requirements of section § 61.87(p) and is proficient to make solo flights in a Cessna 150 Enterprise. Rod Machado 10/13/15, Rod Machado 123456 CFI, Exp. 4/30/16		

Fig. 18A

Student pilots need an endorsement in their logbook every 90 days from an instructor to fly solo flights at night.

REMARKS, PROCEDURES, MANEUVERS	NO. INSTR APP.	NO. LDG.
I certify that Mr. James T. Kirk has received the required presolo training in a Cessna 150 Enterprise. I have determined he has demonstrated the proficiency of § 61.87(o) and is proficient to make solo flights at night in a Cessna 150 Enterprise. Rod Machado 10/13/15, Rod Machado 123456 CFI, Exp. 4/30/16		

Fig. 18B

your flight instructor, a designated pilot examiner or directly at your local FAA office (your instructor is your best bet here). Your instructor will accept either a paper application (an FAA 8710 form) or help you fill out the web-based IACRA (Integrated Airman Certification and/or Rating Application) form (Figure 19). It will take about three weeks for your student pilot certificate to arrive as the TSA does its typical background checks (I don't mean they check your backyard, either). When it arrives, you'll have a nice, new, shiny, solid plastic, student pilot certificate that has no expiration date.

Several years ago, I came across a student pilot with an extraordinary amount of time. He had over 10,000 hours of flight time spaced over a 20 year period. In 1968, he soloed in his own airplane, flew away from the airport, and never flew back. I can only imagine his instructor standing by the runway watching this guy fly off into the sunset and disappear like those six TBM avengers over the Bermuda Triangle. The way he told the story he didn't think he had to fly with another instructor once he soloed. Always make it a point to keep your instructor informed about your solo flight activities.

The FAA's IACRA (Integrated Airman Certification and/or Rating Application) site is where you'll fill out the application for your student pilot certificate under your instructor's supervision. Visit Google.com, type "IACRA" into the search bar and visit this site.

Fig. 19

FAR 61.89 General Limitations

As a student pilot you must adhere to several limitations. First, you can't carry passengers. No, your flight instructor isn't a passenger. He or she is your guru, teacher and your ticket down. Flying for hire isn't allowed, either. You can't use an airplane to make money as a student pilot, nor may you use an airplane in any business pursuit.

During the cross country flight phase of his training, one of my students decided to spend time at his destination soaking up the sights. I became suspicious when he spent an entire day at the desert airport of Needles, California. After all, how many cacti, sand dunes and lizards can you drink in during an eight hour period? I discovered he was plying his trade as an appliance repairman during these solo excursions. It was an illegal activity. As punishment I made him repair all my appliances.

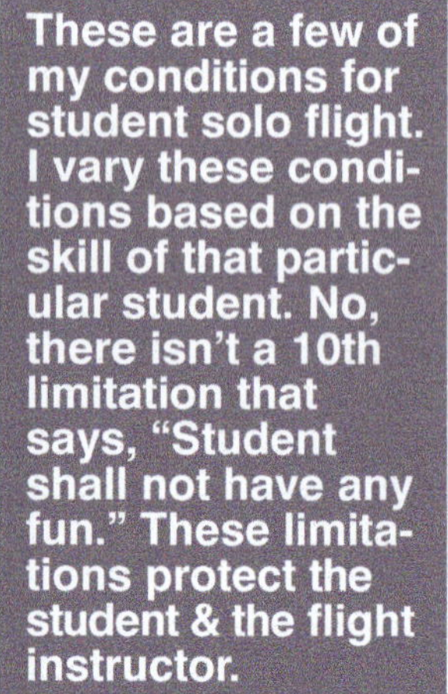

These are a few of my conditions for student solo flight. I vary these conditions based on the skill of that particular student. No, there isn't a 10th limitation that says, "Student shall not have any fun." These limitations protect the student & the flight instructor.

REMARKS, PROCEDURES, MANEUVERS	NO. INSTR APP.	NO. LDG.
Requirements for solo flight:		
1. Student must notify CFI at least 24 hours before any solo flight.		
2. Solo flight to be conducted only in flying club's airplanes.		
3. No solo flight if 90 degree crosswind component exceeds 7 knots (based on x-wind chart placed at end of this logbook).		
4. No solo flight between sunset and sunrise.		
5. No solo flight if wind gusts exceed 15 knots.		
6. No solo flight if visibility less than 5 miles.		
7. Airplane will have full fuel tanks before every solo flight.		
8. No solo flight unless student has obtained an abbreviated weather briefing (even for pattern work). (800) WX-BRIEF		
9. Student must follow additional requirements listed at the back of this logbook pertaining to X-C flying, night flight, practice area, etc.		
PAGE TOTAL		

Fig. 20

Student pilots are not allowed to fly when flight or surface visibilities are less than three miles during the day or less than five miles at night (see page F4 for the official definition of *night*). Students may not fly without visual reference to the surface. In other words, no flying on top of the clouds if you can't see the ground. Think about it this way. If you were on top of a cloud layer and had to make an emergency descent, cloud penetration would be inevitable. Since you don't have an instrument rating, you can't fly in the clouds.

Good instructors will stipulate conditions for solo in their student's logbook. For instance, I wrote the conditions shown in Figure 20 in one student's logbook. These are reasonable limitations for initial solo. One of my students added an additional item at the bottom of the list that said, "No solo if student expects to have any fun!"

Students are required by the regulations to adhere to any limitations their instructor places in their logbook. It's not unusual for instructors to list these and similar restrictions. Instructors are not attempting to prevent you from having fun. They're attempting to minimize your exposure to risk.

FAR 61.93 Solo Cross Country Flight Requirements

As a beginning student pilot, you are on a 25 mile leash. That's the farthest you can go without obtaining an endorsement for cross country flight (Figure 21). You are also required to land at the airport where you took off (in other words, no stops at the edge of your 25 mile world for a Coke and burger).

POINTS OF DEPARTURE & ARRIVAL
Date
AIRCRAFT MAKE & MODEL
AIRCRAFT IDENT.
FROM
TO
REMARKS, PROCEDURES, MANEUVERS
NO. INSTR APP
NO. LDG.
Solo cross-country flight: § 61.93(c)(1) and 61.93(c)(2)
I certify that Mr. Hue Gottalan Sumtime has received the required solo cross-country training. I find he has met the applicable requirements of § 61.93, and is proficient to make solo cross-country flights in a Cessna 172, airplane.
Rocket Rod 987654321 CFI Exp. 04-31-18
PAGE TOTAL
AMT. FORWARD
TOTAL TO DATE

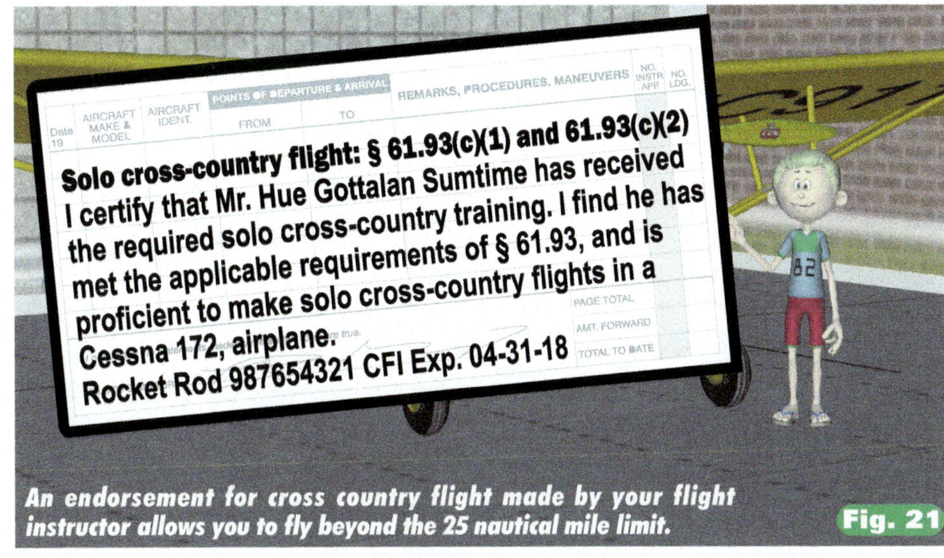

An endorsement for cross country flight made by your flight instructor allows you to fly beyond the 25 nautical mile limit. **Fig. 21**

Cross country endorsements require additional training. Navigation, weather, and traffic pattern entries are just some of the skills required for cross country flight. The main objective of cross country flight training is to keep you from getting lost. The next most important objective is teaching you to find out where you are if you manage to get lost. If you do get lost once in a while, though, don't feel too bad. It happens to everybody. As a student pilot, I got lost so many times that I had to keep changing where it was I wanted to go. The flight school finally bought a St. Bernard and named it *Rod*. With proper training you'll have no problem finding your way around.

There is a provision in the regulations that allows a student pilot to practice solo takeoffs and landings at another airport without having a cross country endorsement. If the airport is within 25 nautical miles of the departure airport at which instruction is received, the instructor can endorse your logbook for these solo landings. The only requirement is that the instructor must determine that you are competent and proficient to make takeoffs and landings at that airport. To do this, the instructor must give you training in both directions over the route and endorsed your logbook for that operation (Figure 22). This is the only time you, as a solo student, can land at another airport (other than the point of departure) without a solo cross country endorsement.

A solo cross country endorsement in your logbook is not a *carte blanche* authorization to fly when and where you wish. Before any cross country flight you'll need to have your flight planning checked by an instructor. This can be any flight instructor, not just the one from whom you're taking flight instruction.

Simply present your flight planning for the proposed cross country flight to an instructor. He or she will examine it, make sure it contains proper headings, checkpoints, fuel consumption figures, and several other important items. Then the instructor will endorse your logbook for that specific flight. This endorsement, shown in Figure 23, usually states that you can make the flight safely as planned.

In the endorsement, instructors can also specify conditions that must be followed. One time I stipulated in a logbook that a student should return to his home base if clouds were present over a mountain range notorious for its cloud buildups. I knew that clouds, in this instance, meant a little more turbulence than he could comfortably handle. Remember,

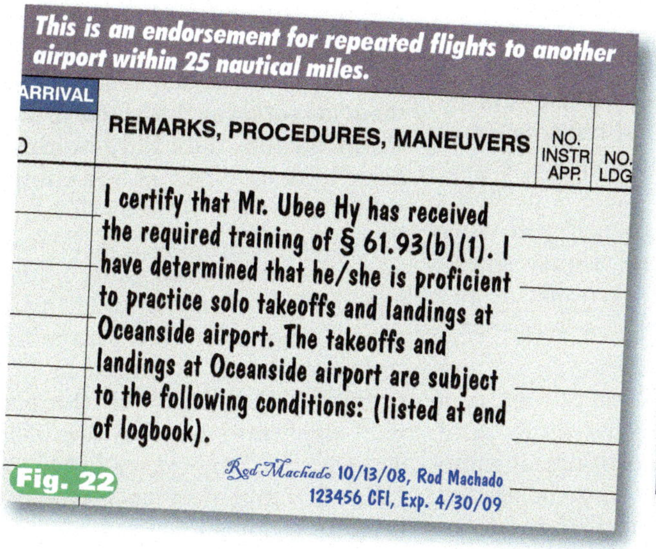

ARRIVAL
REMARKS, PROCEDURES, MANEUVERS
NO. INSTR APP.
NO. LDG
I certify that Mr. Ubee Hy has received the required training of § 61.93(b)(1). I have determined that he/she is proficient to practice solo takeoffs and landings at Oceanside airport. The takeoffs and landings at Oceanside airport are subject to the following conditions: (listed at end of logbook).
Rod Machado 10/13/08, Rod Machado 123456 CFI, Exp. 4/30/09

This is an endorsement for repeated flights to another airport within 25 nautical miles. **Fig. 22**

REMARKS, PROCEDURES, MANEUVERS
NO. INSTR APP.
NO. LDG.
I have reviewed the cross country planning of Mr. Paul Gofar. I find the planning and preparation to be correct to make the solo flight from Palomar airport to Chino airport via CRQ direct OCN VOR direct Chino with landings at Chino in a Cessna 152.
Rod Machado 10/13/08, Rod Machado 123456 CFI, Exp. 4/30/09
PAGE TOTAL

This is an endorsement given by an instructor indicating your cross country flight planning has been checked and found satisfactory for that flight. **Fig. 23**

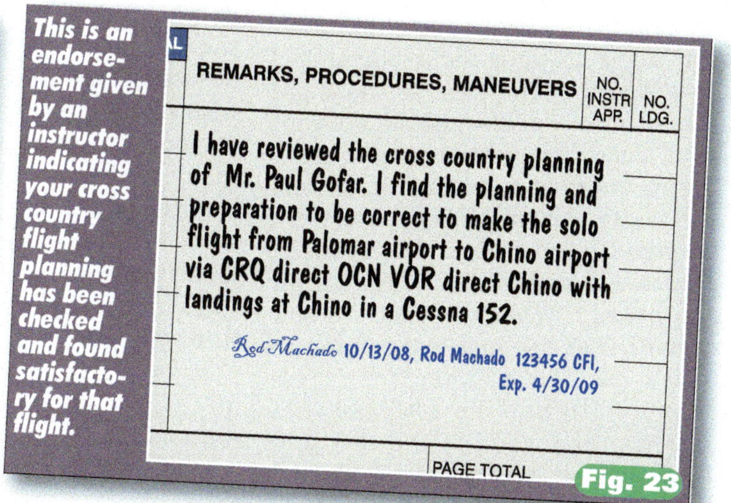

The blimp prepares for landing by chasing people off the runway.

After takeoff the blimp climbs out at the best angle of bag.

Due to some optical effect, the blimps looks big when far away and really small when viewed close up.

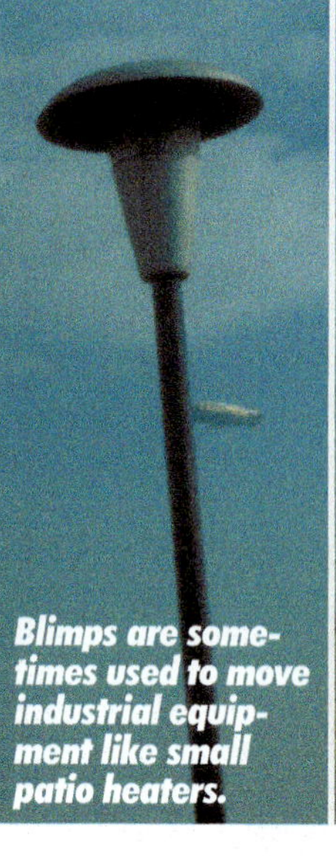
Blimps are sometimes used to move industrial equipment like small patio heaters.

A strong wind came up and this lady got a blimp caught in her hair. It could be said that she's having a bad "blimp" hair day.

these individual endorsements are made in the student's logbook for every cross country flight.

A cross country endorsement in your logbook allows you the additional privilege of making repeated solo cross country flights. If your instructor approves, you can make repeated solo cross country flights to an airport within 50 nautical miles from the point of departure. See, your leash is getting longer. You must have been given instruction in both directions over the route, including takeoffs and landings at the away-from-home airport. You must also adhere to any conditions specified by the instructor in the logbook. This privilege is different from solo takeoffs and landings within 25 nautical miles because it requires a cross country endorsement in your logbook.

Make sure it's a flight instructor who signs off your flight planning. I was watching the desk at the flight school many years ago. A student pilot walked in, took a look at a fellow in the corner, walked up to him, and began chatting. Some paperwork changed hands, then the student departed. I walked over to the corner and asked, "What did that student want?" "Oh, he just wanted me to review his flight planning for a cross country flight," he quipped. "It looked pretty good to me so I told him to go give it a try." I said, "Hey, I didn't know you were an instructor." He replied, "I'm not, I'm just a student myself." "Then how come you signed that other student off for his cross country flight?" I said. "Because he asked me to. Besides, I learned a few good tips for my next cross country flight." (I made $5 on that deal.)

Try and keep in mind that if you goof up, both you *and* your instructor will suffer the consequences. Remember Rod's Rule of Rules—just follow it.

FAR 61.301 Sport Pilot Requirements

See Postflight Briefing #6-1.

FAR 61.103 Private Pilot Requirements

A minimum age of 16 is required to solo an airplane. For balloons and gliders, the minimum age is 14. Why the difference? Apparently the FAA perceives the privileges associated with flying gliders and balloons to be less susceptible to problems of immaturity. The risk to others is probably less in a balloon; even if you were doing bag-and-goes on a busy street, most people could dive out of the way. I'm being facetious here, but I think you get the point.

Private pilot certificates require a minimum age of 16 for glider and balloon pilots and 17 for airplane and helicopter pilots. You must be able to read, speak, write and understand the English language. Yes! You must be capable of writing English. Apparently those flight plans written in Tagalog or Swahili are real show stoppers on your private pilot checkride.

You need to pass a knowledge examination before you can take a flight check for the private pilot certificate. A grade of 70% is the minimum to pass. The knowledge exam is good for 24 calendar months from the date the test is taken. If you don't take your flight test before this deadline, you'll have to retake the knowledge exam.

When I first went to the FAA to take the knowledge exam for my Airline Transport Pilot certificate, I had a little fun with the private pilot applicants in the room. I had been teaching ground school and had access to a large, six foot, wooden, E6-B type computer (basically a round slide rule, for those who haven't yet encountered this instrument of torture). I walked in for the examination. The lady behind the desk took one look at the thing and said, "No way!" I said, "Yes, way." She called Mr. Allen, the FAA chief, over. He said, "Good golly, I'd like to see the airplane that thing goes with." They eventually let me take it in the room. As I walked in I could immediately tell who all the private pilot applicants were. A few of them dropped their jaws and said, "Wow, I'm going to have to get me one of those!"

FAR 61.109 Flight Experience

In preparation for the private pilot's certificate, certain minimum flight requirements must be met. First, you must meet the basic aviation knowledge requirements found in FAR 61.107 (b)1(i-xii). These minimums specify the aeronautical knowledge required to make you an educated pilot.

The FAA requires a minimum of 40 hours total flight time to be eligible for the private certificate. This must include a minimum of 20 hours of flight training (that's time with an instructor), and 10 hours solo flight training (that's time alone in the airplane). Realistically, most people take anywhere from 45 to 70 hours of total time to obtain their certificates. This varies depending on where the training occurs. If you learn to fly in Los Angeles, for instance, you will probably need a few extra hours of preparation. L.A. is a beautiful place (during a cease fire), but it's also one of the most complicated, crowded, and communication-intensive chunks of airspace in the country.

The dual flight time must include three hours of cross country instruction and three hours of night instruction with 10 takeoffs and landings and one night cross country flight of over 100 nautical miles total distance. At least three of the 20 hours of dual time must be used in preparing you for the flight test within 60 days prior to that test. Additionally, you'll need three hours of instrument instruction (this is where the instructor clamps a plastic device to your head and limits your vision to the instrument panel).

The 10 hours of solo time must include at least three solo takeoffs and landings to a full stop at an airport with an operating control tower. Writers of the regulations are interested in exposing you to control tower operations before you get your pilot certificate. Most pilots experience a little anxiety when talking with air traffic control. Often, is seems that as soon as the microphone button is pushed, the human brain disconnects from the mouth. One instructor in Portland, Oregon told me about a student he had just introduced to the radio. The instructor said to the student, "Simply tell the controller who you are, where you are and what you want to do." The student nodded in acknowledgment, transmitted and said, "Ahhh, tower, this is 32 Bravo, Who am I? Where am I at? And, what do I want to do?" A calm came over the tower and a voice said, "Well, 32 Bravo, we give up! You stumped us!" Find solace in knowing that everyone has trouble understanding tower controllers at first, but you'll soon become used to their staccato speech and special aviation language.

A minimum of five hours of solo cross country flight time is also required for the private pilot certificate. To count as cross country flight time for this certificate, there must be a landing at an airport that's at least a *straight-line distance* of *more than* 50 nautical miles away from the *original departure airport*. In other words, there can be numerous stops between these two airports, but the distance between them must be *more than* 50 nautical miles.

As *part* of this five hour solo cross country flight requirement, you must make one solo cross country flight that's at least *150 nautical miles* in total length. Full-stop landings are required at a minimum of three points, and one *segment* of the flight must consist of a straight-line distance of *more than* 50 nautical miles between the *takeoff* and *landing* locations. This is unofficially known as the "big cross country." Figure 24 depicts several variations of this requirement. (Note: I recommend *every* solo cross country flight have a stop more than 50nm from the original point of departure so that the cross country time is applicable toward the instrument rating and commercial pilot certificate.)

Figure 24, Example A shows a flight with landings at three different airports having a total distance of 150 nautical miles. This flight meets the "big cross country" requirement since one segment (X to Y), has a straight-line distance of more than 50 nautical miles. Figure 24, Example B also meets these requirements despite having more than three stops (you only need three but can have as many as you want as long as one segment's straight-line distance is more than 50 nautical miles). Figure 24, Example C depicts a flight not meeting the requirements of this section. Although it has a total distance of 150 nautical miles, there is no straight-line segment more than 50 nautical miles in length.

THE "BIG" 150 NAUTICAL MILE CROSS COUNTRY FLIGHT REQUIREMENT

Example A

Total distance is 150 nm with 3 stops (the departure airport is considered one of the stops). One segment (X to Y) being more than 50 nautical miles between the takeoff and landing location.

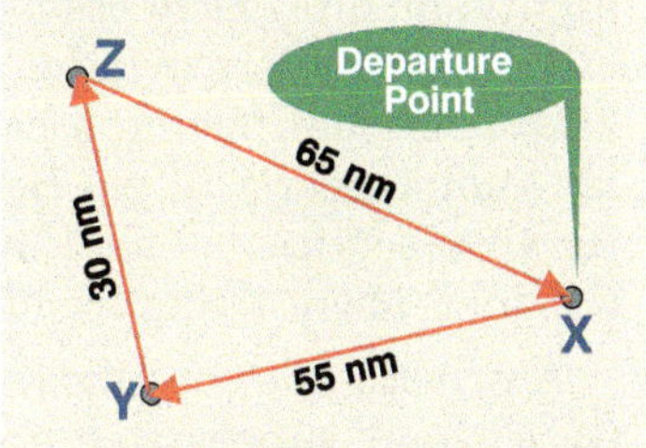

Example B

Total distance is 150 nm with 5 stops and one segment (Z to V, the last segment of the flight) is more than 50 nm. (Note: you can have as many stops as you desire as long as one straight-line segment is more than 50 nautical miles in length.)

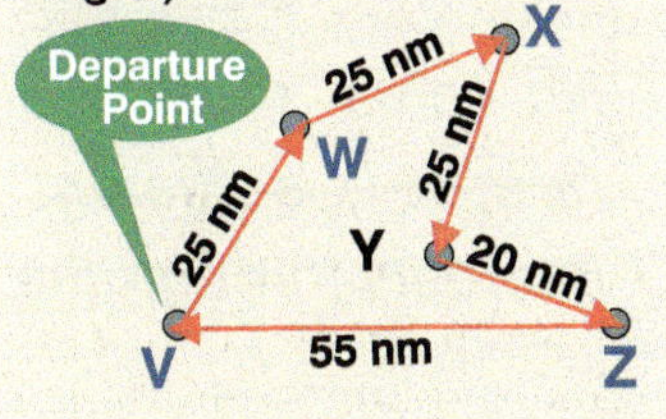

Example C

Total distance is 150 nm with 4 stops but there is no straight-line segment more than 50 nm distance between any two airports (X to Y to Z doesn't count since it's made up of two segments, not one). This flight doesn't meet the "big cross country" requirement.

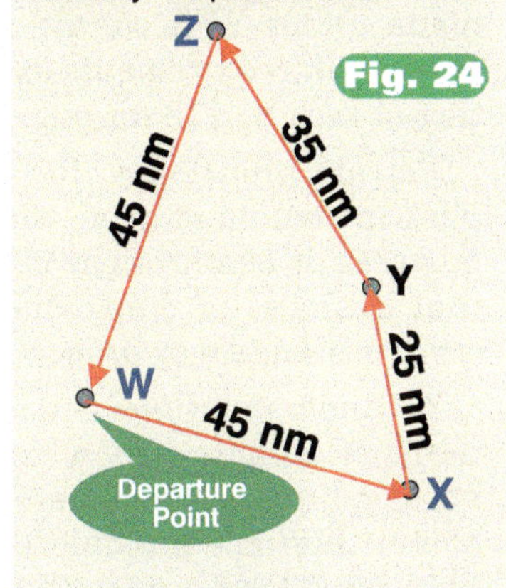

FAR 61.113 Private Pilot Privileges And Limitations: Pilot in Command

Drachmas, yen, shillings, moolah, bucks, dinero. What do all these have in common? All are forms of legal tender which can be exchanged for goods or services. If the service happens to be the piloting of an airplane, then it's a dream come true for most pilots.

Not unreasonably, the FAA rules are both specific and demanding about the training, experience, and capabilities of anyone who hopes to fly for hire.

Many pilots, unfamiliar with the rules governing flights for hire, have created damaging blotches on their otherwise spotless aviation records. It's a blotch that can keep you from having a career in aviation, or limit how far your career will go. Before ever exchanging a nickel for your services as pilot in command, know (and follow) the rules about flying for hire.

A private pilot certificate allows you to do two things: fly without supervision and carry passengers. Notice I didn't say anything about carrying *paying* passengers. You may not act as pilot in command of an aircraft carrying passengers or property for compensation or hire nor may you, for compensation or hire, act as pilot in command. It all boils down to this: furthering your economic interest by transporting passengers or property smacks of a commercial flight operation.

No actual profit need be shown to constitute compensation or hire; it is sufficient that the pilot be furthering his economic interests through the operation.

Official NTSB Case Statement

There is only one exception which allows a private pilot to act as PIC while carrying passengers who exchange money for the flight. If the flight is sponsored by a charitable organization and the FAA is notified at least seven days before the event, then passengers may make a donation to the organization for the flight. This private pilot must have logged 500 hours of flight time, no aerobatic or formation flights are allowed, and the flight must be made under VFR conditions during the day. (Several other FAR requirements exist here. Refer to the complete text of FAR 61.113 for more information.)

Private pilots may, for compensation or hire, act as pilot in command of an aircraft in connection with any business or employment if the flight is only incidental to that business or employment and the aircraft does not carry passengers or property for compensation or hire.

To understand *incidental* it's best to think about it in terms of its antonym, which is *fundamental*. If you cannot conduct your business without the use of your airplane, then it's possible flying is fundamental to your livelihood. Such activity would likely fall under the domain of commercial flying. If flying is subordinate to your business activity as a private pilot, then it is probably not a major enterprise for profit and a commercial pilot's certificate isn't necessary.

Yes, believe it or not, this is a four engine, two place ultralight. This is actual photographic proof that someone wasn't mowing their lawn on the day this picture was taken.

Flying cargo (property) in your Cessna 150 stretched-heavy for compensation or hire is specifically prohibited as a private pilot. Several years ago, a private pilot was operating a dog running business in Southern California. He would fly small animals to a Central California veterinary clinic for specialized medical treatments and be paid by the doctor for doing so. The local FAA got curious about what was going on in the airplane when they heard a downwind call to the tower that went, "Ahhh, tower, ruff, ruff, ruff, this is, ruff, ruff, ruff, 2132 ruff, ruff, Bravo, we'd like a, ruff, ruff, ruff, full stop, over, ruff." Upon landing, his airplane sprouted furry creatures of all sizes and shapes. At no time did he believe he was in violation of the FAR's since he didn't consider dogs to be cargo. Dogs are cargo. They are the kind of cargo that comes when you whistle, but cargo nevertheless. He was advised to modify his activity.

Let's suppose this pilot didn't accept money, but received pick of the litter as compensation for transporting man's best friend. Would he keep clear of the law? Not likely. According to Webster, in his best selling book (the dictionary), compensation is defined as anything given or received as an equivalent for services, debt, loss, injury or suffering. A similar interpretation seems to be held by FAA legal counsel. If you provide the service of transporting persons or property and receive any form of personal gain for doing so, you're probably flying for compensation. This may be money, personal favors, or livestock. Even if you've seen pilots around the airport wearing cardboard signs reading, "I will fly for food," I'm pretty sure a cheeseburger would be considered compensation.

Private pilots *are* allowed to share the operating expenses of the flight with their passengers. Specifically,

Don't Even Think About It!

...The subjective intent relates to the actor, whereas the objective result relates to the act itself. It is only natural that good will results between individuals and businesses when a party accommodates and assists another, and it is unlikely that a free ride would have been given to any stranger off the street who happened by. Here, the individual wanted to get to Honolulu to catch a flight to the mainland. However, because of the lateness of the hour, there were no scheduled flights nor any jets available for charter. Thus, not only would the flight be appreciated for the transportation it provided when there was no other desirable means, but in addition, the individual believed it would essentially be a complimentary flight. His natural appreciation no doubt produced good will which likely would lead to future business and referrals. Therefore, the flight did result in compensation, at least in the form of good will, even if the gratuity is discounted. As a result of the above reasons, the flight was found to be operated for compensation or hire.

Official NTSB Case Statement

the rule states that a private pilot may not pay less than the pro rata share of the operating expenses of a flight with the passengers, providing the expenses involve only fuel, oil, airport expenditures or rental fees. An operating expense is not the mortgage on your home or the alimony payments you must pay to keep your ex-spouse from strapping chains on your airplane. The FAA is very specific on this point. In a May, 1978 letter of clarification that is still applicable, the FAA said:

It remains our opinion that only the direct costs such as gas, oil, landing and parking fees and the like are operating expenses of a flight within the meaning of FAR section 61.113(c).

That's the FAA's way of saying that if you do pay less than your proportional share of the expenses, they're likely to bust your chops.

In the mid 1970's, a Cessna 150 touched down at what was then Orange County airport in Southern California. This wasn't a normal touchdown. Smack once! Smack twice! Whoomp, whoomp, whoomp flapped the landing gear. The pilot had ground looped his airplane, nearly ripping the right wing off his bird. He had turned his Cessna 150 into a Cessna 75. What was so unusual was, when the doors popped open, two of his paying passengers could be seen running from the airplane. What's interesting about this is that a Cessna 150 only holds a pilot and *one* passenger!

The PIC lost his pilot certificate, his plane and his wife (she divorced him). Had he been a country western singer he would have made millions, considering the amount of tragedy he experienced. As it was, he never flew again. Take the extra step to ensure your flying activities are legal and above board. If in doubt, talk to your local FAA representative. There's so much to lose by doing it wrong; there's more than enough to be gained when it's done right.

Professionalism

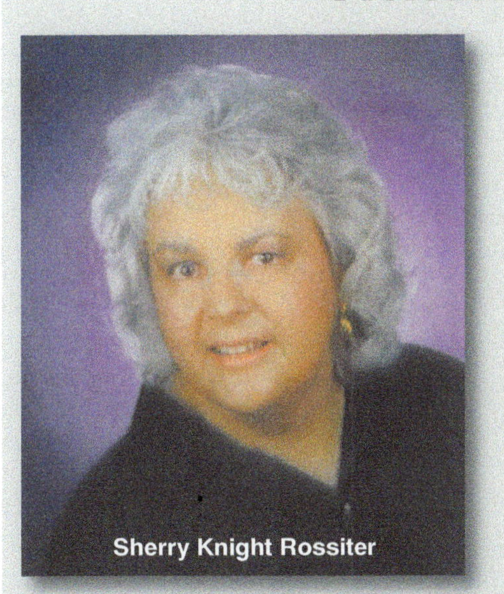
Sherry Knight Rossiter

I'm often asked when it was that I became a professional pilot. The answer may be surprising because it wasn't the day I first earned money as a commercial pilot. It was actually a few years after that on a day when I turned back from a flight because of very bad turbulence that had my Cessna 182 every which way but rightside up!

The dictionary defines "professional" as a person who is expert at his or her work. Professionalism involves using methods and practices different than those used by amateurs. It also involves exercising better-than-average judgment in all situations.

Recently, a 60-hour private pilot flew a Cessna 172 into the side of a 12,000 foot mountain in Montana under adverse weather conditions. He had been told by the FSS that his chosen route was not advised for VFR flight, yet he thought he knew better. A true "professional" would have mentally assessed his or her skills, reviewed his or her knowledge and experience, and concluded that 60 hours was "amateur status" under those weather conditions. Sixty hours might be enough flight time to successfully pass a private pilot checkride, but it's not enough to consistently exercise sound judgment (in every situation), which is based not only on skill and knowledge, but also experience.

The bottom line is that one must evaluate all factors before making a flight. Are you current as a pilot? Are you proficient enough to tackle the flight contemplated under the existing weather conditions? Is the aircraft's performance capability adequate for the route of flight? "Professional" pilots are not afraid to say "NO GO" when appropriate.

Sherry Knight Rossiter is an ATP and CFII rated pilot as well as a licensed counselor living in Los Lunas, NM.

PART 91 GENERAL OPERATING AND FLIGHT RULES

FAR 91.3 Responsibility And Authority of the Pilot In Command

Greetings, Captain, and welcome to FAR 91.3, one of the most powerful regulations in the book. Essentially, it gives you, the pilot of a small airplane, the same authority as the captain of a Boeing 747. The regulation states that you, the pilot in command, are directly responsible for, and are the final authority as to the operation of the aircraft. It doesn't get much simpler than that.

Declaring an emergency is one of the most important options of this rule. For instance, you might be experiencing engine problems and need tower assistance to clear the runway for landing. Stating, "I'm declaring an emergency" puts all available resources at your beck and call. When experiencing an emergency requiring immediate action, this regulation allows you to deviate from any rule to the extent required to meet that emergency.

Let's say the tower controller gave you a specific heading to fly while on your approach to an airport. Suddenly your engine starts running rough. You're calm, but the passengers are saying, "Hello Allah, come in Buddha, speak to me Krishna!" You decide to turn in a different direction, toward terrain more suitable for an off airport landing should the engine quit completely.

Flying a different heading than one given by Air Traffic Control is a deviation from a regulation. ATC says to you, "32 Bravo, why are you changing heading?" You respond by saying, "I'm having engine problems and I'm going to fly over a field on my way to the airport." ATC may ask, "32 Bravo, are you declaring an emergency?" In which case I would recommend you say, "Affirmative!"

Tower controllers now have more flexibility to help you with the problem. They can move other traffic, clear runways and summon ground emergency equipment if necessary. Don't ever be afraid to declare an emergency if you need help. Do this whether or not you think you may break a regulation.

Pilots are sometimes reluctant to declare an emergency. I remember one pilot at a Southern California airport who reported downwind with smoke coming from his engine. The tower called and said, "911 Charlie X-ray, would you like to declare an emergency?" The pilot immediately replied, "No, no way, I mean, no possible way. I'd just like to land as soon as possible!" I spoke with this fellow and asked why he didn't want to declare an emergency. He said, "I was afraid of having to do a lot of paperwork." I guess he wasn't afraid of a smoking airplane.

In refusing to declare an emergency, the pilot completely deprived himself of a very useful service. Even though it was only a leak in an oil cooler, his engine might have caught fire. Tower personnel could have launched fire trucks with fire suppressing foam that can save a burning airplane and its pilot.

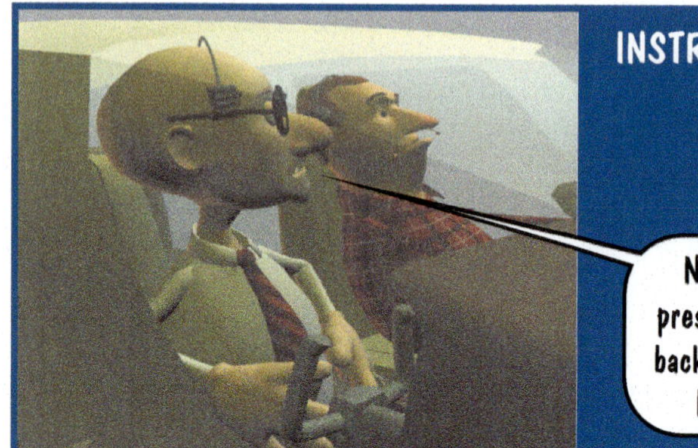

INSTRUCTOR COMMUNICATION FAUX PAS #1

The only time you must send in a written report is when requested to by the administrator. This request could come from tower personnel, FAA inspectors or anyone else operating in an official capacity for the FAA. At seminars across the country I constantly ask how many people in the audience have ever declared an emergency. Then I ask how many have had to send in paperwork. Of those declaring emergencies, only two to three percent have had to send in paperwork. They did so because of the administrator's request.

Such a request is often made when the events surrounding the emergency seem unusual enough to warrant inspection. Sometimes paperwork is necessary for ATC personnel to justify their actions in helping you with your problem.

FAR 91.7 Civil Aircraft Airworthiness

The next time you think about doing a less-than-thorough preflight, think again. This regulation states you may not operate an aircraft unless it's in an airworthy condition. It also makes you responsible for terminating a flight any time you believe the airplane is not airworthy due to the failure of a mechanical, electrical, or structural component. Personally, I think both of these are great rules!

You, the pilot in command, are personally responsible for determining whether the airplane is in a safe condition for flight. Disassembling the airplane prior to each flight isn't practical. The next best bet is to walk around the aircraft, preferably with a written checklist, prior to every flight (always be thorough and systematic, especially if this is the first flight of the day). This ensures that all necessary items are checked in a logical sequence. Checklists are provided by the aircraft manufacturer or they may be constructed and personalized with the help of your flight instructor.

A thorough preflight is especially important if the aircraft has been stored for an extended period of time. In this instance you should also make a special check for damage or obstructions caused by animals, birds or insects. As strange as it may seem, I've found birds' nests inside an airplane's engine cowling on several occasions. Had I not done a thorough preflight, all those little birdies would have had to solo a lot earlier than expected.

Several years ago, at an airport in the Los Angeles area, an unsuspecting pilot had an interesting experience with airworthiness. The senior partner in their Cessna 182 had taken the elevator off to have it painted. The junior partner wasn't notified about this. He showed up at the airport in a rush to make a business flight. With only a cursory preflight, he untied the airplane, taxied out and lined up for takeoff. Halfway down the runway he pulled back on the controls. Nothing happened. "Thump, thump, thump" went the airplane into the grass. It didn't take long for the FAA inspector to arrive and look the bent airplane over. "What happened?" asked the inspector. The pilot replied, "Ahhh, I think my elevator blew off while I was accelerating down the runway." Nice try! An improper preflight caused this gentleman a great deal of unnecessary grief. I believe the inspector said, "Well, this looks like the easiest $5 I've ever made."

If there is anything that looks like it might pose an airworthiness problem, get it checked out. Willingness to do this is one of the qualities separating mediocre pilots from aviators who think professionally.

Color codes are operating limitations. **Placards list operating limitations.** **.Approved Flight Manuals list operating limitations**

Fig. 25

FAR 91.9 Civil Aircraft Flight Manual, Markings And Placard Requirements

The next time you walk onto an elevator, notice the placard next to the door. It usually says, "Weight not to exceed 3,000 pounds." The elevator can't safely hold more than ten 250 pound guys and a 500 pound gorilla. This is known as an operating limitation. Airplanes have similar limitations.

Airplane operating limitations come in the form of color codes, placards, and approved Airplane Flight Manuals (Figure 25). You, as pilot in command, are required by this regulation to comply with all the operating limitations specified in any of these ways.

Operating limitations are seldom expressed in only one form. Most airplanes use several means to express these limitations. For instance, a typical general aviation airplane has color codes (which represent limitations) on the airspeed indicator; placards to identify maneuvering speed for turbulence and other maneuvers; and information on these limits in the Pilot's Operating Handbook (POH). An approved Airplane Flight Manual (AFM) usually identifies the maximum gross weight for the airplane. No matter how these limitations are expressed, they must be followed. Exceeding specific operating limitations is a violation of the FARs. It's also an act of profound mental ineptitude.

FAR 91.15 Dropping Objects

I recall a discussion among several pilots where the topic was about the legality of throwing things out of airplanes. One pilot said his instructor threw a roll of adding machine paper out of an airplane and chased it earthward. Another pilot suggested that real macho pilots might throw out the entire machine and chase it earthward. Is such activity legal?

According to the regulations, the pilot in command may not drop any object in flight if it creates a hazard to persons or property. Since even a tiny object rapidly accelerates to bullet-like speed, and can cause as much damage as a bullet when striking a person, pet, or property, it's pretty hard to argue that tossing anything out of an airplane doesn't at least cause a hazard, whether or not it actually strikes something. Unless you're capable of seeing everything from spotted salamanders to Spot the dog from several thousand feet up, I'd suggest keeping everything that's in the airplane in the airplane.

That Runway Has a Short on It!

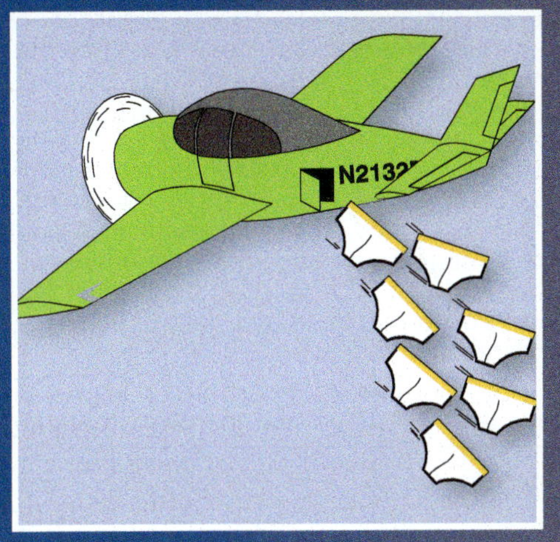

It was a warm summer morning at Fullerton airport when a Piper Arrow taxied into position for takeoff. My friend John, a tower controller, cleared the pilot for a right turnout after departure and the airplane started its takeoff roll. As soon as it was airborne John noticed something leaving the aircraft. It seems that the rear baggage door had popped open and clothing was slowly leaving the airplane. Apparently, the pilot's luggage had also popped open and his undergarments were being sucked out. John tried calling the pilot but he had apparently switched frequencies and wasn't monitoring the tower.

91.17 Alcohol or Drugs

We've already talked about alcohol and drugs, but let's do a brief review here. Regulations strictly prohibit you from acting as a crewmember of any aircraft within eight hours after consuming any alcoholic beverages. This regulation also prohibits you from acting while under the influence of alcohol. In other words, if you'd had several of those "World's Fair" cocktails—drink two and make an exhibition of yourself—you might still be tanked long after eight hours have passed. Having an alcohol concentration of .04 or greater in blood or breath specimen is prohibited according to this regulation.

If a law enforcement officer notices or suspects a pilot is affected by alcohol or drugs, he or she can request a blood test. The pilot must, by law, submit to this test. A law enforcement officer probably isn't going to become suspicious just because he sees your airplane weaving on final approach. If that were the case, I would have had so many blood tests that I would have surely died from anemia. On the other hand, if you smell like a microbrewery while telling the nice officer about why you landed on the taxiway instead of the runway, expect to make a blood donation.

If the FAA suspects that someone acting as pilot in command or as a required crewmember might be under the influence of alcohol, then that person must furnish to the FAA the results of an alcohol-blood concentration test (or authorize the release of such a test), taken within four hours of attempting to act as PIC or as a required crewmember.

Be very careful about carrying intoxicated passengers aboard your airplane. The regulation states that, except in an emergency, you may not carry a person who appears to be intoxicated or under the influence of drugs or alcohol on your airplane. This obviously excludes a medical patient under proper care (and not under the care of Doctor Jack Daniels either).

A Proper Preflight Prevents Problems

Bob carefully considers the importance of the item seen underneath his airplane.

91.103 Preflight Action

Before you begin any flight you are required to become familiar with all the available information concerning that flight. This is one of the many catchall regulations with enough loops in it to snare almost anybody who messes up. "All available information" is a bit broad, but it's clear that several critical items are *de rigueur*. For a flight not in the vicinity of the departure airport, you must check the weather reports and forecasts, fuel requirements, alternatives available if the flight cannot be completed, and any known traffic delays advised by ATC (*vicinity* is defined as more than 5 miles from the airport according to a 1982 copy of *FAA General Aviation News*.)

What does all that mean? Basi-cally, before every flight you must obtain a weather briefing. This is normally accomplished by calling the Flight Service Station (this is a weather service, not where you go to get windows cleaned) or by using a computer briefing service like the Leidos web portal at *www.1800WXbrief.com*. Not only do you want the current DUATweather, you want forecasts (weather to be expected). Alternate airports are technically not required for VFR pilots. The official language states that the pilot must have *alternatives* available if the planned flight cannot be completed. A 180 degree turn is a reasonable alternative. However, any pilot who doesn't figure out where he or she would go if they can't get where they're going is simply one fry short of a Happy Meal.

Traffic delays are available as NOTAMS (notices to airmen) from the Flight Service Station (FSS). You are required to get this information not because the FAA is concerned you'll be late to dinner if the airport is shut down, but because such a shutdown can put you and any passengers in an awkward situation. *Awkward* is a polite description of what happens when you arrive somewhere short on fuel, with marginal weather, only to discover the airport has been closed to resurface the only available runway and it will be open a week from Sunday.

You are also required to check the runway lengths at the airport you'll use. Now, this is one of those "Duuuh" sort of things, but you'd be

THE HEAT IS ON: Talk to Those Passengers

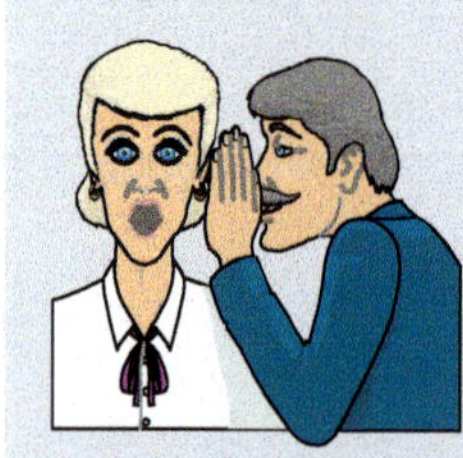

A new flight instructor decided to treat his wife to a flight on a clear cold winter's night. As with a car, in small planes the heater works best when you pour on the power. They both felt cold while taxiing, so the pilot had the heater adjusted to high. Pushing the throttle in for takeoff brought the heater to life with a hearty blast of hot air. Feeling uncomfortable with this rush of heat, the wife reached down and turned off the heater. When only a few hundred feet in the air, the engine sputtered and died. The pilot landed in the trees with no damage to the occupants; unfortunately the aircraft sustained a great deal of damage. Have you deduced what killed the engine, Dr. Watson? The knob that the nonpilot wife pushed was not the heater at all. It was the fuel control knob and she switched it off!

Moral: Before the engine is started, all nonpilot passengers should be given a thorough briefing that they shouldn't touch ANYTHING without the pilot's permission. This would be a good time to also explain the importance of a sterile (no-talking-to-the-pilot) cockpit below 1000 feet (airlines use 10,000 feet) during takeoff and landing.

D.T.

surprised how many pilots every year manage to make a 3000 foot landing on a 2000 foot runway. You have to know how long the runway is, and you have to figure out whether your airplane, loaded as it will be loaded, can take off, land, and take off again from the runways you intend to use.

For airplanes with approved flight manuals containing takeoff and landing distance information, simply check the airplane performance for the runway lengths and conditions of the flight. If your airplane has no approved flight manual, you can use any reliable information concerning takeoff and landing performance data that considers elevation, runway slope, gross weight, wind and temperature to compute takeoff and landing distances. Checking runway performance is required when taking off or landing at *any* airport, whether it's within or beyond the vicinity of the departure field.

The intent of the takeoff and landing regulation is to prevent you from using gut feel to estimate airplane performance. Your gut has no brains. Neither does the seat of your pants. Keep that in mind. It will save you much aviation grief. If the performance chart says the takeoff requires 1,713 feet and the runway is 1,500 feet long, take a taxicab instead of a taxiway.

FAR 91.105 Flight Crewmembers at Stations

During takeoff, landing, and while enroute, you, the pilot in command, shall be in your seat (sometimes called a station). On big airliners, all the other command performers (copilot, flight engineer) have to be in their places, all with smiling faces, as well. You are required to keep your safety belt fastened while seated, and if your airplane is equipped with a shoulder harness and wearing it doesn't interfere with your duties, it must be kept fastened during takeoff and landing. The rules do not demand that a shoulder harness be worn while enroute, but doing so is good practice. Besides, anything that protects you from becoming tossed salad in turbulence is good. One bang of your head against the roof of the cockpit can be incapacitating. It can also leave an enormous lump on your melon which always prevents a headset from fitting correctly.

There are only two times when you are not required to be in your seat as a required flight crewmember. First, you may leave the seat when your absence is necessary to perform duties in connection with the operation of the airplane. This could happen if you're a flight crewmember on a Boeing 727. It's highly unlikely on anything you'll probably fly with a private pilot certificate. Besides, where are you going to go in a Katana DA-20, outside to check the engine oil?

The other time you can get up and go is to get up and go. As the regulations delicately put it, you are permitted to leave your seat to attend to your *physiological needs.*The vast majority of private aircraft have no bathroom, so I don't expect to bump into the PIC in the aisle while flying in a Piper Warrior.

LOOK MOM—NO FINGERS!

The folly of propping an airplane with nobody in the cockpit was observed when the engine started. Chocks and rope slipped their grip; the airplane rolled and the prop struck hangar. There was damage to the hangar door, prop and left wing tip. (Perhaps a course in knot-tying for the reporter?)

ASRS Report

Safety tip: Don't even think about hand propping an airplane unless a *qualified pilot is at the controls.* Even then, you should be trained in the proper techniques for hand propping before attempting such an act.

Wearing seatbelts and shoulder harnesses is good for your pilot health. Please keep in mind that most of the time you are not only the pilot in command, you are the *only* pilot on board. A whack up the side of the head from unexpected turbulence can leave the airplane without a pilot and the passengers without a way to get home safely. They will bear a grudge.

Sometimes people feel trapped when strapped in their seats. I had one student who was emphatic about not wearing a shoulder harness. We argued about this for almost 15 minutes. Then, in a sing-song voice she quipped, "I want to be free, I've got to move around; I'm a butterfly, and you don't strap butterflies down!" Slapping my hand to my forehead, I looked at her and said, "If you're a butterfly, why are you taking flying lessons?" She buckled up.

FAR 91.107 Use of Safety Belts

What about passengers and seatbelts? Prior to takeoff, the PIC is required to brief each passenger on how to fasten and unfasten their seatbelt and shoulder harness. Getting into and out of an aviation seatbelt and shoulder harness is not always the most obvious thing in the world, as you will see from Figure 26. Keep in mind that your passengers are counting on you to keep them safe. Do not assume they know how to operate the seatbelts. You are also required to notify the passengers prior to moving (taxiing), takeoff, and landing to fasten their safety belts and shoulder harnesses (if installed).

Some seatbelt buckles are a little more complex than others.

Fig. 26

Actually Heard...

Pilot: "Golf Sierra Bravo, request instructions for takeoff."

Unknown Person: "Open the throttle smoothly, check temperatures and pressure rising, keep the aircraft straight using...."

One brand of safety belt requires pulling a lever to unlatch the belt. Several years ago a young lady went for a ride in an older, open cockpit biplane having this unusual belt lock. Her boyfriend strapped her in without showing her how to unlatch the belt. Parking at a refueling stop, he went for a quick snack while she remained strapped in the airplane. The gas person (liquid fuel liberator) was fueling the airplane from on top when the gas nozzle stuck. Gasoline rained down on her. Unable to release the belt, she was stuck until her friend returned. She had serious irritation to her mucous membranes. Be smart; inform all passengers about the use of their seat belts.

During taxi, takeoff and landing all passengers should be in their seats with safety belts and shoulder harnesses on (if the airplane has shoulder harnesses). Roaming around the airplane isn't allowed, and in most general aviation aircraft it also isn't possible. The first exception to this rule is that if the passenger has not yet reached his or her second birthday, that person may be held by an adult who is occupying an approved seat or berth. Parachutists are the second exception. They may use the floor as a seat since they usually leave before landing.

Our family had a close friend who insisted on never using safety belts when driving. I asked him why. He said, "If I crash, I want to be thrown clear." I replied, "Then you might want to ride on the hood. That way, if you crash you don't have to go through the windshield!" He still doesn't wear seatbelts, but I did make $5 off his answer.

FAR 91.111 Operating Near Other Aircraft

No person may operate an aircraft so close to another aircraft as to create a collision hazard. In other words, don't even think about buzzing another airplane in flight or on the ground. There is no such thing as a buzzing license. This is a very unsafe practice.

No person may operate an aircraft in formation flight except by prior arrangement with the pilot in command of each aircraft in the formation. You're not allowed to join up with another airplane in flight without letting the pilot know about it beforehand. Think how jolting it would be to look out your left window and view another pilot waving at you!

Have you ever wondered why you've never seen two passenger-carrying airliners in close formation? This regulation also states that no person may operate an aircraft carrying passengers for hire in formation flight. Nothing would scare me more than having the captain of my jetliner roaming the sky, looking for one of his or her buddies to play with.

FAR 91.113 Right of Way Rules: Except Water Operations

Now comes the mother of all rules. This is It, folks. The Big One, the Whopper of the FAA liturgy.

See and avoid. I want you to read and remember *see and avoid.*

To make a complicated bunch of words easy, the FAA says it is your responsibility above all else to see and avoid airplanes and obstacles. If you munch, crunch, or otherwise run into something in the air, the FAA says you're responsible under 91.113 for "failure to see and avoid."

Several right of way rules exist that determine who gets to go first in case of conflict. When a pilot must give the right of way to another aircraft, that pilot shall give way and may not pass over, under or ahead of the aircraft unless well clear. Just because you must legally maneuver to avoid an aircraft, you shouldn't return to your original course so quickly that you scare the daylights out of the other pilot.

Distress – Remember our discussion a while back about declaring an emergency? Aircraft in distress have the right of way over all other air traffic. If you had an engine failure and needed to land, you'd appreciate this rule. It would be quite scary if you called the tower, told them your engine quit and they said, "Roger 32 Bravo, we can't let you land right now because we're busy!" Fortunately, they are not going to say that for two reasons. First, because they really want to help you, and second, because of 91.113.

Converging – When aircraft of the same category are converging at approximately the same altitude, except head on or nearly so, the aircraft to the other's right has the right of way. This scenario is shown in Figure 27. Airplane B is to the right of airplane A, giving B the right of way. Airplane C is to the right of airplane D, giving C the right of way. Avoiding collisions while converging is best handled by climbing, descending, maneuvering or any combination of these. Personally, I prefer to maneuver in such a way that I never lose sight of the converging airplane.

CONVERGING AT THE SAME ALTITUDE

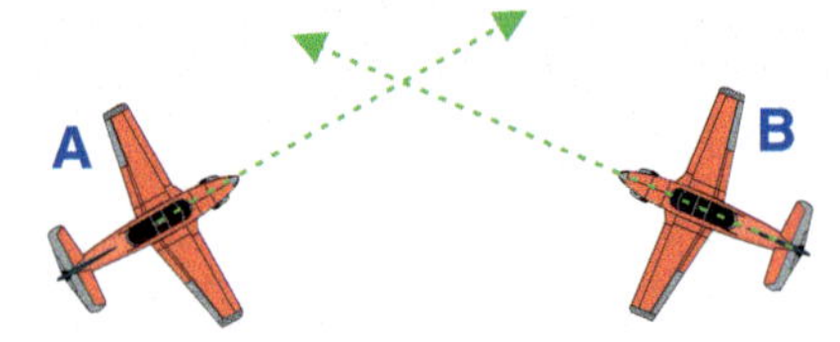

Airplane B has the right-of-way since it's to the right of airplane A.

Fig. 27

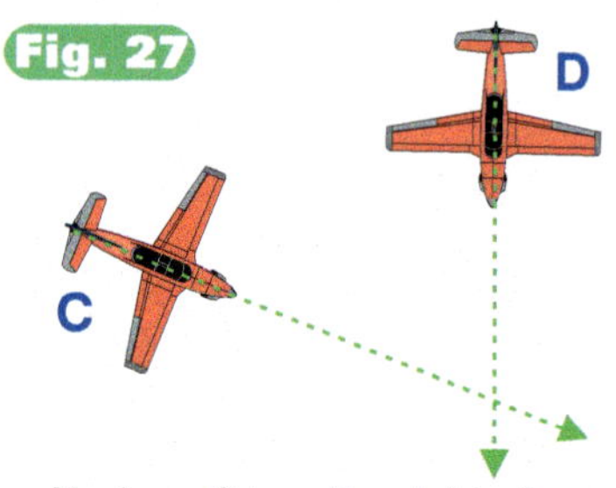

Airplane C has the right-of-way since it's to the right of airplane D.

AIRCRAFT CONVERGING HEAD ON OR NEARLY SO

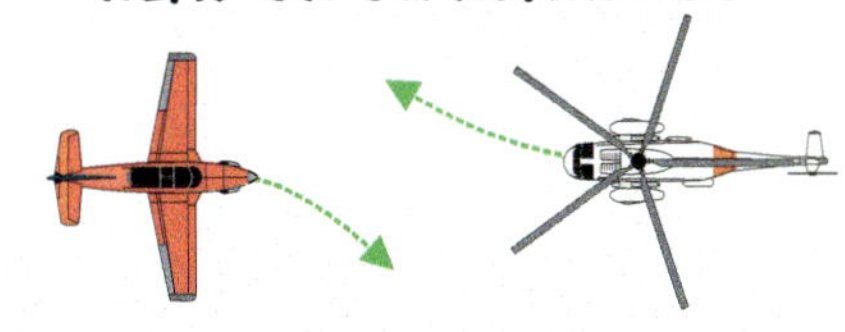

Since both aircraft are approaching each other head on, or nearly so, each shall alter their course to the right and pass well clear. Fig. 28

Aircraft approaching head on, or nearly so, shall alter their course to the right to avoid a collision (Figure 28).

Even though you may have the right of way, be careful about insisting on it. Pig headed pilots are a danger to themselves, their passengers, and others in the sky and on the ground (falling airplane pieces can cause serious damage). Be reasonable, be sensible, be safe.

Aircraft Categories – Aircraft of different categories on a converging course offer different right of way possibilities. The right of way usually belongs to the least maneuverable category of aircraft. For instance, a balloon has the right of way over any other category of aircraft. This makes sense, since you can't do steep turns in a balloon to avoid traffic. Balloons just sort of hang in midair, hoping no one will hit them. Since no evasive action is possible, balloons have the right of way over all other aircraft.

A glider has the right of way over an airship, airplane, rotorcraft, powered parachute and weight-shift-control aircraft. An airship (blimp) has the right of way over an airplane, rotorcraft, powered parachute and weight-shift-control aircraft. However, an aircraft towing or refueling other aircraft has the right of way over all other engine driven aircraft. Don't expect to see a glider towing an airplane. (If you do see such a thing, take a picture of it and immediately send it to me. It's worth millions!)

AIRCRAFT OVERTAKING EACH OTHER

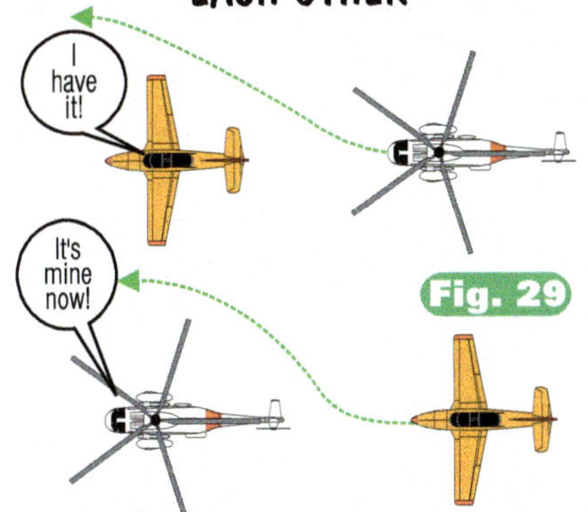

Fig. 29

Each aircraft that is being overtaken (regardless of its category) has the right-of-way. The pilot of the overtaking aircraft shall alter his course to the right and pass well clear.

Overtaking – One aircraft overtaking another presents its own right of way solution. The aircraft being overtaken has the right of way. The pilot of the overtaking aircraft must alter her course to the right to pass well clear of the slower aircraft (Figure 29). Fortunately, this is one regulation the Goodyear blimp doesn't have to worry about. The only time the blimp worries about this is when it's following a slower, fatter blimp. In this case the overtaking process may take hours and hours!

Landing – Landing presents yet another right of way scenario. Aircraft, while on final approach to land or while landing, have the right of way over other aircraft in flight or operating on the surface (Figure 30). Assume that airplane B has just taxied onto the runway. Therefore, airplane A has the right of way. Airplane A also has the right of way over helicopter C that's performing crop dusting short of the runway. Pilots should not take advantage of this rule to force an aircraft, that has already landed, off the runway.

When two or more aircraft are approaching an airport for the purpose of landing, the aircraft at the lower altitude has the right of way

RIGHT-OF-WAY DURING LANDING

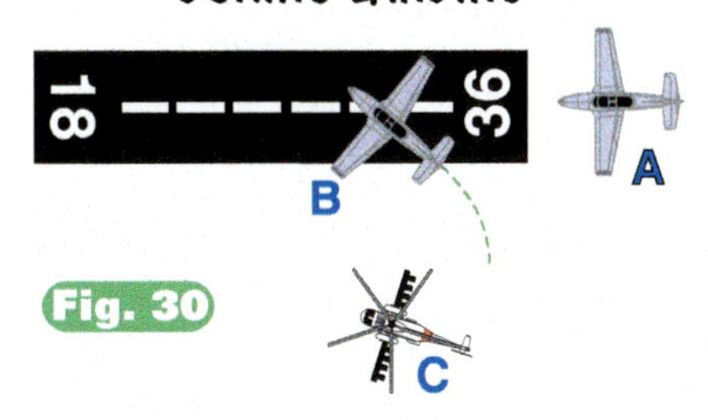

Fig. 30

Airplane A has the right-of-way over airplane B (which is taxiing onto the runway for takeoff) and helicopter C, which is crop dusting next to the runway.

(Figure 31). Airplane B has the right of way over airplane A because it's at a lower altitude. An alternate way of thinking about this is to consider the right of way as belonging to the airplane that's most committed to landing. Once again, pilots should not take advantage of this rule to cut in front of or overtake another aircraft that is on final approach to land.

Pilots are generally a very courteous group. Unfortunately, a few bad apples exist. Over the years I've come across a few pilots who were so ornery that they couldn't get along with dead people. These were the type of folks capable of rubbing entire cities the wrong way. I've actually witnessed two aviators coming to blows over who had the right of way in the pattern. Several flight instructors gathered around and no one knew what to do. One instructor actually suggested we jump in and help the bigger guy. Like cats twirling in heated frenzy, they eventually climbed into their airplanes and flew off to lick their wounds. It's a good policy never to insist on the right of way. Take it if it's yours, but demanding it is dangerous business.

RIGHT OF WAY DURING LANDING

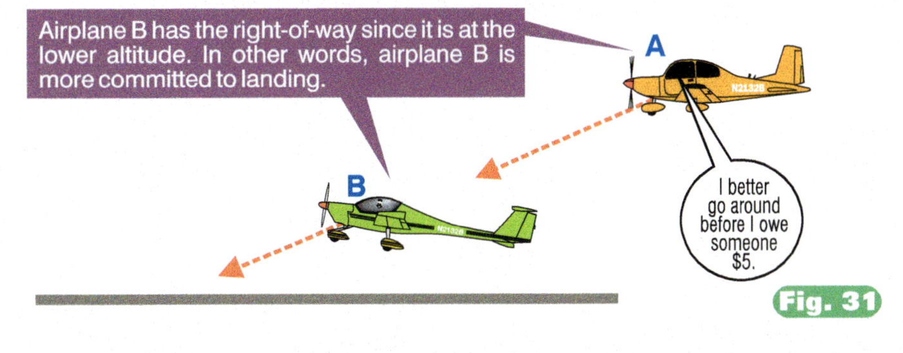

Fig. 31

FAR 91.115 Right of Way Rules: Water Operations

If you're landing a seaplane, you're required to keep clear of all vessels and avoid impeding their navigation. The notion here is that boats belong on the water, while airplanes are sort of odd ducks.

If you're on a crossing course with another aircraft or surface vessel, the aircraft or vessel on your right has the right of way. While approaching head on, or nearly so, each vessel should alter its course to the right to keep well clear. If you are overtaking another aircraft or vessel, you should alter your course to keep well clear (either a right or left turn is acceptable). This last regulation is different from overtaking in the air, where the overtaking aircraft should alter its course to the right. Operations on water may not allow you the option of passing on the right. There could be scuba divers or water skiers in that direction. There's nothing like going for a little scuba dive and getting conked on the head with the float of a big Cessna.

FAR 91.117 Aircraft Speed

Speed limits exists in the air as they do on the ground. Regulations state that no person may operate an aircraft below 10,000 feet MSL at an indicated airspeed of more than 250 knots (288 MPH). Why? Think about it for a second. Two aircraft flying toward each other at 250 knots have a combined closing speed of 500 knots (576 MPH). That works out to covering approximately 10 miles every minute! Remember, it is your job to "see and avoid." That task gets more difficult as airspeeds increase. Most small aircraft fly below 10,000 feet, generally under VFR conditions (without radar control and other niceties that generally accompany IFR flight). It's not safe for fast jets to fly at these altitudes while scattering the small fry like frightened quail.

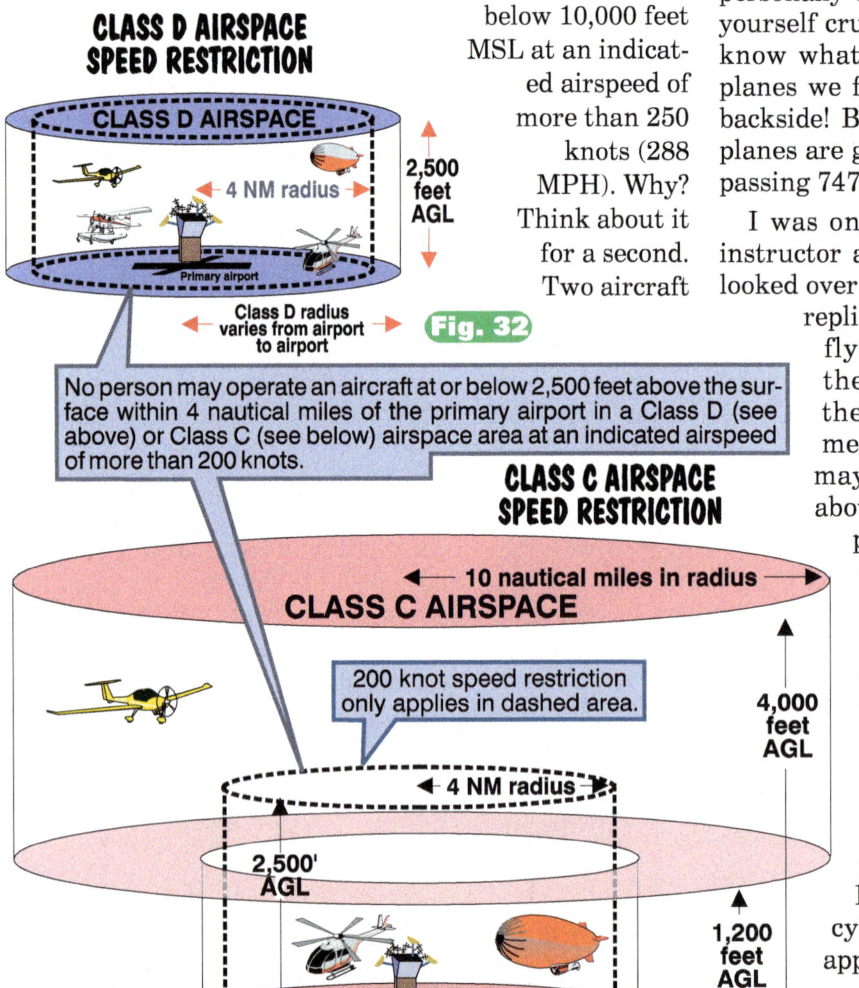

Most of us, unfortunately, don't have the equipment to personally bust the 250 knot speed limit. If you do find yourself cruising that fast in a Cessna 152, please let me know what kind of fuel you're using. Most of the airplanes we fly are so slow they get bird strikes from the backside! But things are changing. General aviation airplanes are getting faster. It won't be long before you'll be passing 747's on every flight.

I was on a cross country flight with my first flight instructor and was having trouble finding the airport. I looked over at him and said, "I can't find the airport." He replied, "Could it be where all those airplanes are flying over there?" I said, "That's just what they'd expect me to think!" Of course, where there are airports there are usually airplanes, meaning the sky is busy. Therefore, no person may operate an aircraft at or below 2,500 feet above the surface within 4 nautical miles of the primary airport in Class C or Class D airspace at an indicated airspeed of more than 200 knots (230 MPH).

Class C or D airspace is a cylindrical shaped area around airports having an operational control towers (we'll be talking more about airspace structure in Chapter 9). These areas are more likely to be occupied by a wide variety of aircraft. A 200 knot speed restriction makes it easier for aircraft intending to take off and land to see and avoid each other. Figure 32 shows the basic dimensions of these cylindrical areas where the speed restriction applies.

This regulation doesn't apply to any operations within Class B airspace. Class B airspace is a special type of airspace shaped somewhat like an

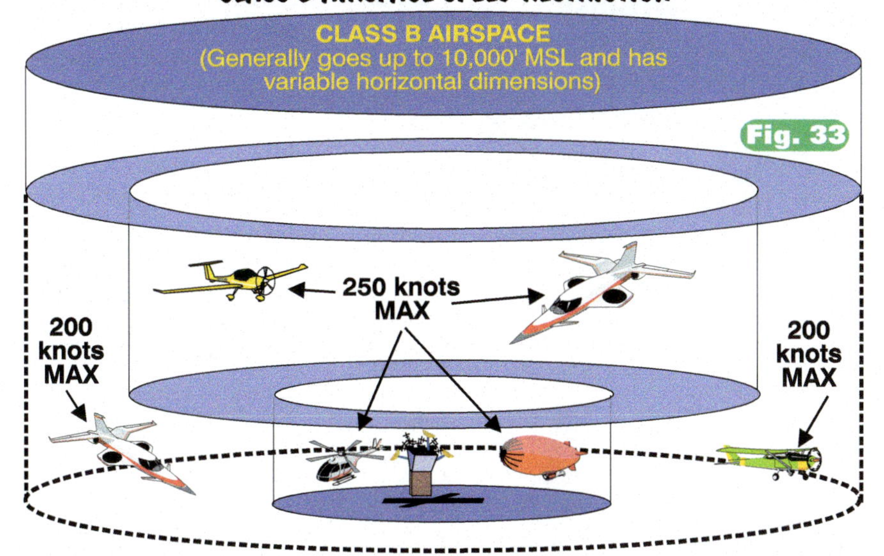

Underneath the lateral limits of Class B airspace (dashed lines) the maximum indicated airspeed limit is 200 knots. This also applies to any corridor through Class B airspace. Inside class B airspace the indicated airspeed limit is the same as it is below 10,000' MSL– 250 knots.

inverted wedding cake, as shown in Figure 33. It's designed to keep aircraft, usually the larger ones, under tighter control while landing or taking off at a very busy primary airport. Within Class B airspace the speed limit is 250 knots. Underneath the lateral limits of this airspace, however, the speed limit is 200 knots (230 MPH). Many aircraft try to avoid Class B airspace, which means they're likely to be found at its outskirts, making the lower limit a prudent one.

Some airplanes are just plain fast. The SR-71 (Blackbird) is one of the most impressive airplanes of this type. Diane, one of my trusty editors, who was also a radar controller in Houston, told me about a call she got from an SR-71. The pilot, with a Texas twang stated, "Ma'am, this is Blackbird 431 Charlie. We want to go to Beale Air Force Base. And, ma'am, we don't do turns!" Or windows. He was really saying that the aircraft moves so fast that one turn could put them in a different time zone.

FAR 91.119 Minimum Safe Altitudes

The rules designate certain minimum altitudes that you must maintain under given circumstances. These altitudes are designed to protect people on the surface as well as the pilot and passengers on the aircraft. For some aircraft, the risk associated with flying too low is greater than for others. Airplanes must be operated higher than helicopters because they require more distance to land. As a student pilot, I always thought helicopter pilots liked to fly low because it was easier to stop and ask for directions. (OK, I was wrong).

None of the following minimum altitude rules pertain to takeoff or landing at an airport. Taking off or landing obviously requires climbs and descents at closer than normal altitudes to the surface. Don't try stretching the rule by flying at treetop height 50 miles from the airport and then claiming you were just setting up your approach (you're going to owe someone $5 on that deal). Also, don't delay your normal climbout after takeoff just so a passenger can check her house for holes in the roof.

Here are some of the most important rules about how low you can go:

Rule No 1: No person may operate an aircraft below an altitude allowing an emergency landing to be made without undue hazard to persons or property on the surface in the event of an engine failure. This is another of the famous FAA catchall rules. On land, there's always a "basic speed law" that says that no matter what the posted speed, you can't drive faster than is prudent under the circumstances. In aviation, you can't fly any lower than it is safe, and if something bad happens, that proves you weren't high enough. You'll have a difficult time convincing an FAA inspector that flying 50 feet above a crowded beach on July 4th is a safe practice (besides, you never want to give someone a moving target to aim a bottle rocket at).

Prior decisions which the NTSB therein cited include those which concerned situations of (1) 10 houses and a school as a "small congested area," a university campus not shown to be part of a city or a town, and (3) a group of 60 to 70 cottages.

Official NTSB Case Statement

Common sense and good piloting practice dictate flying high enough so you can glide to an acceptable landing site. Professional pilots think this way and they never allow themselves to become trapped by circumstances and altitude.

Rule No. 2: When flying over any congested area of a city, town or settlement or over any open air assembly of persons, the aircraft must be

Plucky Bird

A Navy pilot called the radar controller and said, "Center, we've just taken a bird strike and are declaring an emergency." The controller working the flight made radar identification of the aircraft and asked for additional details on the bird strike. "It was a northeast bound chicken hawk," the navy pilot said. "He was big, too. He hit our canopy head-on at 300 knots." Maintaining his composure, the controller replied, "Roger, and how fast were you going, sir?"

ASRS Report.

operated at an altitude of 1,000 feet above the highest obstacle within a horizontal radius of 2,000 feet of the aircraft.

Figure 34 depicts a building in a congested area topping out at 750 feet MSL. An aircraft operating horizontally, within 2,000 feet of that building, needs to fly at a minimum altitude of 1,750 feet MSL for legal flight. The question pilots frequently ask is, "What is the definition of a congested area?" FAA officials have yet to define this concept. Frankly, it's often the NTSB (National Transportation Safety Board) that defines these concepts by legal precedent when pilots are called into an NTSB hearing to explain their actions. One thing is clear though: you'll have a lot of explaining to do if you violate this regulation.

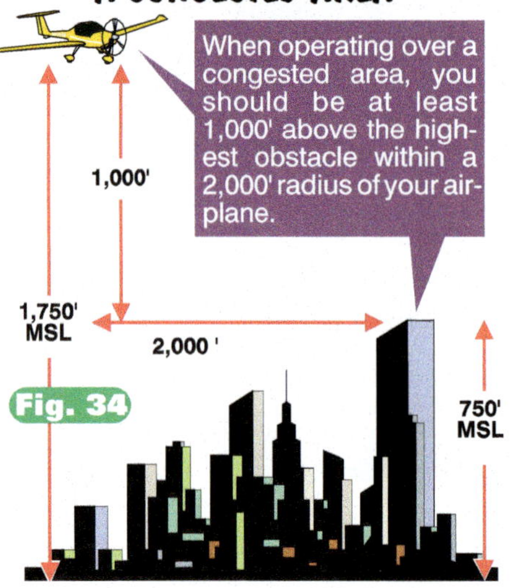

While a precise definition of *congested area* is lacking, we can understand what the FAA considers a congested area by examining a few NTSB court decisions. On one occasion, a pilot was cited for operating an airplane within a radius of 2,000 feet and less than 1,000 feet above a few isolated homes with smoke rising from their fireplaces. Smoke was a vital factor, since, by its presence, it implied the homes were occupied. On another occasion, a pilot wasn't cited for flying within a few hundred feet of an industrial warehouse. The reason? It was Sunday and no cars were in the parking lot. The implication here is that the presence of people is the major factor in determining the congestion quotient of an area. You'll need to use your good judgment on this one because of the vague definitions involved. Be conservative. Don't fly too low where there are lots of people.

One old timer summed it up very well when he said, "Never fly low enough so someone can get your aircraft tail number." Of course, that was the intelligent part of the statement. He went on to say, "Always fly an airplane with a two-tone paint job so that you can have conflicting eye witness reports."

Where the landing conducted by a pilot involved a final flight path under the bridge which was both unnecessary and inappropriate, the operation within 500 feet of structures was not excused by the prefatory clause of FAR 91.119 ("Except when necessary for takeoff or landing...").

Official NTSB Case Statement

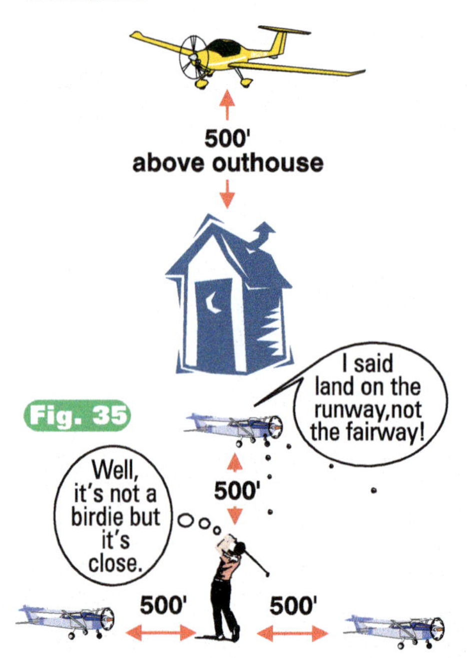

Rule No. 3: When operating an aircraft over other than a congested area, no person may operate below an altitude of 500 feet above the surface, except over open water or sparsely populated areas. In those cases, the aircraft may not be operated closer than 500 feet to any person, vessel, vehicle or structure.

When over open water or a sparsely populated area you may take your plane right down on the deck if you wish. But do so only if you can land safely in an emergency (see Rule 1). The moment you spot a person, boat, car or structure, you need to move away by a distance of at least 500 feet vertically or horizontally as shown in Figure 35.

In Honolulu, Hawaii, the pilot of a small aerobatic biplane had an unusual collision. He was flying just above the water when he collided with a surfboard. Smack! It was a direct hit on the leading edge of his wing. After landing at the airport, the pilot called the local FAA office and reported the encounter. He must have thought that the surfer intentionally tossed the surfboard toward his airplane during the fly-by. Otherwise, why report it to the FAA? Unless this was a particularly strong surfer, I hardly think it's possible to throw a surfboard 500 feet into the air (the minimum distance the airplane should have been from the surfer). Personally, I think the surfer saw the airplane and dove into the water to avoid being hurt. Imagine the conversation with the FAA inspector. "Is this the FAA?" "Yes, it is." "I was flying along minding my own business when some dude threw a surfboard at my airplane." "Oh, really, what's your name...?" Perhaps this pilot didn't think carefully before he made this call. One thing is sure, the FAA inspector was $5 richer at the end of the day.

FAR 91.121 Altimeter Settings

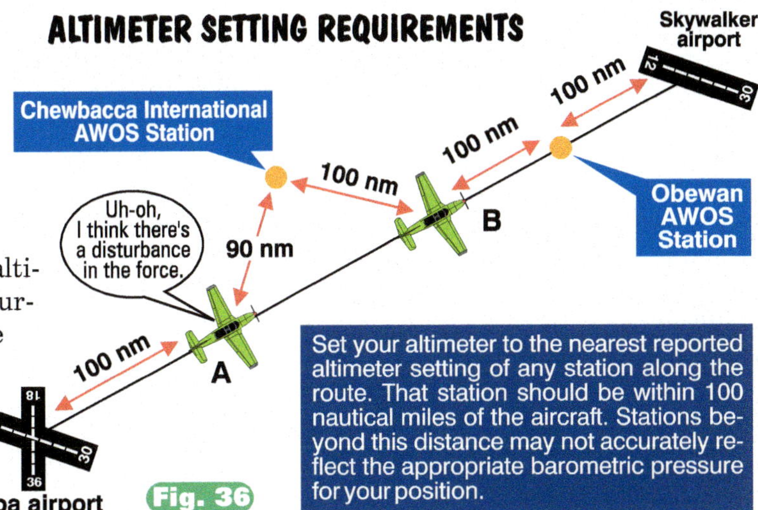

Fig. 36

In Chapter Five we discussed setting the local barometric station pressure into the altimeter's Kollsman window. We did this so the altimeter would correctly read our height above sea level. Of course, as we move away from the last altimeter setting source we need to update this setting.

Regulations require that you maintain a cruising altitude by reference to an altimeter that is set to the current reported altimeter setting of a station along the route and within 100 nautical miles of the aircraft. This regulation applies to aircraft operating below 18,000 feet MSL.

Aircraft operating at or above 18,000 feet MSL set their altimeters to 29.92" Hg. Fast moving jet-type aircraft are usually found operating at these high altitudes. Having to readjust altimeters every 100 miles or so would send most jet pilots to their carpel tunnel specialist.

Figure 36 depicts a typical cross country flight and the associated altimeter adjustment points. Assume your altimeter is set to the altimeter setting for Jabba International (the departure airport). You may fly for 100 nautical miles along the route before needing an altimeter update.

At position A, the Chewbacca International AWOS Station is within 90 nautical miles of your airplane. You set your altimeter to Chewbacca's altimeter setting and continue on to position B, where you are now 100 nautical miles from this source. A new altimeter source within 100 nautical miles of the aircraft is needed. Fortunately, the Obewan AWOS Station is along the route and within 100 nautical miles of the aircraft. Setting the altimeter to Obewan's altimeter setting, you continue to Skywalker Airport. On the last part of the flight, you should be within 100 nautical miles of Obewan. Therefore, you'll only need to keep the altimeter set to Obewan's station pressure.

What Did You Do That For?

After a particularly lousy landing by the copilot of an Australian airliner, that copilot heard the captain announce, "Ladies and gentlemen our airline wishes to apologize for the copilot's rough landing."

Some months later, the same crew was together and, you guessed it, the captain did an even worse landing. The first officer immediately jumped on the intercom and announced, "Ladies and gentlemen, our airline would like to apologize for the captain's rough landing."

The captain responded angrily, "What did you say that for?"

The copilot replied, "Remember a couple of months ago? I owed it to you."

The captain said, "But I never keyed the microphone!"

Source: The First General Aviation WWW Server

Realistically, try to update the altimeter every chance you get. This prevents altimeter errors and keeps pilots safely separated by using the same barometric pressure source.

FAR 91.123 Compliance with ATC Clearances and Instructions

This regulation states that when an ATC clearance has been obtained, no pilot in command may deviate from that clearance unless an amended clearance is obtained, an emergency exists or in response to a traffic alert and collision avoidance system resolution advisory.

Like many adolescents, some pilots have trouble with the concept of authority. They hate to admit someone else has the right to control their actions. In the case of Air Traffic Control, the authority is clear; your job is learning how to follow directions.

ATC clearances are authorizations to proceed under specific traffic conditions in controlled airspace. These clearances come in all sizes and shapes. Most commonly, they are headings to fly. When receiving VFR vectors from ATC, it's not unusual to be given a heading that puts you on a collision course with a cloud. Since ATC radar can't see clouds and VFR pilots are prohibited from flying into clouds, what do you do if you find yourself being vectored toward one?

You are required to follow the ATC clearance unless an amended clearance is obtained. Given the above situation, the only logical thing to do is to request another heading. ATC is almost always accommodating in these cases. Simply call the controller and say, "Sir (or Ma'am), this is N2132 Bravo, I'm unable that heading due to clouds." They may respond by saying, "32 Bravo, will a heading of such-and-such keep you away from the clouds?" You'll be surprised how helpful ATC is when they're not too busy. Remember, since you are a VFR pilot, under no circumstances should you fly into a cloud.

This regulation goes on to say that if a pilot is uncertain of the meaning of an ATC clearance, the pilot shall immediately request clarification from ATC. Simply stated, if you don't understand, ask.

A friend of mine took a fellow pilot on a demonstration sales flight in his cherried-out Cherokee 140. When asked what she did for a living the pilot stated she was a controller. "Excellent," my friend thought, "I can relax while she flight tests the airplane. After all, she's probably a controller at some big airport and is very familiar with airplanes, airspace and procedures."

She started up the airplane, taxied out and requested a clearance out of the Class C airspace. Her departure proved interesting. She flew the wrong headings, the wrong altitudes, and was smitten with confusion over ATC's directions. My friend was perplexed but didn't intervene. After all, she was a controller. He thought she must have known something he didn't. Finally, he couldn't take it any longer. When she wouldn't ask for clarification of an ATC clearance, he grabbed the controls and immediately followed ATC's directive. Looking over at her he asked, "Why are you having such trouble? I thought you were a controller!" She replied, "I am a controller—at Woolworth's!" Being an accountant with limited piloting experience, she certainly had her hands full.

Sometimes it's necessary to deviate from the rules in an emergency situation. This regulation also states that, except in an emergency, no person may operate an aircraft contrary to an ATC instruction in an area in which air traffic control is exercised. All this statement does is clarify that an emergency situation allows deviation from an ATC clearance.

Each pilot in command who, in an emergency, deviates from an ATC clearance or instruction is obligated to notify ATC of that deviation as soon as possible. Let's assume you just departed from a tower controlled airport when you notice smoke billowing up from under your panel. An electrical fire is the likely cause so you immediately turn off your master switch and follow the electrical fire procedure. Not wanting to fly away from the airport, you turn back to the field. You're supposed to call ATC but you've got a burning problem that keeps you from doing that. Stay cool, you're not in trouble, and the FAA is not about to fan the flames. This is an emergency, and your obligation is simply to call ATC as soon as possible after things are under control.

Under certain conditions you might not need to deviate from a rule or declare an emergency. You might only need priority handling by ATC.

There's one last section to this block of regulations that I've always found fascinating. Unless otherwise authorized by ATC, no person operating an aircraft may operate that aircraft according to any clearance or instruction that has been issued to another aircraft for radar air control purposes.

Who'd fly someone else's headings? This rule dates back to a time when equipment was much more archaic. To identify which blip was which on the radar screen, a controller would have an aircraft fly a series of specific headings. If the blip turned right/left/left/right as directed, the controller felt pretty sure he knew what he was looking at. Who else would fly like that?

Well, as it turns out, student pilots did. Instructors, for practice, would sometimes have their students respond to the controllers' commands. On several occasions aircraft were misidentified and vectored in the wrong direction, perilously close to other airplanes or higher terrain. That's how the rule came to be. The moral is, don't do what you're not told.

Emerging From An Emergency

I departed John Wayne airport many years ago and immediately had a partial power failure in a small airplane. My student looked over at me and said, "OK, knock it off; what did you do this time?" He thought I was playing one of my little educational tricks on him. I wasn't (you might think the large beads of sweat accumulating on all my skin surfaces would have tipped him off).

Barely able to maintain altitude, I turned back toward the airport. I called the controller and requested an immediate landing on the runway opposite that used for takeoff. I glanced over at my student and noticed his lips were moving but no sound was coming out. He looked like a fish freshly pulled from water that was still trying to breathe. We landed without incident, and my student regained his speech.

Although not deviating from any rule, I was given priority handling. Under priority conditions, where no deviation from a rule has occurred, the pilot in command must submit a detailed report of that emergency within 48 hours to the manager of that ATC facility *if requested to do so*. Sometimes they ask, sometimes they don't. It sort of depends on how much commotion is created and whether it demands a paper explanation. If they have to close down JFK for half an hour to accommodate your priority condition, expect to write a letter. If you had to awaken the controller at Prozac International for priority handling (his second operation of the month), it's unlikely a report will be requested.

The controller didn't request a report from me so I didn't send one in, and that was the end of the matter.

Rod Machado

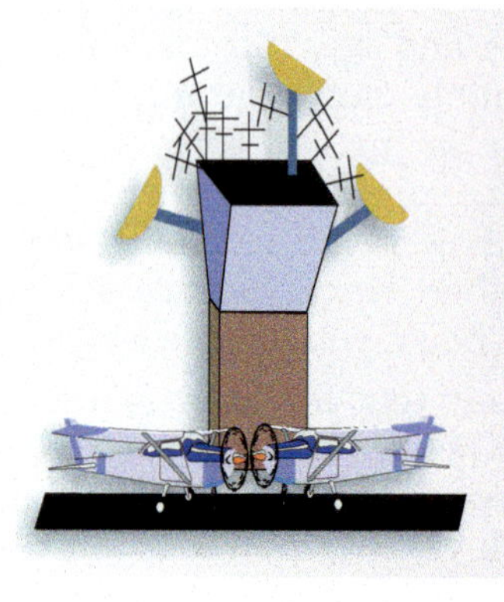

A Cessna 172 landed at a tower-controlled field and came to a complete stop on the runway. The pilot then made a 180 degree turn and commenced to taxi back on the runway while two airplanes were on final to land. The controller yelled, "Hey, 2132 Bravo, we don't allow one-eighties on the runway." The pilot replied, "Well what are you getttin' in a huff about? I'm a 172!"

FAR 91.125 ATC Light Signals

When radios stop working, tower controllers fall back on a primitive but effective means of communication to control traffic in the landing pattern—light signals. These signals are shown in Figure 37. Holding a small but powerful light gun (Figure 38), controllers can direct a concentrated beam of light directly at your aircraft. Using one of three colors—red, green, white—controllers can communicate several important commands to pilots.

Light Signals in the Air – If your radio fails under VFR conditions, simply enter the traffic pattern at a tower controlled field after observing the flow of traffic (not going with the flow could result in a few unusual signals from the pilots in the other airplanes). Keep an eye on the tower cab for a light signal. If, while airborne, you receive a steady green light, this means you are cleared to land. Think of a steady green light as being similar to the three green landing gear lights on a retractable geared airplane. If they're all indicating green, then it's OK to land.

If you saw your three green landing gear lights flickering or flashing instead of painting a steady green, you'd probably go around and solve the problem. Likewise, a flashing green light from the tower means you should return for landing, to be followed by a steady green light at the proper time. This is essentially a go-around command.

Fig. 38

LIGHT GUN SIGNALS FROM THE TOWER

Color & Type Of Signal	Meaning With Respect To Aircraft on The Surface	Meaning With Respect To Aircraft in Flight
Steady green	Cleared for takeoff	Cleared to land
Flashing green	Cleared to taxi	Return for landing (to be followed by steady green at proper time)
Steady red	Stop	Give way to other aircraft and continue circling
Flashing red	Taxi clear of runway in use	Airport unsafe, do not land
Flashing white	Return to starting point on airport	Not applicable
Alternating red & green	Exercise extreme caution	Exercise extreme caution

Fig. 37

A steady red always means stop. At least that's what it should mean to you at a stoplight. Of course, the only way to stop in the air is to give way to other aircraft and continue circling. Controllers might use this signal if they see you (a non-radio airplane) approaching the traffic pattern and are unable to sequence you into the flow of traffic. They'll hold you in your present position until they can clear you to land. At that time you'll probably receive a steady green light.

Whenever you see a flashing red light in the air, it indicates danger. Think of all those red flashing beacons you see on tall TV towers. Tower controllers send out a flashing red light when the airport is unsafe for landing. The runway could be torn up, there could be a disabled plane on the runway, or perhaps there are deer and antelope at play. Whatever is wrong, the controller is telling you that bad things will happen to your good airplane if you land there. It's time to head for the next closest airport.

Alternating red and green lights, on the ground or in the air, mean exercise extreme caution. There might be another no-radio airplane in the pattern. Or, there might be wild animals running across the runway. Don't think that this can't happen. A fellow pilot in Florida had an alligator crawl onto the runway during landing. I'm not sure what would happen if you hit one of these big guys. Perhaps you'd leave a trail of boots, assorted baggage and Gucci belts scattered along the runway.

Light signals also apply to surface movement at tower controlled fields. Radios do go on the fritz occasionally, though many general aviation airplanes have a double set of communications radios. If there is no avionics repair shop at your home field, you'll need to fly somewhere to get it fixed. If you have no communications capability, simply call the tower by phone and tell them you want to depart the airport. They'll probably tell you to taxi out and visually monitor the tower for light signals.

Light signals also serve as your taxi instructions after a no-radio landing.

Light Signals on the Ground – A steady green light on the ground means the same to an airplane as it does to a car—go. A steady green light means that you're cleared for takeoff (in your airplane, not your car). A flashing green light on the ground means that you're cleared to taxi. If you look in your rear view mirror and see a steady red light you'd better stop. It's the law and they want to talk to you. A steady red light from the tower means you should stop. The controller wants you to hold your position. When the time is right, they'll provide you with a flashing green signal to continue taxiing.

A flashing red light in your rear view mirror usually belongs to an emergency vehicle. Your natural response in a car is to get off the road. In an airplane a flashing red light from the tower is a signal to taxi clear of the runway in use. You might have just landed without a radio and are taxiing down the active runway. The controller may have another airplane waiting to land. A flashing red light is a signal to clear the runway on which you've landed. Simply find the nearest taxiway and get on it.

The last light signal is the flashing white light. It only pertains to operations on the surface. If the airport suddenly becomes very busy, your no-radio takeoff might be more appropriate at a later time. Controllers will signal their desire to have you return to your starting point on the airport with a flashing white light. Think of the newer automobiles that have flashing headlights to warn you that you must return to your starting point to turn them off (my original car had headlights that flashed, not because of new technology, but because of a bad circuit. It did have a heated rear window that kept my hands warm on those cold days when I had to push it in for repairs).

FAR 91.126 Operating on Or In the Vicinity of an Airport In Class G Airspace

As you have probably already guessed, we're using letters to describe certain types of airspace. In order to understand regulations 91.127, 91.129, 91.130, 91.131, 91.135, 91.155, 91.157 and 91.215, it might be better for you to jump ahead to the chapter on airspace (Chapter 9). You might also choose to skip these regulations and return to them after reading the airspace section. Even though it's not mentioned in the following material, landing at any airport requires a minimum flight visibility and distance from any clouds. These VFR requirements are also described in the airspace chapter.

With only a few exceptions, airports lying in Class G and Class E airspace don't have control towers (we won't discuss the exceptions). These airports have been called *uncontrolled airports*, but can also be described as *nontower airports*. Since there are no operating control towers at these airports, pilots must follow specific procedures to prevent bumping into each other.

When approaching to land at an airport without an operating control tower in Class G airspace, each pilot of an airplane must make all turns to the left. The exception to this is when the airport displays visual markings (at/on the segmented circle) indicating turns should be made to the right. In that case, the pilot must make right turns. Why are left turns the norm? The answer is standardization. Someone decided a long time ago that if everyone made a left traffic pattern, there'd be less chance of confusion. Shown in Figure 39, these patterns make it easy to sequence yourself with the flow of traffic.

A segmented circle, shown in Figure 40, sometimes shows a nonstandard, right hand traffic pattern is in effect (you'll find out why in Chapter 7). Pilots can see these large segmented circles from several thousand feet in the air. Mountains, towers or noise sensitive areas often dictate that a pattern be flown on the opposite side of the field.

IT'S THE LITTLE THINGS...

I lost radio contact with Tower. By accident my daughter disengaged my hand-mike jack from its receptacle enough to cut off communication, but I could not tell. She was in right front seat with a blanket over her legs that prevented my noticing anything wrong. After landing I discovered the problem and contacted Ground Control for taxi instructions. Tower said they gave me a red signal when our communications went out, but unfortunately I did not see it.

Moral: If you are NORDO (no radio) near a controlled airport, keep a sharp eye out for lightgun signals. Even in this high-technology era you sometimes have to fall back on the old reliable methods.

ASRS Report

AIRPORT TRAFFIC PATTERNS (FOR RUNWAY 18)

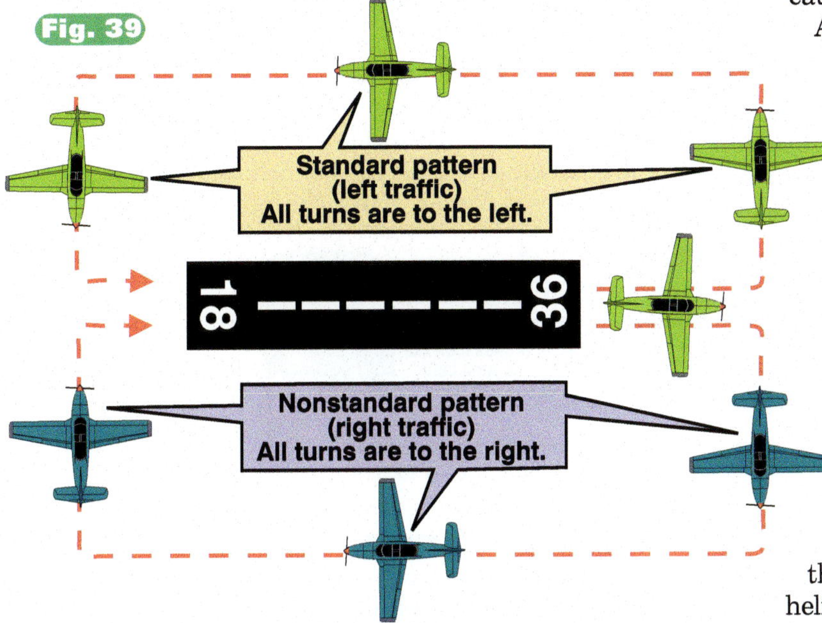

SEGMENTED CIRCLES SHOWING NONSTANDARD RIGHT-HAND TRAFFIC PATTERNS

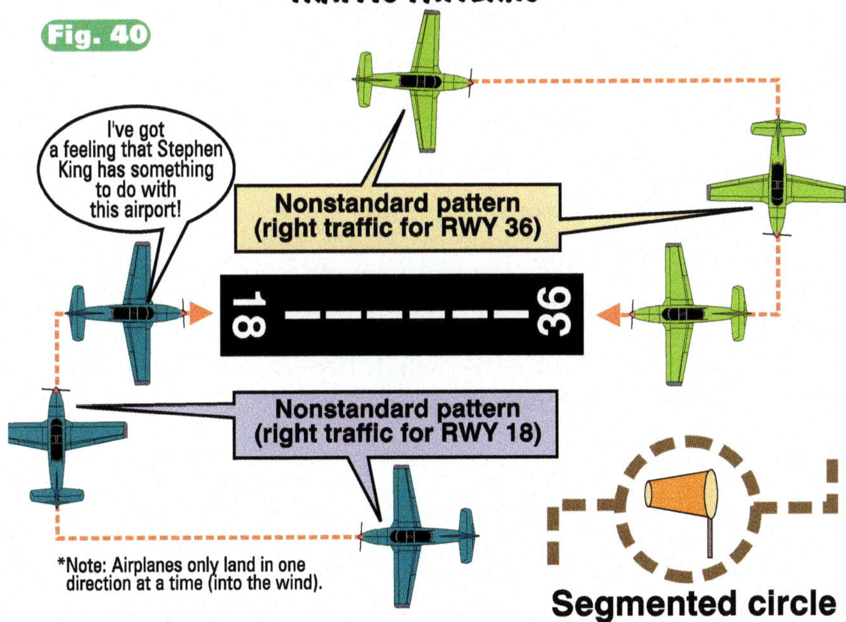

HOW CAN THAT BE?

The controller sitting next to me (a fellow controller) is trying to change Mooney 45Q to my frequency, but gets no response. Thinking that the Mooney may have already switched to my frequency since he's a local pilot who knew it was coming, he asks me to check:

Me: "Mooney 45Q, are you on this frequency?"

45Q: "Negative, but I should be any time now."

Pilots not flying the correct traffic pattern often cause dramatic adrenaline rushes in those who do. At Corona airport in Southern California, a pilot entered the pattern the wrong way opposite seven other airplanes in the lefthand circuit. They scattered like frightened chickens with the Colonel close behind. This pilot was probably thinking, "Hey, look at all those guys going the wrong way! What's the matter with them?" Fortunately he finally got the idea, switched his pattern and landed. Several new EKG records were set that day!

Another part of this regulation requires that all helicopters and powered parachutes approaching to land should avoid the flow of fixed-wing aircraft. This means you shouldn't see a helicopter at your altitude in the traffic pattern because they usually fly lower and slower. Perhaps this explains why a friend once said that the Bible specifically states that all pilots should fly helicopters. I asked him to quote me the specific passage. He said the Bible clearly states, "Lo, I am with you always." I replied, "Five dollars. Pay up now."

FAR 91.127 Operations on or in The Vicinity of an Airport in Class E Airspace

For all practical purposes, this regulation is the same as FAR 91.126 for Class G airspace. Similar to airports within Class G airspace, there are only a few airports lying within Class E airspace that have control towers. Therefore, we won't bother discussing the exceptions. The only significant difference between airports within Class E and Class G airspace is a FAR Part 93 departure requirement. FAR Part 93 contains noise abatement requirements.

Many people around airports are quite vocal about airport noise. They want to reduce the noise by getting rid of airplanes. Some of these folks have mentioned to me that they don't care if airplanes fly as long as they don't use their engines. To them, the only good aircraft is a glider. Be very careful about adhering to local noise abatement procedures at the airport. Good relations with airport neighbors keeps aviation alive in your community.

At the Los Alamitos (CA) airport several years ago a C5A galaxy transport airplane was practicing touch and goes. The tower controller heard the phone ring and picked it up to find a local resident saying "Hey, why don't you let that man land his airplane?" Don't think this doesn't happen. The same tower controller told me that he once received a noise complaint about one of the gliders operating out of the same field! (Truth is stranger than fiction because fiction must make sense.)

FAR 91.129 Operations in Class D Airspace

If you've read the airspace section, you know that Class D airspace generally extends upward from the surface to 2,500 feet above the airport elevation as shown in Figure 41. Its radius around the primary airport varies based on the instrument procedures for which the controlled airspace is established. I've seen the radius vary from a little less than 3 nautical miles to 7 nautical miles with the typical radius being a little less than 5 nautical miles. You'll be able to determine the specific size of an airport's Class D airspace by looking at the aeronautical sectional chart. The Class D airspace, shown in Figure 41, looks somewhat like a can of tuna since it has a short, cylindrical shape. Let's refer to Class D airspace as the *tuna can.*

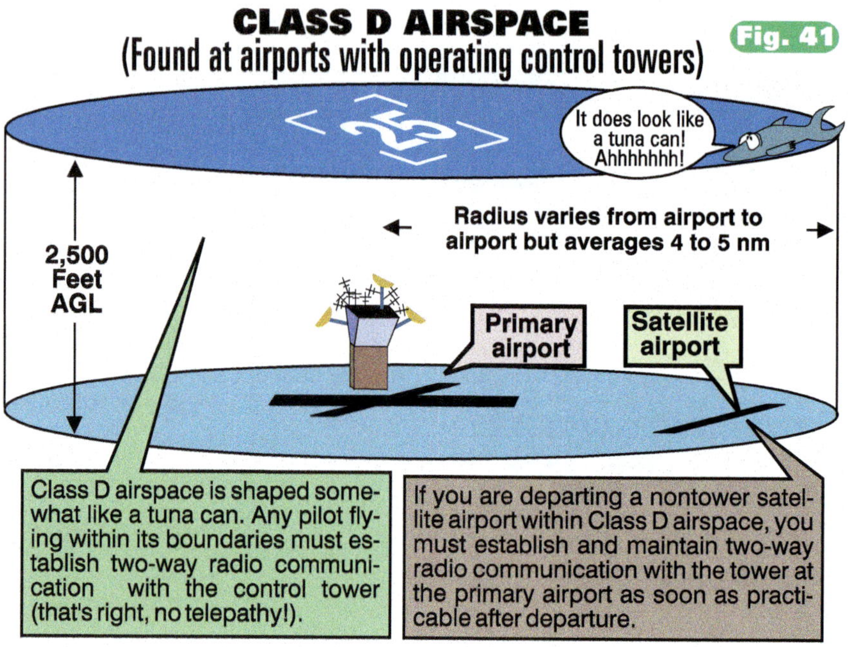

CLASS D AIRSPACE
(Found at airports with operating control towers)

Fig. 41

It does look like a tuna can! Ahhhhhhh!

Radius varies from airport to airport but averages 4 to 5 nm

2,500 Feet AGL

Primary airport

Satellite airport

Class D airspace is shaped somewhat like a tuna can. Any pilot flying within its boundaries must establish two-way radio communication with the control tower (that's right, no telepathy!).

If you are departing a nontower satellite airport within Class D airspace, you must establish and maintain two-way radio communication with the tower at the primary airport as soon as practicable after departure.

Airports in Class D airspace have an operating control tower. The purpose of a control tower is to provide information and instructions to airplanes taking off or landing at the primary airport within that airspace. The primary airport (the one that's usually in the center of the tuna can) is the airport for which that airspace (Class D) is designated. It's possible to have one or more additional airports lying within Class D airspace. These airports are often called "satellite" airports (signifying that they "orbit" or lie close enough to the primary airport to be within its Class D airspace).

Equipment Required – The minimum equipment required to operate within Class D airspace is a two-way radio. You can, however, request permission from ATC to fly into or out of this airspace without a radio. You might, for example, need to take your airplane to another airport to have the radio repaired. By calling ATC (the tower controllers) on the phone, they'll provide you with instructions for departing and/or arriving at the airport without two-way radio communication.

Arrivals and Fly-Throughs – If you want to fly through this airspace or land at the primary airport, you must establish two-way radio communication with the ATC facility that is responsible for that Class D airspace. Normally, this ATC facility is the control tower located at the primary airport. Once established, you must maintain communication with the air traffic control tower while in this airspace. In other words, you must give the tower controller a call before entering the tuna can boundaries, have them acknowledge you, and once inside the can you must maintain communication at all times.

Pilots sometimes become confused about the precise definition of *establish communication.* Technically, you've established communications anytime ATC acknowledges your aircraft call sign (the airplane's N number, such as N2132B). For instance, on your initial call, while outside or above the physical dimensions of the tuna can, you give the tower your position, altitude, destination and any requests you have. They'll normally call you back using your aircraft call sign and give you directions for entering the traffic flow around the airport.

If the controller says, " N2132B, stand by," you've technically established communications and may continue into the tuna can toward the airport. If the controller says, "Aircraft calling Onfire Tower, standby" (that is, if you aren't called by your N-number name) then you have not established communications and should remain outside or above the tuna can. Of course, if the controller says, "N2132B, remain clear of Class D airspace" (they don't say *tuna can*), then you must follow their instructions even though two-way communication has been established.

These communication requirements are in force even if you are landing at one of the satellite airports within Class D airspace. In other words, if another airport lies within the boundaries of the tuna can (typically an airport without an operating control tower) and you're interested in landing there, you must establish two-way radio communication with the air traffic control tower at the primary airport before entering this airspace. You must maintain these communications during your flight to this airport.

Departures – If you're departing from the primary airport, you must establish and maintain two-way radio communication with ATC within Class D airspace. In other words, don't take off without calling the tower and listening to them while in the tuna can.

Suppose you're taking off from a non-tower satellite airport within Class D airspace? Do you still need to call the ATC facility for the primary airport? Yes. You must establish and maintain two-way radio communication as

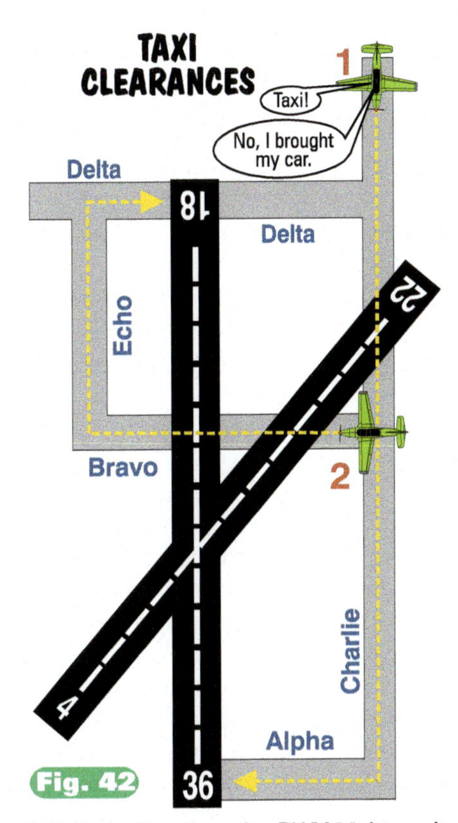

If Airplane 1 is cleared to RWY 36, it needs a clearance to cross RWY 22. With this, the pilot may taxi to but not onto RWY 36. If Airplane 2 is cleared to RWY 18, it needs a clearance to cross RWY 22 and RWY 18 with each clearance being issued only after the first runway is crossed.

soon as practical after departing. In other words, take off and give the tower at the primary airport a call as soon as it's reasonable for you to do so. Let them know what you're doing, follow their directions and keep listening to them while you're anywhere within the tuna can.

Communications Failure – Your radios could give up the ghost enroute. Does this mean you can't fly back into the Class D airspace you departed from? Not necessarily. A provision in this regulation allows you to enter Class D airspace under VFR conditions (we'll explain VFR in more detail in Chapter 9). In other words, you can get back into the tuna can as long as you have weather conditions at or above basic VFR minimums. How do you do it? Simply fly to the airport, enter the traffic pattern, watch the tower for light signals and land when you receive a steady green light from the tower.

Minimum Altitudes – The important section here is the part saying that you must stay at or above the glideslope (until a lower altitude is necessary) when approaching to land on a runway served by a visual approach slope indicator (VASI). We'll discuss VASIs in Chapter 7. For now, accept the fact that a VASI consists of light bars that tell you if you're on the proper glideslope for the runway you're approaching.

Takeoff, Landing, Taxi Clearance – No person may, at an airport with an operating control tower, operate an aircraft on a runway or taxiway, or take off or land an aircraft, unless an appropriate clearance is received from ATC.

If this ATC clearance is to a runway via a specific taxi route, and if a runway (closed, active or inactive) intersects your path along the way, then the controller must also issue (and you *must obtain*) a clearance to cross that runway before proceeding. In fact, you must receive a specific crossing clearance for *each runway* that your route crosses. This applies even if you're told to follow another aircraft to a specific runway.

For example, airplane #1 (Figure 42) will be cleared to departure Runway 36 as follows: *StingSport 714CT, Runway 36, taxi via Charlie and Alpha, cross Runway 22, hold short of Runway 36*. Airplane #2 will be cleared to departure Runway 18 as follows: *StingSport 714CT, Runway 18, taxi via Bravo, Echo and Delta, cross Runway 22, hold short of Runway 18 at Bravo*. To cross Runway 18 at the midfield point, 714CT must obtain another clearance which would eventually lead it to the Runway 18 departure threshold via taxiways Bravo, Echo and Delta.

Since ATC is required to obtain a readback of all *runway hold short instructions*, ATC will consider your readback of those instructions containing runway assignments as confirmation of those runway assignments. When ATC is ready for you to taxi onto the departure runway, the controller will instruct you to, *lineup and wait Runway 18*. At this point you are expected to taxi onto the departure runway and line up, then wait for your takeoff clearance.

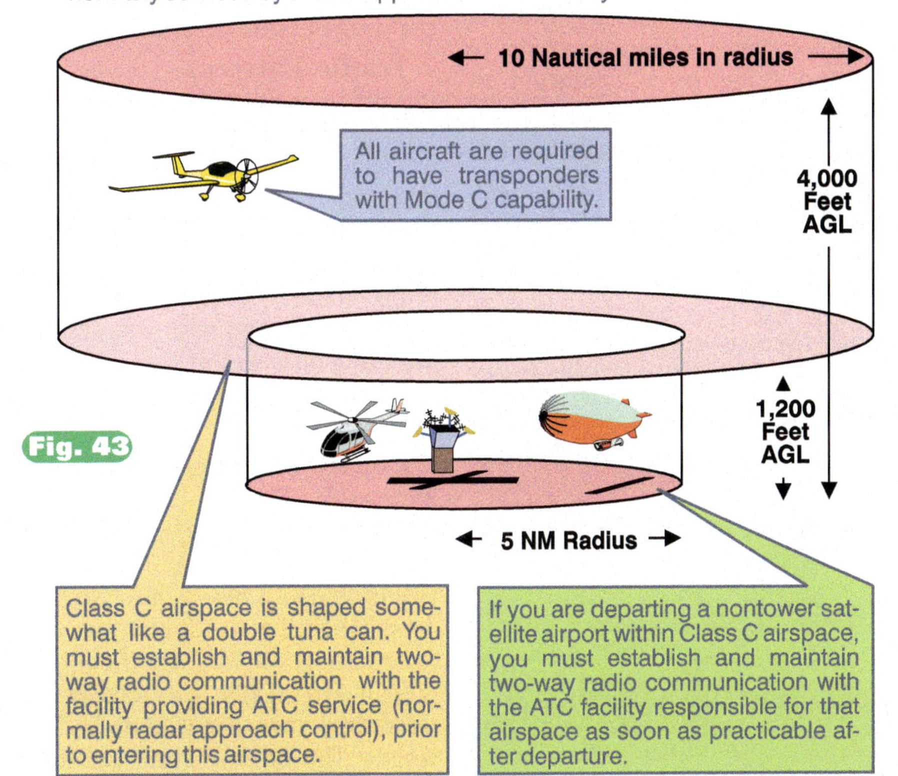

FAR 91.130 Operations In Class C Airspace

An example of Class C airspace is shown in Figure 43. This type of airspace is larger than Class D airspace in that it has two cylindrical components instead of the single, tuna-can-shaped Class D airspace. Class C is a double-decker tuna can. The physical dimensions of Class C airspace consist of a lower tuna can having a radius of 5 nautical miles and extending vertically from the ground to 4,000 feet above the airport elevation. The upper and larger tuna can has a radius of 10 nautical miles. It starts at 1,200 feet and extends vertically to 4,000 feet above the airport elevation. For the sake of continuity, we'll refer to Class C airspace as the *double tuna can.* (I do feel it's necessary to mention that no dolphins have been hurt, injured or eaten in the writing of this material.)

Simply stated, Class C airspace goes with airports that handle larger, faster airplanes (generally this means significant quantities of commercial traffic). It's established to keep the small airplanes and bigger airplanes from bumping into one another. Since there are faster airplanes involved, it makes sense that the airspace must cover more area (refer to Chapter 9 for more information on Class C airspace).

As with Class D airspace, there is a primary airport in the center of the double tuna can. This is the airport for which the Class C airspace was established. The double tuna can usually sits directly over this airport. As with Class D airspace, there may be satellite airports within the boundaries of Class C airspace. In other words, there may be other airports, with and without control towers, within the surface area covered by the double tuna can.

You're going to find there is very little difference between the requirements for flight in Class C airspace compared to Class D airspace. Whether you're in the single or double tuna can airspace, the requirements are essentially the same. The main difference is that the airport tower typically has a *clearance delivery* (a controller dedicated to providing you a route to fly when departing the airport). There is also radar associated with the airport in the form of approach and departure control. Let's examine the Class C requirements.

General Requirements – All operations in Class C airspace must comply with the previous regulation—FAR 91.129. In other words, the operating rules are essentially the same as in Class D airspace. This makes sense since both Class D and Class C airspace have primary airports with operating control towers. Therefore, they should have similar requirements for aircraft operations.

Traffic Patterns – If you're taking off or landing at a satellite airport within Class C airspace, you must comply with the FAA arrival and departure traffic pattern established for that airport. There's nothing new here. Just because the primary airport is a little bit busier, there's no reason why you should do anything different at one of the satellite airports than you would for Class D airspace.

Communications - Arrival or Through Flight – If you want to land at the primary airport in Class C airspace, or if you just want to fly through that airspace, you must establish and maintain two-way radio communication with the facility providing air traffic services prior to entering that airspace. In other words, the double tuna can of airspace may be controlled by either a tower, an approach control facility, or a combination of both. Your aeronautical sectional chart (charts used for aerial navigation) will generally instruct you to contact Approach Control on a specific frequency within 20nm from the primary airport having Class C airspace (of course, you're *required* to establish and maintain two-way radio communication prior to *entering* Class C airspace).

Communications - Departing Flight – If you're departing the primary airport within Class C airspace, you must establish and maintain two-way radio communications with the tower prior to departure. If the controller hands you off to Departure Control, talk and listen to the departure controller until you're out of the double tuna can (Class C airspace). If you're departing a nontower satellite airport lying within the surface boundaries of Class C airspace, you must establish and maintain two-way radio communications with the Approach or Departure Control facility having jurisdiction over that airspace. Do this as soon as practicable after departure. (An approach or departure control facility is usually the ATC facility having jurisdiction over Class C airspace.) In the rare event the satellite airport has an operating control tower, do exactly as you would do if you were departing the primary airport having an operating control tower. In other words, establish communications with the tower at the satellite airport and follow their instructions.

Equipment Requirements – The minimum equipment required to operate within Class C airspace is a two-way radio, a transponder with altitude reporting capability (per FAR 91.215), and ADS-B (out) capability (see page I31). You'll learn more about transponders shortly. These are electronic devices that allow your airplane to be identified on the approach or departure controller's radar scope. The altitude reporting capability allows the controller to see your altitude on his or her radar screen.

FAR 91.131 Operations In Class B Airspace

Class D airspace was small (a single tuna can). Class C airspace was slightly larger because there were bigger and faster airplanes there (a double tuna can). Class B airspace is the biggest of these tuna can stacks of airspace. It usually extends up to 10,000 feet MSL and often has horizontal dimensions of many miles as shown in Figure 44. This airspace is larger than Class C or D airspace because its primary airport has many very large and fast airplanes like Boeing 747s and DC-10s and much IFR activity.

In some cases Class B airspace (Figure 44) looks like several stacked cans of tuna. Actually it looks more like an inverted wedding cake with individual tiers or floors contributing to its structure. Extra tiers allow faster jet airplanes to make long arrivals and departures into and out of the primary airport while remaining within the protected airspace. The following are the requirements to take off or land at the primary airport or operate within the wedding cake airspace.

Operating Rules – First, you must follow all the rules of FAR 91.129 (Class D airspace) while in Class B airspace. In addition, before you can enter Class B airspace you'll need a *clearance* from the ATC facility having jurisdiction over that airspace. A clearance is essentially verbal permission for entry into this airspace. This is different from the entry requirements for Class C or D airspace which only required that you establish and maintain two-way radio communication before entry.

Pilot Requirements – You need to be at least a private pilot to take off or land at any airport within Class B airspace. If, however, you are a student pilot or recreational pilot seeking private pilot certification and have met the requirements of FAR 61.95, then you may take off or land as well as fly in Class B airspace (FAR 61.95—not included in this book—identifies the requirements for student pilots to enter Class B airspace. Your instructor will give you the details if she/he intends to have you tooling around with 747's). No matter how confident you may be as a student pilot, there are some primary airports within Class B airspace that are just too darn busy for you to take off or land at unless you have a private pilot certificate or better. (See Appendix D of FAR 91, Section 4, for a list of these airports—not included in this book.)

CLASS B AIRSPACE

Exists at some of the nation's busiest airports. Its shape and size are customized to accommodate the arrival and departure paths of the many airplanes using this airport. Because the airport is so busy, Class B airspace almost always exists on a 24 hour basis.

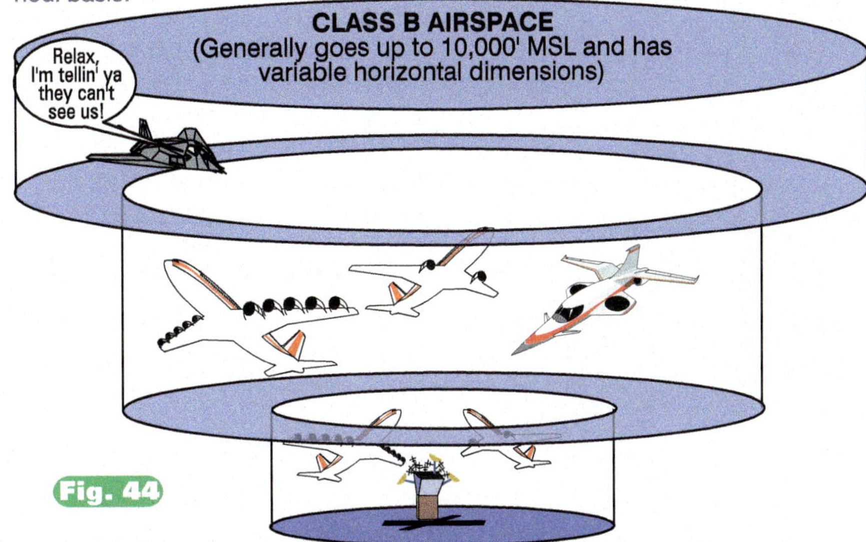

Fig. 44

An ATC clearance is required (usually from radar Approach Control) before entering this airspace. All aircraft must have a two-way radio with the appropriate frequencies, mode-C equipped transponder & a VOR for IFR operations. To land at the primary airport, pilots must have at least a *private pilot certificate (students can enter and land if they meet the requirements of FAR 61.95). *Airports listed in section 4, appendix D of FAR 91 require a private pilot certificate to land.

Equipment Required – The minimum equipment required to operate within Class B airspace is a two-way radio with all the frequencies needed for ATC communication, a transponder with altitude encoding capability, and ADS-B (out) capability (see page I31), and, for IFR operations, a functioning VOR receiver or RNAV system (i.e., think GPS unit here).

FAR 91.133 Restricted And Prohibited Areas

Across the United States you will find areas known as *special use airspace*. Restricted and prohibited areas (Figures 45 & 46) are part of this special use airspace group. *Restricted areas*, while not wholly prohibited, subject flights to certain restrictions. These restrictions may be based on

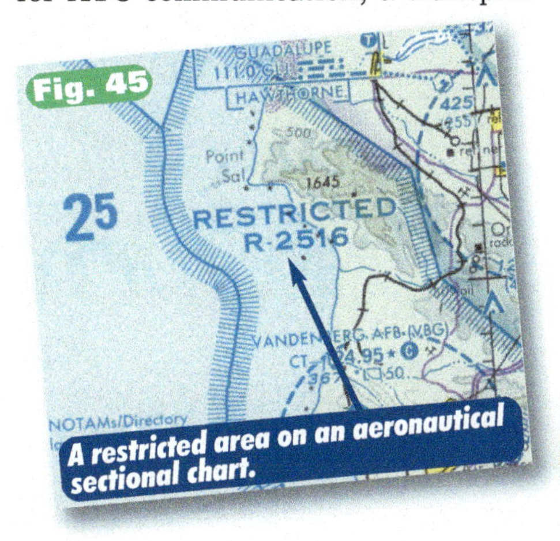

Fig. 45 A restricted area on an aeronautical sectional chart.

Fig. 46 A prohibited area on an aeronautical sectional chart.

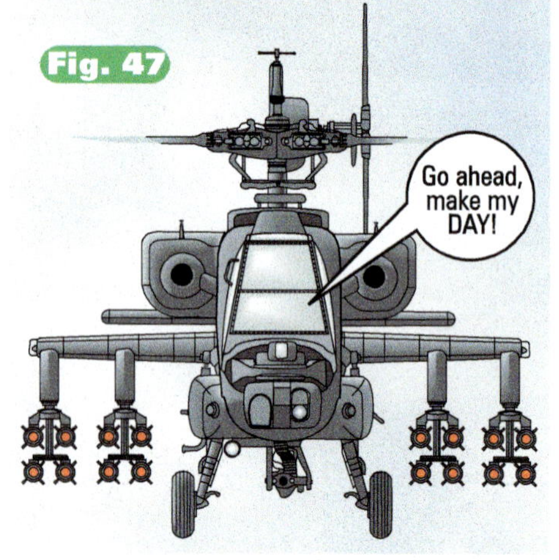

time, altitude, or other requirements. Operations within a restricted area assume that pilots have the permission of the controlling agency responsible for that area. It also requires that pilots follow whatever restrictions are imposed by the agency.

A restricted area is often used for military activities. Fighter pilots might be performing their tactical maneuvers and wild aerial dances designed to frighten off an archenemy (Figure 47). These dances often frighten off little general aviation pilots too. You should avoid these areas unless you have permission to enter.

What can you do in a prohibited area? It's reasonable to say you can do a lot less than in a restricted area. There are certain areas of the country where flight is prohibited. For instance, the capital of the United States in Washington, D.C. is surrounded by a prohibited area. I doubt that you'll get permission from the U.S. government to fly into this prohibited area. This is usually the case with most prohibited areas. They're prohibited for a good reason.

A friend living on the east coast played a nice little practical joke on one of his first flight instructors. He obtained a few large color aerial photographs of the capitol building and had them converted into smaller 3 inch by 5 inch photographs. He flew a solo cross country near the Washington, D.C. area and took a few actual photographs of the trip.

When he met his instructor the following week he interspersed his Capitol dome shots in with the scenic shots. Giving them to his instructor he said, "Here are a few aerial photographs I took from the plane." When his instructor saw the capital shot his eyes bugged out and he said, "Oh man, you're going to owe me a few bucks for this one." What is aviation if you can't have a little fun with your instructor?

FAR 91.135 Operations In Class A Airspace

Class A airspace is airspace starting at or above 18,000 feet MSL. You can't be in Class A airspace without an instrument rating, so I won't even discuss it here. I will, however, discuss it in Chapter 9 (airspace).

FAR 91.137/141/145 Temporary Flight Restrictions (TFRs)

See Postflight Briefing #6-3 for detailed information on TFRs.

FAR 91.151 Fuel Requirements for Flight In VFR Conditions

This regulation states that no person may begin a flight in an airplane under VFR conditions unless (considering wind and forecast weather conditions) there is enough fuel to fly to the first point of intended landing and, assuming normal cruising speed, during the day, to fly for at least an additional 30 minutes. During night flight, the required fuel reserve is increased to 45 minutes. Obviously, the risks in running out of fuel at night are greater than during the day, so a larger cushion is desirable.

FAR 91.155 Basic VFR Weather Minimums

As you'll discover in Chapter 9, a VFR pilot must always maintain a minimum visibility and clearance from any clouds while flying. Known as *Basic VFR Weather Minimums,* these visibilities and cloud clearance requirements vary depending on the particular class of airspace in which you are flying. I've listed these VFR requirements in Figure 48 and I'll offer detailed explanations in Chapter 9.

FAR 91.157 Special VFR Weather Minimums

We'll leave the discussion of special VFR for Chapter 9.

FAR 91.159 VFR Cruising Altitude or Flight Level

The *lambada* is often the forbidden dance at high school proms because it involves close physical contact and wild gyrations of the hip that might easily dissolve the pelvis of anyone over 40. Likewise, there are forbidden altitudes that you want to avoid in preventing close physical contact with another airplane

Fig. 48

BASIC VFR WEATHER MINIMUMS IN CONTROLLED AIRSPACE

Altitude or Airspace	Flight Visibility	Distance From Clouds
Class A	not applicable	not applicable
Class B	3 statute miles	clear of clouds
Class C	3 statute miles	500' below 1,000' above 2,000' horizontal
Class D	3 statute miles	500' below 1,000' above 2,000' horizontal
Class E		
Less than 10,000' MSL	3 statute miles	500' below 1,000' above 2,000' horizontal
At or above 10,000' MSL	5 statute miles	1,000' above 1,000' below 1 statute mile horizontal

BASIC VFR WEATHER MINIMUMS IN UNCONTROLLED AIRSPACE

Altitude or Airspace	Flight Visibility	Distance From Clouds
Class G 1,200' or less above the surface (regardless of MSL altitude)		91.155(b) allows you to operate an airplane at night clear of clouds and within a half mile of the runway in an airport traffic pattern when the visibility is at least one statute mile but less than the three normally required.
Day, except as provided in FAR 91.155 (b)	1 statute mile	clear of clouds
Night, except as provided in FAR 91.155 (b)	3 statute miles	500' below 1,000' above 2,000' horizontal
More than 1,200' above the surface but less than 10,000 feet MSL:		
Day	1 statute mile	500' below 1,000' above 2,000' horizontal
Night	3 statute miles	500' below 1,000' above 2,000' horizontal
More than 1,200' above the surface and at or above 10,000 feet MSL	5 statute miles	1,000' above 1,000' below 1 statute mile horizontal

(otherwise known as "preventing a mid-air collision"). The altitudes you're allowed to fly will keep VFR aircraft separated vertically by 1,000 feet and they are based on the aircraft's direction of flight. In this way, altimeters become vertical traffic separators that prevent pilots from bumping into one another.

This regulation states that during VFR flight, when operating more than 3,000 feet above the surface, you are to fly at an altitude appropriate for your direction of flight. If you are on a magnetic course of 0° through 179°, you should fly any odd thousand foot MSL altitude plus 500 feet. Altitudes such as 3,500 feet, 5,500 feet, 7,500 feet, etc., are appropriate for that direction. While on a magnetic course of 180° through 359° you should fly at an even MSL altitude plus 500. Altitudes such as 4,500 feet, 6,500 feet, 8,500 feet, etc., are appropriate for this direction. This provides you with a minimum 1,000 foot clearance from other VFR airplanes heading in opposing directions (Figure 49).

Are you wondering who uses the even (4,000, 6,000, etc.) or odd thousand (5,000, 7,000, etc.) foot altitudes? IFR pilots do. If you're flying on an airway you can probably expect some IFR traffic 500 feet above or below your airplane. Since you'll be in VFR conditions, you should be able to see and avoid these airplanes, and in VFR conditions they have the same obligation toward you. Comforting, isn't it, to know that everyone is looking out for everyone else?

Remember, these cruising altitudes apply only if you're operating at more than 3,000 feet AGL (above ground level). Operations at and below 3,000 AGL can be flown at whatever altitude you choose. These rules don't apply if the airplane is turning. If you're maneuvering while practicing your stalls, steep turns and other activities, you're not required to maintain a specific altitude.

HEMISPHERICAL CRUISING ALTITUDES (For VFR Flight)

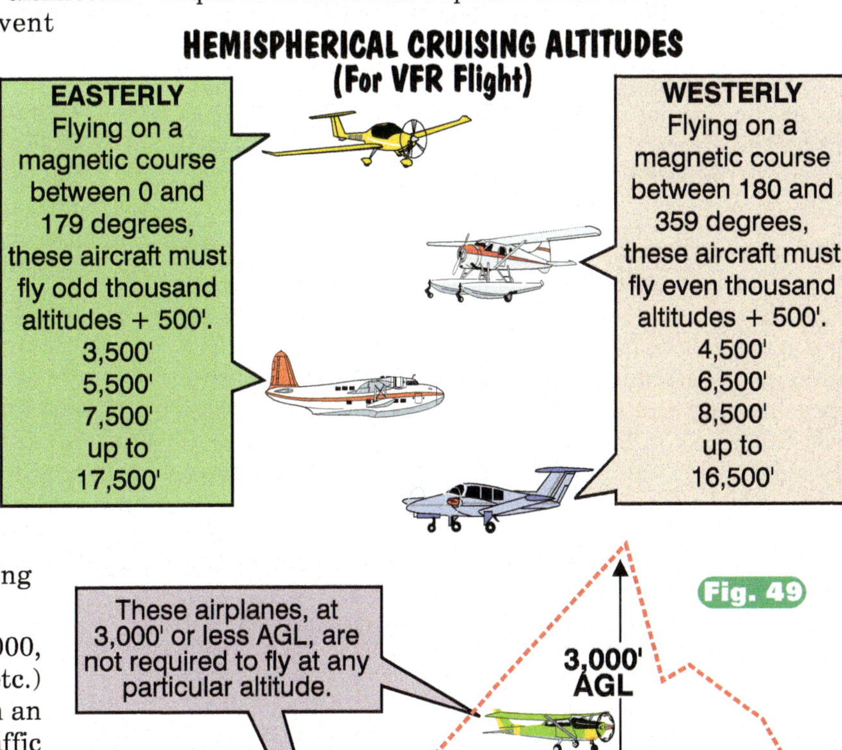

Fig. 49

FAR 91.203 Civil Aircraft: Certifications Required

Several years ago I wanted to discover if a student of mine knew what documents were required to be carried on board the aircraft. I said to him, "Hey Bob, what things are required to be in the airplane for it to be legal for flight?" He looked at me, scratched his head and said, "Ahh, the pilot?" I gave him the same look that I gave the seafood waiter who was supposed to bring me a twin lobster dinner. Instead he brought me a lobster and a crab. I said, "Hey what gives? I ordered twin lobsters." He said, "Well, they're fraternal twins." In both cases I lifted a single eyebrow and radiated one of those "You're going to owe me $5" looks.

There are four items that must be on board the aircraft at all times when it's being operated. Two of these are certification documents: the *airworthiness certificate* and the *registration certificate*. The other two items are the airplane's *operating limitations* and its *weight and balance information*. These last two items may be found in the approved Airplane Flight Manual (AFM) or in approved manual materials, markings and placards, or any combination thereof in the airplane. (Note: The specific requirement to keep weight and balance information in the airplane is found under FAR 23.1583.)

The first certification document is the airworthiness certificate (Figure 50A). This is issued for a specific aircraft at the time of manufacture, and it remains valid as long as the aircraft receives the required annual inspection by a licensed mechanic and meets other legal requirements.

The airworthiness certificate must be displayed at the cabin or cockpit entrance so that it is legible to the passengers or crew. Take a look the next time you get on board a commercial airliner. There, in the vicinity of the smiling cabin attendant and the cockpit, will be a plastic pouch bearing the airworthiness certificate. It's supposed to make you feel secure. Frankly, I'd feel better if they showed me the pilot's license. I *know* the airplane can fly.

Note: Aircraft registration certificates must be renewed every three years.

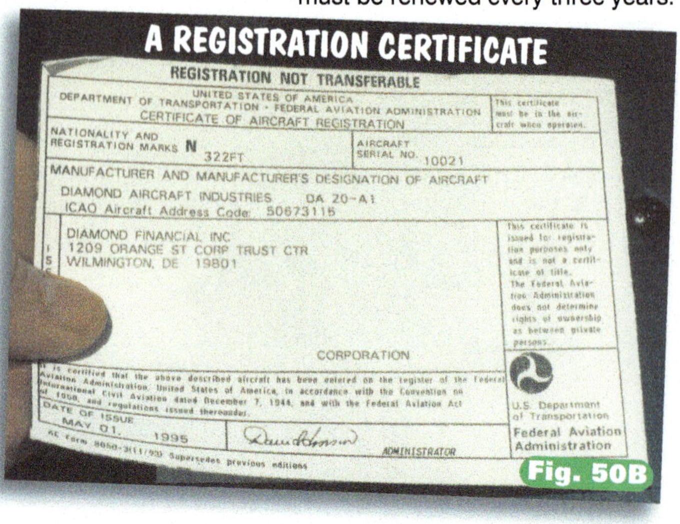

A REGISTRATION CERTIFICATE

Fig. 50B

A STANDARD AIRWORTHINESS CERTIFICATE

Fig. 50A

The second certification document that must be on board is the registration certificate issued to the owner of the aircraft. The registration (Figure 50B) need not be displayed; it just needs to be in the aircraft.

FAR 91.207 Emergency Locator Transmitters

All U.S. registered civil airplanes must be equipped with an automatic-type emergency locator transmitter or ELT (Figure 51). The ELT must be in operable condition. These transmitters are impact-activated devices that send out pulsed transmissions on the emergency frequency (121.5 MHz & 243 MHz). Should you land hard enough (usually a 5G or greater impact) or crash, an inertial arm on the transmitter is activated and the transmission begins. Satellites and search and rescue pilots can easily track ELT signals to find downed pilots.

As a flight instructor, I've heard of students landing hard enough during practice to activate the ELT. Although the airplane wasn't damaged (airplanes can take a lickin' and keep on tickin') the ELT went off. Like Pinnochio's nose, ELT's don't lie. Imagine a student returning from touch and go practice. Tires are smoking (not really) and the instructor is suspicious. He asks, "Did you have a hard landing?" The student straightens and replies, "No way, they were all greasers." The instructor says "Well let's see how greasy they were," as he tunes the airplane radio to 121.5 (the emergency frequency). Suddenly the speaker wails with, "Whewwww, whewwww, whewwww..." It seems like you can't get away with anything nowadays!

The most important thing to remember about your ELT is that the batteries must be replaced or recharged if the device has been in use for more than one cumulative hour, or when 50% of their useful life (or life of charge) has expired. If you want to manually test the airplane's ELT on the ground you may do so during the first five minutes past the hour (you're limited to three audible sweeps during the test).

Additionally, each ELT must be inspected within 12 calendar months after the last inspection for: proper installation, operation, battery corrosion and for the presence of a sufficient signal radiated from its antenna.

As a final note on ELTs, you might not have heard that there is a new kid on the block known as a 406 MHz ELT. This newer type of ELT is superior to its older (121.5 MHz) cousin in that it has a more precise signal and is compatible with our present search and rescue satellite system (current satellites no longer monitor 121.5 MHz). The newer ELT system makes search and rescue (SAR) operations easier and more efficient, leading to a greater chance of rescue in the event of an emergency. The 406 MHz ELT can also be coded with the airplane owner's identification or coding. There is, however, no requirement for airplane owners to replace their older ELT systems with the newer 406 MHz systems. This remains a voluntary operation on the part of airplane owners.

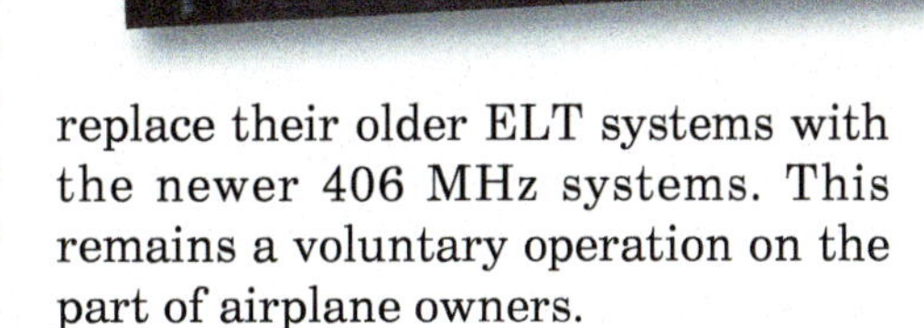

Fig. 51

AIRPLANE LIGHTING

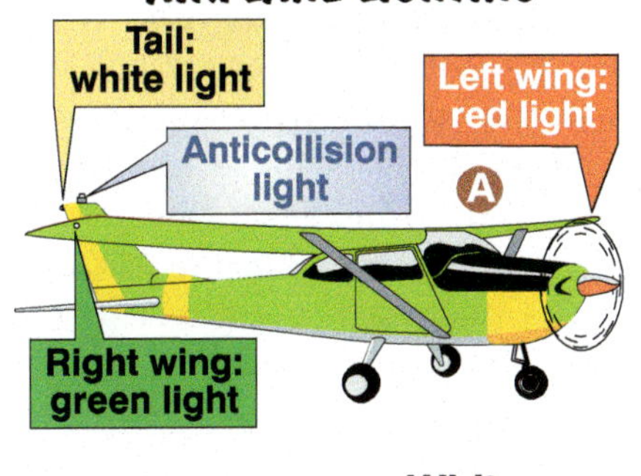

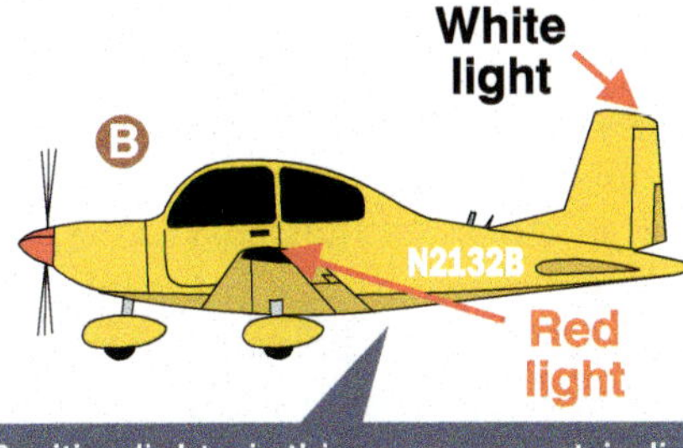

Position lights, in this arrangement, indicate the airplane is moving from right to left.

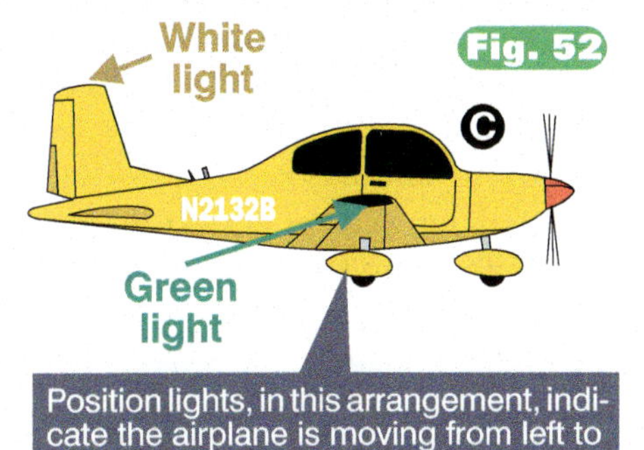

Fig. 52

Position lights, in this arrangement, indicate the airplane is moving from left to right.

FAR 91.209 Aircraft Lights

Several years ago a truck driver was driving beyond official sunset with his headlights off. A highway patrol officer gave chase. Feeling a little ornery, the truck driver didn't stop for several miles. When he did stop, the officer was fuming as he exited his vehicle. The truck driver knew he was in trouble. Approaching the truck the officer said, "Hey buddy, I've been chasing you for several miles to tell you your lights need to be on past sunset. Why didn't you stop?" The truck driver thought fast and said, "Well officer, several years ago my wife ran off with a fellow from the highway patrol and, quite frankly, I just thought you were trying to bring her back!" The moral to that story is—turn your lights on from sunset to sunrise.

Official night time for airplanes is from sunset to sunrise. No person may operate an aircraft during this period unless it has lighted position lights (Figure 52). These are the lights that make it easier for pilots to see each other at night. An easy way to remember the color of these lights for airplanes is to ask the following questions. What color means it's all RIGHT to go? Yes, a green light and that's the color light on the RIGHT wing, as shown in Figure 52A. What do we call the radical LEFT-wingers in our political system? Yes, we used to call them Commies or Reds. Therefore, LEFT wings have a red position light. The tail carries a white light.

These lights are called position lights for a good reason. Since it's difficult for someone outside the airplane to tell which way an airplane is headed at night, specific colors are needed to help get the job done. For instance, suppose you see a white light and a red light as shown in Figure 52B. Which direction is the airplane traveling? Of course, it's moving from right to left. A white light and a green light means the airplane is moving from left to right as seen in Figure 52C. A red light on the right and a green on the left means the airplane is coming toward you. This becomes especially obvious if the distance between these lights is increasing.

Airplanes with an anticollision light system must have these lights on at *all* times when the airplane is in operation. This typically consists of white strobe lights or a red rotating beacon. Pilots are allowed to turn off the anticollision lighting system if the pilot in command determines, because of the operating conditions, it is unsafe. In hazy conditions at night, strobe lights can be quite distracting. But don't turn them off unless it presents a real serious problem. On one flight where we were in the clouds my right seat, nonpilot passenger became annoyed by the flashing white light on the right wing. He looked over at me and said, "Hey, turn your blinker off if you're not going to make a turn."

If you're piloting a seaplane, you may not anchor an aircraft unless it has lighted anchor lights or is in an area where anchor lights are not required on vessels. A friend had a student who was a crusty old mariner. He spent so much time on boats that he'd show up for the flight lesson with clams, mussels and lobsters still attached to his jeans. During one preflight, he untied the ropes and, out of habit, threw them away from the airplane while yelling, "Cast off, cast off!"

If you're in Alaska, where night time and day time take on different meanings, another method of determination is used. Read the next sentence only if you're an Alaskan (in an igloo wearing seal furs). In Alaska, during the period a prominent unlighted object cannot be seen from a distance of three statute miles or the sun is more than six degrees below the horizon, the aircraft must have lighted position lights and an anticollision lighting system in operation. In these northern territories the sun could shine for 20 hours at a stretch in the summer months. That sure adds some excitement to those Fourth of July fireworks shows, doesn't it? You can hear the explosions, but you don't know where they're coming from.

FAR 91.211 Use Of Supplemental Oxygen

It is in your best interest, not to mention your passengers', to have full mental capability while piloting an airplane. Reducing oxygen flow to the brain is one of the quickest ways to get it to act really weird. To keep us from acting any weirder than we're genetically programmed to be, the regulations require the PIC (and any required flight crewmembers) to use supplemental oxygen when flying for more than 30 minutes above 12,500 feet up to and including 14,000 feet. If you go above 14,000 feet, you must use oxygen from the moment you exceed that altitude.

Over the years, I've had pilots come up to me and say, "Hey, couldn't I be at 13,500 feet for 29 minutes, descend to 12,500 feet for a few seconds, then immediately climb back to 13,500 feet, thereby avoiding the use of oxygen?" Legally, the answer is yes. But a question like this makes me think that the pilot's brain has already suffered the debilitating effects of oxygen deprivation.

The only people we haven't talked about yet are the passengers (hopefully they're not in back asleep because you forgot to provide them with oxygen!). According to the regulations you (the pilot in command) are required to provide each occupant of the aircraft with supplemental oxygen when operating at altitudes above 15,000 feet MSL. The rule specifically states *provide,* not *use.* Common sense dictates that it should be used, of course, but it's the old "You can lead a horse to water" situation. You will notice that if some of your passengers choose not to use oxygen above 15,000 feet, they will be very, very quiet. That's because they've probably dozed off or are unconscious.

All these altitudes are MSL altitudes. Since you might someday fly a pressurized airplane, these rules also apply to cabin pressure altitudes. For instance, if you pressurize the cabin to an altitude simulating 13,000 feet, then you and the flight crew are required to use supplemental oxygen for that portion of the flight exceeding 30 minutes at that cabin altitude.

One last word on the use of supplemental oxygen. Don't get it near fire. That's deadly! The airlines are always telling their passengers to extinguish their cigarettes before putting on the oxygen mask (yes, they still smoke on international flights). Frankly, I'm amazed that we need to tell anyone this. After all, who would smoke in an oxygen tent? Perhaps an even more appropriate question to ask is, "Who would do it a second time?"

A PROTEIN A DAY KEEPS THE DOCTOR AWAY

ASRS Pilot and Flight Surgeon: *GA pilot became confused during approach after a 1.5 hour flight at 12,500 - 13,500 feet. He porpoised on landing, made a go around, and struck the prop before finally landing successfully. Pilot suspected oxygen deficiency following the time at altitude. The pilot's last meal before takeoff had consisted of clear broth and a candy bar. Story fits a diagnosis of either hypoxia or hypoglycemia (low blood sugar). I favor the latter because confusion persisted to a low altitude in an acclimatized person and because symptoms cleared rapidly after the pilot became frightened during initial attempt to land. Surge of adrenaline in such a situation will produce a very rapid increase in blood sugar level. It must be noted that hypoxia could have made the problem worse. The reporting pilot was counseled about the avoidance of hypoglycemia by use of protein meals. Using supplemental oxygen on long flights at those altitudes would be wise too.* **ASRS Report**

Be sure to preflight the pilot before flight too. Make time for nutritious meals. In your flight case, have a plastic bag stocked with natural almonds (no salt) and cartons of juice. These are perfect for emergency in-flight refueling of the pilot.

FAR 91.215 ATC Transponder And Altitude Reporting Equipment and Use

Transponders are electronic devices that allow an aircraft's position to be precisely identified on radar. Transponders absorb radar energy, modify it with a special numerical code, then send that numerical code back to the radar. Controllers, asking pilots to squawk (set in the transponder's window) a four digit code, can see those exact numbers on the radar screen (Figure 53). This makes for positive identification of each airplane.

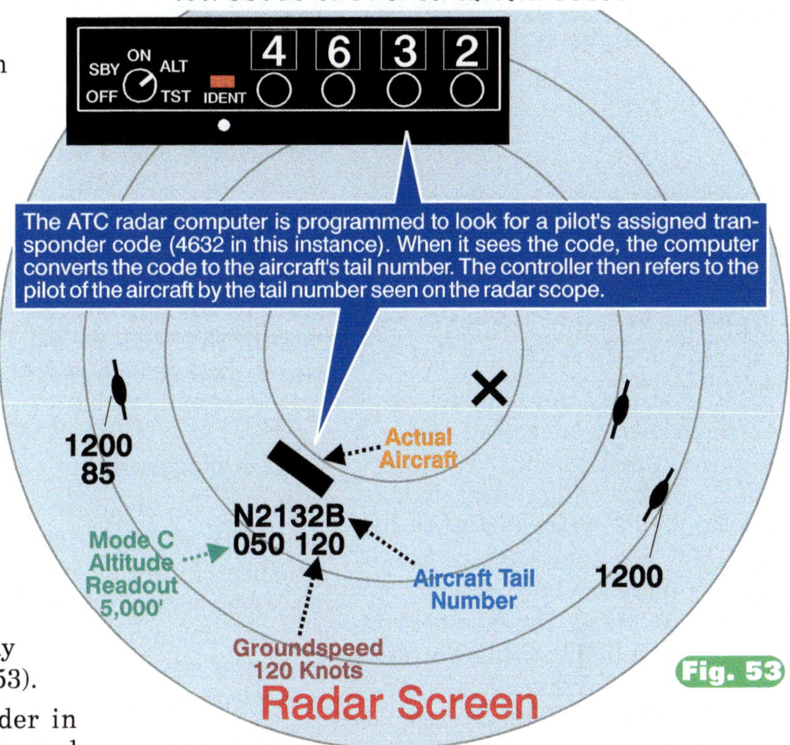

Fig. 53

These transponders are known as Mode 3/A 4096 code capable transponders. The 4096 represents the number of possible combinations of codes capable of being set in the transponder. (For the math maniacs, there are four window each with 8 possible numbers. $8^4=4096$.) Some transponders have *Mode C* or *Mode S* capability otherwise known as *altitude reporting capability*. This means they can display the airplane's altitude on the radar screen (Figure 53).

You'll learn more about using the transponder in Chapter Eight. For now, let's understand when and where we're required to use the transponder. We'll also assume you aren't flying either a balloon or glider and that your airplane was originally certified with an engine-driven electrical system (or hasn't been subsequently certified without such a system). After all, if there's no electrical source on board, a transponder isn't going to work. Transponders with Mode C capability (ALT mode) are required if operating in any of the following:

1. In Class A, Class B and Class C airspace areas as well as in all airspace above the ceiling and within the lateral boundaries of a Class B or Class C airspace upward to 10,000 feet MSL

2. In all airspace within 30 nautical miles of certain airports listed in appendix D, section 1 of FAR Part 91, from the surface upward to 10,000 feet MSL. (I won't bother to list these airports since they can be identified from your aeronautical sectional charts by thin, magenta, circular rings.)

3. In all airspace of the 48 contiguous states and the District of Columbia at and above 10,000 feet MSL, excluding the airspace at and below 2,500 feet above the surface.

4. In the airspace from the surface to 10,000 feet MSL within a 10 nautical mile radius of any airport listed in appendix D, section 2 of FAR Part 91. This also excludes the airspace below 1,200 feet outside the lateral boundaries of the surface area of the airspace designated for that airport. (At the time of this writing, there are no longer any airports listed in this section of appendix D.)

One last thing about this regulation. It requires you to keep your transponder turned on (ALT mode) while in the airspace listed above, or in any controlled airspace, as well as prior to movement on the airport surface (so you'll be visible to ATC surveillance systems). In addition to keeping it turned on, you must also operate it in Mode C (the altitude mode) if you are so equipped.

You are probably wondering, "What do I do if my transponder, or Mode C, fails in flight or fails at some intermediate stop on a cross country flight?" Well, fear not. ATC can waive the transponder requirements, regardless of the airspace in which you're flying. ATC can honor this request at any time. Simply call the Center or approach controller with your request. If, however, you don't have a transponder, ATC wants at least a one hour notice before they approve a flight in an area requiring a transponder. In other words, if you want to depart the primary airport in Class C airspace, you should call the tower at least one hour before departure and request a waiver if your aircraft is not transponder equipped.

FAR 91.303 Aerobatic Flight

Aerobatic flight is defined as an intentional maneuver involving an abrupt change in an aircraft's altitude, an abnormal attitude, or abnormal acceleration, not necessary for normal flight (from that description, it sounds like I was doing aerobatic flight on every solo flight as a student pilot). If you intend on doing aerobatic flight as it's defined, then you must comply with the following rules.

First, you may not conduct aerobatic flight over a congested area of a city, town or settlement. Nor can you conduct aerobatic flight over an open air assembly of persons or when less than 1,500 feet above the surface or when the flight visibility is less than three statute miles. You may not conduct aerobatic flight within the lateral boundaries of the surface areas of Class B, C, D or E airspace designated for an airport. (The surface area for these classes of airspace is identified on your aeronautical sectional chart by dashed or solid lines. You'll learn more about airspace identification in the airspace chapter.)

If you're thinking about doing aerobatic flight within four nautical miles of the centerline of a Federal Airway, think again. This isn't allowed. The last thing the FAA wants is some guy doing loops on a crowded highway-in-the-sky.

Aerobatics is plane fun and you'll be easily hooked. In fact, it's amazing to me that there isn't a special wing at the Betty Ford Center for aerobatic withdrawals! Trust me, you'll have tons of fun, even with these restrictions.

Aerobatics: Pure Fun!
Sean Tucker

I often tell people that I had an opportunity to go up with the famed Bob Hoover, an extraordinary airshow pilot, at Oshkosh in 1992. As I say this, I watch the other pilots wilt with envy. Then I tell them that we went up in an elevator at the Oshkosh Hilton. Even there, Bob Hoover made a typically smooth elevator takeoff and landing. I'm not sure he was current to carry passengers in that Otis model 1301, but it was a great ride anyway!

FAR 91.307 Parachutes And Parachuting

Pilots often confuse the parachute rule with the aerobatic flight rule. The parachute rule states that unless each occupant of the aircraft is wearing an approved parachute, no pilot carrying any person, other than a crewmember, may execute any intentional maneuver that exceeds a bank of 60° relative to the horizon or a nose-up or nose-down attitude of 30° relative to the horizon.

The aerobatic flight rule (FAR 91.303) never mentions the aircraft's pitch or bank. It only talks about abrupt or abnormal maneuvers or accelerations. It's technically possible to perform an aerobatic maneuver and not be required to wear a parachute. Simply pointing the nose downward at a 29° angle and radically pulling up to 29° might be considered an aerobatic maneuver since it's abrupt and certainly abnormal. It doesn't, however, require a parachute. I use this example only for clarification; do not attempt to do this at home. Without a doubt, a snap roll, loop or Cuban Eight is an aerobatic maneuvers requiring parachutes.

If you are by yourself in an aircraft, parachutes are never required regardless of the aircraft's pitch and bank. The FAA figures that you have enough common sense to measure risk for yourself. When it comes to the passengers, though, they aren't betting on your risk assessment abilities.

Parachutes are not required when on flight tests for pilot certification. They are not required when practicing spins or other flight maneuvers required by regulations when given by a certified flight instructor.

Unless you're doing aerobatics, your instructor shouldn't come to the airport dressed like this!

If you're thinking about carrying any parachute in your airplane, then it must be an approved type and have been packed by a certificated and appropriately rated parachute rigger within either 180 days (if its canopy, shrouds, and harness are composed exclusively of nylon, rayon, or other similar synthetic fiber or materials that are substantially resistant to damage from mold, mildew, or other fungi and other rotting agents propagated in a moist environment) or 60 days (for silks, pongees or other natural fibers).

A fellow pilot (we'll keep him anonymous) had an unusual occupation: he threw people out of airplanes (parachute jumpers). Flying a Cessna 206 with the door removed, he would hold the brakes as jumpers exited the plane. These folks would grab onto the strut and stand on the locked wheel. Upon the jumpmaster's command, these jumpers would let go of the strut, and sink into an ocean of air.

On one flight, the last jumper got cold feet, literally and figuratively. He stood on the wheel, holding the strut, but refused to let go. The jumpmaster yelled, "Jump! Jump!" The reluctant jumper said, "No, no, I'm not going!" Both the jumpmaster and the pilot looked at each other and the pilot knew exactly what to do. He let go of the brakes (what a rat). While this is not what pilots normally mean when they refer to *rotation,* it worked. The strut-clinger suddenly became a skydiver.

FAR 91.313 Restricted Category Civil Aircraft: Operating Limitations

When an airplane is given its airworthiness certificate, it is assigned a category. Most airplanes are certified as *standard category,* but some are committed to special or *restricted* category. This means they are to be used for one purpose only. Cropdusting aircraft are one example of this. A few of these aircraft are certified to fly carrying 50% more weight than would be permitted under standard category limits. That's why there are restrictions.

A restricted category aircraft can only be used for the special purpose for which it was certificated. It cannot be used for flight involving compensation or hire when a passenger is being carried. If you show up at the airport for flight training and your flight instructor shoves you into a cropduster, something is definitely wrong. He shouldn't be providing you with basic flight training while dusting a few crops on the way home.

Cropdusting aircraft cannot be operated over a densely populated area, on a congested airway or near a busy airport where the airlines fly. Frankly, the thought of a cropduster flying over my house doesn't exactly thrill me. If I have bug problems at home, I'm calling the ground-bound pest control people.

AN EXPERIMENTAL AIRPLANE

An aircraft certified in the experimental category.

FAR 91.319 Aircraft Having Experimental Certificates: Operating Limitations

Some aircraft have *experimental* certificates. This doesn't mean you can do experiments in these airplanes either. It means the airplane was constructed according to rules different than those under which a standard production airplane is built. Amateur-built aircraft (kit planes) fall into this category.

Until it's proven to the FAA that an Amateur-built aircraft is safe to fly, no person can operate that aircraft outside a designated area. Passengers may be carried but passengers and property can't be carried for compensation or hire. The pilot is required to advise each person carried of the nature of the aircraft. In other words, he or she must say something like, "By the way, I just wanted to let you know that I built this thing and there's nothing wrong with it...any more." This statement is usually followed by, "Hey wait, come back, don't run away, I was only kidding, geesh." Amateur-built aircraft, constructed correctly, are quite safe.

Flight operations may be conducted under day VFR conditions only, unless the FAA specifies otherwise. When operating out of airports with operating control towers, the pilot must notify the tower of the experimental nature of the aircraft. These experimental aircraft may only be used for the purpose for which their certificate was issued.

An experimental aircraft can not be operated over a densely populated area or on a congested airway. Pilots of experimental aircraft may apply for a waiver to these two rules.

Perhaps you've seen one of those large promotional (and experimentally certified) hot air balloons that drifts around the country touting various companies and products. There is one in particular that impresses me. It's a large cow, hundreds of feet tall. I suppose if you listen carefully enough, you could probably hear the instructor saying, "More right udder! Give it more right udder!"

A RESTRICTED CATEGORY AIRPLANE

A cropdusting airplane falls into the restricted category.

FAR 91.403 Aircraft Maintenance: General

One reason flying an airplane is a safe activity (there are many reasons, too) results from the FAA's strict maintenance policy. That's why it's extremely rare for modern aircraft to suffer mechanical difficulty. Regulations place primary responsibility for maintaining an aircraft in an airworthy condition on the owner or operator.

The owner is the person who has legal title to the aircraft. But this isn't always the person in charge of its maintenance. When an airplane is leased back to a flight school, the fixed-base operator is now the person legally responsible for maintaining that aircraft.

FAR 91.407 Operations After Maintenance, Preventive Maintenance, Rebuilding Or Alteration

This regulation states that no person may operate any aircraft that has undergone maintenance, preventive maintenance, rebuilding, or alteration unless it has been approved for return to service by a qualified mechanic and a maintenance record entry is made in the aircraft's logbooks. Airplanes have airframe, engine and propeller logbooks as shown in Figure 54. These are the maintenance records where the required inspections and return to service statements are logged.

PROPELLER, AIRFRAME AND ENGINE LOGBOOKS

Fig. 54

Have you ever wanted to be a test pilot? Well, here's your chance. This regulation also states that no person may carry another person (other than crewmembers) in an aircraft that has been maintained, rebuilt or altered in a manner that may have appreciably changed its flight characteristics, or substantially affected its operation in flight, unless the following is done. An appropriately rated pilot with at least a private pilot certificate must fly the aircraft, make an operational check of the maintenance performed or alteration made, and log the flight in the aircraft records. Translation: anyone with a private pilot certificate can become the test pilot.

Suppose you put a waterbed, disco strobe light and wet bar in the back of your Cessna 172. This would certainly be a major alteration requiring a flight check before passengers are carried. Realistically, you wouldn't put these things in your airplane. But you might have previously suffered major wing damage requiring a test flight of the wing repair prior to the carriage of passengers. The maintenance records is where the operational check must be logged.

LOGBOOK ENTRY OF MAJOR ALTERATION/REPAIR

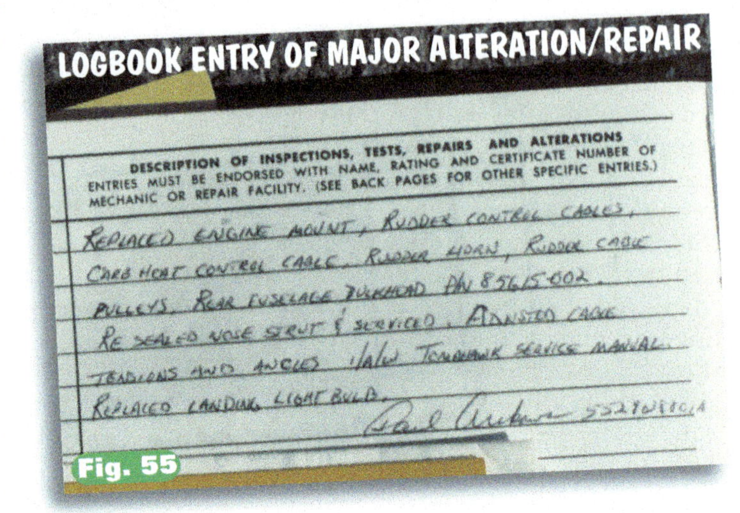

Fig. 55

FAR Part 43 (not shown in this book) allows *airplane owners* to do specific preventive maintenance tasks on their airplanes. This doesn't mean major overhauls and airframe repairs. (An FAA inspector doesn't expect to see pistons and cylinders lying around on your hangar floor.) It does, however, mean that a *private pilot* or *higher* can do things like changing sparkplugs, replenishing hydraulic fluid, and servicing landing gear and wheel bearings. The entire list is spelled out in the regulations. If you're doing preventive maintenance on your airplane, you're required to complete specific paperwork. This entry must include the signature, certificate number and kind of certificate held by the person approving the work (that could be you, the person doing the work). A description of the work must be entered in the aircraft maintenance records as shown in Figure 55.

FAR 91.409 Inspections

If you elect to operate an aircraft it must have had an inspection within the preceding 12 calendar months by a qualified mechanic and been approved for return to service. This is typically called the annual inspection (Figure 56). Since gliders don't have engines, they have only an airframe maintenance logbook. Airplanes actually have three logbooks, one for the airframe, one for the engine and one for the propeller. Required inspections and maintenance must be logged in the appropriate logbook(s).

In addition to the annual inspection, a 100 hour inspection is sometimes required. If you are carrying any person (other than a crewmember) for hire, or if you are giving flight instruction for hire in an aircraft, that aircraft must have had an inspection within the preceding 100 hours of time in service. This is known as a 100 inspection (who names these things?) and is usually less intensive than a typical annual inspection. Of course, if you had an annual inspection, this obviously counts as a 100 hour inspection. The 100 inspection must be entered in the aircraft maintenance records (Figure 57).

LOGBOOK ENTRY OF THE ANNUAL INSPECTION

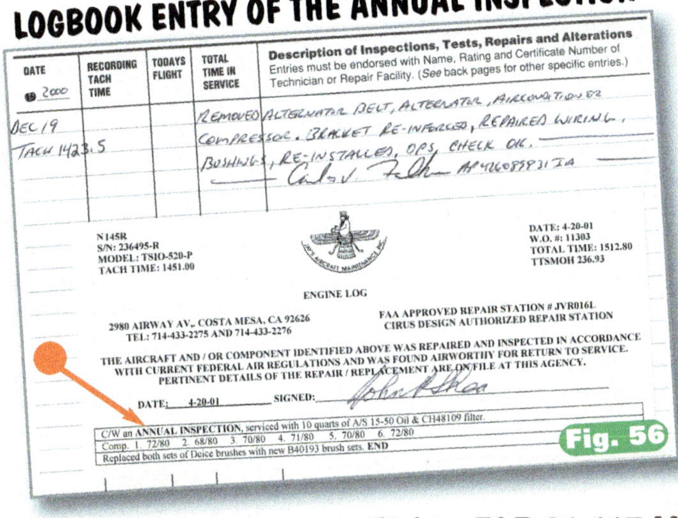

Fig. 56

LOGBOOK ENTRY OF THE 100-HOUR INSPECTION

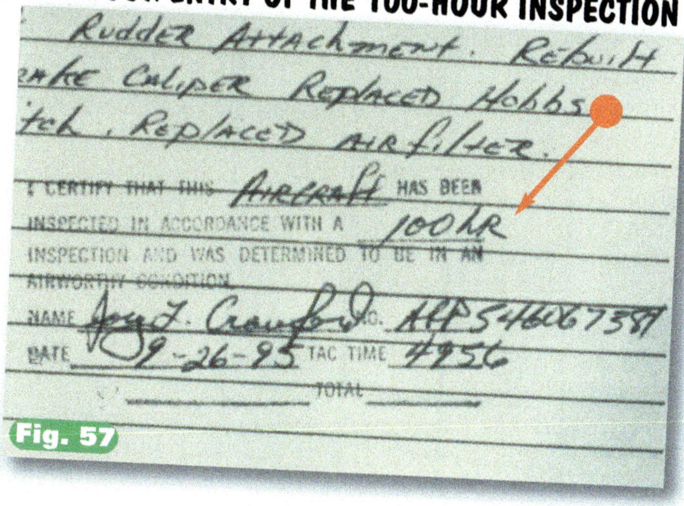

Fig. 57

On several occasions our flight school had to exceed the 100 hour limit to fly the airplane to an airport where the maintenance was performed. Such activity is perfectly legal although the 100 hour time limit may be exceeded by not more than 10 hours. The excess time used to reach a place where the inspection is done must be included in computing the next 100 hours of time in service. In other words, if we exceeded the 100 hour limit by three hours, the next 100 hour inspection was due in 97 hours.

FAR 91.413 ATC Transponder Tests and Inspections

Transponders may not be operated unless they have been tested and inspected within the preceding 24 calendar months and found to comply with the appropriate regulations. Completion of this inspection is shown in the aircraft logbook (Figure 58).

FAR 91.417 Maintenance Records

Each registered owner or operator of an aircraft is required to keep records of aircraft maintenance. These are the records containing the annual inspection, the 100 hour inspection, major alterations or repairs, and the completion of other required maintenance. A frequent and additional inspection that might be performed on an aircraft often results from something known as an airworthiness directive.

When a particular mechanical problem occurs with an aircraft, the FAA may issue an *airworthiness directive* or AD (ADs are issued under FAR Part 39). This is sent to the owner or operator of the aircraft. It's the owner or operator's responsibility to provide the maintenance required by that AD. When the mechanic completes this maintenance, an entry is made in the aircraft logbooks identifying the AD as having been complied with (Figure 59).

National Transportation Safety Board Regulations

The National Transportation Safety Board (NTSB) is the agency responsible for aircraft accidents, incidents and overdue aircraft. Under certain conditions, you may have to notify them or file a report if you are involved in an aircraft accident in which any person receives serious injury or the aircraft receives substantial damage. Part 830 of the Board's regulations governs the reporting of accidents, incidents, and damage to aircraft, cargo, mail, or injury to required crewmembers.

NTSB 830.2 Definitions

It's important that you know the definitions of serious injury and substantial damage, since many of your reporting obligations depend on

A logbook entry indicating the transponder has been tested and inspected (this entry is usually found in the airframe logbook). Airplanes with encoding altimeters must have signoffs for FAR 91.411 and 91.413.

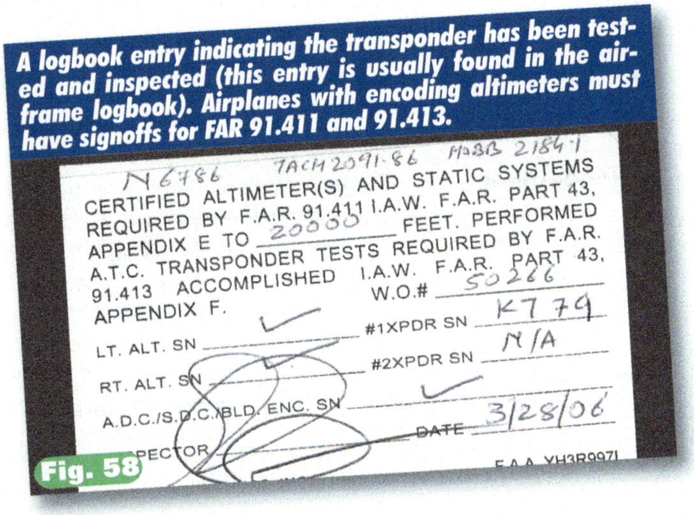

Fig. 58

Logbook entries below reflect compliance with several airworthiness directives (AD). ADs are mandatory and the owner or operator must comply with them. Don't plan on flying an airplane that isn't in compliance with an AD (unless the AD allows it, of course).

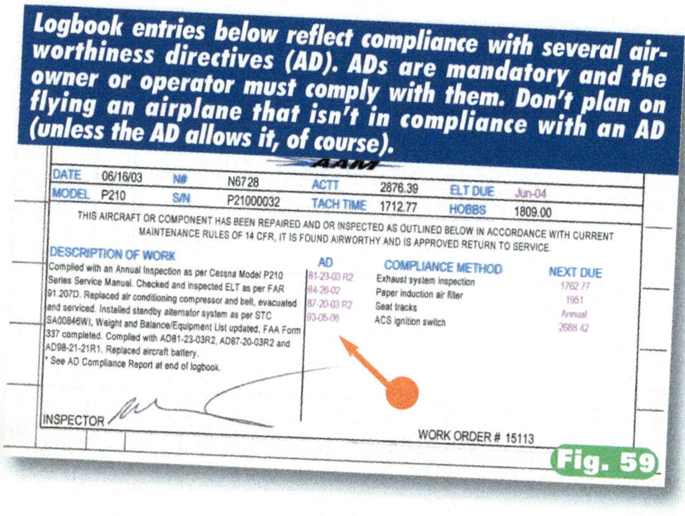

Fig. 59

The 16 Greatest Lies in Aviation

1. I'm from the FAA and I'm here to help you.
2. Pardon me ma'am, I seem to have lost my jet keys.
3. I have no interest in flying for the airlines.
4. All that turbulence spoiled my landing.
5. I'm a member of the mile high club.
6. I only need glasses for reading.
7. Don't worry about the weight and balance—it will fly.
8. If we get a little lower I think we'll see the lights.
9. Oh sure, no problem, I've got over 2,000 hours in that airplane.
10. Sure I can fly it—it has wings, doesn't it?
11. I'm always glad to see the FAA.
12. It just came out of annual—how could anything be wrong?
13. I thought you took care of that.
14. I've got the field in sight.
15. Of course I know where we are.
16. I'm SURE the gear was down.

deciding whether someone has sustained a serious injury, or an aircraft has sustained substantial damage.

The NTSB has five specific definitions for a serious injury. Looking at them closely, they appear to be what you might see at any hockey game. A *serious injury* is any injury that:

1. Requires hospitalization for more than 48 hours, commencing within 7 days from the date the injury was received.

2. Results in the fracture of a bone, except simple fractures of the fingers, toes or nose (such as what you get if you miss our first loan payment to a guy named Vinny).

3. Causes severe hemorrhages, nerve, muscle, or tendon damage.

4. Involves any internal organ.

5. Involves second- or third-degree burns, or any burns affecting more than 5 percent of the body surface.

Substantial damage is defined as damage or failure that adversely affects the structural strength, performance, or flight characteristics of the aircraft and which would normally require major repair or replacement of the affected component. The following are NOT considered to be substantial damage for the purposes of this part:

1. Engine failure or damage limited to an engine if only one engine fails or is damaged.

2. Bent fairings or cowling, dented skin, small puncture holes in the skin or fabric

3. Ground damage to rotor or propeller blades and damage to landing gear, wheels, tires, flaps, engine accessories, brakes, or wingtips.

An *accident* is an occurrence associated with the operation of an aircraft which takes place between the time any person boards the aircraft with the intention of flight and all such persons have disembarked, and in which any person suffers death or serious injury, or in which the aircraft receives substantial damage.

An *incident* means an occurrence other than an accident, associated with the operation of an aircraft, which affects or could affect the safety of operations.

NTSB 830.5 Immediate Notification

The operator of an aircraft must immediately and by the most expeditious means available notify the nearest NTSB field office when an aircraft accident or any of the following listed incidents occur:

1. Flight control system malfunction or failure.

2. Inability of any required flight crewmember to perform his or her normal flight duties as a result of injury or illness.

3. Failure of structural components of a turbine engine excluding compressor and turbine blades and vanes.

4. In-flight fire.

5. Aircraft collide in flight.

6. Damage to property, other than the aircraft, estimated to exceed $25,000 for repair or fair market value in the event of total loss (i.e., you land on a large house or a small Mercedes).

(7) Release of all or a portion of a propeller blade from an aircraft, excluding release caused solely by ground contact.

(8) A complete loss of information, excluding flickering, from more than 50 percent of an aircraft's cockpit displays which you know as your primary flight display (PFD), primary navigation display (PND), electronic flight information systems (EFIS), and other integrated displays.

(9) An aircraft is overdue and is believed to have been involved in an accident.

NTSB 830.10 Preservation Of Aircraft Wreckage, Mail, Cargo and Records

This regulation basically says that if you are the operator of an aircraft involved in an accident or incident, it's your job to protect the wreckage and everything associated with that wreckage until the NTSB arrives and assumes responsibility. Avoid disturbing the wreckage. Do so only if it's necessary to help persons injured or trapped, to protect the wreckage from further damage, or protect the public from injury. If you need to move the wreckage or anything associated with it, make notes, take photographs, or draw sketches to detail its original condition.

NTSB 830.15 Reports And Statements to Be Filed

The operator of an aircraft must file a report *within 10 days* after an accident or *after 7 days* if an overdue aircraft is still missing. A report on an incident for which immediate notification is required shall be filed *only as requested* by an authorized representative of the Board.

Those are some of the important regulations necessary for flying safety. Of course, some of you may be thinking there's only one thing more boring than studying the FARs and that's listening to golf on the radio. OK, let me make this a little more exciting for you by introducing you to our next subject: Airport Operations.

Postflight Briefing #6-1

Sport Pilot Certificate

On page F16 we discussed the requirements for a private pilot certificate. There is, however, another type of pilot certificate you might want to consider. It's a step up from the student certificate and a step sideways from the private pilot certificate. It's called the *sport pilot certificate* and it's a heck of a deal. Here's an overview followed by the details. Let's begin by examining the upside of this license.

First, a sport pilot license doesn't require that you have an FAA issued third-class medical certificate. It only requires that you have a valid U.S. drivers license without having an official *denial* or *revocation* of an FAA medical certificate on file with the FAA. This means if you have a drivers license then the FAA considers you medically qualified to fly as a sport pilot in a sport airplane.

Second, the sport pilot license requires only 20 hours of flight time in preparation for your license compared to 40 hours minimum preparation for a private pilot certificate. This means you can meet the sport pilot license requirement with as little as 15 hours of dual instruction from a certified flight instructor and five hours solo flight time. While a written (knowledge) test and a practical flight test are still required for the sport license, there's no doubt that you'll dramatically reduce the cost of learning to fly, perhaps as much as 60% as compared to that for private pilot licensing.

So what's the downside to obtaining a sport pilot license? The downside (if you want to call it that), is that as a sport pilot you're limited to flying a single- or two-place *light sport aircraft* (LSA) during daylight hours and you can't ever carry more than one passenger. There are other limitations that I'll cover later, but these are the most relevant ones. Now, this isn't necessarily a big downside. As a general rule, most folks only fly with one person at a time anyway. And while flying at night is an aesthetic experience, you'd be surprised how little night flying most pilots really do. Nevertheless, these are limitations to be considered.

So what are the light sport aircraft available to a sport pilot to fly?

The Cessna SkyCatcher is a light sport airplane and is one of many wonderful models of LSAs from which to choose.

A J-3 Cub having a standard airworthiness certificate can be flown by a sport pilot.

The following are six categories of light sport aircraft (LSA): airplane, glider, gyroplane, lighter-than-air (balloon or airship), powered parachute and weight shift control.

In the airplane category of light sport aircraft (the one I'm assuming that you're interested in flying since you're reading a book on airplanes), the airplane must weigh no more than 1,320 pounds and have a top speed of no more than 120 knots (138 mph). It can have no more than two seats and must have fixed landing gear. There are other requirements but these are the important ones. There are many manufacturers making light sport aircraft today and some of these are pretty sexy looking and a real blast to fly (Figure 60).

On the other hand, there are several airplanes with standard airworthiness certificates that also fall into the LSA category. With a sport pilot license you can fly any of these airplanes (the ones that would normally require a regular private pilot license to fly). I'm speaking of a handful of airplanes like: Aeronca Chiefs and Champs, Piper Cubs (Figure 61), Luscombes and Taylorcrafts.

On the whole, flying an LSA as a sport pilot might better accommodate your aviation desires as compared to training for a private pilots license. If, however, you desire greater utility with the machine you fly, then you should consider private pilot training. This allows you to fly bigger and faster airplanes and also allows you to earn an instrument rating, which makes weather delays less of a factor.

There is, however, another strategy you might consider. There's absolutely nothing wrong with obtaining your sport pilot license as an intermediate step in preparation for the private pilot license. This strategy is a good one if you want to fly as a private pilot but presently don't have the $5,000-$7,000 you need for the training. After all, LSAs are generally a bit less expensive than renting standard, non-LSA machines.

It's reasonable to assume that obtaining your sport pilot license in a sport airplane would allow you to fly with a passenger sooner and have more fun quicker. That means having someone with which to share the operating expenses of the flight. That means that flying is overall less expensive, even if you don't wear overalls when you fly (sorry, I really love that line).

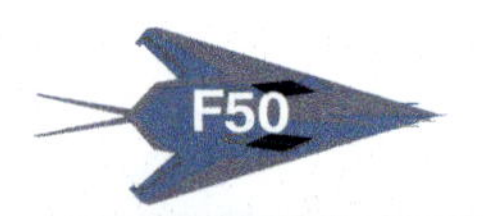

Postflight Briefing #6-2

Why Are NASA Forms A Pilot's Best Friend?

The reports sprinkled throughout this book are from the Aviation Safety Reporting System (ASRS). Staffed with controllers, flight surgeons, aviation lawyers and pilots from every aviation arena, they analyze safety related reports from pilots and controllers.

If you have been involved in a less-than-safe situation or feel you have accidentally been in violation of an FAR, immediately complete and mail a NASA ARC Form 277B or fill out the electronic version for submission (Figure 62). Always have one or two of these forms in your flight bag or glove box.

The NASA form should be thoroughly completed, using additional paper as necessary. Typed is great, handwritten is okay. They'll accept cranberry juice on birchbark, but attempt legibility. Before the strip at the top of the report is removed to de-identify you from the report, one of their experts may call for further clarification.

These folks have been doing this since the 70's without a breach of confidentiality, so rest easy. They even black out all names, places and times from the report body, like a war-time letter. When NASA has a full understanding of the incident, they separate the time-stamped top portion, returning it to you. It is important to keep this portion! Read on.

FAA Advisory Circular 00-46D affirms and clarifies the principles underlying the establishment of ASRS and the responsibilities of NASA in its administration.

The filing of a report with NASA concerning an incident or occurrence involving a violation of the FARs is considered by the FAA to be indicative of a constructive attitude. Such an attitude will tend to prevent future violations. Accordingly, although a finding of a violation may be still be made, neither a civil penalty nor certificate suspension will be imposed if: (1) The violation was inadvertent and not deliberate; (2) The violation did not involve a criminal offense or accident nor action which discloses a lack of qualification or competency; (3) The person has not been found in any prior FAA enforcement action to have committed a violation since initiation of the ASRS of the Federal Aviation Act or any regulation promulgated under that act; and (4) The person proves that, within 10 days after the violation, he or she completed and delivered or mailed a written report of the incident or occurrence to NASA under ASRS.

This information (without your identity) will be used to correct problems within our aviation system. Portions of reports are used in the newsletter, CALLBACK. Reading ASRS reports can be a positive learning experience. Learning from others' mistakes is less painful and less expensive.

NASA ARC Form 277 may be obtained from a FSS, tower, FAA office or your flight school. If you need a supply for your club or flight office write to: FAA, Aeronautical Center, Distribution Section, AAC-45C, P.O. Box 25082, Oklahoma City, OK 73125.

You can also submit your NASA ARC form via the internet. Visit the ASRS web site at the address shown below and follow the links for electronic submission.

For a free monthly copy of CALLBACK write to: CALLBACK, NASA Aviation Safety Reporting System, P. O. Box 189, Moffett Field, CA 94035. Visit NASA's home page at: http://asrs.arc.nasa.gov/.

THE ASRS FORM

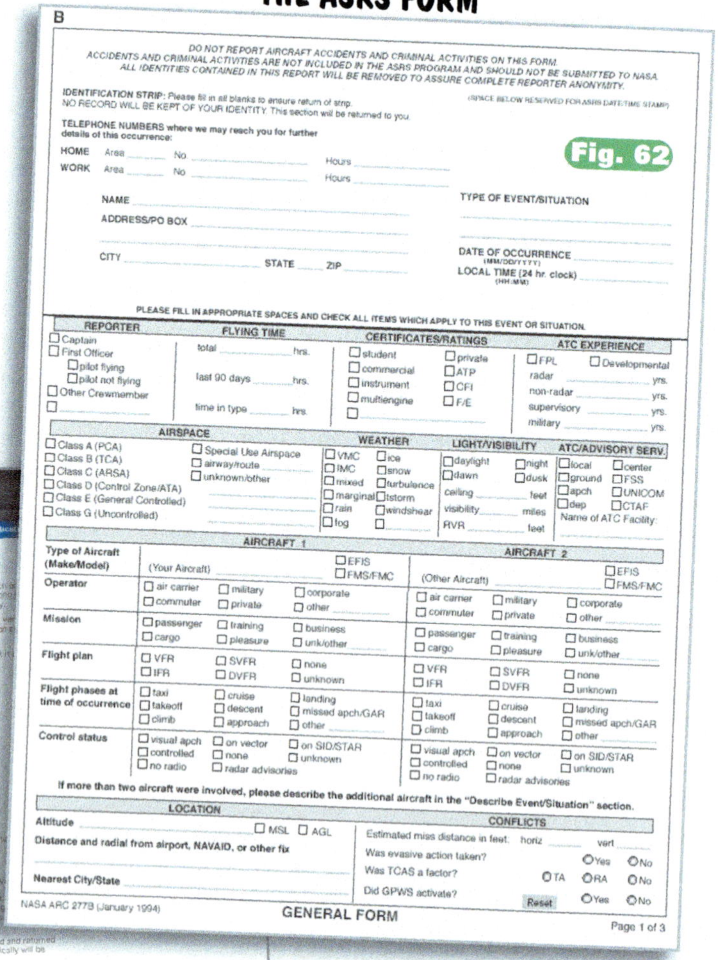
B
DO NOT REPORT AIRCRAFT ACCIDENTS AND CRIMINAL ACTIVITIES ON THIS FORM.
ACCIDENTS AND CRIMINAL ACTIVITIES ARE NOT INCLUDED IN THE ASRS PROGRAM AND SHOULD NOT BE SUBMITTED TO NASA.
ALL IDENTITIES CONTAINED IN THIS REPORT WILL BE REMOVED TO ASSURE COMPLETE REPORTER ANONYMITY.

IDENTIFICATION STRIP: Please fill in all blanks to ensure return of strip.
NO RECORD WILL BE KEPT OF YOUR IDENTITY. This section will be returned to you.
(SPACE BELOW RESERVED FOR ASRS DATE/TIME STAMP)

TELEPHONE NUMBERS where we may reach you for further details of this occurrence:
HOME Area ____ No. ____ Hours ____
WORK Area ____ No. ____ Hours ____

Fig. 62

NAME
ADDRESS/PO BOX
CITY ____ STATE ____ ZIP ____

TYPE OF EVENT/SITUATION
DATE OF OCCURRENCE (MM/DD/YYYY)
LOCAL TIME (24 hr. clock) (HH:MM)

PLEASE FILL IN APPROPRIATE SPACES AND CHECK ALL ITEMS WHICH APPLY TO THIS EVENT OR SITUATION.

REPORTER	FLYING TIME	CERTIFICATES/RATINGS		ATC EXPERIENCE	
☐ Captain	total ____ hrs.	☐ student	☐ private	☐ FPL	☐ Developmental
☐ First Officer	last 90 days ____ hrs.	☐ commercial	☐ ATP	radar ____ yrs.	
☐ pilot flying	time in type ____ hrs.	☐ instrument	☐ CFI	non-radar ____ yrs.	
☐ pilot not flying		☐ multiengine	☐ F/E	supervisory ____ yrs.	
☐ Other Crewmember		☐		military ____ yrs.	
☐					

AIRSPACE		WEATHER		LIGHT/VISIBILITY		ATC/ADVISORY SERV.	
☐ Class A (PCA)	☐ Special Use Airspace	☐ VMC	☐ ice	☐ daylight	☐ night	☐ local	☐ center
☐ Class B (TCA)	☐ airway/route	☐ IMC	☐ snow	☐ dawn	☐ dusk	☐ ground	☐ FSS
☐ Class C (ARSA)	☐ unknown/other	☐ mixed	☐ turbulence	ceiling ____ feet		☐ apch	☐ UNICOM
☐ Class D (Control Zone/ATA)		☐ marginal	☐ tstorm	visibility ____ miles		☐ dep	☐ CTAF
☐ Class E (General Controlled)		☐ rain	☐ windshear	RVR ____ feet		Name of ATC Facility:	
☐ Class G (Uncontrolled)		☐ fog	☐				

	AIRCRAFT 1			AIRCRAFT 2		
Type of Aircraft (Make/Model)	(Your Aircraft)		☐ EFIS ☐ FMS/FMC	(Other Aircraft)		☐ EFIS ☐ FMS/FMC
Operator	☐ air carrier ☐ commuter	☐ military ☐ private	☐ corporate ☐ other	☐ air carrier ☐ commuter	☐ military ☐ private	☐ corporate ☐ other
Mission	☐ passenger ☐ cargo	☐ training ☐ pleasure	☐ business ☐ unk/other	☐ passenger ☐ cargo	☐ training ☐ pleasure	☐ business ☐ unk/other
Flight plan	☐ VFR ☐ IFR	☐ SVFR ☐ DVFR	☐ none ☐ unknown	☐ VFR ☐ IFR	☐ SVFR ☐ DVFR	☐ none ☐ unknown
Flight phases at time of occurrence	☐ taxi ☐ takeoff ☐ climb	☐ cruise ☐ descent ☐ approach	☐ landing ☐ missed apch/GAR ☐ other	☐ taxi ☐ takeoff ☐ climb	☐ cruise ☐ descent ☐ approach	☐ landing ☐ missed apch/GAR ☐ other
Control status	☐ visual apch ☐ controlled ☐ no radio	☐ on vector ☐ none ☐ radar advisories	☐ on SID/STAR ☐ unknown	☐ visual apch ☐ controlled ☐ no radio	☐ on vector ☐ none ☐ radar advisories	☐ on SID/STAR ☐ unknown

If more than two aircraft were involved, please describe the additional aircraft in the "Describe Event/Situation" section.

LOCATION	CONFLICTS
Altitude ____ ☐ MSL ☐ AGL	Estimated miss distance in feet: horiz ____ vert ____
Distance and radial from airport, NAVAID, or other fix	Was evasive action taken? ○ Yes ○ No
Nearest City/State	Was TCAS a factor? ○ TA ○ RA ○ No
	Did GPWS activate? ○ Yes ○ No

NASA ARC 277B (January 1994)
GENERAL FORM
Reset
Page 1 of 3

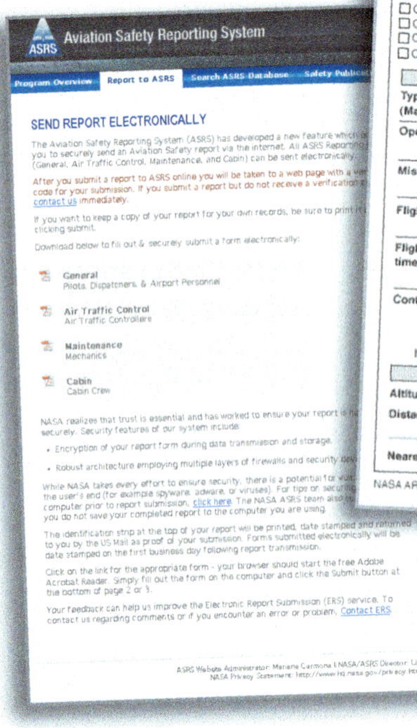

NASA's aviation safety reporting form can be downloaded directly from their web site and physically mailed. Or it can be downloaded, filled out then submitted electronically via the internet.

Postflight Briefing #6-3

One type of airspace restriction that's temporary in nature is called, not surprisingly, a *temporary flight restriction* (TFR). These are typically generated by disaster/hazard areas, presidental visits or airshows. Let's examine all three.

FAR 91.137 Temporary Flight Restrictions (TFRs) In Disaster/Hazard Areas

In the event of either a disaster or a hazard, the FAA might find it necessary to restrict aviation activities to protect persons or property on the ground, to provide safety for those involved in the disaster relief or to prevent sightseeing congestion due to intense public interest. This regulation (FAR 91 .137) specifically deals with *disasters and hazards*. A NOTAM will describe the TFR restrictions. You may not operate within the TFR without meeting one of the specific exceptions in this regulation.

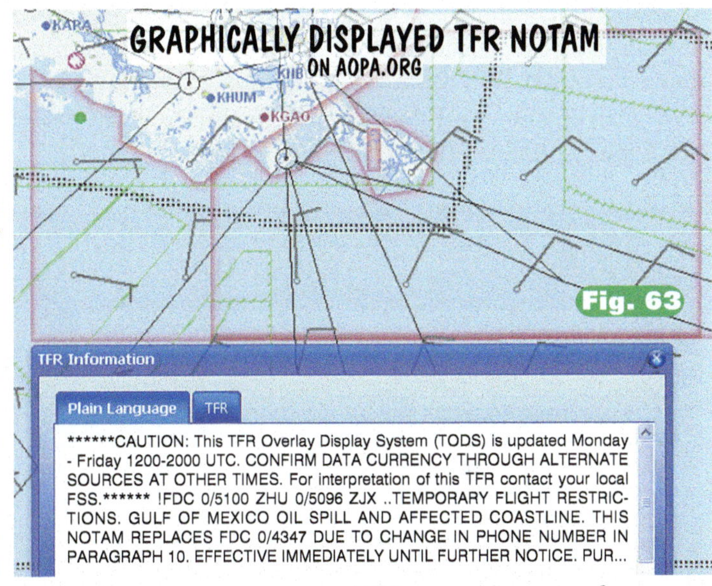

The exception that's relevant to you as a private pilot says you may not enter a TFR involving disasters or hazards *unless* the operation is conducted directly to or from an airport within the area, or is necessitated by the impracticability of VFR flight above or around the area due to weather or terrain, and the operation is *not* conducted for the purpose of observing the incident or event that generated the TFR. You must also give notification to the AFSS or ATC facility specified in the TFR'd NOTAM to conduct this operation. This is necessary so you can receive advisories concerning TFR operations in that area. This is the type of TFR that won't necessarily restrict you from your home airport lying within the disaster/hazard area.

FAR 91.141 Presidential TFRs

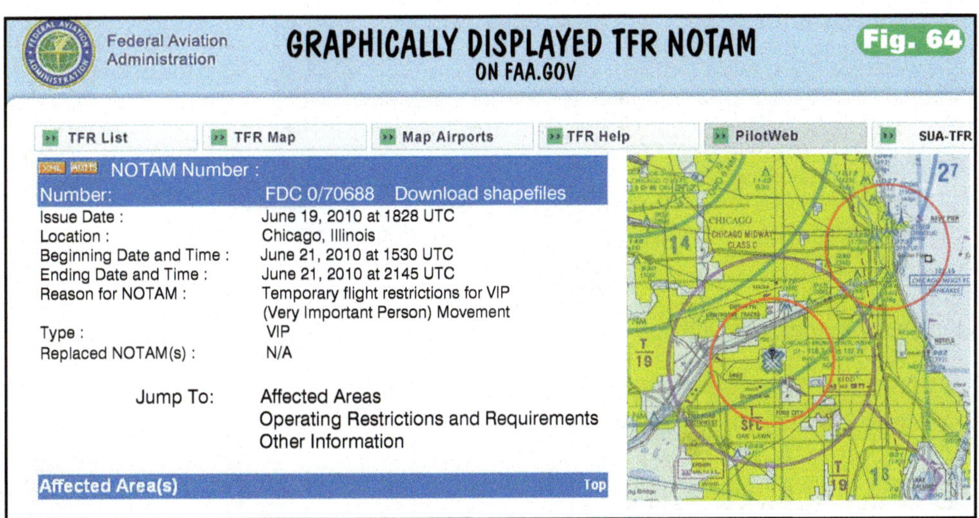

On the other hand, some TFRs pertain to the *president of the United States*, and his associates. This regulation says that you may not operate an aircraft in the vicinity of any area to be visited by the president, vice president, or other public figures contrary to the limitations in the TFR NOTAMs. This essentially means "stay away" unless you want to engage in aquatic sports with the Secret Service, such as *water boarding*. OK, it's not that severe, but you get the point, right? As with all TFRs, you'll find this one described fully in the appropriate NOTAMs.

FAR 91.145 TFRs Covering Aerial Demonstrations and Sporting Events

TFRs are also issued for *aerial demonstrations* (think airshows) or *major sporting events*. These TFRs protect persons or property on the surface, help maintain safety and prevent congestion in the vicinity of these events.

When TFR NOTAMs are issued for aerial demonstrations, the restricted airspace will usually be limited to a five nautical mile radius of the event and less than 17,000 feet MSL (or 13,000 feet AGL for parachute operations). And no, you can't just join up with the Blue Angles during an airshow with your Whifferdill Six, either.

For sporting events, the TFR-restricted airspace will usually be limited to a three nautical mile radius from the center of the event and 2,500 feet above the surface. So avoid these TFRs. It's pretty hard to deny that you flew over a TFR'd sporting event when NBC shows the nation your instant "violation" replay on national TV. These NOTAMs are normally issued at least 30 days in advance of the aerial demonstration or sporting event. Keep in mind that all TFRs can be found by calling the automated flight service station (1-800-WXBRIEF), or via the AFSS web portal.

Postflight Briefing #6-4

Inoperative Equipment: What Now?

Here's the situation. You walk out to the airplane and notice a piece of equipment is inoperative. Can you legally fly the airplane? The answer is: it depends. Of course, if the engine's inoperative, you're staying put. But what if it's the clock? or the magnetic compass? Or the number two communication radio? Or the...? Let's find out.

Figure 65 shows a Pilot Decision Sequence chart useful for answering questions about inoperative equipment.

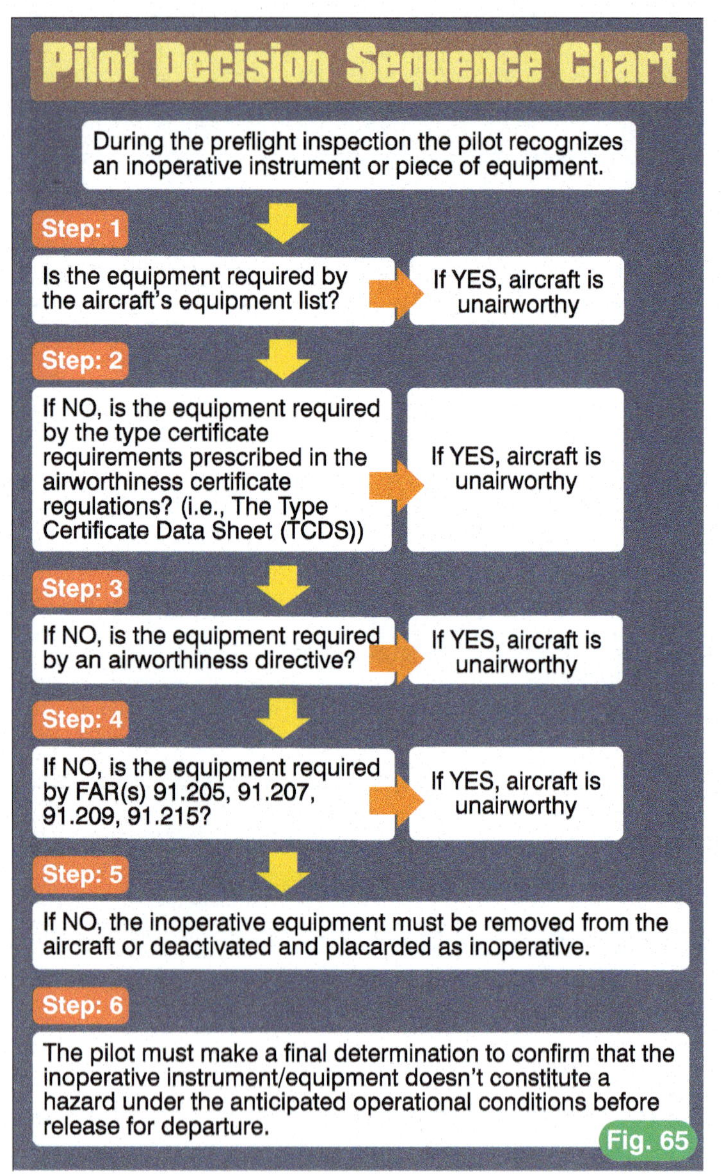

Fig. 65

Step #1:

Step #1 asks if the equipment is required by the aircraft's *equipment list*. Does your airplane have an equipment list? Probably so. If the airplane was manufactured after March 1, 1979, then the FAA says it must have an *Aircraft Flight Manual* (AFM), which includes an equipment list. Figure 66 shows the *AFM* that Cessna provides

The Aircraft Flight Manual

Fig. 66

for the 1985 Cessna Centurion. (Note: for airplanes manufactured prior to this date, the airplane manufacturer might be able to provide an equipment list for that particular airplane's make, model and serial number. Contact the manufacturer to find out.)

Looking in section 6 of the *AFM* (the *Weight and Balance/Equipment List* section), you'll see a long list of airplane equipment (Figure 67). While different

The Weight and Balance Equipment List

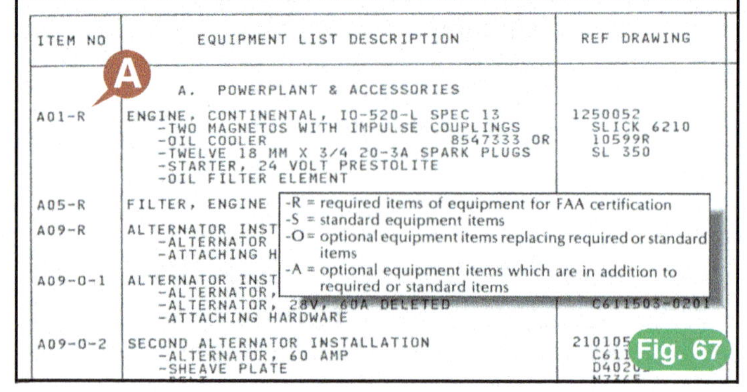

ITEM NO	EQUIPMENT LIST DESCRIPTION	REF DRAWING
	A. POWERPLANT & ACCESSORIES	
A01-R	ENGINE, CONTINENTAL, IO-520-L SPEC 13 -TWO MAGNETOS WITH IMPULSE COUPLINGS -OIL COOLER 8547333 OR -TWELVE 18 MM X 3/4 20-3A SPARK PLUGS -STARTER, 24 VOLT PRESTOLITE -OIL FILTER ELEMENT	1250052 SLICK 6210 10599R SL 350
A05-R	FILTER, ENGINE	
A09-R	ALTERNATOR INST -ALTERNATOR -ATTACHING H	
A09-0-1	ALTERNATOR INST -ALTERNATOR, -ALTERNATOR, 28V, 60A DELETED -ATTACHING HARDWARE	C611503-0201
A09-0-2	SECOND ALTERNATOR INSTALLATION -ALTERNATOR, 60 AMP -SHEAVE PLATE	210105 C611 D402

Fig. 67

manufacturers vary the way this information is presented, all *AFMs* provide some means of identifying whether individual equipment is required or is optional for that airplane.

For instance, Cessna provides four designators next to each piece of equipment to identify whether it's a

required, *standard*, or *optional* item for that airplane (see the shadow box in the center of Figure 67, position A).

In the top left corner of Figure 67, the first equipment item under the *Powerplant and Accessories* section is the engine. It has an *R* next to the designation *A01*. Therefore, the engine is a *required* item for original FAA certification of this airplane. Thank goodness they cleared this one up for us. Nevertheless, if the engine or any other *required* item is inoperative, you can't go flying until it's repaired or replaced.

The Weight and Balance Equipment List

ITEM NO	EQUIPMENT LIST DESCRIPTION	REF DRAWING
D16-A-5	ALTITUDE ENCODER, BLIND -ENCODER	2101011-1 C744001-01
D16-A-6	ALTITUD	-3
D16-A-7	ALTITUD -ENC -ALT -CAB	-5 013-10 -0000
D16-A-8	ALTITUDE -ENCODING ALTIMETER (LIGHTED) -ALTITUDE ALERTER -CABLES & MISC ITEMS	-5 2101013-21 43310-0000
D25-S	ELECTRIC CLOCK	C664508-0102
D25-O	ELECTRIC CLOCK, DIGITAL (NET CHANGE) -CLOCK/CHRONOMETER	0770776-3 C664511-01
D28-R	COMPASS, MAGNETIC	C660501-0102
D38-R	GAGE, FUEL QUANTITY, (IN DISTAL)	C6
D67-A	HOURMETER INSTALLATION	C66

-R = required items of equipment for FAA certification
-S = standard equipment items
-O = optional equipment items replacing required or standard items
-A = optional equipment items which are in addition to required or standard items

B C D

Fig. 68

Further down the list, under the *Electrical System* section, you'll see the designation *D25-S* for the electric clock (Figure 68, position B). This is a *standard* item which wasn't required when the airplane was originally certified. Therefore, it's not a mandatory part of this airplane's equipment list but it may be mandatory according to the other steps on our flow chart.

One step below this is the designator *D25-O (Figure 68, position C)*. This indicates that a digital electric clock is an *optional* equipment item which is an *allowable replacement* for a standard or required item. In other words, no sundials, hourglasses, or ancient Aztec calendars are allowed as an optional means of measuring time in the cockpit.

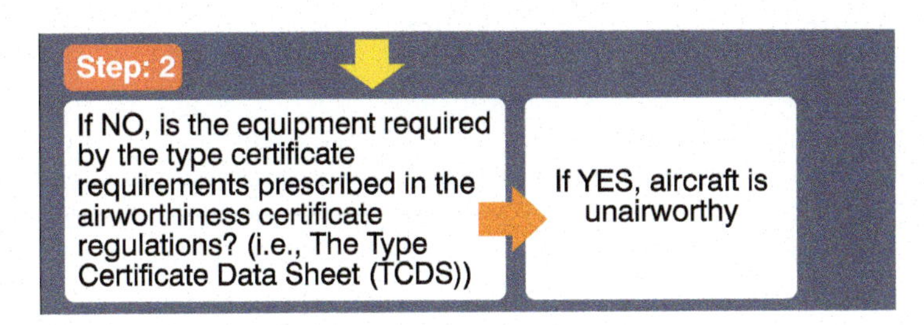

And a few steps below that in Figure 68 is the designation *D28-R*. This indicates that the magnetic compass is a required item for this airplane. According to this list, you can't operate the airplane if the magnetic compass isn't working.

Step #2:

Let's assume that Step #1 indicated that the inoperative equipment isn't mandatory. Step #2 asks if the equipment is required by the airplane's *type certificate data sheet* or the airworthiness regulations as per FAR 91.213 (d) (2) (ii). If it is, then the airplane is unairworthy until that equipment is replaced or repaired. Here's what all this means.

The *Type Certificate Data Sheet* (*TCDS*) provides a listing that shows the specific equipment required for that particular type, make and model of airplane (Figure 69).

In fact, the *TCDS* lists the equipment required for that airplane based on its particular serial number. Some airplanes (a particular model of Cessna 150 for instance) don't require a propeller spinner. Yet, another model (a Cessna 152, for example) or the same model with a different serial number may require a propeller spinner be installed.

The Type Certificate Data Sheet

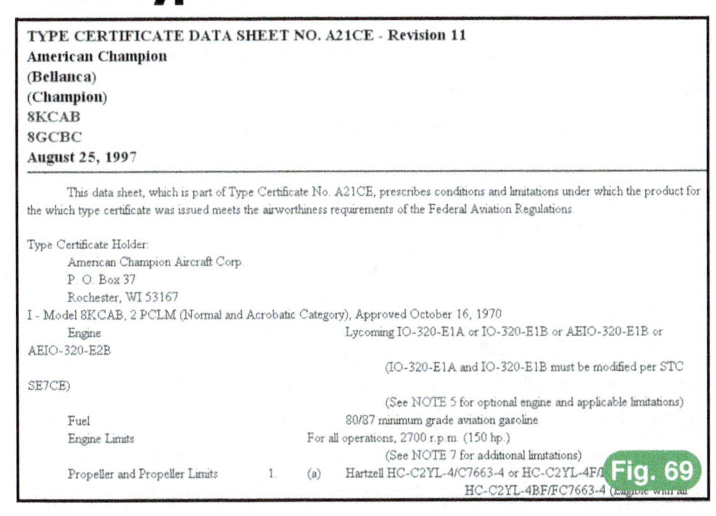
TYPE CERTIFICATE DATA SHEET NO. A21CE - Revision 11
American Champion
(Bellanca)
(Champion)
8KCAB
8GCBC
August 25, 1997

This data sheet, which is part of Type Certificate No. A21CE, prescribes conditions and limitations under which the product for the which type certificate was issued meets the airworthiness requirements of the Federal Aviation Regulations.

Type Certificate Holder:
American Champion Aircraft Corp.
P. O. Box 37
Rochester, WI 53167

I - Model 8KCAB, 2 PCLM (Normal and Acrobatic Category), Approved October 16, 1970

Engine: Lycoming IO-320-E1A or IO-320-E1B or AEIO-320-E1B or AEIO-320-E2B
(IO-320-E1A and IO-320-E1B must be modified per STC SE7CE)
(See NOTE 5 for optional engine and applicable limitations)

Fuel: 80/87 minimum grade aviation gasoline

Engine Limits: For all operations, 2700 r.p.m. (150 hp.)
(See NOTE 7 for additional limitations)

Propeller and Propeller Limits: 1. (a) Hartzell HC-C2YL-4/C7663-4 or HC-C2YL-4F/... HC-C2YL-4BF/FC7663-4 ...

Fig. 69

So the big question is: where does the average pilot find the *TCDS*? One source is the FAA's *Regulatory and Guidance Library* located at: http://rgl.faa.gov/. This is an excellent source of aviation information. Another source is a mechanic with an IA (Inspection Authorization). You can also call or visit the FAA to get this information.

Let's assume that you called the FAA and asked an inspector about an inoperative piece of equipment. If he or she looks over the *TCDS* and tells you that this equipment is required for your airplane, then it must be repaired or replaced before you fly. If it's not required, then you should proceed to Step #3.

Airworthiness Directives

85-02-07 CESSNA: Amendment 39-4991. Applies to Models 205, 205A (S/Ns 205-0001 thru 205-0577); 206, U206, U206A, U206B, U206C, U206D, U206E, U206F, U206G, TU206A, TU206B, TU206C, TU206D, TU206E, TU206F and TU206G (S/Ns 206-0001 thru U20606827); P206, P206A, P206B, P206C, P206D, P206E, TP206A, TP206B, TP206C, TP206D and TP206E (S/Ns P206-0001 thru P20600647); 207, 207A, T207, and T207A (S/Ns 20700001 thru 20700773); 210G, 210H, 210J, 210K, T210K, 210L, T210L, 210M, T210M, 210N and T210N (S/Ns 21058819 thru 21064535); T210G, T210H, T210J, (S/N T210-0198 thru T210-0454) and P210N (S/Ns P21000001 thru P21000760) airplanes certificated in any category.

Compliance: Required within 100 hours time-in-service after the effective date of this AD, unless already accomplished.

To eliminate the possibility of loss of the fuel selector roll pin installation, accomplish the following:

(a) Visually inspect the fuel selector for free play. If free play exceeds 15 degrees, replace any components that exhibit loose or worn conditions, as necessary, to reduce the free play to this limit.

(b) Safety the fuel selector shaft to yoke roll pin installation by installing safety wire through the roll pin in accordance with Cessna Single Engine Customer Care Service Information Letter SE84-5.

(c) The airplane may be flown in accordance with FAR 21.197 to a location where this AD may be accomplished provided fuel tank selection during flight is not performed.

(d) An equivalent means of compliance with this AD may be used if approved by the Manager, Aircraft Certification Office, Federal Aviation Administration, 1801 Airport Road, Room 100, Mid-Continent Airport, Wichita, Kansas 67209; telephone (316) 946-4400.

This amendment becomes effective on March 6, 1985.

Step #3

If you aren't grounded by Step #1 or 2, then Step #3 requires you to check and see if the equipment is required by an *Airworthiness Directive* (*AD*) as shown in Figure 70.

The big question that pilots face is how to know if and when an *AD* requires a specific piece of equipment to be operable in the airplane? Certainly the owner or operator of the airplane receives the *ADs*, but suppose it's a rental airplane? How would you know? After all, most pilots don't have easy access to *ADs*, do they? In some cases, they do.

For instance, you can look up all the *ADs* pertinent to an airplane on the FAA's web site at: http://rgl.faa.gov/. You can even subscribe to these ADs while at this site, too. Unfortunately, reading an *AD* is often as easy as reading *Finnegan's Wake* on a moonless night, during an electrical storm while huddled down in a ship's swaying

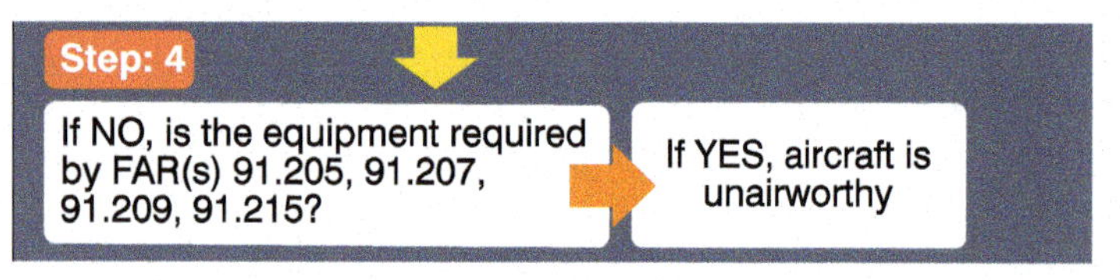

crow's nest. *ADs* are not always easy to understand. Once again, you're almost forced to consult a qualified mechanic to determine if the inoperative equipment is required for this flight.

Let's assume the mechanic tells you that he knows of no *AD* limiting flight with the referenced equipment inoperative. What next? You go to Step #4.

Step #4

Step #4 requires you to reference FAR 91.205, 91.207, 91.209 and 91.215 to determine if the inoperative equipment is required for this flight (see Page 56). For instance, 91.205 is the *Instrument and Equipment Requirements* regulation. It lists all the equipment that must be on board for *Day VFR flight*, *Night VFR flight*, *Instrument flight*, etc. It's an easy regulation to understand and doesn't require a crypto-linguist to interpret.

Step: 5

If NO, the inoperative equipment must be removed from the aircraft or deactivated and placarded as inoperative.

At this point, however, without a functioning magnetic compass, we're unable to operate VFR as per FAR 91.205(b)(3). For training purposes, let's say that Steps #1-4 do not prohibit flight based on the equipment that's inoperative. What next? It's time for Step #5.

Step #5

At this point you must either *remove* the inoperative equipment from the airplane or *deactivate* it. Hmmm. Let's examine the first option.

Equipment Removal

Suppose the landing light is inoperative. Can you remove the bulb from the airplane? The way to know what you can or cannot do to the equipment on the airplane is to check the definition of *preventive maintenance*. As a pilot you're allowed to perform preventive maintenance without being a licensed mechanic or being supervised by that mechanic. Preventive maintenance is defined in FAR 43, Appendix A (it's a long list so I won't print it here but you can find it in any good FAR source). Therefore, you're allowed to remove the landing light bulb in this instance (hopefully, you'll do this in accordance with the manufacture's maintenance manual).

Maintenance Record Entry

Placard (Minimum 1/8 inch high letters)

Landing Light Inoperative

PREVENTIVE MAINTENANCE ENTRY:

(DATE) Total time ________ hours. Landing light bulb removed in accordance with (manufacturer) maintenance manual, Chapter ____, ________page. Landing light switch placarded inoperative.

Pilot's Signature ____________ Certificate Number ____________

Placard (Minimum 1/8 inch high letters)

Landing Light Inoperative

Fig. 71

Additionally, anytime a pilot performs preventive maintenance, he or she must make an entry in the *maintenance records* in accordance with FAR 43.9. Figure 71 shows what this entry should look like. In other words, you shouldn't have an entry that reads something like, *"Took out bulb, taped on a big flashlight with duct tape in its place and hooked string to the switch so I could activate it in flight. Looks good to me as long as you don't mind the rattlin' noise during flight. Signed: Bubba."*

Next, you must write the word **INOPERATIVE** on a piece of tape with letters a minimum of 1/8th inch tall. Then place this tape over or near the inoperative piece of equipment (in case you're a comedian, don't even think about placing it on the pilot's forehead). In this instance, you should place the tape above or near the landing light

switch (don't place it over the landing light cover on the outside of the airplane).

It's fair to say that anytime you remove an item from an airplane, it's best to consult a qualified mechanic first (and I'm not talking about the guy who works on your Toyota, either).

As a personal note, I'd leave the landing light installed and simply deactivate it. How do you do that? Read on.

Equipment Deactivation

In maintenance circles, deactivating a piece of equipment implies removing it from its power source. Suppose the airplane's gas heater is inoperative. This is a difficult item to remove, so you decide to deactivate the heater instead. Unlike a landing light (which you can deactivate yourself) the heater's deactivation isn't covered by the definition of preventive maintenance. A mechanic *must* be consulted. (Even if it's not required, I'd recommend that you always consult a mechanic anytime you decide to deactivate a piece of the airplane's equipment.)

Maintenance Record Entry

Placard (Minimum 1/8 inch high letters)

Aircraft Heater Deactivated

PREVENTIVE MAINTENANCE ENTRY:

(DATE) Total time ________ hours. **Aircraft Heater Deactivated** in accordance with (manufacturer) maintenance manual, Chapter ____, ______page. **Heater Switch** placarded inoperative.

Mechanic's Signature ______________ Certificate Number ______________

Placard (Minimum 1/8 inch high letters)

Aircraft Heater Deactivated

Fig. 72

Let's say, upon examination, the mechanic elects to cap the heater's fuel lines as a means of deactivating the device. FAR 43.9 requires that the mechanic make an entry in the maintenance records that looks something like that in Figure 72.

Additionally, you or the mechanic must still write the word **INOPERATIVE** on a piece of tape with letters a minimum of 1/8th inch tall. This tape must be placed over or near the inoperative piece of equipment (the *heater switch* in this instance).

Is that all there is to this? Nope, one more thing.

Step #6

Step: 6

The pilot must make a final determination to confirm that the inoperative instrument/equipment doesn't constitute a hazard under the anticipated operational conditions before release for departure.

If you remove or deactivate a piece of inoperative equipment, you (the PIC) must make a final determination that the equipment doesn't constitute a hazard under the anticipated conditions of flight.

Whew! Are we there yet?

Nope, you have one additional thing to consider.

How long can the inoperative equipment remain inoperative? FAR 91.405 says that the owner or operator of the aircraft shall have any inoperative equipment repaired, replaced, removed, or inspected at the next required inspection. For most airplanes, this refers to the *annual inspection*. If the airplane is operated for hire, then the next required inspection also refers to the next 100 hour inspection in addition to the annual inspection. (As a side note, the landing light is a required equipment item if the airplane is operated at night for hire.

Despite the six steps mentioned above, your local FAA inspector may require an additional step(s) when removing or deactivating equipment. For instance, he or she may require a placard be placed in the airplane if the landing light is removed. The placard might read, "Day-VFR Flight Only." I suggest you make a call to your local FAA office just to make sure the work you're doing is acceptable to them.

Heck, it seems like it would be a lot easier to sell the airplane every time something stops working and buy a new one. Indeed, I realize that all this can be confusing. No argument here. But, there is some good that can come out of all this. If you follow these procedures, pilots will have a better idea about what equipment is or is not working when they enter an airplane.

So this is life in the big city when it comes to inoperative equipment. Yes, it's a bit troublesome, but if you're ever ramped check by the FAA, I wouldn't plan on using the old ruse, "Hey, the compass was working when I took off this morning." Difficult as it may be, it's better to jump through the hoops and make sure you're completely legal before hitting the airways.

Postflight Briefing #6-5

FAR 91.205—Powered Civil Aircraft with Standard Category U.S. Airworthiness Certificates: Instrument and Equipment Requirements

It doesn't get much more down than this, the mother of all rules. This is the one that says what instruments you need up and running in order to fly VFR during the day or at night.

Notice I said "up and running." Having your co-pilot hold the aircraft's sole altimeter in her lap does *not* constitute having it function.

To understand what instruments are necessary for VFR flight (day and night), you need to poke your nose into FAR 91.205. So let me focus your nose-poke on the specific part of this regulation that pertains to you (Figure 73).

The instruments/equipment necessary for day VFR flight are:

- Airspeed indicator
- Altimeter
- Magnetic direction indicator
- Tachometer for each engine
- Oil pressure gauge for each engine using pressure system
- Temperature gauge for each liquid-cooled engine
- Oil temperature gauge for each air-cooled engine
- Manifold pressure gauge for each altitude engine
- Fuel gauge indicating the quantity of fuel in each tank
- Landing gear position indicator, if the aircraft has a retractable landing gear.

Fig. 73

Equipment Required for Night VFR Flight

• For small civil airplanes certificated after March 11, 1996, in accordance with Part 23 of this chapter, an approved aviation red or aviation white anti-collision light system (I would prefer an anti-collision force field if one were available, but it isn't). In the event of failure of any light of the anti-collision light system, operation of the aircraft may continue to a location where repairs or replacement can be made.

• If the aircraft is operated for hire over water and beyond power-off gliding distance from shore, approved flotation gear readily available to each occupant and at least one pyrotechnic signaling device. As used in this section, "shore" means that area of the land adjacent to the water which is above the high water mark and excludes land areas which are intermittently under water.

• An approved safety belt with an approved metal-to-metal latching device for each occupant two years of age or older (fortunately, this doesn't apply to pilots who act younger than two years of age according to their pediatrician).

• For small civil airplanes manufactured after July 18, 1978, an approved shoulder harness for each front seat. The shoulder harness must be designed to protect the occupant from serious head injury when the occupant experiences the ultimate inertia forces specified in FAR Part 23.561(b)(2). Each shoulder harness installed at a flight crewmember station must permit the crewmember, when seated and with the safety belt and shoulder harness fastened, to perform all functions necessary for flight operations.... (There are additional details listed in this reg that aren't pertinent to this chapter so I won't cover them. But if you're upset by this and your name is Blayde, give me a call and I'll personally interpret them for you. Just don't hit me.)

The instruments/equipment necessary for night VFR flight are: (Figure 74)

• The instruments and equipment previously specified for day VFR flight

• Approved position lights

• An approved aviation red or aviation white anti-collision light system on all U.S.-registered civil aircraft. In the event of failure of any light of the anti-collision light system, operations with the aircraft may be continued to a stop where repairs or replacement can be made.

• If the aircraft is operated for hire, one electric landing light (sorry, save those candles for the solstice).

• An adequate source of electrical energy for all installed electrical and radio equipment (who moved my hamster?)

• One spare set of fuses, or three spare fuses of each kind required, that are accessible to the pilot in flight (not the kind of fuses you light, but the kind that let the lights work).

Postflight Briefing #6-6

I'm sure at one time or another you've seen an airplane towing a glider. This might seem quite reasonable, since gliders don't have engines. It would appear that a glider pilot must rely on the generosity an airplane pilot to tow him from airport to airport. Well, not quite. Gliders are towed aloft, then released to do what they do best—glide. As a private pilot, you can be the one towing the glider or UPUV (unpowered ultralight vehicle) as long as you meet a few specific requirements. While these are discussed in detail in FAR 61.69, here are a few that you should be familiar with.

To tow a glider or UPUV you need at least a private pilot certificate with a category rating for powered aircraft. I'm sorry to disappoint you, but this means you won't be towing gliders in your hot air balloon. To act as pilot in command for towing a glider or UPUV, you must have logged at least 100 hours of pilot-in-command time in the aircraft category, class, and type (if a type rating is required) used to do the towing. You also need to have logged at least three flights as the sole manipulator of the controls of an aircraft towing a glider or simulating glider-towing flight procedures while accompanied by a qualified pilot. Towing gliders or UPUVs is a great way to build flight time and polish those stick and rudder skills.

Postflight Briefing #6-7

FAR 61.23 - BasicMed for Pilots

No doubt there are some private pilots who enjoy visiting their aviation medical examiner once every two to five years, especially if this AME is friendly and popular. I remember visiting one AME who was so popular that the guy in line ahead of me had a musket wound. Well here's some good news for you.

Thanks to the lobbying efforts of the AOPA we have had a reform of the basic medical requirements pilots must meet to act as PIC of an aircraft. This effort is known as *BasicMed*.

In a nutshell, what does BasicMed mean to you? It means that you may now act as PIC without having to have a current FAA medical certificate as long as you meet certain requirements. Let's examine the details.

To qualify for BasicMed you need to meet the following requirements:

•You must hold a valid U.S. driver's license and comply with any of the restrictions shown on that license. No, I don't mean that you can't operate an airplane having more than four axles, either. I'm speaking of limitations such as corrective lenses, prosthetic aids and so on. And yes, even a driver's license issued from a state that is "non-REAL ID compliant" meets this requirement.

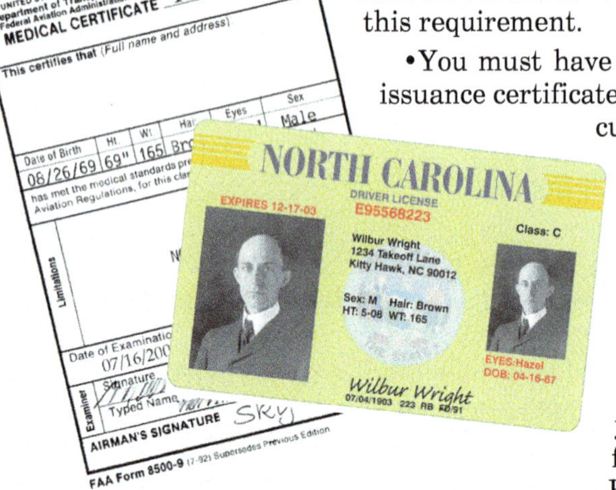

•You must have held a valid FAA medical certificate, either a regular or special issuance certificate, on or after July 15, 2006. No, this certificate does not have to be current, either. If you obtained an FAA medical certificate on July 16th, 2006 and let it expire after 24 to 60 months, you're good to go with BasicMed. If this medical certificate was a "special issuance" certificate and you let it expire, you're still good to go for BasicMed as long as you haven't newly developed any of the medical conditions that I'll list shortly since the last time you received your medical certificate. You're also good to go for Basic Med if you never had a special issuance medical certificate for any of the medical conditions I'll list shortly. If otherwise, then you'll need to obtain a special issuance medical certificate for the following medical conditions before you can operate under BasicMed.

Mental Health:

(i) Personality disorder severe enough to have repeatedly manifested itself by overt acts

(ii) Psychosis

(iii) Bipolar disorder

(iv) Substance dependence within the previous two years

Neurologic:

(i) Epilepsy

(ii) Disturbance of consciousness without satisfactory medical explanation of the cause

(iii) A transient loss of control of nervous system functions without satisfactory medical explanation of the cause

Cardiac:

(i) Myocardial infarction (heart attack)

(ii) Coronary heart disease that has required treatment

(iii) Cardiac valve replacement

(iv) Heart replacement

•If your most recent medical certificate has been suspended or revoked, or your application for a special issuance medical certificate was withdrawn or denied, then you need to obtain a new medical certificate before you can operate under BasicMed.

To operate under BasicMed you need to:

1. Visit a state-licensed physician at least once every 48 months (to the date of your exam) for an examination sufficient to determine the absence of any medical conditions that could interfere with the safe operation of an aircraft. This exam must have been performed on or after April 24, 2017.

2. Take a free online medical education course every 24 calendar months (for example, AOPA offers such a free course).

The limitations for aircraft and pilot operating under BasicMed:

1. You may fly an aircraft having up to a 6,000-pound maximum certificated takeoff weight.

2. This aircraft is authorized to carry no more than six occupants (that's five passengers plus you, the pilot).

3. You may conduct VFR or IFR flights within the United States only.

4. You may fly at an indicated airspeed of 250 knots or less and fly at an altitude that's at or below 18,000 feet mean sea level.

5. You cannot fly for compensation or hire except as permitted by FAR 61.113.

6. You may fly in connection with a business only if the flight is incidental to that business and does not carry any passengers or property for compensation or hire.

7. You must keep a copy of the Medical Education Course certificate of completion and the Completed Medical Examination Checklist in your logbook (no, you are not required to carry your logbook with you when acting as PIC).

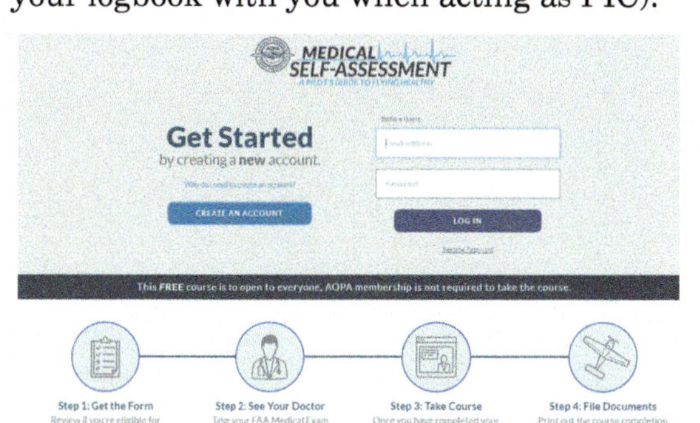

8. You may act as a safety pilot under BasicMed but only if you are the PIC of the airplane.

9. Flight instructors may give flight instruction under BasicMed, including instruction to others not holding an FAA medical certificate.

Steps to take to operate under BasicMed:

1. Complete the FAA self-assessment form prior to your examination.

2. Schedule a physical examination with your state-licensed physician who will complete the FAA form.

3. Complete the Online Medical Education Course.

4. Print the completion certificate from the course and keep it in your logbook along with the completed Medical Examination Checklist.

Postflight Briefing #6-8

FAR 91.519 - Passenger Briefings

This regulation applies to the operators of large airplanes (not you), turbojet powered multi-engine airplanes (not you), and fractional ownership programs (maybe you...someday). Fractional ownership refers to aircraft with multiple owners who share the costs of purchasing, leasing, and operating the aircraft. These programs are becoming quite popular in general aviation (mainly because the word "share" is involved here). Should you decide to participate in a fractional ownership program, here are a few additional items required of the pilot in command (PIC) of the aircraft.

Aside from telling your passengers about how to use the seat belts, exit doors (and barf bag, if you think this is necessary, although this isn't required), there are several other items that you must include in your preflight passenger briefing.

First, if your passengers are planning on smoking during the flight, the PIC must brief the passenger on when, where, and under what conditions smoking is allowed. No, the passengers don't need to see a Surgeon General's warning about smoking, either. Then again, if you happen to have a plastic model of a lung that many pilots carry around in their flight bag, it might not hurt to point out how cigarettes will affect its alveoli over time.

As we've previously discussed, the PIC is responsible for briefing the passengers on when, where and under what conditions it's necessary to use their seat belt and shoulder harness.

Of course, you should have also briefed your passengers on the location of the aircraft's entry door and emergency exits as well as how to use these exits. This keeps your passengers from having to grab onto your ankles as a means of cockpit egress during an emergency evacuation. It's less humiliating for the passengers, too.

If your airplane has survival equipment (flotation devices, flares, dinghies, portable submarine, etc.), you are required to brief your passengers on the location of this equipment. You are also required to brief your passengers on the proper procedures for ditching as well as the use of any flotation equipment on the airplane. You might also mention that you, the pilot, are not considered a flotation device despite having lettered in swimming during the 11th grade.

Finally, you must brief your passengers on the use of any oxygen equipment that might be installed on the airplane. This means how to activate the oxygen system and how to use it to actually breathe. In other words, the nasal cannula doesn't go underneath the arm since there are no nostrils down there (thank goodness!), and the mask doesn't go on top of anyone's head (irrespective of whether or not it's party time and you've run out of hats).

Keep in mind that, despite these additional requirements for operators of fractional aircraft, they should be applied to every flight on every airplane. Yes, that means in your Cessna 172 or Piper Warrior. The items in this regulation are just common sense. Please use them.

Have you ever wondered what all those small trucks at airports—the ones with the flashing yellow lights—do? I thought I knew. For a long time I was convinced they brought sandwiches to the student pilots who became lost on the airfield. After all, even students need sustenance while attempting to navigate from taxiway to runway to parking spot.

An airport's signage and markings are one situation where consistency makes for confidence, and the FAA lends a helping airfoil by specifying in great detail how airport runways, taxiways, and other aircraft movement areas are to be laid out, marked, and lit. While it's not quite true that if you've seen one airport you've seen 'em all, there *is* a method to the apparent madness. As with a Buck Rogers secret decoder ring, you just have to decipher what's in front of you.

Let's take a look at the airport in Figure 1. The airport is graced with two runways capable of handling takeoffs and landings in four different directions (two directions on each of two runways, for the geographically and mathematically challenged).

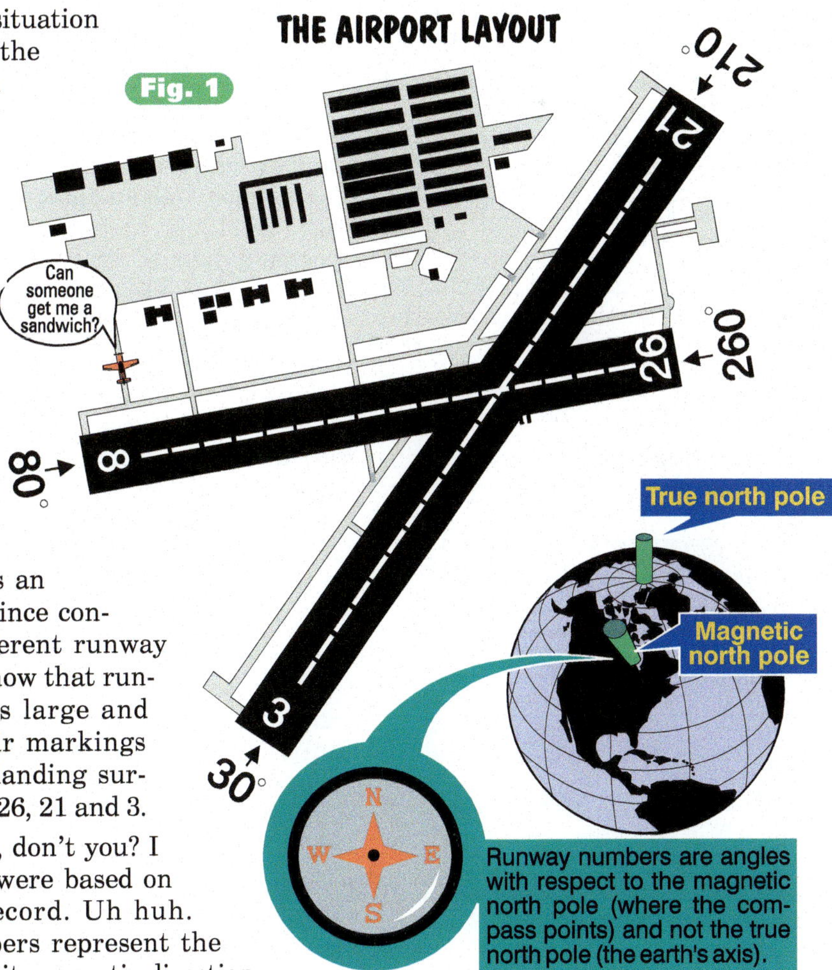

If we assume that the airport in Figure 1 is an airport with an air traffic control tower, and since controllers get so upset when you land on a different runway from the one *they* had in mind, it's helpful to know that runways come with numbers, which are always large and painted in white. Runway numbers and their markings help distinguish them from the airport's nonlanding surfaces. The runways in Figure 1 are numbered 8, 26, 21 and 3.

You think they just make those numbers up, don't you? I had a student who thought runway numbers were based on some sort of speed limit or seismograph record. Uh huh. There's a method to the madness. The numbers represent the first two digits of the runway's actual three digit magnetic direction.

Speaking of Runways

There are three ways to say anything. The right way, the wrong way, and the runway.

Let's learn the runway. In order to sound like a pilot, you need to know that real pilots like runways so much they always say each digit in a runway's name separately. Thus *Runway 26* become *Runway Two Six* when spoken. *Runway 3* is *Runway Three.*

There's actually a reason the numbers are spoken in this manner. English is the international language of aviation. Every tower handling international traffic must, by treaty, have at least one English-speaking controller on duty at all times. In order to avert international chaos, as well as crashes, it has been agreed that a certain controlled English vocabulary will be what everyone speaking Aviation English uses. Part of the deal is that instead of having to learn all the numbers from 0 to 360 in English, only the numbers 0-9 will be used in referencing runways and headings. That's how Runway 21 comes to be *Runway Two One,* and why headings are given as three single digits, rather than *one hundred seventy five.*

Essentially, a runway's numbers are its direction, rounded off to the nearest 10 degrees. A runway oriented at 211 degrees becomes Runway 21 (pronounced *runway two one* when speaking to controllers and other aviation-savvy people). A runway pointed 076 degrees becomes *Runway eight* (rounding up).

There are two sides to almost every issue, and two ends to every runway. With rare exceptions (usually having to do with terrain), you can theoretically land or take off from either end. This means each piece of runway pavement has numbers on each end. Those who are way ahead of me will realize these numbers, when expressed as three digit figures, differ by a value of 180. Makes sense, since the two directions are 180 degrees apart.

All runway angles are oriented to the magnetic north pole, where the magnetic compass points, and not the true north pole, where Santa Claus (a pilot) lives. When your airplane is pointed down any runway, the airplane's magnetic compass should approximately indicate that runway's direction. Figure 2 shows what the compass and the directional gyro might look like when aligned with Runway 26. In Chapter 14 you'll learn more about magnetic and true direction. For now, just remember this when operating at an airport: wind direction, landing direction and any headings ATC asks you to fly are all based on magnetic direction.

Both the heading indicator and the magnetic compass show the magnetic direction when pointed down the center of Runway 26.

Fig. 2

Runway Lighting

Painted white runway markings are easy to identify during the day, but what about at night? Don't look for Day-Glo orange any time soon. The airport has an image to maintain. Besides, the airport would become a magnet for rock stars and flower-painted VW buses.

The answer at night is light. As the sun sinks slowly into the west, the airport often lights up like one of those Disneyland Main Street parades. All kinds and colors of lights, some flashing and some steady, are there to amuse and confuse you. Think of it as color-coded hints and you'll be on the right track.

White lights, shown in Figure 3, border both sides of the runway. Called runway edge lighting, these lights are spaced 200 feet apart. Controllers turn these lights on between sunset and sunrise or when the visibility is poor.

The beginning of the runway is announced with green threshold lights, while the far end of the runway is lit in red. It's an appropriate color to indicate you are running out of usable landing surface (only tractors, bulldozers, and dune buggies beyond those red lights, please!). These lights actually lead a dual life. On one side they're green; on the other, red. Think about it for a second. The beginning (or threshold) of one runway is the end of another. The lights on the threshold of Runway 21 are also at the terminus of Runway 3.

What I've described so far is the basics of runway lighting, which you will encounter at almost any airport that supports night operations. It can and does get a lot fancier. While gathering aviation experience, you're sure to come across airports with sophisticated lighting. In fact, airports with precision instrument runways can have such detailed lighting that it's possible to mistake it for a prairie fire. Some runways have

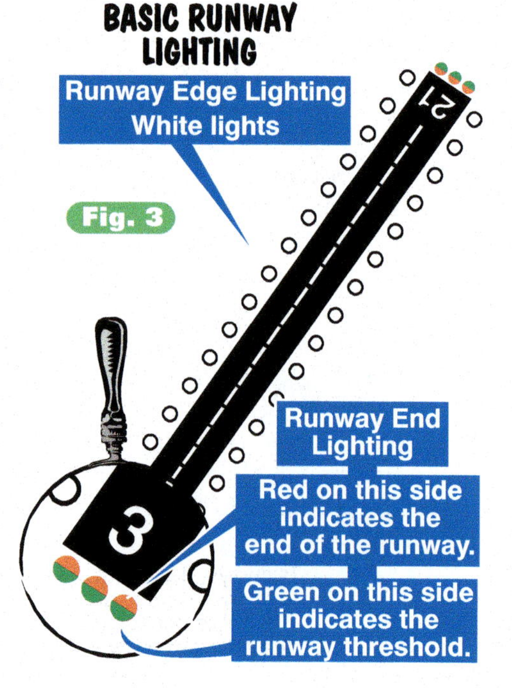

centerline lighting, with embedded lights running the entire length of the runway centerline. Some have brilliant sequenced flashing strobe lights leading to the runway threshold. Others have touchdown zone lighting that looks like a gigantic Christmas tree was squished into the first 3,000 feet of the runway. One of my students said it was so pretty he wasn't sure he should land on it. You can! See the Aeronautical Information Manual for additional information on these lighting systems.

Taxiway Markings

There are few things as pitiful as a pilot on the ground, even in the daytime. The King or Queen of the Airways can easily become the Lost Platoon when the gear hits the ground. It is a common misconception that pilots are endowed with some superior ability to find their way around airports. This is demonstrably untrue. Most pilots can find a vending machine blindfolded, but many of us have trouble getting from the runway to the tiedown spot at an unfamiliar airport. Pilots and their airplanes have been extracted from some very unusual places (like the time a fellow pilot accidentally taxied into a secret military hangar at a combo civil/military airport. It obviously wasn't much of a secret, since they were in the habit of leaving their doors open.)

Figure 4 shows a drawing of taxiway markings from an airport chart. Taxiway D (Delta) parallels the north side of Runway 8L-26R and Taxiway C (Charlie) parallels the northwest side of Runway 3-21. There are several intersecting taxiways with individual phonetic names.

At larger airports, and even at smaller ones when ground traffic or construction exists, it's not unusual for a tower controller to offer a complex taxi clearance. Here's such a clearance: "November 2132 Bravo, taxi to Runway 21 via Charlie, southwest to Delta, turn left; cross Runway 21, left on Golf, hold short of Runway 21 at Golf." Students normally respond to this clearance with a, "Huh?" If you had an airport chart out you could easily navigate from position A1 to position A2 in Figure 4 without getting lost. Figure 5 is an airborne view of the airport in Figure 4. Many varieties of airport charts (similar to the one in Figure 4) are available to make airport ground navigation easier.

Bravo, Charlie

Remember our international English lesson a bit ago? Here's Part 2.

Pilotspeak includes a phonetic alphabet. Some letters and numbers can sound a lot like others, especially when spoken over an aviation radio by a non-native speaker of English. The phonetic alphabet is there to save the day. It permits unambiguous communication. It's also what verbally distinguishes pilots from those controlling other types of moving vehicles.

Every letter in the alphabet has a phonetic pronunciation. By speaking the word, instead of the letter, pilots make themselves heard and understood under some pretty non-optimal conditions. It's easy to mistake *B* for *C*, or *E*, but there's little chance of mixing up *Bravo*, *Charlie*, and *Echo*.

After a surprisingly short time, you will speak phonetic like a native.

A	Alpha
B	Bravo
C	Charlie
D	Delta
E	Echo
F	Foxtrot
G	Golf
H	Hotel
I	India
J	Juliet
K	Kilo
L	Lima
M	Mike
N	November
O	Oscar
P	Papa
Q	Quebec
R	Romeo
S	Sierra
T	Tango
U	Uniform
V	Victor
W	Whiskey
X	Xray
Y	Yankee
Z	Zulu
1	WUN
2	TOO
3	TREE
4	FOW-er
5	FIFE
6	SIX
7	SEV-en
8	AIT
9	NIN-er
0	ZEE-RO

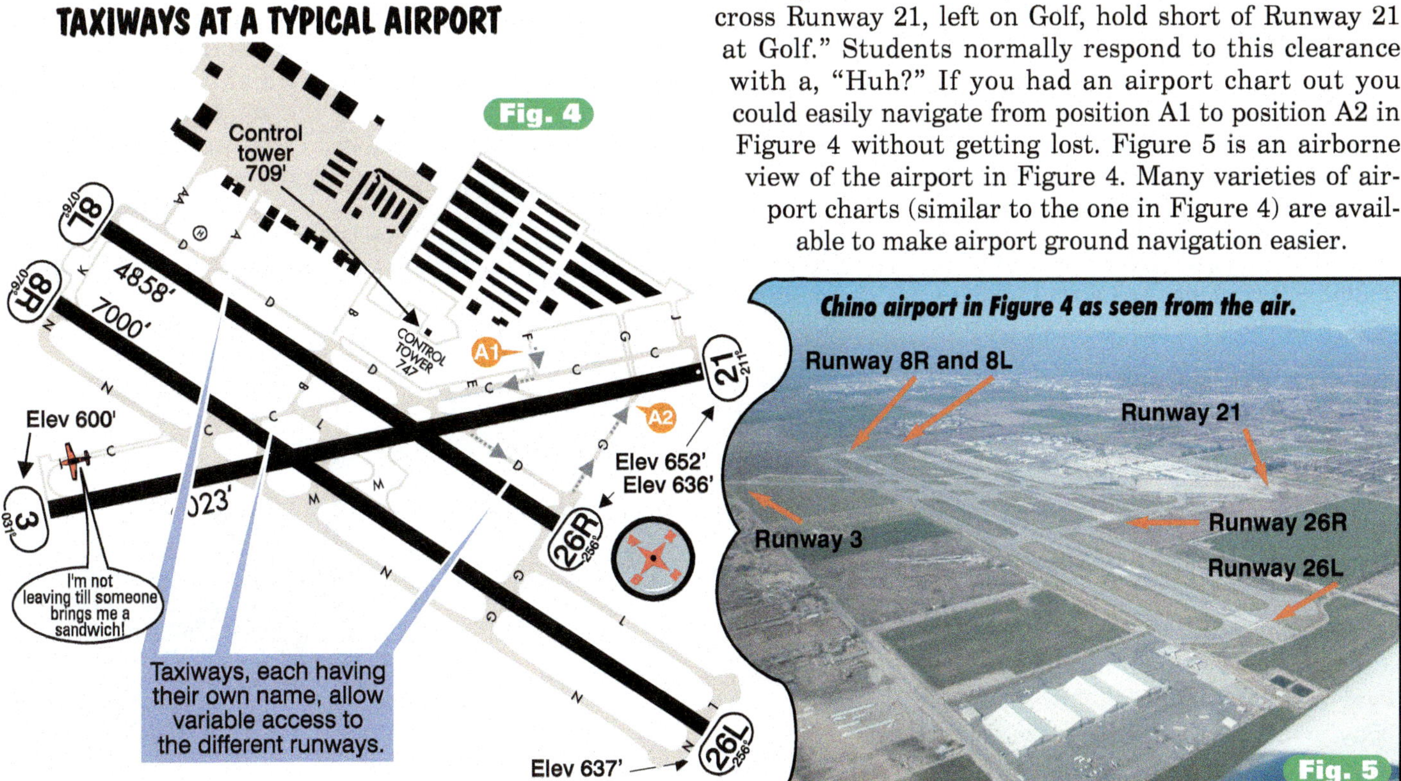

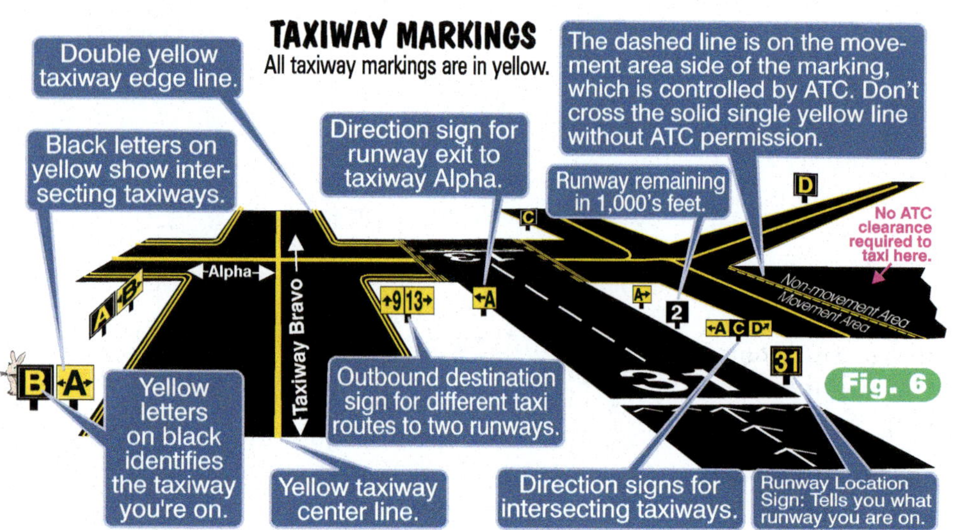

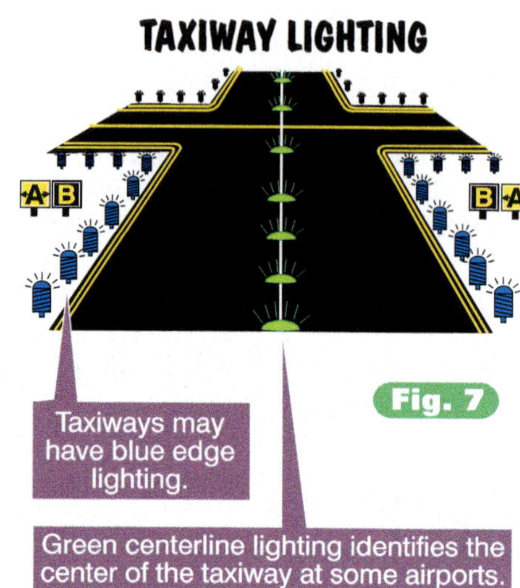

Taxiways are identified by a continuous yellow line with parallel double yellow lines on the outer edges of the taxi surface (Figure 6). Taxiway names are shown by small signs (Figure 6). Placed along the side of the taxiway, these signs consist of yellow lettering on a black background. Signs containing black lettering on a yellow background indicate the position of intersecting taxiways. Arrows indicate the relative direction of these intersecting taxiways. At night, many (not necessarily all) taxiways have blue omnidirectional sideline lighting (Figure 7). At some airports, taxiways may have embedded green centerline lighting.

One time I caught an empathetic and sensitive student of mine weaving between the embedded green taxiway lights. I thought she was having a Nyquil flashback until I found out that she was afraid of damaging either the lights or the tires. You won't hurt the lights or the tires, but feel free (if you wish) to keep the nose wheel a few inches to the side of the embedded lighting.

As a pilot you must be able to identify the point where the taxiway ends and the runway begins. This transition is identified by four yellow lines—two solid and two dashed—crossing perpendicular to the taxiway and running parallel to the runway (Figure 8). These markings are known as *runway hold markings*. If the two solid lines are on your side, then, at a tower-controlled airport, a clearance is required to enter the runway. If the double broken dashed lines are on your side, then you should cross those lines to clear the runway and enter the taxiway. (From now on we'll assume that a *controlled airport* is one having an operating control tower.)

Assuming you have just landed and are taxiing off the runway, you should taxi across the double broken dashed lines and clear the runway. The FAA assumes that your airplane hasn't cleared the runway until the entire airplane (down to the last rivet) is on the other side of those broken double yellow lines. The reason for this is to prevent the tails of long airplanes (like a stretched DC-8) from poking out onto the runway. This could make landing quite challenging for another pilot and possibly give him or her an extra EKG blip.

At airports without an operating control tower (meaning the airport has no control tower or the tower has shut down for the night), entering an active runway is done at the discretion of the pilot. (From now on, an airport having no control tower or one at which the tower is not in operation will be referred to as an *uncontrolled airport.*) In this instance, you should hold short of the runway, behind the solid runway-hold lines. Taxi onto the runway only when it's

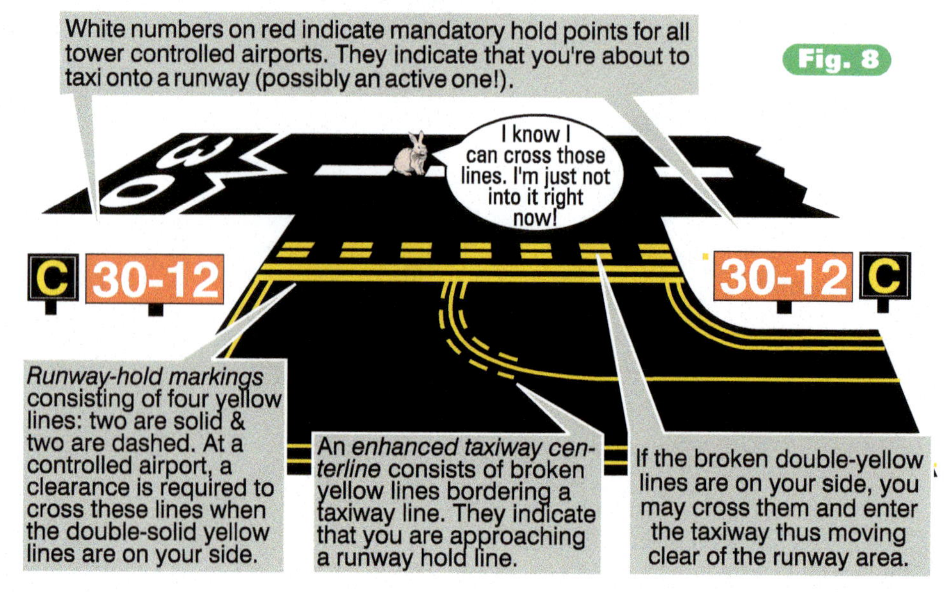

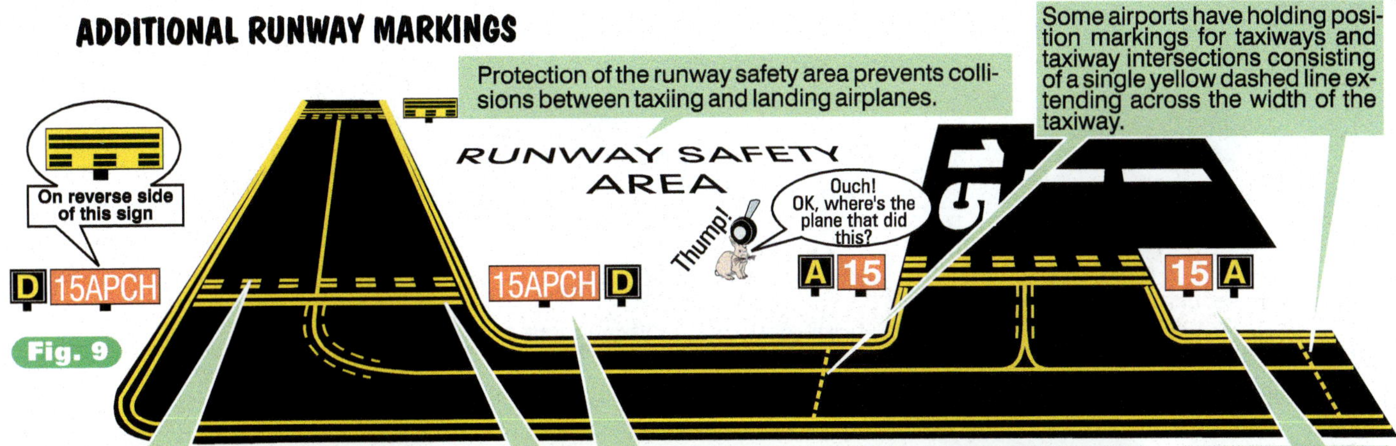

clear of traffic and no airplanes are on a short final (getting ready to land). In other words "look carefully before taxiing onto the runway." The last thing you want is for someone to do a touch and go on you. And making another pilot go around won't win you too many friends at the airport. It's also a good idea to broadcast your intentions on something known as the Common Traffic Advisory Frequency (CTAF) when no tower is in operation. This lets other pilots in the traffic pattern know what you're doing. More on this later.

Another way to identify where the runway begins is the presence of a white-on-red sign next to the dashed and solid double yellow lines (Figure 8). These information billboards are called *runway holding signs,* though they don't actually hold anything. They exist to inform you when you're about to enter an active runway. They also indicate the runway direction. In Figure 8, *30-12* indicates Runway 30 is to the left and Runway 12 is to the right (in other words, go to the left to find the beginning of Runway 30, etc.). At controlled airports, these signs are your cue to hold your position unless a clearance has been given to enter or cross the runway. Figure 9 shows a single runway holding sign indicating that the taxiway intersects the beginning of the takeoff runway.

At uncontrolled airports, the runway hold signs indicate that you can proceed across or onto the runway when you've assured yourself no traffic conflict exists (an airplane preparing to take off or land is most definitely a conflict). At a tower-controlled airport, these signs are coupled with the double solid and dashed runway-hold lines, providing ample warning that you're crossing into the action area.

Holding position markings for a taxiway, consisting of a single dashed yellow line as shown in Figure 9, are installed at some airport. When a tower controller instructs you to hold short of a taxiway intersection, you should stop so that no part of the airplane crosses the dashed yellow line.

Some airports may have taxiways that interfere with the runway safety area, as shown in Figure 9. Taxiway Delta is located directly behind the beginning of Runway 15. Airplanes landing on Runway 15 could approach low enough to present a problem to both the approaching and taxiing airplane. This is more likely to be a problem for big airplanes, but the rules take into account the worst-case scenario. Holding position signs for this peripheral runway are shown by white on red lettering. The term *15APCH* next to the solid double yellow lines indicates a mandatory hold point at tower controlled airports (this means any aircraft on the following taxiway might affect aircraft on approach to Runway 15). On the opposite side of the runway, on taxiway Delta, on the back side of the runway hold sign, is a runway safety area sign (normally only found at only tower controlled airports). This consists of the same marking shown on the taxiway (double solid and dashed lines). These signs can be used as a guide in deciding when to report back to a controller that you are clear of the runway. Remember, at uncontrolled airports pilots must decide for themselves whether to enter or cross a runway.

It's difficult, but not impossible, for pilots to accidentally taxi onto an active runway at a tower controlled airport. One pilot at a very busy airport taxied right into the middle of an active runway and just sat there (probably waiting for one of those yellow trucks to bring him a sandwich). Completely confused about the tower's directions and unwilling to ask for clarification, he stopped his airplane while a jet was on final approach. The tower controller said, "32 Bravo, do you know where you are?" The pilot replied, "Burbank Airport?" The controller said, "Yes, that's good, but do you see that big Boeing 707 out there on final approach headed directly for you?" The pilot replied, "Yes." "Do you want him to do a touch and go on you?" The pilot replied, "No." The controller said, "Then you'd better get off his runway." The pilot, not wanting to get bounced on by a Boeing 707, immediately exited the runway.

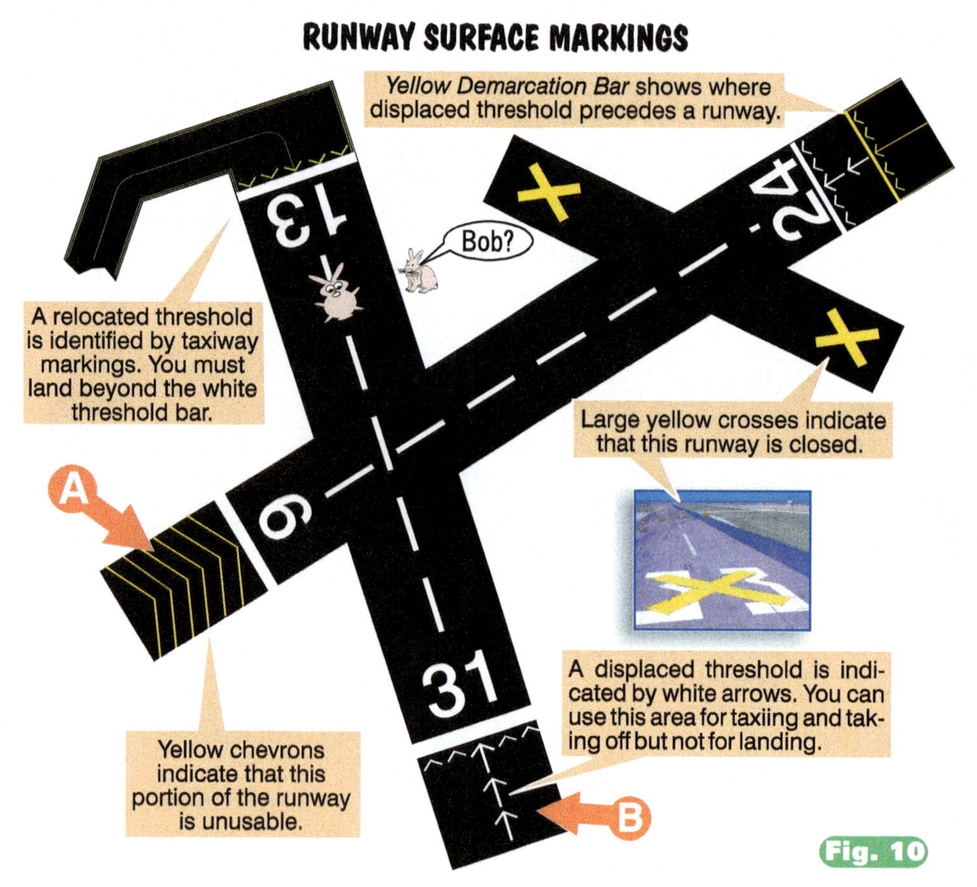

Fig. 10

Additional Runway Markings

Just because there is concrete in the shape of a runway doesn't mean that it can be used for landing. Some runways have yellow chevrons painted on them (Figure 10, position A). This signals that the surface is unsuitable for either taxiing, taking off, or landing. It's basically an airplane no man's land. Don't use any portion of this area. It might be off limits because the surface won't support the weight of an airplane even for taxiing, let alone landing, or because the surface is otherwise unsuitable. Planes that venture onto chevrons can find themselves up to their axles in asphalt, trapped like a gigantic fly on a No-Pest strip.

White arrows pointing in one direction form what is called a *displaced threshold* (Figure 10, position B). This is a runway area that is not to be used for landing, but on which you can taxi, take off, or roll out after landing. Displaced thresholds often exist as part of a noise abatement effort. By forcing you to land farther down the runway this causes you to maintain a higher altitude on the approach than you would if landing at the very beginning of the runway. A displaced threshold can exist for other reasons, such as the presence of a surface that will support the weight of an airplane, but not the impact of an airplane landing. (There's a big difference. I know this since one of my instructors used to call out Richter scale values following my touchdowns.)

I won't mention any names, but on occasion professional airline pilots have been known to land at the wrong airport, with a full load of passengers. Nothing like bringing your own audience to a *faux pas*. Several years ago, a pilot did this at an east coast airport. He accidentally landed at a small training field with nothing but itty-bitty Cessnas and Pipers fluttering around the pattern. As he touched down and came to a stop, his wheels punched holes in the thin runway surface. He knew he was in trouble when it took full power just to taxi. A few of the locals came out and said, "Hey! Look what you did to our runway! You put divots in it. Geesh!" The only way they could get the airplane out was to completely strip it down to barebones metal, making it light enough to take off without further runway damage. The same could not be said for the pilot's career. (See Postflight Briefing #7-2 for more information on airport lighting.)

Airport Beacons

Airports have rotating beacons to make them easier to find at night. Civilian airports with runway lights have a two-color rotating beacon that alternately flashes green-white, green-white... Military airports, on the other hand, have rotating beacons that alternately flash green-white-white, green-white-white (the two white lights flash very quickly). A lighted heliport has a rotating beacon that flashes green-yellow-white. I mention the heliport lighting because if you try to land at a heliport I can guarantee the runway will be extremely short.

Figure 11 shows Taft Kern County airport with a small star (point A) near the airport symbol. This star indicates the presence of a rotating beacon at the airport. Elk Hills airport (point B) doesn't have a star; therefore, no rotating beacon is present (and the airport doesn't have runway lights either). Figure 12 shows the actual rotating beacon found at many airports.

The small star (position A) at Taft Kern County indicates the airport has a rotating beacon. Elk Hills airport (position B), does not have a rotating beacon.
Fig. 11

An Airport's Rotating Beacon
Some beacons are omnidirectional capacitor-discharge devices that flash instead of rotate.

Fig. 12

Rotating beacons (some flash instead of rotate) are normally on between sunset and sunrise. If an airport's beacon is up and running during daylight hours, it means that the airport is below basic VFR conditions (ceiling less than 1000 feet AGL and/or visibility less than 3 miles). Of course, if the visibility is that bad you probably can't *see* the beacon until you've violated all kinds of airspace, but they turn it on anyway. In such conditions, a special VFR clearance is required if Class B, C, D, or E airspace exists at the airport (see Chapter 9 for more info on special VFR operations).

The Traffic Pattern

If you've ever seen moths dancing around a light bulb, you'll understand why airports have traffic patterns. If it weren't for some organization, airplanes might fly frenetically over, above and to the side of runways, vying for a position to land. Fortunately, it's not like that. We have traffic patterns that impose a respectable and safe order on the flow of traffic at airports. These patterns are usually rectangular in shape with each portion having a specific name, for easy identification (Figure 13).

All airports—controlled and uncontrolled—have traffic patterns. At controlled airports, air traffic controllers manage the flow of aircraft. This becomes especially important when the airports are extremely busy. While it's obvious that airports such as Los Angeles, Chicago, and New York need towers, there are many general aviation airports that also have a very heavy volume of traffic. At such airports, pilots simply fly the established traffic pattern while controllers verbally coax them into an orderly sequence.

At airports with less activity, it's difficult to justify establishing an air traffic control tower. At these non-tower airports, pilots typically fly the airport's traffic pattern on their own. They are left to their own devices in deciding their landing direction and sequence among other aircraft in the pattern.

If the idea of a lot of pilots flying around near an airport without someone telling them what to do raises a few questions, then you have at least a modicum of common sense. Believe it or not, things work out remarkably well because pilots are reasonably adept at following rules. Much of aviation depends on there being a high degree of predictability. Knowing what pattern another pilot is flying or is likely to fly is the key to making the system work for everyone.

Where Are We?

It's important to know which airports have beacons, since this helps prevent an accidental landing at the wrong airport. I'm not proud of my mistakes, but everyone makes them (the secret, of course, is not to make the same one twice, unless of course you've had your name changed). As a newly rated private pilot, I took a friend to Watsonville (CA) airport late one evening. It was a clear night except for a few patches of low stratus. Watsonville, located on the Pacific coast, was visible many miles out. I kept my eye on the airport beacon, flew over the airport, identified the appropriate traffic pattern and direction for landing, then landed.

We touched down, taxied off the runway and pulled back the canopy of the American Yankee TR-2. I looked at my friend and said, "Hey Phil, when did Watsonville get all these army tanks?" Phil replied, "Rod, Watsonville (a civilian airport) doesn't have any army tanks." Then I said, "Well, maybe the guy pointing a gun at us can give us some information." I had accidentally landed at an army base a few miles south of Watsonville. I hadn't even noticed the double-peaked white light signifying a military airport.

Fortunately, the military tower had shut down 30 minutes earlier. The young military guard said, "What are you guys doing here?" The only thing I could say was, "Ahhhh, we were wondering if you know how to get to Watsonville?" He said, "This ain't no gas station so you fellows better leave now." Poof! We were gone. No sandwich, either. David Copperfield couldn't have gotten rid of our airplane so fast. A big mistake and certainly one I learned from. **Rod**

THE TRAFFIC PATTERN Fig. 13

Decision Point (for turn to base leg) D
Downwind leg C
Crosswind leg B
E
Wind direction
A
F
Base leg
Final approach
Upwind leg (parallel & offset) G
Departure leg

That's why the concept of the *traffic pattern* is so important. The traffic pattern represents a very standardized way for pilots to depart from or land at an airport. If everyone does what they're supposed to do in the traffic pattern, then everybody's actions become quite predictable. Once you know where you fit in the sequence of traffic, you will know what is going on and when it is your turn to take a particular action.

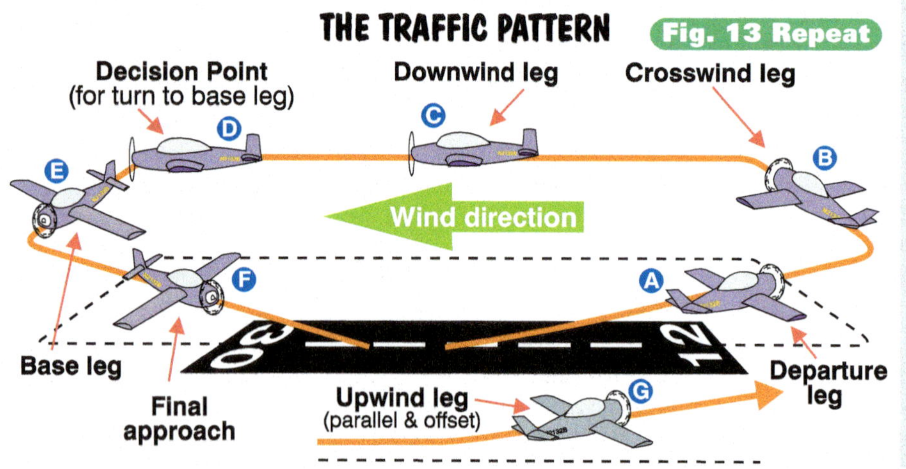

Left Wing Pilots

Traffic patterns are, unless posted otherwise, made with a series of left turns. This is referred to as flying *left traffic.*

Given a choice, pilots generally favor left turns because their visibility is better when the airplane is tilted toward the side they're sitting on. This is another example of a way in which flying is completely unlike driving. In a car, no matter which way you turn, your visibility from the driver's seat is pretty much the same. An airplane, however, operates in three dimensions. All things being equal, a pilot would rather have things rolling his or her way when it comes to turns.

Let's take a closer look at the airport traffic pattern, and what you will do once you're in one.

Traffic Pattern Components

Traffic patterns are rectangular in shape and consist of six segments: *departure leg, crosswind leg, downwind leg, base leg, final approach* and *upwind leg* (Figure 13).

Airplane takeoffs are made into the wind, and the takeoff flight path is thus called the *departure leg* (point A). After takeoff, you have two major choices—you can either depart the airport traffic area, or you can *remain in the pattern,* which means you will fly a prescribed path, come around, and land on the runway you just departed from. This is done by pilots who enjoy very short flights, as well as by pilots who are practicing landings. From time to time, we pilots remain in the traffic pattern in order to polish our skills and minimize the explanations to passengers for our occasional bad landings.

If you're remaining in the pattern, a turn (generally a left turn) to the *crosswind leg* (point B) will be made when the airplane is beyond the departure end of the runway and within 300 feet of the traffic pattern altitude. This portion of the pattern is called the crosswind leg because the flight path is perpendicular to the runway and generally crosswise to the wind direction (one time I asked a student what leg he was on in the traffic pattern. He replied, "I'm on my right leg, but plan on using my left leg once the right one gets tired" (I, of course, immediately asked if anyone had delivered him a sandwich lately).

As the airplane continues its climb, another 90 degree turn is made. This places the airplane parallel to the runway and traveling opposite to the direction of landing. This is called the *downwind leg* (point C) because your direction is with the wind. Throughout the upwind, crosswind and even a part of the downwind leg, the airplane continues to climb until reaching traffic pattern altitude. This altitude varies from one airport to the next because of terrain, obstruction and noise concerns. Expect traffic pattern altitudes to range from 600 to 1,500 feet above the airport elevation, typically averaging about 1,000 feet AGL. The downwind leg is flown approximately 1/2 to one mile out from the landing runway. This keeps you comfortably close to the runway. In the event of an engine problem, you can glide to a safe landing.

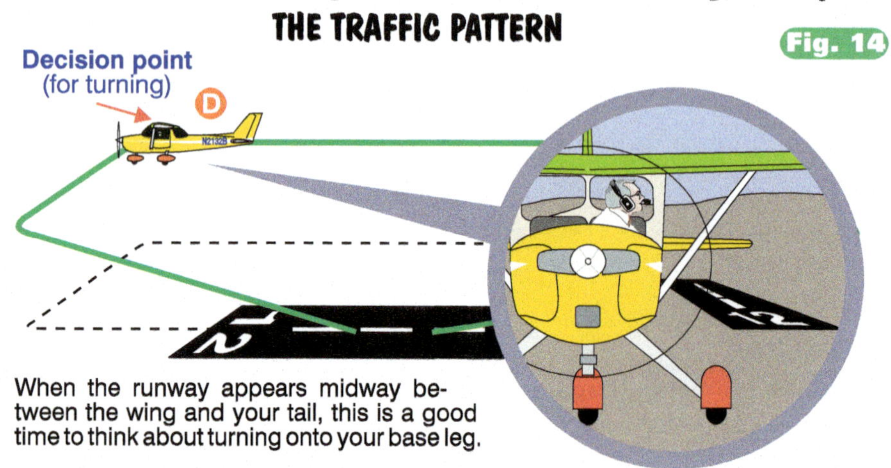

When the runway appears midway between the wing and your tail, this is a good time to think about turning onto your base leg.

You continue downwind until passing a point abeam the beginning of the landing threshold of the runway. Then it's another 90 degree turn and you're on *base leg* (point E). From here you make one more 90 degree turn, onto *final approach* (point F). The *upwind leg* (point G) is flown parallel to the runway in the direction of landing. It's often used during go-arounds or overflights to avoid departing traffic.

Assuming traffic isn't a factor, it's convenient and practical to start your turn onto base leg when the landing threshold appears 45° between the wing and the tail of your airplane. In other words, as you look out the left window (Figure 14, point D), the threshold appears to be at a 45° angle to the left of the wing (or midway between the wing and the tail). This provides you with a symmetrical, rectangular-type pattern and gives you enough distance from the runway to make a comfortable approach.

Aviation is one place where it is not good to become a homeboy or homegirl. Some student pilots fudge by using familiar landmarks on the ground to tell them when to make

TURNING ONTO BASE LEG

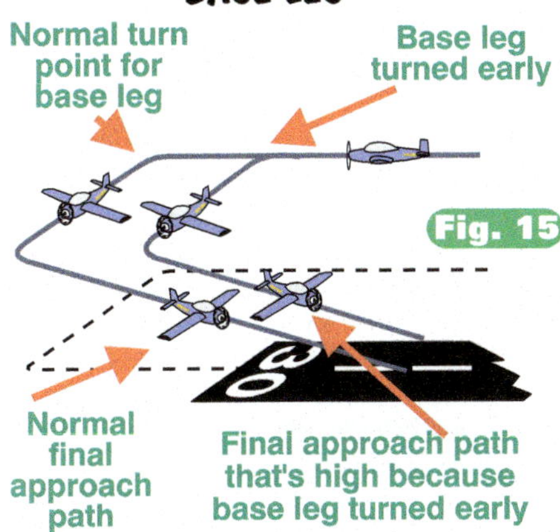

their turns. This is bad because it leads to a lack of flexibility. If you need the local Burger Boy restaurant to land, what will you do when you go to a new airport? There's nothing more pitiful than a pilot who can only fly to and from his or her home airport comfortably!

I've seen student pilots come absolutely unglued when they weren't allowed to turn base at "their" landmark. You will *not* always be able to turn base or final at an ideal time, and the ability to make adjustments is crucial. When traffic is heavy, you may have to fly the downwind leg for some distance past the airport before turning base leg. In fact, I was once in a traffic pattern with 19 other airplanes. One pilot was so far downwind that the controller called and asked, "45 Charlie, what time zone are you in now?"

Base leg is a point of transition for landing. It's the place where important adjustments are made in the airplane's speed and landing configuration. This is why, even when there is little or no traffic, you should avoid turning base too early, as shown in Figure 15. Things happen mighty fast as you approach the runway. You want to give yourself enough time to adjust your airspeed, flaps, and glidepath. The descent for landing is normally started on base leg and continues throughout the final approach.

TURNING BASE TO FINAL

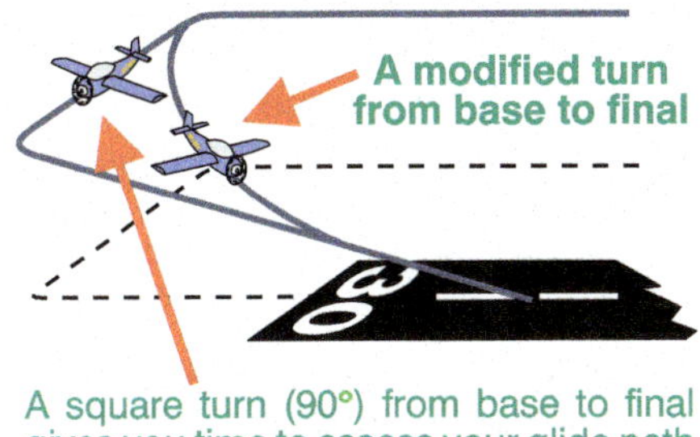

A square turn (90°) from base to final gives you time to assess your glide path and the effects of any crosswind.

Fig. 16

The *final approach* (sometimes just called *final*) is a critical part of the landing sequence. Generally, a square turn from base onto final approach is best (Figure 16). This provides you with enough time to observe your airplane's descent path and alignment with the runway. You can observe and correct for the effect of crosswinds on the airplane if you give yourself a reasonably long final approach. During the final approach, the airplane's glide path can be adjusted (using flaps, slips, or S-turns), making it easier for you to land on any selected runway spot.

When turning from base leg onto final approach, you have an additional opportunity to correct your glidepath (Figure 17). Let's assume that you are making a power-off approach from the base leg. After turning base, you retard the power and commence a descent. Your objective is to land on the runway numbers (the ones at the beginning, not the end of the runway—unless you want a sandwich!). If you're too low, you can cut short the turn from the base leg to final approach as shown in Figure 17A. Flying path 1 allows you to fly less distance during the descent, thus increasing your chances of making the runway numbers. Path 2 is longer, and path 3 is a nice square turn onto final.

If you're too high, you can deliberately overshoot the turn onto final approach giving you more distance to cover during your descent as shown in Figure 17B. Another option is to S-turn on final as shown in Figure 17C. S-turns are simply a series of alternating turns left and right of the direct glide path. Since the shortest distance between any two points is a straight line, anything you do to fly *other* than a straight line lengthens the trip. Assuming a constant rate of descent, taking the long way home will allow you to lose more altitude.

S-turns, coupled with forward slips and use of flaps, provide you with several ways of adjusting your glidepath. This knowledge becomes especially important when a precision landing is necessary, such as on a short field or in the event of an engine failure when you generally get only one opportunity to hit the safe landing spot you've chosen. With a little practice you will be able to put the airplane down in the precise place you want. (We won't discuss forward or side slips in this book. Any good aviation procedures book should have information on this.)

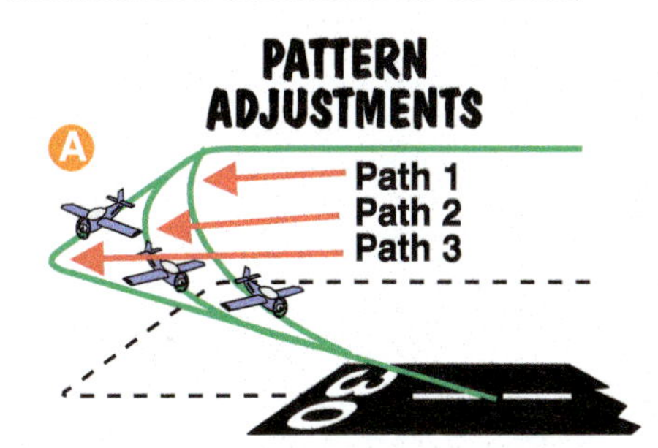

If you're attempting a power-off glide, you can purposely modify your pattern (the distance you travel) to allow you to make the runway.

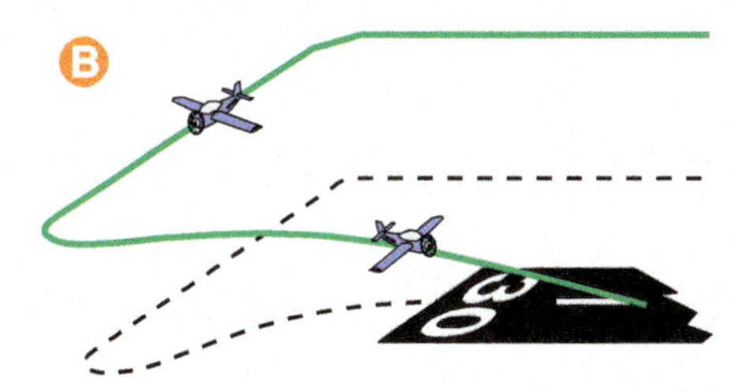

Another way of modifying the distance you travel is to purposely overshoot your turn to final.

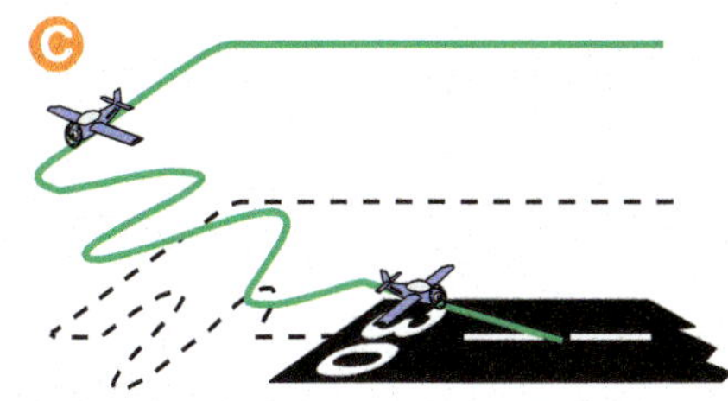

Another very effective way to modify your pattern is to make S-turns while on final approach. This is also very effective if you're following slower traffic ahead.

Fig. 17

Crabbing in the Pattern

No, this isn't what happens when your instructor doesn't get enough sleep, though it definitely describes how the instructor, the tower, and other pilots will act if you don't learn how to take account of the wind and adjust for its effects on your airplane.

The path your airplane traces over the ground is called its *ground track*. If you sit there fat, dumb, and happy with your compass showing a 165° heading, you will track a 165° heading over the ground from any given point only when there is no wind (or the wind blows directly on your nose or tail).

Think of the wind as being a giant hand. Because the airplane doesn't have its feet on the ground, it gets pushed around by the wind. Depending on how much wind there is and what angle the hand is pushing from, the effect can be anywhere from slight to considerable.

The only way to create a straight ground track is to compensate for whatever wind there is by pointing the airplane's nose (slightly or more so, depending on conditions) into the wind (Figure 18). If you head the plane to the right a bit, and the wind pushes to the left a bit, everything balances and you make your intended straight line over the ground. The term "crabbing" comes from the fact that crabs walk in a direction other than the one where they're facing.

Fig. 18

CORRECTING FOR WIND DRIFT WITHIN THE TRAFFIC PATTERN

B

C

Wind direction

A

D

8

26

Who are you looking at?

In positions A & C the airplane crabs (points) into the wind to maintain a rectangular ground track in the traffic pattern. The stronger the wind, the greater the crab angle needed to fly a rectangular ground track.

It's called crabbing because the crab points one way and moves another, just like airplanes A and C.

Crab moves this way

Crab points this way

How do you know the precise amount to crab? You simply make a slight turn (say 5° or 10° at first) into the wind, level the wings and watch the results. If the airplane is crabbed properly, it will make a rectangular ground track about the runway as shown by the dashed line in Figure 18. The airplane's ground track is now perpendicular to the runway, as flown by Airplane A. Airplane C is crabbed to the left, into the wind, to maintain the desired ground track while on base leg. Of course, if the wind is not directly aligned with the runway you'll have to crab on all five segments of the traffic pattern to maintain a rectangular ground track (Figure 19).

If you let yourself get pushed around by the wind, you won't be where you're supposed to be. This is a particular problem in the traffic pattern. Remember a while ago I said predictability was important? Other pilots and the tower expect you to fly a traffic pattern that tracks straight on each leg, and crabbing to take account of the wind is the only way to do it.

Entering the Traffic Pattern

So far we've been talking about taking off and staying in the pattern, and we've been talking about flying at a tower-controlled airport. What happens when you are arriving at an airport to land, and there's no tower to issue instructions?

Before entering the traffic pattern at uncontrolled airports, you are expected to observe the flow of traffic and conform to the traffic pattern in use. In other words, you shouldn't be going in a direction different from everyone else. Doing so is not polite, smart, safe, or sanctioned. So, avoid doing this unless you want to end up on one of those TV shows like *Cops*, *Rescue 911* or *America's Most Wanted*.

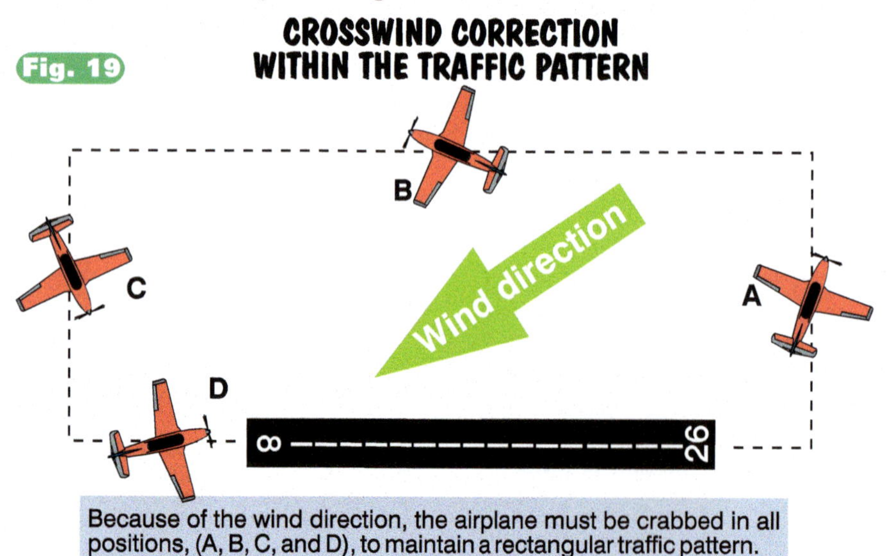

Because of the wind direction, the airplane must be crabbed in all positions, (A, B, C, and D), to maintain a rectangular traffic pattern.

TWO MISSES...

Having my own small airplane at a private strip gives me a privilege few people get to enjoy, of being able to fly when I please. I always do a complete preflight before moving the airplane; however, this time I was preoccupied with worldly matters during my check. I taxied out, did a quick runup, and headed for the blue. After climbout, I wanted to turn left but was unable. Then it struck me. How stupid. I had forgotten to remove the wooden wedges used as rudder gust locks. Fortunately, a large open field near my runway provided ample room to land in any direction I desired by using ailerons only. It was an uneventful landing. A rather embarrassed but wiser pilot removed the gust locks.

ASRS Report

Forget the elevator lock, rather than rudder locks, and you will find yourself with even less control. A proper pre-takeoff check for freedom and direction of movement is imperative. Not doing so, this pilot missed his second chance to catch his walk-around foul.

...AND A HIT

"If I have been interrupted for any reason, or feel that my full attention has not been given to the task of an aircraft preflight walkaround, I will start again from the beginning." (Ahh, Grasshopper can learn much from this wise man.)

Dave Gwinn
Airline pilot, CFII, aviation educator and author

OK, you want to do what's right. How do you find out what that is? You need two pieces of information in order to figure out a traffic pattern—the runway in use, and the direction of turns in the pattern (left or right traffic).

The runway in use is normally determined by the wind direction. With rare exceptions, you take off and land *into* the wind. The exceptions (very rare) would be situations where the airport is situated in such a way that you can only land in one direction no matter what the wind (this generally has to do with terrain obstruction or other geographical oddities).

You don't need a weatherman to know which way the wind blows. You do, however, need either a wind sock or a report from the ground.

Wind socks look like brightly colored nets for capturing butterflies on steroids (See Figure 24, position A). They are supposed to be easily visible from the air. This is one of those aviation secrets, but I'm going to tell because you've been nice enough to read this far. Wind socks are *not* usually easy to spot, and when they are, it isn't always easy to figure out what they're telling you. In theory, the fat end is facing into the wind and the narrow end is pointed toward the end of the runway where you'll land. This is most easily seen while standing on the ground next to the wind sock. Trying to discern it while 1000 or more feet in the air, traveling 150 miles an hour and keeping the airplane upright, is a bit more of a challenge.

There is often an easier way to get the info. Many uncontrolled airports have what is called a *unicom*(short for *universal communications*). This is an authorized frequency on which someone—usually the operator of one of the refueling and repair operations (fixed base operators, or *FBO's* in pilotspeak)—provides information on the wind and traffic pattern directions. The unicom information is advisory in nature only. Unicom operators are *not* air traffic controllers. They cannot issue commands, sequence traffic, etc. though they will usually advise you if there are other aircraft in the pattern or inbound.

Another option is a *multicom* frequency. This is a frequency approved for air-to-air use. Other pilots in or around your destination airport will generally help out with information on request.

If information is not available from either unicom or multicom, then you have to take clues from wherever you can on wind direction (smoke, waves on a lake or ocean), and should refer to the *segmented circle* located at the airport for directions on the type of traffic pattern to fly.

Segmented circles are often constructed of large white blocks, bricks or ground paintings. Figure 20 shows how a segmented circle looks from the air. These circles contain several additional items to help you decide upon the proper runway for landing as well as the appropriate traffic pattern to fly (I'll show you how to interpret the segmented circle shortly).

Segmented circles are segmented so they are easier to identify at higher altitudes. If you are unaware of the proper traffic pattern, simply fly over the airport and look for the segmented circle. The proper way to do this at uncontrolled airports is to overfly the field, above traffic pattern altitude and observe the indicator. Usually 1000 feet above the established traffic pattern altitude is sufficient to avoid the flow of airport traffic. In other words, if the traffic pattern altitude is 700 feet AGL and you're an additional 1,000 feet above that, this puts you at 1,700 feet AGL. At this altitude, you can easily observe the segmented circle without unexpectedly bumping into people who are minding their own business and trying to land.

At controlled airports, air traffic controllers will inform you of the runway on which to land and the appropriate traffic pattern to be flown. Some people are just born do-it-yourselfers, and they want to determine for themselves the lay of the land. It is often very helpful to see which way the runways run before attempting a landing, especially if visibility is less than optimal. In fact, I prefer that students unfamiliar with the complex taxiway and runway layout of an airport overfly the field and observe its runway and taxiway layout before attempting to enter the pattern. Things can get pretty confusing down close to the ground and the overflight helps orient you to a runway direction. Once you gain a little experience, you can plan on skipping this overflight and enter the downwind at a 45 degree angle. To overfly a controlled field for a preliminary "look see," just ask the controller for permission to overfly at whatever altitude you want that is safely above the traffic pattern. Such a request will almost always be approved.

If you really want to take a look first, before even engaging the controller, keep in mind that Class D airspace normally ends at 2500 feet AGL. You can overfly at any altitude above that boundary without the need to tell anyone what you're doing. Then, when you're ready to enter the traffic pattern, you simply establish and maintain communication with the tower and enter the pattern (more later on how to call the tower and what to say). Remember, we're talking about overflying an airport in Class D airspace here, not Class C or B airspace, which extends to higher altitudes.

EVERYTHING'S COMING UP ROSES...

I watched as my aircraft was refueled with 35 gallons of 100 octane fuel. After going inside, I came back out to look in tanks and drained a sample. Imagine my surprise at seeing a pink sample! I was ready to yell and scream when I realized my eyeglasses (brown-rose colored) had changed the color. Suppose I had worn blue sunglasses and looked at clear fuel? Moral: Look at fuel samples without sunglasses.

REMINDER: 80 octane=red, 100 octane=blue, Jet fuel=clear

ASRS Report

A few years ago, a student pilot got hopelessly lost on a solo cross country. He spotted a controlled airport and commenced circling the field a few hundred feet above the tower. Fortunately, the pilot knew enough to transmit on the emergency frequency of 121.5 MHz. The tower heard a transmission that went like this, "Will the tower that has a small airplane circling above it, with me in it, please identify yourself." The tower replied, "This is Long Beach airport. What are you doing up there?" The pilot replied, "I'm lost. Well, I was lost; but thanks to you, I think I just found myself." They cleared him to land on Runway 25 Left. When the pilot said he wasn't familiar with the runways, the tower said to pick out any piece of asphalt at the airport and land on it (of course, I'm sure all the controllers were placing bets on what kind of sandwich this pilot liked).

The Segmented Circle

The segmented circle shown in Figure 21 contains several useful pieces of information, once you know how to read the hieroglyphics. Attached to the segmented circle (A) are the landing strip indicators (D) and the traffic pattern indicators (B and C). The landing strip indicators are aligned with and represent the airport's runway(s). These are shown by the two strips (D) located on either side of the segmented circle. Attached to each end of landing strips are the traffic pattern indicators (B and C). Because of this combination, the landing strip and traffic pattern indicators take on an L shape when viewed from the air.

Basically, the traffic pattern indicators (B and C) point to the side of the runway on which the traffic pattern is flown. For instance, pilots

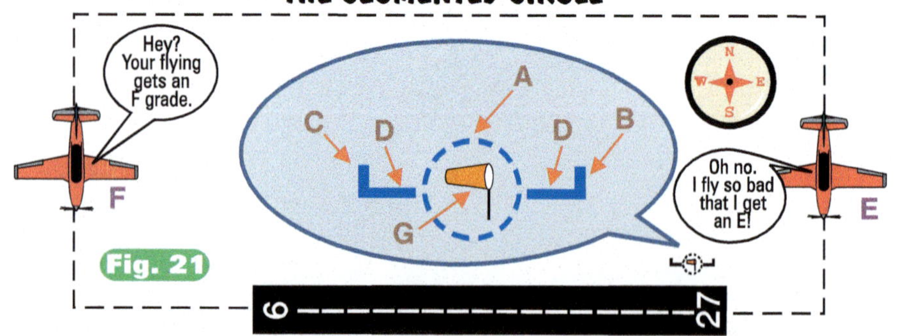

The segmented circle has several elements associated with it. These may include the landing-strip indicator (D); the traffic pattern indicator (B and C) and some form of wind or landing indicator (G) usually found inside the circle (A). According to the segmented circle's information, left traffic is made to Runway 9 with a wind from the east (Airplane F) and right traffic is made to Runway 27 with a wind from the west (Airplane E). Of course, pilots land into the wind whenever possible. The wind or landing indicator identifies the appropriate runway on which to land (G).

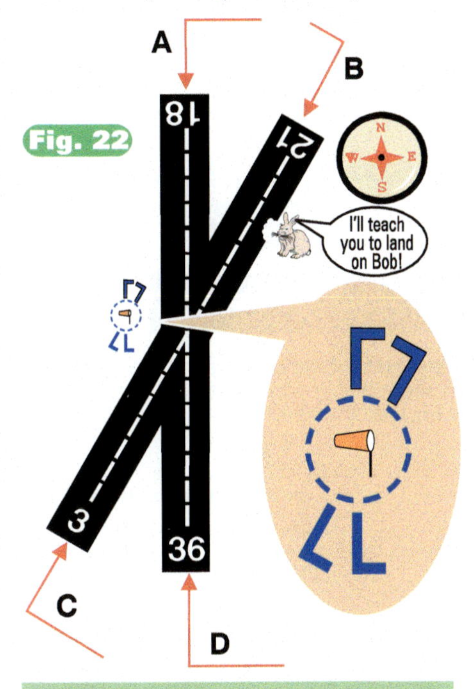

The landing strip & traffic pattern indicator informs the pilot that the pattern for:
Runway 18 (A) is left traffic,
Runway 21 (B) is right traffic,
Runway 3 (C) is right traffic and
Runway 36 (D) is right traffic.

Actually Heard at the Airport...

Situation: A student pilot was on final approach to land with a Cessna jet (called a Citation) following close behind.

Tower: "Cherokee 43511, keep your speed up and make the first turnout, Citation to follow."

Cherokee 43511: "Hey, what did I do wrong?"

landing on Runway 27 should make their pattern to the north of the airport, since the traffic pattern indicator (B) is on the north side of landing strip (D). This results in Airplane E making right traffic for Runway 27 (all right turns). Pilots landing on Runway 9 should, likewise, make their pattern north of the runway as shown by traffic pattern indicator (C). Consequently, Airplane F makes left traffic (all left turns) to Runway 9.

Where two or more runways exist, multiple L shaped bars may protrude from the segmented circle as shown in Figure 22. Landing on Runway 3 requires a right hand traffic pattern; Runway 21, a right hand pattern; Runway 18, a left hand; and Runway 36, a right hand pattern.

What happens if no landing strip indicators or traffic pattern indicators protrude from the segmented circle, as shown in Figure 23? Is this a sign of airport vandalism? No. Segmented circles without these indicators imply that you should fly a standard left hand traffic pattern for the runway in use. Left hand traffic is considered standard and pilots should make all turns to the left in the absence of other indications. Right hand traffic patterns, by default, are considered to be nonstandard patterns.

Wind and Landing-Direction Indicators

Knowing whether it's a right or left hand traffic pattern is one thing, but what about deciding which way to land? Within the segmented circle you'll normally find some type of wind or landing direction indicators. Either one of these help you select a runway for landing that's most nearly aligned with the wind. We want to land into the wind whenever possible. It slows our touchdown speed and makes landings safer as well as easier.

Three types of indicators are used to identify the proper direction for landing. The first two are known as wind direction indicators and the last is called a landing direction indicator.

THE SEGMENTED CIRCLE
(indicating standard, left-hand traffic)

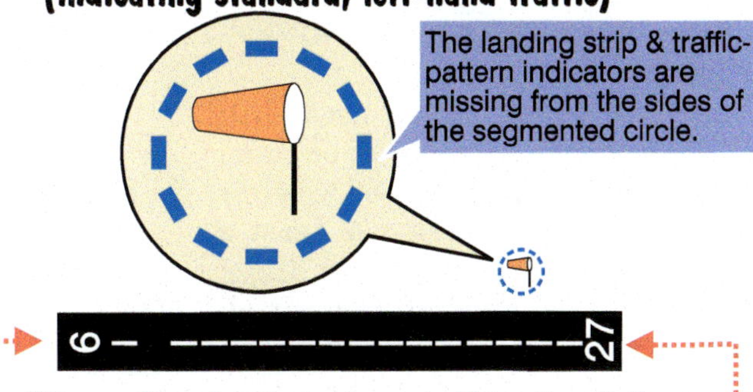

When neither landing-strip nor traffic-pattern indicators are shown along with the segmented circle, make all turns in the pattern to the left.

The first type of wind direction indicator is the wind sock, which I discussed earlier. It's a big help—if you can see it. Study Figure 24A, so you'll at least know what you're looking for.

The *wind tee,* shown in Figure 24B, is another means of determining landing direction. This device looks like a little airplane. It's free to rotate around its base and is aerodynamically constructed so the small airplane points into the wind. Sometimes the device isn't free to rotate and airport personnel manually place it in the proper direction of landing. Either way, you can determine the appropriate landing direction by imagining the wind tee as a small airplane pointing in the direction (or nearly so) that you should land. Simply land on the runway most nearly aligned in the direction the wind tee points. The wind tee in Figure 24B suggests a landing on Runway 9 would head you into the wind.

A more direct means of determining landing direction is with a *tetrahedron* (this isn't a prehistoric dinosaur). Figure 24C shows what appears to be an arrow located within the segmented circle. This is a tetrahedron (a four sided object—three sides on top and one side on the bottom) and is technically called a landing-direction indicator instead of a wind indicator. It's a three dimensional structure that's usually free to rotate about its base. When it can rotate freely, it points into the wind; when it can't, it is also manually rotated by airport personnel to point in the appropriate landing direction. Determining landing direction is simply a matter of landing on the runway most nearly aligned with the direction the tetrahedron points (children seen playing on the tetrahedron should arouse suspicion as to the actual direction in which to land).

The tetrahedron should be used with caution when the winds are light or calm. These things are large hunks of wood or metal, not ballerinas. It takes at least a modest puff of wind to move one. It's a good rule in general aviation to treat all information with a high index of suspicion until you can confirm it in another way. I've had students who were crabbing 60° into the wind while insisting it had to be coming from another direction because they'd heard it on the radio or seen it on the tetrahedron. The airplane is the ulti-

LANDING & WIND DIRECTION INDICATOR Fig. 24

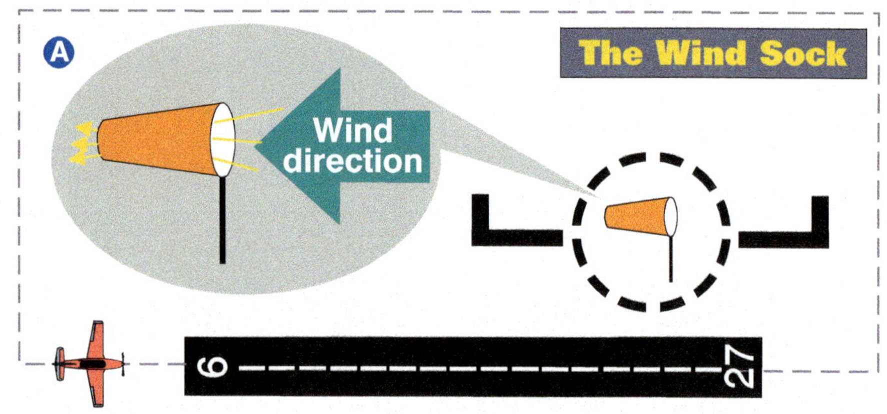

The wind cone (or wind sock) aligns itself parallel to the wind. The small end or opening points downwind and the big end (the opening) is upwind. To decide on wind direction, simply look at which way the small end points. This is the direction the wind is blowing. You'll land into the wind.

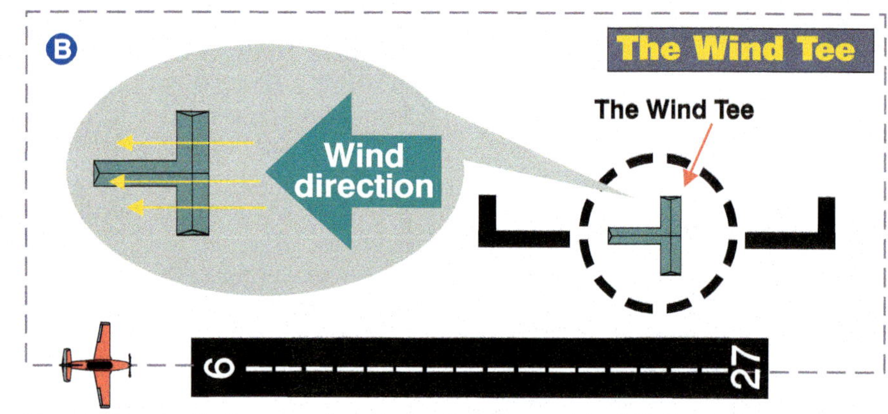

The wind tee looks like a small airplane placed on a swivel. It's free to rotate into the wind. Think of its shape as an airplane that points in the direction you should land (into the wind). The wind tee may be manually rotated by airport personnel to identify the proper landing direction. It may also be tethered, unattended and completely inaccurate! Use caution when using it to assess landing direction.

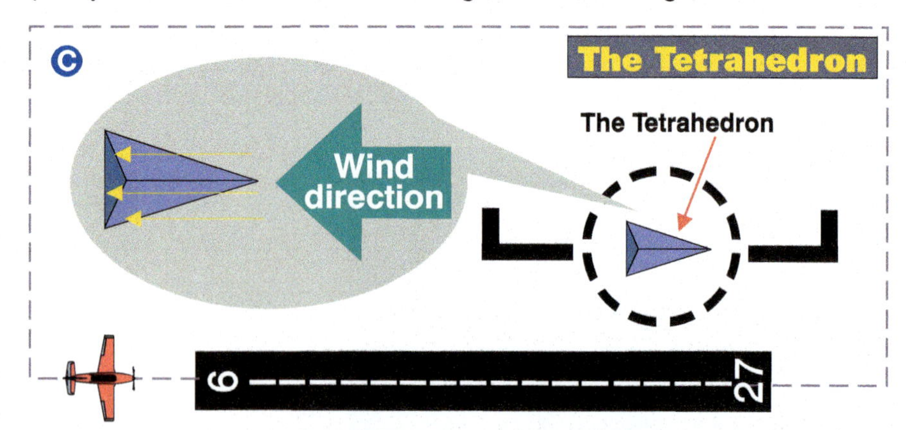

The tetrahedron points in the direction you should land (or it is manually pointed in the direction you should land). It is mounted on a swivel and can pivot, and like the wind tee, its reliability is questionable during light winds.

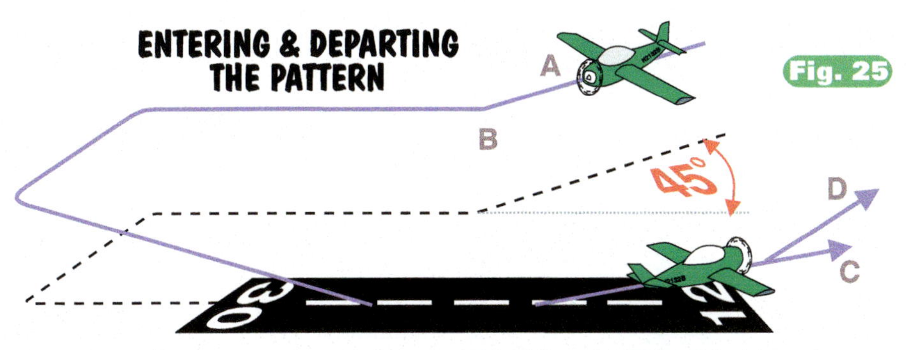

Enter the traffic pattern at a 45 degree angle (A) to the downwind leg about midfield (B). When departing an airport, make either a straight out (C) or a 45 degree turn in the direction of the pattern (D) when reaching pattern altitude.

mate authority on what's really happening!

Some airports have a designated *calm wind runway* (usually the runway that's less noise sensitive). Under calm wind conditions, airport personnel may manually point the tetrahedron in the direction of the calm-wind runway. Be sure and maintain special vigilance during landings at uncontrolled airports when the winds are calm. This is necessary for two reasons. First, another pilot might have chosen another runway, since the wind didn't enforce its will. Second, keep in mind that *calm* doesn't necessarily mean *none,* so be prepared for the possibility of a breeze from any angle.

Many times the landing or wind direction indicators aren't aligned with any specific runway. This means a crosswind exists at the airport. In these conditions, pick a runway that's most nearly aligned with the wind. With a little practice you'll have no difficulty handling these crosswind landings. Honest!

The 45° Entry Point

Once you know the direction of the landing runway and the appropriate traffic pattern to use, you're ready to enter the pattern in an organized way. The best way to do this is to enter the traffic pattern in level flight at a 45° angle to the downwind leg at the approximate midpoint of the runway, as depicted in Figure 25, point A. This doesn't have to be exactly 45° but it should be close. This angle of entry allows you to more easily see traffic on the crosswind and downwind legs of the traffic pattern. Seeing these airplanes makes it easier for you to blend into the flow of traffic. A 45° entry also makes it easier for other airplanes in the pattern to see and blend in with you. Of course, if it's a controlled airport, tower controllers will usually advise you of traffic in the pattern. Once again, keep in mind that *predictability* is important. The controllers expect you to make a standard pattern entry, at the standard pattern place. They don't like surprises very much, perhaps because they're responsible for what happens on their shift (they're concerned too!).

Aim to enter the pattern abeam the midpoint of the runway (point B). And always enter the pattern at the specified pattern altitude for that airport. This allows everyone to be at the same height, making it easier to see other airplanes. If no traffic pattern altitude is established, it's usually best to fly the pattern at 1000 feet AGL if no tower is available to advise otherwise.

I do want to make it clear that we're talking about an entry at a 45° angle and not a 45° bank to the downwind leg. I gave a phase check to a student pilot who didn't quite understand this. We were approaching the pattern when I reminded him to use a 45° entry. He immediately rolled the airplane into a 45° bank (then he asked me for a sandwich). How novel! I'm just glad the FAA doesn't recommend a 90° entry!

It should come as no surprise to you that the majority of midair collisions occur within five miles of an airport at an altitude of less than 3,000 feet AGL (79% in one study). Makes sense, since that's where the majority of the airplanes are. The same study found nearly half of all midair collisions occurred within 5 miles of an airport at an altitude of 500 feet or less AGL (49% to be specific). This is a common altitude for base leg and final approach, isn't it? A word or three to the wise should be sufficient here. *Pay close attention.* Look with your eyes and ears (i.e., listen for the call and position of other aircraft).

Departing the pattern also requires that you avoid interfering with traffic entering and remaining in the pattern. Figure 25, points C and D, depict two common methods for departing an airport. First, a departure can be made straight out as in position C. A 45° turn on the pattern side of the runway (the left side of Runway 30 in this case) is also recommended after the airplane has reached traffic pattern altitude. Of course, if there are parallel runways, noise sensitive areas, or obstructions, then you should follow the recommended procedures for departing that particular airport. These recommended procedures are sometimes found posted near the departure end of the runway (Figure 26). They may

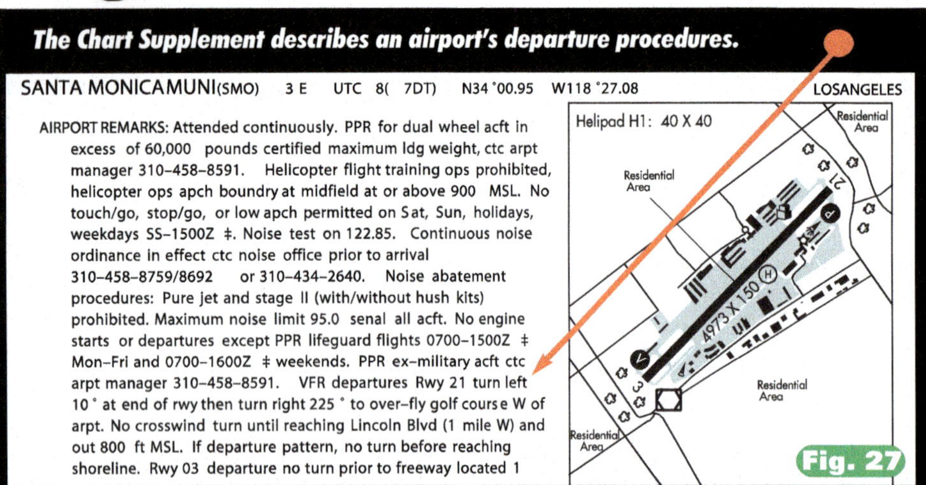
The Chart Supplement describes an airport's departure procedures.

SANTA MONICA MUNI (SMO) 3 E UTC 8(7DT) N34°00.95 W118°27.08 LOS ANGELES

AIRPORT REMARKS: Attended continuously. PPR for dual wheel acft in excess of 60,000 pounds certified maximum ldg weight, ctc arpt manager 310–458–8591. Helicopter flight training ops prohibited, helicopter ops apch boundry at midfield at or above 900 MSL. No touch/go, stop/go, or low apch permitted on Sat, Sun, holidays, weekdays SS–1500Z ‡. Noise test on 122.85. Continuous noise ordinance in effect ctc noise office prior to arrival 310–458–8759/8692 or 310–434–2640. Noise abatement procedures: Pure jet and stage II (with/without hush kits) prohibited. Maximum noise limit 95.0 senal all acft. No engine starts or departures except PPR lifeguard flights 0700–1500Z ‡ Mon–Fri and 0700–1600Z ‡ weekends. PPR ex-military acft ctc arpt manager 310–458–8591. VFR departures Rwy 21 turn left 10° at end of rwy then turn right 225° to over-fly golf course W of arpt. No crosswind turn until reaching Lincoln Blvd (1 mile W) and out 800 ft MSL. If departure pattern, no turn before reaching shoreline. Rwy 03 departure no turn prior to freeway located 1

Fig. 27

also be found in a useful document known as the *Chart Supplement (CS)* or its digital version, the *d-CS* as it's affectionately known to pilots,Page G1 as shown in Figure 27. More on the *d-CS* in Chapter 17.

CTAF (Common Traffic Advisory Frequency)

The airports you'll land at and depart from will be either controlled or uncontrolled. Operations at controlled airports are accomplished by communicating with an air traffic controller. We'll discuss how to do this shortly. For now, let's examine the proper communication techniques when operating into or out of an uncontrolled airport (remember, this is an airport without a control tower or one whose tower isn't in operation).

At uncontrolled airports, pilots are not required to use their radio to communicate with other traffic during takeoff or landing. Simple see-and-avoid vigilance is considered satisfactory. Common sense, however, dictates using a radio if one is on board. Airplanes with radios tuned to the same (common) frequency can broadcast their intentions to each other while operating in the traffic pattern. This makes the airport a safer and more harmonious place.

At many uncontrolled airports a frequency known as the *Common Traffic Advisory Frequency* (CTAF) is available for pilots to communicate their intentions and receive information during takeoff or landing. It's called *common* simply because all pilots communicating at a particular airport use that frequency. The CTAF may be either a unicom, multicom, or tower frequency (if the airport has a tower but it's not in operation at the time).

Getting from Overhead to Over There

Many student pilots overfly an uncontrolled airport and take a look to see what's where. Then they say "OK big fella', now how do I get from way up here to over there for a standard 45° entry?"

ENTERING THE PATTERN

There are two common ways to enter the traffic pattern at an uncontrolled field from overhead. You can observe the segmented circle at 2000 feet AGL then fly from A to B to C to D, then inbound to the runway at a 45 degree angle (D to E). Another way is to start at 2,000 feet AGL and fly from A to F to G to H to D. The descent from 2,000 feet AGL to traffic pattern altitude is started from D to E. Traffic and terrain permitting, the descent can be done earlier at the pilot's discretion (from G to H, H to D or C to D.

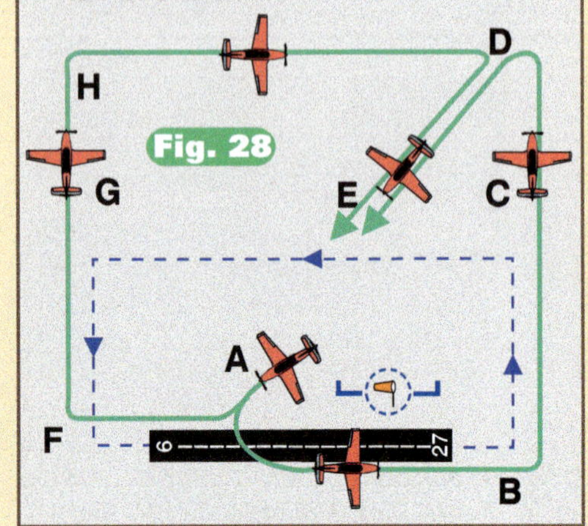

Fig. 28

Some of the more creative students might think about flying to the entry spot at several thousand feet above the pattern altitude and diving into the pattern (after one too many reruns of *Tora, Tora, Tora*). This earns a Swiss cheese sandwich, for having enormous holes in their judgment.

Here are two options. Overfly an uncontrolled airport at a *minimum* of 2000 feet AGL to observe the runways and traffic pattern indicator. Once you've identified the runway you'll be using, fly parallel to the runway direction and off to one side as shown in Figure 28. Flying from A to B allows you to keep the runway in sight out of your left window. When the airplane is beyond the crosswind leg (point B), make a left 90° turn. This allows you to keep departing traffic and pattern traffic in sight.

Make sure you keep your eyes out for high performance airplanes departing the runway. These aircraft climb like a big hungry bat whose sonar is locked on the moon. It's no problem if you maintain a good scan, as pilots are supposed to do at all times.

Continue beyond the downwind leg until reaching point C. You can start your descent here or start it at point D as you turn toward the midpoint of the runway. Descend so as to enter the traffic pattern at traffic pattern altitude. Point D is chosen far enough from the runway to lose the excess altitude you had while overflying the airport. On the return to the airport, enter the downwind at a 45° angle, at traffic pattern altitude. Adjust your flight path, speed or timing to follow any traffic in the pattern or entering the pattern.

Another method is to fly from A to F while keeping the runway in sight out your left window. Point F is chosen far enough from the airport to keep the runway visible over your right shoulder as you fly from F to G to H. You can start your descent to traffic pattern altitude at position G, which is beyond the downwind leg

These methods of pattern entry allow you to keep the airport in sight at all times. The same procedures apply to a right hand traffic pattern. These procedures also work at tower controlled airports when the controller hasn't provided you with

CTAFs are found in several aviation publications as well as being printed on aeronautical sectional charts.

While a unicom frequency can also be the CTAF, this is not always the case. At airports with towers, the tower frequency will usually be the CTAF that's used when the tower isn't in service. Most airports with a tower will also have one or more unicom frequencies; these are *not* CTAFs, but they can be used to obtain airport and runway information from the provider. (See the *d-CS* or the aeronautical chart for this frequency.)

Using Unicom and Multicom For Information

If you're landing at an uncontrolled airport, at about 10 miles out it's time to talk, using the CTAF.

If the CTAF is a unicom station, the following phraseology is appropriate:

"Corona Unicom, Cessna two one three two Bravo is 10 miles southeast descending through 3,000 feet landing Corona, request wind and runway information Corona, over."

At airports without an established unicom station, you may ask for landing advisories from traffic that may already be in the pattern. On the CTAF simply state:

"Sun Hill traffic, Cessna two one three two Bravo is 10 miles southeast descending through 4,000 feet landing Sun Hill, request landing advisories Sun Hill, over."

Without an operating control tower to help inform pilots of each other's position, the CTAF is used to make position reports while in the pattern. In addition to the call 10 miles from the airport, report your position entering the pattern, when downwind, on base and on final approach. This keeps other airplanes at the airport apprised of your whereabouts. Since there may be another airport in the vicinity on a similar unicom or multicom frequency, state the airport name during these transmissions. For instance, the following is a typical report for such an airport:

"Corona Unicom, Cessna two one three two Bravo entering left downwind for Runway 25 for touch and go at Corona." Notice that you announce whether you're making left or right traffic. This provides an opportunity for everyone to yell at you if you're going the wrong way.

You should also broadcast your intentions on the CTAF when departing an uncontrolled airport. Make a broadcast before taxiing and on the runway before departure. The following self-announce phraseology should be used, "Sun Hill traffic, Cessna two

Finding Out What's Common

A CTAF isn't much good unless it's common knowledge. If a unicom *can* be a CTAF, but it isn't always a CTAF, how are you supposed to know what's what?

There are several ways to determine the CTAF for any airport.

Since you will always have a navigational chart on board (that's a polite hint, a request, and a plea all rolled into one), look at it. The information is printed there. The chart depiction in Figure 29 shows how Circle Town is presented on an aeronautical sectional chart. The small reverse-bold "C" under the airport tells you that 122.8 MHz is the CTAF.

The *Digital Chart Supplement* is another handy resource. It will tell you the CTAF. If there's no tower, but a unicom frequency exists, that fact appears in the *d-CS*, as shown in Figure 29. The following frequencies are usually reserved for unicom: 122.7, 122.8, 122.725, 122.975, 123.0, 123.050 and 123.075 MHz.

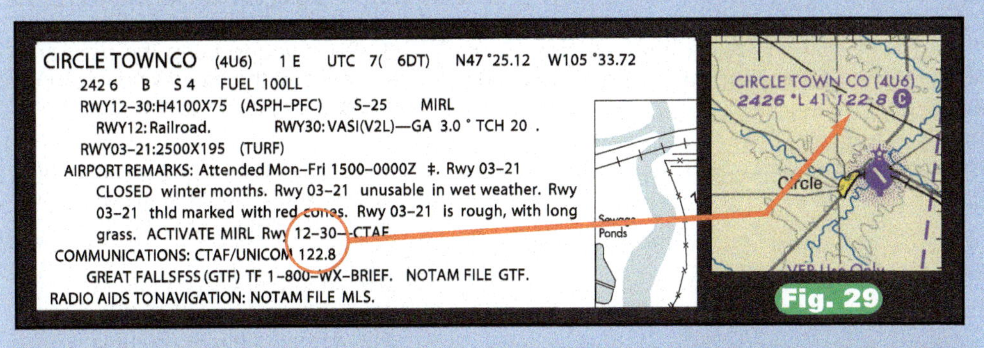
CIRCLE TOWN CO (4U6) 1 E UTC 7(6DT) N47°25.12 W105°33.72
2426 B S4 FUEL 100LL
RWY12-30:H4100X75 (ASPH-PFC) S-25 MIRL
RWY12: Railroad. RWY30: VASI(V2L)—GA 3.0° TCH 20 .
RWY03-21:2500X195 (TURF)
AIRPORT REMARKS: Attended Mon-Fri 1500-0000Z ‡. Rwy 03-21 CLOSED winter months. Rwy 03-21 unusable in wet weather. Rwy 03-21 thld marked with red cones. Rwy 03-21 is rough, with long grass. ACTIVATE MIRL Rwy 12-30—CTAF.
COMMUNICATIONS: CTAF/UNICOM 122.8
GREAT FALLS FSS (GTF) TF 1-800-WX-BRIEF. NOTAM FILE GTF.
RADIO AIDS TO NAVIGATION: NOTAM FILE MLS.

Fig. 29

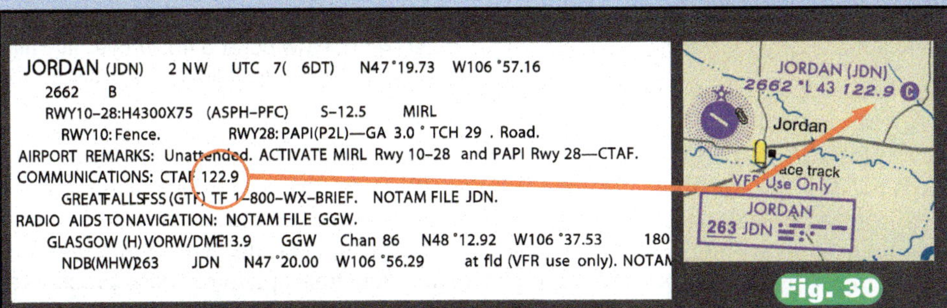
JORDAN (JDN) 2 NW UTC 7(6DT) N47°19.73 W106°57.16
2662 B
RWY10-28:H4300X75 (ASPH-PFC) S-12.5 MIRL
RWY10: Fence. RWY28: PAPI(P2L)—GA 3.0° TCH 29 . Road.
AIRPORT REMARKS: Unattended. ACTIVATE MIRL Rwy 10-28 and PAPI Rwy 28—CTAF.
COMMUNICATIONS: CTAF 122.9
GREAT FALLS FSS (GTF) TF 1-800-WX-BRIEF. NOTAM FILE JDN.
RADIO AIDS TO NAVIGATION: NOTAM FILE GGW.
GLASGOW (H) VORW/DME 113.9 GGW Chan 86 N48°12.92 W106°37.53 180
NDB (MHW) 263 JDN N47°20.00 W106°56.29 at fld (VFR use only). NOTAM

Fig. 30

If there's no tower or unicom frequency being used as the CTAF, are you left speechless? Nope. Just tune your aviation radio to 122.9. This frequency is referred to as multicom, because it's shared by many pilots at many places. It's sort of the pilots' airport party line frequency, and is used primarily for communications at airports with no tower, FSS or unicom. Without a unicom (or tower or FSS), the only airport information you're likely to receive will come from other pilots flying the pattern.

An aeronautical sectional chart excerpt (Figure 30) shows that 122.9 is the CTAF for Jordan airport. Figure 30 shows an *d-CS* excerpt of Jordan airport indicating that no unicom, tower or FSS is available at the airport (all these are missing from the communications line). By a process of elimination, you know it has to be multicom.

one three two Bravo, at Bob's Bean Palace (this is your location on the airport), taxiing to Runway 25, Sun Hill."

"Sun Hill traffic, Cessna two one three two Bravo departing Runway 7, departing the pattern to the (direction) climbing to (altitude), Sun Hill"

Just because there is no tower doesn't mean that you should use nonstandard phraseology. I heard one pilot call the control tower and say, "Man in the tower this is the man in the bird, I'm ready to go so give me the word."

The controller responded, "Man in the bird this is the man in the tower, you talk funny, the delay's an hour." The moral to this story is save the poetry for smoky midnight cafes. Avoid slang and stick with accepted word usage. Remember that *predictability* is important. Other pilots and controllers expect to hear certain information in a certain order.

There are airports without an established CTAF. Normally, these are private (PVT) airports, as shown in Figure 31. This doesn't mean that you have to be a private pilot to use it, either. It just means that it's privately owned and you should seek permission from the owner if you want to land there.

When landing at a private airport, broadcast your intentions on 122.9 MHz. This is the frequency for air-to-air communications at airports without a control tower, FSS or Unicom. If you're landing at a non-privately owned airport without any CTAF listed in the *d-CS* or on a sectional chart, also use 122.9 MHz to broadcast your intentions.

Fig. 31

On Being an Air (Man or Woman) of Few Words

Learning to speak well on the radio is one of the most important piloting skills you can acquire.

Speaking well means speaking clearly and using *standard phraseology* to say the most with the least number of words.

The quickest route to being a royal pain in the prop is to be long-winded on the radio. I've heard pilots who had more hems than a recycled party dress. A few tips that will make you a microphone pro:

- Your initial callup in most cases should consist of who you are calling (Kennedy Tower, Alabaster unicom), and your call sign. I've heard pilots do a 60-second monologue only to be told "Stand by" because the controller was busy.
- Be patient. When you call a tower or ground controller, he or she can be talking to another controller on the phone (the *landline* in controller terms), working another frequency, or otherwise occupied. If you don't get an instant reply, wait 10 to 15 seconds before calling again.
- Listen before talking. Some pilots feel they have to start talking as soon as they tune in a frequency. Make certain you aren't in the middle of someone else's conversation. You will not be popular if you *step on* other pilots by talking over them.
- Think before talking. Don't key the microphone and then start pondering what to say. Key your brain first.

The airwaves are a very limited resource. You're sharing a frequency with a lot of other people who may also need to communicate. Be considerate by being concise and precise.

So far we've discussed operations at uncontrolled airports. Uncontrolled airports require that you, on your own, identify the wind direction, runway landing direction as well as the appropriate traffic pattern to fly. At controlled airports (those with operating control towers) the air traffic controller provides you with this information. This information includes traffic pattern direction, runway to use, directions to fly as well as position reports to make when approaching the airport. An important point to remember is that you must establish two-way radio communication before entering the controller's airspace (Class C or D) or obtain a clearance if it's Class B airspace.

Automatic Terminal Information Service (ATIS)

At many controlled airports there is a recorded broadcast of airport information known as *Automatic Terminal Information Service (ATIS)*. This service, which is pronounced *A-TIS,* provides noncontrol information to help relieve frequency congestion. In other words, ATIS keeps the controller from having to repeat the same airport information (ceiling, wind, visibility, etc.) over and over again to pilots landing or departing the airport.

Figure 32A shows the sectional chart depiction for Long Beach airport. The control tower (CT) frequencies are 119.4 and 120.5 MHz; 119.4 MHz is the CTAF (indicated by the reverse bold "C" after the frequency) and is used whenever the tower isn't in operation. The ATIS frequency is 127.75 MHz. Figure 32B shows where ATIS information is found in the *Digital Chart Supplement*. There's even a phone number available if you are so inclined to call and listen to the ATIS before departure. When approaching Long Beach or any other airport with an ATIS, you should listen to the ATIS broadcast when you're approximately 25 miles from the airport. If you're departing the airport, you should listen to the ATIS broadcast prior to contacting the tower for taxi instructions. A typical ATIS broadcast might sound like this:

"This is Long Beach airport information Hotel, 1300 Zulu weather.

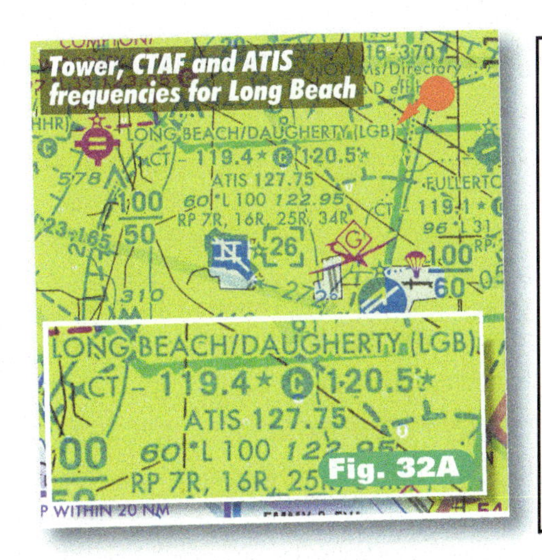

CALIFORNIA

LONG BEACH (DAUGHERTY FLD) (LGB) 3 NE UTC–8(–7DT) N33°49.07′ W118°09.10′ LOS ANGELES

clsd—CTAF. Rwy 12-30 HIRL lighted during hours tower clsd. REIL Rwy 12, Rwy 25R, and Rwy 25L, MIRL Rwy 07L-25R, HIRL Rwy 07R-25L, CL TDZL lgts Rwy 12-30 not avbl when ATCT clsd. VASI Rwy 25R and PAPI Rwy 25L opr 1500-0600Z‡ only. VASI Rwy 12 and PAPI Rwy 30 opr continuously. NOTE: See Special Notices — Air Carrier Operations Vicinity of Long Beach (Daugherty Fld), CA.

WEATHER DATA SOURCES: ASOS (562) 424-0572.

COMMUNICATIONS: CTAF 119.4 ATIS 127.75 (562) 595-8564 UNICOM 122.95 **Fig. 32B**

Ⓡ SOCAL APPCON 124.65

Ⓡ SOCAL DEP CON 127.2

LONG BEACH TOWER 119.4 (Rwy 30 apch, Rwy 12 dep) 120.5 (Rwy 12 apch, Rwy 30 dep) (1415-0745Z‡)

GND CON 133.0 CLNC DEL 118.15

AIRSPACE: CLASS D svc 1415-0745Z‡ other times CLASS G.

RADIO AIDS TO NAVIGATION: NOTAM FILE HHR.

SEAL BEACH (L) VORTACW 115.7 SLI Chan104 N33°47.00′ W118°03.29′ 278° 5.3 NM to fld. 23/15E. HIWAS.

BECCA NDB (LOM) 233 LG N33°45.40′ W118°04.64′ 301° 5.2 NM to fld.

ILS 110.3 I-LGB Rwy 30. Class IT. LOM BECCA NDB. Unmonitored when twr clsd. MM unmonitored.

Thirteen hundred scattered, measured ceiling three thousand broken, visibility 4 smoke and haze, wind 230 at 10. Altimeter 30.04. ILS Runway 30 in use. Landing and departing on Runways 30 and 25L. Contact Ground Control on 133.0. For Runway 30 contact tower on 119.4. For Runway 25R contact tower on 120.5. Inform the controller on initial contact you have information Hotel."

Once again, predictability is paramount. ATIS broadcasts always contain the latest weather sequence, active runways and other pertinent remarks in that order (ceilings and visibilities are not broadcast when they are above 5,000 feet and more than five miles). The first few times you hear one of these beasts, it sounds like a transmission from Mars. You soon figure out that it's always airport name, followed by the phonetic designator, followed by the time, etc. In addition to basic weather and frequency information, the ATIS broadcast may have other important tidbits tagged on at the end such as taxiway closures, temporary restricted areas, birds in the vicinity, etc. One time the ATIS said there was a large, 200 foot crane south of the airport. My student looked over and said, "Wow, now that's a big bird!" (I immediately liberated the sandwich from his hand.)

ATIS broadcasts are updated when any significant change occurs at the airport or upon the receipt of any official hourly or special weather information (typically received from electronic weather sensing devices). Each new recording gets the name of the next phonetic alphabet letter in order. Delta becomes Echo, Hotel becomes India, etc.

One time I called the controller and told him we had information Delta. He replied, "32 Bravo, how can you have Delta when we've just issued information Bravo?" I thought about my mistake and said, "Well, we have a psychic on board." The controller, with a bit of humor, said, "Well, what does that psychic say about your chance of getting touch and goes today?" As you can see, controllers are intelligent people, often with a very sharp sense of humor.

Listening to the ATIS may not be as much fun as tuning in the Superbowl, but it can be a lot more helpful. From the ATIS you can find out if the airport is VFR or IFR (VFR meaning that you can fly and IFR meaning that you can't as a student pilot); what direction you will be landing; whether there are any problems on the ground or special procedures (such as newly installed large obstacles around the airport like a construction crane or advertising balloon) and whether you have to take into account a nasty crosswind, etc.

At about 15 miles out, it's talk time. If you're approaching an airport in Class D airspace, you'll make your initial call to the tower controller. If you're approaching an airport within Class C airspace, you'll make your initial call to the radar approach control facility responsible for that airspace. An early call means you have more time to establish communication in the event the frequency is congested or the tower controller's workload prevents an immediate response to your initial call.

Your initial contact with any air traffic controller should contain the following information:

1. The name of the facility you're calling.

2. Your full aircraft call sign as filed in your flight plan (if you filed a flight plan).

3. The type of message to follow, or your request, if it's short.

4. The word *over* if required.

When contacting Long Beach Tower, your initial should sound like this:

"Long Beach Tower, Cessna two one three two Bravo, 15 miles southeast at 3,500 feet for landing, information Whiskey received, over."

The tower might reply with:

"Cessna two one three two Bravo, this is Long Beach Tower, make right traffic for Runway 7 right. Report entering downwind."

I was sitting at the local flight school when a student came back from a cross country to a busy tower-controlled airport. He was obviously flustered so I asked him what the problem was. He said, "I tuned in the tower frequency and they never stopped talking. All they did was blab, blab, blab. I couldn't get a word in edgewise and finally had to return home." I asked him to point out the tower frequency on the chart. Guess what? He pointed to the ATIS frequency (between taking big bites out of his sandwich). His instructor had never taken him to an airport with an ATIS, so he knew nothing about it. I suppose if the tower ever asked him if he had the ATIS (sounds like "A - TIS") he might of thought they were talking about some sort of tropical skin rash.

Speaking When Spoken To

When a controller speaks, you are expected to acknowledge the communication orally. The acknowledgment consists of nothing more than the last three letters of your call sign. If the tower says "Cessna two one three two Bravo, report turning final" your reply is "32 Bravo."

There is one situation in which a longer reply is *mandatory.* When a controller issues instructions to taxi to but not enter a runway, you *must* acknowledge with your call sign and the fact that you understand you are to hold short of the runway. It might sound like this:

"Cessna two one three two Bravo, hold short of Runway 21."

"Cessna two one three two bravo, will hold short Runway 21."

Pilot Control Of Airport Lighting

At a few very busy airports the runway edge lights are kept on from sunset to sunrise. Figure 33 shows a sectional chart excerpt of Hogeland airport. Notice that next to the numbers "3138" (this is the airport's elevation above sea level) there is the letter "L." This indicates that lighting (specifically—runway edge lighting) is in operation from sunset to sunrise.

At many airports, though, you get to turn the lights on yourself. No, it doesn't take really long arms. In fact, all you need is a short thumb, because you can activate the lights by clicking the microphone.

Figure 34 shows a sectional chart excerpt of Turner airport. An asterisk (*) next to the lighting symbol (the "L") on the sectional chart means *lighting limitations exist.* In this instance, the limitation refers to the fact that "pilot control" of airport lighting is in use (available) at this airport. So don't expect to see Turner's airport lights on at night unless you or another pilot activated them. Figure 35 shows an excerpt from the *Digital Chart Supplement* for Turner, indicating that pilots should activate the MIRL (medium intensity runway lighting) on the CTAF of 122.9 MHz. The words, "ACTIVATE," followed by the specific type of lighting system, indicate that pilot control of airport lighting exists at that airport. The *d-CS*, not the sectional chart, is where the appropriate frequencey for lighting activation is found. (The "*L" symbol may also mean lighting is available on *request* or the lighting is *part time*. If it's available on request, the *d-CS* will identify who to contact for light activation. Always check the *d-CS* if you see the "*L" symbol.)

Three different intensities of runway edge lighting (high, medium and low) are available at many airports. To activate runway lighting from the cockpit, key (click) the microphone button on the appropriate CTAF frequency. How many times should you click it? If all three intensities of lighting exist at an airport, simply click the mike 7 times within 5 seconds for the high intensity runway lighting (HIRL), 5 times within 5 seconds for the medium intensity runway lighting (MIRL) and 3 times in 5 seconds for the low intensity runway lighting (LIRL). Once activated the lights will stay on for 15 minutes.

The "L" in Hogeland's airport information line indicates lighting is in operation from sunset to sunrise. Fig. 33

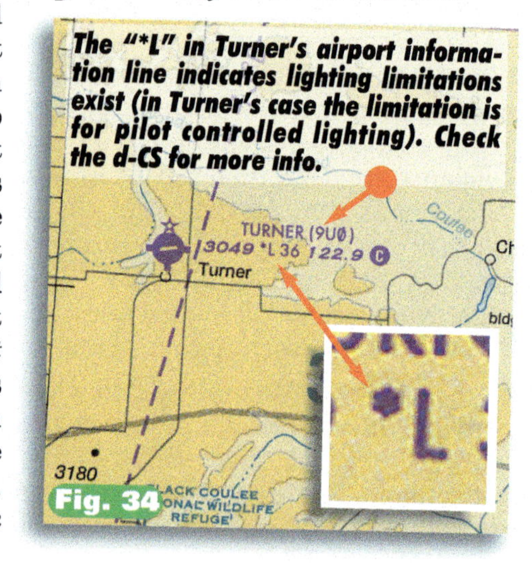

The "*L" in Turner's airport information line indicates lighting limitations exist (in Turner's case the limitation is for pilot controlled lighting). Check the d-CS for more info. Fig. 34

Light of My Life

According to one reliable source, this really happened.

A pilot who flew freight at night got to be familiar with the controllers at the numerous airports where he made stops.

Slightly bored with the repetitious nature of his work, he liked to key the microphone and say "Guess who?" to the controllers as his first callup.

One night the tower controller at a small airport was just waiting for his opportunity. Right on time came "Guess who?"

The tower controller turned out the airport lights, and said "Guess who? Guess where!!"

If you're approaching the airport at night and it's approximately 15 minutes since you've last activated the lights, you might want to re-click the microphone the appropriate number of times to reactivate them for an additional 15 minutes. Personally, I re-key the microphone the appropriate number of times when I'm on final approach just to make sure the lights don't go off by surprise. Imagine being on short final when the airport disappears. Not only will this make you nervous, but imagine what it'll do to the passengers.

Figure 35 shows only MIRL is available at Turner (look after the word "ACTIVATE" at point A). Keying the microphone more than 5 times in 5 seconds will only activate the medium intensity setting since it doesn't have high intensity capability.

If HIRL lighting exists and it's too strong for your eyes (some pilots say you can cook chicken on the bulbs of those high intensity lights), simply re-key the mic 3 or 5 times within five seconds to step down the lighting system to lower intensity lighting (if it is available). The FAA suggests that, when approaching an airport, you should key the microphone 7 times in 5 seconds just to activate all the airport's controlled lighting. After this, you can re-key the mike and lower the lighting intensity (if MIRL or HIRL are installed) or deactivate other lighting systems (VASI, REIL, PAPI, approach lights) that may be wired into the control system (more on these other lighting systems shortly).

The *d-CS* excerpt in Figure 35, point B also shows a Precision Approach Path Indicator (PAPI) is wired into the pilot controlled lighting system at Turner (I promise, I'll cover the PAPI shortly, honest!). Make it a point to activate airport lighting when close to the field. Activating the system at high altitudes far from the airport might needlessly activate another airport's lighting systems. It may also change another pilot's light system settings while on approach.

At some airports there are two small stroboscopic lights near the runway's threshold. These are called *Runway End Identifier Lights.* The acronym is *REIL,* pronounced like the word *real.* REIL lights help identify the beginning of the runway threshold, making it easier to see.

Highway to Heaven

On final with gear down and full flaps, I noticed a movement out of the corner of my eye. Another aircraft was turning final ahead and to our left. We took evasive action and went around. The aircraft took forever to get off the runway and we thought we might have to go around again. We didn't, but on short final, right before we landed, the pilot of the other aircraft said, "Tower, were you trying to call me?" We decided that we ought to talk with this pilot about the close call. He was apologetic. His excuse was that he had his personal tape player headset on and couldn't hear the tower over the music. **ASRS Report.**

New pilots are sometimes surprised at how hard it can be to spot an airport from the air, day *or* night.

Re-keying the mike button may allow you to step down or turn off the REIL system. At one airport, a tower controller called a pilot on approach and asked him if he wanted the REIL lights activated. The pilot replied, "Well, how can I tell the difference between the real lights and the imitation ones?" It wouldn't have surprised me if the controller said, "Well, I guess that all depends on what kind of sandwich you're having."

Visual Approach Slope Indicator (VASI)

Under poor visibility conditions or at night, the lack of outside visual clues sometimes makes a determination of the proper landing glidepath difficult. Fortunately there is something known as a *Visual Approach Slope Indicator* (VASI) that provides you with a visual clue as to the proper glidepath to fly. (By the way, VASI is pronounced *VAZ-eee*. It is not something in which you put flowers).

A VASI usually consists of two pairs of lightbars along the side of the runway (it's often called a *two bar VASI* for this reason). The two VASI bars are usually 500 to 1,000 feet from the approach threshold as

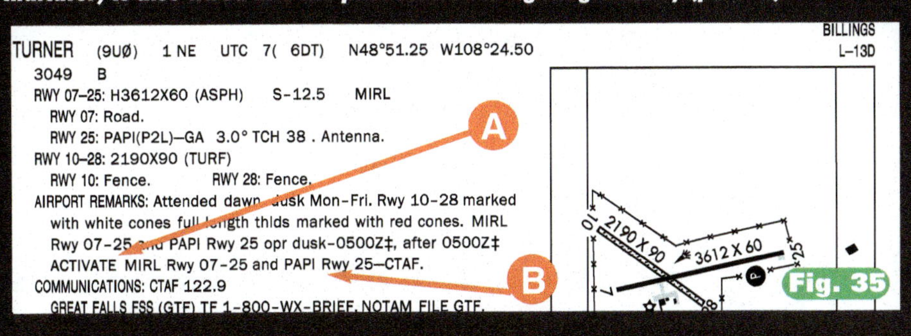

The word ACTIVATE in the d-CS excerpt for Turner indicates MIRL (Medium Intensity Runway Lighting) is available (point A). The PAPI (Precision Approach Path Indicator) is also wired into the pilot controlled lighting circuitry (point B).

BILLINGS
L–13D

TURNER (9UØ) 1 NE UTC 7(6DT) N48°51.25 W108°24.50
3049 B
RWY 07–25: H3612X60 (ASPH) S-12.5 MIRL
RWY 07: Road.
RWY 25: PAPI(P2L)—GA 3.0° TCH 38 . Antenna.
RWY 10–28: 2190X90 (TURF)
RWY 10: Fence. RWY 28: Fence.
AIRPORT REMARKS: Attended dawn-dusk Mon-Fri. Rwy 10-28 marked with white cones full length thlds marked with red cones. MIRL Rwy 07-25 and PAPI Rwy 25 opr dusk-0500Z‡, after 0500Z‡ ACTIVATE MIRL Rwy 07-25 and PAPI Rwy 25—CTAF.
COMMUNICATIONS: CTAF 122.9
GREAT FALLS FSS (GTF) TF 1-800-WX-BRIEF. NOTAM FILE GTF.

shown in Figure 36. These lights project either a red or white color, depending on your altitude. The colors are constant and don't actually change within the box. What changes is your height, which allows you to look at the VASI from different angles and see different colors.

When you are below the proper glideslope, both VASI bars show red. Some pilots remember that this signals trouble by thinking of it as *Red over red, you'll conk your head.* Level off until you see red over white. Red over white means that you're above the glidepath for the bar closest to you and below the glidepath for the bar farther away. This is a complicated way of saying you're on the glidepath that will plunk you down halfway between the two bars. A good way to remember this is *Red over white, you're all right.* Of course, if you're too high, both bars will show white. A good memory aid for this is *White over white, you'll soon be out of sight.* Increase the descent rate until the upwind bar turns red. You can expect the VASI's red and white bars to transition through a pink color as your altitude in relation to the proper glideslope changes.

If you see flashing red over flashing white, then you're making an approach to a police car. Now you're in really big trouble (besides, it's not natural for the VASI bars to chase other cars down the highway).

VASIs are visible from 3 to 5 miles during the day and up to 20 miles or more at night. You can count on safe obstruction clearance for 10° either side of the runway centerline when using the VASI. Obstruction clearance is guaranteed for a distance up to 4 miles out along the centerline of the runway (Figure 37). If, however, you're nearing your turn onto final approach, it's best not to start a descent using the VASI until you are aligned with the runway. Personally, I wouldn't start my descent until aligned with the runway even if I was within 10° of the runway centerline. You never know what's out there, and I'm not about to turn my airplane into some sort of probe whose mission is to find a newly installed obstruction.

Keep in mind that regulations require you to fly at or above the glideslope when approaching a runway equipped with a VASI in Class B, C and D airspace. Be cautious about

THE 2-BAR VISUAL APPROACH SLOPE INDICATOR

THE 2-BAR VASI (Visual Approach Slope Indicator)

A "red over red" indication on the VASI means you're below glide path. Think, "Red over red, you'll soon conk your head."

A "red over white" indication on the VASI means you're on the proper glide path. Think, "Red over white, you'll be all right."

A white over white indication on the VASI means that you're above the proper glide path. Think, "White over white you'll soon be out of sight."

VASI PROTECTED AREA

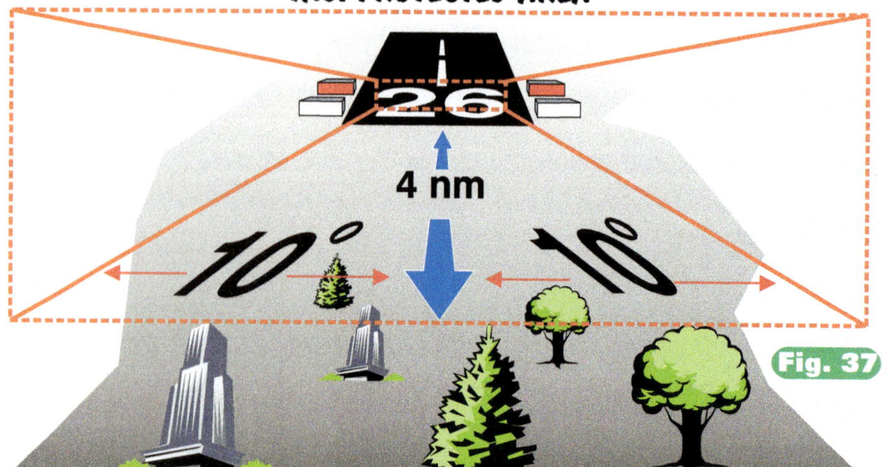

The VASI provides you with obstacle clearance for plus or minus 10 degrees either side of the runway centerline for 4 nautical miles.

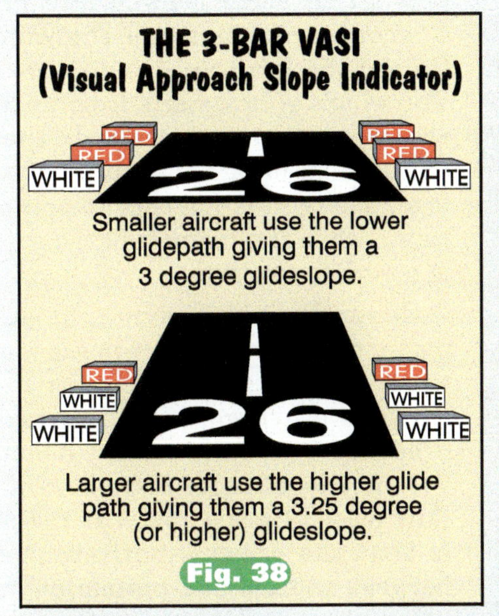

Fig. 38

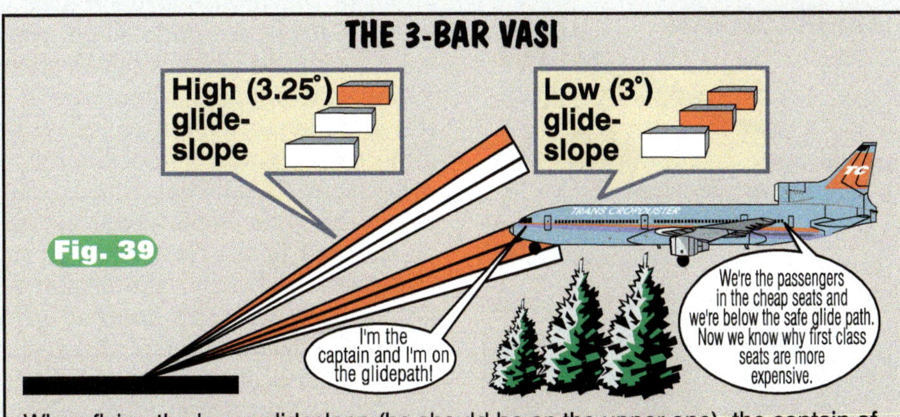

Fig. 39

When flying the lower glideslope (he should be on the upper one), the captain of this airliner is on glidepath while the rest of his long-bodied airplane is below glideslope. This is why many large aircraft use the high glideslope for landing.

3-Bar VASI

Some of the larger air carrier airports have a 3-bar VASI. This exists to serve the jumbo jet crowd, as shown in Figure 38. Problems arise in long-bodied aircraft when the captain is on a safe glideslope but the passengers behind him or her are not, as shown in Figure 39. If pilots of jumbo jets landed this way, obstructions in the flight path might intrude on passengers seated in row 38 through L (lavatory).

Three-bar VASI's have two glideslopes. One is angled at 3° and is identified by a bar combination of red/red over white as shown in Figure 38. The higher glideslope is angled at approximately 3.25° (1/4 degree steeper than the lower glideslope). Long bodied aircraft use this and see a color combination of red/white over white. VASI glideslope angles vary depending on the obstructions located along the approach path. It's possible to have VASI glideslopes as steep as 4.5°. Even if you're in a Cessna 152 pretending to be a Boeing 747, it's best to use the lower glideslope to avoid steep descents. Look for red/red over white as the appropriate on-glidepath indication for this lower (3°) glideslope.

making premature descents below the glideslope. In addition to safety, VASIs aid in keeping pilots from descending over noise-sensitive areas along the flight path.

Precision Approach Path Indicator (PAPI)

The precision approach path indicator (*PAPI*, pronounced *PAP-pee*) is another version of a visual glideslope indicator, as shown in Figure 40 (no, it's not that nice guy who's paying for your flying lessons either—that's your *pappy*). The PAPI uses red and white signaling colors in an arrangement of four horizontal lights to identify the correct glidepath. These four horizontal light units appear to change color as your glidepath varies. If you're above a 3.5° glide slope, the PAPI shows all four light units as white. When on a 3° glideslope the right two lights are red and the left two lights are white. When below a 2.5° glideslope, all four light units show red. A pink transition between lights doesn't exist as it does with a two- or three-bar VASI.

PAPI
Precision Approach Path Indicator

Below a 2.5 Degree Glide Path

On a 3 Degree Glide Path

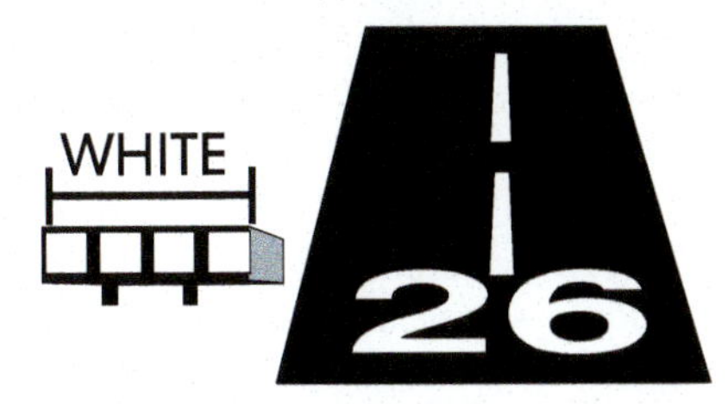

Above a 3.5 Degree Glide Path

Fig. 40

RIDE 'EM COWBOY!

A very hot pilot was Henry Hightowers,
Who boasted of having two hundred hours.
To prove it, he dove on this girl's house one day;
They would have been married the fifteenth of May.

After departure, I remained in ground effect to the end of the runway, then pulled up sharply, turning to the left. Remaining in the pattern, I made a steep 60° turn and come down along the runway for a low pass. Flew the length of the runway and repeated the pattern. I put the airplane in a high forward slip and came in low. When I pulled up, the airplane's nose exceeded a safe angle of attack. The airplane flipped and rolled. I had to recover at low altitude. I was so shook that it took me a half hour to stop shaking. This is a lesson in lack of judgment and common sense. Low passes and subsequent pull-ups are more dangerous than they appear. NEVER, NEVER AGAIN!!

Unlike the cowboy in the poem, this one survived and seems to have learned a lesson conducive to longevity. Don't horse around in an airplane.

ASRS Report

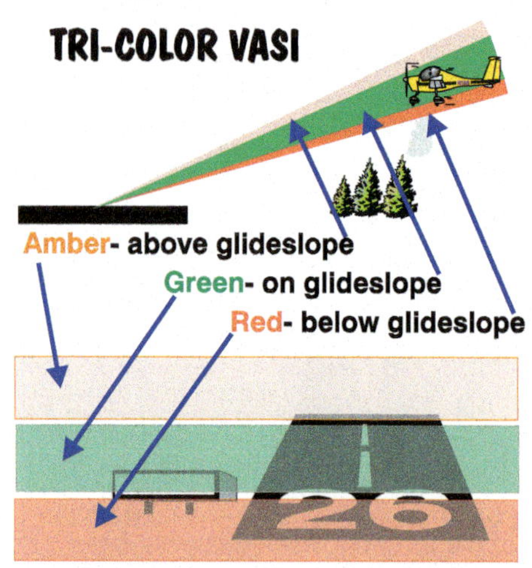

The Tri-Color VASI is a single-light unit whose projected colors change in appearance based on your relation to the glideslope.

Fig. 41

Tricolor VASI

The tricolor VASI is not as common as the two- and three-bar VASIs. It normally consists of a single light unit projecting a three-color visual approach path into the final approach area of the runway (Figure 41). Red is the *below glideslope* indication. The *above glideslope* indication is amber, and the *on glideslope* indication is green. When the airplane descends from green to red the pilot may see a dark amber color during the transition. Tricolor VASIs have a useful range of approximately one-half to one mile during the day and up to five miles at night.

Pulsating VASI Systems

The last type of the fairly common VASI systems is the the Pulsating Light Visual Approach Slope Indicator (PVASI, Figure 42). A pulsating VASI consists of a single light unit projecting a two-color signal to pilots in the final approach area. If you are above the glide slope, you'll see a pulsating white light. A steady white light appears when you're on the glide slope. If you're below the glide slope, you'll see a steady red indication. If you descend further below the glide slope, you'll notice a pulsing red light. The pulsating rate increases the further the airplane is above or below the desired glide slope. The useful range of this system is approximately four miles during the day and up to ten miles at night (depending on the visibility).

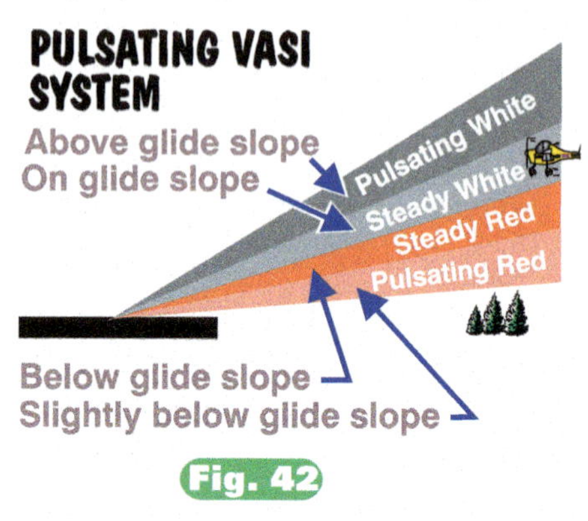

Fig. 42

Wake Turbulence

One of the unseen hazards of flight is something known as *wake turbulence*. This can be any form of airplane-generated disturbance of the atmosphere. The most common and hazardous type of wake turbulence is known as *wingtip vortices*. Wingtip vortices pose quite a hazard to other airplanes. An airplane caught in wake turbulence can experience a rolling motion so severe that there isn't enough control capacity to fight it. Wake turbulence can roll a small plane inverted and, quite frankly, passengers often become very upset when suddenly placed upside down in an airplane.

If that's not enough, the rolling motions and turbulence produced by the vortices can damage aircraft components. This doesn't mean that your airplane is necessarily going to go to pieces upon encountering vortices, but it's a risk not worth the gamble.

Wingtip vortices come not from somebody's shoes, but as an unwanted byproduct of lift. Wingtip vortices are generated by the differential pressure which exists over and under the wing's surfaces (Figure 43). High pressure air under the wing attempts to sneak over the tip of the wing, toward the low pressure air above. The wing's vortex starts from under the wing, moves outward, then upward and inward toward the fuselage. The vortex appears to coil or rotate while trailing behind the wing of a moving airplane.

Generally, the heavier the airplane, the stronger the wingtip vortex (there are a few exceptions to this). In other words, the vortices produced by a fully loaded Boeing 747 are a lot stronger than those of a fully loaded Cessna 152. The reason is that the pressure differential between the top and bottom of the 747's wing is a lot greater than the pressure differential of a Cessna's wing. After all, the 747 has a lot more to lift. A greater difference in pressure implies air at the wingtip rotates faster.

Fig. 43

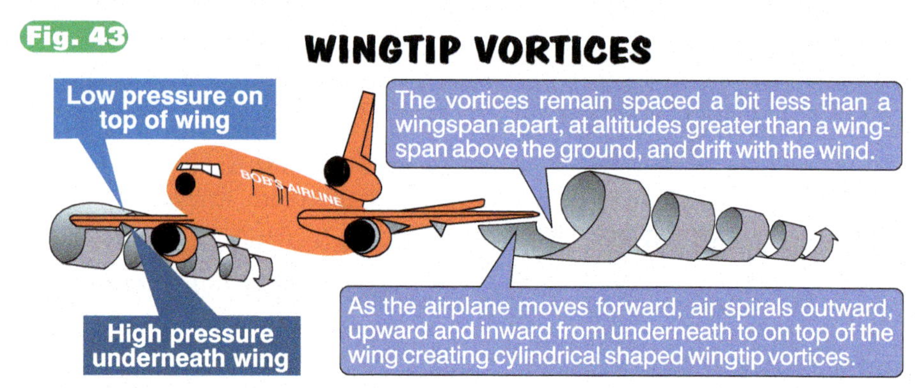

When an airplane's gear and flaps are retracted, there is a tendency to produce stronger vortices. An airplane in this no-gear-and-flap configuration is said to be *clean* (no, this isn't a newly washed airplane). Couple a cleanly-configured airplane with slow airspeed and you've got a condition that normally produces the strongest wingtip vortices. Slow speed means a higher angle of attack, which results in a greater lift differential between the bottom and the top of the wing. Any large airplane that's flying heavy, clean and slow could produce more serious wingtip vortices.

As a small-airplane pilot, you must watch out for airplanes that produce hazardous wingtip vortices. Some are

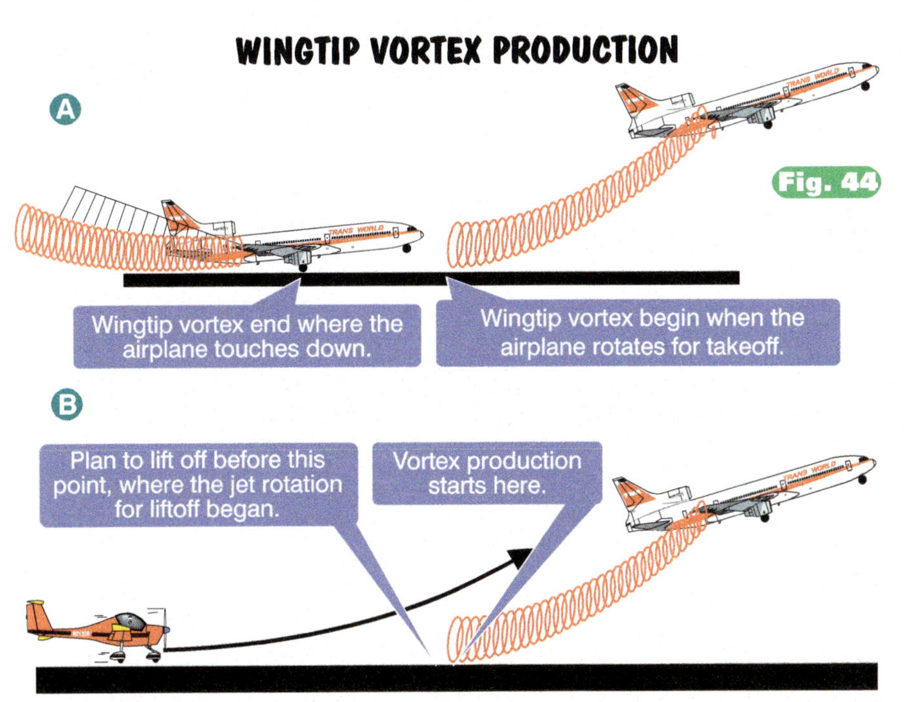

Wingtip vortices begin at the point where the heavier airplane rotates for takeoff (this is the point where the nosewheel first lifts off the runway). Make sure you lift off long before this point and avoid flying directly into the path of the vortices. You may need to turn left or right to avoid the vortices.

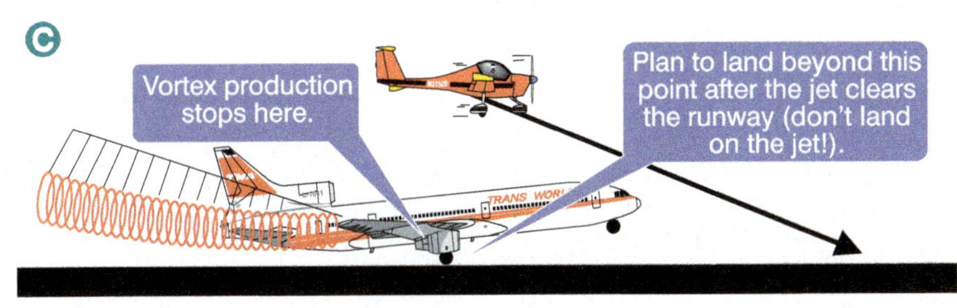

When landing behind a heavier airplane, plan to land beyond the point where the airplane touched down. And make sure you don't sink into the the vortices while on the approach.

famous, or infamous, as generators of these horizontal tornadoes. Beware of Boeing 747, 757 and 767's, and DC-10's. Even other large airplanes try to avoid the vortices of these mammoth jumbos. But don't be deceived by the airplane's size. Lear jets, although small in size, can produce serious wingtip vortices.

Always remember that wingtip vortices are a byproduct of lift. The moment an airplane rotates for takeoff, lift is generated and vortices are produced. So expect vortices at and beyond the point of airplane rotation, as shown in Figure 44B. Likewise, as soon as the airplane's wheels touch down, wingtip vortice production stops (Figure 44C).

If you are departing behind a larger airplane, it's best to lift off before the point where that airplane raised its nose (rotated) and commenced climbing. Once off the ground, avoid flying into the flight path of the departing airplane as shown in Figure 44B. In a small airplane with limited performance, it's unlikely you will climb above the glide path of the larger airplane. Turn right or left to avoid climbing into the larger airplane's departure path (and its vortices), as shown in Figure 44B. Let the tower controller know what you're doing (if departing a controlled field).

The unique thing about wingtip vortices is that they tend to descend at a rate of several hundred feet per minute and normally level off at 500 to 1,000 feet below the generating airplane (Figure 45). They also tend to remain a little less than a wingspan apart and drift with the wind. It's *always* wise to avoid the area 1,000 feet below any large airplane. So maneuver laterally (preferably upwind) to avoid flying below and behind these large aircraft.

While vortices diminish with time as well as with atmospheric turbulence (this helps chop them up and disrupt their rotational energy), they remain a threat for many minutes after the passage of a large airplane. Vertical separation of at least 1,000 feet below the airplane is considered safe by the FAA. Personally, I'd recommend you avoid flying directly beneath and parallel to the flight path of a large transport airplane even if you're more than 1,000 feet below it (vortices can remain formed 8 to 10 nautical miles behind an airplane). It never makes sense to thumb your nose at any in-flight hazard.

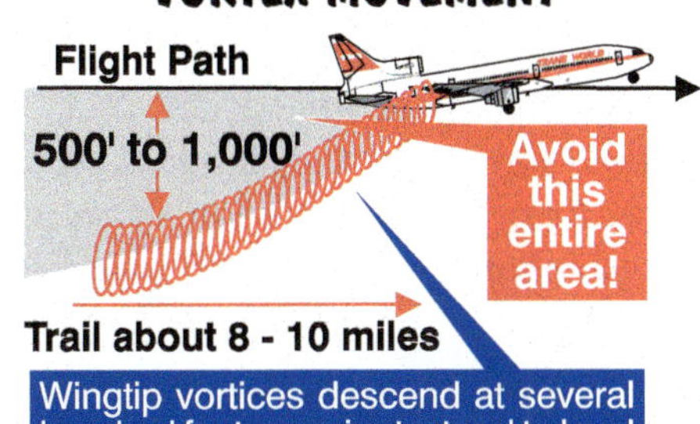

Wingtip vortices descend at several hundred feet per minute, tend to level off at 500' to 1,000' below the generating airplane and can trail for as much as 8-10 nautical miles behind.

Fig. 45

Be prepared for vortices to drift when crosswinds exist at the airport. Figure 46(A) shows the typical behavior of a drifting vortex near the surface. When vortices sink to within 100 to 200 feet above the ground, they tend to move sideways at a speed of 2 to 3 knots. A crosswind will decrease the sideways movement of the upwind vortex and increase the movement of the downwind vortex as shown in Figure 46B. Expect the upwind vortex to remain over or near the touchdown zone if a light crosswind component of 1 to 5 knots exists.

A light quartering tailwind can move the vortices forward into the touchdown zone as shown in Figure 46C. You must be especially cautious because this increases the possibility of lingering vortices in the touchdown area. Be especially cautious when departing on close, parallel runways when a large airplane is upwind of your runway as depicted in Figure 46D. The vortices may drift directly into your flight path.

Another area of concern is when a larger airplane makes a low approach, missed approach or a go-around and flies directly over your airplane during the climbout. This is most common on parallel, closely spaced runways. It's also a problem on runways that intersect at a small angle. If you experience such an event and feel the airplane will pass less than 1,000 feet over your airplane during the go-around, move out from under the airplane's flight path. Your job is to protect you and your passengers. Call the tower and explain that you'd like to turn right or left in the interest of wake turbulence avoidance (if it's critical, turn first, talk later). I have never been refused a request to do something in the interest of "safety."

In many cases ATC will issue a "caution wake turbulence" warning when such a hazard presents itself. Even if ATC issues no warning, adjust your flight path as necessary to prevent encountering these dangerous wingtip vortices.

WINGTIP VORTEX DRIFT

When the vortices of larger aircraft sink close to the ground (within 100 to 200 feet), they tend to move sideways over the ground at a speed of 2 or 3 knots if no wind is present.

Vortex movement near ground—no wind present

A crosswind will decrease the sideways movement of the upwind vortex and increase the movement of the downwind vortex. Thus a light wind with a cross-runway component of 1 to 5 knots could result in the upwind vortex remaining in the touchdown zone for a period of time and hasten the drift of the downwind vortex toward another runway.

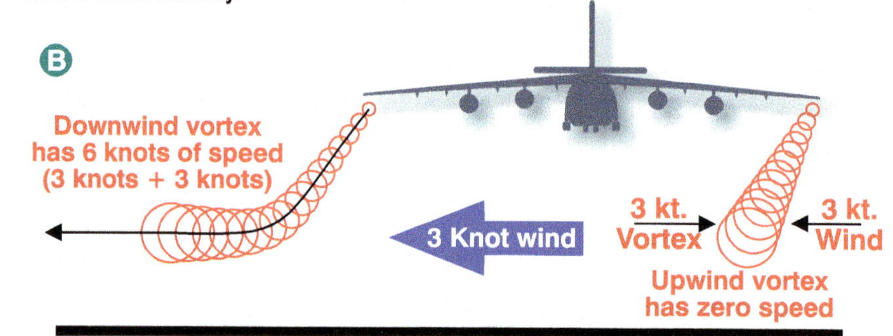

Vortex movement near ground—with crosswind

A tailwind condition can move the vortices of the preceding aircraft forward into the touchdown zone. The light quartering tailwind requires maximum caution. Pilots should be alert to large aircraft upwind from their approach and takeoff flight paths (especially when the runways are closer than 2,500 feet).

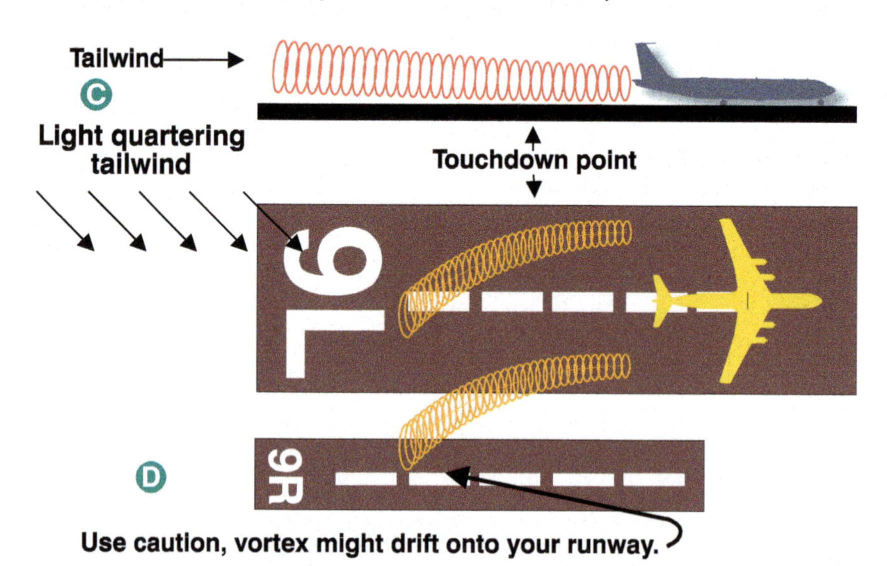

Use caution, vortex might drift onto your runway.

And always be prepared for the unexpected. One of my friends in a Cessna 421 (a twin-engine airplane) was cleared for takeoff when a small rabbit pulled out on the runway. He radioed the tower that he couldn't takeoff until the rabbit moved. The tower replied, "The rabbit on the runway is now cleared for takeoff. And Cessna 421, you're cleared for takeoff too, caution wake turbulence from the departing rabbit." This is what happens when tower controllers have a lot of free time on their hands.

ATC Wake Turbulence Separation Requirements

For the purposes of wake turbulence separation minima, ATC classifies aircraft as *super*, *heavy*, *large* and *small*.

Heavy aircraft are aircraft capable of takeoff weights of more than 300,000 pounds regardless of their weight during any particular phase of flight. *Large* aircraft are aircraft of more than 41,000 pounds maximum certified takeoff weight up to 300,000 pounds. A *super* aircraft is either an Airbus A-380-800 or an Antonov AN-225. *Small* aircraft are aircraft of 41,000 pounds or less maximum certified takeoff weight. (For the purposes of an aircraft type rating, a *large* aircraft is one weighing more than 12,500 pounds. See Page F3.)

Be especially alert to the word *heavy* when used by transport-type airplanes. This means the airplane can weigh nearly a third of a million pounds. And don't be fooled by the words *small* either. A Falcon 50 jet is a three-engine business jet that packs tremendous wake turbulence potential and it is classified as a small aircraft under these definitions.

If you're *landing* your small airplane behind a heavy aircraft, ATC will ensure that at least a six mile separation exists between you and that heavy aircraft (or four miles for a B757) by the time it crosses the runway threshold. If you're *following* (not landing behind) a heavy aircraft, ATC will keep you either 1,000 feet below or at least six miles behind the big fellow. These distances tell something about how smaller airplanes are affected by wingtip vortices. And if ATC provides *traffic* information, issues a *visual approach clearance* or asks you to maintain *visual separation* from an airplane and you accept these instructions, then you immediately become responsible for your own distance and wake turbulence separation.

When departing directly behind a heavy aircraft or when your projected flight paths will cross, ATC provides a two minute wait for wake turbulence. ATC may state, "2132 Bravo, hold for wake turbulence avoidance." The controller can't waive these holding times for you. Nor should you want him/her to, either. Doing so is about as risky as accidentally honking your horn while riding behind a Hell's Angels biker gang.

Taking off from a runway intersection poses significant hazards if a *large* or *heavy* aircraft has just departed. Your departure path could put you directly into this airplane's descending vortices. Controllers *request* a 3 minute wait for wake turbulence separation in these instances (or 4 minutes for a super aircraft). You can waive the hold time if it's a large aircraft but not if it's a *super* or *heavy* aircraft or a B757 jet. Then again, this isn't always a wise thing to do even if you're wearing a helmet.

WHERE TO PLACE THE FLIGHT CONTROLS WHILE TAXIING IN A QUARTERING HEADWIND

The wheel is turned into the wind (to the left) which moves the left aileron up and keeps the left wing (upwind wing) from lifting. The elevator is held in a neutral position.

WHERE TO PLACE THE FLIGHT CONTROLS WHILE TAXIING INTO A QUARTERING TAILWIND

In a left-quartering tailwind while on ground, move the controls as if you were diving with the wind–wheel forward and to the right.

Fig. 48

Left quartering tailwind

WIND

N2132B

The wheel is turned with the wind (to the right) which moves left aileron down. This keeps the left wing (upwind wing) from lifting as the wind pushes down on this aileron. Elevator is pushed forward so that the wind pushes down on the tail instead of pushing it up and tipping the airplane to the right or left.

Taxiing in Crosswind Conditions

Strong crosswinds present quite a challenge when landing as well as when taxiing. I've always felt much more comfortable flying an airplane than taxiing one. Why? Airplanes were meant to fly; cars were meant to taxi. Frankly, airplanes are a little awkward on the ground. It's possible, with a strong enough wind, coupled with a mishandling of the flight controls, for an airplane to tip over resulting in wingtip or propeller damage. If, however, you know how to position your flight controls to compensate for these strong crosswinds, your airplane will always remain upright.

When taxiing in strong winds, the proper placement or movement of the flight controls helps keep downward pressure on the airplane's wings. Remember, wind wants to lift the wing up. Your job is to keep it forced downward until you're ready to fly.

When taxiing into a quartering headwind in a tricycle-gear airplane, turn the ailerons into the wind and put the elevator in a neutral position (Figure 47). This forces the upwind wing downward. Keeping the elevator neutral (instead of back or forward) keeps the nose from coming up or going down and exposing more wing surface to the wind. If you are

in a taildragger, position the ailerons in the same way but keep the elevator stick pulled full aft. This keeps the tailwheel stuck to the ground for more effective steering.

Quartering tailwinds are handled a little differently. Do you remember when you rode your first tricycle as a child? When you fell (and I know you did), you fell forward to the right or left. Tricycles are unstable in this direction. Unfortunately, a quartering tailwind tends to push in the direction the airplane's most unstable. Therefore, the ailerons should be positioned so that the upwind aileron is deflected downward (Figure 48). This aileron position allows the quartering tailwind to push downward on the upwind wing instead of lifting it and tipping the airplane. Applying down elevator allows the wind to push the tail down. A downward push on the tail means that the airplane is less likely to roll forward to the right or left. With quartering tailwinds, think of moving the control as if you are diving with the wind. This helps you to properly place the aileron and elevator controls. If you're in a taildragger and have a quartering tailwind, keep the elevator well forward to prevent that tail from lifting.

Knowing how to handle yourself around an airport is important. This chapter provides you with much of the information you'll need to successfully cope during your first solo and continuing operations. But don't be surprised if something new arises. After all, isn't that what makes flying so novel? New experiences imply new learning.

A while back, Long Beach airport had a spectacular airshow with displays of several large aircraft. One of these was a C5A Galaxy aircraft—one of the largest transports in the world. As the show ended these large airplanes readied themselves for departure. A student pilot was number one in position on Runway 30 for departure. He was listening on 119.4 MHz—the tower frequency. Behind him was a C5A Galaxy whose pilots were listening on both the tower (119.4) and ground control (133.0) frequency. The C5A pilot had forgotten to load a jeep. So the pilot called ground control (unbeknown to the student) and requested permission to load it right there on the taxiway, while holding in the number two position for takeoff.

C5As load their equipment by raising the nose of their airplane and sticking out a large metal pallet that looks like a big tongue. As the student pilot looks behind him he sees something his instructor never told him about. The student calls the controller and says, "Hey tower, what's that guy doing?" Before the tower could respond the C5A pilot says, "Hey little buddy, we're going to eat you." The student says, "Tower, what's he going to do?" The tower replied, "Well, it sure does look like he's going to eat you, 32 Bravo!" The student pilot in that Cessna 150 made one of the fastest takeoffs ever recorded in Long Beach history.

Having covered airport operations at controlled and uncontrolled airports, we'll discuss the specifics of radio communication in the next chapter.

Postflight Briefing #7-1

LAHSO (Land And Hold Short Operations)

At some controlled airports, LAHSO (Land And Hold Short Operations) provides visual signage for you to *land and hold short* of intersecting *runways, taxiways* or other *designated points on a runway*. Two solid yellow lines followed by two rows of dashed yellow lines along with runway number identifiers on each side depict the designated LAHSO hold point as shown below. For instance, in the figure below, you're in Airplane B and are landing on Runway 8. ATC clears you to land but instructs you to hold short of Runway 15 for crossing traffic, a Boeing 767 (Airplane A). This means that if you accept the LAHSO clearance, you can't use the full length of Runway 8. So check the available landing distance (ALD) in the *Special Notices* section of the *Chart Supplement* to ensure you can land and stop safely. You should land and exit by the first convenient taxiway short of the LAHSO hold lines. If you can't exit the runway, then hold at the LAHSO hold lines. A LAHSO clearance doesn't preclude a rejected landing (a go-around). If this is necessary, then go around, but maintain safe separation from other traffic and promptly notify the controller. A ceiling of 1000' and 3 miles visibility is required for a LAHSO clearance. Student pilots and pilots who are not familiar with LAHSO should not participate in this program. The available landing distance on a LAHSO runway is found in the *Chart Supplement*. It's very important that you give the controller a *full readback* of the LAHSO clearance. This lets the controller know that you know what's expected of you. And, if you need the full length of the runway, then don't accept the clearance. Remember, you're the PIC!

LAND AND HOLD–SHORT OPERATIONS

LDG RWY	HOLD–SHORT POINT	AVBL LDG DIST
RWY 08:	15-33	3550

RUNWAY DECLARED DISTANCE INFORMATION

Postflight Briefing #7-2

ADDITIONAL AIRPORT & RUNWAY LIGHTING & MARKINGS

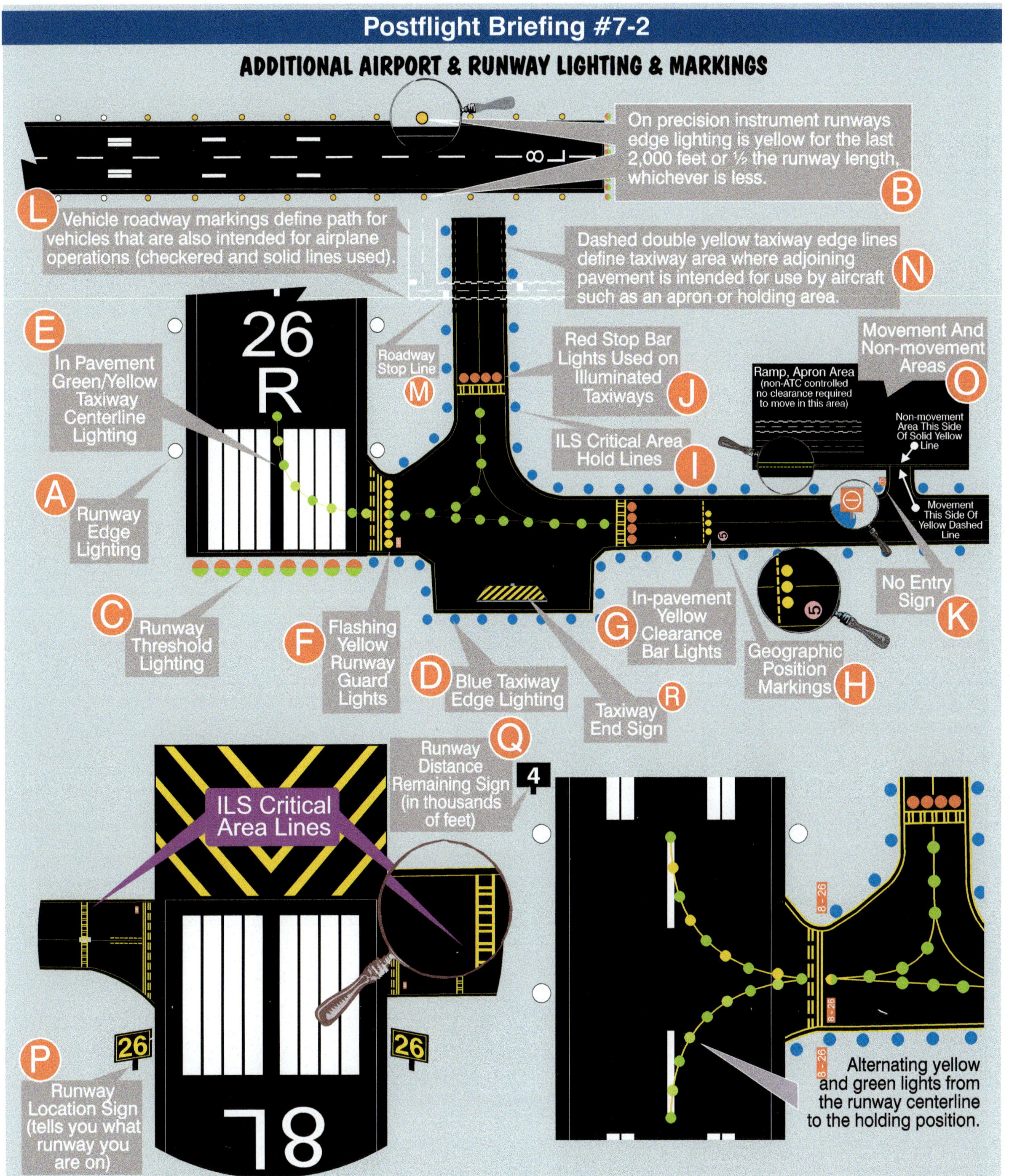

The ILS (instrument landing system) critical area is identified by double-double solid yellow bars. When the weather is poor and pilots are flying instrument approaches (one of which is called an ILS approach), then the controller might protect the ILS critical area, meaning that your airplane shouldn't cross these double-double lines unless you're instructed to do so. This prevents your airplane from interfering with the navigation signal used by pilots flying instrument approaches. Since the weather is quite poor when the ILS critical area is in use, you probably won't be flying and thus won't have a reason to use these lines. It's nice to know about them, nevertheless.

Postflight Briefing #7-3

THE RUNWAY STATUS LIGHT SYSTEM (RWLS)

The RWLS is a fully automated system (using multiple airport sensing devices) that provides runway status information to pilots on final approach as well as to pilots during taxi and when holding in position for takeoff. The RWLS is based on red illuminated lights that tell pilots to either stop or remain stopped until a runway conflict is resolved. The operation of this system depends on your transponder being on at all times when departing the parking area and until engine shutdown.

Runway Intersection Lights (RIL)

- Flush mounted, one-directional red lights just like THLs (see below).
- Lights are directed toward the arriving end of runway and extend for 3,000 feet in front of aircraft approaching an intersecting runway.
- RILs end at LAHSO light bars or the hold short line for the intersecting runway.
- RILs illuminate for departing aircraft or aircraft in position to depart when there is high speed traffic operating on the intersecting runway. Once traffic passes the intersection, the RILs will extinguish.
- RILs illuminate for an aircraft that has landed and/or is rolling and there is high speed traffic on the intersecting runway that's within 5 seconds of meeting at the intersection. Once traffic passes, the RILs will extinguish.
- If you observe RILs illuminate, you will stop before LAHSO bars or the hold short line for the intersecting runway.

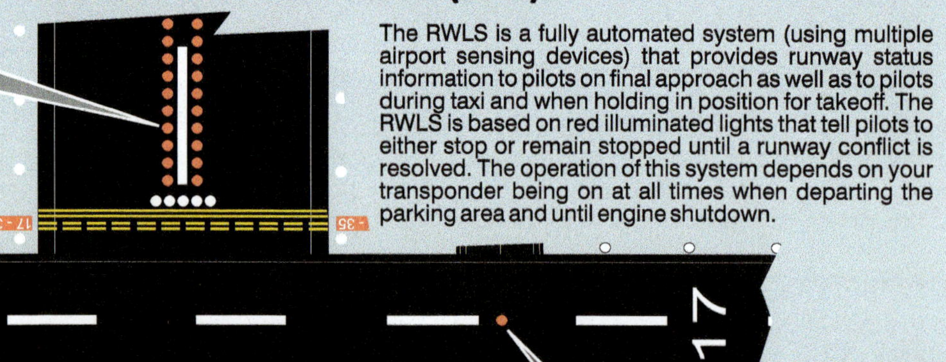

RELs consist of one light before the hold line followed by a series of evenly spaced lights to the runway edge. One additional light is located in line with other lights at runway centerline

NOTE: The RWLS system uses *Airport Surface Detection Equipment* (ASDE). Therefore, at any airport (with or without ASDE), your transponder should be on "ALT" mode at all times when moving on the airport surface.

Takeoff Hold Lights (THL)

- Flush mounted lights directed toward the arriving end of the runway at the line-up-and-wait point.
- THLs extend for 1,500 feet in front of holding aircraft.
- When illuminated (red color), THLs signal pilot that takeoff is unsafe because the runway is occupied by another aircraft or vehicle.
- Once other aircraft or vehicle exits runway, the red THL lights extinguish.
- When you observe red THLs illuminate, you should stop or remain stopped and contact ATC for a resolution if your clearance is in conflict with the lights.
- NOTE: When THLs extinguish, this is not a clearance for takeoff! Only ATC can give you a clearance for takeoff!

Runway Entrance Lights: REL

- RELs are flush mounted, one-directional red lights directed toward the pilot at the runway hold line.
- RELs turn red when activated, indicating that high speed traffic is on the runway or an aircraft is on final approach within the designated activation area.
- When departing traffic on Rwy 26 reaches 30 knots, all intersection RELs ahead of the aircraft turn red then extinguish 3-4 seconds before aircraft reaches RELs.
- When aircraft landing on Rwy 26 is one mile from the threshold, all RELs on Rwy 26 illuminate. Lights extinguish 3-4 seconds before aircraft approaches RELs.
- Pilots would see RELs illuminating then extinguishing in relation to an airplane or vehicle operating on runway.
- If you observe RELs illuminated red, you must stop at hold line or remain stopped (regardless of what your clearance says) and contact ATC to ask why your clearance is in conflict with illuminated lights.

Precision Approach Path Indicator Lights

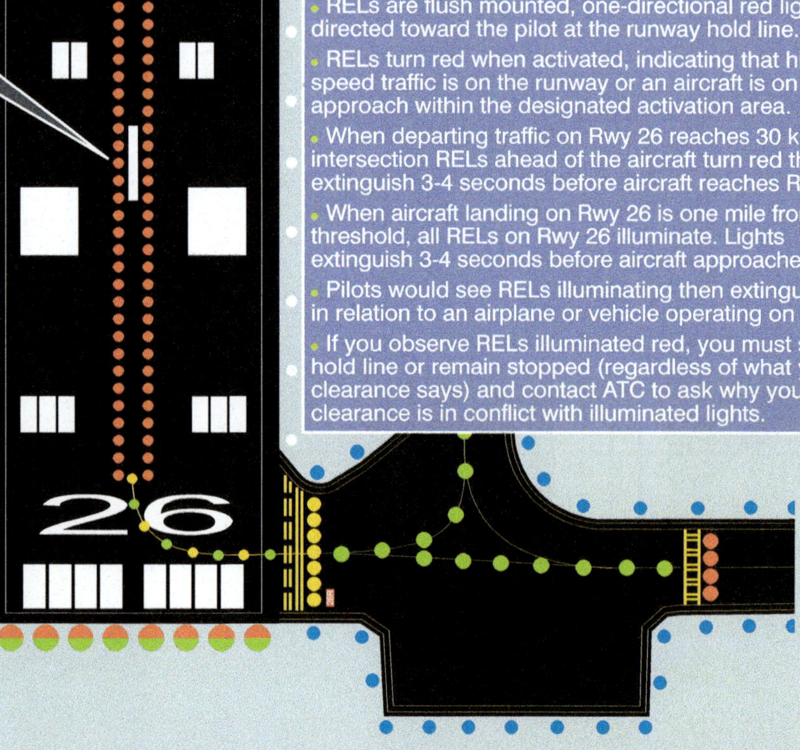

Final Approach Runway Occupancy Signal (FAROS)

- When activated, the PAPI lights flash or pulse to indicate to the pilot on final approach that the runway is occupied and may be unsafe for landing.
- PAPI lights will stop flashing or pulsing when traffic moves outside of the runway hold short lines.
- If PAPI lights are flashing, you must look for and acquire runway traffic at 500 feet AGL. At 300 feet AGL you must contact ATC for a resolution if PAPI are flashing.
- If PAPI is flashing below 300 feet AGL & pilot can't determine if safe to land, then he must immediately execute a go-around.

RIL, THS and REL are in-pavement flush lights. These lights have no distinct color when not illuminated; they are bright red when lit. ATC can adjust the settings of these lights to one of five brightness levels. Never cross illuminated red lights! Red means stop, so stop!

Postflight Briefing #7-4

GROUND REFERENCE MANEUVERS

Gettin' Down With the Ground

When does reference to the ground become important during flight training? If you answered, "When the pilot is close to it," then you've just found the second best answer. The very best answer is, *when a pilot tries to put his or her airplane on the ground*. I'm speaking of putting the airplane on the runway during a landing, of course. A landing is nothing more than the ultimate ground reference maneuver, and it's the primary reason we practice to gain proficiency in the following two maneuvers.

The Rectangular Course

One of the venerable ground reference maneuvers that all pilots learn is called the *rectangular course*. Its purpose is to show you how wind affects your operations in the airport traffic pattern and that's the reason I'm presenting it here.

You'll enter the maneuver at a 45 degree angle to the downwind leg (position 1). From here you'll turn and fly parallel to a previously chosen rectangular course (position 2), remaining a small horizontal distance from the course boundary. The horizontal offset chosen is primary determined by the steepness of the bank required while turning from one course leg to another.

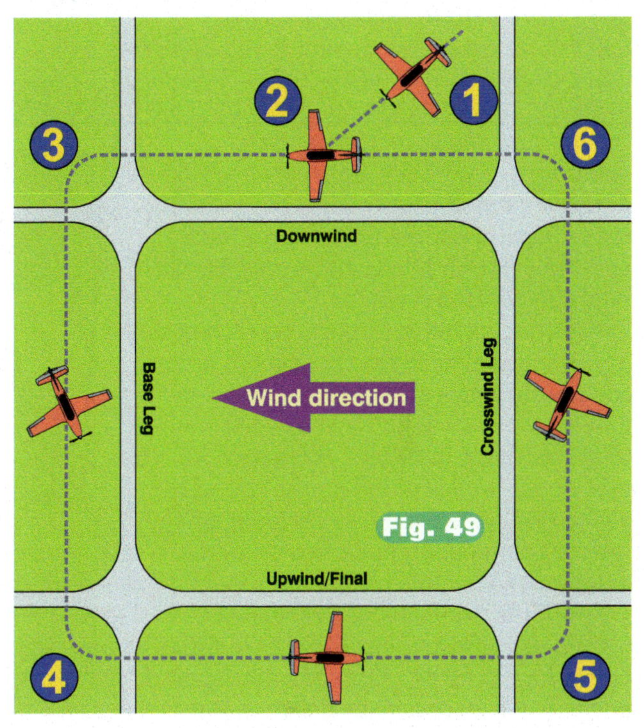

Fig. 49

On the turn from downwind to base leg (position 3) your groundspeed is the maximum experienced throughout the entire maneuver. Therefore, to remain the same distance from the course boundary, you'll initiate a steep bank that gradually transitions to a medium bank during the turn. Because you must crab into the wind to maintain the desired ground track, you must turn more than 90 degrees during downwind to base transition.

On the turn from base leg to final, you'll start with a medium bank then transition to a shallower bank angle since your groundspeed decreases as you turn into the wind. The base to upwind turn is less than 90 degrees since no crab angle is necessary on the upwind leg. When initiating a turn from upwind to crosswind, you'll start with a shallow bank then transition to a medium bank as your groundspeed increases slightly when turning away from the headwind. The turn here is less than 90 degrees. Finally, on the turn from crosswind to downwind, you'll turn more than 90 degrees and go from a medium bank to a steep bank as your groundspeed increases with the turn downwind.

S-Turns Across a Road

S-turns across a road looks like you're using the "catch and release" method of holding a heading. Actually, this is another one of those great ground reference maneuvers that sharpens your skills by having you fly half-circles on each side of a road that's perpendicular to the wind. You'll enter the maneuver by flying downwind (position 1). At position 2, your groundspeed is at its maximum, so you'll need the steepest bank angle to begin the turn. At position 3, the bank is shallower and the airplane crabs into the wind to maintain the lower half-circle track. At position 4 the wings are level as you cross the road and the groundspeed is at a minimum for this maneuver. You'll begin a shallow bank at this point, and maintain the half-circle track by crabbing the airplane into the wind through position 5. From position 5 to position 6, the bank angle increases to its maximum with an increase in groundspeed.

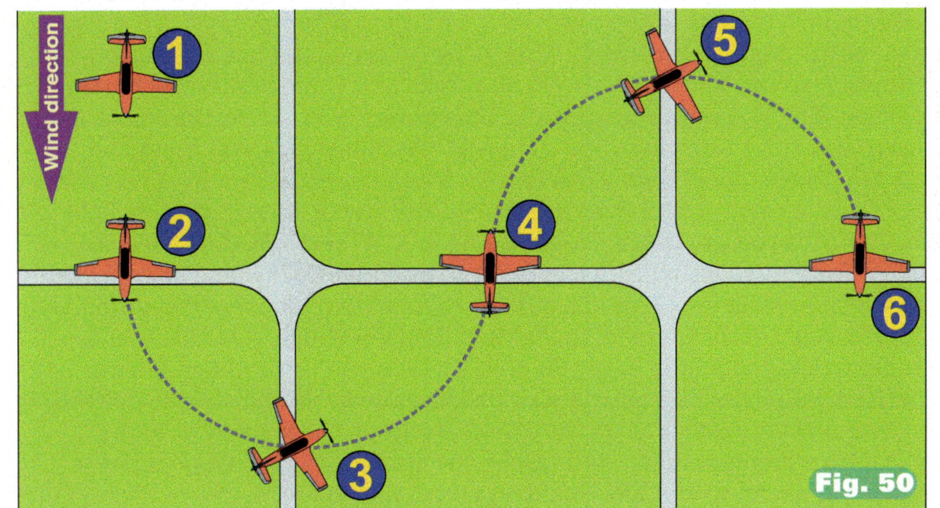

Fig. 50

Become proficient at this maneuver and no one will ever doubt your flying skills.

Postflight Briefing #7-5

AVOIDING RUNWAY INCURSIONS

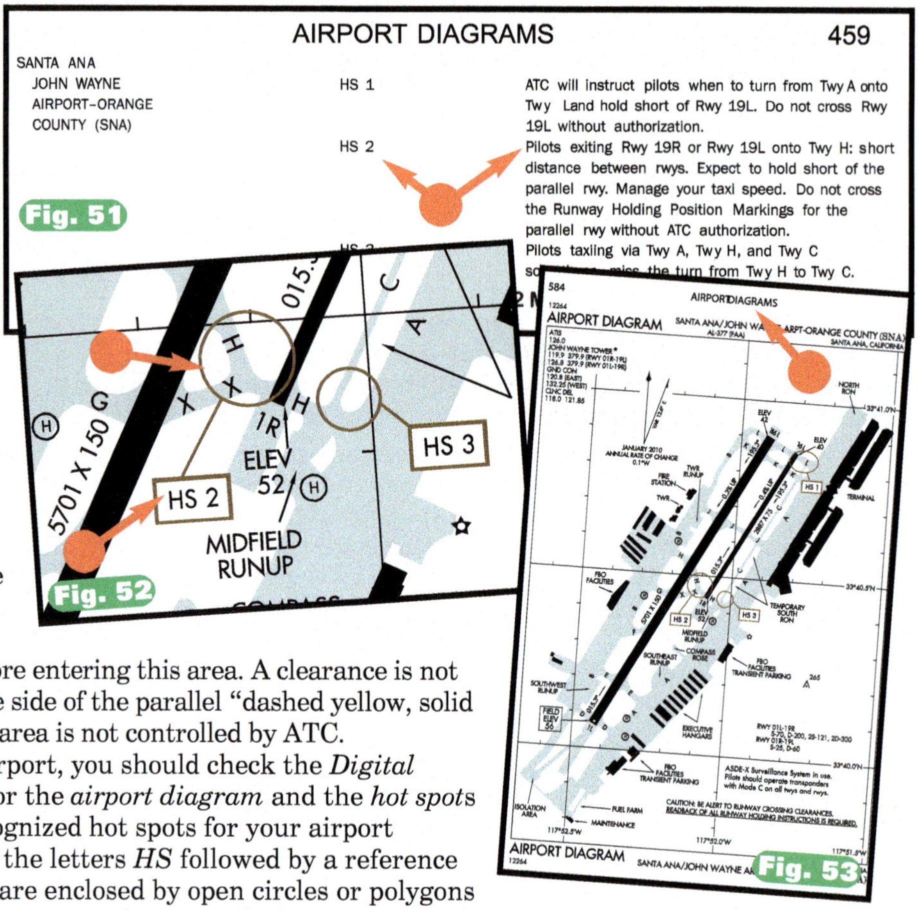

The FAA is very concerned about something known as runway incursions. They don't want airplanes to bump into each other (and not because airplane's don't have bumpers, either). Runway incursions are events involving the unauthorized presence of an aircraft, vehicle or person on a protected area designated for the landing and takeoff of aircraft. According to the FAA, approximately 65% of these incursions are caused by pilots, three-quarters of the 65% are caused by general aviation pilots. Let's see how we might avoid this problem.

AIRPORT DIAGRAMS 459

SANTA ANA
JOHN WAYNE
AIRPORT-ORANGE
COUNTY (SNA)

HS 1 ATC will instruct pilots when to turn from Twy A onto Twy Land hold short of Rwy 19L. Do not cross Rwy 19L without authorization.

HS 2 Pilots exiting Rwy 19R or Rwy 19L onto Twy H: short distance between rwys. Expect to hold short of the parallel rwy. Manage your taxi speed. Do not cross the Runway Holding Position Markings for the parallel rwy without ATC authorization.

Pilots taxiing via Twy A, Twy H, and Twy C

Fig. 51

Fig. 52

Fig. 53

Tower controlled airports have their airport surface divided into movement areas such as taxiways and runways, and non-movement areas such as ramps, aprons, etc. (See Postflight Briefing 7-2, position O.) The movement area is found on the side of the dashed yellow line and is controlled by the tower. You must obtain a taxi clearance before entering this area. A clearance is not necessary to taxi in the area on the solid-line side of the parallel "dashed yellow, solid yellow" line (the non-movement area). This area is not controlled by ATC.

When operating out of an unfamiliar airport, you should check the *Digital Chart Supplement* "supplemental" pages for the *airport diagram* and the *hot spots* page. The *hot spots* page describes any recognized hot spots for your airport (Figure 51). These are areas designated by the letters *HS* followed by a reference number on the airport diagram. Hot spots are enclosed by open circles or polygons on the airport diagram and are areas which are complex or confusing areas of taxiway or runway intersections offering increased risk of runway incursions for the unaware. Make sure you look closely at these areas before taxi and before landing. At John Wayne airport, for instance, HS 2 is an area between parallel runways where pilots have been known to turn off one runway and directly onto another without a clearance (Figure 52).

Once you're familiar with any hot spots that exist you'll want to use the airport diagram (Figure 53) to plot your assigned or planned taxi route to the departure runway. That's right. Run your finger along the route you were assigned as if it's a miniature airplane (just don't make the engine noise...unless you really want to).

If at any time you become uncertain about your position or the instructions you were given, ask ATC to say them again or request *progressive taxi instructions* (meaning that ATC will give you step-by-step taxi instructions).

ATC will normally give you a clearance to the departure runway. If ATC tells you to hold short of the runway, then you are required to read back all runway *hold short* instructions to the controller, verbatim. When cleared to a runway, I set the heading bug (on the DG) to the number of the departure runway. This helps ensure that when ATC clears me onto the runway, I'm actually on the correct runway (some runways intersect at a small angle and it's possible to confuse one with the other if you're not careful). When ATC wants you to taxi onto the runway, you'll hear the words *line up and wait*. And if you're waiting on the runway and don't hear anything from ATC for 90 seconds, call them and remind them of where you are. Yes, controllers are people too, and they can forget about you. Additionally, ATC wants pilots to state their position on the airport when calling the tower for takeoff from a runway intersection. This helps ensure that the tower controller knows precisely where you are instead of engaging in a "Where's Waldo?" scenario.

Whatever you do, don't taxi onto a runway unless you've been given clearance to do so. Period! Doing so becomes extremely dangerous if that runway is being used by another airplane. This is the reason that pilots are requested to illuminate all external airplane lights when crossing any runway (landing and taxi lights, nav lights, strobe lights, etc.). It simply makes it easier for other airplanes to see you just in case you aren't where you're supposed to be or someone else isn't where one of you should be. And when you line up and wait on the runway at night, do so a little to the left or right of the centerline. This makes your airplane easier to identify (and avoid) on the runway at night.

So keep your eyes open, ask ATC for clarification when necessary, and before you start taxiing, always use your airport diagram to make certain you know where you're going and how you are going to get there.

Chapter Eight

Radio Operations: Aviation Spoken Here

Controllers are real people, just like you and me.

I'm telling you this before we start talking about talking on the radio because the people you will usually be talking to on an aviation radio are controllers. For some reason the simple act of communicating with one strikes terror in the heart of most student pilots. Even lawyers become speechless when asked to push and talk.

Radios make us nervous because we're afraid of embarrassing ourselves. Mouthing a mistake when speaking to controllers who sound like radio announcers seems unbearable. It's voices like those of the controllers that got Noah into boat building and gave Moses the 10 Commandments.

It never fails to amaze me how normally-loquacious people can become completely tongue-tied when confronted by the microphone in an airplane. I've had student pilots who, on their first attempt at radio work, just moved their mouths without emitting a sound, kind of like a large goldfish at feeding time. I usually set a 30 second limit on such behavior for my students or they'll hyperventilate.

There are actually several factors at work here simultaneously. First, new pilots usually have their brains pretty well tied up with the mechanics of handling the airplane. They literally have trouble flying and talking at the same time. Second, there is a definite aviation language, and at first it does sound quite foreign. Nobody wants to say the *wrong* thing, so some student pilots hope to get around it by saying *nothing*.

It won't work. Communication is crucial, especially in today's increasingly-controlled airspace. I'm convinced that learning to fly might be the cure for teenagers who spend too much time on the phone. Nothing will shut them up quicker than telling them they have to talk.

Students, and even experienced pilots, often find it difficult to believe controllers will be nonjudgmental. As a result, it's easy to become self-conscious about our radio behavior. In fact, most controllers are eager to help beginners, and they'll do everything they can to assist you, including slowing down a bit if you ask.

Visit the tower and meet some real controllers. You'll see for yourself. As a courtesy, call in advance. Don't just show up and start banging on the tower. Given enough notice, they might let you plug in and listen to traffic under their control (but don't for a second think they'll let you control a few airplanes, even if you have Nintendo experience). As an added bonus, you'll gain some real insight into how the air traffic control function operates, and what can (and can't) be done and seen from the controller's perspective.

THE AIR TRAFFIC CONTROL TOWER

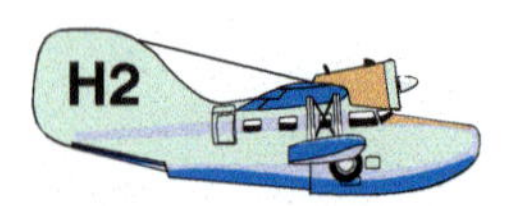

Radio Technique

Using the radio is no great mystery. When transmitting, move the mic close to your mouth (Figure 1). Don't slobber on it. Don't lick it. Just hold it close and speak in a normal voice. Whatever you do, don't yell. You'll blast the headset off the controllers' ears.

Fig. 1

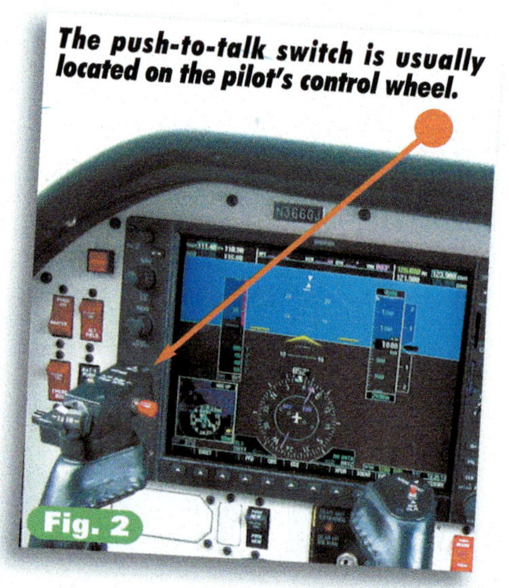

Fig. 2

Unlike telephones, aviation radios cannot transmit and receive at the same time. To transmit, simply push the microphone button and speak. To listen, you must let go of the button. With headsets, the process is the same. You simply push the *transmit button* to speak, and release it to listen. This button, sometimes called the *push-to-talk switch,* or *PTT,* is usually located on the flight control column as shown in Figure 2. Be careful. Sometimes the electric pitch-trim switch is located next to the radio's push-to-talk switch. One of my students accidentally confused these switches in the traffic pattern. Every time he called the tower, the airplane's nose dropped.

Many women and some men have high-pitched voices. The excitement of flying, mixed with the anxiety of talking to controllers, tends to raise such a voice an octave or two. Radios often provide another boost in pitch. You've now gone ultrasonic, and your voice is probably causing bats to fly into walls or killing cockroaches for hundreds of miles in every direction.

To avoid being cited by the SPCA, and shunned by others on the airwaves, it's a good idea to develop a *radio voice* that is deliberately lower in pitch. Emulate those deep-toned FM DJ's from late night radio. You may not believe this, but a controller once told me that he turned down a pilot's request for radar service (something it is within a controller's discretion to do under certain circumstances) just to keep this guy's screeching voice off the frequency.

The secret to sounding like a pro on the radio is knowing what you want to say, saying it in the shortest, most efficient manner, then getting off the microphone. Brevity is the hallmark of an experienced pilot. Follow Rod Machado's Linguistic Legerdemain Law which states:

- Speak low
- Tell' em only what they need to know
- Let go

Practice this by having your instructor write out on 3x5 cards all of the common communication statements you're likely to encounter. If you're operating at a controlled airport, these exchanges might include calls to ground control, to the tower for departure, to the tower for entry into the pattern, etc. Operating at an airport without an operating control tower, these statements might include departing advisory, traffic pattern position calls, etc.

How do you get good on the radio? Practice! Purchase a little VHF receiver (you can get them real cheap) and listen to the tower. Make recordings and listen to them over

Shhhh.

Over the years I've witnessed some unusual cockpit behavior relating to the radio. Once, while sitting in the runup area (a place where the engine and airplane are checked and readied for takeoff), I overheard the following exchange between a student and a tower controller who had a quick mind and wonderful sense of humor. The instructor was coaching his student on proper use of the radio when the student apparently keyed the microphone (pushed its button to transmit) before the instructor was finished giving directions. The following conversation in its entirety was transmitted over the airwaves:

Student (whispering): "What do I say? What do I say?"

Instructor (whispering): "Tell him you want to take off."

Student (in loud voice close to mike): "I want to take off."

Student (whispering): "What do I do now?"

Instructor (whispering): "Nothing. Let go of that button, dummy."

The controller, after hearing all this, decided to have a little fun.

Tower controller (whispering): "What do I say? What to I say?"

Same controller pretending to be another person (whispering): "Tell him he's cleared for takeoff."

Tower controller (in loud voice): "You're cleared for takeoff."

Tower controller (whispering): "What do I do now?"

Same controller pretending to be another person (whispering): "Nothing. Let go of that button, dummy."

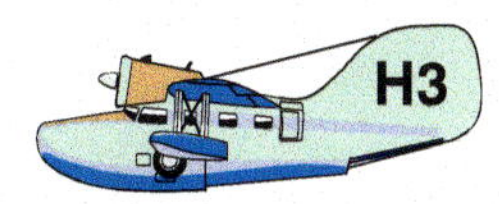

Listen to Learn and Learn to Listen

Learning good radio work is part and parcel of being a good pilot. One of the fastest ways to learn is to listen (that's a good general rule). Invest in a small battery-operated radio that receives aviation frequencies. Then listen to the tower controllers. Listen to the ground controllers. Listen to the ATIS. Listen whenever and wherever you can (in some urban areas you can pick up a dozen or more frequencies throughout the city; in other places you'll have to get near the local airport to listen in).

You can teach yourself to talk, too. Just don't do it on the radio. I know one person who used to practice in the shower. He'd give himself clearances to taxi, then acknowledge the transmission. He'd clear himself for takeoff, give himself permission to change frequencies, then he'd call up approach control and ask for in-flight traffic advisories, carefully providing his call sign, position, altitude and request. On some of his coast-to-coast shower flights his skin got a bit shriveled, but he was *very* good on the radio (especially while flying in the rain).

As in much of aviation, practice really does make perfect.

and over again. You can learn to listen and interpret at a rate 10 times the rate of normal speech with a 40% distortion of the transmission (to a student, this is exactly what controllers sound like). All it takes is practice.

If you find the controllers talking too fast for you, tell them you're a student pilot. When driving down the road and seeing an automobile with *student driver* written on the side, don't you watch it a little closer than the other cars? If it's swerving all over the place, you're sure to keep an eye on this target. Tower controllers do the same thing with student pilots.

I prefer that all my students inform ATC they are *students* by saying, "Tower, this is November 2132 Bravo, ready for takeoff, student pilot." At a local airport in California, I had a student with me who mentioned to the controller that he was a student pilot. Replying without missing a beat the controller said, "Hey, don't worry, I'm a student controller. We can mess each other up." Be advised, some controllers have a wild sense of humor.

VHF Transmissions

Aviation transmissions are usually on the very high frequency (VHF) portion of the radio spectrum. Like most things in life, this has its good and less-good points. Operation in this frequency range minimizes interference from atmospheric static and can provide excellent range. The downside is that the range is limited by the *line of sight* nature of VHF signals. There must be an unobstructed path between the transmitting antenna and the receiving antenna in order to communicate (Figure 3). While lower-frequency signals will bend and bounce, VHF is strictly point-to-point. Line-of-sight limitations are one of the biggest problems pilots face in communicating. The solution is to climb. The higher you are, the less chance there is of some obstacle interfering with your radio's reach.

The Federal Communications Commission (FCC) assigns frequencies ranging from 118.0 MHz to 135.975 MHz for aviation use. (*Hertz* is the international unit for frequency. One *Hertz* is one cycle per second. One *megahertz*, abbreviated MHz, is one million cycles per second.) VHF radio frequencies are spaced at 25,000 Hertz (.025 MHz) intervals: 118.000, 118.025, 118.050, etc. All radio frequencies have six digits even though it's not apparent that we're using all six of them. For instance, the frequency of 118.0 MHz is actually 118.000 MHz and 118.05 is MHz is actually 118.050 MHz.

If you're using a handheld microphone, please be careful about where you place it. When it's not in use, put the mic on the hook where it belongs. When it's not being used, don't lay it between your legs. One pilot put the mic between his legs while landing at a very busy airport. Everything after that he said with a thigh. From base to landing, this mic man radiated his landing commentary to the world—and blocked the frequency for everyone else. All the tower heard was, "I can't believe it, what a bad landing, I'm so messed up, I'm really messed up, UH-OOOH!"

Realizing what had happened, the pilot put the microphone back where it belonged. The controller said, "Aircraft that's messed up, please repeat your call number." The pilot came back with, "I may be messed up, but I'm not that messed up."

VHF (very high frequency) transmissions are "line of sight," meaning that there must be no obstacles between the transmitting and receiving stations. Airplane A has line of sight with station C, airplane B doesn't. Therefore, if the pilot of airplane B is having trouble receiving or transmitting, he or she should climb.

High Tech Radios

Many of the radios found in today's technically advanced airplanes are part of the avionics GPS package. Garmin's 530 GPS unit is a popular radio-navigation package commonly found in many airplanes today (Figure 4). The 530, for instance, contains not only a GPS unit, but also a VHF communications transmitter/receiver and a VHF navigation receiver. Using the two knobs in position A, you can select a communication frequency in window B or VHF navigation frequency in window C. Frequency switching buttons (positions D and E) allow you to move the frequency from the *standby* position of either window (the frequency on the bottom of the two) to the *active* position of that window (the frequency on top).

Of course, some pilots prefer to have two *separate* communication radios in their airplane, thus keeping one of their standard VHF radios as a backup (Figure 5, position F).

Fig. 4

Fig. 5

Radio Equipment

Figure 6 shows a radio typical of those found in most general aviation airplanes. The control at position A consists of a small knob on top of a bigger knob. These knobs are used to select the frequency seen in the window (C). On some radios, there are two windows; the *active frequency* (the one you're currently transmitting and receiving on) is on the left; the window on the right shows the *standby frequency*. Pushing a button (D) swaps what's in the two windows. This arrangement allows you to select a frequency and keep it in standby until needed. Even better, it keeps the frequency you just signed off of handy in case nobody is home when you call on the new frequency (sometimes controllers hand out the wrong frequency, or pilots mishear what they're told).

Button B is the on/off/volume control. Turning it clockwise turns the radio on and increases the volume. Of course, if nobody is talking it's difficult to know how loud is loud enough. Pulling the volume button all the way out usually activates the *squelch mode*. The squelch provides a pilot with the sound of static, which can be used to set the volume level (young student pilots will notice that this static is very similar to the tunes of certain heavy metal bands). Once the volume level is set, you simply push the button in to deactivate the squelch mode.

Talking the Talk

College professors sound like college professors; engineers sound like engineers; and pilots sound like pilots. If you are going to be a pilot, you will want to talk the talk. It won't do much in terms of providing lift for the airplane, but it will provide considerable lift for the pilot. If you hear the controller laughing hysterically after you've said something, it doesn't improve your pilot self-image (by the way, they don't really laugh hysterically).

As I've pointed out earlier, aviation has its own language. *Avspeak* consists of acronyms, special vocabulary, and particular shorthand ways of saying things. Much of this has evolved because of the need to communicate on the radio, where it's essential to communicate a lot while saying little.

You'll learn avspeak as you go along, but I want to provide a few basics so you can start sounding good from the get go.

The first and most important item is identifying yourself. Remember, controllers can't see you over the radio, and they hate guessing games.

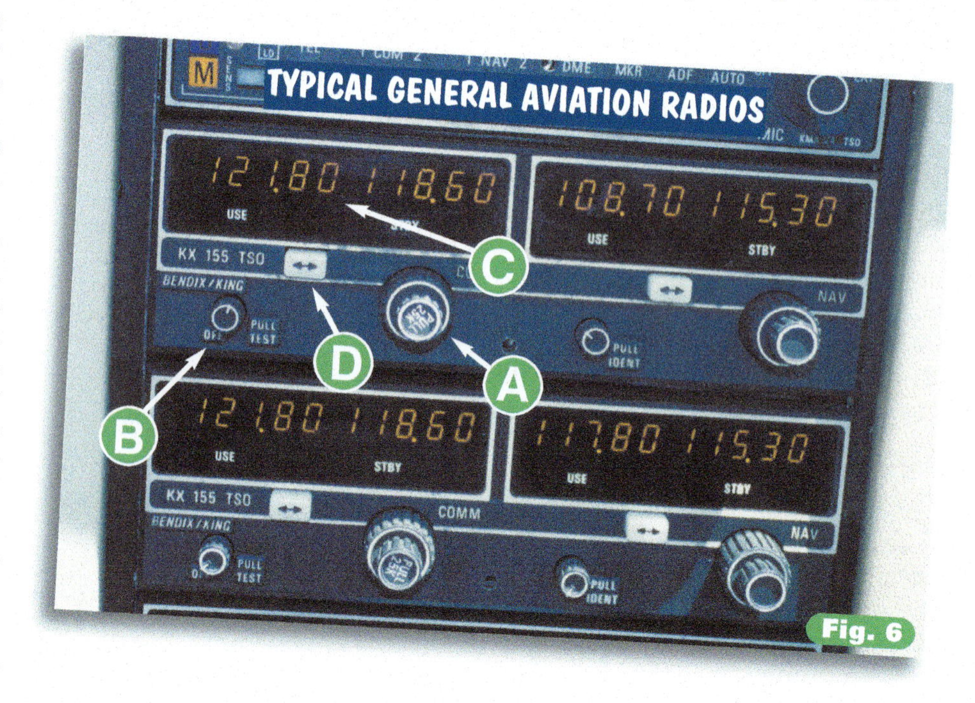

Fig. 6

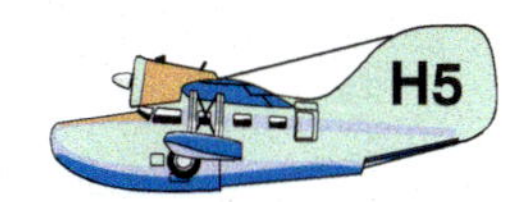

Frequent Flyer Frequencies

The following is a partial list of common aviation communication frequencies. You don't have to memorize all of these, though you should commit the ones **in boldface** to memory, because they're people you need to communicate with for critical information or at critical times.

118.0 to 135.975 MHz - Air Traffic Control general frequency range

121.5 MHz - Emergency frequency and ELT's

121.6 to 121.9 MHz - Ground control at tower airports

122.1 MHz - Flight Service (FS) receive-only and transmit other frequency

122.2 MHz - Flight Service common enroute frequency

122.7 MHz - Unicom at airports without an operating control tower

122.725 MHz - Unicom at airports without an operating control tower

122.75 MHz - Air-to-air communications (private fixed wing aircraft)

122.8 MHz - Unicom at airports without an operating control tower

122.9 MHz - Self-announce on Multicom at airports with no tower or unicom

122.925 MHz - Multicom, forestry management and fire suppression, fish and game management and protection and environmental monitoring and protection

122.95 MHz - Unicom at airports with a control tower

122.975 MHz - Unicom at airports without an operating control tower

123.0 MHz - Unicom at airports without an operating control tower

123.025 MHz - Air-to-air communication general aviation helicopters

123.05 and 123.075 MHz - Airports without an operating control tower.

123.3 MHz - Aviation instruction, glider, hot air balloon (not an advisory service)

123.5 MHz - Aviation instruction, glider, hot air balloon (not an advisory service)

You'll have to tell them who you are. Actually, they're not interested in who *you* are; they want to know the number of the airplane they're talking to. Controllers don't really talk to people, they talk to airplanes. So don't expect statements like, "OK Bob, cleared to land Bob, and Bob, contact ground control after you've cleared the runway. Have a good day Bob."

Suppose your aircraft number is N794CT and you want to call an ATC facility. Using the phonetic alphabet I described in Chapter 7, your call would be:

"Ontario Approach, this is Cessna seven niner four Charlie Tango, over."

The prefix *N* is dropped when the aircraft manufacturer's name or model number is stated. After initial communication is established, ATC may use an abbreviated call sign and refer to your aircraft by the prefix N and your last three digits or letter. In the above example, ATC may refer to you as *November four Charlie Tango,* or more commonly just *four Charlie Tango.*

Knowing how to refer to yourself on the radio is a good starting point in learning to talk avspeak. By the way, most aircraft have their call sign posted on a small placard somewhere among the instruments, or right above them. Many pilots fly multiple aircraft — especially instructors — so it's handy to be able to look and know who you are at the moment!

When informing ATC of your altitude, aviation phraseology should be used in the following manner (I'll assume that you are flying below 18,000' MSL):

If your altitude is 6,500 feet, state this as *six thousand five hundred.*

If your altitude is 10,500 feet, state this as *one zero thousand five hundred.*

If you're referring to a frequency like 125.6 MHz, it's properly stated as *one two five point six.* Decimals are identified by the word *point.*

Over is often used at the end of a transmission, although it is not essential if the context and pattern of your communication makes it obvious when you're done talking. When you use *over* at the end of your statements, it means that a reply is expected. It's also an effective way of telling the receiving party that you're done talking. If we were to use such language at a cocktail party, there would be much less confusion about

Tower, I Don't Know Who I Am...

A student reported downwind during a slow traffic morning at Riverside airport. The small plate with the airplane's identification number had fallen off the panel and he couldn't remember his aircraft call. The transmission went like this:

Student: "Ah Riverside tower, this is November... ahhh, ahhh, ahhh, I don't know who I am."
Tower: "Whoever doesn't know who they are, what's your name if you have one?"
Student: "My name is Bob, I'm at your airport and I still don't know who I am."
Tower: "We know who you are. You are Bob and you're cleared to land, over."
Student: "Tower, this is Bob, I understand I'm cleared to land. Thank you."
Tower: "Ah Bob, after landing, you're cleared to taxi to your destination so you can find yourself, over."
Student: "This is Bob, roger, wilco."

A wise man says, "Pilot who doesn't know who he is, probably doesn't know where he's at."

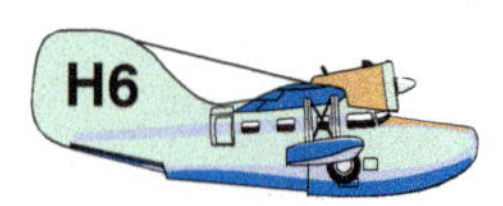

who's still talking. "Well Bob, how are you doing, over?" "To tell you the truth Frank, I'm not sure, over."

The word *roger* is used to let the transmitting party know their transmission has been received. It should not be used to answer a question requiring a *yes* or *no* answer. Speaking of *yes* and *no,* these become *affirmative* and *negative* in avspeak. Once again, the goal is to create clarity and eliminate (as much as possible) any chance of confusion. *No* can sound like too many other words when said over an aviation radio, which degrades speech considerably (no matter how silver-tongued you are). *Yes* could be *I guess,* or *What a mess.*

When the tower says to do something and you agree that you can and will accept the instruction, the proper response is *wilco,* which means you have received the message, understand it and *will comply*. Sometimes pilots are a little lazy and use *roger* instead of *wilco*. I can assure you that the words *roger dodger* are not part of the aviation communication lingo, so please don't use them. If you're carrying around any leftover CB lingo, get your ears on for a second good buddy, and listen up. Drop it, lest you become the laughingstock of the aviation airwaves.

Flight Service Station is a nice name, but a bit long for throwing around on the radio. That's why we call a Flight Service Station *Radio*. Hawthorne FSS becomes *Hawthorn Radio* on a radio call.

Other ground stations have their own nomenclature:

Airport unicom ..... *Corona Unicom.*

EFAS - Enroute flight Advisory Service (Flight Watch) ..... *Hawthorne Flight Watch.*

Air Traffic Control Tower ..... *Lambert Tower.*

Ground Control ..... *Boise Ground.*

Clearance Delivery ..... *Ontario Clearance Delivery.*

Approach Control ..... *New York Approach.*

Departure Control .... *St. Louis Departure.*

Air Route Traffic Control Center ..... *Miami Center.*

Some instructors have a very unusual way of helping their students overcome radio fright.

Trapped by the Talk

A man comes home and thinks his wife has been messing around with the airline pilot who lives down the street. He confronts her and says:

Man: "Hey Betty, have you been messing around with that pilot down the street?"
Betty: "Negative."
Man: "Are you sure you haven't?"
Betty: "That's affirmative, over."

Then there's the matter of time. Pilots have lots of it. *Zulu* or *UTC (coordinated universal time)* time is the time in Greenwich, England. Who cares? You do, because many aviation times are stated as Zulu (or Z) times. Weather reports are stated in Zulu time, and the flight plans you file will give departure and arrival times in Zulu time. By using a clock in one place, pilots who sometimes cross large amounts of space in a relatively brief period don't wrestle with local time zones and conversions. When it's 0300 Zulu, it's 0300 Zulu *everywhere in the world,* although what it comes out to be in *local time* varies.

Another type of pilot time is the 24-hour clock (like that used in the military). In this system, the hours of the day are numbered from 1 to 24; 1 a.m. is 0100 hours, and 1 p.m. is 1300 hours. Local time is expressed on the 24 hour clock in aviation. Of course, this can be a bit of a mystery to non-aviators. One time I was on my way out of a parking garage. The young attendant looked at my ticket, subtracted 1300 (1 p.m., when I'd entered) from 1500 (3 p.m., when I was leaving) and announced the bill as 200 hours times $3/hour, for a total of $600. No checks or credit cards accepted (ouch!).

There's lots more avtalk to learn, but this will get you started.

Controlled Airports

As you learned in Chapter 7, some airports have control towers and others don't. The purpose of a control tower is to manage the flow of traffic into and out of the airport. The government usually installs a control tower when there is enough traffic to justify its existence. You can reasonably assume that an airport graced with a tower is (or has the potential to be) a busy place.

Most towers are staffed by at least two controllers at any time—one to control airborne traffic, and one to control ground traffic (and perform other duties). The ground controller is responsible for seeing that planes don't have any unexpected meetings on the ground, and that they don't intrude unexpectedly onto runways. That's why pilots are required to call and obtain permission—a *clearance*—before taxiing the airplane beyond specific areas at a controlled field.

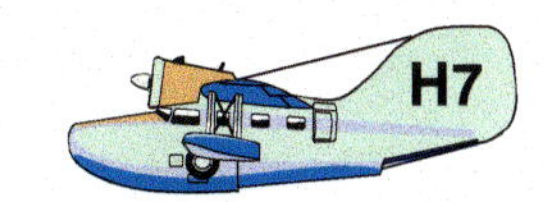

When making your initial call to ground control, you will usually have listened to the ATIS recording. You'll tell the controller you have *information Bravo,* and he or she will clear you to taxi to the runway or some intermediate point. If it's a very large airport, you might be given a specific routing via particular taxiways.

Ground control frequencies are usually between 121.6 MHz and 121.9 MHz. After landing, it's not unusual to hear the controller say, *32 Bravo, contact ground point niner.* They're assuming that you know the beginning part of the frequency is *121* for 121.9 MHz. I realized how confusing this could be when one of my students, having just landed, taxied off the runway when the tower controller said, "32 Bravo, contact ground point six." He sat there, twirling the radio's frequency dial. I said, "Bob, what are you doing?" He replied, "I'm trying to get these first three numbers to go away." I immediately loosened his tie, thinking it might be restricting the flow of oxygenated blood to his brain.

After you've landed and taxied off the runway, don't automatically switch from tower to ground control frequency. Wait until you've been advised by the tower controller to do so. The tower controller may need you to maneuver on the taxiway to make room for other airplanes. If you're on a different frequency, you won't hear these instructions.

Some busier airports have an additional person in the tower known as a clearance delivery controller (we'll explain more about this controller later in this chapter). Essentially, he or she is the person providing you with detailed instructions on how to depart that airport's airspace (typically Class C or B airspace). These instructions are essential when specific routes or departure procedures are necessary for traffic management.

I Have Hotel

If you don't listen to the ATIS, then the controller must spend additional time giving you information. This results in the clogging of the airwaves, to the inconvenience of all pilots. One fellow, obviously an out-of-towner, called John Wayne (Orange County, California) tower and commandeered the frequency. He said, "John Wayne tower, this is 2132 Bravo, we're 15 miles south of the airport for landing. We got mom, dad and a few kids and are planning on having a good time, hope we can..." (on and on and on).

John Wayne is a very busy urban airport with considerable commercial traffic, and the controller was stunned at the thought of a few big jets running into each other because this guy was yakking his head off.

Finally the pilot let up and the controller asked, "32 Bravo, do you have information Hotel?"

"Naw," said Mr. Visitor, "we won't be needing no hotel, you see we got us a big mobile home ....blah, blah, blah."

And we wonder why controllers act weird sometimes.

Control Tower Communications

Figure 7 shows how control tower frequencies are portrayed on an aeronautical sectional chart. Columbia Regional's control tower frequency is 119.3 MHz. The *(CT)* identifies this as the tower frequency. The ATIS is found on 128.45 MHz. There is a unicom station at the field on 122.95 MHz (this is the unicom frequency for an airport with a control tower or FSS on the field). You can call for fuel, transient parking availability, or other general information on the unicom frequency. It's usually staffed by one of the large FBO's (fixed based operators) having fuel services on the field. The small star next to the control tower's frequency means this tower is in operation only part time (usually closed from late evening until early morning).

At the bottom of every aeronautical sectional chart is a listing of the towers' hours of operation, ground and tower frequencies, ATIS frequencies, as well as ASR or PAR radar information for each airport, as shown in Figure 8. (ASR—Airport Surveillance Radar and PAR—Precision Approach Radar are services that provide radar guidance to the very beginning of the runway.) Columbia Regional's tower is in operation from 0700 to 2300 local

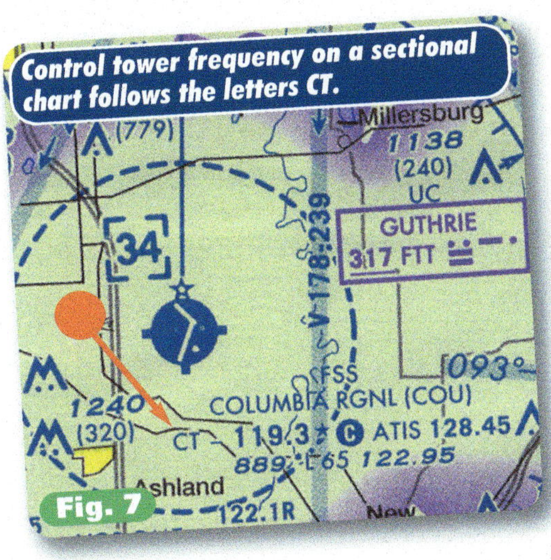

Control tower frequency on a sectional chart follows the letters CT.

Fig. 7

Tower information is shown on a tab of the sectional chart.

CONTROL TOWER FREQUENCIES ON KANSAS CITY SECTIONAL CHART

Airports which have control towers are indicated on this chart by the letters CT followed by the primary VHF local control frequency. Selected transmitting frequencies for each control tower are tabulated in the adjoining spaces, the low or medium transmitting frequency is listed first followed by a VHF local control frequency, and the primary VHF and UHF military frequencies, when these frequencies are available. An asterisk (*) follows the part-time tower frequency remoted to the collocated full-time FSS for use as Local Airport Advisory (LAA) during hours tower is closed. Hours shown are local time. Ground control frequencies listed are the primary ground control frequencies.

Automatic Terminal Information Service (ATIS) frequencies, shown on the face of the chart are primary arrival VHF/UHF frequencies. All ATIS frequencies are listed below. ATIS operational hours may differ from control tower operational hours.

ASR and/or PAR indicates Radar Instrument Approach available.

"MON-FRI" indicates Monday thru Friday.

CONTROL TOWER	OPERATES	TWR FREQ	GND CON	ATIS	ASR/PAR
BILLARD NF	0700-1900	118.7 257.8	121.9		
COLUMBIA REGIONAL	0700-2300	119.3*	121.6	128.45	
DRAKE	0600-2200	128.0 371.9	121.8	133.1	ASR
FORBES	0545-2200	120.8 255.9	121.7 275.8	128.25	
FORNEY AAF	0830-1630 MON-FRI	125.4 241.0		118.7 237.5	

Fig. 8

The Chart Supplement

COLUMBIA RGNL (COU)(KCOU) 10 SE UTC–6(–5DT) N38°49.04′ W92°13.08′ KANSAS CITY
889 B ARFF Index—See Remarks NOTAM FILE COU H–5D, L–27B
RWY 02–20: H6501X150 (CONC–GRVD) S–92, D–125, 2S–159, IAP, AD
2D–215 PCN 26 R/D/W/T HIRL
RWY 02: MALSR. RVR–T
RCO 122.65 (CO
®MIZZU APP/DEP CON 124.375
TOWER 119.3 (1300–0300Z‡) GND CON 121.6
AIRSPACE: CLASS D svc 1300–0300Z‡ other times CLASS E.
RADIO AIDS TO NAVIGATION: NOTAM FILE COU.
(L) VORW/DME 110.2 COU Chan 39 N38°48.65′ W92°13.10′ at fld. 883/0E HIWAS.
VOR unusable:

Fig. 10

The operational hours of the control tower at Columbia Regional airport are provided in the Chart Supplement and are referenced as Zulu or UCT.

time (7 a.m. to 11 p.m.). Operational hours of the tower can also be found in the *Chart Supplement* (or *digital Chart Supplement*) as shown in Figure 9 (more on the *Chart Supplement* later). The *Chart Supplement* for Columbia Regional airport (Figure 10, position A) indicates that the control tower is in operation from 1300 to 0300 Zulu (UTC or coordinated universal time). Keep in mind that the operational hours of the tower posted on a sectional chart are referenced to local time while the *Chart Supplement* posts these hours in Zulu.

In addition to the tower frequency, the *Chart Supplement* is where you can find the frequency for ground control and clearance delivery (should one exist at this airport). Keep in mind that the *Chart Supplement* can often be purchased as a booklet from your local pilot supplier or downloaded free from the FAA's web site. It's also available as part of a subscription service for many of the flight planning softwares used on cockpit tablet computers (iPads, iPhones, Android phones or tablets, etc.).

Suppose you want to call a Leidos Flight Service facility while enroute for weather information? It's true that uplinked weather information is available to pilots using ADS-B (covered in Chapter 17) or some other weather service such as XM Weather, however, you can obtain weather directly from a weather specialist at Leidos Flight Service. (Leidos Flight Service is the result of the FAA's consolidation of its many individual Flight Service Stations that once existed across the country, occasionally residing on an airport.)

Figure 11, position A, shows a sectional chart excerpt of Austin-Straubel airport. Position B shows a blue-lined VOR frequency box (VORs will be covered in Chapter 11). Below the frequency box in an "L" shaped support brackets is the name "Green Bay" shown at position C. On top of the box are several VHF frequencies: 122.2 MHz and 122.55 MHz (243.0 and 255.4 are UHF frequencies that you don't use). These are the frequencies used to contact Leidos Flight Service when you are near Green Bay VOR.

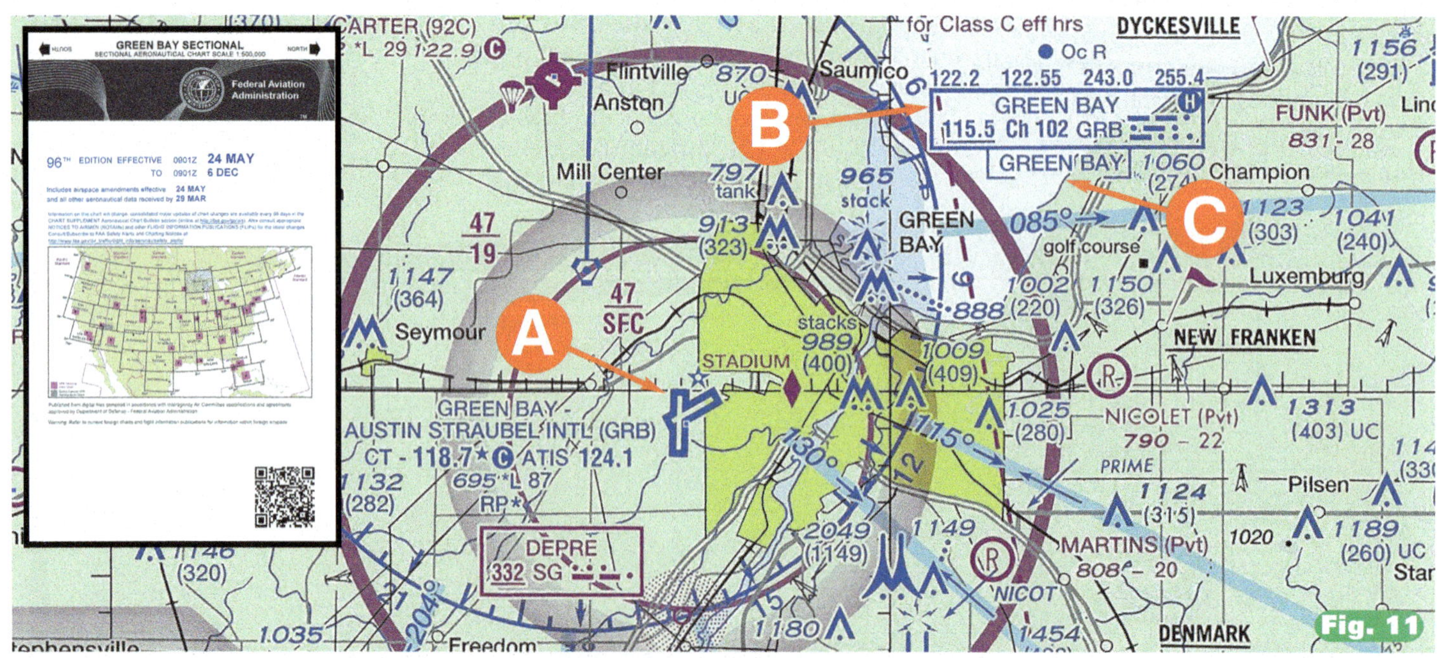

To communicate with a Leidos Flight Service specialist while in the Green Bay area use any one of the frequencies shown above the Green Bay VOR box (position B). Address the Leidos specialist as "Green Bay radio."

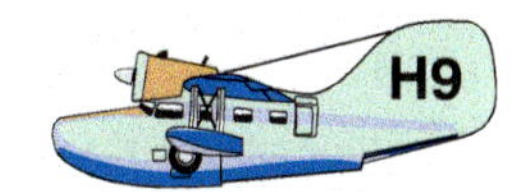

The name "Green Bay" underneath the VOR frequency box is the Leidos Flight Service facility responsible for providing weather and general flight information to pilots in the Green Bay area. No, Green Bay is not where the Leidos Flight Service facility is located. Leidos facilities are located at three hubs (soon to be two hubs) in the United States (one in Leesburg, VA and the other in Fort Worth, Texas with a hub in Prescott, AZ that's soon to be decommissioned). The name "Green Bay" simply tells you how to address the Leidos Flight Service Specialist when initiating communication for aviation information.

To make contact with Leidos, you'd simply transmit and receive on 122.2 MHz or 122.55 MHz and say, "Green Bay Radio, this is Cessna 2132 Bravo on one two two point two, Green Bay VOR, over." Notice that we tell the Leidos specialist what frequency we're using. Why? Unlike a typical tower controller, the Leidos specialist is often monitoring several frequencies that broadcast and receive over a large geographic area. If you don't announce which one you're on and your general location (i.e., Green Bay VOR) then the specialist might have to push five transmitter buttons saying, "Hello? Hello? Hello? Hello? Hello?" before finding you.

Flight Service Frequencies

Another means of communicating directly with Leidos Flight Service is shown above the Waycross VOR frequency box of Figure 12. The 122.1R above the box (position A) means that Macon Radio (the Leidos specialist in charge of this area) receives on this frequency. To communicate with Macon, you'd simply transmit on 122.1 MHz and listen on the VOR frequency of 110.2 MHz (the *R* stands for "receives" so don't look for an *R* on the radio dial). Your transmission should go something like this: "Macon radio, this is Cessna 2132 Bravo, on one two two point one, listening Waycross VOR, over." The Leidos

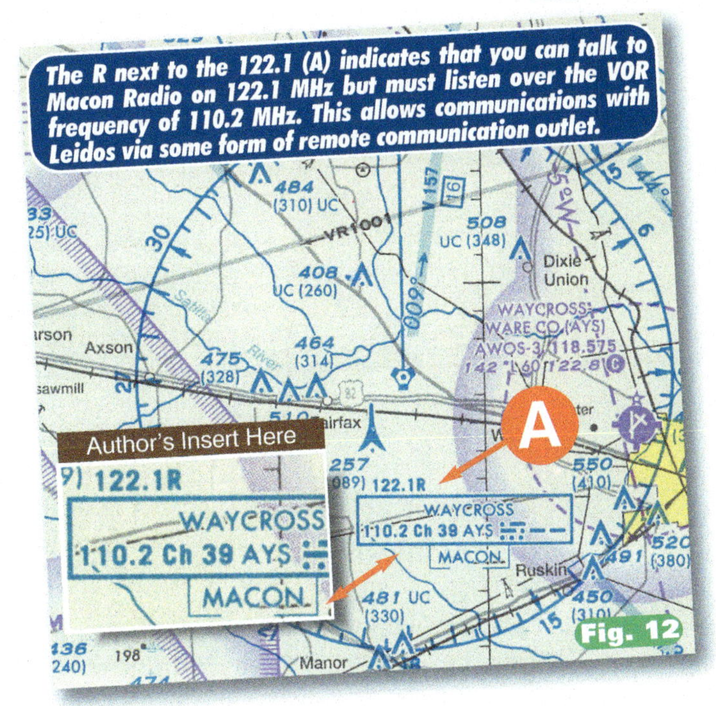

specialist would immediately know which transmitter to use. You simply turn the VOR receiver volume up and listen to Leidos Flight Service on the VOR frequency while transmitting on 122.1 MHz.

Figure 13 and 14 show that VOR frequencies for the El Dorado VOR (position A) and Julian VOR (position B) are underlined. An underline means no voice is available on this frequency. Fortunately, you don't need to listen over the VOR frequency when communicating with either Jonesboro or San Diego radio. Remember, underlining usually means someone is trying to attract your attention to something. That's why I don't have a mustache. My wife said, "With a nose that big, why underline it?"

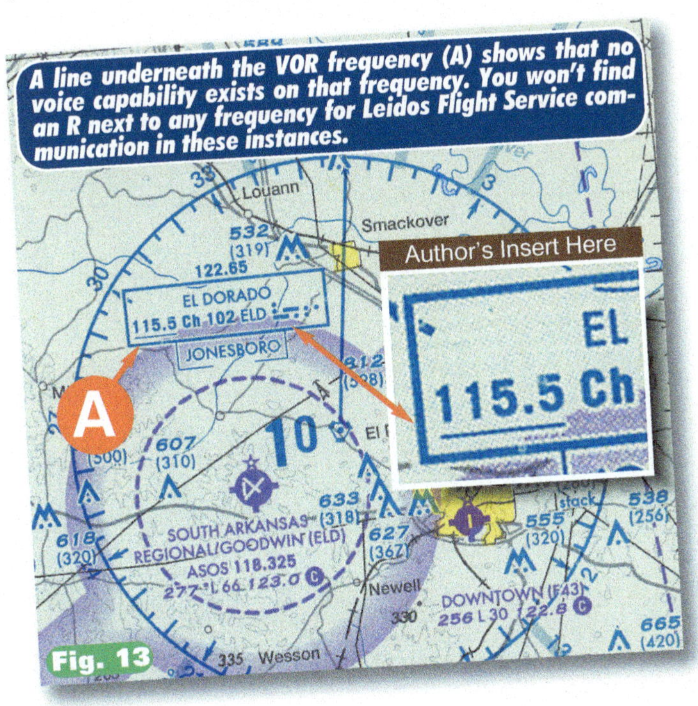

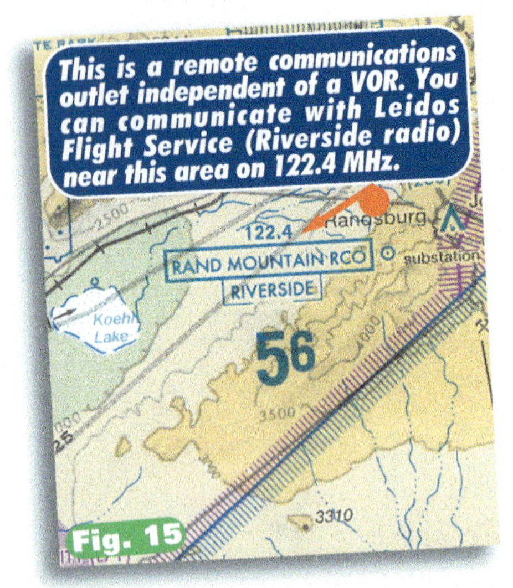

Figure 15 shows an RCO (remote communication outlet). This is a communication outlet separate from a VOR. In other words, at some locations the Leidos Flight Service specialist can only transmit over a VOR frequency while you transmit on 122.1 MHz. It's true that this method of communication is a relic from the earlier days of aviation. At some locations, however, there are dedicated remote communication outlets (RCOs) such as Rand Mountain. This RCO is a remote transmitter and receiver that connects you to a distant facility. In this instance, you can communicate with Riverside radio (Leidos) through the RCO even though you're some distance away.

If you were near this site you would simply dial 122.4 MHz on your communications radio and make the following call: "Riverside Radio, this is Cessna 2132 Bravo, on one two two point four, listening Rand Mountain, over." Give the Leidos specialist a few seconds (perhaps even a minute or longer) to establish communication. Be patient. These folks at Leidos may be talking with other pilots who you can't hear because they're on a different frequency.

Not knowing how to find and use all the communication frequencies available is a little like not knowing what all the dials and buttons in the cockpit do. Not smart. Not safe. Not fun. It's very comforting to have someone to call on when you're not certain what the weather's doing up ahead, or if your engine starts sounding a bit unusual a million miles from anywhere. Modern communications capabilities mean you will rarely be out of calling range of *someone,* as long as you know how to read the available information and put it to use.

ASOS and AWOS

Sounds like the two guys Simon and Garfunkel wouldn't let into their band, doesn't it? Your ability to obtain weather information while airborne is what separates you from early 20th century barnstormers

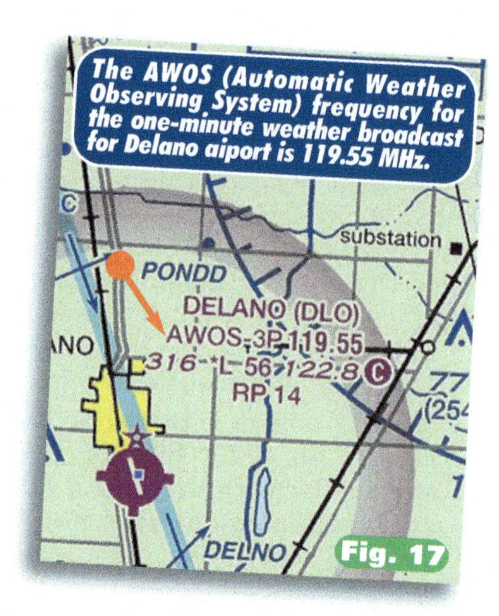

(OK, you also don't wear scarfs and goggles while flying. Or do you?). The only way these pilots obtained the weather was by looking outside their open cockpit biplane. While we'll talk in detail about all the weather services available to you shortly, there is one source of recorded weather that provides you with minute-by-minute local weather within 25 NMs of an airport from the surface up to 10,000 feet AGL. This service is known as ASOS (Automated Surface Observing System) or AWOS (Automated Weather Observing System).

You'll see frequencies for these ASOS or AWOS stations on sectional and terminal charts near the airport

Switch Hitter

We'll be discussing the use of VOR equipment for navigation a bit later, but it has a non-navigation feature you need to know about. Figure 16 shows a typical VOR receiver in the airplane. It has a switch with three positions: OFF, VOICE, IDENT.

Every VOR transmits a three-letter, Morse code identifier which permits you to confirm that what you see in the frequency window is what you've got. To receive the VOR's Morse code identification, you simply switch to the *IDENT* position. In this position, the Morse code is emphasized and voice transmissions (if any) can be heard weakly in the background.

The *VOICE* position is used to move voice transmissions to center stage and quiet the Morse code. This is the position in which you leave the switch whenever you are receiving or are expecting to receive voice transmissions over the VOR's frequency.

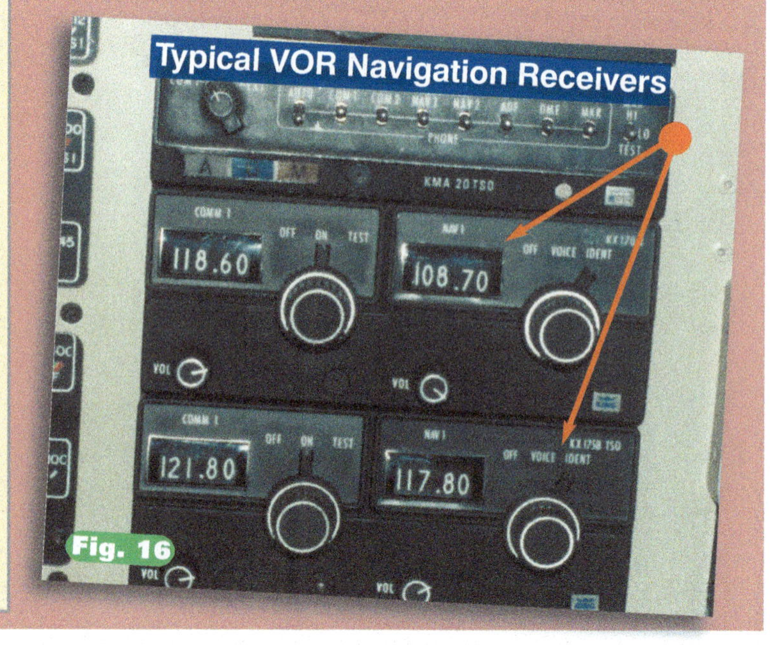

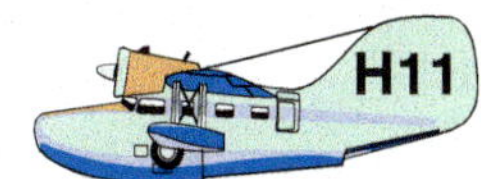

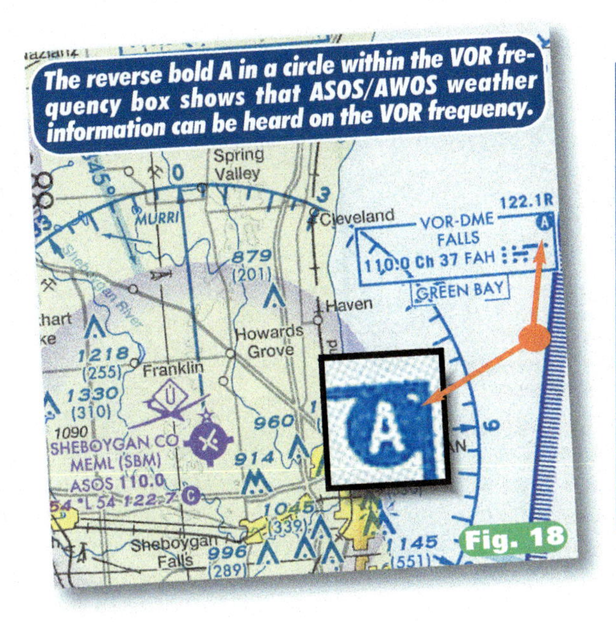

The reverse bold A in a circle within the VOR frequency box shows that ASOS/AWOS weather information can be heard on the VOR frequency.

Fig. 18

Mayo Emergency

Several years ago, a pilot had an emergency. In his anxious state, he forgot the word *Mayday*. He got as close as he could, yelling, "*Mayonnaise, mayonnaise, mayonnaise.*" Someone (probably from the Mayo clinic) responded immediately.

The Chart Supplement contains valuable aviation information about airports and pilot services.

Fig. 19

model as shown in Figure 17. By tuning in 119.55 MHz in your communication radio you can hear something known as the *one-minute weather* for Delano Airport. This allows you to learn about the visiblity, density altitude, sky conditions, temperature, wind, altimeter, and other important information at the field before you land.

Figure 18 shows a VOR frequency box having a black circle with a white "A" (a reverse-bold "A") inside. This indicates that the ASOS or AWOS "one minute" weather information associated with the airport nearest the VOR (Sheboygan, in this instance) can be heard on Falls' VOR frequency. While you'll learn more about ASOS and AWOS in Chapter 13, it's important to know that you can listen to the local airport weather information at Sheboygan on 110.0 MHz. This information is broadcast minute to minute (thus the reason it being called the "one minute" weather information), and it may contain information on ceiling and sky cover, visibility, precipitation and so on.

Can't Raise the Controller On the Radio?

1. Check for stuck mic.
2. Check frequency—try another frequency or facility.
3. Check connections/plugs on mic.
4. Try another mic.
5. Check circuit breakers.
6. Check facility hours of operation
7. Use spare handheld radio.
8. In the air—look for light gun signals.
9. On the ground—shut down, phone tower.

The Emergency Frequency

121.5 MHz is the international emergency frequency. Whether you're flying in Florida or France, Iowa or Italy, a call on 121.5 will usually get you help.

There is a tremendous bond between people in the aviation community, especially in times of trouble. A pilot declaring an emergency is entitled to—and receives—the undivided attention and assistance of anyone and everyone within radio range.

This doesn't mean you *must* be having an emergency to use 121.5. This frequency can be used if you know of no other frequency on which to communicate with someone, though it should be used that way as a last resort. You should be able to figure out another frequency that will permit you to communicate with someone, leaving 121.5 available for a pilot who has an emergency.

If you *do* have an emergency, 121.5 MHz is the frequency to use. Of course, this assumes you are not talking to someone else at the time of the emergency, such as a tower controller, radar controller or FSS specialist. In this instance, it's obviously best to stay with the person to whom you're speaking.

The international distress call is *Mayday* repeated three times. This will get the attention of everyone listening on *any* frequency (it goes without saying that the words, "ahhhhhhhh!, ahhhhhhh!, ahhhhhhh!," screamed loudly into the microphone will also get someone's attention, but it's not as professional). Having said the magic word, you just sit back and wait. Usually help will be at hand (or ear) in microseconds. Someone will usually come on the frequency and say, *Aircraft transmitting Mayday, please identify yourself.* After that, you identify and explain the nature of the problem. We'll talk more about emergencies when we get to transponders.

The Chart Supplement

The *Chart Supplement* (*CS*) or its digital version (*d-CS*), shown in Figure 19, is a booklet published every 56 days by the National Oceanic and Atmospheric Administration (NOAA). This is kind of a guidebook for pilots. Instead of listing tacky motels and hot nightspots, the *CS* contains valuable information on airports, seaplane bases, heliports open to the public, communications data, navigational facilities, certain special notices and procedures, and even information on parachute jump areas and areas having glider operations. Figure 20 shows a sample excerpt from the *CS*.

Why would you want to know where parachute jump areas are? There's a good reason. You don't want to hit or come close to hitting one of these folks. It's bad enough they've already fallen out of an airplane; you certainly don't want to frighten them. For a *skydiver,* as they like to be known, seeing an airplane coming at them is sort of like seeing a food processor from the inside, with the blade set to *dice*. You will find that most pilots are appalled at the thought of deliberately jumping out of a perfectly good airplane. They can't get past the notion that the first part of the word *parachute* sounds like *perish.*

Let's talk about the *CS* excerpt below. Area 1 in Figure 20 gives runway information. Unless otherwise stated, left traffic is assumed for the runway. Area 2 identifies the frequencies for ATIS, unicom, approach and departure control, tower, ground, clearance delivery and pretaxi clearance delivery. This section contains almost every frequency you'd need for the airport. The times these facilities operate are usually given in Zulu time.

Area 3 describes the airspace in which the facility is situated. This becomes important when you're attempting to determine the type of ATC service you can expect when arriving or departing this airport. As you'll soon see, each class of airspace (B, C and D) offers a different type of service.

The *CS* will be covered in additional detail in later chapters. For now, understand that it is a valuable aid in finding information about specific airports and their services. Each *CS* booklet covers a different region, usually consisting of several states. The value of the *CS*'s information far, far exceeds its very modest cost. You can subscribe and have the *CS* mailed to your door as soon as it's published. The *d-CS* is also available online for viewing and download at *naco.faa.gov*.

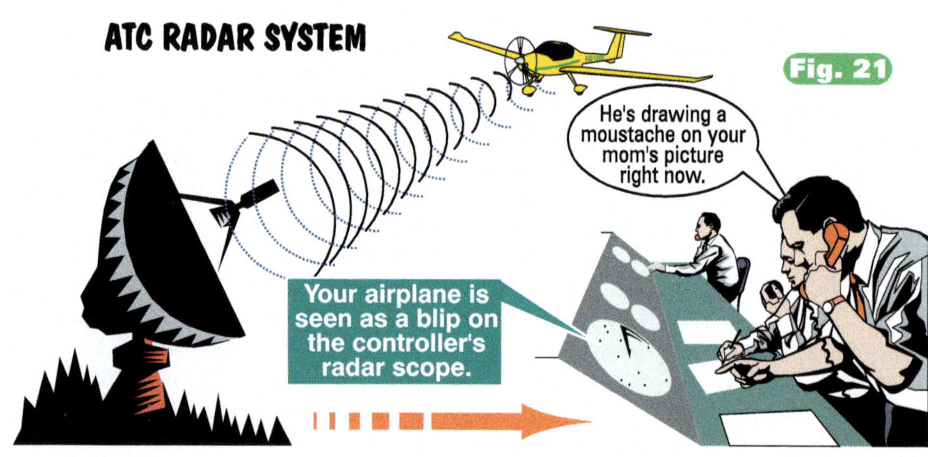

Fig. 21

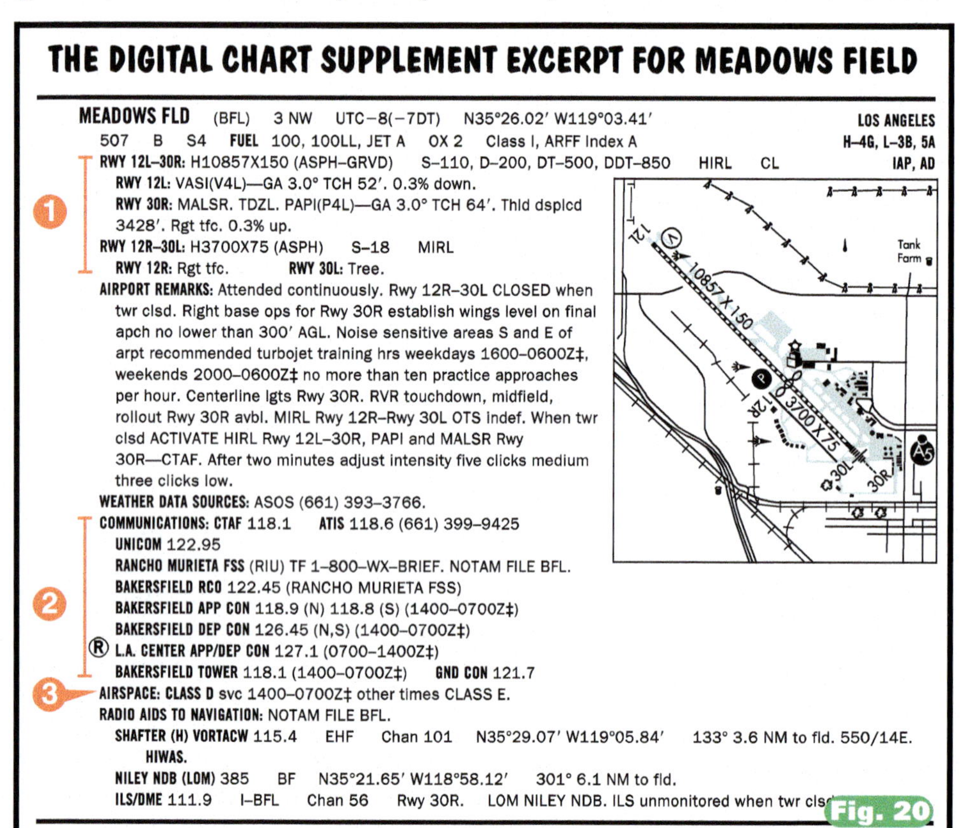

THE DIGITAL CHART SUPPLEMENT EXCERPT FOR MEADOWS FIELD

MEADOWS FLD (BFL) 3 NW UTC–8(–7DT) N35°26.02′ W119°03.41′ **LOS ANGELES**
507 B S4 **FUEL** 100, 100LL, JET A OX 2 Class I, ARFF Index A **H–4G, L–3B, 5A**
RWY 12L–30R: H10857X150 (ASPH–GRVD) S–110, D–200, DT–500, DDT–850 HIRL CL **IAP, AD**
RWY 12L: VASI(V4L)—GA 3.0° TCH 52′. 0.3% down.
RWY 30R: MALSR. TDZL. PAPI(P4L)—GA 3.0° TCH 64′. Thld dsplcd 3428′. Rgt tfc. 0.3% up.
RWY 12R–30L: H3700X75 (ASPH) S–18 MIRL
RWY 12R: Rgt tfc. **RWY 30L:** Tree.
AIRPORT REMARKS: Attended continuously. Rwy 12R–30L CLOSED when twr clsd. Right base ops for Rwy 30R establish wings level on final apch no lower than 300′ AGL. Noise sensitive areas S and E of arpt recommended turbojet training hrs weekdays 1600–0600Z‡, weekends 2000–0600Z‡ no more than ten practice approaches per hour. Centerline lgts Rwy 30R. RVR touchdown, midfield, rollout Rwy 30R avbl. MIRL Rwy 12R–Rwy 30L OTS indef. When twr clsd ACTIVATE HIRL Rwy 12L–30R, PAPI and MALSR Rwy 30R—CTAF. After two minutes adjust intensity five clicks medium three clicks low.
WEATHER DATA SOURCES: ASOS (661) 393–3766.
COMMUNICATIONS: CTAF 118.1 **ATIS** 118.6 (661) 399–9425
UNICOM 122.95
RANCHO MURIETA FSS (RIU) TF 1–800–WX–BRIEF. NOTAM FILE BFL.
BAKERSFIELD RCO 122.45 (RANCHO MURIETA FSS)
BAKERSFIELD APP CON 118.9 (N) 118.8 (S) (1400–0700Z‡)
BAKERSFIELD DEP CON 126.45 (N,S) (1400–0700Z‡)
Ⓡ **L.A. CENTER APP/DEP CON** 127.1 (0700–1400Z‡)
BAKERSFIELD TOWER 118.1 (1400–0700Z‡) **GND CON** 121.7
AIRSPACE: CLASS D svc 1400–0700Z‡ other times CLASS E.
RADIO AIDS TO NAVIGATION: NOTAM FILE BFL.
SHAFTER (H) VORTACW 115.4 EHF Chan 101 N35°29.07′ W119°05.84′ 133° 3.6 NM to fld. 550/14E. **HIWAS.**
NILEY NDB (LOM) 385 BF N35°21.65′ W118°58.12′ 301° 6.1 NM to fld.
ILS/DME 111.9 I–BFL Chan 56 Rwy 30R. LOM NILEY NDB. ILS unmonitored when twr clsd.

Fig. 20

Radar and the ATC System

When you ask anyone what the word "radar" means, they're likely to say something about a popular TV show from the mid-70s and early 80s. Radar O'Riley knew what was going to happen before it occurred. In a vaguely similar way, Radar allows air traffic controllers to do the same. Through the use of microwave radar energy, controllers can identify solid objects (aircraft, for example) at great distances as well as determine their direction, speed and altitude (altitude if Mode-C transponder equipped). Radar lets controllers "see" far beyond the range of their eyes. Now, you can easily see the meaning behind the name Radar which stands for *radio detection and ranging*.

Radar works on the echo principle. Microwave energy pulses are sent out over an antenna arrangement, as shown in Figure 21. Some of the energy bounces back to the originating antenna, and is reported as a visual blip on a screen. Through the use of radar, controllers can identify solid objects (aircraft, for example) at great distances.

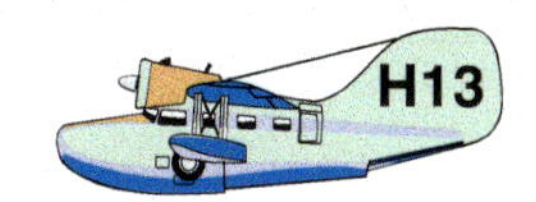

If all the system has to work with is the unadulterated bounceback of the radar signal, the blip is referred to as a *primary return* (which is not an election result). This would let a controller know *something* was there, but wouldn't provide much information beyond that.

Modern air traffic control is based on aircraft being equipped with *transponders,* which take the incoming radar beam, add coded information to it and return a stronger signal. This hyped-up bounceback is referred to as a *secondary return.* It permits the identification of a specific aircraft and the display on the controller's screen of a blip that is both brighter and more informative. For a further discussion of how ATC radar works, see Postflight Briefing #8-1 (page H21).

Transponders

On several occasions, I've mentioned the word *squawk.* This is official language for setting a specific, numerical code in the transponder or rotating the transponder's function switch to a specific selection. In other words if the controller told you to *squawk 2154,* you would set this code in the transponder's windows by twisting the number-code selection knobs, as shown in Figure 22. Then you would turn the function selection switch to the *ALT* position. If the controller said to *squawk standby,* you would move the function-selection switch from the *ALT* position it normally rests in during flight to the *SBY* position (in a moment I'll explain what these positions do).

VFR CODES SHOWN ON RADAR SCOPE

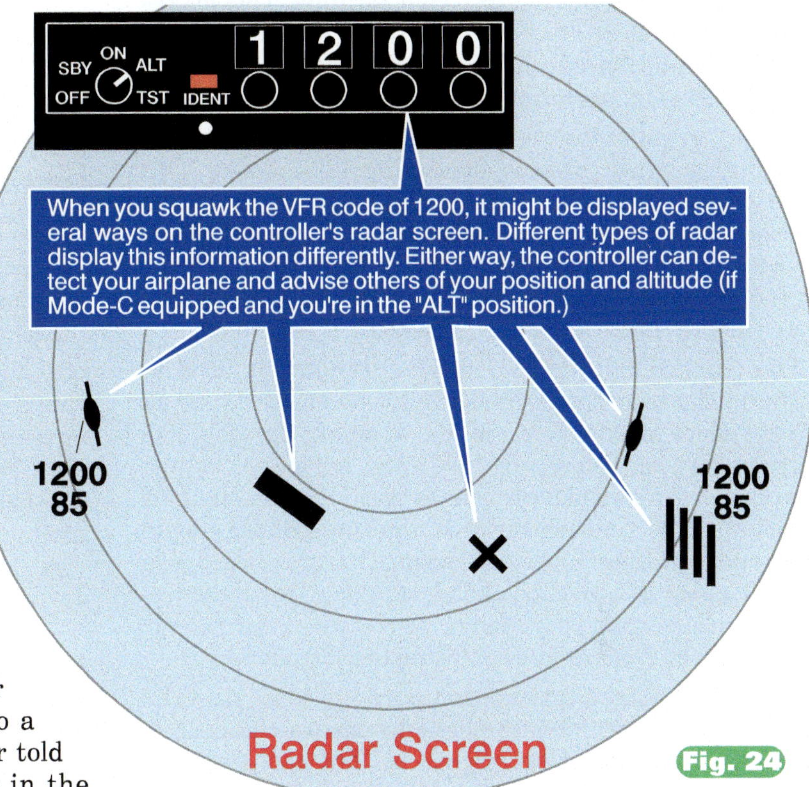

When you squawk the VFR code of 1200, it might be displayed several ways on the controller's radar screen. Different types of radar display this information differently. Either way, the controller can detect your airplane and advise others of your position and altitude (if Mode-C equipped and you're in the "ALT" position.)

Fig. 24

SQUAWKING A CODE Fig. 22

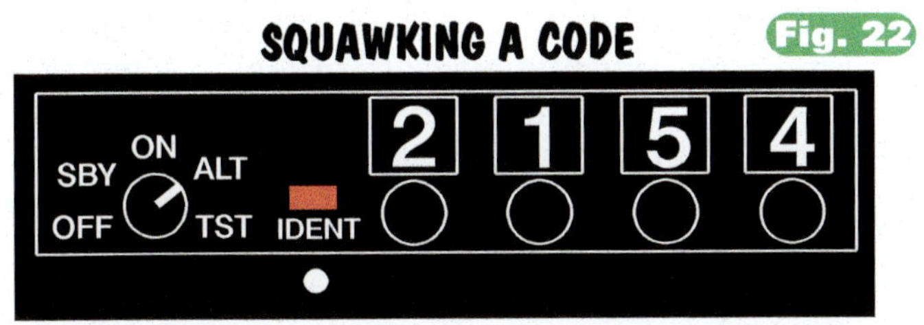

ATC told the pilot to squawk 2154. The pilot complies by dialing the numbers 2154 in the windows and making sure the function switch is set to the "ALT" position.

The transponder allows your airplane to be easily identified by air traffic control on their radar screen.

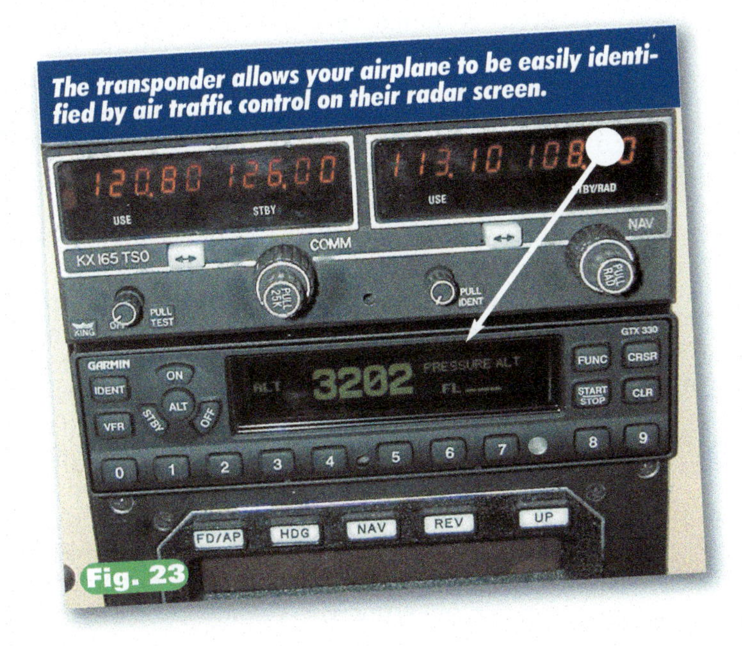

Fig. 23

The transponder is a necessary component of the secondary radar beacon system. This little device has several interesting features. First, the typical transponder, shown in Figure 23, is called a 4096-code transponder because it has 4,096 code combinations that can be set in the windows. Radar controllers normally assign aircraft specific codes, but some codes are standard.

For instance, if you're flying VFR, whether you are talking to a radar controller or not, you should squawk the code 1200. This allows your airplane and the 1200 code (or a symbol representing that code—like an *x*) to appear on the controller's radar screen as shown in Figure 24. Traffic avoidance becomes easier when other airplanes, in contact with the radar controller, are alerted to your position.

The transponder's function switch has an *ALT* selection (meaning ALTitude). Unless ATC instructs otherwise, you should always operate your transponder in the ALT mode since your airplane most likely has something known as an encoding altimeter (a device that tags your altitude onto the signal and sends it along as part of the transponder's return). Selecting the altitude mode allows your altitude to show up with the airplane's data block on the controller's radar screen. Now the controller knows not only your position, but also your altitude. This makes it easier for him or her to inform other aircraft of your exact position. Operation in the altitude mode is also known as *Mode C operation.*

In fact, regulations require that if you have Mode C capability, you use it while squawking 1200 during VFR flights in controlled airspace. Sometimes controllers will ask you to *squawk altitude.* This means your transponder is probably being operated in the *ON* position and the controller wants you to turn the function switch one more click to the altitude (*ALT*) or Mode C position.

The transponder's *SBY* feature (Standby) is used to warm up the transponder and/or altitude encoder (not all transponders or encoders require warming up). It's like warming up a car before you drive away, except no exhaust is produced. Anytime an airplane is positioned on any portion of an airport movement area, the transponder should be on and operating in the *ALT* mode. On rare occasions, a controller may ask you to *squawk standby.* This most frequently occurs when your Mode C or S readout seems inaccurate and thus potentially confusing to controllers.

The *TST* or test feature temporarily activates the transponder's reply/monitor light to ensure the bulb is working and to adjust its brightness. The reply/monitor light flashes when the transponder is being interrogated by a ground-based radar unit.

Under the reply/monitor light is the *IDENT* (identification) button. This is pushed when the controller requests that you *ident.* Pushing this button makes the radar blip bloom temporarily, causing it to stand out, as shown in Figure 25. The ident feature is simply the transponder's way of saying to the controller, "Hey, look, I'm over here!"

Don't push the ident button unless told to do so by the controller. It's interesting to note that when the controller tells one specific aircraft to ident, sometimes another pilot, not listening carefully, pushes his ident button. As a student pilot, I accidentally did this a number of times. If other airborne students were like me, I'm sure the controller's radar screen probably lit up like fireflies at a recharging center. Certainly this makes it a little confusing for controllers.

The code 7700 should be used in the event of an emergency. Selecting this code in your transponder visually alerts the controller that you are in distress. Essentially, your data block lights up, making it easier for the controller to identify you, as shown in Figure 26. Students, lost on cross country flights, have set 7700 in the transponder and tuned 121.5 MHz (the emergency frequency) on their radios and asked for help. It usually doesn't take long before someone replies on this frequency and offers assistance (and you didn't even need to yell, *"Mayonnaise, mayonnaise, mayonnaise."* Of course if you're in an area where there is no radar coverage, the emergency transponder code won't be seen. This is one of the reasons why it's important to climb (if possible) when you're lost. It increases your chances of being seen on someone's radar as well as communicating with them.

This Buzzz's for You

Removed two wasps from the cabin during preflight. On takeoff at 100 feet a wasp flew into my vision and distracted me. I tried to hold altitude and prevent a stall as I pulled my wits together. It stung me on the hand as I waved it away. My flight path had diverted close to a skydiving operation so I made a sharp climbing turn away from the trees.

Preflighting the cabin doesn't mean just removing the gust lock. It takes only a minute for a small creature to move its home (in fact, a wasp can build a nest overnight). I assumed there were only two wasps. The next day I found a centipede under the step. I'm glad I'm looking harder now as I could have found him hidden in my plush sheepskin cover as I sat down.

Remember, no matter what's crawling down your leg, fly

VFR CODES SHOWN ON RADAR SCOPE

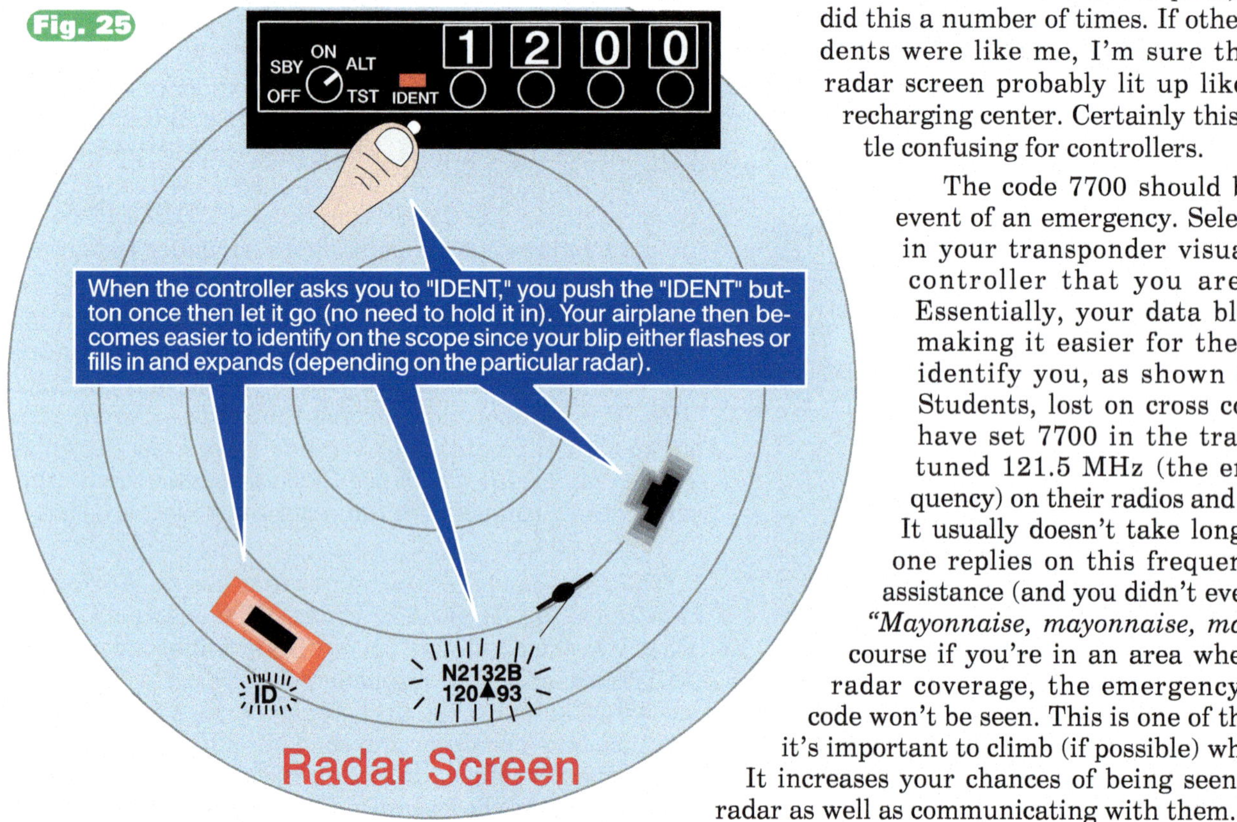

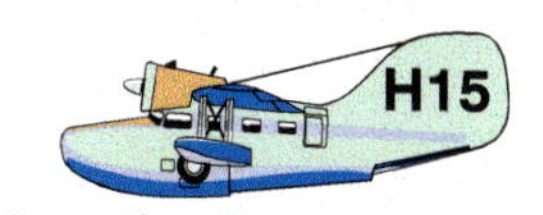

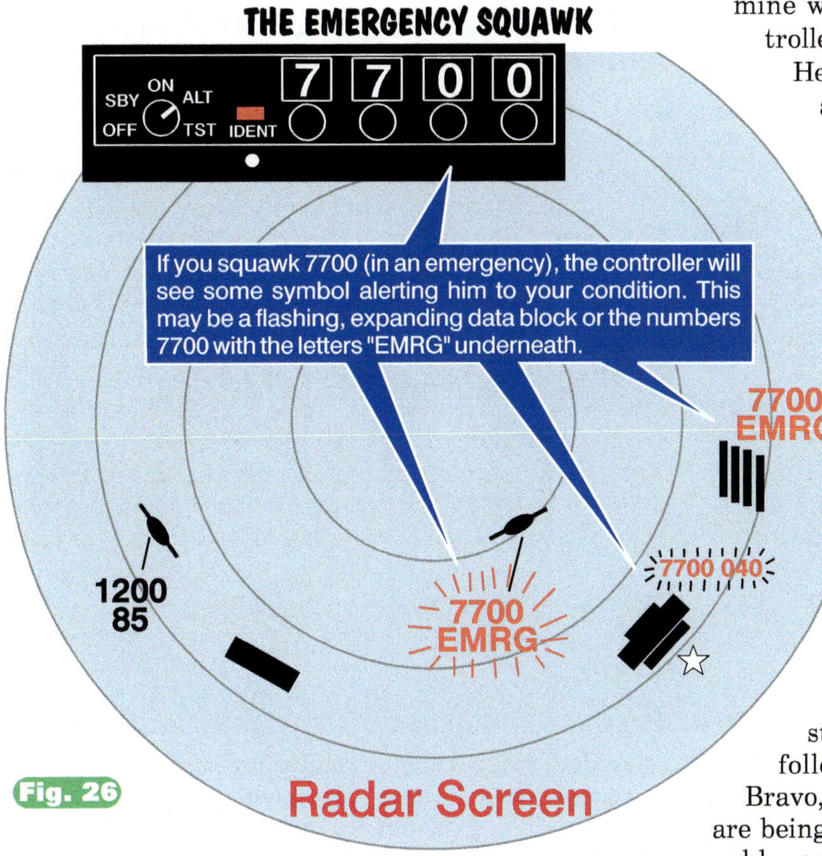

Fig. 26

When I was a student, I was never lost. Temporarily unsure of my present position, perhaps, but never lost. These days it's more politically correct to call it *location challenged* instead of being lost (that's a joke). A friend of mine was lost and decided to land at the first uncontrolled airport he observed underneath his airplane. He taxied up to the gas pump, got out of his airplane and walked across the street to the hamburger joint to find out what town he was in. He asked the hamburger cook (the sliced protein thermal coordinator) how he pronounced the name of this place. The fellow looked at him and said, "BURR-GURR-KING." Ouch! After a few more questions and a Coke, he finally discovered where he was.

If you are hijacked, which is relatively rare in a Cessna 172, squawk code 7500 and tell your guest you can't go nonstop from California to Cuba. The 7500 code flashes a warning on the controller's radar screen. Of course the controller, seeing 7500 on the scope, won't say, "Hey 32 Bravo, why are you squawking the hijack code?" If the hijacker were listening, he might not be too happy with you and may request an impromptu wing walking demonstration. There is a certain protocol controllers follow when they see 7500. Usually they ask, "32 Bravo, verify squawking 7500?" In which case, if you are being hijacked, you calmly reply, "Ahhhh, ut, ahhhh, ughh, gulp, errrr, roger." Once it's established that the code selected is for real, you'll get some really incredible radar service, and a very nice landing reception with guests from the FBI, FAA, and local law enforcement agencies.

Automatic Dependent Surveillance Broadcast

ADS-B or *automatic dependent surveillance broadcast* is a revolutionary new way of controlling/observing air traffic and is now mandatory for all aircraft operating in certain types of airspace (see page I31 for details). The concept is simple. ADS-B equipped aircraft broadcast their precise position via a digital datalink along with their airspeed, altitude, direction of movement (up, down, right, left). Air traffic control or other aircraft with ADS-B can identify targets in real time for air traffic control to avoid a traffic conflict.

As a simplified example, consider an air-traffic control secondary radar. The radar measures the range and bearing of an aircraft. The bearing is measured by the position of the rotating radar antenna when it receives a reply to its interrogation from the aircraft. The range is measured by the time it takes for the radar to receive the reply. Unfortunately, the antenna's projected radar beam gets wider as the aircraft get farther from the antenna, thus making the measured position information less accurate.

An ADS-B based system, on the other hand, would listen for position reports broadcast by the aircraft. These position reports are based on accurate navigation systems, such as satellite navigation systems (e.g., GPS). The accuracy of the system is now determined by the accuracy of the navigation system, not measurement errors. The accuracy is unaffected by the range to the aircraft. With the radar system, detecting aircraft velocity changes requires tracking the received data. Changes can only be detected over a period of several position updates. With ADS-B, velocity changes are broadcast almost instantaneously.

The diagram to the right shows how ADS-B information is exchanged. A communications satellite helps provide voice capability between the aircraft and the ATC facility. The GPS satellite system provides position and altitude information and this information is relayed directly to the ATC facility via ground lines. Additionally, there is an airplane-to-airplane exchange of information (data).

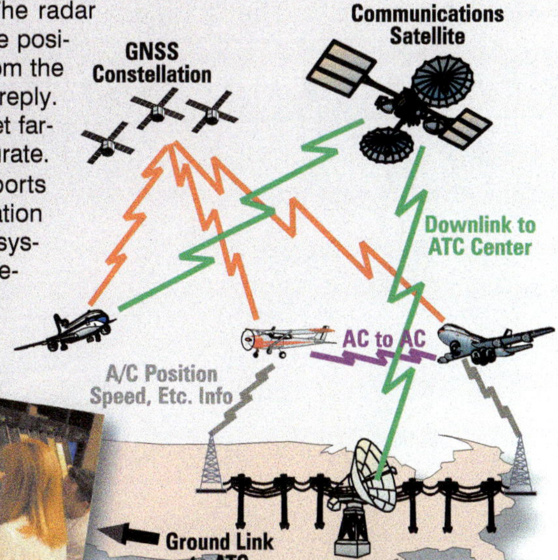

Another transponder code exists for pilots experiencing lost communications. (*Lost communications* means the radio has failed, not that you have lost your voice or have gotten yourself lost.) Squawking 7600 tells the controller that you've lost two-way radio capability. Normally, this code is used by IFR pilots experiencing communication failure (i.e., it's used by pilots flying in the clouds). VFR pilots, however, could also find it useful. For instance, if you were approaching an airport lying within class D airspace, in VFR conditions, with a failed radio, you might squawk 7600 hoping to get the attention of the tower controller. Even if the tower controller doesn't have radar, an observant radar controller, noticing the 7600 code on his or her screen, might alert the tower controller to your problem. In this instance, you would enter the pattern and look for the appropriate light signals from the tower. Code 7777 is for military intercept. Use this code if you are intercepted by military aircraft.

When switching transponder codes, be careful to avoid switching through the codes 7500, 7600 and 7700. You don't want to trigger a false alarm on the controller's screen. Controllers have enough excitement in their lives just from the regular stuff some pilots do.

Finally, the military uses several types of transponders. The type that corresponds to civilian Mode A and C is Mode A/3 and C/3. The "3" indicates a military transponder. I say this to satisfy the curious among you.

Fig. 27

Radar Services for Pilots

When you make contact with a radar facility and they identify you and provide in-flight advisories, the service is referred to as "flight following." It's an extra set of eyes that help you watch for traffic, and something you'll want to make use of as often as possible.

Men are notoriously reluctant to ask for directions when driving. I suppose if we had aerial gas stations, we'd still be reluctant to use them for directions. Manhood and directionhood seem intimately bound. Uncouple them when you get in the air, and ask the nice controller for *vectors to the airport* when you can't see because of poor visibility, or when you just can't find the darn thing.

He or she will be more than happy to help.

Flight following also provides you with the location of in-flight traffic. This becomes very helpful during hazy flight conditions or in and around busy airports. When using this service, controllers call out the traffic's position using the 12-hour clock, with the airplane's nose being 12. If the controller says, "Cessna 2132 Bravo, you have traffic at two o'clock, three miles," you start looking for traffic a bit to the right of the nose, as shown in Figure 27. If you see the traffic, inform the controller that you have "traffic in sight." If you don't see it, say, "negative contact." If you don't see it and are still looking, say to the controller "looking for traffic." In other words, don't sit silently after a controller calls traffic for you. A reply is mandatory, traffic permitting.

If the target airplane has Mode C capability (altitude encoder) then the controller will provide you with the airplane's altitude (otherwise, you'll be told *altitude unknown).* The controller might say, "Cessna 2132 Bravo, you have traffic at eleven o'clock, four miles, southbound at 3,000 feet." This clarifies how much of a concern the target aircraft is to you. If you're at 4,500 feet, then you have reasonable separation. If you're at 3,000 feet, you really want to find that puppy—and sooner, rather than later. If the traffic is a factor for you, the controller will usually continue making these calls. You can sometimes get an approximate distance by listening to the rising tone and urgency of the controller's voice. At about high C, it's time to ask the controller to vector you out of harm's way.

If the traffic is not in sight, don't let the controller think you see it. Several years ago, late one evening, I heard a controller rapidly call three targets in a row for a pilot. Each time the controller said, "Cessna 2132 Bravo, traffic at..." the pilot immediately replied, "contact." Suspicious, the controller paused then said, "OK, traffic at twelve o'clock." The pilot immediately said, "contact." The controller said, "Hey, 32 Bravo, I was just kidding about that one." The pilot replied, "Hey, so was I."

Keep in mind that the controller has no idea which way your airplane is pointing. All the controller can visually discern on the screen is the path the aircraft is making across the ground (its ground track). If a strong wind exists, you will be crabbed into the wind. Your nose would point in one direction, while the airplane moved in another. Look at Figure 28. The controller sees you as having traffic at 12 o'clock. But you aren't pointed exactly where you're headed, so for you the traffic is going to be found at two o'clock. When ATC calls traffic, you must look in the general area of the traffic advisory. In other words, you must look to the right or the left of the given position (we'll discuss this in greater detail in Chapter 17).

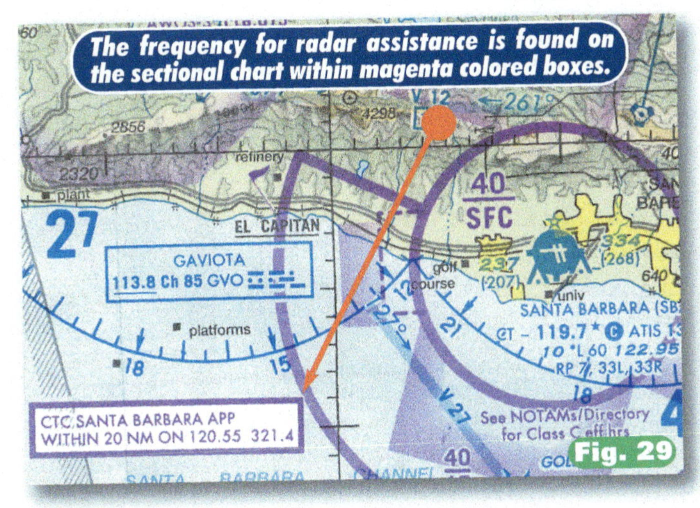

Fig. 29

WIND EFFECT ON TRAFFIC CALLS

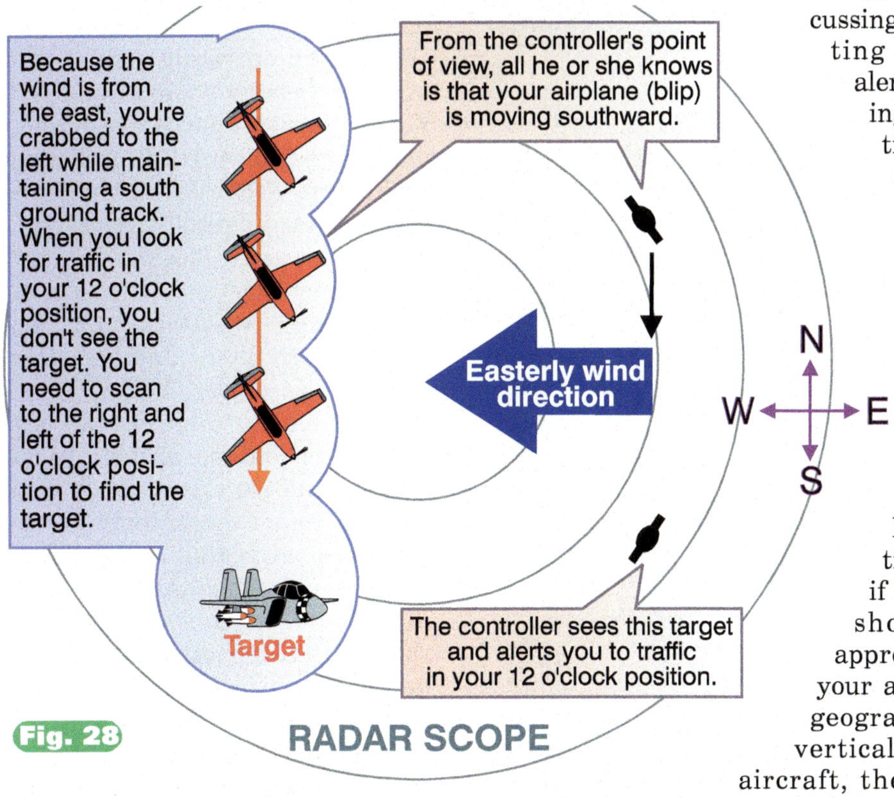

Because the wind is from the east, you're crabbed to the left while maintaining a south ground track. When you look for traffic in your 12 o'clock position, you don't see the target. You need to scan to the right and left of the 12 o'clock position to find the target.

From the controller's point of view, all he or she knows is that your airplane (blip) is moving southward.

Easterly wind direction

N

W

E

S

Target

The controller sees this target and alerts you to traffic in your 12 o'clock position.

RADAR SCOPE

Fig. 28

Radar Assistance to VFR Aircraft

Radar assistance to pilots is available in several different forms. These include:

1. Basic radar service
2. TRSA service
3. Class C service
4. Class B service

Basic Radar Service

Basic radar service is what we've been discussing. Radar controllers, on a workload permitting basis, provide VFR pilots with safety alerts, traffic advisories, limited radar vectoring and sequencing at specific terminal locations. The *primary* purpose of radar control is to provide control and separation for aircraft on instrument flight plans (IFR flights). Assistance to VFR pilots is also provided if the controller can do so without compromising the level of service to the IFR aircraft he or she is handling.

If you want basic radar service after departure, then inform ground control upon initial contact. If you're airborne and want radar vectoring to an airport, call Approach Control on the frequency listed on the appropriate aeronautical sectional or terminal area chart. For instance, if you were near Santa Barbara airport, as shown in Figure 29, you'd simply call approach control on 120.55 MHz. Give them your aircraft call sign, altitude, position (that's geographical and not whether you're sitting vertical or sideways in the airplane), type of aircraft, the transponder code you're squawking, destination and your request. If you're arriving at an airport with ATIS, let the controller know that you've received the latest information. The call might go something like this:

YOU: "Santa Barbara Approach, Cessna 2132 Bravo."

SBA APPROACH: "Cessna 2132 Bravo, Santa Barbara Approach. Go ahead."

YOU: "32 Bravo is a Cessna 172, 4,500 feet over Gaviota VOR, squawking 1200, requesting vectors to Santa Barbara airport, information Whiskey received."

If you aren't planning on landing and just want radar traffic information only, your callup might go like this:

YOU: "Santa Barbara Approach, Cessna 2132 Bravo."

SBA APPROACH: "Cessna 2132 Bravo, Santa Barbara Approach. Go ahead."

YOU: "32 Bravo is a Cessna 172, 4,500 feet over Gaviota VOR, squawking 1200, transition to the north, requesting traffic advisories."

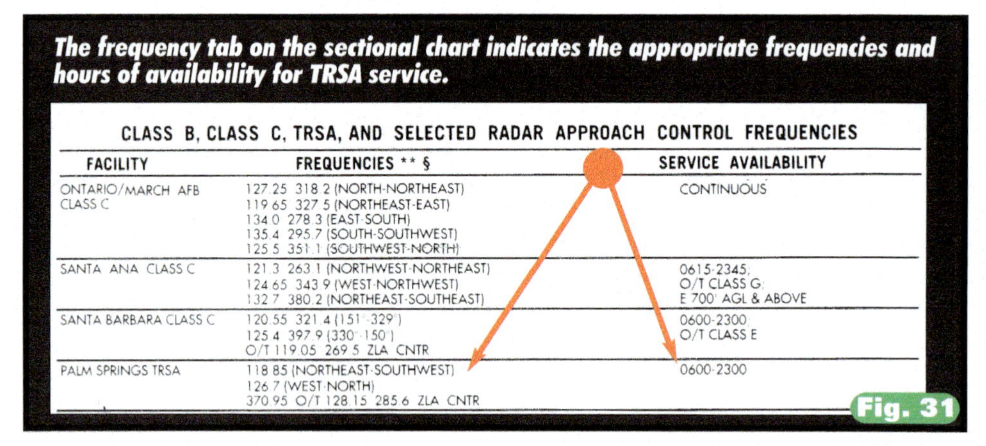

The frequency tab on the sectional chart indicates the appropriate frequencies and hours of availability for TRSA service.

CLASS B, CLASS C, TRSA, AND SELECTED RADAR APPROACH CONTROL FREQUENCIES

FACILITY	FREQUENCIES ** §	SERVICE AVAILABILITY
ONTARIO/MARCH AFB CLASS C	127.25 318.2 (NORTH-NORTHEAST) 119.65 327.5 (NORTHEAST-EAST) 134.0 278.3 (EAST-SOUTH) 135.4 295.7 (SOUTH-SOUTHWEST) 125.5 351.1 (SOUTHWEST-NORTH)	CONTINUOUS
SANTA ANA CLASS C	121.3 263.1 (NORTHWEST-NORTHEAST) 124.65 343.9 (WEST-NORTHWEST) 132.7 380.2 (NORTHEAST-SOUTHEAST)	0615-2345; O/T CLASS G; E 700' AGL & ABOVE
SANTA BARBARA CLASS C	120.55 321.4 (151°-329°) 125.4 397.9 (330°-150°) O/T 119.05 269.5 ZLA CNTR	0600-2300 O/T CLASS E
PALM SPRINGS TRSA	118.85 (NORTHEAST-SOUTHWEST) 126.7 (WEST-NORTH) 370.95 O/T 128.15 285.6 ZLA CNTR	0600-2300

Fig. 31

Terminal Radar Service Area (TRSA) Service

At certain busy airport locations a special type of airspace known as a Terminal Radar Service Area (TRSA) exists. Once widespread, TRSA's are rapidly fading from the aviation scene as they're replaced by Class C airspace.

Dark gray lines represent the borders of the Palm Springs TRSA as shown on an aeronautical sectional chart (Figure 30). For instance, position A shows the border of the Palm Springs TRSA. Position B shows the altitude limit for the TRSA in that area. It starts at 3,500 feet and extends vertically to 10,000 feet. If you're flying within the TRSA, you are encouraged to participate in TRSA service (although participation isn't mandatory). Figure 31 shows the frequency tab located on the bottom of every aeronautical chart. This tab lists the appropriate frequencies on which to call for TRSA service when you're approximately 25 miles from the TRSA-served airport. (We'll cover aeronautical sectional charts in greater detail in Chapter 10.)

The borders of a Terminal Radar Service Area (TRSA) are shown on sectional charts by dark gray lines.

Fig. 30

TRSA service provides radar sequencing and separation between all participating VFR aircraft and all IFR aircraft operating within the airspace defined as the TRSA. Separation standards are based on one of the following: 500 feet vertical separation, visual separation between pilots or target resolution (a process controllers use to keep radar targets from touching—now that's a good idea isn't it?). (See Figure 32.) If you are asked to follow another aircraft into or out of the TRSA, you are responsible for maintaining a safe distance behind this aircraft. In other words, don't get close enough so that you can watch the in-flight movie in the other airplane. If you suspect wake turbulence could be a problem, give yourself more room. Even though ATC applies greater distances between large and small airplanes for wake turbulence separation, ask for more if you feel it's necessary. You *are* the pilot-in-command.

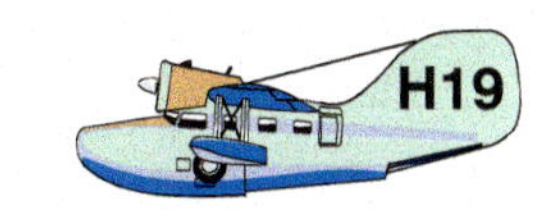

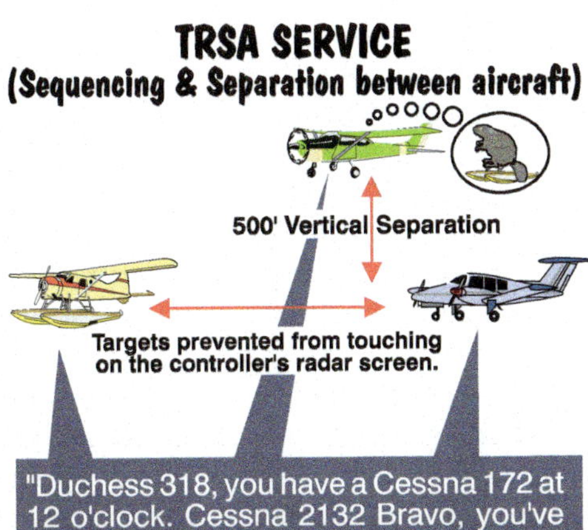

Fig. 32

Here's an important caveat about TRSA service. As you're being vectored by ATC, be cautious about adhering to the required VFR minimums relating to clouds and altitude requirements. Remember, ATC's radar doesn't show clouds—clouds aren't solid and don't show up on the screen. The controller simply can't tell if the heading he or she gives you will put you in a cloud. Since you're not instrument rated, you can't be in the clouds. Avoid them! Immediately ask for an amended clearance—a new heading—if your present one will take you into a cloud. Even if ATC hasn't given you a new heading, turn as necessary to avoid flying into that cloud. The best thing to do is keep the radar controller advised of the weather conditions along your route if it looks like clouds or other obscuring phenomena are a problem.

Sometimes, when arriving or departing a TRSA, I prefer obtaining radar advisories from ATC, but not having the formal separation efforts that TRSA service entails. In this case I'll state *negative TRSA service* on my initial callup with approach control or ground control, as appropriate. This becomes especially important when departing. Suppose, barring any departure restrictions, you wanted a straight out departure after takeoff. We'll assume this heads you directly toward your destination. If you don't say, "negative TRSA service" on your initial callup, the controller might have you call Departure Control after takeoff. Now the radar departure controller, thinking you want TRSA service, could give you vectors that are anything but the shortest direction to your destination. These types of delays are most common at busy airports on busy days.

When departing the TRSA (or any other class of airspace), the controller will sometimes say, "Cessna 2132 Bravo, radar service terminated." Don't take it personally. This either means you are leaving the boundaries over which the controller exercises control, or the controller is too busy to continue providing service. Either way, this is your clue to squawk VFR by setting the code 1200 in your transponder. Since you're no longer being given radar service, the controller has no need to keep you on a specific code or his or her frequency.

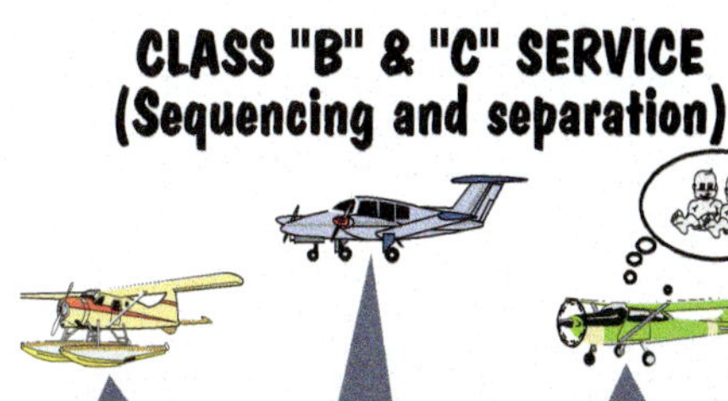

Fig. 33

Cartoon by Bob Stevens

Reprinted with the permission of Mrs. Bob Stevens

Class C Service

In Chapter 9, you'll learn more about Class B and C airspace. For now, understand that these airspace types belong to increasingly busy airports with operating control towers. Class C service provides basic radar service, separation between all IFR and VFR aircraft, and sequencing of the VFR arrivals to the primary airport as shown in Figure 33.

Class B Service

Class B service provides basic radar service, separation between IFR and VFR aircraft, and sequencing of VFR arrivals to the primary airport.

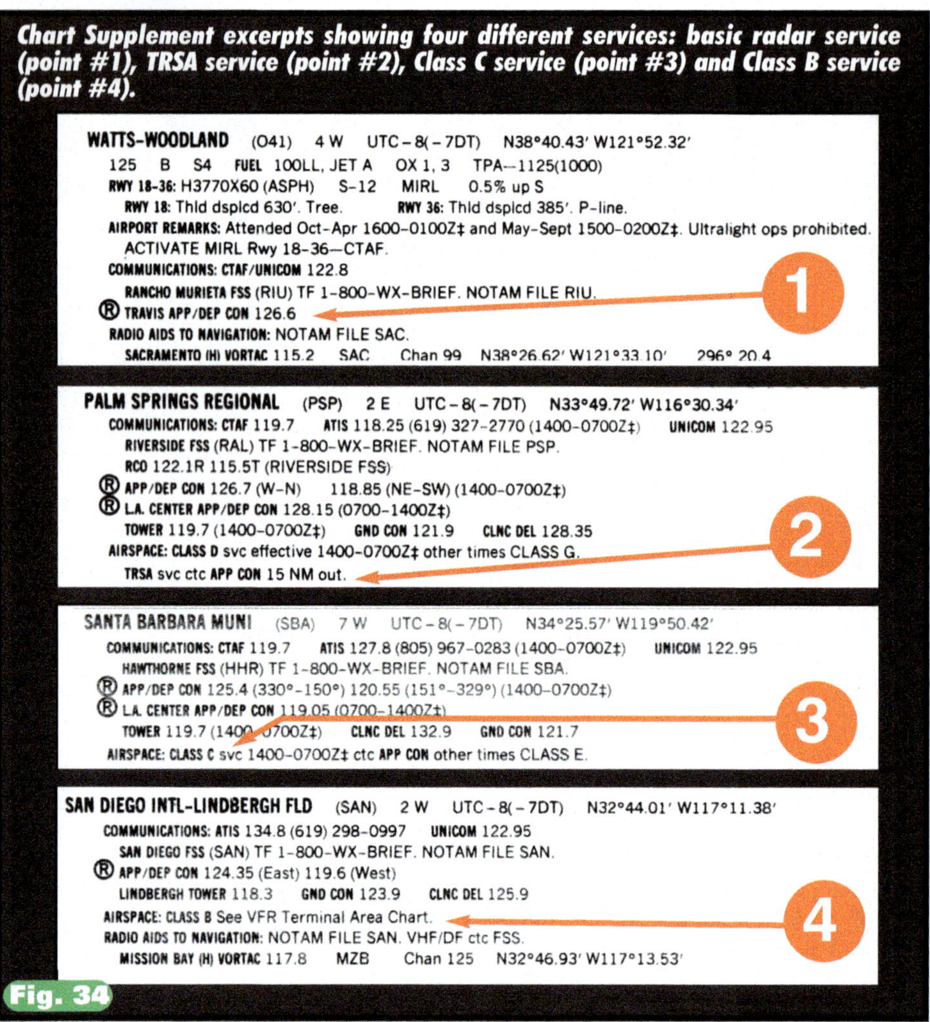

Chart Supplement excerpts showing four different services: basic radar service (point #1), TRSA service (point #2), Class C service (point #3) and Class B service (point #4).

WATTS-WOODLAND (O41) 4 W UTC–8(–7DT) N38°40.43′ W121°52.32′
125 B S4 **FUEL** 100LL, JET A OX 1, 3 TPA—1125(1000)
RWY 18-36: H3770X60 (ASPH) S-12 MIRL 0.5% up S
RWY 18: Thld dsplcd 630′. Tree. **RWY 36:** Thld dsplcd 385′. P-line.
AIRPORT REMARKS: Attended Oct–Apr 1600–0100Z‡ and May–Sept 1500–0200Z‡. Ultralight ops prohibited. ACTIVATE MIRL Rwy 18–36—CTAF.
COMMUNICATIONS: CTAF/UNICOM 122.8
RANCHO MURIETA FSS (RIU) TF 1-800-WX-BRIEF. NOTAM FILE RIU.
Ⓡ **TRAVIS APP/DEP CON** 126.6
RADIO AIDS TO NAVIGATION: NOTAM FILE SAC.
SACRAMENTO (H) VORTAC 115.2 SAC Chan 99 N38°26.62′ W121°33.10′ 296° 20.4

PALM SPRINGS REGIONAL (PSP) 2 E UTC–8(–7DT) N33°49.72′ W116°30.34′
COMMUNICATIONS: CTAF 119.7 **ATIS** 118.25 (619) 327-2770 (1400–0700Z‡) **UNICOM** 122.95
RIVERSIDE FSS (RAL) TF 1-800-WX-BRIEF. NOTAM FILE PSP.
RCO 122.1R 115.5T (RIVERSIDE FSS)
Ⓡ **APP/DEP CON** 126.7 (W–N) 118.85 (NE–SW) (1400–0700Z‡)
Ⓡ **L.A. CENTER APP/DEP CON** 128.15 (0700–1400Z‡)
TOWER 119.7 (1400–0700Z‡) **GND CON** 121.9 **CLNC DEL** 128.35
AIRSPACE: CLASS D svc effective 1400–0700Z‡ other times CLASS G.
TRSA svc ctc **APP CON** 15 NM out.

SANTA BARBARA MUNI (SBA) 7 W UTC–8(–7DT) N34°25.57′ W119°50.42′
COMMUNICATIONS: CTAF 119.7 **ATIS** 127.8 (805) 967-0283 (1400–0700Z‡) **UNICOM** 122.95
HAWTHORNE FSS (HHR) TF 1-800-WX-BRIEF. NOTAM FILE SBA.
Ⓡ **APP/DEP CON** 125.4 (330°–150°) 120.55 (151°–329°) (1400–0700Z‡)
Ⓡ **L.A. CENTER APP/DEP CON** 119.05 (0700–1400Z‡)
TOWER 119.7 (1400–0700Z‡) **CLNC DEL** 132.9 **GND CON** 121.7
AIRSPACE: CLASS C svc 1400–0700Z‡ ctc **APP CON** other times CLASS E.

SAN DIEGO INTL-LINDBERGH FLD (SAN) 2 W UTC–8(–7DT) N32°44.01′ W117°11.38′
COMMUNICATIONS: ATIS 134.8 (619) 298-0997 **UNICOM** 122.95
SAN DIEGO FSS (SAN) TF 1-800-WX-BRIEF. NOTAM FILE SAN.
Ⓡ **APP/DEP CON** 124.35 (East) 119.6 (West)
LINDBERGH TOWER 118.3 **GND CON** 123.9 **CLNC DEL** 125.9
AIRSPACE: CLASS B See VFR Terminal Area Chart.
RADIO AIDS TO NAVIGATION: NOTAM FILE SAN. VHF/DF ctc FSS.
MISSION BAY (H) VORTAC 117.8 MZB Chan 125 N32°46.93′ W117°13.53′

Fig. 34

If you want to know what stage of radar service is available at an airport, simply look in the *Chart Supplement*. Figure 34 shows four *CS* excerpts indicating the individual services at an airport. Item #1 identifies an approach and departure control with a circled *R* next to the radar frequencies. This implies basic radar service is probably available at this airport. Item #2 shows TRSA service is available and that you should contact approach control 15 miles out from the airport for this service. Item #3 shows Class C service is available. Item #4 shows Class B service is available at this airport; you should look at the VFR Terminal Area Chart to determine how to make contact (this chart is discussed in Chapter 10).

Clearance Delivery

Some airports lying within class B or C airspace require you to have a *clearance* prior to departure. In this type of airspace you will generally be assigned very specific routing and altitude directions, as well as a frequency on which to make contact with a controller after a handoff from the tower.

Since you have to know before you go, that means getting a clearance from somewhere. The somewhere is called *clearance delivery*. A special frequency exists with a controller awaiting your call and request for a clearance. If there is a clearance delivery frequency, it will generally be part of the ATIS broadcast. The information can also be found in the communications section of the *CS*, as shown in Figure 35. At some less-busy airports, ground control functions as a clearance delivery.

When you contact clearance delivery, give them your complete aircraft number, tell them you have the current ATIS information, give them your destination and direction of flight, and tell the controller you're a VFR aircraft. A typical call may sound like this:

YOU: "Palm Springs Clearance Delivery, Cessna 2132 Bravo."

CLEARANCE DELIVERY: "Cessna 2132 Bravo, go ahead."

YOU: "Cessna 32 Bravo with information Hotel, VFR to Ontario, over."

A typical clearance out of a busy airport may sound like this:

CLEARANCE DELIVERY: "Cessna 2132 Bravo, after departure fly heading 230 degrees, climb and maintain 3,500 feet, departure control frequency will be 124.3, contact ground control on 121.9 when ready to taxi."

THE LOCATION OF CLEARANCE DELIVERY FREQUENCIES IN THE "CS"

NORTH PLATTE REGIONAL (LBF) 3 E UTC–6(–5DT) N41°07.56′ W100°41.23′ **OMAHA H-1D, L-11A IAP**
2778 B S4 **FUEL** 100LL, JET A ARFF Index Ltd.
RWY 12L-30R: H8000X150 (CONC-GRVD) S-75, D-110, DT-190 HIRL
RWY 12L: VASI(V4L)—GA 3.0° TCH 55′. **RWY 30R:** MALSR. Rgt tfc.
RWY 12R-30L: H4925X100 (ASPH) S-42, D-58, DT-106 MIRL
RWY 12R: Rgt tfc.
RWY 17-35: H4436X100 (ASPH) S-28, D-48, DT-86 MIRL
RWY 17: Road. **RWY 35:** REIL. VASI(V4L)—GA 3.0° TCH 41′. Thld dsplcd 234′. Berm.
AIRPORT REMARKS: Attended 1200–0500Z‡. 5 foot dike 100′ from approach end Rwy 35. Waterfowl and deer on and in the vicinity of the arpt. PPR 24 hours for unscheduled air carrier ops with more than 30 passenger seats call arpt manager 308-532-1900. ACTIVATE HIRL Rwy 12L–30R, MIRL Rwy 17–35, VASI Rwy 12L and Rwy 35, MALSR Rwy 30R and REIL Rwy 35—CTAF. For MIRL Rwy 12R–30L ctc arpt manager 308-532-1900.
COMMUNICATIONS: CTAF/UNICOM 123.0
COLUMBUS FSS (OLU) TF 1-800-WX-BRIEF. NOTAM FILE LBF.
LEE BIRD RCO 122.5 (COLUMBUS FSS)
Ⓡ **DENVER CENTER APP/DEP CON** 132.7 **CLNC DEL** 132.7
RADIO AIDS TO NAVIGATION: NOTAM FILE LBF. VHF/DF ctc FSS.
(L) VORTACW 117.4 LBF Chan 121 N41°02.92′ W100°44.83′ 019° 5.4 NM to fld. 3050/11E.
PAMBE NDB (HW/LOM) 416 LB N41°04.10′ W100°34.35′ 295° 6.3 NM to fld. Unmonitored.

Fig. 35

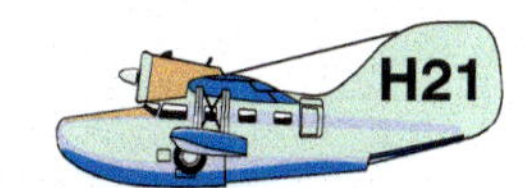

It's customary to read back clearances to controllers to ensure the accuracy of the communication. Sometimes this makes pilots a bit nervous. Especially, if the controller spoke at 60 knots (fast!) with peak gusts to 90 knots (that's real fast!) and the clearance wasn't copied in its entirety. One fellow, after receiving a rapid fire clearance, picked up his microphone and said (very slowly), *Hey fellows, do you hear how fast I'm talking? Well, this is how fast I listen.* The controllers laughed and repeated his clearance slowly. If you have trouble understanding the clearance, ask the controller to slow down. One of these days some pilot is going to record his clearance with a portable recorder and play it back to the controller as his readback. I'm sure the controller, after hearing his own clearance, will say, *Hey, 32 Bravo, you're going to have to speak a little slower if you want me to understand any of that.* Gottcha!

Fig. 36

Well, I've been promising you for quite a while that we're going to begin studying airspace. It's time to pay off on the promise. The next chapter is all about airspace and how it works. I hope you are ambitious enough to learn all you can about airspace. It's the one area in which I find pilots to be consistently in need of further study. Understanding how the airspace is arranged, and what you can (and can't) expect in each kind of airspace is absolutely vital to a safe flight.

Fasten your seatbelt. Here we go.

Postflight Briefing #8-1

How ATC Keeps An Eye on You

Radar is the air traffic controller's eye on the sky. A radar antenna sends out a microwave length radio signal. Encountering a solid object, these energy pulses bounce back to the originating antenna, where they are identified and converted to visual blips on a radar scope. One of my students said, "How can that same pulse bounce off an airplane and return to the antenna if the antenna has rotated slightly?" My student didn't quite understand that electromagnetic pulses travel out and back at 186,300 miles per second (that's millions of miles per hour). A rotating antenna doesn't have much of an effect on the radar return. The target's distance from the radar antenna is determined by the signal's roundtrip time, based on the known speed of light.

Visual radar blips are called *primary radar returns* and are shown in Figure 36. Primary radar was the basis of early radar detection. But primary radar was inefficient since smaller targets (those with a less-reflective surface) were often difficult to identity. Weather (suspended water or ice) often interfered with target identification. With advances in technology, we now use something known as *secondary surveillance radar*. This system is known officially as the Air Traffic Control Radar Beacon System or ATCRBS.

Essentially, secondary surveillance radar is a separate system from primary radar because it uses an aircraft's transponder to identify

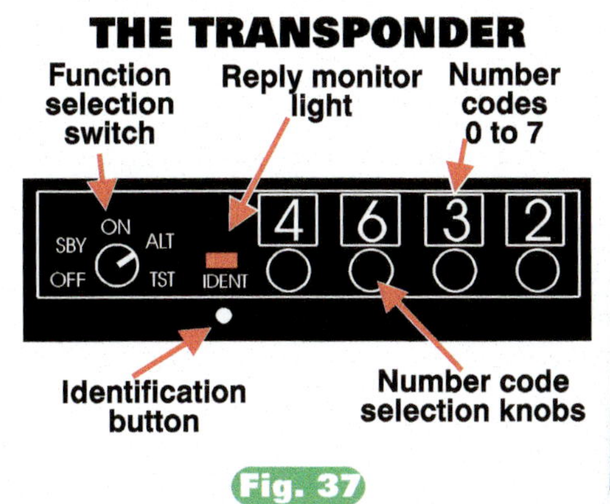

Fig. 37

A secondary radar return and its data block.

Fig. 38

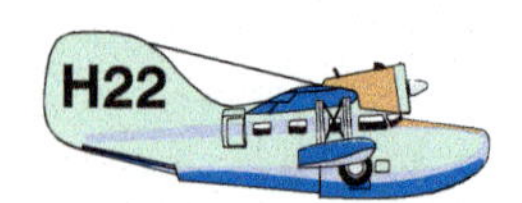

aircraft. A transponder is similar to the bell on a cow. Farmers hear the bell and know the location of the cow (which is also why cows can no longer play their favorite game called "let's sneak up on the other cows"). Transponders provide an electrical signal that the radar unit hears (receives) to determine your position.

Figure 37 shows a typical aircraft transponder. With the secondary radar beacon system, the ground-based radar sends out a coded signal which is received by the transponder, modified, then transmitted back to the radar unit where it's decoded by the ground facility. This allows ATC to identify your airplane among many other targets on the radar scope, based on the specific four-digit, discrete transponder code the controller assigned you.

If you are told to squawk a transponder code of "4312," you set those numbers in the code selection window, then turn the transponder function switch to the "alt" position. Controllers watching the scope might see your airplane as a secondary radar return in the form of a "blip" (also knows as a data block) with numbers along side as shown in Figure 38. These numbers might be 4312 (your assigned code) which makes it easy for the radar controller to identify you. Depending on the controller's type of radar equipment and the mode selected, the radar screen may show your groundspeed, altitude and aircraft call sign alongside the blip. Another advantage of the secondary system is that non-useful, scope-cluttering information can selectively be edited out.

Strangely enough, scope-clutter could be in the form of freeway traffic near the radar antenna. If it weren't for the secondary radar beacon system, the controller might have to visually ignore these extraneous targets. These targets don't show up on the secondary beacon system's screen because they don't have transponders. Therefore, you'll never hear ATC say, "32 Bravo, you have a U-Haul truck at twelve o'clock, opposite direction, turn right for an avoidance vector; and watch out, those guys make wide right turns!"

Radar is truly ATC's eye on the sky. It permits large volumes of traffic to move safely and efficiently. Which is not to say ATC radar is perfect. Far from it. Most facilities are using sadly outdated equipment, driven by computers that should be in museums. A multibillion dollar upgrade effort in the mid-90s bogged down in bureaucratic inertia, and the FAA is now scrambling to find a way to bring its system up to snuff as quickly as possible.

Chapter Nine

Airspace

The Wild Blue, Green & Red Yonder

In this chapter we're going to discuss how the airspace in the United States is constructed. We'll concern ourselves with the weather minimums and equipment requirements when flying in several varieties of airspace. I'll do my best to simplify the subject and make myself perfectly clear. (When one of my early flight instructors asked if he made himself perfectly clear, I wanted to run my hand up and down behind him and say, "Hey everyone, come here, look, Bob's perfectly clear now!")

Airspace rules sound and look worse than they are in practice. The fact of the matter is that 99% of the time 99% of the pilots will need to know only a handful of basics. Some of what you're about to read covers situations that, quite honestly, are *not* very prevalent. You need to be aware that certain rules exist, though, so you'll know when it's time to refresh your memory.

Bright student of aviation that you are, you might be asking yourself useful questions such as "Why?" Why is it so complicated, why are there so many rules, why do I care?

You care because the airspace structure is there to assure the maximum safety for everyone. Knowing where you can fly and under what conditions is essential to keeping yourself, your passengers, and lots of other people healthy and happy. You also care because I guarantee you that this stuff will show up on all the FAA aeronautical knowledge exams you ever take, both computerized and oral.

One more question. Why is the V-formation of ducks longer on one side than the other? Well, of course, one side has more ducks. Despite the asymmetric display, our fine-feathered friends are pretty good at keeping themselves from bumping into one another. They are their own air traffic control system. This is all the more remarkable when you consider that they have slightly less mental computing power than an Etch-a-Sketch.

Even if a few ducks were to collide, what's the worst that could happen? Some ruffled feathers? A headache, resulting in a duck coming in on a wing and a Bayer (I had to do that).

Pilots, on the other hand, can't afford a collision. Megatons of metal hurtling through the air at enormous speeds means any encounters will be of a very unfortunate type. Let's see how that can be avoided.

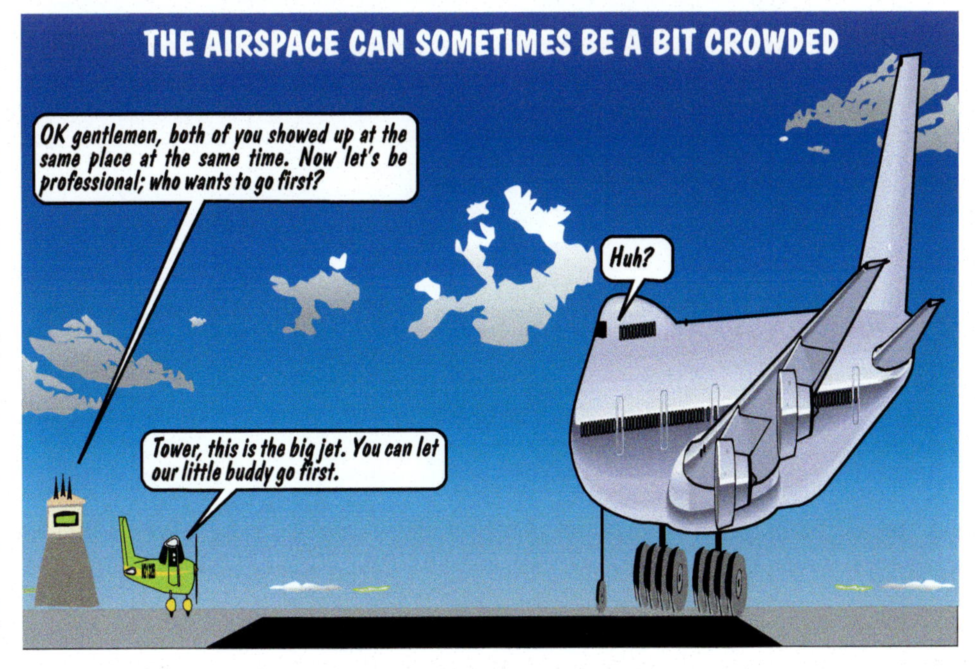

Eye See

Our modern airspace system has evolved to protect you (the pilot) from bumping into other aircraft and various solid objects (mountains, trees, antennas. etc.). This is accomplished by having rules that determine how and where you can (and can't) fly under given conditions. The rules vary depending not only on weather conditions, but also on the type of airspace in which you're flying. In order to maximize safety, the airspace has been divided into different types of areas, which generally reflect how busy that patch of airspace is and thus how demanding the flying is within it. Once upon a time, these had names like *airport traffic area,* and *terminal control area.* They've been renamed with snappy titles like Class A, B, C, D and E airspace. These are simple but they're not too descriptive. By whatever name, your job as a pilot is to know at all times what kind of airspace you're in and what its rules are.

BAD JOKE!

...it was only then that I realized our transponder was set to 7700 instead of 1200. Someone set the emergency signal into the transponder as a practical joke prior to our flight. Neither my student nor I had noticed the error. I regret that the military was called on to do an intercept as escort. I guarantee that I will check my transponder carefully preceding future flights.

ASRS Report

Any time you are flying, you will be operating under one of two primary sets of rules: visual flight rules (VFR) or instrument flight rules (IFR). Generally speaking, VFR flight is fair-weather flying based on the concept of being able to look out the window and see any obstacles or other aircraft at all times. IFR is flight when clouds, fog, rain, dust and other kinds of natural phenomena reduce visibility. IFR flight is, of course, more demanding. It requires additional training for the pilot (an *instrument rating)* and additional equipment for the airplane. A VFR flight is a pretty hang-loose proposition. No flight plan is required (although it's suggested), you can get from hither to yon via any route you want, and you don't need to talk to anybody except perhaps tower controllers at your departure or arrival airport.

IFR, on the other hand, is a tightly-controlled exercise. You file a flight plan prior to departure, in which you propose a very specific route, including altitudes, based on electronic highways in the sky. You receive a *clearance,* which may contain modifications to your proposed route, and you follow it from takeoff to landing, communicating constantly with air traffic controllers on the ground. With rare exceptions, you are under constant radar surveillance.

The exact flight visibility and required distances from clouds for VFR flight vary, depending on the type of airspace in which you're flying. In other words, flying in busy airspace requires greater flight visibility and distance from clouds than flying in less-busy airspace. These minimum requirements, known as *basic VFR weather minimums,* allow you ample time to see and avoid other aircraft. See and avoid is the basis of all VFR flight. When you can't see and avoid, you're no longer flying VFR. Keep that in mind, please, because far too many needless accidents occur every year when pilots qualified only for VFR flight continue on into bad (IFR) weather and create business for a metal salvage dealer.

You might be wondering, "What keeps an IFR pilot from popping out of a cloud and bumping into a VFR pilot?" A VFR pilot, adhering to the minimum distance-from-clouds and flight visibility requirements, should have adequate time to see and avoid an IFR aircraft emerging from a cloud. That's why, in the types of airspace used by IFR pilots, the basic VFR weather minimums make collisions highly unlikely. This assumes, of course, that pilots are looking out their windows and making an effort to see and avoid other aircraft.

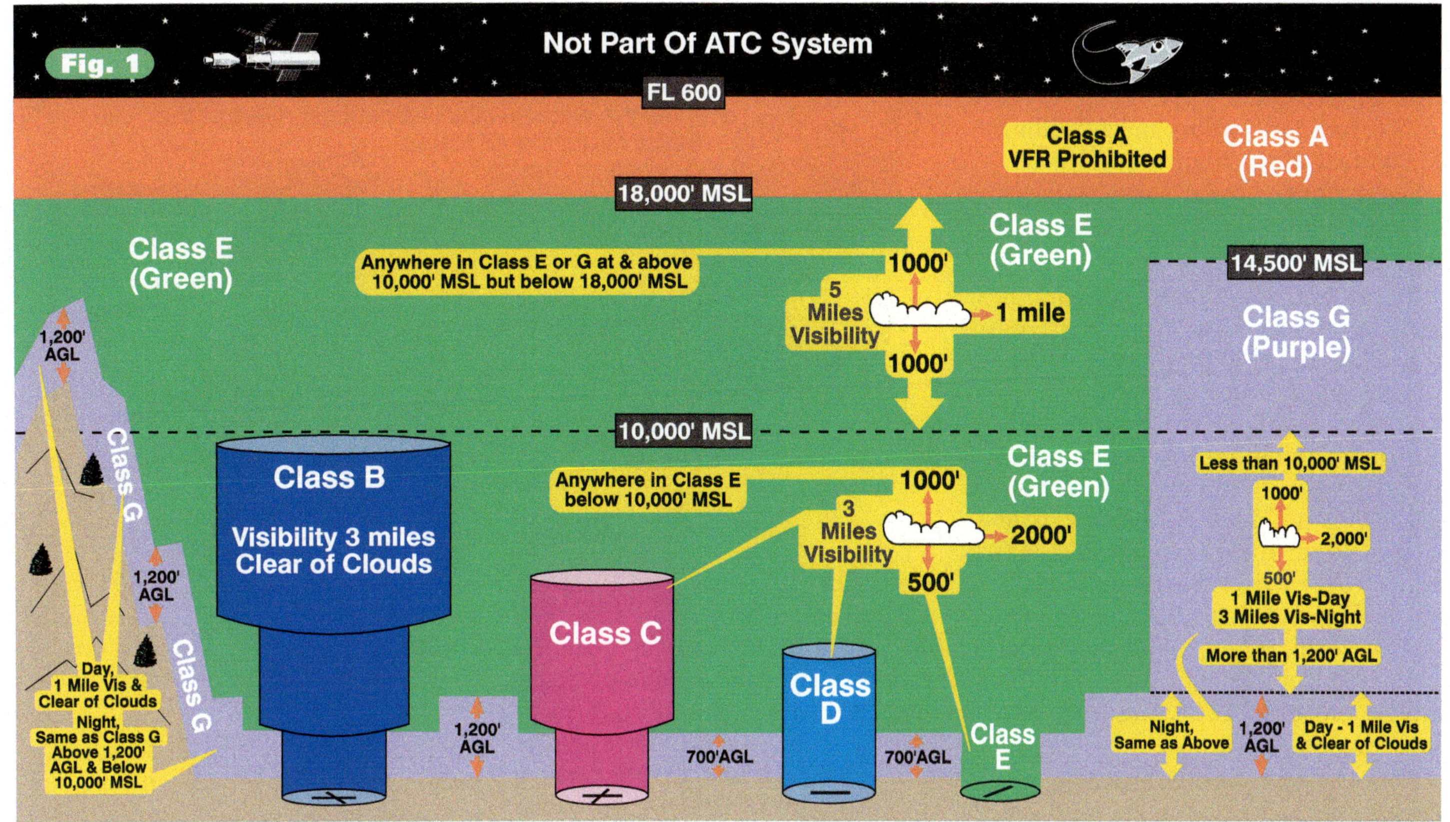

Controlled and Uncontrolled Airspace

Two basic types of airspace exist in the United States, *controlled* and *uncontrolled*. The major difference between the two can be distilled down to one very important point: controlled airspace is likely to be used by more aircraft (especially aircraft on IFR flight plans) than uncontrolled airspace. That's why controlled airspace typically has greater cloud distance and flight visibility requirements than uncontrolled airspace.

That makes sense, doesn't it? After all, if more airplanes use controlled airspace, the risk of a collision is higher. It's a numbers game. Greater flight visibility and cloud distance minimums make it more likely that pilots will see and avoid each other.

Uncontrolled airspace, on the other hand, is less active. It's normally found close to the surface, away from busy airports, and in areas devoid of airways (airways are the electronic highways in the sky I mentioned a few paragraphs ago, on which IFR flights are conducted and along which many VFR pilots also navigate). Since uncontrolled airspace is used less often, you can typically fly in this airspace with a lower flight visibility and cloud distance minimums.

If you've ever watched fish in an aquarium, you'll agree they swim around completely confused. If they think at all, it's to contemplate whether the Almighty is really an enormous nose that occasionally appears overhead and always precedes the sudden and inexplicable appearance of fish food falling from the sky. It's obvious that fish can't understand anything because they don't have the big picture. I don't want you to suffer the fish's dilemma. Let's take a look at airspace from the big picture perspective (just for the halibut).

The Big Picture

Figure 1 represents the big picture overview of the national airspace system. Don't be alarmed. This will all make a great deal of sense to you soon (and we won't need to do a Vulcan mind meld to get you through this). As you can see, the airspace is made up of several layers, shapes and sections. Each layer or section has a letter designation of either A, B, C, D, E, and G. Yes, I know, the *F* is missing. That's because there is no F-type airspace in the United States.

Because the people in charge didn't want any, that's why.

Class A, B, C, D and E is *controlled airspace*. Class G is *uncontrolled airspace*. Your job is to know the minimum flight visibility, cloud distance, aircraft equipment, and pilot qualifications for each class of airspace.

With the use of an aeronautical sectional chart and a little knowledge, it's easy to identify the weather minimums needed for any class of airspace. Just because the designations for airspace run from A to G (less F) doesn't mean we need to learn about them in alphabetical order, and a fair argument can be made that taking them out of order actually makes more sense.

Let's try this. We'll start with Class A (at the very top), then move on to Class E, then Class G airspace. There's a method to my madness (at least this portion of it). Class A airspace overlies Class E airspace, which, in turn, overlies Class G airspace.

Class A Airspace

Class A airspace consists of controlled airspace extending from 18,000 feet MSL up to and including 60,000 feet MSL (Figure 2). This airspace stretches from coast to coast with an additional 12 nautical mile extension over ocean waters.

CLASS A AIRSPACE

Class A airspace starts at 18,000' MSL and extends vertically to 60,000' MSL. It extends offshore and overlies the waters within 12 nautical miles of the coast within the 48 states and Alaska.

Alaska

Top of Class A 60,000' MSL

Base of Class A 18,000' MSL

18,000' MSL

18,000' MSL

Class A extends over water within 12 nm of the coast.

Fig. 2

Flight in Class A airspace requires that you have an instrument rating and be on an IFR flight plan. Why? Let me put it this way. When you're flying at and above 18,000 feet, you're flying where the heavy metal usually goes. Think about two 300,000 pound airplanes closing in on each other at a closure rate of 1,000 knots or more. *See and avoid* becomes something of a moot point. At this level, what keeps the metal monsters apart is flight plans and Air Traffic Control (ATC), the nice people at the radar screens.

At and above 18,000 feet MSL we don't refer to altitudes with *MSL* values. All pilots flying in Class A airspace set their altimeters to 29.92 inches of mercury, rather than local station pressure. These altitudes are referred to as flight levels (FL) as shown in Figure 3. Class A airspace starts at 18,000 feet MSL and officially tops out at FL600 (pronounced "flight level six zero zero") or 60,000 feet (add two zeros onto the flight level value to obtain the five digit altitude value in feet).

There's a good reason pilots don't use local station pressure at and above 18,000 feet. Imagine the pilot of a jet aircraft flying at hundreds of miles per hour having to reset the altimeter to the local station pressure every 100 miles or so. That pilot would be changing numbers in the altimeter's window faster that a teenager channel surfing with the TV's remote control. This pilot would need carpel tunnel surgery after each flight. It was decided that all pilots flying in Class A airspace would simply agree to use 29.92 as the altimeter setting and revert back to local station pressure when below 18,000 feet. At least everyone operating at and above 18,000 feet MSL is flying by the same altitude reference.

As a nice bonus, flight at and above 18,000 feet MSL will clear all terrain in the United States with the exception of Mt. McKinley in Alaska. With a few exceptions that ATC handles, pilots can set their altimeters to 29.92 at the transition altitude of 18,000 feet MSL and not worry about terrain.

Since Class A airspace doesn't come anywhere near the surface, it's not designated on any aeronautical sectional chart. In other words, the only way you know you're in Class A airspace is when your altimeter indicates 18,000 feet. (Frankly, the only time I can imagine someone unintentionally stumbling into Class A airspace is when they're flying the family's F-16 and accidentally hit the afterburner switch.)

Up to this point, we've only discussed the performance of civilian airplanes. Military airplanes also use the airspace system. Often, they operate secretly at high altitudes,

Why So High?

Why was 18,000 feet MSL chosen for the beginning of Class A airspace? When the airspace system was originally conceived back in the 1950's, designers thought few general aviation airplanes would fly above 18,000 feet MSL. At the time, private airplanes commonly went no higher than 15,000 feet MSL. Things have changed. We now have general aviation airplanes that climb like homesick angels and can easily ascend to 41,000 feet or more. Airspace operational specifications, however, haven't changed much since the 1950's.

Why does Class A airspace only go up to 60,000 feet? Similar reasoning applies. There weren't (and still aren't) very many commercial airplanes that can reach such lofty heights, though the late British Concorde jet did come pretty close to topping this altitude, while traveling at twice the speed of sound (that's why you can't hear the in-flight movie until two hours after you land—just kidding!). With the development of the Space Plane, it won't be long before this rule, too, is outdated.

CLASS A AIRSPACE SHOWN IN RED

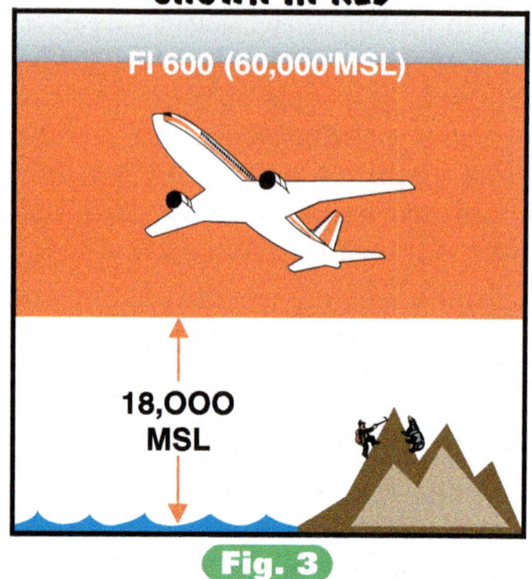

Fig. 3

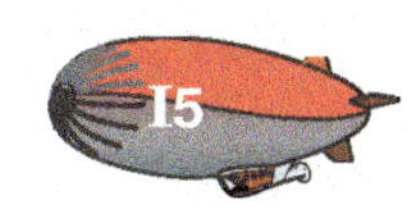

CLASS E AIRSPACE

Class E airspace starts at 1,200 feet AGL (sometimes higher or lower) and extends up to but not including 18,000' MSL—the base of Class A airspace.

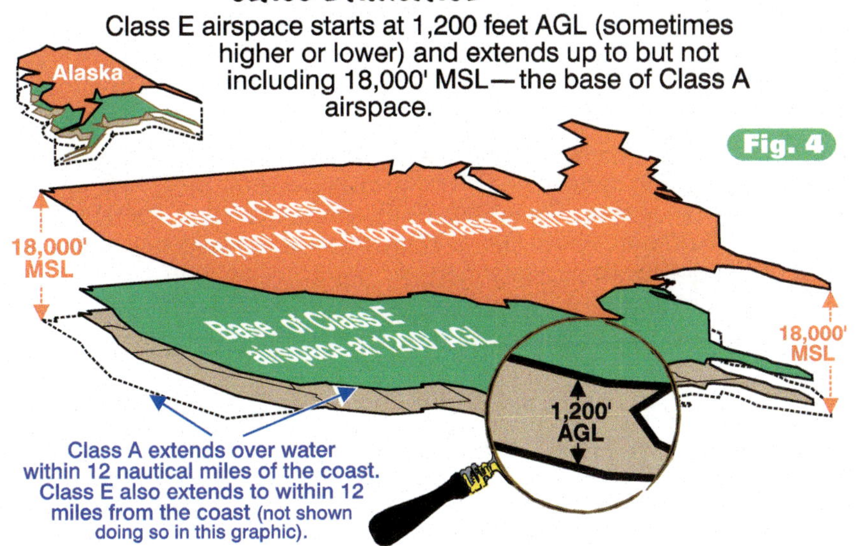

doing their own thing. In the early 1980s, a radar controller at the Los Angeles Center had an experience with a military pilot flying an SR-71 (the *Blackbird,* once used for secret aerial reconnaissance around the world). This aircraft is so fast and flies so high that its performance is still classified. Even the controllers don't know how high it flies. The pilot of this SR-71 called the controller and said, "L.A. Center, this is Blackbird 431 Charlie, request Flight Level 850" (that's 85,000 feet!). The controller started laughing and replied, "Hey 431 Charlie, if you can get up there, you can have it." There was a pause, then, in his best Clint Eastwood voice, the pilot replied, "We'll be coming down to Flight Level 850!" Now that's performance.

Class E Airspace

The airspace lying directly below Class A airspace is Class E airspace (Figure 4). Class E airspace overlies the 48 United States and Alaska (including a 12 nautical mile extension off the coastline).

Class E airspace is controlled airspace, implying that quite a few pilots are likely to use it. It's made up of airways, commonly flown routes, and those areas between busy airports.

You'll probably do the majority of your flying in Class E airspace, so let's cover it thoroughly. After all, if you use something regularly, you should know a lot about it, shouldn't you? Unfortunately, I have a friend who regularly eats at a Mexican restaurant but still doesn't know the proper Mexican names for food. He ordered a burrito and asked the waiter if it came with any Guatemala on it (it's actually called *guacamole).* The waiter said, "No, sir, but I do have some Nicaragua and conquistador that is mighty tasty." It pays to learn all about the things you use.

Our modern airspace system has evolved to protect you (the pilot) from bumping into other aircraft and various solid objects (mountains, trees, antennas, etc.).

Figure 5 provides a better understanding of the vertical structure of Class E airspace. This figure shows a plot of land over which lies Class E airspace. The Class E airspace in this figure starts at 1,200 feet AGL. Note that this is above ground level, not above sea level. Where there are hills or mountains, Class E airspace starts at 1,200 feet above the variable rising and descending surface as shown by position 1.

Class E airspace can also drop down to 700 AGL as shown in position #2. Class E airspace can also descend all the way down to the surface around an airport. When Class E airspace touches the surface, it's identified by a dashed magenta line in the shape of a circle, possibly with rectangular attachments, as shown at position #3. In just a while I'll explain why it drops to the surface and why this airspace is shaped the way it is. For now, our objective is to understand what Class E airspace means to you as a pilot. To do that, let's divide Class E airspace into two sections: a section at and above 10,000 feet MSL and a section less than 10,000 feet MSL.

CLASS E AIRSPACE

Class E (controlled) airspace (green) generally begins at 1,200 feet above ground level (#1) and extends vertically up to but not including the base of Class A airspace. Within the area of the magenta faded border (#2), Class E begins at 700 feet AGL. Within the red dashed lines (#3), Class E beings at the surface. Therefore, it's surface-based Class E airspace in this area.

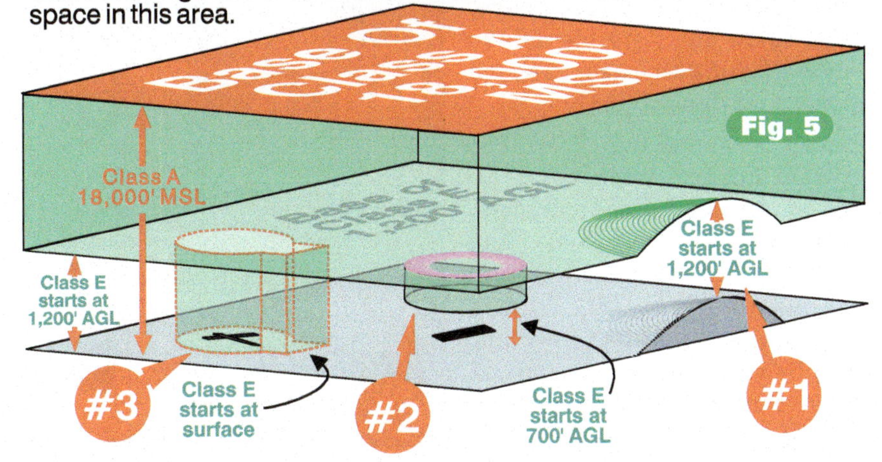

Too High in the Sky

The electronic highways in the sky I've referred to are called Victor airways below 18,000 feet, and jet routes (JR's) at 18,000 feet up to a maximum of FL450 (45,000 feet).

Jet routes stop at FL450 because above 45,000 feet the aircraft's VOR equipment, which receives the signals that define where the highways are, can pick up signal interference from other VOR stations. There are only a certain number of VOR frequencies to go around. VOR's near one another always have different frequencies. Remember, VOR communication is line-of-sight. The higher you are, the farther you can "see." Above FL450, it is possible to see farther than the amount of territory where frequency exclusivity can be guaranteed.

Above FL 450 aircraft use point-to-point navigation, like radar vectors, inertial navigation systems or GPS (global positioning systems). These systems don't rely on the VOR system for navigation.

Class E at and Above 10,000 Feet MSL

To operate VFR in Class E airspace at and above 10,000 foot MSL you need the basic VFR minimums shown in Figure 6. You're required to operate at least 1,000 feet above, 1,000 feet below and one statute mile to the side (horizontally) of any cloud formation. This means that if you see a cloud directly in front of you, you must maneuver to climb over it by at least 1,000 feet, go below it by at least 1,000 feet or go to the side of it by at least one statute mile (5,280 feet). You're also required to have a minimum of five statute miles of flight visibility at all times. These minimums make it easier for you to see and avoid other (and possibly faster) aircraft.

Here's Rod Machado's Airspace Simplification Rule #1: If you're flying at and above 10,000′ MSL, you could find fast jet fighters like the F-111. This reminds you that the minimum flight visibility is five (*F*) statute miles and the minimum distance above, below and to the side of a cloud is *111* or 1,000 feet above, 1,000 feet below and 1 statute mile to the side. To make this easy to remember, just think 5V/111.

You may be wondering, "How do I know when I'm one statute mile to the side of a cloud?" Good question. You must take your best guess. The reason you are required to be one statute mile horizontally from a cloud at these altitudes is to prevent being hit by emerging IFR aircraft. If you're at or above 10,000 feet MSL and a jet (traveling at 450 knots) on an IFR flight plan pops out of a cloud, your entire vocabulary would be reduced to two words: "Bad thing." Do you have any idea how scary it is to look out your window and see a jet coming directly at you at 450 knots? It's probably as scary as having Stephen King as a flight instructor. Being at least one mile to the side of a cloud provides you with a better chance of seeing and avoiding other aircraft.

*Rod Machado's Airspace Simplification Rule #1: If you're flying at and above 10,000′ MSL, you could find fast jet fighters like the **F-111**. You need **5** miles Visibility, **1**,000′ above, **1**,000′ below and **1** mile horizontally from any cloud formation.*

One way to make a practical judgment on distance from clouds is to always ask yourself "If a jet were to pop out of there at about 500 knots right now, aimed directly at me, would I have time and space to do something about it?" With that thought in mind, you should always have sufficient clearance from clouds, and it will be a heck of a lot more than one mile.

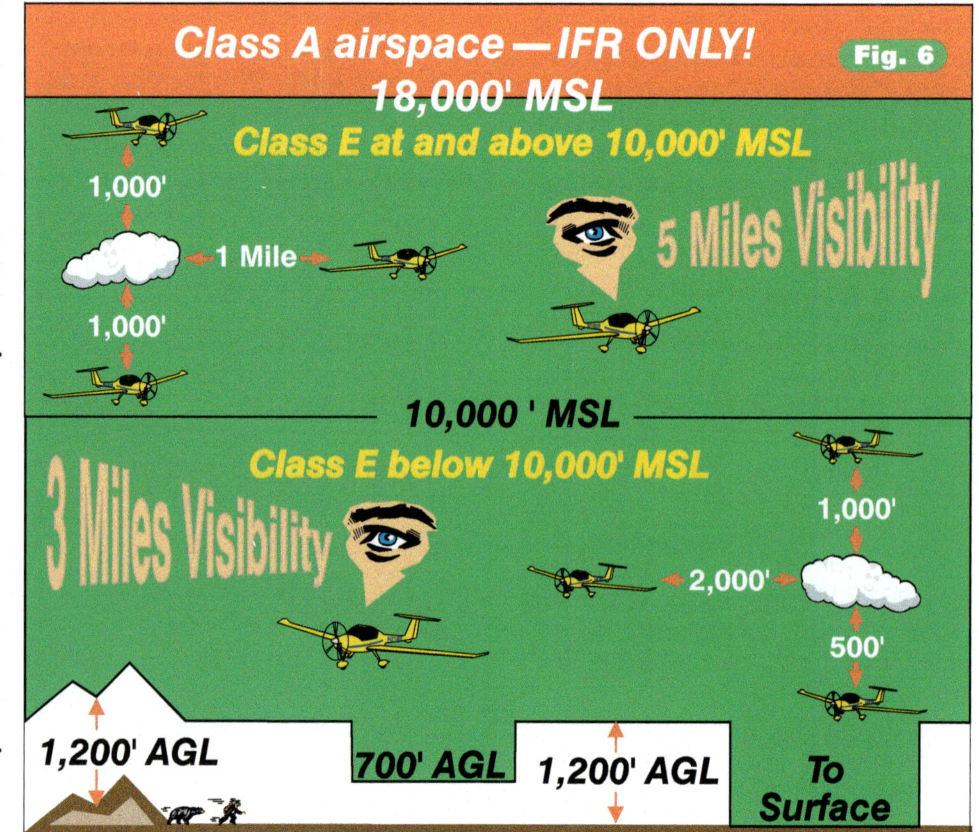

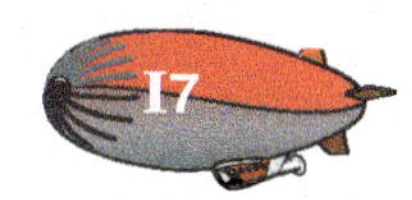

Since there is no aircraft speed restriction at and above 10,000 feet MSL, jets and other fast flying aircraft typically move at or near their top speed. Over land, however, jet pilots must avoid flying faster than the speed of sound (if you're breaking the sound barrier in your Piper Cub, please send me a little note with information on what power setting you're using).

Class E Below 10,000 Feet MSL

Most recreational flying is done below 10,000 feet MSL. It's not that our airplanes can't fly higher than this, but the performance of the majority of general aviation airplanes drops off pretty rapidly as you get above 10,000 feet. For short flights, it's just not worth the time and fuel it takes to fly high.

DON'T MAKE LOW PASSES, UNLESS WEARING GLASSES

Approaching the airport, neither the pilot nor passenger could visually verify the gear down. The pilot then opened the window for a closer look. At that point the pilot's eyeglasses were blown from the aircraft. After losing eyeglasses, pilot turned final and resumed pumping of gear. On what appeared to be a normal glidepath the pilot encountered a ridge line. After an abrupt pull-up maneuver to avoid the ridge, all emergency pumping of the landing gear ceased. With a smooth flare the main landing gear failed and the aircraft slid to a stop. Moral: It is a mistake for a pilot who relies on eyeglasses to open the window and look for the landing gear.

ASRS Report

Figure 6 shows the VFR cloud distance and flight visibility minimums below 10,000 feet MSL. Any altitude in Class E airspace below 10,000 feet MSL requires that you fly at least 1,000 feet above, 500 feet below and 2,000 feet horizontally from any cloud formation. Three miles of flight visibility is also required. Here's Rod Machado's Airspace Simplification Rule #2: Since you're likely to see at least three Cessna 152's below 10,000 feet, let's encode the minimums in an easy-to-remember formula: 3V/152.

Why are the cloud distance and flight visibility minimums below 10,000 feet MSL less than those at and above 10,000 foot MSL? There is a 250 knot (288 MPH) indicated airspeed limit for all aircraft operating below 10,000 feet MSL. A 250 knot airplane could still pop out the side of a cloud and you'll be as shocked as a pig seeing someone eating a ham sandwich. Maintaining a distance of no less than 2,000 feet horizontally from any cloud formation minimizes the risk of a collision. To repeat myself for a good cause, stay as far away from any cloud as you need to in order to feel really, really safe. Two thousand feet might not do it for you; it certainly doesn't for me. I prefer three, four or even five thousand feet (big feet too).

Why is a greater distance required above a cloud than below? Many high performance airplanes typically climb faster than they descend. Small jet aircraft, like Learjets, can climb at several thousand feet per minute after takeoff (Learjets feel like someone strapped a little rocket onto your back). Being higher above the cloud tops helps reduce the risk that you will unintentionally become a hood ornament for a Learjet.

*Here's Rod Machado's Airspace Simplification Rule #2: Since you're likely to see at least **three** Cessna **152**'s below 10,000 feet. You need **3** visibility, **1**,000' above, **5**00' below and **2**,000' horizontally from any cloud formation. Let's encode the minimums in an easy-to-remember formula: **3V/152.***

Pilots of jet aircraft, particularly big ones, rarely descend at thousands of feet per minute when they are below 10,000 feet MSL. Why? Trying to arrest a 6,000 foot-per-minute sink rate in a fully loaded Boeing 747 would take hundreds of feet. Boeing 747's (also known as "aluminum overcasts") have such inertia that descents in excess of 1,000 feet per minute while close to the ground are done with great care. Since pilots generally descend at lesser rates than they climb, required distances below clouds are typically less than those above.

The minimum flight visibility of three statute miles is less than that required above 10,000 feet. Once again, because of the speed limit, somewhat less margin is acceptable. Allowing more than the minimum is certainly the wise thing to do.

CLASS E AIRSPACE AT 700' AGL

Within the borders of the magenta faded area surrounding an airport, Class E (controlled) airspace starts at 700 feet above ground level (AGL) instead of the normal 1,200 feet AGL. The lower base of Class E airspace (i.e., 700' AGL), keeps airplanes flying instrument approaches in controlled airspace as they descend to the airport.

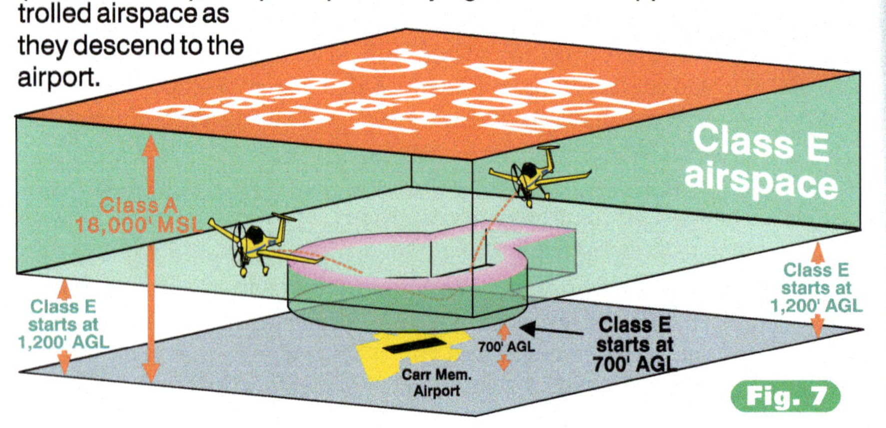

Fig. 7

Carr airport as shown on an aeronautical sectional chart.
Fig. 8

Class E Airspace Starting At 700 Feet AGL

When Class E airspace starts at 700 above ground level, it will be surrounded by a magenta faded line, as shown in Figure 7. Anywhere within this magenta faded area, controlled airspace starts at 700 feet AGL. An aeronautical sectional chart shows this magenta faded border quite clearly in Figure 8, position 1. Outside the border of the magenta fade, controlled airspace starts at 1,200 feet AGL.

Within the borders of the magenta fade, at and above 700 feet AGL, Rod Machado's Airspace Simplification Rule #2 applies. In other words, you need a minimum of 3V/152 for VFR flight.

Why would an airspace designer want to lower Class E airspace to 700 feet AGL around or near an airport? To keep VFR pilots from bumping into IFR pilots who are making instrument approaches.

The keyhole type extensions of Class E airspace starting at 700 feet AGL in Figure 8 identify descent paths followed by IFR airplanes during their instrument approaches. The keyhole slot is shown on the aeronautical sectional chart excerpt in Figure 8, position 1. IFR pilots on an instrument approach typically descend to altitudes of 700 feet AGL (and lower). They remain in Class E airspace during most of their IFR approach. If they see the airport, they land; if they don't see it, they fly off to another airport (hopefully one that has fewer clouds and better visibility).

Remember that in Class E airspace *below* 10,000 feet MSL, VFR pilots should be flying with no less than 3V/152. This means if an IFR pilot pops out of the clouds, there should be ample time for the VFR and IFR pilots to see and avoid each other (IFR pilots are equally responsible to see and avoid whenever they are not in instrument meteorological conditions).

Some airports have instrument approaches that bring IFR pilots down closer than 700 feet AGL, as shown in Figure 9. There are airports allowing IFR pilots to come within 200 feet AGL or less while still in the clouds. Since controlled airspace

CLASS E AIRSPACE AT THE SURFACE

Within the borders of the magenta (red) dashed line, Class E airspace descends all the way to the surface surrounding McComb-Pike airport. Since some instrument approaches bring pilots real close to the surface of an airport, this lower Class E surface area keeps them in controlled airspace during their descent.

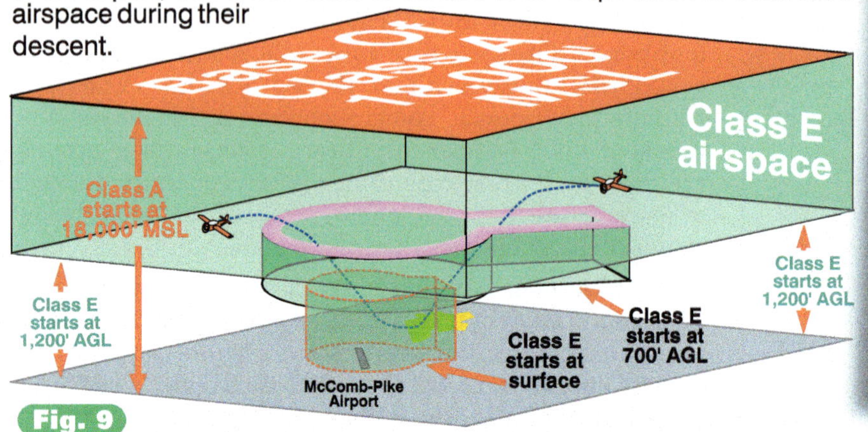

Fig. 9

Fig. 10

helps VFR pilots see and avoid other pilots, these airports have Class E airspace lowered all the way to the surface. (There are other reasons why controlled airspace is lowered, but these are beyond the scope of this book.)

Figure 10 shows how surface-based Class E airspace is shown on an aeronautical sectional chart. A dotted magenta line defines the lateral boundaries of the controlled airspace surrounding McComb-Pike County airport (position 1). Airports without air traffic control towers use a magenta dashed line to represent this surface-based Class E airspace. (Airports with established control towers, as you'll see a little later, use blue-dashed lines to represent controlled airspace in contact with the surface around that airport.)

What does this surface-based Class E airspace mean to you as a VFR pilot approaching and departing McComb-Pike airport? It means Rod Machado's Airspace Simplification Rule #2 applies all the way to the surface within the boundaries of the magenta-dashed line. The only thing different here is that the controlled airspace normally existing at 700 feet or 1,200 feet AGL drops to the surface within the boundaries of the magenta dashed line.

WHY 1,000 FEET WAS CHOSEN AS THE MINIMUM CEILING

If you think like a flight instructor (we're attracted to bright, shiny objects and trinkets that rattle), then you're probably wondering why 1,000 feet was chosen as the minimum ceiling for basic VFR within any surface-based controlled airspace. Well, as famed undersea explorer Jacques Cousteau says, "We do not know, but we shall soon find out." (Although, come to think of it, I've never actually seen him go into the water).

In Class E airspace, less than 10,000 feet MSL, you need to remain at least 500 feet below any cloud formation. Regulations also require that you remain at least 500 feet above the surface over a noncongested area. For the sake of rulemaking, the airport is assumed to be built around a noncongested area (you and I know that this isn't always true, but it's general enough to make this point). Adding the 500 foot minimum altitude requirement to the 500 foot minimum clearance beneath a cloud gives you a minimum ceiling height of 1,000 feet. These values are shown in Figure 11.

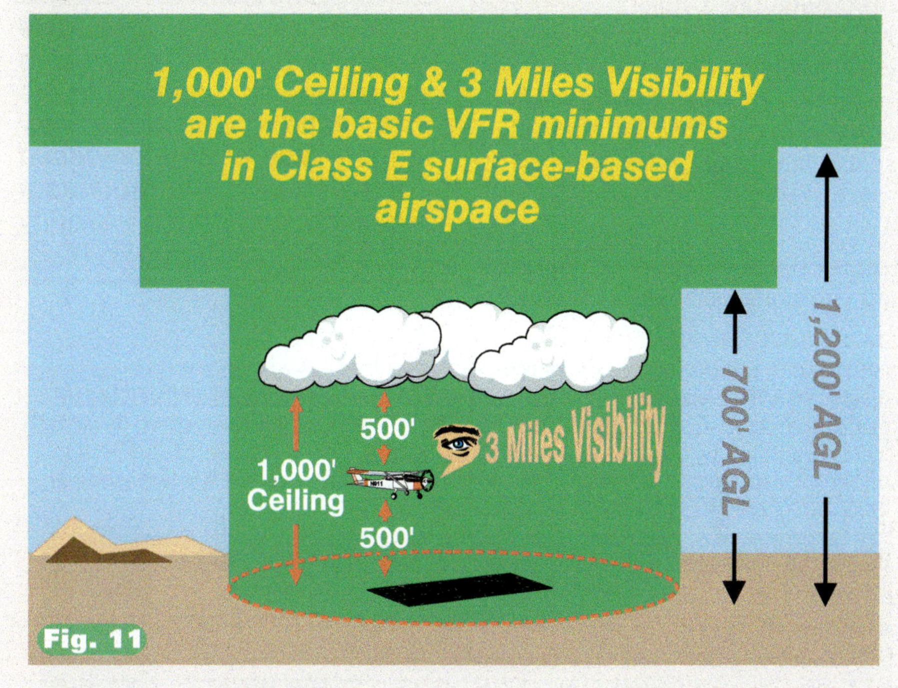

Fig. 11

Additional Requirements In Surface-Based Controlled Airspace

There are two additional requirements when operating at an airport having *any* type of surface-based controlled airspace established for it (Class E in the case of McComb-Pike):

1. The reported ground visibility at the airport must be at least three statute miles. If the ground visibility isn't reported, then the flight visibility during takeoff, landing or when operating in the traffic pattern must be at least three statute miles. (The *flight visibility* is always determined by the pilot on the honor system.)

2. If a ceiling exists at that airport, it can be no lower than 1,000 feet AGL if you desire to operate beneath it. If you want to take off, land or operate in the traffic pattern, the ceiling (if one exists) must be at least 1,000 feet AGL or more.

A *ceiling* is defined as the height above the earth's surface of the lowest layer of clouds reported as *broken* or *overcast*, or any reported *vertical visibility* into obscuring phenomena. We'll be talking more about these terms in Chapter 13. For the moment, consider a ceiling as being anything in the sky you can't readily see through (like clouds for instance).

To summarize these requirements, remember this. To operate to, from, or at an airport within the boundaries of any surface-based controlled airspace, you need a minimum of three miles reported visibility (flight visibility if none reported) and no less than a 1,000 foot ceiling (if a ceiling exists). Let's symbolize these basic VFR requirements as *3V/1C*. (As you'll soon see, in addition to Class E, there are three other types of controlled airspace that can surround an airport at the surface: Class D, C and B.)

Here's Rod Machado's Airspace Simplification Rule #3: Taking off, landing, or operating in the traffic pattern of an airport having *any* type of surface-based controlled airspace requires basic VFR minimums of at least three miles visibility and, if a ceiling exists at that airport, it can be no lower than 1,000 feet. We'll symbolize this rule as 3V/1C.

I specifically chose the words above to indicate that surface-based controlled airspace is established for a specific airport (usually the one in the center of that airspace). We call this the *primary airport*. Sometimes, other airports lie within the boundaries of the primary airport's surface-based controlled airspace. These are called *satellite airports* (think of them as orbiting the primary airport, although they really don't move!). As you'll soon see, the above simplification rule #3 also applies to satellite airports, with one exception.

The *Chart Supplement* indicates that McComb-Pike's Class E surface area operates continuously.

Mc COMB-PIKE CO-JOHN E LEWIS FLD (MCB) 4 S UTC–6(–5DT) **NEW ORLEANS**
N31°10.71′ W90°28.31′ **H-5C, L-17D**
413 B S4 **FUEL** 100LL, JET A **IAP**
RWY 15-33: H5000X100 (ASPH) S-25, D-30, DT-60 MIRL
RWY 15: PAPI(P2L)—GA 3.0° TCH 38′. Trees. **RWY 33:** PAPI(P2L)—GA 3.0° TCH 46′. Trees.
AIRPORT REMARKS: Attended 1400Z‡-dusk. For attendant and fuel after hours call 601-684-7070 or ctc FSS. ACTIVATE MIRL Rwy 15-33—CTAF. For MALSF Rwy 15 ctc FSS. Ground drops abruptly both ends Rwy 15-33 starting 200′ from thld.
COMMUNICATIONS: CTAF 123.6 **UNICOM** 122.95
Mc COMB FSS (MCB) on arpt. 123.6 122.4 122.2 122.1R. LC 684-7070 NOTAM FILE MCB.
Ⓡ **HOUSTON CENTER APP/DEP CON** 133.5
AIRSPACE: CLASS E svc effective continuously.
RADIO AIDS TO NAVIGATION: NOTAM FILE MCB.
(H) VORTAC 116.7 MCB Chan 114 N31°18.26′ W90°15.49′ 233° 13.3 NM to fld. 440/03E. **HIWAS**
FERNI NDB (MHW/LOM) 413 MC N31°15.27′ W90°30.63′ 153° 5 NM to fld.
ILS 109.1 I-MCB Rwy 15. LOM FERNI NDB. LOC unusable byd 25 degrees E of course.

Fig. 12

Just because Class E airspace exists at the surface of an airport doesn't mean it stays that way 24 hours a day. In other words, the surface-based portion of that controlled airspace can revert back to Class E airspace starting at 700 or 1,200 feet AGL.

Normally, any type of surface-based controlled airspace requires a federally certificated weather observer or weather-observing system be present to make visibility and cloud height determinations. These weather observers or observing systems can be tower controllers, flight service station personnel, licensed weather observers, or federally certificated automated weather observing stations known as AWOS-3 (Automatic Weather Observing System). Some means of pilot-to-ATC communication is also required. Either direct communications with ATC, relayed communication through an FSS, or communication via a remote communication outlet is acceptable.

*Rod Machado's Airspace Simplification Rule #3: Taking off, landing or operating in the traffic pattern of an airport having any type of surface-based controlled airspace requires a minimum of 3 miles visibility and a 1,000′ ceiling or **3V/1C**.*

The official weather observer's hours of operation normally coincide with the hours during which the surface-based controlled airspace exists. I said *normally*, not *always*. The actual hours that surface-based controlled airspace exists are shown in the *Chart Supplement* (CS) as shown in Figure 12. If the weather observer leaves before these hours, the surface-based airspace is still in effect. This is one reason why ground visibility might not be reported, yet three miles of flight visibility is still required for landing.

SPECIAL VFR (SVFR)

A special VFR clearance applies only within the lateral limits of the Class E surface area (B,C & D also) below 10,000 feet MSL. It allows you to fly with 1 mile visibility while remaining clear of clouds. The purpose of SVFR is to allow you to depart toward VFR weather or to land when the weather is less than basic VFR.

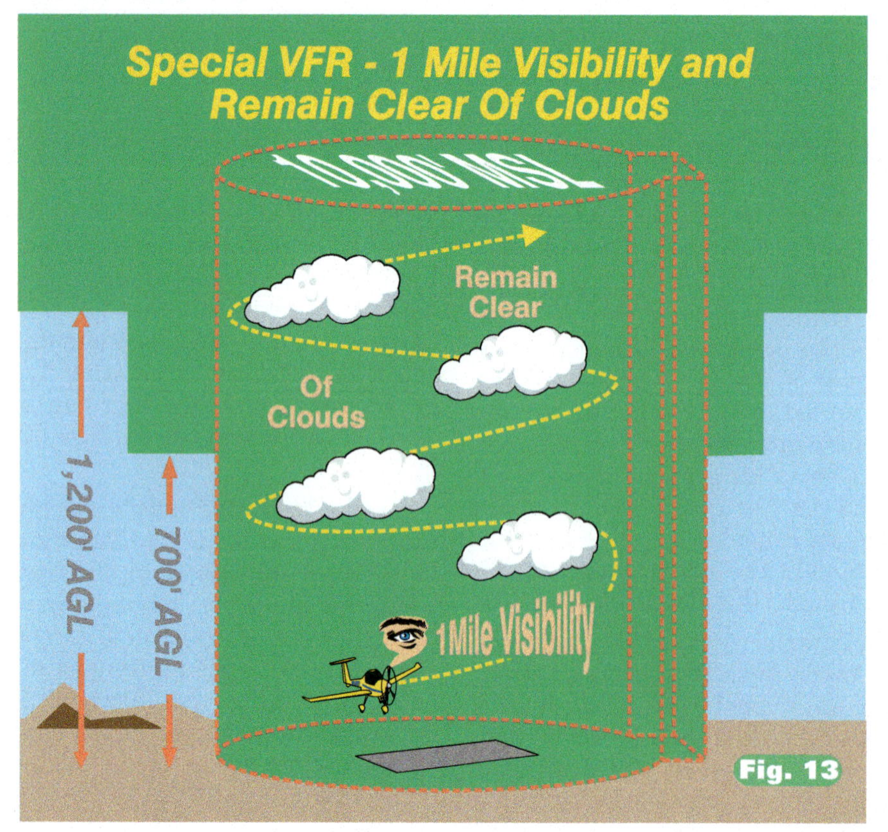

Fig. 13

Special VFR Clearance

What happens if you want to land or depart McComb-Pike airport and the reported ground visibility is less than three miles or the ceiling is less than 1,000 feet? Do you circle, eating a sandwich, until the cows come home or the clouds blow away? Not necessarily.

Report Reaching

Hey! We're backin' up.

One of the things making special VFR *special* is that you get the airspace all to yourself. Until you report reaching VFR conditions, or clear of the lateral limits of the surface-based controlled airspace, all other traffic is barred. If you reach VFR conditions 30 seconds after departure, *say so.* Pick up the nice microphone, summon your best radio voice, and say "SoCal Approach, Cessna 2132 Bravo is VFR."

One of the quickest ways on or off earth to become highly unpopular is to fail to report reaching VFR, especially when 19 other people are backed up waiting.

The only thing worse is to depart the frequency without reporting clear. For some reason, there is a subgroup of pilots who think that they only have to take care of themselves and everything else will be fine. They take their special VFR clearance, depart the airport, and without so much as an *adios* they flip the dial and tune in the baseball game. Down below, some controller is calling every 30 seconds, while considering whether to order a missile strike from a nearby Air Force base.

Until ATC can confirm that you are out of the airspace, they can't do a thing with all the other people other than try and harness the steam coming from their ears. Don't be a special VFR abuser.

You can request something known as a *special VFR clearance (SVFR)* from the nearest ATC facility. This is permission to operate within the surface-based controlled airspace at less than basic VFR minimums.

An SVFR clearance allows you to operate below 10,000 feet MSL down to the surface, within the lateral boundaries of surface-based controlled airspace (Class E in this instance at McComb-Pike) under the following conditions:

1. The pilot must have a clearance from ATC.

2. The reported ground visibility (by the official weather observer) must be at least one statute mile. If the ground visibility isn't reported, then the flight visibility must not be less than one statute mile.

3. The pilot must remain clear of all clouds and maintain one mile flight visibility.

Despite the lowered visibility that SVFR permits, this is considered a safe operation from the perspective of ATC. Since ATC is responsible for providing separation between aircraft during SVFR conditions, they usually allow only one aircraft to operate within the lateral boundaries of the surface-based controlled airspace at any one time during SVFR operations. Remember, SVFR applies to any surface-based controlled airspace (Class E as well as three other types we haven't discussed yet: B, C and D).

The whole purpose of SVFR is to get into or out of an airport that's surrounded by surface-based controlled airspace when the weather conditions are less than basic VFR minimums. This clearance is not intended to let you fly to a far-off destination, halfway around the globe, with a minimum of one mile flight visibility while remaining clear of all clouds. The SVFR clearance is only applicable within the horizontal boundaries of the vertically extended, surface-based airspace at that airport, as shown in Figure 13. The SVFR clearance is good below 10,000 feet MSL unless ATC assigns a lower altitude restriction.

SVFR is a very handy tool, and when used properly, a safe one. It is the answer to the phenomenon, observed by every pilot, that if there is one cloud in the sky it will hang over the airport. You can use SVFR to depart or arrive at an airport when there is some local obscuring phenomena such as fog, haze or low clouds and the enroute weather is above basic VFR minimums for the airspace in which you'll fly.

Let's examine how you go about getting a SVFR clearance.

Obtaining an SVFR Clearance

Special VFR clearances are usually obtained by contacting the nearest ATC facility (tower, FSS, approach or departure control.) For instance, let's suppose the reported ground visibility at McComb-Pike is two miles and you need to obtain an SVFR clearance. You can obtain this clearance by calling the FSS using the remote communication outlet shown in Figure 10, position 2. As an aside, you could also attempt to call the

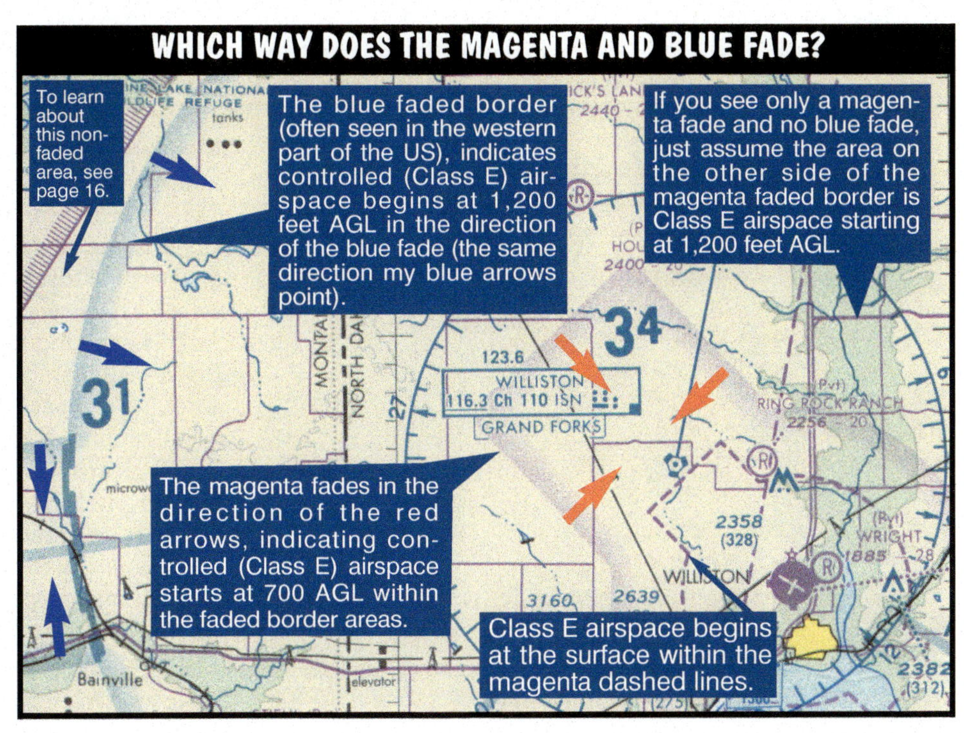

local ATC facility (typically the departure control facility) from the ground at McComb-Pike using the radio frequency or the listed ATC phone number found in the chart supplement. Either one works.

After contacting the FSS specialist using the remote communication outlet, the FSS specialist would contact the ATC facility in charge of the surface-based controlled airspace (Class E in this case) at McComb-Pike and obtain an SVFR clearance for you. Since no control tower exists at this airport, the nearest approach and departure control or air traffic control center will normally have jurisdiction over this airspace. The clearance may sound something like this:

"Cessna 2132 Bravo is cleared to climb to VFR within the Class E surface area within 4 miles of McComb-Pike airport, maintain special VFR conditions until reaching VFR. Report reaching VFR."

This is a typical SVFR clearance issued when conditions of restricted visibility exist near the airport. When cleared for takeoff, you must maintain at least one mile flight visibility and remain clear of clouds within 4 miles of McComb-Pike. The assumption is that you will reach VFR conditions (3V/152 when operating below 10,000' MSL) by the time you depart the controlled airspace.

An altitude limitation may be given in an SVFR clearance when it's necessary to keep you separated from IFR traffic in the vicinity of the airport. For example, ATC may issue the following SVFR clearance:

"Cessna 2132 Bravo is cleared to maintain special VFR conditions at or below 2,000 feet within the Class E surface area of McComb-Pike airport."

By the time you reach 2,000 feet, it's expected that you will be in VFR conditions. If not, the clearance forbids you to continue your climb in special VFR conditions. If you haven't reached VFR conditions by 2,000 feet, you should contact the ATC facility responsible for that airspace and request further instructions. In this instance, I

Fig. 14

would ask ATC for my SVFR clearance to be amended with a higher altitude restriction.

If you were approaching McComb-Pike airport and the reported ground visibility was 2 miles, you could call the nearest ATC facility (typically approach control in this instance) and request an SVFR clearance into Class E airspace. The clearance might sound something like this:

"Cessna 2132 Bravo is cleared into Class E airspace from the west, toward McComb-Pike airport, in special VFR conditions at or below 2,500 feet, maintain SVFR conditions until reaching McComb-Pike."

Now, don't go out and fall on your sword or throw yourself in front of an onrushing glacier, but student pilots are limited in the SVFRs they can obtain. Student pilots can't fly when the ground or flight visibility is less than three miles during the day and five miles at night (no exceptions!). Students can, however, obtain a clearance for SVFR operations when the ceiling is less than 1,000 feet (I'm not recommending you do this, either. Let your flight instructor be the judge of this. Check and see if he or she will allow such activity).

No pilot (student or otherwise) can obtain an SVFR clearance from sunset to sunrise unless they have an instrument rating and an airplane equipped for instrument flight. This obviously means no SVFR at all for student pilots at night. Clouds are difficult to see at night, making them much easier to accidentally fly into. An instrument rating provides good insurance for SVFR operations at night in case you accidentally fly into a cloud.

Satellite Airports Lying Within the Primary Airport's Surface-Based Controlled Airspace

Sometimes an additional airport (a satellite airport) lies within the surface-based airspace originally established for another airport (the primary airport). Port Angeles (Figure 14) is an example of such an airport. It lies within the Class E surface area established for Fairchild International airport. If Fairchild reports less than three miles visibility, an SVFR clearance isn't required for operations at Port Angeles as long as the pilot has a minimum of three miles flight visibility (or ground visibility—if it's reported at the satellite airport). However, if Fairchild (the primary airport) reports a ceiling less than 1,000 feet AGL, then an SVFR clearance is required for operations anywhere within that surface-based controlled airspace. Simply stated, visibility is determined by pilots on the honor system but ceilings are determined by the official weather observer at the primary airport. This rule pertains to *any* type of surface-based controlled airspace (B, C, D as well as E).

Figure 15A and 15B provide a quick summary of the VFR weather minimums for flight in Class E airspace.

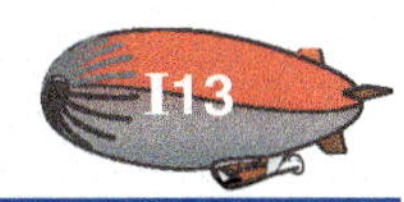

Fig. 15A

SUMMARY OF VFR WEATHER MINIMUMS FOR CLASS E AIRSPACE

Airspace/ALtitude	Visibility	Cloud Clearance
Class E airspace at & above 10,000' MSL	5 Miles Visibility	1,000' above, 1 Mile horizontal, 1,000' below
Class E airspace below 10,000' MSL	3 Miles Visibility	1,000' above, 2,000' horizontal, 500' below
Basic VFR in Class E surface area	3 Miles Visibility	1,000' ceiling (min)
Special VFR in Class E surface area	1 Mile Visibility	Clear Of Clouds

AVIATION'S PRIORITIES

1. **Aviate: Always fly the airplane.**
2. **Navigate after the airplane is under control.**
3. **Communicate: Don't lose control or lose positional awareness just to talk to ATC.**

VFR REQUIREMENTS IN CLASS E AIRSPACE

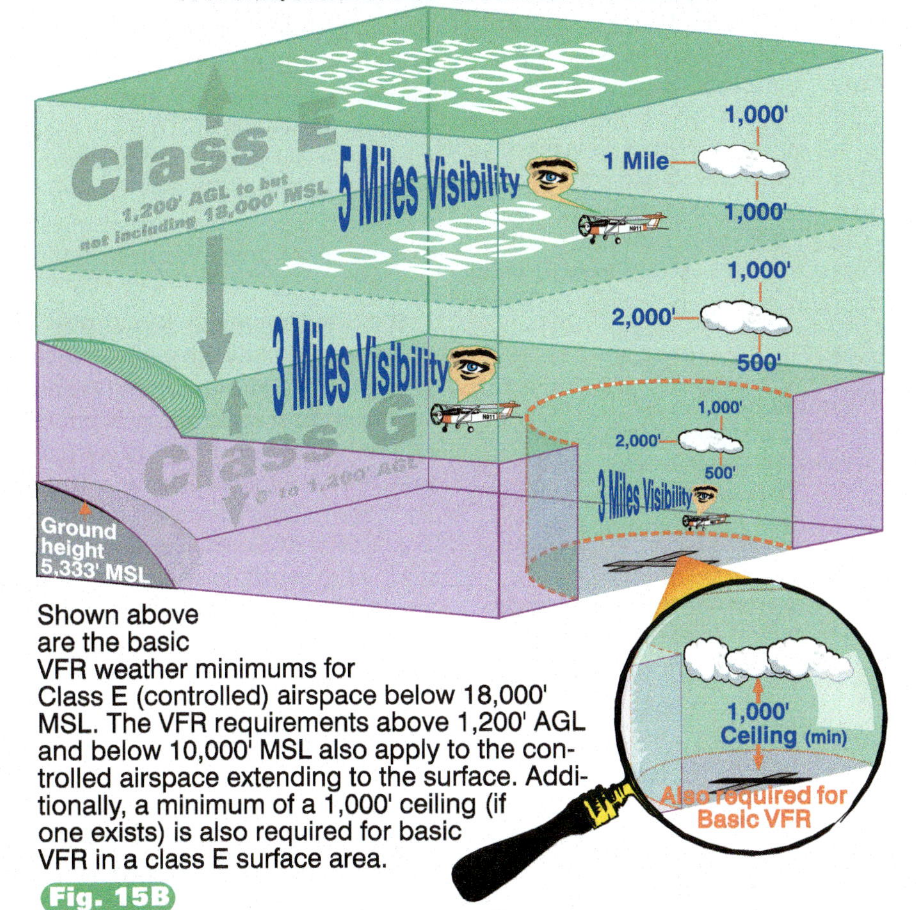

Shown above are the basic VFR weather minimums for Class E (controlled) airspace below 18,000' MSL. The VFR requirements above 1,200' AGL and below 10,000' MSL also apply to the controlled airspace extending to the surface. Additionally, a minimum of a 1,000' ceiling (if one exists) is also required for basic VFR in a class E surface area.

Fig. 15B

TO ERR IS HUMAN—BUT NOT COMPULSORY

Reporting over XYZ (last foreign point before entering USA), the controller asked us to contact the American center on 125.65 and squawk 7500. We acknowledged and complied. Center asked me to confirm squawking 7500. I confirmed without it reminding me that this was the hijack code. The approach was curious in that we received (sort of), special handling. There didn't seem to be anybody else on the frequency and everything went very smoothly.

Tower asked us to roll out all the way to the end of the long runway, which seemed odd. I taxied off the runway and was surrounded by a phalanx of vehicles (police cars, airport vehicles, FBI, Border Patrol, M-16 carbines, sirens, lights, and customs people). The whole world was there to greet us. It was only when someone asked if I knew the meaning of Code 7500, that it dawned on me what had happened. It was then difficult to convince the authorities that the flight was in no way abnormal. Unfortunately, in the papers the next day they correctly spelled my name.

Our foreign controller friends could use a refresher on emergency codes like the one these company pilots received.

ASRS Report

CLASS G (UNCONTROLLED) AIRSPACE

Class G (uncontrolled) airspace starts at the surface and ascends upward until reaching the base of Class E (controlled) airspace. Class G airspace may extend upward to 700 or 1,200 feet AGL or even higher. Generally, Class G airspace contains fewer big and fast airplanes (except in the vicinity of certain airports). Therefore, the visibility and cloud clearance requirement is usually not as great as in controlled airspace.

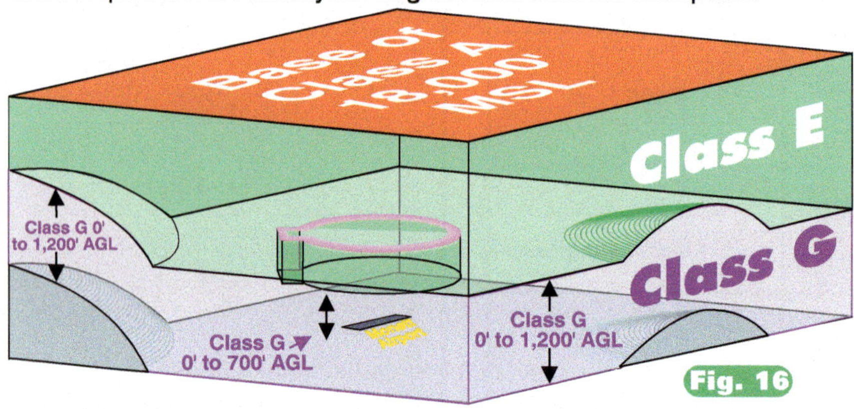

Fig. 16

Fig. 18

Class G Airspace

We're about to do much ado about nothing.

Welcome to the short course on *Class G,* or *uncontrolled* airspace. This is a tiny sliver of airspace whose rules are thicker than its depth, and whose practical importance to most pilots on most occasions is vanishingly small unless you routinely fly from Point A to point B at or below 1200 feet above the ground.

While there are several types of controlled airspace (Class B, C, D and E), there is only one type of uncontrolled or Class G airspace. It's generally found below Class E airspace at altitudes less than 1,200 or 700 feet AGL. Figure 16 depicts Class G airspace. In fact, the only place near the surface where you *won't* find Class G airspace, is within the surface-based controlled airspace that surrounds an airport.

Think about Class G airspace as a thin layer of water resting over the entire, continental United States. In other words, any place other than an airport having surface-based controlled airspace must have a thin layer of Class G airspace lying on top of it. Those airports having surface-based controlled airspace in the United States couldn't possibly cover even 1% of the nation's surface (believe me when I say it's much, much less than that, but we'll use 1% anyway). Simple math indicates that over 99% of the United States surface area must have Class G airspace lying on top of it and extending vertically to 700 or 1,200 feet AGL. As you can imagine, Class G airspace within 700 or 1,200 feet AGL is quite common. That's why it's nice to know something about the basic VFR minimums in Class G airspace.

To understand what Class G airspace means to you, it's necessary to think back to the introduction of this chapter. Our airspace discussion revolves around the idea that controlled airspace is likely to be used by more aircraft (especially aircraft on an IFR flight plan) than uncontrolled airspace. Therefore, the basic VFR weather minimums are stricter in controlled airspace.

Have you noticed how the basic VFR weather minimums change with altitude? Generally, the lower you go, the less restrictive the weather minimums become. At low altitudes (say less than 1,200 feet AGL), fewer airplanes, and certainly fewer fast airplanes, fly close to the surface for long periods of time (except for taking off and landing at airports of course). There is less threat of a collision at these lower altitudes between airports.

With fewer airplanes flying long distances at low altitudes between airports, it's reasonable to conclude that the VFR weather minimums in these areas should be the least restrictive. That is precisely the case. In Class G airspace at and below 1,200 feet AGL, the basic VFR minimums for daylight operations are one statute mile flight visibility while remaining clear of all clouds as shown in Figure 17. We'll simplify this with the symbol *1V/COC*. (COC stands for clear of clouds.)

Monett airport, shown in the aeronautical sectional chart excerpt in Figure 18, position 1, is in Class G airspace. During the day you may depart or land at Monett with a mini-

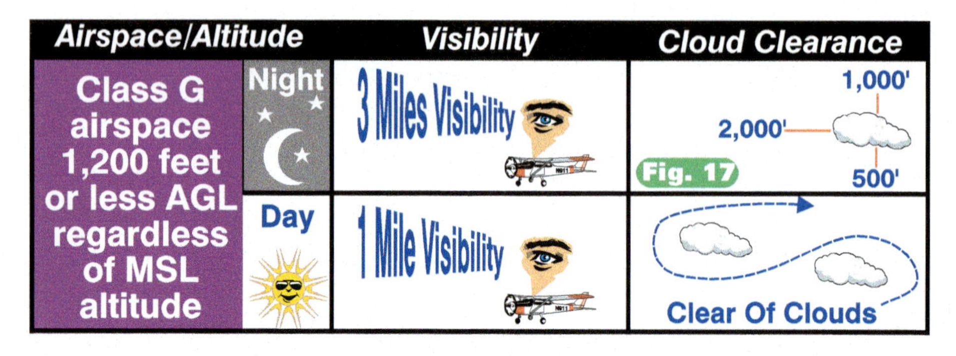

Airspace/Altitude		Visibility	Cloud Clearance
Class G airspace 1,200 feet or less AGL regardless of MSL altitude	Night	3 Miles Visibility	1,000' above, 2,000' horizontal, 500' below
	Day	1 Mile Visibility	Clear Of Clouds

Fig. 17

mum flight visibility of one mile, while staying clear of all clouds, as long as you remain at or below 700 feet AGL. Class E airspace starts at 700 feet AGL within the magenta faded borders above Monett (position 2). For flight above 700 feet AGL, within the magenta border's lateral limits, you must have the basic VFR minimums for Class E airspace operations below 10,000′ MSL (3V/152).

Outside the lateral limits of the magenta fade, at what altitude does Class E airspace start? I hope you said it starts at 1,200 feet AGL, as shown in Figure 16. Let's assume you want to take off or land at Mt. Vernon airport (position 3, Figure 18). You can do so during the day with a minimum of one mile flight visibility and remaining clear of clouds as long as you ascend no higher than 1,200 feet AGL. Climbing higher than 1,200 feet AGL above Mt. Vernon puts you in Class E airspace which requires 3V/152.

Most pilots do *not* routinely fly around at 1200 AGL or below. That's because most pilots realize there's not much margin of safety in case of engine failure when you're 1200 AGL, there's a good chance of bumping into something tall (like a basketball player or TV antenna), and you probably couldn't convince the FAA that this met the standard for sensible altitude when over a densely occupied area. For these reasons, and many others, Class G airspace is not something in which you will spend a lot of your pilot life. In fact, you'll probably spend more time trying to memorize the rules about Class G airspace than you will using them to fly within such airspace.

Remember, the airspace designations and the basic VFR weather minimums for each are there for a reason—to protect you and other pilots. Rules are often created for just that purpose. In fact, that's why you now see little signs on Coke machines saying, "If you lose money in this machine, don't shake it, call the manager." Apparently people without much common sense were shaking the machines, causing them to tip over and squish these folks graveyard dead. (If you've been injured by a falling Coke machine, you probably shouldn't be flying an airplane. I always check for Coke imprints on the forehead before I fly with anyone.)

*Rod Machado's Airspace Simplification Rule #4: When flying in Class G (uncontrolled) airspace at or below 1,200′ AGL during the day you're low enough to knock over **1 COC** machine (sounds like Coke). You need **1** mile visibility and must remain **c**lear **o**f **c**louds.*

Night Operations in Class G Airspace at 1,200 Feet AGL And Below

To offer you additional protection, the FAA has established slightly stricter basic VFR minimums at night in Class G airspace. If you are operating in Class G airspace at or below 1,200′ AGL, from sunset to sunrise, the Class E (less than 10,000 feet) airspace minimums apply—3V/152.

Why the increase in basic VFR minimums at night? Simply stated, it's more difficult to see and avoid objects when it's dark outside (perhaps that's how Neanderthals received their sloped foreheads—by walking into stationary objects at night. If they were around today, they'd probably be found under Coke machines). The additional flight visibility and cloud clearance minimums lessen the risk that pilots will hit terrain, obstructions, or other aircraft when it's dark. Figure 17 also depicts the minimums for night operations in Class G airspace at or below 1,200 feet AGL.

One exception to nighttime minimums exists for airplanes operating in Class G airspace while in the traffic pattern. If the flight visibility is less than three statute miles but not less than one statute mile during night hours, an airplane may be operated clear of clouds if it is flown in the airport traffic pattern within one-half mile of the runway. The assumption is that if a pilot is close to the runway, it's unlikely that he or she will hit an obstruction.

Here's Rod Machado's Airspace Simplification Rule #4: When flying in uncontrolled airspace at or below 1,200 feet AGL during the day, you're low enough to knock over 1 COC machine (COC sounds like Coke) and end up wearing a night-E. Therefore, the weather minimums for Class G airspace below 1,200 feet AGL during the day are 1 mile visibility and remain clear of clouds. At night, they become the same as for the Class E airspace directly above—3V/152.

At this point, you know more about Class E and G airspace than most pilots will know throughout their entire career. That's the truth. You could skip the following section dealing with Class G airspace above 1,200 feet AGL and probably never have a need for the information. Nevertheless, I challenge you to master this subject. If you do, you'll become a guru. Pilots will sacrifice headsets and training aids in your honor. Hobbs meters will run slower in your presence. Most of all, I'll be proud of you for the attempt.

Operations In Class G Airspace Above 1,200 Feet AGL

Class E airspace begins at 700 feet AGL within the magenta faded area as shown in Figure 19, position 1. Directly outside the magenta fade, Class E airspace begins at 1,200 feet AGL as shown by position 2. How do I know this? Because these positions are all surrounded by a blue-tinted line that fades in one direction and has a solid border on the other (position 3). The blue tint fades in the direction where Class E airspace begins at 1,200 feet AGL. This is shown by the direction of arrows marked by the number 4.

On the other side of the blue-tinted line, opposite the direction that it fades, is Class G airspace. Normally, Class E airspace begins at 1,200 feet AGL, but not in those areas shown at position 5. Here, Class G airspace actually rises vertically to more than 1,200 feet AGL, as shown by the direction of the white arrow pointing toward the area of position 5. In fact, Class G airspace in this area rises up to but not including an altitude of 14,500 feet MSL as shown in Figure 20 (this is an approximate 3-D representation of Figure 19).

3-D VIEW OF BISHOP'S AIRSPACE (Fig. 20)

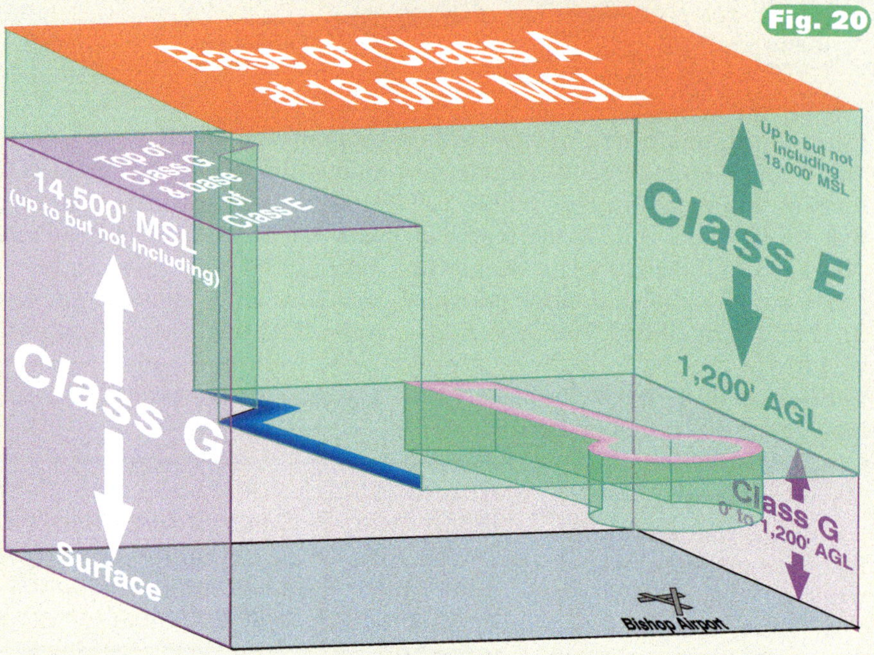

The direction the blue tinted line fades indicates where Class E (controlled) airspace begins at 1,200' AGL. On the opposite side of the blue tinted line is Class G (uncontrolled) airspace from the surface, up to but not including 14,500' MSL.

Now, I must admit that Class G airspace extending more than 1,200 feet AGL is rare in the central and eastern United States. It is, however, more common in the western and north-central parts of the United States. The way to find it is by looking for the border of the blue tinted line on aeronautical sectional charts (Figure 19, position 3). On the opposite side of the blue fade, will be Class G airspace extending more than 1,200 feet AGL. Despite the presence of Class G airspace more than 1,200 feet AGL, it's a reasonable assumption that most of your flying will be done in Class E airspace.

OK, I've pushed you where no mammal has gone before, beyond normal vertebrate endurance. So why stop now? I only have one last thought for you. We've already concluded that Class G airspace above 1,200 feet AGL is not very common. Why not make it all Class E airspace starting at 1,200 feet AGL over the entire United States? The reason is that air traffic control can't use some portions of the airspace above 1,200 feet AGL for IFR flights. In other words, there's no way to use the navigational facilities (VOR navigation for instance) because of restrictions imposed by other types of airspace, navigation station limitations or, as is frequently the case, by terrain-created signal limitations.

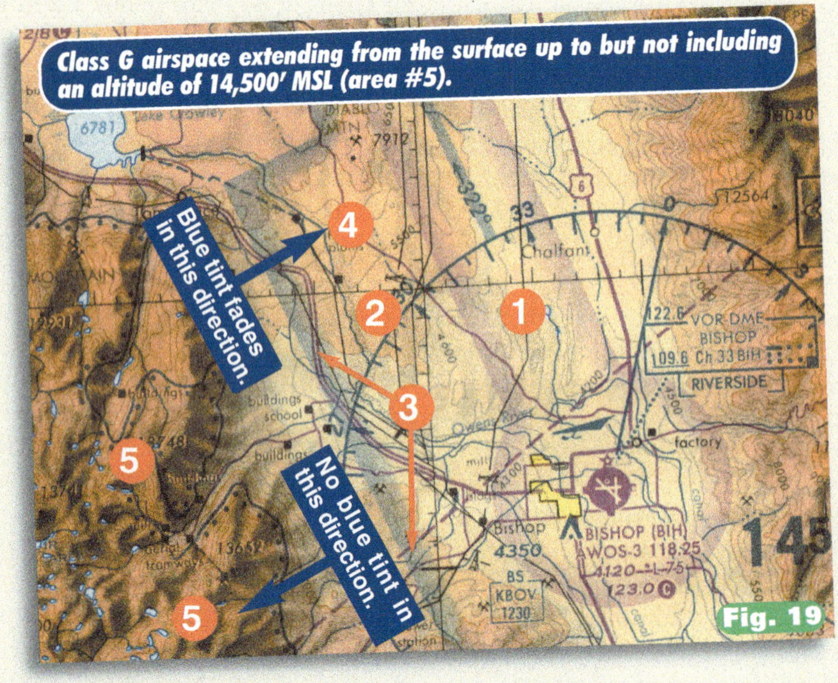

Class G airspace extending from the surface up to but not including an altitude of 14,500' MSL (area #5). (Fig. 19)

There is an interesting point here. The highest mountain in the 48 contiguous United States is Mount Whitney, at 14,491 feet MSL. If you're at or above 14,500 feet MSL anywhere in the United States, you're not likely to have a problem with mountains interfering with navigational signal reception. That's why Class G airspace more than 1,200 feet AGL, extends up to, but not including 14,500 feet MSL as shown on the left hand side of Figure 20. At and above 14,500 feet MSL, it's Class E airspace (at least until reaching the base of Class A airspace).

On occasion, the floor of Class E airspace starts at altitudes higher than 1,200 feet AGL. See Postflight Briefing #9-4 for advanced information on this topic.

BASIC VFR MINIMUMS IN CLASS G AIRSPACE

Shown below are the basic VFR weather minimums within Class G (uncontrolled) airspace for three altitude levels: from the surface up to and including 1,200' AGL, more than 1,200' AGL but less than 10,000' MSL and at or above 10,000' MSL up to but not including 14,500' MSL.

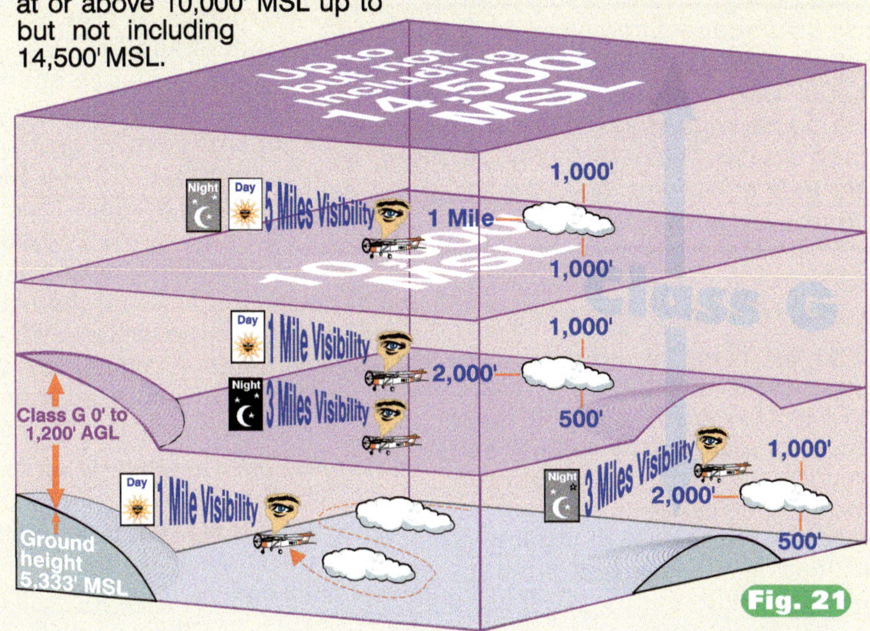

Fig. 21

VFR Weather Minimums For Class G Airspace

Figure 21 is a 3-D depiction of the VFR weather minimums for all Class G airspace. Notice that in Class G airspace at 10,000 feet MSL and above, the weather minimums are the same as they are for Class E airspace at this altitude. There is, however, a difference between night and day basic VFR minimums at altitudes less than 10,000 feet MSL but more than 1,200 feet AGL. At night, all Class G airspace basic VFR minimums are the same as those for Class E below 10,000 feet MSL—3V/152 (is this starting to sound like a familiar tune? I wrote the words—you do the music).

Of course, at this stage you're probably checking your forehead for a Coke machine imprint. It's not there, it just feels like it. I'm proud of you for sticking with this. It gets easier from now on. Honest!

General Conclusions About Class A, E and G Airspace

Here are some general conclusions that make understanding VFR minimums easier. First, the lower you go, the less restrictive the weather minimums for VFR flight (Figure 22). In Class A airspace (at and above 18,000 feet MSL) there is no VFR flight allowed. How much more restrictive can you get? Below Class A airspace and at or above 10,000' MSL, the flight visibility minimum is five miles. Below 10,000' MSL the visibility minimum drops from five miles to three miles, then finally to one mile within Class G airspace next to the surface (daytime assumed). Cloud clearance minimums also become less restrictive at lower altitudes.

Second, at night, the Class G airspace minimums increase to those of Class E airspace. In other words, if you're flying VFR at night in Class G airspace, you need the same VFR minimums as you do in Class E airspace for similar altitudes. Frankly, if you like to fly long distances at night at 1200 AGL or less, you should probably be wearing a *vacancy* sign on your forehead, right above the Coke imprint.

Third, when flying at and above 10,000 feet MSL, while higher than 1,200 AGL, the VFR weather minimums are the same, regardless of whether you're in Class E or G airspace. Postflight Briefing #9-2 provides you with a useful memory aid in recalling these minimums.

Here's Rod Machado's Airspace Simplification Rule #5: If you're flying more than 1,200 feet AGL and your altimeter indicates 10,000 feet MSL or higher, the basic VFR minimums are the same regardless of the class of airspace in which you're flying (5V/111). At night, all Class G

GENERALIZATION OF LOWERING VFR MINIMUMS

As a general rule, the basic VFR weather minimums decrease as you get closer to the surface. At night, the VFR requirements all become the same below 10,000' MSl: 3 miles, 1000'/2000'/500'.

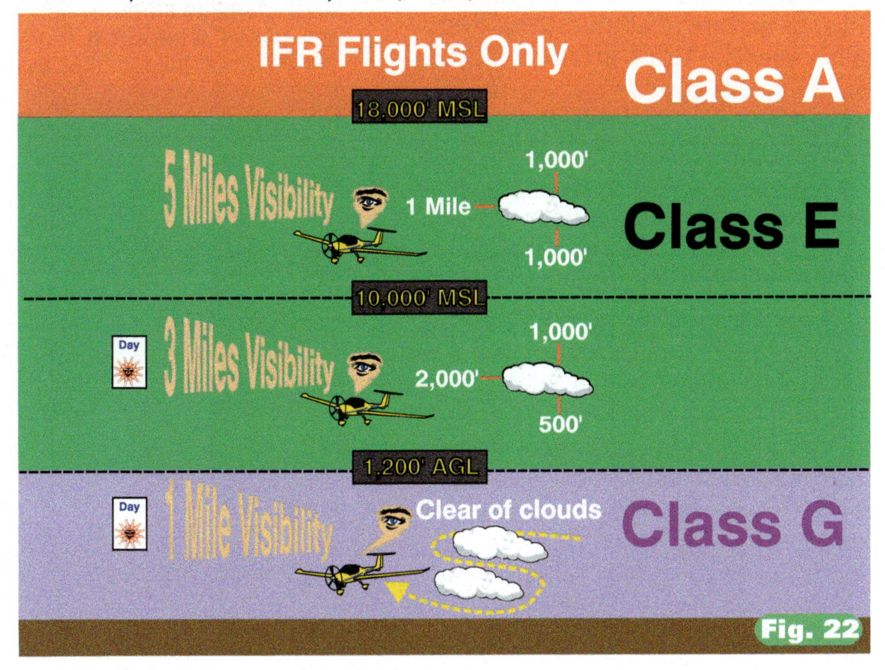

Fig. 22

basic VFR minimums become the same as Class E minimums for similar altitudes.

You might be wondering, "Do all pilots who fly remember all these rules?" Yes, in varying degrees. What's perhaps most important is that you are aware they exist, so you'll at least think to check in situations where there might be a question. A pilot with a good understanding of airspace seldom finds him- or herself in trouble with the FAA. Not only will you impress other pilots with your practical knowledge, you'll sail right through those flight reviews and phase checks.

It's also the case that the vast majority of pilots do *not* spend much time flying around VFR in marginal conditions, so the precise letter of the law about VFR minimums doesn't really come into play for them on all that many occasions. If you want to fly in marginal weather conditions, please get an IFR rating and use it. You'll be flying more often and more safely.

Remember, if you're interested in a visual memory aid to help remember all these airspace rules, please see Postflight Briefing #9-2 at the end of this chapter.

Several years ago, at an FAA office in Santa Monica, a student was taking the private pilot knowledge exam. This was his third attempt, having failed on his first two tries (the airspace section gave him trouble). Finally, this student decided to cheat. The observing FAA inspector became suspicious when he noticed the student kept opening and closing the bread on his bologna sandwich.

Walking quickly into the testing room, the inspector attempted to catch the student in the act of cheating. The inspector testified he had never witnessed anyone eating a bologna sandwich so fast in his life. When the inspector asked the student why he shoved an entire bologna sandwich into his mouth, the student replied, "A sudden surge of hunger came over me." Considering the state of intelligence of this fellow, the inspector should have simply provided him with a few bent quarters and told him to go get a Coke.

Rod Machado's Airspace Simplification Rule #5: If you're flying more than 1,200' AGL and your altimeter indicates 10,000' MSL or higher, the basic VFR minimums are the same regardless of the class of airspace in which you're flying (5V/111). At night, all Class G basic VFR minimums become the same as Class E minimums for similar altitudes.

Class B, C and D Airspace

The last three variations of controlled airspace are Class B, Class C and Class D airspace. All three types of airspace start at the surface and surround those airports that have an operating control tower. Each class of airspace serves the single purpose of coordinating takeoffs and landings between individual aircraft. That's why an operating control tower is required. Geometric versions of these three different types of airspace are shown in Figure 23.

In Chapter 6 we referred to Class D and C airspace as having the shape of a single and double-stacked tuna can. We referred to Class B airspace as looking like an inverted wedding cake. Now it's time to upgrade this simile to an analogy.

It's safe to generalize here and say that the taller the airspace structure, the busier the airport with which it is allied. The word *busy* implies more as well as bigger and faster airplanes. A good way to understand how big and small airplanes operate within these three types of airspace is to think about fish. If you have goldfish, you put them in a small bowl. They certainly don't need a large living area. Sharks, on the other hand, need bigger aquariums. Whales need giant tanks. Airplanes are like fish, in that larger ones need more space in which to operate.

Think about these three airspace shapes as aquariums or water tanks (Figure 24). Class D airspace is small in comparison, meaning (most of the time) that smaller airplanes (goldfish) like Cessnas, Pipers and Beechcraft swim there. Class C airspace, being slightly larger, means that bigger and faster airplanes like Learjets and Boeing 737's (sharks) may be found there. Class B airspace (big tanks) means that aircraft like Boeing 747's and DC-10's (whales) may loom within this airspace. Let's examine each class of airspace starting with Class D (the goldfish bowl).

CLASS B, C, OR D AIRSPACE

An airport with an operating control tower can have either Class B, C, or D airspace at its surface. The Class of airspace depends on several factors: how busy the airport is, the types of airplanes using the airport, the number of IFR flights, the facilities available at the airport, etc.

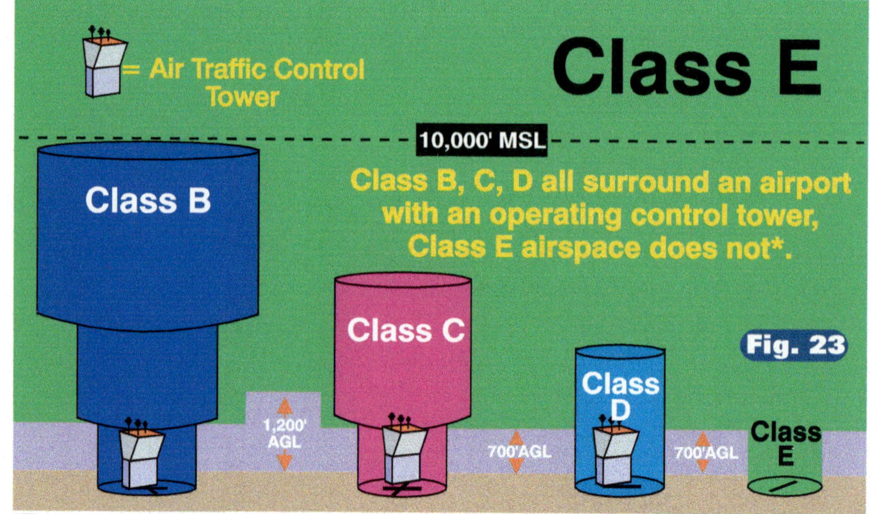

*There may be a few exceptions where a Class E or G surface area actually does have an operating control tower. These exceptions are minor and shouldn't ever concern you.

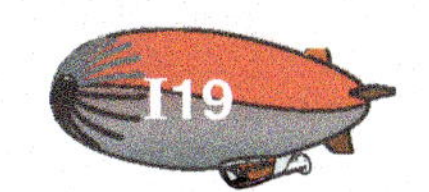

Class D Airspace

Class D airspace is controlled airspace starting at the surface of airports having an operating air traffic control tower (Figure 25 shows its dimensions). It's established to help air traffic controllers provide an orderly flow of traffic taking off or landing at airports within this airspace.

The blue dashed line surrounding Chico airport in Figure 26 (position 1) represents the lateral dimensions of Class D airspace. The radius of Class D airspace varies with individual airports and is individually tailored to the instrument approach procedure for which the controlled (Class D) airspace is established. It averages 4.3 nautical miles (5 statute miles). The top of the airspace cylinder generally extends to heights of approximately 2,500 feet AGL. The height also varies, depending on local needs. Position 2 in Figure 26 identifies the actual top of Class D airspace in hundreds of feet above sea level as shown by the bracketed value of 27 (2,700 feet MSL). As you can see, the 2,700 foot MSL top of Chico's Class D airspace is approximately 2,500 feet above its elevation of 238 feet MSL.

Class D airspace is established at airports having sufficient traffic to justify the presence of a control tower. Normally, numerous general aviation airplanes are found taking off or landing at the primary airport within this airspace. The primary airport shown in Figure 26, position 3, (the one with the control tower) is usually found at the center of the blue dashed circle. This doesn't mean you won't find the occasional larger aircraft (shark or whale) at this airport. It does mean, however, that there may be quite a few smaller airplanes (goldfish) in the vicinity.

All aircraft operating within Class D airspace are required to establish and maintain two way radio communication prior to entering and when operating within this airspace. In other words, you must talk to the control tower before taking off, landing, or flying through this airspace. Of course, if you overfly Chico airport at more than 2,700 feet MSL, or operate beyond the lateral limits of the blue dashed line, you're not in Class D airspace and no communication is required. (See Chapter 6, FAR 91.129 for the precise definition of *establishing and maintaining communication.)*

AIRSPACE AS A FISH TANK

Think of different classes of airspace as fish tanks. The bigger the tank, the bigger the critter found within the tank. Similarly, larger classes of airspace usually contain larger airplanes. Of course, smaller fish (propeller airplanes) can also be found swimming in larger tanks.

Fig. 24

DIMENSIONS OF CLASS D AIRSPACE

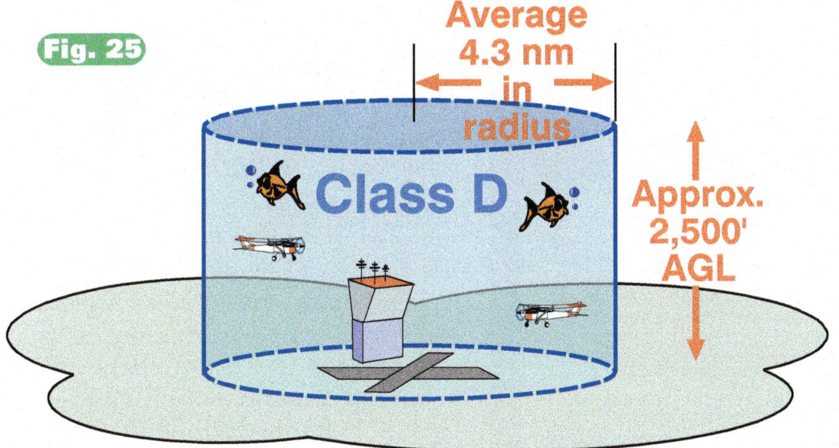

Fig. 25

Operating anywhere within the boundaries of Class D airspace requires that you establish and maintain communication with the Air Traffic Control tower prior to entering this airspace. While controllers don't provide separation between aircraft, they do provide sequencing as well as information about known air traffic.

CLASS D AIRSPACE AT CHICO

Fig. 26

Chico airport (Figure 26, position 3) is solid blue in color. This identifies the airport as having a control tower. Remembering this is easy, since blue is the color your face usually turns when you're attempting to understand what fast-talking controllers are saying. Communication with the air traffic controller is made on the tower frequency of 121.0 MHz shown next to the symbol CT (control tower). Realize that Class D airspace only exists when the control tower is operating. This means the control tower has someone in it. After all, there's no way you can establish communications without controllers (the night cleaning staff will not answer your calls). When the tower shuts down, the airport is treated like a non-tower (uncontrolled) airport.

This is the CS excerpt for Chico showing the effective hours of operation for Class D airspace (point A). Notice that these are the same as the operating hours of the air traffic control tower (point B).

CHICO

CHICO MUNI (CIC) 4 N UTC–8(–7DT) N39°47.72' W121°51.51' SAN FRANCISCO
238 B S4 **FUEL** 100, 100LL, JET A TPA—See Remarks ARFF Index A H-1A, 2A, L-2G
RWY 13L-31R: H6724X150 (ASPH-PFC) S-63, D-100, DT-170 HIRL 0.5% up NW IAP
RWY 13L: MALSR. VASI(V2L)—GA 3.0° TCH 54'. Rgt tfc (when twr clsd).
RWY 31R: REIL. VASI(V4L)—GA 3.0° TCH 50'. Rgt tfc (when twr open).
RWY 13R-31L: H3005X60 (ASPH) S-25
RWY 13R: Rgt tfc.
AIRPORT REMARKS: Attended 1530-0330Z‡. For fuel services after hours call 916-896-6122. TPA—1500(1262) jet/heavy acft opr E of fld, 1000(762) lgt acft opr W and E of fld. Rwy 13R-31L is part of an asphalt pad 3000'X1500'. When twr clsd ACTIVATE HIRL Rwy 13L-31R and MALSR Rwy 13L-121.0.
WEATHER DATA SOURCES: LAWRS.
COMMUNICATIONS: CTAF 121.0
RED BLUFF FSS (RBL) TF 1-800-WX-BRIEF. (1400-0600Z‡). NOTAM FILE CIC.
RANCHO MURIETA FSS (RIU) TF 1-800-WX-BRIEF. (0600-1400Z‡).
RCO 122.1R 109.8T (RED BLUFF FSS)
Ⓡ **OAKLAND CENTER APP/DEP CON** 132.2
TOWER 121.0 (1500-0300Z‡) 121.9
AIRSPACE: CLASS D svc effective 1500-0300Z‡ other times CLASS G.
RADIO AIDS TO NAVIGATION: NOTAM E CIC.
(T) **VOR/DME** 109.8 CIC Chan 35 N39°47.39' W121°50.83' at fld. 220/16E. VOR/DME without voice when FSS cls
NORDE NDB (LOM CI N39°53.22' W121°55.99' 132° 6.5 NM to fld.
ILS 111.3 I- Rwy 13L LOM NORDE NDB. Unmonitored when twr clsd.
COMM/NAVAID REMARKS: Emerg frequency 121.5 not avbl at twr.

A B C

Fig. 27

Figure 27 shows an excerpt from the *CS* for Chico airport. Class D airspace is effective from 1500 to 0300 UTC. This is the same as the operating hours of Chico's control tower (0700 to 1900 local time), as shown on the aeronautical sectional chart's side panel in Figure 28. According to the *CS* (Figure 27, point C), when Class D airspace is not in effect, the airspace reverts to Class G airspace.

Figure 29 identifies the Class E airspace extensions added onto Class D airspace. As I've mentioned before, extensions of Class E airspace are added when it's necessary to keep IFR airplanes in controlled airspace during their instrument approaches.

Tower controllers give the impression of being pretty serious, yet most of them have a great sense of humor. For instance, one of our airport's more senior pilots had his false teeth fall out during a landing (he sneezed and flared at the same time and blew his teeth out of his mouth). The tower called but he couldn't reply. He finally got his teeth back in and said, "Tower, I'm sorry about the delayed response but my teeth fell out on landing. The controller said, "Well, you might think about pulling back on the wheel a little sooner next time." I think the controller also said, "and make sure you stay away from those Coke machines, OK?"

CONTROL TOWER FREQUENCIES ON THE SECTIONAL'S TAB

The operating hours of an air traffic control tower (Chico in this instance), are also found on the sectional chart's frequency tab.

CONTROL TOWER FREQUENCIES ON SAN FRANCISCO SECTIONAL CHART

Airports which have control towers are indicated on this chart by the letters CT followed by the primary VHF local control frequency. Selected transmitting frequencies for each control tower are tabulated in the adjoining spaces, the low or medium transmitting frequency is listed first followed by a VHF local control frequency, and the primary VHF and UHF military frequencies, when these frequencies are available. An asterisk (*) follows the part-time tower frequency remoted to the collocated full-time FSS for use as Local Airport Advisory (LAA) during hours tower is closed. Hours shown are local time. Ground control frequencies listed are the primary ground control frequencies.

Automatic Terminal Information Service (ATIS) frequencies, shown on the face of the chart are primary arrival VHF/UHF frequencies. All ATIS frequencies are listed below. ATIS operational hours may differ from control tower operational hours.

ASR and/or PAR indicates Radar Instrument Approach available.

"MON-FRI" indicates Monday thru Friday.

CONTROL TOWER	OPERATES	TWR FREQ	GND CON	ATIS	ASR/PAR
NAS ALAMEDA	CONTINUOUS	127.05 384.4	121.65 352.4	284.2	ASR/PAR
BEALE AFB	CONTINUOUS	119.4 276.15	121.6 228.4	273.5	ASR/PAR
BUCHANAN	0600-2200	119.7 123.9 257.8	121.9	124.7	
CHICO	0700-1900	121.0 239.3	121.9		
NALF CROWS LANDING	MON-FRI AS SKED	125.05 328.1			

Fig. 28

Weather Minimums For Class D Airspace

The weather minimums for Class D airspace are exactly the same as they are for Class E airspace below 10,000 feet MSL. Therefore Rod Machado's Airspace Simplification Rule #2 applies here. You need to maintain the VFR minimums of 3V/152—3 miles visibility, 1,000 feet above any clouds, 500 feet below clouds, 2,000 feet laterally from clouds—while airborne. Since Class D airspace is surface-based controlled airspace, Rod Machado's Airspace Simplification Rule #3 also applies. Taking off, landing or operating in the traffic pattern of an airport having any type of surface-based controlled airspace established for it requires a minimum of 3V/1C—3 miles visibility, 1000 foot ceiling.

As with Class E airspace, this is *reported* ground visibility. When it's not reported, the pilot must maintain at least three statute miles *flight visibility*. If weather conditions at that airport are less than three miles reported ground visibility or less than a 1,000 foot ceiling (if a ceiling exists), an SVFR clearance is required before taking off, landing, or entering the traffic pattern within the surface-based portion of Class D airspace (and its Class E extension).

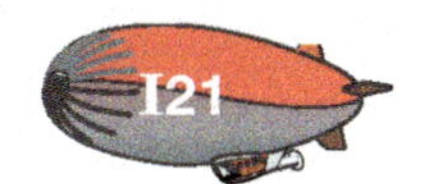

CHICO'S CLASS D AIRSPACE

Class D (blue cylinder) airspace starts at the surface of an airport with an operating control tower. It extends vertically to approximately 2,500' feet above the airport elevation. Chico airport, shown below, has an elevation of 238' MSL. This makes the top of the Class D airspace approximately 2,700' MSL ([27]). The radius of Class D airspace is approximately 4.3 nautical miles (but this varies from airport to airport).

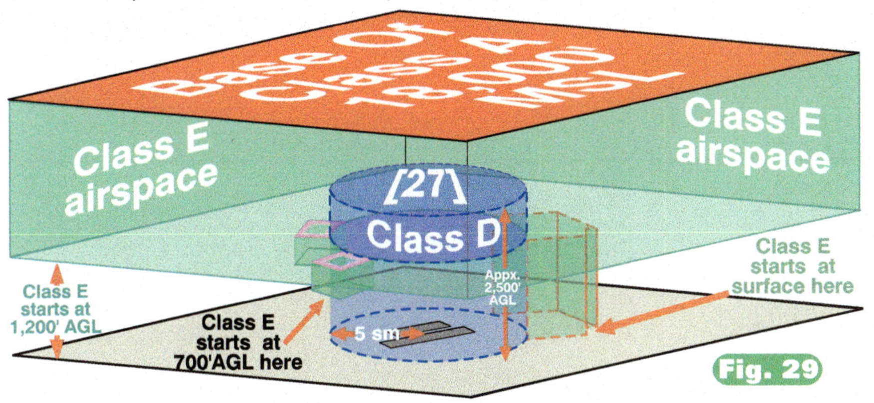

Fig. 29

During the day, you can usually tell if the primary airport is below basic VFR minimums by looking at the airport's rotating beacon. The beacon, which flashes white and green as it rotates, is normally activated at night to help identify an airport with runway lights. When it's activated during the day, it means that an existing ceiling is less than 1,000 feet or the visibility is less than three miles, or both. Either way, an SVFR clearance (or an IFR clearance if IFR rated) is required to operate into or out of the surface-based controlled airspace under these conditions.

Satellite Airports Within Class D Airspace

On occasion, another airport lies within the lateral boundaries of Class D airspace, as seen in Figure 30. Martha Lake airport (position 1), an uncontrolled airport, lies within the Class D airspace of Snohomish County airport (position 2).

If you're landing at Martha Lake, you need to establish and maintain two way radio communication with the primary airport (Snohomish Tower) prior to entering Class D airspace. If you're taking off from Martha Lake airport, you must establish contact with Snohomish tower as soon as practicable after departing.

Sometimes a special arrangement is made with the control tower concerning satellite airports within its Class D airspace. This provision is known as a *letter of agreement.* It's somewhat like a prenuptial agreement that attempts to prevent the uppercuts, headlocks and general mayhem associated with divorce hearings. For example, a letter of agreement with the tower might allow pilots from a particular flight school at a satellite airport to take off or land in a specific direction without first establishing communications with the tower. Unless you know that you are covered by this procedure, you should always establish and maintain two way radio communications with the tower prior to entering Class D airspace.

Fig. 30

Class C Airspace

Smaller jet-type aircraft (sharks) as well as propeller driven aircraft (goldfish) are normally found in Class C airspace. Radar services are available to ensure traffic separation between this mixture of fast and slow, IFR and VFR aircraft. An operating control tower (as found in Class D airspace) as well as radar approach control services are associated with the existence of Class C airspace. Figure 31 shows the typical dimensions of this airspace.

Class C airspace is geometrically shaped like two cylinders—a larger one on top of a smaller one (the double tuna can, remember?). The surface-based inner cylinder (the core surface area) extends upward to approximately 4,000 feet AGL and has a five nautical mile radius from the center of the primary airport. The upper cylinder (the shelf area) normally begins at 1,200 feet AGL and has a 10 nautical mile radius from the center of the primary airport. The upper limit of the top cylinder is generally found at 4,000 feet above the elevation of the primary airport. Remember, the Class C airspace fish tank is larger because it must hold sharks as well as goldfish. Dimensions of Class C airspace may vary depending on local terrain and traffic considerations.

Class C airspace is depicted on an aeronautical sectional chart by solid magenta rings surrounding the primary airport, as shown in Figure 32. Beale Air Force Base is the primary airport in this case. Positions 2 and 3 show both the inner and outer cylinders of this airspace. Elevation numbers (positions 4 and 5) show that the two sections of the outer cylinder start at 2,600 feet and 1,600 feet MSL respectively and extend vertically to 4,100 feet MSL (that's approximately 4,000 feet above Beale's airport elevation of 113 feet MSL).

DIMENSIONS OF CLASS C AIRSPACE

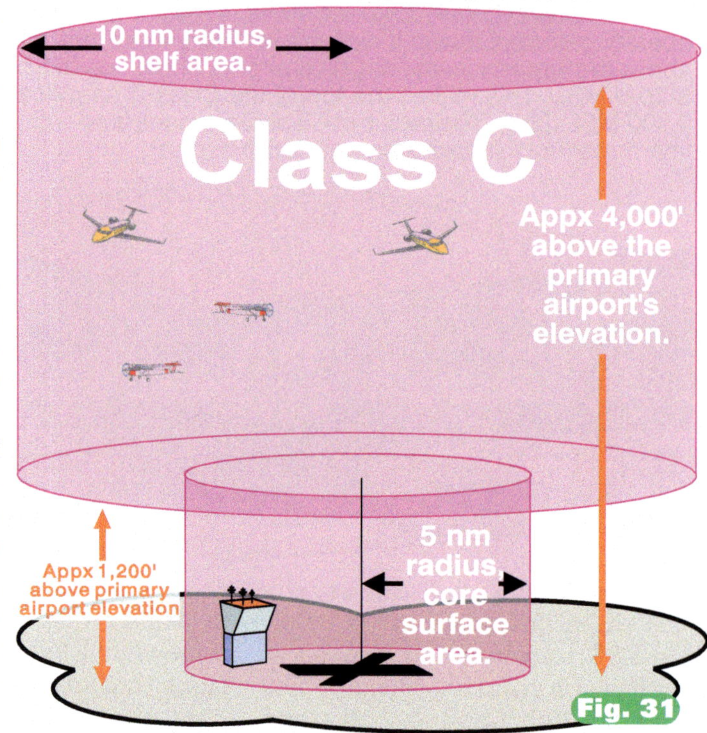

Fig. 31

Operating anywhere within the boundaries of Class C airspace requires that you establish and maintain communication with the appropriate ATC facility (usually Approach Control) prior to entering this airspace. ATC provides *basic radar service*, *sequencing* and *separation* between VFR and IFR aircraft. It also provides this same service within a 20 nm radius of the primary airport (often defined as the *outer area*). A mixture of faster ( ) and slower aircraft ( ) is common in Class C airspace.

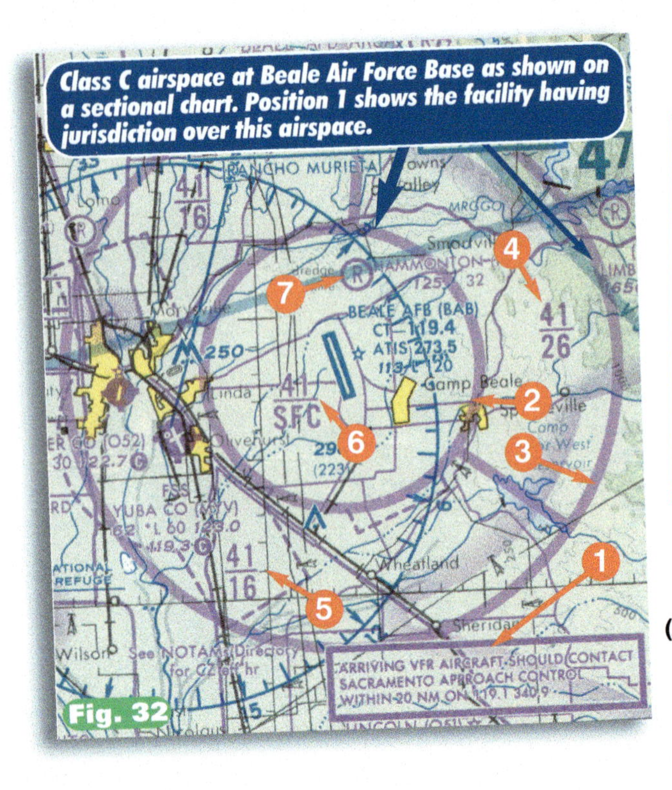

Class C airspace at Beale Air Force Base as shown on a sectional chart. Position 1 shows the facility having jurisdiction over this airspace.

Fig. 32

BEALE'S CLASS C AIRSPACE STRUCTURE

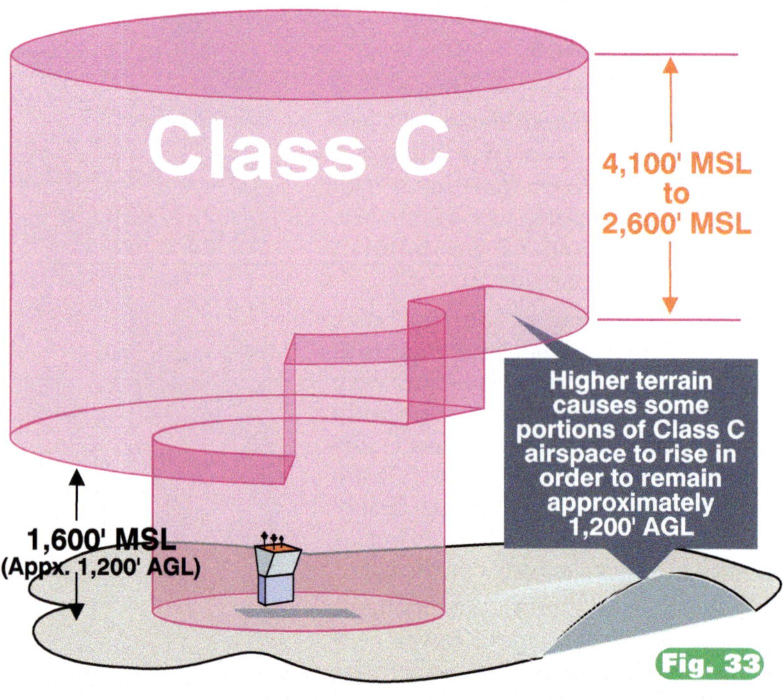

Fig. 33

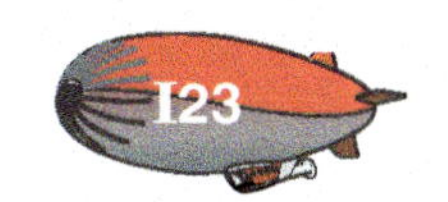

Because of higher terrain east of the airport, a section of the outer cylinder begins at a higher MSL altitude (position 4), yet it's still approximately 1,200 feet AGL. The inner cylinder elevation limits (position 6) extend from the surface (SFC) to 4,100 feet MSL. Figure 33 shows a 3-D view of Beale's Class C airspace.

Will The Flier Please Fly?

Do make it a point to have your radios in good working order when dealing with busy air traffic controllers. One pilot was attempting to call the tower for departure without much success. All the controller heard was, "Bzzzz, bzzzz, bzzzz." The controller said, "Aircraft calling the tower, your transmission is inaudible." Once again the controller heard "Bzzzz, bzzzz, bzzzz." This time the controller got upset and said, "Aircraft calling tower, get that radio fixed, you sound like a fly." Suddenly, from somewhere, the controller hears another pilot's high pitched voice saying, "Bzzz, bzzz, I am a fly, bzzz, bzzz." Never let it be said that pilots don't have a sense of humor.

Equipment Requirements To Operate Within Class C Airspace

If you are planning on entering Class C airspace (to land at any airport within the inner cylinder, or to fly through the area) you must establish and maintain two way radio communication with the appropriate ATC facility prior to entering this airspace. The facility you must communicate with is the one providing air traffic services for that airspace. Normally, this will be the local approach control facility for that area. Position 1 in Figure 32 shows the frequencies for the ATC facility having jurisdiction over this airspace.

Two-way radio communication is required in Class C as well as Class D airspace. In addition, operations within Class C airspace require a transponder with Mode C capability (an encoding altimeter) and ADS-B (out) capability. This transponder and ADS-B (out) requirement also applies if you are flying anywhere above the ceiling and within the lateral boundaries of Class C airspace upward to 10,000 feet MSL. In other words, even though you're above the top of Class C airspace, as long as you are within its lateral boundaries and below 10,000 feet MSL, you need a transponder with an encoding altimeter. This helps keep ATC aware of potential traffic conflicts as pilots exit and enter the top of Class C airspace.

Class C Service

Within Class C airspace you'll receive Class C service. It's really first class service for Class C airspace. It means ATC provides you with basic radar service, sequencing to the primary airport, and separation of VFR aircraft from IFR aircraft.

Although *not shown* on the sectional chart, there is an *imagined* outer area to Class C airspace that's assumed to extend to a 20 nm radius from the primary airport. It's considered good operating practice (although not mandatory) to contact the approach control facility within 20 nm of the primary airport. This gives the controller more time for sequencing and separating you from IFR aircraft. (An aircraft doesn't need to be operating in the clouds to be considered an IFR aircraft. It need only be on an IFR flight plan, regardless of the weather conditions. IFR aircraft are in constant contact with ATC and these are the aircraft Class C service sequences you with and separates you from.)

Let's assume you're departing the primary airport within Class C airspace. Obviously you must establish and maintain two way radio communication with the control tower just as you did in Class D airspace. After departure, you must communicate as instructed by ATC while operating within this airspace. This means you'll probably be handed off from the tower to Departure Control when leaving the airport. The tower might say, "Cessna 2132 Bravo, contact Bay Departure Control on 121.3." When departing the primary airport in Class C airspace, the ATIS will often require you to contact Clearance Delivery for departure instructions. Normally you will be given the departure control frequency, a transponder squawk code and instructions on how to depart the area (such as a heading or a route to be flown).

Satellite Airports Within Class C Airspace

Figure 32, position 7, shows that Hammonton airport is an uncontrolled, satellite airport within the inner circle of Beale's Class C airspace. You can depart a satellite airport without an operating control tower if you establish and maintain two-way radio communication with the appropriate ATC facility (usually approach or departure control) as soon as possible after departing. In other words, you may take off and, as soon as it's feasible, contact Sacramento Approach Control on one of the frequencies shown in the red tabbed box (position 1).

GOOD GRIEF, WILL SOMEONE TALK TO THIS GUY!!!

A small aircraft was observed maneuvering low within Class D airspace with no contact with the tower. The tower controller suspected the aircraft was NORDO (no radio) and was planning to maneuver traffic around it. Pilot finally called tower when entering downwind and was cleared to land on Runway 15L. Airplane landed on 15R, necessitating a go-around for another airplane on short final to 15R. After landing, the pilot said he was taking pictures and didn't know he was supposed to establish communications with the tower before entering Class D airspace. He THOUGHT he had landed on 15L. He said he didn't carry his private pilot license or medical certificate because it was getting wrinkled in his wallet.

That license should not get wrinkled during its possible suspension. Pilot might benefit by reading the FARs since he will probably have some spare time. **ASRS**

Variations in Class C Airspace

Figure 34 shows Class C airspace for Santa Barbara airport. A portion of the outer cylinder on the eastern side of Santa Barbara's Class C airspace is missing (no, this has nothing to do with UFO cattle mutilations). Steeply rising terrain east of the airport necessitated removal of this section.

The inner cylinder of Santa Barbara's Class C airspace is controlled airspace touching the surface. As we've previously seen with surface-based Class E airspace, a keyhole extension is sometimes necessary to accommodate instrument pilots making approaches into the airport. An extension of Class E airspace (position 1) is added onto the inner cylinder of Class C airspace at Santa Barbara (Figure 34). Within this small segment of the magenta dashed line, Class E airspace extends from the surface upward to the overlying shelf of Class C airspace (the overlying shelf begins at 1500 feet MSL in this case).

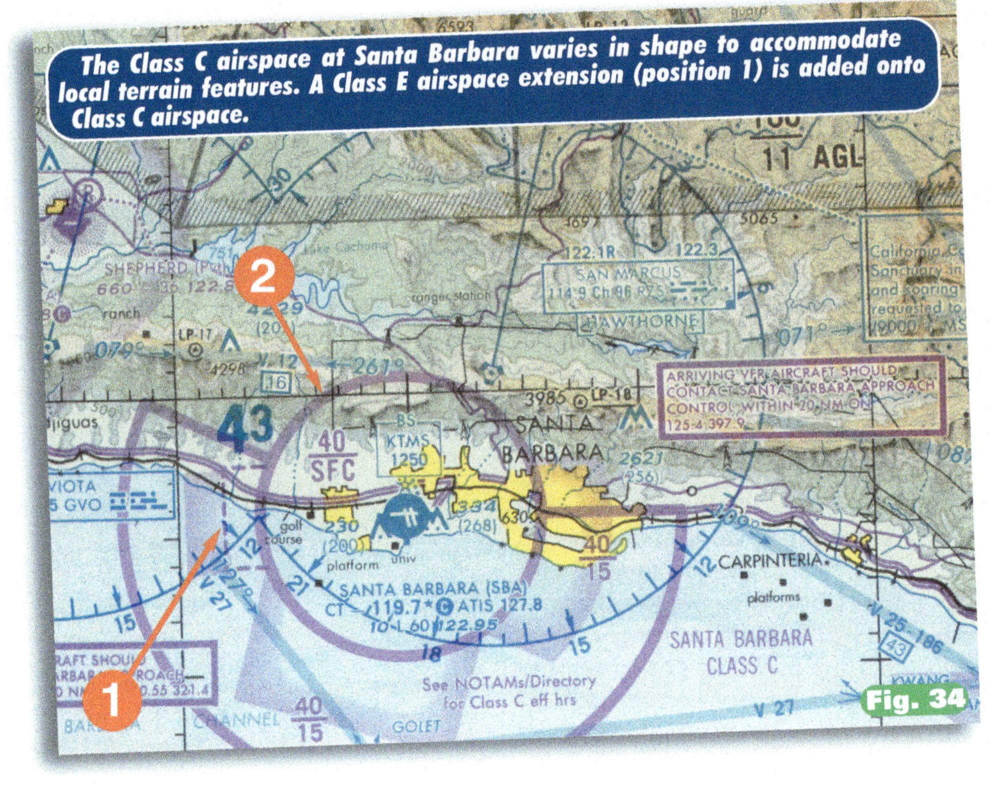

Fig. 34

Weather Minimums For Class C Airspace

The weather minimums for Class C airspace are exactly the same as they are for Class D airspace and Class E airspace below 10,000 feet MSL. Rod Machado's Airspace Simplification Rule #2 applies here. You need to maintain the VFR minimums of 3V/152 while airborne. Since Class C airspace is surface-based controlled airspace, Rod Machado's Airspace Simplification Rule #3 also applies. Taking off, landing, or operating in the traffic pattern of an airport having *any* type of surface-based controlled airspace established for it requires a minimum of 3V/1C. As with Class D and E surfaced-based airspace, an SVFR clearance is required if these minimums don't exist.

If an SVFR clearance is necessary, contact Santa Barbara Clearance Delivery (if on the ground) or Approach Control (if airborne). This clearance allows operations below 10,000 feet MSL, within the lateral boundaries of the Class C surface area as shown by position 2 (not the boundaries of the upper cylinder), as well as to any Class D or E airspace extension (position 1). As with all SVFR clearances, an ATC-issued altitude restriction supersedes the 10,000 foot MSL limit.

An excerpt from the *CS* (Figure 35) shows that Santa Barbara's Class C airspace is in operation from 1400Z to 0700Z. These are also the hours of operation of the control tower. Outside these times, the *CS* says that Class E airspace exists at the airport. Therefore, there is always some type of surface-based controlled airspace existing at SBA.

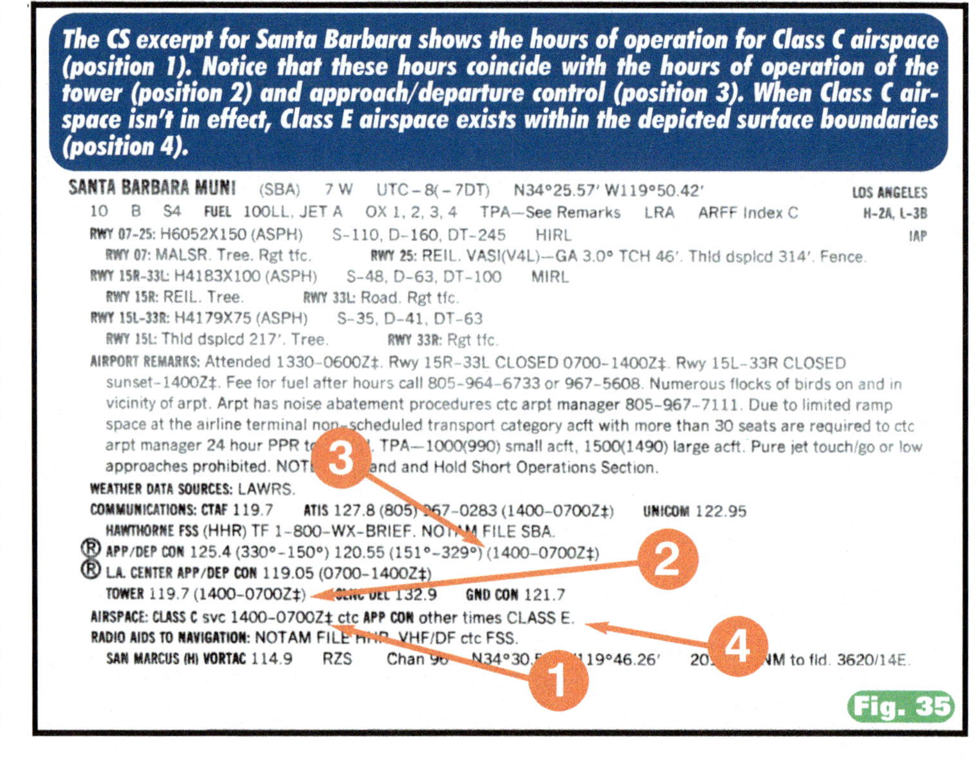
The CS excerpt for Santa Barbara shows the hours of operation for Class C airspace (position 1). Notice that these hours coincide with the hours of operation of the tower (position 2) and approach/departure control (position 3). When Class C airspace isn't in effect, Class E airspace exists within the depicted surface boundaries (position 4).

SANTA BARBARA MUNI (SBA) 7 W UTC–8(–7DT) N34°25.57′ W119°50.42′ LOS ANGELES
10 B S4 FUEL 100LL, JET A OX 1, 2, 3, 4 TPA—See Remarks LRA ARFF Index C H-2A, L-3B
RWY 07-25: H6052X150 (ASPH) S-110, D-160, DT-245 HIRL IAP
RWY 07: MALSR. Tree. Rgt tfc. RWY 25: REIL. VASI(V4L)—GA 3.0° TCH 46′. Thld dsplcd 314′. Fence.
RWY 15R-33L: H4183X100 (ASPH) S-48, D-63, DT-100 MIRL
RWY 15R: REIL. Tree. RWY 33L: Road. Rgt tfc.
RWY 15L-33R: H4179X75 (ASPH) S-35, D-41, DT-63
RWY 15L: Thld dsplcd 217′. Tree. RWY 33R: Rgt tfc.
AIRPORT REMARKS: Attended 1330–0600Z‡. Rwy 15R-33L CLOSED 0700–1400Z‡. Rwy 15L-33R CLOSED sunset–1400Z‡. Fee for fuel after hours call 805-964-6733 or 967-5608. Numerous flocks of birds on and in vicinity of arpt. Arpt has noise abatement procedures ctc arpt manager 805-967-7111. Due to limited ramp space at the airline terminal non-scheduled transport category acft with more than 30 seats are required to ctc arpt manager 24 hour PPR to ... TPA—1000(990) small acft, 1500(1490) large acft. Pure jet touch/go or low approaches prohibited. NOT... and and Hold Short Operations Section.
WEATHER DATA SOURCES: LAWRS.
COMMUNICATIONS: CTAF 119.7 ATIS 127.8 (805) ...67-0283 (1400–0700Z‡) UNICOM 122.95
HAWTHORNE FSS (HHR) TF 1-800-WX-BRIEF. NOTAM FILE SBA.
Ⓡ APP/DEP CON 125.4 (330°–150°) 120.55 (151°–329°) (1400–0700Z‡)
Ⓡ L.A. CENTER APP/DEP CON 119.05 (0700–1400Z‡)
TOWER 119.7 (1400–0700Z‡) ... 132.9 GND CON 121.7
AIRSPACE: CLASS C svc 1400–0700Z‡ ctc APP CON other times CLASS E.
RADIO AIDS TO NAVIGATION: NOTAM FILE ... VHF/DF ctc FSS.
SAN MARCUS (H) VORTAC 114.9 RZS Chan ... N34°30.... 119°46.26′ 20... NM to fld. 3620/14E.

Fig. 35

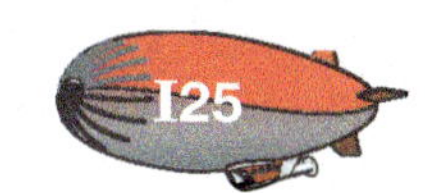

Class B Airspace

Now let's talk about where the whales swim (747's, DC-10's, etc.). Airports like Los Angeles, Chicago, San Francisco, New York-JFK and others are home to these metallic sky mammals. Class B airspace is established to separate the whales from each other as well as from any small goldfish or sharks that might swim with them during takeoff or landing at the primary airport.

As we've already learned, the shape of Class B airspace is like an inverted wedding cake. It usually starts with a circular-based surface area surrounding the primary airport. Ever widening circular cylinders lie on top of lower cylinders, creating the inverted wedding cake (with a squished bride and groom) appearance, as shown in Figure 36.

CLASS B AIRSPACE

10,000' MSL

Class B

Some Class B airspace structures have a corridor allowing flight that's exempt from Class B airspace entry requirements.

Fig. 36

Class B airspace resembles an inverted wedding cake. Its multiple tier structure is designed to keep larger aircraft ( ) and small aircraft ( ) separated as they approach or overfly the primary airport. This is why an ATC clearance is required when operating anywhere within Class B airspace.

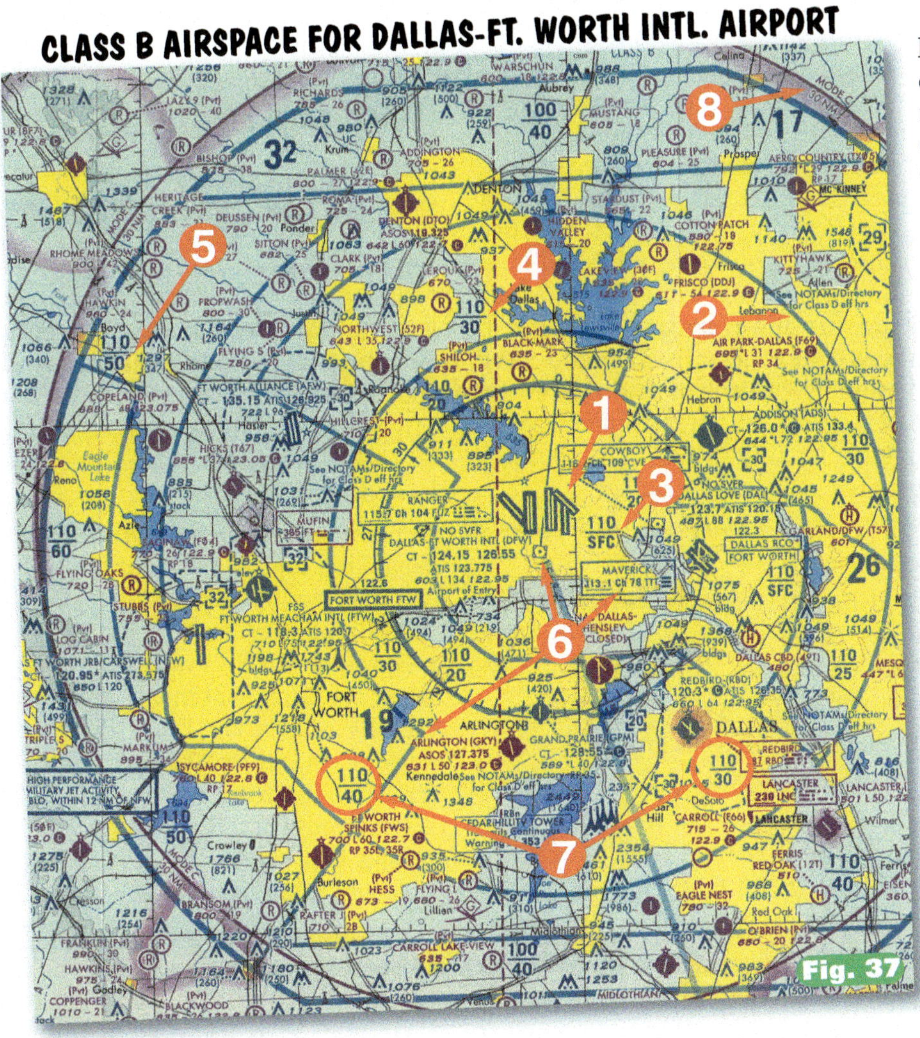

Class B airspace is designed to keep larger aircraft in a protective tank without unnecessarily restricting the movement of smaller aircraft below. Special extensions of the tank are nothing more than approach and departure paths into and out of the primary airport. These sections establish boundaries that prevent other aircraft from straying into the path of larger and faster aircraft.

Typically, Class B airspace has a radius of 15 to 30 miles from the primary airport and it extends vertically from the surface to 10,000 feet MSL. Figure 37 shows how Class B airspace for the Dallas-Ft. Worth International Airport (position 1) is displayed on an aeronautical sectional chart. The boundaries of Class B airspace are defined by solid blue lines surrounding the primary airport (position 2)

Position 3 shows that Class B airspace in the innermost ring extends vertically from the surface (SFC) to 11,000 feet MSL (DFW's Class B airspace is a little taller than normal. Most Class B airspace extends to about 10,000 feet MSL). Position 4 shows another section where Class B airspace starts at 3,000 feet MSL and extends to 11,000 feet MSL. Position 5 shows a section starting at 5,000 feet MSL and extending vertically to 11,000 feet MSL. Sections of Class B airspace may vary in altitude and shape to accommodate arriving and departing traffic (probably from airways or high altitude transitions).

An important thing to be aware of is that the rings and segments of Class B airspace are often made up of DME arcs and/or radials or bearings from local navigation stations. (DME, or *distance measuring equipment*, is an electronic instrument that tells you your distance from a navigation station, which is often a VOR.) For instance, the 207 degree radial from the Maverick VOR (position 6) makes up the line that identifies where the floor of Class B airspace changes from 4,000 feet to 3,000 feet on one of the inner rings (see the values circled in red at position 7). The arcs or rings of Class B airspace are determined by distances from the Maverick VOR (position 6). Since many airplanes have GPS or DME capability, pilots can tell their position relative to the individual rings of this Class B airspace.

Requirements to Enter Class B Airspace

Now that you know what Class B airspace is and how it's depicted on an aeronautical sectional chart, you are inevitably curious about what it takes to swim with the big ones. First, in order to take off or land at an airport within this airspace, or to simply fly through the airspace, you must hold at least a private pilot's license (an exception exists for student and recreational pilots seeking private pilot certification who were given the instruction and appropriate logbook endorsement required by FAR 61.95).

Second, an ATC clearance is required before operating in Class B airspace. This clearance must be obtained from the ATC facility having jurisdiction over that area. Normally, it's the local approach and departure control serving the primary airport. This assumes you'll have a two way radio capable of communication with the appropriate ATC facility.

The communication requirement for Class B airspace is different than the communication requirement for Class C or D airspace. While you need only establish and maintain communication for Class C or D airspace, you need to obtain a *clearance* to enter Class B airspace. In other words, if you contact the controller to enter Class C or D airspace and that controller says, "Roger 2132 Bravo, stand by," you've established communication. You can enter that airspace. If, however, the controller in charge of Class B airspace says, "Stand by," this is most definitely *not* a clearance, You must remain on the outside looking in until permission is granted to enter the tank.

A typical clearance into Class B airspace will be:

"Piper 2132 Bravo is cleared to enter Class B airspace via direct to the Los Angeles VOR, maintain 5,500 feet while in Class B airspace."

Departing Class B airspace:

"Piper 2132 Bravo is cleared out of Class B airspace via radar vectors to MATWA intersection, climb and maintain 3,500 feet while in Class B airspace."

The arrival clearance would probably be provided by approach control and the departing clearance by clearance delivery or ground control. Sometimes controllers will clear you to a specific intersection on or off an airway as part of your clearance. These intersections, consisting of five letters, are usually shown on an aeronautical sectional chart. MATWA is the name of a typical intersection. One time, a pilot asked a controller (who was in a good mood) to "call MATWA" for him. (In avspeak, a request to "call" something means "Please tell me when I reach that spot, or when you want me to make that turn.") Without hesitation the controller said, "Here MATWA, here MATWA, here boy, whistle, whistle, whistle." Who said controllers don't have a sense of humor?

Third, a transponder with Mode C capability, and ADS-B (out) capability are also required (see page I31 for ADS-B details). For IFR pilots, a VOR receiver or RNAV system is required when operating within this airspace. If for any reason the Class B airspace doesn't extend to 10,000 feet MSL, a transponder with Mode C capability is required when operating above the ceiling and within the lateral boundaries of Class B airspace.

It's interesting to note that while Class B airspace is controlled airspace, it actually has slightly less stringent VFR weather minimums (you knew there had to be one exception, right?). Three miles visibility is still required within Class B airspace. However, you only need to remain clear of clouds instead of the typical 1,000′/500′/2,000′ distance minimums. The reason for this is that all aircraft operating within this airspace are being sequenced and separated while under ATC control. There is little chance of another pilot popping out of a cloud and creating a collision threat to nearby aircraft. This cloud distance reduction prevents pilots from having to fly evasive headings (often to the surprise of ATC) while trying to maintain a minimum distance of 2,000 feet from any cloud.

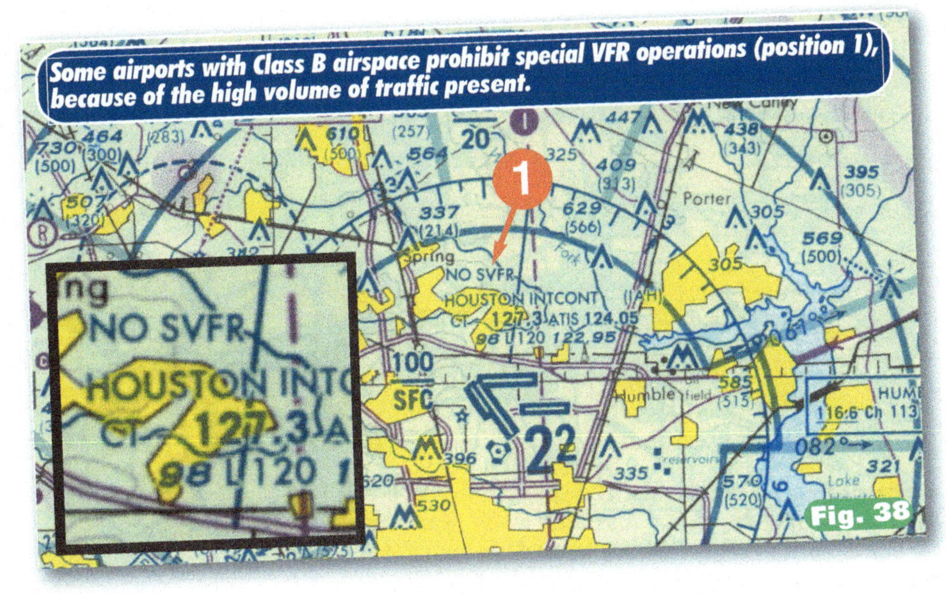

Some airports with Class B airspace prohibit special VFR operations (position 1), because of the high volume of traffic present.

Special VFR Within Class B Airspace

Since Class B airspace is surface-based controlled airspace, Rod Machado's Airspace Simplification Rule #3 applies. Taking off, landing or operating in the traffic pattern of an airport having *any* type of surface-based controlled airspace requires a minimum of 3V/1C. A special VFR clearance is required if these minimums don't exist.

Because of the high volume of traffic as well as the type of traffic operating within Class B airspace, special VFR (SVFR) operations may be unavailable. Figure 38 shows the letters *NO SVFR* for the primary airport in Houston's Class B airspace. Pilots without an instrument rating would need to wait until VFR conditions existed at the airport before they would be permitted to take off or land.

Corridors And Circumnavigating Class B Airspace

Because of the numerous airplanes in, near, and around Class B airspace, you should be cautious when circumnavigating this area. Pilots often elect to fly underneath the floors or individual shelves of Class B airspace, thus avoiding the need for an ATC clearance. To enhance the opportunity for seeing and avoiding other aircraft, a speed limit is established in these areas. FAR 19.117C requires that pilots not exceed 200 knots indicated airspeed when operating below the lateral limits (or through a VFR corridor) of Class B airspace area.

At a few locations, a VFR corridor has been implemented to assist pilots transiting the Class B airspace. Figure 39 depicts the LAX VFR corridor. This opening or tunnel through the Class B airspace is called the *special flight rules area.* Basically, it is an exception to the Class B airspace that allows pilots to fly either north or south, directly over Los Angeles International Airport without having to meet some of the operational requirements of Class B airspace. You don't need a clearance to use this corridor. You may need to meet other requirements, such as having a VFR terminal area chart, specific navigation equipment, etc. Just follow the requirements listed on the VFR terminal area chart for the area's Class B airspace. (You'll learn about terminal area charts in Chapter 10)

A VFR corridor exists through Class B airspace (Los Angeles in this instance) to assist pilots in transiting this airspace without an ATC clearance.

More than one of these special routes may exist within the borders of Class B airspace. At the time of this writing, Los Angeles has two additional routes allowing passage through Class B airspace. Unlike the special flight area mentioned above, these require that you meet all the operational requirements of Class B airspace (i.e., FAR 91.131). Therefore, an ATC clearance is necessary, as well as minimum equipment and pilot qualifications.

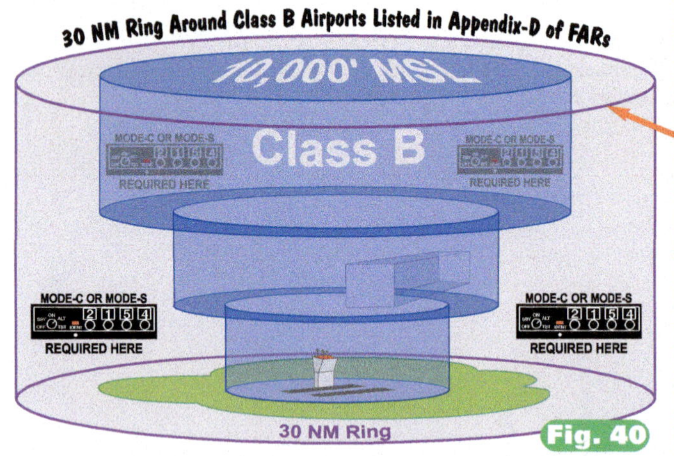

A transponder having Mode C or S capability is also required from the surface to 10,000 feet MSL, when operating within 30 nm of certain high-capacity airports having Class B airspace. This requirement is identified by the presence of a magenta ring around these airports as shown in Figure 41, position A.

Transponder and Mode C or S Within 30 NM Of Certain Airports in Appendix 1 of FAR Part 91

In addition to the requirement for a transponder with Mode C or Mode S capability in Class A, B and C airspace, FAR 91.215 also requires this equipment in other areas. Several airports listed in appendix D, section 1 of FAR Part 91 require a transponder with Mode C capability from the surface to 10,000′ MSL when operating within 30 nautical miles of that airport (Figure 40). You can tell if an airport requires this by looking at the aeronautical sectional chart. You'll see a magenta colored ring surrounding the primary airport listing this Mode-C requirement, as shown at George Bush Intercontinental Houston airport, Figure 41, position A. The ring is slightly off-center from the Class B airspace, because the Class B airspace is centered at the Humble VOR (Figure 41, position B), while the ring is centered at the airport (position C).

Transponders & Mode C or S Above 10,000′ MSL

A transponder with Mode C is also required in all the airspace of the 48 contiguous United States and the District of Columbia when operating at and above 10,000 feet MSL, excluding the airspace at and below 2,500 feet AGL (Figure 42). If you're flying at or below 2,500 feet AGL above Mt. Whitney (standing at 14,491' MSL), you don't need a transponder with Mode C (although you should bring a parka and mittens).

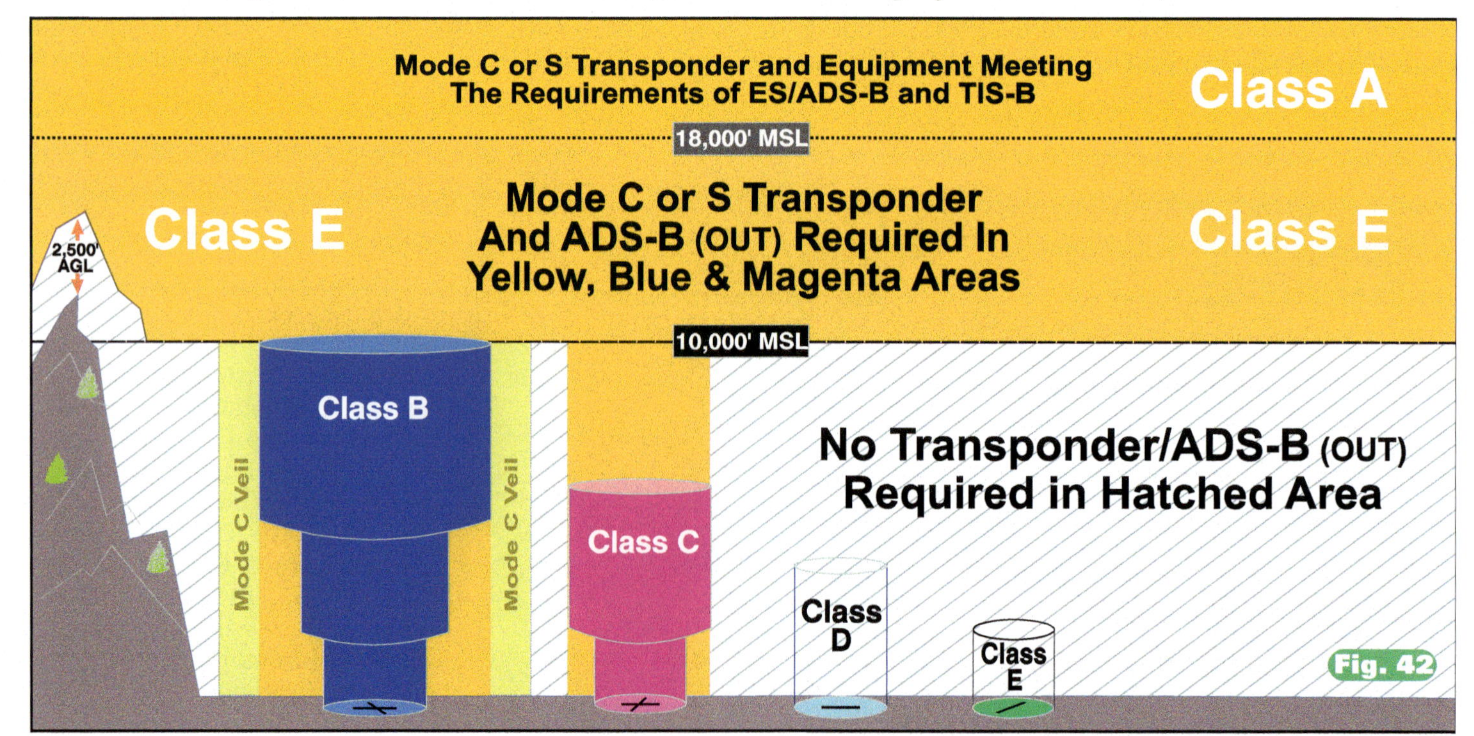

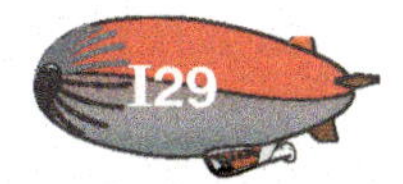

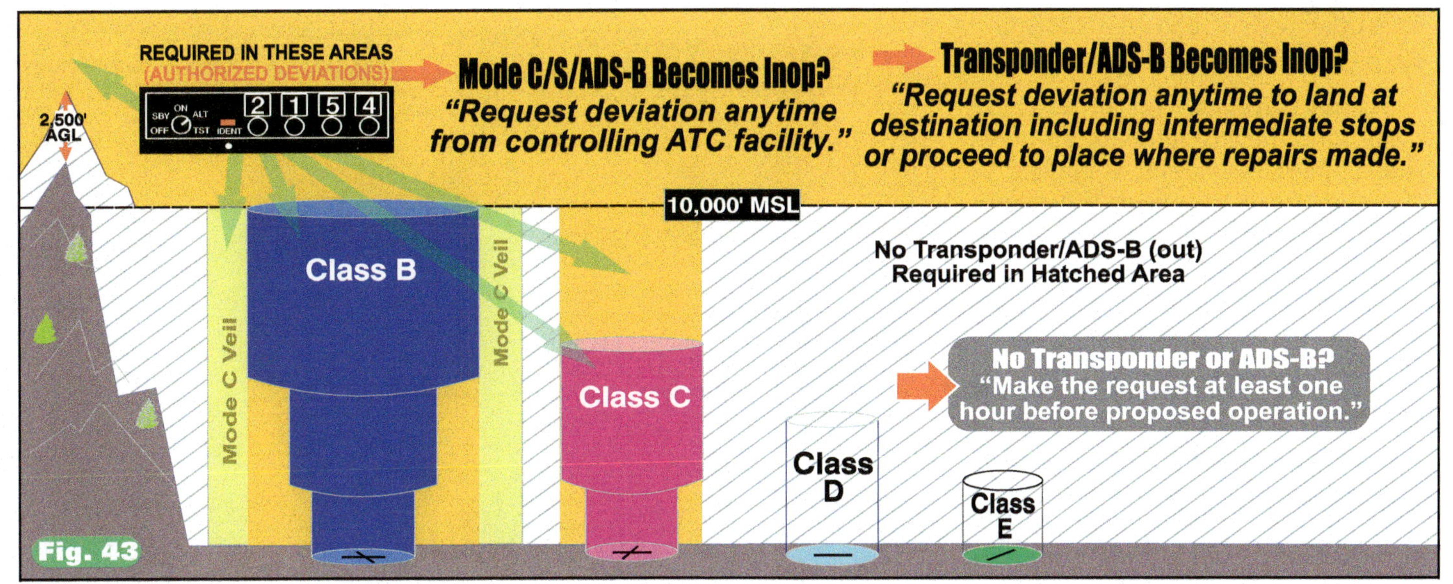

Transponders In Controlled Airspace

If your airplane has a transponder (and most do), the rules require that it be turned on including the Mode C, Mode S and ADS-B *out* capability any time you are operating in controlled airspace (we'll talk about ADS-B *out* soon). This is to be done even when it's not required by the specific type of airspace in which you're operating. You should use the code assigned by ATC, or the VFR code (1200) when not in contact with ATC.

Transponder and Mode C Deviations

Occasionally, electrical equipment ceases to operate. It's possible that, one day, you might see a big puff of white smoke come from the transponder (and the inside of your cockpit could go to less than basic VFR minimums). The transponder has probably failed.

According to FAR 91.215, if you have a transponder lacking Mode C capability, you can request a deviation to operate within airspace requiring Mode C at any time (Figure 43). Such a request is made with the ATC facility having jurisdiction over that airspace (typically, the tower or approach control has jurisdiction). If you have a transponder that is temporarily inoperative and you need to continue to your destination, just let the controller know of any intermediate stops you'll be making. He or she can OK the flight on the spot. If, however, your airplane doesn't have a transponder at all, a request must be submitted at least one hour in advance.

One day an air traffic controller at Van Nuys airport received a call from a hang glider using a handheld radio. This guy called up and said, "Van Nuys Tower, this is, ahh, hang glider Bob, over your airport for landing." The controllers didn't know what else to do, so they cleared him to land in the grass, next to the runway. I mentioned to my friend that they should be glad I wasn't in the tower at the time. My friend asked why. I said that I would have made him go around!

The ADIZ (Air Defense Identification Zone)

The ADIZ is a boundary along the eastern and western coasts of the United States and the U.S./Mexican border and around land-based areas where national security is a concern. Unauthorized penetration of this zone is sure to arouse the suspicion of the military and/or drug enforcement agencies. Pilots penetrating the ADIZ without following proper procedures have been known to end up with a military jet escort for a portion of their flight. If you're thinking about either leaving the U.S., entering the U.S. or just entering any ADIZ, you must meet several requirements. A DVFR (Defense VFR) flight plan must be filed for coastal and domestic ADIZs and position reports must be made. A transponder (Mode C) and two-way radio are also required (see the AIM for more information on ADIZ entry requirements and position reporting). For VFR entry into a land-based ADIZ you must have a transponder (Mode C), two-way radio and must file and activate a VFR (or IFR) flight plan then you must contact ATC to obtain a transponder code, maintain two-way communications at all times within the ADIZ as well as maintain your discrete transponder code until you have landed or are outside the ADIZ boundary. You must also close that VFR flight plan after landing.

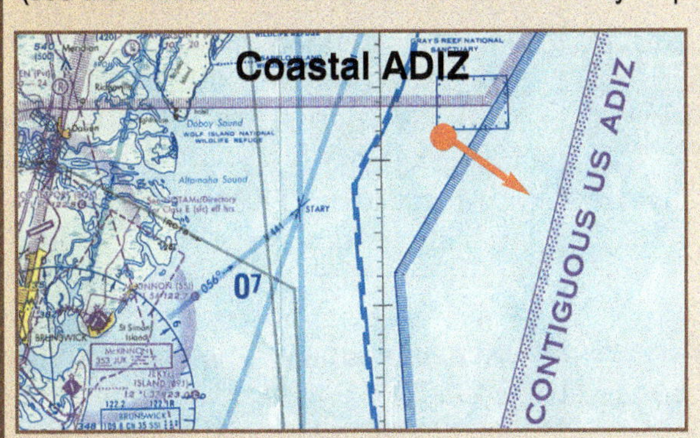

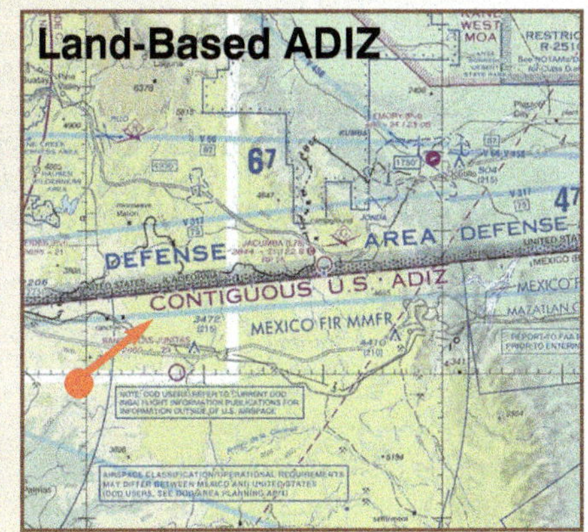

Speed Restriction In Class C And D Airspace

To help prevent faster aircraft from gobbling up goldfish, an additional speed restriction is applied to Class C and D airspace. When any aircraft is within four nautical miles of the primary airport in Class C and D airspace and at or below 2,500 feet AGL, a 200 knot speed restriction applies.

Terminal Radar Service Area

In Chapter 8 I briefly mentioned the *Terminal Radar Service Area* (TRSA). Let's fly by for a closer look at a type of airspace that's unusual by virtue of having nothing about it that's mandatory!

Recall that in a TRSA, ATC provides sequencing and separation between all participating VFR aircraft and all IFR aircraft. Figure 44 depicts a typical TRSA. Its boundaries are identified by a black line. TRSA's take on variable sizes and shapes but they usually contain a surface-based layer around the primary airport with one, two or more elevated cylinders of airspace. Altitudes for the different layers are shown within the individual rings as with Class B airspace.

Suppose you're approaching Binghamton airport and you want TRSA service (refer back to Chapter 8 for more detail on TRSA service). You would refer to the frequency tab on the edges of the aeronautical sectional chart to identify the appropriate approach control frequencies. Figure 45 shows the frequencies for the Binghamton TRSA. If you're approaching anywhere from the surface to 5,000 feet, then you'd contact Approach Control on 118.6 MHz (Note: if bearings are shown instead of altitudes, then these bearings are from the station.) The *Chart Supplement* (Figure 46, position 2) also contains this information.

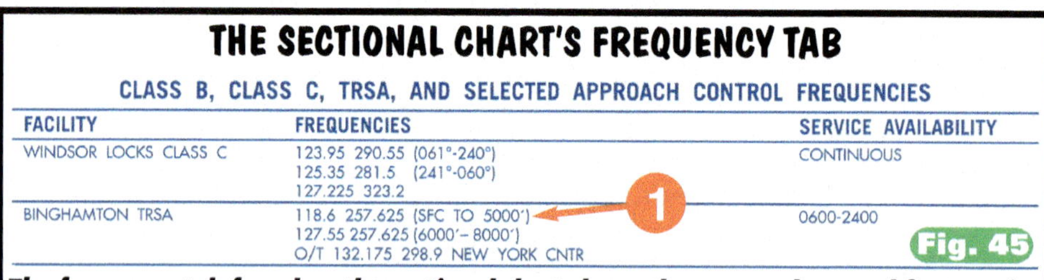

THE SECTIONAL CHART'S FREQUENCY TAB

CLASS B, CLASS C, TRSA, AND SELECTED APPROACH CONTROL FREQUENCIES

FACILITY	FREQUENCIES	SERVICE AVAILABILITY
WINDSOR LOCKS CLASS C	123.95 290.55 (061°-240°) 125.35 281.5 (241°-060°) 127.225 323.2	CONTINUOUS
BINGHAMTON TRSA	118.6 257.625 (SFC TO 5000') 127.55 257.625 (6000'- 8000') O/T 132.175 298.9 NEW YORK CNTR	0600-2400

Fig. 45

The frequency tab found on the sectional chart shows the approach control frequencies for TRSA service at Binghamton (position 1). These frequencies are based on the listed bearings from the primary airport (Binghamton in this instance).

The Chart Supplement also contains similar information about the Binghamton TRSA and contact location information based on altitudes at Binghamton (position 2).

BINGHAMTON

GREATER BINGHAMTON/EDWIN A LINK FLD (BGM)(KBGM) 7 N UTC–5(–4DT) NEW YORK
N42°12.51´ W75°58.78´ H–10H, 11C, 12J, L–30J, 32F, 33A
COMMUNICATIONS: CTAF 119.3 ATIS 128.15 UNICOM 122.95 IAP, AD
BINGHAMTON RCO 122.1R 112.2T (BUFFALO RADIO)
Ⓡ BINGHAMTON APP/DEP CON 118.6 (Sfc–5000´) 127.55 (6000–8000´) (1100–0500Z‡)
Ⓡ NEW YORK CENTER APP/DEP CON 132.175 (0500–1100Z‡)
BINGHAMTON TOWER 119.3 (1100–0500Z‡) GND CON 121.9 CLNC DEL 125.0
CLEARANCE DELIVERY PHONE: For CD if una to ctc on FSS freq, ctc New York ARTCC at 631-468-1425.
AIRSPACE: CLASS D svc 1100–0500Z‡; other times CLASS E.
TRSA svc ctc APP CON

Fig. 46

If you're departing Binghamton, you can also elect to use the TRSA service. Usually, the ATIS or the ground controller will provide you with the appropriate departure control frequency to use after departure.

In short, the TRSA is a good thing. It helps pilots approach and depart busier airports in a safer manner. Having ATC call traffic for you enhances safety. Pilot participation in the TRSA service is recommended, but not mandatory. If you happen to

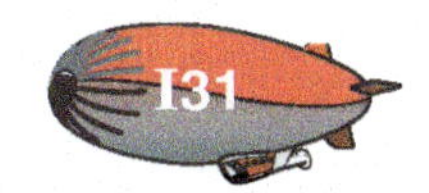

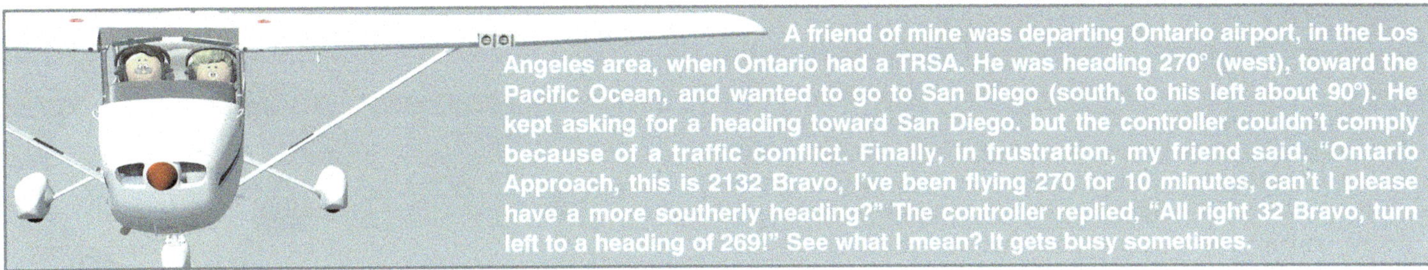

be talking to approach control (when approaching) or ground control and don't want TRSA service, you should state, "Negative TRSA service." There may be times when you want to fly your own (and perhaps more expeditious) route to the airport and have ATC provide only traffic information for you. At times like these, when it's real busy, TRSA service can entail extensive delay vectoring. In this instance you might say:

"Binghamton Approach, this is 2132 Bravo, negative TRSA service, request traffic advisories enroute to Binghamton airport, over."

When approaching and before entering Binghamton's Class D airspace, you'd cancel traffic advisories with approach control, then establish communication with Binghamton Tower and request landing instructions.

Conversely, when departing an airport, you can state, "Negative TRSA service" to the ground controller. This tells the controller that you want to fly your own route out of the airport.

You might be wondering why we have TRSAs when we have Class B and C airspace that seem to serve a similar function. TRSAs belong to airports that don't qualify for Class B or C airspace, yet have enough traffic to justify the presence of some sort of radar service.

Automatic Dependent Surveillance Broadcast or ADS-B (And TIS-B/FIS-B)

ADS-B or *automatic dependent surveillance broadcast* is cutting edge technology that is already present in the cockpit of many airplanes. It's a revolutionary new way of identifying and controlling air traffic. The concept is simple. Here's how it works. (Here the term ADS-B implies both "in" and "out" capability. I'll discuss these shortly.)

Unlike radar, which bounces radio waves from ground-based antennas off airborne targets and then captures the reflected signals for interpretation, ADS-B uses conventional Global Navigation Satellite System (GNSS) technology and a relatively simple broadcast communications link as its fundamental components (Figure 47). It does this with a UAT or *universal access transceiver*. Garmin's GLD82 (position 1) or the GTX335 Mode S transponder (position 2) is are examples of UATs that interfaces with a multi-function cockpit display (position 3). This UAT is remotely mounted in your airplane and is designed to transmit, receive, and decode ADS-B messages sent from other airplanes and from ADS-B ground stations (called GBTs). This data link broadcasts your aircraft's position, velocity, projected track (all derived from GPS), and flight identification to other ADS-B equipped aircraft in your area, as well as to GBTs.

Fig. 47

It's important to remember that ADS-B allows airplane-to-airplane information exchange (Figure 48, airplanes 1 and 2). No GBTs are required for ADS-B equipped airplanes to talk (exchange data) with each other. This is what allows ADS-B equipped airplanes to identify each other's position, direction of flight, speed, and altitude. Unfortunately, resolution advisories (which way to turn, climb or descend to avoid traffic) are not provided by ADS-B units at this time.

The interesting thing about the GBTs is that they can uplink the traffic information shown on ATC's secondary surveillance radar (Figure 48, positions 3 and 4). This means that in addition to identifying other ADS-B equipped airplanes, you can see the Mode A/C/S targets that the controller sees on his or her radar screen (between airplanes 2 and 3 in Figure 48). In fact, there is a special name for this very specific uplink activity. It' called TIS-B or *traffic information service-broadcast.*

So, if you're asked what TIS-B is, you should say that it's the ability to see traffic information uplinked from ATC radar and from airplanes with ADS-B out capability. Figure 49 shows how TIS-B information is typically presented on a cockpit moving map display.

Traffic Information Service Broadcast (TIS-B)

GNSS Constellation
Communications Satellite
1090ES ADS-B OUT
1090ES ADS-B OUT
1090ES ABS-B IN
1090ES TIS-B
18,000' MSL
NO ADS-B
ADS-B OUT/IN
UAT TIS-B
ADS-B OUT/IN
Traditional Radar
ATC System And (Cross Link Rebroadcast)
Ground Link to ATC

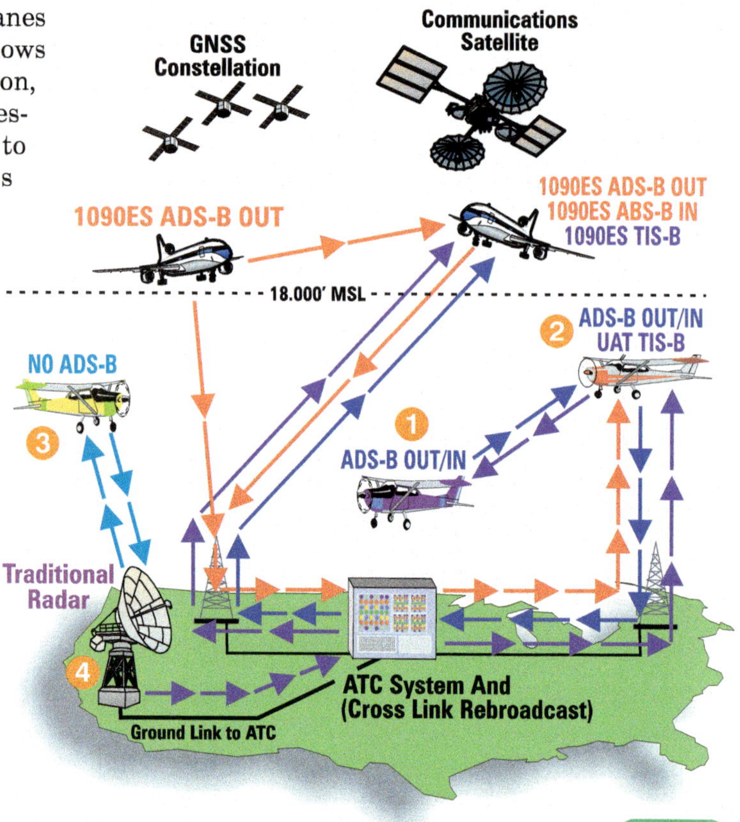

Fig. 48

ADS-B accuracy does not seriously degrade with range, atmospheric conditions, or target altitude. And update intervals do not depend on the rotational speed or reliability of mechanical antennas. It is also a relatively simple, cost-effective technology that works well at low altitudes and on the ground. It's completely effective in remote areas or in mountainous terrain where there is either no radar coverage, or where radar coverage is restricted by problems with elevation, or line of sight. In fact, ADS-B proved itself successful during its early tests conducted in Alaska. Now that's mountainous and isolated terrain.

TIS-B Information Presented on Garmin's Cockpit Display

Fig. 49

TIS-B traffic information is typically presented on a cockpit's moving map display (positions #1, #2, #3). This information often identifies the position, altitude, and direction of travel for the referenced traffic.

So what gives with the "out" part of the ADS-B "out" unit, and just exactly where is ADS-B out required? Let's find out.

ADS-B "out" means that your airplane's ADS-B unit *sends* information on your airplane to ATC and to other airplanes. I'm speaking of information such as your airplane's identification, current position, altitude, and velocity (not how clean it is or if it's for sale). It doesn't, however, receive information from those other airplanes.

If your airplane is equipped with both ADS-B out and in, then you can also receive something known as TIS-B and FIS-B, or *traffic information service broadcast* and *flight information service broadcast.* TIS-B offers you the same position-type information on other aircraft while FIS-B offers you such things as "subscription-free" textual weather, weather graphics, TFRs, NOTAMS, etc., assuming, of course, you have some sort of cockpit map display on which to view this information. You're able to obtain uplinked weather information from your ADS-B (in) unit is because it's a data link unit using a

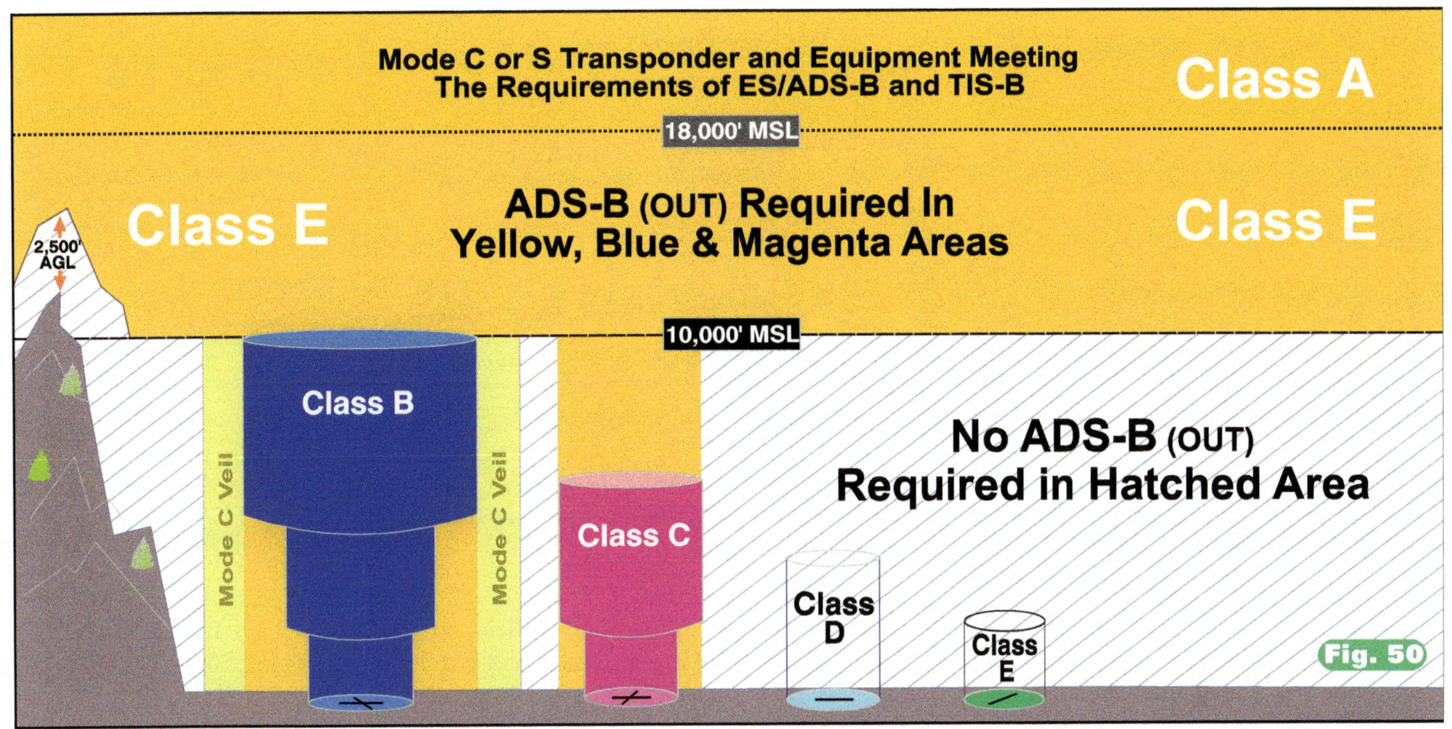

universal access transceiver or UAT. While there are many portable ADS-B "in" units that you can put in your airplane to receive TIS-B and FIS-B, there are no portable ADS-B "out" units that meet the FAA's ADS-B requirement. To meet this requirement, your ADS-B "out" unit must be certified by the FAA and installed by an FAA license mechanic or avionics technician.

For example, Garmin's GDL82 is an FAA-approved and installed ADS-B "out" unit that uses a UAT that transmits or "squits" on 978 MHz. This frequency limits aircraft to operations within the United States and below 18,000 feet MSL. To operate at and above 18,000 feet MSL and/or outside the United States, an airplane must have an ADS-B unit based on a 1090 MHz Mode S "extended squitter" transponder, referred to as *1090ES* (Figure 50). Given that "squitter" refers to random pulses of data used to maintain a regular signal from ADS-B ground stations, we could say that "extended squitter" means more "squits" and more carried data.

Keep in mind that the regulations now require all aircraft (with the exception of those aircraft not originally certified with an electrical system) to have ADS-B "out" when operating in the following areas.

•Class B, and C airspace (operations in Class A airspace require a Mode C or S transponder meeting the requirements of Extended Squitter ADS-B and TIS-B);

•Class E airspace at or above 10,000 feet MSL, excluding airspace at and below 2,500 feet AGL;

•Within 30 nautical miles of a Class B primary airport (within the "Mode C" ring found at some Class B airports);

•Above the ceiling and within the lateral boundaries of Class B or Class C airspace up to 10,000 feet MSL;

•Class E airspace over the Gulf of Mexico, at and above 3,000 feet MSL, within 12 nm of the U.S. coast (Figure 51).

If for some reason, your ADS-B "out" unit stops working while enroute, you can request a deviation from these ADS-B requirements at any time to proceed to your destination airport, including any intermediate stops, or to proceed to a place where suitable repairs can be made (vs. unsuitable repairs). However, if you don't have an ADS-B unit or your unit is inoperative, then your request must be made at least one hour before the proposed operation. These are the same deviations permitted with Mode C and Transponders failures (see Figure 43, Page I29).

ADS-B *out* equipment required at and above 3,000 feet MSL over the Gulf of Mexico from the coastline of the United States extending to 12 nautical miles off the cost.

ADS-B (Out) Required Here

12 Miles

3,000' MSL

Gulf of Mexico

Fig. 51

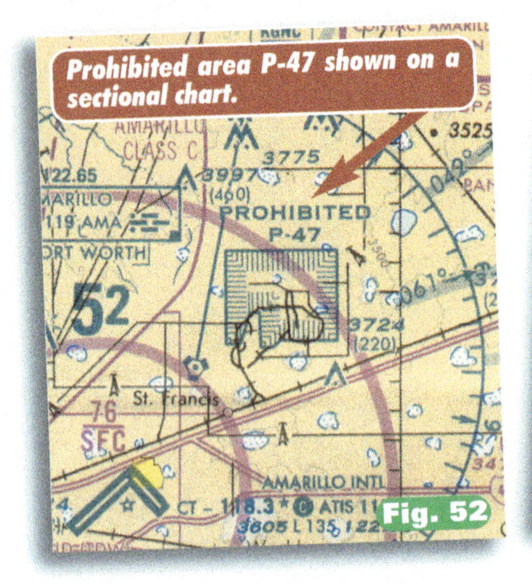

Prohibited area P-47 shown on a sectional chart.
Fig. 52

THE SECTIONAL CHART'S SPECIAL USE AIRSPACE TAB

The sectional chart's special use airspace tab provides information on prohibited area P47.

Fig. 53

SPECIAL USE AIRSPACE ON DALLAS-FT. WORTH SECTIONAL CHART

Unless otherwise noted altitudes are MSL and in feet; time is local.
Contact nearest FSS for information.
†Other time by NOTAM contact FSS

The word "TO" an altitude means "To and including."
"MON-FRI" indicates "Monday thru Friday"
FL – Flight Level
NO A/G – No air to ground communications

U.S. P-PROHIBITED, R-RESTRICTED, A-ALERT, W-WARNING, MOA-MILITARY OPERATIONS AREA

NUMBER	LOCATION	ALTITUDE	TIME OF USE	CONTROLLING AGENCY**
P-47	AMARILLO, TX	TO 4800	CONTINUOUS	NO A/G
R-5601 A	FORT SILL, OK	TO 40,000	CONTINUOUS	ZFW CNTR
R-5601 B	FORT SILL, OK	TO 40,000	CONTINUOUS	ZFW CNTR
R-5601 C	FORT SILL, OK	TO 40,000	CONTINUOUS	ZFW CNTR
R-5601 D	FORT SILL, OK	500 AGL TO 16,500	SR-SS TUE-SAT†	ZFW CNTR
R-5601 E	FORT SILL, OK	500 AGL TO 6000	SR-SS TUE-SAT†	ZFW CNTR
A-561	FREDERICK, OK	TO 4000	0700-2300 MON-FRI	NO A/G

Special Use Airspace (SUA)

As if A, B, C, D, E and G weren't special enough, there are a few more special surprises out there in the air. *Special use airspace* is pretty much what it says it is—airspace that is set aside for a particular purpose. Some of it you can use, though with caution, while some of it is strictly off limits without specific permission.

Prohibited Areas – Prohibited areas are just that—areas where flight is simply prohibited. Figure 52 shows prohibited area P-47. This area is defined by blue-hatched lines within the prohibited area. Under the special use airspace section shown on the sides of the aeronautical sectional chart, Figure 53, there is a listing of different special use airspace segments as well as their limitations. P-47 extends to 4,800 feet MSL and is in continuous operation.

Like many things, *prohibited* is a somewhat relative term. Some prohibited areas function only during limited hours. Make the worst case assumption—that prohibited really means prohibited—and you can't go wrong. This is one of those situations where making a mistake will probably get you a bushel basket full of trouble. Prohibited areas protect sensitive sites ranging from the White House to national security areas or secret military installations. Unless you have a lot of free time on your hands, don't even think about trying to get permission to cross a chunk of prohibited airspace. Go around it!

Restricted Areas – Restricted areas are much more numerous than prohibited areas. Unlike prohibited areas, they restrict flights due to the unusual activities conducted within them. These areas often contain invisible hazards to aircraft such as the firing of artillery, aerial gunnery, guided missiles or, in the case of the restricted area in Figure 54, big rockets. Restricted areas are identified by blue-hatched lines similar to those defining prohibited areas. You can tell the difference by the listing of either a *P* or an *R* next to its identifying number.

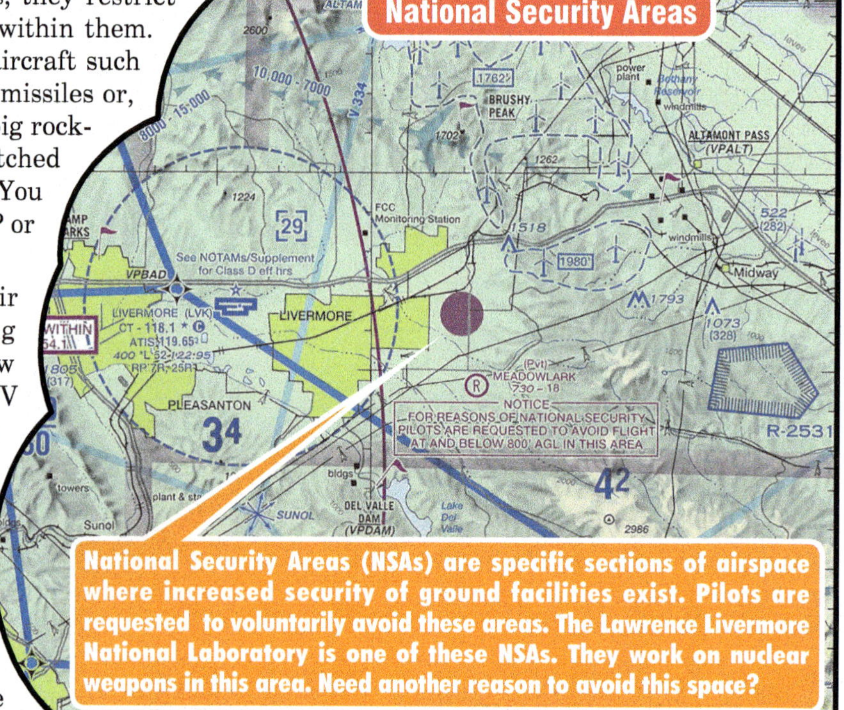

National Security Areas

National Security Areas (NSAs) are specific sections of airspace where increased security of ground facilities exist. Pilots are requested to voluntarily avoid these areas. The Lawrence Livermore National Laboratory is one of these NSAs. They work on nuclear weapons in this area. Need another reason to avoid this space?

Rockets are often fired from Vandenberg Air Force Base located in R-2516. There's nothing more unsettling than looking out your window and seeing yourself in formation with a Saturn-V rocket booster. The special use airspace section on the aeronautical sectional chart (Figure 55) shows R-2516 is in use continuously and extends to an unlimited height. *Unlimited* is really, really high so you can forget about climbing above it.

Before you can enter or fly through a restricted area, you need permission from the controlling agency (this is often obtainable through the local Air Route Traffic Control Center-

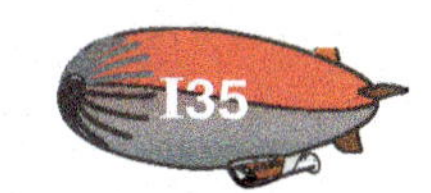

Restricted area R-2516 as shown on a sectional chart. Fig. 54

SPECIAL USE AIRSPACE ON LOS ANGELES SECTIONAL CHART

Unless otherwise noted altitudes are MSL and in feet. Time is local.
"TO" an altitude means "To and including."
FL – Flight Level
NO A/G – No air to ground communications.
Contact Flight Service for information.

Note: Special Use Airspace (SUA) NOTAMS are issued when SUA is active outside scheduled/published times. NOTAMS to be discussed in last chapter.

U.S. P-PROHIBITED, R-RESTRICTED, W-WARNING, A-ALERT, MOA-MILITARY OPERATIONS AREA

NUMBER	ALTITUDE	TIME OF USE	CONTROLLING AGENCY/ CONTACT FACILITY	FREQUENCIES
R-2501 A, B, C	UNLIMITED	CONTINUOUS	LOS ANGELES CNTR	126.35
R-2501 D, E	UNLIMITED	CONTINUOUS	LOS ANGELES CNTR	128.15
R-2502 A	TO 16,000	CONTINUOUS	LOS ANGELES CNTR	
R-2512	TO 23,000	0600-2300 †24 HRS IN ADVANCE	YUMA MCAS/YUMA INTL	124.15
R-2513	TO FL 240	CONTINUOUS	OAKLAND CNTR	128.7 307.0
R-2515	UNLIMITED	CONTINUOUS	JOSHUA CON FAC	120.25 133.65
R-2516	UNLIMITED	CONTINUOUS	LOS ANGELES CNTR	119.05
R-2517	UNLIMITED	CONTINUOUS	LOS ANGELES CNTR	119.05
R-2519	UNLIMITED	CONTINUOUS	LOS ANGELES CNTR	135.5
R-2524	UNLIMITED	CONTINUOUS	JOSHUA CON FAC	120.25 133.65
R-2534 A, B	500 AGL TO UNLIMITED	INTERMITTENT BY NOTAM 4 HRS IN ADVANCE	LOS ANGELES CNTR	119.05
R-2535 A, B	TO 100,000	0600-2200 MON-FRI †24 HRS IN ADVANCE	LOS ANGELES CNTR	132.15
W-285 A	TO FL 450	0630-2100 MON-FRI†	OAKLAND CNTR	134.15 355.6 (N) 134.55 290.5 (S)
W-285 D	TO FL 190	0630-2100 MON-FRI†	OAKLAND CNTR	134.15 355.6 (N) 134.55

Fig. 55

—ARTCC). Some restricted areas have designated hours or days of operation (as opposed to being active *continuously*). It's unlikely that you're going to get permission to enter a restricted area when it's in use.

Many times restricted areas aren't in use. The controlling agency for R-2516 is ZLA CNTR (Los Angeles ARTCC). Contact them for this permission. If you don't know how to establish contact with the center, call the nearest FSS for help in doing this.

Be cautious when flying in, near, or around restricted areas. A friend once unknowingly penetrated an active restricted area and saw red tracer shells whisking past his window. He had entered a gunnery range at a low altitude. Since they don't make bulletproof flight jackets (and seats), he felt pretty uncomfortable. Until bulletproof airplanes become popular, avoid flying in active restricted areas unless you have permission from the controlling agency.

In the early 1970s one of my students accidentally entered an active restricted area. He thought the top of the restricted area was 1,500 feet instead of 15,000 feet. A crease in his chart had rubbed off the last zero in 15,000. Upon entering the area, he scattered a covey of F-4s like frightened quail. The flight leader joined up on him and tried to give him hand signals to switch to 121.5 MHz. My student simply thought the guy was waving at him so he waved back. Finally, out of frustration, my student pulled his power to slow down and assess the situation. Unable to maintain the slow speed, the jet sped off into the distance. The moral to the story is to get a new chart if wrinkles make it unreadable.

Warning Areas – Warning areas are another type of special use airspace where hazards may exist for pilots. Think of warning areas as restricted areas for airspace over which the U.S. doesn't have the right to impose a restriction because it's beyond the country's boundaries. These areas are identified by a blue-hatched line, similar to restricted and prohibited areas, as shown in Figure 56. Warning areas contain hazards similar to those found in restricted areas (things that go *bang* in the night, and day; hyperactive fighter aircraft at low altitudes; and unescorted test rockets).

Penetration of a warning area when it's in use can be very interesting. The Aeronautical Information Manual states that warning areas may contain hazards to "non participating" aircraft. Participation, by the way, is on a strictly invitational basis, and you are not invited. It's best to avoid warning areas if at all possible. The special use airspace section on the sectional chart (Figure 57) shows that W-291 extends to 80,000 feet and is intermittently in operation. Calling the controlling agency listed (ZLA—Los Angeles Center) is a good idea if you're planning on entering this area.

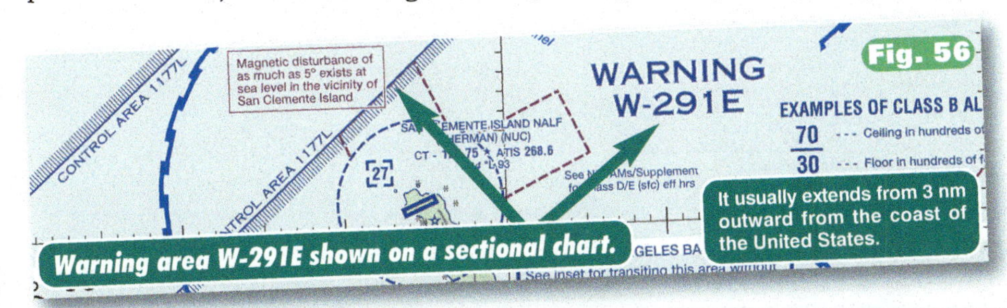

Warning area W-291E shown on a sectional chart. Fig. 56

Warning area information on the sectional chart's special use airspace tab. Fig. 57

U.S. P-PROHIBITED, R-RESTRICTED, W-WARNING, A-ALERT, MOA-MILITARY OPERATIONS AREA

NUMBER	ALTITUDE	TIME OF USE	CONTROLLING AGENCY/ CONTACT FACILITY	FREQUENCIES
W-289 S, E, W	UNLIMITED	INTERMITTENT BY NOTAM	LOS ANGELES CNTR	132.15
W-2[illegible]9 N	TO FL 240	INTERMITTENT BY NOTAM	LOS ANGELES CNTR	132.15
W-291 E	TO FL 800	INTERMITTENT BY NOTAM	LOS ANGELES CNTR	132.15 (E OF 120 W)
W-292 E, W	UNLIMITED	INTERMITTENT BY NOTAM	LOS ANGELES CNTR	132.15

Alert Areas – Alert areas are shown on sectional charts to help identify areas where there is a high volume of pilot training or an unusual type of aerial activity. These areas are shown in a magenta color using the same symbolic hatching used by restricted, prohibited or warning areas. Figure 58 shows a typical alert area. Figure 59 shows the special use airspace box on the sectional chart that provides information on this airspace (the text used here is also magenta). You are not prohibited from entering an alert area, but as the name suggests, you should maintain added vigilance (remember, all pilots have a responsibility for collision avoidance). An alert area can be a place where a lot of student military drivers are practicing, but instead of cars they have airplanes that go hundreds of miles per hour. Got the picture?

Military Operations Areas – Known as a MOA (as in *mow-ahh*), military operations areas are designed to separate or segregate certain nonhazardous military activities from IFR traffic (outside of Class A airspace). Figure 60 depicts the military operations area outlined with a magenta hatched line. MOAs are often given names instead of numbers (the military has always liked secret code names). Figure 51 shows the MOA airspace listing found on the aeronautical sectional chart. It lists altitude for all the MOAs. These are the MOAs' base altitude. All MOA's are assumed to extend vertically to FL180 (18,000 feet) unless stated otherwise. The Bakersfield MOA, according to Figure 61, consists of the airspace starting at 2,000 feet AGL and extending up to flight level 180, between the hours listed. The ZLA (Los Angeles Center) is the controlling agency for the Bakersfield MOA.

Unlike restricted or prohibited areas, a MOA doesn't restrict or prohibit the flight of VFR aircraft. You can enter a MOA without permission. I suggest, however, that you contact the nearest FSS and ask about the status of that particular MOA. If it's active (also referenced to as hot), I also suggest you contact the controlling agency prior to entry and ask for traffic advisories.

Be aware that you will find all types of military training activities within this airspace. It's possible that military pilots will be doing aerobatics, dog fighting (I don't know why they're so angry at dogs), or high speed runs (no military speed limit in a MOA). The last thing you want to do is get in the way of a bunch of battle thirsty pilots who haven't seen combat in a while.

> **SAY AGAIN!**
>
> Reason pilot gave for taking off without a clearance: "We may have been distracted by trying to be extra vigilant."
>
> **ASRS Report**

Take note of the red circle around Kern Valley airport in the Isabella MOA. The note attached to this circle (known as an *aerodrome traffic zone*) states that the MOA excludes the airspace below 1,500 feet AGL within the circle. In other words, you can do touch and goes in peace below 1,500 feet at Kern Valley. I had one student in a ground school class who suggested that if a military pilot were chasing you (they don't do that) you could make for the red circle. At least they can't go in there. I retorted that if he really wanted to get you, he'd be circling outside that circle until you made a break for your home field. Don't worry, the military guys are friendly, they don't chase us small guys—at least on purpose, anyway.

My recommendation is to avoid active MOA's when and where possible. Sometimes you have no choice but to fly through them. If so, do keep your eyes open. One student of mine claimed he discovered why they're called MOA's. Apparently, if you get frightened by a military jet while in one of these areas, you won't want to go back "no moah."

Military Training Routes (MTRs) – Military training routes are highways for military jet aircraft. They usually come in two brands: IFR or VFR military training routes. IFR military training routes are designed to be flown above 1,500 feet AGL. VFR military training routes exist at and below 1,500 feet AGL. Figure 62 shows how MTRs are depicted on an aeronautical sectional chart.

MTR's have the letters "IR" or "VR" identifying whether they are

Fig. 58

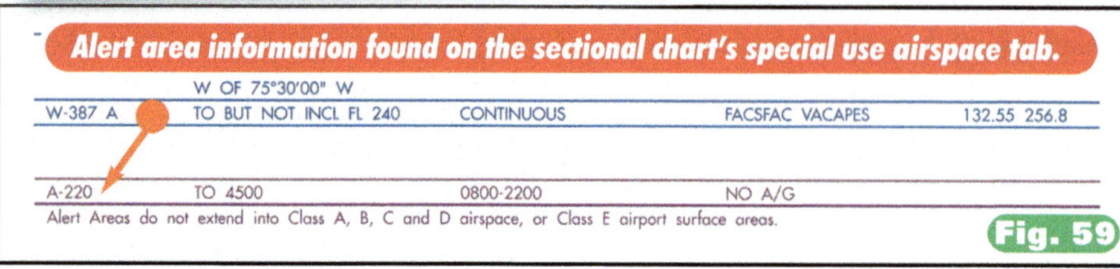
Alert area information found on the sectional chart's special use airspace tab.

	W OF 75°30'00" W			
W-387 A	TO BUT NOT INCL FL 240	CONTINUOUS	FACSFAC VACAPES	132.55 256.8
A-220	TO 4500	0800-2200	NO A/G	

Alert Areas do not extend into Class A, B, C and D airspace, or Class E airport surface areas.

Fig. 59

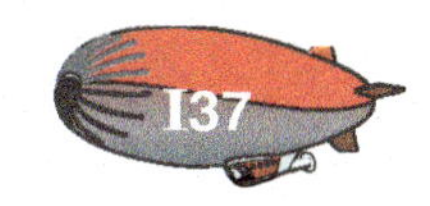

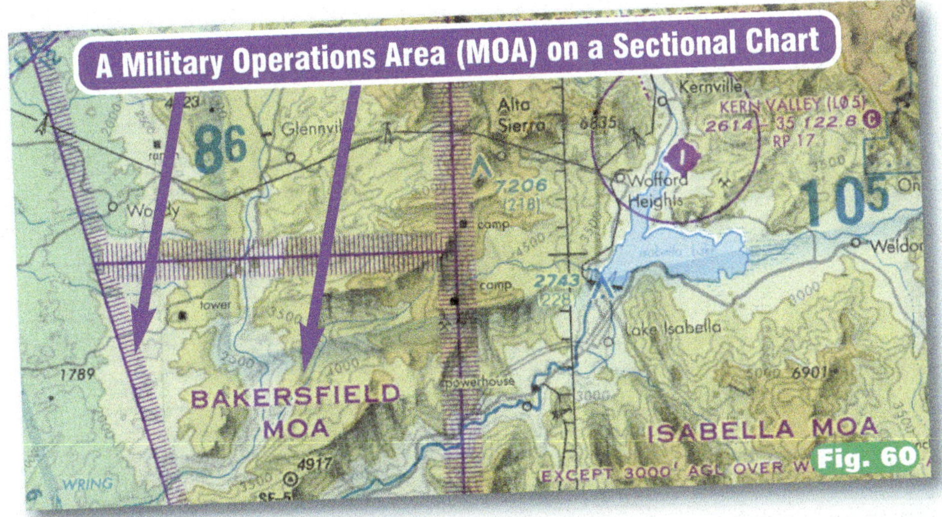

Fig. 60

MOA INFO ON THE SPECIAL USE AIRSPACE TAB

MOA information found on the sectional chart's special use airspace tab.

MOA NAME	ALTITUDE OF USE*	TIME OF USE†	CONTROLLING AGENCY**
ABEL BRAVO	7000	0500-2200 MON-FRI	ZLA CNTR
ABEL EAST	5000 TO BUT NOT INCL 13,000	INTERMITTENT BY NOTAM	ZLA CNTR
ABEL NORTH	7000	0500-2200 MON-FRI	ZLA CNTR
ABEL SOUTH	7000	0500-2200 MON-FRI	ZLA CNTR
BAKERSFIELD	2000 AGL	0600-2200 MON-FRI	ZLA CNTR

Fig. 61

IFR or VFR routes. If either route has a four digit number next to it, it was designed to be flown at and below 1,500 feet AGL (i.e., VR1266). If the route has only three numbers next to it, it was designed to be flown above 1,500 feet AGL (i.e., IR216). Arrows point in the direction these routes are usually flown.

While you are not prohibited from flying along or near an MTR, it's a great idea to avoid them whenever possible. Consider that there are no speed restrictions for military aircraft along an MTR. Military jet aircraft may be flying at many hundreds of miles per hour just a few hundred feet off the ground, scaring all kinds of terrestrial-dwelling animals (groundhogs, ducks, mice, humans, etc.). Don't be one of them! A simple call to the nearest FSS will give you information on the status of MTR's in your area. In other words, the FSS should know whether the MTR is in use.

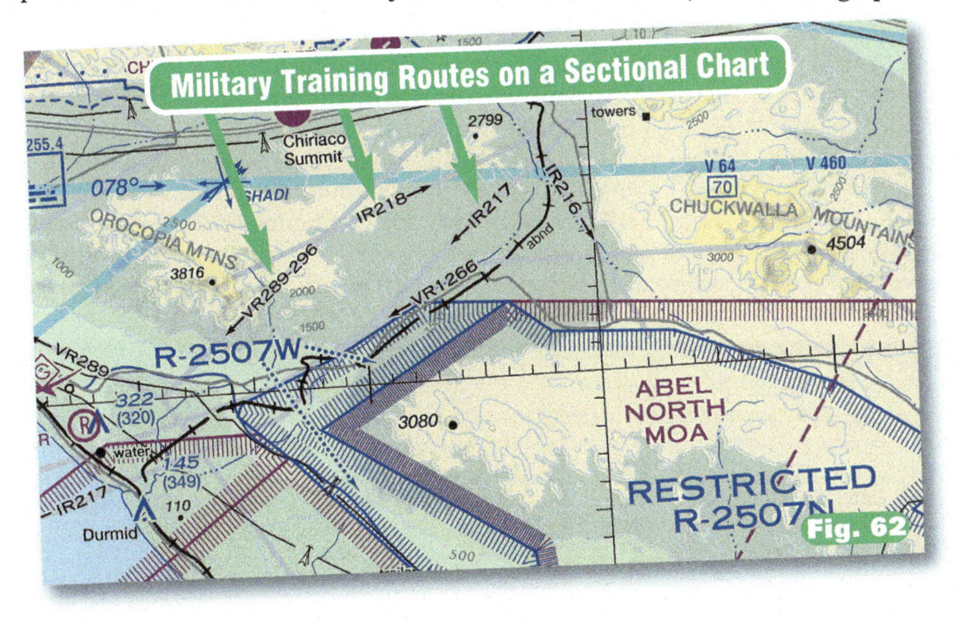

Fig. 62

Temporary Flight Restrictions – When an unusual situation arises (natural disaster, events of high public interest, forest fires, national security, etc.) the FAA will often issue a TFR or *temporary flight restriction* for that area. Such a restriction helps protect persons or property on the surface, protect those providing disaster relief from the hazard of low flying sightseeing type aircraft, protect the President, Vice President or other public figures or provide a safe environment for space operations.

These temporary flight restrictions are usually issued in the form of a notice to airmen (NOTAM). NOTAMs designate an area and altitude in which the restrictions apply.

After the attack on September 11, 2001 numerous TFRs have been established for security reasons. This is one reason you need to check all NOTAMs during flight planning. TFRs are changing and new ones are being created frequently. Before every flight, check with the local FSS, or a reliable NOTAM internet source for TFR information about the area in which you'll fly. The following is a typical temporary flight restriction:

Flight Restriction - Julian, California due to fire fighting activity. Effective 1100 UTC August 28, 2009, until further notice pursuant to 14 CFR Section 91.137 (a)(1). Temporary flight restrictions are in effect within a three mile radius of the 20 DME fix on the 223 degree radial from Julian VOR at and below 4,000 feet MSL. San Diego FSS is the FAA coordinating facility.

SFRAs and FRZs

Just in case you thought airspace couldn't get more complicated, think again. For some time, the FAA has used a charting symbol to designate a SFRA (Figure 63, position 1) or *special flight rules area* surrounded by a blue line containing regularly- spaced blue blocks (position 2). In this figure, we see the SFRA for the area around Washington, D.C. SFRAs can also be found in and around locations at the Grand Canyon and certain areas in Florida, Alaska and New York.

Flight Restricted Zone (FRZ), Special Flight Rules Area (SFRA) in Washington, D.C. Airspace

Flying within 60 nautical miles of the centerpiece VOR for the SFRA, or landing at an airport within the boundaries of a SFRA, requires you to meet both awareness training and equipment requirements as specified in *14 CFR Part 93* (sorry, but you cannot substitute Zen meditation for the awareness training, either). For instance, to operate within the DC SFRA, you'll file and activate a DC SFRA flight plan. Within the DC SFRA, you'll find the DC FRZ or *flight restricted zone* (Figure 65, position 3). The FRZ is essentially a no-fly zone with exceptions for those airports unfortunate enough to be located within its boundaries. Flight to or from these airports require that a DC FRZ flight plan be filed and activated. No, these aren't VFR flight plans, either. They are special flight plans discussed in the awareness training you'll receive for this airspace.

Should you decide on a flying trip to Washington, D.C., (or any other SFRA) make sure you check the AIM, FARs and all the other information that might be necessary for operations within that area. It's also wise to call the FAA in that area and ask for additional advice.

Spaced Out

Now that we've charted the airspace, it's time to chart the charts. That means learning how to identify the symbology on aeronautical charts and use this information to help you navigate. Not knowing how to read an aeronautical chart is like having your limo driver show up wearing a neck brace—a very unsettling experience. So, fasten your seatbelts as we set off to discover how to make sense of those squiggles, squirts and markings on popular aviation charts.

Controlled Firing Areas

A *controlled firing area* (CFA) is where the military (most likely) conduct certain activities that could be hazardous to non-participating aircraft (no, you can't participate, either). Fortunately, any activity in the CFA will be suspended immediately when a spotter airplane, radar or a ground-observer spots an aircraft in the area. For this reason, CFAs aren't shown on sectional charts. However, info on them can be found in the Special Notice section (in the rear section) of the *Chart Supplement*.

CONTROLLED FIRING AREA (CFA) EAST OF YUMA, AZ

The military has established a controlled firing area (CFA) east of Yuma, AZ. The CFA is bordered by the following fixes: BZA058015 - BZA068035 - BZA072034 - BZA075030 - BZA075015 - BZA058015. Operations will be conducted at or below 3000´AGL. The hours of operation are Monday through Saturday from sunrise to sunset.

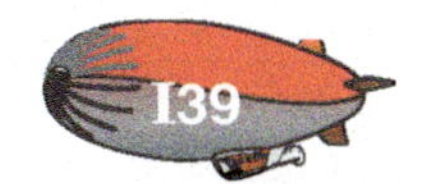

Postflight Briefing #9-1

More on TFRs

Given the importance of TFRs in today's airspace, it makes sense to know where they are and how to avoid them, or enter them if it pleases you. Of course, some of today's wonderful electronic equipment makes this easy to do. Take the iPad, for instance (Figure 66). There are several varieties of navigation and flight-planning software available for these devices. One of the more popular programs is Foreflight. As you can see from Figure 66, position 1, Foreflight shows TFRs as magenta circles on the map display. By tapping your finger on the magenta circle, you'll see a box pop up with details on the TFR (Figure 67, position 2). Now that's nice, right? Yes, expecially if you're an ant and can read letters at a scale of one-half your body length. Nevertheless, this is good information to have. It's also a good reminder to read the TFR specifics before departure.

The Disneyland TFR extends from the surface to 3,000 feet AGL within a three nautical mile radius from the theme park. It has been in effect since October 27th, 2014. These are known as Charted (or "Blanket") TFRs since they're relatively permanent fixtures at other locations such as Camp David and Disneyland in California. As stated in the TFR NOTAM, you can enter this TFR if you are in contact with ATC, perhaps while using flight following or while on an IFR flight plan.

Other forms of "blanket" TFRs that aren't charted are those that appear during major sporting/speedway events held at prominent stadiums (Figures 68 and 69). While stadium symbols are now shown on sectional charts, any accompanying TFRs is not depicted. It's assumed that a blanket-NOTAM'd-TFR covers all major sporting/speedway events at stadiums with a seating capacity of 30,000 or more people. This TFR is in effect within +/- one hour of the scheduled event. It's also assumed that you'll avoid flying within 3 NM of these stadiums at 3,000 feet or less AGL.

So how do you know if a blanket TFR is present? Well, if you look down and see a major sporting event taking place, you'd better be more than 3,000 feet above the ground. Fortunately, it doesn't take amazing eyesight to identify a major sporting activity from the air long before reaching the 3 NM limit.

As an important and final note on TFRs, I want you to exercise extreme caution when using your GPS (don't deny it, I know you have one) to avoid and circumnavigate TFRs. Yes, it's tempting to decrease the range on your GPS's moving map display and fly "one pixel" away from the border of the TFR as depicted on the screen. Well, while your chart is certainly important, it's the chart that ATC looks at that determines whether or not you violated the boundary of TFR airspace, even if his chart has less accuracy than yours. Sorry, but that's a fact. So please avoid all TFRs by a reasonable distance and several hundred feet (at least) to avoid an airspace violation.

Postflight Briefing #9-2

Memorizing Visibility Minimums

It was the best lucid dream a flight instructor could have. The setting was ground school, the subject was FARs and I was the instructor. Unrestricted by space, time and dimension, I wasted no time in satisfying a lifelong wish of being able to install FAR knowledge by smacking the foreheads of my students with the palm of my hand (just like those TV evangelists). "Feel the power of the FARs," I yelled. SMACK! They'd topple backwards and be gently lowered to the ground by their previously anointed classmates (double SMACK if the installation required the definitions listed in the FARs.) Alas, it was only a dream.

Teaching the FARs isn't that simple in the wide-awake world. If it were, students would have few problems remembering the visibility minimums in Part 91. With the memory aid shown in Figure 70, however, this process becomes much simpler.

Before I explain how to use this mnemonic artifact, take a good look at it. In an oxygen rich atmosphere, how long would it take you to commit it to memory? Perhaps 10 minutes? Maybe 15 minutes? The short investment of time involved in memorizing this illustration will serve you well. It provides you with the required visibility and cloud clearance requirement for every airspace classification in which you'll fly. Let's see how it works.

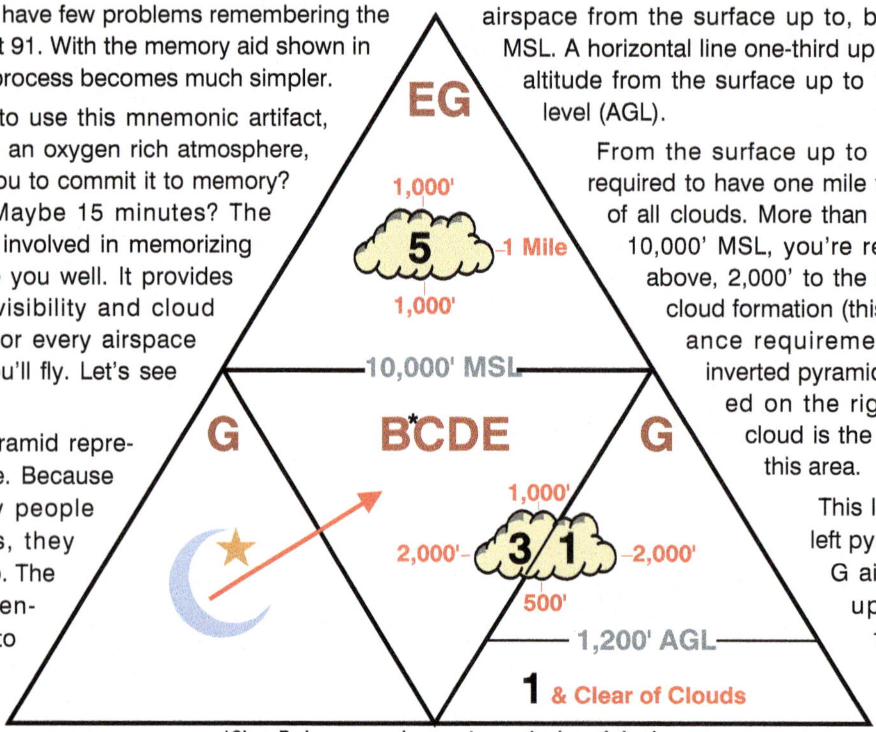

The bottom of the pyramid represents the Earth's surface. Because pyramids were built by people with diminishing goals, they taper to a point at the top. The pyramid's vertical dimension—from the surface to the apex—represents the altitudes flown by VFR pilots. In other words, the pyramid's top extends up to, but not including 18,000' MSL (the upper limit of Class E—controlled airspace). Flight at and above 18,000' MSL requires no VFR minimums since only instrument pilots on IFR flight plans should be up there (it's all Class A airspace up there).

Fig. 70

*Class B airspace requires you to remain clear of clouds

The larger pyramid contains a smaller, inverted pyramid within itself. This smaller pyramid allows the larger pyramid to be divided into four separate sections. Each of the four triangular sections is marked with a letter representing one or more types of airspace. We'll refer to each of the four smaller triangular sections as the top, bottom-left, bottom-right and middle (inverted) pyramid.

The top pyramid and its contents represent the VFR minimums for Class E or G airspace at and above 10,000' MSL, extending up to, but not including 18,000' MSL (other classes of airspace don't usually extend above 10,000' MSL). The cloud within this triangle identifies a cloud-clearance requirement of 1,000' above, 1 statute mile (sm) to the side and 1,000' below. The number "five" is the required flight visibility in statute miles.

The middle pyramid represents Class B, C, D and E airspace (with one exception). The cloud bisected by the middle and the bottom-right pyramid represents the cloud-clearance requirements for these two sections of airspace. Below 10,000' MSL and extending to the surface, you're required to remain 1,000' above, 2,000' to the side and 500' feet below any cloud formation in the above mentioned classes of airspace. The one exception is Class B airspace where you only need remain clear of clouds (remember this as "Be Clear").

A small line bisects the numbers 3 and 1 located in the cloud. The 3 on the left side of the bisecting line is the required flight visibility in Class B, C, D and E airspace below 10,000' MSL.

The bottom right pyramid represents Class G (uncontrolled) airspace from the surface up to, but not including 10,000' MSL. A horizontal line one-third up this triangle identifies the altitude from the surface up to 1,200 feet above ground level (AGL).

From the surface up to 1,200' feet AGL, you're required to have one mile visibility and remain clear of all clouds. More than 1,200' AGL but less than 10,000' MSL, you're required to remain 1,000' above, 2,000' to the side and 500' below any cloud formation (this is the same cloud clearance requirement found in the middle inverted pyramid). The number "1," located on the right side of the bisected cloud is the required flight visibility in this area.

This leaves us with the bottom left pyramid. It represents Class G airspace from the surface up to but not including 10,000' MSL. The moon and the star in this section represent nighttime. The arrow points directly to the middle pyramid. Symbolically, this tells us that, in this section of Class G airspace at night, the VFR requirements are the same as they are in the middle pyramid. By default, the bottom-right triangle represents the day VFR requirements for Class G airspace.

Here are a few additional tips for interpreting this memory aid. First, the lowest visibility and cloud clearance in which private pilots can fly is 1 mile while remaining clear of clouds. Consequently, this represents the minimums for special VFR flights. Second, if Class B, C, D or E airspace touches the surface surrounding an airport, an additional cloud clearance requirement must be met. You must have a 1,000' ceiling in addition to the required 3 miles visibility for basic VFR flight underneath that ceiling.

I remember my first karate class as a high school student. The instructor said, "Mr. Machado, in karate we use our feet instead of our hands." I replied, "That's good, because I can run much faster on my feet." The instructor mumbled a comment in Chinese, then proceeded to chase me around the karate school.

OK, I was confused. I didn't understand karate's "big-picture." Our visual mnemonic allows you to quickly capture a "big-picture" understanding of the required VFR flight minimums. I guarantee you'll experience much less confusion over these minimums if you take the time to memorize my memory artifact. It will serve you well throughout your piloting career.

Postflight Briefing #9-3

Airspace: Dimension, Equipment and Pilot Entry Requirements Memory Aid

Here's a memory aid that allows you to memorize the pertinent equipment and entry requirements as well as the dimensions of Class A, B, C and D airspace. (Class E and G airspace require no special equipment or entry requirement, so we won't concern ourselves with them.) Like many memory aids, this one initially appears rather complex. It's not. After just 15 minutes of study you'll have complete command of these airspace requirements.

This aid is based on the use of similar sounds and commonplace items to help memorize these requirements for each of the four different airspace types. In other words, forklift reminds you of the letter *four* and a dozen eggs reminds you of the number *12*.

Draw a square approximately 4 inches on each side and divide it into four smaller squares. Label the top left hand corners of each square with the letters A,B,C and D (representing the four types of airspace we're concerned with) as shown in Figure 71.

Let the sound of each letter represent a similar sounding reference noun for each square (nouns are easy to visualize since they are persons, places or things). The letter *A* sound like *Hay*; *B* sounds like *Bee*; *C* sounds like *Sea* and *D* sounds like *Deer* as shown in Figure 71. Draw these items in the upper middle part of each square (use stick figures and basic drawings. Remember, they only need be identifiable by you).

Starting clockwise from box A, let's associate the specific items to be memorized with the reference nouns in each square.

Square A

A *teenager* jumps on the *hay* causing a *cloud* to pop out the side of the bushel. The teenager is holding a *missile* that crosses into square B as shown in Figure 72 (Any item that crosses the borders of a square, i.e., the missile" applies to both squares.)

Square B

A *bee* stands on a *tent* as it holds onto the other end of the *missile.* An army *private* runs out of the tent holding a *clarinet* as his weapon.

Square D

A *comb* is on the head of the *deer.* A *leash* runs from the comb to a *stable* (crosses both squares). Under the stable is an *operation* in progress (crosses both squares). The patient is on a *table* (crosses both squares) with *25* cents on his *feet.*

Square C

The patient's *five* fingered hands rest on each side of a *dozen* eggs. On top of the eggs is a *forklift* with two *tennis* rackets on either side. Out of the patient's mouth shoots a *train* with a *panda* that pushes a little section of the *sea* with it as it moves up. It hits the hay and turns right into the tent (it also crosses squares A & B).

That's it. Here's what it means. Class A (**hay**) airspace starts at 18,000 (**hay teen**) thousand feet MSL (**missile**). It requires that you be qualified to fly IFR (in a **cloud**).

Class B (**bee**) airspace ascends to 10,000 feet (**ten**t) MSL (**missile**). It requires a private (army **private**) pilot certificate and a clearance (**clarinet**) to enter.

Class D (**deer**) airspace requires that you have an operating (**operation**) control tower and that you establish (**stable-leash**) communications (**comb**). This requirement also applies to Class C airspace since the operation and stable crosses both squares. It ascends to 2,500 (**25** cents) feet (guy's **feet**) AGL (**table**). The table crosses squares C and D therefore, the AGL reference also applies to the dimensions of Class C airspace.

Fig. 71

The dimensions of the lower section of Class C (**sea**) airspace ascends to 1,200 feet (**12** eggs) AGL (**table**) and has a radius of 5 miles (**five** fingers on each side egg carton's center). The upper section ascends to 4,000 (**for**-**k**-lift, "K means 1000") feet AGL (**table**) and has a radius of 10 miles (**ten**nis on either side of center). This airspace also requires a transponder **(train panda)** with mode C (**sea**) capability. Class A and B also require the transponder with mode C since the train panda moves into these two squares.

When you arrive for the knowledge exam, take out a piece of paper, draw the big square, the subsquares, the letters and the noun reference items for each square. If you find it difficult to draw, simply write the names of the reference items in their approximate relative position. You'll be surprised how easy it is to recall all of the airspace requirements using this aid.

Remember, as with all memory aids, this one allows you to memorize items by brute force. Once you start using it, you'll need it less and less as the information finds its way into your long term memory.

AIRSPACE EQUIPMENT, PILOT REQUIREMENTS AND DIMENSIONS MEMORY AID

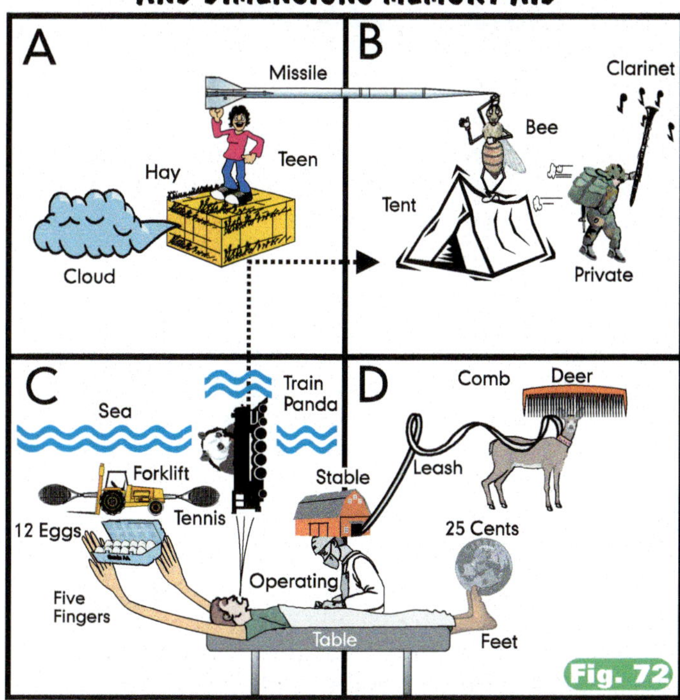

Fig. 72

Postflight Briefing #9-4

Variable Floors Of Class E Airspace

The sectional chart excerpt (Figure 73) and its 3-D representation (Figure 74) depict several airways and their variable floors of controlled airspace. These are called Federal Low Altitude airways and are identified by a V (standing for the word *Victor)* followed by a number (position 1 in Figure 73). These are the routes pilots typically file on their VFR flight plans.

Of course, you don't have to fly these airways, just as you don't have to take major highways when you travel. You can take side streets (travel off airways in a direction of your choosing). Nevertheless, airways are convenient for flight planning. These low altitude airways are normally 8 nautical miles wide and begin at the base of the Class E airspace, continuing up to but not including 18,000 feet MSL.

Look at airways V-12 and V-538 (position 1 in Figure 73). The blue line fading toward the center of the airway indicates that controlled (Class E) airspace begins at 1,200 feet AGL within these borders. The solid blue wavy (serrated) symbols at position 2 indicate that the floor of controlled airspace (Class E) has changed within these symbols. Position 3 shows 7,500 feet MSL as the new altitude for the floor of this airway. Thus, the Class E airspace, within the area bordered by blue faded and wavy symbols, begins at 7,500 feet MSL instead of 1,200 feet AGL. Why raise the floor of controlled (Class E) airspace? Mountains in the local area may make VOR reception unreliable below 7,500 MSL within these borders. Therefore, Class G exists below 7,500 feet MSL at and around position 3. Compare Figure 73 with its 3-D representation in Figure 74.

HIGHER FLOORS OF CLASS E AIRSPACE

The blue serrated figure indicates that the base of Class E (controlled) airspace has changed. Within the borders of two or more serrated figures is an altitude value (shown in blue). This altitude (normally an MSL altitude) is the base of controlled airspace for that area. In the area listed below, the Class E airspace under Victor airway 538, is a section with a base of 7,500' MSL. A large mountain is responsible for raising the base of this airspace since, below 7,500' MSL, it would be difficult to receive the airway on your VOR equipment.

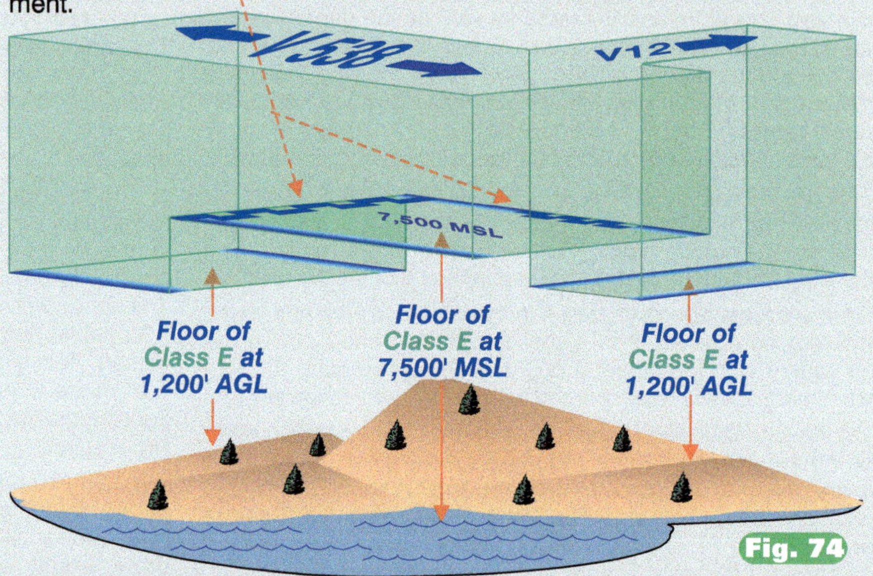

Fig. 74

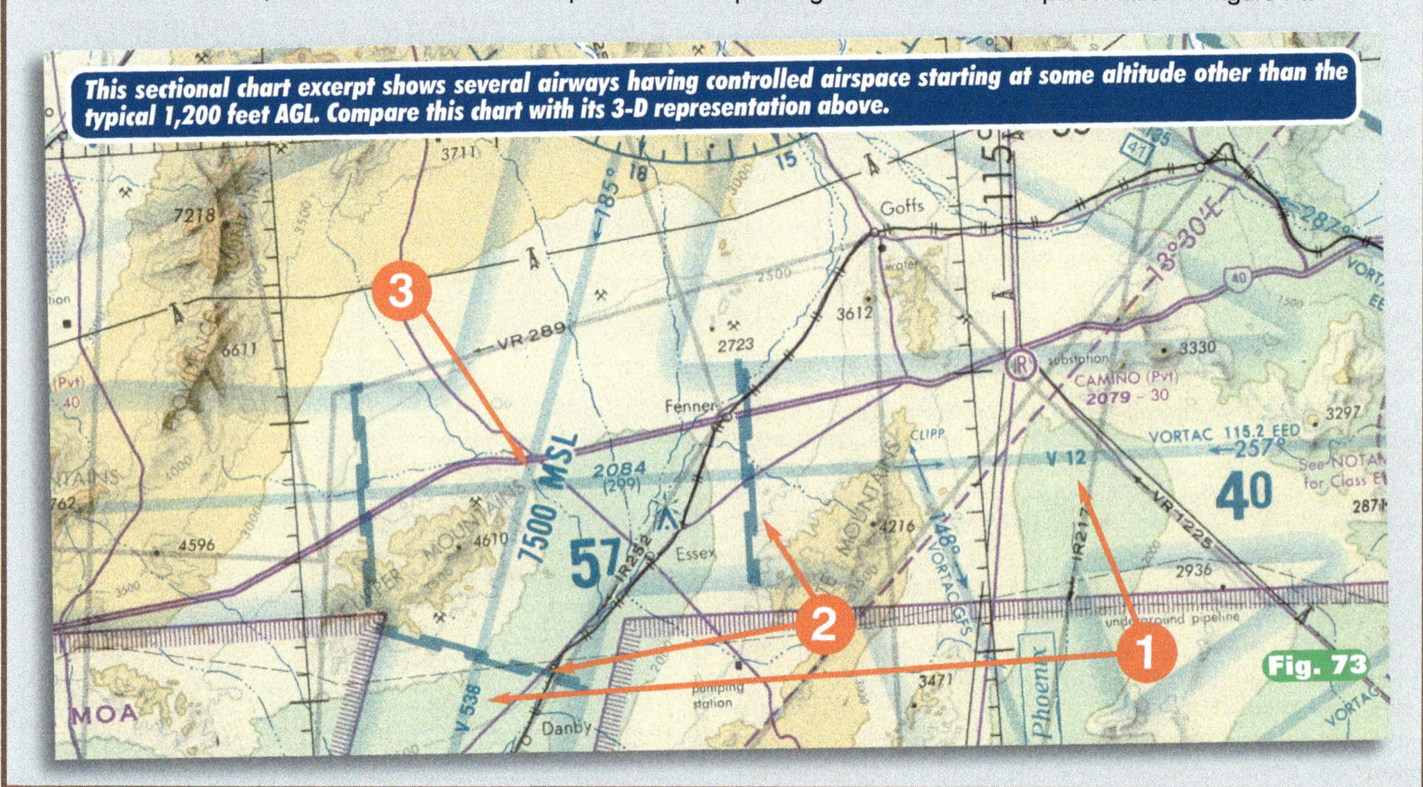

Fig. 73

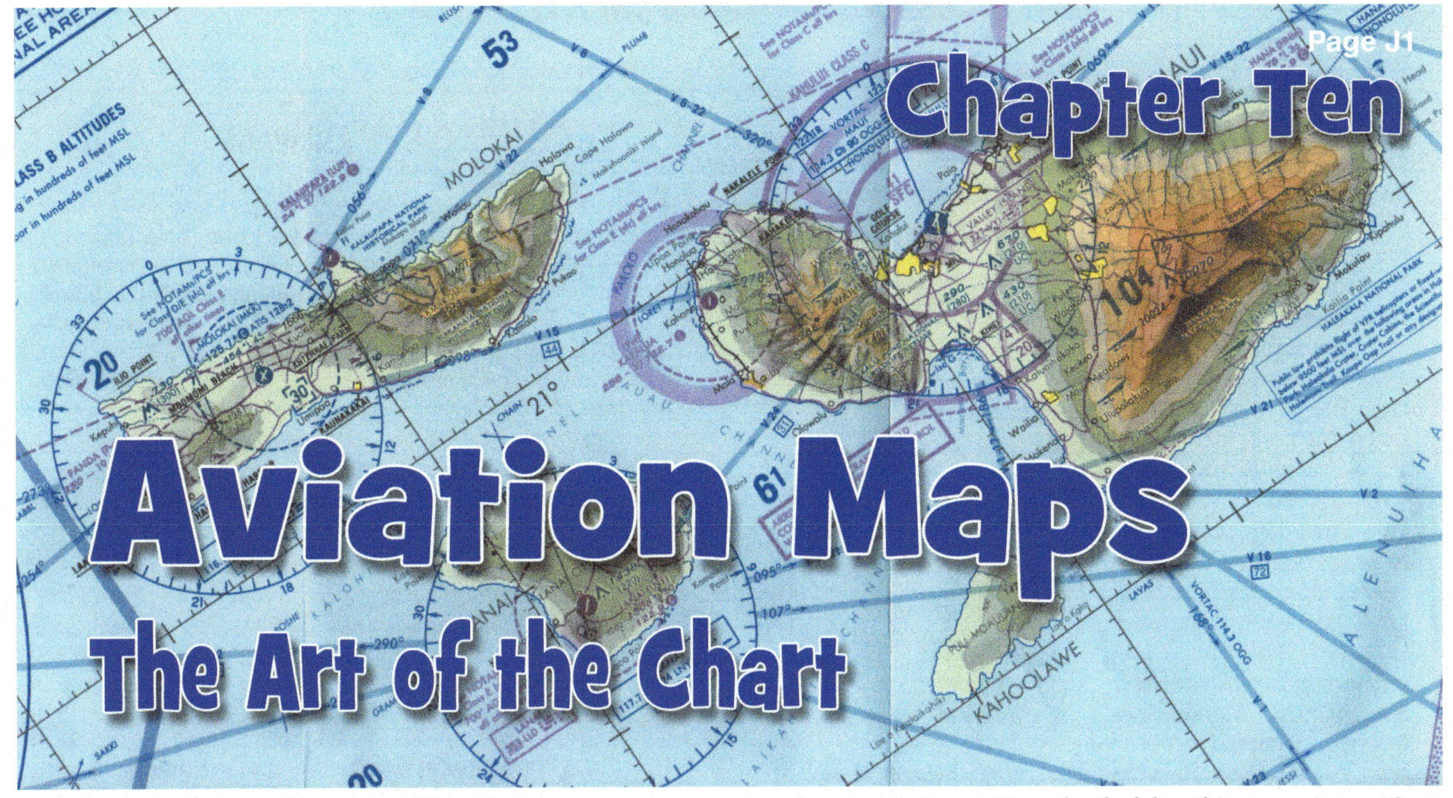

Chapter Ten

Aviation Maps

The Art of the Chart

Maps aren't something new. They began many years ago when one of our Neanderthal brothers or sisters first etched the location of a cave on a deerskin. This really upset the deer, of course, causing him to run away. That produced the world's first moving map display.

Many advances have come along since that time. We now draw maps on ground-up trees, which are easier to sneak up on than deer, come in several exciting shades, and leaf a good impression.

Maps are simply representations of the earth's surface and its topographic features—the bumps and holes that are mountains and lakes, hills and valleys, deserts and forests. In the case of aviation maps, there is also information about a variety of manmade features, such as cities, towns, roads, railroad tracks, and the other evidence of human existence. The challenge of mapmaking is to translate a three dimensional reality into a two dimensional map. Despite the age-old injunction about not fitting a round peg in a square hole, that's exactly what every mapmaker has to do. Like it or not, the earth is round and bumpy; maps are flat. Therein lies the rub.

A good map does several things at once. First, it minimizes the distortion that is inevitable in converting a 3-D world to a 2-D map. Second, it conveys at a glance crucial information. What's crucial? As a pilot you need to know where the land rises and falls (lest it rise up and smite thee), and what the major landmarks are, so you can figure out where *you* are.

Pilots use a wide variety of maps (or *charts,* as they are often called) to tell them where to go, or where they've been. Each type has specific information, and being able to select the right chart for the right job is an important pilot skill.

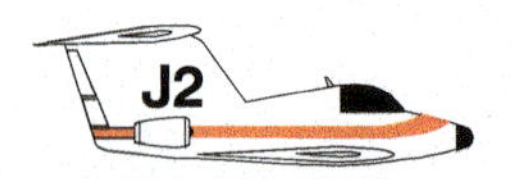

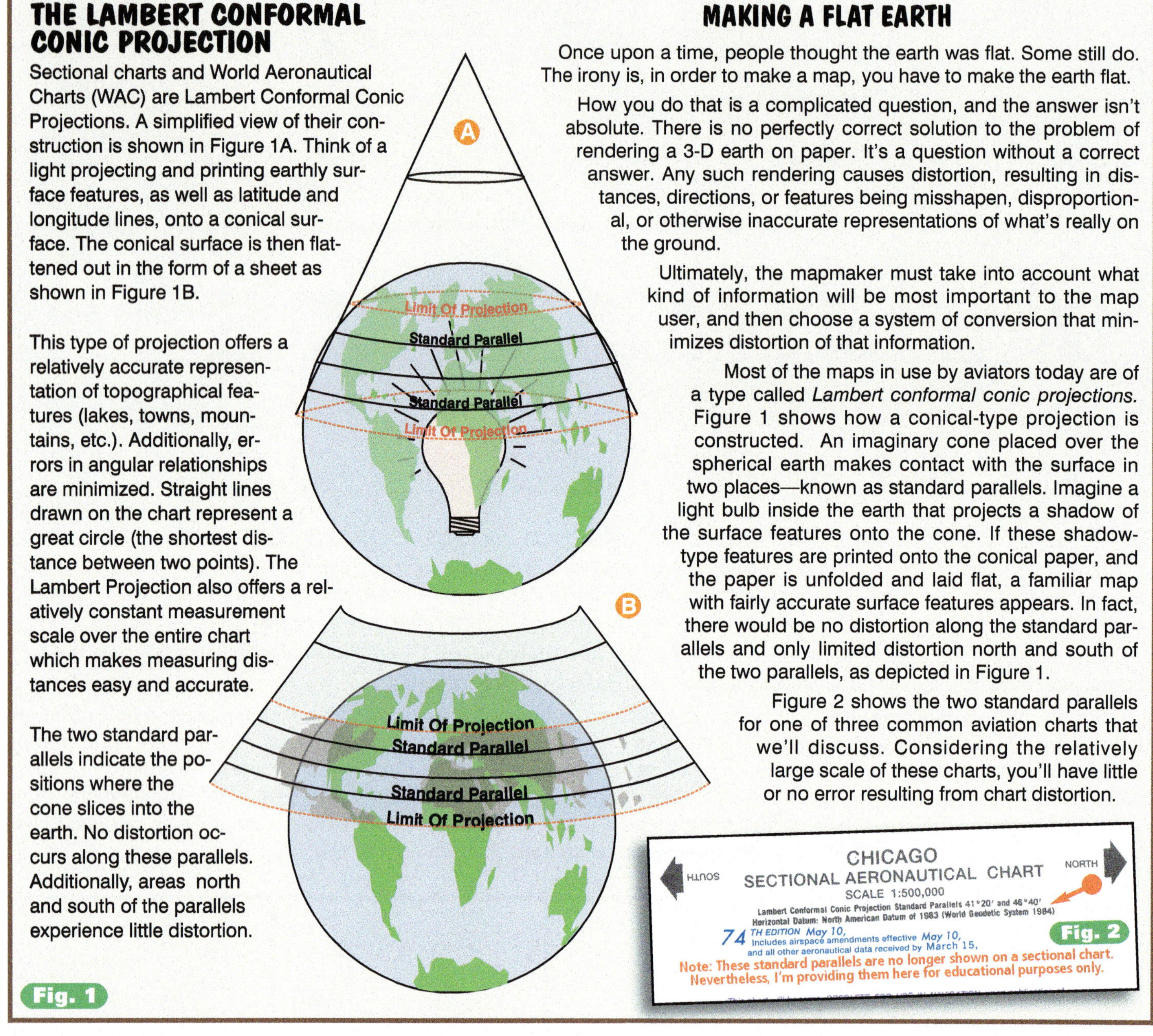

THE LAMBERT CONFORMAL CONIC PROJECTION

Sectional charts and World Aeronautical Charts (WAC) are Lambert Conformal Conic Projections. A simplified view of their construction is shown in Figure 1A. Think of a light projecting and printing earthly surface features, as well as latitude and longitude lines, onto a conical surface. The conical surface is then flattened out in the form of a sheet as shown in Figure 1B.

This type of projection offers a relatively accurate representation of topographical features (lakes, towns, mountains, etc.). Additionally, errors in angular relationships are minimized. Straight lines drawn on the chart represent a great circle (the shortest distance between two points). The Lambert Projection also offers a relatively constant measurement scale over the entire chart which makes measuring distances easy and accurate.

The two standard parallels indicate the positions where the cone slices into the earth. No distortion occurs along these parallels. Additionally, areas north and south of the parallels experience little distortion.

Fig. 1

MAKING A FLAT EARTH

Once upon a time, people thought the earth was flat. Some still do. The irony is, in order to make a map, you have to make the earth flat.

How you do that is a complicated question, and the answer isn't absolute. There is no perfectly correct solution to the problem of rendering a 3-D earth on paper. It's a question without a correct answer. Any such rendering causes distortion, resulting in distances, directions, or features being misshapen, disproportional, or otherwise inaccurate representations of what's really on the ground.

Ultimately, the mapmaker must take into account what kind of information will be most important to the map user, and then choose a system of conversion that minimizes distortion of that information.

Most of the maps in use by aviators today are of a type called *Lambert conformal conic projections.* Figure 1 shows how a conical-type projection is constructed. An imaginary cone placed over the spherical earth makes contact with the surface in two places—known as standard parallels. Imagine a light bulb inside the earth that projects a shadow of the surface features onto the cone. If these shadow-type features are printed onto the conical paper, and the paper is unfolded and laid flat, a familiar map with fairly accurate surface features appears. In fact, there would be no distortion along the standard parallels and only limited distortion north and south of the two parallels, as depicted in Figure 1.

Figure 2 shows the two standard parallels for one of three common aviation charts that we'll discuss. Considering the relatively large scale of these charts, you'll have little or no error resulting from chart distortion.

Fig. 2

The Aeronautical Sectional Chart

The sectional chart is a pilot's most common tool for VFR navigation. Figure 3 shows a typical sectional chart. It is one of 37 such charts covering the entire continental United States. Each one is issued with an effective date and an expiration date (Figure 4). Sectional charts are good for approximately 6 months, then reissued. It's very good practice to avoid using an outdated chart. While terrain doesn't move all that much (not even in California), airports, obstructions, navigational aids and airspace can change. The last thing you want to do is attempt to navigate using a VOR that's been shut down or moved.

Many years ago a friend was using an old sectional chart (outdated by more than a year) for navigation to a Louisiana airport. The chart indicated the VOR was located on the airport. Arriving over the VOR, all my buddy saw was swampland. He finally called the tower and asked them what happened to their airport. They said the VOR had been moved 15 miles north of the field seven months earlier. He's lucky the FAA wasn't moving it the day he flew this cross country. (Imagine the confusion he'd feel at seeing a VOR cruising down the street on a flatbed truck!)

Cautious pilots know chart information can change within the 6 month publishing cycle. Fortunately, the *Chart Supplement* provides you with information on these changes, as shown in Figure 5. The only way you can be completely assured a sectional chart (or any other aeronautical chart) is up to date is by checking the *Chart Supplement* for these changes.

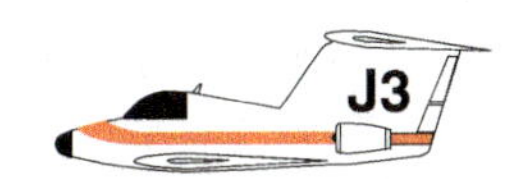

A TYPICAL VFR SECTIONAL CHART

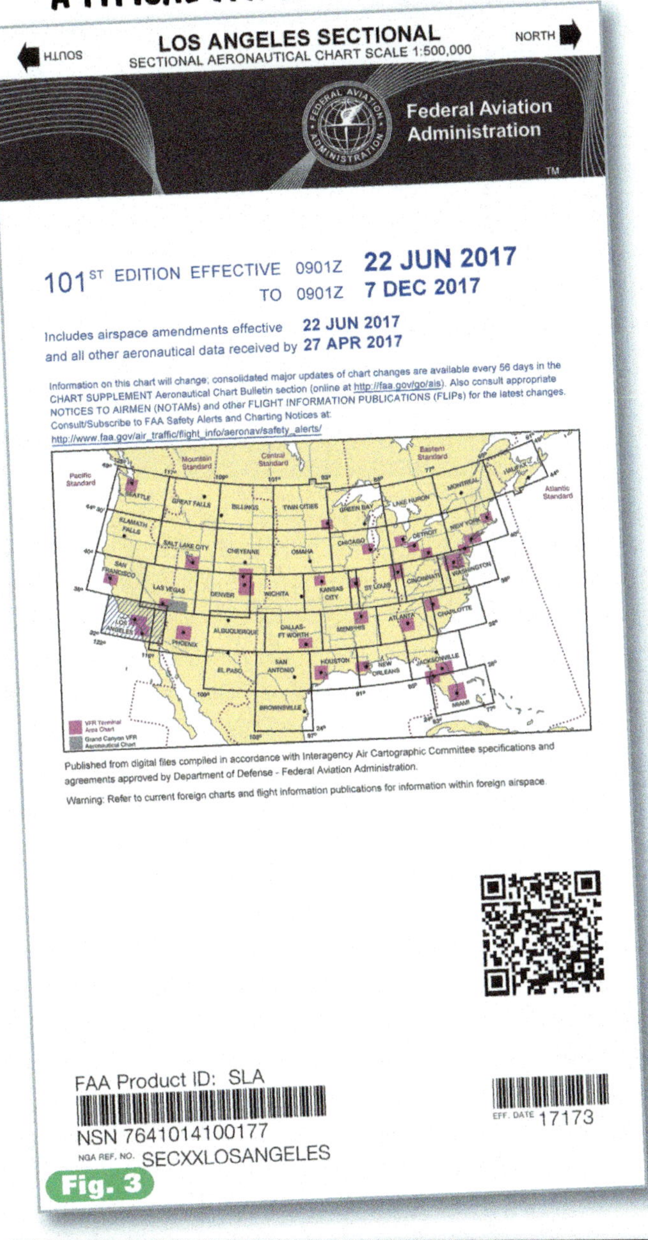

Fig. 3

EACH SECTIONAL IS ISSUED WITH AN EFFECTIVE AND AN EXPIRATION DATE

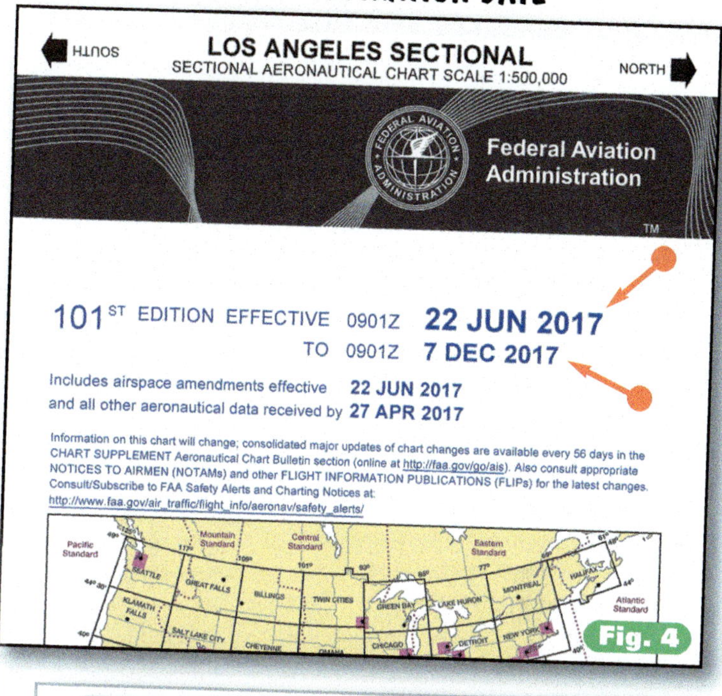

Fig. 4

The Digital Chart Supplement lists changes that affect aeronautical sectional charts.

LOS ANGELES SECTIONAL
101st Edition, 22 Jun 2017

OBSTRUCTIONS
22 Jun 2017 –17 Aug 2017 No Major Changes.

AIRPORTS
22 Jun 2017 No Major Changes.
17 Aug 2017 Delete BELRIDGE arpt, 35º28´05"N, 119º43´19"W.
Delete REIDER arpt, 32º38´17"N, 116º38´21"W.
Delete LLOYDS arpt, 34º54´20"N, 118º18´06"W.

NAVAIDs
22 Jun 2017 No Major Changes.
17 Aug 2017 Shutdown PRIEST VOR, 36º08´25"N, 120,deg>39´54"W.

AIRSPACE
22 Jun 2017 –17 Aug 2017 No Major Changes.

SPECIAL USE AIRSPACE
22 Jun 2017 –17 Aug 2017 No Major Changes.

MILITARY TRAINING ROUTES

Fig. 5

A VFR sectional chart comes with its own mileage scale.

Fig. 6

CAUTION: This chart is primarily designed for VFR navigational purposes and does not purport to indicate the presence of all telephone, telegraph and power transmission lines, terrain or obstacles which may be encountered below reasonable and safe altitudes.

10 | 0 NAUTICAL MILES | 10 | 20 | 30
10 | 0 STATUTE MILES | 10 | 20 | 30
10 | 0 KILOMETERS | 10 | 20 | 30 | 40 | 50 | 60

The sectional chart has a scale of 1 to 500,000. This means every inch on a sectional chart represents 500,000 inches on the actual earth. Fortunately, we can leave our rulers at home because sectional charts (and others) carry their own mileage scale, as shown in Figure 6. This scale is consistent for all sectional charts and equates to 1 inch=6.86 nautical miles. You can also measure using the two-knuckle method, as described in Chapter 11, though this is generally a bit less accurate.

NOT YOUR GRANDPA'S NAVIGATION SYSTEM

Paper cuts be gone. That's right. Today's private pilots typically do not carry paper-type sectional charts in their airplanes. So, when a private pilot gives blood, it's given at the Red Cross center and not in the cockpit.

The availability of tablet iThingy devices (iPhones, Android phones, iPads, Android tablets, etc.) and robust navigation softwares such as *ForeFlight*, *WingX* and others are now acceptable substitutes for paper charts. These softwares are offered on a subscription basis and provide data-driven moving maps (care of the phone's or tablet's internal GPS) in the form of scaleable sectional charts (and IFR charts) along with airport diagrams from the FAA's *Digital Chart Supplement*.

Wait, there's more. Nearly all of today's popular navigation softwares have flight planning ability, weather briefing ability, current NOTAM briefing ability as well as the ability to file flight plans direct from the device itself. With ADS-B in your airplane, your phone or tablet device can also display active traffic information in your area.

If you like science fiction, then you'll find something that looks just like it in your navigation software's computer generated synthetic vision. Several companies offer synthetic vision as a 3-D moving map display. Flying across mountainous terrain at night can be done with greater certainty and comfort when using this data-driven moving map technology.

Then again, should you not carry current sectional charts in your airplane? Call me old school, but I've never known a paper chart to become unreadable because its batteries went dead. My recommendation is to always carry backup paper charts for the type of navigation you're doing. It's just cheap insurance for those times when electrons misbehave.

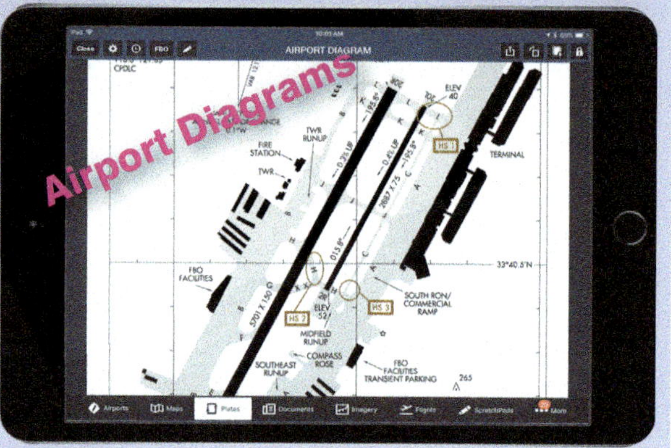

VFR Terminal Area

THE VFR TERMINAL AREA CHART

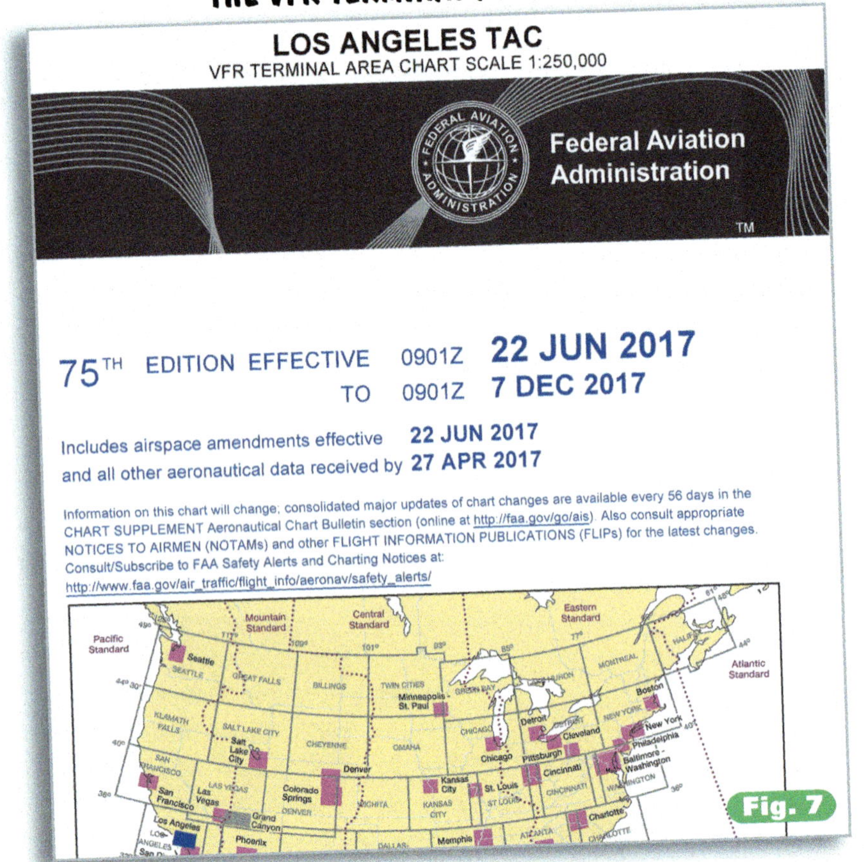

Fig. 7

Charts

I never liked the word terminal. It's a tad scary if you think about it. I once told a student I'd be taking him into a terminal area on our next flight. He didn't show up! Rest easy. Terminal areas are simply places with busy (such as Class B) airspace, usually with a major commercial airport right about in the middle. Many of these areas have a VFR terminal area chart associated with them (Figure 7). The area covered by the VFR terminal area chart is indicated by a white bordering rectangular line on a sectional chart as shown in Figure 8.

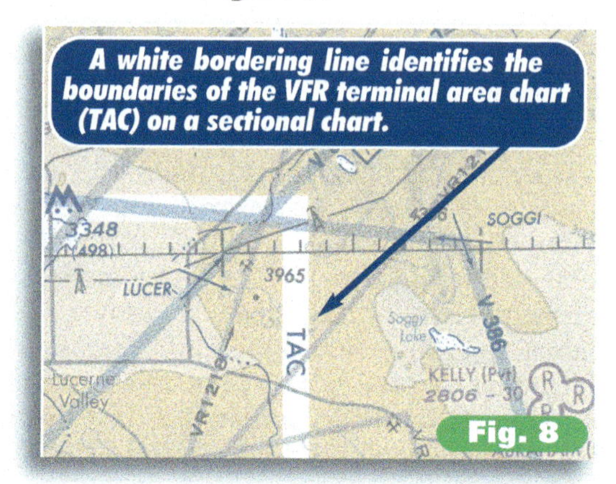

Fig. 8

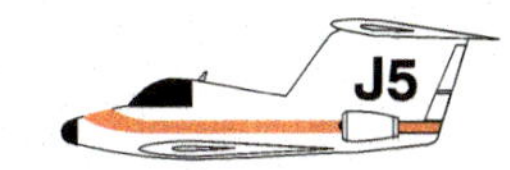

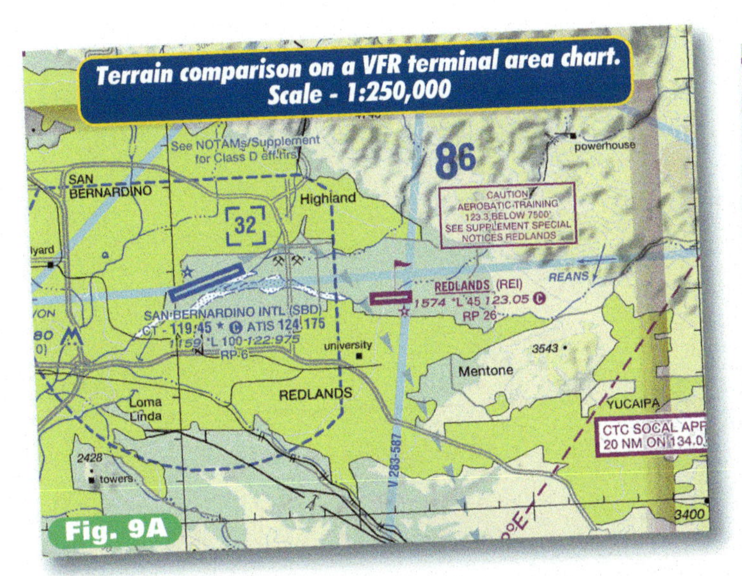

VFR terminal area charts are exceptionally detailed, with a scale of 1 to 250,000 (1 inch=3.43 nautical miles) which provides much more detail than sectional charts. These charts, revised once every 6 months, are very useful for pilots operating from airports within or near a major terminal area. For instance, they allow you to more precisely identify terrain features that help you physically avoid the shelf of Class B airspace. Figures 9A and 9B show a comparison of both charts and their different information detail.

Topographical Information On A Sectional Chart

Topographical (ground) features on a sectional chart are of great value to the VFR pilot, if she or he knows what to look for. Pilotage is most often accomplished by use of the sectional chart, but learning to translate the shadings and markings on the chart into a mental picture and match it up with what's outside is definitely a learned skill. It's also a skill you definitely should learn.

Not all features are created equal, especially on a chart. The big stuff is pretty easy. Most of my students don't have a problem figuring out the Pacific Ocean. It's big, it's blue, and they've usually seen it before. Deciphering the contour features of a mountain or the alluvial fan of small streams takes a little more skill.

Here are some of the major topographical features you should be familiar with. Keep in mind that not all features on the ground are shown on the chart. What mapmakers show on the chart, however, is almost always found on the surface. (I say *almost always* because, over time, some landmarks disappear by erosion, construction, etc.)

Relief (the sloping of terrain) – Depicting three-dimensional hilly and mountainous terrain on a two-dimensional chart presents some difficulty. Mapmakers partially solve the problem with the use of contours to depict terrain elevations. Contours are lines joining areas of equal elevation—somewhat like the isobar on a weather map connecting areas of equal pressure. Figure 10 is an example of how contours depict terrain elevation.

TERRAIN CONTOUR LINES

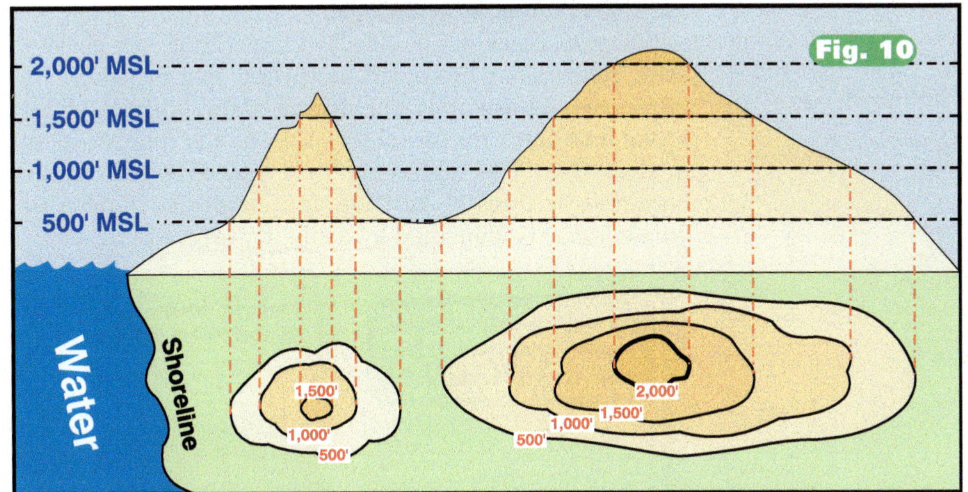

Contour lines allow you to interpret terrain height and gradient above mean sea level on a sectional chart. The contour lines above are spaced at 500 foot intervals while other maps may use 100 or 250 foot terrain intervals.

Fig. 11A

Fig. 11B

On a sectional chart, contour lines are spaced at 500 foot intervals, as shown in Figures 11A and 11B. Occasionally, contours may be shown at 250 foot, 100 foot or even 50 foot levels in areas of relatively low relief (slope). You can tell a lot about the slope of the terrain by examining the spacing between the contour lines in Figure 11A. Closely-spaced contour levels indicate rapidly rising terrain, while contours spaced farther apart indicate less precipitous terrain.

Color – An additional aid in determining the height and slope of terrain is color. Every sectional chart has a terrain color bar on its front side (see Figure 12). The color bar shows a specific color representing the maximum and minimum elevations of terrain. These colors range from light green for the lowest elevation to dark brown for higher elevations. For instance, the dark yellowish-color shown at position A in Figure 12 represents terrain rising between 5,000 and 7,000 feet above sea level. Remember, a specific color doesn't precisely indicate the height of terrain, it indicates a range of altitudes (i.e., 5,000′ to 7,000′) through which terrain can be found in those areas. More precise indications of terrain are identified by something known as *spot elevations*.

The terrain color bar on VFR charts helps identify terrain height and slope.

Fig. 12

Spot Elevation Symbols – Figure 13A shows a spot elevation used on VFR charts (Figure 13B shows the actual terrain features from the air). Normally, spot elevations (shown as *small* black dots) are chosen by mapmakers to indicate the high point on a particular mountain range or ridge. Next to the small black dot is the elevation of that spot above sea level. Remember, there can be several spot elevations in a local area. These spot elevations show heights of local peaks and don't necessarily represent the highest terrain in that area. The highest terrain located within an area bordered by lines of latitude and longitude (known as a *quadrangle*) is identified by a slightly *larger* black dot.

Fig. 13A

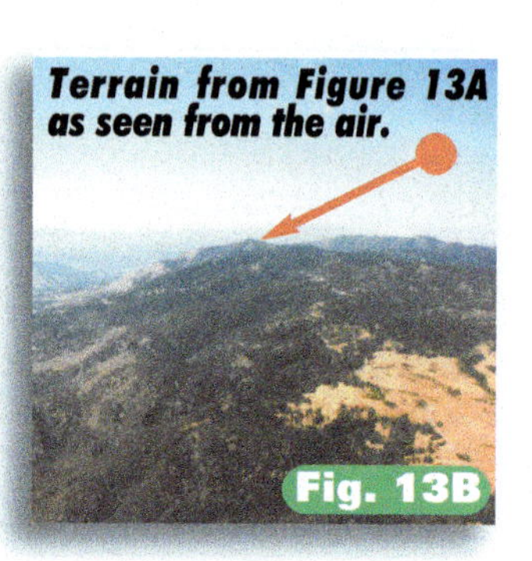

Fig. 13B

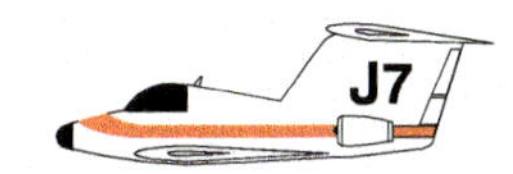

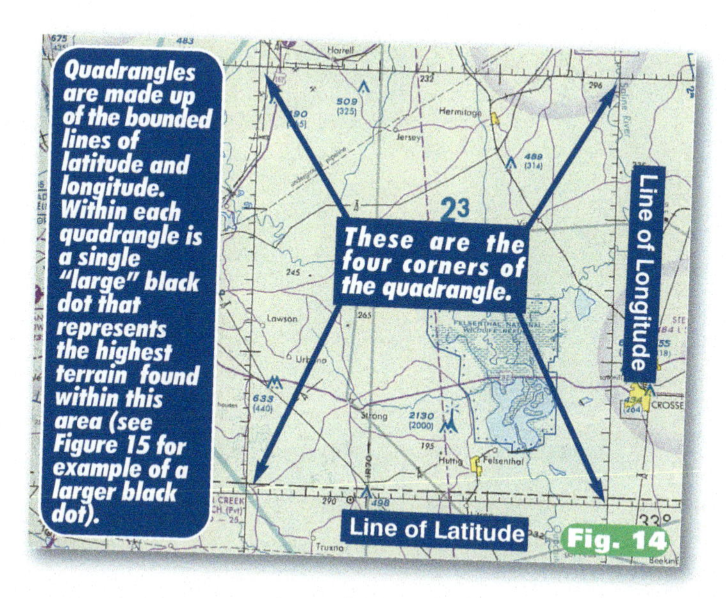

Fig. 14

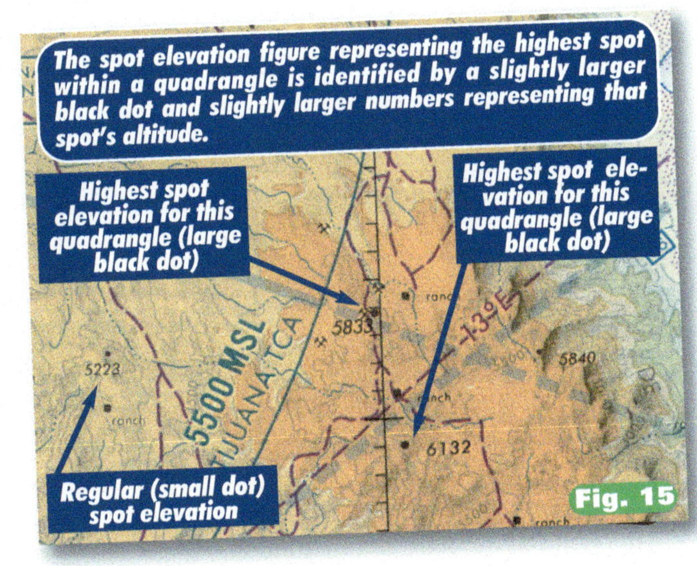

Fig. 15

Spot Elevations Showing Highest Terrain – *Quadrangles* are the rectangular areas bounded by printed lines of longitude and latitude, as shown in Figure 14. Within each quadrangle there is a single *large* black dot. This dot is a special spot elevation figure that locates the highest *terrain* within that area and shows its height above sea level (see Figure 15). While there may be several spot elevation figures (small black dots) within a quadrangle, there will only be one represented by a larger black dot.

Maximum Elevation Figures (MEF) – Maximum elevation figures (MEFs) represent the highest elevation of terrain and other obstacles (towers, trees, etc.) within a quadrangle. Figure 16 shows the MEF value (point A) from the quadrangle containing the spot elevation identified by point B. The two-digit number represents the MEF value in hundreds of feet with the last two zeros missing. Figure 16 (point A), shows an MEF value of 6,700 feet MSL.

MEF values are slightly higher than the obstruction within the quadrangle it represents. How much higher? Cartographers (people who make maps) have a specific formula for figuring MEF values. To understand how this is computed, you must first understand that only manmade obstacles standing more than 200 feet AGL are generally charted. Those 200 feet or less are charted if they are considered critical by cartographers (i.e., in the vicinity of an airport). Cartographers then add a minimum of 100 feet onto the highest elevation shown on the chart. Then they round up to the nearest whole-number hundred value. Finally, they add an additional 200 feet for those manmade obstructions that may not be shown.

For instance, the MEF value in Figure 16 is 6,700 feet MSL (point A). The critical elevation figure for that quadrangle is 6,378 feet MSL (point B). Adding 100 feet onto 6,378 equals 6,478. Rounding this up to the nearest whole number hundred value equals 6,500. Adding an additional 200 for uncharted obstruction equals 6,700 feet MSL.

The MEF is calculated in a similar manner if a manmade obstacle standing more than 200 feet AGL is located on the highest peak in a quadrangle. In this instance, only 100 feet is added to the top of the obstacle, then this value is rounded up to the nearest whole number hundred value to calculate the MEF. The point here is the MEF is not the minimum altitude you should fly within this quadrangle. You should be at least a minimum of 1,000 to 2,000 feet higher (or more) than any MEF value shown along your route. This becomes especially important at night when it's difficult to see terrain or obstacles, even if these obstacles are lit (you don't want to hit one and light it up even more).

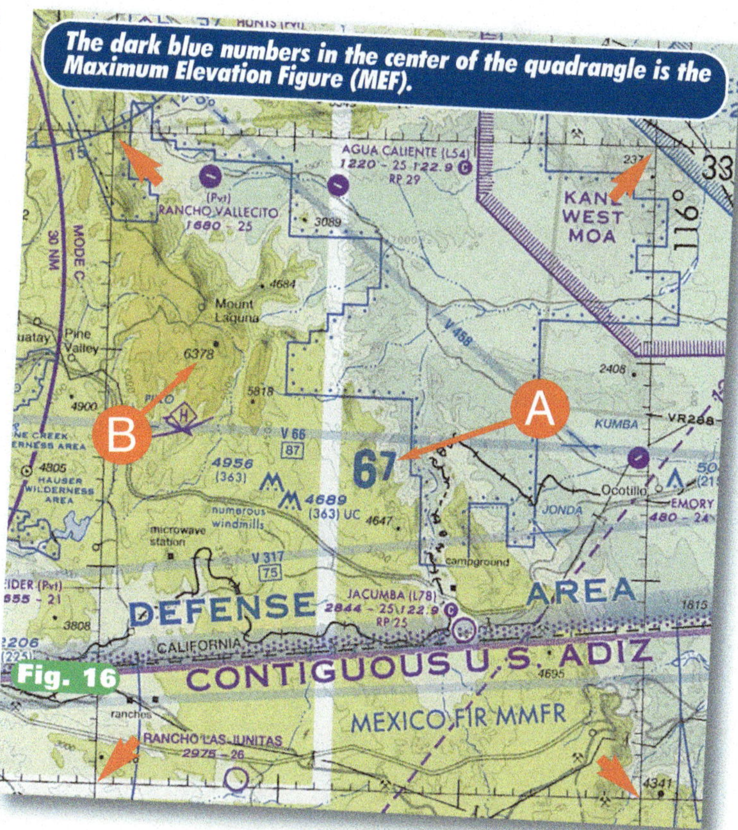

Fig. 16

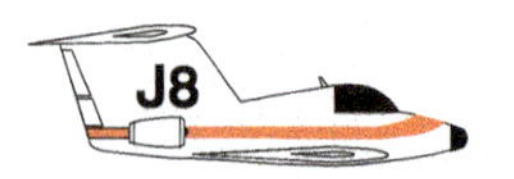

Fig. 17A

Fig. 17B

Symbols that look like large tepees are obstacles standing 1,000' or more AGL.

Fig. 18

Obstacles – At first glance, the item in Figure 17A looks like the tepee (or bingo temple) on an Indian reservation. It's not. This symbol represents obstacles standing less than 1,000 feet AGL. The bold number represents the height of the top of the obstacle above sea level. The number contained within the parentheses is the height the obstacle stands above ground level. If you're ever asked to find the height of the *base* of the obstacle above sea level, you only need to subtract the obstacle's AGL height from its height above sea level. (Be careful when taking a knowledge exam. Test makers have often graduated from "Trick Question Graduate School" and will try and confuse you with AGL and MSL values.) Figure 17B shows the same obstacle as seen from the ground.

Obstacles standing 1,000 feet and higher above ground level are portrayed by a more elongated obstruction symbol, as shown in Figure 18. The bold numbers and those within parentheses represent heights MSL and AGL, respectively. Sometimes these obstacles will have light-ray symbols emanating from the top of the obstruction symbol, as shown in Figure 19. This indicates the obstacle has a high intensity strobe lighting system associated with it. Sometimes an obstacle has the letters "UC" next to it, as shown in Figure 20. This means the obstacle is under construction. If the eventual height above ground that the obstacle will stand is known, it will be shown in parentheses (even though the building of the obstruction isn't completed).

Roads – Roads and highways make excellent VFR reference points, as shown in Figure 21A and 21B, and many pilots claim that *IFR* really stands for "I follow roads." Highways, especially major ones, are relatively easy to identify from the air. VFR charts often distinguish between single and multi-lane roads. Some major interstates even have their route numbers listed on the sectional chart.

Actually Heard!

A pilot calls the Flight Service Station and says:

Albuquerque Flight Service Station, this is Cessna 714 Sierra Bravo. I'd like to file a flight plan...depending on where I am.

Fig. 19

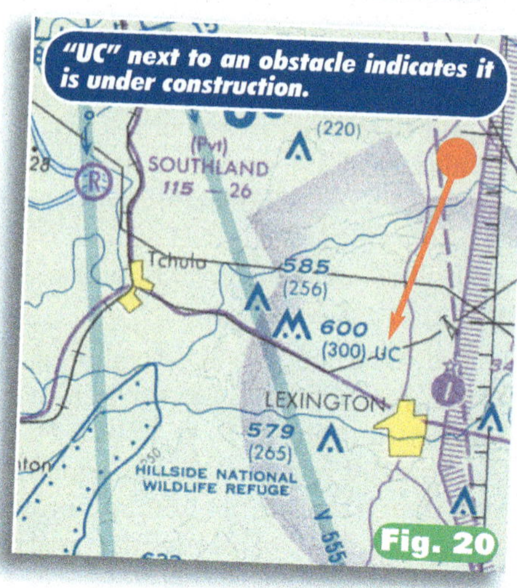

Fig. 20

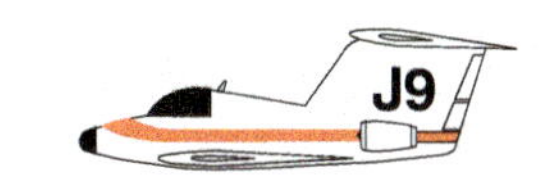

Roads are excellent visual checkpoints for navigation by pilotage.

Fig. 21A

The arrow points to the same road shown in Figure 21A.

Fig. 21B

Railroad Tracks – Railroad tracks (Figure 22A) are often relatively easy to identify from the air (see Figure 22B), especially if you're at a fairly low altitude. This is particularly true when a train lopes along the tracks (it's rare to see trains moving without tracks. If you see one, take a picture and send it to me—it's worth millions).

Railroad tracks can make good checkpoints.

Fig. 22A

Railroad tracks from Figure 22A as seen from the air.

Fig. 22B

Wires – Power transmission wires and telephone lines are depicted on charts as shown in Figure 23A. These wires are usually a lot easier to see on the chart than they ever are from the air (Figure 23B). They're not very wide, and they tend to blend in with the terrain below, though you might have some success spotting the supporting towers. I'd be cautions about relying on them as my sole source of VFR landmarks or checkpoints for any cross country flight.

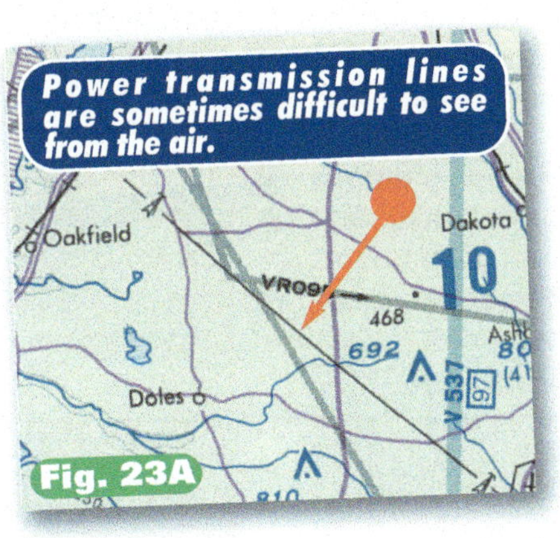

Power transmission lines are sometimes difficult to see from the air.

Fig. 23A

Power lines similar to those in Figure 23A.

Fig. 23B

Shorelines, Rivers & Streams – Shorelines for coastal areas along with piers, wharves and jetties are excellent landmarks as shown in Figure 24A and 24B. Other large

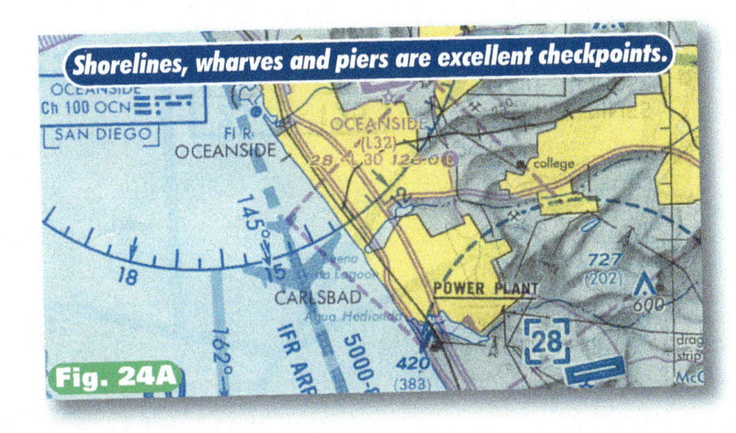

Shorelines, wharves and piers are excellent checkpoints.

Fig. 24A

Shoreline from Figure 24A as seen from the air.

Fig. 24B

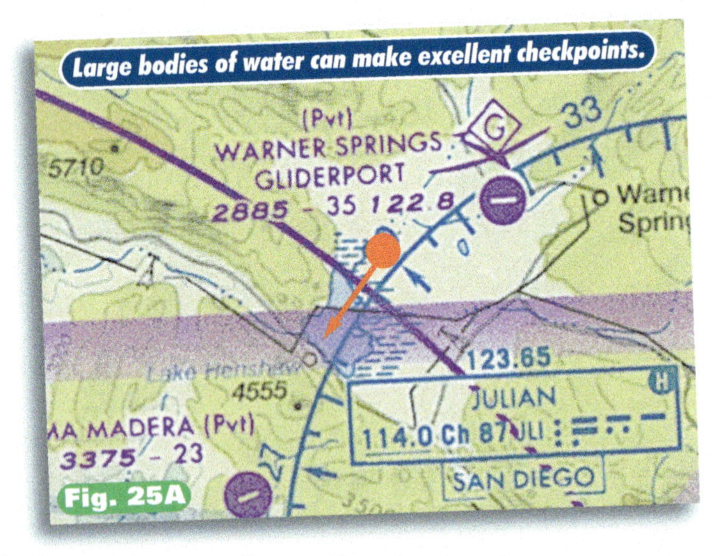

Fig. 25A

Fig. 25B

bodies of water make excellent landmarks as shown in Figure 25A and 25B. Of course, this assumes a drought hasn't made the shoreline unrecognizable. You'll probably have more difficulty in recognizing streams and small rivers from the air, as shown in Figures 26A and 26B. Frankly, unless you're using major rivers (the Colorado River for example), you'll be better off using larger bodies of water, roads or other references for VFR checkpoints.

Populated Areas – On sectional and VFR terminal charts, populated areas in the form of cities and large towns are outlined in yellow, as shown in Figure 27A. As long as you don't become too hung up on comparing the actual city to the yellow borders on the sectional, you'll find them a useful VFR reference point. Cities often grow faster than cartographers update their charting information. This can cause the city to have a very different outline than that shown on the chart (Figure 27B). Smaller towns and villages are shown by an empty circle (Figures 28A and 28B). These areas also make useful VFR landmarks. You'll find cities and towns even more useful at night, where their lights provide extremely helpful landmarks for VFR navigation.

Fig. 27A

Fig. 27B

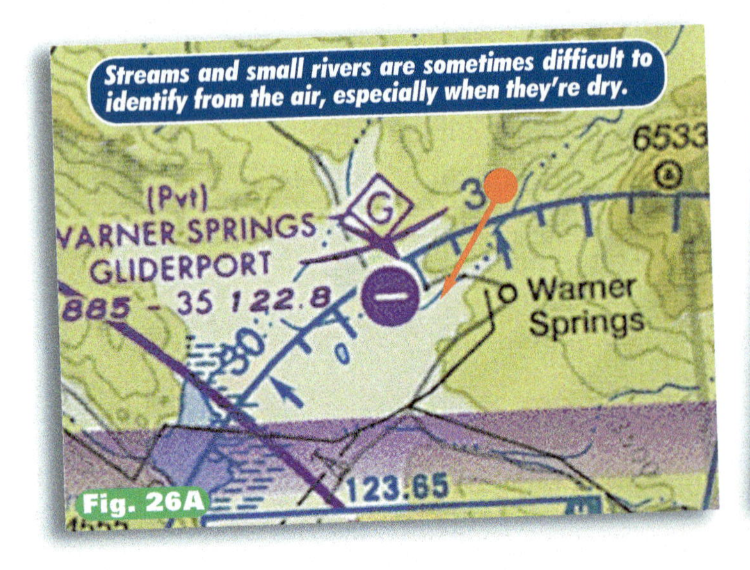

Fig. 26A

Fig. 26B

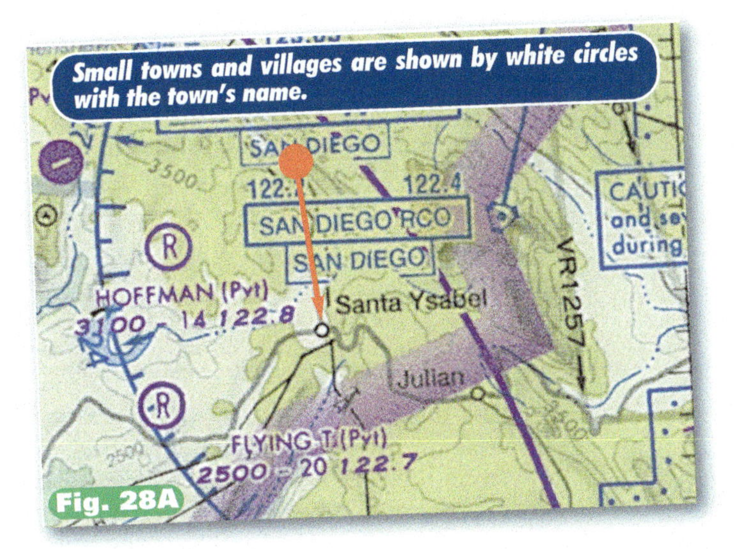

Small towns and villages are shown by white circles with the town's name.

Fig. 28A

The same small town in Figure 28A, as seen from the air. At night the light clusters from these towns make good checkpoints.

Fig. 28B

Airports colored in magenta don't have air traffic control towers.

Fig. 29

Airports colored in blue have air traffic control towers.

Fig. 30

Airports (magenta or blue) with hard surface runways longer than 8,069' take on a more realistic look.

Fig. 31

Airports – Frankly, there are few VFR reporting points better than airports. I like them for VFR navigation because I like having a place to land in the event of engine, weather or (human) bladder problems. Airports are divided into colors on the map (they are *not* really painted these colors, just like the states aren't painted the colors you saw on your junior high school maps). Magenta colored airports (Figure 29) don't have an air traffic control tower (ATCT). Those shown in blue have a tower (although it may not be in operation 24 hours a day—most aren't). Figure 30 shows an airport associated with an ATC tower. All recognizable runways, including closed runways, are pictured within the airport symbol, for visual identification.

Normally, both the magenta and blue airport symbols are circles unless the airport has a hard surfaced runway greater than 8,069 feet. In that case, cartographers place an enclosed box around the runway periphery, as shown in Figure 31.

A current aeronautical chart is a like a good aviation mechanic. It has the most up-to-date information to help you get to where you're going.

Airports with a solid circle (blue or magenta) have at least a 1,500′ to 8,069′ hard surface runway.
Fig. 32A

This is the hard surface runway from Figure 32A as seen from the air.
Fig. 32B

Airports having other than hard surfaces at least 1,500′ long or soft surfaces are shown by an open symbol.
Fig. 33A

This is a typical soft surface runway seen from the air.
Fig. 33B

Any airport having a darkened circle, with the runways in reverse-bold white, has a hard surface runway between 1,500 and 8,069 feet in length, as shown in Figure 32A and 32B. Airports with soft surface runways (grass, dirt, etc.) or with hard surfaces less than 1,500 feet long are shown by an open symbol without the runway(s) depicted (Figure 33A and 33B). Military airports are shown by a double circle (Figure 34).

An open dot within a hard-surfaced runway configuration indicates the approximate position of a VOR located on the field, as shown in Figure 35. Airport symbols on VFR charts having four square protrusions around the airport indicate that fuel services are available during normal working hours (Mon.-Fri. 10 a.m. to 4 p.m., local time). (See Figure 35.)

Some airports are restricted to emergencies or by special authorization. These airports are identified by the airport symbol containing the letter "R" if they have soft surface runways or hard surfaced runways less than 1,500 in length or the letters "PVT" if they are not for public use (Figure 36).

Next to an airport symbol you'll find the airport data (Figure 37, position A). The official airport name is located above the control tower frequency (identified by the letters "CT"). Some airports have more than two control tower frequencies (this isn't for pilots who really like to talk, either). Different frequencies are for use by aircraft approaching from different directions, or using different parallel runways (at very large airports). The Automatic Terminal Information Service frequency, which is listed, will provide the proper frequency. In lieu of the ATIS, other airports such as Chico (Figure 37, position B) have AWOS or ASOS installations that provide a repeating, one-minute automatic recording of the local airport weather. (Read more about AWOS and ASOS in Chapter 13, page M13.)

The last line of information starts with the airport's elevation in dark bold numbers. An "L" following this number means lighting is available from sunset to sunrise. The next number is the length of the longest runway, in hundreds of feet (the useable runway may be less) and the unicom frequency. The letters "RP" followed by a number indicate the runway(s) that have a non-standard right hand traffic pattern.

Unicom stations at tower controlled airports usually provide fuel service while those at nontower airports usually provide traffic information (and may provide fuel service, too). Figure 38 shows the typical airport data for a nontower airport. Notice that the letter "*L" has an asterisk next to it. This means airport lighting limitations exist. Runway lights for night landings may be available part time or on request. Refer to the *d-CS* to find out more about the airport's lighting.

Military airports with other than hard surface runways are shown by a double circle.
Fig. 34

An open dot within a hard-surface runway configuration indicates the position of a VOR on the airport. Square protrusions indicate fuel services are available during normal business hours.
Fig. 35

Restricted airports (not open to the public) are shown with an "R" in the airport circle or by "PVT."
Fig. 36

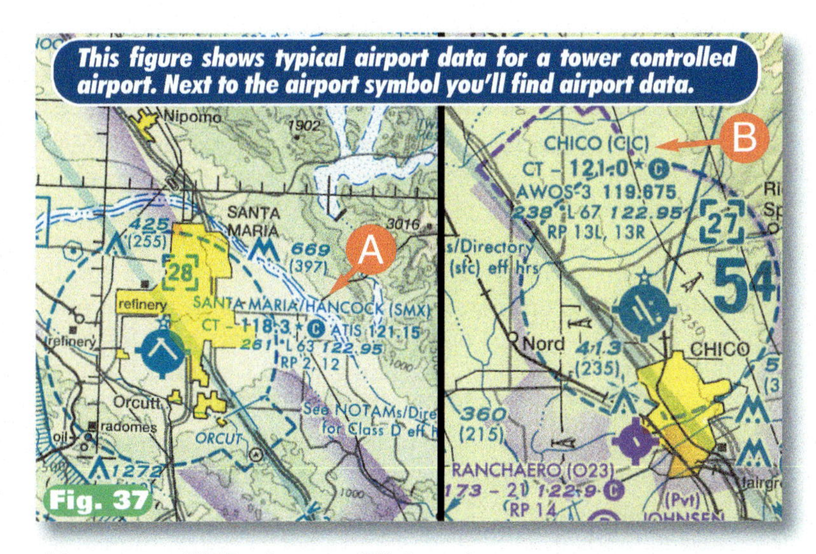

This figure shows typical airport data for a tower controlled airport. Next to the airport symbol you'll find airport data.

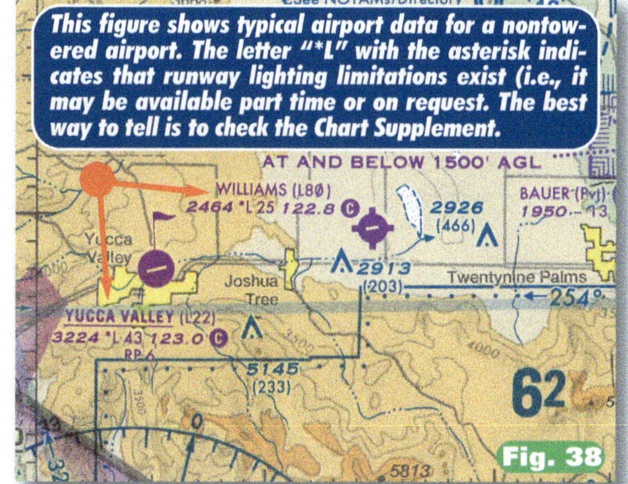

This figure shows typical airport data for a nontowered airport. The letter "*L" with the asterisk indicates that runway lighting limitations exist (i.e., it may be available part time or on request. The best way to tell is to check the Chart Supplement.

Airways – VFR airways (Victor airways) are depicted on sectional charts as shown in Figure 39. Each airway typically extends from one VOR to the next and is identified by its own unique number. These are the numbers used on a flight plan to describe your route of flight. A square box with a number inside shows the airway distance between VOR stations, in nautical miles.

VFR Checkpoints – Visual checkpoints are shown on sectional and terminal charts by a magenta flag (Figure 40). Their names are underlined and in bold capital letters. These are prominent landmarks visible from the air. Air traffic controllers may ask you to report your position in reference to these landmarks when contacting them for landing. (See Postflight Briefing #10-1 for more information.)

A student pilot once approached a major psychiatric hospital, which was a designated visual checkpoint. He called the tower for landing instructions and said, "San Jose Tower, this is 2132 Bravo inbound from the north for landing, over." The tower replied, "Ahh, 32 Bravo, are you headed for the mental hospital." The student said, "No. Why? Is my flying that bad?" You must pay attention to these symbols.

Airborne Vehicle Symbols – In addition to airplane activity, other airborne vehicles use the airspace. Figure 41 shows those areas containing ultralight activities, hang gliders, gliders, parachutists and stadium TFRs. The symbols simply remind you to be extra vigilant.

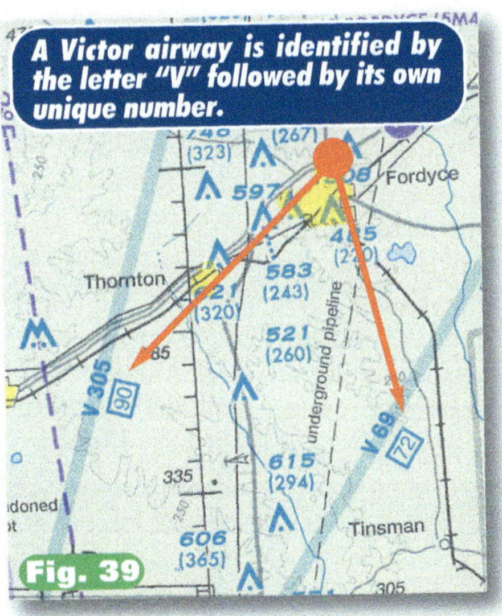

A Victor airway is identified by the letter "V" followed by its own unique number.

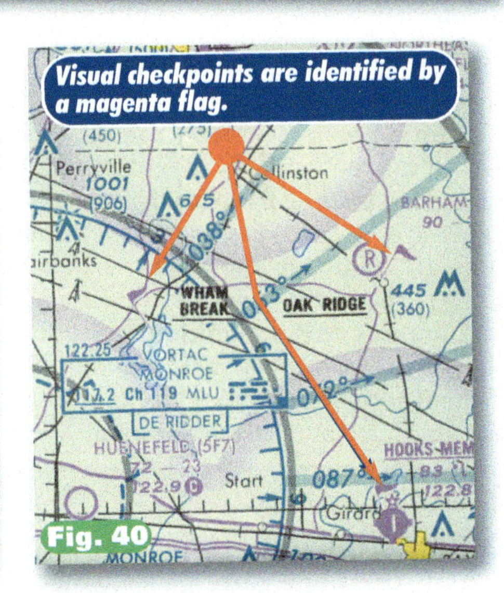

Visual checkpoints are identified by a magenta flag.

Airborne vehicle symbols identify glider (1), hangglider (2), unmanned aerial vehicles (3), parachute areas (4) and ultralights (5), aerobatic practice areas (6), and space launch activity areas (7). Symbol #8 (stadium TFR) represents an intermittent stadium TFR which prohibits all aircraft and parachute operations at or below 3,000 feet AGL within a 3 nm radius of any stadium with a seating capacity of 30,000 people or more when a major sport event is occurring.

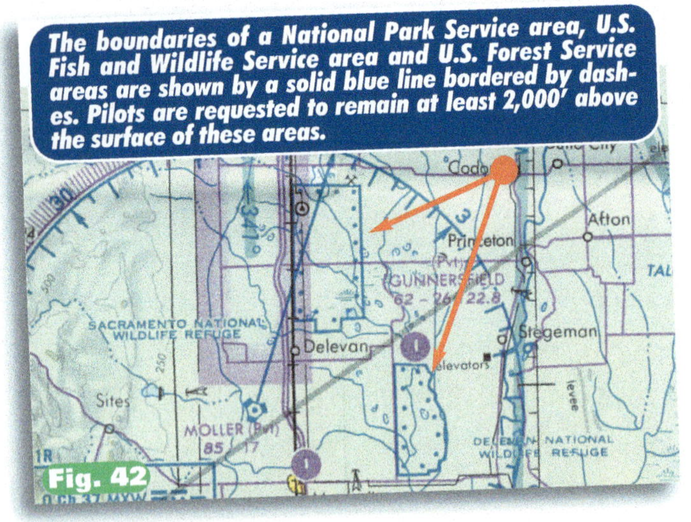

The boundaries of a National Park Service area, U.S. Fish and Wildlife Service area and U.S. Forest Service areas are shown by a solid blue line bordered by dashes. Pilots are requested to remain at least 2,000′ above the surface of these areas.

Fig. 42

Park, Wildlife, Forest, Wilderness and Primitive Areas – Figure 42 identifies the boundaries of either a National Park Service area, U.S. Fish and Wildlife Service area or U.S. Forest Service Wilderness or Primitive area. Aircraft operating within one of these areas are often requested to maintain a minimum altitude of 2,000 feet above the surface within these areas (unless the chart specifically notes a different altitude). Maintaining these minimum altitudes prevents destruction or damage to our national wildlife. It also helps prevent people from thinking pilots are unconcerned about anyone but themselves. General aviation depends to a substantial degree on public tolerance for its existence, and disrupting the solitude of backpackers or annoying wildlife to death is not a defensible act.

Sometimes, of course, the wildlife defends itself. Many years ago, a fellow in Alaska decided wildlife wasn't all that sacred. He was piloting a helicopter when he spotted a grizzly bear. Descending to only a few feet above the grizzly, he taunted the beast with the helicopter's landing skid. In a surprise move (it was a surprise to the pilot) the bear rose up, grabbed the skid and retrieved his lunch from room service (if you know what I mean). Pay close attention to the minimum altitudes for these areas.

While there are many other symbols to discuss on the sectional chart, we've covered some of the most important ones. Take time to study the VFR charts in greater detail. With a little practice in chart symbol interpretation, you'll be able to fly anywhere using pilotage as your single navigational tool.

We've reached the Great Divide in our introduction to aviation. The next subject allows us to put our charts to use. After all, if you don't know how to navigate you're not likely to go anywhere (at least anywhere you intended to go) and charts will have little significance to you. In the upcoming chapter, we'll discuss the most common means of navigation. You'll find this chapter quite valuable since you'll need to have some knowledge of the subject before your instructor lets you zip off on solo cross country flights.

Postflight Briefing #10-1

GPS Identified VFR Checkpoints

Some VFR checkpoints are collocated with GPS waypoints as shown in Figure 43, positions A, B, C and D. The name of the checkpoint is listed above its five letter GPS identification. To navigate to any of these collocated checkpoints, just tune the five letter identifier into your GPS and proceed direct to the waypoint as shown in Figure 44.

In this instance, the GPS is set to track directly to the Queen Mary VFR checkpoint which is collocated with the GPS waypoint identified as VPLQM (Figure 44, position E).

Since it's not always easy to recognize these VFR checkpoints from the air, especially if you're from out of town, using your GPS to identify them makes navigation much easier in these instances. The GPS also provides you with the ability to inform ATC of your position and distance relative to any of these checkpoints.

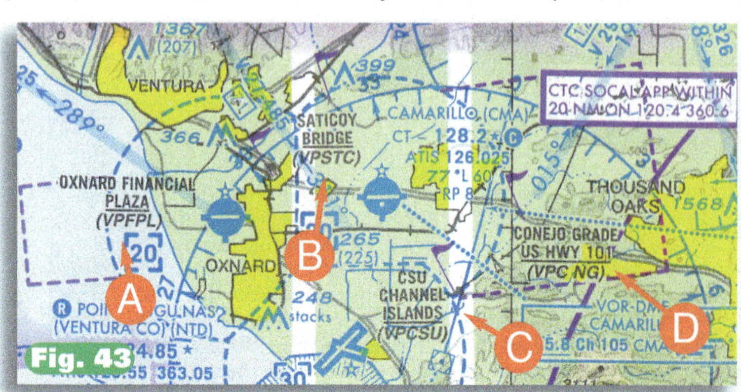

Fig. 43

Fig. 44

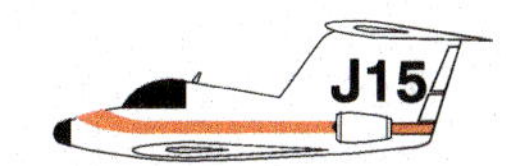

Postflight Briefing #10-2

The Terminal Area Chart

The Terminal Area Chart (TAC) shown in Figure 45, is provided to show more chart detail in known high density traffic areas. Areas covered by the terminal area chart are identified as magenta shaded blocks on the front panel of the sectional chart (Figure 46, position A). Each block represents an individual terminal area chart. Inside the terminal area chart you'll find the detailed area coverage of these areas along with whatever VFR Flyway and special airspace information is available for that particular area of coverage.

For instance, the Los Angeles terminal area chart contains several navigation inserts that provide information on published routes through the Los Angeles Class B airspace (Figure 47) as well as the special flight rules area that provides easy transit directly across Los Angeles International airport (Figure 48). The VFR Flyway routes (Figure 49) shown on the chart are very useful when you're operating in a high density traffic area like the Los Angeles basin.

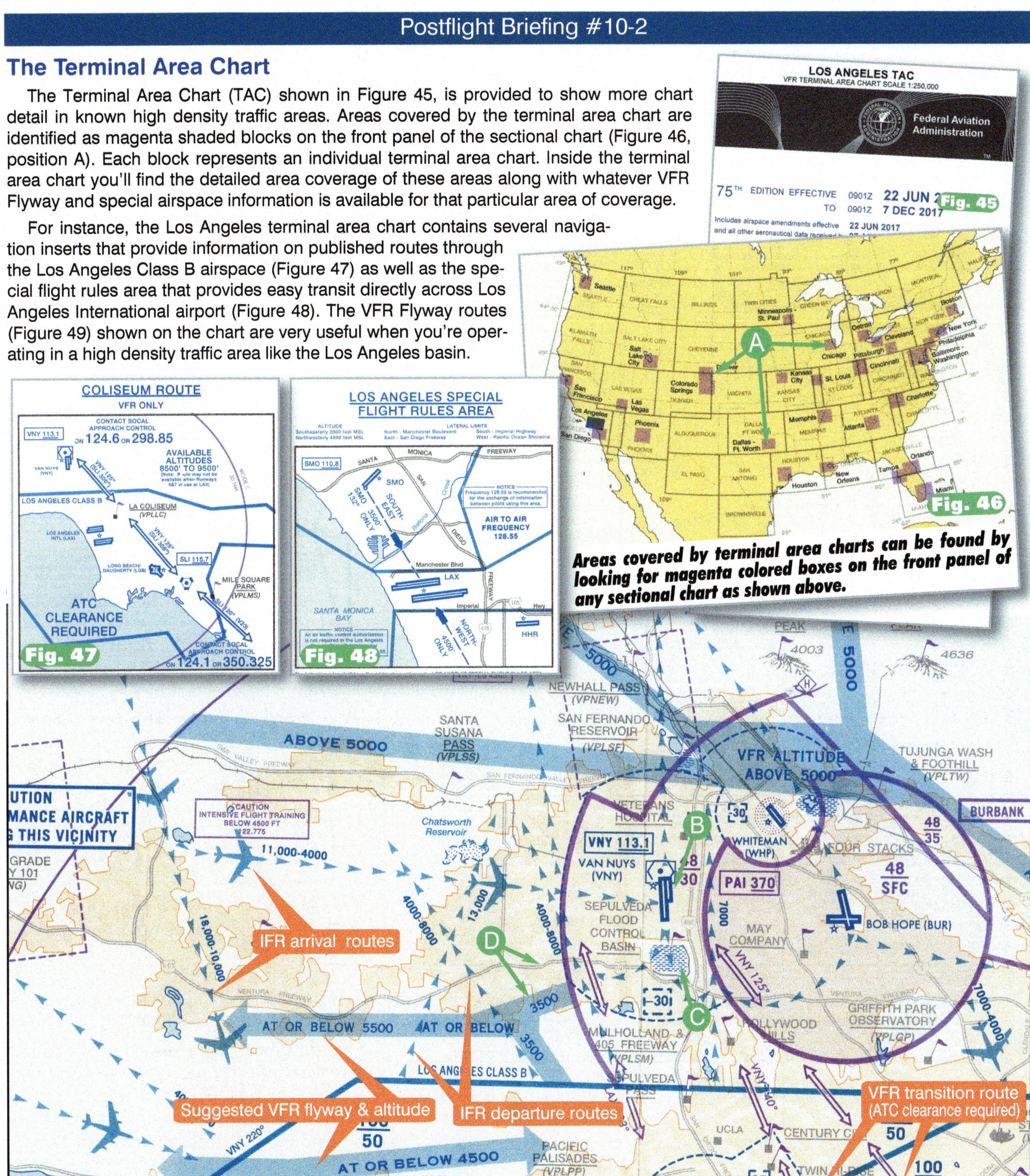

Areas covered by terminal area charts can be found by looking for magenta colored boxes on the front panel of any sectional chart as shown above.

This chart helps you identify VFR flyways, which are designed to help VFR pilots avoid major controlled traffic flows. For instance, when departing Van Nuys airport (Figure 49, position B) to the west, it's probably wise to fly toward the Sepulveda flood control basin (position C) then follow the flyway found just south of the 101 Ventura freeway (position D). Flying at or below 3,500 feet then at or below 5,500 feet westbound should keep you out of major traffic flows (the routes with small blue arrows and accompanying altitudes). Ground references shown on the chart make visual navigation easy.

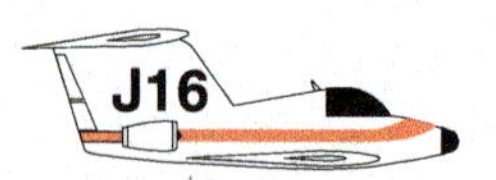

Postflight Briefing #10-3

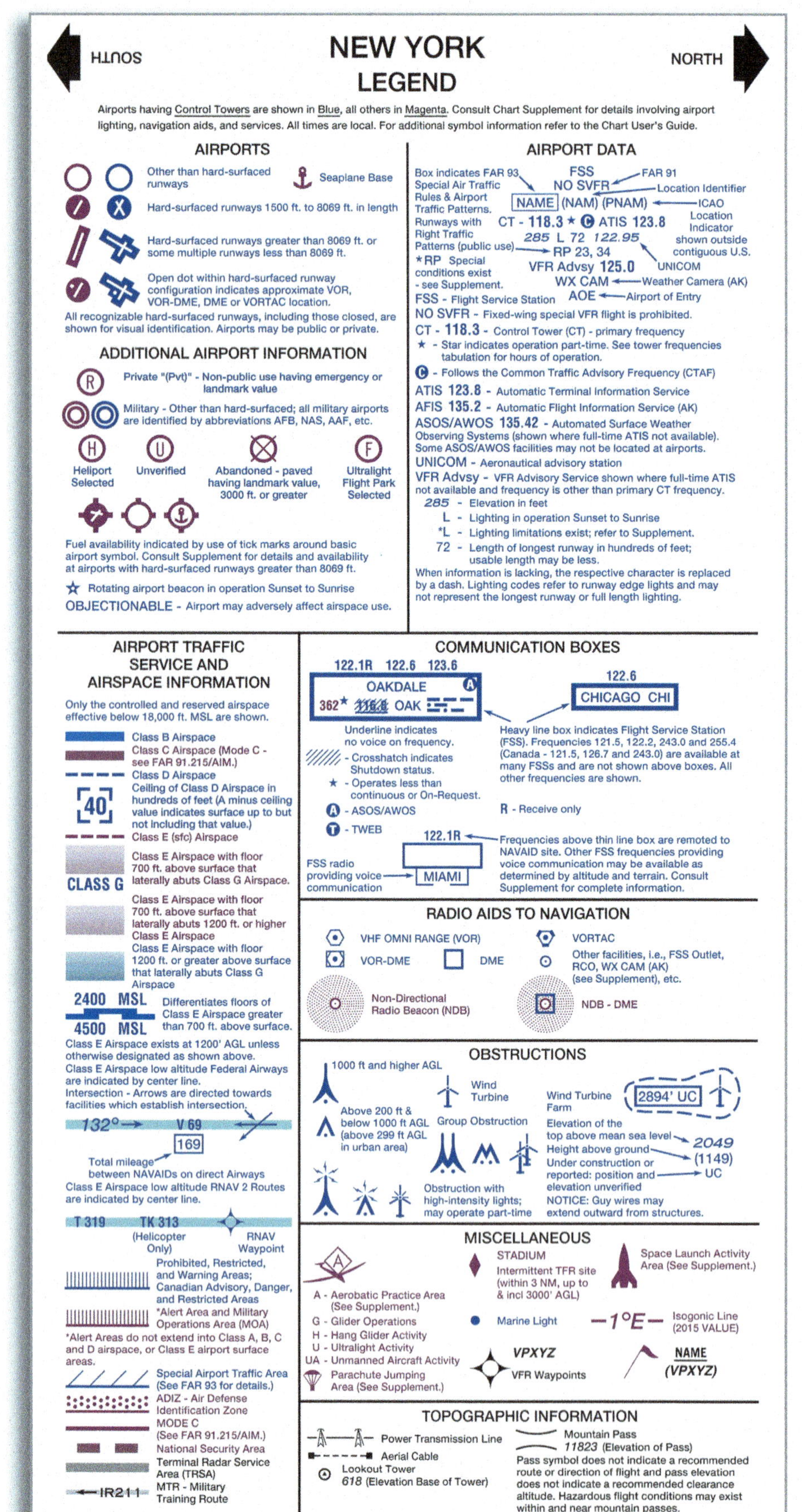

Postflight Briefing #10-4

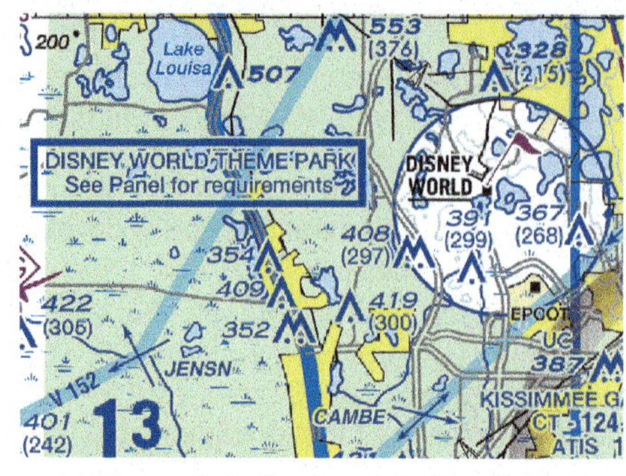

Special Security Notice Permanent Continuous Flight Restriction Areas

After the terrorist attacks of September 11, 2001, Congress mandated that the FAA issue permanent airspace restrictions over our country's two Disneyland facilities. These facilities are located in Orlando, Florida and Los Angeles, California.

These permanent airspace restrictions are now identified on sectional and terminal area charts by a blue circle containing a slightly lighter (subdued) terrain colored background as shown above.

Information on the restrictions associated with these areas can be found somewhere on the charting panel as shown below.

DISNEY WORLD THEME PARK
Pursuant to Public Law 108-199, Section 521, aircraft flight operations are prohibited at and below 3,000 feet AGL within a 3 nautical mile radius of the Disney World Theme Park (282445N/0813420W or the Orlando (ORL) VORTAC 238 degree radial at 14.8 nautical miles) except as specified. See Chart Supplement for details.

If you're thinking that this information might be easy to find on the chart, think again. Charts are often crowded with detail. Looking for this information is almost like playing a game of Where's Waldo?

It's clear from the charting panel insert above (once you've found it), that the restrictions in this area prohibit aircraft from operating at or below 3,000 feet AGL within this 3 NM "blue-ring" radius.

To help you identify this area before you stumble into it and knock someone off a Mr. Toad Wild Ride, the notice also identifies its center point, located at 14.8 NM on the Orlando VORTAC's 238 degree radial.

Pilots need good navigational skills. They need to find airports. After all, that's where the fuel is. The sandwiches, too. Until aerial refueling of light airplanes is standard, navigational skills will always be a necessity, and even aerial refueling won't solve the sandwich challenge. While getting there is definitely more than half the fun of flying, finding the airport is pretty darn satisfying.

It's interesting to watch people learn aviation navigation. Some people who can find a white ostrich in a snowstorm on the ground can't seem to locate the airport when they're in the air—even when they're still in the pattern. Others, who've spent their lives asking "Where am I?" suddenly find that being airborne gives them the perspective they need to discover where they are, where they've been, and where they're going.

As a student pilot, it seems as though I got lost on every trip (it felt that way). The FBO bought a St. Bernard puppy and promptly named it "Rod." If I knew then what I know now, I'd never be lost. I'd just keep changing where it was I wanted to go (I'd be in a constant state of destination flux).

I envied my hot air balloon brothers and sisters who weren't the least bit concerned about landing at an airport. Their flight instructors would ask, "Where are you going?" "That way" was the reply, as they pointed with the wind. Much to the happiness of insurance companies, airplane navigation is more sophisticated.

The world of aviation navigation is changing rapidly. In flying's early days, pilots navigated by looking out the window and spotting familiar landmarks. The first big breakthrough was maps, which enabled pilots to go where they hadn't gone before. Then came simple forms of radio navigation, in which an electronic signal is used as a guidepost. Today, highly sophisticated satellite navigation is well on its way to being the main means by which pilots determine their position. As incredible as it may seem a private pilot can today buy a device for just a few hundred dollars that tunes five or more satellites simultaneously and displays where the airplane is to within a few hundred feet.

Toward the end of the chapter we'll be taking a look at the gee-wizardry of satellite navigation, but before that I want to introduce you to some of the more basic forms of navigation. These are still the most frequent ways by which pilots get around, and they're likely to be with us for many more years.

Pilotage

The most elementary form of navigation is *pilotage,* in which you look out the window and combine your observations with information from an aviation map to locate your position.

Having seen and heard about all the fancy navigation gadgets, you're probably wondering why anybody would want to navigate by just looking at where they're flying. I can think of several good reasons. One is that it might save your rawhide one day. Electronic toys are great when they're working, but like any good guppy, they can and do go belly up. A total electrical failure means that all the nice electronic toys go to sleep. You're left with the compass and pilotage.

Aviation is a very peculiar mix of something old, something new. Some of the technology and techniques represent the cutting edge; others are throwbacks to a different era. We still put magnetic compasses in airplanes, and teach pilotage to pilots, because these things are virtually bulletproof. When all else literally fails, pilotage can and will get you through.

How Far? How Fast?

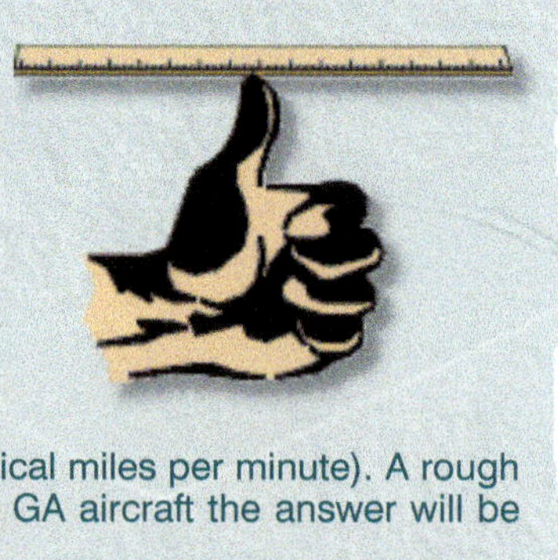

"Where are we now?"

This is one of those deceptively simple questions asked by generations of flight instructors. One of the things we love to do is stick a sectional chart in front of a student who's flying and say the four magic words: "Where are we now?"

I've heard and seen some mighty creative replies over the years. What always amazes me is just how wrong people can be. I've had students who didn't know what state they were in, other than a state of confusion.

What's amazing about this is how easy it is to be at least close to right.

Pay attention. I'm about to let you in on a tip for avoiding embarrassment.

Find out how fast your airplane generally flies per minute (at 120 knots, you're flying two nautical miles per minute). A rough approximation is all that's needed here, rounded to the nearest half mile per minute. For most GA aircraft the answer will be between two and three.

Now, by knowing when you took off (you'll find a clock somewhere in that assortment of dials on the front panel) and multiplying it by 2, 2.5, or 3 as appropriate, you will know how far you've flown since taking off. Airborne for 25 minutes in a 120 knot airplane, you've flown about 50 miles (a little less if you allow for the climbout, which was at a slower speed).

Now look at the second and third fingers on your hand. Fold the other fingers out of the way for a moment. Nice, huh? You can use them for either the Cub Scout salute, or to find out where you are. The width of the two fingers you're looking at, measured at the first knuckle down from the tip, represents approximately ten miles on a standard sectional chart. (Make adjustments if you're particularly ham handed or if you model for hand commercials on TV). If you have even a vague idea of which way you headed after leaving the airport, lay your dexterous digits down on the sectional and figure out approximately where you are.

It's not high science, but it will get you close enough to not be a laughingstock.

There's an important lesson here. Learning to approximate solutions is a crucial aviation skill. Quick rules of thumb will often keep you from doing something dumb.

A second very important reason for developing your skills at pilotage is that you should always be checking and double checking what any bunch of circuit boards is telling you. Some years ago, a commercial airliner strayed into forbidden airspace and was shot down because the pilots had misprogrammed their zillion dollar inertial navigation system. Redundancy is second only to predictability on the list of important things that make airplanes fly. Wherever and whenever possible, you will find that good pilots check one thing against another, and resolve any discrepancies.

Pilotage is the ultimate navigational check. No electronic system of navigation is foolproof. Its electronic circuits can freeze, fritz, or fry; its CPU can be out to lunch. Some types of electronic signals can be affected by atmospheric variations, local electronic interference, or perhaps secret Martian ray guns.

When all else fails (and it does), pilotage suddenly looks very good. It's also a very satisfying skill to develop. If you don't have map reading experience, the first few hours will take some concentrated effort (on the ground) in order to translate the map into a visual representation of what's on the ground.

Once you learn to do that, the map will prove to be your friend. Don't leave home without it. One of the things that sends chills up and down the spines of flight instructors is students raised on electronic goodies who think they can fly without maps. You should never leave the ground without having in hand at least the *sectional chart* (an aviation map covering an area that is generally several hundred miles across) for the entire area you will traverse. We've already discussed these charts in Chapter 10. I hope you realize how valuable they are as navigational tools. Make sure you carry one on every flight and learn how to read them in order to become proficient at pilotage.

A final benefit to pilotage is that it encourages pilots to look out the window. The flowering of the electronic era in navigation has brought with it head-in-cockpit disease. This affliction can strike any pilot of any experience level. The symptoms are an obsessive preoccupation with the glowing readouts in the cockpit, and

Some places treat airplanes with the respect they deserve!

Courtesy: Maggie & Jim Ash

VOR RECEIVING EQUIPMENT FOUND IN MANY AIRPLANES

Fig. 1

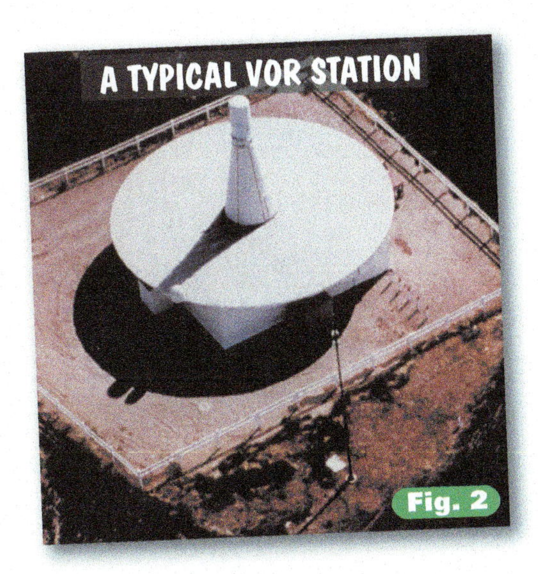

A TYPICAL VOR STATION

Fig. 2

the failure (sometimes terminal failure) to look outside and pay attention to what's going on.

I've noticed this disease becoming more frequent as the MTV generation has progressed into pilothood. Some recently minted pilots think that if they tune their satellite navigation receiver just right, it will play a Madonna rock video.

My advice to all pilots is to look out—look out the window. Not just for the purpose of avoiding other airplanes (though that's an important reason), but also to gain the full enjoyment and wonder of aviating. We're privileged to be able to fly, and the greatest wonders are to be seen out the window. Enjoy them by practicing pilotage.

Electronic Elucidation

There's more to modern navigation than meets the eye, so let's move on to some of the radionavigational devices that grace the cockpit of most GA aircraft.

The mainstay of the aviation navigation system since the late 1940's has been the ground-based *very high frequency* ***o****mnidirectional* ***r****ange (VOR)* system. While GPS is the new kid on the block, VOR navigation is sure to be around for decades because it's a good backup in case all our GPS satellites decide to strike out on their own for the Klingon homeworld. Nevertheless, the VOR system is being reduced in size via a program known as MON or *Minimum Operational Network*. For the moment, however, VOR is very much with us. So let's see how to use it.

Dotted around the country, the VOR stations on the ground emit a signal that is received and displayed in the cockpit. Properly used, this VOR information enables pilots to navigate to or from any of the hundreds of VOR stations. It's the designated paths between these VOR stations that constitute the electronic highways in the sky we discussed earlier.

At the time VOR was developed and deployed, the FAA suggested no one would ever get lost again. They underestimated us. As simple a device as it is to use, VOR is still capable of tying some pilots into complete navigational knots.

The Big Picture

VOR navigation requires two things: airborne VOR equipment (Figure 1) and a ground transmitting station (Figure 2). The ground transmitter radiates 360 electronic spokes, called *radials,* from its center. Each radial (think of it *radiating* away from the station) represents one degree on the compass, with 0 degrees being due north from the station. The 90 degree radial reaches eastward, etc. Using their airborne VOR equipment, pilots can navigate either directly to or from a VOR station on any of its 360 radials. Pilots can also obtain position fixes using two or more VOR stations. Of course, knowing where you are in relation to a VOR station does no good unless

Faked Out by High Tech Gear!

I was cleared direct to destination airport. On a five-mile final, Approach advised me that I appeared to be lined up with Runway 21 at the military field adjacent to destination airport. Be darned if they weren't right! This also explains why I couldn't find the aircraft I was to follow. Made a correction to Runway 22 at the destination airport and landed. Got faked out because I lost sight of the big picture. On approach is no time to tinker with high tech gear, stick with raw data.

In a similar scenario, with a full load of passengers, an air carrier landed on the military runway. Quick witted Captain announced on the P.A., "Ladies and Gentlemen, we have decided to take off again and land closer to the terminal, so you will have a shorter walk to your baggage." Very considerate. Would have worked, too, but the smug flight crew was eventually nailed. Chief Pilot called them in at their home base. Clairvoyant Chief? Nope. The aircraft was equipped with ACARS, the device that reports automatically to the company—time off, time-on location, and other operational data. Ain't progress grand?

ASRS Report

VOR RADIALS

Think of the VOR as a transmitter that radiates 360 individual radials from its center. These radials are oriented to the magnetic north pole. You may navigate to or from the station on any of these radials via your airborne VOR equipment.

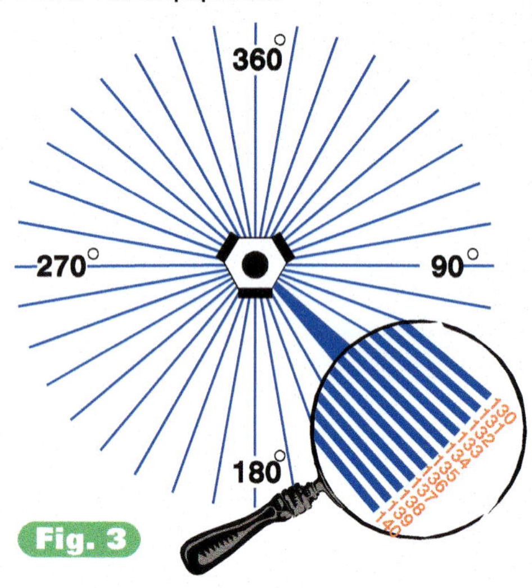

Fig. 3

This is a VOR compass rose on a sectional chart. The actual VOR station is located in the middle of the compass rose (position 1). The VOR frequency and its Morse code identifier are shown in the box (position 2).

Fig. 4

you know where the VOR station is. That's why pilots always fly with aeronautical sectional charts that depict these stations and their locations.

To make understanding the VOR easier, imagine the ground station transmits specific directional signals for every degree of the compass. Figure 3 shows some of these signals. Since there are 360 degrees in the compass rose, there are 360 specific signals radiating from the station. (The VOR actually transmits two signals that define radials, but hey, we're not trying to get a Ph.D. in astroelectronics are we?)

VOR Stations Shown on a Sectional Chart – Figure 4 shows how VORs are depicted on a sectional chart. The VOR station is located in the middle of the surrounding *compass rose* (position 1). Individual radials aren't shown on aeronautical sectional charts, but they can be approximated by using the outer ring of the compass rose (Figure 5). The VOR compass rose has a marking every 5 degrees, a larger marking every 10 degrees and numbers every 30 degrees.

A box below the compass rose lists the name, Morse code identification and frequency of the station (position 2). Each VOR station transmits its signals on frequencies ranging from 108.0 to 117.95 MHz. These frequencies are just below the VHF frequencies used for aircraft communications (118.0 to 135.975 MHz).

Why does every VOR station have a Morse code identifier? It allows you to positively confirm the station is the one you think it is. Remember me telling you a few moments ago to never completely trust the dashing electrons? Sometimes what you see *isn't* what you get. Just because a frequency is tuned in and showing on the display does not absolutely guarantee you are receiving that frequency. Things can go wrong. You want to make sure the VOR you're using for navigation is the one you think you're using. You simply turn up the volume on your VOR receiver long enough to match the dots and dashes you hear with what you see on the chart. There's no requirement to memorize the Morse code (Whew! Thank goodness). Some VOR stations also have a repetitive voice identification along with the Morse Code.

Several years ago, I took a student who was reluctant to identify navigational stations on a cross country flight. All he had to do was select the frequency in the navigation radio, turn up the volume for a moment, and compare the Morse code he heard with what he saw on the chart. This was apparently too much effort

VOR COMPASS ROSE

The VOR compass rose has markings every 5 degrees, with larger markings at 10 degree increments. The compass rose is numbered at 30 degree increments.

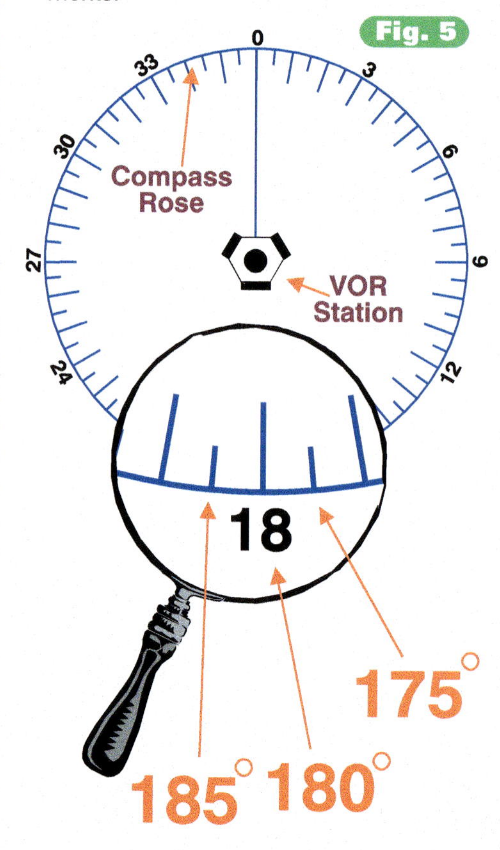

Fig. 5

for him. He was too lazy (the only exercise he ever did was a "get-up" that he did every day at the crack of noon). One time, when he became slightly distracted, he misdialed the frequency and selected the wrong VOR station. I did nothing but watch. We were supposed to be heading towards Palm Springs (inland toward visibly higher mountains). Approximately 5 miles off the coast of California, over the Pacific Ocean, I said, "Hey, what's that down there?" He looked down, looked up, and said, "Ahhh, ahhh... lake?" Astounded, I replied, "Look! Look! There's an oil supertanker down there. What does that mean?" He glanced over and said, "Oh man, it must be a really big lake!" His pilotage wasn't very good, either.

Identifying navigation stations via their Morse code identifiers is important for another reason. Stations sometimes malfunction, or are taken off the air for maintenance. The absence of a Morse identifier, or the broadcast of a TEST code *(dash, dot, dot dot dot, dash),* tells you the VOR is not reliable for navigation.

VORs operate on VHF frequencies. While VHF transmissions are relatively free from interference, they don't bend or curve around obstacles like low frequency signals. Recall from our previous discussion of radio transmission that a VHF signal depends on line of sight. If there isn't a clear path from transmitter to receiver, the signal can't get through. Practically speaking, if mountains, hills, or even buildings are between you and the VOR station, the navigational signal can be lost. You might be able to hear the Morse code, but the onboard VOR equipment's warning device—the OFF flag—will be activated. Adequate reception is only assured when you hear the audio identification with no OFF flag visible (we'll discuss this flag shortly).

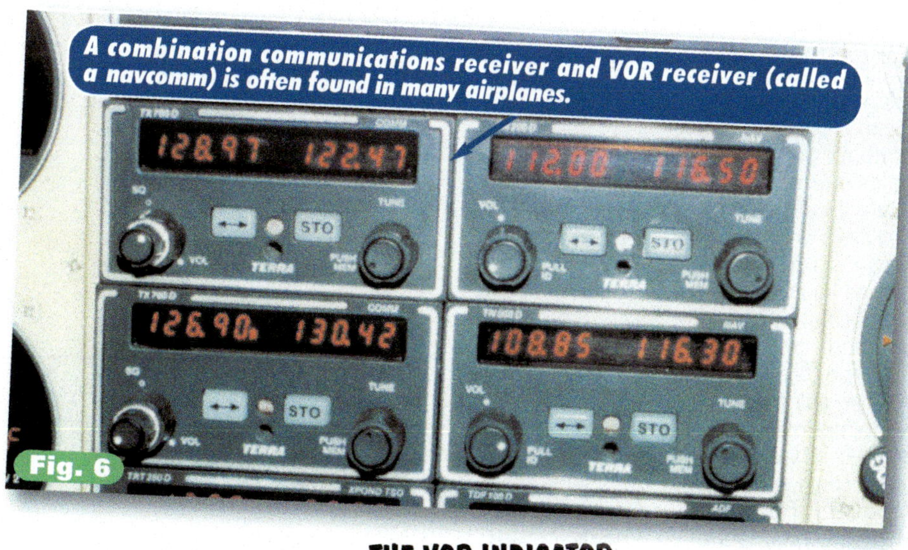

THE VOR INDICATOR

By rotating the OBS knob, the compass rose moves until a course is selected under the index (white triangle) located at the top of the instrument. The CDI (needle) swings left or right, indicating the direction of the selected course. The ambiguity indicator shows whether the selected course would take you to or from the VOR station.

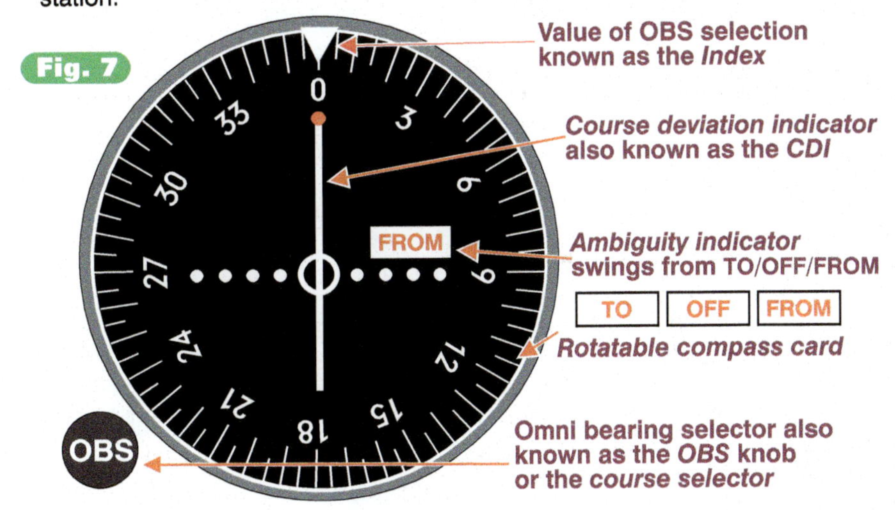

Your VOR Equipment

Airplanes usually have one or more VOR receivers on board. A typical receiver is shown in Figure 6. Usually this is a combination of a navigation receiver and a communications transmitter/receiver in one package, which is referred to as the *navcomm.*

The VOR receiver is connected to the VOR indicator, shown in Figure 7. When pilots refer to "the VOR in their airplane," they are usually talking about the display, though the display is simply a graphic representation of what the radio receiver is getting. The VOR consists of :

- a vertical needle (also known as a *course deviation indicator,* or *CDI)* that swings right or left;
- a *flag* (also known as an ambiguity indicator) with three possible indications: TO, FROM or OFF, and
- an *omni bearing selector* or *OBS* knob (from now on we'll assume the OBS is the knob that you turn).

Surrounding the needle is a circular, moveable compass rose controlled by the OBS. Rotating the OBS causes a different compass value to move under the inverted white triangle or index at the top of the instrument.

VORs and Airborne Freeways

Let's begin our discussion with a recollection of your last car trip when you drove through a small town (it was so small that the Baskin Robbins surprise flavor of the week was vanilla). Let's also say the freeway

VOR RADIALS AND AIRBORNE FREEWAYS

The freeway at position (A) takes the car into and out of town. The car's direction is due north (or 360 degrees) on its journey through town. If we give the freeways entering and leaving town separate names as in position (B), the car still heads due north on its passage through town. We can say that we went into town on *freeway one-eighty* and out of town on *freeway three-sixty*. Regardless of what we name the freeways, the car still heads 360 degrees as it passes through town. If we're tracking to and from the VOR as shown in position (C), we track inbound on the 180 degree radial and outbound on the 360 degree radial. Either way our airborne freeway points in a direction of 360 degrees (just like our car). For convenience, we'll refer to the direction our airborne freeway points as its *course*. The airplane's VOR equipment (D) can be set to any one of 360 different courses.

A North Town North

B North Freeway three-sixty Town North Freeway one-eighty

C 360° North Town VOR North 180°

D **VOR COURSE SELECTION**

We've selected a course of 0° or (360°) by rotating the OBS so this value appears under the index.

Fig. 8

pointed due north as it passed straight through town as shown in Figure 8, position A. While entering and leaving town, your car pointed north (360 degrees), in the same direction as the freeway. If the portion of the freeway exiting the town had a different name than the portion entering the town, would this affect the direction your car pointed while passing through town? Of course not. Let's call the portion of the freeway exiting the town to the south, *Freeway 180* and the portion exiting to the north, *Freeway 360* (position B). Now we can say that we went to town on *Freeway 180* and exited on *Freeway 360*. Our direction never changed despite giving the freeway different names.

Navigation by VOR is basically the same, as shown by position C. If we're headed northbound to the Town VOR, we travel inbound on the 180 degree radial and outbound on the 360 degree radial. Either way, our airborne freeway points in a direction of 360 degrees, just like the ground freeway. Referring to a single freeway by radials going to and from a VOR station is sometimes awkward. So let's refer to our freeways as *courses*. The course is simply the direction our airborne freeway points.

OK, now you're ready to see how we can select and fly any one of 360 individual courses (airborne freeways) by using our VOR equipment.

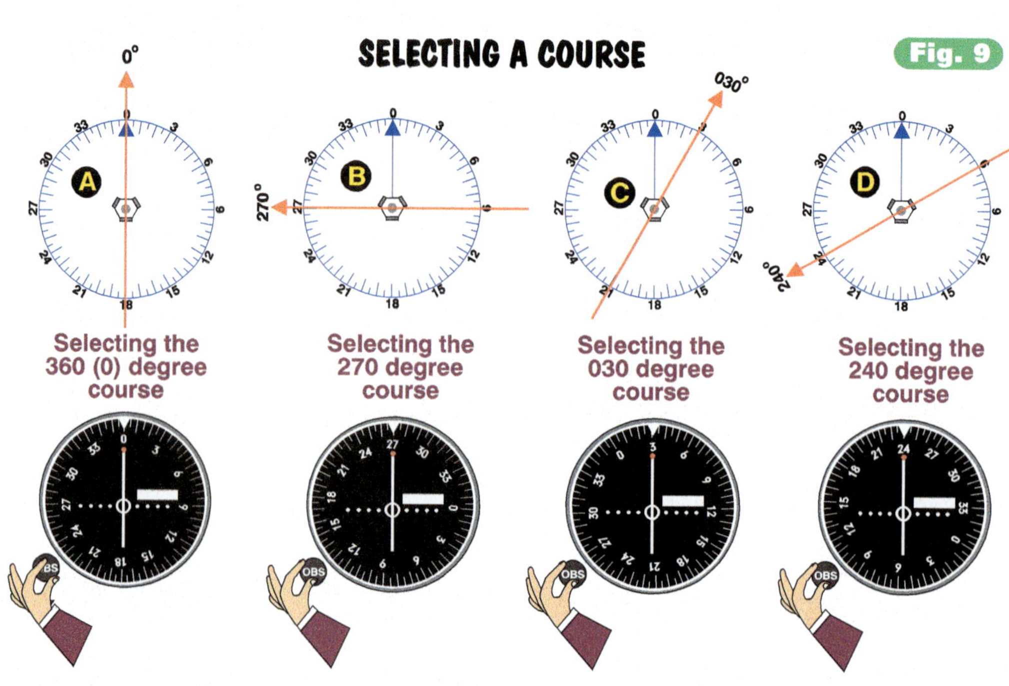

Rotating the OBS to a specific course number, orients your airborne VOR equipment to tell you where you are in relation to that course. You may chose any one of 360 different courses using the OBS.

How to Navigate With VOR

To navigate by VOR, the first thing you do is tune and identify the VOR station on which you wish to navigate. After putting this frequency in the appropriate nav receiver and checking the Morse code, you're ready to dial for courses (airborne freeways).

Rotating the OBS to a specific number allows you to select any one of the VOR's 360 flyable courses. Let's suppose you selected 360 degrees (0 degrees, same thing) with the OBS as shown in Figure 8, position D. Your airborne VOR equipment now automatically orients itself to tell you where the 360 degree course is located, as shown in Figure 9A. As you can see, the 360 degree course runs completely through the VOR in a direction of 360 degrees just like the freeway running through town. If you had selected the 270 degree course, your VOR equipment would orient itself to the 270 degree course as shown in Figure 9B. Selecting 030 degrees with the OBS orients you to the course shown in Figure 9C. And selecting 240 degrees orients you to the course shown in Figure 9D.

In Figure 10, we've selected the 360 degree course with the OBS. To fly this course, you should head your airplane in a magnetic direction of 360 degrees on the heading indicator. Assuming you've done this, and your airplane is in position A, the VOR indicator shows a centered needle with a TO flag indication.

As you fly along the selected course, the TO flag automatically changes to a FROM flag on the other side of the station (Airplane C). When directly over the station (Airplane B), the flag reads OFF, indicating a position of ambiguity (you're neither going to nor from the VOR at the time). Simply stated, the TO or FROM flag lets you know whether you'll be going to or from the VOR station if you point in the direction of the course set into the OBS while keeping the needle centered.

Fig. 10

SELECTING 0° (360°) WITH THE OBS AND FLYING A HEADING OF 360°

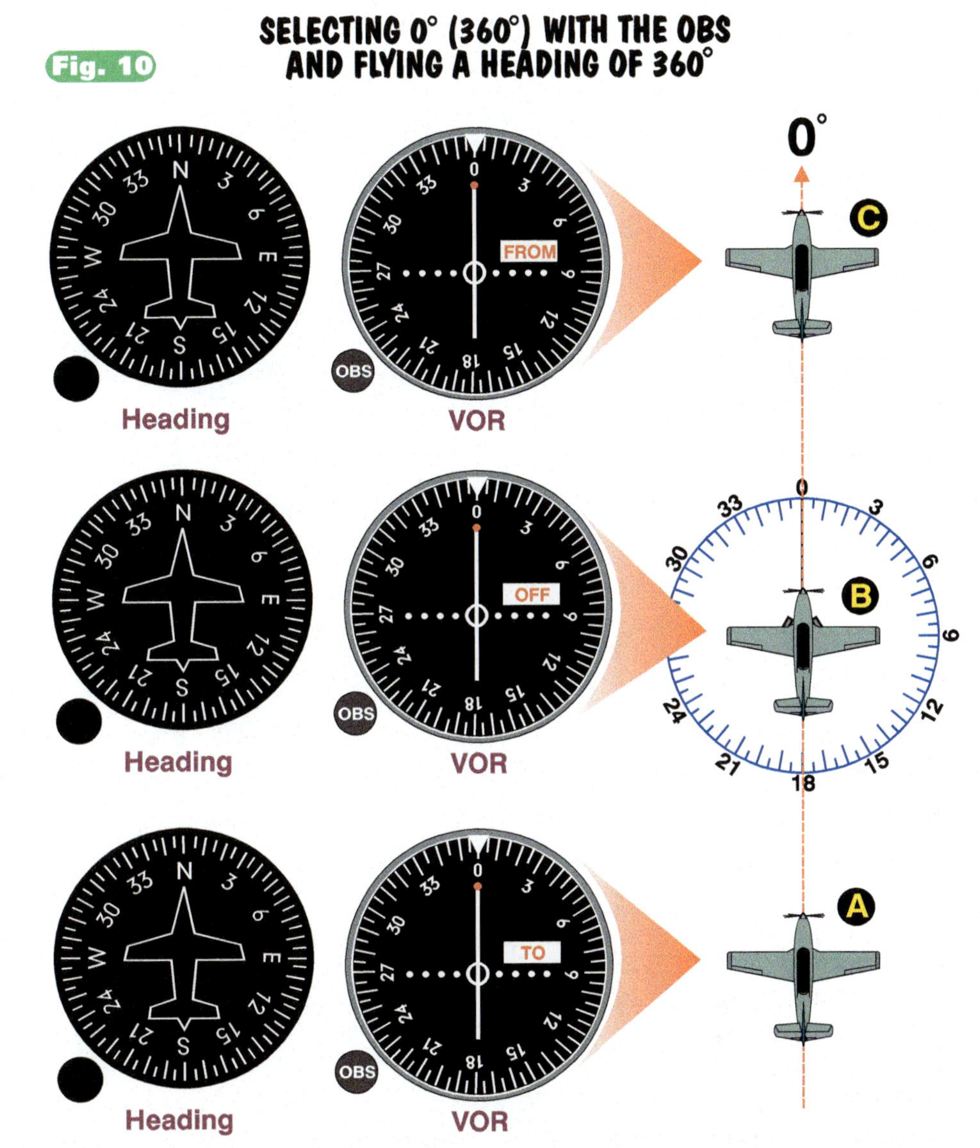

VOR NEEDLE INDICATIONS

All airplanes are heading 360 degrees. Airplanes (A), (C) and (E) have a right needle indication, implying the 360 degree course is to their right. They would turn right to get on the selected course. Airplanes (B), (D) and (F) have left needles, indicating the 360 degree course is to their left. They would turn left to get on the selected course. Airplanes (C) and (D)_have "OFF" shown by their ambiguity indicators. This implies they are abeam the station in a zone of ambiguity.

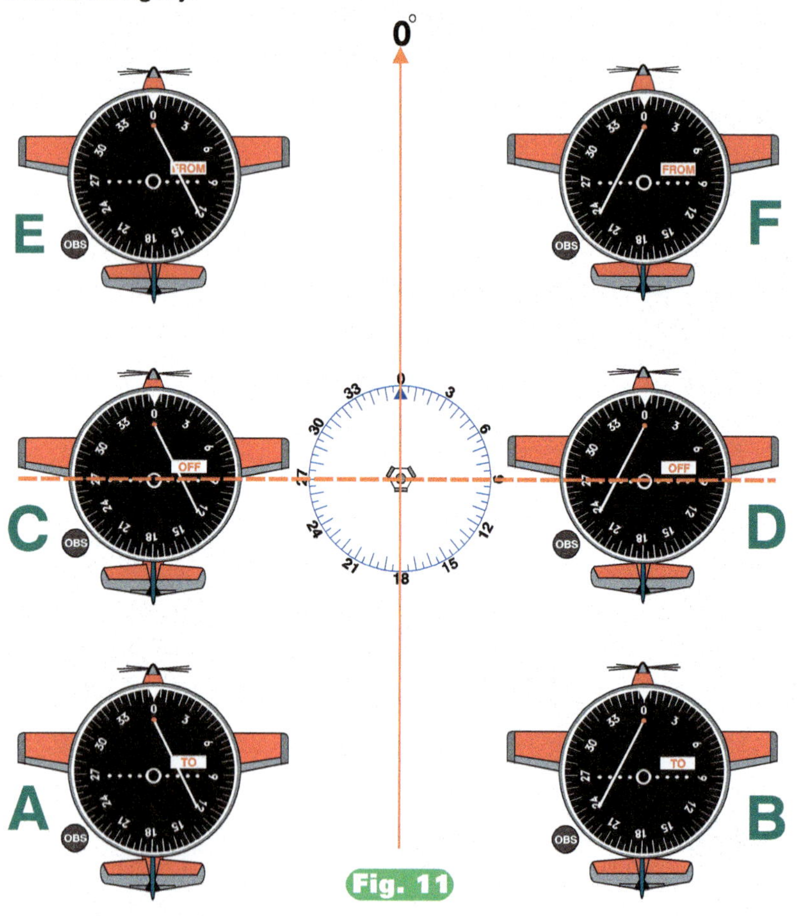

Figure 11 shows several VOR indications in relation to airplane positions. Airplane A is heading 360 degrees (the direction of the selected course). Its airborne VOR equipment shows a right needle with a TO indication. This means that the selected course is to the right and, if Airplane A were on the course, it would be headed to the station. Airplane A must turn to the right to intercept the selected course. So must Airplanes C and E. Airplanes B, D and F must turn left to intercept. Notice that when you are abeam (90 degrees to the side of) the station, the ambiguity indicator shows OFF. This means that you are in the zone of ambiguity and are going neither to nor from the station.

Let's say Airplane A in Figure 12 turns right to a heading of 045 degrees to intercept the 360 degree course to the VOR. As it approaches the course, the VOR needle begins to center, as shown in positions B and C. Once the needle is centered, the airplane should be heading 360 degrees to fly the selected course to the station. Airplanes E, F, G and H show a similar sequence of intercept with a FROM indication. Airplanes F and G intercept the 360 route at a 45 degree angle (an intercept heading of 315 degrees is 45 degrees to the left of 360 degrees).

INTERCEPTING A VOR COURSE

After turning to intercept a selected VOR course, watch the movement of the CDI (the needle). When the needle is centered, you should fly the heading of the course selected by the OBS (360° or 0° in our case).

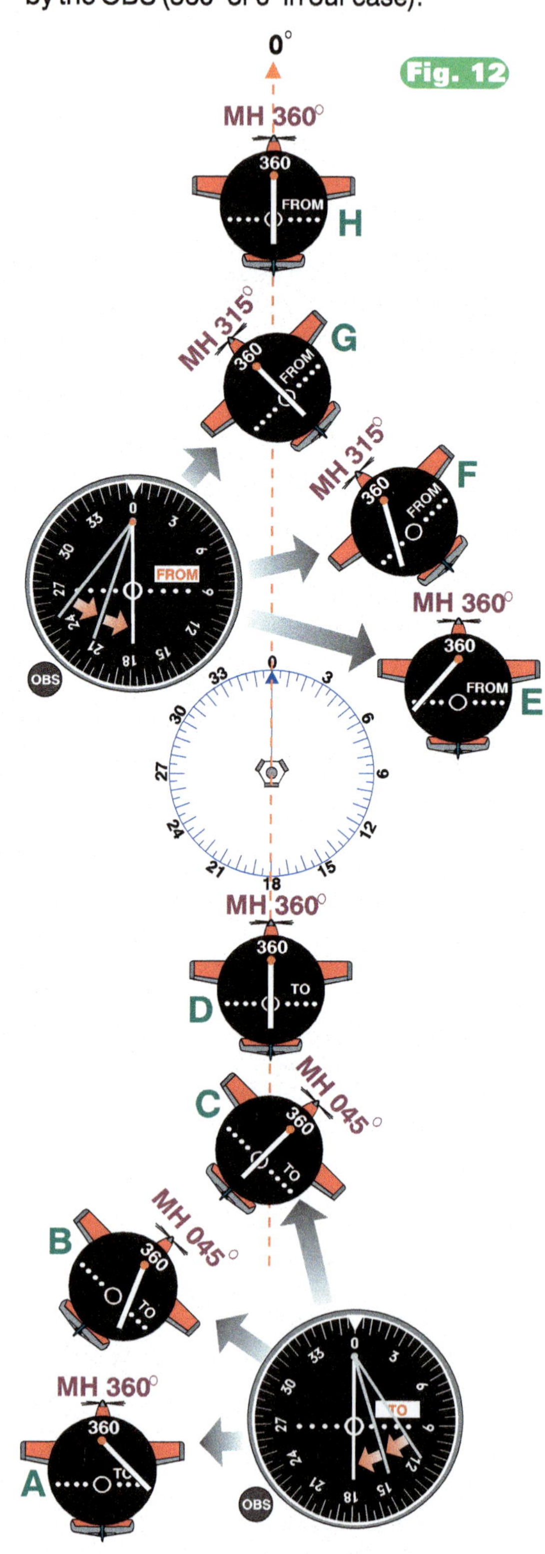

MH = The Airplane's Magnetic Heading

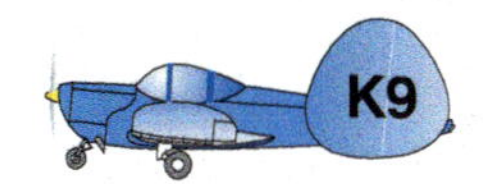

VOR INDICATIONS INDEPENDENT OF YOUR HEADING

The VOR needle and ambiguity indicator (TO/FROM/OFF flag) are completely independent of the airplane's heading. All airplanes in each of the four quadrants (A, B, C or D) have the same ambiguity flag indications and needle deflections. The only way to make sense of a right or left needle indication is to head the airplane in the direction of the selected course (360° in this case). Then and only then does a right or left needle make sense.

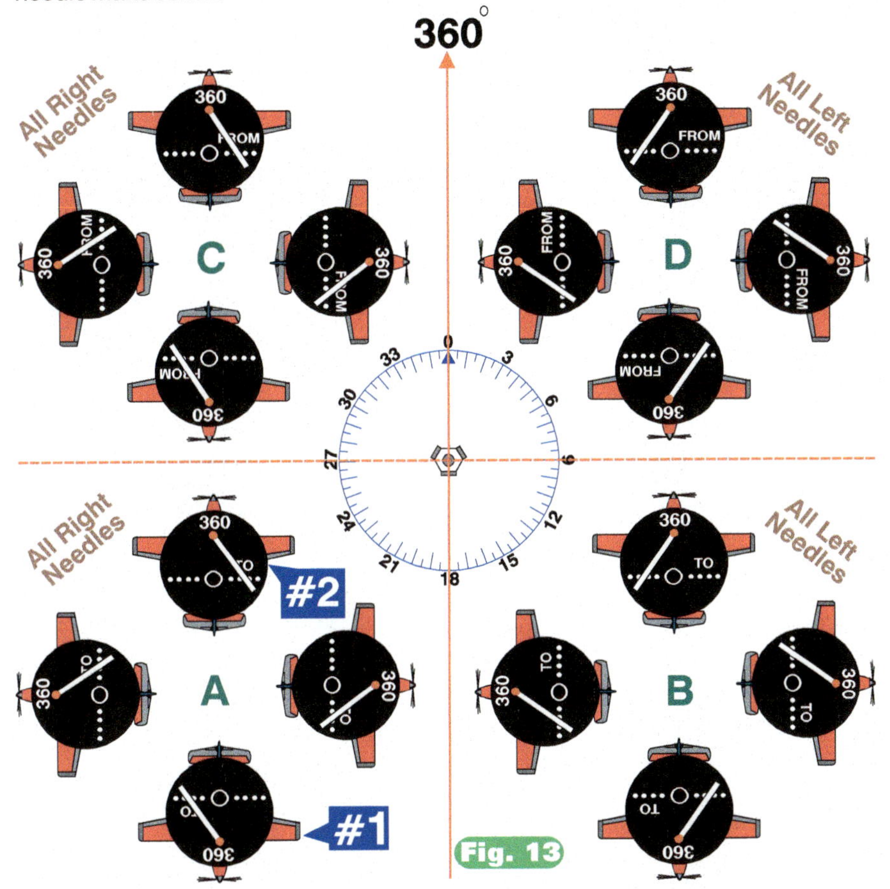

Fig. 13

A right or left needle indication doesn't tell you on what side of the airplane the selected course is located *unless* you physically point the airplane in the direction set into the OBS or you imagine yourself pointed in this direction. Why? The VOR needle and flag indications are completely independent of the airplane's heading.

With the OBS set to 360 degrees, the VOR indication on the airplanes in Figure 13, (quadrant A) all show the same thing—a right needle with a TO indication. Airplanes in quadrant B all show a left needle with a TO indication, regardless of which way the airplane's heading. Airplanes in quadrant C all show a right needle with a FROM indicator. And all airplanes in quadrant D show a left needle with a FROM indication.

The point is that a left or right needle deflection and a TO or FROM flag indication only have meaning if you are pointed (physically or mentally) in the direction of the selected course. VORs don't know which way your airplane is heading. That's because the airborne VOR equipment is programmed to think of itself as always pointing in the direction of the course selected by the OBS. It only knows if it's to the right or left of a selected course and if the selected course takes it to or from the station.

If the airplane also physically points in the same direction as the selected course or you at least visualize it pointed that way, then a right or left needle literally means that the selected course is to your right or left. For instance, Airplane 1 in Figure 13 shows a right needle and TO flag indication. It's obvious that the selected course isn't physically located off the right wing of Airplane 1. If the pilot were to physically turn the airplane to 360 degrees as shown by Airplane 2, or at least imagine being pointed in that direction, then the needle reflects the side of the airplane on which the course is located (the right side). Let's put our knowledge to practical use with a real-life problem.

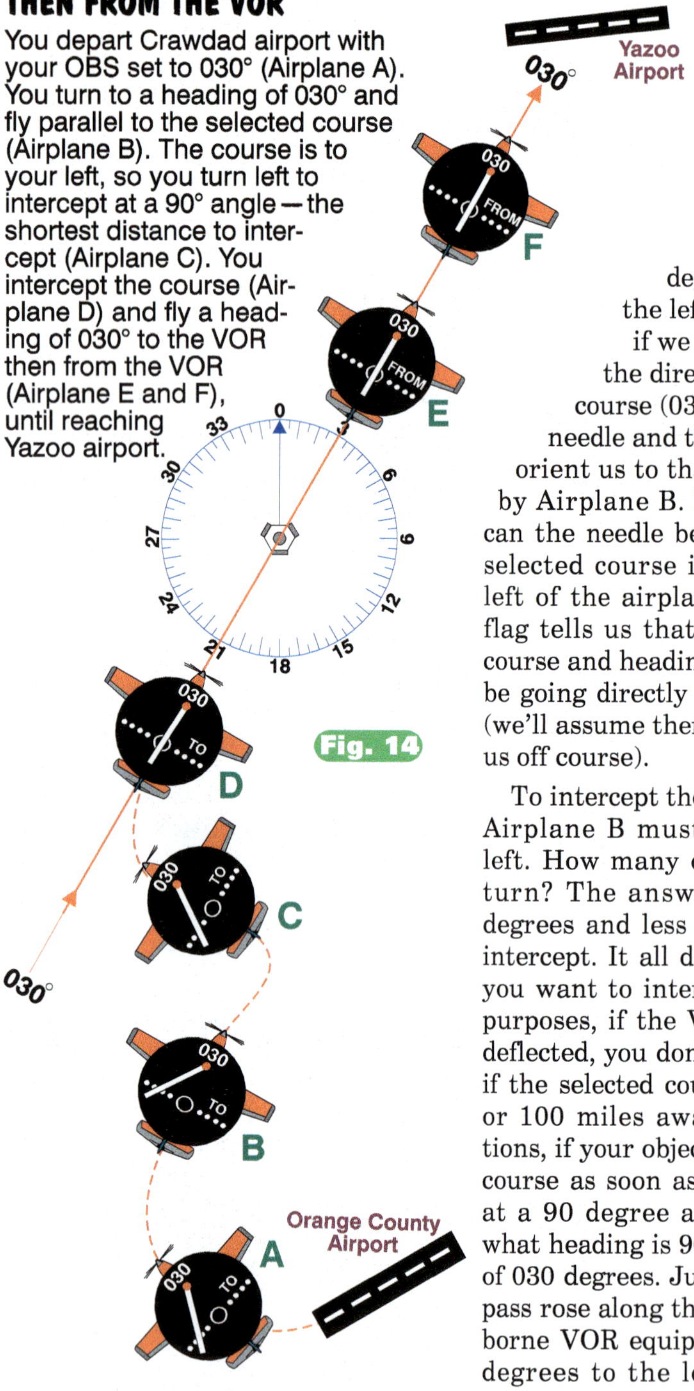

FLYING A SELECTED COURSE TO, THEN FROM THE VOR

You depart Crawdad airport with your OBS set to 030° (Airplane A). You turn to a heading of 030° and fly parallel to the selected course (Airplane B). The course is to your left, so you turn left to intercept at a 90° angle—the shortest distance to intercept (Airplane C). You intercept the course (Airplane D) and fly a heading of 030° to the VOR then from the VOR (Airplane E and F), until reaching Yazoo airport.

Fig. 14

Intercepting a VOR Course

You depart Orange County airport and want to fly the 030 degree course to and beyond the VOR as shown in Figure 14. (To be precise, degree values less than 100, are shown with a "0" in front of them. This prevents thinking that a value of "30" is 300 degrees. We pronounce "030" as "zero-three-zero.") Your destination is Yazoo airport, which is directly on the 030 degree course from the VOR.

You set your OBS to 030 and depart Orange County as shown by Airplane A. The VOR face in Airplane A shows a left needle with a TO indication. Obviously the 030 degree course is not to the left of Airplane A. But if we turn the airplane to the direction of the selected course (030 degrees), then the needle and the flag will properly orient us to that course, as shown by Airplane B. Now and only now can the needle be said to tell us the selected course is physically to the left of the airplane. The TO/FROM flag tells us that once we're on the course and heading 030 degrees, we'll be going directly to the VOR station (we'll assume there's no wind to blow us off course).

To intercept the 030 degree course, Airplane B must be turned to the left. How many degrees should you turn? The answer is more than 0 degrees and less than 90 degrees of intercept. It all depends on how fast you want to intercept. For practical purposes, if the VOR needle is fully deflected, you don't necessarily know if the selected course is 1 mile away or 100 miles away. In these situations, if your objective is to get on the course as soon as possible, intercept at a 90 degree angle. Ask yourself what heading is 90 degrees to the left of 030 degrees. Just look on the compass rose along the outside of the airborne VOR equipment and count 90 degrees to the left of the selected course (030 degrees), as shown in Figure 15. Flying a heading perpendicular to the selected course (300 degrees), as shown by Airplane C in Figure 14, will allow you the shortest intercept time.

A young student named Bob was on his private pilot checkride performing a similar 90 degree intercept to a course. He wanted to show the examiner how skillfully he could turn to the desired course and end up with a centered needle. As he flew through the course the first time, the needle swung from left to right. He made a right 90 degree turn to intercept. The examiner looked at Bob and said, "Hey partner, what heading are you using?" In frustration Bob replied, "All of them, sir!" He finally realized his error and used a smaller intercept angle (20 to 30 degrees).

Airplane C in Figure 14 should plan to turn in the direction of the selected course as the radial is intercepted. A precisely completed interception and turn is shown by Airplane D. Notice how the VOR needle of Airplane D centers as the airplane heads 030 degrees (the selected course direction). Don't worry if you can't do this precisely at first. How quickly the needle centers is a function of how close you are to the station. A little bit of experience will teach you to estimate the rate at which the needle approaches the center and how much (before centering) to begin your turn to the on-course heading.

Airplane D will eventually pass over the VOR and its VOR flag will

VOR COURSE INTERCEPT ANGLE

To find an angle to intercept the selected VOR course, look to the left or right of the present course selection on the VOR's compass rose. A heading of 300° provides the shortest distance to intercept the 030° course.

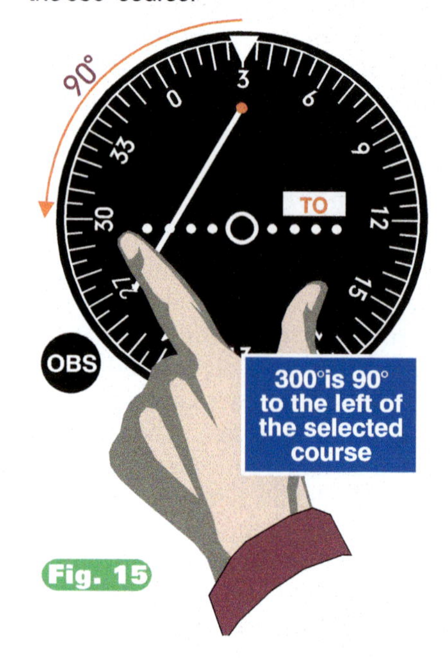

Fig. 15

VOR NAVIGATION FROM FAITH TO CHEYENNE EAGLE

Tuning your OBS to 068° takes you direct to the Dupree VOR from Faith airport. To fly to Cheyenne Eagle airport, select the 096° course on your OBS when over the VOR, then track outbound to Cheyenne Eagle.

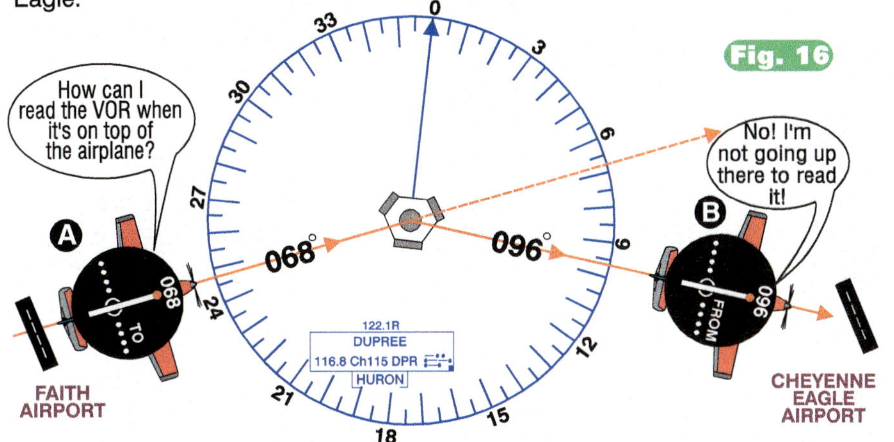

automatically go from TO to OFF, and then to FROM. Obviously, the airplane is now on the 030 degree course from the station. Keeping the needle centered will eventually put Airplane D directly over Yazoo airport.

Many VOR stations have as part of their installation a second piece of navigational gear called distance measuring equipment (DME). A receiver in the airplane converts the DME signals into a readout of exactly how far you are from the VOR station. Suppose the airplane has airborne DME equipment, and you know Yazoo's distance from the VOR. If you fly the selected course until that distance shows on your equipment, you'll be directly over the airport. This provides a very accurate way of finding an airport. More on DME later.

Flying From the VOR On A Selected Course

Let's make VOR usage even more practical. Suppose after departing Faith airport as shown in Figure 16, we wanted to fly directly to the Dupree VOR, then fly outbound on the 096 degree course to Cheyenne Eagle airport. How would we do this? First, look at the VOR compass rose in Figure 16 and decide what route runs directly from the center of Faith airport to the Dupree VOR. Draw a line from the center of Faith airport through the center of the Dupree VOR and out the side of the compass rose. The line intersects 068 degrees on the compass rose. We'll rotate our OBS to 068 degrees and fly this course to the VOR immediately after departure, as shown by Airplane A. Once over the VOR, when the flag switches from TO to OFF, we'll turn to a heading of 096 degrees, then rotate our OBS to 096 degrees, as shown by Airplane B. We'll track this new route to Cheyenne Eagle.

Pretty slick eh? Well, if you think that's slick, think about this. Suppose you're airborne in the vicinity of Ulost airport and desire to fly to Wongway airport as shown by Airplane A in Figure 17. Since you're not exactly sure of your position, what's the best way to get to the Bigfoot VOR? You can always assume you are on *some* course going to the VOR. How do you know which course it is? Simply tune in the Bigfoot VOR frequency on your navigational radio, identify the station, rotate the OBS until you get a TO flag indication and the needle centers as shown by the VOR indication of Airplane A in Figure 17. Look up at the index to see what the course is. In our case, we're on the 305 degree course to the Bigfoot VOR. Now turn to a heading of 305 degrees on your heading indicator and fly that course to the VOR, as shown by Airplane B. When you're over the station, follow the same procedure outlined previously to get to Wongway airport, as shown by Airplane C.

FINDING THE SHORTEST ROUTE TO AND FROM A VOR

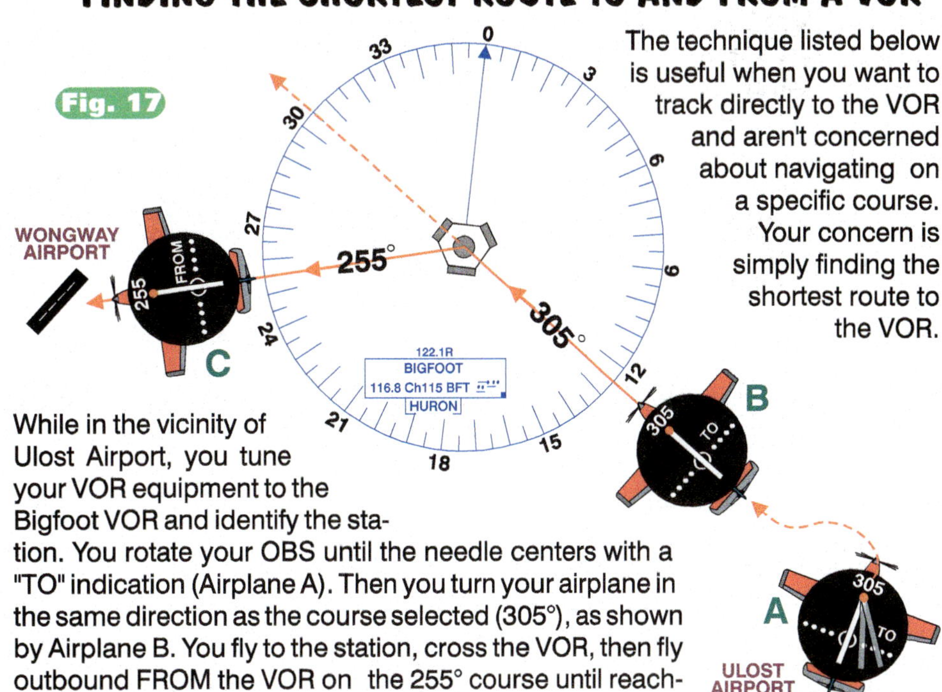

The technique listed below is useful when you want to track directly to the VOR and aren't concerned about navigating on a specific course. Your concern is simply finding the shortest route to the VOR.

While in the vicinity of Ulost Airport, you tune your VOR equipment to the Bigfoot VOR and identify the station. You rotate your OBS until the needle centers with a "TO" indication (Airplane A). Then you turn your airplane in the same direction as the course selected (305°), as shown by Airplane B. You fly to the station, cross the VOR, then fly outbound FROM the VOR on the 255° course until reaching Wongway Airport.

USING YOUR NUMBER 2 VOR FOR POSITION IDENTIFICATION

Airplanes A, B and C are tracking outbound from Birdtalk (BRD) VOR on the 080° radial as shown by their No.1 VOR. The No.2 VOR is set to receive the 025° course from Rocket (RKT) VOR. When Airplane C is on the 025° course "FROM" the station, the No. 2 VOR needle should center, indicating a position directly over Yazoo airport. This form of VOR cross-referencing is an excellent way to help identify your position. It's customary to use a course from a VOR to identify your position rather than a course to a VOR.

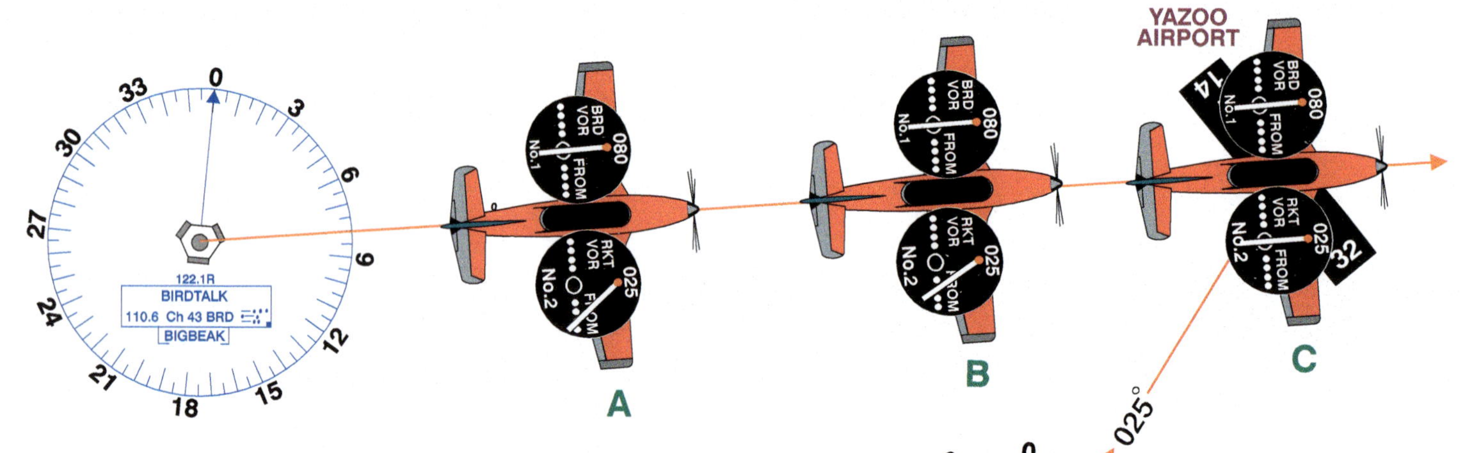

Fig. 18

I hope this makes sense, because many things don't. For example, while taxiing to the arrival gate on a commercial airline flight, the flight attendant said, "Will those passengers requesting wheelchairs please remain seated." This didn't make much sense to me. I hope VORs are making more sense to you by now.

Basic orientation in hand, it's now time to really put the VOR to work. The next trick requires two VORs, which most airplanes these days have. Figure 18 shows an expanded, scaled representation of Yazoo airport. If the No. 1 VOR receiver were set to allow you to navigate from the Birdtalk (BRD) VOR to Yazoo, could the No. 2 VOR receiver be used to inform you when you're over Yazoo? Absolutely!

Dual VORs for Position Fixing

Find another station in the vicinity of Yazoo by looking at your aeronautical sectional chart. Figure 18 shows that Rocket (RKT) VOR is nearby. Draw a line from the center of RKT VOR through the center of Yazoo airport. Ask yourself, "What course runs through Yazoo airport to the VOR?" The compass rose around RKT VOR shows this to be approximately the 025 degree course from the station. Set this into the No. 2 VOR receiver and tune that receiver to RKT VOR.

Figure 18 shows the airplane in three positions while outbound from BRD VOR to Yazoo airport. Airplane A is outbound from BRD VOR to Yazoo airport. Its No. 2 VOR shows a right needle with a FROM indication. To make sense of the needle and flag, imagine Airplane A facing in a direction of 025 degrees (i.e., parallel to the 025 degree course from RKT). You can clearly see that the 025 degree course is to airplane A's right side. If Airplane A was on the 025 degree course, it would be going FROM the RKT VOR. Therefore, the No. 2 VOR for Airplane A shows a right needle with a FROM indication. (Remember, the VOR's needle and flag indication are independent of the airplane's heading.) As we approach Yazoo airport, the needle in VOR No. 2 moves toward the center of the instrument, as shown by airplane B's VOR indication. When the No. 2 VOR needle centers, we know we're over Yazoo airport, as shown by Airplane C.

Considering the ample supply of VORs in most parts of our country, it's pretty difficult not to know exactly where you are most of the time. And always remember that we pilots are never really lost, we're just temporarily unsure of our present position.

You can use courses going TO or FROM the VOR for position fixing. It is, however, customary to use FROM courses to cross check positions. Why? Perhaps it's because most people ask, "Where are you from?" rather than asking, "Where are you to?" (Besides, only a New Age guru would understand such a metaphysical question.) In other words, it's a matter of convention to state your position *from* a specific reference (a VOR in this case).

Reverse Sensing

One of the insidious traps of VOR navigation occurs when pilots attempt to orient themselves or travel *to* a VOR with a FROM flag showing on the instrument (or the other way around). If you do attempt to do such a thing, you're going to be as lost as a 13-year-old at a sock hop. Why? Because the VOR needle will show your selected course in reverse of its actual position.

When you visit the doctor and say, "Doc, it hurts when I do this" (you move your arm, for instance). The

WIND CORRECTION WHILE TRACKING A VOR COURSE

Airplane (A) has just intercepted the 030° course to the station and is flying a parallel heading of 030°. Wind from the west blows Airplane (B) right of course. Airplane (C) turns left to reintercept the original course at a 20° angle on a heading of 010°. When established back on course, Airplane (D) uses a wind correction angle of 10° to the left of the selected course. A magnetic heading of 020° carries Airplanes (D & E) to the VOR station.

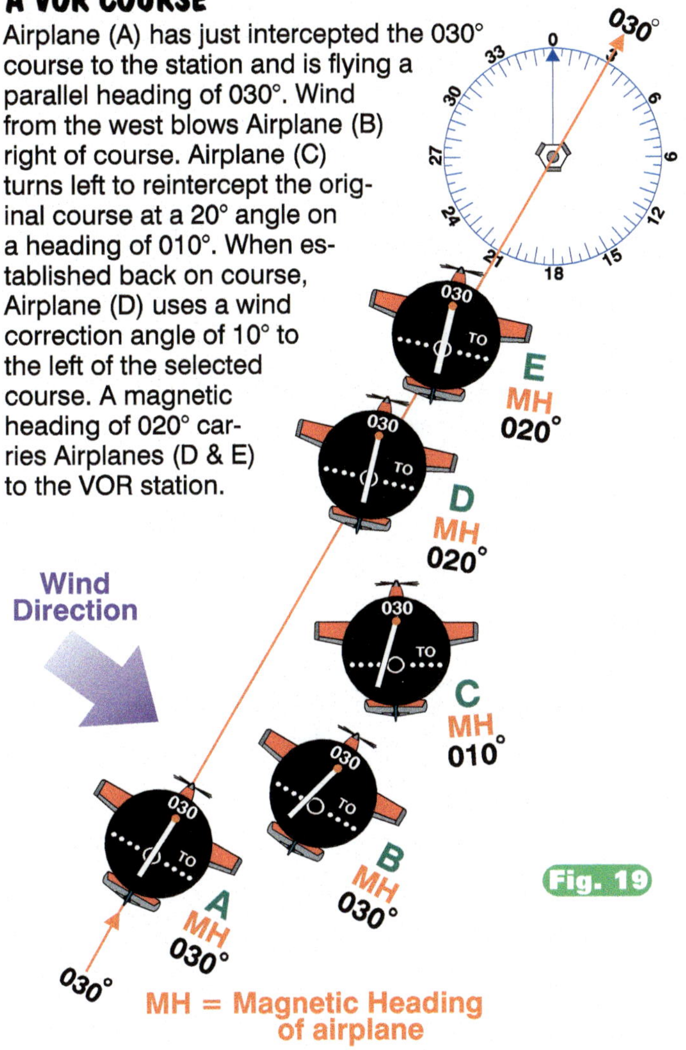

Wind Direction

MH = Magnetic Heading of airplane

Fig. 19

doctor says, "Well, don't do that." So I'm telling you don't try to navigate or orient yourself *to* a VOR station unless a TO flag is showing. Similarly, don't try to navigate or orient yourself *from* a VOR station unless a FROM flag shows in the window. These rules sound simple, but you'd be surprised how often pilots forget this.

For more about reverse sensing, see Postflight Briefing #11-1.

Tracking a Selected VOR Course

Until now we've discussed VOR navigation in a wind-free environment. Such an environment seldom exists in the real world. Let's examine how to correct for wind.

Wind correction is broken down into four components: Identifying the effect of wind on the airplane, reintercepting the course, applying a wind correction, and adjusting the correction. Let's see how it works.

1. Identifying the Effect of Wind – Figure 19 depicts Airplane A as having just intercepted the 030 degree course to the VOR. Under a no-wind condition, Airplane A could hold a 030 degree heading and fly to the VOR with a centered needle. But with wind, Airplane A is going to drift off course. Determining wind direction and making the proper correction is thus paramount to successful navigation.

To determine wind effect on the airplane, you should fly the value set by the OBS (030 degrees in this example). Now, just wait. If there is no wind, the needle will stay centered (or nearly so). If a crosswind exists, the needle will eventually show a deflection, as depicted by Airplane B. How much of a needle deflection should you allow before applying a correction? Realistically, you should correct for wind as soon as you notice any needle movement. Unfortunately, some needle movement can be attributed to the difficulty beginners have in holding a heading. As a student pilot I used the catch-and-release method of heading hold. In other words, I'd finally get on the desired heading, then the next thing I knew, I'd let it go. When it came to courses, I was always letting them go (like fish). I was a real conservationist. I should have joined that famous environmental vegetable group, Green Peas. Perhaps the best advice in these instances is to let the needle move just a little (to the end of the circle—doughnut—in the center of the VOR's face) before making a correction.

2. Reintercepting the Course – If the needle moves to the left, then the selected course is to the left, as shown by Airplane B. The airplane has been blown to the right of the course (implying the crosswind is from your left). Once you've identified wind direction, the second step is to get back on course before applying a wind correction. The best way to get back on course is to intercept the course at some angle less than 90 degrees (say around 20 degrees or even 40 degrees if the wind is strong) and fly toward the desired course, as shown by Airplane C. Attempting to reintercept at too large an angle could cause you to fly through the selected course. In one respect, it's really no big deal if this happens because you would simply reintercept the course. Serpentining along a selected VOR course will get you to your destination but it's not a professional way to aviate (and it makes your passengers suspicious of your flying skills).

3. Applying a Wind Correction – Once reestablished on course, the third step in tracking is to apply a wind correction. As we previously discussed, the airplane must be angled (turned) by some amount into the wind. How much? That depends on the wind speed and wind angle as well as your airspeed. But none of that really matters. Just use one-half of your intercept angle—10 degrees in this case. Try it and see if it works. It's just like going to the movies. You never quite know how good or bad the film might be, so you try it (the last movie I watched was so bad that I walked out. Unfortunately, it was on TV and I walked out of my own home). Once you're on course, simply turn the airplane 10 degrees to the right (for a heading of 020 degrees), as shown by Airplane D, and wait to see what happens.

Airplane D has a wind correction angle of 10 degrees while heading 020 degrees. Airplanes D and E are tracking directly *to* the VOR station on the 030 degree course.

The needle hasn't moved. Congratulations! You've successfully corrected for wind. And you're darn lucky if you, or for that matter any experienced pilot, can find the proper wind correction angle on the first attempt. Realistically, you're probably going to make a *minimum* of two attempts at determining a wind correction angle before you find the right one.

4. Adjusting the Wind Correction – Figure 20 depicts a situation similar to Figure 19. The difference is that you're now tracking *from* a station using the previous 10 degree wind correction angle, as shown by Airplane A. Soon the airplane begins to drift, as shown by Airplane B. It's now obvious your wind correction angle must be changed. Return to 010 degrees, the original intercept angle, and reintercept the course, as depicted by Airplane C. Since a heading of 020 degrees (10 degree wind correction to the left) didn't keep you on course, increase the wind correction angle by 5 degrees.

Flying 015 degrees, as shown by Airplane D, might be a satisfactory correction. If, however, the needle moves to the right, showing that the airplane was flying across the 030 degree course to the left, then we'd know that our wind correction angle was too large. At least now you would know the wind correction angle was between 10 and 15 degrees.

Sometimes, if the wind varies, the entire flight consists of constantly changing the wind correction angle. This is especially true if you're changing altitudes or flying near mountainous terrain where wind is often variable. As you become more skilled at tracking you'll find that you can apply small corrections to stop the needle from moving before it ever gets away from the center. With that kind of skill the wind can shift every minute and it won't faze you. Soon you'll become a high priest of VOR tracking, master of meteorological forces, and reign as a king over airway navigation. You'll be required to walk around the flight school in white robes. Pilots from all over will come seeking your guidance. Wow, TV shows! Live appearances! Think of the possibilities. If not, at least you'll get to your destination with ease.

Chasing the Needle

While on a VOR training flight, my student Bob was having a devil of a time keeping the VOR needle centered. I looked over at him and said, "Bob, don't chase the needle." In a moment of frustration he looked back and said, "Hey, my friends are pilots and this is the way they do it." A small smile stretched across my face as I thought of the countless times I've tried to use that type of logic on my father. I couldn't resist. I said, "Bob, just because your friends jump off a bridge, that doesn't mean you should jump off too." I couldn't believe it. The logic worked. He looked at me like a dog looking at a fan and said, "Duuuhh! OK, I guess you're right." (I'm glad he never heard about bungee jumping.) It's also logical to have a little patience with the VOR needle, since patience will probably solve all your tracking problems.

WIND CORRECTION WHILE TRACKING A VOR COURSE

Airplane (A) has just flown past the VOR, tracking outbound on the 030° course. Airplane (A) has a 10° wind correction angle to the left, which originally held it on course. With a change in wind direction or velocity, Airplane (B) drifts to the right of course. After the needle reaches the edge of the inner circle (donut), Airplane (C) turns left to the original course intercept heading of 010° and reintercepts the 030° course from the station. Upon reintercepting the 030° course, Airplane (D) now applies a 15° wind correction angle by turning 5° to the right of its 010° intercept heading. Now Airplane (D) is heading 015°. This correction is sufficient to allow Airplane (E) to track the course.

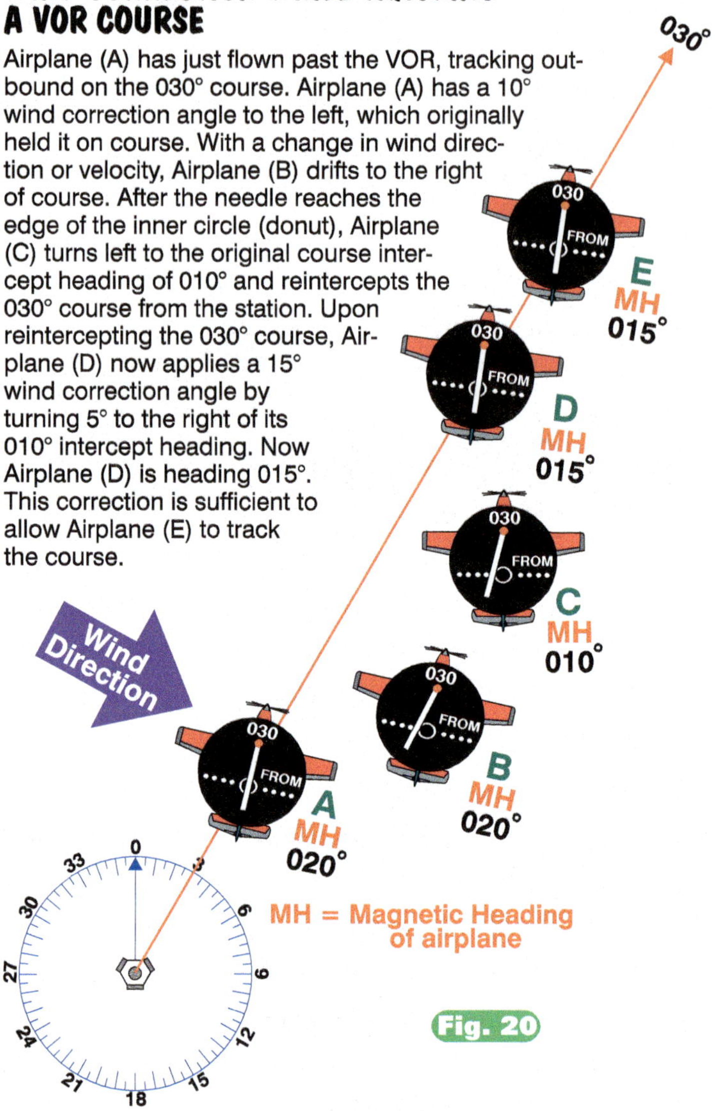

MH = Magnetic Heading of airplane

Fig. 20

VOR needles become quite sensitive when closing in on VOR ground stations. Rapid needle movements are not uncommon within 1/2 mile of a VOR transmitter. In this situation most students are likely to hear a thumping sound. Yes, it's the sound of the passengers' heads bumping against the windows as you chase the VOR needle to the right, then left, then right again. Don't do it. When you get close to the station, settle on a heading and fly it until station passage.

A Nifty Technique

If you're having trouble keeping the VOR needle centered, try the following technique. As the needle is moving away from center, turn toward it to stop the needle's movement. Keep increasing the angle slightly, then watch the result. As soon as the needle stops, note your heading. This value approximates the wind correction

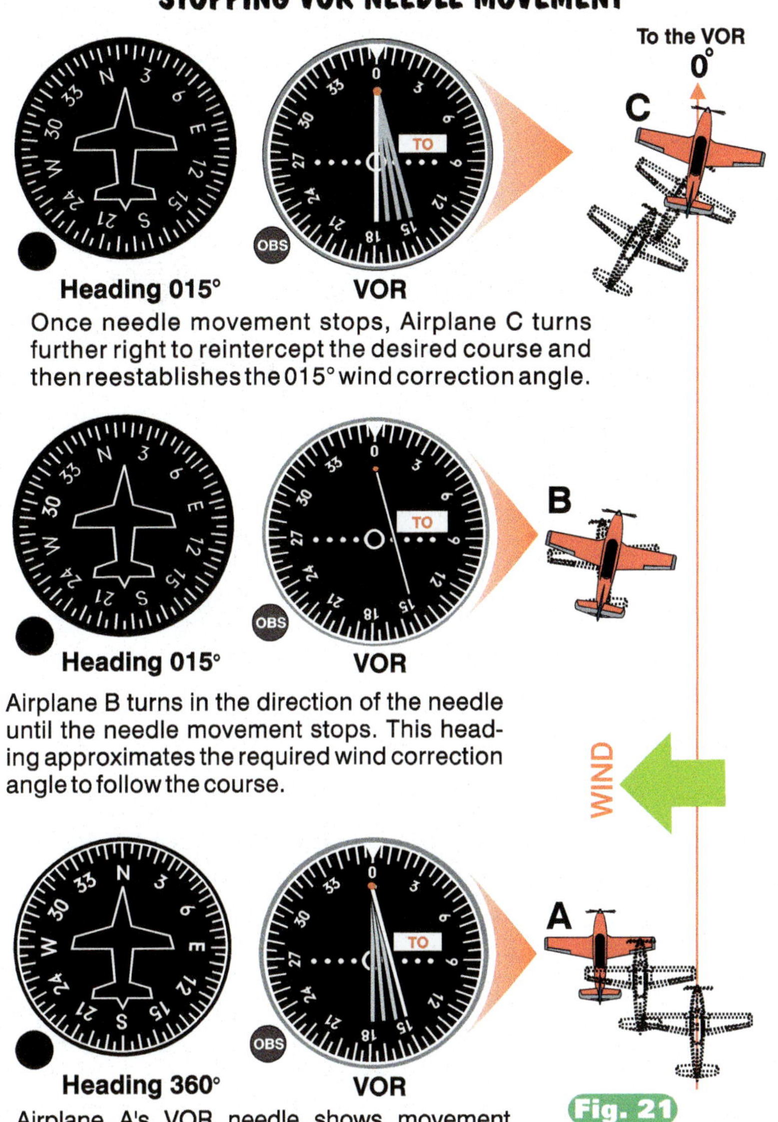

Fig. 21

Freaked Out!

I planned a cross country flight in excess of 300 miles. My map and notations were checked by my instructor and approved. Weather briefing showed broken and scattered clouds, visibility 10 miles. During my flight, about 10 minutes past ABC the clouds thickened greatly. I decided not to continue and instead to land at ABC. I consulted the sectional on my lap for the ABC Tower frequency and called the tower, now in sight. There was no response, so I repeated my call a second and third time. I assumed that the Tower was not in operation so I chose a runway and landed. I tried the Tower again before taxiing out and before taking off. No response either time. After landing at home, I was told the frequency at ABC had recently been changed. **ASRS Report**

While attempting to call an airport tower, stay out of their airspace. If the facility is unfamiliar to you, call any nearby facility to verify the tower's frequency and hours of operation. A pilot should use all available tools. "XYZ Tower, 444C, VFR, 10 miles north of ABC, requesting the frequency for ABC Tower?" On the ground, verify tower frequencies before going to your plane. If you cannot raise the tower during normal hours, call them on your cell phone. **D.T.**

heading required to stay on course. Now, reintercept the course at some larger angle. Fly the wind correction heading once you're reestablished on the desired course, as shown in Figure 21.

Yes, as with all maneuvers in aviation, this does take a little practice. Pilots chase VOR needles out of impatience. They keep turning toward the needle until they see it moving back to the center. By then, it's too late. The needle ends up swinging across the face of the instrument faster than a Samurai warrior's sword in the heat of combat. Thinking about stopping needle movement first, instead of moving it back to the center, will minimize rapid needle movement. With a little patience, the needle will move slower than a turtle with sore feet on a double dose of Prozac.

As a flight instructor, I hear some mighty strange ideas about navigation. I was giving a navigational phase check to a student pilot and had such an experience. We were about 10 miles from the VOR and supposedly tracking directly to it. The needle was pegged and this young fellow seemed to think everything was OK. I asked, "Why is that needle pegged against the side of the instrument?" "Because we're close to the station and the needle is too sensitive to chase," was his reply. My mouth dropped open and my eyes bugged out as if I had just seen those six TBM Avengers lost in the Bermuda triangle. I felt my eyes to make sure they hadn't popped completely out of their sockets, then patiently replied, "You're too far from the station to be satisfied with a deflected needle. If you're a couple of miles horizontal to the station, sensitivity might be an acceptable excuse for not pursuing a rapidly moving needle. However, even under those conditions you should be using smaller angles of intercept (5 degrees or so) to recapture that needle." He looked at me and said, "Hey, all the other pilots I fly with do it this way." He should have known better than to say that. I had him....

Actually seen written in an airplane squawk sheet:
"This airplane has a tendency to overshoot."

Proper Names

Why is it that when Elvis is spotted, it's always in some strange pizza parlor or laundromat in Kansas or Mississippi? How come he's never spotted at Mensa headquarters? That's a true mystery to some people (me). Of course, VOR navigation is not without its own mysteries. For instance, what would you do if asked to track to the VOR on the 180 degree radial? What course would you select with the OBS? The answer is 360 degrees. Let me explain why.

Throughout this chapter I've mentioned that we select VOR courses with the OBS. Those courses are either to or from the VOR. There is another way of expressing the same thing. Earlier we learned that VORs can be thought of as transmitting 360 individual directional signals spaced one degree apart. Since these signals radiate from the station, they're called radials.

VOR RADIALS vs VOR COURSES

You can say you're going to or from a VOR on a specific course. The course is also the heading you'd fly to get to or from the station (assuming no wind). You can also say that you're going to or from the station on any one of its 360 radials. You must be careful when saying this since, going to a VOR on any radial implies that you set your course selector (OBS) and fly a heading 180° opposite of that radial.

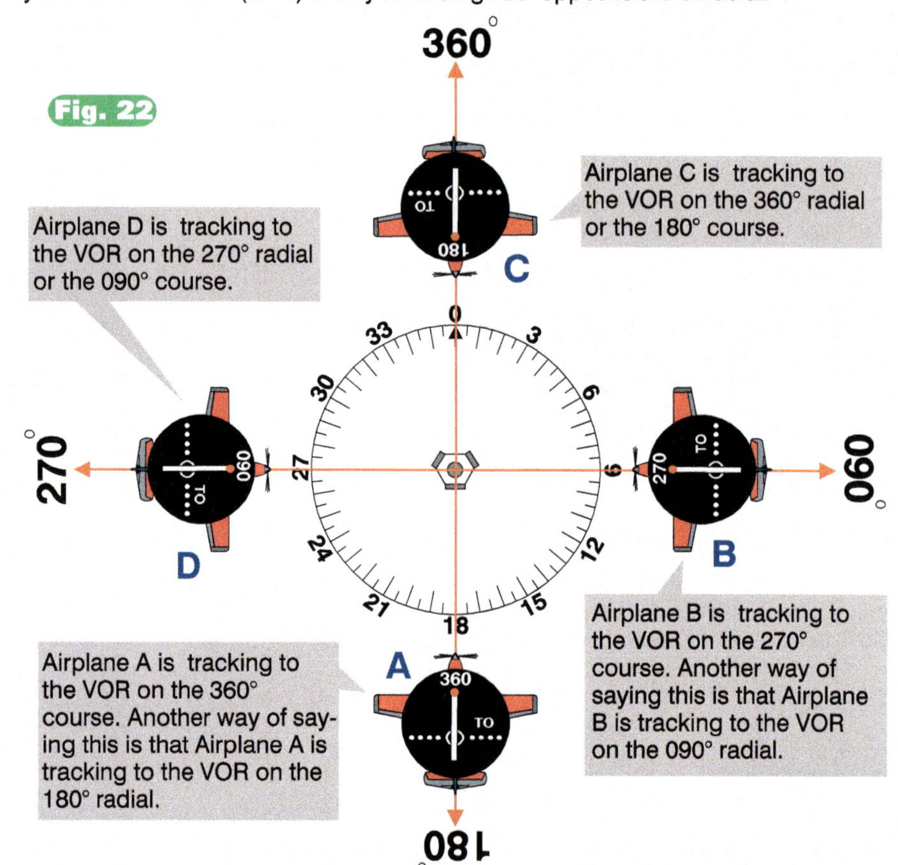

Figure 22 shows four of these radials. Airplane A is tracking to the station on the 360 degree course. Another way of describing this is by saying Airplane A is tracking to the station on the VOR's 180 degree radial. As Airplane A crosses over the station it would be tracking outbound on the 360 degree radial. Airplane B is tracking to the VOR on the 090 degree radial, Airplane C is tracking to the VOR on the 360 degree radial and airplane D is tracking to the VOR on the 270 degree radial.

To minimize the confusion, think about it this way. Whenever you're asked to track *from* a station on a specific radial, simply set your OBS to that radial. After all, radials radiate from the station and this is the same direction you would fly them. When asked to fly *to* a VOR on a radial, set the OBS to the reciprocal (add or subtract 180 degrees) of that radial.

All the airplanes in Figure 22 are flying to the VOR on specific radials and each OBS is selected to the reciprocal of the radial it's on. Complex? A mystery? Yes! It's a mystery why we refer to radials when we can refer to courses to and from a station. Well, did anyone ever say that everything in aviation is easy to understand? It's not only aviation that can be confusing. I recently bought satin sheets for our guest bedroom. I got them home and they had pentagrams stitched all over the fabric. It turns out I was confused and in the wrong department store. I had actually purchased Satan sheets. This is proof that men should only be allowed to shop at Radio Shack. Confusion in shopping, as with VOR navigation, is lessened if you pay close attention to our mistakes. Don't be satisfied with being a mediocre navigator. Try your best to keep those needles centered. Make every flight an opportunity to become more proficient. Soon you'll be so skilled at needle tracking that fellow pilots will think the instrument has been turned off (needle drops to center when off).

One last word here. Don't get the impression that pilots only look at the VOR equipment when they navigate. They look outside too! See and avoid, remember?

The next two pages contain sidebars having a few nifty ideas you need to explore. First, there is an easy way to help you answer VOR questions on the FAA knowledge exam (use it for the computer exam only. I don't recommend that you use it in the airplane). It's called the VOR orienter. You can draw it on scratch paper during the test and use to solve VOR problems. Next is the HSI or horizontal situation indicator. This is a very popular device found in many airplanes. You should become familiar with it. It makes VOR orientation extremely easy. The radio magnetic indicator (RMI) is another device you may use for navigation. See Postflight Briefing #11-2 for information on the RMI.

The VOR Orienter

I've always looked for the easiest way to do things—minimum energy expended for maximum gain is my motto. Of course some people are just plain lazy. A bachelor friend of mine is very much like that. If a button falls off his jacket, he'll sew up the hole. If he spills liquid on his kitchen floor, he handles the problem organically—he lets it evaporate. Well, the little device you see here will allow you to discover the answer to VOR problems with minimum energy. It's called a VOR orienter.

Practice drawing it exactly as it's pictured. When you're taking an aeronautical knowledge exam, draw the orienter on a small 2 inch by 2 inch square sheet of paper. Place the orienter over the VOR referenced in the test. Face the arrow on the orienter in the direction set by the OBS. Now you can easily answer any question about VOR orientation. For example, on a flight from Findme International airport to Ubhere Municipal airport, the 340 degree radial identifies the halfway point of the journey as shown in the accompanying figure.

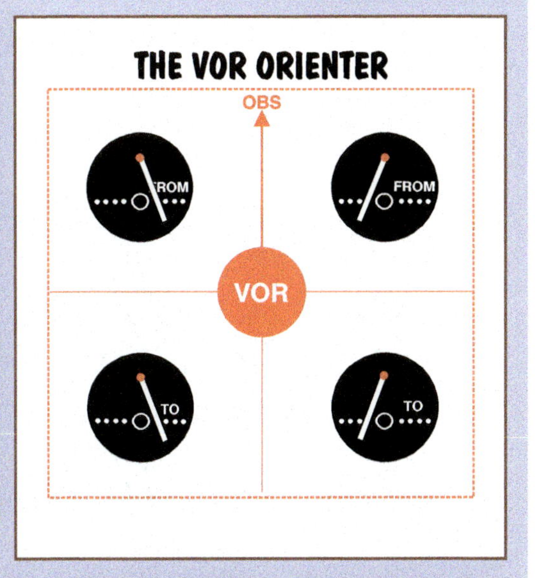

VOR ORIENTER IN ACTION

The VOR Orienter is a useful tool for answering written test questions. You simply place the VOR orienter that you drew on a 2"x2" piece of paper over the VOR you're referencing. Face the Orienter's arrow in the direction of the OBS referred to in the test question. The orienter has four quadrants, each having a specific VOR indication associated with it. The airplane's VOR receiver will read exactly like that shown for a particular quadrant.

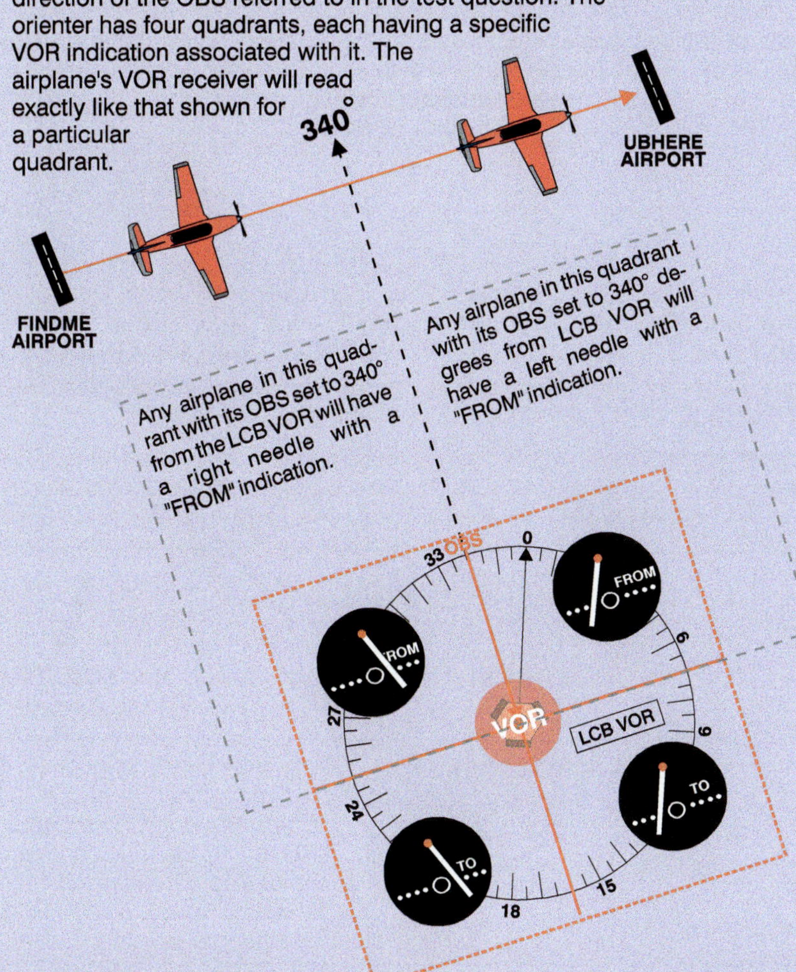

Assume your VOR receiver is tuned to the LCB VOR and the OBS is set to 340 degrees. If you have a right needle with a FROM indication, have you crossed the halfway point of your flight?

To solve the problem, simply place your VOR orienter over the LCB VOR and face it to a heading of 340 degrees, as shown by the dashed lines. The four quadrants of the VOR orienter represent the VOR indications for airplanes in each of those four quadrants. Find the quadrant on the orienter with a right needle and a FROM indication. This shows you where you are in relation to the selected course. From the looks of it, your airplane hasn't crossed the halfway point. The VOR orienter isn't practical for use in flight, but makes perfect sense for aeronautical knowledge exams.

The same navigational problem also turns up on exams phrased this way: "While on a flight from Findme International to Ubhere Municipal airport, what will your VOR indicate if you haven't crossed the halfway point as defined by the 340 degree radial from LCB VOR?" Set your orienter up the same way you did previously. Look at the side of the orienter to the left of the halfway point (to the left of the 340 degree radial). It shows a right needle with a FROM indication. If you had crossed the halfway point, you'd have a left needle with a FROM indication.

THE HORIZONTAL SITUATION INDICATOR

THE HORIZONTAL SITUATION INDICATOR - HSI

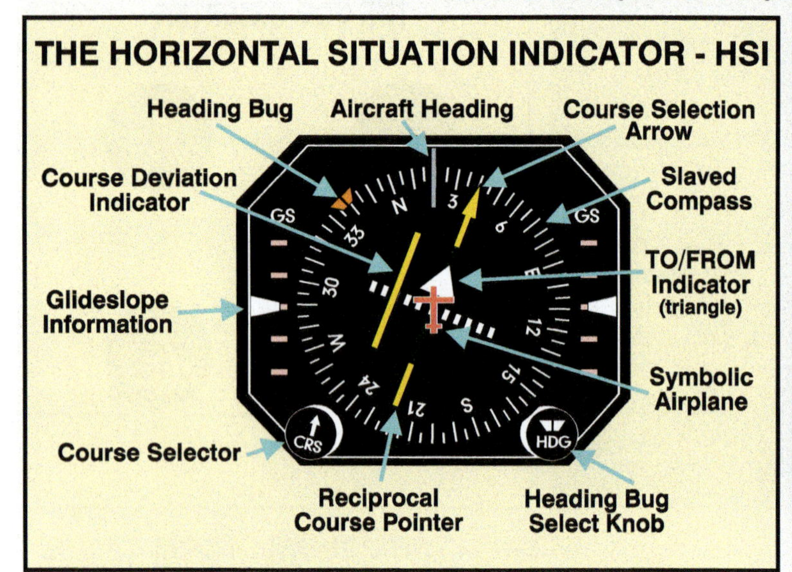

HSI AND VOR SIMILARITIES

The horizontal situation indicator (HSI) is VOR unit combined with a heading indicator (electrically slaved to a compass). Instead of a needle that swings, its course deviation indicator (CDI) slides sideways, away from the course selection arrow, to indicate the direction and amount of course deviation. The TO/FROM indicator is a single white triangle that automatically flips toward the head or tail of the course selection arrow, depending on whether the selected course takes you to or from the station. The heading bug is simply a heading reminder that can be set on any heading value. The small symbolic airplane always points straight ahead, in the direction the airplane is headed. Course interception is made easy by turning until the symbolic airplane is pointed toward the horizontally displaced CDI. Thus, the HSI provides a picture of your airplane, relative to the selected course.

When Airplane B intercepts the course, the CDI aligns itself with the course selection arrow. The airplane now heads in the direction of the selected course (068°) and flies to the station. Upon station passage the TO/FROM triangle will automatically flip and point toward the bottom of the course selection arrow.

Airplane C flies over the VOR and turns to a heading of 150° to intercept the 110° radial from the station. The pilot rotates the course selection arrow to 110° (the desired outbound radial). The TO/FROM triangle automatically flips and points toward the bottom of the course arrow, indicating that the course selected is from the station. The symbolic airplane is pointed toward the displaced CDI indicating that, under a no wind condition, the airplane will intercept the 110° radial.

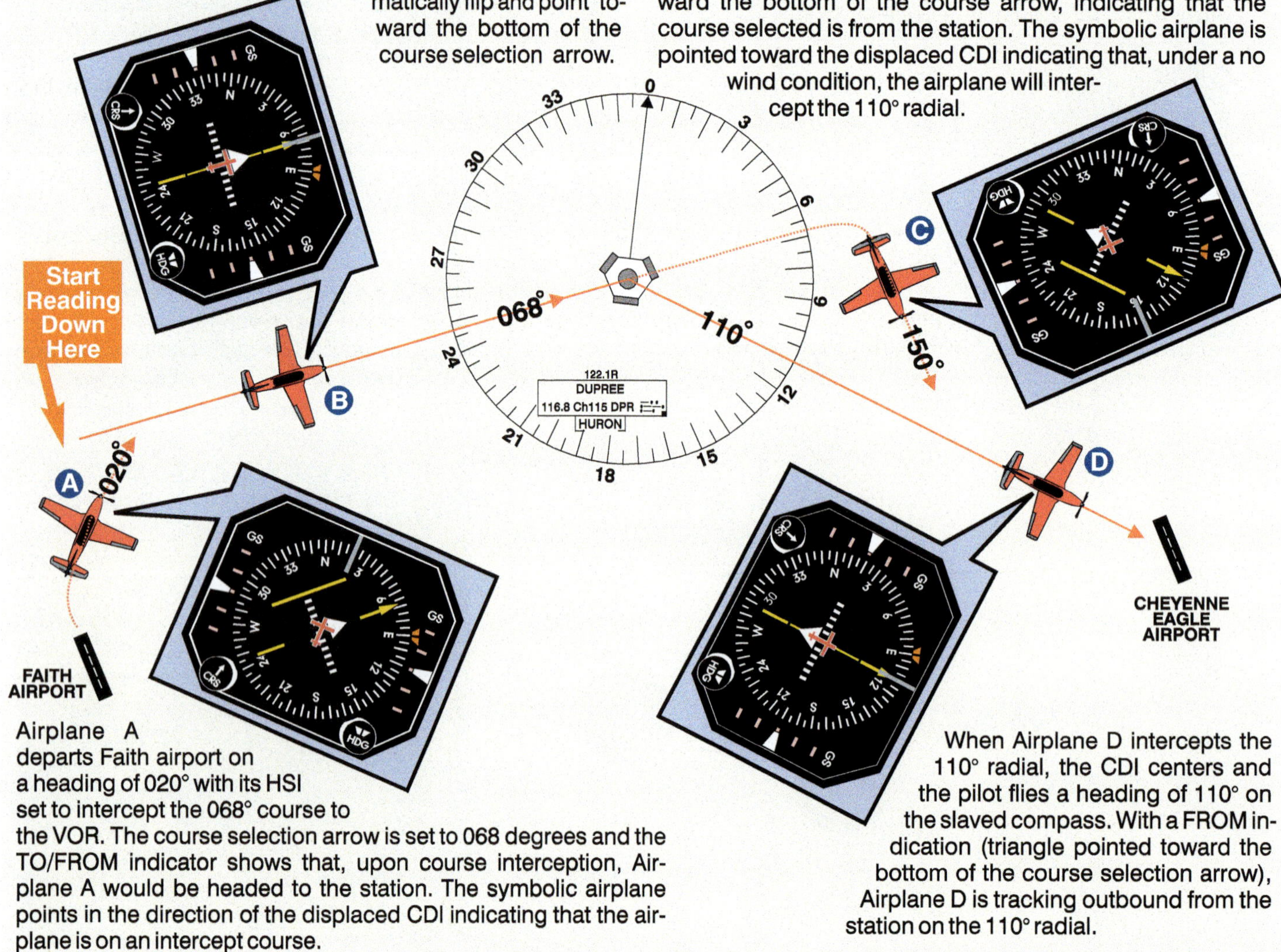

Airplane A departs Faith airport on a heading of 020° with its HSI set to intercept the 068° course to the VOR. The course selection arrow is set to 068 degrees and the TO/FROM indicator shows that, upon course interception, Airplane A would be headed to the station. The symbolic airplane points in the direction of the displaced CDI indicating that the airplane is on an intercept course.

When Airplane D intercepts the 110° radial, the CDI centers and the pilot flies a heading of 110° on the slaved compass. With a FROM indication (triangle pointed toward the bottom of the course selection arrow), Airplane D is tracking outbound from the station on the 110° radial.

Distance Measuring Equipment (DME)

I stop looking at product advertisements after I've purchased something. To continue looking is like saying, "I bet I was pretty dumb for buying this thing, so let me look in the sales literature for some evidence to support this theory." Yes, at periodic moments of weakness all of us have made regrettable purchases. I have never heard, however, of a pilot regretting the purchase of distance measuring equipment (DME).

DME, shown in Figure 23, provides you with nautical mile distances from many VOR stations. This equipment usually displays groundspeed as well. It's a wonderful device, making cross country flying and position fixing considerably easier. Let's examine how it works.

DME is one of those great devices that does so much and demands so little. The DME equipment in the airplane operates by sending out paired pulses at a specific spacing. These pulses are received at the ground station, which then transmits paired pulses back to the aircraft at the same pulse spacing but on a different frequency. The round trip time for the signal exchange is measured in the airborne DME unit and translated into distance from the aircraft to the ground station.

DME EQUIPMENT FOUND IN MANY AIRPLANES

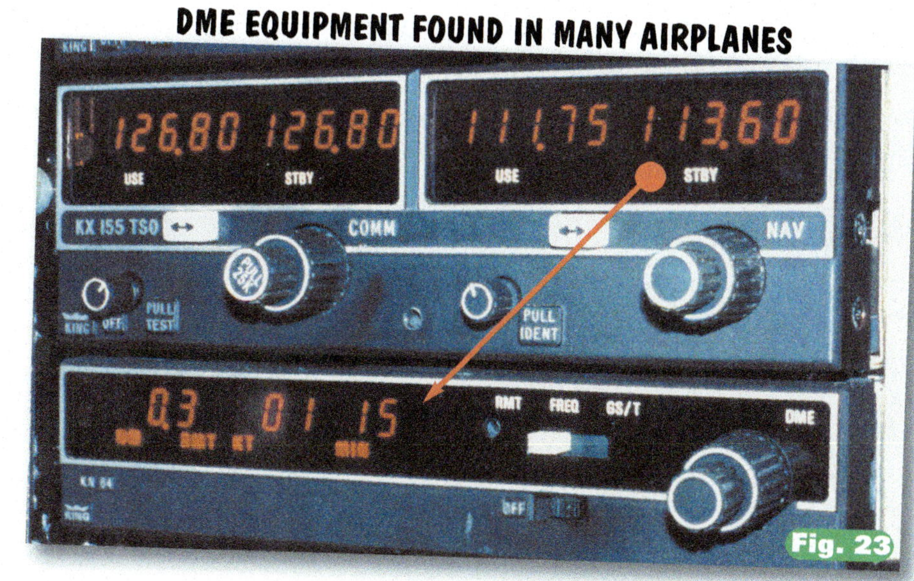

Fig. 23

DME provides you with the distance (in nautical miles) to whatever VOR station you've selected. It's quite easy, and it's remarkably helpful.

Not every VOR has a DME station associated with it. How can you tell which ones do? VOR station symbology depicts the presence of DME, as shown in Figure 24. Symbol A shows a VOR station without DME. Symbol B is the symbol for a VORTAC. While VORTAC sounds like the name of a Klingon starship captain, it's actually the combination of a civilian VOR station and a military navigation station called a TACAN (Tactical Air Navigation station). TACAN stations operate on higher frequencies, but what's important to you is that they always include DME capability. Symbol C depicts a combination VOR and DME station.

Figure 25 shows the VOR frequency box for the Los Angeles VORTAC (it's perfectly proper to refer to VORTACs as VORs). Sitting to the right of 113.6 MHz is the DME frequency (shown as *Channel 83*) that a military pilot would dial on his UHF receiver to obtain navigation information. The only significance the word *channel* has for you is the implication that the VOR station has DME capability.

What DME Really Tells You – If you stretched a piece of string (a very long piece of string) between the airplane and the VOR, then measured it, you'd have the distance shown on the DME. This is the *slant range*

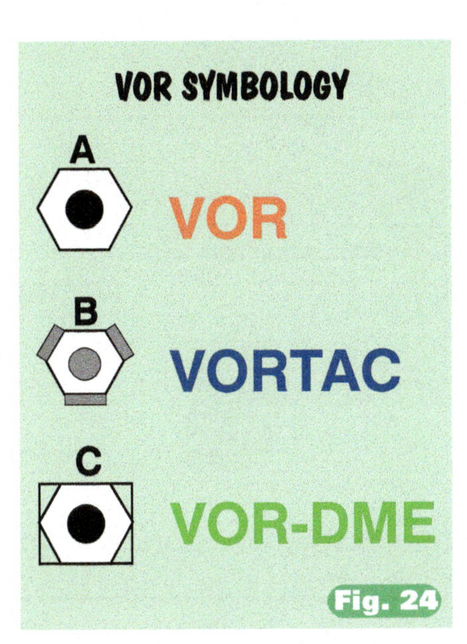

Fig. 24

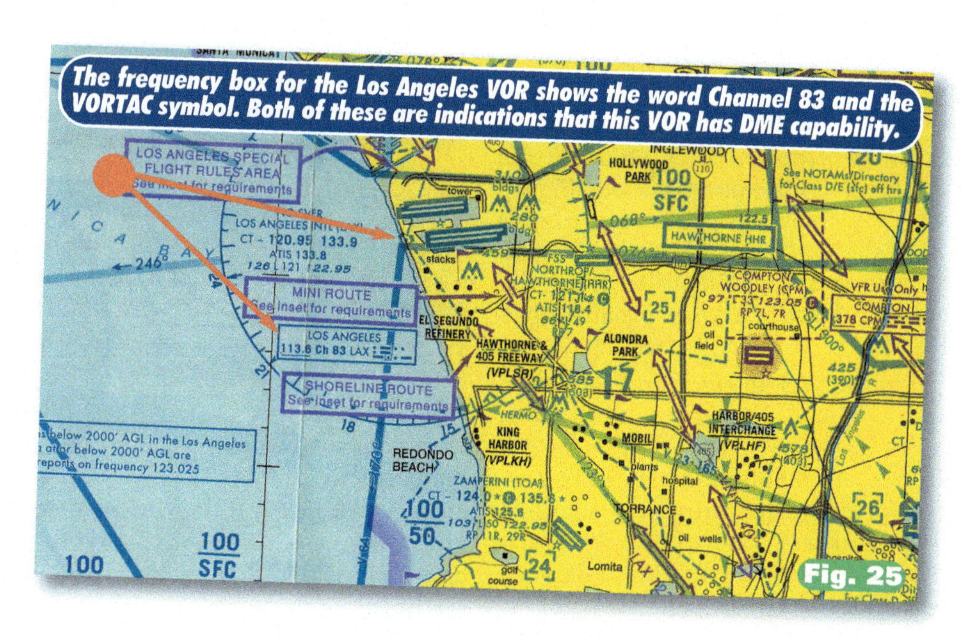

Fig. 25

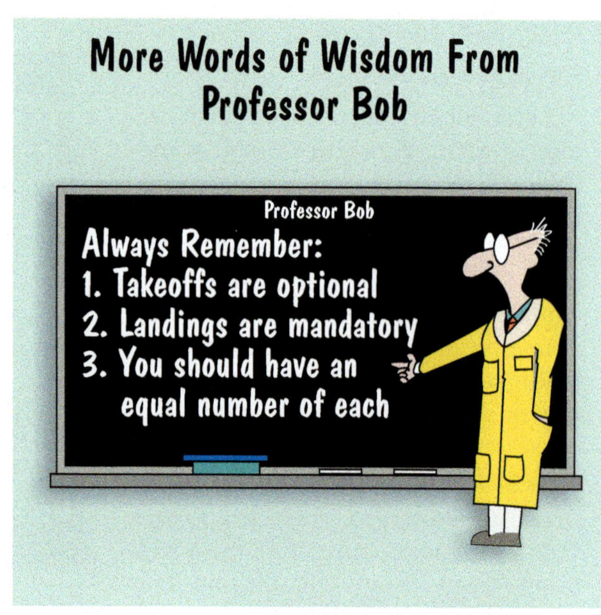

distance, as shown in Figure 26. This is not your precise horizontal distance from the station. If you're more than a few nautical miles from the station, slant range can be considered equal to horizontal range. However, if you're directly over the station, then DME errors can be rather large. Airplane B's DME reads one nautical mile (approximately 6,000 feet) yet it is directly over the station. Be cognizant of large horizontal errors when close to the station.

Position Fixing With DME – Do you have to be tracking a VOR radial to obtain DME information? Absolutely not. You need not be tracking to or from any VOR (VORTAC or VOR/DME) station to obtain your distance from that station. Simply select the VOR frequency in the DME receiver and read the DME display.

DME offers several possibilities for identifying your position. Figure 27 shows several examples. Figure 27A shows an airplane on the 130 degree radial at 10 miles from the station. That's a very precise position fix.

Figure 27B shows the airplane on the LCB 200 degree radial at seven miles from the BAD VOR. Figure 27C shows the airplane at the intersection of two DME arcs from separate VOR stations. Use whatever combination of navaids you like to fix your position.

With VOR and DME it sure is difficult to get lost. But pilots still do it. A sly thinking pilot called air traffic control and said, "Hey fellows, this is 2132 Bravo, I was wondering if you folks could help me out a little." He was lost and ATC knew it. ATC responded with, "32B, are you lost?" He replied, "No sir. Why I just purchased some new navigational equipment and wanted to confirm its indication with what you have on your screen. So, how about telling me where you think I'm at, huh?" No doubt about it, he was lost. If you think VOR and DME is wonderful, just wait until you read about something known as area navigation or RNAV equipment.

Area Navigation – RNAV

Area navigation or *RNAV* (pronounced *R-nav*) is a navigational process allowing point-to-point navigation without requiring that you overfly any navigational aids. Simply stated, if you have RNAV equipment on board you can fly *direct* from one airport to another without having to follow traditional navigational routes, i.e., airways.

While airways are nice to have, they are not always the fastest route between two places. They often don't connect the places between which you want to travel, at least not directly. Instead of your path being a string directly connecting the two

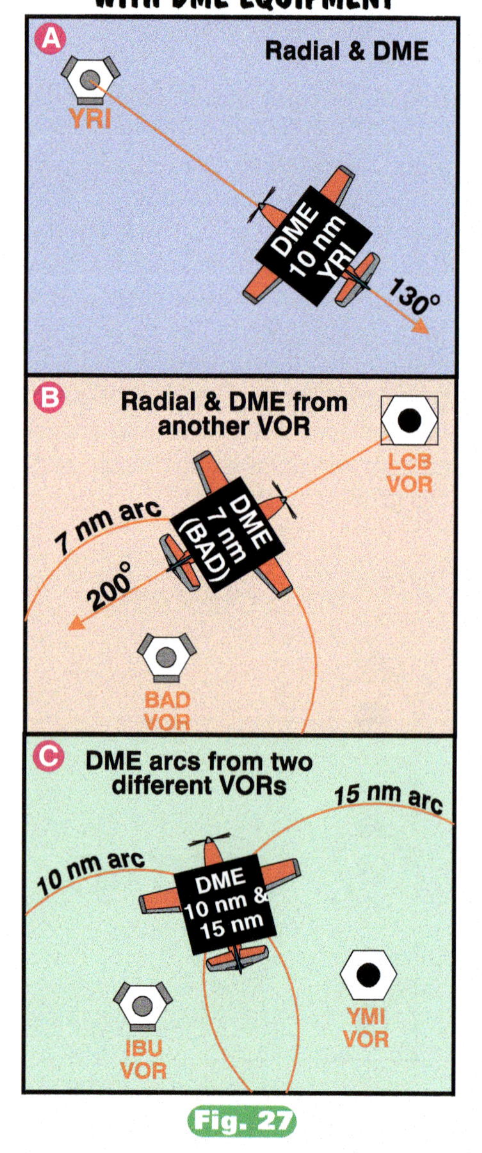

GLOBAL POSITIONING SYSTEM (GPS)

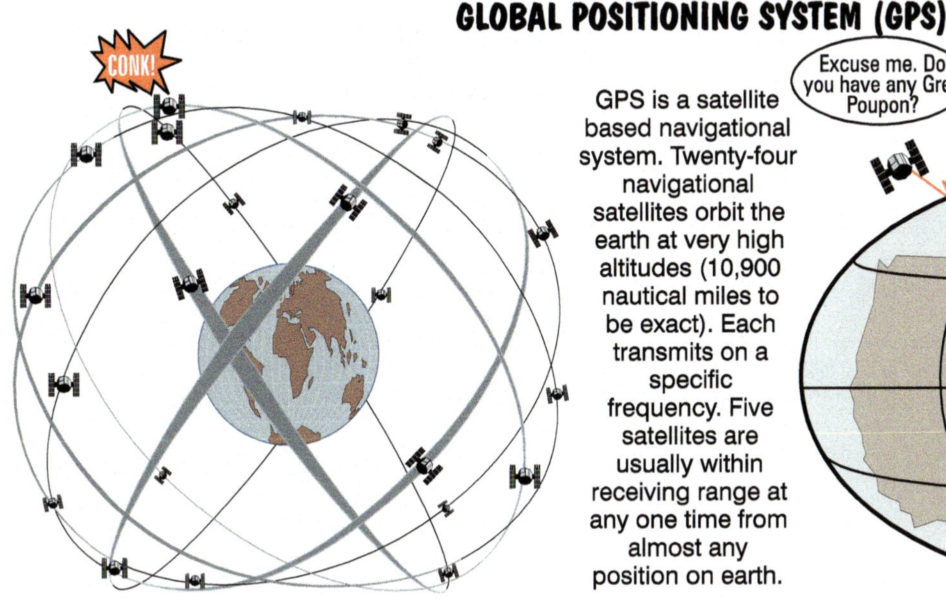

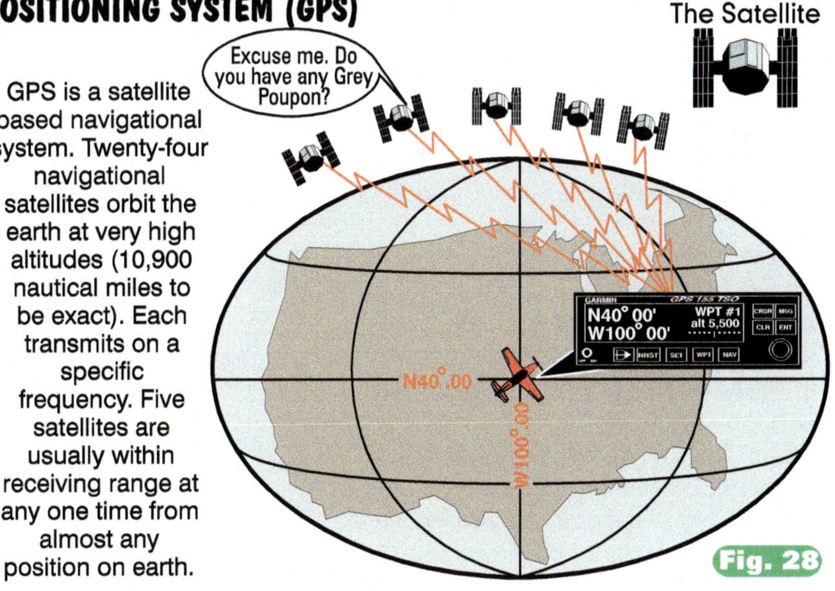

Fig. 28

points, following airways can make your route look more like a piece of spaghetti that's been used to play crack-the-whip.

Pilots are odd creatures. They love to fly, which should mean they want to spend as long as they can in the air. Which they do. Except they always want to get where they're going as quickly as possible. Yes, it *is* a contradiction.

RNAV offers the opportunity to pull the string taut and get from Point A to Point B by the most direct route possible.

In today's modern airspace system, RNAV is accomplished by use of the Global Positioning System or GPS. Let's take a look at how this marvelous satellite navigation system works.

The Global Positioning System—GPS

It's a bird, it's a plane, it's a . . .satellite?

Start the 2001 theme. Beam me up, Scotty. We now glide from science fiction to science fact. You can, today, at low cost and no fuss, navigate using satellites, and more and more pilots are doing it every day. There is no doubt that the Global Positioning System (GPS) has become the dominant form of navigation worldwide.

Originally developed by and for the military, GPS was radionapped by the civilian population. It's easy to understand why. GPS provides highly accurate position information, a signal that's subject to very little distortion, and certainly no line-of-sight problems. Besides that, it's cool.

GPS is in many ways like taking all the ground-based navigation stations and launching them into orbit. The receiver in your airplane (or in your hand) locks onto signals from several satellites all at once. By knowing the exact location of each satellite and precisely matching timing with its onboard atomic clock, the GPS receiver can figure out where *it* is and do so with an accuracy of less than three meters horizontally. (My friend, if you manage to get lost while using GPS, then you're REALLY lost.)

For your GPS receiver to determine a three dimensional fix (latitude, longitude and altitude), at least four satellites must be in view (although a minimum of five satellites are usually in view by a user anywhere on earth). The receiver can compute its position with only three satellites in view but it must be provided with altitude information to do so.

GPS is *much more* accurate than other forms of navigation. As a student of mine said, "Wow, with GPS you know exactly where you're lost at!" I looked at him and said, "Hey, just because your friends say weird things doesn't mean..."

Not only does GPS locate your latitude and longitude position, it can also locate you vertically (provide altitude information above sea level). Figure 28 shows a typical GPS system and a few of its associated satellites. GPS can do everything VOR does for you and much, much more.

GPS allows you to navigate to and from points in space known as *waypoints*. Waypoints are defined by both latitude and longitude coordinates. You can dial these coordinates directly into your GPS, or you can list the letter/number identifiers of the airport or intersection to which you desire to travel since your GPS has preprogrammed coordinates for these locations (Figure 29).

The Digital Chart Supplement provides you with the latitude and longitude coordinates of an airport (position 1).

PORTLAND-TROUTDALE (TTD) 10 E UTC–8(–7DT) N45°32.96′ W122°24.08′ **SEATTLE**
35 B S4 **FUEL** 100LL, JET A **H-1A, L-1C**
RWY 07-25: H5400X150 (ASPH) S-19, D-25 MIRL **IAP**
RWY 07: REIL. VASI(V4L)—GA 3.0° TCH 50′. Tree. **RWY 25:** REIL. VASI(V4L)—GA 3.0° 1 . Tree.
AIRPORT REMARKS: Attended 1500-0600Z‡. CAUTION: Migratory flocks of waterfowl on and in vicinity of arpt.
ACTIVATE MIRL Rwy 07-25—CTAF.
WEATHER DATA SOURCES: LAWRS

Fig. 29

For instance, if you wanted to fly cross country on a flight from Rod's Municipal airport to Bob's International airport, you might program your GPS unit for two waypoints as shown in Figure 30. Waypoint No. 1 takes you to the outside of the restricted area and waypoint No. 2 is located at Bob's International airport.

After departure, you'd fly directly to waypoint No. 1, thus avoiding the restricted area. Then you'd fly directly to Bob's International airport on waypoint No. 2. With GPS, when following a predetermined flight plan, you typically track from waypoint to waypoint, known as To-To navigation. Once over a waypoint, you select the next waypoint along your navigation route. On GPS units, you'll see bearing, track and distance information as well as a course deviation indicator, as shown in Figure 31.

AVOIDING RESTRICTED (or other) AREAS WITH GPS NAVIGATION

Two waypoints are used for this flight: Waypoint #1 helps avoid the restricted area and waypoint #2 is located at Bob's airport. Both waypoints are defined by latitude and longitude coordinates. You can find the latitude and longitude coordinates required to designate your own waypoints by looking at your aeronautical sectional chart.

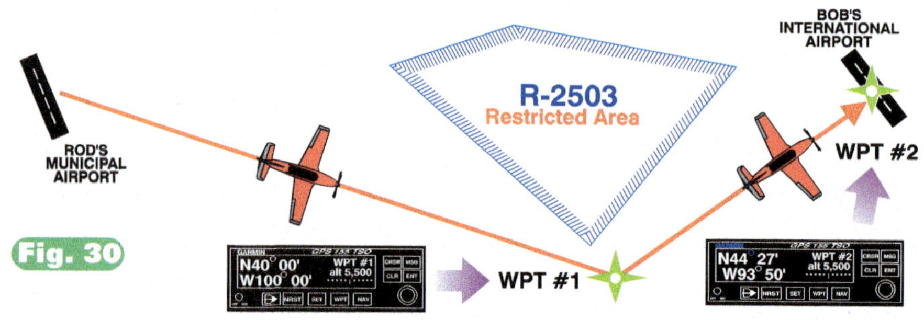

Fig. 30

HOW GPS UNITS PRESENTS INFORMATION

GPS units vary in their display of information of distance, groundspeed, bearing and estimated time enroute. Directly below is an example of the Garmin 150 display and below that is the newer Garmin 530W display. Same information, but in a slightly different format.

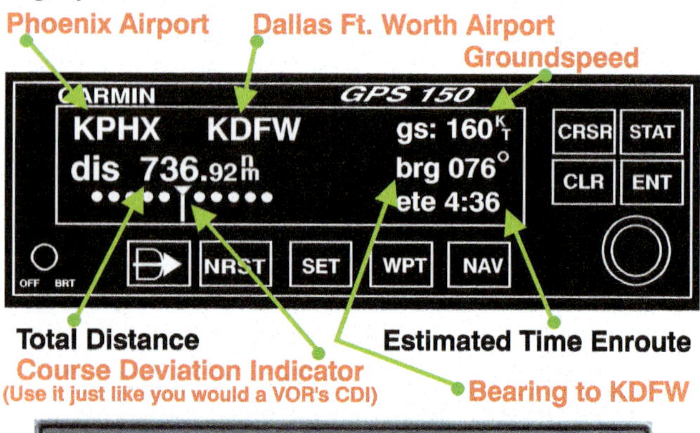

With Garmin's modern 530W GPS unit, track information can be read on the screen or on the airplane's HSI.

Fig. 31

One of the things that distinguishes GPS from VOR-based RNAV, is that GPS works virtually everywhere on the planet. Its operation is virtually unaffected by distance from the station (thank goodness, since the station is in outer space!), location, or weather. You can be out in the Sahara desert or on top of Everest and still obtain accurate GPS signals for navigation (of course, if you're on the top of Mt. Everest, you shouldn't need GPS to tell you where you are). In fact, many backpackers now carry handheld GPS units.

A friend of mine has a small Cherokee 140 with 3 VORs, 2 GPS units on board. He parks his airplane at Long Beach International airport, goes away for two days, comes back, and can't remember where he parked his plane. He needs GPS (or a LoJack system) to tell him where his airplane is.

The Global Positioning System

GPS: Details, Details

GPS is the most sophisticated form of area navigation. By telling your GPS that you want to go from your present position (the GPS always knows its current lat and long after you turn its power on) to a distant waypoint, it electronically knows where to point your airplane's nose in order to get there. GPS units typically tell you where to go by showing the bearing to that waypoint, or by providing a course deviation indicator on a display similar to that of a common VOR (or the GPS may be slaved to the omni display—VOR or HSI—in your airplane).

Now, if you had to look up the latitude and longitude of the destination waypoint for every trip, you'd go wacko and probably never go anywhere. Fortunately, GPS units have databases with the lat/long information for nearly all important airports, aerial intersections, navigation aids and other significant places. You need only select the name or letter/number identifier of any airport, intersection, or navaid in the GPS, push a few buttons/knobs, and bingo (that magic word you learned in church), you're on your way to that place (Figure 32).

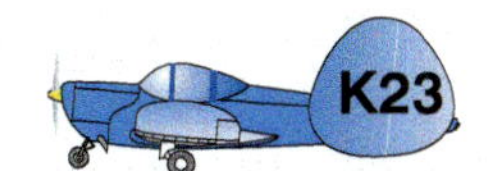

How GPS Works Inside

The Mask Angle

The little GPS receiver in your panel (or hand) is a rather remarkable device. It's doing all the things you wished you'd done in math class, such as getting the right answer, and it's doing them a *lot* quicker than you and I ever did.

Ranging and calculation of position from a group of satellites in space, which act as precise reference points, is the basis of operation for GPS operation. GPS receivers use data from a minimum of four satellites above something known as the *mask angle,* as shown to the right (the lowest angle above the horizon at which the GPS unit can use a satellite). The GPS takes complex information from four or more satellites and in a virtual instant calculates where it and you are. Try doing *that* in your head, whiz kid.

GPS receivers measure what we might best call a "working distance" from a satellite, using the travel time of a radio signal (even though no actual radio may be involved). Because the clock in the airborne receiver is not nearly as accurate as the atomic clock carried on each satellite, the elapsed time for the signal to reach the receiver is not known with perfect accuracy. However, the answer is equally incorrect for each satellite being observed, which is what enables the receiver to eventually calculate the correct answer.

Multiplying the approximated elapsed time by the speed of light (the rate at which the signal traveled from satellite to receiver) yields the working distance also known as the *pseudorange*.

In addition to knowing the pseudorange to a satellite, your little GPS receiver needs to know the satellite's exact position in space, which is known as its *ephemeris*. Sounds temporary, doesn't it? Each satellite transmits information about its exact orbital location, which the GPS receiver uses to precisely establish the position of the satellite.

Using the calculated pseudorange and position information supplied by the satellite, the GPS receiver/processor mathematically determines its position by calculating the one precise spot (accurate to within about 60 feet) at which a mathematically-constructed sphere (actually, a hyperboloid, for those who really liked math class) around each of the satellites' intersects. This sphere has a radius equal to the time delay between the satellite and the receiver multiplied by the speed of light, and you need a minimum of four hyperboloids to mathematically arrive at one unique point in space.Yes, really. And frequently, too. While doing that calculation once would probably take you all day (or the rest of your life) with pencil and paper, your GPS unit repeats it many times every minute and it never gets tired or wants to go to recess.

While it's at it, and to keep from getting bored while onboard, the GPS receiver computes navigational values (e.g., distance and bearing to a waypoint, groundspeed, crosstrack error, dinner time, etc.) by using the aircraft's known latitude/longitude and referencing these to a database built into the receiver.

Let's say, for instance, that you wanted to go to WACKO intersection, as shown in Figure 32, position A. Select the letters WACKO in the GPS's window, and push the appropriate buttons. Now you legitimately have the means to go WACKO. If your GPS has a moving map display, you can see your track to WACKO (or, your tracko to wacko) along with other information such as groundspeed, track, crosstrack error (more on this in a bit) and so on (Figures 32B and C).

GPS is only one form of area navigation. For instance, airliners have LNAV (lateral navigation) equipment. Airliners also have flight management systems (FMS), VLF/Omega, and the others we've already discussed. GPS is the most common form in use by general aviation IFR pilots. So it's the one we'll spend a lot of time discussing. From now on, if you see the term RNAV (GPS), it means area navigation based strictly on GPS.

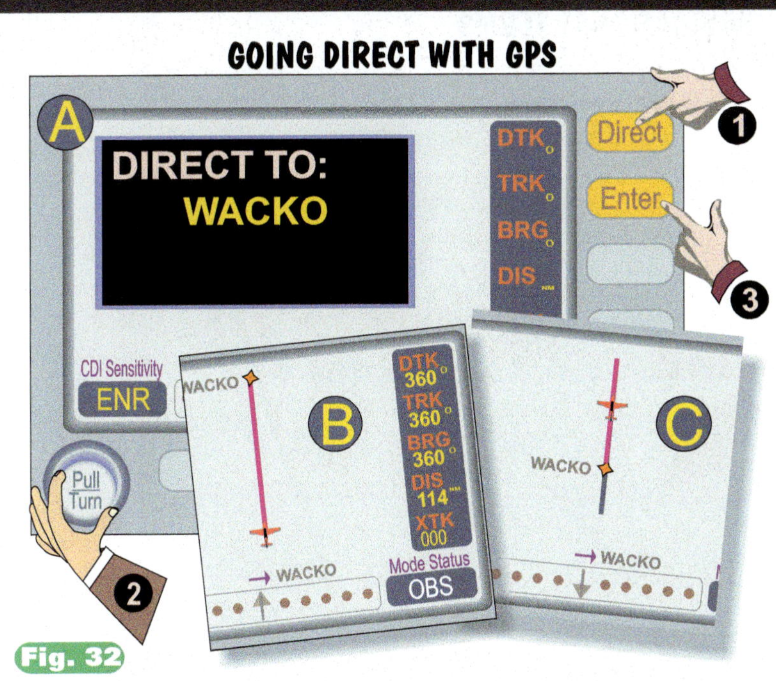

Going direct to an intersection is a fairly simple process with many GPS units, often involving no more than a few steps.

Terms You Need to Know: The Basics

Discussing RNAV (GPS) approaches requires us to come to terms with a few terms. Vocabulary is important here if you're going to get the concepts etched in your cranium. Figure 33 identifies some of the basic GPS navigation terms.

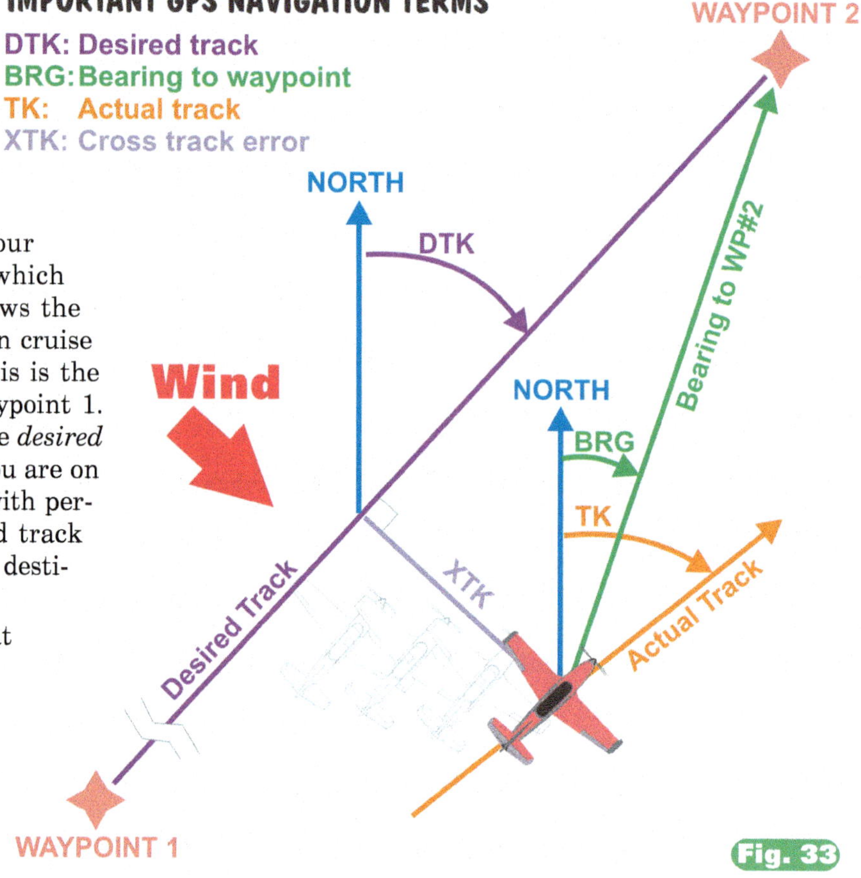

Fig. 33

Let's assume that you've programmed your GPS to take you to a destination airport, which we'll call Waypoint 2. Because the GPS knows the lat/long of the starting point (even if you're in cruise flight somewhere), it always assumes that this is the departure waypoint. We'll call this point Waypoint 1. The line between these two points is called the *desired track* (no doubt your instructor desires that you are on this track, too). Under a no-wind condition, with perfect navigational skills, you'd fly the desired track (DTK) heading and eventually arrive at your destination.

As you know, our universe is very good at amusing itself. One way it does this is by allowing your airplane to be blown around by the wind. The universe really gets a kick out of this, as your empennage gets a kick out of the wind. The airplane's *actual track* (TK) has now diverged from the DTK.

The universe just can't contain itself with all the fun it's having at your expense. GPS units show your actual track (TK). If this value is different from the desired track (DTK), then the universe has just scored big time. How far are you off course? The GPS will tell you by expressing the discrepancy in terms of something known as the *cross track error* (XTK).

IMPORTANT GPS NAVIGATIONAL TERMS

DTK: Desired track
BRG: Bearing to waypoint
TK: Actual track
XTK: Cross track error

WAYPOINT 2
Desired Track
Actual Track
Bearing to WP#2
Wind
NORTH
BRG
TK
WAYPOINT 1

Fig. 34

Figure 33 shows that the airplane is to the right of the desired track. For example, if the GPS says Fly Left 2.7 miles (different GPS units have different ways of displaying this), it means that you are offset to the right from your original course, the desired track (DTK), by 2.7 miles. You should obviously turn left to get back on course.

The XTK measurement is very important to you for several reasons. Obstacle-protected airspace is the primary one. If an airway's MEA provides protection for four nautical miles on each side of centerline, then an XTK of five nautical miles should raise your blood pressure to a little above that found in a fire hose. That's one reason XTK messages are written in terms such as *Fly left 5 miles.* And I would have no problem if they read, *Fly left 5 miles, you're about to hit a guy on a mountain bike.* XTKs are also valuable when flying RNAV (GPS) instrument approaches, where there is less tolerance for deviation from obstacle-protected airspace as you approach the airport.

If your airplane were off course to the right, as shown in Figure 33, then you'd have the option of going directly from your current spot to Waypoint 2, in lieu of re-intercepting the original desired track (DTK). Pilots often do this by pushing the GPS's Direct button (the one that's really worn down) and establishing a new desired track (DTK) to Waypoint 2. Of course, a pilot who keeps establishing new desired tracks every few minutes is homing to the station, not tracking to it. It's best not to keep homing, even if you're homely. Instead, you should use the GPS's bearing (BRG) information to help you identify and correct for wind.

THE AIRPORT IDENTIFIER

CARLSBAD
McCLELLAN–PALOMAR (CRQ) 3 SE UTC–8(–7DT) N33°07.70′ W117°16.81′
331 B S4 FUEL 100LL, JET A OX 3, 4 TPA—See Remarks ARFF Index A
RWY 06–24: H4897X150 (ASPH–PFC) S–60, D–80, DT–110 HIRL
LOS ANGELES
L–3C
IAP, AD

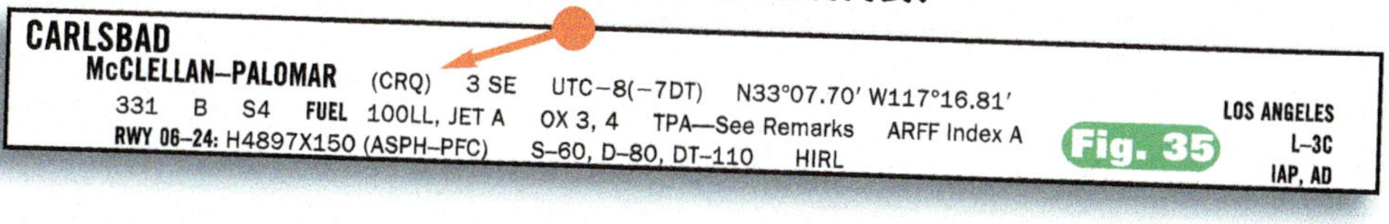

Fig. 35

The BRG is the heading you must fly to get to your next waypoint in a no wind condition. Suppose the pilot of the airplane in Figure 34 flies the bearing to the station on his heading indicator. Under a no wind condition, the bearing and the actual track (TK) should be the same. If these two values begin to differ, then wind is blowing the airplane off course. So, do something about it. Apply a wind correction. You'll know the wind correction is sufficient when the bearing to the station (BRG) remains the same as the airplane's actual track (TK). Now you're on your way directly to Waypoint 2, rather than using the ancient Greek philosophy of aerial navigation which was written by some guy name Homer for his skills at homing (OK, I made this one up).

Your GPS in Action

Let's take a look at how to use GPS for basic navigation. We'll do so by seeing how a generic GPS unit is operated to go to a place and to fly a flight planned route. The intent here is not to teach you how all GPS units work. Instead, it's to show you what's common to most IFR-certified, panel-mounted GPS units. Keep in mind that for an installed GPS to be used for IFR enroute and approaches, your flight manual supplement must indicate that this unit is approved for IFR flight. Handheld GPS units are not legal for IFR enroute and approaches, although you can certainly use one for situational awareness.

Your GPS receiver (I'll just say GPS from now on) can take you to any point on the globe. Doing so requires it to figure out where it is at the moment, and know the latitude and longitude coordinates of the point to which you want to go. That's why we use aviation databases that include the names and letter/number identifiers for all the important spots on the globe (except for your house). We need only dial the letter/number identification for the airport, navaid, intersection, or user-defined waypoint into our GPS, push a button or two, and we're off (no, not off course, but off as in ready). Let's see how to find the airport identifier for our destination, so we don't get off course, off key, or off color.

Figure 35 shows a *Chart Supplement* excerpt for Carlsbad's McClellan-Palomar airport. Next to the airport's name is its identifier (CRQ) in parentheses. If your GPS requires that you manually enter the airport letter by letter (instead of spinning through a list of alphabetized airport identifiers), then you add a "K" in front so that it looks like KCRQ (Figure 36). If the airport's identifier contains numbers (e.g., L66, Q49, S52), place these identifiers directly into the GPS without the special K prefix. Keep in mind that the letter "K" identifies an airport in the continental United States while the letter "P" identifies airports in Alaska (with a few exceptions) and "C" identifies airports in Canada. If you're inserting a three-letter navaid identifier (as opposed to a four letter airport identifier) into the GPS, don't worry about the GPS confusing it with any three-number-letter airport identifiers. Navaid identifiers don't use numbers. Remember, there are many ways to look up airport and intersection identifiers. The *CS* is only one of many resources.

THE FIRST STEP IN GOING GPS DIRECT

DIRECT TO:
KCRQ
McClellen-Palomar
DTK
TRK
BRG
DIS
XTK
000
Direct
Enter
CDI Sensitivity
ENR
Mode Status
OBS
Pull Turn
Pull Turn
1
2
3

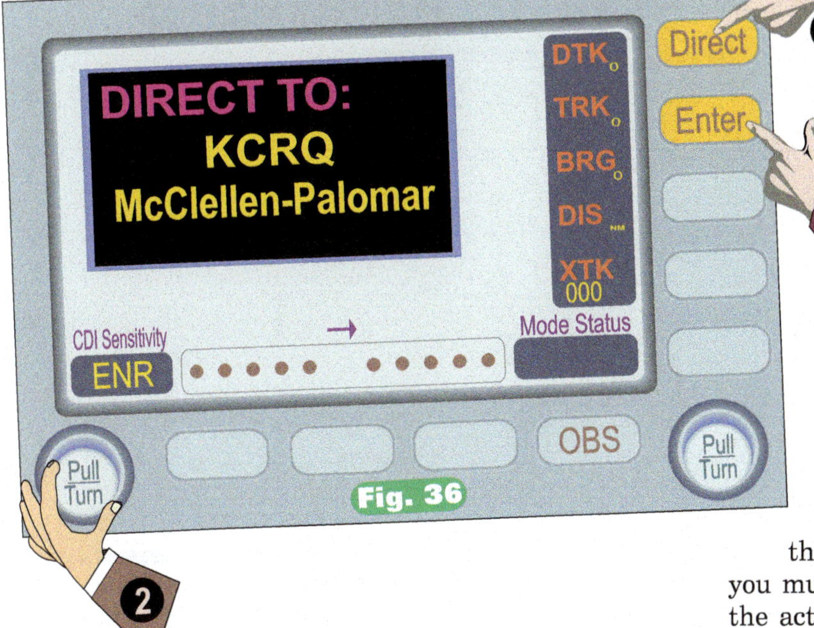

Fig. 36

Putting the GPS to use, let's go direct from our present position to KCRQ. With the GPS warmed up and a current database that's ready for use, we push the Direct button to activate a direct-to menu, as shown in Figure 36. The pull-turn knobs allow us to select KCRQ in the menu. Now we press Enter to make the airport the active waypoint. On some GPS units you must press Enter twice to confirm your selection as the active waypoint (and not because someone dropped and then kicked the box the GPS came in, either).

Along Track Distance (ATD): Getting the Right Point

Your GPS is not a DME, but sometimes the difference is lost on pilots, who in turn become lost when flying a GPS flight planned route.

One of the differences in a GPS operating in Leg Mode is that its mileage counter always counts down to the active waypoint (the one you're currently tracking to). This count is known as ATD or *along track distance*. Unlike a DME, the GPS is so smart that when it reaches the active waypoint in a flight planned route consisting of several waypoints, it automatically tees up the next waypoint for you so it's always counting down a distance to someplace ahead.

The figure on the right shows a flight planned route from JABAL to GUGEC to JLI to RICEE. When you fly this route in Leg Mode, the mileage you see on your GPS unit will be your distance "to" the active waypoint along the final approach course. If you're over JABAL, then GUGEC is the active waypoint (GPS window A) and the distance to the next waypoint, or 10 nm, is shown in the GPS window. As you fly from JABAL to GUGEC, the distance will count down, eventually reading 0.0 miles when you reach GUGEC. At that point, the distance countdown would start again (GPS window B), counting down until you reach the next active waypoint (JLI), and so on. When using GPS to fly to a selected series of waypoints, the distance you read in the GPS window will always be the along track distance to the active waypoint.

Our DTK, TRK, and BRG to KCRQ are 360 degrees at a distance of 114 nautical miles, as shown in Figure 37. The CDI built into the GPS shows an up arrow with a centered needle. This means we're going TO the active waypoint. The active waypoint (the one to which you're presently navigating) is shown above the CDI and right of the horizontal arrow. Enroute (ENR) is shown as the current flight mode; the CDI is operating with *enroute sensitivity*. This means that each dot on the built-in CDI scale represents one nautical mile off course (enroute sensitivity is the default sensitivity for most GPS units).

Notice what happens to the CDI's up/down triangle when you fly beyond KCRQ (Figure 38). The triangle flips downward, behaving just like the TO/FROM flag in an ordinary VOR, indicating that you've flown beyond the chosen waypoint. This is called *to/from* navigation, and it's one of two course status modes common to GPS units. This is known as the "OBS Mode."

The other tracking mode is called *to/to* navigation (referred to as "Leg Mode"). This is not something done only by a peg-leg pirate. In this case, you're flying from one waypoint to another in a sequence, just as if you were following a flight plan consisting of several segments, or flying an instrument approach made of up several waypoints. With to/to navigation, the GPS arrow references only the waypoint ahead of you, not the one you've just flown over. In to/to navigation you're always looking ahead. What's left behind is left behind for good. This is a very happy navigation mode, because you'll only see up arrows.

Your GPS not only takes you direct to any waypoint, it also lets you select any course you want to that waypoint.

GOING GPS DIRECT TO KCRQ

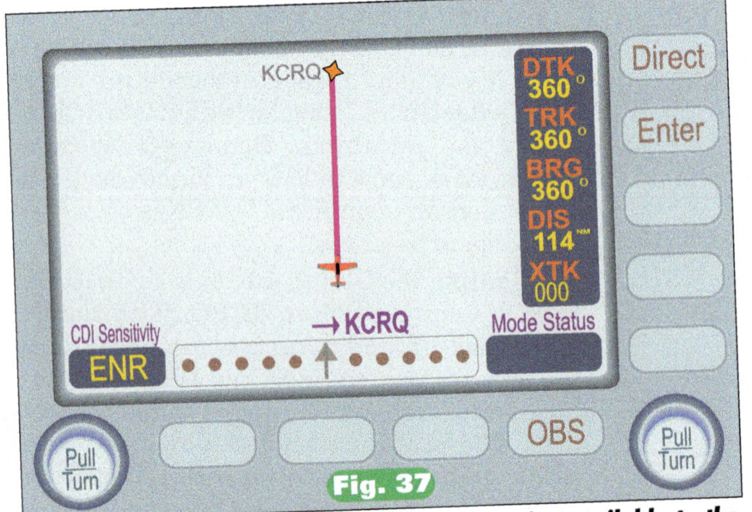

The GPS unit above shows the typical information available to the pilot when going direct to a waypoint. Heading, distance, groundspeed, and CDI info are available.

TO/FROM NAVIGATION

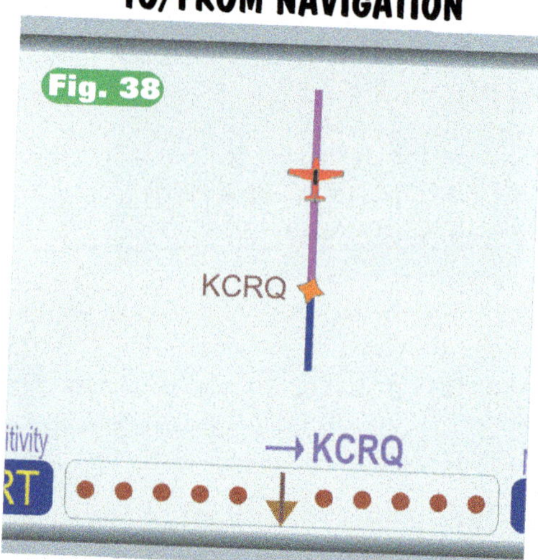

In OBS Mode you're using to/from navigation. Your GPS now acts similar to a VOR with the typical To/From indications in the form of a flipping triangle on the CDI.

For instance, Figure 39 shows that I've pushed the OBS button. Now the selection of a particular course to the active waypoint that's shown on the moving map is dependent on what I select with the HSI's OBS. In other words, the GPS unit is now allowing you to track to KCRQ as if this waypoint were a VOR station. With the OBS knob, you can select any of 360 individual courses to or from this waypoint. Are you impressed or what?

Let say you want to intercept and track the 330 degree course to this waypoint instead of flying direct to KCRQ, as you were doing in Figure 37. Perhaps you're opting for this specific course to avoid restricted airspace that's directly ahead of you (mainly because your airplane and your skivvies aren't made from bulletproof Kevlar). Reason is irrelevant here. First, you'll need to push the OBS button and rotate the HSI's OBS to 330 degrees (Figure 39). From the look of the HSI, it appears that you're a little less than five miles to the left of the course, based on a fly-right cross-track error of 4.9 miles (remember, a five dot deflection on the CDI represents five nautical miles deviation to the side of the selected course). On many GPS units with a moving map capable of color, the map will show a difference in color between the course to the active waypoint and the one beyond this waypoint. In this case, we'll show the course to the active waypoint in a lighter color than other courses shown on this map.

When you intercept the 330 course, the needle in the HSI will, once again, center with a TO (up triangle) indication, as shown in Figure 40. This GPS is set to read track-up on its display. Some can be set to read north up, which can make you throw up if you don't know how to select the desired option. Once you intercept and are tracking the course, that course is shown vertically on the map.

As you fly beyond the waypoint, as shown in Figure 41, the HSI shows a FROM (down triangle) indication. I'm showing you this again because I want to remind you that when the GPS's OBS function is selected, the active waypoint acts somewhat like a VOR station. This allows you to pick and choose any course you want, and track either to or from it just as you would when tracking to or from a VOR station.

With this basic understanding of GPS in hand (and in mind), let's take a look at flying from waypoint to waypoint as you'll typically do on a VFR flight with several flight planned legs. Once you learn how to do this, you'll be able to get a leg up on everyone who navigates without benefit of GPS.

Flight Plans Made of Several Waypoints

Most GPS units allow you to enter a flight plan by pressing the FPL button. I'm not speaking of an FAA flight plan here. Instead, I'm referring to a series of waypoints that make up a longer route of your choosing. From here, you enter waypoint after waypoint, using the

TO/FROM NAVIGATION WITH GPS

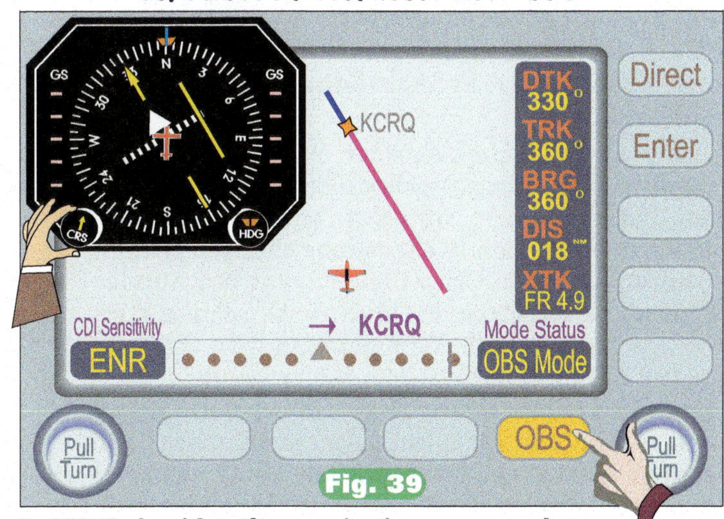

In OBS Mode with to/from navigation, you can select a specific course on which you can fly to or from a particular waypoint.

TO/FROM NAVIGATION WITH GPS

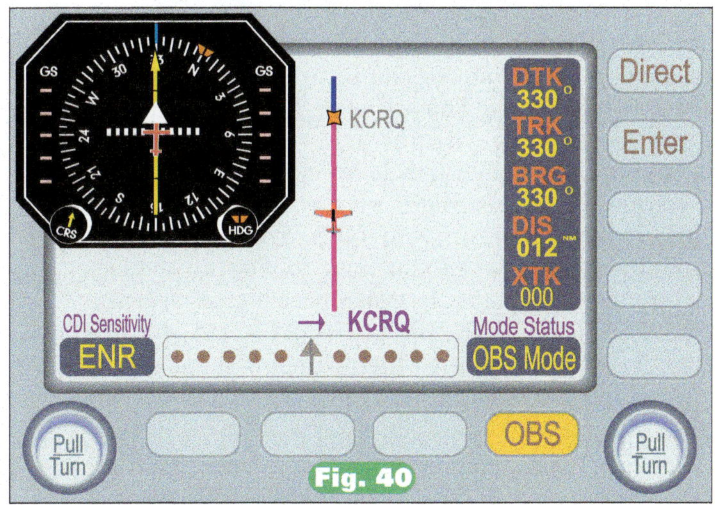

When intercepting the desired bearing, you'd turn inbound and track it as you would a VOR course.

GPS IN OBS MODE

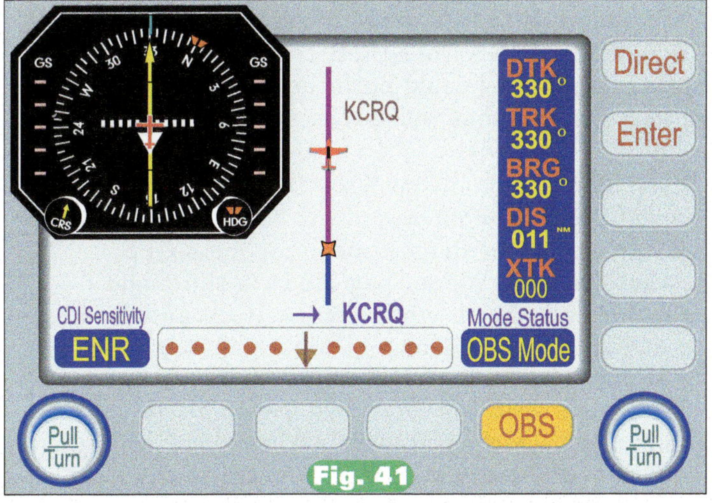

When flying beyond the active waypoint the TO/FROM triangle flips to a FROM indication.

method offered by the personality of your particular GPS (Figure 42). These waypoints can be made up of VORs, intersections, and/or points you choose on a sectional chart defined by their latitude and longitude coordinates.

Let's say you were over John Wayne airport and wanted to fly to Long Beach airport, and then on to Santa Barbara airport, with San Francisco airport as your final destination (we'll assume that you're high enough to avoid the Class B airspace at Los Angeles and won't need a clearance to enter it). In most GPS units, you can activate the flight plan with the push of a few buttons/knobs. (Note: the active flight plan window shows you the route you're currently flying. On most GPS units, you can have several other flight planned routes stored for future use. Using them simply means bringing these routes to the active flight plan window by pushing a button or two or three or four.) After you enter the waypoints or activate a stored flight plan, you can begin the trip, as shown in Figure 43.

In our GPS unit, the waypoint identifiers KSNA and KLGB, found above the internal CDI, show the leg you're flying. The active flight plan window shows the same leg with the arrow indicating that the current leg of the flight is from KSNA to KLGB. Of course, the active flight plan window may not be continuously visible in your GPS. You may have to manually select it when you want to view all the legs in your planned flight. It's also possible to view the route data (DTK, TRK, BRG, DIS, XTK, etc.) for the active leg of your planned flight. I show these values as already selected and active on our virtual GPS unit.

Figure 43 shows something that is very different and very important. The Mode status indicator now depicts something called Leg Mode. Recall that when we push the OBS button, the Mode status indicator reads OBS Mode. This means that we can manually choose the specific route we want to fly to any specific waypoint. In other words, if the direct route shown from KSNA to KLGB took me near restricted airspace, I could push the OBS button and select a route that would take me around it, as shown in Figure 44.

If you didn't manually push the OBS button to enter OBS Mode, what would the Mode status indicator read? The default mode for most GPS units is often Leg Mode. Leg Mode is the mode you'll normally be in when you activate and fly a stored flight plan, as shown in Figure 45. It's called Leg Mode because the GPS automatically creates direct legs between the individual waypoints in your planned flight. After you overfly a waypoint in Leg Mode, the GPS automatically sequences to the next waypoint in your flight. Remember, this is what is meant by the term "to/to" navigation.

CREATING A GPS FLIGHT PLAN

GPS can be used to create a series of flight planned legs. When the flight plan is activated, you'll fly from one leg to the next in to/to navigation in Leg Mode.

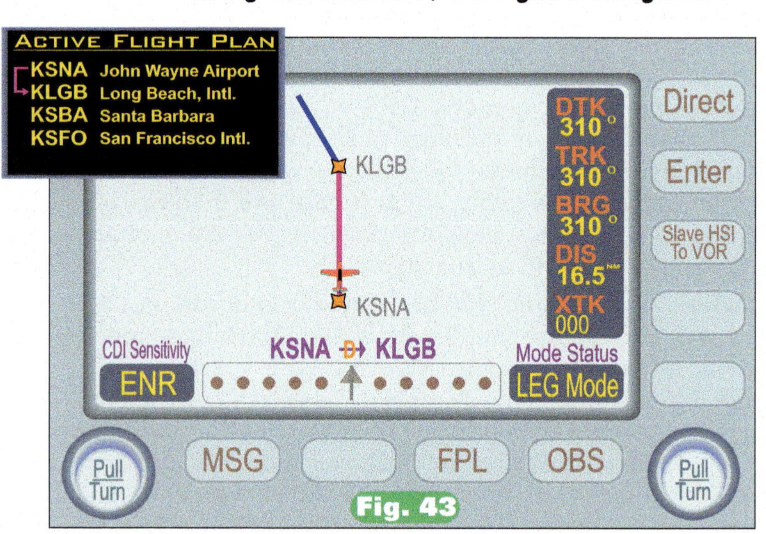

Once the GPS flight plan is activated (meaning that you push the appropriate buttons in the GPS window), you'll see the active leg in one color while the next leg to be flown will usually be identified by another color.

Sometimes it's necessary to leave Leg Mode for OBS Mode to accomplish a specific navigational task.

In Leg Mode, the moving map always shows your relationship to the waypoint ahead of you, not from the waypoint behind you. That's why the arrow in the CDI points up (a TO indication) and continues to point up as the GPS references the next waypoint in the route.

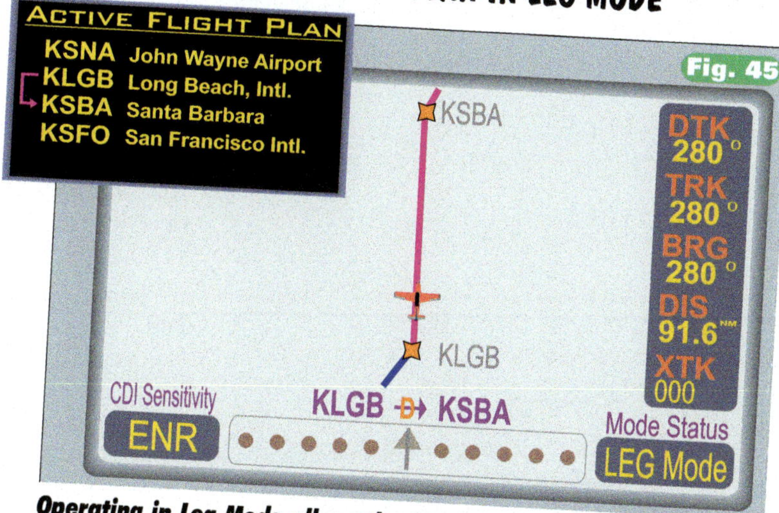

Operating in Leg Mode allows the GPS unit to automatically display the next waypoint and leg of flight (thus, the name Leg Mode).

Figure 45 shows this process in action, as KLGB is crossed. This is why the continued referencing to the next waypoint in the flight plan is sometimes called *auto-sequencing*. After you cross over a waypoint in your flight plan, the GPS literally puts that behind you and automatically sequences to the next waypoint in the flight plan.

You can suspend Leg Mode at any time by pushing the OBS button. Doing this suspends the GPS's auto-sequencing between waypoints in your active flight plan. Why would you want to suspend the Leg Mode? As stated earlier, you might want to use OBS Mode to select a different course to avoid a temporary flight restriction that just became active. Once you've avoided the flight restriction, pushing the OBS button returns the GPS to Leg Mode, resumes auto-sequencing and continues your flight planned route to San Francisco.

Now that you understand flight plans, you're ready to fly any of the flight planned routes stored in your GPS's database. That's right. You can sit on the ground and create all types of flight planned routes in your GPS unit and store them for future reference. You might, for instance, create a route that takes you around Class B airspace when departing your local airport. Prior to departure, all you need to do is load the flight planned route, activate it and fly it. Easy, right? Keep in mind that not all GPS units are alike. They do, however, have many similarities and most of what I'm describing is true for most units. I can't overemphasize how important it is for you to study the GPS owner's manual and learn all the details peculiar to the unit you're flying with. It's also very helpful to download the GPS PC simulator that many manufacturers make available for their products.

Automatic Direction Finding (ADF) Navigation

Well, I've left the first for last.

Automatic Direction Finding (ADF) equipment is the oldest type of radionavigational aid still in use. It is not cool. It is not slick. It is not particularly precise. But it *is* found in many airplanes, from trainers to jumbo jets, and it's a major item in places such as Alaska, where VORs are about as frequent as housebroken caribou.

ADF has persisted because of its simplicity and reliability. Yes, I realize that few airplanes today have ADF equipment, but many primary flight displays have the ability to portray an RMI needle that's slaved to your GPS. So even with modern technology, you have the option of using an ADF needle superimposed on a rotating magnetic compass (known as an RMI or radio magnetic indicator). How's that for an example of technological longevity? But let's get back to basic ADF navigation.

Because the ADF operates on a relatively low-frequency (long wavelength) signal, these signals can travel very long distances. The ADF isn't subject to the line-of-sight limitations of VOR, and you don't need very sophisticated equipment to decode it. Perhaps the *real* reason ADF has persisted for so many years is that it receives standard AM broadcast frequencies, enabling you to hear the baseball game or country-and-western wails while enroute. You'll see why this is of more-than-obvious significance in a second.

THE AUTOMATIC DIRECTION FINDER (ADF)

The ADF (automatic direction finder) receiver (bottom) receives signals from non directional radio beacons (dashed circles). The ADF indicator's needle points directly to that NDB. The top of the ADF indicator always represents The nose of the airplane.

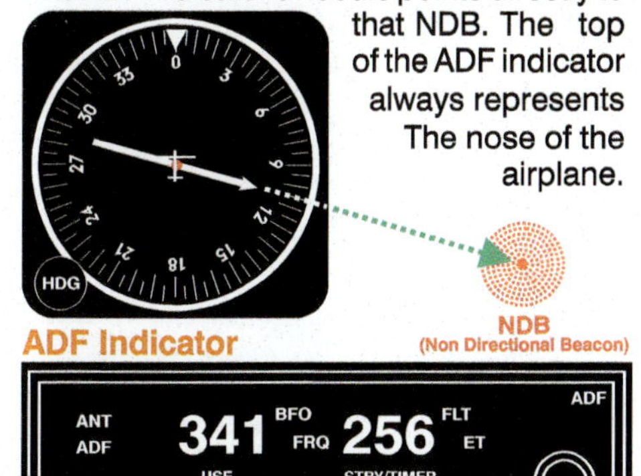

Figure 46 shows a typical ADF set. Airborne ADF equipment consists of a rotating needle resting over a fixed or manually rotated compass card. The needle always points to a nondirectional beacon (NDB), which is the source of the ADF signal. It's a *nondirectional* beacon because the signal is radiated equally in all directions. There are no NDB radials.

The ADF sense antenna is long because the low frequency wavelengths it receives are long.

Fig. 47

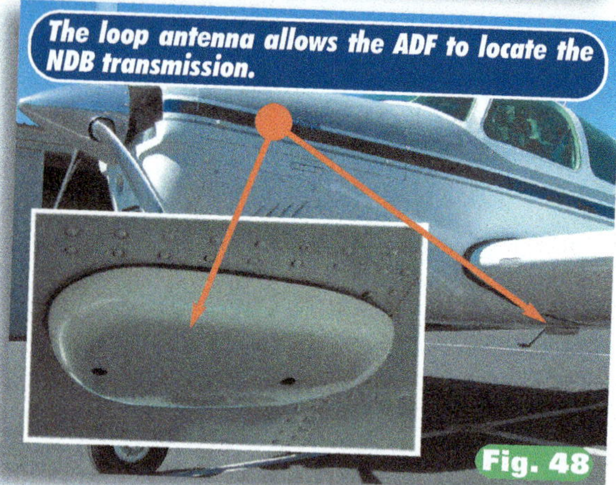

The loop antenna allows the ADF to locate the NDB transmission.

Fig. 48

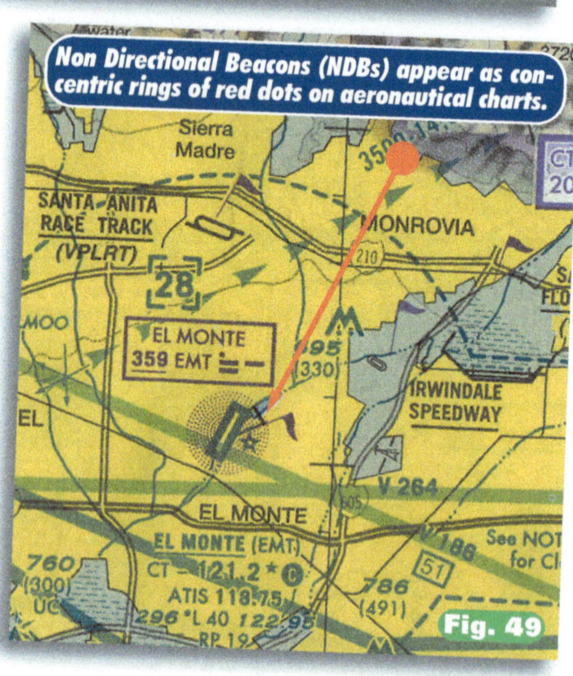

Non Directional Beacons (NDBs) appear as concentric rings of red dots on aeronautical charts.

Fig. 49

There is one other source of signals for your ADF. Yup, those radio stations playing that country music or the baseball game. If you can receive it on the ADF, you can fly to it. Every AM radio station in the country is an unofficial nondirectional beacon. During a cross country flight, one of my students insisted on listening to ball scores over the ADF. I called the Flight Service Station for a weather update. The FSS specialist delivered a less-than-happy weather forecast, then heard my student yelling at his favorite team in the background, "AH, FOR CRYING OUT LOUD, YOU CAN DO BETTER THAN THAT. GEESH!"

"Hey, I only report the weather, I don't make it," the specialist said.

Since even the smallest of towns usually has a radio station, you can home in on almost anywhere using the ADF. *Homing* is exactly what ADF does. In no frills terms, ADF takes you to the transmitting station (NDB). Enter the frequency for an NDB where (or near where) you want to go, then turn the plane until the ADF needle is pointing straight ahead. Follow it. When the needle gets erratic, then swings back in the opposite direction, you've just flown over the NDB (or station WXYZ).

There are a few subtle details, but if you get the concept that the needle points like a good hound dog on the trail of Porky the Pig, you've got the basics. Tune it and aim it.

Figure 46 shows a modern ADF unit with two frequencies selected: 341 kilohertz (KHz—thousands of cycles per second) and 256 KHz. One frequency (341 KHz) is in use and the other (256 KHz) is set for standby use. Many older ADFs you encounter will have three windows into which you dial the three numbers of the frequency you want, using mechanical switches.

Several other switches are present on typical ADF equipment. The switch marked *ADF* activates the ADF function (sometimes things actually are what they say they are). The needle will point to the NDB or radio station, and you will hear the station's audio transmission. Pilots often listen for the Morse code identification of the NDB as their only means of knowing the station is on the air. (Radio stations, of course, transmit rock 'n roll instead of Morse code.) ADFs don't have OFF flags to warn the pilot of signal reception loss. You can electronically disconnect the needle from the circuitry and still listen to NDB transmissions by selecting the ANT or antenna position.

Last, but not least, if you're looking for a good reason to keep the ADF in your airplane, remember this. The ADF needle can point to the location of those big airplane-catching radio antennas (assuming you've tuned your ADF equipment to their transmissions).

The TEST position allows you to determine if the ADF needle is indeed pointing to any NDB or simply drifting without being locked onto a transmission.

ADF antennas are easy to spot on the airplane. They're usually a long wire, strung almost from end to end on the airplane. The long wire is needed to receive the longer wavelength signal, as opposed to the higher frequencies used by VOR, DME and other radionavigational gear. The long, wire-type antenna shown in Figure 47 is the signal antenna. Underneath the aircraft is a loop antenna (Figure 48). This antenna establishes a signal direction. Sometimes both of these antennas are combined in a signal unit.

Figure 49 shows how NDBs (low frequency) non directional beacons appear on aeronautical charts. NDBs appear as concentric rings of expanding dots (normally red in color). Frequency and identification information is shown in the accompanying rectangular box.

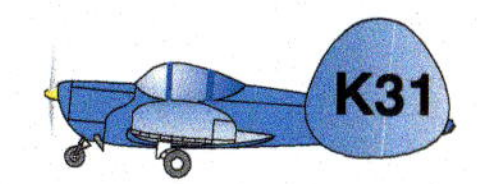

Remember, you never know when you might need the ADF for navigation assistance. For a closer look at the best ways to use the ADF, be sure and take a look at Postflight Briefings #11-2, #11-3 and #11-4.

Are We Where Yet?

Good job. You've gotten oriented (by now you certainly won't pardon the pun) to the basic types of radionavigational equipment you're likely to meet. Now you're ready to learn something about the weather, which can often keep you from getting to all the wonderful places your equipment can take you.

Postflight Briefing #11-1

REVERSE SENSING OF THE VOR NEEDLE

If you are attempting to go to the VOR with a FROM flag indication, the needle will indicate the course in the opposite or reverse direction as is shown by Airplanes D and E. If you mentally rotate Airplanes D and E in the direction of their OBS setting (or 140°), you'll see that their needles are correctly sensing course direction. For proper sensing, you must rotate the OBS of Airplanes C, D and E to 320°, since this is the direction of the inbound course to the VOR.

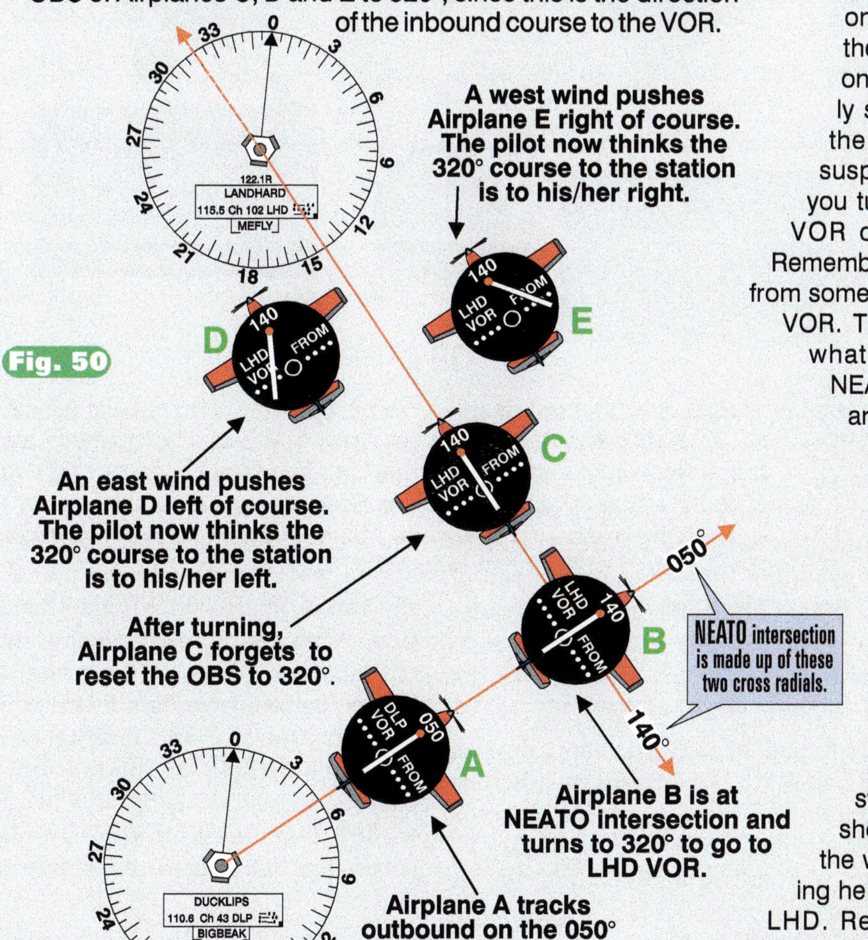

VOR REVERSE SENSING

Reverse sensing occurs when you try to go *to* a VOR with a FROM indication (or vice-versa). If you try to do this, the VOR needle will work opposite (reverse) of the way it normally does. In other words, if the selected course is shown to the left, it's actually to the right of the airplane. Figure 50 shows how this could happen.

Assume you have been instructed to fly outbound on the 050 degree course from DLP VOR to NEATO intersection as shown by airplane A. At NEATO you are to track to the LHD VOR on the 320 degree course (the reciprocal of the 140 degree course from the station). You only have one VOR in the aircraft and it's initially set to the DLP VOR with 050 degrees set in the OBS as shown by airplane A. When you suspect that you are near NEATO intersection you tune in the 140 degree course from the LHD VOR on your OBS as shown by airplane B. Remember, most pilots prefer to know their position from someplace when identifying an intersection with a VOR. There's nothing wrong with this, but watch what happens as your airplane approaches NEATO with your VOR tuned to the LHD VOR and the OBS set to 140 degree.

The VOR needle starts to center as shown by airplane B. As it does, most pilots will turn toward the LHD VOR attempting to fly the 140 degree course to LHD as shown by airplane C. The problem is that they often forget to rotate their OBS from 140 to 320 (the 180 degree reciprocal), which selects the same course *to* the station, instead of *from* the station.

If wind blows the airplane slightly southwest of the 320 degree course to the station as shown by airplane D, the needle shows a left deflection. This is reversed from the way it should be. The pilot may fly left thinking he or she will intercept the 320 degree route to LHD. Remember, if you're going to a VOR the TO/FROM flag should read TO not FROM. The heading you're flying and the course you've selected by the OBS should be similar, not 180 degrees in error.

If the pilot is slightly northeast of the route as shown by airplane E, the VOR shows a right needle with a FROM indication. This needle and flag indication makes sense if the airplane is heading 140 degrees. The pilot of airplane E will probably turn right, attempting to capture the route. You shouldn't need a burning bush to tell you that the most important rule in VOR navigation is, *The heading you are flying should be very similar to the number set by the OBS*. When flying a specific route TO or FROM a VOR there is one time when the heading and OBS setting won't be "precisely" the same—*when wind exists*.

Postflight Briefing #11-2

The Radio Magnetic Indicator (RMI)

Ever been in a Chinese restaurant with a large group? You get the food on a huge lazy Susan. The food spins round and round, the sauce stands still in the middle, and you pick what you want. It's egg roll on a roll, wonton on a turn.

The *radio magnetic indicator (RMI)* is the aviation version of this device. What it serves up is information. While not common in smaller GA aircraft, if you are fortunate enough to fly in something that has an RMI, you'll want to make full use of it.

An RMI is essentially a rotating needle mounted over a slaved compass, as shown in Figure 51. (A *slaved* compass is one where the rotating compass card is electronically connected to a magnetic compass.) The rotating needle is slaved to the compass card so that it always indicates the course to the VOR station with the head of the needle. The tail of the needle points to the course or radial from the station. The slaved compass card rotates like a heading indicator would. The airplane's heading can be found under the index at the top of the RMI. (The RMI needle information is correct only if the slaved compass is correct. Check it against the wet compass occasionally.)

The easiest way to learn how to use the RMI is to observe how the instrument's display orients you to a VOR station. Airplane A in Figure 52 is on a heading of 060 degrees, as indicated by the RMI's slaved compass. The RMI needle is pointing directly to the VOR station. Notice that Airplane A is physically located on the 360 degree course to the station (or the 180 degree radial from the station). Also notice that the RMI needle points to 360 degrees on the slaved compass and the tail points to 180 degrees.

OK, can you feel those neurons firing and synapses welding to form new ideas? This is really easy. The RMI needle always points to the course TO the VOR station. The tail of the RMI needle always points to the radial you're on FROM this station. What course is Airplane C on to the station? Yes, it's on the 180 degree course (needle's head) to the station and the 360 degree radial (needle's tail) from the station. Of course, Airplane C is flying a heading of 300 degrees and will fly right across the 360 degree radial from the station.

Airplane B, on the other hand, is headed directly toward the station on a heading of 270 degrees. Its RMI needle is pointing dead ahead at 270 degrees. Airplane B is headed to the station on the 270 degree course or inbound on the 090 degree radial (same thing). Airplane D is headed toward the station on the 090 degree

HOW THE RMI INDICATES COURSES AND RADIALS

The head of the RMI indicates your course to the VOR station. Simply turn to center the RMI needle at the top of the instrument and you'll be headed directly to the station. The tail of the RMI needle always tells you what radial you're on from the station.

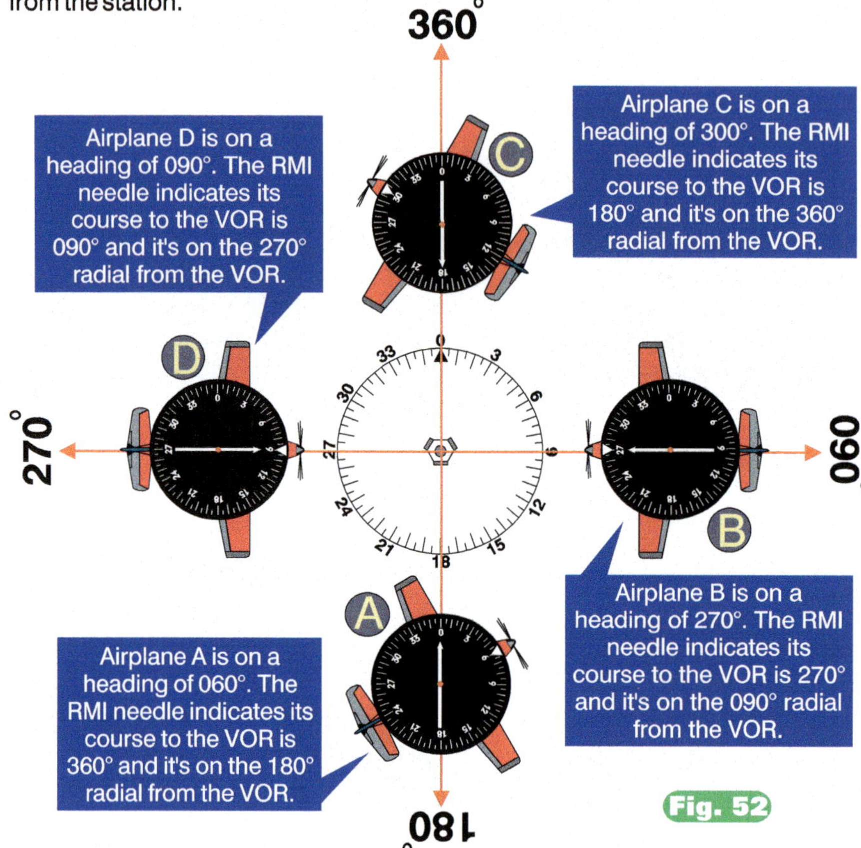

Fig. 52

THE RADIO MAGNETIC INDICATOR

The RMI (radio magnetic indicator) is essentially a heading indicator with a rotating needle on its face. The top of the needle points to the VOR station. The number the needle points to is the bearing or course to the VOR. The number the tail of the needle points to is the radial the airplane is on from the VOR.

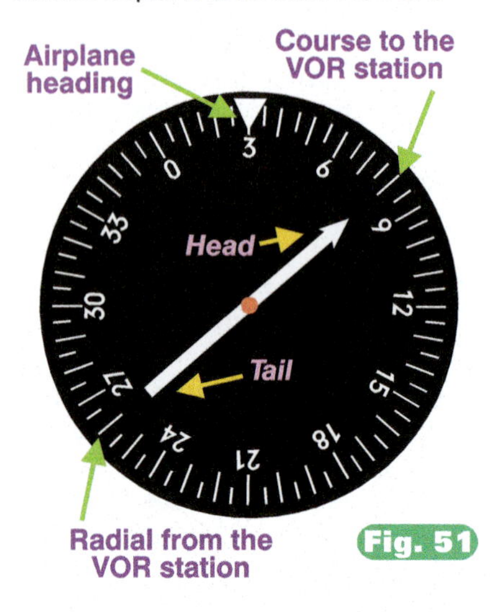

Fig. 51

DOUBLE NEEDLE RMI

The double-needle RMI can have either needle set to point to an NDB (non directional bearing) or a VOR station. Two selectors, each marked to represent a specific needle, are located at the bottom of the instrument.

Fig. 53

course or inbound on the 270 degree radial (same thing).

Orientation with the RMI is really simple. If you want to know what your course is to the station, just look at the number to which the RMI needle points. If you want to know what radial you're on from the station, simply look at the tail of the RMI needle. One last thing. Sometimes RMIs have two needles instead of one. To keep them from being confused with one another, the second needle is different, as shown in Figure 53. Each needle can be selected to represent VOR or ADF information. This is accomplished by the selection switches at the bottom of the instrument. We'll learn more about RMI usage when we cover ADF navigation next.

Before I begin Postflight Briefing #11-3, let me say that I was tempted to eliminate most of the ADF information that follows from this book. REALLY TEMPTED! Frankly, if you know how to determine the relative bearing and magnetic bearing to a station by using the formula on page K34, you can answer 99% of the knowledge exam questions on ADF. I'm leaving the information in simply because if you take the time to understand ADF principles, you'll never have trouble with any type of navigation.

Postflight Briefing #11-3

ADF: Bearing Down On Homing In

Look at the numbers on the compass card of the ADF display in Figure 54. They're fixed, in that the card doesn't automatically rotate like the compass card of an RMI. You can manually rotate the card, as we'll discuss later. For now, however, forget those numbers! Yes, that's right, forget them! As far as you're concerned right now, those numbers only identify 30 degree incremental positions to the left and right of the nose. Don't attach any significance to them. Treat each of these numbers like most people treat the Surgeon General's warnings on a cigarette package—know that it's there but don't look at it.

OK, here is one of the most powerful and simplest rules you'll ever see for navigation with the ADF. To go to any NDB station, simply tune in that station's frequency, identify it (usually by Morse code) and turn the airplane so the ADF needle points to the nose of the symbolic airplane on the ADF display, as shown in Figure 55, Airplanes A and B. The symbolic airplane represents the real airplane's orientation. It's always pointed

THE AUTOMATIC DIRECTION FINDER (ADF)

The numbers found around the ADF compass card must be manually rotated by turning the "HDG" knob. They are not part of a slaved (electric) gyro and do not reflect the airplane's heading. We normally leave the compass card set with a "0" under the index for basic ADF work. The "0" represents the actual airplane's nose.

Fig. 54

HOMING WITH THE ADF

The ADF indicator's needle points directly to the NDB. For Airplane A to go to the NDB it must turn right to center the needle on the ADF's nose (the "0" under the index). Keeping it there, the airplane travels to the NDB as shown by Airplane B. When over the station, the needle reverses direction pointing to the ADF's tail as shown by Airplane C.

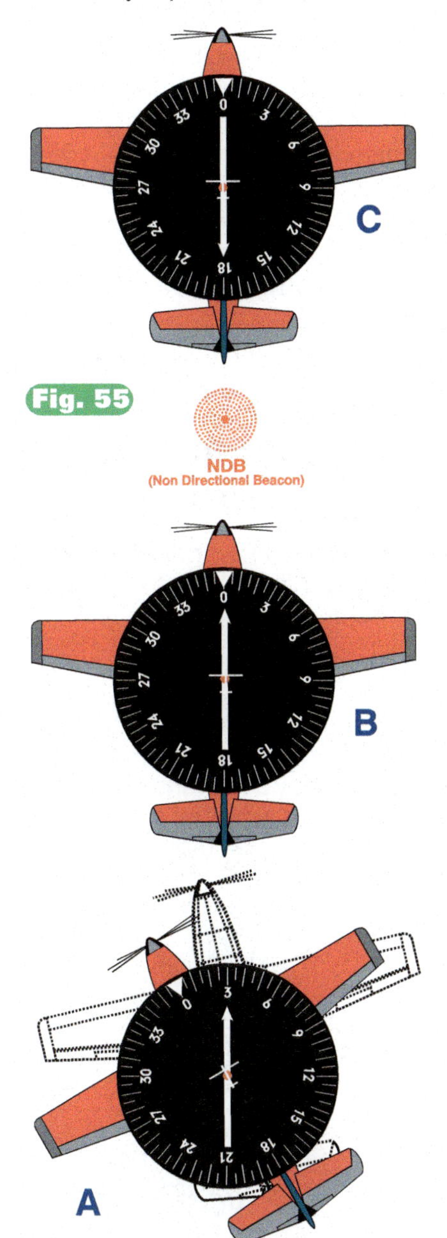

Fig. 55

toward the white triangle at the top of the ADF indicator, which represents the airplane's nose. Simply turn toward the tip of the needle to go to the station.

If you keep the needle centered at the top of the display you will eventually end up over the station. As you fly over the station the needle will swing to the tail as shown by Airplane C in Figure 55. This type of tracking is known as homing. It involves no wind correction, but it works every single time. Don't forget it. Figure 56 shows airplanes A, B and C homing directly to the Flynice NDB. Airplane E is flying directly away from the station by keeping the needle on the tail of the ADF display.

Airplane D's ADF needle points to the left of the nose. Making a left turn will center the needle at the top of the display. Airplane F's ADF needle shows the NDB station to the right of the airplane's nose. Turning right will center the needle at the top of the display.

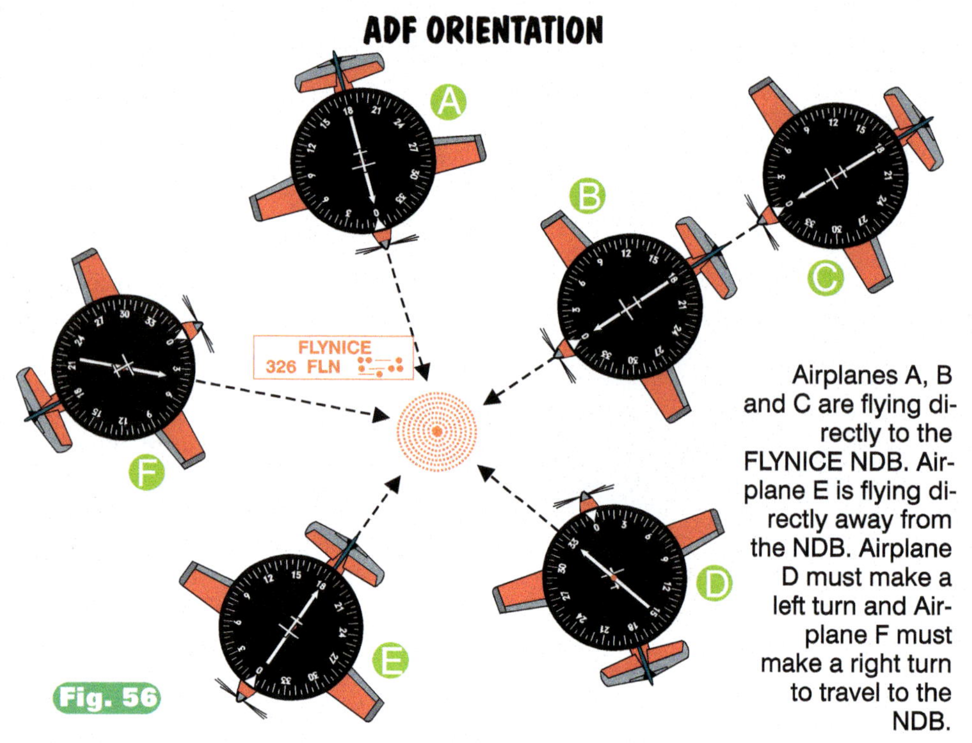

Airplanes A, B and C are flying directly to the FLYNICE NDB. Airplane E is flying directly away from the NDB. Airplane D must make a left turn and Airplane F must make a right turn to travel to the NDB.

Fig. 56

NDB AND VOR SIGNAL DIRECTIONS

The NDB signal is nondirectional in that it radiates its energy outward, in all directions, from its center.

NDB
Non Directional Beacon

VORs, on the other hand, are designed to radiate electromagnetic radiation by a reference and a variable phase signal so that 360 specific "directional" radials are identifiable.

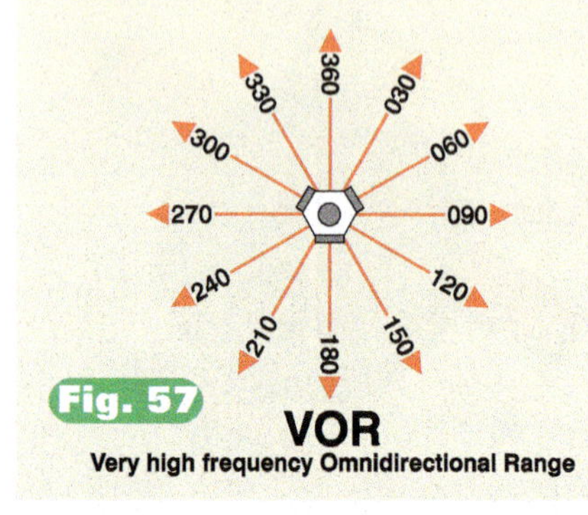

Fig. 57

VOR
Very high frequency Omnidirectional Range

Frankly, if I had my way, we'd stop here and consider ourselves done with the ADF discussion. All you really need to understand about ADF navigation is to know how to home with it. The private pilot knowledge exam, however, demands a slightly more sophisticated knowledge of ADF navigation. Study the following and find some solace in knowing that this information will help you become an overall better navigator (not a navigator who wears overalls).

Tracking a Magnetic Bearing – Homing is the easiest method of ADF navigation (perhaps it's called homing because pilots can always find their way home using this technique). There is another method, however, that allows you to intercept and track magnetic bearings directly to and from an NDB. This is done in much the same way as the RMI is used. Let's start from the beginning.

Figure 57 shows an NDB and a VOR station. NDBs are unlike VORs in that their signal is nondirectional. This means the NDB's signal radiates outward in all directions while VORs have 360 specific radials on which we can navigate. We can, however, imagine 360 bearings running through an NDB in much the same way courses run through a VOR. First, we need to define what a bearing is.

Examine the diagram in Figure 58. If you were instructed to fly from position A directly to position B, you could do so with great precision by using the VOR. You would track inbound on the 270 degree radial and outbound on the 090 degree radial. You would know your exact position with respect to these radials by looking at the VOR needle. Suppose you were asked to fly from position X directly to position Y using your

NDB vs. VOR ROUTES

Traveling along a VOR route is relatively easy. You simply select the appropriate course from A to B (the OBS is set to 090°) and keep the needle centered. Traveling along a similar route to and from an NDB isn't as simple as with VOR navigation. NDB navigation requires that you understand the concept of bearings to and from the station.

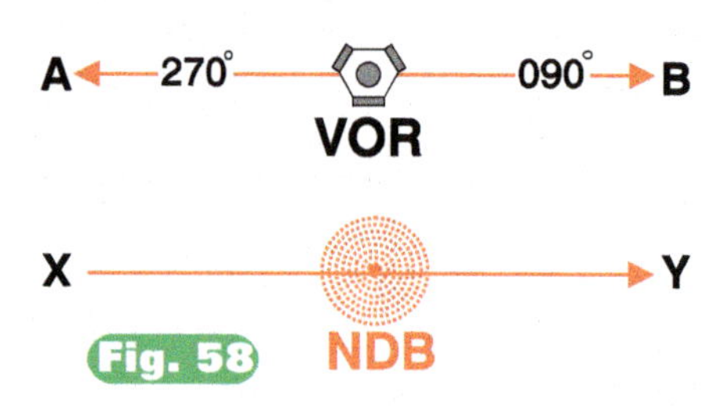

Fig. 58

ADF. How would you know your airplane is tracking directly along the specified course?

You need to know two things before answering this question. First, the airplane must be heading in a direction of 90 degrees (we'll assume no wind for these examples). Heading 90 degrees will certainly point you in the direction of location Y, as shown in Figure 59A. However, heading 90 degrees will also allow you to fly a parallel course offset from the originally desired path, as shown in Figure 59B. We need one additional bit of information. If the ADF needle points to the nose of the display airplane while it is heading 090 degrees, then it is precisely on the course from X to Y, as shown in Figure 59C.

After crossing the NDB station in Figure 59C, the airplane will be flying the targeted course to Y if its heading is 090 degrees and the ADF needle points directly to the tail. Airplanes flying a parallel route between X and Y in Figure 59D don't meet both requirements to be on the specific course.

In Figure 59D, both airplanes flying from X to Y are heading 090 degrees but the ADF needle points somewhere other than to the nose or the tail. A very important principle has just been uncovered. Even though NDBs are non directional in their signals, we can still fly specific directional routes using the ADF and our heading indicator. These routes are called magnetic bearings and they may be flown to or from an NDB.

Oh Baby, What a Flight!

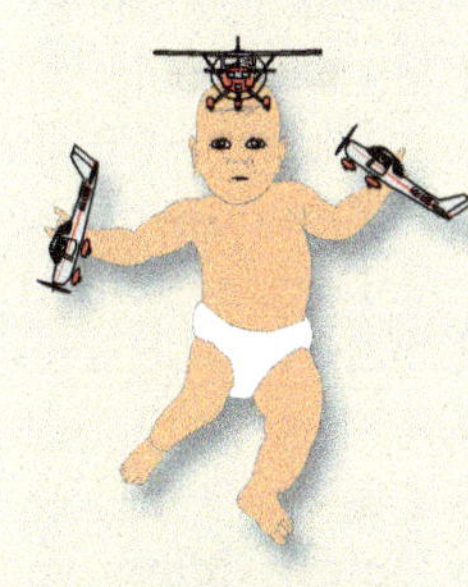

My toddler (2 years, 1 month) had been demanding that I take him for an airplane ride. I moved the passenger seat full aft and strapped the car/aircraft infant seat into the airplane and my headstrong passenger into the infant seat. During takeoff, as the airplane neared flying speed, I eased back on the yoke. When my son saw the yoke on his side moving aft he lunged forward against his shoulder straps, grabbed the yoke with both hands and pulled with all his (not insubstantial) might. The aircraft over-rotated into a "soft field" takeoff. I pushed forward to overcome my passenger's unauthorized control inputs but was afraid that if he suddenly released the yoke I would push the airplane back onto the runway. I sternly reminded my passenger of the gravity of his actions but the attraction of manipulating the controls was too strong. At 50 feet I pried his fingers off the yoke and pushed over into a cruise climb to keep the yoke out of his reach. At altitude he discovered he could push the yoke and the throttle with his outstretched foot. He also tried to fight me for the handheld microphone while I was trying to talk to approach control. After 20 minutes aloft he fell asleep. I landed, now even wiser that a good backseat passenger can't always be trusted within grabbing distance of the controls—especially when he's big for his age but still in the "terrible twos"....

ASRS Report

TRACKING TO AN NDB WITH ADF

We want to discover how to fly a specific track from X to Y, to and from the NDB, using our ADF equipment (position A). Flying a heading of 090° allows you to fly parallel to the desired track (we'll assume no wind in this example). But how do you know if this parallel route is directly over the desired track from X to Y?

After all, your airplane may be a little north or south of the intended route from X to Y despite flying parallel to it as shown below.

If, while flying a heading of 090°, the ADF needle points directly to the nose (#1) or the tail (#2), then you can be sure that you're tracking directly from X to Y.

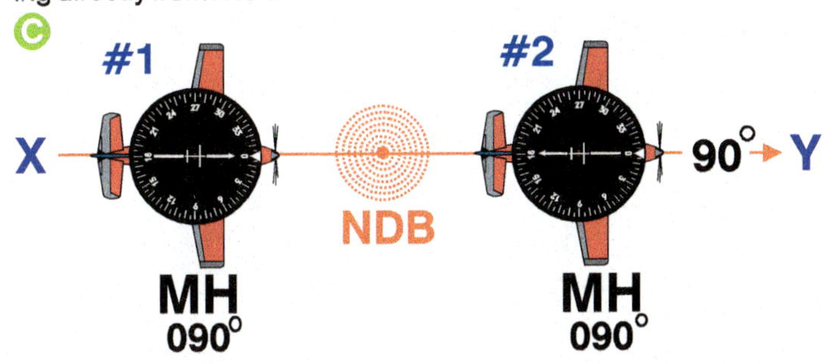

If the ADF needle of airplane #3 or #4 isn't pointed directly toward the nose or tail of the ADF, then, despite a heading of 090° the airplane is parallel to, rather than on, the desired course from X to Y.

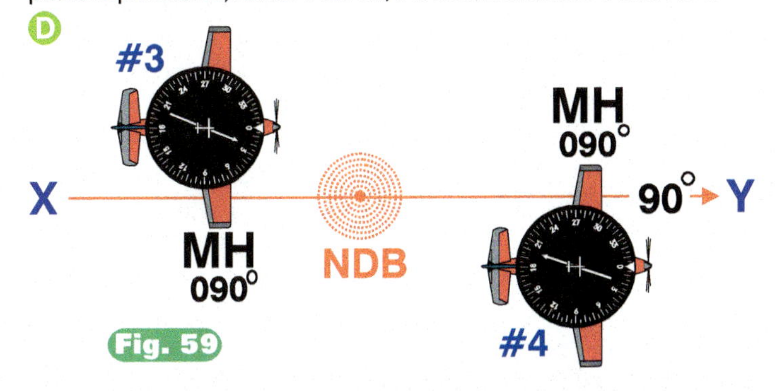

Fig. 59

The Aviator's Awareness Code:
Beware!
Be Wary!
Be Awake!

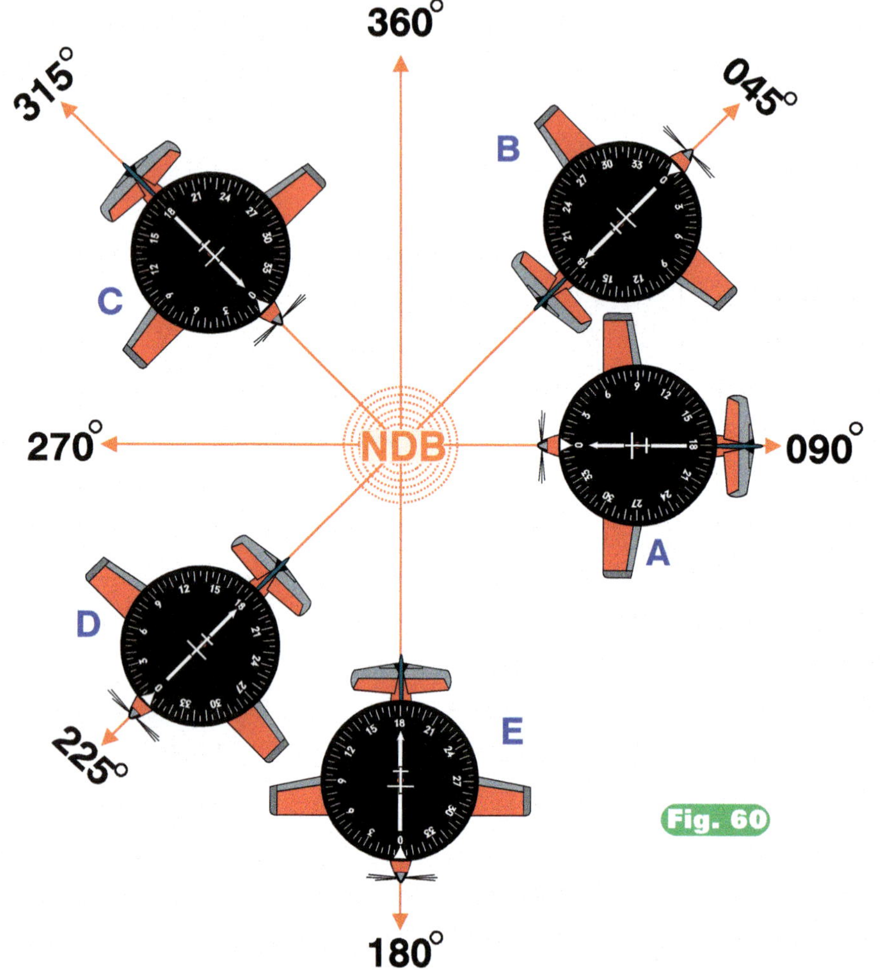

Fig. 60

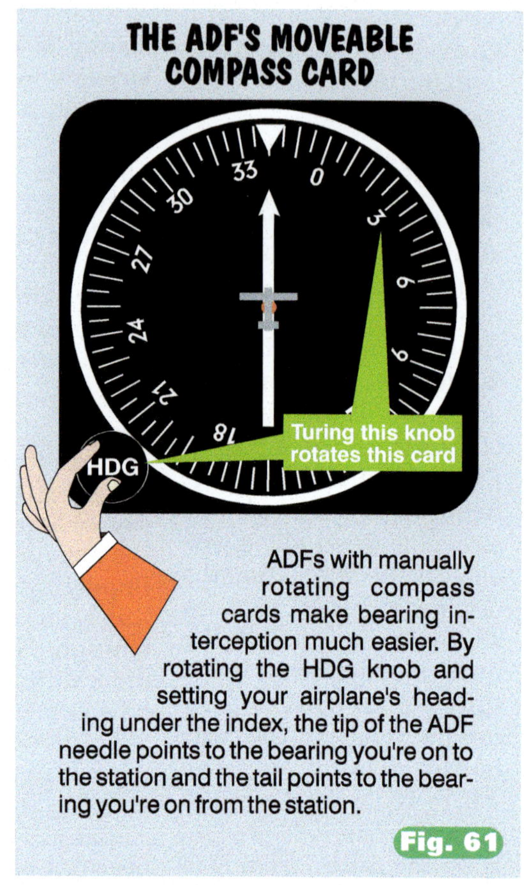

Fig. 61

Now you're ready for two nifty techniques. First, I'm going to show you how to use the ADF's rotating compass card to identify the bearing you're on to or from an NDB. You'll do a backflip when you see how easy this is. Second, I'll show you an easy formula you can use to solve any written test question concerning ADF navigation (and there will be some, I can promise you that).

Figure 60 shows several airplanes, all of which are on specific magnetic bearings to and from a station. Airplane A is heading 270 degrees with the ADF needle pointed to its nose. It's on the 270 degree magnetic bearing to the station. Airplane B is on the 045 degree magnetic bearing from the station and Airplane C is on the 135 degree magnetic bearing to the station. Of course, we don't have TO/FROM/OFF flags on an ADF. It should be obvious whether you're going toward or away from any station since the needle is pointed either to the nose or the tail of the ADF's compass card.

Airplane D is flying the 225 degree magnetic bearing from the NDB and Airplane E is on the 180 degree magnetic bearing from the NDB. Make sure you understand this important principle: when the needle is pointed directly to the nose or the tail of the ADF, the direction the airplane is heading is also its magnetic bearing to or from the NDB (we're still assuming a no-wind condition).

The ADF's Moveable Compass Card – I'll have to admit that practical jokes run in my family. Many years ago my girlfriend wanted me to take her out for her birthday. She said she didn't care where we went as long as it was "expensive." I took her to the airport for a sandwich. I promised we'd do something really exciting after dinner. I got out my blackboard and started to describe how to use the ADF's moveable compass card. She loved it (but not me). But you'll probably love it (if not me) when you see how easy the moveable compass card makes ADF navigation.

Most ADFs have numbered compass face cards that rotate. Let's examine the utility of this manually rotating compass card, as shown in Figure 61.

A rotating compass card allows you to set the airplane's heading under the heading index (white triangle at the top of the instrument). Unlike the RMI which had a slaved gyro compass, the moveable ADF card must be

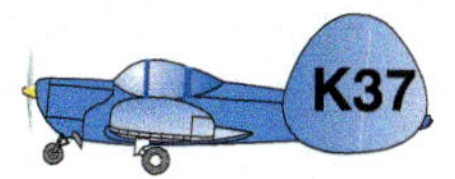

USING THE MOVEABLE ADF COMPASS CARD TO INTERCEPT A BEARING "TO" THE NDB

Airplane A has a moveable compass card set to the airplane's present heading of 090°. The head of the ADF needle now points to the bearing the airplane is on to the NDB and the tail points to the bearing the airplane is on from the NDB. Airplane A is on the 060°/240° bearing to and from the NDB respectively. Airplane B has intercepted the 360° bearing to the NDB. Airplane C is on the 300°/120° bearing to and from the NDB respectively.

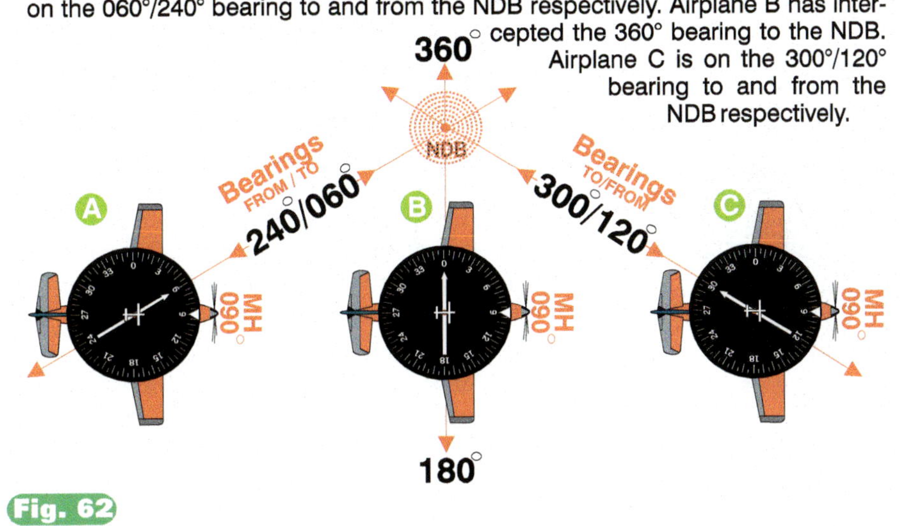

Fig. 62

manually rotated to the airplane's current heading. Nevertheless, it has a practical use. Rotating the ADF compass card to the airplane's heading results in the needle pointing to the bearing the airplane is on to or from the NDB. The ADF's needle is then interpreted in exactly the same way as the RMI's needle.

If you manually rotate the ADF card to the airplane's magnetic heading of 090 degrees, the ADF needle always points to a number that's the magnetic bearing *to* the NDB (that's right, now, and only now, is it OK to pay attention to the numbers on the face of the ADF card). Airplane A in Figure 62 is on the 060 magnetic bearing to the NDB. Airplane B is on the 360 degree (0 degree) bearing to the NDB and Airplane C is on the 300 degree bearing to the NDB.

Pretty easy to use, isn't it? If you were instructed to identify crossing the 360 degree bearing to the NDB you would wait until the ADF needle pointed to 360 degrees or 0 degrees. If you were in Airplane A, you would know you hadn't crossed the 360 degree magnetic bearing to the station since the needle doesn't point to 360 degrees. You know you will eventually cross the bearing if your heading is held constant. Why? Because the ADF needle always moves toward the tail if your heading is constant (any NDB station in front of you will always end up behind you if you hold a constant heading). Airplane C has flown beyond the 360 degree bearing to the NDB because the head (point) of the ADF needle has fallen past the 360 value on the ADF's card. That needle will not move back up as long as the airplane's heading is maintained.

These same procedures apply when intercepting a magnetic bearing from the NDB with a moveable ADF card. In Figure 63, Airplanes A, B, and C are on a magnetic heading of 320 degrees. Suppose you are asked to report crossing the 020 degree magnetic bearing from the station. The moveable compass card has been rotated so that your heading of 320 degrees is set to the top of the compass card. How will you know when you're crossing the designated bearing? You'll know when the tail of the ADF needle points to 020 degrees, as is shown by Airplane B. In this instance, the tail of the ADF's needle points to the magnetic bearing from the NDB. Of course, Airplane C has flown beyond the 020 degree bearing. How do you know? If the head of the ADF needle always moves aft on a constant heading, the tail can only rise. There's no room for argument here: head falls, tail rises.

USING THE MOVEABLE COMPASS CARD TO INTERCEPT A BEARING "FROM" THE NDB

Airplane A is on a heading of 320° to intercept the 020° bearing from the NDB. The tail of Airplane A's needle indicates it is on the 070° bearing from the NDB. If the head of the needle always falls when a constant heading is maintained then the tail must always rise. Airplane A continues on its heading until reaching position B where the rising tail points to the 020° bearing from the NDB. If Airplane B continues on its present heading, the ADF tail will continue to rise and eventually indicate a position on the 355° bearing from the NDB as shown by Airplane C.

355°

020°

070°

MH 320°

NDB

Fig. 63

MEASURING RELATIVE BEARINGS

The relative bearing is simply the number the ADF needle points to. It's measured on a fixed ADF card to the right, relative to the nose or the "0" on the card.

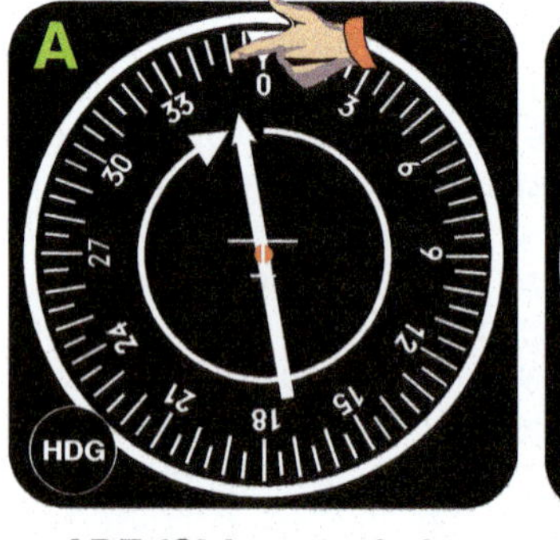

ADF (C) has a relative bearing of 270°

ADF (D) has a relative bearing of 330°

Fig. 64

The tail of airplane C's ADF needle has risen above 020 and it certainly won't move back down. Knowing the ADF tail will rise allows you to determine what magnetic bearing you'll intercept from any NDB station. The only problem with using a moveable compass card is that you must constantly keep twisting it as your heading changes.

Hey, you can't believe everything you hear. A friend of mine told me that watching fish is relaxing. Well, that surely explains why I doze off when I'm snorkeling. You can, however, believe that ADF navigation is made very simple when you use the rotating compass card to help determine your magnetic bearing to and from the station.

The ADF Fixed Compass Card – At the very beginning of our discussion I said to think about the numbers on the ADF's fixed card as index marks. I didn't want you to think they represented anything useful at that stage of the presentation. However, the numbers on the fixed card (the card with "0" set at the top), do have value, especially when solving knowledge exam questions. The following information is for doing just that—answering written test questions *only*. Don't attempt to navigate this way in an airplane. It's just not practical. If you do try it in the air, I guarantee your mind will come to a stop quicker than a lawnmower cruising over a tree stump. We only do practical things in airplanes. It's like the old sage advice to yell "fire" if you're being attacked. This surely works a lot better than, "Help, this guy has a gun!"

First let's define a few terms. The *relative bearing* is not a round metal ball underneath your Aunt Mabel. It is the actual number the needle points to on the face of the ADF's fixed compass card. It's called *relative* because it's measured clockwise from 0 degrees to 360 degrees to the right of the nose. In other words, if the needle were pointed 10 degrees left of the top of the compass card, as in Figure 64, we could say its relative bearing is 350 degrees. ADF card B shows a relative bearing of 70 degrees; Card C shows a relative bearing of 270 degrees and Card D shows a relative bearing of 330 degrees. Remember, relative bearings are "relative" or counted to the right of the top (nose) of the ADF compass card.

During a written test, there is a nifty way to find your bearing to the NDB station using the relative bearing and the airplane's magnetic heading. By adding the relative bearing, shown on the face of the ADF compass card, to the airplane's magnetic heading, found on the heading indicator, you can find your magnetic bearing to the NDB. In other words:

RB + MH=MBTS

Relative Bearing + Magnetic Heading = Magnetic Bearing To the Station

Don't be scared. This is a very simple math formula. I know! I know! Many people have difficulty with math. In fact, a friend who has math phobia once said, "Hey Rod, did you know that 5 out of 4 people have trouble with math?" As you can see, he *really* has trouble with math.

To understand how to use this formula, examine Figure 65. Airplane A has a relative bearing of 080 degrees showing on the face of its ADF compass card. Its heading is 310 degrees. Use the formula to find its magnetic bearing to the station. First we add, RB + MH=MBTS or (080 degrees) + (310 degrees) = 390 degrees —the magnetic bearing to the station. As we've previously learned, any magnetic bearing greater than 360 degrees means a complete circle has already been made and the heading count should begin anew. So, subtract 360 degrees from 390 degrees to find the 30 degree magnetic bearing to the station, as depicted Figure 65.

Suppose we wanted to know our magnetic bearing *from* the station. Simply add or subtract 180 degrees from the bearing *to* the station to get its reciprocal. If we are on the 030 degree magnetic bearing *to* the station, the magnetic bearing *from* the station is (30 degree + 180 degrees)=210 degrees.

What is the magnetic bearing to the station of Airplane B in Figure 65? Adding the relative bearing of 300 degrees to a magnetic heading of 270 degrees gives us a magnetic bearing to the station of 210 degrees (570-360; your answer always has to be 360 or less). What is airplane

MAGNETIC BEARING TO THE STATION

Airplane B
Relative Bearing = 300°
Magnetic Heading = 270°
Magnetic Bearing To Station (MBTS)
(270° + 300°) = 570° (- 360°) = 210°

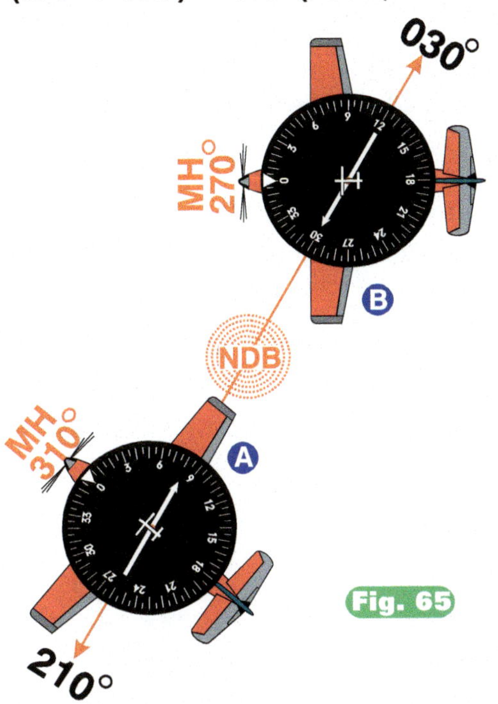

Fig. 65

Airplane A
Relative Bearing = 080°
Magnetic Heading = 310°
Magnetic Bearing To Station (MBTS)
(080° + 310°) = 390° (- 360°) = 030°

B's magnetic bearing from the station? Simply subtract 180 degrees from 210 degrees to get 030 degrees, as shown in Figure 56.

Would you ever use this formula in flight? Probably not. I have never met a competent pilot who pulled out his abacus and started flipping beads to find his location with an ADF. I have, however, met some who used beads to pray with because they didn't have an easy way to solve knowledge exam questions.

Postflight Briefing #11-4

Advanced ADF Navigation

Now that we understand determination of when an airplane is on a specific NDB magnetic bearing, let's examine what happens when the airplane's heading changes. Airplanes A, B, C and D in Figure 66 are all situated on the 360 degree magnetic bearing to the NDB. Conversely, we can say that all four airplanes are also on the 180 degree magnetic bearing from the station. For this discussion, let's talk about magnetic bearings *to* the station. Of course, because these airplanes are not flying 360 degrees, they will eventually move away from this magnetic bearing. Let's assume they remain stationary, as shown in Figure 66.

Airplane A's ADF needle points to the left wing or 90 degrees to the left of the nose. How many degrees would Airplane A have to turn to the left to get its ADF needle on the nose? Yes, the answer is 90 degrees. As Airplane A turns left the ADF needle will continue pointing to the NDB. If Airplane A's heading is east or 90 degrees, at the completion of a 90 degree left turn its new heading will be 360 degrees and the needle will be on the ADF's nose.

Airplane B is heading 270 degrees and the ADF needle is pointing directly off the right wing. If Airplane B turns 90 degrees to the right, the ADF needle will end up pointing to the nose and the airplane's heading will be 360 degrees. Sound familiar? This means that both Airplane A and B, if they immediately turned to a heading of 360 degrees, would be flying to the NDB station on the 360 degree magnetic bearing.

These same principles apply on a magnetic bearing *from* the station. The ADF needle on Airplane E is 30 degrees to the left of the tail. If Airplane E is turned 30 degrees to the right, where would the ADF needle be? Yes, right on the tail. Remember, the needle will remain pointing directly to the NDB and the airplane (our ADF compass card) appears to rotate around the needle. To clearly understand this point, look at all the airplanes in Figure 66. The ADF needle points to the NDB despite all the variations in airplane headings. Which way and how many degrees would Airplane F need to turn to establish itself outbound on the 360 degree magnetic bearing? The answer is 30 degrees to the left.

NDB BEARINGS

The 360° and 180° bearings to and from the NDB station are shown below.

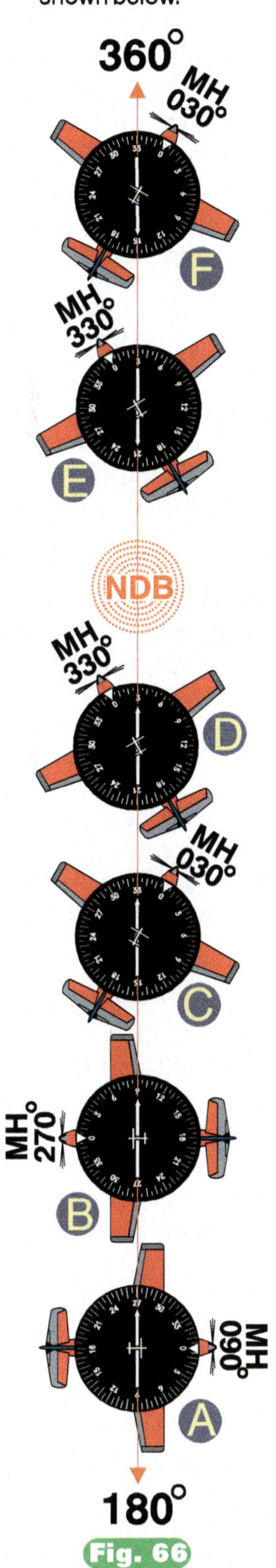

Fig. 66

Now you understand how the airplane can be established on a magnetic bearing while the ADF needle points to the right or left of the nose or tail. This becomes important when making corrections for wind while remaining on the specified magnetic bearing.

Another Way of Determining Your Magnetic Bearing to or from an NDB – Figure 67 shows ADF indications on several different airplanes. Each airplane is obviously on one of the marked magnetic bearings to or from the station. Yet each airplane is headed in a direction different from that magnetic bearing. Here's the question. Is it possible to determine your magnetic bearing to or from the station by examining the airplane's heading and the angle the needle is deflected to the right or left of the nose or tail? Yes, it is. To find your magnetic bearing to or from any NDB station, simply ask yourself the following two questions:

1. How many degrees must you turn the airplane to the right or left to center the ADF needle on the nose (if you want a magnetic bearing to the NDB) or the tail (if you want a magnetic bearing from the NDB)?

2. What is the airplane's new heading after turning by this number of degrees?

The answer to question two is your magnetic bearing to or from that specific NDB. Let's see how this works. Using the method above, what magnetic bearing is Airplane H on from the NDB? Since we're dealing with a magnetic bearing *from,* we'll concern ourselves with the angle between the needle and the tail. The ADF needle in Airplane H is 75 degrees to the left of the tail. A right turn of 75 degrees puts the needle on the tail (this answers question 1). Since Airplane H is heading 330 degrees, a right turn of 75 degrees puts the airplane on a new heading of 405 degrees. Remembering that directional answers must always be 360 degrees or less, you subtract 360 from 405. This give you a value of 45 degrees, which answers question 2.

What is Airplane D's magnetic bearing to the NDB? Airplane D must turn 45 degrees to the left to center the ADF needle on the nose (this answers question 1). Starting on a heading of 090 degrees, a 45 degree turn to the left puts the airplane on a new heading of 045 degrees with the needle centered on the nose (this answers question 2). Airplane D's magnetic bearing to the NDB is 045 degrees.

Use the preceding two questions to determine the other airplanes' magnetic bearing to and from the NDB. Remember, if you obtain a value greater than 360 degrees, subtract 360

BEARING TO AND FROM AN NDB

Each of the airplanes below is on a specific bearing to and from the NDB. To determine which bearing the airplane is on to or from the NDB, you must ask two questions. First, how many degrees must the airplane turn (either right or left) to center the ADF needle on the nose of tail of the ADF display (for either a bearing to or from the NDB, respectively)? Second, what is the airplane's new heading after turning by this number of degrees? This heading represents the airplane's bearing to or from the NDB.

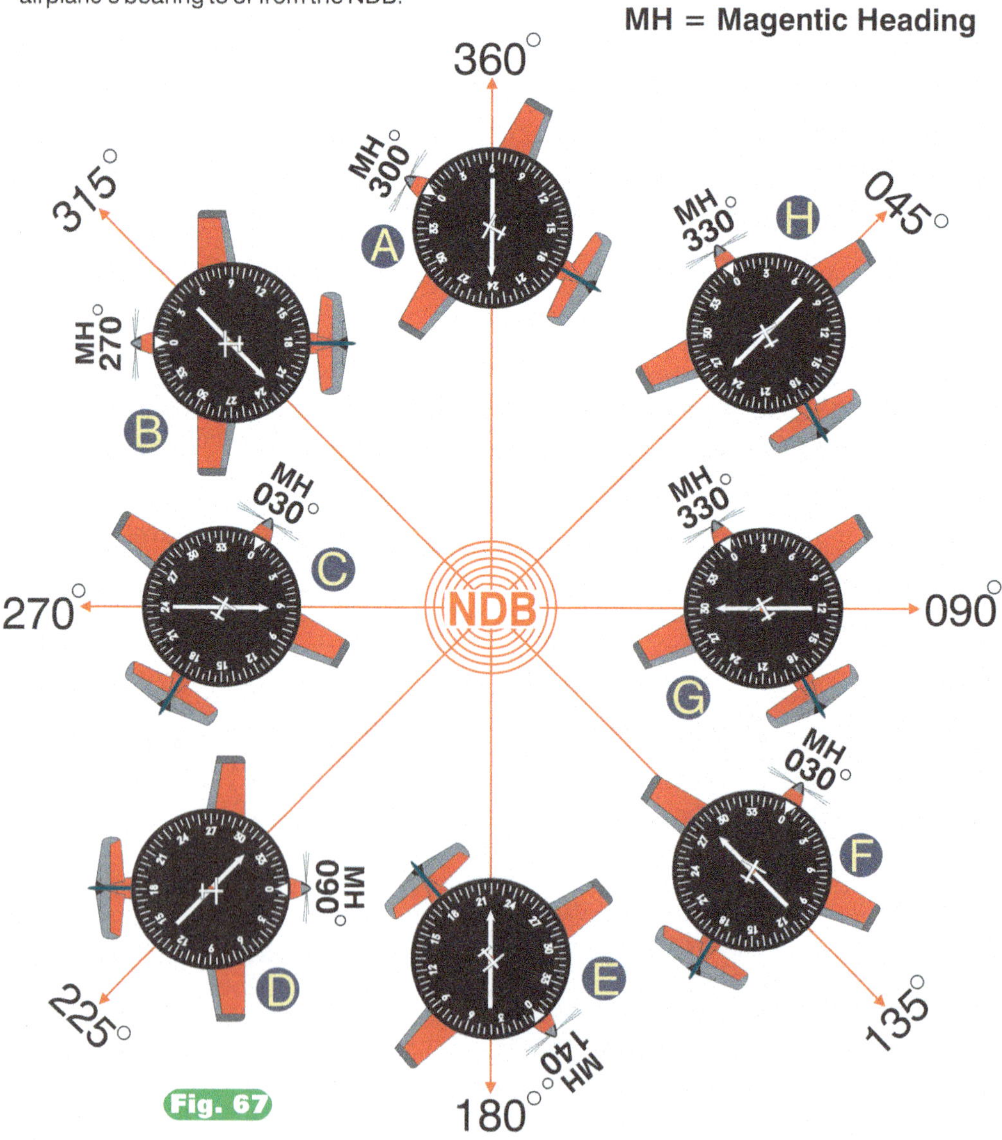

Fig. 67

from the number. There's no such thing as a heading of 400 degrees. If a controller ever asks you to turn left or right to 400 degrees, be very suspicious. If an instructor asks you to do this, tell him or her to get their gyro stabilized and their bearings dry lubed. Coming from an instructor, this is roughly the equivalent of being sent out to find a left-handed monkey wrench. Don't go.

Correcting for Wind – Is it possible to do everything in aviation and never make a mistake? No way. It's not possible in aviation or in life. Perhaps this explains why many pilots are not sure they are going to heaven, but they sure hope that God grades on a curve. It's important to think of your first few times navigating with ADF as being graded on a curve, because you're going to make a few mistakes. This is especially true if you're attempting to track NDB bearings in strong winds. Fortunately we can apply some of the same philosophy that worked for making VOR wind corrections to ADF navigation.

Figure 68 shows several airplanes tracking to and from the NDB on the 360 degree magnetic bearing. The wind conditions vary for all four airplanes. Notice that Airplane A has a wind from the left (west) and is angled 15 degrees into the wind. Even though the airplane is flying a heading of 345 degrees, the airplane remains on the 360 degree magnetic bearing to the station. Since the NDB station is to the right of Airplane A's nose, the ADF needle remains deflected 15 degrees to the right. A general rule about ADF wind correction is, If your wind correction angle is sufficient, the angle between the ADF needle and the nose or tail remains equal to that wind correction angle. In other words, if your wind correction angle is 15 degrees, the ADF needle deflects 15 degrees on the appropriate side of the nose or tail.

Airplane B has a wind from the right (east). Crabbing into the wind on a heading of 015 degrees, Airplane B tracks directly to the NDB. Consequently, the ADF needle deflects 15 degrees to the side the station is on. In this instance, the station is to the left of Airplane B's nose and the needle deflects 15 degrees to the left of the ADF's nose.

Airplane C is experiencing a wind from the left (west) as the pilot attempts to track outbound on the 360 degree magnetic bearing from the NDB. The pilot applies a 15 degree wind correction angle to the left by turning to a heading of 345 degrees. The ADF needle deflects 15 degrees left of the tail—the side of the tail where the NDB is located. If this wind correction angle is sufficient, Airplane C will remain on the 360 degree magnetic bearing while on a heading of 345 degrees.

Airplane D experiences a wind from the right (east) as the pilot attempts to track outbound on the same magnetic bearing from the NDB. A 15 degree wind correction angle is applied to the right. Even though the airplane is heading 015 degrees, it remains on the 360 degree magnetic bearing from the station. The ADF needle shows this wind correction angle by deflecting 15 degrees to the right of the tail—the side of the tail where the NDB is located.

Figure 69 shows a smaller and more common wind correction angle, experienced under light wind conditions. Airplanes A and B need to angle only 5 degrees into the wind to remain on track to and from the NDB.

Here's the most important thing I want you to understand about wind correction with the ADF. When a wind exists, the airplane can track a specific magnetic bearing to and from an NDB while pointing in a direction different from that of the bearing. This is the basic premise for wind correction regardless of whether you're using the VOR, ADF or any other means of navigation.

I'm often asked if private pilots really need to be masters of ADF navigation. Perhaps this is similar to the question, "Do hunters really need assault rifles?" I suppose they do if they are really bad hunters. If you are really bad at VOR navigation, don't have VORs where you come from, and the airplane you use isn't

WIND CORRECTION WITH THE ADF

A wind correction angle of 15° is applied under different wind conditions on bearings to and from the NDB.

Fig. 68

equipped with GPS, then you'd better have good ADF skills. Fortunately, most of the 48 contiguous states in the U.S. are well equipped with VOR stations.

While modern navigational methods are rapidly pushing ADF into the background, at least a working knowledge of this stalwart system could prove to literally be a beacon in the night for you when other methods fail. Being a good pilot means knowing how to use everything at your disposal to navigate. ADF remains one of those tools.

Besides, it's the only radionavigational aid that receives baseball games.

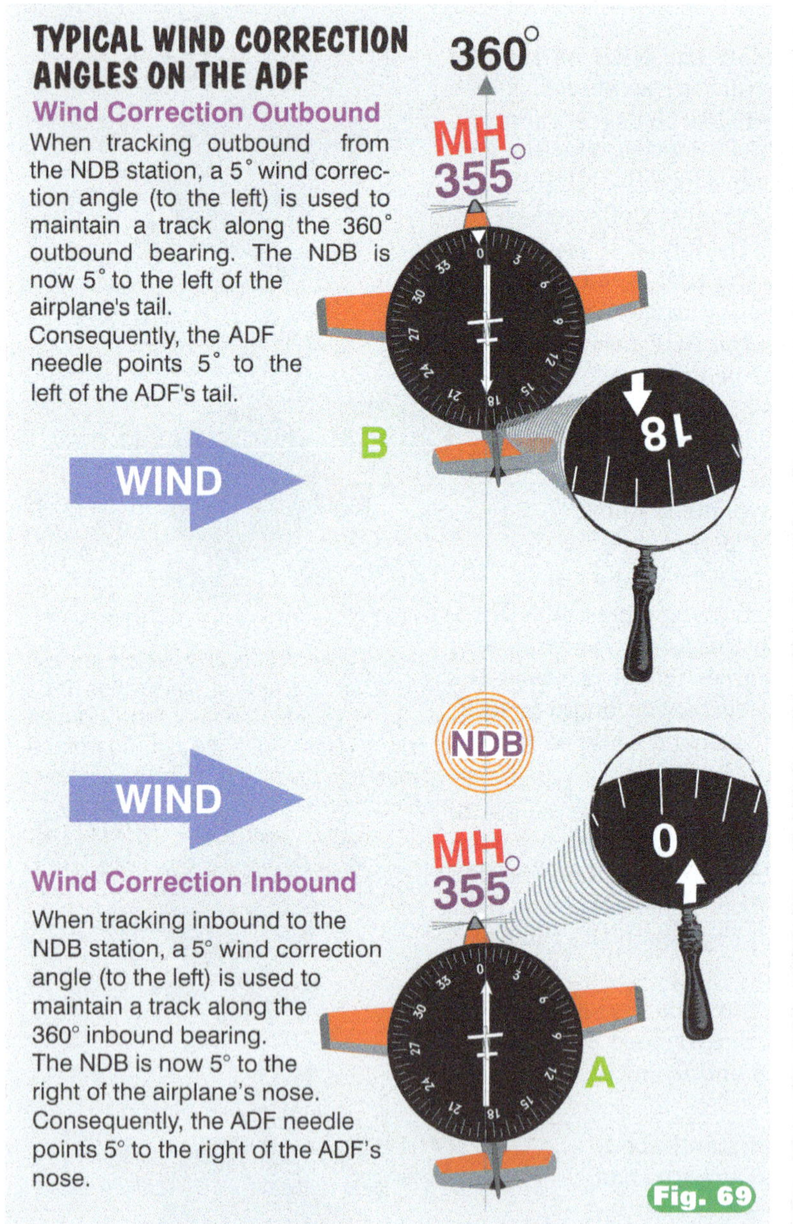

Fig. 69

Postflight Briefing #11-5

VOR TEST SIGNAL

Since VOR is still a common means of navigation, it's nice to have a way of checking the airborne equipment's accuracy. A VOT or *VOR test facility* allows you to conduct this test regardless of your position in relation to the VOT signal. The VOT only broadcasts a signal for the 360 degree radial. Selecting 360 degrees with your OBS should result in a centered needle and a *FROM* indication. Selecting 180 degrees should give you a centered needle with a *TO* indication. If the needle doesn't center, you can determine the error by rotating the OBS until it does. Instrument pilots are not allowed to use their VOR equipment for navigation if the airborne equipment's error is greater than 4 degrees. The equipment should be accurate within +/- 1 degree. Here's how to make the test:

Step 1: Check the *Chart Supplement* for the VOT frequency.

VOR TEST FACILITIES (VOT)

Facility Name (Airport Name)	Freq.	Type, VOT Facility
Centennial .... Colorado Springs	108.2	G

Step 2: Select the VOT frequency and rotate OBS to 360. Look for a FROM indication and a centered needle.

Step 3: Rotate the OBS to 180. Look for a centered needle and a TO indication.

Step 4: If your VOR equipment isn't accurate to within +/- 4 degrees, you should have it checked by an avionics technician.

Postflight Briefing #11-6

Antennas Galore

As an instrument pilot, you need to know two basic principles about antennas. Their size is related to their function and they have to be properly placed on the airplane if they are to work correctly.

An antenna's size is related to the wavelength and frequency of the equipment it supports. Higher frequencies mean shorter wavelengths and that means shorter antennas for better reception. Transponders operate in the higher frequency range of 1,030-1,090 MHz. This means they need short antennas (about 3 inches long) as shown in Figure 70.

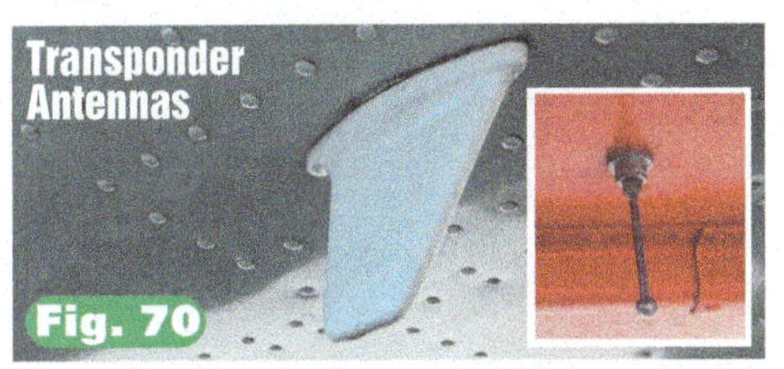

Fig. 70

DME equipment also operates on higher frequencies in the range of 960 to 1,215 MHz. Thus, DME antennas are similar in size to transponder antennas (about 3 inches in length) to better receive these shorter wavelength signals (Figure 71). Both transponder and DME antennas are typically found on the bottom of the airplane for better line-of-sight reception with the transmitting/receiving ground station.

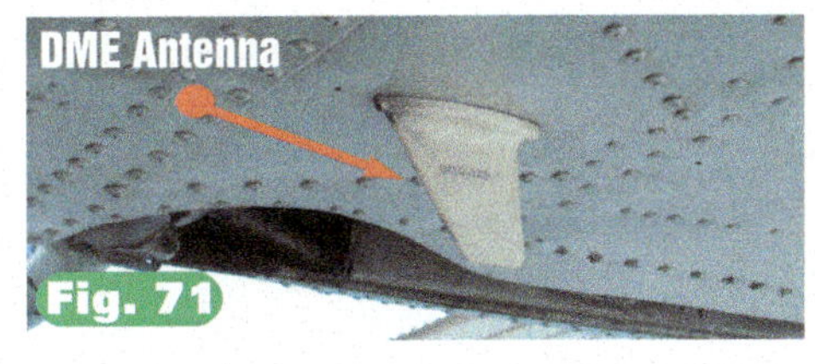

Fig. 71

Communication antennas receive signals in the frequency range between 118.0-136.975 MHz. Their relatively lower frequency means slightly longer wavelengths, thus requiring antennas larger than that used with your transponder and DME (Figure 72). These antennas are often found on the top of the airplane's fuselage. Since VHF requires line-of-sight with the receiving station, this antenna location prevents shielding the VHF signals.

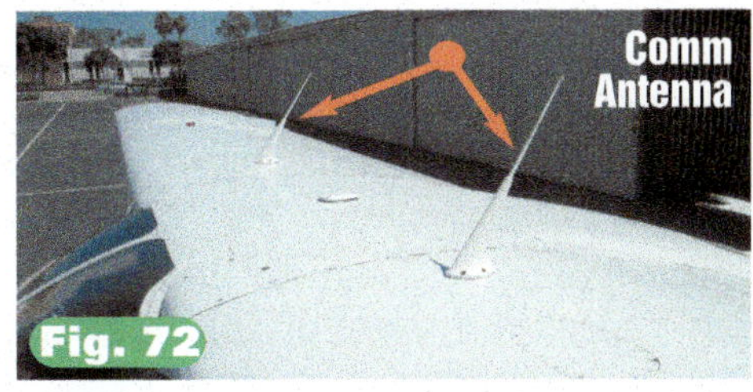

Fig. 72

VOR navigation antennas operate in the 108.0-117.95 MHz frequency range. These antennas are similar in size to the comm radio antennas and are often located at the top of the airplane's vertical stabilizer (Figure 73). These antennas can either look like two thick wires, a looping tube or blades. It's common, however, for these VHF nav antennas to also provide reception for the airplane's glideslope. This is possible because many nav receivers have glideslope receivers built into them. Despite the higher frequency of the glide- slope (in the 330 MHz range), signal reception isn't a problem since the glideslope signal is directional (toward the airplane that's on final approach) and the glideslope transmitting station is often close to the airplane when it's used (0 to 20 miles).

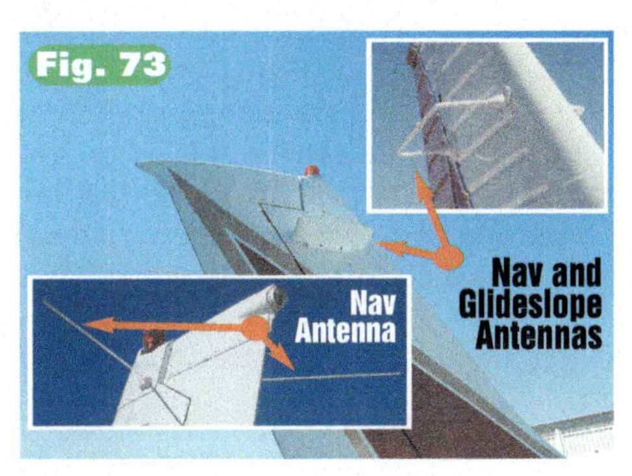

Fig. 73

The airplane's marker beacon equipment operates on a frequency of 75 MHz. Since airplanes fly over the marker beacon transmitter (not under it), the marker beacon antenna is located on the bottom of the airplane (Figure 74). Of course, you might assume that the lower frequency would make this antenna longer than the VHF antennas. Since airplanes fly at 200 to 3,000 feet above the marker beacon transmitter, this antenna can be made small because of its proximity to the transmitting station.

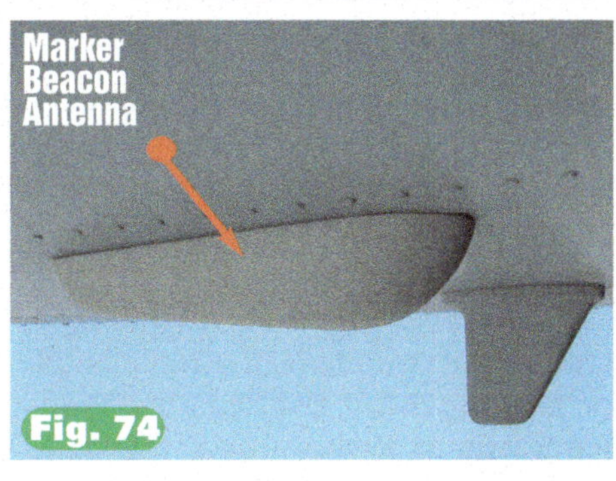

Fig. 74

The ADF antenna is a combination of both a loop and sense antenna as shown in Figure 75 (not long ago the sense antenna was separate from the loop antenna). The Stormscope antenna is nothing more than a loop antenna (Figure 76). Both ADF and Stormscope use low frequencies for reception, thus the similar appearance of each antenna.

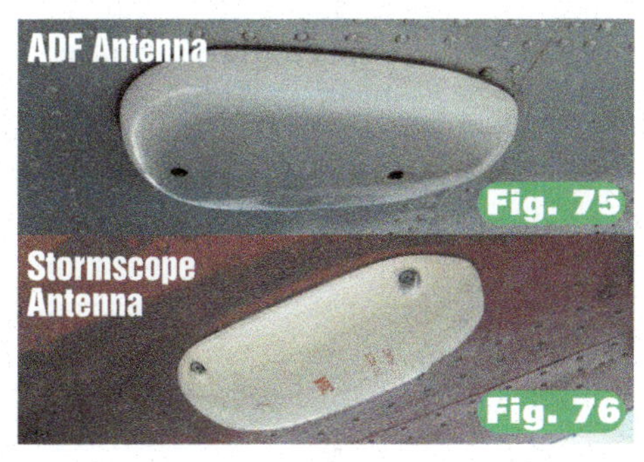

Fig. 75

Fig. 76

Your airplane's GPS antenna is normally located on top of the airplane's fuselage giving it an excellent view of the horizon and space (Figure 77). It's also one of the shortest antennas on the airplane since its operating frequency is so high. Combined GPS/comm antennas are now available, too.

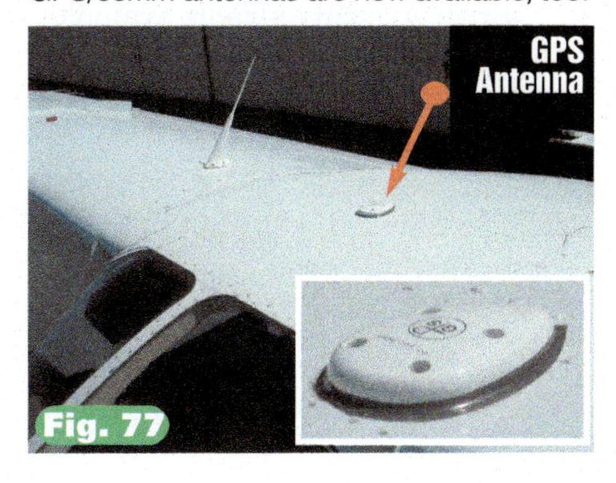

Fig. 77

Postflight Briefing #11-7

The Moving Map Display

Unless you've been working underground running piping at the Cern Acceleration Laboratory for the past 15 years you've probably heard the term TAA or *Technically Advanced Aircraft*. Popularized by the FAA in the early 2000s, the TAA is defined as an airplane having a moving map display.

Believe it or not, every airplane comes with several moving map displays, which are also known as "airplane windows." However, the moving map displays of which I speak are those driven by GNSS (GPS) technology. These devices are part of electronic flight displays found in today's modern airplanes. If there's anything that has revived excitement in aviation over the past few decades it's the upgrading of airplane avionics to moving map technology.

So, just what exactly are the benefits of moving map technology? First and foremost, pilots who are properly trained in the use of this equipment will have an increase in situational awareness. They'll be able to glance at their moving map and immediately know where they are in relation to their destination airport as well as any other airports within the scaled range of their display. Not only will these same pilots know where the airports are, but they'll also know where natural (mountains) and man-made (towers) obstructions are in relation to the airplane. When you couple this ADS-B (Automatic Dependent Surveillance-Broadcast) technology (discussed in Chapter 17), you'll be able to identify the proximity of airborne traffic on your screen as well as view free weather information provided by the ADS-B system. As part of a multi-function display, the map screen can also show engine instruments, flight progress, terrain information and synthetic vision (meaning you'll see a computer generated image of what's typically seen through your forward cockpit windscreen), flight route, fuel management, airspace and checklists, to name a few. That's everything except TV (most likely Netflix access will arrive soon). There are many other benefits associated with having a moving map display, but there are also many drawbacks.

For instance, your moving map display does not take the place of your airplane's primary navigation system, such as VOR or GPS. In other words, the moving map display should not be used as the primary means of navigation (i.e., flying direct to a tiny airport symbol on the screen by following a magenta—direct course—line). You've been trained in pilotage and dead reckoning navigation and that requires the use of your airplane's window. You've also been trained to track a course and that means correcting for wind. Unfortunately, the moving map display makes it easy to point your airplane toward the destination airport (as shown on a scaled map display) until reaching that airport. This is known as homing, irrespective of whether you call the destination airport home. Your moving map display should be used as a supplement to navigation, not as a substitute for it.

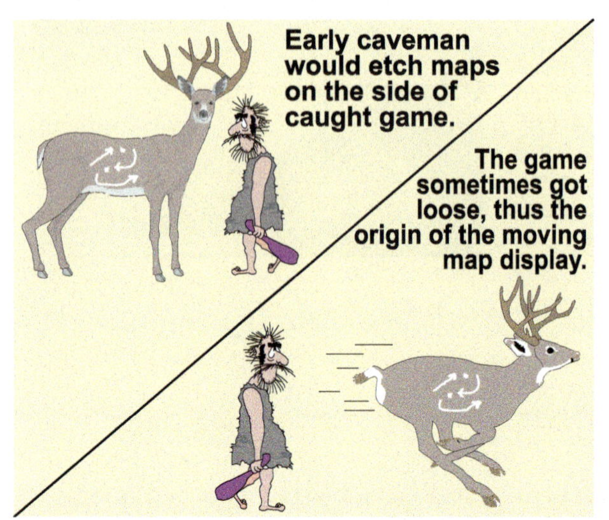

Additionally, the moving map display has a way of attracting and distracting your attention to the detriment of flight safety. For instance, it's far too easy to rely on the traffic altering system (TAS, TIS or ADS-B) typically incorporated into the moving map than it is to rely on your personal EYE-BALL system for observing traffic.

Finally, the moving map display is not a substitute for missing or weak piloting skills. Reliance on a moving map display by pilots with poor piloting skills might actually increase their risk of danger aloft. So, be wise, be smart and use our new cockpit technology as a supplement to help you fly better and not as a substitute for poor piloting skills.

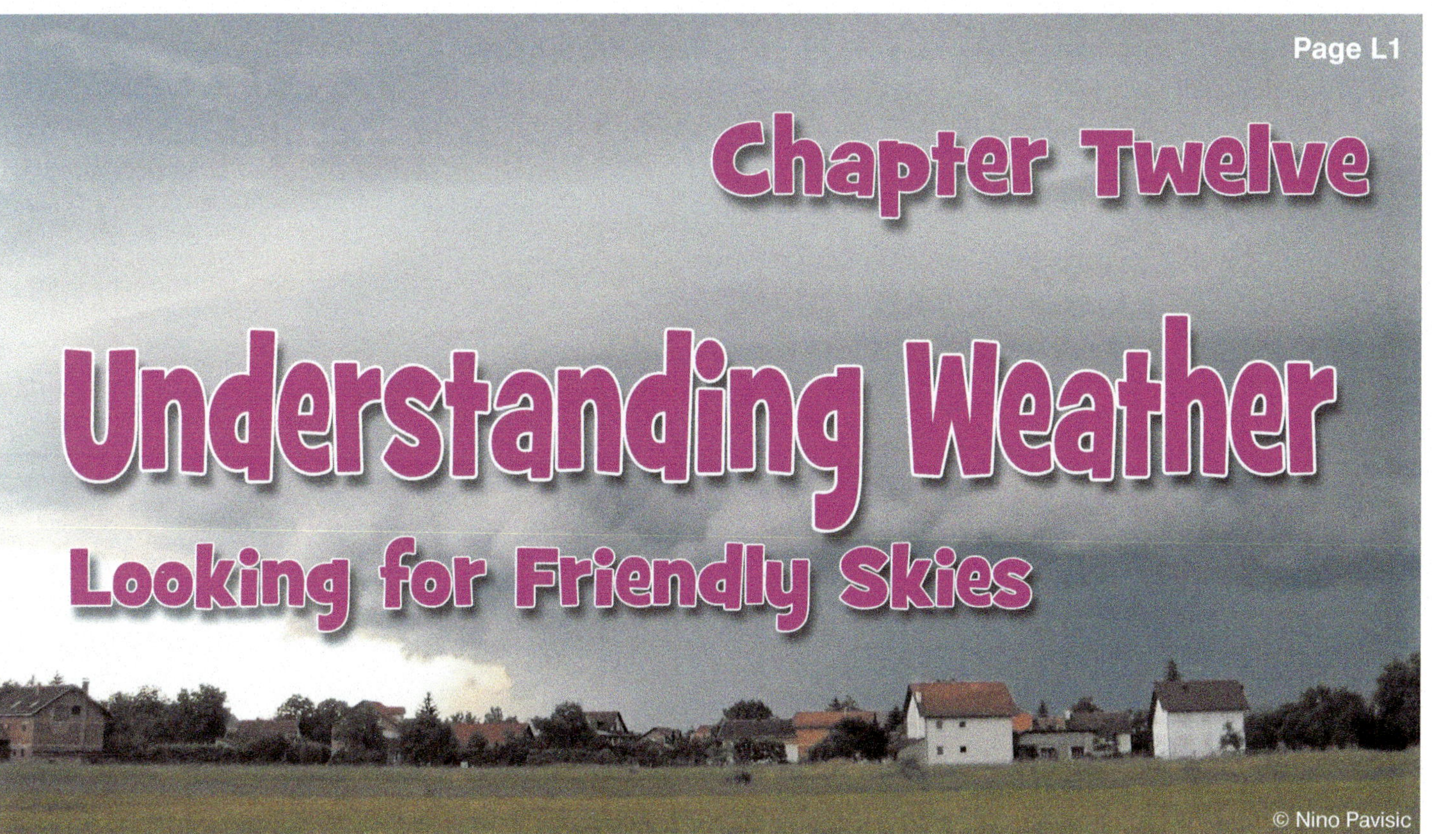

Chapter Twelve

Understanding Weather

Looking for Friendly Skies

© Nino Pavisic

Introduction

An airline pilot friend was seven miles from the airport on approach to Lambert Field in St. Louis when he made his first call to the air traffic control tower. “Lambert Tower, this is TWA 413, outer marker inbound, over.” No reply from the tower.

“Lambert Tower, this is TWA 413, outer marker inbound, over.” The tower controllers still didn’t respond.

“Lambert Tower, this is TWA 413, how do you hear, over?”

Finally the tower controller replied, “TWA 413, this is Lambert Tower, please stand by, we’re changing controllers down here” (meaning a controller shift change).

Not wanting to miss an opportunity, my TWA pilot friend replied, “Lambert Tower, this is TWA 413. Tell me, what do you folks use, Huggies or Pampers?” Everyone had a good laugh as the airliner landed uneventfully.

Isn’t it interesting that tower controllers and pilots can get along with each other despite the tensions and anxieties of their jobs? Sure there are moments of frustration, but it ultimately works because of knowledge and understanding.

Knowledge and understanding is exactly what you need in order to cope with another relationship—the one you as a pilot must have with the weather. Unlike most relationships, this isn’t one about which you have a whole lot of choice. If you fly, you will face weather, unless you confine your flying to outside the atmosphere. Learning about the weather, and your relationship to it, is what we’re setting out to accomplish in this chapter. As a bonus, when you graduate from this chapter you will be able to really understand what the person on the Eyewitness News is doodling on the weather map.

Weather accounts for 25% of the aviation accidents and almost 40% of all aviation fatalities. Getting along with the weather machine is essential for safe, successful flying. As with all relationships, understanding the other party allows us to survive and thrive in a comfortable, safe atmosphere. Understanding meteorological forces begins with identifying how uneven heat distribution across the planet’s surface creates weather.

Atmospheric Circulation

I will now teach you the basics of weather:

1. Air is heated unevenly by incoming solar radiation.

2. Heated air rises and moves.

That’s it. The rest is just filling in the details. Class almost dismissed.

And you thought learning about weather was difficult.

Uneven heating is the ultimate weather engine. It's what makes weather go. It causes rain, wind, thunder, clouds, and all the other excitement that makes up the weather show on earth.

Have you ever seen a cat on a metal roof in summer? There was once a play about it—Cat on a Hot Tin Roof. Instead of pussyfooting around, the animal stays on the move. Air does the same. It's air today, gone tomorrow, moving restlessly around the earth in a never-ending (and futile) attempt to evenly distribute heat. As the air moves, it creates the things we collectively refer to as *weather*.

For the sake of discussion, let's assume our earth doesn't rotate. (This is not true, just in case you're confused on the concept. I'll make the earth move for you in a minute.) Figure 1 shows how a portion of the earth at the equator receives a great deal more solar heat than the area near the poles. Equatorial air, resting over a warmer surface, is eventually heated from below, just like the cat's feet on a hot tin roof. The air becomes less dense, and rises. The engine is running.

Up to a certain altitude in the atmosphere (called the *tropopause)*, temperature decreases with altitude. Therefore, our equatorial (heated) air rises until it finds air of a similar temperature near the tropopause (position A). Once it's at equilibrium with the air around it, the air stops rising, but it won't stop moving. Unable to ascend further, the air begins a journey north and south toward the poles, where it eventually cools and descends (position B). The airflow cycle in this simple illustration is complete when cold, descending polar air moves toward the equator, replacing the rising equatorial air (position C). This simple, single-cell circulation would be the way things were *if* (there always seems to be an *if)* the earth didn't rotate.

If the earth didn't rotate, this would be the end of our discussion on atmospheric circulation (and this chapter would be incredibly short). The earth, however, rotates, which literally introduces a new twist into the calculations.

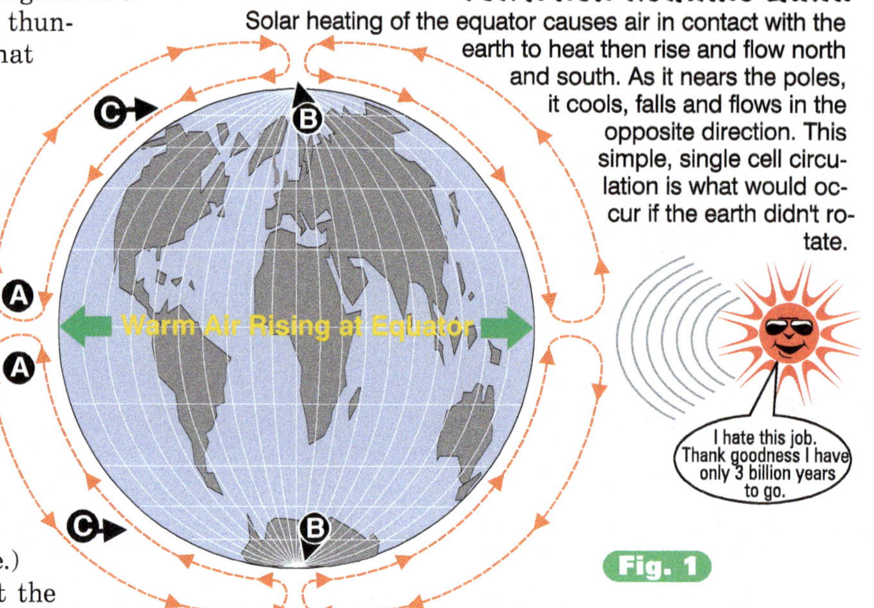

Fig. 1

The Coriolis Force

When viewed from above the north pole, the counterclockwise rotation of the earth causes air to curve or twist to its right (relative to the terrain) in the northern hemisphere (and to the left in the southern hemisphere). No matter which way the air moves, it will have a right curve or twist added to its direction of motion.

Air is forced to curve by something known as the *Coriolis force*. This isn't a real force similar to that which you feel when a big thug punches you in the snoot. It's an apparent force. In other words, the earth rotates under a moving parcel of air which gives the air the appearance of being deflected to the right in the direction it was moving. What appears to be magic is actually sleight of land.

You can demonstrate the Coriolis force quite nicely as shown in Figure 2. Simply take an old record (Ethel Merman records are easiest to find since they sell like hotcakes—$2 a stack) and spin it in the direction the earth rotates (counterclockwise) as if you're looking down from over the north pole. Have a friend hold a ruler one-half inch above the rotating record. Take a piece of chalk and move

IT'S AN ILL WIND

After landing at the cabin, I parked my airplane and walked a short distance. There was no wind, so I didn't tie my plane down. While away, the wind picked up within five minutes and turned my plane upside down. To prevent this occurrence pilots should always tie their plane down even if they are going to leave it only five or ten minutes. Very little damage was done. A lot of lost time could have been saved by just taking a minute to tie the airplane down.

ASRS Report

EFFECT OF CORIOLIS FORCE IN THE NORTHERN HEMISPHERE

To demonstrate the effect of the Coriolis force, draw several lines along a straight edge over a rotating record. Make sure record rotates in the direction shown, since this simulates the direction of earth's rotation as seen from over the north pole in the northern hemisphere.

As you can clearly see, the line always curves to the right in the direction of its motion because of the Coriolis force. A moving mass of air will also curve to the right in the direction of its motion in the northern hemisphere.

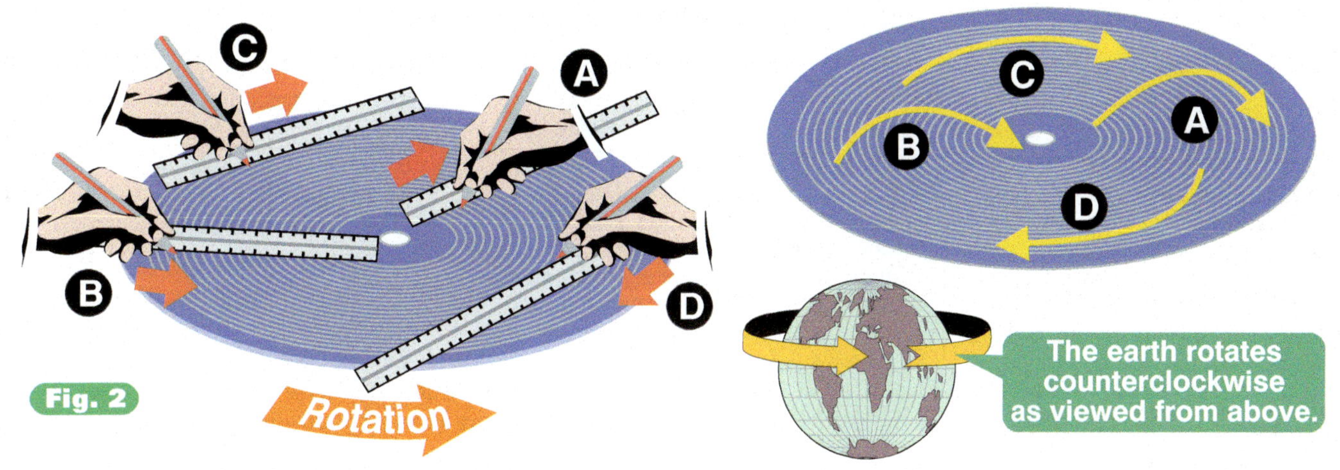

it along the straight edge of the ruler drawing a line on the rotating surface. Do it first from the exact center outward, as in position A. Then do it from the edge to the exact center, as in position B. Finally, do it in a sideways direction, as in positions C and D.

After each marking, notice how the chalk path curves. Each path is curved to the right in the direction the chalk moves. No matter which way you move that chalk, a right curve is apparently added to its motion. North of the equator, the Coriolis force curves the air to the right. South of the equator, the Coriolis force adds a left curve to the motion of the air. We'll limit our discussion to events in the northern hemisphere.

Little, if any, movement escapes the effects of the Coriolis force. One-way railroad tracks experience more wear on the right side of the track than the left. Rockets, planes, spitballs, boats and cars all, to some degree, experience the effects of the Coriolis force.

Remember, no matter which way the air moves in the northern hemisphere (right, left, sideways or diagonally), it will have an apparent right curve or twist added to it by the Coriolis force.

An easy way to remember this is to recall the movie *The Godfather*. You might remember Don Coriolis (actually it's Corleone). If things weren't going RIGHT he'd make them RIGHT, by doing the RIGHT thing. Perhaps Don Coriolis would grab a tough guy's RIGHT arm and make him say "uncle," then talk to him about fish heads, RIGHT? Hopefully this makes it easier to associate the Coriolis force with a curve or twist to the RIGHT.

Now let's take a look and see how the Coriolis force alters the simple, single cell atmospheric circulation previously presented in Figure 1. In the northern hemisphere, rising warmer air is curved to the right in an easterly direction by the Coriolis force (Figure 3). Eventually, the high altitude rising air moves in an easterly direction and starts to bunch up, much like a freeway crowded with cars. This bunching up occurs most noticeably at about 30 degree north latitude. As the air rises, some of its heat is lost through radiation during the ascent.

SINGLE CELL CIRCULATION TO 30 DEGREES NORTH LATITUDE

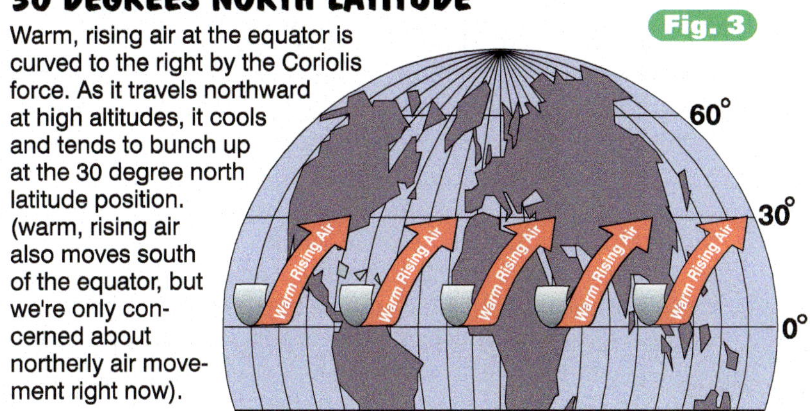

Warm, rising air at the equator is curved to the right by the Coriolis force. As it travels northward at high altitudes, it cools and tends to bunch up at the 30 degree north latitude position. (warm, rising air also moves south of the equator, but we're only concerned about northerly air movement right now).

HOW MUCH DOES A CLOUD WEIGH?

According to atmospheric physicists, the water in an average cloud weighs about 500,000 pounds. That's roughly the same weight as a 747 jumbo jet. A typical cloud contains somewhere around 2.8 million water droplets per cubic foot of space. These droplets don't fall to earth because of friction between the droplets and the air surrounding them. This force is greater than the force of gravity which keeps these droplets suspended until they become larger than .04 inches. At this point, they overcome friction and fall to earth as rain.

CIRCULATION OF AIR AT 30 DEGREES NORTH LATITUDE

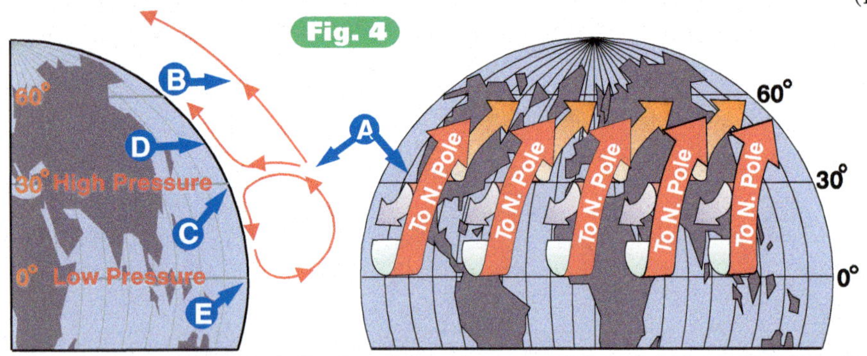

High altitude, northeasterly flowing air bunches up at 30° north latitude (position A). Some of this high altitude air continues northward (position B), while some of it falls, creating a permanent band of high pressure air around the globe at approximately 30 degrees of latitude (position C). The air at this latitude splits, some moving north (position D) and some moving south, back to the equator (position E).

MULTI CELL CIRCULATION OF AIR IN THE NORTHERN HEMISPHERE

Fig. 5

As high altitude air (position B) flows north, it finally reaches the North Pole (position F) where it cools, falls and flows southward (position G). The cold polar air flowing southward (position G) eventually makes contact with the warmer air flowing northward (position D). This warmer air flows up and over the cooler air, forming the polar front (position H). Three individual circulation cells are now apparent in both the northern and southern hemispheres (not shown here).

WIND BELTS OF THE NORTHERN HEMISPHERE

Surface winds, resulting from three individual circulating cells in the atmosphere, form three permanent wind bands across the northern hemisphere. Effects of the Coriolis force cause these winds to curve to their right in the direction in which they move.

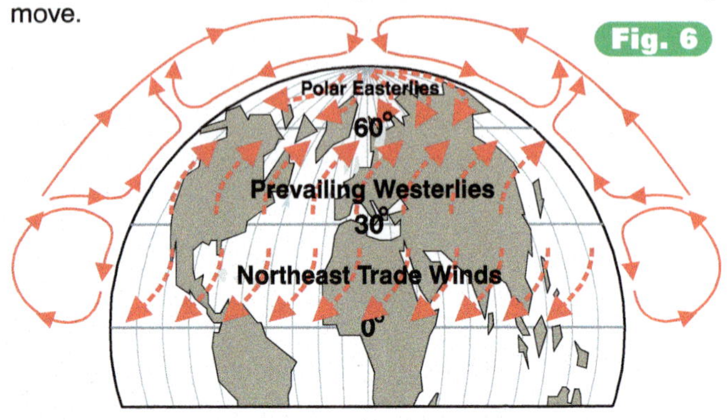

Both bunching up and cooling cause some (not all) of this air to slowly descend at the 30 degree north latitude location, shown in Figure 4, position A. Bunching up increases the air mass above and thus causes a higher surface pressure at the 30 degree latitude position. As the air descends toward the surface it warms, causing clear skies (usually) and warm surface temperatures. Some of this high pressure air flows southward toward lower pressure at the equator (position E). The rest of this warm, low altitude air at position D moves northward.

Some of the high altitude air that didn't descend at 30 degrees latitude continues to move northward toward the pole, as shown by position B in Figure 5. As it continues to cool, it falls, and travels southward from the north pole (position F). At approximately the 60 degree north latitude (position G), this southward-moving colder air meets the northward moving warmer air (position D). These two air masses have different temperatures, and thus different densities. We know that things with different densities tend not to mix. For example, crude oil and water have different densities and certainly don't mix (that's why California, with all its oil spills, now has three different types of beaches—regular, super and unleaded).

When very cold polar air bumps into cool tropical air, the result is a transition zone, shown at position H. This zone is known as the *polar front* (a front is simply a zone where air masses with different densities meet). Some of the northward-moving, cool air flows upward over the colder (denser) polar air (position H). This ascending air is carried northward, toward the pole, with the rest of the high altitude winds. Three separate cells of circulation are now evident. In a while, we'll discuss fronts and their movement. Right now, just notice how winds in these three cells are affected by the Coriolis force.

Figure 6 depicts a profile of these three individual circulation cells. Between 0 and 30 degrees latitude, the northeast tradewinds blow. From 30 to 60 degrees, the prevailing winds are westerlies, and from 60 to 90 degrees the winds are the polar easterlies.

Notice that meteorologists always talk about winds in terms of the direction they blow *from*, not to! Meteorologists do this because winds, like people, are better understood when you know their origins. If winds come from the north, they're likely to be cold; from the south, they're likely to be warm. If a mean looking guy comes from a bad neighborhood, you know a lot about him. If he said he not only grew up on the wrong side of the

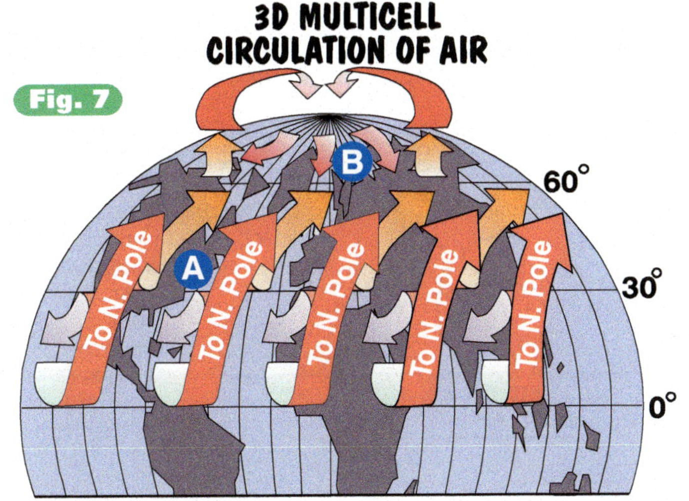

Three wind belts are seen from above in 3-D perspective. Notice how warmer, northward moving air from 30° latitude (position A) confronts colder, southward moving air from the north polar region (position B). This confrontation is the source of much of the nasty weather we experience in the United States.

tracks, but grew up underneath them, you know he was a bad dude. Figure 7 depicts this circulation on a multidimensional level.

While the issue of air is weighing on your mind, let's see how it weighs on the earth.

Air Pressure and Vertical Air Movement

Air has weight. This weight exerts a pressure on the earth's surface in much the same way a professional wrestler exerts pressure on your body by standing on your chest (I hope this doesn't happen to you a lot). Changing the air's temperature, however, changes its density and the pressure it exerts on the earth's surface.

For example, along the equator there exist areas of warmer (less dense) rising air, as shown in Figure 8, position 1. Rising air certainly wouldn't create as much pressure on the surface as descending air. After all, one moves upward while the other pushes downward. Warmer (less dense) rising air provides less push or pressure on the surface. We call large areas of warm rising air *low pressure centers*. Near the equator, it's quite common to find permanent belts of low pressure air wrapped around the earth.

Conversely, permanent high pressure areas exists at the poles (Figure 8, position 2). Colder (more dense) air descends, creating more pressure on the earth's surface. Now you know why cold air falls on your toes during those nocturnal refrigerator raids. Think of cold air as an anvil resting on your chest, as shown in Figure 9. Gravity pulls the anvil downward as it does with cold air, increasing the pressure on your body. Let's attach helium balloons to the anvil, making it lighter. Now the anvil moves upward (off your chest), in the same manner as rising warmer air moves upward off the earth's surface. Pressure at the surface decreases as warm air rises. Of course, as warm air rises, cold air moves in underneath to replace it. Thus, atmospheric circulation consists of high pressure air moving toward lower pressure air (Figure 8, position 3). This simple air circulation model is a fundamental key to understanding weather.

Now that you understand major wind patterns, it's time to examine exactly what makes the wind blow.

Getting Water in the Air

Weather (meaning clouds, rain, thunderstorms, etc.) wouldn't exist if there wasn't a means of putting water into the air. Television meteorologists would be forced to entertain their flock with hand-puppet shadows and benign patter. Nearly half of all pilot fatalities would disappear, and any remaining Flight Service Stations could be retrofitted as bowling alleys.

HIGH AND LOW PRESSURE CENTERS ON A NONROTATING EARTH

Fig. 8

Higher pressure found at poles. (Cold, falling air)

Lower pressure found at equator. (Warm, rising air)

1 2 3

When looking at a simplified, single-cell circulation of the atmosphere we see that the cold air descending at the poles (#2) creates higher pressure on the surface. This air (#3) moves toward the equator to fill in the lower pressure created by the rising, warmer air (#1). Of course, as the earth rotates, the circulation become a tad more complex as you've already seen.

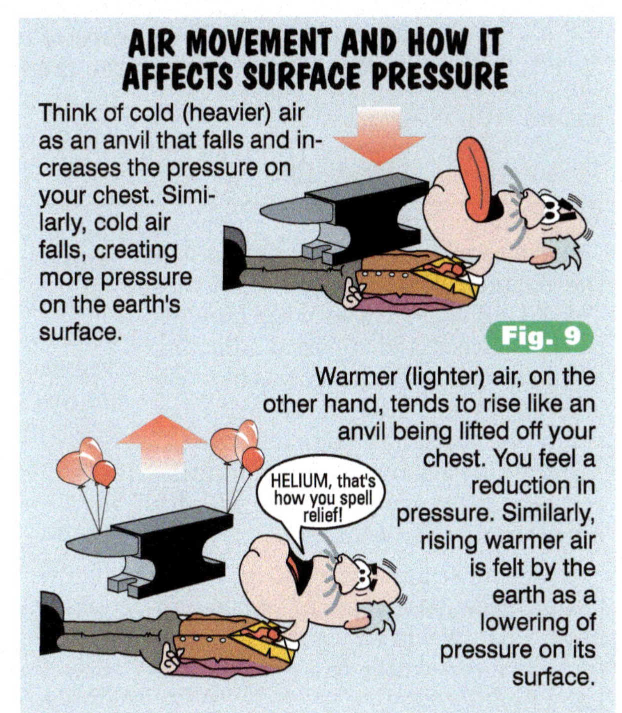

Think of cold (heavier) air as an anvil that falls and increases the pressure on your chest. Similarly, cold air falls, creating more pressure on the earth's surface.

Warmer (lighter) air, on the other hand, tends to rise like an anvil being lifted off your chest. You feel a reduction in pressure. Similarly, rising warmer air is felt by the earth as a lowering of pressure on its surface.

Weather is water. There's a good chance the room you're sitting in right now contains several pints of water suspended in the air. You can't see it, but it's there. It got there through one of two different processes: *evaporation* or *sublimation*. Either of these processes cause water molecules to absorb heat energy and enter the atmosphere.

Water exists in three states: solid (ice), liquid, and gas (water vapor). Changing from ice to water vapor (or water vapor to ice) while bypassing the liquid state is known as *sublimation*. For instance, snow or ice can sublimate directly from a solid to the gaseous state. This increases the water vapor content of the atmosphere, as shown in Figure 10.

A more common means of adding water to the atmosphere is through evaporation. As water molecules absorb heat energy, they eventually become energetic enough to jump into the air (Figure 11). More heat means more evaporation.

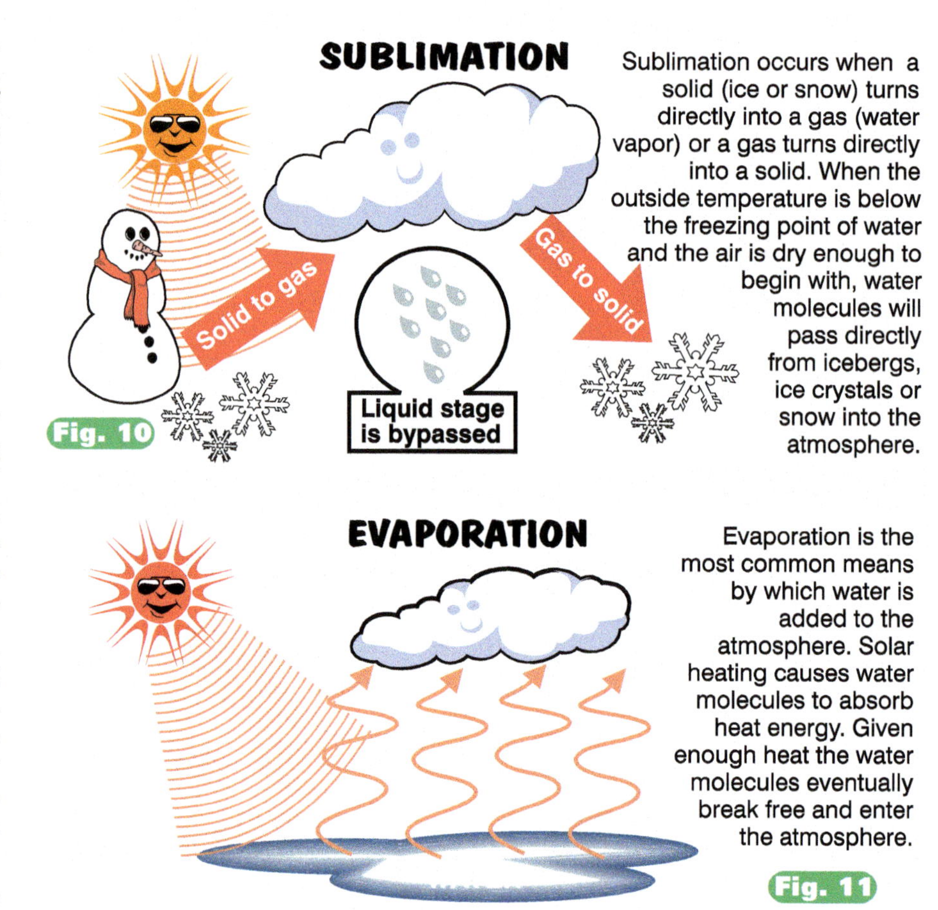

Given enough heat and a large enough water supply, the atmosphere can fill with water vapor. For a given temperature, however, the air can only hold a certain amount of water, just as a theater has only so many seats. The air is said to be *saturated* when additional water vapor is unable to enter the air. Saturated air is very much like the packed theater, in that no one else can get in without someone else leaving. The place is packed.

The Water Content Of Warm and Cold Air

Anyone who has spent time along the eastern coast of Florida or the Texas Gulf coast knows what humidity is. I once asked a friend what his summer visit to Houston was like. He replied, "Well, Rod, have you ever tried to breathe pound cake?" Apparently he found the humidity stifling. Why are summers usually more humid than winters?

Summers are generally more humid because the air is warmer to begin with. Warm air has the capacity to hold more water than colder air. Let's find out why.

To understand why warm air can hold more water vapor than cold air you need to understand a little quirk about water molecules. Unlike air molecules, water molecules like to cling to one another. This explains why you're more likely to find puddles of water than puddles of air on the ground. Water molecules are like aging, out of shape, one-too-many-Twinky-a-day prize fighters who always seem to grab onto each other in the 14th round (of course they might do this simply because they like each other).

Heating the air causes both air and water molecules to vibrate faster (Figure 12A). Water molecules that bounce and ricochet off each other with sufficient impact are less likely to stick together. Thus, you can put more water molecules into warmer air without them clinging to each other and forming clouds (*sky puddles*).

As the air cools, water molecules move slower and vibrate less (Figure 12B). Collisions between water molecules are now gentle enough to let them stick together. These clinging water molecules now become visible in the form of a cloud. In other words, the water molecules can't remain as vapor (gas), so they return to the liquid state in the form of something visible (a cloud). Additional cooling allows the water droplets to grow in size, as shown in Figure 12C.

The process of water vapor becoming visible is called *condensation* and it results in the formation of fog or clouds. When water vapor condenses it means that the air is *saturated* and can't hold any more water in vapor form. Now you know why cold air can hold less water vapor than warm air. It reaches its point of saturation sooner.

Keep in mind that the process of condensation is the opposite of evaporation. When it comes to water, what goes around definitely comes around.

This explains The Mystery of the Sweating Glass. Why does a glass get damp on the outside when you pour cool lemonade in it on a hot summer's day? Hot air, carrying lots of

WATER HOLDING ABILITY OF WARM AND COLD AIR

A In warmer air, water molecules (large circles) vibrate and move faster. Thus, they tend not to stick together (as they like to do). This allows more water molecules to enter the air before it becomes completely saturated with water vapor.

B Cooling the air slows the speed and impact of colliding water molecules, allowing some of them to stick together, thereby returning to the liquid state in the form of a cloud (sky puddle). This leaves fewer unattached "invisible" water molecules in the now saturated air.

C As cooling continues, the smaller droplets grow and merge into larger "visible" droplets of water. The colder air is still saturated, but even fewer water vapor molecules remain in the air. Thus, colder air can hold less water vapor than warm air.

Warm, Unsaturated Air

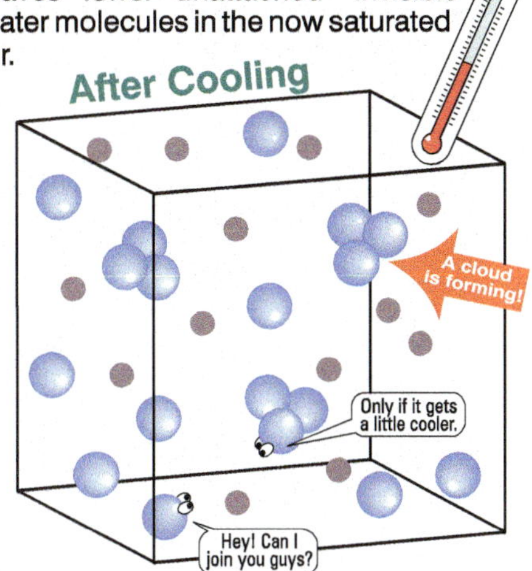

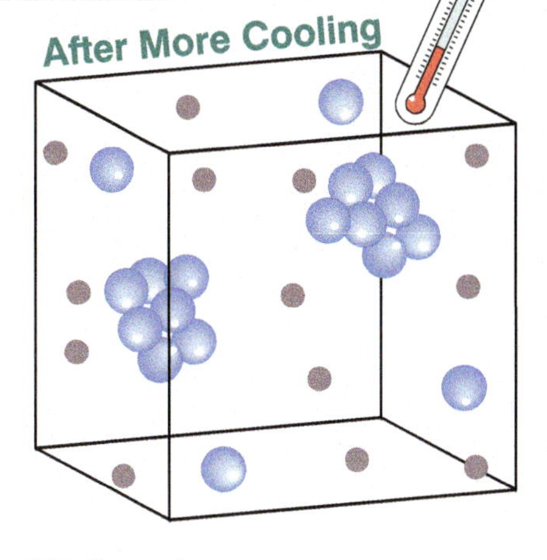

Fig. 12

= Water Molecule = Air Molecule

moisture, comes in contact with the cool surface of the glass. The suddenly-chilled air can't hold its water.

Do you recall your last flight on an air conditioned airliner? Cool, wasn't it? Dry, too. Very dry. Air conditioning cools the air and dries it, making your eyes feel like tiny shriveled prunes rattling around in oversized sockets (just like the last Tic Tac in the pack). Contact lenses dry and stick as if they've been arc welded to your corneas. This explains why several people on my last flight requested a ginger ale with a Visine chaser.

Two Ways to Cool Air

There are two ways to cool air and condense water vapor. First, you can put the air in contact with a cooler surface or environment. Second, you can lift the air and let it cool by expansion. Let's examine the first process.

Have you ever been to Minot, North Dakota in the winter? It's a beautiful place but it's memorably cold (a preacher friend says that's where you'll find all of God's frozen people). And that's why they call it Minot—you go there for one winter and you minot want to go back. Talk with anyone on those cold winter mornings and you'll see visible breath shafts (clouds) coming from their mouth, as shown in Figure 13. Warm air from their lungs contains a lot of moisture. As this warm air comes into contact with the colder surroundings, the breath shaft becomes saturated with water vapor, condensation occurs, and a cloud forms. This is how clouds form by coming into contact with a cooler surface (an added benefit is that if the person speaking to you has bad breath, you can see it coming and take evasive action).

Fog formation is often based on air coming into contact with a cooler surface. Water vapor condenses, forming visible moisture in the form of clouds that touch the ground. But what about clouds that don't touch the ground? How do clouds form in the atmosphere?

If you lift air, you'll cool it. You'll have to go a bit farther than from your desktop to the top of your head to have any noticeable effect, so this isn't an experiment you can do at home. Rising air undergoes a decrease in pressure because of the decrease in weight (thus pressure) of the atmosphere above it. This is similar to the reduction in body pressure experienced when ascending from the bottom of a swimming pool. Air molecules expand when they are subject to less pressure. Since there's no other source of energy available, the air molecules must use their own energy to expand. This slows them down, which results in a lower temperature. Air that rises always expands and cools. What happens to cooler air? It doesn't hold as much water as warmer air. Out it comes. This creates visible

HOW A CLOUD FORMS

On cold days a visible breath shaft is often seen when warm, moist air from the lungs is cooled by coming into contact with the cold, ambient (outside) air. As the air in the breath shaft cools, its water vapor condenses (returns to its liquid state), resulting in visible moisture in the form of a cloud (a mouth cloud).

Fig. 13

moisture, in the form of clouds, as shown in Figure 14.

In fact, air is not the only thing that expands as it ascends; the human body also does this. Decreasing air pressure with increasing altitude is one reason why flight attendants are told to wear looser clothing on the ground. Bodies expand slightly with altitude, making tight fits uncomfortable. I have never been trapped in pantyhose (honest!) but I understand it's very uncomfortable (hey, that's my story and I'm sticking to it).

Fortunately, the process of condensation is rather predictable. Without the amazing Kreskin or a Ouija board, we can still determine the temperature at which clouds begin to form. This is certainly a handy thing for pilots to know. Before we can do this, however, we need to know something about the percentage of water in the air, otherwise known as the relative humidity.

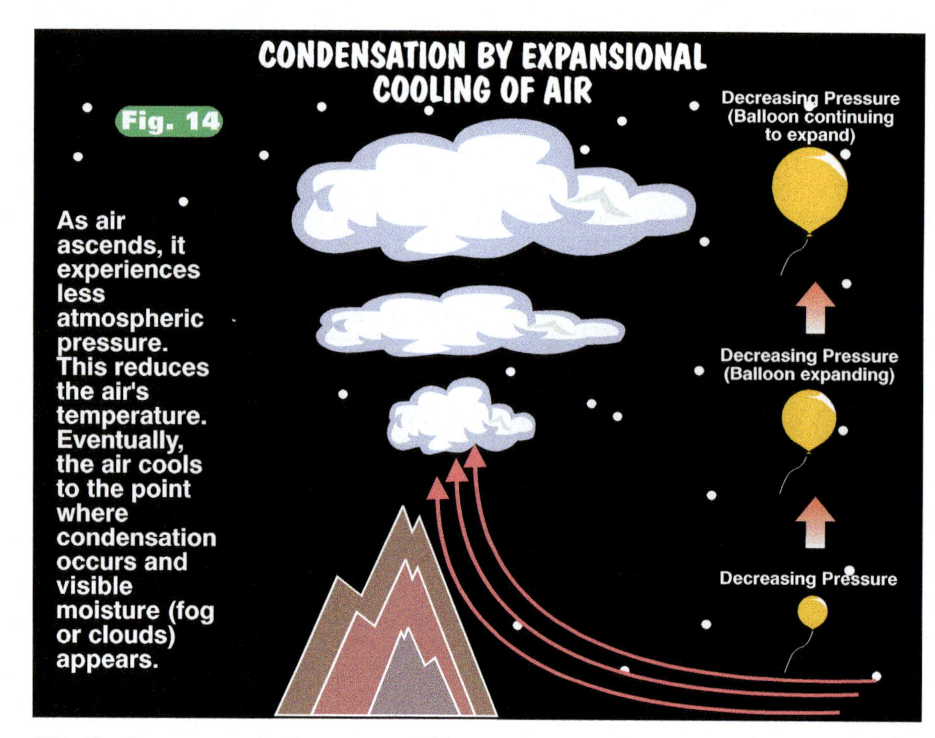

Similarly, evaporation or sublimation can add only so much moisture to the air before things reach a saturation point. And when the air is saturated, you're not going to coax any more water vapor into it. Evaporation or sublimation is just one way air becomes saturated, but it's not the most common way.

Relative Humidity

Relative humidity is not a description of your family who are all wet. It's a number that tells us how much water vapor the air is holding in relationship to how much it could theoretically hold at its current temperature.

Rush hour in Los Angeles, California helps us visualize this. At 3 in the afternoon, each moving automobile on the freeway is spaced about three car lengths behind the next. With greater space between vehicles, it's easy to slip in and move with traffic (especially when no weapons are involved). It might be said that the freeway currently holds only 25% (1 of a total capacity of 4) of the number of automobiles it's capable of holding. We might say the freeway's relative capacity is 25%.

But what happens at 5 p.m.? Space between automobiles decreases until bumpers are nearly touching. The freeway is now 100% saturated with cars. No more will fit. Nothing is moving. Its relative capacity is now 100%. If a car tries to get onto the freeway, another has got to go over the railing (Hey! It could happen!!).

RELATIVE HUMIDITY

The parcel of warm air (A) is holding 50% of the water vapor it's capable of holding. We say its *relative humidity* is 50%. As the air cools, its capacity to hold water vapor diminishes. Water molecules begin to stick together, condense and return to the liquid state (form a cloud). Remember, if water molecules are leaving the vapor state for the liquid state, you're not going to get more water vapor into the air (and that is that). Eventually the air cools to the point where it can't hold any more water. The *relative humidity* has increased to 100% as shown by parcel B.

Fig. 15

Warm Air: Relative Humidity - 50%

The container of air at this temperature can actually hold an additional 10 water molecules in the vapor phase (for a total of 20). Relative to the 20 that are possible, the *relative humidity* is 50%.

Cold Air: Relative Humidity - 100%

As the air cools, its water holding ability decreases. Now it can't hold any more water in the vapor phase because the water molecules want to cling and form a cloud. Relative to this container, the relative humidity is now 100%.

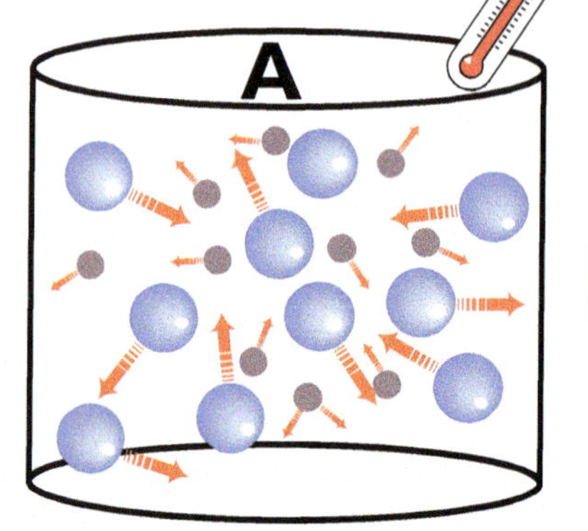

B

Hey! Can I come in?

There's no more room for water vapor in here man. Can't you see we're returning to the liquid state? We're going to see our ancestors in the Big Lake that everyone talks about.

A cloud is forming!

= Water Molecule

= Air Molecule

Fig. 16

The psychrometer is a device used to determine the dew point and relative humidity.

All Dew Determination

Dew point is determined by use of a wet and dry bulb thermometer—also called a psychrometer (Figure 16). Both are identical, mercurial thermometers. One measures air temperature; the other is encased in a wet sheath, permitting moisture to evaporate and cool the thermometer. Both thermometers are connected by small rope and are swung around for a few seconds. Then their temperatures are read.

Based on the readings from the two thermometers, the dew point, relative humidity and other measures can be calculated.

The first time I saw a weather specialist do this I thought he was a Bruce Lee protegee doing a nunchuka demo. In actuality, he swung them for a few seconds, took a reading, then retired with his data to the weather room.

It was a calculating move.

Cooling the air is the most common way for it to become saturated. Suppose air parcel A in Figure 15 contains only half the moisture it's capable of holding. We can say this parcel is 50% saturated, relative to the amount of moisture it can hold at its current temperature. Another way of expressing this is to say its *relative humidity* is 50%. The numerical value of 50% is relative to that particular parcel of air only.

What happens to the relative humidity when the air temperature decreases? Yes, the relative humidity goes up. It's just like the freeway losing a few lanes. It loses its capacity to handle traffic. When the temperature drops, the air loses its capacity to hold water.

As air parcel B in Figure 15 is cooled, its water molecules start clinging to one another and begin to return to the liquid state. The air eventually becomes saturated and can't hold additional water molecules with further cooling. Parcel B's relative humidity has now increased to 100%, condensation occurs, and water molecules are forced out of the air.

Notice that the actual amount of water (vapor and liquid) in parcel B didn't change. Only the ability of the air parcel to hold *additional* water vapor has changed.

While relative humidity informs us about the air's capacity to hold water vapor, it doesn't allow us to predict when clouds will form. After all, relative humidity just tells us the state of the air right now, not what it will be in the future. There is, however, a meteorological value known as the dew point which provides us with cloud-predicting ability.

The Dew Point

The *dew point* is the temperature to which a parcel of air must be cooled to become 100% saturated. It's a predictor of when condensation will begin for a particular parcel of air. Assume a meteorologist (that's a weatherperson, not an asteroid technician) says the air's dew point is 60 degrees Fahrenheit (F). If our thermometer shows the air's temperature is 75 degrees F, then we immediately know the air is not completely saturated. In other words, its relative humidity is less than 100%. But cool the air down to its dew point of 60 degrees F and the relative humidity increases to 100%. Condensation occurs, and fog or clouds form.

Meteorologists refer to the actual temperature difference between the temperature and the dew point as the *temperature-dew point spread*. Sounds like a nifty name for a Texas cattle ranch. The process of condensation can actually begin about 5 degrees F (2.8 degrees C) *before* the air temperature cools to its dew point (otherwise stated as a temperature-dew point spread of 5 degrees).

Dew points are handy numbers for pilots to have for several reasons. It's important to understand that the dew point is a great indicator of the atmosphere's water content. High dew point temperatures indicate a lot of water in the air. Low dew point temperatures indicate little water in the air. The temperature-dew point spread also tells you whether the humidity is high or low.

Assume, for instance, you're planning a short flight to arrive at an airport about a half hour after sunset. Air temperature often drops noticeably at sunset—sometimes 10-15 degrees F (or more) within the first half hour. Your weather briefing shows the air temperature at the airport is 65 degrees F and the dew point is 55 degrees F. Would you anticipate any problems? Despite a 10 degree F degree spread between the temperature (65 degrees F) and the dew point (55 degrees F),

A wise man observes that all pilots should use their superior judgment to avoid situations that may require use of their superior skill.

atmospheric cooling after sunset could easily drop the air's temperature to within five degrees of its dew point. That means fog or low clouds. Nothing is more frustrating for a VFR pilot than to navigate directly to where the airport should be, look down, and see the area covered by clouds.

Be aware that fog or low cloud formation can even occur with temperature-dew point spreads of as much as 6 degrees F. Also, water vapor condenses more easily when the air contains an abundance of airborne particles (also known as *condensation nuclei).* A large number of atmospheric particles makes it easier for very small particles of water vapor to collect, helping to form larger water drops. Airports downwind from an area of industry (smog = particulate matter) are more likely to have fog or low clouds form at larger temperature-dew point spreads.

Air in places like Los Angeles contains a lot of particulate matter. In the Los Angeles basin, it's not unusual for fog or low clouds to form at temperature-dew point spreads of 6 degrees F. Not only are there salt crystals from the ocean suspended in the air, but dust and photochemical smog are often available in abundance. As one friend said, "L.A. is a great place to be... if you're a muffler" (it is, however, a beautiful place... during a cease-fire).

Keep in mind the dew point varies with such items as geographic location and atmospheric pressure. It can change considerably during the day. A simple call to the Flight Service Station (FSS), accessing a computer weather program, calling an air traffic control facility, hearing the ATIS broadcast, or listening to an automated weather observation station, provides instant temperature-dew point information.

Condensation and Cloud Formation

If clouds are present, does that mean it's going to rain? Definitely not. But if you have rain, or some other form of precipitation (hail, snow, etc.), clouds are definitely nearby. If you're driving along and see water coming from the sky without clouds, there's a good chance that you've just hit a fire hydrant or driven under an elephant.

For significant precipitation to occur, clouds must generally be around 4,000 feet thick. Precipitation can take the form of rain, hail, snow, ice pellets or grains, or freezing rain. Essentially, precipitation is any or all forms of water particles, whether liquid or solid, that fall from the sky and reach the ground. It is distinguished from clouds, fog or dew in that it falls and makes contact with the earth's surface. When flying near any airport reporting precipitation of light or greater intensity, expect clouds to be at least 4,000 feet thick.

Lapse Rates and Temperature Inversions

Suppose your family acquires an electric hedge clipper, and you're an only child. The very next day, the family cat suddenly sports a new haircut. Does it take Sherlock Holmes to solve this mystery? Hardly. Most weather mysteries are equally easy to solve once you understand the relationship between lapse rates and temperature inversions.

The sun heats the earth. That's a fact. Very little of the sun's energy directly heats the air. That's also a fact. Then how does the air become warm? To incoming light, the atmosphere acts much like a pane of glass on a greenhouse (Figure 17). It lets solar radiation easily pass through without absorbing much heat itself. This heat is absorbed by the earth's surface. It's this heated surface that is primarily responsible for the atmosphere's heat content.

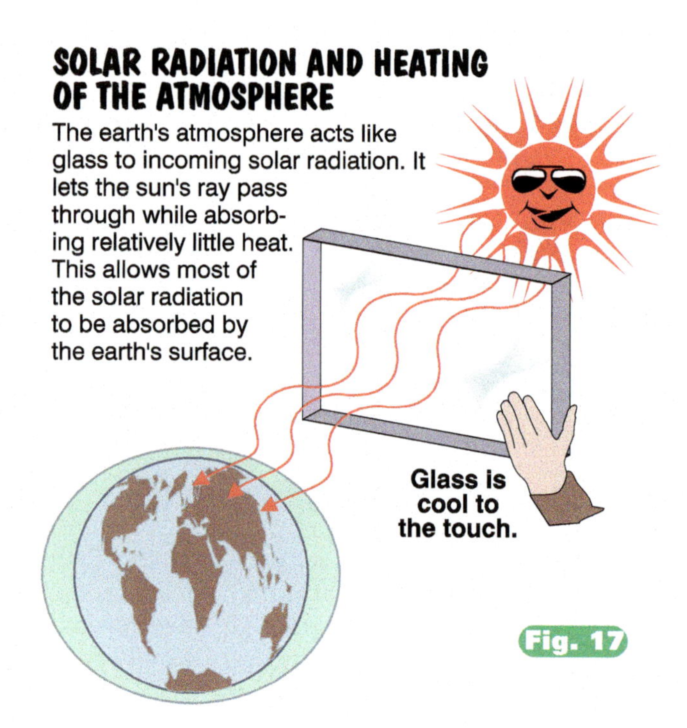

Fig. 17

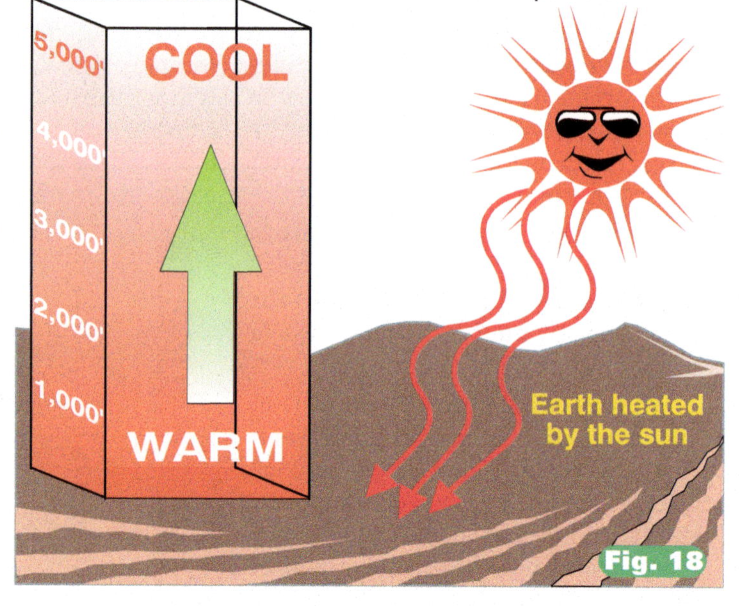

Fig. 18

As we learned in the beginning of this chapter, it's the surface of the earth that heats or cools the air directly. On clear days, when the earth absorbs an enormous amount of heat, the air in contact with the surface is warmed by touching (Figure 18). As we move away from this heated surface, the air cools. We might say the temperature lapses or changes with an increase in altitude. Meteorologists call this the *temperature lapse rate.* It is one of the most important items in the science of meteorology.

No one can guess exactly how much the temperature will change with altitude. In fact, meteorologists don't know, and they're paid to make scientific guesses. A few people think it changes at a steady 3.5 degrees F (2 degrees C) per thousand feet, but that's not quite true. This is a misconception on the order of believing Pluto is a large dog orbiting the sun. There are many variables affecting the rate temperature changes with altitude.

To identify the rate of temperature change, weather specialists across the nation send up atmospheric test probes hooked to weather balloons twice daily. These probes, called radiosondes, provide information on wind, pressure, humidity and temperature.

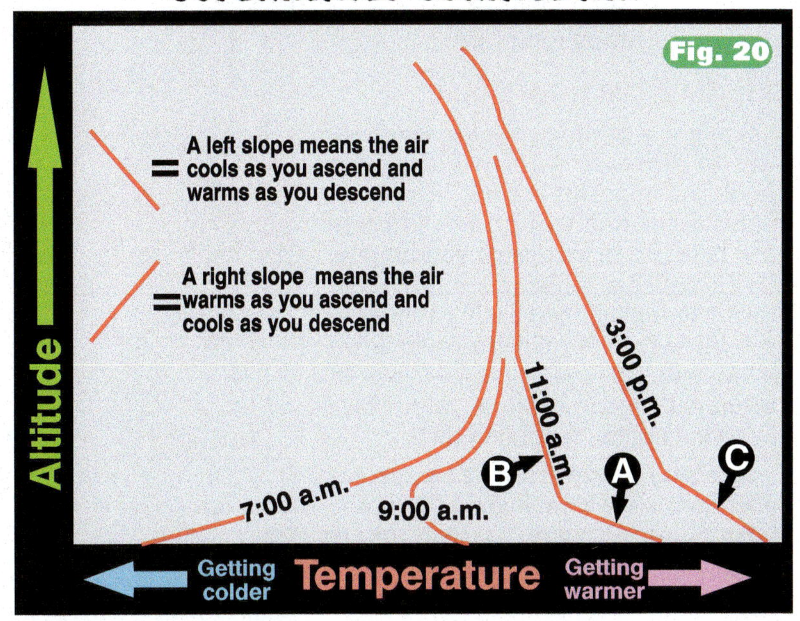

A left sloping line indicates a temperature drop with altitude. Slope (A) and slope (C) both indicate the presence of a superheated layer of air close to the surface. The surface air of slope (C) starts off warmer because it's later in the afternoon. Above the surface, the air at slope (B) shows a normal lapse rate.

Using this information, meteorologists are able to determine an exceptionally important measurement called the *environmental temperature lapse rate.* This lapse rate is essentially a vertical temperature profile of the atmosphere.

Temperature change with altitude can vary considerably. It's anything but consistent. On a very hot day, the desert surface can reach temperatures of 150 degrees F, as shown in Figure 19 (it's so hot that small animals, standing too long in one spot, can be seen exploding right in front of you). Four to five feet above the surface the air temperature may be only 90 degrees F .

That's an incredible lapse rate! Airplanes entering this shallow, heated layer of air during landing might experience turbulence as well as a decrease in air density. The turbulence is caused by *thermals* or updrafts, which are small, rising parcels of warmer air that your airplane bumps into. This could make for a slightly less smooth landing if the pilot wasn't prepared (it's also a great excuse to use with passengers if you land hard).

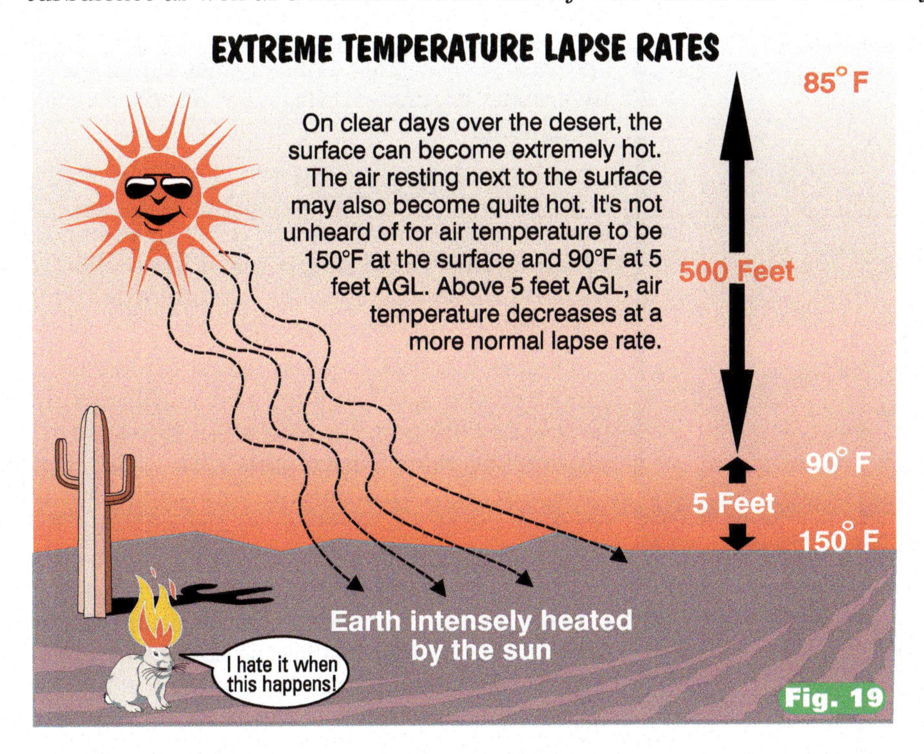

Above the heated layer of air, this super lapse rate reverts to a rather normal, less dramatic temperature decrease with altitude. The depth (height) of this superheated layer can increase during the day as warm air from below rises and mixes with the cooler air aloft.

Figure 20 depicts several temperature-altitude plots for a clear day. At 11 a.m., the temperature plot tilts to the left immediately above the surface, showing a dramatic temperature drop with altitude (point A). This is the result of a super-high lapse rate found over very hot surfaces.

As altitude increases, the temperature decrease at a more normal, less dramatic lapse rate (point B). Later, at 3 p.m., the surface temperature starts off warmer and a quick temperature drop is even more noticeable because of intense afternoon heating (point C).

Temperature Inversions

While it's common for air temperature to decrease with height, sometimes the opposite occurs. There are many occasions when the temperature actually increases as you ascend. This is called a *temperature inversion,* since the normal-decreasing temperature lapse rate is turned upside down or inverted. There are two types of temperature inversions, a surface inversion and an inversion aloft.

SURFACE BASED INVERSION

Altitude
Temp
Top of Inversion
Bottom of Inversion
Air starts to cool again
Air becomes warmer
Air starts to get warm
Air next to ground is cool
Ground cools quickly as evening progresses
I knew I shouldn't have eaten that!
Fig. 21

A surface inversion occurs as the ground cools and the air next to it also cools. The air at altitude still contains heat from earlier in the day. With a further increase in altitude the air decreases in temperature.

Surface Inversion—The surface inversion, shown in Figure 21, is the most common type. It frequently forms around sunset and lasts until midmorning. A setting sun allows the surface temperature to drop quickly, especially on cloudless, calm nights. In the absence of a cloud cover, the earth cools quickly in much the same way a heated waterbed cools when the covers are left off. There is nothing above the surface to absorb the radiant heat (Clouds, somewhat like blankets, prevent rapid surface cooling. The water droplets in them absorb radiant heat from the surface. As they warm, they re-radiate this heat back toward the ground, which absorbs the heat energy again. This exchange continues all night long and keeps surface temperatures warmer than they would be on a clear night).

As the earth cools, the air next to it starts to cool. In situations where there is not a lot of mixing, the layer adjacent to the earth cools while the air above remains at or near daytime temperatures. The result is a temperature inversion.

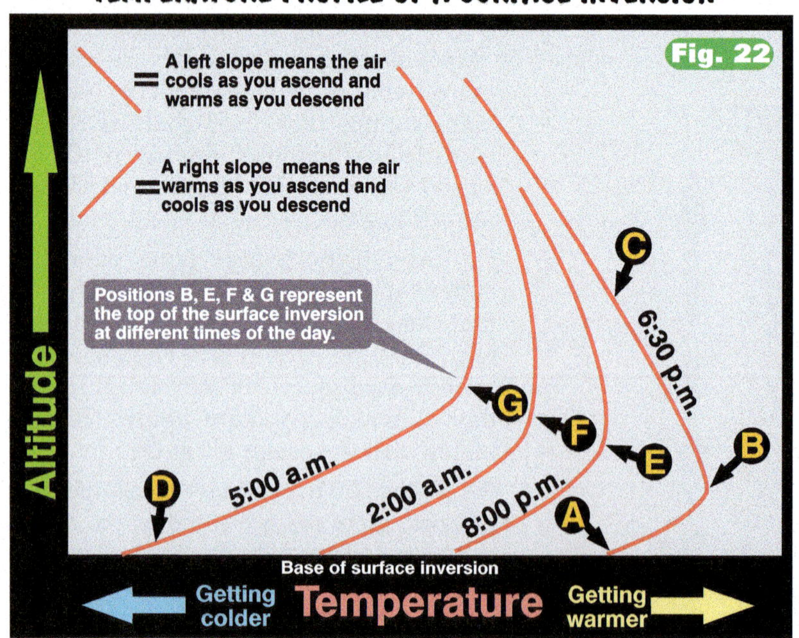

A surface inversion starts at the surface and is characterized by an increase in air temperature with altitude (a right sloping line). The top of the inversion occurs where temperatures resume their normal decrease with altitude (a left sloping line). As day progresses into night the top of the inversion increases in height, as shown by positions E to F to G.

The base of a surface inversion (where the temperature starts to increase with height) is located at the surface (I'm just making sure this is clear). The top of the inversion occurs where the temperature lapse rate resumes its normal decrease with height. Typically, the top of surface inversions occurs within a few hundred feet of the ground.

In case you think surface inversions involve sissy, wimpy little temperature changes, think again. Surface inversions can result in a temperature increase of 25 degrees F with a 250 foot increase in height above the surface (even larger temperature differences are possible).

Figure 22 shows several temperature/altitude plots for the late evening and early morning hours. At 6:30 p.m., a little after sunset in this profile, the temperature plot tilts to the right (position A). This means the temperature increases with an increase in altitude—up to a point—then the temperature plot bends back to the left (position B). Where the curve bends to the left, the air is the warmest (position B). This is the location of the top of the surface inversion. Above the inversion, the air has a normal (decreasing temperature) lapse rate (position C).

The 5 a.m. temperature plot tells a similar story. The plot line starts at the far left of the diagram, indicating the surface temperature has cooled noticeably during the late evening and early morning (position D). As night progresses, the top of the inversion occurs at progressively higher altitudes (points E to F to G) as the layer of colder surface air grows. (Remember, Figure 22 is a microview of the atmosphere. The altitude scale is in hundreds of feet.)

During winter, in parts of Alaska, surface inversions can be quite impressive. Air at the surface can be minus 45 degrees F, while at 200 feet AGL the air temperature can be minus 5 degrees F. This is a 40 degree F temperature increase in 200 feet—a very dramatic temperature change (somewhat like a Pompeian with a front row seat at the Mt. Vesuvius volcano trials). Long nights and short days contribute to this type of dramatic surface inversion.

Inversions with extreme temperature differences can cause pilots serious problems. Reports of very cold airplanes climbing into the warmer, moister air aloft warn of instantaneous *frost* formation on the windshield. This occurs because the temperature of the collecting surface (the airplane) is at or below the dew point of the air and the dew point is below freezing. Here the atmospheric moisture sublimates (bypasses the liquid state, going from gas in the atmosphere to solid on the glass) directly onto the aircraft's cold surface as ice crystals. At only a few hundred feet AGL, with no visual reference and no instrument rating, this has proven deadly to some pilots.

Without wind to mix the warm and cold air together, a surface inversion is more likely to form. Winds of about seven knots or greater can start mixing the warm and cold layers of air, causing the inversion to disappear. Little parcels of rising warm air (called *convective* currents because the motion is mostly vertical) from hotspots on the surface can help break up an inversion. This is why surface inversions forming over the desert seldom last past midmorning, which is the time when convective currents typically start forming and begin mixing the air.

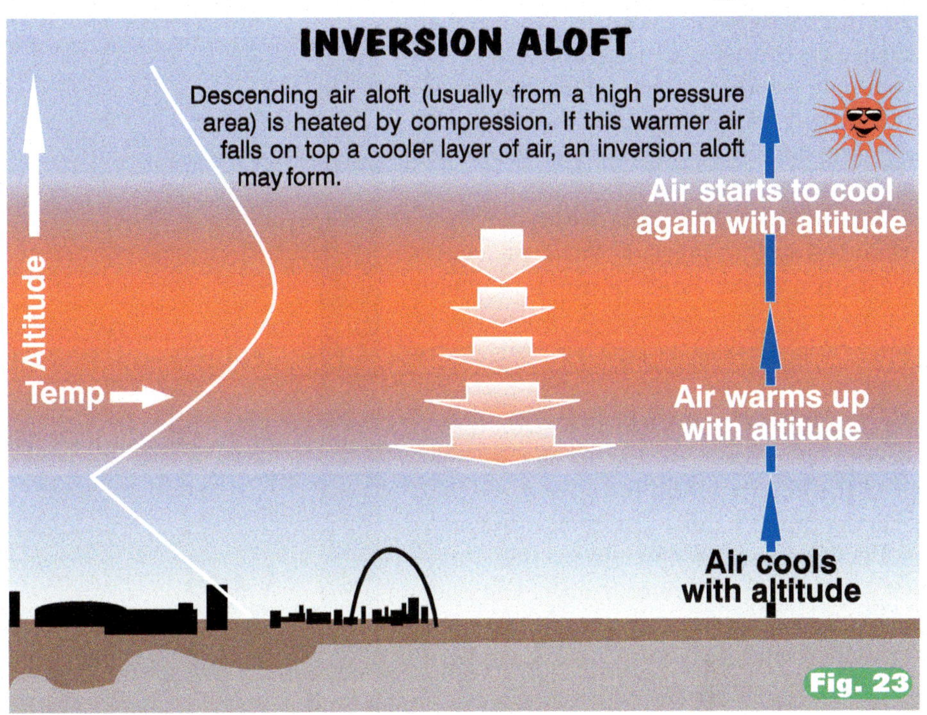

I've always thought of convective currents as little, unruly children who run up and down stairs in the house breaking things up. Several years ago one of these little guys visited our place and tore things up. I told the little guy, "You better stop it or the devil is gonna get you!" He looked at me and said, "Why should I stop? I'm doing what he wants!" Ouch!

Inversion Aloft—The other type of inversion is called an *inversion aloft*. These inversions are caused by warmer air moving horizontally over colder air or by air aloft that is descending and heated by compression (Figure 23). Unlike surface inversions, these inversions are typically found at higher altitudes (thus the word *aloft*).

High pressure centers in the atmosphere consist of large masses of air descending at rates of hundreds to thousands of feet per day. As this subsiding air descends, it experiences the same effect divers experience when descending to the bottom of a swimming pool—an increase in pressure.

DATE WITH THE DUST DEVIL

It was the last pass spray run on an irrigated corn field. I started to pull up to clear the wires. A dust devil turned the aircraft nose down and to the left. I straightened the plane just before impact with wire. Damage: 18 inches of leading edge slapped with wire, paint scratched off nose bowl, 2 wires broke. These whirlwinds sometimes occur before a front moves through. They are 10' to 100' across and very powerful. Only way to keep out of them is to not fly when present. They are visible, except where the ground is wet— no debris for the whirlwind to pick up.

ASRS Report

An increase in air pressure produces an increase in temperature for the same reason dough becomes warm when it's kneaded (I'm not talking about the $dough$ everyone needs). Compressing dough (or air) increases its temperature. The harder the dough is squeezed, the warmer it gets. If this descending layer of warm air comes to rest on a cooler layer of air, a temperature inversion can form aloft. This type of inversion is sometimes called a subsidence inversion.

In the summer months, a subsidence inversion is more common in the western half of the country than in the eastern half. In particular, it's quite common on or near the Pacific Coast. When warm, high pressure air subsides (lowers) onto the cool, moist inflow of air from the ocean, an inversion aloft forms, as shown in the temperature-altitude profiles of Figure 24.

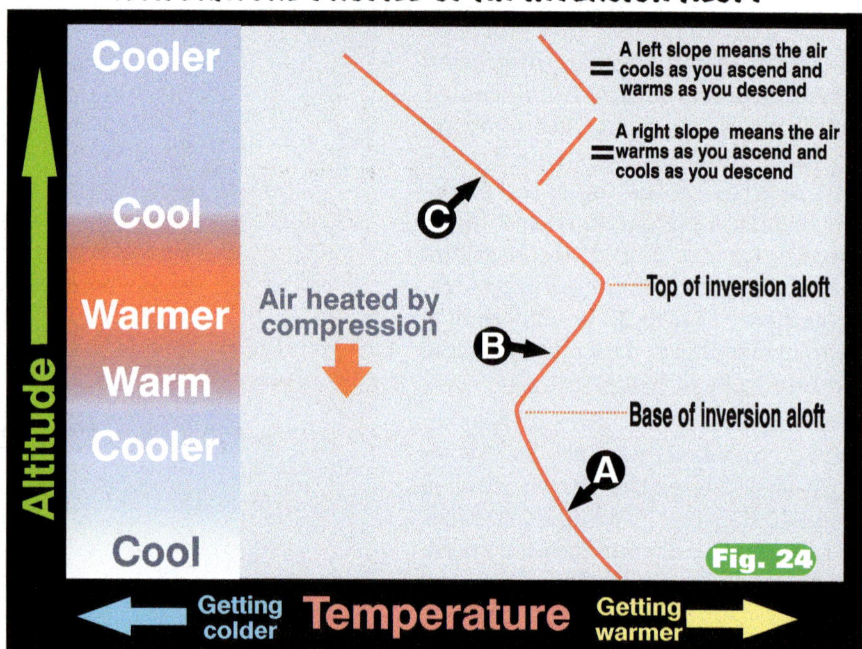

An inversion aloft is characterized by a temperature profile that starts decreasing at the surface (position A), increases (position B), then finally decreases again at the top of the inversion (position C). When air aloft is forced to descend (as in a high pressure area) it heats by compression. If warmer air comes to rest over a colder layer of air, an inversion aloft may form.

A pilot faces a decreasing temperature lapse rate when departing an airport beneath the inversion. The climb is initially made in cool air (position A). Upon entering the bottom of the inversion the air becomes warmer as altitude is gained (position B). At the top of the inversion, a decreasing temperature lapse rate once again prevails (position C).

Effects of Temperature Inversions

Recently, a friend and I went flying in a hot air balloon. We departed immediately after sunrise and ascended through the cool, morning air. We rose so quickly it appeared that we were climbing at the best-angle-of-bag (if there were such a thing—there isn't). Suddenly, at approximately 1,500 feet AGL, the balloon ceased climbing (Figure 25A).

Reaching the base of a temperature inversion aloft nullified our lift. The middle or top of a surface inversion can produce the same effect on a balloon but at an altitude closer to the surface (Figure 25B). We just skipped along horizontally, beneath the base of the inversion, until more heat was applied to the balloon. In much the same way a temperature inversion impedes the ascent of a balloon, it can also prevent parcels of warmer air on the surface from ascending any higher.

Have you ever noticed smoke coming from a chimney in the early morning or evening hours? Sometimes this smoke ascends for a short distance then spreads out horizontally, as shown in Figure 26. The flattening of smoke is a sure indication of a temperature inversion (since it's often seen closer to the surface in the evening, it's probably a surface inversion).

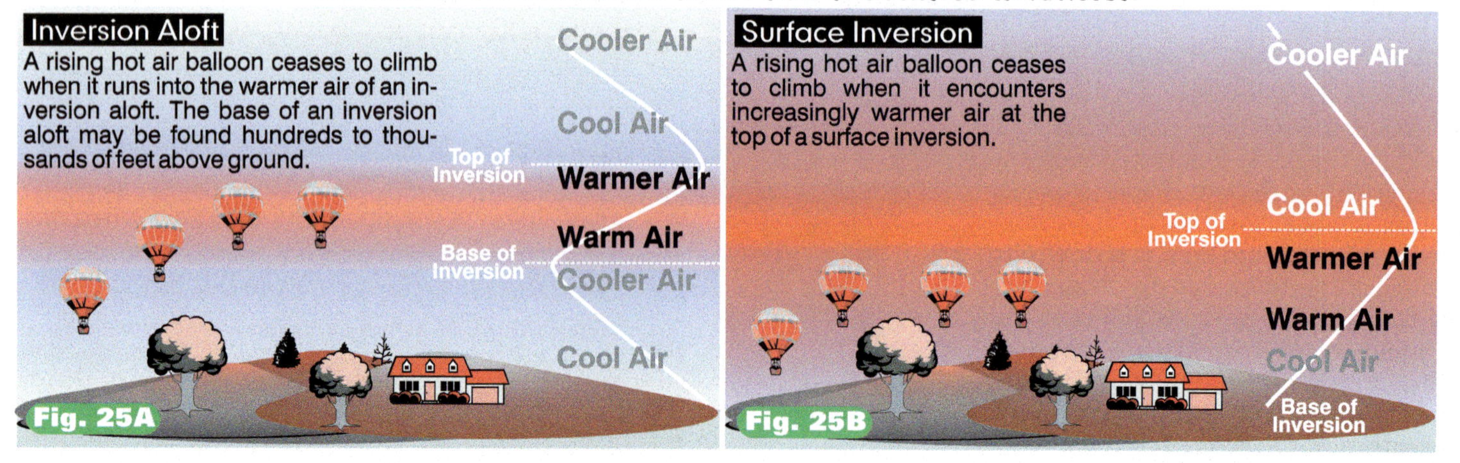

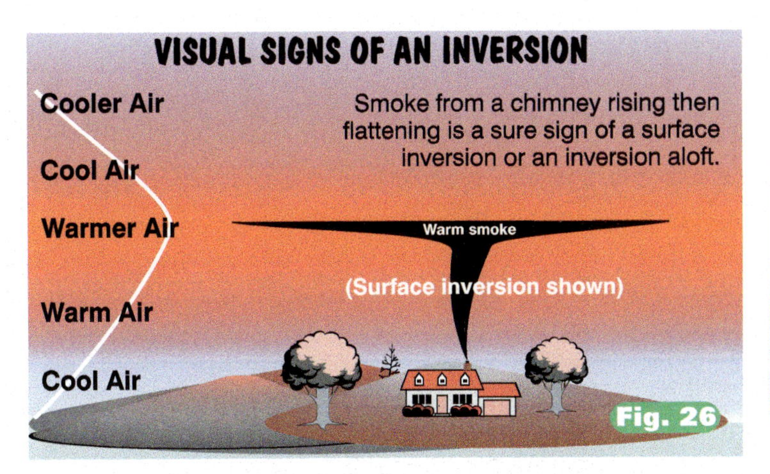

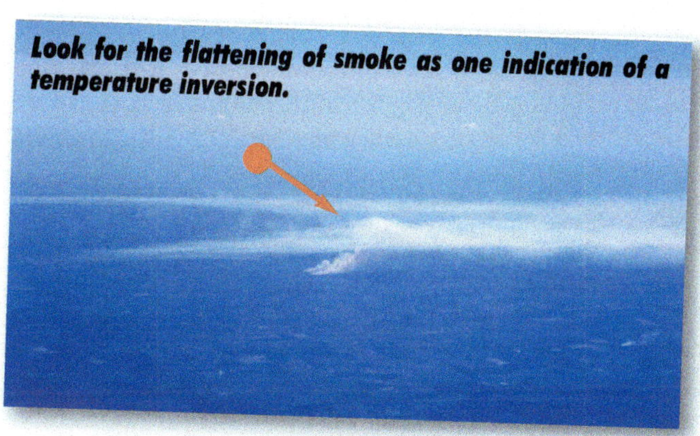

STRATUS CLOUDS ARE A SIGN OF A TEMPERATURE INVERSION

As warm parcels of air rise, expand and cool they may eventually form clouds. The inversion acts like a lid that keeps these rising parcels from ascending into the warmer air of the inversion. The parcels form clouds having *straight* tops, called *stratus* clouds.

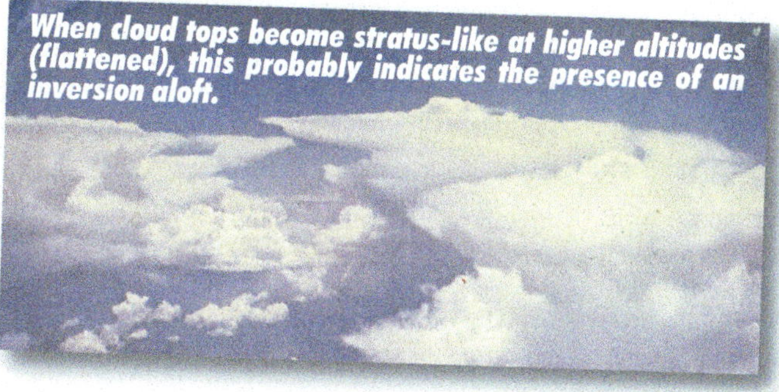

POOR VISIBILITY IN AN INVERSION

A temperature inversion (surface or aloft) acts like a lid on the atmospheric pollutants beneath it. Unable to rise and disperse, the pollutants remain in a lower layer and restrict visibility.

Warm, rising puffs of smoke, much like a hot air balloon, cannot ascend through the warmer air of an inversion. In a very similar way, the presence of a temperature inversion acts to flatten cloud tops. Therefore, layer-type clouds (otherwise known as stratus or straight type clouds) are another visible indication of a temperature inversion, as shown in Figures 27A and 27B (more on stratus clouds later).

The inability of smoke, haze or pollution to move vertically and be carried away by winds at higher altitudes reduces the local flight visibility. This is especially true in areas of industry, as shown in Figure 28. Mexico City rests in a large valley and is notorious for its temperature inversions. Trapped pollution from the city can become so bad that asphyxiated birds have been known to fold their wings, croak, and just fall to earth. I wonder how many needless hours are spent plucking pigeons from sombreros?

What to Expect in an Inversion

The visible signs of an inversion should cue pilots to expect several possible flight conditions. First, temperature inversions mean an increase in the likelihood of cloud formation. Since cool air exists at the surface, the air might start to condense, forming fog or low clouds.

Second, visibility beneath the inversion can be quite low. Objects look farther away than they actually are. The mind equates something that is difficult to see with being farther away. A natural response to this situation is to get closer to the item you're attempting to see.

For example, under lower visibility conditions, pilots, thinking they are flying five miles away from the airport, are in all probability closer. They might be within the lateral limits of Class C or D airspace while thinking they're avoiding these areas. (In good visibility conditions, the opposite effect occurs. Pilots think they are flying closer to a specific point than they are and they tend to move farther away from a specific reference in good visibility conditions.)

Third, temperature inversions can indicate the presence of low-level windshear. An inversion can allow a warmer, faster layer of air aloft to move, unrestricted by surface friction (Figure 29). Since warmer and colder air have different densities, they tend not to mix (that's why fancy restaurants like Jacques en de Baux keep oil and vinegar salad dressing in separate bottles; they have different densities and don't mix). Given the proper conditions, the warmer air aloft can easily slip across the top of the cooler air, like skis on snow. Such a condition is conducive to the formation of a low level jet stream. This is where air, within a few hundred to a few thousand feet above the surface can be moving at speeds up to 100 MPH.

In the presence of an inversion, if surface winds are calm, and winds at a few hundred to a few thousand feet AGL are in the 25 knot range, be prepared for possible *windshear*. Windshear is a condition where the velocity of the wind changes drastically over a small distance vertically. It can occur at all altitudes and in all directions and result in a sudden loss of lift. Large crab angles on approach to an airport that's reporting calm surface winds are another clue to the presence of this windshear. In other words, if the tower reports the winds as calm, yet you're having to substantially crab to keep aligned with the runway, be prepared for strong windshear as you descend. I can think of no better time to add a few extra knots onto the approach speed for safety.

Fourth, temperature inversions indicate the presence of stable air. Stability is the tendency of the atmosphere to resist vertical motion. In much the same way an inversion impedes the vertical progress of a hot air balloon, it

WINDSHEAR IN A TEMPERATURE INVERSION

Windshear in a temperature inversion can occur in the zone where warm air aloft and cold air below meet. The greater the difference in velocity between the warm and cold air, the greater the turbulence found in the shear zone (the warm and cold air in the shear zone don't mix well). It's possible to have sudden changes in airspeed when climbing or descending through windshear.

STABLE AIR IN A TEMPERATURE INVERSION

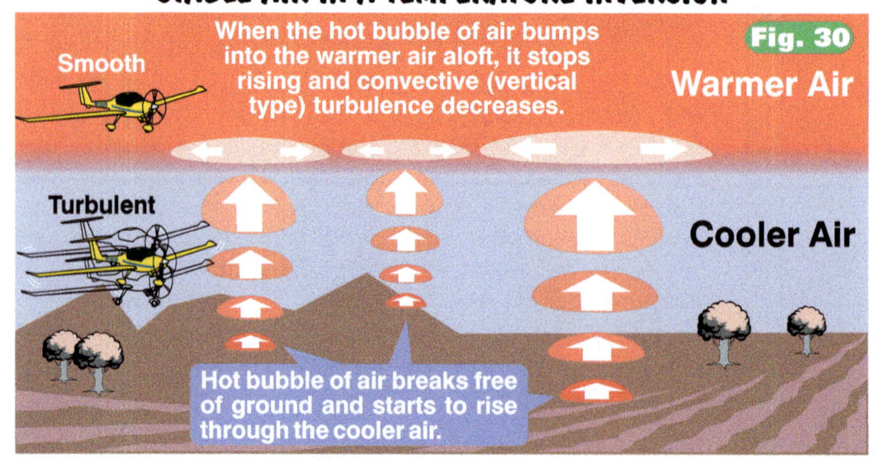

Stable air is air that suppresses vertical motion. In a temperature inversion, a warm bubble of air rises through the cooler air but can't rise into the warm air aloft (the bubble must be hotter than its surroundings for it to rise). Vertical air motion is suppressed. Therefore, temperature inversions are associated with stable air since they suppress the vertical motion of rising bubbles.

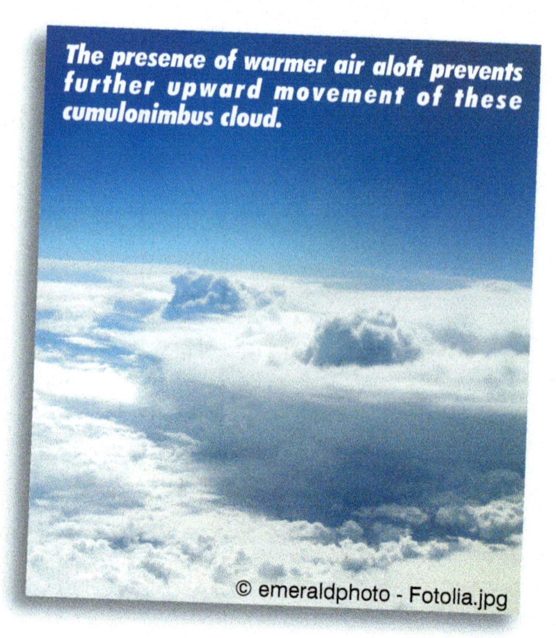

A warmer layer of air above a cooler layer of air is a stable condition. This is called a temperature inversion and it forms in stable air. These two layers don't want to change places. In unstable air, however, a warmer layer of air is found below a cooler layer of air. These two layers want to change places. This is an unstable condition and vertical motion (convection) occurs between these two layers.

also impedes the ascension of warmer air in the atmosphere, as shown in Figure 30. This is one of the most important points in the understanding of atmospheric stability.

Little parcels of warm air attempt to rise but they cannot ascend into the increasingly warmer layers of air aloft (just like the smoke stops rising when it hits warmer air aloft). This means the atmosphere becomes smoother, because the warm parcels of air stop rising. A smoother, more comfortable ride is the net result. This is especially true when you're flying within the warmer air that rests on top of the cooler air at the bottom of the inversion. At this point, there is probably very little air rising within the warmer air, and you are not likely to experience any turbulence.

Professional pilots know the most important tools for analyzing weather are visual clues, particularly haze layers, flattened cloud tops and smoke levels. These are all flags signaling the existence of a temperature inversion.

As the GPS is primary for navigational positioning, the thermometer is primary for meteorological understanding. Pay attention to the temperature when climbing or descending.

Perhaps Abraham Maslow summed it up very well when he said, "If the only tool you have is a hammer, then everything looks like a nail." The more tools in your toolkit, the better chance you'll have of building a complete picture of the weather at hand. One of the tools you'll most certainly want is knowledge of how slight changes in the lapse rate affect atmospheric stability.

Atmospheric Stability: Warm Over Cold, And Cold Over Warm

The atmosphere is stable when it resists the upward movement of air. It is unstable when it permits or amplifies this upward movement. In other words, stable air, if given an upward shove, sinks back to its original level. Unstable air, if shoved upward, continues to climb on its own.

Atmospheric stability can be roughly visualized in two different scenarios. Figure 31A consists of a warm layer of air resting on top of a colder layer of air. Do these two layers want to change places? In other words, will the cold air on the bottom want to rise up through the warm air on top? This is unlikely. Cold air is heavy (more dense) and warm air is light (less dense). The atmosphere is stable, since these two layers are content to remain where they are.

This explains why, after sunset, the air is usually stable. As the earth cools, so does the air resting next to it. An upper layer of the atmosphere remains warm from heat acquired during daylight hours. Cold (heavy) air is on the bottom and warmer (lighter) air on top, a very stable condition. We know this condition to be a temperature inversion and it explains why inversions are associated with stable air.

Figure 31B consists of a colder layer of air resting on top of a warmer layer of air. Does the warm layer of air on the bottom want to rise up through the colder air above? Do Golden Retrievers want to eat dinner? You bet. Warm air rises, cold air falls. It's sort of like sitting on a balloon in the bathtub (you're on your own if you try this at home). You know that balloon wants to rise, and it will at the first opportunity. Warm air surrounded by cooler air will do exactly the same thing (I can't predict what the Golden Retriever will do). Cold on top of warm is a very unstable condition.

Here's an excellent example showing how the earth is unevenly heated. Cloud formation occurs over the land because of the lifting from warmer, rising parcels of air.

Courtesy NASA

As we've already seen with super lapse rates, a layer of air resting next to the heated surface of earth can become quite warm. The vertical motion of unstable air produces turbulence. It also produces good visibility as the rising air causes atmospheric mixing and helps disperse airborne pollutants.

The earth isn't heated evenly. The air next to the earth's surface isn't heated evenly either. If it were, then entire layers of air in the atmospheric environment would move up and down together. In reality, layers of air don't do this. What actually happens is that some chunks of air become hotter than others. These air parcels break off from the surface and ascend individually, as small blobs of variable sizes. Dust devils or isolated thunderstorms are often visual evidence of this happening. Glider pilots look for these rising columns of air with the same enthusiasm of young people on Spring break. So do hot air balloonists, who count on rising air for a free lift. Discovering one of these rising elevator shafts of air is their version of finding an engine in flight.

Part and Parcel

When lifting occurs, only a small chunk of air—a parcel—is lifted. Nature moves a lot more parcels every day than U.P.S. In studying the weather, what we're really trying to figure out is, Who's shipping what to whom?

Parcels of air are made, not born. Something happens to lift a small section of the air in the environment upward. Lifting can be caused by a weather front, a mountain, or a hot spot on the surface.

The size of an air parcel varies. It can be a few feet across, or even miles in diameter. A parcel is this small portion of air that differs in temperature from its surroundings. Meteorologists use the parcel theory as a convenient way of explaining nature's behavior.

The Environmental Lapse Rate

I previously mentioned the environmental temperature lapse rate. This is the actual rate at which atmospheric temperature changes with altitude. Meteorologists also refer to the environmental lapse rate as the ambient lapse rate. These terms are used synonymously. I don't know why they don't just call it the real lapse rate, because that's what it is. Too simple, I guess.

No one can predict what this environmental lapse rate will be. If they could, meteorologists wouldn't need to send up radiosondes at locations around the nation twice a day.

Many aviation books will tell you the average lapse rate is 3.5 degrees F (2 degrees C) per thousand feet, and this number is often used in calculations. Even the FAA uses it. Fine and dandy, but I want you to know it is as much a work of fiction as "Jaws or New York on $3 a Day." This 3.5 degree number is an average that conceals a huge amount of variation, both horizontally and vertically. The 3.5 degree figure might hold true for 10,000 or 20,000 feet, then change to a different rate; it might remain true for 50,000 feet straight up over a shopping mall in Topeka, but be different if measured 15 or 50 miles away (see Figures 31 A and B). The lapse rate is highly variable from place to place, time to time, and even moment to moment. You can guess at it, you can approximate it, but in the end if you want real information, you must measure it.

With an understanding of the environmental lapse rate under your seatbelt, you're ready to use your airplane's thermometer to obtain a rough approximation of atmospheric stability. On your next cross country flight, take vertical temperature measurements every thousand feet of climb. Ask yourself, "Am I climbing into air that's becoming warmer or colder?" If you're climbing into warmer air (a temperature increase with altitude), then a temperature inversion is present. This is a stable condition (see Figure 31A), and no fancy calculations or advanced thinking are necessary. Enjoy your flight.

If you're climbing into colder air (the temperature decreases with altitude), then atmospheric stability is dependent on how quickly the temperature decreases. If the air cools

The Meaning of Adiabatic Cooling

We've been speaking of air cooling from expansion as it's lifted, and heated by compression as it's forced downward. Meteorologists have a more precise word for this. It's called *adiabatic cooling* (or heating). Many pilots think that adiabatic is a Greek word meaning "you're not going to pass the weather portion of your written test." I can assure you it doesn't mean that. It literally means "without gain or loss of heat." In other words, adiabatic cooling or heating occurs without having to take heat away or add it to the parcel.

Expanding a parcel of air by lifting will move its molecules farther apart, keeping them from bumping into one another. Air molecules not being forced to bump into one another create less friction. Energy has been used in expanding the parcel, which causes the molecules to slow down a little. Thus, air temperature decreases. The parcel has cooled, yet no heat has been taken from it.

Conversely, compressing a parcel of air by downward motion moves its molecules closer together and increases their speed, which increases the air's temperature. No heat has been added to this parcel, yet it becomes warmed. Whenever you hear about adiabatic cooling or heating you can assume it involves the lifting or falling of air and the resultant temperature change.

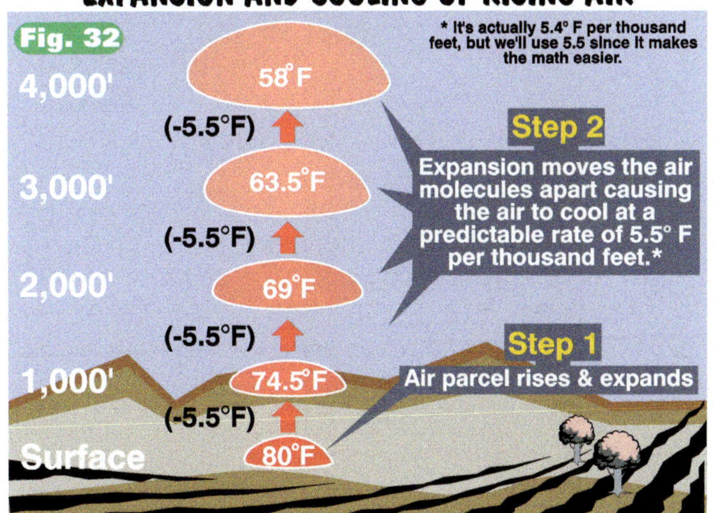

As long as a rising parcel of air doesn't start to condense and form a cloud, it will cool at a rate of approximately 5.5°F per every thousand feet of altitude gain (it's actually 5.4°F/1000' but we'll use 5.5° for convenience). This is a constant that occurs everywhere on earth (similarly, as the unsaturated parcel descends it compresses and heats at a rate of 5.5°F per thousand feet altitude change).

quickly as you ascend, then the cold air is above you and the warmer air is below (see Figure 31B). You can be sure these two layers want to change places. Some instability is sure to be present.

Rising Parcels of Air

Let's consider those individual parcels of rising warm air we previously discussed. A warm parcel breaks away from the surface and rises into the cooler air aloft. As this parcel ascends it expands, as shown in Figure 32.

The air parcel expands much like a sealed bag of Fritos corn chips found in the back of your ascending airplane (eventually you reach the CFH or Critical Frito Height and the bag goes Frito-Nova). Frito bags, like air parcels, expand because atmospheric pressure decreases with a gain in altitude.

Basic physics decrees that as a parcel of air expands, it also cools. This is one of the reasons why using a spray-on deodorant early in the morning can cause you to moonwalk and make the Michael Jackson sound, "Eeeeooooowwwww!" The spray, which is rapidly expanding after being freed from its confinement in the can, cools quickly on its brief journey and forms a little glacier under your arm. A solitary parcel of air, moving vertically, also expands and cools with similar predictability.

Here is an amazing and crucial fact of atmospheric physics:

A rising parcel of air expands and cools at a constant rate of 5.4 degrees F for every thousand feet of climb as long as that parcel remains unsaturated (doesn't form a cloud).

Just to make the math a bit easier we'll round that figure off to 5.5 degrees. For all practical purposes, no matter where you are on earth (even the Bermuda Triangle!), if you lift a parcel of unsaturated air, it's going to cool at about 5.5 degrees F for every thousand feet of altitude change, as shown in Figure 32.

"But wait," I hear you saying, "Doesn't the rising parcel of air move through an atmosphere that also changes temperature?" Yes, it does. But the *rate* at which the atmosphere (the environment) changes temperature is, you will recall, inconsistent. It's inconsistencies that make things interesting, including the weather.

Suppose we measure the environmental lapse rate with the airplane's thermometer, as shown in Figure 33. Our thermometer shows a decrease in temperature as we gain altitude. Which will cool most quickly, the environment or the rising parcel of air? As the Kung Fu Master Cain would say, "Ahhhh Grasshopper, read on."

The airplane's thermometer in Figure 33 shows that, at this spot, at this time, there is a temperature decrease of 6 degrees F per thousand feet. The parcel, shown resting on the surface, rises because it is 1 degree warmer (at 71 degrees F) than the surrounding air (70 degrees F). This differential can be caused by the air parcel lying over a portion of the ground that is warmer, perhaps because it's paved, or because it's rock as opposed to the soil of surrounding areas. For whatever reason, there's a difference in temperature, and the air is on the move. Fasten your seatbelt and hang on tight.

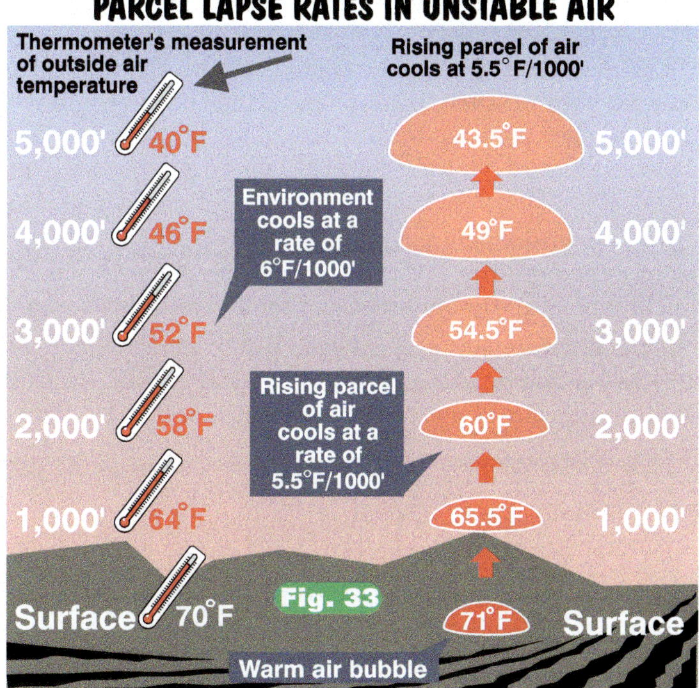

A warm bubble of air at the surface starts to rise because it is 1 degree warmer than its environment. As the bubble ascends, it cools at the constant rate of 5.5°F per thousand feet. The environmental lapse rate (as measured by a thermometer in the airplane) changes 6°F per thousand feet. As the bubble rises it remains warmer than the environment. Thus, the bubble continues to climb indicating that the air in the environment is unstable.

Keep in mind that this air is going to cool off at 5.5 degrees per thousand feet, because that's a law and air is very law abiding. By 5,000 feet above the ground, it will cool to 43.5 degrees (5.5 [drop per thousand feet] × 5 [thousands of feet] = 27.5; 71-27.5 = 43.5). The surrounding air, meanwhile, has cooled to 40 degrees F (5 [thousands of feet] × 6 [degree F drop per thousand feet] = 30; 70-30 = 40).

As long as there is a temperature differential, our air parcel will keep moving. In fact, because the temperature differential is now greater than it was at ground level, the air packet will move even faster and accelerate its journey to equilibrium. When it gets there is all a matter of degree. The atmosphere depicted in Figure 33 is *unstable,* since it encourages upward motion of individual air parcels.

Let's examine a situation where the atmosphere is cooling at a lesser rate of, say, 3 degrees F per thousand feet (Figure 34). Same starting conditions, but this time look what happens at just 1000 feet AGL. The rising parcel has cooled to 65.5 degrees, or 1.5 degrees *cooler* than the surrounding air. It becomes a sinker that would be the envy of any major league pitcher. The South may rise again; the air won't, at least not far, because in this instance the atmosphere is *stable.*

The important fact you need to take away from this explanation is that the *environmental lapse rate determines the stability of the atmosphere.* Don't forget this concept. It's extremely important.

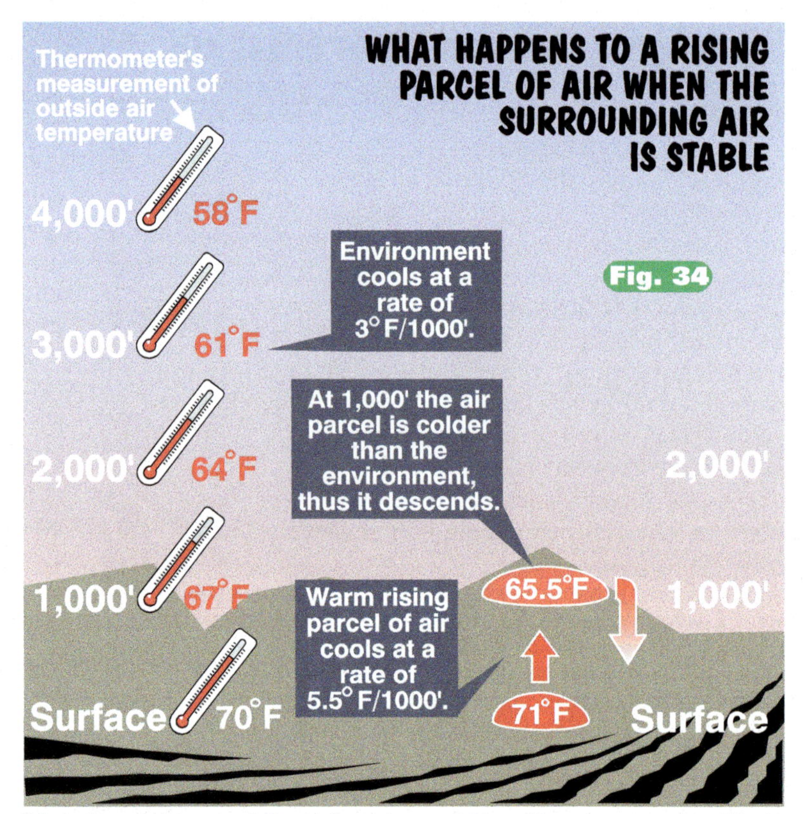

When the environment doesn't cool as quickly with an increase in altitude (i.e., remains warmer longer), it is more stable. In this example, the environment cools at only 3°F/1,000'. A warm, rising parcel of air cooling at an expected rate of 5.5°F/1,000' can only ascend to 1,000' before it becomes cooler than its environment. Thus, the environment (the surrounding atmosphere) is stable and the cooler air bubble now descends.

The next time you're on a flight, observe the thermometer during the climb. By noting the rate that temperature changes with altitude, you're measuring the environmental lapse rate in much the same way a radiosonde does (no, you can't get paid for the information). If the environment cools quicker than 5.5 degrees F per thousand feet, as shown in Figure 33, then the atmosphere is potentially unstable, because a rising parcel of unsaturated air can't cool as quickly as the environment. You've located the stairway to heaven (but please don't play it for us).

If the environment cools at a rate less than 5.5 degrees F per thousand feet, or even becomes warmer with altitude (as in a temperature inversion), the atmosphere is potentially stable. A rising parcel of unsaturated air will cool more quickly than its surroundings and tend to fall back to earth, as shown in Figure 34.

If the environment cools at exactly 5.5 degrees F per thousand feet, then a parcel of air will have the same temperature as its surroundings if it's physically moved up or down. The atmosphere would be *neutrally stable.* In other words, a parcel will neither climb nor descend on its own.

Saturated Parcels of Rising Air

So much for unsaturated air. Now, let's get wet.

Once these rising parcels cool to within a few degrees of their dew point, condensation occurs and clouds form. Now things get really interesting, because when clouds form, heat is released as the water goes from vapor to visible moisture. Think about it for a second—what is an ice cube if not a big drop of water with the heat sucked out? Same goes for water that materializes out of water vapor. In the course of rearranging themselves in a new formation, the water molecules shed heat. You can take my word for it, or take three years of physics. Your choice. This *latent heat,* as the physics people call it, gets released into the atmosphere.

An air parcel that's busy chugging out clouds *doesn't cool as quickly* as one that isn't engaging in puffery. In fact, *saturated* parcels of air cool at rates between 2 degrees F and 5 degrees F per thousand feet, depending on how much water vapor (and thus how much trapped heat) was in the air to begin with.

Water Vapor and Instability

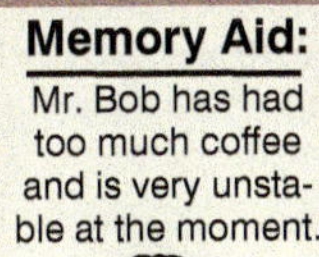
Memory Aid:
Mr. Bob has had too much coffee and is very unstable at the moment.

He makes himself stable by getting rid of the moisture (you figure it out).

If the atmosphere contains a great deal of water vapor, then the temperature of a *saturated*, rising parcel of air within the atmosphere might decrease at only 2 degrees F per thousand feet. This means the air parcel is being kept warm by the release of its latent heat as water vapor condenses (essentially, the parcel cools at a slower rate than its environment, making it want to keep rising). If the atmosphere contains very little water vapor to begin with, then a rising parcel of *saturated* air can decrease at a rate of as much as 5 degrees F per thousand feet.

A moist atmosphere is potentially more unstable than a dry one. Instability, however, is predicated on the condition that a rising air parcel within the atmosphere is lifted enough to reach saturation. This is why very moist air is called conditionally unstable air. It is stable as long as air parcels rising within it don't become saturated (i.e., form a cloud). The moment these parcels reach saturation, they can readily become warmer than their surroundings and start rising on their own. The atmosphere is then said to be unstable. Saturation is the *condition* upon which stability or instability is based.

Blowing In The Wind

Put a little water on your hand and blow on it, as shown in Figure 35. What does it do? It should cool your hand as the moisture evaporates (if it doesn't you've been eating too many Jalapeño peppers!). Heat, taken from your hand, is used in evaporating the saliva (that's why your hand feels cool—it lost some of its heat). Blowing simply accelerates this process. This heat (known as the *latent heat of vaporization*) is now trapped as energy in the water vapor above your hand. It's in a different energy state known as latent heat.

Try not to become overwhelmed by this concept of different forms of energy (energy states). Remember, whenever you put gasoline in your tank you're converting ancient vegetables and dinosaur lips into movement energy. Your automobile is nothing more than a fancy energy converting device much like that of the atmosphere.

Think of evaporation as a process opposite that of condensation. While evaporation puts *water* into the atmosphere, condensation gives the *water* back. If evaporation takes *heat* away, condensation must give *heat* back. The heat given back is known as *latent heat* (the *latent heat of condensation* to be precise). When water vapor condenses, latent heat is given back to the parcel, making that parcel slightly warmer.

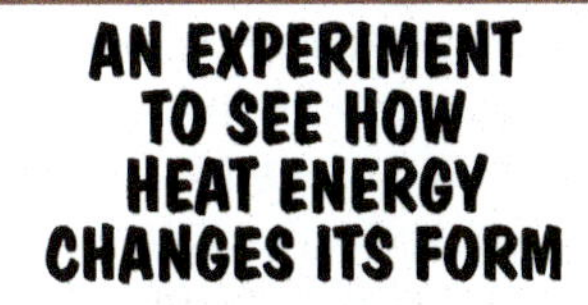

Fig. 35

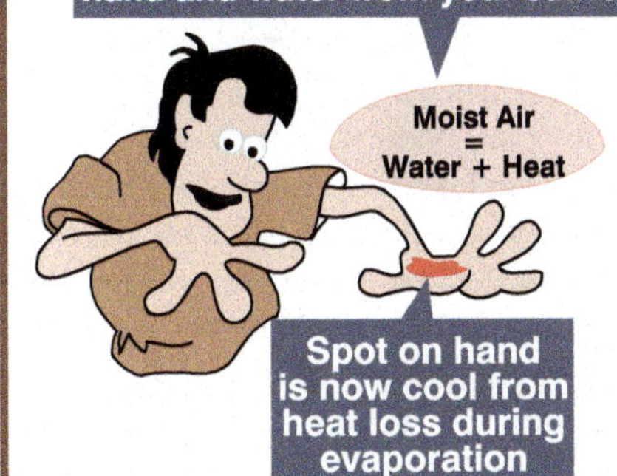

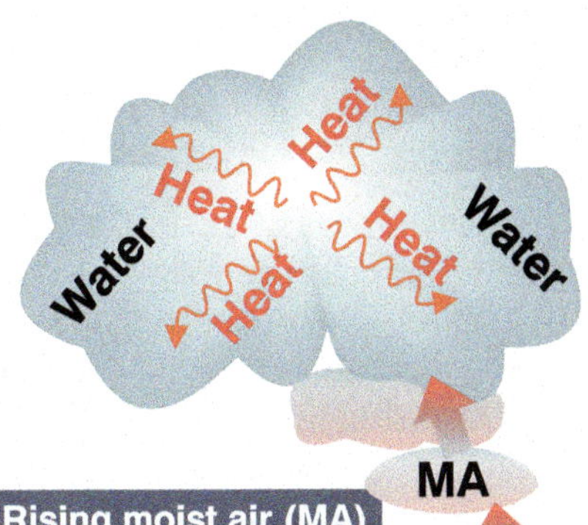

Figure 36 shows what happens when a rising parcel of air becomes saturated. Let's assume a parcel of unsaturated air is pushed up the side of a mountain. As it ascends, it cools at the unsaturated rate of 5.5 degrees F per thousand feet. The environmental lapse rate, as measured by our airplane's thermometer, also happens to be 5.5 degrees F per thousand feet. At 1,000 feet, this air parcel's temperature is the same as the surrounding air (its environment). It has neutral stability, since the parcel neither wants to rise nor descend.

Pushed aloft by The Force (the wind against rising terrain), at 2,000 feet the parcel cools to within a few degrees of its dew point and the moisture starts to condense. The parcel now becomes saturated. Latent heat is released, causing the rising air parcel to cool at a slower rate of only 3.5 degrees F per thousand feet. Push this baby up the mountain just a tiny bit more and a big difference in temperature will appear between the parcel and the surrounding atmosphere.

At 3,000 feet, the parcel has only cooled another 3.5 degrees F, while the surrounding air has dropped by 5.5 degrees. There is now a 2 degree F differential, and the air is about to do the locomotion. It rises on its own because it's warmer than the surrounding air. There may not be a free lunch, but there is a free ride. While the atmosphere was neutrally stable with respect to the unsaturated parcel of air, it is now unstable due to saturation of the rising parcel.

UNSTABLE AIR WITH RESPECT TO A CONDENSING PARCEL

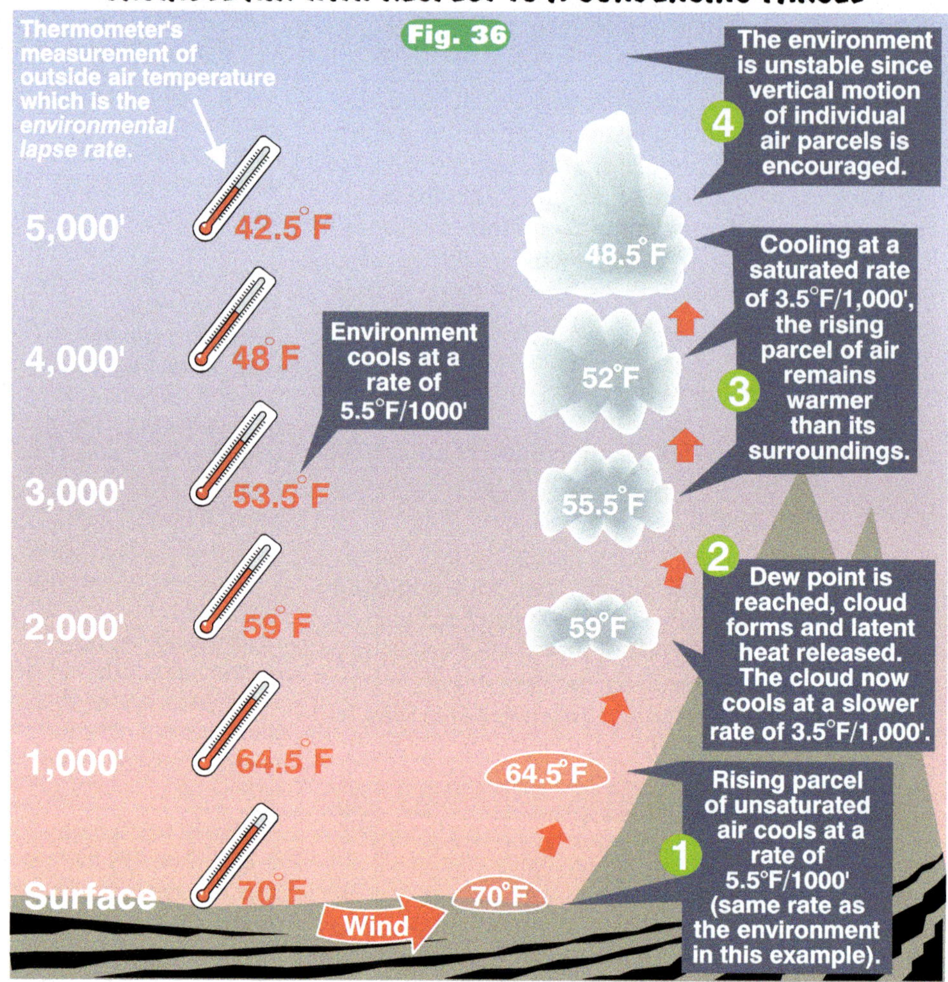

A rising parcel of unsaturated air (i.e., no cloud forming) being moved up a mountain slope cools at the same rate as the environment (step 1). So far the atmosphere (the environment) is neither stable nor unstable; it's neutrally stable. When the parcel becomes saturated and a cloud forms (step 2), it releases its latent heat, which warms the body of the rising parcel (the cloud). Thus, the cloud remains warmer than its environment since this particular cloud parcel cools at only 3.5°F/1,000' (step 3). The parcel now rises on its own without the help of wind. The atmosphere is considered unstable since it encourages the parcel (once it's given a shove upward, of course) to rise.

Clouds and Atmospheric Stability

By now you want to know what you know, and know why you care. You're ready to make a synaptic jump and begin contemplating some of the atmosphere's great mysteries.

Have you ever wondered why *cumulus clouds* (Figure 37) are associated with unstable air and *stratus clouds* (Figure 38) go with stable air? Maybe you've looked at clouds all your life and *not* known there was such an association. Chalk one up for learning and latent heat.

Your Guess Is as Good as Mine

Meteorologists can predict the stability of the atmosphere by examining the environmental lapse rate, the amount of moisture in the air, and the opportunities for the air being lifted. While this isn't an exact science, they do fairly well with their predictions.

At least they are more accurate than seismologists (earthquake scientists). A friend from Ohio was visiting me in Los Angeles when a large earthquake struck. He remembered reading about what to do in a quake, so he ran under a door frame. The quake immediately stopped. He replied, "Hey, this stuff really works."

Geesh! I fell over laughing...in my newly sunken living room.

When an air parcel moves within unstable air, its direction is upward. Cloud formations tend to accumulate vertically, as you can see in Figure 37. Cumulus accumulate. As these clouds build, they eventually release their condensed water in the form of intermittent, showery-type precipitation. It's not unusual to see rain appear beneath a cumulus and, shortly thereafter, disappear.

Since cumulus clouds form in unstable air, there is a lot of vertical motion in the atmosphere. Dirt, dust, haze and other pollutants are drawn upward and redistributed to neighboring areas. That's why cumulus clouds normally correlate with decent-or-better visibility. All this vertical motion, of course, produces turbulence, which is a common phenomenon near or under cumulus clouds. Figure 37 also lists the conditions typically encountered when cumulus clouds are present.

When an air parcel moves in stable air, the resulting motion is more horizontal than it is vertical. The parcel of air doesn't develop the temperature difference with its environment that encourages vertical motion. If an air parcel is given a shove up the side of a mountain, it can eventually cool enough to condense and form a cloud. Then, when given an opportunity, the parcel of air sinks back to its original level on the other side of the mountain. During the process, stratus, or straight type, clouds develop, as shown in Figure 38.

Fig. 37

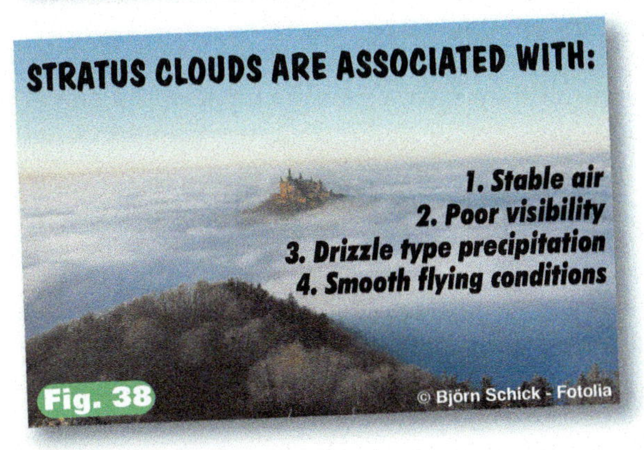

Fig. 38

Nearer My Cloud to Thee, But How High Are You?

Just how high up *is* that cloud? Good question. Sometimes you can get an ATIS answer, but there's a way to figure out for yourself the approximate height of the bottoms of cumulus clouds.

Because atmospheric pressure affects the dew point, the dew point will decrease approximately 1 degree F for every thousand foot altitude gain. Couple this with the understanding that a rising parcel of unsaturated air cools at a rate of 5.4 degrees F per thousand feet (3.0 degrees C per thousand feet), and you get the dew point and temperature converging at a rate of 4.4 degrees F per thousand feet.

So what? Well, when the temperature and dew point come together, water vapor condenses in the parcel and clouds form. To *estimate* the height of the cloud bases, simply find the difference between the temperature and dew point and divide this by 4.4 degrees F (or 2.5 degrees C if using Celsius). The number you get is the height of the cloud bases in thousands of feet.

This method of estimating is only reliable with cumulus clouds, since they are usually formed by lifting and thus subject to the effects of changing lapse rates.

Determining Bases of Cumulus Clouds From Surface Temperature & Dew Point

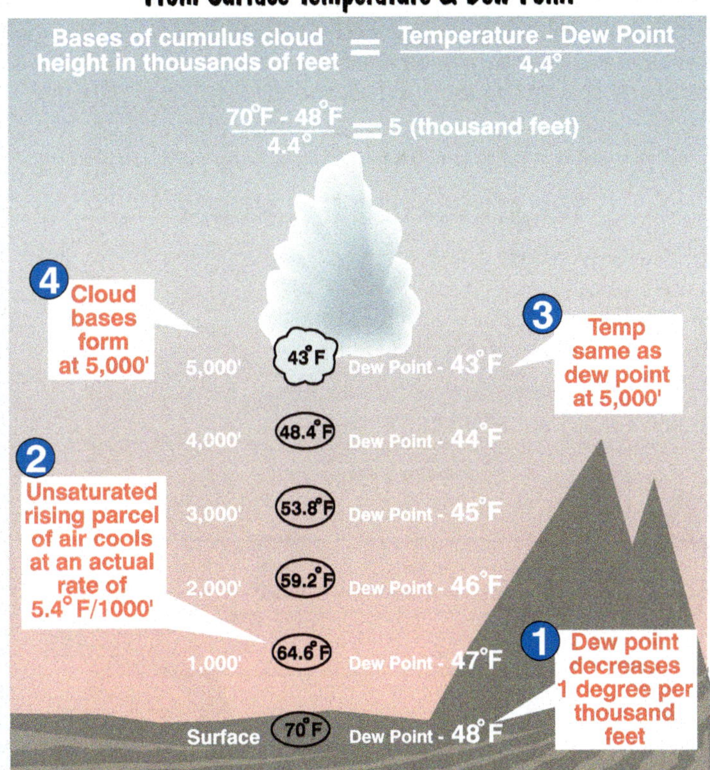

You can estimate the bases of cumulus clouds by using the formula listed above. The dewpoint decreases approximately one degree Fahrenheit for every thousand feet of altitude gain. The actual temperature lapse rate in a rising air parcel for non saturated air is 5.4°F/1000'. Given this information, we can estimate where the temp and dew point will come close enough to form cloud bases (the 4.4° value in the denominator is the air parcel's lapse rate with 1° subtracted from it for a decrease in the dew point).

Stratus clouds are the result of water vapor condensing in air parcels that have little vertical movement. For instance, if the atmosphere becomes warmer with height (such as in an inversion), parcels of warm air are prevented from rising. Since these air parcels can't move vertically they tend to be flat on top, and any cloud tops present will take on a straight or stratified appearance. To see this in action in your very own kitchen, take a stick of cool but not cold butter in your hand and ram it into a plate, narrow-end first. Turn upside down, remove the plate, and you will have a fine model of a stratus cloud. Moving object meets immovable object. Squish. This is the Butterball explanation of stratus cloud formation, and no meteorologist has ever made it public. It is *not* a turkey.

It's no accident that stratus clouds often signal the presence of a temperature inversion. Limited vertical air movement in stable air means poor visibility. Pollutants, dust, dirt, and haze become trapped under the inversion much like dirt under a carpet. Any precipitation associated with stratus clouds is usually in the form of a continuous type of drizzle because stratus clouds typically contain smaller water droplets than those found in cumulus clouds and the clouds usually cover a wider area for a longer period of time. Figure 38 depicts the conditions typically found when stratus clouds are present.

Weather-wise pilots understand that water in the atmosphere is the enemy. When the atmosphere contains lots of moisture, there is great potential for atmospheric mischief once lifting gets going. For instance, the area around Texas has a great deal of water vapor in the air (I should know, I go to Houston every summer for the humidity festival). The area around the Texas panhandle is called tornado alley because some of the world's nastiest thunderstorms swoop through this area. The Gulf of Mexico adds so much water vapor to the air that a fast moving cold front from the north often provides enough lift to create squall lines (lines of thunderstorms) hundreds of miles long. In other words, the fast moving cold front acts like a snow plow in that it scoops or pushes up large parcels of moist air that eventually become warmer than the atmosphere surrounding them. The results are thunderstorms that belch fire, hail, and electricity the like of which make a T. rex. dinosaur look like a sandbox sissy.

NOW IS THE WINTER OF DISCONTENT

This problem is not restricted to wintertime, but seems to occur more frequently, and to be fraught with more serious consequences at that time of year. ALTIMETER SETTING, Kollsman Number, the old timers called it, but they meant the same thing: Station barometric pressure corrected to sea level. Elementary, you think. The voice in the speaker says, "Altimeter two niner four zero." So you turn the little knob until the numbers in the little window say "29.40." Don't you? Well, not always or we wouldn't receive any reports about it and we wouldn't have to deliver this sermon. If you set in the correct numbers, the altimeter tells you your altitude above sea-level. If you don't, it tells you something else, and that something else may turn out to be unhealthy.

Obtained ATIS. I mistakenly copied the altimeter setting as 30.59. We leveled at what we thought was 11.000'. The controller didn't advise us that we were at 10,000'. When we were given clearance to 3500' we descended and leveled off at 2500'. Controller advised we were at 2500'. We climbed back up to 3500' after resetting our altimeter. OVERLOOKED THE FACT THAT WE WERE GOING INTO A FAIRLY DEEP LOW PRESSURE SYSTEM. Fortunately, nothing serious happened this time.

ASRS Report

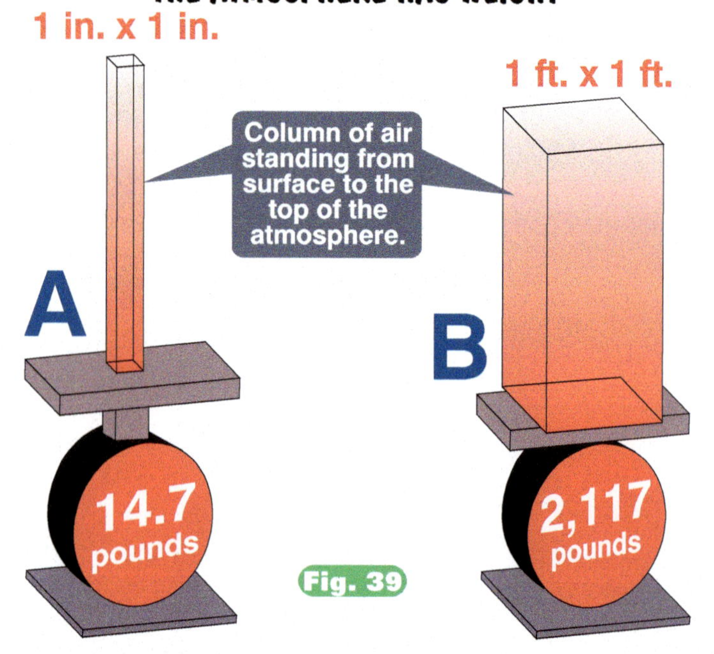

Air has weight. One square inch of air (scale A), standing from the earth's surface to the top of the atmosphere weighs 14.7 pounds. It also produces 14.7 pounds per square inch of pressure on the surface. A square foot of air (scale B), standing the same height weighs 2,117 pounds and produces 2,117 pounds per square foot of pressure on the surface.

Understanding the difference in lapse rates between the environment and a rising parcel of air is perhaps the most important concept to comprehend. You're well on your way to being a real meteorological monster. Before you get too carried away with yourself, though, I must warn you that like most scientific models, the parcel concept is an attempt to make a simple statement about a remarkably complex real world. As a generalization, it works, and provides useful insights.

Differences in atmospheric pressure are just as important as temperature differences when it comes to making weather. For years you've listened to the nightly weather report and nodded when the weatherperson spoke of highs and lows. Now you're about to get the lowdown on what these terms *really* mean.

High and Low Pressure Areas

In a philosophy class I once took, the professor asked a very difficult question during our final exam. He really put the pressure on when he pointed to a chair at the front of the room and said, "Prove that that chair doesn't exist."

My buddy immediately asked, "What chair?" We laughed, the pressure was reduced and... and my friend failed. We speak of pressure metaphorically as compelling us to act or move in a certain, almost predictable way. Atmospheric pressure causes air to do the same thing—to move in a certain way.

The tropical storm results from an enormous low pressure system.

As you might have noticed from our discussion of temperature and air parcels, there is a ceaseless, restless attempt to equalize any differentials in the atmospheric system. This applies to pressure differentials, as well. Pressure differences are another way in which the atmosphere gets moved around, helping to create wind and weather.

AIR MOVEMENT FROM HIGH TO LOW PRESSURE WITHIN A VACUUM CLEANER

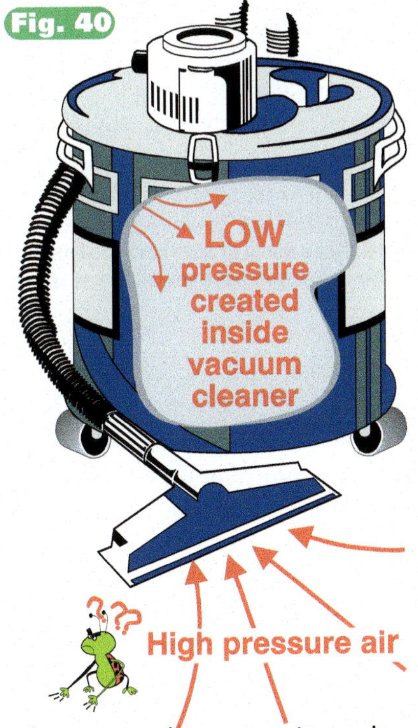

A vacuum cleaner creates a low pressure center inside its container. Air outside the container exists at a higher pressure by comparison. This high pressure air rushes into the vacuum's hose toward the area of lower pressure dragging dirt along with it.

Our atmosphere is composed of mega-billions of air molecules. There may even be more air molecules than the number of hamburgers cooked by McDonald's (but maybe not). Each air molecule is affected by gravity. This is why air has weight.

At the earth's surface, air pushes down with a pressure of 14.7 pounds for every square inch, as shown in Figure 39. That's a lot of pressure. The next time you tell someone that you're under a great deal of pressure, you won't be lying.

While gravity provides a constant tug on the air, the atmosphere still experiences variations in the pressure it exerts on the earth's surface. Sometimes, individual sections of air are forced upward or downward. Mechanical or thermal forces are often responsible for this movement. Regardless of the cause, small changes in atmospheric pressure can still be felt at the surface of the earth.

We've previously learned that air over the north pole is cooled and sinks. As the cool, descending air pushes on the surface, its weight is felt as higher atmospheric pressure. Conversely, at the equator, air is heated by warm surface temperatures and rises. Rising air reduces the pressure it exerts on the surface, creating extensive areas of low pressure around the globe.

Variations in temperature, over water and land, cause changes in atmospheric pressure. Wherever there's a differential in the atmosphere, be alert, because I guarantee you *something* will happen to try and equalize it. In the case of pressure, the air moves from areas of higher pressure to areas of lower pressure. Moving air is what we call *wind*. You are probably the first person on your block (unless you live near a weatherperson) to truly understand what wind is.

Vacuum cleaners are wonderful inventions. They absorb dirt, dust, and small insects and do it by creating pressure inside the machine that's lower than the pressure outside, as shown in Figure 40. Air moves from the area of high pressure (outside the vacuum) to the area of low pressure (inside the vacuum), carrying the crud with it. Of course, it takes a motor and fan (which means noise) to do this. That's why my mother used to drive my dad crazy by vacuuming while he watched football. He'd become so upset that he would get up and move to another part of the stadium.

Sea and Land Breeze Circulation

Everyone knows it's usually breezy by the sea, but hardly anyone knows why.

Figure 41 shows a typical daytime sea breeze. Remember, it's called a *sea breeze* because that's the direction from which the air blows (from the sea). The sea breeze forms because land warms faster than water. Heating the land heats air lying next to it, causing the air to rise. This creates a small land-based low pressure area. Air rising over the land eventually cools by expansion and moves toward the ocean, where it begins to settle. It continues to cool (becomes heavier) as it makes contact with the cool water, thus forming an area of high pressure over the ocean. Higher pressure over the ocean forces air to move toward land, creating a breeze from the sea. A single-cell circulation pattern is established.

Later in the evening, after the land has had a chance to cool, airflow near the beach reverses direction (Figure 42). After sunset, the ocean retains more of the day's heat than the land. Land isn't generally heated to the depth water is, so it has less heat to lose and cools more rapidly. In the late evening hours, the low pressure center that was once over land is now over the water. High pressure now exists over the land where the air has cooled. A land breeze (blowing from the land) forms and airflow moves toward the water. The original single-cell circulation pattern is reversed.

HOW A SEA BREEZE FORMS

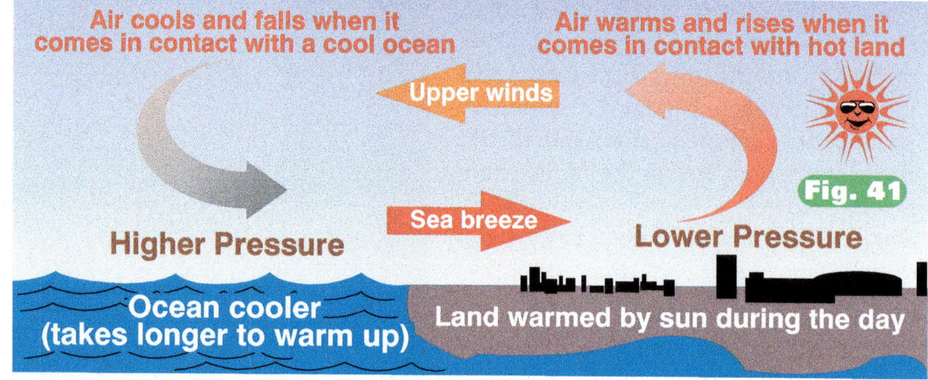

As land is heated by the sun during the day, the air next to the surface becomes warm and rises. Water takes longer to heat because water can absorb more solar energy before a temperature increase occurs. Therefore, during the day the ocean remains cooler than the land. Air over the ocean that's in contact with the cool water also cools and falls, creating higher pressure. Airflow is from the water toward the land, where the pressure is lower (thus it's called a *sea breeze*).

HOW A LAND BREEZE FORMS

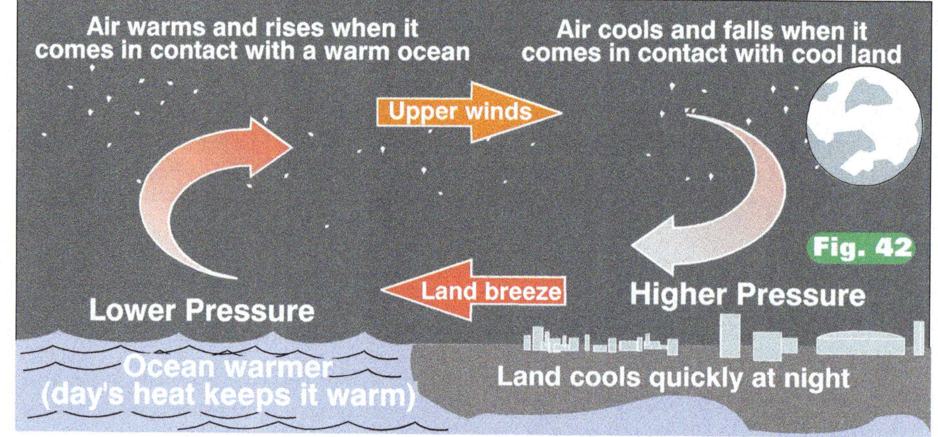

The ocean heats to a greater depth than the land during the day. Thus, at night, the ocean remains warmer than the land. Descending high pressure air over the land moves toward the rising low pressure air over the ocean. Since the breeze is from land it's called a *land breeze*.

HIGHS AND LOWS

HIGH HIGH LOW HIGH HIGH

High and low pressure areas are measured by comparison. If the center of an air mass is slightly lower in pressure, it makes the surrounding areas higher in pressure. Similarly, if the surrounding areas are slightly higher in pressure, it makes the center area lower in pressure. **Fig. 43**

These two types of airflow—land and sea breezes—are miniature models of atmospheric circulation. Magnify them thousands of times and they become the large high and low pressure centers talked about by meteorologists.

Keep in mind that the terms *high* and *low* are relative. One man's ceiling is another man's floor. A low pressure center can exist simply because there are several higher pressure centers around it, as shown in Figure 43. Here's another way of thinking about the concept of pressure centers being relative to one another. You can spend a lot of time working out, pumping iron to look tough. Or you can just hang out with a bunch of sissies and weaklings and look tough by comparison. It's all relative. If the area surrounding a parcel of air becomes slightly cooler, this makes the central parcel of air warmer, thus lower in pressure by comparison. Air would then flow in the direction of this lower pressure, as shown in Figure 43.

Keeping It in Perspective

Keep high and low pressure areas in their proper perspective. High and low pressure centers are large masses of air—sometimes thousands of miles across—that descend and rise slowly, descending at rates from a few centime-

ters per second to thousands of feet per day. Within these slowly moving oceans of air, smaller air parcels move up and down, playing out any of the previously discussed stability scenarios.

It's important to remember that these high and low pressure oceans of air are the environments that smaller parcels of air move within. The environment is constantly changing (albeit slowly) because high and low pressure air moves. If the environment is slowly changing, atmospheric stability also changes. This is one reason why the atmosphere can be stable one day and unstable the next. *Tempest fugit,* and stability, too.

Highs and Lows on Weather Maps

On weather maps, high pressure and low pressure systems are represented by a series of contour lines (see Figure 44). High pressure centers are cooler and denser masses of air. Moving downward and outward, they rotate in a clockwise direction. Low pressure centers are typically warmer, less dense masses of air. Air moves inward and upward and rotates counterclockwise in a low pressure system. Right now you must be thinking, "Why does the air circulate counterclockwise in a low?" Hold onto your retrorockets Captain Midnight, we're going to cover that in detail on the very next page.

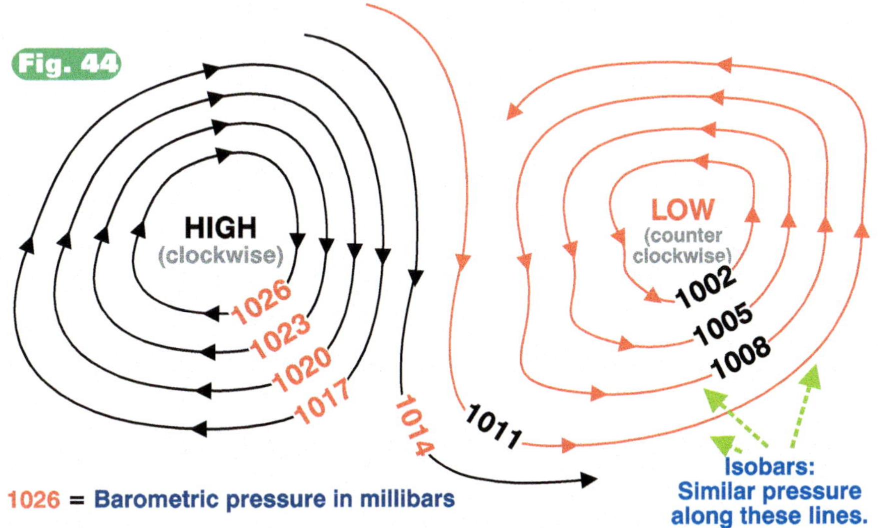

Pressure centers on weather maps are created by barometric pressure readings from weather stations across the United States. The lines shown above are called *isobars*. The prefix *iso* means *equal* and *bar* represents *barometric pressure*. Therefore, anywhere along the isobar the pressure is the same.

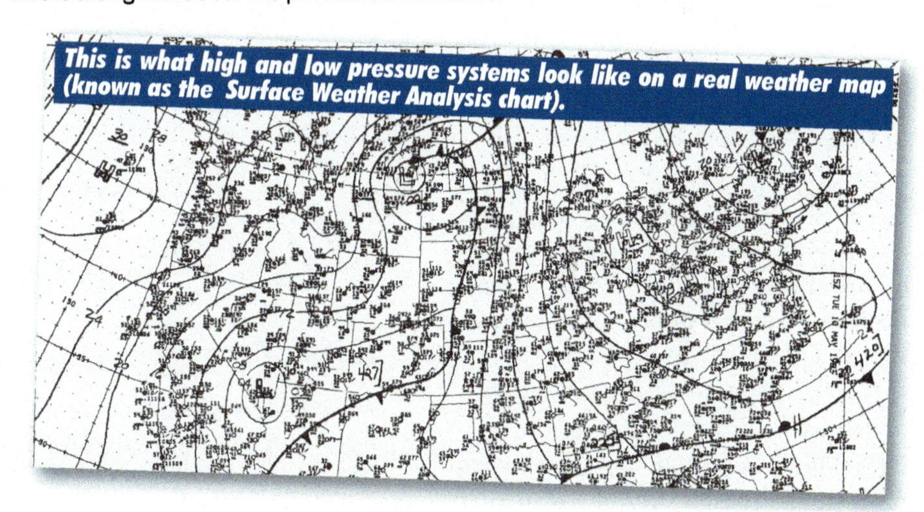

These contour lines surrounding the highs and lows are called *isobars* (that's not an Italian ice cream cone, either). An isobar is a line connecting areas of equal barometric pressure. This is similar to the contour lines on an aeronautical sectional chart connecting areas of equal altitude. *Iso* means *equal,* and *bar* represents *barometric pressure.* Weather computers can automatically connect areas having similar surface pressure with lines. (People can do this, too, but people aren't used much to draw weather maps any more.) The result is a pattern like the one shown in Figure 44, which depicts atmospheric pressure distribution on a typical surface weather map.

Placed along each isobar in Figure 44 is a pressure value, stated in *millibars* (thousandths of a bar, which is the international unit of pressure). The isobar in the very center of the high pressure system depicted here connects all areas having a pressure of 1,026 millibars. Moving toward lower pressure (anywhere away from the high's center), the pressure decreases until the isobar connects pressure of 1,002 millibars in the center of the low.

Perhaps you've been feeling a little uncomfortable with Figure 44? Perhaps you wonder why the air doesn't flow directly from the high to the low as it does in a vacuum cleaner hose? Perhaps you have the latest copy of *Playpilot* hidden between the pages of this book and didn't think to ask this question?

Circulation in Highs And Lows: Going With the Flow

Air should flow directly from the high to the low because of something known as a *pressure gradient force.* This is the basic pushing force exerted on the air, causing it to move from a higher to a lower pressure, as shown in Figure 45A. Were it not for the Coriolis force, air would do just that. But it doesn't. As the descending high pressure air settles and spreads outward, the Coriolis force adds a right curve to its motion (Figure 45B). This explains the clockwise circulation shown in Figure 45E. The low pressure system, on the other hand, has air converging toward it. As air moves inward toward the center of the low, the Coriolis force also curves it to the right (Figure 45C). Eventually, the air is forced into a counterclockwise circulation around the low as shown in Figure 45D.

Because of these two forces—pressure gradient and the Coriolis forces—air circulation around a high or low flows parallel to the isobars instead of across them, as shown in Figure 45E.

Surface friction also has an effect on winds within 2,000 feet of the surface. This has a tendency to decrease wind speed as air is tugged on by mountains, trees and other terrain features. But as the air slows down it is less affected by the Coriolis force. This means the right curve added to the air diminishes slightly. This gives the wind the appearance of turning slightly left of the isobars within 2,000 feet of the surface, as shown in Figure 46. Over water, where there is less surface friction, wind curves left of the isobars by about 10 to 15 degrees. Over land, with greater friction, wind can curve 25 to 45 degrees left of the isobars.

Surface friction explains why weather maps depicting winds for high altitudes (more than 2,000 feet AGL) show isobars aligned differently from maps showing surface isobars. Figure 47 depicts this difference with a constant pressure chart for 10,000 feet MSL and one for the surface.

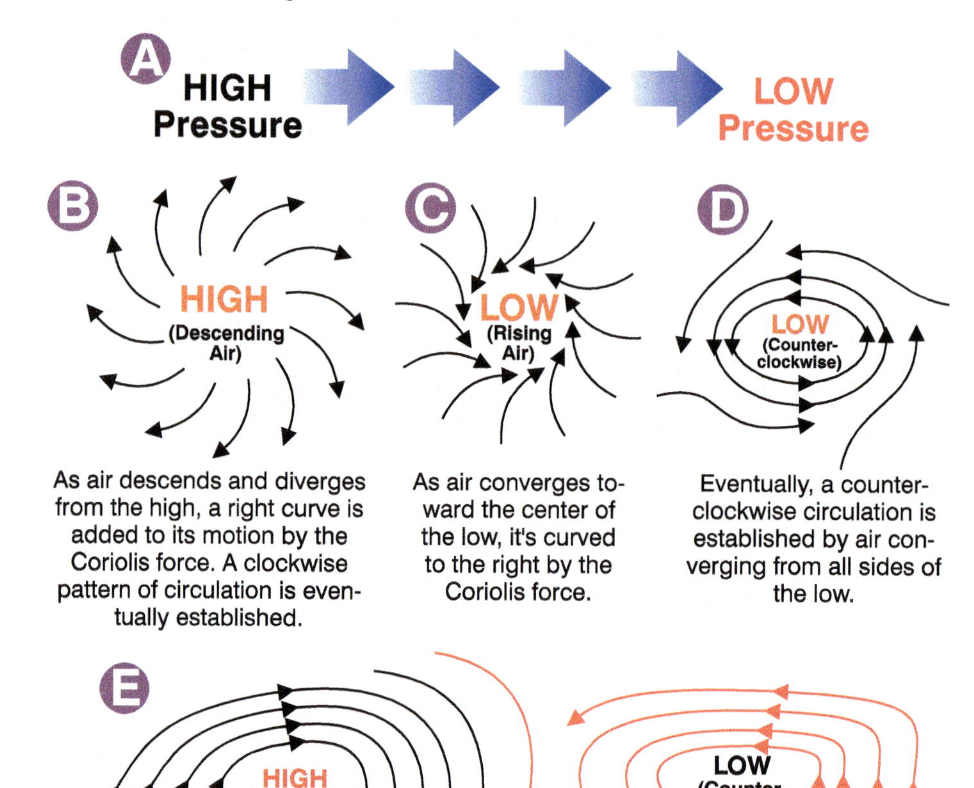

Any parcel of air that moves is acted upon by two forces: the pressure gradient force (the push from high to low) and the Coriolis force (the right twist in the direction it moves). Therefore, instead of flowing straight air flows parallel to the isobars, rather than across them.

As you'll see later, surface winds can give a false appearance of what the wind a few thousand feet above the surface is doing. Windshear is common when surface winds are calm and the wind at higher altitudes (a few thousand or even a few hundred feet AGL) is moving quickly.

Sometimes pilots are like surface winds—they give false appearances. There was a fellow who hung around our airport with a terrible reputation for bragging. His mouth was so big that he could smoke a Duraflame log. He had the highest ratio of talking to listening in aviation, and claimed to have flown everything flyable. One day I asked him if he had some time in a tetrahedron (that's the big wind pointer resting on the ground). He said he had 30 or 40 hours in a tetrahedron. Must have been one that had hot air in it.

The Answer is Flowin' In the Wind

Sharp pilots on long cross country flights know how to take advantage of high altitude airflow to gain a tailwind and avoid a headwind. On west-

EFFECT OF SURFACE FRICTION ON WINDS

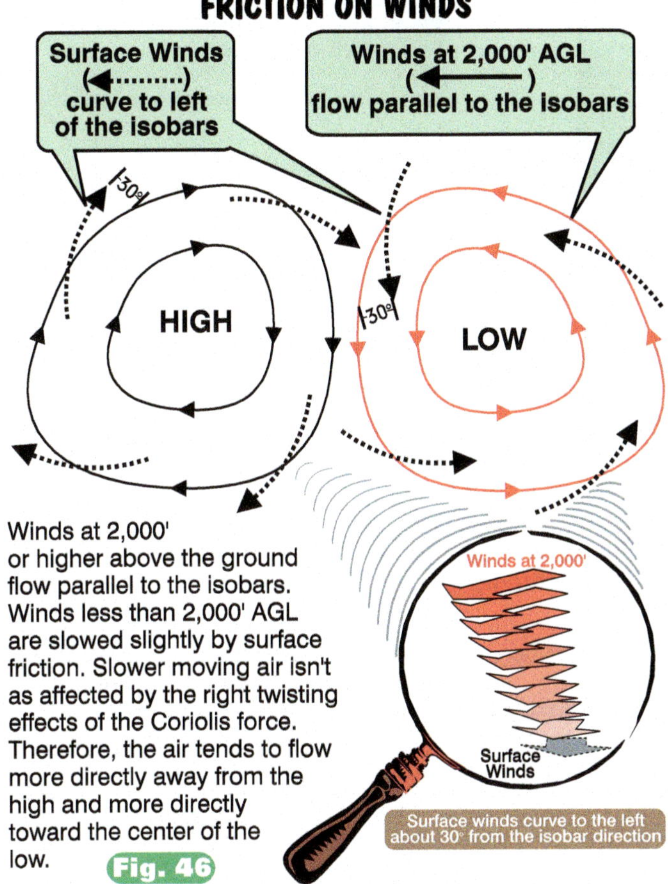

Winds at 2,000' or higher above the ground flow parallel to the isobars. Winds less than 2,000' AGL are slowed slightly by surface friction. Slower moving air isn't as affected by the right twisting effects of the Coriolis force. Therefore, the air tends to flow more directly away from the high and more directly toward the center of the low. **Fig. 46**

SURFACE WINDS VS. WINDS AT 10,000' MSL

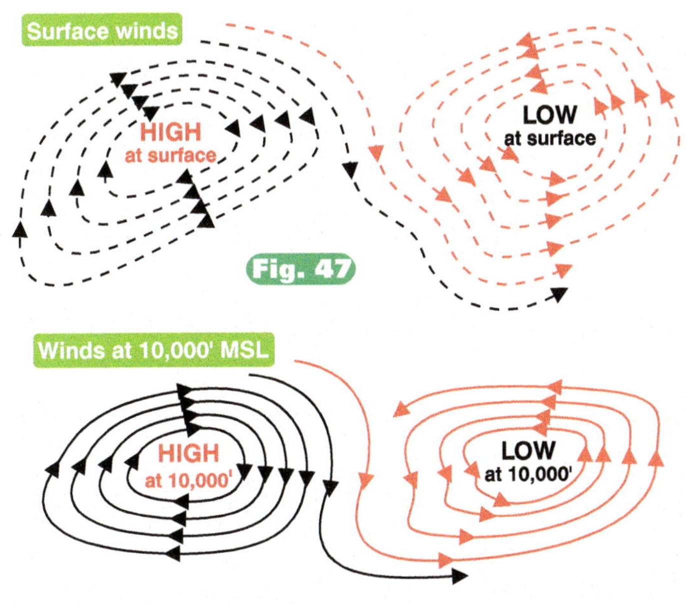

Fig. 47

Examination of these wind patterns indicates that the surface winds flow in a slightly different direction than winds at altitude (10,000' MSL). Surface friction causes this difference to be 10° to 15° over water and as much as 25° to 45° over land with 30° being typical (depending on how rough the terrain is).

TAKING ADVANTAGE OF HIGH ALTITUDE WINDS

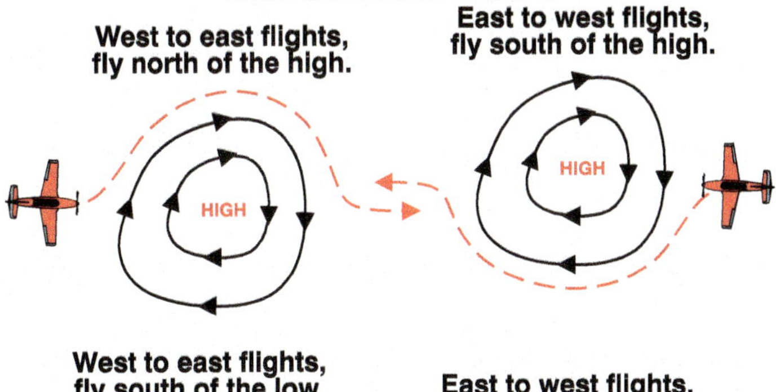

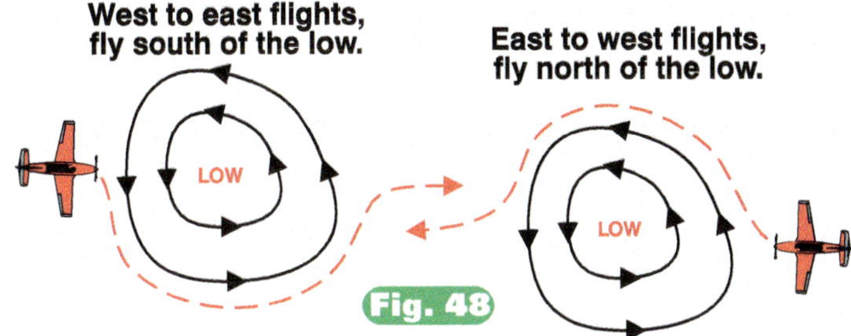

Fig. 48

WIND CORRECTION ANGLES IN HIGHS AND LOWS

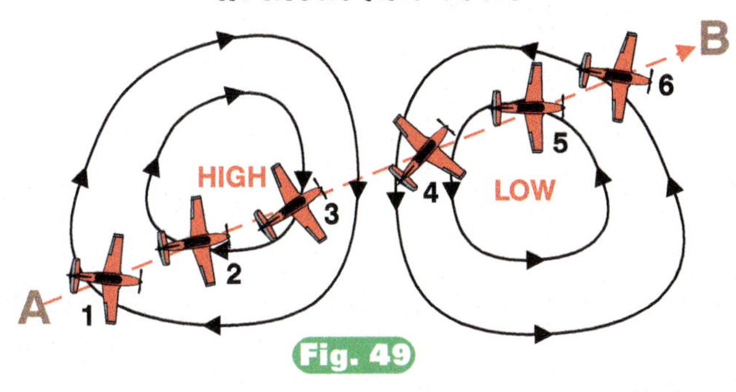

Fig. 49

Our airplane wants to maintain a ground track from A to B. Flying toward a high pressure area requires a wind correction to the right of the desired ground track (Airplane 1 and 2). Flying away from a high is like flying toward a low. Thus, a left wind correction is required (Airplane 3 and 4). Flying away from a low is like flying toward a high, thus requiring a right wind correction angle (Airplane 5 and 6).

to-east flights, plan to fly north of the high and south of the low as shown in Figure 48. You'll have a tailwind most of the way using this method. On east-to-west flights, plan on staying south of the high and north of the low. This is called *pressure pattern flying.*

Pilots can tell whether they're approaching a high or low based on the relationship between their wind correction angle and their ground track. For instance, in Figure 49 the airplane is flying a ground track from position A to B. Airplane A flies into a high pressure area. Thus, in positions 1 and 2, it needs a wind correction to the right to maintain its ground track. As the airplane flies away from a high, it must be flying toward a low. Approaching a low requires an increasing left wind correction as shown in positions 3 and 4. Flying out of a low, the air-

plane moves toward another high with the expected wind correction angle to the right of the ground track, as shown in positions 5 and 6.

You will always make a wind correction to the right when approaching a high, and to the left when approaching a low. If you ever want to determine the position of a low pressure center, simply stand with your back to the wind, rotate 30 degrees to the right (to compensate for the effects of ground friction) and stick out your left hand. It will point in the direction of the low, as shown in Figure 50.

ISOBAR SPACING AND WIND SPEED

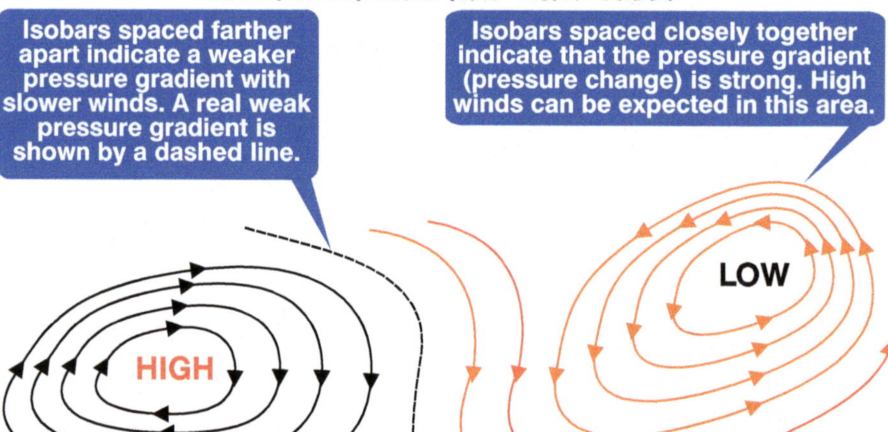

Fig. 51

As high pressure air descends, it eventually makes contact with the surface. Since it can't penetrate the ground, it spreads out in all directions. Meteorologists call this *divergence.* As we've already learned, the air spreads out away from the center of the high and the Coriolis force causes it to curve to the right, thus setting up a clockwise circulation.

DETERMINING THE LOCATION OF A LOW

Fig. 50

You can determine the location of a low pressure system by standing with your back to the wind and sticking out your left hand. Rotate 30° to the right to compensate for the wind's left shifting tendency due to surface friction. You're now approximately aligned with the isobars above the friction level. Your left hand now points toward the general location of the low pressure system.

Low pressure air converges near the center of a low. Having nowhere else to go as it converges from all directions, it begins to rise. Interestingly, convergence in the low accelerates the air. In much the same way a spinning ice skater picks up speed by bringing his or her arms in toward the body, wind speed in a low increases because air converges (is brought in) toward its center. This explains why wind velocities are generally higher around a low than a high.

Notice how the isobars are spaced in Figure 51. They are more closely spaced around the low than the high. Closely spaced isobars indicate a rapid pressure change. Rapid pressure changes mean faster winds. Isobar comparison around the high and low provides you with a good indication of wind speed in that system.

Weak pressure gradients (areas where there isn't much horizontal pressure change) are depicted with dashed lines, as shown above the high in Figure 51. Expect light winds in this area.

Weather Associated With Highs and Lows

In addition to wind direction and speed, high and low pressures centers have their own weather associated with them. As high pressure air descends, it tends to warm up slightly, decreasing the relative humidity. Clouds are less likely to form with decreasing relative humidity, and clouds that are present are likely to dissipate. Highs are generally associated with clear skies.

Lows, on the other hand, have rising air that expands and cools. If the air within the low approaches its dew point, condensation occurs. If this happens, clouds appear and the weather usually gets worse. Air that condenses in a low pressure system releases its latent heat, which adds to the heat content of the low pressure system. The low pressure area is now slightly warmer, causing it to rise faster. This further increases the chance that the weather in a low pressure area will continue deteriorating.

Remembering that you make a left wind correction when flying toward a low, you can use the Rule of L—left, low, lousy—to help remind you what weather to expect.

Keeping It in Perspective

Let's back off for a second in order to see the big picture. Large masses of air circulate around high and low pressure areas. Within these large masses, which heat or cool due to rising and falling air, individual parcels of air can in turn rise and fall, driven by changes in the environmental lapse rate.

Once again, you can see that the stability of the atmosphere is affected by several interacting variables.

Ridges and Troughs

Pressure patterns can take on rather unusual, elongated shapes. To the novice, they're just pretty; to the trained eye, they're pretty important. Figure 52 shows an extended area of a high and a low pressure center.

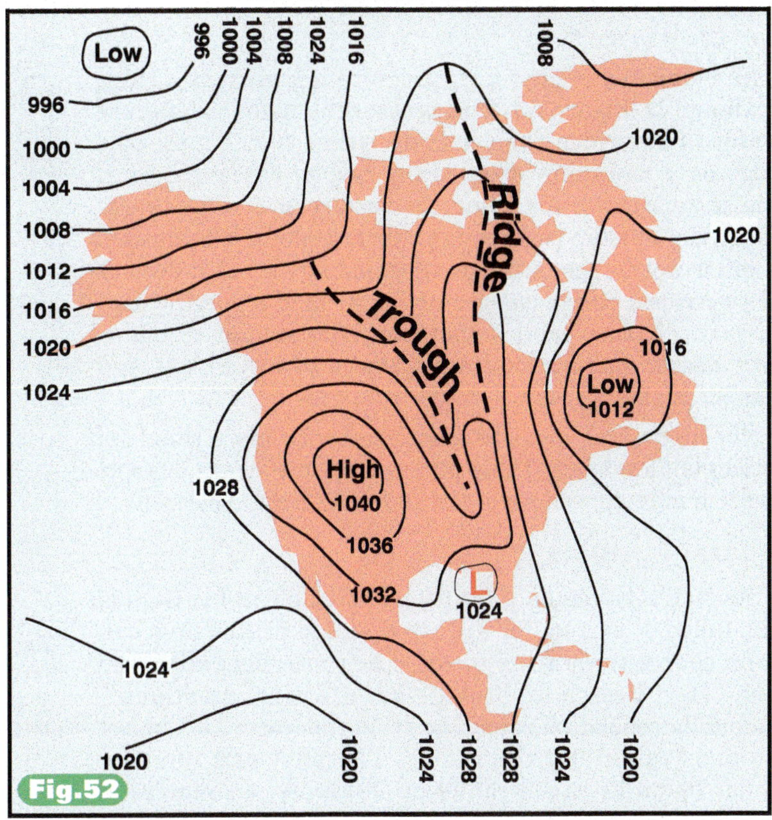

A trough is an extended area that's lower in pressure than the area on either side of it. Circulation is counterclockwise but not closed since the isobars aren't connected. A ridge is an extended area of pressure that's higher than the pressure on either side of it. Circulation is clockwise and, like the trough, isn't closed because the isobars aren't connected.

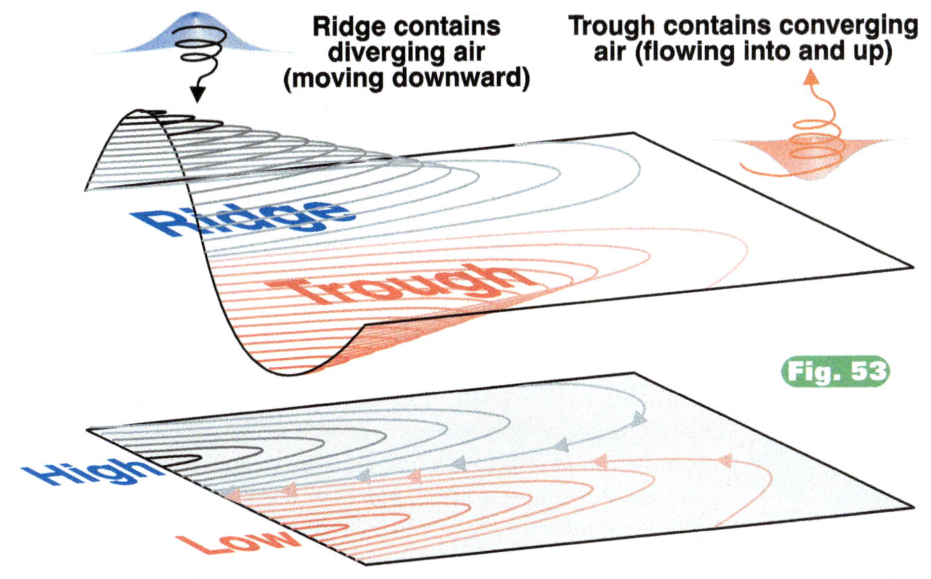

A trough is a "V" or "U" shaped, extended area of low pressure. Think of it being similar to a valley or depression that draws air into it in much the same way a low pressure area draws air into it. This drawing-in or "convergence" causes air to ascend and, depending on its stability, might be the source of poor weather. A ridge, on the other hand, can be thought of as a "V" or "U" shaped, extended mound of descending, high pressure air. Good weather is usually associated with a ridge.

An elongated area of low pressure is known as a trough (pronounced *TROFF*). The pressure along this line is lower than the pressure on either side. Notice how the isobars show counterclockwise circulation at the trough line but don't form a closed circulation pattern. A trough frequently delineates the boundary between two different pressure centers. Just as pigs gather at a pig trough, storms gather at an atmospheric trough.

Perhaps the best way to think about a trough is to consider it, metaphorically, to be like a valley, as shown in Figure 53. The floor of the valley is lower than the mountains bordering it. Given the chance, water would easily flow into this valley. In a similar way, a trough allows air to converge (to flow into it). Of course, the air doesn't really sink into the trough, it just flows toward the lower pressure and rises. The concept of a trough simply makes it easier for meteorologists to visualize the way air flows.

An elongated area of high pressure is known as a ridge as shown in Figure 53. The pressure is higher along the center of the ridge than it is on either side. Think of a ridge as a mountain of piled up, heavy, descending air. The circulation of air along the isobars at a ridge line is clockwise, but the isobars don't form a closed circulation. In other words, they still have descending air but it doesn't follow typical clockwise circulation around a specific center point. Ridges exhibit characteristics similar to highs, with descending air and a minimum of cloudiness and precipitation.

But highs and lows are associated with more than the horizontal flow of air. These pressure centers attract or repel massive moving wedges of air known as frontal systems.

Frontal Systems

Several years ago a pilot friend lifted off in his Cessna 152, failed to correct for a crosswind and drifted on a collision course toward the tower. The controller called and said, "Hey! Cessna 32 Bravo, what are your intentions?" My buddy replied, "I intend to avoid the tower...if I'm not too busy talkin' on the radio!" The pilot and the controller had a little confrontation. Likewise, air masses of different densities that bump into one another can also cause a confrontation. We call this confrontation a *front*, which is the battleground where these air masses meet.

Frontogenesis is about frontal formation (as *Genesis*, the first book of the Old Testament, is about how the universe formed). It's about two air masses, having different properties, that bump into one another and battle it out.

At first glance, you'd think the air would just sort of mix itself together and everything would even out. It doesn't work that way because the differences in temperature result in a difference in density. Things of different densities, such as oil and water, don't mix readily.

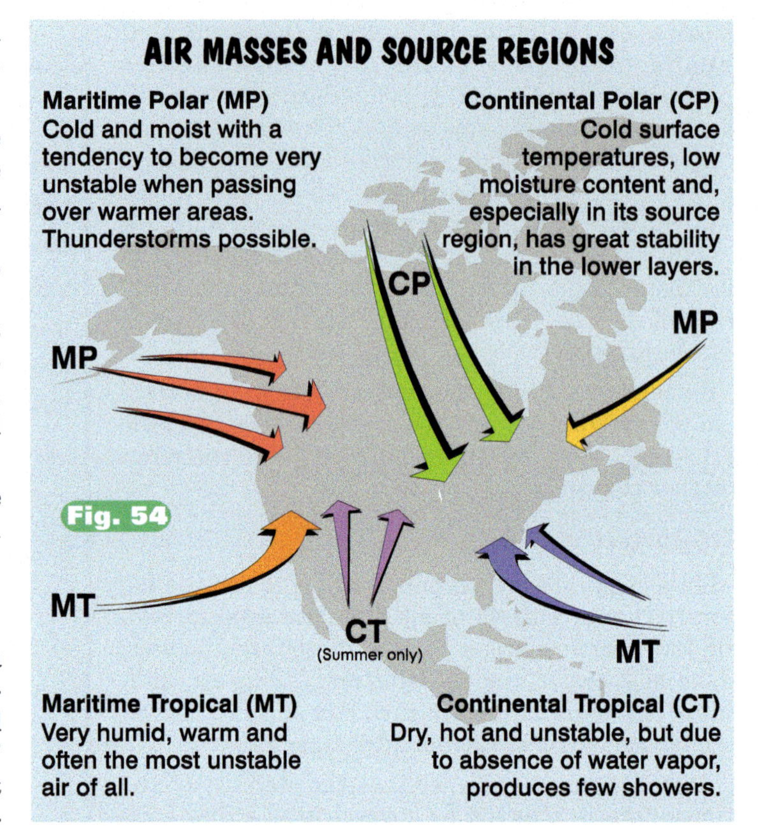

The zone of transition between air masses of different densities is called a *front*. Think of it as the place where the weather action is, and often the place you as a pilot *don't* want to be. This is one kind of action you can definitely live without.

Frontal systems start with large air masses. These masses of air take on the characteristics of their source region (the land or water over which they form and originate). This occurs in much the same way people take on dialects of the local culture. I had a friend who spent 10 years in Texas and took on some of the local dialect. I still catch her saying, "fixin' to." I asked her if she was working on her instrument rating and she said, "I'm fixin' to." I replied with, "Well, then why don't you fix another one, that way you can be fixin' three." I'm lucky I'm not fixin' my tooth.

Fronts, like people, are often very different. Figure 54 depicts the source regions for the different air masses that affect weather in the United States. *Continental polar* air masses come from where Santa Claus lives—near the north pole. These are dry, cold air masses. *Maritime polar* comes from the same latitudes but the air is more moist because it originates over water. *Maritime tropical* air masses are born over heated, moist tropical waters, meaning they are hot and full of water vapor. This also means there is a tremendous amount of latent heat energy trapped inside the air (look out for thunderstorms). And *continental tropical* air masses are typically hot, dry, and unstable at low levels. The instability makes for bumpy flying but good visibility. Rain showers are virtually nonexistent as afternoon relative humidities drop to 10% or less.

The Polar Front

A cap of dense, cold air sits over the north polar region (Figure 55A). This undulating, amoeba-shaped mass of cold air comes from the cool air descending at the poles. Moving southward, this cap of cold air flows from the east, forming a band of winds known as the polar easterlies. The *polar front* is the zone between the cold polar easterlies and the warmer prevailing westerlies.

Several protrusions or waves of cold air occur along this frontal zone. There can be three to seven long waves existing globally at any one time. These long, protruding waves of cold air are anything but stationary. Plunging and retreating like the probing tentacles of an octopus, these waves advance southward in one area and retreat northward in another. It's this advance and retreat that we, as ground observers, experience as frontal movement.

THE POLAR FRONT

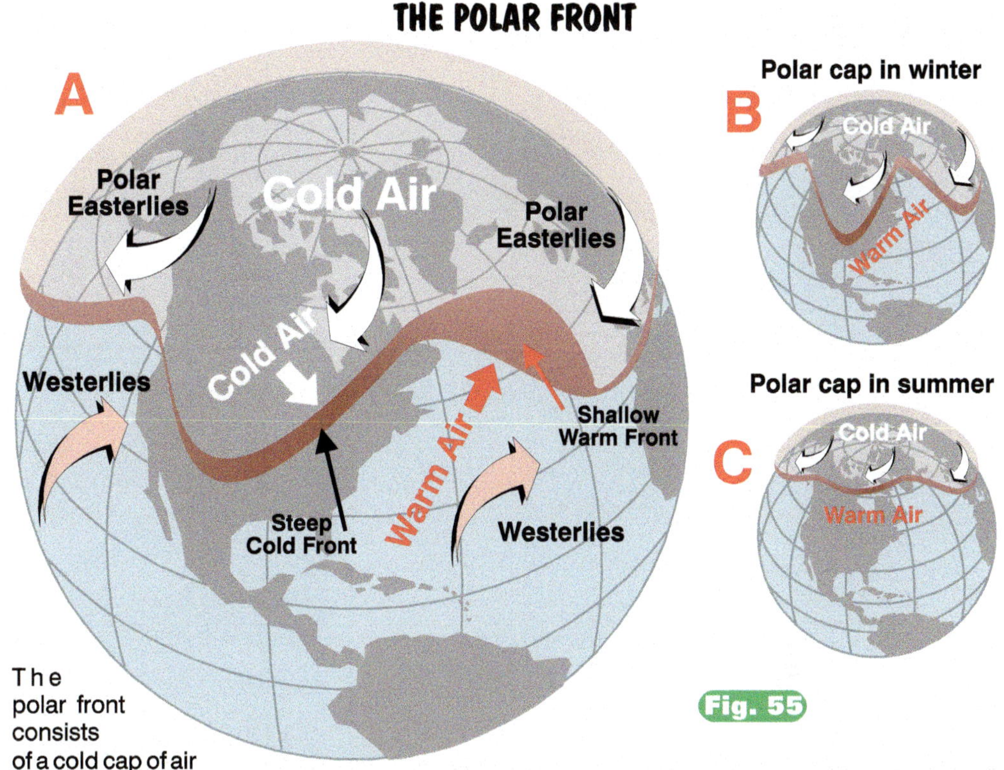

Fig. 55

The polar front consists of a cold cap of air centered over the north pole. Air over the pole descends and is cooled by a cold source region. Moving southward, this descending, high pressure air curves to the right, forming winds known as the polar easterlies. This mass of air is responsible for much of the weather we experience in North America. Cold air overtaking the warmer air of the westerlies forms steep-sloped cold fronts as shown by Globe A. Warmer air replacing receding cooler air forms shallow-sloped warm fronts as shown in Globe A. In the summer months the polar front doesn't extend as far south as it does in winter as shown by Globes B and C.

Fig. 56 **FRONTAL TYPES**

Icicles (triangles) represent the cold front and point in the direction it's moving (A). Half-suns or beads of sweat (B), represent the warm front and similarly point in the direction it's moving. A stationary front is indicated by icicles and beads of sweat on opposite sides of a frontal line (C). Beads of sweat and icicles pointing in the same direction indicate that the faster moving cold front has overtaken and undercut the slower moving warm air (D). This is called an *occluded front*.

An *occluded front* results when a cold front (A) overtakes the warm front (B). (See page L55.)

During winter, a long cold wave of this air can plunge down into the tropics, as shown in Figure 55B. A cold wave advancing southward in one area can allow the introduction of warm tropical air moving northward. Winter weather is characterized by a longer, more protruding polar front, as shown in 55B. The polar front is less wave-like in the summer (Figure 55C).

If you're really interested in how small storms form along the polar front see Postflight Briefing #12-1.

Different Types of Fronts

As a plunging long wave of cold air moves southward, it overtakes warmer, moister air. Hello, *cold front* (Figure 56, position A). Little blue triangles (think of them as icicles) represent the direction of cold front movement. Warm tropical air fills in the receding side of the long cold wave, forming a *warm front* (position B). Warm fronts are represented by red half circles (think of these as beads of sweat). As cold and warm fronts advance and retreat, weather constantly takes on new faces. Sometimes the warm and cold air butt up against one another and neither moves. This is called a *stationary front* (position C). Sometimes the cold front catches up to and lifts the warm air ahead of it forming an *occluded front* (position D).

Pressure falls as fronts approach. If you've ever spent time with a barometer, you will have seen this effect firsthand. It happens because fronts are often found along low pressure

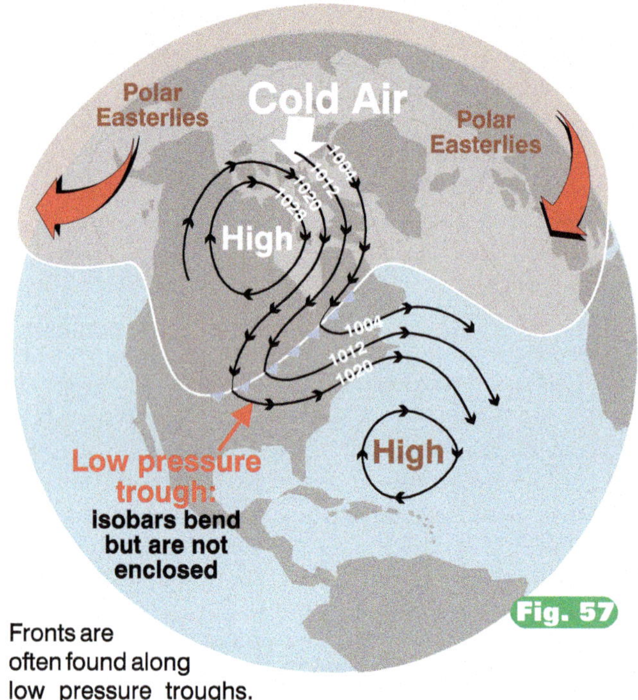

Fronts are often found along low pressure troughs. According to our definition, a trough is an extended "V" or "U" shaped area of low pressure. Circulation in a trough is counterclockwise but not closed (i.e., the isobars don't connect). As you can see, the trough shown above meets these requirements. Because of the convergence in a trough, it's usually associated with bad weather (such as the cold front within it).

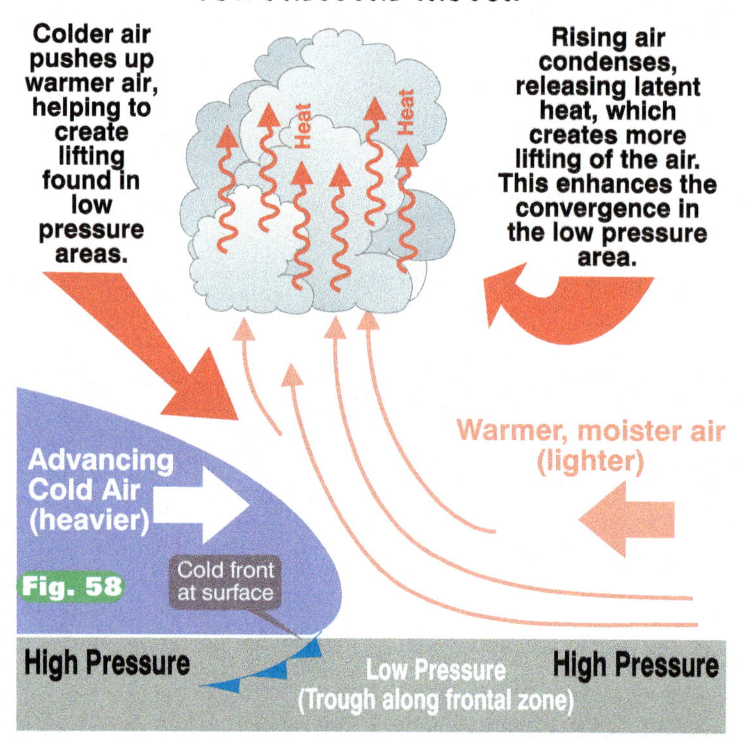

When birds and other airplanes are flying in the opposite direction, this should cause you concern.

troughs. Figure 57 depicts this process. Notice that the cold front lies along the border between two high pressure areas. As the front approaches, the pressure falls. It increases after frontal passage, since a high pressure area lies behind the front. But, why is the area along the front associated with a trough or area of low pressure?

Figure 58 shows the cold front air mass approaching a warmer air mass. Cold air is heavy, so it easily slips under the warmer air. As it does, it lifts the warmer air (which usually contains a lot of moisture). Given sufficient lift and lapse rate, it condenses and releases its latent heat. Heat released into the air enhances upward movement, intensifying the low pressure along the front. Simply stated, the frontal zone itself helps intensify the trough's low pressure. (While there are other reasons for trough formation, this gives you a basic understanding of how troughs form and what they do).

Remember, the trough is a line where the pressure is lower than on either side of the line, and where the isobars form a counterclockwise curvature but don't form a closed circulation. Along the cold front in Figure 57, the isobars are elongated diagonally in a downward and upward direction. Air flows in a counterclockwise circulation but it's not the typically smooth, circular flow of a low pressure center. In other words, the isobars look pinched and bent along the trough axis.

Polar cold fronts tend to move toward the low pressure trough, as shown in Figure 59. Keep in mind that high and low pressure centers move, so their associated

POLAR FRONT MOVES TOWARD LOW PRESSURE TROUGH

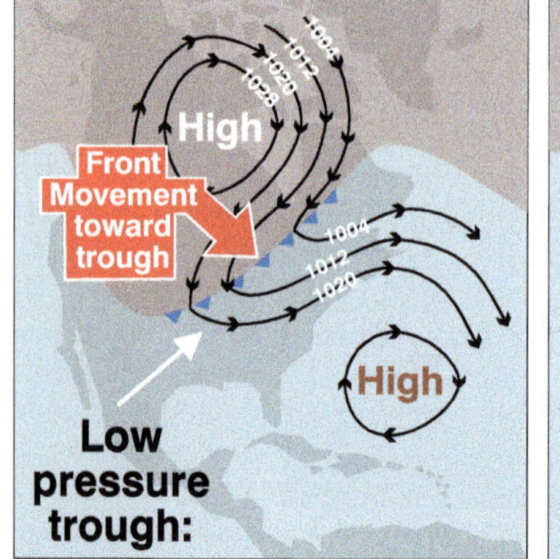

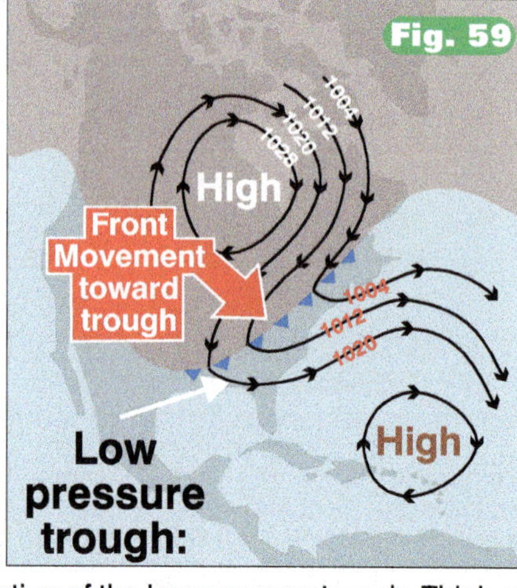

Polar cold fronts tend to move in the direction of the low pressure trough. Think of the trough as drawing the frontal system into it as water might be drawn into a trough or depression on the earth's surface.

WIND SHIFT ACROSS A FRONT

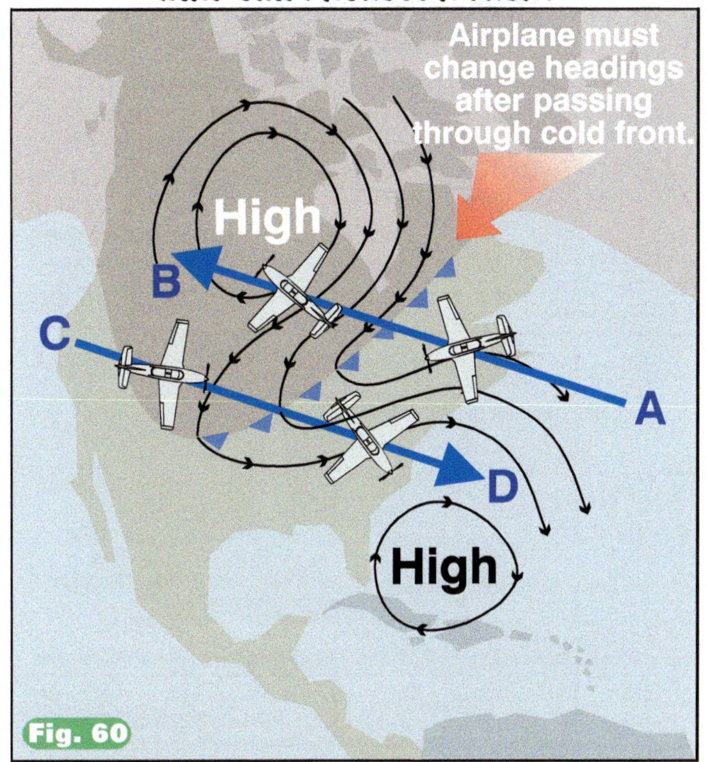

One of the indications of frontal passage is a wind shift. The airplane above, flying from position A to B and from C to D, must change its heading to the right to stay on course.

troughs move. You can think of the front being drawn along with the trough, much like a horse is drawn to a carrot (or as renter pilots are drawn to airplanes with broken Hobbs meters). There are many variables affecting the intensity of a low pressure trough—high altitude winds, intensity of upper-level convergence, latent heat of the air, to name just a few. Meteorologists go to school for many years to figure out how all these variables interact. So, if you can't predict the weather perfectly after reading this chapter, don't feel bad (the meteorologists can't either, and they paid for all that schooling).

Your job is to gain enough knowledge about weather to make some basic predictions. This is why I went to school to study psychology—to allow me to predict human behavior. A friend of mine used to work as a baggage handler for an airline when people used stairs instead of jetways to board airliners. During the boarding process, he delighted in making the passengers very nervous. He would walk over to the engine with a broom handle, hit the jet engine three times, then walk under the cockpit and yell, "OK, try it now." As I originally predicted, he's no longer working for the airline.

You'll become equally good at predicting weather by understanding a few basic weather principles.

Discontinuities Across a Front

Recall that a front is a boundary or transition zone separating air masses having different properties. As you cross a front, these properties change or become discontinuous. When in an airplane, temperature is the most easily recognized discontinuity across a front.

Pilots flying across a front are likely to notice a sharper temperature change at lower altitudes than higher ones where air tends to become more homogenous. Since relative humidity varies with the moisture content of the air, as well as the temperature of the air, you should also expect changes in dew point with frontal passage. (My grandpa always got upset after cold frontal passage when we left the house door open. He'd yell, "Hey, I'm not paying to heat the neighborhood." You can probably tell that he desperately needed a course in thermodynamics!)

A change in wind direction and intensity is another good indication of frontal passage. Figure 60 shows an airplane flying from A to B across a cold front. On the east (right) side of the cold front the wind is from the left, requiring a left crab angle to maintain a straight ground track. On the west (left) side of the cold front the wind is from the right, requiring a right crab angle to maintain a straight ground track. Wind shifts from left to the right are an additional way pilots know they are crossing a frontal area. Direction of travel is irrelevant. Notice that a pilot flying from C to D still experiences a wind shift from left to right.

A stationary observer on the ground will notice a shift in wind with frontal passage. By the time the cold front in Figure 60 moves past position A, the wind will shift from a southerly (from the bottom of the page) to a northwesterly (from top of page) direction.

Aside from temperature, dew point, and wind shift, a falling then rising barometer is another good indication of frontal passage. As the front approaches, barometric pressure lowers. In other words, the altimeter settings for local airports along your flight path are reporting consistently lower altimeter settings. Altimeter settings rise as the high pressure air behind the front approaches.

The infamous aviation weather lecture has always been known to produce a carnival-like atmosphere in the classroom.

Cold Front Characteristics

A cold air mass overtaking a warm air mass is called a cold front. Cold air, being heavier than warm air, moves along the surface, pushing warmer air up in a bulldozer-type action. Because of its consistency and surface friction, the leading edge of the cold air tends to stick to the surface, forming a steeply sloped frontal edge, as shown in Figure 61. Faster moving cold fronts have steeper frontal slopes than slower ones.

Frontal steepness is relative. To me, a set of stairs leading up to a children's slide is steep. To a mountain climbing friend, the face of Yosemite's El Capitan is steep (at least that's what he told me in the hospital emergency room). Cold frontal slopes range on a meteorological scale of 1/50 (that's steep) to 1/150 (not too steep) and average about 1/80. A slope of 1/80 means that 80 miles behind the point where the cold front is at the surface, the top of the cold air would be 1 mile above the ground (Figure 61).

Figure 61 shows a cross sectional view of the cold front. The diagram is exaggerated for clarity, since the cold air is nowhere near as tall, relative to its length in this picture. A more realistic vertical versus horizontal view of this front is shown at the bottom of the diagram. With tops of cold air ranging up to 25,000 feet, the cold front occupies a relatively small vertical slice of the atmosphere.

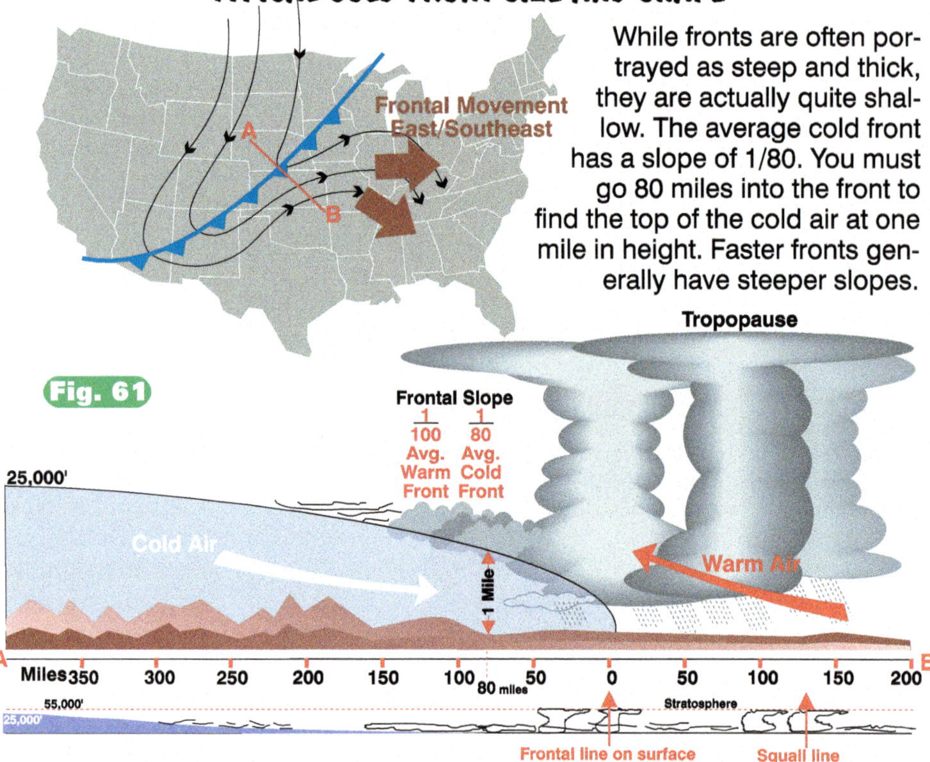

Fig. 61

While fronts are often portrayed as steep and thick, they are actually quite shallow. The average cold front has a slope of 1/80. You must go 80 miles into the front to find the top of the cold air at one mile in height. Faster fronts generally have steeper slopes.

In the Northern Hemisphere, strong cold fronts are usually oriented in a northeast to southwest direction and move toward the east and southeast, as shown in Figure 61. They are often followed by colder and drier weather. The cloudiness and weather associated with the front depends on the degree of stability and moisture content of the air mass ahead that's being lifted by the front.

Keeping It in Perspective

Earlier we talked about how parcels of air are lifted within their environment. Keep in mind that it's not the environment that's lifted, it's a parcel that's somehow pushed upward. Cold fronts provide an excellent means of lifting these parcels. Of course, the longer and steeper the front, the larger the number of parcels lifted. Therefore, the effects of stability or instability of the air are more widespread.

Two Types of Cold Fronts

Cold fronts can be divided into two general types: fast-moving and slow-moving.

Fast moving cold fronts have been clocked in excess of 60 MPH, which means you can be doing the legal freeway speed limit in some states and get run over by a speeding cold front. On average, they usually move at half that speed. Their speed is generally faster in winter than in the summer months.

Most of the cloudiness and precipitation associated with a cold front is located along and ahead of the area where warm and cold air meet, as shown in Figure 62. Because of the cold front's high speed, this weather is often the most hazardous that pilots encounter. Couple a fast moving, steep-sloped cold front with

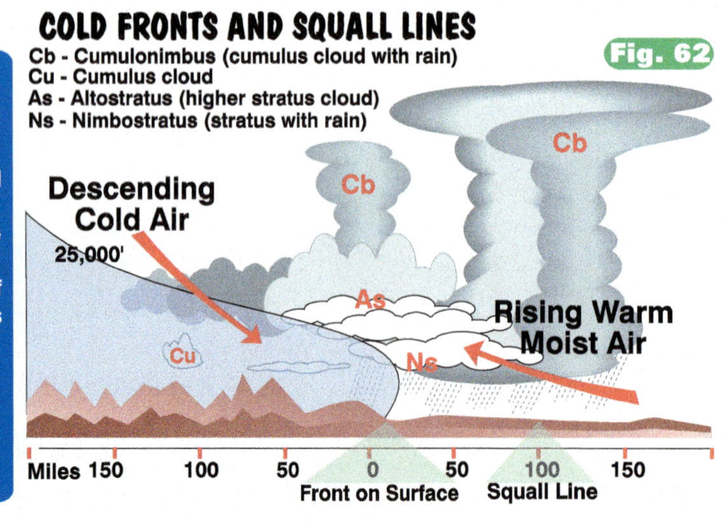

Fig. 62

Fast moving cold fronts may generate a line of thunderstorms up to and beyond 150 miles in advance of the actual front. This line of thunderstorms is called a *squall line* and contains some of the nastiest weather pilots can imagine.

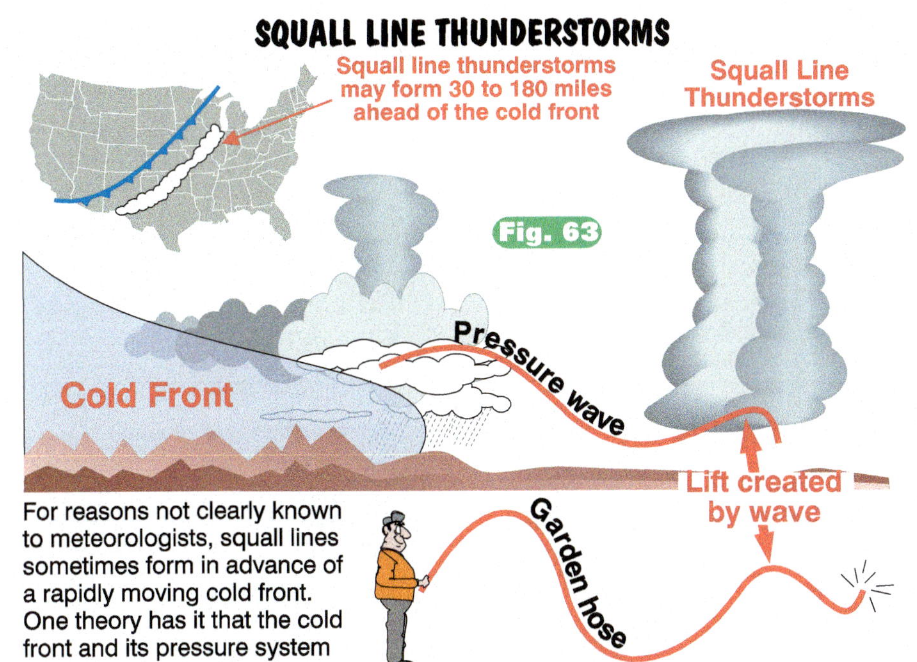

For reasons not clearly known to meteorologists, squall lines sometimes form in advance of a rapidly moving cold front. One theory has it that the cold front and its pressure system might generate a wave form (also known as a *gravity wave*) that moves in advance of the actual front. This is similar to the wave generated when you shake a garden hose. The wave travels along the hose. In a similar manner, pressure waves might travel ahead of the cold front, generating lift and creating thunderstorms in the unstable air.

unstable, moist air and you have the possibility for cumulonimbus (nimbus means rain) clouds, scattered thunderstorms and rain showers in advance of the front, as shown in Figure 62.

Fast-moving cold fronts can generate squall lines 30 to 180 miles in advance of and parallel to the front, as shown in Figure 63. Squall lines are lines of thunderstorms containing some of the most turbulent weather known to pilots.

Some meteorologists speculate that an isolated wave form may cause prefrontal lifting in the warm, moist air preceding the cold front. Think of this prefrontal wave (called a gravity wave) as the form appearing in a long garden hose that's given a good shake. This ripple of energy moves along the hose. A wave of air, moving in advance of the cold front, can generate enough prefrontal lifting (lifting in advance of the actual front) to instigate squall line thunderstorm weather.

Cirrus clouds have a thin, white feathery look and often form in patches or narrow bands.

Cloud Families

Clouds are divided into four families: High clouds, middle clouds, low clouds and clouds with extensive vertical development. The first three families of clouds have further classifications based on the way they are formed. They are classified as either cumulus, stratus, nimbus (meaning *rain*) and fractus (meaning *fragmented*).

High clouds are the cirriform family: cirrus, cirrocumulus and cirrostratus. Their bases typically range from 16,500 to 45,000 feet. The middle cloud family contains altostratus, altocumulus and nimbostratus.Their bases range from 6,500 feet to 23,000 feet. The low cloud family contains stratus, stratocumulus and fair weather cumulus clouds. Their bases range from near the surface to 6,500 feet. Clouds with extensive vertical development have bases ranging from 1,000 feet or less to above 10,000 feet.

These clouds are transparent, whitish, smooth in appearance and often produce halos.

These clouds are grayish or bluish sheets or layers and are often thin enough to partially reveal the sun.

These clouds are gray, dark and often block out most of the sun. They are rain clouds.

SLOW MOVING COLD FRONTS AND STABLE AIR

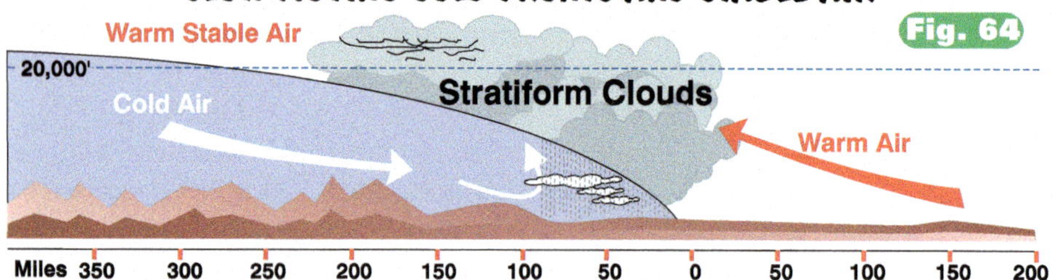

Slow moving cold fronts are likely to generate more benign weather than their faster moving cousins. With a shallower slope, less intense lifting occurs. If stable air is being lifted, stratiform type clouds may occur over a large area.

Stratiform clouds associated with stable air in a slow moving cold front.

SLOW MOVING COLD FRONTS AND UNSTABLE AIR

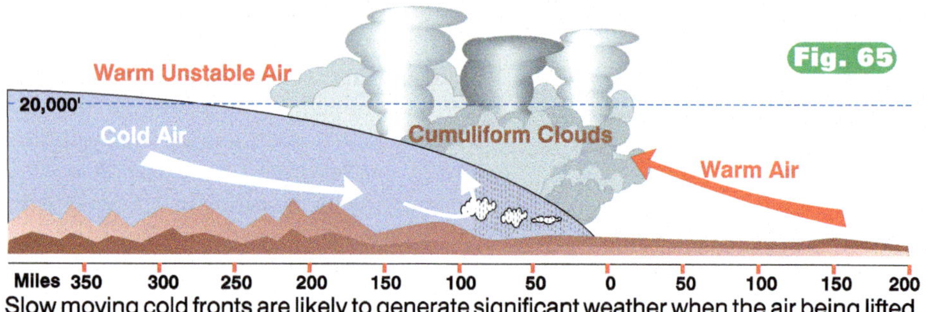

Slow moving cold fronts are likely to generate significant weather when the air being lifted is unstable. Cumulus clouds are likely along the frontal line.

Cumuliform clouds associated with the unstable air of a slow moving cold front.

Slow-moving cold fronts, on the other hand, generally generate less-hazardous weather. Slower moving cold air forms a shallower slope, with less intense lifting of air (see Figure 64). Precipitation and cloud formation occurs in a rather broad band behind the cold front's surface position. Because the lifting is less intense, stratiform clouds are more likely to form if the air is relatively stable. Fog can also form in the rainy area. Unstable air, on the other hand, forms cumulus clouds and thunderstorms. Either way, the weather is confined to a rather narrow band along the front, as shown in Figure 65.

Warm Fronts

Warm fronts are typically associated with the small wave patterns moving along the polar front, as shown in Figure 66. Retreating cool air in the upper part of a small frontal wave is replaced by warmer, moister air from the south. Being heavier and denser, the retreating cool air is tugged by surface friction as it moves. Warm front orientation is more north-south or northwest-southeast, with the frontal position moving in a northeasterly direction, as shown in Figure 66.

Tugging creates a long shallow slope over which warm air rises gradually as it replaces the cooler air.

WARM FRONTS AND MOIST STABLE AIR

Warm fronts consist of warmer air overriding and replacing cooler air in the retreating part of the wave cyclone. Warm front slopes are very shallow, thereby producing less dramatic lifting as compared to a cold front. Additionally, warm fronts move slower (about 15 MPH on the average). Warm frontal weather is, therefore, distributed over a larger area for a longer time.

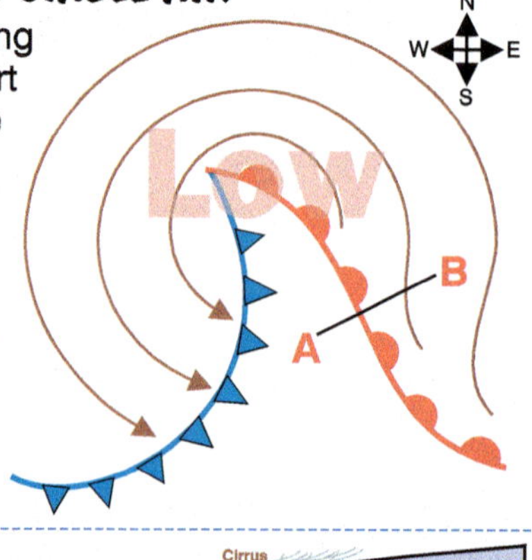

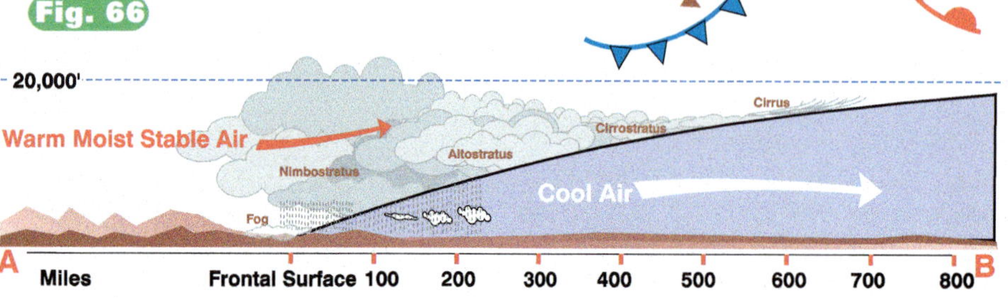

Stratiform clouds associated with warm fronts and moist stable air.

Embedded thunderstorms (viewed from space) associated with warm fronts and conditionally unstable air.

Courtesy NASA

WARM FRONTS AND MOIST CONDITIONALLY UNSTABLE AIR

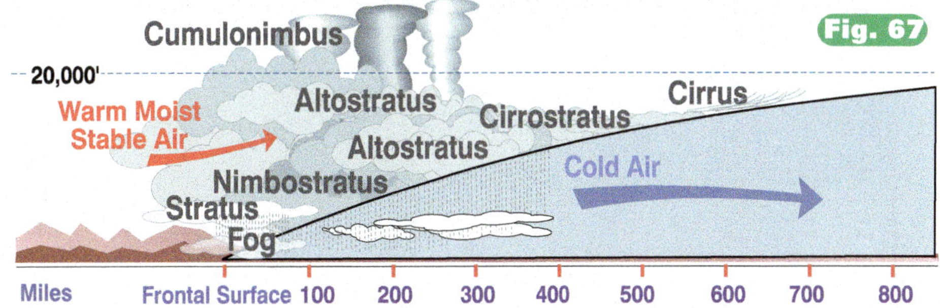

Embedded thunderstorms are likely to be found in warm fronts containing moist, conditionally unstable air. Widespread precipitation is also likely to be found ahead of the warm front which generates fog and low stratus clouds. The frontal zone is also likely to have extensive fog and stratus because of high humidities induced from precipitation ahead of the front.

Because cool air is reluctant to give way to lighter, warmer air, warm fronts usually move at 15 MPH or half the speed of the average cold front. Warm front slopes typically range between 1/50 to 1/200 with an average of 1/100. A shallower slope means that warm frontal weather is distributed over a larger area than that of a cold front.

If the rising warm air is moist and stable, stratiform-type clouds develop in the warm front. The sequence of cloud formation encountered in advance of the warm front is cirrus, cirrostratus, altostratus and nimbostratus. Precipitation increases gradually with the approach of the warm front and usually continues until it passes. This sequence is seen in Figure 66. It's not unusual to have thunderstorms embedded in the stratus cloud mass if the air being lifted by the warm front is warm, moist, and conditionally unstable, as shown in Figure 67.

Widespread precipitation ahead of a warm front often causes low stratus and fog to form. The precipitation raises the humidity of the cold air to saturation. This and other related effects produce low ceilings and poor visibilities over a wide area. The warm frontal zone itself often has wide areas with ceiling and visibility reports of zero (such a condition is called *zero-zero* in pilot talk, or *not with me in the airplane you don't* in passenger lingo).

If the retreating cold air has below-freezing temperatures, the precipitation can take the form of freezing rain or ice pellets (freezing rain accumulates quickly on airplanes making it very dangerous to pilots). This occurs because raindrops from the warmer air aloft freeze as they fall into the colder air below. In fact, freezing rain or ice pellets are usually good indicators that there's warmer air aloft.

Frontolysis

If you go in for electrolysis, you expect to see hair disappear (you should also expect to see a great deal of your money disappear). *Frontolysis* is the process of frontal dissipation.

Have you ever wondered where fronts go? (If you haven't then you're probably still reading that Playpilot magazine.) As air masses travel from their source regions, they are modified by the type of surface over which they move. The winds aloft determine the trajectories of these air masses. Sometimes an air mass will control the weather in a region for a while. These persistent weather conditions are known as air mass weather. Yet even while controlling the weather, they are continually being modified. Eventually, cold air masses heat up and warm air masses cool down. With time, their differences disappear and they blend in with the local environment. They become one of the boys, so-to-speak (hey, girls too!).

Stationary Fronts

Sometimes the opposing forces exerted by air masses of different densities are of similar strength and little or no movement occurs between them. With little or no movement at the air mass boundary, a stationary front forms, as shown in Figure 68. Wind on either side of the boundary blows parallel to the front rather than across it.

While stationary fronts are seldom (precisely) stationary, they usually move at a rate of less than 5 knots. The type of weather that forms is similar to that of a warm front, but it's less intense because very little lifting of warm air over cold occurs. An annoying feature of stationary fronts is that their weather patterns usually persist for several days, driving VFR pilots to new depths of frustration. Frankly, there's nothing worse than having bad weather persist for days as it often does in Europe. This is why the British definition of a UFO is called—the sun.

STATIONARY FRONT ON SURFACE WEATHER MAP

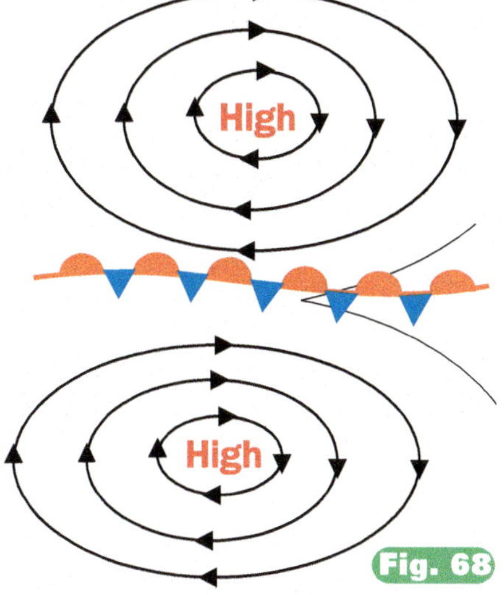

When opposing air masses of different densities meet and no movement occurs, a stationary front forms. Wind on either side of the front blows parallel to the front's boundaries.

Thunderstorm Truth!

Captain James P. Johnson

Thunderstorms are a weather event that capture the attention of most aviators. Many pilots tell me that lightning is the most captivating feature. Lightning—the gunpowder of the Gods. It's nature's biggest spark. It's also nature's most deadly event.

Lightning kills 100-200 Americans every year. It kills more people in an average year than tornadoes, hurricanes and floods combined. Lightning strikes the earth over 14 million times a year. While its beauty can be truly striking, its striking power can be deadly.

Thunderstorm precautions should begin well before you get into your aircraft. As you know, a thunderstorm's gust front can affect a runway that is up to 15 miles away. As with gust fronts, so it is with lightning—the thunderstorm doesn't have to be overhead for lightning to strike. Lightning can discharge miles away from the thunderstorm into the rain-free area, where even patches of blue sky appear.

The mere presence of a thunderstorm near an airport should cause concern. As you study the storm, be aware that the most frequent cloud to ground lightning occurs just prior to the heaviest rainfall during the mature stage. Be cautious about disconnecting tie-down chains and other pre-flight activities at this time. Especially as you walk around a 20 foot lightning rod called the vertical stabilizer...

James Johnson, aviation meteorologist, Glenview, Illinois

Thunderstorms are one of Mother Nature's bad boys!

The Jet Stream

The *jet stream* is not a trout habitat funded by Boeing. The jet stream consists of one or more tubes of very fast moving air flowing west to east across the United States (other places, too, but we'll start close to home). The jet stream does several things (kind of like lowering your bird feeder to within 6 inches of the ground—now it's a combo bird and cat feeder). High altitude winds direct storm track movement across the United States, as well as providing tailwinds to pilots moving in an easterly direction.

It's kind of interesting to understand how jet streams form. If you share my interest, take a look at Postflight Briefing #12-2 for more information.

Thunderstorms

Thunderstorms are Mother Nature's bad boys.

Are we paying attention now? Good, because turbulence is unpleasant, rain is a pain, clouds make you crabby, but thunderstorms can and do cause pilots lots of grief. Along with ice, thunderstorms are something *every* pilot in *every* size of airplane is taught to avoid. It's not a question of "My plane isn't big enough to do that." In the case of thunderstorms, *nobody's* plane is big enough.

That's not to say that if you're caught in a thunderstorm, you are absolutely fillet of soul. Let's just say your survival opportunities languish.

A thunderstorm is one of the most impressive displays of raw power in existence. There are around 40,000 of these lightning-bolt, thunder-belching creatures roaming the planet on a daily basis. Your job is to avoid them.

If you could purchase a Mattel thunderstorm kit, it would include three items: moisture, unstable air, and some type of lifting force.

Moisture is a necessary ingredient of thunderstorms simply because it contains trapped energy, in the form of latent heat. The more moisture available in the air, the taller the thunderstorm monster can grow.

All the moisture in the world, however, won't help thunderstorm growth if the air is stable. A strong temperature inversion (very stable air) acts like a lid on cumulus clouds and stunts their growth. In the presence of unstable air, building cumulus clouds can heat up well beyond the temperature of their surroundings, creating conditions ripe for thunderstorm formation.

Finally, thunderstorms, like people, sometimes need a good kick in the pants (a push) to commence the growth process. A lifting force, in the form of wind blowing up a mountain, frontal lifting, surface heating or convective activity is often sufficient to start thunderstorm formation.

The (Not So Secret) Life Of a Thunderstorm

Thunderstorms have life cycles ranging from 20 to 90 minutes. They usually form in clusters of two or more cells, each in various stages of development. Thunderstorm cells have three stages: cumulus, mature, and dissipating. You can think of

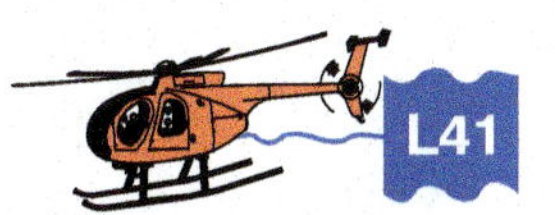

these as the beginning, middle, and end of a brief but very electric story. Let's examine each stage.

Cumulus Stage—The first stage of a potential thunderstorm is the cumulus stage. Although cumulus clouds don't always become thunderstorms, the initial stage is always a cumulus cloud, as shown in Figure 69A. Air parcels, given an initial shove by a lifting force (front, mountain or convective heating), form a small cumulus cloud in the unstable air. As the cumulus cloud grows, updrafts draw in more moist air from below. Latent heat is released as this moisture condenses. This makes the cloud warmer and accelerates its growth. The cumulus stage is characterized by updrafts that can be in excess of 3,000 feet per minute.

Have you ever heard of frozen birds falling from the sky? This is one of those "uh-huh, sure they do" stories that's true. Ducks (and other birds) flying beneath a building cumulus cloud can be drawn up into the cloud's belly. I'm sure the little guys have their power off and landing gear down, but they are unable to keep from ascending. They are promptly de-quacked, frozen solid, and spit out the top or side of the cloud, where they fall to earth.

Mature Stage—Thunderstorms are their nastiest when mature. This stage is characterized by updrafts, downdrafts, turbulence (sometimes severe), low level windshear, hail at times, ice, rain and lightning. This is the most dangerous stage of a thunderstorm's life cycle.

Toward the end of the cumulus stage, just before the mature stage, there is a lot of water in the cloud. The cloud droplets are very close together and give the cloud its crisp, well defined appearance. As more low level, moisture-laden air is drawn into the cloud, the condensation process continues producing additional cloud droplets in the updrafts. Pretty soon the cloud droplets begin bumping into each other and start combining, growing larger and larger. In fact, it takes about 1 million tiny cloud droplets to produce a respectable size rain drop. Gravity pulls on these droplets just as it does your airplane (and beltline). So, what's holding all of them up

The first sign of rain at the earth's surface indicates the beginning of the thunderstorm's mature stage.

in the cloud? The only thing keeping the raindrops aloft is the updraft. As long as they are not too heavy, they are held aloft. The faster the updraft velocity, the larger the raindrops.

Eventually, a point in time is reached where the raindrops become so heavy that the updraft can no longer support their weight and they begin to fall. Yet, they're still growing as they collide with other cloud droplets. Once they get bigger than 5 millimeters, atmospheric drag breaks them apart into two smaller raindrops. Your first visual clue that the thunderstorm has reached the mature stage will be rain at the surface.

Falling water creates downdrafts, because rain drops tend to drag air along with them as they fall. The greater the rainfall rate, the greater the downdrafts. If you don't believe this, try an experiment the next time you're in your home-based karaoke club system—your shower. Run the water and notice how air currents swirl as droplets shoot from the shower head. This same principle is responsible for the downdrafts found within the cumulus cloud. With a combination of updrafts and downdrafts, the mature stage offers the greatest amount of turbulence and windshear. Hail is most likely to occur during this stage.

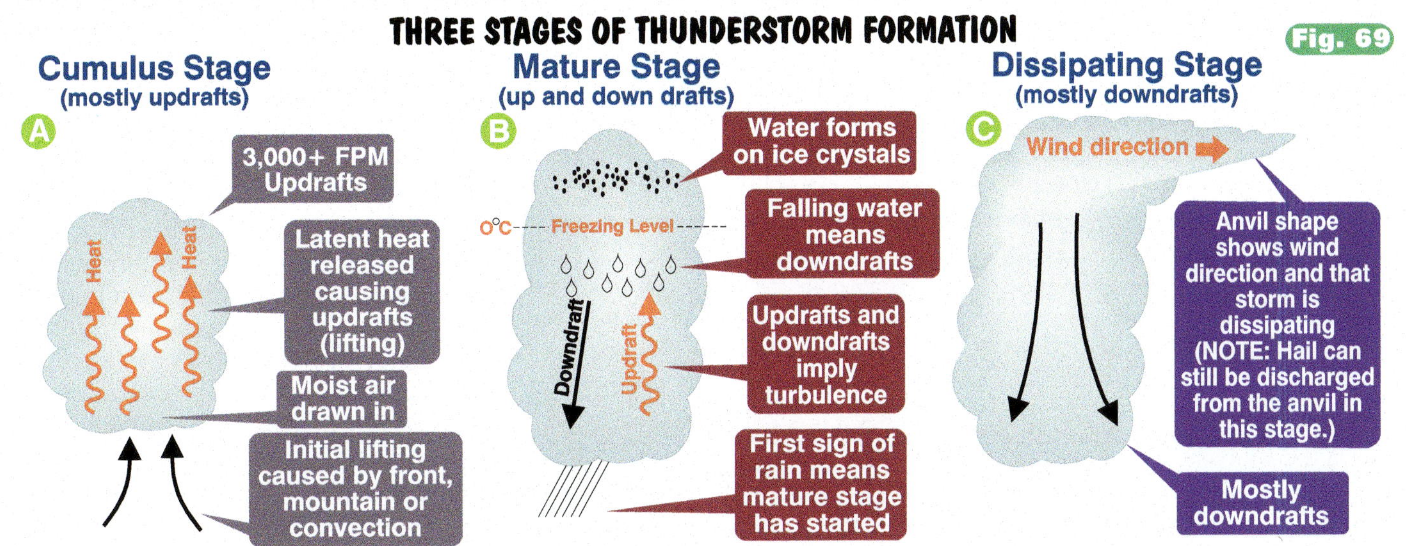

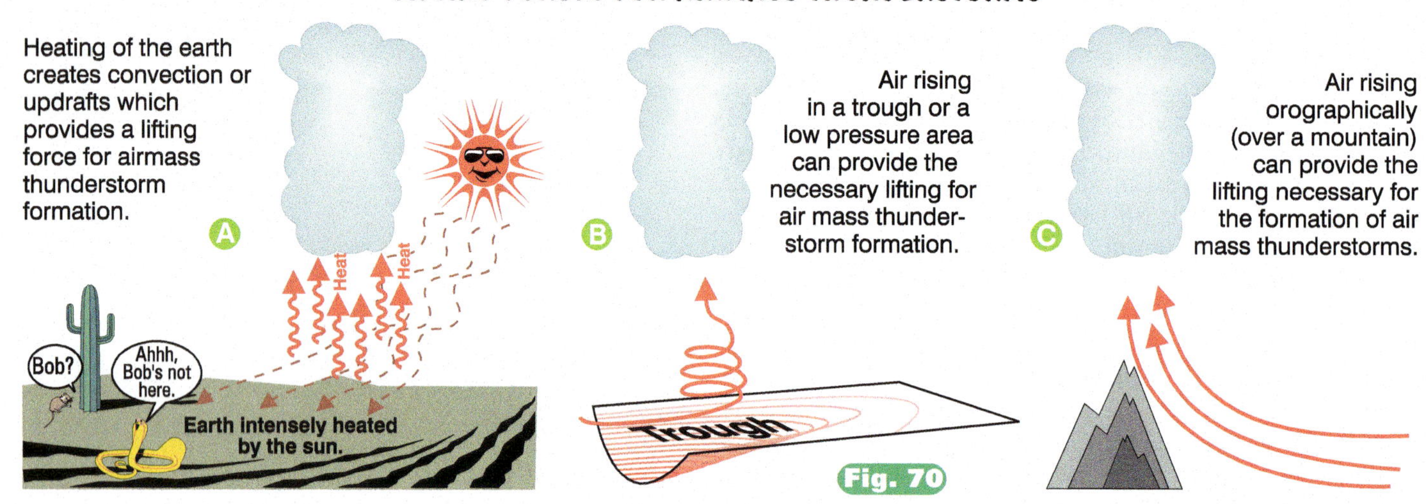

It's not unusual for thunderstorms to grow to 25,000 to 35,000 feet. In certain parts of the country they can tower to 50,000 to 60,000 feet, extending into the tropopause.

Airline pilots try to avoid being anywhere near thunderstorms. It's simply uncomfortable (and sometimes dangerous) for passengers. Consider that most airline lavatories have places to dispose of razor blades. How would you like to be shaving at 29,000 feet, hit turbulence, and come out looking like Van Gogh?

Dissipating Stage—Throughout the mature stage, downdrafts develop and updrafts weaken. Ultimately, downdrafts are all that's left in the once-mighty thunderstorm cell. But don't be fooled. Although aged on a meteorological scale, this geriatric cloud still packs a powerful wallop of gusts and turbulence.

The dissipating stage is often characterized by an anvil top (Figure 69C). Without continued vertical development, the thunderstorm's top is blown over by high altitude winds. The upper part of the cloud resembles a blacksmith's anvil, which points in the direction the storm is moving. These same winds begin to disassemble the cloud's structure. With most of the water gone, the cloud is composed almost entirely of ice crystals, which changes its appearance. The crisp, sharp edges now look soft and fuzzy. Rain at the surface is now light.

Thunderstorm Types

The lifting action required for thunderstorm formation can be furnished by any of four sources: heating from below (creating convective currents), lifting by a front, air movement up a mountain, or convergence of air. Typically, thunderstorms form in air masses, in fronts, or over mountains.

Air Mass Thunderstorms—Air mass thunderstorms generally form within a warm, moist air mass and are not associated with fronts. They are usually classified as convective (heated from below) or orographic (mountain induced) thunderstorms. They are usually isolated and widely scattered enough that pilots can safely navigate around them. The most important characteristic of an air mass thunderstorm is that it moves very slowly, making it relatively easy to avoid. What makes them tricky is that they are very hard to forecast.

During the afternoon or early evening, land masses can provide enough heating for air to begin rising and condensing. Figure 70A illustrates this process. With enough moisture and instability, thunderstorms form. Troughs or areas of decreasing pressure can also provide the necessary lifting for thunderstorm formation, as shown in Figure 70B.

Orographic Thunderstorms—Orographic thunderstorms occur when moist, unstable air is forced up mountain slopes, as shown in Figure 70C. When heating from below works in conjunction with other lifting forces (orographic lifting for instance), air mass thunderstorms tend to increase in frequency, especially during afternoon and early evening.

Sometimes thunderstorms are scattered along mountain peaks and safe passage around them is possible. When the conditions are right, however, you can have entire mountain ranges obscured by orographic thunderstorms. It's not unusual to have violent thunderstorms preventing passage for substantial distances in mountain ranges such as the Rockies.

LIGHTNING FACTS

When the discharge of electricity between the cloud and the ground (known as lightning) occurs, it may release as much as 3.75 billion kilowatts, stretching from 1,000 to 9,000 feet in length. Every second, 100 bolts of lightning strike the earth. In an average week, the odds are 1 in 2.6 that the Empire State Building will be struck. Each year, it attracts an average of 20 lightning bolts. A human getting hit by lightning is much less likely. On any given day the odds of a human taking a lightning strike are 1 in 250 million. In any given week, 1 in 35 million. In any given year, 1 in 685,000. Over an average lifetime, 1 in 9,100.

Source: National Oceanic and Atmospheric Administration

Frontal Thunderstorms—Because fronts vary in slope and speed, thunderstorms associated with them vary considerably in intensity. Faster moving fronts usually produce the nastiest thunderstorms.

Thunderstorms associated with cold fronts are normally the worst, except for those found in squall lines. Both of these are associated with movement. Frontal thunderstorms usually form in continuous lines, as shown in Figure 71, and are relatively easy for pilots to identify.

Problems arise for pilots when thunderstorms extend along the frontal line. Circumnavigation is often impossible since the frontal line can extend several hundred miles and be packed with thunderstorms. The pilot's best option is to park the airplane, have a soda, and tell tall tales to older and wiser pilots waiting on the surface for frontal passage. I've done this on several occasions when thunderstorms loomed along my flight path. One time I landed at Garden City, Kansas (a real small town) and decided to rent a car to tour the neighborhood until the weather cleared. I walked into the car rental shop and said, "Ma'am, I'd like to rent a car." The agent said, "Ahhh, Bud's got it."

Thunderstorms can also be found in warm fronts. The gentleness of warm frontal lifting produces stratiform type clouds. These clouds can hide thunderstorms, as shown in Figure 72. These hidden pilot pokers are called *embedded thunderstorms*. Embedded thunderstorms are not easily visible to pilots. Fortunately, because of the shallow lifting, thunderstorms associated with warm fronts are usually the least severe of all frontal-type thunderstorms.

Warm occlusions can also produce thunderstorms. Rapid lifting of warm air occurs along the upper cold front, which sets off thunderstorm development, as shown in Figure 73. These thunderstorms are usually more severe than those found in warm fronts. And, in a similar fashion, they are usually embedded in stratiform clouds.

FRONTAL THUNDERSTORMS

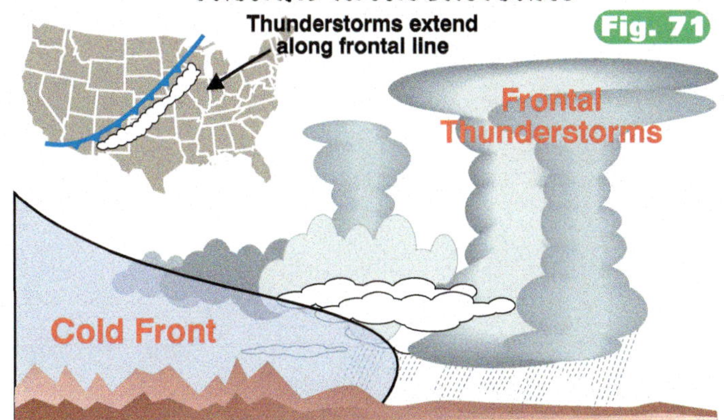

Tremendous lifting occurs along the boundaries of a fast moving cold front. Given unstable air and a fast moving cold front, you could have thunderstorms stretching for hundreds of miles ahead of the front. This may require that you either sit out the storm or plan an extensive deviation (best to sit it out!).

EMBEDDED THUNDERSTORMS

Fig. 72

Embedded Thunderstorms

Warm Air

Cold Air

Embedded thunderstorms are likely to be found in warm fronts containing moist, conditionally unstable air. They present a problem in that you may fly under the stratus clouds of the warm front and encounter extensive areas of downdrafts associated with the thunderstorms. Fortunately, thunderstorms associated with warm fronts are the least severe of frontal thunderstorms.

THUNDERSTORMS IN A WARM OCCLUSION

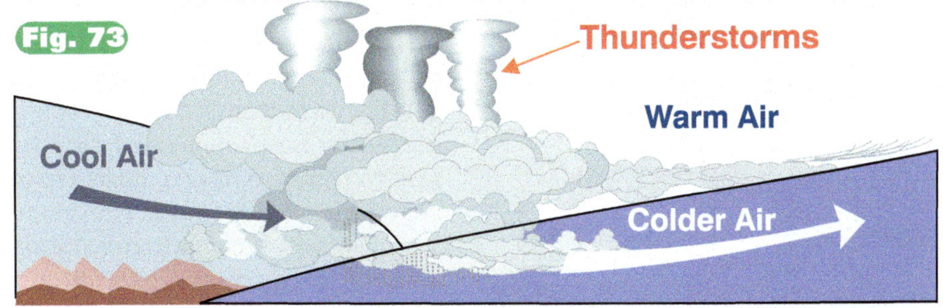

The rapid lifting of warm air by the upper (overriding) cold front can set off thunderstorm development. This type of thunderstorm is usually more severe than those found in warm fronts and has the additional hazard of being embedded (hidden) by the stratus cloud mass.

BUCKLE UP—TIGHTLY

In cruise flight while enroute I was enjoying a normal flight on a nice VFR day. With the autopilot engaged, the last I recall was dialing up the VOR/DME about 60 miles out. My groundspeed was 180 knots. I awoke 5.8 miles north of the VOR at 6,500 feet. I had encountered light chop, then a severe area of clear air turbulence. My seatbelt was not as tight as it should have been and when encountering the turbulence, I was thrown up against the ceiling of the aircraft striking my head on the overhead console. When I regained consciousness, I had a small gash on my forehead. Moral: keep the belt tight.
ASRS Report

SQUALL LINE THUNDERSTORMS

Squall line thunderstorms may form 30 to 180 miles ahead of the cold front

Squall Line Thunderstorms

Fig. 74

Pressure wave

Cold Front

Lift created by wave

Squall line thunderstorms can form many miles in advance of a cold front.

Courtesy NASA

Squall Lines

As if one thunderstorm weren't enough (it is), these electric shows sometimes appear in extended lines—sort of a chorus line of trouble. Squall lines are associated with the most severe of weather conditions—large hail, destructive winds, tornadoes. Squall lines often develop 30 to 180 miles ahead of and roughly parallel to a fast-moving cold front, as shown in Figure 74.

Squall lines frequently accompany cold fronts, but a cold front is not an absolute requirement for their existence. Low pressure troughs, easterly waves, or atmospheric convergence can also produce squall lines.

Thunderstorm Turbulence

By now I hope you've gotten the idea that thunderstorms are *not* a party we wish to attend. Most thunderstorms have the capability to produce extreme turbulence, and up- and downdrafts that far exceed the capability of most light aircraft to cope. You do not ever want to fly *into* a thunderstorm, but with a little understanding and a lot of respect, you can often safely circumnavigate these airborne bullies.

One of the significant hazards produced by thunderstorms is something known as the *first gust*, which is illustrated in Figure 75. During the mature stage, when rain begins falling from beneath the cell, a massive gust of cold air shoots down to ground level and spreads out in a horizontal direction. Winds of 20 to 50 knots and higher, within 150 feet of the ground, have been reported. Although most intense within 10 to 15 miles from the storm, the effects of these winds have been known to travel distances of 50 miles from the generating cell.

If you are on the ground (where you should be), the passage of a gust front resembles a miniature cold front. As it passes, the wind shifts and becomes strong and gusty; temperatures drop sharply; and because the air in the downdraft is cold and heavy, surface pressure rises. This cold air can linger close to the ground for several hours after the thunderstorm dissipates.

Seasoned pilots expect rapid changes in both wind direction and velocity. They watch for several signs of the first gust when thunderstorms are present. They keep an eye out for the first signs of rain beneath the cell. This usually indicates rapid changes in wind direction or velocity. Rising dust and flailing trees also indicate the presence of this gust. Before the arrival of a gust, the very best place to be is on the ground. Think carefully about taking off or landing in the presence of an anticipated thunderstorm. Sometimes it's better to wait for the storm to dissipate or move before taking off or to head for another thunderstorm-free

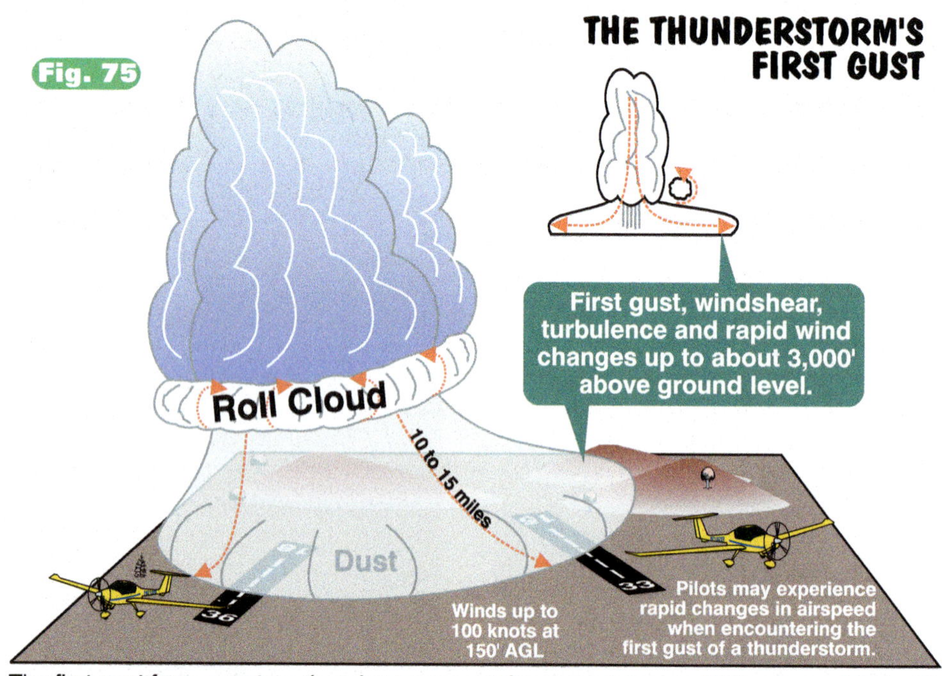

The first gust from a mature thunderstorm contains many hazards. With winds of 20 to 50 knots at 150 feet above ground level, this gust may cause dangerous airspeed changes close to the surface. Blowing dust, flailing trees and a sudden downburst of rain sometimes provide a visual clue to the presence of first gust hazards.

Fig. 76

airport for landing. Patience is the most often rewarded virtue in aviation.

Virga

Virga (variable intense rain gradient aloft) is virgin rain. It's called virgin because the rain doesn't touch the ground, as shown in Figure 76. Virga occurs when rain falls from a cumulus cloud (usually an altocumulus cloud) and evaporates before hitting the surface.

Think of virga as a "do not disturb" sign. As rain falls into the drier and warmer air beneath the cloud, it evaporates, as shown in Figure 77. You know it takes heat to evaporate water. Where does this heat come from? It comes from the air the rain falls through. This makes the air cold. The cold air falls, picking up speed as it descends. You can expect moderate turbulence and high-velocity downdrafts beneath virga.

My advice to you is to avoid flying directly underneath and near virga. You're thumbing your nose at the gods of turbulence and windshear if you do. If you see either virga or the downburst from a thunderstorm near the airport, I'd recommend making friends with your car until the phenomena dissipate.

HOW VIRGA FORMS

Cumulus Cloud

Altocumulus clouds (12,000' to 16,000') are known to produce virga.

Cumulus cloud produces rain.

Rain falls from a cloud into dry air (air with a large temperature-dew point spread).

Rain begins to evaporate.

Cold Air

Heat is taken from the air to evaporate water and air is now cold.

Cold air falls into warmer air and continues to accelerate downward creating very strong downdrafts.

Temporary increase in airspeed

Downdrafts

Downdrafts

A

Increasing headwind

Increasing tailwind

B

Temporary decrease in airspeed

Virga is "virgin rain" or rain that evaporates before being touched by the ground. It's sometimes associated with a severe downdraft phenomenon known as a "microburst." Microbursts produce downdrafts containing winds up to 150 knots that typically last from two to five minutes. Unlike a thunderstorm's downburst, which can cover areas of 10 miles or more, the microburst usually covers an area less than two and a half miles at the surface. An airplane attempting to take off into or land into a microburst might experience a temporary increase in indicated airspeed (A) as it flies into an increasing headwind. As it flies through the core of the microburst it may experience an increasing tailwind (B) which temporarily lowers its indicated airspeed. Fig. 77

Thunderstorm Avoidance

No one wants to get beat up. One time, while at school, a big sixth-grader came up, grabbed me and demanded my lunch money. I gave it to him and decided that would be the last time I'd hire on as a substitute teacher. What I needed was some form of defense, similar to what pilots need against thunderstorms. The best means of defense is avoidance.

Avoid thunderstorm cells by at least 20 miles (Figure 78). That may seem like a lot, but it isn't. Thunderstorm cells have tentacles of turbulence reaching out many miles. While turbulence is more frightening to pilots than it is structurally damaging to airplanes (assuming you're flying at or below maneuvering speed), it should be avoided. Besides, it bothers passengers and makes them think you don't know how to fly smoothly.

Flying between two cells is recommended only if enough distance separates them. Most pilots use a minimum of 40 miles separation between big cells for this minimum distance. Avoid flying directly underneath a thunderstorm cell. Once the cell becomes mature and rain falls, you can expect substantial downdrafts in the core of the rain shaft. Small airplanes don't have sufficient power to even think about out-climbing these downdrafts.

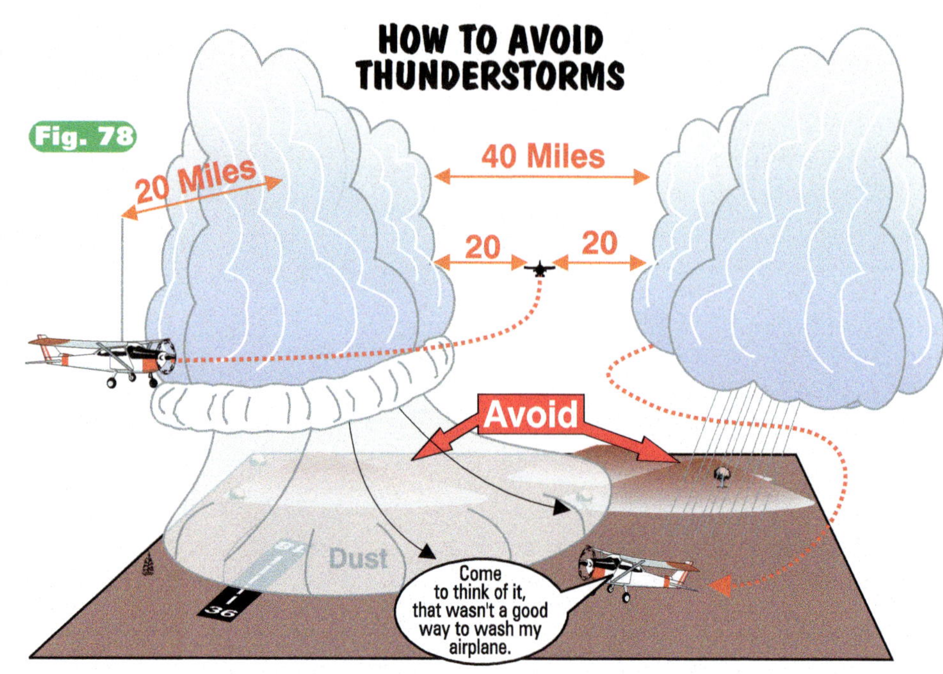

Avoiding thunderstorm hazards means that you stay at least 20 miles away from the side of any thunderstorm. Additionally, if you must fly between thunderstorms, make sure they are horizontally separated by at least 40 miles. Flying in the first gust or under the rain shaft of a thunderstorm is a very dangerous idea. Powerful downdrafts near a cumulus cloud could easily exceed the airplane's ability to climb safely.

Lightning

Lightning is a phenomenon associated with every thunderstorm (without lightning you'd have no thunder). While not much of a problem during the day, it's a real thriller at night. The most important thing to understand about lightning is that it seldom affects airplanes in flight. What it does affect is you, the pilot. A reduction in night vision occurs when your pupils close as a reaction to the intense light display. It's not unusual for pilots to experience varying degrees of night blindness from lightning many miles away. Turning the white cockpit lights up as bright as possible is usually the best remedy for acclimating yourself to future flashes. This simply gets the eyes used to an elevated light intensity.

Turbulence and Windshear

Nothing bothers people more than an unsettling force they can't see. After all, isn't that what horror movies are made of? (Actually, the scariest part of the movie is that the producer took $7.00 from you.) Pilots experience the same thing with turbulence: it's there, but they don't know where. There are, however, several ways to anticipate and avoid turbulence and windshear. Let's start with an understanding of windshear and find out when and where it might occur.

Windshear occurs when wind makes a rapid change in direction or velocity (or both). If you're standing by the roadside and a truck goes by, your pants or skirt start to wiggle. In one instant, the wind was calm; in the next, it changed in direction and/or velocity with truck passage. If it was a big enough and fast enough truck, the windshear might have ripped your pants clean off and taken a toupee along with it.

Windshear and its associated turbulence can become a factor during landing when winds flow over uneven terrain. Figure 79 shows how this

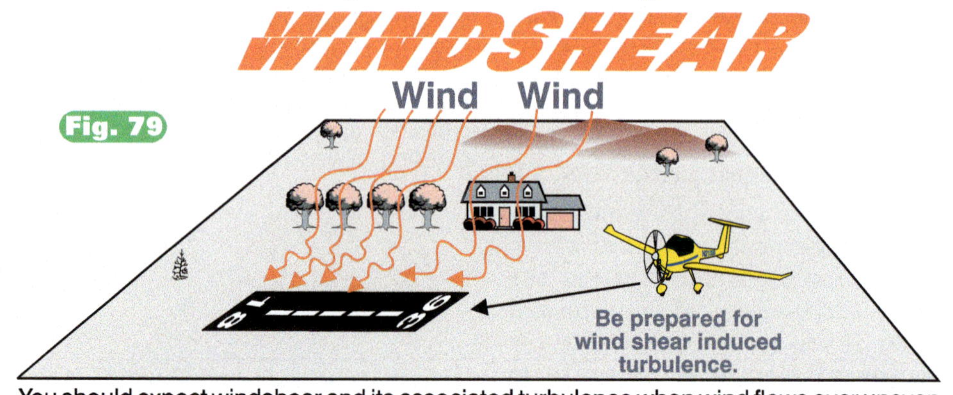

You should expect windshear and its associated turbulence when wind flows over uneven terrain, buildings and trees. If you suspect windshear while on approach, increase your approach speed a few knots above normal for better controllability.

can occur. Like water flowing over rocks on a creek bed, wind is upset, tumbled and churned as it flows over buildings, trees and other structures near the runway.

Often, windshear is hardly felt as more than a bump in low wind conditions. But given enough wind speed, say 10 to 15 knots, turbulence can be quite noticeable. Anticipating bumpiness, most pilots add a few knots onto their approach speed (perhaps 5 knots or more) for better controllability during landing. Of course, they'll make sure the extra speed doesn't cause them to run out of runway. Knowing where to expect turbulence prevents you from being shocked when it appears.

Convective currents are the most common form of turbulence you're likely to encounter in flight. As we've already seen, convective activity is often responsible for the start of thunderstorm formation. On a smaller scale, it becomes quite noticeable at low altitudes during approach to landing, as shown in Figure 80.

The uneven heating of land along your approach path causes variable concentrations of heated air near the surface. When the air is hot enough or when it's disturbed, heated air parcels rise, creating vertical currents of air. Air parcels cool as they rise, eventually falling back to earth. It's these rising and falling parcels that upset or disturb your glidepath.

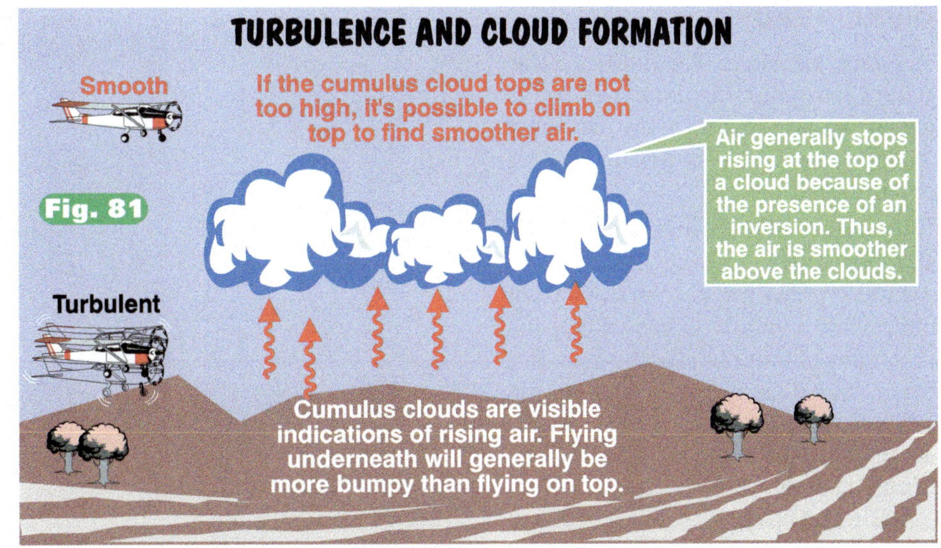

Darker surfaces, such as plowed fields and paved roads, warm up quickly, producing rising currents of air. Conversely, green fields and small bodies of water remain cooler, creating downward currents of air. On approach, the glidepath you anticipate can require noticeable changes in pitch and power depending on the how strong the up- and downdrafts are.

The territory beneath cumulus clouds is a place that's almost guaranteed to give you the elevator effect (Figure 81). While not necessarily severe or extreme, it's often uncomfortable for passengers. Fair weather cumulus clouds are generally visible indications of rising and condensing air. The smoothest ride is generally found above these clouds. Of course, when cumulus clouds reach many thousands of feet in height, getting on top presents some difficulty for those airplanes without turbocharging. Therefore, circumnavigation of cumulus clouds is often the best means of avoiding turbulence.

Frankly, the only people who love turbulence are airline flight attendants. When it's bumpy, they don't have to serve food. This explains why flight attendants can sometimes be found in the back of the airplane jumping up and down, creating artificial turbulence.

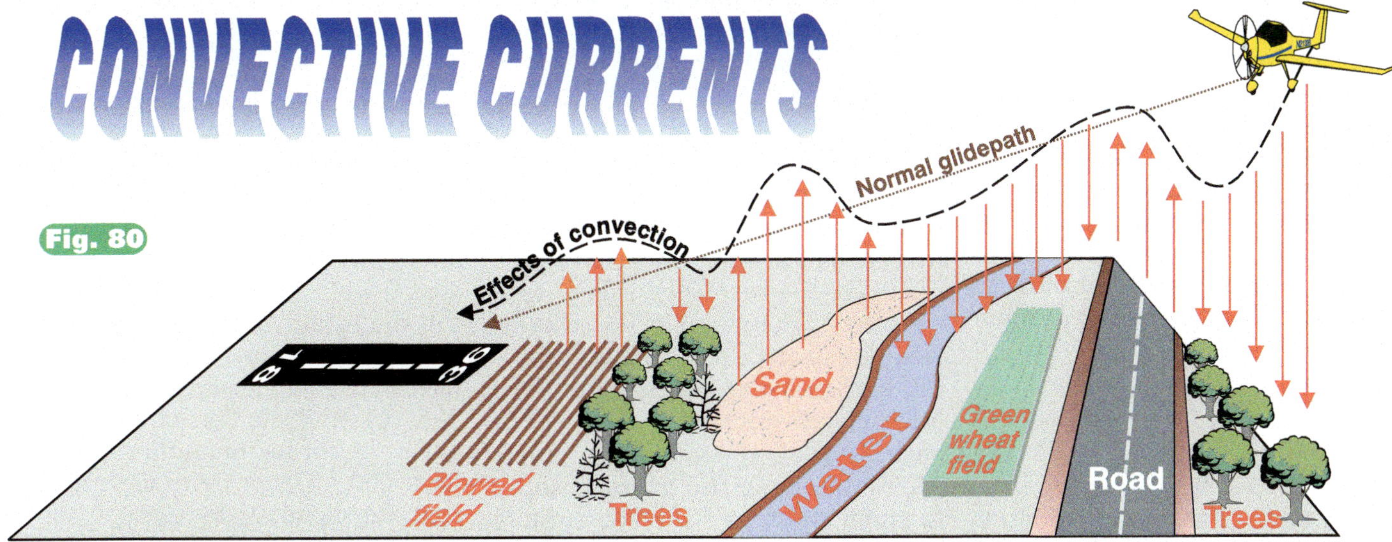

Convective currents caused by differences in terrestrial heating are quite common. Where different terrain exists, it's not unusual for pilots to experience considerable up- and downdrafts while on approach. Perceptive pilots can identify these convective currents by observing that plant life and water generally absorb heat and create downdrafts. Terrain, on the other hand, generally radiates heat and creates updrafts.

Mountain Waves

A mountain wave is not something you do from your airplane while flying over backpackers in the Rockies. A mountain wave is something much more interesting.

Throw a pebble in a still pond and wave patterns radiate outwardly, eventually traveling across the entire pond. If we move water over a pebble, a curve is added to the flowing stream. When air moves over a larger pebble—a mountain range for example—it also has a curve added to its motion, as shown in Figure 82. Given enough wind speed and large enough mountains, these wave patterns can travel hundreds of miles from their generating source.

Very stable air, moving above the level of surface friction, usually flows in a laminar or smooth, layered pattern. But when it encounters a large enough obstacle (a mountain range for example) a standing or mountain wave pattern is established in the mass of moving air. The standing wave is very similar to the wave that appears when a long rope is given a good shake at one end. The wave pattern appears to travel the length of the rope, eventually dissipating in a flip at the end. Mountain waves do something very similar.

As wind, usually with a velocity of 40 knots or more, encounters a sufficiently large mountain, a perturbation or shake-of-the-rope occurs. A wave pattern is induced in the once smooth-flowing (laminar) air. This pattern sets up a series of waves, in the downwind direction, with valleys and peaks that remain stationary. Given enough moisture in the stable air, condensation (from air cooling as it rises) occurs at the peaks of these waves.

Directly over the mountain top, a *pileus* or *cap cloud* occurs above the rough mountain surface (that's not Pontius Pileus either—wrong guy, wrong story). Farther downwind almond or lens-shaped clouds form at the wave crests. These clouds are called *lenticular clouds* because of their lens shape.

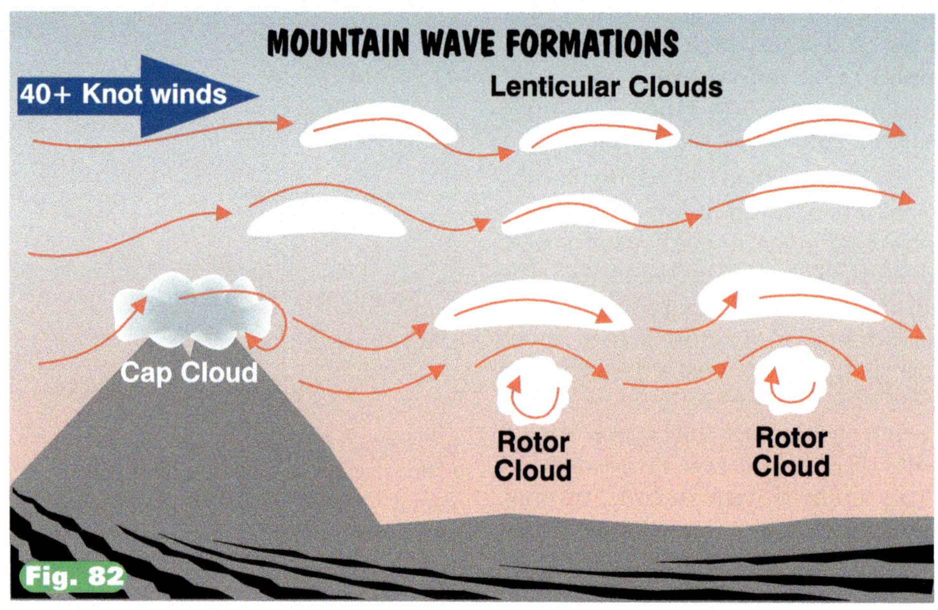

When very stable air moves across a mountain at velocities of 40 knots or more, a standing wave pattern may form. Similar to the shaking of a garden hose, airflow across the mountain sets up waves with crests and valleys. At the peak of this wave, the air is lifted, cooled and condensation occurs if there is sufficient moisture available. Lens shaped or *lenticular* clouds may form and appear to stand in one position. Underneath the lenticular cloud small rotor clouds may appear. Rotor clouds contain massive turbulence.

The formation of lenticular clouds is shown in Figure 82. As moist air rises on the upwind side of the wave, it cools and condenses, producing a cloud. On the downwind side of each wave crest, the air sinks and warms, resulting in the cloud droplets evaporating. Lenticular clouds differ from other clouds not only in shape, but because they appear not to move. This is because the air is rushing through them as they continually form on their western edges and evaporate away on their eastern edges. This is why they are sometimes called *standing wave clouds.*

When the air between the cloud-forming layers is too dry to produce clouds, lenticular clouds will form one above the other. Sometimes, when a strong wind blows perpendicular to a tall mountain range, the wave pattern extends up into the stratosphere. This produces a dramatic display resembling a fleet of UFO's. It is quite typical for mountain waves to form 100 miles or more downstream from the mountain barrier.

Directly underneath the lenticular clouds, a small *rotor cloud* can frequently be found at altitudes lower than the peaks over which the air

flows. Rotor clouds result from the frictional effects of the surface and a lifting action from the rising crest of air. Air velocity is slowed near the surface, yet flows faster at higher altitudes. This adds a rolling motion to tubes of air, similar to the forward motion of a baker's rolling pin. Long cigar-shaped clouds form, each containing severe turbulence. These clouds are to be avoided like cooties were avoided in sixth grade. Violent turbulence will also be found in the up- and downdrafts associated with lenticular clouds.

Pilots must be especially cautious when flying near or around mountain waves. Many varieties of turbulence appear in these wave patterns. Keep in mind that mountain waves can and do form in dry air. The only problem is you can't see them. In other words, telltale lenticular clouds are not visible. With the lack of clouds in dry, fast moving air, pilots sometimes expect little or no hazard when approaching a mountain. Smart pilots, however, understand that winds in excess of 25 knots at mountaintop altitudes are sure to bring some degree of turbulence as well as up- and downdraft hazards.

Approaching a mountain on the windward side (the upwind side), as shown in Figure 83, you might find yourself climbing at several thousand feet per minute with power completely reduced. While this produces one heck of a ride, it's not as dangerous as approaching a mountain from the leeward side (downwind side) with insufficient altitude.

Approaches to mountains with strong winds present should be made with caution, because the strong downdrafts can easily exceed the ability of a light airplane to climb. One way to minimize the risk if you are uncertain of conditions is to approach the ridge at a 45 degree angle. If downdrafts are encountered, you need only make a 90 degree turn to avoid the mountain instead of a 135 degree turn, as shown in Figure 84.

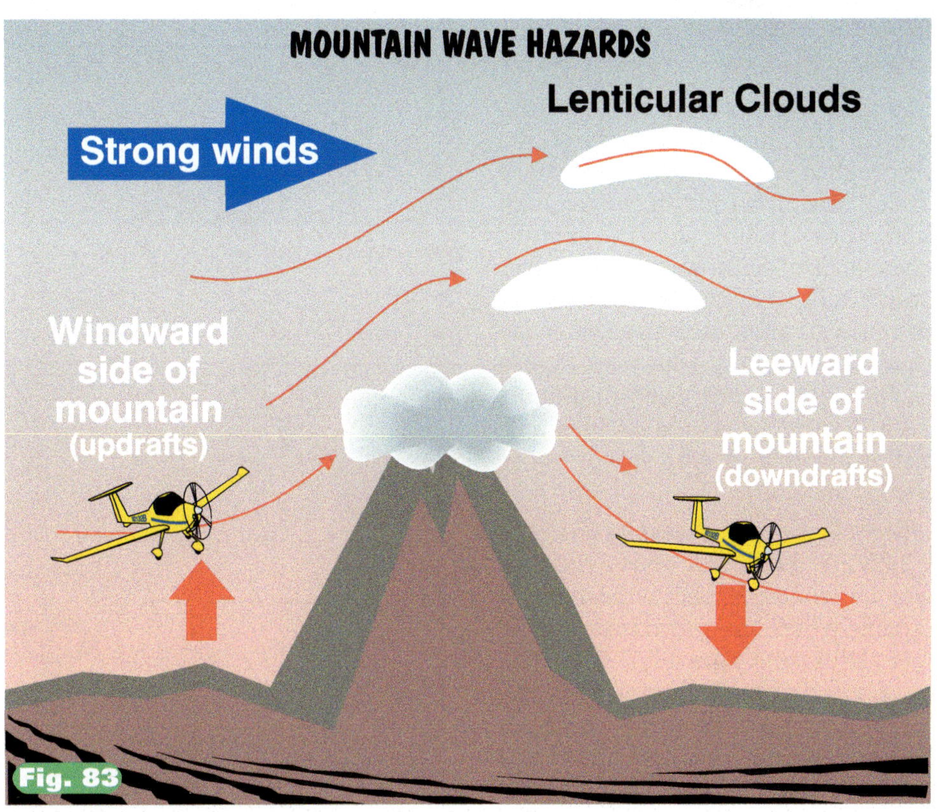

Approaching the mountain on the windward side (the upwind side) you could encounter strong updrafts. On the leeward side (the downwind side), it's possible to encounter strong downdrafts that your airplane might not be able to out climb.

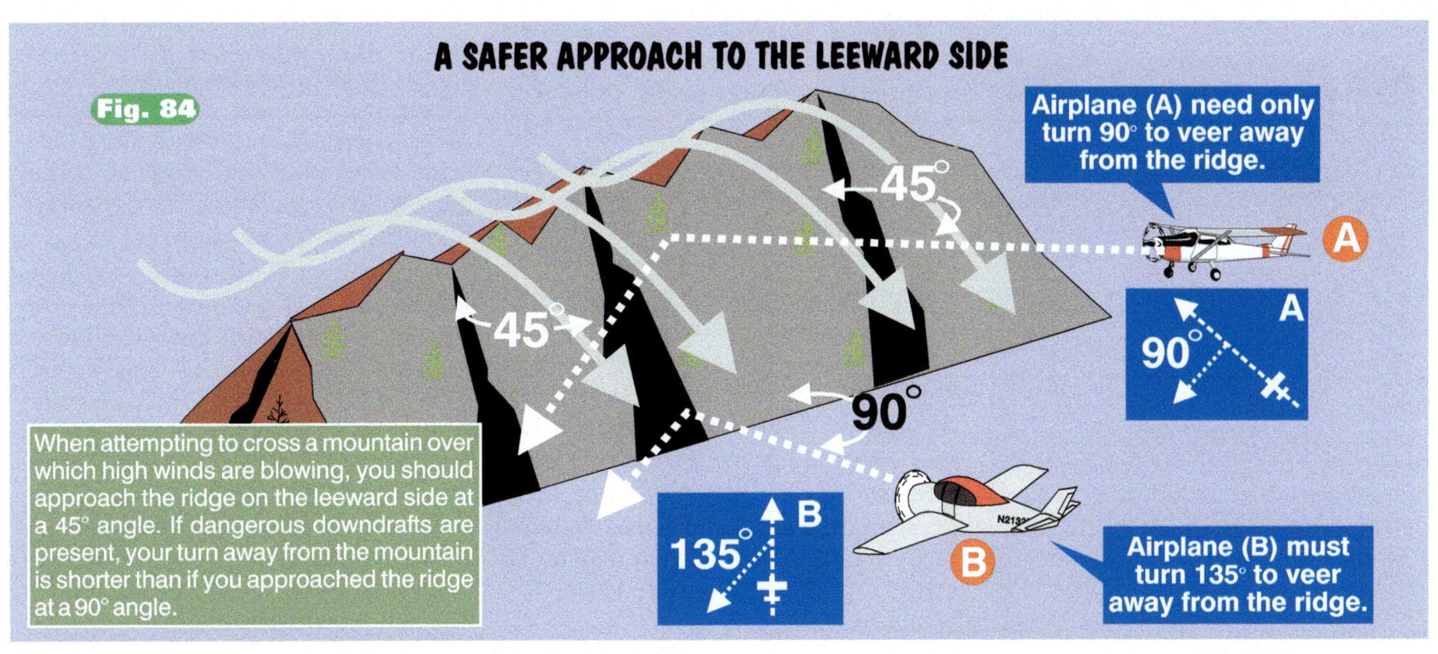

When attempting to cross a mountain over which high winds are blowing, you should approach the ridge on the leeward side at a 45° angle. If dangerous downdrafts are present, your turn away from the mountain is shorter than if you approached the ridge at a 90° angle.

Temperature Inversions And Windshear

Temperature inversions are common on the surface during clear, calm nights with little or no surface winds. Strong winds, however, can exist just above the inversion. Because air of different temperatures doesn't mix well, the warmer air on top tends to slide over the colder air below. This sliding, shown in Figure 85, becomes even more apparent when strong pressure differences exist, causing high wind speeds in the warmer air aloft.

If winds move in excess of 25 knots at 2,000 to 4,000 feet above the surface, you should expect windshear in the zone where the warm and cold air meet. Differences in wind velocities cause a tearing or churning of the air, producing eddies or turbulence in the shear zone. Pilots climbing or descending at slow speeds might find the windshear bad enough to induce a stall at low altitudes close to the ground.

If the inversion occurs within a few hundred feet above the ground, windshear can be a significant hazard. Imagine approaching an airport in a strong temperature inversion. Surface winds are calm at the airport, but you notice the winds at your altitude are quite strong. This often becomes apparent because of the rather large crab angle required to remain aligned with the runway. Noticeable differences between your airspeed and groundspeed is another clue to the possibility of windshear.

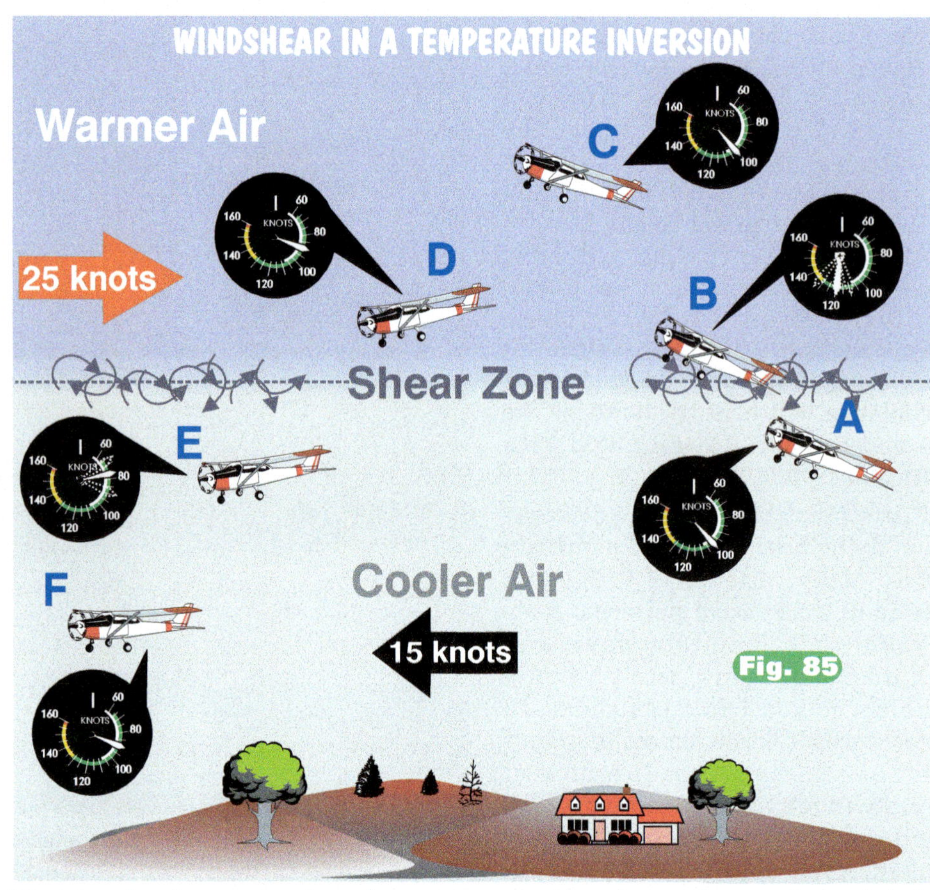

Windshear in a temperature inversion can cause sudden changes in your airplane's indicated airspeed. Airplane A is climbing through the inversion into an increasing headwind. At position B the indicated airspeed temporarily increases. As the airplane adjusts to the new wind direction, the indicated airspeed returns to normal at position C. Airplane D is descending into an increasing tailwind. At position E the indicated airspeed temporarily decreases, then returns to normal at position F. These indicated airspeed changes are more pronounced in heavier airplanes with large differences in wind speed.

Suppose you encounter a sudden tailwind while descending through an inversion (Figure 85, D to F). Differences in wind velocity might cause you to lose a slight amount of airspeed as you descend into a tailwind (Airplane E). A sudden tailwind acts like a burst of wind from behind the airplane. Airspeed is momentarily lost until the airplane is accelerated by the tailwind, then it returns to the previous speed, as shown by Airplane F. This event becomes even more serious when the airplane is close to its stall speed and the temperature inversion is close to the surface. It's possible for the airplane to stall without sufficient room for recovery.

Suppose you were climbing through an inversion into a headwind as shown by Airplanes A, B and C. A sudden headwind, while climbing through the inversion, might cause a temporary increase in airspeed, as shown by Airplane B. While this isn't as serious as a loss of airspeed, the turbulence it produces can startle a pilot (no sense testing that triple bypass or a pacemaker's overdrive function if you don't have to).

Be cautious. Anticipate windshear within the first few hours after sunset. Also anticipate it before and after sunrise. These are the times when temperature inversions are most common. The presence of winds in excess of 25 knots above the inversion, with calm surface winds, is a good sign that windshear may be lurking. Add a few knots onto your approach speed to reduce the danger of a windshear-induced stall.

Actually Heard! Really!!

A pilot called in and said he was unsure of his position but he had a town in sight. Since they didn't have him on radar, the active controller told him to descend and look for the town's water tower, see what it said on the side, climb back up and tell him. Sure enough in about three minutes the pilot called back and said, "Approach, I found the water." The controller, looking rather pleased, asked, "And what did it say on the side?" The pilot replied, "It said, Seniors 1978."

Fog

Fog is a cloud that touches the ground. Fog comes in on little cat's feet, and casts its gloomy pall over the airport, putting an end to aviating for VFR pilots, and sometimes even for IFR-rated pilots. Fog is one of the most frequent causes of reduced surface visibilities and it's a real pain in the wings for VFR pilots.

Fog presents a serious problem because it can form in a very short time. I've seen airports go from three miles visibility to less than one-half mile in just a few minutes because of fog. Even David Copperfield would be hard pressed to make an airport disappear in as short a period of time. Many a student has raced an approaching fog bank to the airport only to lose the race. Figure 86 shows the reduced visibility experienced in fog.

Remember that the *dew point* is the temperature at which water will condense out of the air. It's a function of humidity, and the number is so crucial that it's one of the things you will hear on the ATIS broadcast. Small temperature-dew point spreads are conducive to fog formation. That's why fog is common in colder months. It can, however, form any time the air contains enough moisture, condensation nuclei, and cooling temperatures.

Unfortunately, there are a lot of ways to brew up a batch of fog. Cooling the air to its dew point is the most common means of fog production. Adding moisture to air near the surface also aids in fog formation. Precipitation from fronts is a common way moisture is added to the air. Fog is classified by the way it forms. Let's examine some of the different types of fogs.

Your forward visibility is dramatically reduced in fog.

© Lars Lindblad - Fotolia

Fig. 86

Radiation fog frequently forms over areas of vegetation.

© Jeffrey Sinnock - Fotolia

Fig. 87

Radiation Fog—This isn't the type of fog that forms near a nuclear power plant (we moved next to a nuclear plant and the farm across the street has 20 head of cattle. What bothers me is that the farmer only had 13 cows). *Radiation fog* is what happens when the ground radiates its heat away. On clear, calm nights, terrestrial radiation of heat cools the ground. This allows the air resting next to the surface to cool quickly. As air is cooled and approaches its dew point, water vapor condenses and forms a shallow layer of fog. Radiation fog is very common at night and early morning hours. Figure 87 shows an example of radiation fog.

Areas of high humidity (rain soaked ground and vegetation) are especially conducive to the formation of radiation fog. This is why golf courses are common places for this type of fog. I've driven by these courses early in the morning and seen golf clubs popping out the top of a 6 foot layer of radiation fog. All you can see are funny little hats floating on the top of a 6 foot layer of fog.

I've even seen control towers standing above a shallow radiation fog layer at the airport. It's VFR for the controller but IFR for taxiing pilots. Bodies of water, despite their moisture potential, aren't a likely place for radiation fog to form. Bodies of water don't cool as quickly at night (compared to land), making radiation fog unlikely.

Winds up to about 5 knots tend to mix and deepen the layer of fog. Higher winds tend to disperse radiation fog. Solar heating of the earth after sunrise tends to dissipate radiation fog. Despite a fog layer, some solar heat makes it to the surface. This warms the ground, which helps dissipate the fog from below. Radiation fog also dissipates around its periphery first, where it's the thinnest. Of course, all this assumes a high altitude cloud layer isn't preventing a reasonable amount of solar heat from reaching the surface.

IT'S A LONG WAY TO A TIP-A-PILOT

The runway was tucked in close and parallel under a row of hills. The windsock was limp, giving no indication of the crosswind and turbulence higher up. Shortly after takeoff, I found myself fighting the turbulence with full and abrupt control movements. I heard my passenger remark that he didn't think my door was latched. It was good that I moved the throttle to its full-open position. My right hand was busy holding me in the seat. I hadn't fastened my seatbelt either!!! **ASRS Report**

HOW ADVECTION FOG FORMS

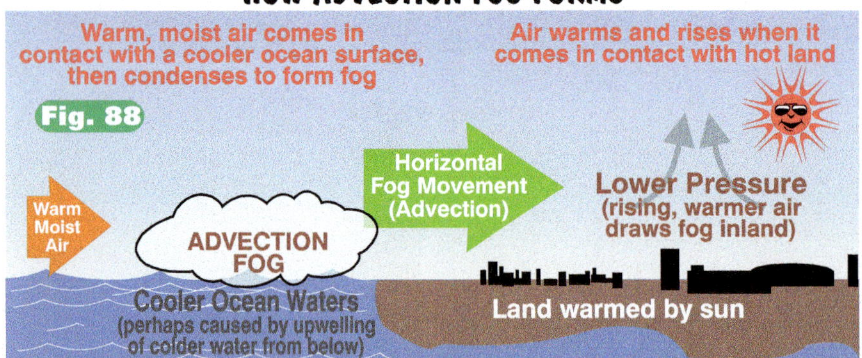

Advection fog, otherwise known as *sea fog* forms along coastal areas. When warm air comes in contact with cooler ocean waters, condensation can occur and form fog. Advection implies horizontal movement, thus this fog typically moves inland toward the area of lower pressure (caused by rising warm air from solar heating). Winds of 15 knots or more tend to lift the fog and form stratus clouds.

Advection fog is very common near the coasts where it can move inland and quickly blanket an airport.

© JENNY SOLOMON - Fotolia

Some people speak of fog *burning off* rather than dissipating. I once told a student we could fly later in the morning after the fog burned off. He went home and told his mother he couldn't fly because there was going to be a fog fire at the airport. Geesh!

Advection Fog – Convection means to move something vertically; advection means moving it sideways. *Advection fog* is fog that forms elsewhere and comes to visit you. Sometimes called sea fog, advection fog is most common in coastal areas, although it can form in inland areas. As warmer, moist air comes in contact with the ocean's surface, air temperatures decrease and water vapor condenses. This process is shown in Figure 88. With slight heating, the pressure over land lowers, drawing advection fog inland. Advection means to move sideways, thus allowing this fog to live up to its name. Advection fog deepens when winds increase to about 15 knots. Winds above this speed tend to lift fog layers into low stratus or stratocumulus-type clouds. (Stratocumulus clouds are a mixture of both stratus and cumulus clouds.)

Advection fog can form quite rapidly and cover extensive areas. Many a pilot has found only a deep white fog where the airport was supposed to be, even though the airport was reporting VFR conditions just a short time earlier. This makes you feel like you showed up at the airport gift shop before a commercial flight only to find them selling items from the luggage you just checked with the Skycap. Of course, plan B is to always have a fog-free airport nearby. Remember, good pilots always have a plan B and even a plan C.

Upslope Fog – When warm, moist air is forced up the slope of a mountain and condenses, it forms upslope fog. Technically, this cloud is considered fog because it touches the surface of the mountain. Upslope fog depends on wind for its existence. Therefore, it's not dependent on terrestrial cooling. This means that upslope fog can form under a higher layer of clouds that usually prevent terrestrial cooling. Expect to see upslope fog in the winter and spring on the eastern side of the Rocky Mountains.

Precipitation-Induced Fog – Warm rain, falling through cooler air can bring the air to the point of saturation, forming fog as shown in Figure 89. Commonly associated with warm fronts, it can occur in slow-moving cold fronts and stationary fronts. Couple this fog with the conditions that produce it—warm, cold and stationary fronts—and you get a double whammy of hazards.

Ice Fog – Ice fog forms under conditions similar to those that cause radiation fog except the air temperature is way below freezing. Instead of fog, you wind up with water sublimating directly into the air as ice crystals. We're talking temperatures around -25 degrees F as being favorable for its formation. This happens

PRECIPITATION INDUCED FOG

Precipitation-induced fog occurs when warm rain falls through cooler air and raises the humidity of the atmosphere to the point of saturation. It's usually associated with warm fronts but can occur in slow moving cold fronts and stationary fronts.

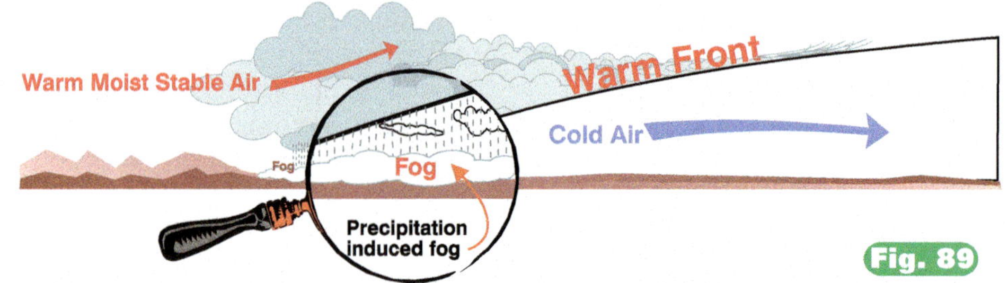

mostly in the Arctic region but is not unknown in the middle latitudes. Ice fog can be quite blinding to someone when it refracts sunlight. If your instructor is sending you to the Arctic regions on your solo cross countries, you might want to check and see if he's upset with you over something.

Steam fog forms over a warm body of water.

© Sylvana Rega - Fotolia

Ice fog forms when the temperature is below zero.

Courtesy NOAA Collection

Steam Fog – Anyone who has seen a heated swimming pool early on a cool morning has witnessed steam fog. As dry, cold air passes over a body of warm water, moisture evaporates rapidly from the surface. Condensation takes place as the cold air is quickly saturated. Water droplets often freeze, falling back into the water as ice crystals. Steam fog is quite conducive to low level turbulence and icing.

Weathering the Weather

Whether you like the weather or not, it's there, a force to be reckoned with. You don't need to get a Ph.D. in meteorology in order to be a good pilot, but you do need to understand and apply a basic knowledge of weather in order to fly safely.

Weather is a contributor to far too many aviation accidents. Most occur not because something came out of nowhere and smote the poor pilot, but because the pilot failed to properly anticipate what the weather would be, and plan accordingly.

Pilots as a group tend to be strong personalities. That's why they're called *pilots in command*. However, when it comes to the weather, a little bit of humility will go a long way toward keeping your skin (and that of your aircraft) intact.

"Know before you go," is the fundamental concept you need to come away from this chapter bearing. Keep in mind that you are legally *required* to obtain a weather briefing for all but the most minor of local flights. That should give you some sense of just how important it is to know what's in the sky before you put yourself there.

Weather is a fascinating subject, and one I think most pilots could profitably spend a lifetime schooling themselves in. Whatever you know, there's always more to learn. Take advantage of every opportunity to talk with flight instructors, Flight Service Station specialists, meteorologists, and others who can advance your education in how weather works.

WHOA NELLIE!!!

Normal approach and landing (wet runway). We could have taken any high speed turnoff but, because there was no apparent traffic immediately behind us, we asked permission to roll to the end. The response was, "OK, expedite to the end." Approaching the turnoff point at the end, I initiated brake application (unfortunately on the painted runway numbers) for final slowing (with allowance for the wet runway) for the turnoff. Braking was nil; came off brakes, tried easing into the turn with nosewheel steering. No reaction. Re-applied brakes; no response. Tried differential braking for pinwheel effect; no positive effect. Released brakes, straightened nosewheel, continued off the runway and 20° angle onto asphalt overrun. Informed Ground about possible/probable runway light strikes. Controller thanked us for the report and said they would check it out. Result: four lights struck. Should not plan to stop or turn on wet painted runway surfaces (even when grooved all the way to the end). A turnoff at one of the high-speeds would have prevented problem. At no time was there any flailing about or other gyrations of the aircraft. In fact, at the gate a flight attendant commented, "Nice landing." Unknowing is bliss, I suppose.

ASRS Report

Postflight Briefing #12-1

Advanced Weather Concepts

For those with a secret longing to challenge the local TV weatherperson, or perhaps just to gain that little edge you need to finally win a hangar discussion over why it's raining, I offer some more details on why the weather does what it does.

You won't need this to pass any pilot test administered by the FAA, but if you know and understand it, you might be able to get a job with the National Weather Service.

Wave Cyclones (Frontal Waves)

Not all fronts are found along low pressure troughs. Sometimes they form as small waves along one of the three to seven larger waves of the polar front. These smaller waves (also known as *wave cyclones* because they rotate in a counterclockwise manner) move along the polar front in an easterly direction. They are blown that way by the prevailing westerlies. Let's examine this process.

(The word *cyclone* indicates low atmospheric pressure having a counterclockwise rotation. Small wave cyclones are also simply called storms because they bring inclement weather).

Discontinuities along the polar front can appear and cause small wave cyclones (sometimes referred to as frontal waves) to form. Figure 90 (on the right hand page) depicts this process. Wave cyclones usually form in slow moving cold fronts or stationary fronts, as shown in Figure 90A. Airflow on each side of the stationary front is parallel to the actual front. Thus, there is little or no reason for the front to bend or twist.

Any small disturbance in the stationary frontal pattern, caused by uneven heating, irregular terrain or high altitude winds (the jet stream), can start a wave-like bend in the front, as shown in Figure 90B. If the wave-like bend is big (energetic) enough, warm air can start to rise over the retreating colder air. This often leads to condensation, and the release of latent heat into the atmosphere which intensifies the low pressure system (in other words, makes the air want to rise more quickly).

As the low pressure deepens, atmospheric pressure decreases. Counterclockwise circulation bends the front, which advances the cold air and forms a cold front, as shown in Figure 90C (position 1). As warmer air slides up and over the receding colder air, a warm front forms, as shown in Figure 90C (position 2). As fronts form, the entire wave cyclone (the storm) moves in an easterly direction, along with the prevailing westerlies.

Advancing cold air (cold front) usually moves faster than retreating cool air (the zone of which is the warm front). Think of the cold air as falling or sliding underneath the warm air. Things that fall are accelerated by gravity. Retreating cooler air tugs at the ground as the warmer air slides up and over it. This tugging or sticking to the ground slows the advancing warm front. Retreating cool air acts like I did during my first visit to the dentist—I got splinters under my fingernails as my mother tried to tug me off the porch.

Figure 90D shows the faster moving cold front catching up, and overtaking the slower warm front. Meteorologists call this an occlusion and it is depicted by warm front and cold front symbols moving in the same direction.

Many parents have had the experience of taking their children to the orthodontist and hearing that little Bobby has maloccluded teeth. What the orthodontist is saying is that his teeth overlap. Translation? You pay megabucks (but little Bobby gets a great set of choppers). Since these fronts overlap, pilots find that an occluded front contains a combination of warm and cold frontal weather, as shown in Figure 90D (we'll discuss frontal weather shortly).

Once the occlusion forms, frontal movement slows down. The low pressure area diminishes in intensity because warm air is no longer rising and condensing over the colder air. In the final stage, shown in Figure 90E, the occlusion dissipates and the two fronts form a stationary front once again. Remnants of the low spin off and usually dissipate in forgotten whirling eddies.

Sometimes multiple storm systems (several wave cyclones) form along the polar front, as shown in Figure 91. It's not unusual for three, four or more of them to appear. These move eastward, with the flow of the westerlies and in the same direction as the high altitude jet stream (which blows from west to east).

Wave Cyclone Weather Patterns

Small frontal systems that occur in wave cyclone patterns offer a large scale mixture of the most interesting weather (a wave cyclone is the storm system that typically

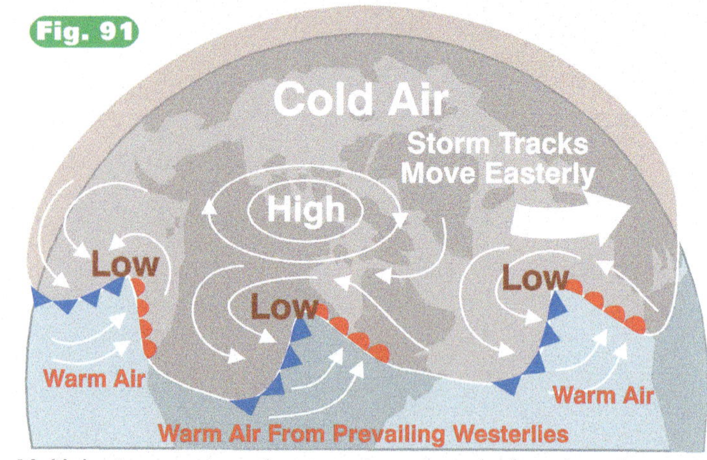

Multiple storm systems (wave cyclones) can be found moving eastward along the polar front. Warm air from the prevailing westerlies and high altitude winds move these storms.

SHORT WAVE (STORM) FORMATION

Fig. 90

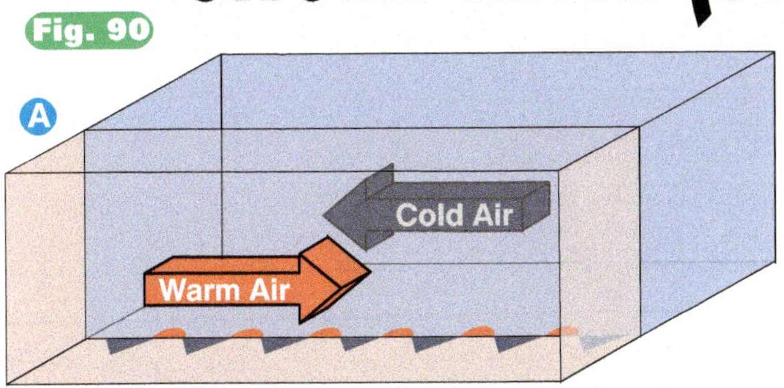

Frontal waves may form along a slow moving cold or stationary front.

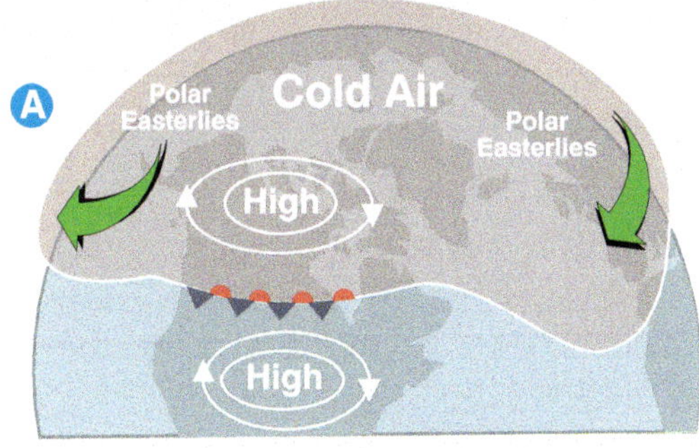

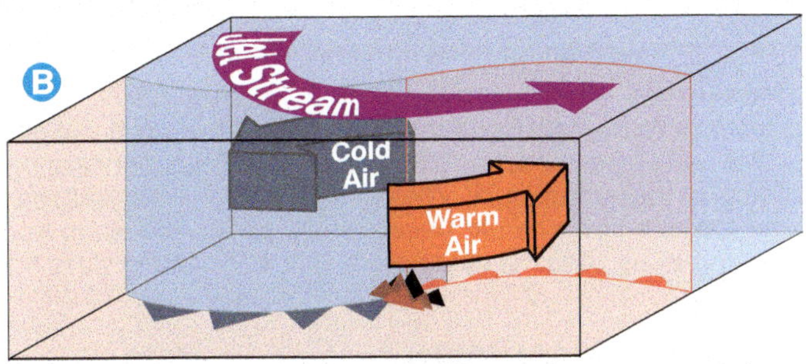

The jet stream or a geographical feature may cause a bend in the front.

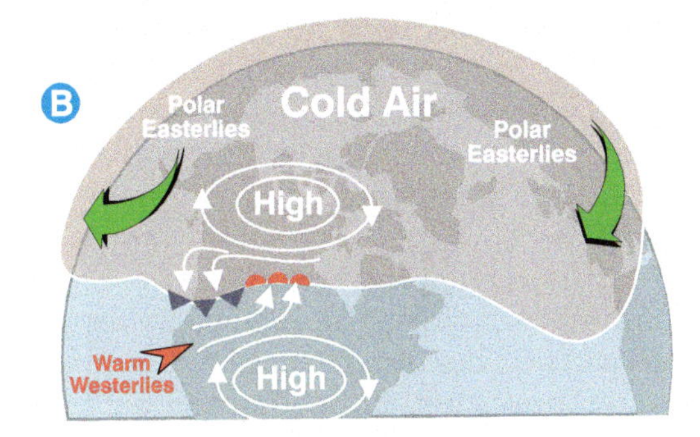

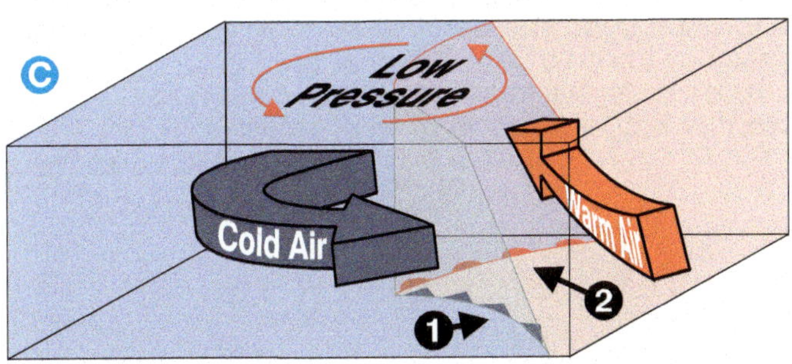

Low pressure forms in the development of distinct cold and warm fronts.

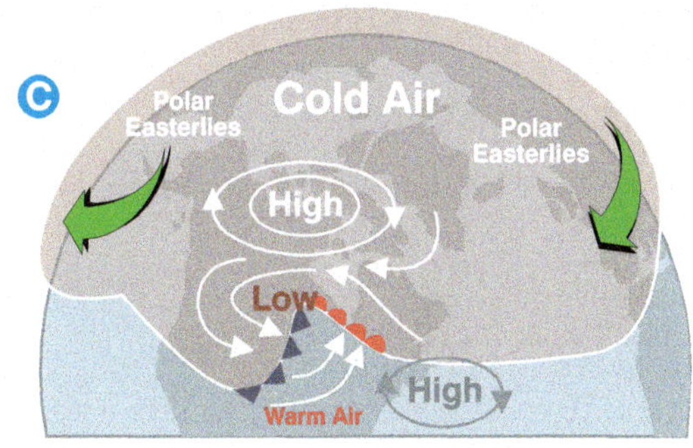

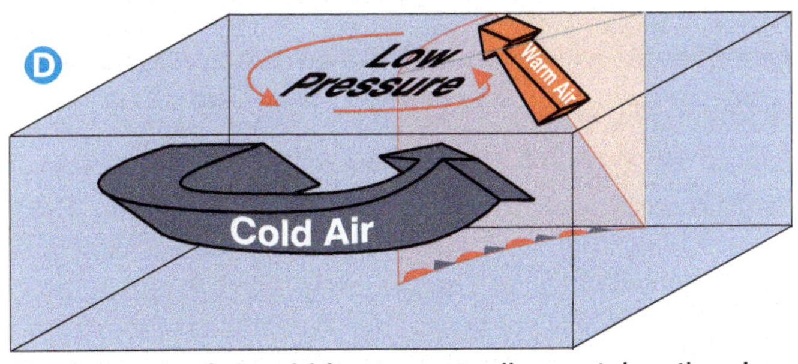

The faster moving cold front eventually overtakes the slower warm front.

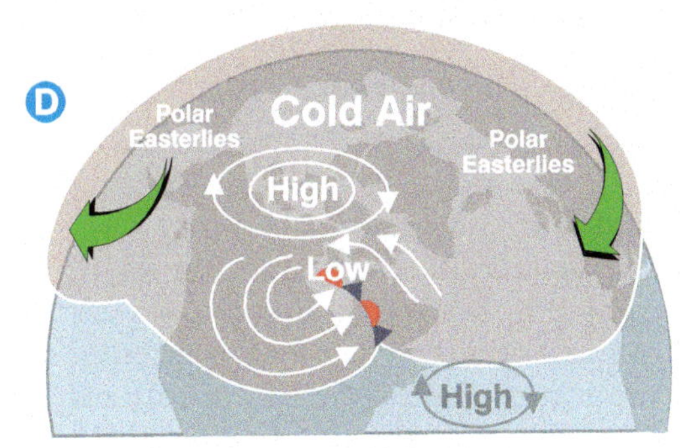

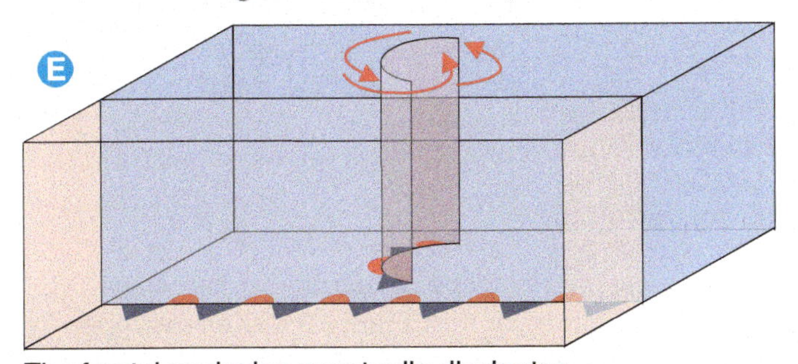

The frontal occlusion eventually dissipates.

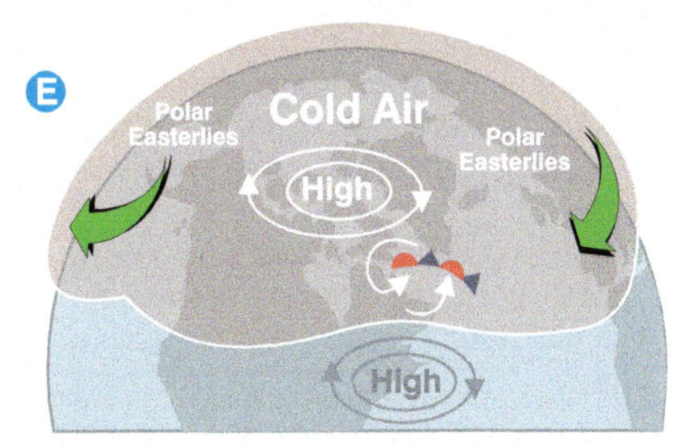

contains fronts, a low pressure system and counterclockwise—cyclonic—circulation). Figure 92 shows one of these wave cyclones in full formation. North of the low pressure center, clouds lower and thicken, producing rain or snow usually lasting 12 to 24 hours. If the storm's warmer air is above you (along path A to B), precipitation usually takes the form of showers or snow flurries, depending on the temperature of the air below.

South of the low (along path C to D), you'll experience the approach of a warm front with lowering stratus, nimbostratus (stratus clouds with rain). With passage of the warm front, the weather clears and the air warms up. Finally the cold front arrives, typically bringing cumulonimbus clouds (these cloud types have the greatest turbulence) and thunderstorms. Following the cold front is cold air, clearing skies and gusty winds.

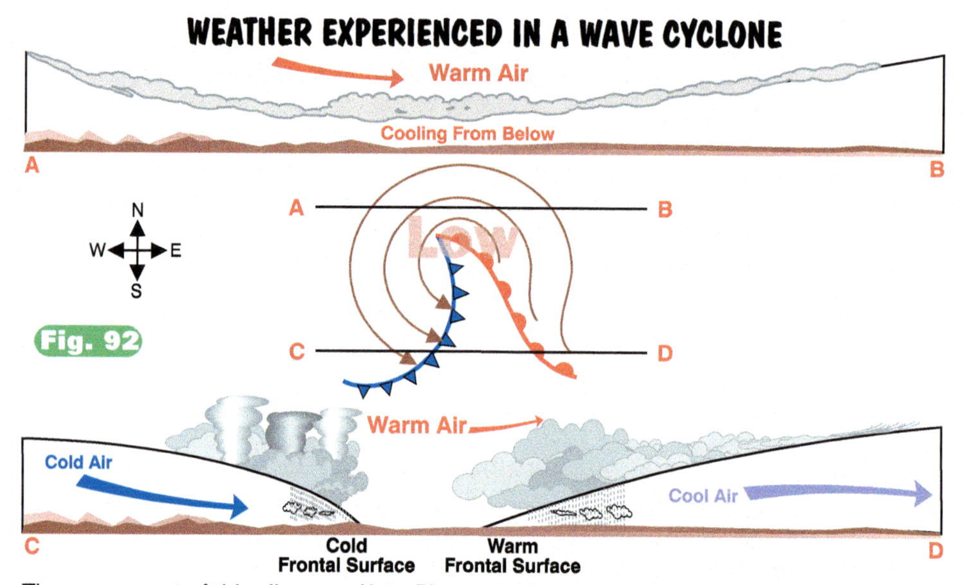

The upper part of this diagram (A to B) represents the north part of the wave cyclone. Warmer air is above you in this part of the wave, implying that you may experience showers or snow flurries, depending on the temperature of the air below. If you were stationary on the surface, south of the low, the fronts would pass from (C to D). The warm front passes first, followed by clearing skies, then the cold front and finally clearing skies and cold air.

COLD OCCLUSION

A cold occlusion occurs when the cold front overtakes and lifts up the preceding warm front. The warm air is lifted entirely off the surface by the cold front. Weather ahead of the occlusion is similar to that in a warm front. Near the surface, the weather is similar to that of a cold front.

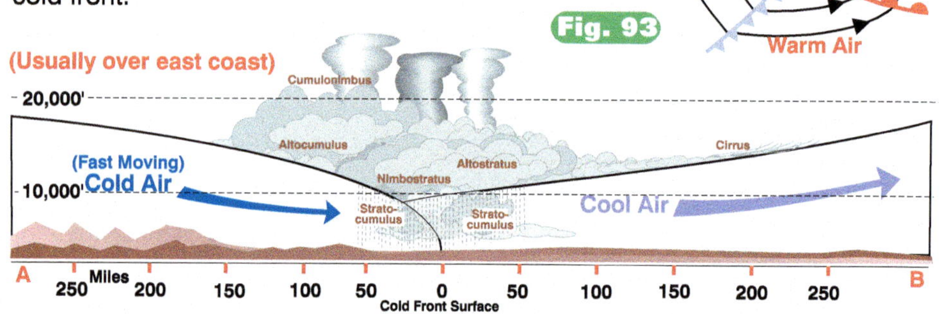

Cold Occlusions

In wave cyclones, cold fronts usually catch up to and overtake slower moving warm fronts. This overtaking produces what is known as a cold-type occluded front or a cold occlusion. Two varieties of occlusions are typical—cold occlusion and warm occlusion.

Cold occlusions occur when the air ahead of the warm front is less cold than the air behind the overtaking cold front, as shown in Figure 93. The cold front overtaking the warm front lifts the warm air up and over the retreating cool air. Essentially, the warm front is lifted entirely off the surface by the undercutting cold front.

The hollowed-out warm front symbols in Figure 93 represent the lifting of the warm front by the colder air. Weather ahead of the occlusion is similar to that associated with warm fronts, while weather near the surface position is similar to that of cold fronts.

As the occlusion develops, warm air is lifted higher and higher. Finally the cloud system associated with the warm front disappears. The weather and cloud system now resembles that of a cold front. Cold occlusions form predominantly over continents or along the east coast and are more common than warm occlusions.

Warm Occlusions

Warm-type occluded fronts (or warm occlusions) are usually found in the northwestern United States. They begin with cold air masses from the Pacific overtaking a retreating colder air mass from the Arctic. Warmer air is caught in between these moving air masses. This process is shown in Figure 94.

The retreating Arctic air mass is colder than the approaching Pacific air mass. The Pacific cold front pushes the warmer air up and over the retreating Arctic air mass. The Pacific air mass is cool, but not as cold as the Arctic air mass, and it moves up the same slope as well. At this point the Pacific cold front becomes an upper cold front. Weather in the cross sectional area from (A) to (B), shown in the insert, is shown in Figure 94.

The structure of the warm occlusion in Figure 94, shows an open-type cold front symbol. This indicates the Pacific front is no longer in contact

WARM OCCLUSION

A warm occlusion occurs when the Pacific cold front pushes the warmer air up and over the retreating Arctic air mass. The Pacific air mass, not being as cold as the Arctic air mass, moves up the same slope. Weather associated with the warm occlusion is similar to that of a warm front, while tropical cold front weather occurs near the upper cold front boundary.

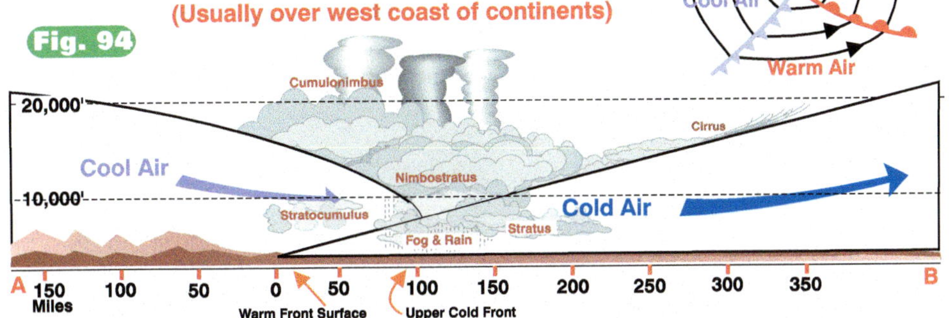

Fig. 94

with the surface. Weather associated with a warm front occlusion has characteristics of both warm and cold fronts. The cloud sequence ahead of the occlusion is similar to that of a warm front, while tropical cold front weather occurs near the upper cold front boundary.

Are we having fun yet? Remember, it takes a lot of study to become intimately familiar with weather. It's not something you're expected to master before you become a private pilot. The study of weather is an ongoing process for pilots. Try to learn a little about it every day. That way you won't be like the pilot who thinks stable air is something you find in a barn.

Postflight Briefing #12-2

How the Jet Stream Forms

To understand how the jet stream forms, we need to know something about the tropopause.

The tropopause is the boundary between the troposphere (where all our weather occurs), and the stratosphere (where very little weather occurs). This boundary surrounds the earth like skin surrounds an onion. The tropopause is shown in Figure 95. Temperatures decrease until reaching the top of the troposphere. Above the tropopause, however, temperatures remain steady and then start to increase.

The tropopause tends to bulge at the middle of the earth as a one-a-day Hostess Twinky man might bulge at the beltline. Normally, the tropopause is located around 30,000 feet MSL in the northern latitudes and bulges at the equator to altitudes of 65,000 feet MSL. It bulges because the warmer air near the equator expands slightly. As we move northward the air cools and shrinks slightly, thus lowering the height of the tropopause. The polar tropopause can vary, but will be typically found at 18,000 to 26,000 feet MSL.

Occasionally, breaks occur in the tropopause. Think back to the last time you witnessed a giant, big, big fellow sit on a waterbed (this guy's so big that when he gets on a scale it says, "Please, one at a time!"). You winced because this fellow's weight caused a large bend or bulge in the mattress. If it bulges too much and tears, water—under pressure—shoots out and swirls around the tear zone, as shown in Figure 96. Uneven weight distribution on the mattress causes a shearing or tearing effect in its thin skin.

In a similar manner, a strong vertical temperature gradient can cause large differences in pressure, resulting in a bulge or tear in the tropopause. Pressure differences occur because warmer air expands

THE TROPOPAUSE

The tropopause is like a thin skin covering the troposphere It's found at lower altitudes over the poles and higher altitudes over the equator. Height varies because of the direct effects of air expanding by heating and shrinking by cooling.

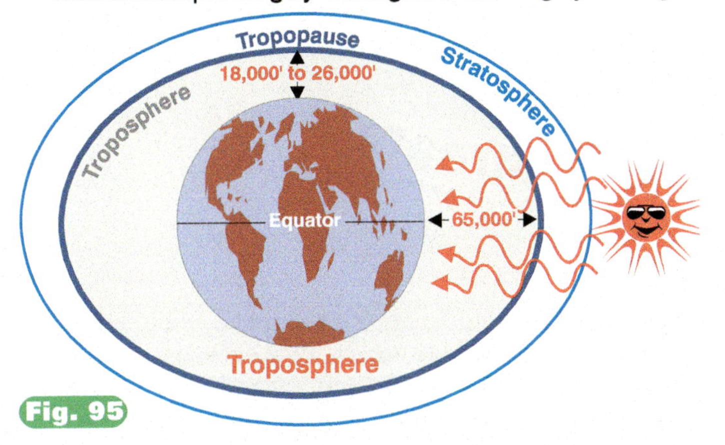

Fig. 95

WATERBED AND THE JET STREAM

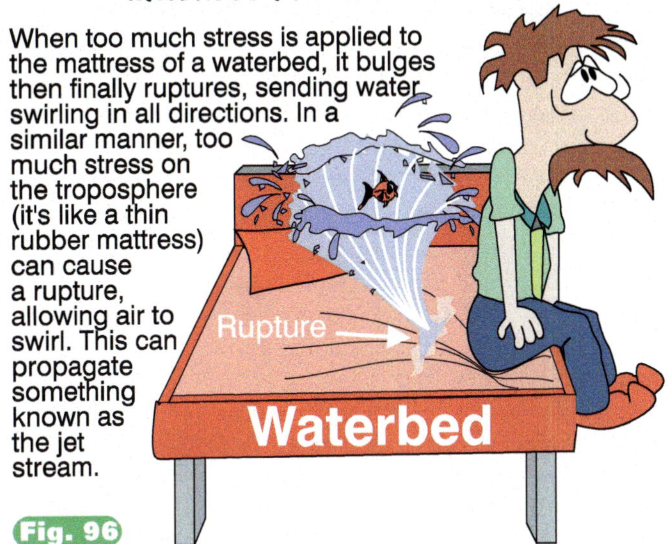

Fig. 96

and cooler air shrinks. Given enough vertical expansion and shrinkage in the troposphere, a break in the tropopause occurs. Air spills around the tear, as shown in Figure 97.

Figure 98 shows warm, tropical air rising at the break in the tropopause. This warm air circulates upward and northward toward the cold polar air. Then it circulates downward as it's cooled. As it circulates upward and downward, it's curved to the right by the Coriolis force. This gives the air a west-to-east rotating motion. The jet stream's tube of fast-moving air is further coaxed into a west to east motion by the prevailing westerlies.

Jet streams, which are usually found along or near the polar front, can have winds in excess of 250 MPH. If you could get your nonturbocharged Cessna 172 up that high (you can't—take pictures if you do) and tried to fly against the jet stream you'd be able to fly it backwards at twice its normal speed!

Jet streams are important because they help meteorologists track the west-to-east migration of wave cyclones and their associated storms. These wave cyclones (and their associated low pressure systems), tend to follow the jet stream's winds at higher altitudes. In addition, jet streams can modify pressure centers near the surface.

Think of a jet stream as a ceiling fan that forces air earthward and forms a high pressure center. At other times, jet streams act like the ventilator fans found in our ceilings. These fans create a sucking action that creates a miniature low pressure center. Jet streams can increase low pressure centers on the earth's surface, modifying local weather patterns. The exact reasons for this are beyond the scope of this book (and most other books, too!). Suffice it to say that meteorologists pay very close attention to the jet stream when forecasting weather.

Studying the jet stream (admittedly advanced for a private pilot) is like playing the slots in Las Vegas. Even if you don't win, it makes doing your wash a lot more fun. Playing with ideas about the jet stream makes studying weather a lot more fun because it helps explain many things that would otherwise seem a complete mystery.

THE JET STREAM

Think of the warmer air to the south standing taller than the colder air to the north. The differences in these heights stretch and eventually tear the tropopause in a manner similar to someone sitting on a water bed and stressing its mattress. At the point of tear, a large difference in temperature exists. This causes air to swirl in a circular manner as shown below. Warmer air rises upward toward the tropical or southern part of the tropopause. Then it cools and descends at the northern part of the polar tropopause. This circular motion is primarily responsible for the formation of the jet stream.

Fig. 97

JET STREAM MOVEMENT

The jet stream contains high speed, high altitude winds flowing from west to east. The flow of this stream normally follows the polar front and, at times, modifies the direction of polar frontal movement. It's not unusual to find winds from 150 to 200 MPH in the jet stream.

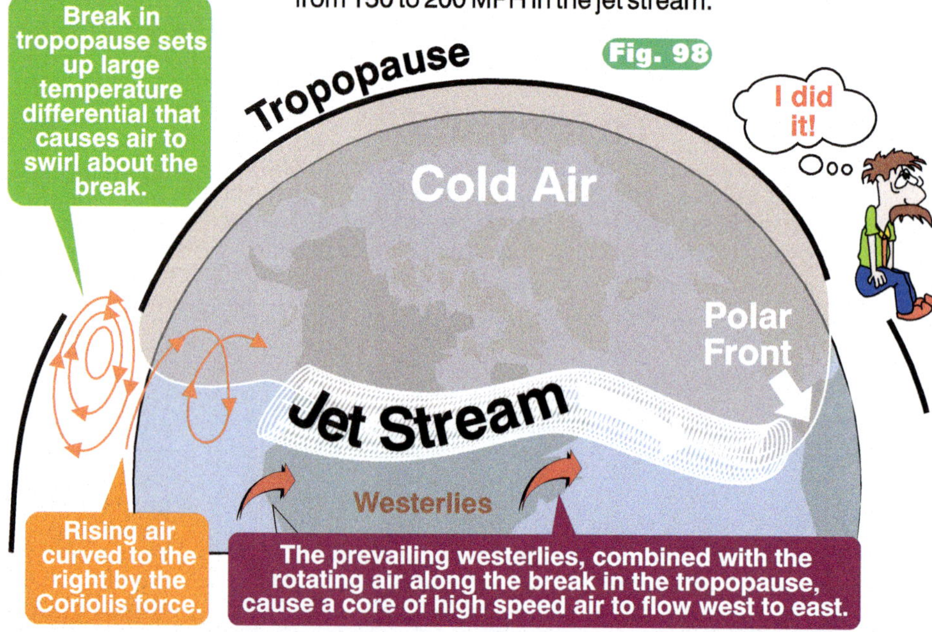

Wisdom comes from experience, and experience from lack of wisdom.

Chapter Thirteen

Weather Charts And Briefings

PIREPS, PROGS and METARS

We all remember a few of the golden rules governing our earthly behavior: Do unto others as you would have them do unto you, judge not lest ye be judged, and always turn your wheel in the direction of the skid (the rules that are important to you may be a little different). Flying, too, has its golden rules, and they're not just bullion, because they often relate directly to the matter of keeping you and your passengers safe and happy.

That's never more true than when it comes to weather. As I hope you understood from reading Chapter 12, nature is not to be trifled with. Good pilots are not fearful, but they are certainly respectful. That's why one of the aviation golden rules is to always obtain a weather briefing before flying . . .anywhere, any time.

Some pilots think weather briefings are for sissies; others think they're just for cross country (long) flights. Both of these attitudes come from pilots who are flying with a fog bank between their ears.

It does *not* take the awesome force of a severe thunderstorm to make flying distinctly unfun and unsafe. Clouds, wind, fog, closed runways, unavailable navigational aids—these are just some of the things you will find out about in a preflight weather briefing—but only if you get one. Any or all of these things can have a direct impact on any flight, no matter what its duration.

I distinctly remember preparing one day, while still a student, to do touch-and-goes. I anticipated only good weather. It was late morning and the skies were clear, without a hint of adverse weather. I knew it was a good day to practice landings for two reasons. First, all the seasoned instructors were away at a flight instructor seminar, so there was no one around to make fun of me. Second, the tower had switched the airport to right traffic and right turns were my specialty. Off I went.

Thirty minutes passed. The winds picked up substantially. Small cumulus clouds developed above the airport, causing turbulence and gusty conditions. I decided to quit early, before the local university called and complained about someone at the airport who kept popping the needle of their seismograph. Keeping the taildragger lined up on final was quite a challenge for an 18-hour student. I thought I did a great job, even though I swerved a little. Apparently the folks in the tower thought I swerved a lot. They called while I was on final and asked, "32 Bravo, are you in need of some assistance or should we just put on a little music?"

In the span of about 30 minutes the sky went from a beautiful blue to a white, cloud-dotted tableau with turbulence-bearing cumulus clouds. It wasn't a significant problem, but it did impress me with just how quickly weather changes. Obtaining a weather briefing before every flight keeps the pilot informed of weather changes that might be far more uncomfortable than what I experienced.

Aviation Weather Services

Think of a huge jukebox. No, even bigger than that. Press F7 and you get "Purple People Eater," while G10 gets you "There Ain't Enough Whiskey in Tennessee to Wipe the Ugly Off of You."

Aviation weather works pretty much the same way, though the titles aren't as interesting. You can obtain a staggering array of information from a large number of places. All you have to do is know which buttons to push. In fact, it's even better than the jukebox, because you don't have to deposit a quarter. Aviation weather services are, for the moment at least, free to pilots. Push the right buttons and *ka-ching*, out comes an hourly weather observation. Push again and *ka-ching*, there's your forecast, pilot reports, hazards, or NOTAMS (notices to airmen).

Lots of people from many agencies of the federal government, as well as private individuals, have a hand in providing the weather services available to pilots. Among the participants are the Federal Aviation Administration, the Department of Defense, and several other groups and individuals, including a huge network of weather volunteers who provide hourly reports.

The main button that lets you rock 'n roll, is the Flight Service Station (FSS), currently run by Lockheed Martin (Leidos FSS). Dial (800) WX-BRIEF for a phone briefing, of contact the FSS on its listed radio frequencies as shown in the *Chart Supplement* excerpt (Figure 1), or log onto this site at: *www.1800wxbrief.com*. Either way you'll be connected to an FSS facility serving up weather.

Figure 2 shows what it looks like at your typical Flight Service Station. Flight Service offer a complete menu of prerecorded weather information accessible to anyone with a telephone or internet access.

Personal computers have become an increasingly popular way of obtaining a weather briefing. In fact, most pilots today obtain all their

What's in an A?

When I tell new pilots there's such a thing as an *Automated* Flight Service Station, they tend to picture an unstaffed facility with synthesized voices. *Dave, I will give you the weather now. Please don't hang up, Dave. Dave, do you hear me?*

Once upon a time, when the nation was young and budgets were big, there were small Flight Service Stations all over the place. You could walk right in, sit right down, and they'd let your briefing hang down. (This was literally true, because once upon a time PC—pre-computer—the weather reports came on long rolls of Teletype paper. Yes! Really!)

Today, the standard FSS is gone! Gone, I say! The FAA has replaced the hole-in-the-wall model with the AFSS (also called *Flight Service*), which is currently manned (and wo-manned) by a company called *Leidos*. Leidos, as of this writing, has three large AFSS centers located around the country (soon to be two large centers). These centralized facilities serve a huge area—did I say huge? Flight Service relies heavily on modern electronic wizardry. It's highly computerized, has telephone and radio tentacles that reach everywhere, and can access almost anything in an instant.

Gone are the clanking, cranky Teletype machines that used to print barely-readable weather reports on rolls of paper. Gone are the hand-generated weather maps.

What's not gone are the people. Today's Flight Service Station is still staffed by very real folks whose expertise you'll learn to appreciate. While many pilots feel that the "local knowledge" has been lost because of the centralized nature of the new facilities, the people who staff them are information experts and certified weather briefers who can provide almost any kind of weather data you might want, and assist you in interpreting it correctly.

Though they're highly automated, Flight Service depend on briefers to use that automation to your advantage before each and every flight.

A lot of time, money, and effort has been invested to gather and disseminate the information. None of it helps, though, if you don't make the call.

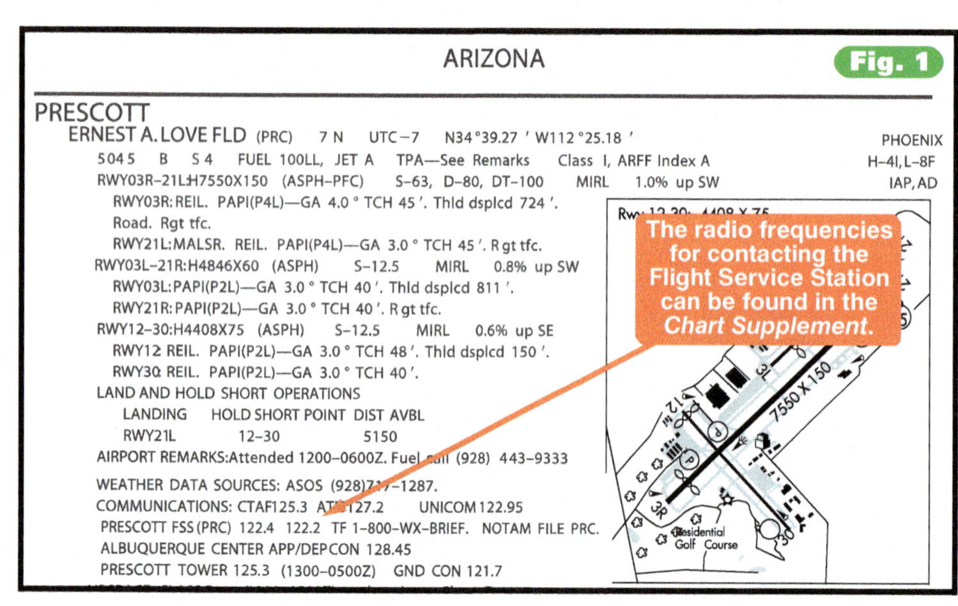

ARIZONA

PRESCOTT
ERNEST A. LOVE FLD (PRC) 7 N UTC−7 N34°39.27′ W112°25.18′ PHOENIX
5045 B S4 FUEL 100LL, JET A TPA—See Remarks Class I, ARFF Index A H-4I, L-8F
RWY03R-21L:H7550X150 (ASPH-PFC) S-63, D-80, DT-100 MIRL 1.0% up SW IAP, AD
RWY03R: REIL. PAPI(P4L)—GA 4.0° TCH 45′. Thld dsplcd 724′. Road. Rgt tfc.
RWY21L: MALSR. REIL. PAPI(P4L)—GA 3.0° TCH 45′. Rgt tfc.
RWY03L-21R:H4846X60 (ASPH) S-12.5 MIRL 0.8% up SW
RWY03L: PAPI(P2L)—GA 3.0° TCH 40′. Thld dsplcd 811′.
RWY21R: PAPI(P2L)—GA 3.0° TCH 40′. Rgt tfc.
RWY12-30:H4408X75 (ASPH) S-12.5 MIRL 0.6% up SE
RWY12: REIL. PAPI(P2L)—GA 3.0° TCH 48′. Thld dsplcd 150′.
RWY30: REIL. PAPI(P2L)—GA 3.0° TCH 40′.
LAND AND HOLD SHORT OPERATIONS

LANDING	HOLD SHORT POINT	DIST AVBL
RWY21L	12-30	5150

AIRPORT REMARKS: Attended 1200-0600Z. Fuel call (928) 443-9333
WEATHER DATA SOURCES: ASOS (928)7[illegible]-1287.
COMMUNICATIONS: CTAF 125.3 ATIS 127.2 UNICOM 122.95
PRESCOTT FSS (PRC) 122.4 122.2 TF 1-800-WX-BRIEF. NOTAM FILE PRC.
ALBUQUERQUE CENTER APP/DEP CON 128.45
PRESCOTT TOWER 125.3 (1300-0500Z) GND CON 121.7

This is your typical Automated Flight Service Station (FSS). The folks are very friendly and they have really good toys for weather watching.

Fig. 2

weather without ever making a phone call to fetch it. They'll typically use their desktop computers or iThingys (iPad, iPhone, Android tablet, etc.) at the time and place of their choosing. Several commercial vendors sell software and access to either government or private weather databases. Combined with apps such as ForeFlight and WingX, these programs offer flight planning capability, enabling you to plan your flight's time, distance, and fuel requirements based on the current winds and the airplane's performance characteristics (see Postflight Briefing #14-5 on Page N47.

For those with a computer, flight planning and preparation is easy, interesting, and informative. Best of all, you can save everything and either review it on the screen or print it out and take it along. One of the downsides of the oral weather briefing has always been the "Whatzat?" factor. This comes into play when you try to read your hastily scribbled notes after hanging up the phone.

There are other means of acquiring weather information. Newspaper weather forecasts, the Internet, the Weather Channel from cable television as well as public television news broadcasts all contain weather information of use, though none of these sources provides anything approaching a full weather briefing. Sometimes, though, all you need is one look at the weather map or the forecast to know it's no go.

The Telephone Briefing

As I mentioned earlier, it's no longer easy (or possible in most instances) to pay a visit to an actual flight service station facility. Yes, there are a few private weather service facilities that you might visit, but these aren't available to the average pilot. Nor are they really necessary, nowadays.

Today's pilot has at his or her fingertips more weather information than the average pilot could even imagine 30 years ago. I'm speaking of internet weather access via your mobile computing device (tablets, phones, pads, iThingy), or your desktop computer. We'll discuss this in more detail shortly.

Then there's the Automated Flight Service Station that can provide you with the same weather but dished up and a friendly and easily consumed format. You can call Leidos Flight Service Station (or log onto their web site as reference on the previous page) to obtain your official weather briefing.

As a student pilot, that first call for a weather briefing might make you a little nervous. Most students have no idea of how they are supposed to act on the phone. This is why I have all my students listen to me on another line as I make a call to the FSS. One of my students decided to try it for himself. He picked up the phone, dialed and got a briefer who said, "Hello, Los Angeles Flight Service, may I help you?" The student replied, "Ahhhhh, ahhhh, ahhhh, my instructor wants to talk to you, gotta go, bye," then he handed me the phone. His following calls were anxiety free once he realized how friendly the briefers were.

What's a Legal Weather Briefing?

You are legally required to have a weather briefing before any non-local flight.

Seems easy, until you ask yourself (or someone else) one simple question. What's a weather briefing, and who can give one?

The rules (FAR 91.103) state that "Each pilot in command shall, before beginning a flight, become familiar with all available information concerning that flight." Should something unpleasant happen, you will have a very hard time convincing the FAA that you didn't get a weather briefing because weather wasn't information that concerned you.

Until fairly recently, the only way to get anything approximating a weather briefing was to call a Flight Service Station. All such calls are recorded both manually and on tape, so it always possible to prove a pilot was (or wasn't) properly briefed.

Many pilots now obtain a briefing via computer from one of several private weather services. Whether or not this constitutes a legal weather briefing for purposes of meeting the letter of the law depends on that service's ability to prove you actually obtained the weather.

If you obtain a weather briefing via computer, make sure the service you're using keeps a record of the briefing. Call them and ask, if you're not sure. If they don't, then it's best to leave a paper trail to protect yourself. Calling your friendly Automated Flight Service Station is a sure way to establish having received a briefing.

Besides, some of them have really great music-on-hold.

Just so you won't wind up with your tongue tangled behind your eye teeth, which would keep you from seeing what you're saying, let's walk and talk through a typical briefing.

We'll begin by dialing (800) WX-BRIEF. You will usually get a recording and a menu of selected items from which to choose. Be patient. The computer that's screening your call needs a little information before it can provide you with the appropriate weather service. For instance, it needs to know the state in which you're located so it can route you to the FSS responsible for that area. You can respond to the nice synthesized computer voice by pushing buttons or with a verbal response (head nodding is not yet recognized by your phone or the computer). Eventually you'll be taken to a live briefer for your weather briefing.

Here's how it will go once you've gone live.

The FSS briefer says:

Good morning, this is Prescott Flight Service.

You respond by saying:

Good morning. I'm a student pilot and I need a standard briefing for a VFR flight.

Tell the briefer what kind of pilot you are and what kind of briefing you need, and the type of flight you're proposing to make.

Weather is responsible for over 25% of aviation accidents and 40% of its fatalities. Why are these percentages so high? It would be easy to put the blame on an inability to accurately forecast the weather. It's more likely the pilot didn't even check the weather. In one FAA study, 55% of the pilots involved in a weather related accident had no record of receiving a weather briefing. It seems more plausible that the real culprit is a pilot's inability to resist the urge to press on in the face of poor or deteriorating weather conditions. Known as "get-home-itis," this Lorelei of the air has probably caused pilots more grief than any other psychological pressure. Resisting the press to push on in bad weather is your greatest challenge as an aviator.

By *kind of pilot,* I don't mean a good pilot or a bad pilot. I mean *student, private, commercial* or *airline transport pilot.* Briefers are trained to tailor their briefing to the pilot's experience level.

A friend of mine called for a briefing once and told the specialist he was an airline transport pilot. Part of the briefing went like this: "... we're expecting logarithmic, neonocturnal katabatic perturbations in the magnetohydrodynamic ectoplasmic weather membrane..." Huh? What? My friend said, "Hey, I've got this piece of paper here with two boxes, one says *go* and the other says *stay.* Which one should I check?" The briefer laughed and they went through it all again—slowly.

If you say *student pilot* they'll talk to you differently. For instance, the briefer will normally speak more slowly, usually using more precise terms. A friend who was a 747 captain for one of the now-defunct airlines (Pan Am) said he used to call the FSS for a weather briefing and always told the briefer he was a student pilot. He just liked to have a little fun at the briefer's expense.

Can you imagine the conversation? "This is the FSS, what can I do for you?" He replies, "Ah, yes sir, student pilot cross country today and I'd like a weather briefing." "OK, where are you going today?" He says, "Ahhh, Los Angeles to Japan." The briefer would pause, then reply, "Wow, this is your long cross country isn't it?" You can imagine what happened from there. It must have gotten real interesting when he wanted the briefer to give him the winds at 39,000 feet!

Briefings now come in three flavors, *standard, abbreviated,* and *outlook.*

A *standard briefing* contains all the important weather and related items of concern. These items include adverse conditions, weather synopsis, current weather, forecast weather, forecast winds aloft, alternate routes if any and NOTAMS. NOTAMS include items concerning airports, navigation aids and hazards, all of which contain essential knowledge for safe flight. More on NOTAMS in Chapter 17.

A standard briefing is the entire enchilada. It's everything, and it assumes you have and know nothing. Always request a standard briefing if you haven't collected any weather information prior to your first call.

If you're calling to update or supplement previously acquired weather information, ask for an *abbreviated briefing,* and request the specific type of information you need. Each type of information has its own rate of change; METARs (hourly surface reports) change hourly, while TAFs (terminal aerodrome forecasts) are produced four times a day. If all you want is an update on the weather at your proposed destination, you don't need to sit through the entire enchilada.

Ask for an *outlook briefing* if you are calling the FSS for weather information six or more hours in advance of your proposed departure time. I usually do this the night before a flight to obtain a general idea about the weather the following day. It's difficult for meteorologists to predict weather accurately more than 24 hours in advance. An outlook briefing is only general information, intended to give you a notion of what's out there, and some sense of whether the weather is so bad (or good) that you should definitely cancel (or plan) your flight. A standard briefing is still necessary as departure time grows nearer.

Then tell the briefer that you'll be on a VFR flight (though the information is redundant in this case, since student pilots are *always* VFR, but it's a good habit to get into—later on you will perhaps be asking for a briefing for an IFR flight, which to the briefer is a whole different container of gumballs).

Say this the following way:

Cessna 1234 Bravo, a Cessna 172, Santa Monica to Santa Barbara via the coast. Departing Santa Monica 2230 Zulu, 1 hour plus 10 enroute at 4,500 feet.

Give the briefer your aircraft tail number or your name, the kind of airplane you're flying, the departure point, destination, the route of flight, your estimated time of departure, the estimated time enroute and the altitude at which you'll fly. At this point the briefer may express utter amazement at your preparation, because this information has to be extracted from most pilots in a process somewhat similar to pulling teeth. Briefers *really* appreciate it when you provide them what they need to get the job done for you.

Now get ready to copy. The briefer is about to do his/her thing. You will receive at least the following information *in this order (omitting items where there is no relevant information, of course):*

1. Adverse conditions

You will first be advised of major items that might cause you to say "Whoa, Briefer. That's enough. I thank you, my passengers thank you, good day and goodbye." This might include such things as runway closure at your departure or destination airport, 6-inch hailstones, a hurricane in progress, IFR conditions when you're not IFR rated, etc.

2. VFR flight not recommended

This is a warning that the weather is not great. The briefer will provide the reason ("Due to mountain obscuration in clouds and dense fog") and you will have to decide if it's reason enough not to attempt a VFR flight.

3. Synopsis

This is the general weather pattern covering the major weather systems and air masses influencing weather in the area where the proposed flight will take place.

4. Current conditions

Current surface observations for the departure and destination airports and pilot reports of enroute conditions.

5. Enroute forecast

The briefer will take you from departure and climbout through landing, summarizing the forecast for the period you'll be airborne. That's why the time of departure and time enroute are important information when requesting a briefing.

6. Destination forecast

The forecast weather for the estimated time of arrival (ETA).

7. Winds aloft

You will be given the winds at the altitude closest to your proposed flight altitude for which there are measurements, which is at 3,000 foot intervals through 12,000 feet. Some briefers will do minor math and interpolate, giving you something halfway in between the 6000 and 9000 figures if you're planning to fly at 7500 feet. I'll tell you how to do the math for yourself in a minute.

8. NOTAMS

Notices to Airmen (NOTAMS) are information of an advisory or cautionary nature. They can include everything from a runway being closed to a navaid being dysfunctional. The ones you'll hear most frequently have to do with navaids (VORs, primarily) that aren't working or are out of service.

A Note About NOTAMS

When there are significant and important changes in aeronautical information, you need to know about them. This becomes especially important when such information might affect the safety of your flight. NOTAMS contain information such as airport or primary runway closures, tower construction, changes in the status of navigational aids, radar service availability and other information essential to planned enroute, terminal or landing operations.

You can ask the Flight Service Station specialist for all pertinent NOTAM information during your weather briefing or just download them when you obtain your weather briefing from an FAA approved service provider, such as Leidos FSS. (See Page Q19, Chapter 17 for more information on NOTAMS.)

Runway Construction

Courtesy FAA

Tower Construction

Courtesy FAA

9. ATC delays

These will be pretty rare for pilots flying to anything other than major metropolitan airports. If you are headed for O'Hare or JFK, the briefer will tell you of any holds due to flow control or other measures designed to keep the traffic humming.

That's it.

Or is it? The briefer will usually conclude by asking you if there's anything else you'd like to know. Speak now or forever hold your wings, unless you call back. Now is the time to ask any questions you might have. Briefers are trained by the FAA to disseminate weather information. They're very skilled at reading charts and forecasts and relaying that information to pilots. They are not, however, meteorologists. They don't forecast weather. They only talk to you about it. And good talk it is! That's why briefers don't tell you whether to go or not. That decision is yours and yours alone. They will, however, tell you all about the highs, lows, squiggles and squirts comprising the aviation weather map. Listen to what they have to say. They do good work.

Briefers are sort of the Dear Abby of flightdom. They will answer almost any question (about aviation, that is; questions about your love life should still be directed to Dear Abby). They'll tell you about Customs, search and rescue, ATC services, preferred routes, and why the computer will take a flight plan for one route and not another. They'll look up phone numbers (for aviation facilities, not for your Aunt Maude in Minneapolis), read the Class D NOTAMS, provide information about Military Training Routes, restricted areas, and other special use airspace.

They will do almost anything they can to get you almost any information you want about the aviation system. Just ask and ye shall receive.

Other Sources Of Weather Information

There is, the proverb says, more than one way to skin an airplane, and there are lots of other places to get information about which way the clouds blow.

NEWSPAPERS – My uncle liked his newspaper because he could swat the dog with it when the little fellow did something wrong. It's no wonder the newspaper started turning up wet (that also explains why the dog started chasing the paperboy). Nevertheless, the paper provides you with some valuable information about weather. Most newspapers publish a weather map showing

major weather systems around the country, and many carry a satellite picture that helps provide a look at what the weather's doing. Weather-wise pilots study weather on a daily basis. Simply take the weather chart and/or satellite photo provided by the paper and examine it every day. These charts are a lot more accurate than they were several years ago. You'll be surprised how weather savvy you'll become with this small investment of time.

Cockpit Weather Uplink – A very useful innovation in aviation technology now allows you to receive uplinked weather information in the cockpit on your GPS moving map screen display (Figure 3A).

For instance, your iPad or Android tablet device might have flight planning software such as ForeFlight (Figure 3B), WingX Pro, FlyQ, etc. With some additional equipment (ADS-B equipment, as discussed on Page Q37), this software allows your device to receive uplinked weather information for free. This uplinked weather contains many products including enroute and destination weather, NEXRAD radar imagery (this is similar to the same type of colorful weather imagery shown by your local weather man/woman on the evening news), station reports (METARs), winds aloft forecasts, and so on, all while in flight.

In addition, this flight planning software also works on your cell phone which makes it easy for you to have the same weather information available to you just before takeoff. And I do mean "just before takeoff" as part of your pre-departure engine runup check. Any chance of flying off into unexpected weather is highly unlikely with today's technology. In fact, you probably will never find yourself using the phrase, "Hey, where did that stuff come from?" except when you eat at an airport restaurant. How nice is that?

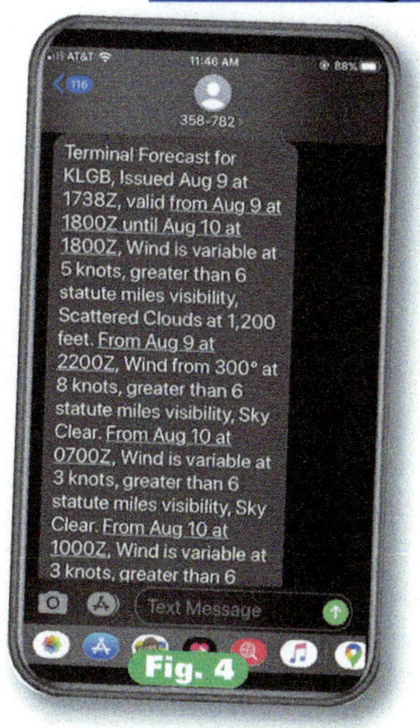

Cellphone weather information is available from the AFSS via the SMX text messaging service.

Cellphone Weather at Your Fingertips – While uplinked cockpit weather is all the rage in aviation today, there's weather available to you at your fingertips that's pure gold from a pilot's perspective. I'm speaking of instant weather information that's available to you via your cellphone's text messaging service (Figure 4).

Of course, your cellphone can probably run any of the popular flight planning apps, but it can also get immediate information on the weather conditions at any airport with weather reporting services. Here's how this works.

Using the Automated Flight Service Station's SMS text messaging service, you'll send a text message to this num-

This portable Garmin GPS unit allows you to receive in-flight weather (NEXRAD imagery in this instance).

Popular Flight Planning Tools Showing Weather

ber 358-782 (FLT-SVC) and include any of the following messages to receive weather.

Text "METAR LGB" and you will receive the latest METAR for Long Beach International Airport.

Text "METAR SNA" and you will receive the latest METAR for John Wayne Airport.

Text "TAF SNA" and you'll receive the latest Terminal Aerodrome Forecast for John Wayne Airport.

Text "MT SNA PT" and you will receive the latest METAR for John Wayne Airport in plain language.

Text "TAF SNA PT" and you'll receive the latest Terminal Aerodrome Forecast for John Wayne Airport in plain language weather (i.e., almost no decoding required).

Now, I realize that you don't know how to interpret this textual weather information yet. However, you'll learn about this shortly. Just realize how unique it is to be able to retrieve the most current airport weather information prior to a flight using your cellphone. Who you gonna text? Try: 358-782 (FLTSVC).

Enroute Weather Information – In addition to the weather information you have via any uplinked cockpit weather, you also have *radio* weather. This is the weather information you obtain by making a call to the Automated Flight Service Station on your radio. Yes, the company providing flight services is Lockheed Martin, but you can still refer to them as *flight service*. The universal frequency that all pilots can use to talk to a flight service station specialist is 122.2 MHz.

Fig. 5

Because flight service covers a rather large area, remote communication outlets have been established to assist pilots in reaching the FSS specialist. Figure 5 depicts the area south and west of Albuquerque. While you can certainly use 122.2 MHz to contact the FSS, it's best to use the specific frequency for the area in which you're flying. What's that frequency? While you'll learn more about this in the chapter on aviation charts, the best frequency to use in this instance is 122.5 MHz. It's shown above the blue box (position A) on the sectional chart excerpt in Figure 5. This is one of the frequencies that the FSS has allocated for communicating with pilots this area. When you make your initial call on this frequency (you'll refer to the FSS as *Albuquerque Radio*), the specialist in charge of that area will see a reference light activate on his/her weather panel indicating that a transmission is being made on 122.5 MHz in that area. The specialist will respond to you on 122.5 MHz and provide you with whatever weather or flight plan information you need.

Pilot Reports (PIREPS) – One of the problems with the weather is that it changes. Weather forecasting is a game of catch-up that can never be won. The closest you can come is *pilot reports (PIREPS)*, which represent actual information on current conditions as reported by pilots in the air. These reports are made to the FSS or an ATC facility, and they can be of immense assistance in helping you to make a go/no go decision, or to avoid problem areas once you're airborne.

When contacting Flight Service, in flight or before takeoff, you will usually be provided current pilot reports as part of the weather briefing.

Radio Check? Check.

Pilot reports are excellent reasons to talk to ATC. When receiving traffic advisories from the radar controller at night, I'm always looking for a reason to talk with him or her. Why? Because there isn't much traffic at night and, with all the silence, I frequently wonder if my radio has died. Instead of asking for time checks, position checks and masculine index voice pitch check (just kidding on that last one), I simply say, "Houston Center, this is 2132 Bravo, I have a pilot report for you." He says, "All right 32 Bravo, go ahead." I reply, "It's clear." Well, at least I know my radio is working.

Airline pilots ask other pilots about the weather on a frequent basis. They're always asking the pilot ahead of them what the ride is like. Is it smooth? Rough? An airline pilot friend of mine said he called the radar controller and asked if he could talk to a Eastern Airlines L-1011 that he knew was 100 miles ahead of him. The weather was turbulent and he needed to find a smooth ride. My friend said, "Eastern 734, this is United 232, how many people are throwing up on your airplane?" The Eastern captain came back with, "Three people throwing up...unfortunately, they're all in the cockpit!" Airline pilots have a great sense of humor!

If they aren't forthcoming, ask for them. These reports give you a good idea how close to reality the forecast is.

In many instances, PIREPS have allowed me to make a decision to go when the forecast painted a very bleak picture. PIREPS become especially important in understanding what's happening in areas where weather reporting stations are few and far between. (Near the end of this chapter I'll show you how to decode PIREPS transmitted by the Flight Service Station.)

Whenever you contact Flight Service or ATC, give them a pilot report. Pilots don't do this often enough. Even if the weather is clear, report it. I make it a point to listen to the ARTCC (Air Route Traffic Control Center) whenever I'm on a cross country flight, whether or not I'm signed on for radar service. Believe me, if there's nastiness ahead, you'll hear it. My rule is that when the male pilots' voices hit a high C or above, it's time to re-evaluate my options. This is one of those cases where it's not just what they say, but how they say it, that counts.

Weather Reports

There are many weather reports available from the National Weather Service and private weather services to aid pilots in flight planning. Knowing what to ask for and how to use the information is an important pilot skill.

The available weather products are of two basic types: *observations* and *forecasts*. Observations are historical. They are the weather conditions that occurred at the time the observation was taken. Forecasts are weather estimates for several hours (sometimes days) into the future. Like all estimates, weather forecasts are subject to change. Sometimes considerable change. If you've ever remodeled your house and remember what the original estimate was, and what you finally paid, you understand exactly what I'm saying.

Let's examine the weather reports you'll need for successful and safe VFR flight planning. Unless the weather report has the word forecast or prognosis in it, then it's probably an observation.

There are some pretty interesting inventions in the world, such as a pager that will summon you when your car is being burglarized, enabling you to get burgled *and* beat up in a single evening. There is, however, no contraption that will interpret the weather for you, though if you do a poor job of it you still might manage to get beat up.

You and only you are responsible for making your go or no-go decisions. It takes training to make good weather decisions. Weather charts are part of this training. There are many times when you'll have access to weather charts without the benefit of an actual briefer. Knowing how to interpret these charts is very important.

Most of the following weather charts are on the private pilot knowledge exam. I have added additional practical information where appropriate. You'll find that a few charts have partial legends accompanying them. These legends help interpret some (not all) of the chart's symbols. For purposes of the FAA knowledge exam, you'll need to memorize some basic chart symbology. As you'll soon see, many of the chart's symbols can be generalized to other charts. I'll specifically advise you when a chart's legend is available for a specific chart on the exam.

International Reports

Airplanes have helped shrink the world, and one of the results is an increasing demand for consistency internationally. This is particularly crucial in aviation, where pilots have the capability to cross numerous national borders within a few hours.

Because weather is so vital to flight safety, it was agreed internationally that consistency in reporting the weather was desirable. A pilot should be able to look at a weather report anywhere in the world and read it. That's why the U.S. now uses the International Civil Aviation Organization (ICAO) weather standard for reporting weather. This format provides a single global format known as METAR (METeorological

Reptile Rattles, Controller Tattles

Several years ago, a friend was working as a controller at Fullerton Tower in Southern California. She was looking at the surface aviation weather reports when she noticed the report for Tucumcari, New Mexico. It read "ROSNOT." She had never seen that particular acronym, so she called the FSS making the report. The phone rang and a briefer answered. She said, "What does ROSNOT mean?" He replied, "It means Rattlesnake On Step, No Observation Taken!"

Must have been a towering snake.

METAR WEATHER REPORTING FORMAT

METAR KINK 081955Z 32014G20KT 1/2SM R30R/2400FT DZ FG OVC006 13/12 A3004
SPECI KMKC 081936Z 20014G24KT 1/2SM R34/2600FT +SN BLSN FG VV008 00/M03 A2898
METAR KBOI 081953Z 23008KT 5SM SCT015 19/13 A2994 RMK SLP156 T01930128
METAR KLAX 081955Z 01013G20KT 3SM HZ SKC 18/11 A2995

Fig. 6

Aviation Report) and TAF (Terminal Aerodrome Forecasts) for weather reporting.

METAR (pronounced *ME - TAR* [as in YOU - JANE]) observations are taken hourly at many reporting stations located across the country. These reports indicate the weather conditions at the time the observation was made. Other than a pilot report, a METAR observation is as close as you can get to the actual weather conditions without sticking your finger out the window. Not only do these reports provide a current weather observation, they also allow you to sense a trend in the weather by observing several of the past hourly reports. Figure 6 shows a typical METAR for several airports (those reports preceded by the letters *SPECI* are special, unscheduled reports as a result of a significant weather change. An example would be when the ceiling goes above or below 1,000 feet or when the visibility goes above or below 3 miles).

When you first look at one of these reports, I'm sure it looks as convoluted and cryptic as Egyptian hieroglyphics. Once you learn the code, though, METARs are easy to understand, and learning the weather-code symbology from one report often makes the others much easier to learn.

You'll notice that these weather reports consist of abbreviations. This is a carryover from the days when weather was sent via Teletype, which was slow. Some personal computer software will automatically decode these abbreviations, providing you with a description of the weather in English (and many internet weather sites will also decode these for you, too). And no, you can't use your IBM or Apple computer on the knowledge exam to interpret weather symbols for you).

To some the METAR looks as convoluted and cryptic as Egyptian hieroglyphics.

Interpreting the METAR requires an understanding of the individual sections contained within the report. Figure 7 is a breakdown of these individual sections. Let's take a closer look at each one.

To better help you understand the order in which a METAR presents the weather, take a look at the following acronym: STWVRWCTDA. This stands for *Should Tina Walk Vera's Rabbit Without Checking The Dog's Appetite?* Each letter represents a particular segment of the weather contained within the METAR as follows:

S Station Identification
T Time in Zulu or UTC
W Wind Direction and Velocity
V Visibility
R Runway Visual Range (if reported)
W Weather
C Clouds
T Temperature
D Dew Point
A Altimeter Setting

By remembering this acronym you'll be able to remember the general order in which the information is presented. Keep in mind that a METAR won't report what isn't happening, nor will it report a segment if the measuring equipment (such as a barometer) is not functional. By knowing what should be there, you'll easily identify any missing section. Let's jump into interpreting the METAR.

Station – The letter S in Figure 7 represents the first section of the METAR and is a four letter/number designation for the station or airport reporting this observation. KLAX is the designator for Los Angeles International Airport (*K* is the international designator that precedes all domestic U.S. location identifiers; Alaska locations start with *PA* and Hawaii locations start with *PH*). You'll learn some of these airport letter designations for your local area as you go along (besides, some of them are easy enough to guess). The only time you need to be really worried is if you're on an airline flight to Los Angeles and the Skycap checks your bag with a PKS (pak-e-stan?) tag—you'll never get it back.

Time – The letter T in Figure 7 is the date and time the weather observation was made. For instance, at KLAX, the observation was taken on the 8th day of the month at 1955 Zulu (also referred to as UTC or Coordinated Universal Time). Weather reports are always given in Zulu time. This is the time in Greenwich, England and not the time certain African tribes use. Using UTC calibrates all the weather reports to one time zone. All you need do is convert from UTC to your local time zone when interpreting weather reports. Refer to Chapter 14, page N4 to review converting between time zones.

Wind – The letter W in Figure 7 identifies the wind direction, velocity, and any gusts. The first three digits represent the wind direction in degrees relative to true north. The next two digits are the wind velocity in knots (as identified by the letters KT). The G followed by a number represents the wind gust in knots. For instance, a wind report of 31015G27KT says that the wind

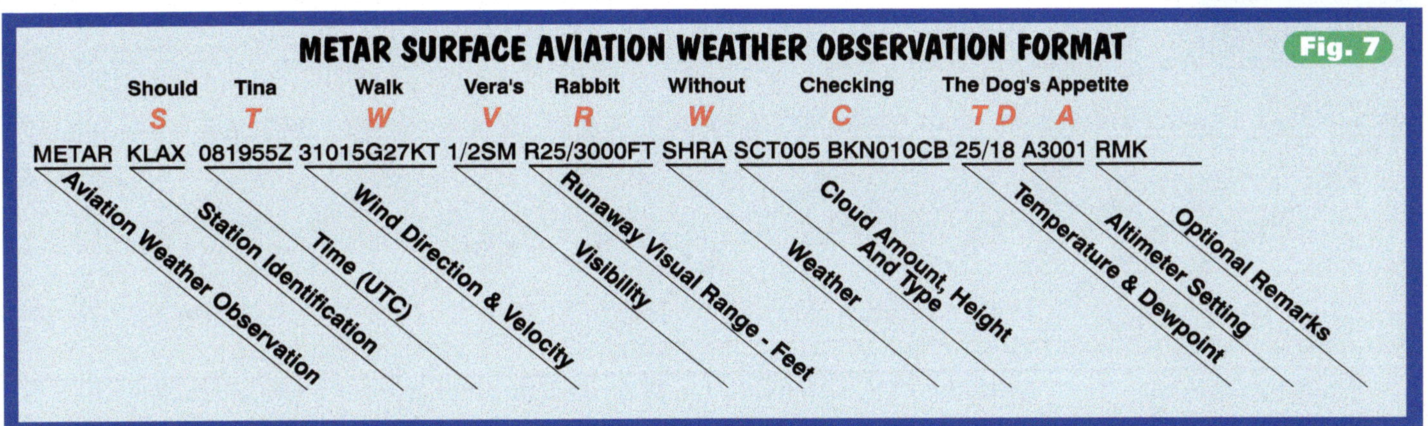

is 310 degrees at 15 knots with gusts to 27 knots. Gusts are reported when a 10 knot fluctuation occurs between the wind's peaks and lulls. A calm wind is reported as 00000KT. The letters VRB may be used if the wind speed is 5 knots or less. If the wind's direction varies by 60 degrees or more and the speed is greater than 6 knots, then variable wind direction values follow the reported wind. For instance, a 280V350 following the wind report indicates that the winds are 280 degrees variable to 350 degrees. The two extremes in direction will be included in clockwise order.

Visibility – The letter V in Figure 7 stands for visibility. Surface visibility is measured in statute miles and fractions thereof. A space divides whole miles and fractions and the letters SM follow the visibility to indicate *statute miles*. In Figure 7 the reported surface visibility is 1/2 mile. If you fly internationally, you should be aware that the U.S. is an exception in reporting prevailing visibility for the full 360 degree area of visibility rather than the *lowest sector* visibility, which is the international standard. In situations where visibility is very poor in one direction but fairly good in others, you can be mislead by what's prevailing, especially if you're flying in the area where visibility is low. (Significant differences in any sector from the prevailing visibility or a differing tower visibility will be stated in the remarks (RMK) section of the METAR.)

Runway Visual Range – The letter R in Figure 7 stands for RVR (runway visual range). RVR is an electronically measured value used to determine the distance down a runway that a pilot can see high intensity runway lights. This shouldn't concern you until you become an instrument rated pilot. Nevertheless, understand that RVR is measured in feet. Figure 7 shows that the RVR along Runway 25 (R25) is 3,000 feet. The letters L, C or R that sometimes follow the runway number are designators for the left, center or right runway. The numbers following the slash indicate the RVR in feet (FT).

Weather – The letter W in Figure 7 represents the weather phenomena presently found at the airport. Figure 8 lists the weather codes used in reporting the weather phenomena. These codes contains five different columns. The first two columns contain qualifiers (intensity or proximity and a descriptor of the weather). The last three columns contain the actual weather phenomena, such as precipitation, obscuration, etc. Up to three separate groups of weather phenomena may be included in the report; the most dominant weather is reported first. Precipitation (water products—rain, snow, hail—reaching the surface) are combined into a single group.

For instance, moderate rain and snow (these are two types of precipitation) present at the airport, is reported as SNRA (snow is the dominant precipitation and is reported first). Both are types of precipitation and are reported as one group. The absence of a + or – sign in front of the precipitation indicates that it's moderate in intensity.

Moderate rain, fog and funnel clouds are three separate groups of weather phenomena and are reported as three separate groups: RA FG FC. If light rain, fog, and volcanic ash were reported, it would look like the following: –RA FGVA. If light drizzle, hail and a sandstorm were reported it would look like the following: –DZGR SS (remember, light drizzle and hail—both are types of precipitation—

WEATHER CODES

Qualifiers		Weather Phenomena		
Intensity or proximity 1	Descriptor 2	Precipitation 3	Obscuration 4	Other 5
- Light	MI Shallow	DZ Drizzle	BR Mist (≥5/8sm)	PO Dust/sand whirls
Moderate (no qualifier)	BC Patches	RA Rain	FG Fog (<5/8sm)	SQ Squalls
	PR Partial	SN Snow	FU Smoke	FC Funnel cloud(s)/
+ Heavy	DR Low Drifting	SG Snow grains	VA Volcanic ash	+FC Tornado/ waterspout
	BL Blowing	IC Ice crystals	DU Dust	SS Sandstorm
VC means: in the vicinity (METAR: between 5 & 10 sm of observation point(s) TAF: between 5 to 10 sm from center of runway complex)	SH Shower(s)	PL Ice pellets	SA Sand	DS Duststorm
	TS Thunderstorm	GR Hail	HZ Haze	
	FZ Freezing	GS Small hail &/or snow pellets	PY Spray	
		UP Unknown Precip		

Fig. 8

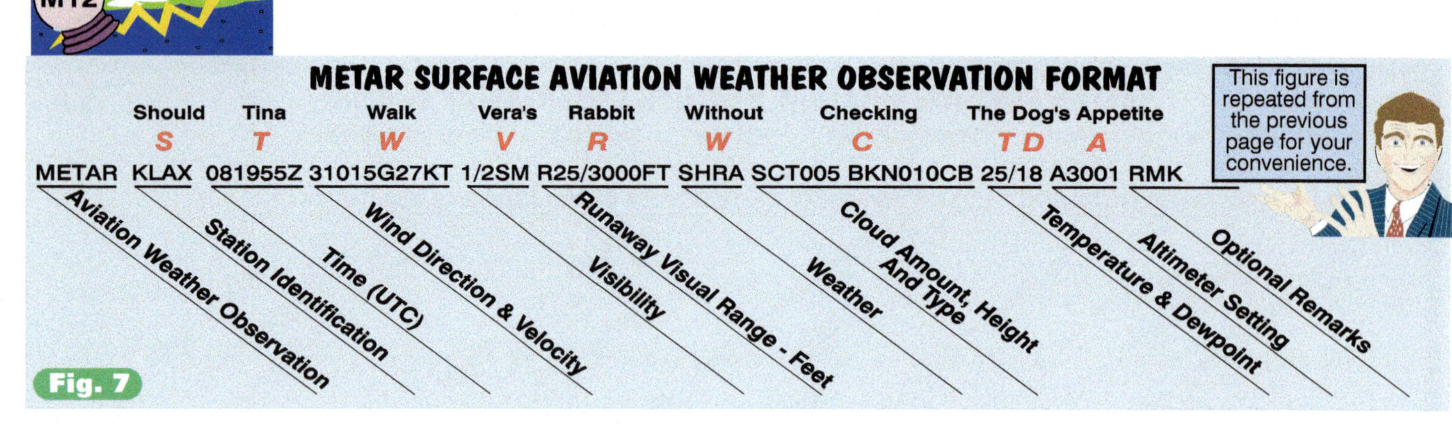

are grouped together). It would also be a hail of a weather report.

The obscuration or second section of the weather phenomena in Figure 8 is only reported in the weather grouping if the visibility is less than seven miles. The presence of smoke (FU) at the airport won't be listed in the weather grouping if the visibility is seven miles or greater.

In Figure 7, the letters SHRA represent showers (SH) and rain (RA). This is spoken as *moderate rain showers*. If it were light rain showers it would be abbreviated as -SHRA.

Clouds – The letter C in Figure 7 represents the cloud coverage, height, and type.

Cloud cover is either SKC (sky clear), indicating no clouds; FEW (reporting more than 0 to 2/8), SCT (scattered), representing coverage of between 3/8 and 4/8 of the sky; BKN (broken), which indicates the sky is between 5/8 and 7/8 covered by clouds; or OVC (overcast) which is complete sky coverage (8/8 coverage). (Automated reporting systems use the letters CLR to indicate no clouds are reported below 12,000 feet.)

A three digit number following the cloud coverage represents the height of the cloud base in hundreds of feet AGL. Three zeros indicates that the cloud height is less than 50 feet AGL.

Cloud types will be provided when towering cumulus (TCU) or cumulonimbus (CB) are observed.

Sometimes weather phenomena based at the surface hide all or part of the sky. This is considered an obscuration. When the sky is obscured and cloud details cannot be assessed, but information on vertical visibility is available, the cloud group is replaced by a five character group. The first two characters are the letters VV followed by the vertical visibility in units of hundreds of feet. VV004 means the vertical visibility is 400 feet (ATIS reports will still broadcast the term *indefinite* 400 feet obscured).

Sometimes an obscuration doesn't obscure the entire sky. In this instance, partial obscurations are reported by the amount of obscuring phenomena (FEW, SCT, BKN), followed by three digits (i.e., BKN001). In the remarks, the obscuring phenomena precedes the amount of obscuration and the three digits (i.e., FU BKN001, which means that the smoke layer, at 100 feet AGL, is obscuring 5/8 to 7/8 of the sky.)

From our study of airspace, we know that a minimum of a 1,000 foot ceiling is required for operations within surface-based controlled airspace. In the METAR, the lowest layer of clouds reported as broken or overcast, or any reported vertical visibility into obscuring phenomena is considered the official ceiling.

In Figure 7, the METAR indicates the presence of a 500 foot scattered layer of clouds, a 1,000 broken layer of clouds (the ceiling), and CB's or cumulonimbus clouds are present.

Fig. 9

REMARKS APPENDED TO METARS

Remarks	Definition
Sky and Ceiling	
FEW CU	Few cumulus clouds.
BINOVC	Breaks in overcast.
LWR CLDS NE	Lower clouds northeast.
CIG 14V19	Ceiling variable between 1,400 feet and 1,900 feet.
Obscuring Phenomena	
FG7	Fog obscuring 7/10 of the sky.
BLSA3	Blowing sand obscuring 3/10 of the sky.
THN FG NE	Thin fog northeast from reporting station.
Visibility	
VSBY S1W1/4	Visibility south is 1 mile, west is 1/4 mile.
SFC VSBY 1/2	Surface visibility is 1/2 mile.

Remarks	Definition
Weather and Obstruction to Vision	
RAB30	Rain began 30 minutes after the hour.
RAE30	Rain ended 30 minutes after the hour.
OCNL DST LTG NW	Occasional distant lightning NW of reporting station.
T OVHD MOVG NE	Thunderstorm overhead, moving northeast.
Wind	
WND 27V33	Wind variable between 270 degrees and 330 degrees.
PK WND 33048/22 ("PK WND" is used whenever the peak winds exceed 25 knots)	Peak wind within the past hour from 330 degrees at 48 knots occurred 22 minutes past the hour.
Pressure	
PRESRR	Pressure rising rapidly.
PRESFR	Pressure falling rapidly.

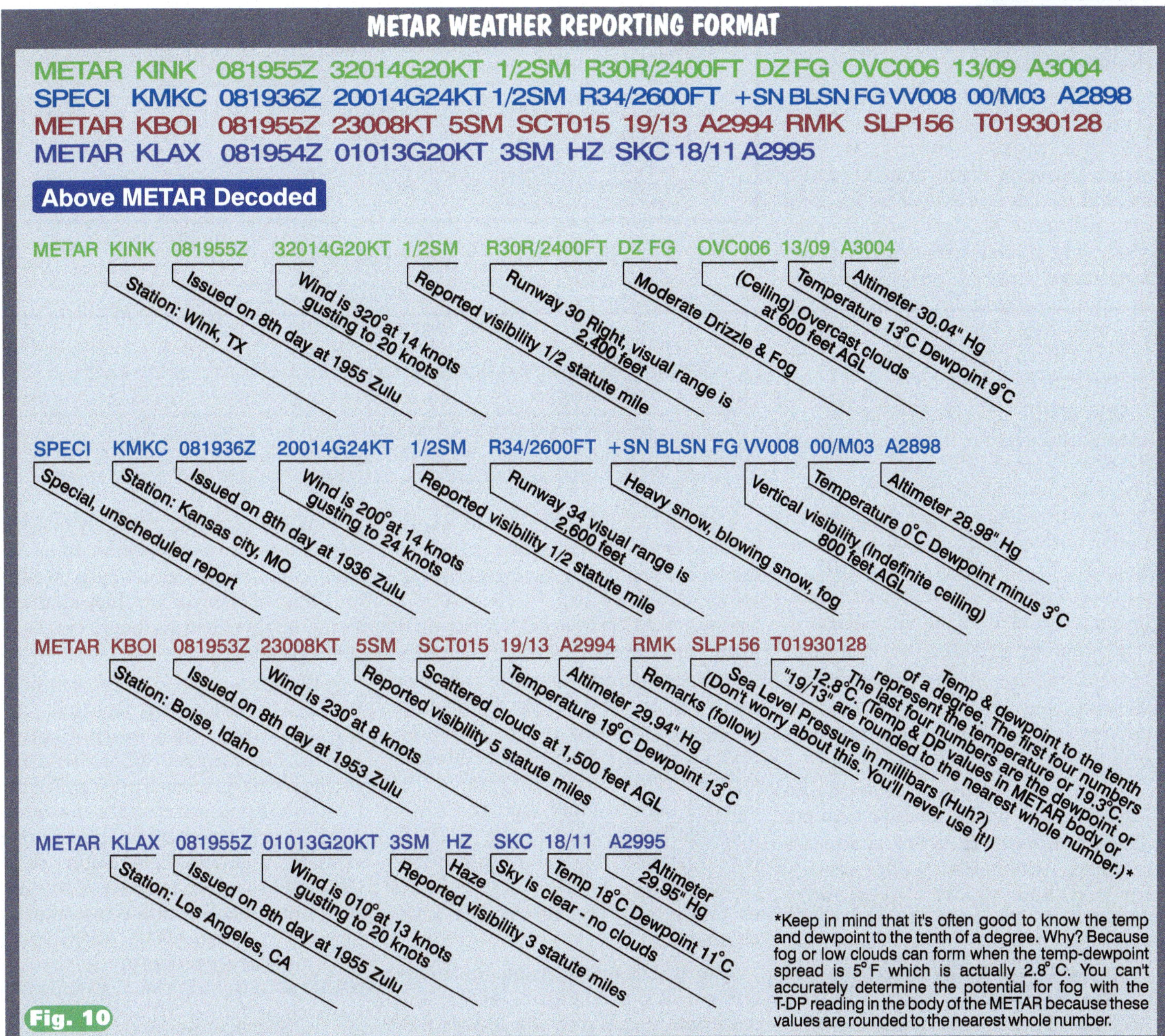

Fig. 10

Temperature/Dew Point – The letters T and D in Figure 7 represent the reported temperature and dew point in degrees Celsius. This is reported to the nearest whole degree using two digits (i.e., 6 degrees C is reported as 06). Sub-zero values are prefixed with an M (e.g., 03/M02). In Figure 7, the temperature is 25 degrees C and the dew point is 18 degrees C.

Altimeter – The letter A in Figure 7 represents the altimeter setting for that location. The altimeter setting is always prefixed with an A, indicating the altimeter setting in inches of mercury. All four digits of the pressure are listed. Simply insert a decimal after the second digit. In Figure 7, the altimeter setting is 30.01 inches of Hg.

At the end of the METAR, you will sometimes find supplementary information in the form of remarks (RMK). This is where the briefer can customize his or her weather observation by adding supplemental information. Figure 9 shows a few of these remarks (see Page M29 for more information on other weather code abbreviations that you'll need to understand different weather reports. These are essential, so don't skip that section). And, don't be overwhelmed. Some of these codes are rarer than a wealthy flight instructor. You'll learn more of them as you encounter them.

Figure 10 shows the decoding of the METAR presented in Figure 6.

Automatic Weather Observing Programs

Automatic weather observing stations will soon serve as the nation's primary surface weather observing network. These weather-watching computers-in-a-can transmit weather information (temperature, pressure, dew point, winds, cloud heights, etc.) directly to you in flight. We'll discuss two types of automatic weather observing systems: Automatic

Surface Observing System (ASOS) and Automatic Weather Observing System (AWOS).

ASOS – ASOS is sort of a hyperactive AWOS. In addition to basic weather measurements, it also reports precipitation and intensity, as well as the occurrence of freezing rain. Situated at airports and other observing points nationwide, these automated stations provide minute-by-minute reports on the ever-changing weather (you would officially report this as having received the *one-minute weather*).

One of the unique benefits of the automated system is that pilots can listen to computer-generated voice observations while airborne (some computer voices sound like Darth Vader with a cold). These transmissions are usually receivable within 25 nautical miles of an airport at a maximum altitude of 10,000 feet AGL.

Figure 11 shows a *Chart Supplement* excerpt for Wiscasset airport showing that ASOS observations can be heard on 135.725 MHz or heard by calling the listed phone number.

Chart Supplement Excerpt

MAINE

WISCASSET (9B9) 3 SW UTC–5(–4DT) N43°57.67'
68 B S4 FUEL 100LL TPA—1068(1000)
RWY 07-25: H3400X75 (ASPH) S-22 MIRL
RWY 07: PAPI(P4L)—GA 4.0°TCH 40'. Trees. RWY 25:
AIRPORT REMARKS: Attended 1300Z‡–dusk. Fuel available 1400–2200Z‡ daily. For fuel after hours call 207–882–6752. No touch and go ldgs Jun–Sep. PAEW S Rwy 25 safety zone. ACTIVATE MIRL Rwy 07–25; PAPI Rwys 07 and 25; REIL Rwy 25—CTAF. Rwy 25 REIL OTS indef.
WEATHER DATA SOURCES: ASOS 135.725 (207) 882–8094.
COMMUNICATIONS: CTAF/UNICOM 122.8

You can hear the ASOS (Automatic Surface Observation System) report on frequency 135.725 as indicated in the Chart Supplement.

Fig. 11

ASOS REPORTS

Fig. 12

METAR KABC 121355Z AUTO 21016G24KT 180V240 1SM -RA FG BKN015 OVC025 06/05 A2990 RMK AO2 PK WIND 20032/25

METAR KINK 130900Z COR 03005KT 21/2SM +SHRA OVC015 15/14 A3000 RMK AO2

The word *AUTO* or *COR* (for *COR*rected) appearing in the METAR indicates that this report was derived from some type of an automatic surface weather observation unit (ASOS, AWOS, etc.). When the ASOS report is augmented by a human observer, the word *AUTO* or *COR* is deleted.

ASOS reports are similar to the METAR that we've already studied. There are, however, a few subtle differences. Automated stations cannot, for instance, report clouds above 12,000 feet. However, the ASOS will report *CLR* (meaning no clouds are reported below 12,000 feet) instead of the *SKC* value shown in the METAR. There could be a solid overcast at 15,000 feet, but the ASOS cannot identify it. Thus, it can't report it. Keep this little idiosyncrasy in mind whenever you see an observation annotated as AUTO, COR (for CORrected) or in the remarks you see AO1 or AO2 (the AO1 or AO2 indicates the level of sophistication of the precipitation discrimination sensors associated with the ASOS unit. AO2, being more sophisticated, can discriminate between different types of precipitation, i.e., rain, snow, etc.).

Remember, if you see or hear of something missing from a ASOS report, it doesn't mean it's not there. It just means that the ASOS unit can't or didn't detect it.

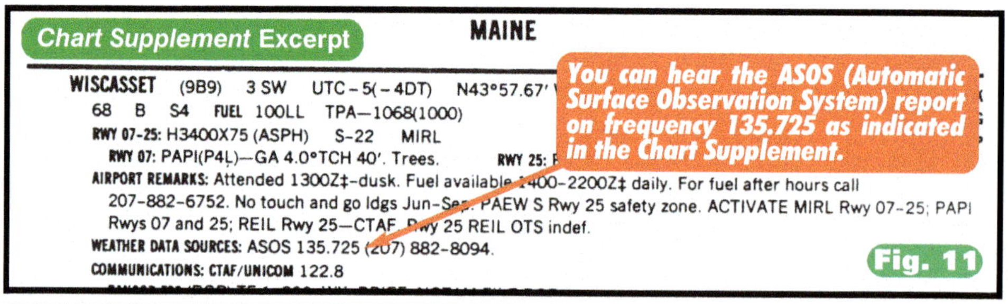

Figure 12 shows two ASOS weather observations. You can tell these are automatic-type surface observations because the letters AUTO (meaning AUTOmated) and/or COR are located directly after the location of the date/time identifier. As you can clearly see, the ASOS observations are provided in the same format as the METARs we've already studied. There's nothing new to be learned here. Simply read the ASOS observations as you do the METAR. (See Figure 9 for a sampling of the codes for the remarks (RMK) found at the end of the ASOS (METAR) observation.)

The ASOS observation for KABC shows AUTO right after the date/time group and the letters AO2 in the remarks section. This indicates that no human oversight backed up or augmented the ASOS report. Some locations have a human observer augment the ASOS report. Whenever the human observer augments or adds to the ASOS report, the AUTO is deleted, because now it is a manual observation. However, the remarks section will still show either an AO1 or an AO2.

Personally, I am inclined to place greater faith in automated weather reports when a human being oversees the process. That's why I don't trust those automated blood pressure machines found at shopping malls and airports. I heard of a pilot who put in his quarter, stuck in his arm and when his reading came up as 390 over 260, it wouldn't let him go until an FAA rep showed up (just kidding). Remember, machines can't detect all the weather.

AWOS – AWOS (Automatic Weather Observing System) are found at more and more airports across the country where weather reports were previously not available. Consisting of various sensors, a processor, a computer-generated voice system and transmitter, these stations broadcast minute-by-minute, real time, local weather information directly to pilots. AWOS/ASOS transmissions are receivable within 25 nautical miles of the transmission site, at or below 10,000 feet AGL. The transmissions can also be received on the airport. Frequencies for AWOS may be found near the airport data on the sectional chart, as shown in Figure 13, and in the *Chart Supplement* as shown in Figure 14.

Four basic levels of AWOS stations are available:

1. AWOS-A reports only altimeter setting.

2. AWOS-1 usually reports altimeter setting, wind data, temperature, dew point and density altitude.

3. AWOS-2 provides the information provided by AWOS-1 plus visibility.

4. AWOS-3 provides the information of AWOS-2 plus cloud-ceiling data.

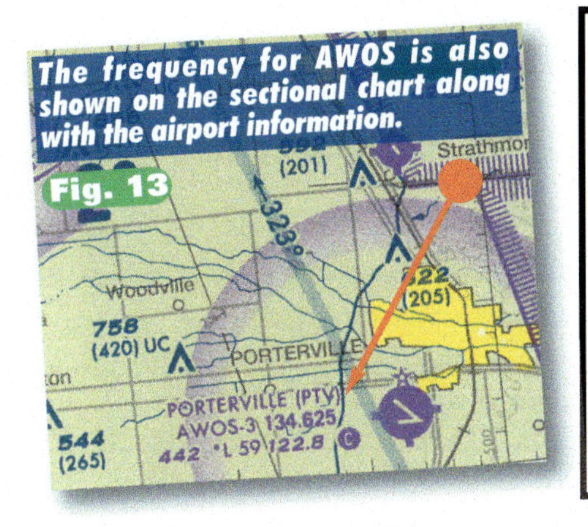

Fig. 13 The frequency for AWOS is also shown on the sectional chart along with the airport information.

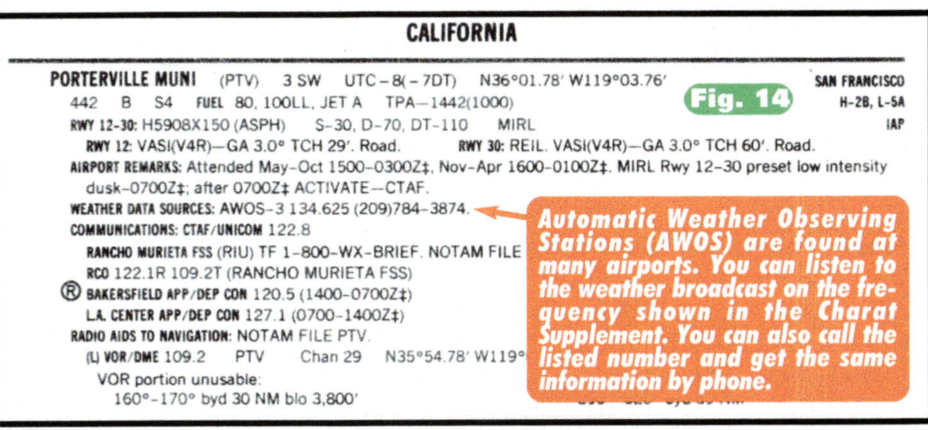

CALIFORNIA

PORTERVILLE MUNI (PTV) 3 SW UTC–8(–7DT) N36°01.78′ W119°03.76′ SAN FRANCISCO
442 B S4 FUEL 80, 100LL, JET A TPA—1442(1000) H-2B, L-5A
RWY 12-30: H5908X150 (ASPH) S-30, D-70, DT-110 MIRL IAP
RWY 12: VASI(V4R)—GA 3.0° TCH 29′. Road. RWY 30: REIL. VASI(V4R)—GA 3.0° TCH 60′. Road.
AIRPORT REMARKS: Attended May–Oct 1500–0300Z‡, Nov–Apr 1600–0100Z‡. MIRL Rwy 12–30 preset low intensity dusk–0700Z‡; after 0700Z‡ ACTIVATE—CTAF.
WEATHER DATA SOURCES: AWOS–3 134.625 (209)784–3874.
COMMUNICATIONS: CTAF/UNICOM 122.8
RANCHO MURIETA FSS (RIU) TF 1-800-WX-BRIEF. NOTAM FILE
RCO 122.1R 109.2T (RANCHO MURIETA FSS)
® BAKERSFIELD APP/DEP CON 120.5 (1400–0700Z‡)
L.A. CENTER APP/DEP CON 127.1 (0700–1400Z‡)
RADIO AIDS TO NAVIGATION: NOTAM FILE PTV.
(L) VOR/DME 109.2 PTV Chan 29 N35°54.78′ W119°
VOR portion unusable:
160°–170° byd 30 NM blo 3,800′

Fig. 14 Automatic Weather Observing Stations (AWOS) are found at many airports. You can listen to the weather broadcast on the frequency shown in the Charat Supplement. You can also call the listed number and get the same information by phone.

A typical ASOS or AWOS voice transmitted observation might sound something like the following:

"Denver, Denver Front Range airport, automated weather observation. One eight three three Zulu. Sky conditions six thousand five hundred scattered. Visibility greater than one zero. Temperature two two Celsius, dew point one niner Celsius. Wind three five zero at zero three (ASOS or AWOS winds received by radio are *magnetic* in direction). Altimeter two niner seven eight. Remarks, density altitude seven thousand five hundred."

Remember, just because it's a machine doesn't mean it won't make mistakes. The entire airport might be surrounded by clouds with a single, solitary hole over the ASOS or AWOS-3 weather unit. You can bet that little puppy reports *all clear*. The entire airport may be shrouded in fog while the ceilometer (cloud height measuring device) reports no clouds at the airport. Fortunately, the visibility would provide a clue to the presence of fog. When a human weather observer supplements mechanical weather observations, these problems disappear. Use a little common sense when using an automated observation of the weather on which to base your decisions.

You would certainly invest one dollar to make a million dollars (we call this the Lotto), but you wouldn't invest half a million dollars to make one dollar. So why then would you risk half a million hours of the rest of your life just to arrive home an hour sooner in your airplane?

Whither the Weather?

Having the current weather for airports along your route is valuable. But this is just one bean short of a hill if you're planning tomorrow's flight. Weather changes from day to day, hour to hour, minute to minute. It also changes while enroute. Pilots need a means of predicting this change.

Since pilots don't have crystal balls (no matter what they may claim), most of them look into the future through more conventional means such as one of several aviation forecasts that are available.

Terminal Aerodrome Weather Forecasts (TAF) – (also referred to as an *Aviation Terminal Forecast*) A terminal forecast sounds like it's the last weather you're ever going to get. Fortunately, this isn't what a TAF is all about. TAFs provide a description of surface weather expected to occur at an airport.

They are an excellent means of identifying the weather you can expect upon arrival at an airport. You can compare forecasts for airports along your route to obtain a better idea of how the weather is expected to change. When used in conjunction with METARs, TAFs provide you with a good idea of the present weather and how it's expected to change.

TAFs are forecast weather for a 24 hour period (30 hours for some locations) and represent the expected weather within a 5 statute mile radius of the airport's runway complex. They are issued four times daily (once every six hours starting at 0000Z). Much of the weather coding is similar to the METAR weather format (I knew that would make you happy). Since it's relatively simple to read, we won't need a memory-type acronym to interpret TAFs. If there are any major differences in the codes used by TAF compared to METAR, I'll let you know. Let's examine the TAF weather shown in Figure 15.

Station: (KLAX)

Same form and format as the METAR.

Date Forecast Issued: (091140Z):

The report was issued on the 9th day (09) at 1140 Zulu (UTC).

TERMINAL AERODROME WEATHER FORECAST (TAF)

Fig. 15

```
TAF
KLAX 091140Z 0912/1012 22020KT 3SM -SHRA BKN020
     FM100300 35014KT 2SM TSRA OVC015
     TEMPO 1006/1012 1SM +RA PROB30 1008/1009 1/2SM FG
```

TERMINAL AERODROME WEATHER FOREC

This figure is repeated from the previous page for your convenience.

TAF
KLAX 091140Z 0912/1012 22020KT 3SM -SHRA BKN020
FM100300 35014KT 2SM TSRA OVC015
TEMPO 1006/1012 1SM +RA PROB30 1008/1009 1/2SM FG

Fig. 15

Time of Forecast: (0912/1012)

This forecast's date and valid times are shown by two four-digit numbers separated by a slash (0912/1012). The first four numbers represent the date and the time the forecast period begins (the 9th at 1200Z). The last four numbers represent the ending time of the forecast period (the 10th at 1200Z). The forecast is valid from 1200Z on the 9th to 1200Z on the 10th (a 24 hour period). If midnight UTC is the beginning time period of the forecast it will be coded as 00. If it is the ending time, it is coded as 24. Therefore, a 24 hour forecast beginning and ending at midnight UTC would be indicated as: 0900/0924.

Forecast Winds: (22020KT)

This is presented in the same format as the METAR. Figure 15 shows winds forecast to be from 220 degrees true direction at 20 knots. Calm winds are encoded as 00000KT and expected gusts are preceded by the letter G.

Forecast Visibility: (3SM)

This is the prevailing visibility expected in statute miles, up to and including 6 miles. Expected visibilities greater than 6 miles are forecast as *P6SM* (*plus six statute miles*).

Forecast Weather: (-SHRA)

The same five categories used in a METAR are used in a TAF for reporting weather phenomena, as shown in Figure 8. The letters -SHRA represent only operationally significant weather that's forecast for the stated time period. In other words, light rain showers are forecast starting at 1200Z.

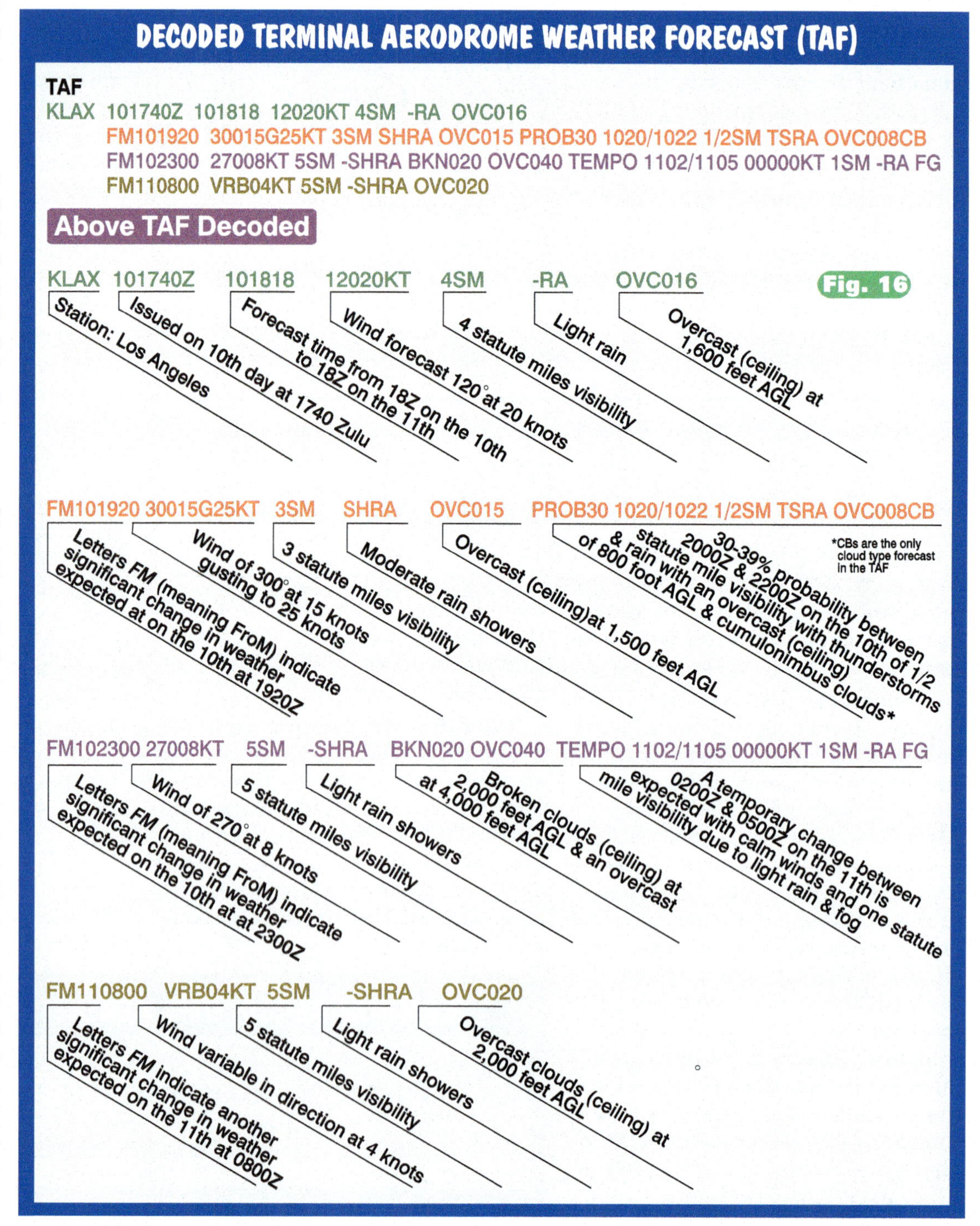

Forecast Cloud Conditions: (BKN020)

This is the same as the METAR format. In this example, broken clouds are forecast at 2000 feet AGL. As in the METAR, ceiling layers are designated by the lowest layer that's BKN, OVC or shows VV (vertical visibility)

30 Hour TAF Formatting

30-Hr. TERMINAL AERODROME WEATHER FORECAST (TAF)

TAF
KLAX 091140Z 0912/1018 22020KT 3SM -SHRA BKN020
FM100300 35014KT 2SM TSRA OVC015
TEMPO 1006/1012 1SM +RA PROB30 1008/1009 1/2SM FG

KOKC 051130Z 0512/0618 14008KT 5SM BR BKN030
TEMPO 0513/0516 1 1/2SM BR
FM051600 18010KT P6SM SKC
PROB30 0600/0606 2SM TSRA OVC008CB

In its desire to remain internationally consistent, the FAA adopted a 30-hour TAF format in lieu of its 24-hour cousin for 32 large airports in the United States. The additional six forecast hours added to the TAF allow long-haul air carriers to better evaluate their flight planned routing.

The date/time value for KLAX 0912/1018 tells us that the TAF forecast period begins on the 9th day of the month at 1200Z and ends on the 10th at 1800 Zulu (30 hours total). Starting at 1200 on the 9th, you can expect winds from 220 degrees at 20 knots with 3 miles visibility and light rain showers. **FM**100300 tells us that on the 10th day, beginning at 0300Z, a rapid change in weather is expected (winds 350 degrees at 14 knots, 2 miles visibility with thunderstorms and rain with a 1,500 foot AGL overcast ceiling. **TEMPO** 1006/1012 means a fluctuation in the weather (lasting less than 1 hour) will occur, resulting in a visibility of one mile and heavy rain. **PROB30** 1008/1009 indicates a 30% probability that, between 0800Z on the 10th and 0900Z on the same day, the visibility will fall to ½ mile in fog.

The date/time value for KOKC 0512/0618 tells us that the TAF forecast begins on the 5th day of the month at 1200Z and ends on the 6th day at 1800Z (30 hours). Starting at 1200Z on the 5th, you can expect winds from 140 degrees at 8 knots, 5 miles visibility in mist with broken clouds (a ceiling) at 3,000 feet AGL. **TEMPO** 0513/0516 tells us we can expect a fluctuation in the weather (lasting less than 1 hour), resulting in a visibility of 1 and 1/2 miles in mist. **FM**051600 tells us that on the 5th day, beginning at 1600Z, a rapid change in the weather is expected (wind 180 degrees at 10 knots and visibility greater than 6 miles [i.e., "plus 6"] and a sky that is clear). **PROB30** 0600/0606 indicates that there's a 30% probability that, between 0000Z and 0600Z on the 6th, the visibility will be 2 miles with thunderstorms and rain along with an overcast ceiling of 800 feet AGL and cumulonimbus clouds.

into an obscuration (see Figure 17 below for a graphic explanation of VV).

Expected Changes: (FM, TEMPO, PROB)

FM is followed by a six digit number (the date and a four digit time value) that indicates the beginning time of a self contained portion of the forecast. This is used when a *rapid* (significant) change in weather (usually occurring in less than one hour) is expected. In our report, the sequence of FM100300 says that on the 10th, from 0300Z the following weather conditions should occur: winds 350 degrees at 14 knots, 2 miles visibility, thunderstorms and rain and an overcast ceiling of 1,500 feet. Weather that's omitted in the FM group isn't significant to aviation. (Since FM implies "one" hour or less of time, it only needs a beginning date and time, thus six digits.)

TEMPO indicates that fluctuations (temporary and usually lasting less than one hour) from the predominant weather conditions are expected. TEMPO is followed by two four-digit numbers separated by a slash (1006/1012) giving the date and time period that these variations are expected. In our report, a temporary condition of 1 mile visibility and heavy rain is expected to occur on the 10th, between 0600Z and 1200Z.

PROB (PROBability) is used when the likely occurrence of any weather phenomena falls in the 30 to 39% (PROB 30) range of expectation.

In our report the sequence, PROB30 1008/1009 1/2SM FG indicates that, on the 10th, between the hours of 0800Z and 0900Z there is a 30 to 39% probability of 1/2 mile visibility in fog. Figure 16 shows a detailed analysis of an airport's TAF. (See Page M29 for more weather code abbreviations.)

Remember, TAFs are issued once every six hours. Make it a point to check the latest TAF for the most current forecast information. I make it a point to check the METAR against the TAF. If the TAF said that this hour was to be clear but the METAR showed clouds, then that particular TAF might be too optimistic. I might then be less inclined to place a great deal of trust in its accuracy. Once something isn't right, you're disinclined to trust it. That's why I never trusted my uncle's communications skills. When I was young he told our neighbor to drop me off at the nursery on her way to work. For an entire day I sat, surrounded by plants and trees.

Horizontal visibility is known as "slant range visibility." The use of VV or "vertical visibility" is the means by which we measure how far we can see straight up into an indefinite cloud ceiling.

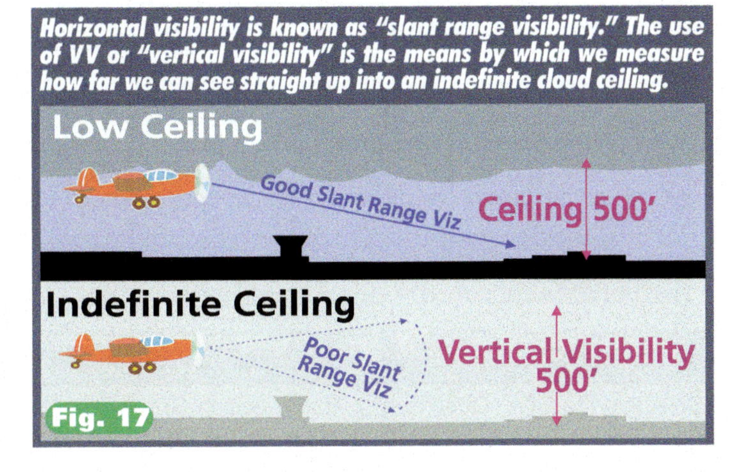

Fig. 17

The Graphical Forecasts for Aviation (GFA) - While the TAF is a valuable tool for evaluating the forecast weather at or near an airport, it doesn't provide you with forecast weather between reporting points (i.e., between airports).

Enter the GFA. This is the "Optimus Prime" of the aviation weather forecasting tools (Figure 18). There are so many useful forecasting and observing tools built into the GFA that I can only offer you a brief introduction to this product here. The GFA is explained in great detail starting on Page M34 and it's absolutely essential you study it carefully. Let's cover a small part of what you'll learn in great detail later.

The purpose of the GFA is to give you a look (graphical, right?) at the weather across the continental United States from 15 hours into the future in the form of forecasts (Figure 20), and up to 14 hours into the past as observational data and warnings (Figure 21). See? I told you it was the Optimus Prime of weather tools. You won't need that DeLorean and hoverboard to time travel 14 hours into the past with the GFA. Just move the slider (Positions I) to see how the weather evolved over time, which helps you evaluate your confidence level in the newest forecast weather.

GFAs provide you with a large assortment of weather products. One of these is forecast ceilings and visibilities for up to 15 hours into the future (Figure 19, position C). Move the time slider (position B) to see 15 hours ahead. Make sure you study the GFA thoroughly.

GFA: https://www.aviationweather.gov/gfa

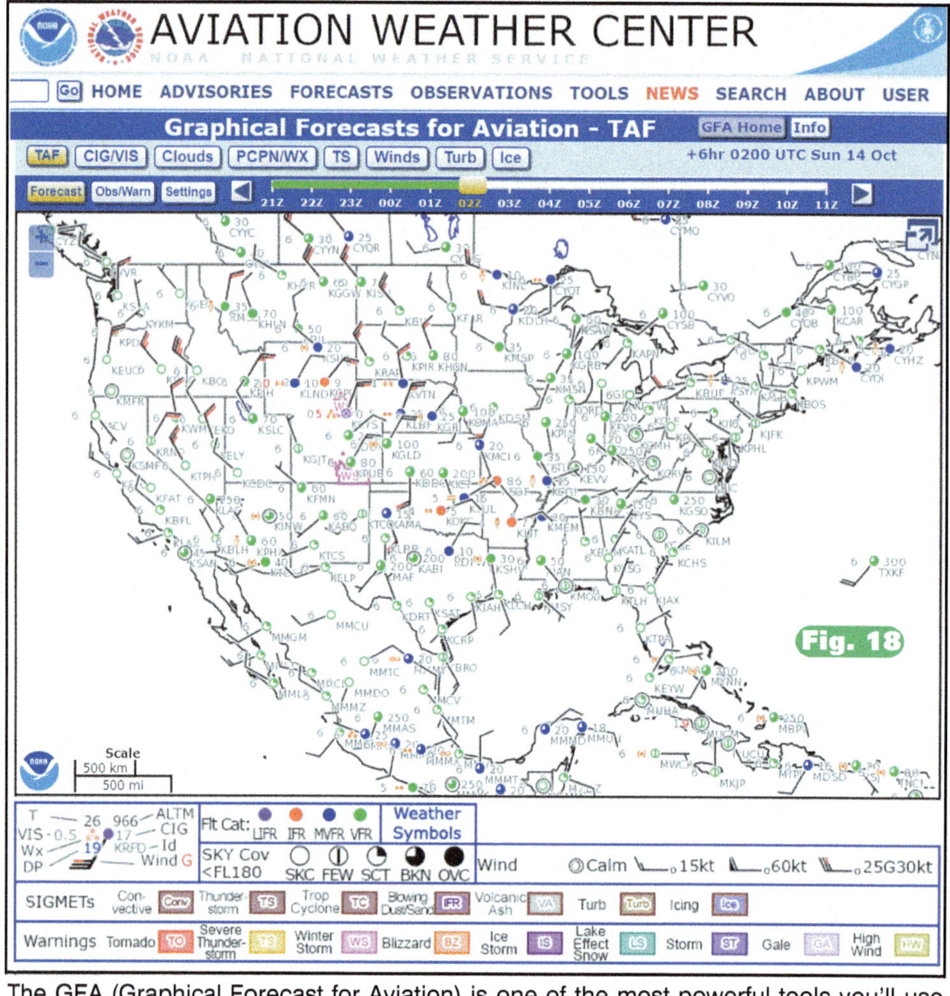

The GFA (Graphical Forecast for Aviation) is one of the most powerful tools you'll use to both observe past, current and forecast weather.

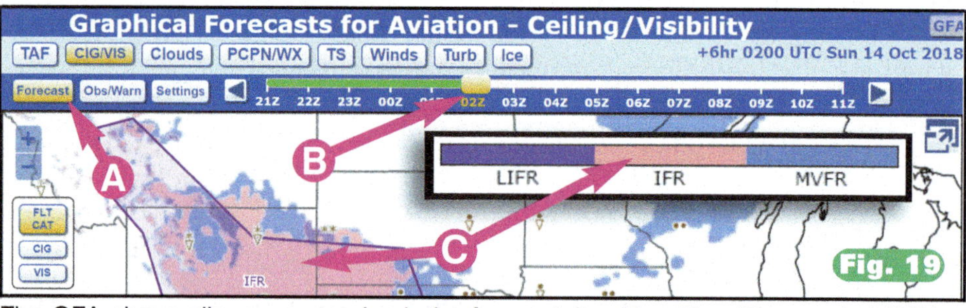

The GFA above allows you to check the forecast (position A) ceilings and visibilities (position B) for the entire time range provided by the time slider (position C).

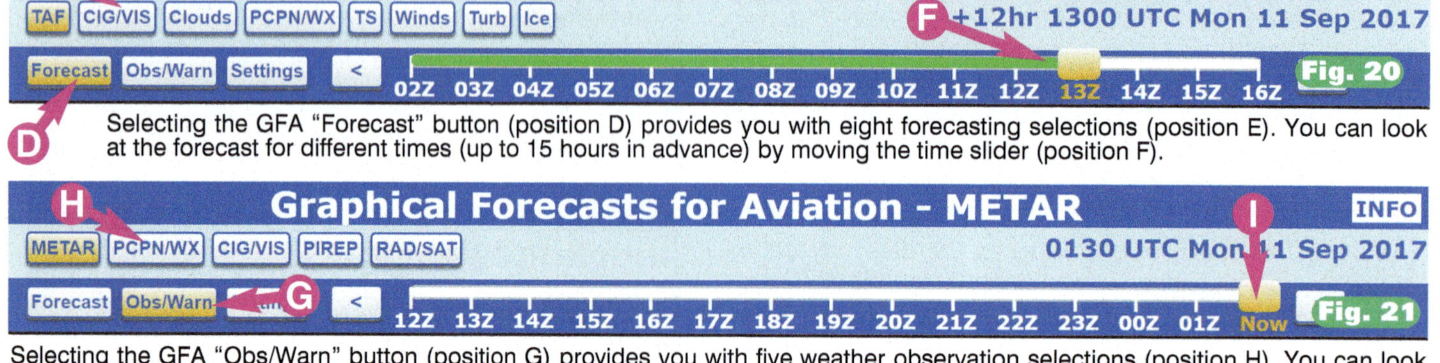

Selecting the GFA "Forecast" button (position D) provides you with eight forecasting selections (position E). You can look at the forecast for different times (up to 15 hours in advance) by moving the time slider (position F).

Selecting the GFA "Obs/Warn" button (position G) provides you with five weather observation selections (position H). You can look back in time up to 14 hours by moving the time slider (position I).

THE WINDS ALOFT FORECAST

FB WBC 151745
BASED ON 151200Z DATA
VALID 1600Z FOR USE 1800-0300Z. TEMPS NEG ABV 24000

Fig. 22

FT	3000	6000	9000	12000	18000	24000	30000	34000	39000
ALS			2420	2635-08	2535-18	2444-30	245945	246755	246862
AMA		2714	2725+00	2625-04	2531-15	2452-27	265842	256352	256762
DEN			2321-04	2532-08	2434-19	2441-31	235347	236056	236262
HLC		1707-01	2113-03	2219-07	2330-17	2435-30	244145	244854	245561
MKC	0507	2006+03	2215-01	2322-06	2338-17	2448-29	236143	237252	238160
STL	2113	2325+07	2332+02	2339-04	2356-16	2373-27	239440	730649	731960

AUTHOR'S NOTE:
When the winds are expected to be in excess of 100 knots the first two numbers of the forecast are greater than 36. To find the direction, subtract 50 from the first two numbers (i.e., 73 - 50 = 23 [winds from 230 degrees]). Add 100 to the next two numbers to find the wind speed (i.e., 100 + 19 = 119 knots).

Winds Aloft Forecasts (FB) – There are certain moments in your life that you just don't forget. A fellow once came up and said he was going to punch my nose in. I said, "Hey, don't you know that you never end a sentence with a preposition?" At that point he proceeded to punch in my nose.

Some folks are pretty tough, but no matter how tough you are as a pilot, you're never going to win a fight with the wind. The way to keep from being beat, however, is to know how fast and from what direction the wind blows. This is extremely important for planning proper fuel consumption, not to mention figuring out whether you'll get to your meeting on time. Fortunately, there is a forecast that provides you with an estimate of winds for up to 24 hours in advance. It's known as the *winds aloft forecast.*

Winds aloft forecasts are very useful to pilots. These forecasts are issued four times daily and are valid for either 6, 12 or 24 hours. Each forecast is issued with a valid time for its use. Figure 22 shows a typical winds aloft forecast.

Winds are forecast for true altitudes starting at 3,000 feet and additional 3,000 foot increments up to 12,000 feet (we won't worry about higher altitudes for the moment). Winds less than 1,500 feet above the reporting station's surface are not forecast. In other words if your airport lies at 5,000 MSL, the 6,000 foot winds aloft forecast will be blank for the area around the airport. Temperature is not forecast for altitudes within 3,000 feet of the surface.

Winds aloft are provided in knots and their direction is always in reference to true north as are other weather reports and forecasts. Figure 22 depicts the forecast winds at 6,000 MSL above AMA (Amarillo, Texas) as 2714. Unlike METAR or TAF, the first two numbers of this four digit value represent the wind direction in tens of degrees; you need to add a zero onto these numbers to get the wind direction. The last two numbers represent the wind's velocity. The wind at AMA is forecast to be from 270 degrees at 14 knots. At 6,000 MSL above MKC, the wind is forecast to be from 200 degrees at 6 knots with a forecast temperature of +3 degrees C.

The – or + after the winds represents a negative or positive temperature value that follows the four-digit wind value. Winds aloft temperatures are in degrees Celsius. At 9,000 feet MSL over DEN (Denver, CO), the winds are forecast to be from 230 degrees at 21 knots with a temperature of -4 degrees C. If winds are expected to be light and variable the identifier "9900" is used. This doesn't mean wind from 990, with no velocity (we can't have a wind with an unknown direction and no speed). Technically, it means that the winds are less than 5 knots. Calm winds are identified by 0000.

Forecast temperatures are useful for several reasons. Many pilots use them to predict where temperature inversions will be. Any time you see the forecast temperature increasing (or not decreasing as much) with altitude, you know you have a stable air situation. Warmer air aloft could act as a lid, trapping industrial pollutants.

If you want the winds at an altitude between those listed, it's time to interpolate, also known as meeting the numbers halfway. Break out the Cray supercomputer. Actually, the math is easy, and you can probably do it either in your head or on your fingers. If the altitude you'll be flying at is halfway between two forecast

A LESSON IN PILOT-DRAGGING

I decided to move the plane. Procedure: open the throttle to establish a fuel flow of 8 GPH with the primer pump, and when the engine starts, pull the throttle back to about 1100 rpm. I entered the plane, set the hand brake and followed the above procedures. The next thing I knew, I was on the ground and the plane was heading for a ditch. I remember hearing the engine start. The cabin door was not closed. The wind that day was 90° at about 20 knots with gusts up to 35. A gust must have lifted the right wing enough to cause me to lose my balance and tumble from the plane. I remember trying to stop the plane from rolling, but it just dragged me with it. In the future, I will secure my seatbelt and close and lock the cabin door every time I start the engine

ASRS Report

levels, the wind and temperature will be about halfway between the numbers given for those two levels. Add the two wind (or temperature) numbers together and divide by 2. Bingo. I told you it wasn't calculus. Actually, halfway is about all you'll ever need to figure; if you're closer than that to one forecast level or another, use it and you'll be close enough for rock 'n roll. If you believe there is a significant difference between the winds at 6,000 feet and the winds at 6,750 feet and that this can be forecast with great precision, then please call me about some low-lying land I have available in Florida.

One of the important items to check during cross country flight planning is the altitude that will provide the most favorable (or at least the least adverse) winds. After studying the winds aloft forecast, you can easily decide on an altitude giving you less of a headwind or more of a tailwind. Sometimes it's advantageous to spend additional time climbing in order to catch a tailwind.

Weather Charts: The Big Picture

OK, you don't like numbers, and you're not real big on words. You bought this book *and* that copy of *Playpilot* you're holding for the pictures. Fortunately, when it comes to weather, you haven't been left out in the cold. Much of the complexity of weather makes a lot more sense presented as pictures, which is the way weatherpeople have been looking at the weather for decades. Even if you can't picture yourself reading charts, join me for a few moments and take a look at what you're missing.

There are a number of weather charts that can prove most informative. Accessing them was easy when there was a Flight Service Station on almost every airport corner. If you have internet access, a personal computer or a cell phone/iPad or any other tablet device, you can now view all these charts electronically. They are available from a variety of sources and come in all shapes, colors and flavors. Today's pilots have all the necessary equipment to provide their own weather briefing from the comfort of their own home.

Surface Analysis Chart - The surface analysis chart (Figure 23) shows the location of pressure patterns and fronts at the time the chart was constructed. This chart is based on reported weather data and is issued every three hours. Individual reporting stations and their associated weather are depicted on the chart. Additional decoding information for the station model on this chart can be found in the FAA's *Aviation Weather Services* manual (AC 00 - 45H).

Even without a detailed understanding of this chart's symbology, you can derive some interesting information from it. Think of the surface analysis as a very large visual portrayal of hundreds of METARs (surface weather reports). Although this chart's information may be older than that of the individual METARs, it can provide you with a big picture

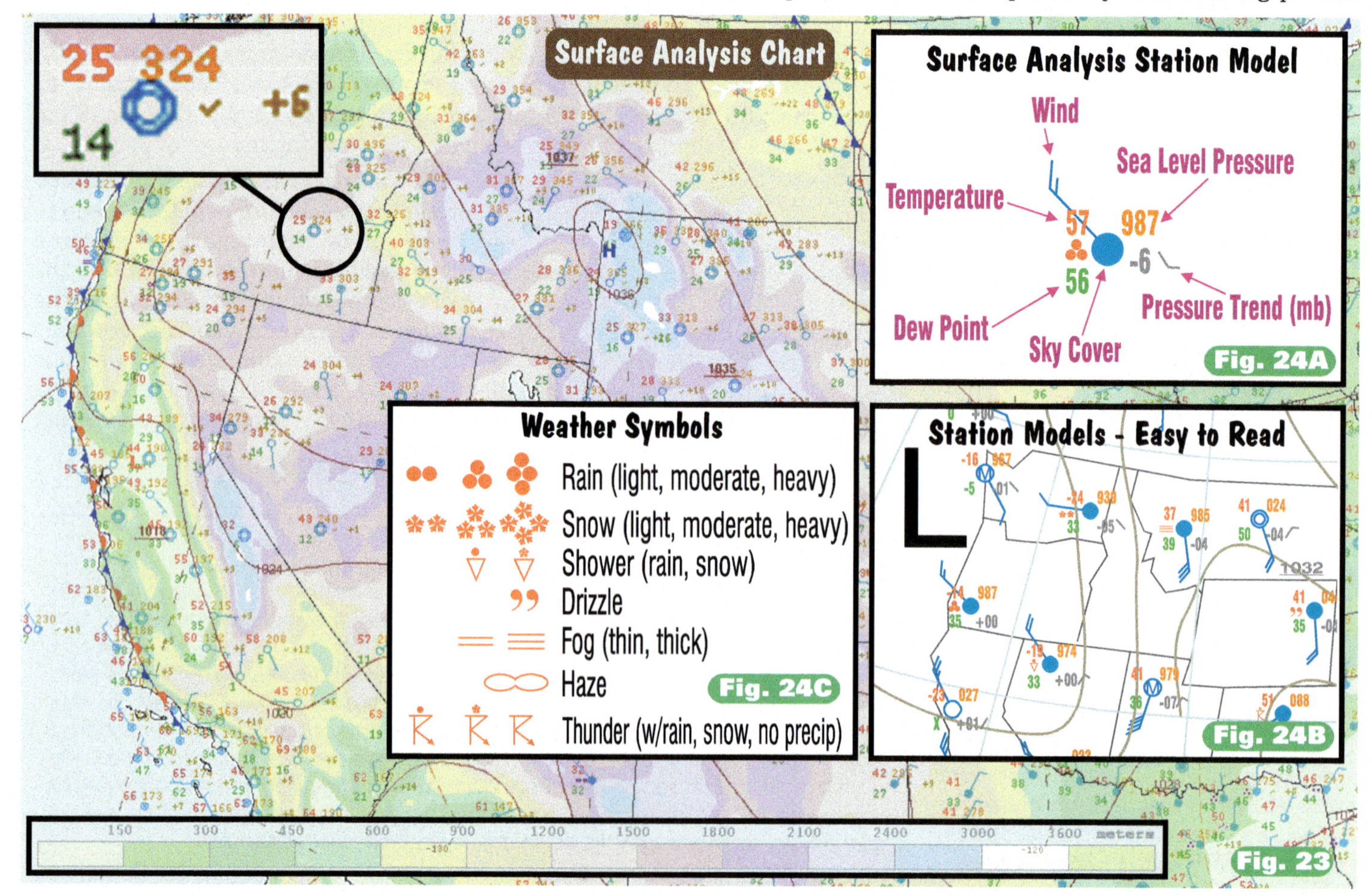

THE PERSPIRATION FACTOR

I was descending from 6000' at night on a vector to the airport and was not using the autopilot. I had spent the day at the beach and had used a sunscreen product on my face at my doctor's recommendation. Apparently night flight has a "perspiration factor" because the sunscreen product ran into my eyes, causing them to sting. While trying to rub my eyes and use a handkerchief to stop the tearing, the airplane went off course by about 100°. I was able to recover quickly, with no damage other than to my pride. The sunscreen product contains a warning about not putting it in eyes, but I had not considered the possibility that perspiration could wash it into my eyes—at a very inconvenient time. Suggestions: try stick or waterproof sunscreen—it tends to stay put, or wear a hat and only put sunscreen below the eyes. **ASRS Report**

of the weather for individual stations along your route. While I'll discuss the symbology next to the individual reporting stations on the chart shortly, let's make a quick overview of this chart's essential features.

For instance, the chart shows the temperature/dew point spread over a large area. From this you can get a good feel for the likelihood of fog or low cloud formation before and after sunset. Orientation of the isobars and the pressure patterns gives you an idea of surface winds. Cloud coverage at the time the chart was constructed is identified by the fill of the individual station circles. In addition, you can determine the types of clouds existing enroute. Much, much more useful weather material exists on the surface analysis chart.

Personally, I like comparing the present location of pressure systems and fronts using the surface analysis with the predicted future locations on the 12 and 24 hour prog chart (See Figure 28). This tells me where these fronts are now and where they're likely to be in the future. I think of this as being similar to the actions of professional boxers, who want to know where their opponent is and where he might move (I've always thought of boxing as being similar to ballet, except that there are no leotards, no music, and the dancers get to hit each other).

SYMBOLS FOR SKY COVER

SYMBOL	TOTAL SKY COVER
	Sky Clear
	Few Clouds - (Less than 12% cover but sky is not clear)
	Scattered clouds (appx. 25% cloud cover)
	Partly cloudy (appx. 50% cloud cover)
	Mostly cloudy (appx. 75% cloud cover)
	Overcast
	Sky obscured
	Sky cover missing

Fig. 25

OK, now let's play with models. No, not those type of airplane models, I'm speaking of the coding and symbols used to build the surface analysis chart. These codes and symbols are assembled into a station model that applies to the surface analysis as well as many of the other charts and weather products you'll access during a weather briefing.

Figure 24A shows a typical station model. Starting at the top and working clockwise, we see a wind barb indicating the direction from which the wind blows (from the northwest in this instance and referenced to true north). Each large feather represents 10 knots of wind and each half feather represents five knots (for a total of 15 knots at this station).

Sea level pressure, shown next, is plotted in tenths of millibars (mb). Since standard pressure at sea level is 1013.2 mb, you'd add either a 9 or 10 before the three number value to obtain the station pressure. For instance, we'd add a 9 in front of 987 for a value of 998.7 mb of station pressure. We wouldn't add a 10 because this would give us a value of 1098.7 mb, which is not a normal pressure value. So add a 9 or 10 to give you something close to the average sea level pressure of 1013.2 mb. (Hint: a value of 410 becomes 1041.0 mb; 103 becomes 1010.3 mb; 872 becomes 987.2 mb.)

The pressure trend reference has two components. The number value represents the change in pressure (mb) during the past three hours. The line graphic represents how the pressure has changed. Reading left to right, let the line's vertical and horizontal direction indicate this pressure change. For instance, a line sloping down then leveling off indicates falling pressure followed by steady pressure. A line sloping upward from left to right indicated rising pressure and so on.

The center of the station model represents the sky cover. A solid circle indicates an overcast condition. A clear circle indicates clear skies. Figure 25 shows the symbols used for station model sky conditions.

The dew point is next. Directly above the dew point is a weather symbol used to describe any precipitation or condition causing reduced visibility at the time of the observation. In our example, three red dots indicates moderate rain. Figure 24C shows the symbols for station model weather and precipitation.

Finally, we have the station temperature shown above any precipitation symbol.

OK, let's get real. Can you fly safely without knowing how to interpret a station model? Yes, of course, but that's not the point. Some fidelity with interpreting these symbols can offer a quick understanding of what's happening at a local airport. For instance, if the atmospheric pressure was decreasing during the last three hours, then falling pressure might be followed by poor weather. Steady pressure might mean whatever weather exists might remain the same. So make it a point to learn how to interpret this model.

NEXRAD—Not Your Daddy's Weather

The revolution in modern avionics has made it possible for the average private pilot to have access to in-flight cockpit weather that not long ago was only a dream. With the appropriate receiver, a moving map GPS display of the portable (Figures 26 and 27) or panel-installed variety and a subscription to one of several weather service providers, it's possible to have airborne access to all sorts of weather data. This includes METAR and TAF information, winds aloft, in-flight weather advisories, radar information and much more. In this chapter we've covered most of the types of in-flight weather available for uplink to the cockpit, but there's one weather product that deserves its own explanation. I'm speaking of NEXRAD or Next Generation Radar.

As a VFR pilot, NEXRAD becomes an extremely valuable source of weather information when making long distance cross country flights. Why? Because it shows you the location of suspended moisture, much like the radar summary chart does. Only NEXRAD does it in more detail and more often. Armed with cockpit uplinked weather, you're now in a much better position to avoid storm systems, areas of precipitation and so on.

Let's take a closer look at how NEXRAD weather information is generated.

Next Generation Radar

NEXRAD is a network of Doppler radars strategically located around the country and tied into a national network (Figure 28). While NEXRAD presents a normal multicolor rain rate display, its Doppler circuits can also depict whirling of droplets that pinpoints turbulence.

NEXRAD is a combination of Doppler radar (WSR-88D to those who know) and conventional radar.

Uplinked weather is available with most panel-mount GPS units (Figure 41) and portable GPS units such Garmin's 496 portable GPS receiver (Figure 42) and a subscription to XM Weather.

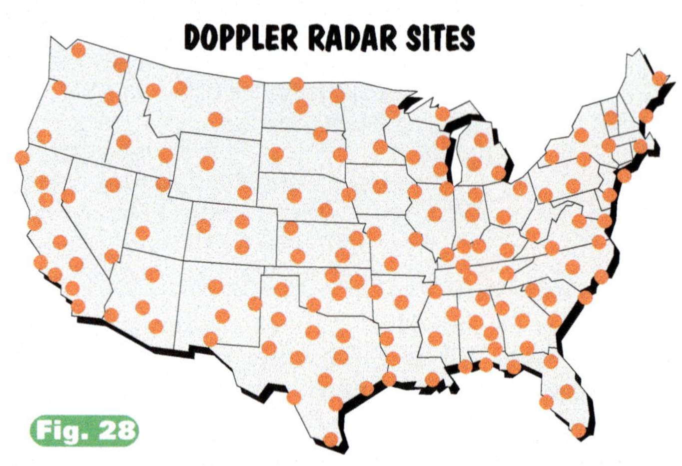

The National Weather Service supports many Doppler radar sites across the United States.

The WSR-88D radar works on the same principle as other radars except that Doppler radar spends more time listening than transmitting. (Airborne radar, for instance, transmits less than 1% of the time and spends 99%+ "listening" for the return of information). Doppler radar spends approximately 7 *seconds* out of each hour of operation in the transmitting mode. The rest of the time (59 minutes and 49 seconds) is spent listening.

What does Doppler radar listen for? Like other radar, it listens for the return of the energy pulse it sent. The difference is that it also listens for any phase shift associated with this returning signal. "Phase shift" is a scientific way of saying that the pitch of a sound changes as it moves closer to or farther from the listener (human or radar). As a train approaches, the sound waves from its horn are compressed, making the pitch higher as the train gets closer. As the train passes, the sound waves from the horn are stretched, which lowers the pitch (Figure 29). This is the "Doppler shift," from which Doppler radar draws its name.

The phase shift of the returning energy pulse allows Doppler radar to detect any change in velocity of an object, either toward or away from the radar. Particles moving toward the antenna impart a minute shift to

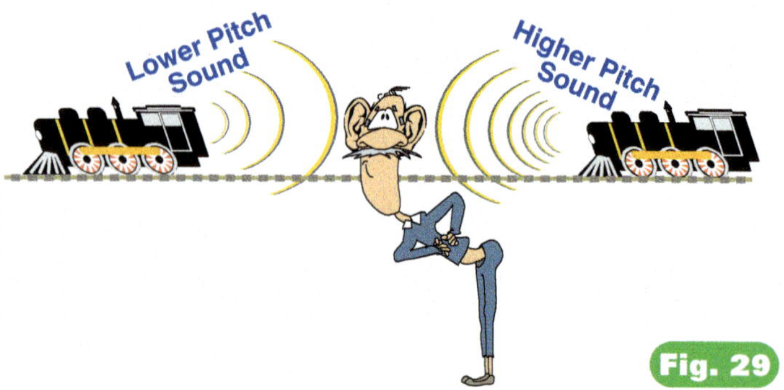

Doppler radar listens for a phase shift to determine the motion of atmospheric particles. You experience a similar phase shift in sound when you listen to a passing locomotive.

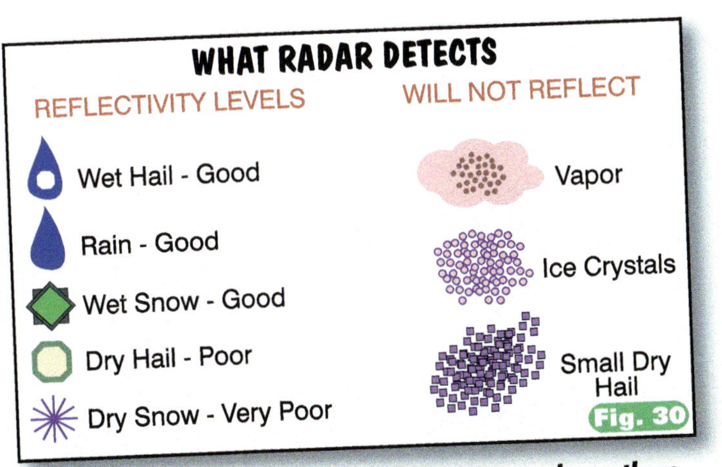

Radar energy reflects off some items better than others. Clouds don't reflect radar energy. It's the moisture in these clouds, in the form of rain, hail or snow, that produces a radar reflection.

higher frequencies; particles moving away from the antenna cause a shift to a lower frequency. The size of the object detectable by Doppler radar depends on the mode in which it's operating. The size of the object and what the particle is made out of also determine how much radar energy it reflects back to the radar screen. Ultimately, it's this reflected energy that determines the colored patterns you seen on your weather radar screen. Let's examine radar reflectivity sufficiently for you to make sense of these weather radar returns.

The absence of a radar return, however, doesn't mean that there are no clouds. Radar energy goes right through a cloud. It takes precipitation size water drops to show up on radar in the form of a precipitation echo.

Radar Reflectivity (dBZ)

At the bottom of many NEXRAD weather charts is a color-number scale, consisting of numerical values paired with chart colors. These values are know as decibels of *reflectivity* or *dBZ* (also called the *reflectivity factor*).

A radar site sends out a pulse of energy, then looks to see what comes bouncing back. Energy is reflected, to varying degrees, by solid objects, as shown in Figure 30. The "object" can be your car, another airplane, or the droplets of water suspended in a cloud (remember, neither water vapor nor clouds reflect radar energy). The more water suspended in a cloud, the greater the radar energy reflected back to the radar antenna. This being science, the reality is of course more complicated than that, but for our purposes this explanation suffices. "Reflectivity" is the industry jargon and an acceptable way to describe radar returns.

It just so happens that the reflected radar energy can be an incredibly small amount or a very large amount, depending on the size of the size of the water droplets and the number of them within the cloud (or if it's a cluster of cars, VWs versus Ford Explorers). The problem is that it's often very difficult to talk about incredibly small numbers and very large numbers in the same conversation. It's like talking about distances that vary from one thousandth of an inch to hundreds of miles. The smaller values tend to lose their meaning (but they are still meaningful, of course). The *decibel* scale is well suited to describing such wide ranges in numbers. That's why radar reflectivity is calculated in decibels, or *decibels of reflectivity*, represented as dBZ (Figure 31, position A).

You're perhaps most familiar with the decibel scale from its use in measuring sound, either for your stereo or of a departing airplane that is being noise-monitored. I could tell you that a decibel is technically defined as the ratio of two numbers converted into a logarithm. I could, but I won't, so forget I said it. Nor did I say or admit to knowing that the *bel* in decibel honors Alexander Graham Bell, who developed the decibel scale.

When speaking of someone's income and wealth, we can say he's either *poor, middle class, upper class,* a *millionaire* or a *billionaire*. The difference between being poor and being a billionaire is humongous. This scale lets you place any person on earth within one of five income slots for easy comparison. You just have to realize that there's a big numerical difference between one slot and the next. Think of decibel values in the same way. The difference between 30 decibels and 60 decibels is not just double, it's actually 100 times greater.

RADAR REFLECTIVITY SCALE ON A CHART

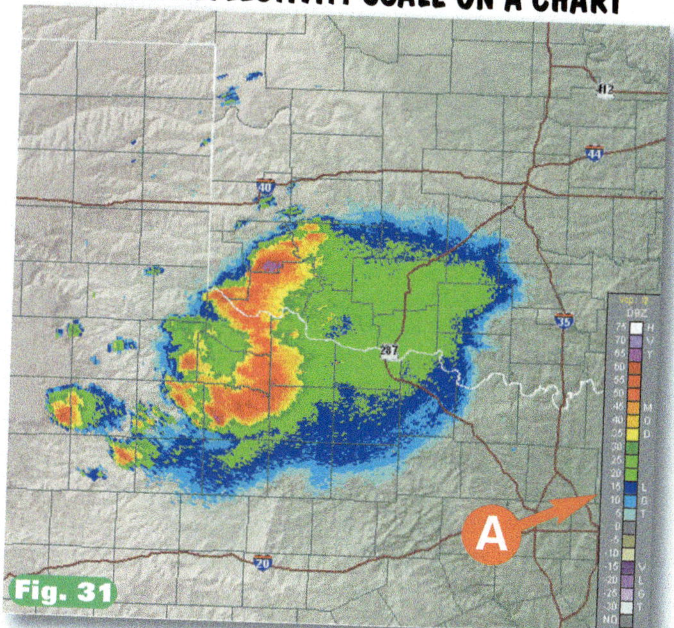

Radar reflectivity values (dBZs) (position A) are often shown on the same chart or WX screen where NEXRAD information is displayed.

What Does dBZ Mean to Me?

So how should you interpret the different color codes you see in a NEXRAD presentation? The answer is simple. The larger the dBZ value, the greater chance of the suspended water in the clouds.

With enough suspended water in the atmosphere, it will eventually rain (Figure 32). A larger amount of suspended water (indicated by a higher dBZ value on the chart) suggests the presence of thunderstorms. As a general rule, weather radar returns with a steady dBZ value of 30 or less aren't associated with convective (storm producing) weather. These lower dBZ values, however, might be an indication of rain and reduced visibilities.

When the dBZ value increases to 40 or above, this is usually a good indication of thunderstorm activity. Remember, the dBZ value is calculated in decibels. Even a small increase in this value means a rather large increase in the return of radar energy. The jump from 30 to 40 dBZs indicates a tremendous increase in suspended water in the atmosphere. There's only one thing that will suspend that much water in the atmosphere—I'm speaking of updrafts, here—which is an indication of highly unstable air.

If the atmosphere is unstable enough to suspend a large amount of water sufficient to produce a 40+ dBZ reading, then thunderstorms are most likely involved (remember, thunderstorms initially form by the production of strong updrafts, also known as the cumulus stage). In Chapter 12, we learned to avoid thunderstorms by at least 20 nautical miles if we don't want to become like Elvis, or *all shook up*.

The general rule, therefore, is to suspect the presence of cloud coverage, reduced visibilities and precipitation where you see radar reflectivity values between 16 and 40 dBZs. Of course, you can't do more than simply "suspect" that poor weather will be present unless you combine the radar information with other weather information such as that from METAR, Prog Charts, PIREPS, etc. Areas of 40 dBZ or greater on NEXRAD presentations not only suggest the presence of cloud coverage, precipitation and reduced visibilities, but should also be treated as thunderstorms or storm areas and avoided by at least 20 nautical miles, unless other information leads you to believe that a closer proximity is safe. In other words, if you see a small, 40 dBZ radar return in one area of the radar presentation, you should treat that area and the area of lesser dBZ returns that are associated with it, as an area of thunderstorms unless you have information to the contrary. Of course, these are just general rules, but they're a good place to being when trying to make sense of NEXRAD information.

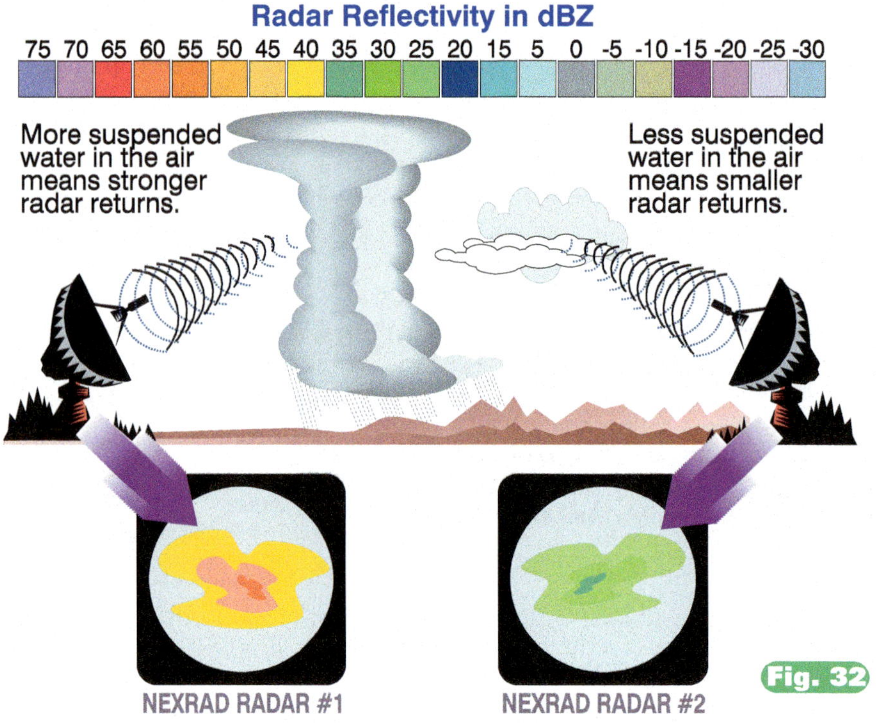

Radar Reflectivity in dBZ

75 70 65 60 55 50 45 40 35 30 25 20 15 5 0 -5 -10 -15 -20 -25 -30

More suspended water in the air means stronger radar returns.

Less suspended water in the air means smaller radar returns.

NEXRAD RADAR #1

NEXRAD RADAR #2

Fig. 32

NEXRAD unit #1 shows that considerable water is suspended in the targeted clouds,so there is a high probability of bad weather associated with these radar returns. NEXRAD unit #2 shows that the examined clouds contain much less water, so there is less chance that these clouds will produce dangerous (thunderstorm-type) turbulence.

Another benefit of NEXRAD is that you can identify stationary storm systems or moving storm systems. When you can see poor weather on a cockpit screen, it should reduce the risk of flying into bad weather. It should also make it unlikely you'll be ambushed by a moving storm system, too. I can't emphasize this last value enough. On your cockpit weather display, you can easily see moving storm systems in sufficient time to land, park the airplane and your derriere, and let the storm system pass. You can even make an estimate of how long you'll stay parked based on how fast you see the storm system moving. Next to the invention of the TV remote, uplinked cockpit weather—specifically NEXRAD—is a VFR pilot's dream come true.

On the other hand, it's important to remember that NEXRAD information isn't presented in *real time*. That's because it takes the radar unit and the computer some time to process the weather information sufficiently to produce NEXRAD imagery. By the time you see it on your cockpit display (or on a paper chart), it can be from five to six minutes old. Measured in terms of the short lifespan of a thunderstorm, this is a long time.

Therefore, what you see on your cockpit weather display can be different from what you see through your airplane's windscreen. Nevertheless,

STORM INTENSITY LEVELS

DIGIT "STORM LEVEL"	PRECIPITATION INTENSITY
1	LIGHT (16-29 dBZ)
2	MODERATE (30-40 dBZ)
3	HEAVY (40-49 dBZ)
4	HEAVY (40-49 dBZ)
5	EXTREME (50-59 dBZ)
6	EXTREME (50-59 dBZ)

The National Weather Service classifies precipitation intensity levels by name and dBZ levels. These are the references that ATC and FSS specialists use when referring to radar returns. Keep in mind that Level 3 represents dBZs values of 40 dBZ or higher. When you hear either "Level 3" or "heavy" precipitation mentioned, suspect thunderstorms. Fig. 33

the information is good enough, in my opinion, to allow you to make practical weather decisions. Keep in mind, however, that NEXRAD is only one of the many bits of information that you'll want to use in making weather decisions enroute.

Finally, also keep in mind that some weather service providers use different color coding calibrations for their dBZ values. Sometimes red represents 40 dBZs, sometimes a dark yellow color represents a 40 dBZ return. However, this really doesn't matter as long as you know how those color codes are calibrated.

Too Many Names?

Given your new understanding of NEXRAD, here's an additional dollop of Doppler information to stick in those cranial folds.

The National Weather Service also references radar returns in terms of precipitation intensity: *light, moderate, heavy,* and *extreme* as shown in Figure 33. Each precipitation level is associated with a specific range of radar reflectivity (dBZ) values. In other words, heavy precipitation is associated with a dBZ value ranging from 40 dBZs to 49 dBZs as shown in Figure 33.

We also know that thunderstorm weather is normally associated with a dBZ value of 40 or more, and is referred to as a Level 3 or 4 radar return. Therefore, when you hear pilots, controllers or a Flight Service Station specialist talking about either a Level 3 radar return or about *heavy* precipitation, you know they're talking about an area that's likely to contain thunderstorm activity.

Of course, you would think that ATC and the FSS would want pilots to report turbulence in pilot reports (PIREPS) by using the same terms used by the NWS to represent precipitation intensity. So sorry, Charlie. Instead, the FAA wants you to report turbulence using the definitions shown in Figure 34.

HOW TO REPORT TURBULENCE

INTENSITY	AIRCRAFT REACTION	REACTION IN A/C
Light	Turbulence that momentarily causes slight erratic changes in altitude and or attitude (pitch, roll, yaw). Report as light turbulence. OR... Turbulence that causes slight, rapid and somewhat rhythmic bumpiness without appreciable changes in altitude or attitude. Report as Light Chop.	Occupants may feel a slight strain against seat belts or shoulder straps. Unsecured objects may be displaced slightly. Food service may be conducted and little or no difficulty is encountered when walking.
Moderate	Turbulence that is similar to light turbulence but of greater intensity. Changes in altitude and/or attitude occur but the aircraft remains in positive control at all times. It usually causes variations in indicated airspeed. Report as moderate turbulence. OR... Turbulence that is similar to light chop but of greater intensity. It causes rapid bumps or jolts without appreciable changes in aircraft altitude or attitude. Report as moderate chop.	Occupants feel definite strains against seat belts or shoulder straps. Unsecured objects are dislodged. Food service and walking are difficult.
Severe	Turbulence that causes large, abrupt changes in altitude and/or attitude. It usually causes large variations in indicated airspeed. Aircraft may be momentarily out of control. Report as severe turbulence.	Occupants are forced violently against seat belts or shoulder straps. Unsecured objects are tossed about. Food service and walking are impossible.
Extreme	Turbulence in which the aircraft is violently tossed about & is practically impossible to control. It may cause structural damage. Report as Extreme Turbulence.	
Duration	Occasional—Less than 1/3 of the time. Intermittent—1/3 to 2/3. Continuous—More than 2/3 of the time.	

Fig. 34

HOW TO GIVE A TURBULENCE PIREP

When encountering turbulence, pilots are urgently requested to report such conditions to ATC as soon as practicable. PIREPs relating to turbulence should state:

1. **Aircraft location.**
2. **Time of occurrence in UTC.**
3. **Turbulence intensity.**
4. **Whether the turbulence occurred in or near clouds.**
5. **Aircraft altitude or flight level.**
6. **Type of aircraft.**
7. **Duration of turbulence.**

EXAMPLES–
1. Over Omaha, 1232Z, moderate turbulence at 9,500 feet, Cessna 172.
2. From five zero miles south of Albuquerque to three zero miles north of Phoenix, 1250Z, occasional moderate chop at 10,500 feet, Cirrus SR-22.

THE LOW LEVEL SIGNIFICANT WEATHER PROGNOSTIC CHART

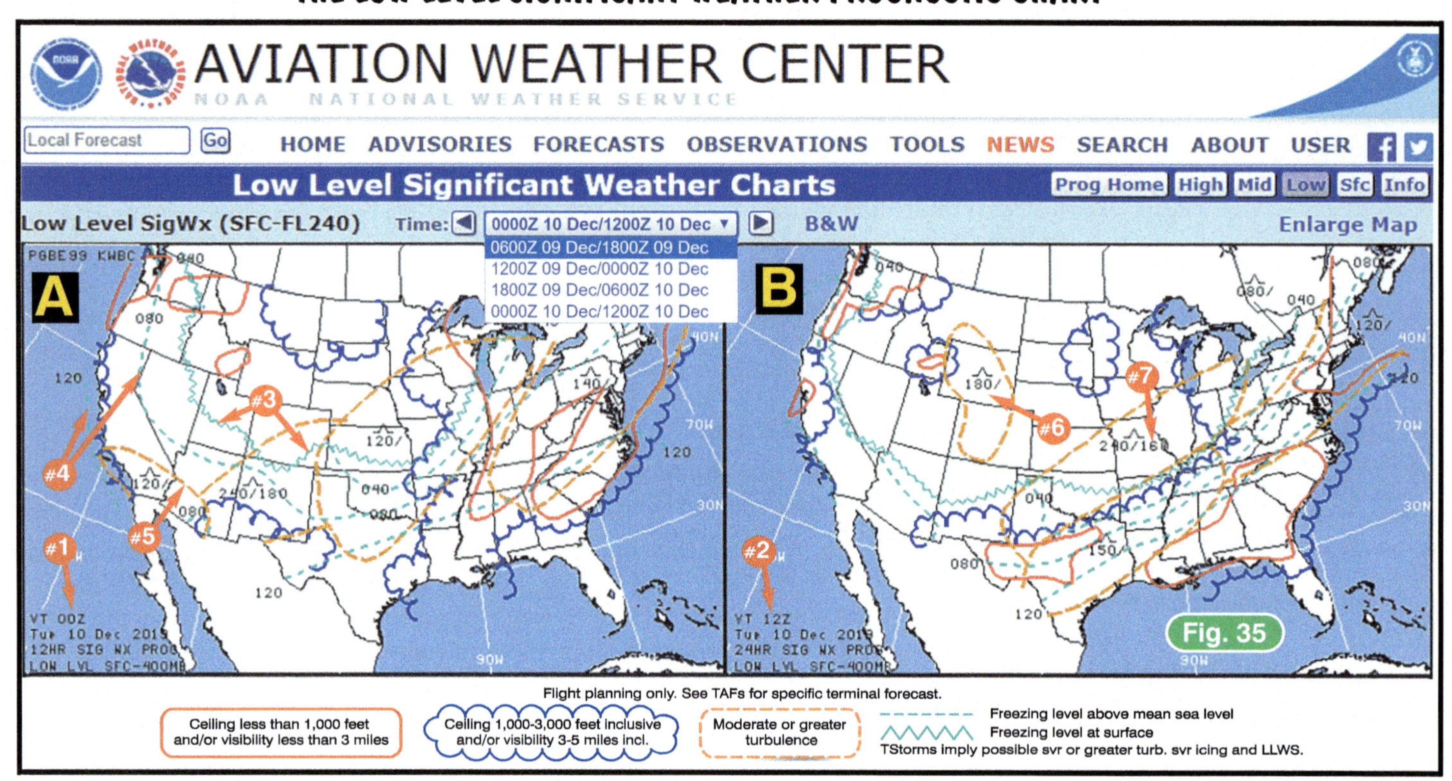

Low Level Significant Weather Prognostic Chart – A doctor told his patient that he had good news and bad news. The doctor asked which the patient wanted to hear first. The patient said, "Give me the good news first." The doctor said, "Well, you've got 24 hours to live." The patient said, "That's the *good* news? What's the bad news?" The doctor said, "I tried to call you yesterday."

Essentially, the doctor gave his patient a *prognosis* or a future outlook. While the terminal aerodrome forecast and winds aloft forecast are all a textual prognosis of the weather, the *low level significant weather prognostic chart* does the same thing in picture form.

The low level significant weather prognostic chart—the *prog chart,* as it's usually referred to by those not wishing to carry supplemental oxygen—can be thought of as a graphic version of textual forecasts, though it differs slightly from the written version, as shown in Figure 35. One of the very unique features of the prog chart is that it is a visual forecast of aviation weather hazards and is primarily intended to be used as guidance for briefing the VFR pilot (that means you). This chart provides a visual display of areas you might want to avoid, such as areas of turbulence and IFR weather. The low level prog chart covers 48 contiguous states (CONUS), southern Canada and the coastal waters for altitudes below 24,000 feet. These charts are issued four times daily and are valid at the fixed times of: 0000Z, 0600Z, 1200Z and 1800Z. Panel A above is valid at 000Z (Figure 35, position 1) and panel B is valid at 1200Z (position 2).

The prog chart typically consists of two panels. The left panel is the 12-hour prognosis and the right panel is the 24-hour prognosis. Both panels predict freezing levels, turbulence, low clouds and ceilings and/or restrictions to visibility.

A key, located on the bottom of the chart panels, helps with interpreting the weather symbols. For instance, all areas surrounded by solid red lines are areas with ceilings less than 1,000 feet and/or visibilities less than 3 miles (i.e., IFR conditions). Areas surrounded by blue scalloped lines are marginal VFR conditions consisting of 1,000 to 3,000 foot ceilings and/or 3 to 5 miles visibility (i.e., MVFR conditions). Areas outside scalloped lines are forecast to have ceilings greater than 3,000 feet and 5 miles visibility (VFR conditions).

Panels A and B of the significant weather prog chart have light blue zig-zag lines that show the location of the freezing level at the surface (panel A, position 3). Light Blue dashed lines on the same panel indicate freezing levels at altitude (panel A, position 4). You'd add two zeros to the three-digit number to obtain the freezing level in thousands of feet. Freezing levels are important for instrument pilots since they want to avoid flying in the clouds when the temperatures are near or below freezing, lest they pick up ice on the plane and turn their aircraft into a giant Snowcone.

An additional and very useful feature of the significant weather prog chart is its forecast of turbulence. The dashed yellow/orange line surrounding the bottom portion of California and extending into southern Arizona indicates moderate or greater turbulence is forecast during the 12-hour time period (panel A, position 5). (Use the key between panels

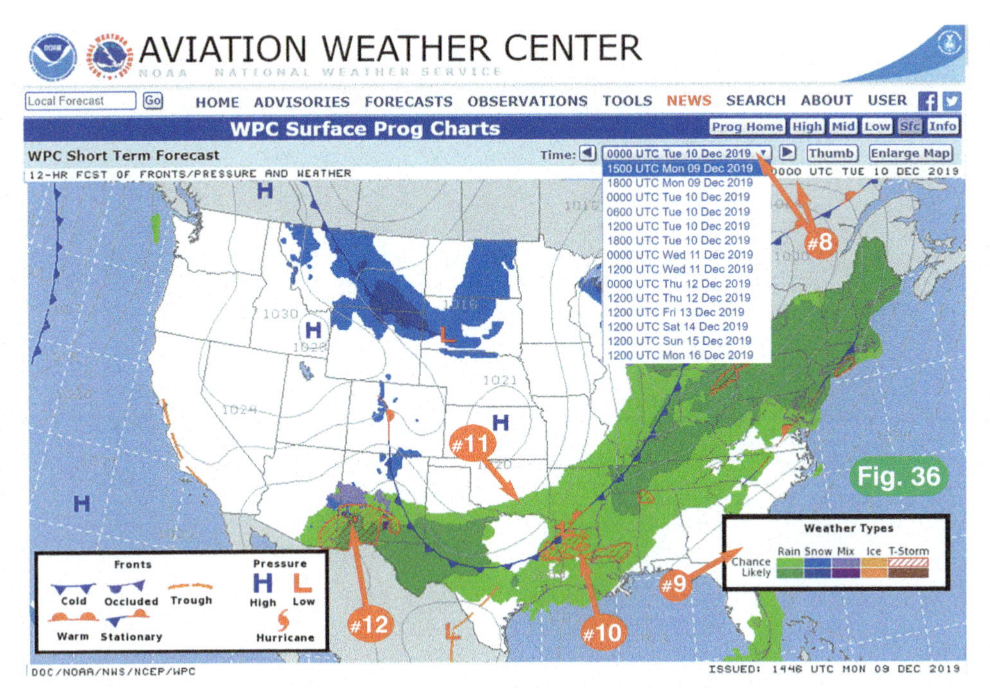

on prog chart.) Within the area surrounded by the yellow/orange dashed line is the number *120* with what appears to be a *witch's hat* symbol above it and a small short diagonal line to the right. The 120 means this turbulence is forecast from the surface up to 12,000 feet. In the 24-hour significant weather prog (panel B, position 6) the *180* tells us that moderate turbulence is forecast for this area from the surface to 18,000 feet MSL during the forecast time. A number to the right of the diagonal line as shown at position 7 (i.e., the "/" that's to the right of 240) states the base of the turbulence when it doesn't begin at the surface. The area of moderate or greater turbulence shown by position 7 indicates that this turbulence is forecast for altitudes between 16,000 and 24,000 feet.

By comparing the 12- and 24-hour significant weather prog, you can visualize the direction of weather movement during the next 24 hours.

In addition to the low level prog chart, you'll certainly want to consult the surface prog chart shown in Figure 36. Yes, it's full of pretty colors, isn't it? But don't be deceived. As a general rule, the more colorful the chart, the worse the weather. So never fly with someone that says, "The prog charts are so pretty today, let's go flying! Ah, maybe not.

Surface prog charts provide the expected (forecast) locations of surface fronts and boundaries, pressure systems and the types of precipitation you can expect at the designated forecast time (Figure 36).

This chart provides forecast information for up to seven days in advance and you'd select the desired forecast interval from the drop-down menu (Figure 36, position 8). The practical utility of this chart occurs when you compare the surface forecast with the 12- and 24-hour low level prog chart. Now you can obtain an understanding of how the weather shown on the prog chart is being generated. A key is provided on the chart to help you interpret the weather you're seeing.

The "Weather Types" key in position 9, uses the terms *chance* and *likely* to describe precipitation. Chance means there's a 25% to less than 55% probability of measurable rain. The term likely means there is a greater than or equal to 55% probability of measurable rain.

For example, the red hatched area in Southern New Mexico, Figure 36, position 10, indicates that there's a chance of thunderstorms in this area during the forecast period. This and the likely chance of rain suggests that clouds and reduced visibility can be expected in the area. In fact, the 12-hour low level prog suggests that you'll experience marginal VFR conditions in this area.

Let's say you are planning a two hour flight from central southern Oklahoma to northern Louisiana (Figure 36, positions 11 to 10) and expect to leave at 0600Z . What type of weather can you expect upon arrival? The surface prog chart shown in Figure 36, position 8, is valid at 0000Z. You expect to arrive at 0800Z. Looking at panel B, it appears that there is MVFR along your entire route with the possibility of thunderstorms upon arrival (the red hatched areas shown in central Louisiana, position 10). The 24-hour prog chart (Figure 35, panel B) also indicates moderate or greater turbulence from the surface to 15,000 feet MSL. Perhaps it's better to call Uber and let the weather improve before departure.

Many of today's weather charts are self-explanatory. Not surprisingly, this is one of the unique features of modern computer/internet weather processing. It's all about the color. When weather charts were black and white, many different symbols were required to describe current and forecast weather. Now you just look at the color, consult the key and make a more informed weather decision.

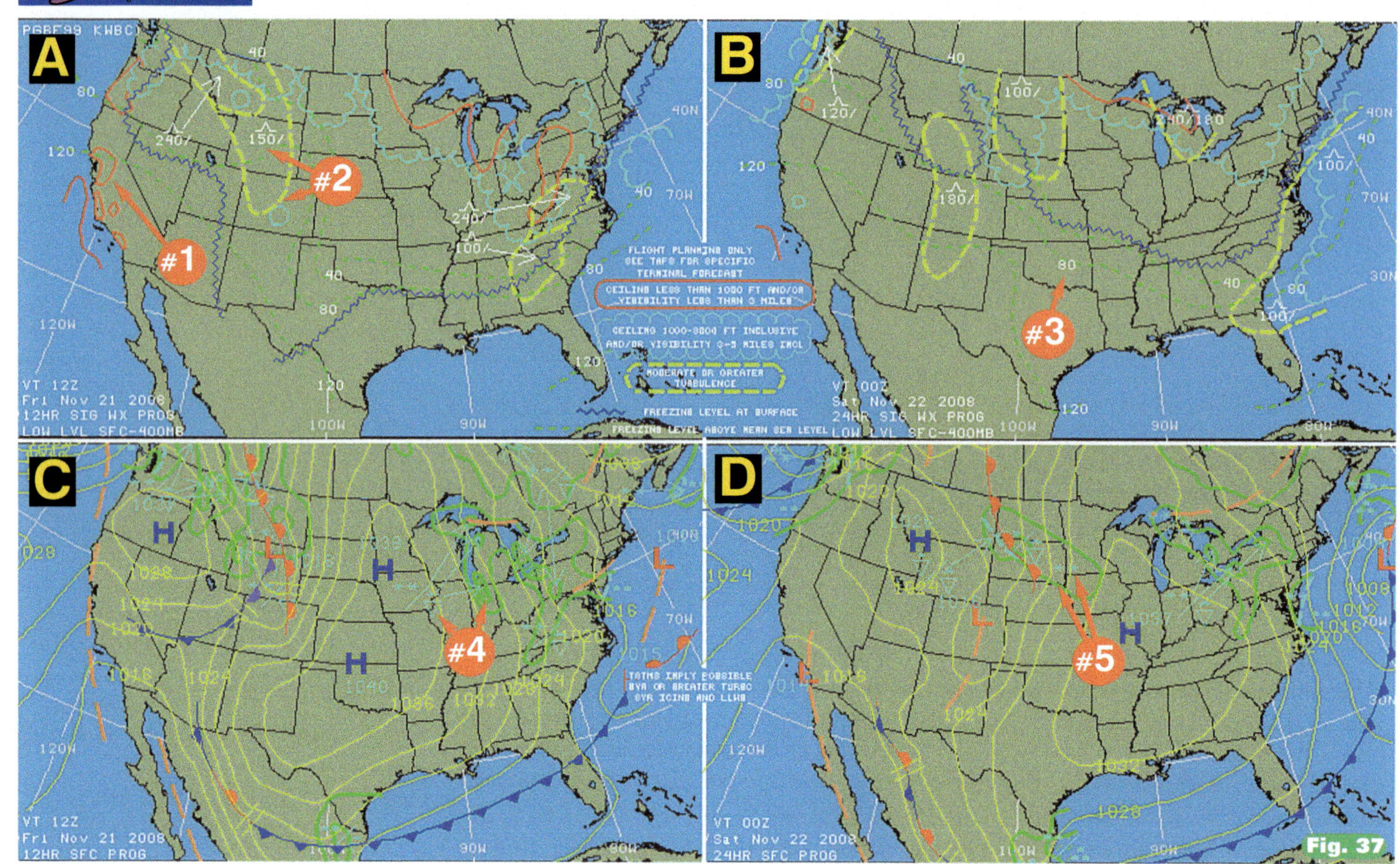

While a two-panel prog chart is most common today, some weather services still offer the four-panel variety. This four-panel chart consists of both the 12- and 24-hour low level prog and the surface prog. Panel A, position 1, shows that during the 12-hour forecast period, the area surrounded by solid red lines is expected to be IFR (see the legend between panels A and B). The thick yellow dashed line in panel A, position 2 indicates that moderate turbulence is expected from the surface to 15,000 feet MSL during the 12-hour forecast period. The thin green dashed line in panel B, position 3 shows that the freezing level over central Oklahoma is expected to be 8,000 feet MSL during the 24-hour forecast period. The solid, thick green line in panel C, position 4 shows a shaded area (it's also called a hatched area) in northern Indiana forecasting mixed precipitation (light snow showers) covering more than half the area.

The solid, thick green line surrounding the non-shaded (non-hatched) area in panel D, position 5 identifies an area where light snow can be expected during the 24-hour forecast period. Since the area isn't shaded (hatched), the snow can be expected to cover half or less of the bordered area.l" (position B).

Your Friendly Automated Flight Service Station www.1800wxbrief.com

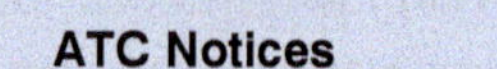

No one can say that today's Flight Service Station isn't cutting edge. Here are a few of the newest services that are available to you when you register at www.1800wxbrief.com.

Since nearly everyone has email and a cell phone, you can register to receive several new flight plan and weather alerting services. Here are a few you should choose.

Adverse Conditions Alerting Services

ACAS provides preflight and in-flight alerts to your email client or cell phone prior to departure or while enroute (if your cell phone can receive while enroute). These alerts include information on TFRs, SIGMETs, AIRMETs, Airport/Runway closures, etc. This service is available for IFR and VFR flight plans.

Easy Activate and Easy Close Flight Plan Service

When you register for this service, you'll receive an email and/or text message with a link for opening a prefiled flight plan 30 minutes prior to your estimated departure time. You'll also receive similar messages 30 minutes after the ETA listed on your flight plan. This service is available for VFR flight plans.

Flight Plan Close Reminders

If you'd rather just have a reminder to close your flight plan (not active it), then this service allows you to receive an email and/or text message 20 minutes after the ETA listed on your flight plan. This service is available for VFR flight plans only.

ATC Notices

This service informs you via email (email only, no text messaging) if and when your IFR flight plan has been accepted by ATC. It also alerts you if ATC makes a change in your flight planned route. This service is for IFR flight plans.

Please note that when you register for these services on Lockheed's web site, you'll see terms such as MIFR, MVFR, ZFR and YFR. The first two terms refer to Military IFR and VFR flight plans (not marginal VFR or IFR as you typically use them). The last two terms are not used in the U.S. at this time. Set up an account today!

Weather Codes You Should to Know

Despite today's advanced computer and software systems (some of which have names such as HAL and Watson) aviation still uses weather abbreviations that were appropriate when Morse code and ancient Teletype machinery was popular. No one uses dots, dashes and older machines to transmit information on weather today. Nevertheless, many aviation weather reports still come with abbreviations, perhaps to make it easier to grasp an eyeful of weather information at one glance. So be it.

Below are some of the most important weather codes you need to know (Figures 39, 40). Study them. They are not optional.

You'll need these codes to interpret the METAR, TAFs, GFAs, PIREPS, and a few other important weather products.

Whoa! Don't fret (unless you want to) because many of these abbreviations are just plain common sense. For instance, OBSCD means "obscured." Easy, right? The letters "PTLY" in front of "OBSCD" means, "partly obscured." FRQ, ISOL and OCNL mean, "frequent, isolated" and "occasional." Not all that tough, right?

Contractions (Fig. 39)

Contraction	*Designator*	*Definition*
CLR	CLR	Sky clear
SCT	SCT	Scattered
BKN	BKN	Broken
OVC	OVC	Overcast
OBSCD	X	Obscured
PTLYOBSCD	-X	Partly obscured
CIG	C	Ceiling

Area coverage of showers and thunderstorms

Adjective	*Coverage*
Isolated -	Single cells (no percentage)
Widely scattered -	Less than 25% of area affected
Scattered -	25% to 50% of area affected
Numerous -	55% or more of area affected

Variability Terms

Variability terms are often included in the remarks and indicate how often a change might occur in ceilings, sky cover, weather, etc.

FRQ **...Consisting of elements with little or no separation between adjacent thunderstorms with a maximum spatial coverage greater than 75 percent of the area affected by the phenomena at a fixed time or during the period of validity.**

OCNL **...An area with a maximum spatial coverage between 50 and 75 percent of the area affected by the phenomena at a fixed time of during the period of validity.**

ISOL **...Consisting of individual features affecting an area with a maximum spatial coverage less than 50 percent of the area affected by the phenomena at a fixed time or during the period of validity.**

Categories (Fig. 40)

Category	*Definition*
LIFR	*Low IFR* - ceiling less than 500 feet and/or visibility less than 1 mile.
IFR	Ceiling 500 to less than 1,000 feet and/or visibility 1 to less than 3 miles.
MVFR	*Marginal VFR* - ceiling 1,000 to 3,000 feet and/or visibility 3 to 5 miles inclusive.
VFR	No ceiling or ceiling greater than 3,000 feet and visibility greater than 5 miles.

Remarks appended to VFR items

Remarks	*Definition*
VFR CIG ABV 100	Ceiling greater than 10,000 feet and visibility greater than 5 miles.
VFR NO CIG	Cloud coverage less than 6/10 or thin clouds and visibility greater than 5 miles.
VFR CLR	Cloud coverage less than 1/10 and visibility greater than 5 miles.

Examples of categorical groupings

Example	*Definition*
LIFR CIG	Low IFR due to low ceiling only.
IFR F	IFR due to visibility restricted by fog.
MVFR CIG H K	Marginal VFR due both to low ceiling and to visibility restricted by haze and smoke.
IFR CIG R WND	IFR due both to low ceiling and to visibility restricted by rain, wind expected to be 25 knots or greater.

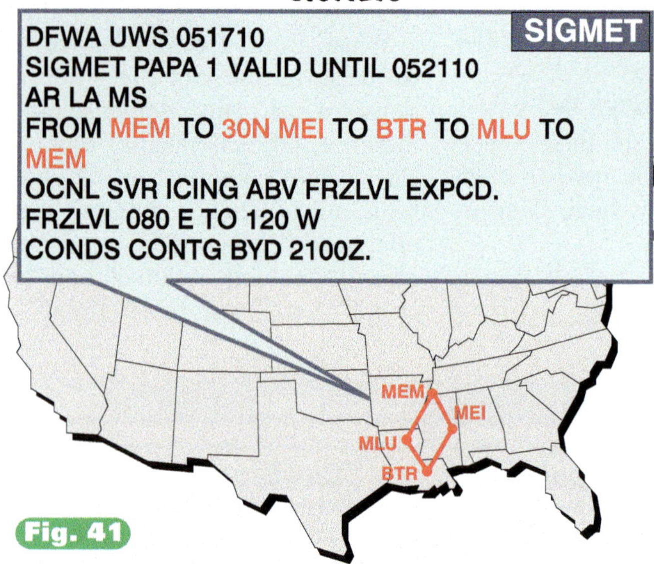

Fig. 41

In-flight Aviation Weather Advisories

Most people want to protect things that are of value to them. For instance, my parents used to have plastic covers on their living room furniture to protect it. My grandfather was different. He tried to make visitors wear plastic leisure suits instead of opting for covers. It didn't work too well (but our guests did lose weight). Pilots want to protect themselves while airborne. They do so by understanding what in-flight advisories are and how they're disseminated.

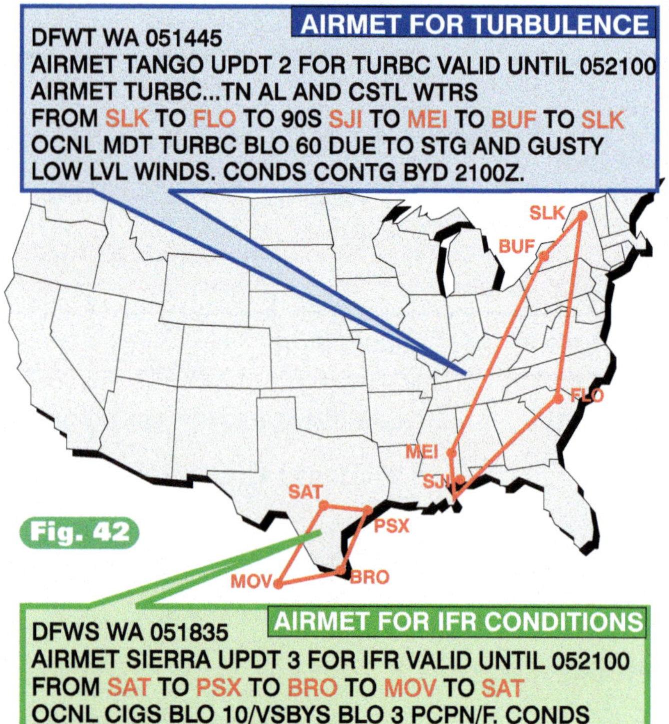

Fig. 42

In-flight aviation weather advisories are forecasts that advise pilots of potentially hazardous weather—some of which might have been forecast, and some of which might have arrived as a complete surprise to everyone involved. These advisories are provided to the FSS and are normally included in your standard weather briefing. Always make it a point to ask the briefer for any in-flight advisories anyway. The FSS also has a full listing of in-flight advisories so you may easily access them in flight via a radio call. There are three types of advisories: Convective SIGMETS, SIGMETS, and AIRMETS.

SIGMET (WS) – A *SIGMET* is an advisory of non-convective weather (non-thunderstorm type weather) that is potentially hazardous to all aircraft, big and small. SIGMETs are issued when any of the following occur or are expected to occur: severe icing not associated with thunderstorms, severe or extreme turbulence or clear air turbulence (CAT) not associated with thunderstorms, dust storms, sandstorms, and volcanic ash that lowers surface visibilities to less than 3 miles and, finally, any volcanic eruption (something we pilots are not trained to handle and don't want to see while it's occurring).

Any of these items certainly affects both large and small airplanes. SIGMETS are named by the phonetic alphabet using designators from November through Yankee, excluding Sierra, Tango and Zulu (these three are AIRMET designators). By knowing the specific phonetic name and number of a SIGMET or AIRMET, you can call the FSS and determine if it has been canceled, continued, amended or updated. Figure 41 shows a typical SIGMET and the area it affects.

This SIGMET was issued for the DFW area at 1710Z on the 5th day of the month and is valid until 2110Z on the same day. The letters UWS (Urgent Weather Sigmet) are included in the first issuance of a SIGMET. SIGMETs have names for identification. This SIGMET is named Papa 1, indicating that this is the first SIGMET issued in that specific area. Issuances for the same weather phenomena will be sequentially numbered using the original name (Papa 2, Papa 3, etc.) until the phenomena end.

The SIGMET in Figure 41 is for Arkansas, Louisiana and Mississippi. From MEM to 30 miles north of MEI to BTR to MLU to MEM, you can expect occasional severe icing above the freezing level (remember, these three letter identifiers are all VORs in the affected area). The freezing level is from 8,000 feet eastward to 12,000 feet westward. Conditions continuing beyond 2100Z. (Four hours is the maximum forecast period of a SIGMET.)

AIRMET (WA) – *AIRMETS* warn of significant weather but describe conditions at intensities lower than those that trigger SIGMETs. They are intended for all pilots in the preflight and enroute phase of flight to enhance safety.

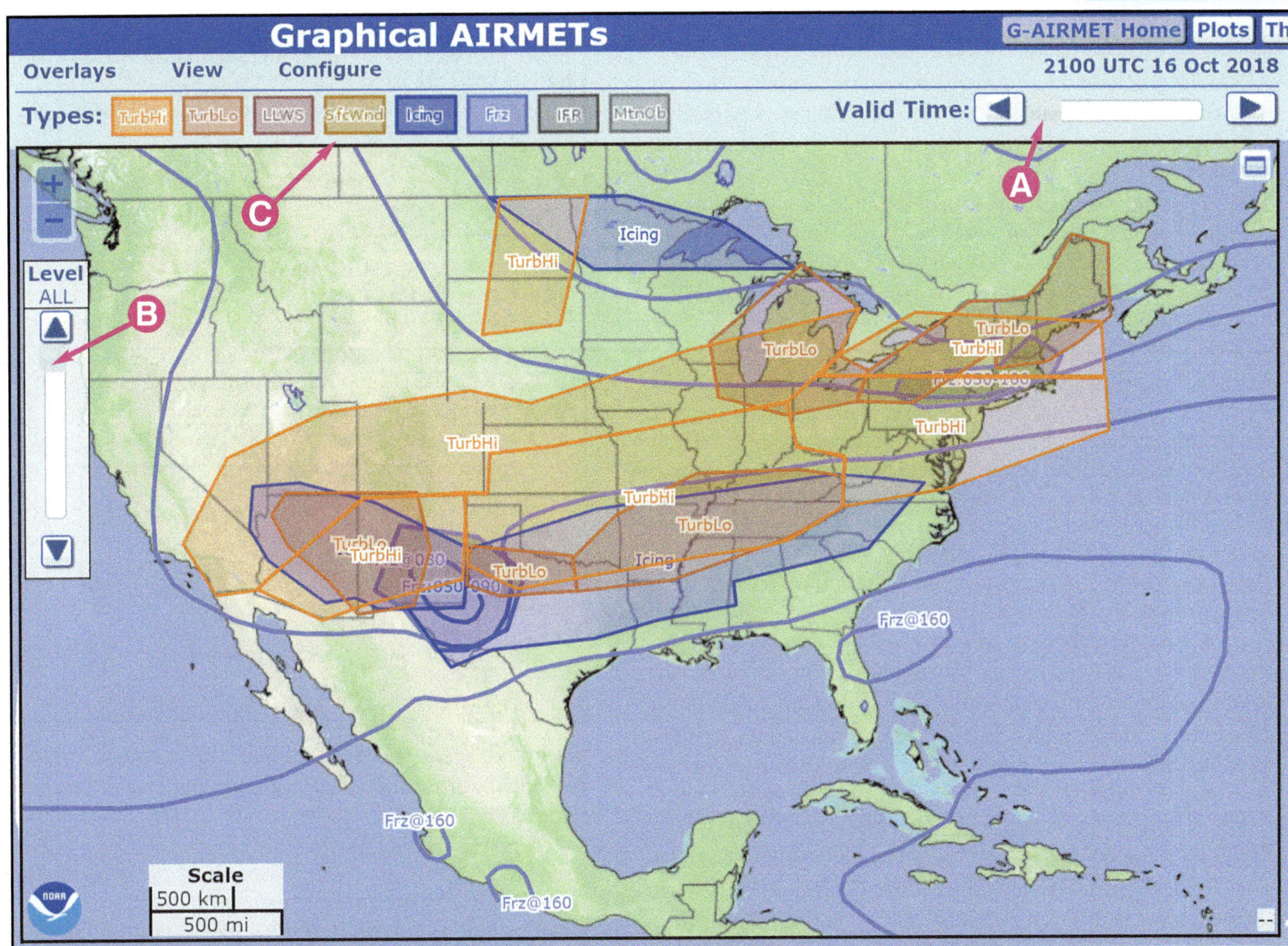

Got graphics? The FAA does and some come in the form of a G-AIRMET (graphical AIRMET) as shown here. You'll learn AIRMETs shortly and when you do, please visit the FAA's G-AIRMET page at (www.aviationweather.gov/gairmet). This graphic allows you to see at a glance AIRMETs for several different parameters such as turbulence, low level wind shear, surface winds, mountain obscuration and more. G-AIRMETs are issued 3 hours apart and a time slider (position A) allows you to see forecast AIRMET conditions for three-hour intervals up to 12 hours into the future. You can also see how an AIRMET affects you at specific altitudes by moving the altitude slider (position B). Specific AIRMET conditions can be selected by pushing any or all of the eight feature buttons (position C).

AIRMETs are issued once every 6 hours on a scheduled basis, with unscheduled amendments issued as required. Each AIRMET issuance contains current AIRMETs still in effect, significant conditions not meeting AIRMET criteria and an outlook for conditions expected after the AIRMET valid period. AIRMETs are valid for a period of 6 hours. They contain one or more of the following weather phenomena when they occur or are forecast to occur: moderate icing, moderate turbulence, sustained winds of 30 knots or more at the surface, ceilings less than 1,000 feet and/or visibilities less than 3 miles affecting more than 50% of the area at one time, as well as extensive mountain obscuration.

The upper portion of Figure 42 shows an AIRMET and the area it affects. It was issued for the Dallas/Ft. Worth forecasting area on the 5th day of the month at 1445Z. The *T* following DFW indicates the type of AIRMET. In this instance it means TANGO (for turbulence). AIRMET TANGO is updated and is valid until 2100Z on the 5th day of the month and applies to the area around Tennessee, Alabama and the coastal waters. The area described in the AIRMET is expected to have moderate turbulence below 6,000 feet MSL due to strong and

gusty low level winds. These conditions are expected to continue beyond the AIRMET's valid time of 2100Z.

AIRMET SIERRA in the lower portion of Figure 42 is on its third update. The S following DFW indicates AIRMET SIERRA (which indicates IFR conditions or mountain obscuration).

The bordered area shown is expected to have occasional ceilings below 1,000 feet and visibilities below 3 miles in precipitation and fog. Conditions are expected to continue beyond 2100Z through 0300Z. If you're planning on doing any traveling to this area during the forecast time, you might think about doing it by car.

AIRMETs have fixed alphanumeric designators. If you see AIRMET SIERRA, this stands for IFR and mountain obscurations; TANGO stands for turbulence (because that's what you feel you're doing in strong turbulence), strong surface wind and low level wind shear; and ZULU stands for icing and freezing level. AIRMETs can be a very big asset during the pre-departure stage of flight because they're issued and updated (as necessary) frequently. Always check for AIRMETs that may affect your flight.

Convective SIGMETs (WST) – Another version of the SIGMET is the *convective SIGMET* (WST). This is the granddaddy of in-flight advisories and present hazards to all aircraft. A convective SIGMET is an advisory associated with convective activity such as severe thunderstorms. Any convective SIGMET implies severe or greater turbulence, severe icing, and low level windshear. A convective SIGMET may be issued for any of the following items:

1. A line of thunderstorms at least 60 miles long with thunderstorms affecting at least 40 percent of its length,

2. An area of active thunderstorms affecting at least 3,000 square miles covering at least 40 percent of the area concerned and exhibiting a very strong radar reflectivity intensity or a significant satellite or lightning signature.

3. It is also issued for embedded or severe thunderstorm(s) expected to occur for more than 30 minutes during the valid period regardless of the size of the area.

Figure 43 is an example of a convective SIGMET. This SIGMET was issued on the 22nd day of the month at 1855Z. It is the 20th consecutive SIGMET (20C) issued on this day in the central U.S. The SIGMET references a line in the vicinity of GLD to CDS. It forecasts a line of thunderstorms developing by 1955Z and moving eastward at 30 to 35 knots through 2055Z. Hail to one and one-half inches is also possible. That's pretty serious weather. You better be on the ground wearing a hard hat and a roll bar if you experience hail that size.

Convective SIGMETs also contain an outlook. This is a forecast for thunderstorms that are expected to require convective SIGMET issuance during a time period 2-6 hours into the future. The convective SIGMET outlook in Figure 43 predicts isolated strong thunderstorms will develop over southwestern Kansas through the forecast period as an upper level trough moves northeastward over very unstable air.

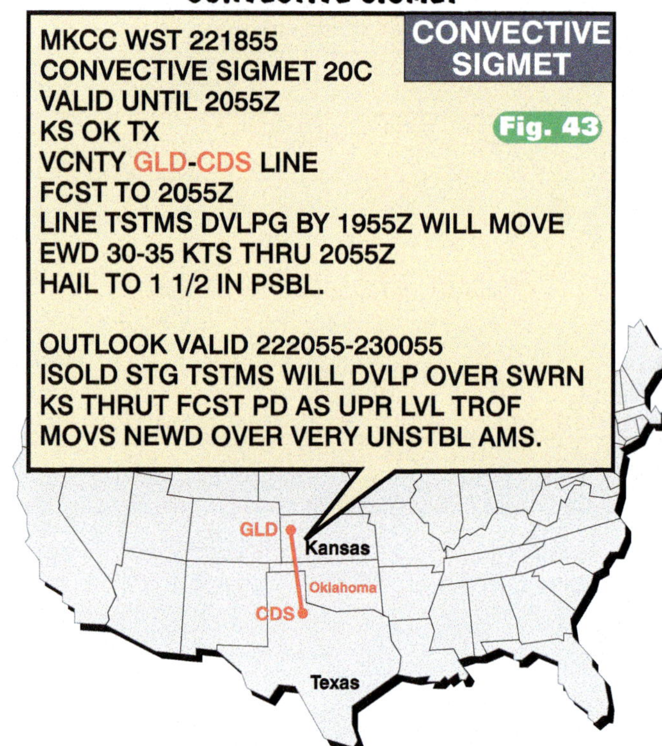

Pilot Reports (PIREPs) – *Pilot reports* provide pilots with some of the best real-time weather information available. PIREPs provide an excellent means of finding current weather between reporting stations. The FSS and other ATC specialists, long for pilots to give reports of weather and other items of interest, particularly any unforecast conditions you might encounter. Pilot reports don't have to only relate to weather information. Reports of flocks of birds, balloons, and other items affecting flight are helpful.

I remember seeing the following pilot report distributed by a midwest FSS (decoded for your convenience):

Pilotless airplane (Aeronca Champ) last seen heading northeast of Goodland at 3,000 feet.

It seems the airplane was being handpropped without a qualified pilot aboard. The engine started and, with the throttle set too high, the airplane zoomed off through a field and became airborne (after nearly giving the pilot a crewcut). It remained airborne for a little over an hour before slamming into a farmer's field. Shouldn't this be called a *nonpilot* report or a *no-pilot-aboard* report?

Pilot reports are officially coded, then disseminated through the ATC system for use in flight planning. The official format for this coding is shown in Figure 44. Figure 45 shows how PIREPs are encoded. Let's examine a few reports.

Figure 46 shows a typical pilot report. It reads: a routine PIREP (UA meaning *routine,* it doesn't mean United Airlines either; UUA means *urgent*)/ from Oklahoma City

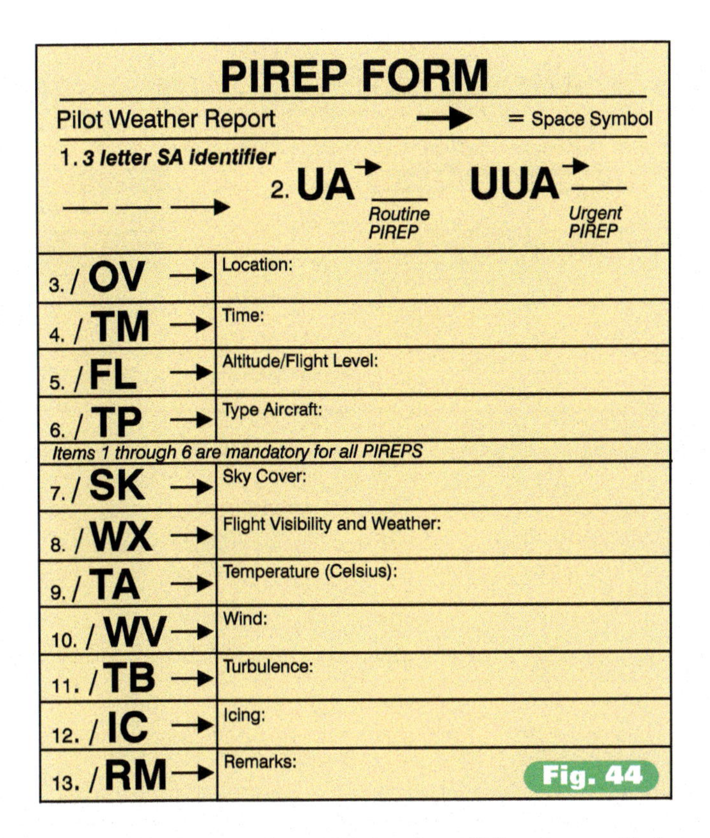

PIREP FORM

Pilot Weather Report → = Space Symbol

1. 3 letter SA identifier ———→ 2. UA→___ (Routine PIREP) UUA→___ (Urgent PIREP)

3. /OV →	Location:
4. /TM →	Time:
5. /FL →	Altitude/Flight Level:
6. /TP →	Type Aircraft:
Items 1 through 6 are mandatory for all PIREPS	
7. /SK →	Sky Cover:
8. /WX →	Flight Visibility and Weather:
9. /TA →	Temperature (Celsius):
10. /WV →	Wind:
11. /TB →	Turbulence:
12. /IC →	Icing:
13. /RM →	Remarks:

Fig. 44

to Tulsa/ at 1800Z/ at 12,000 feet (FL means *flight level* and is used for any altitude)/ reported by a Beech 90. (The type of aircraft is important. If a 747 reported light turbulence it could mean moderate or severe for a small airplane.)/ the base of the first cloud layer is at 1,800 feet MSL broken with tops at 5,500 MSL (since a pilot reported this he or she is referencing the altimeter which displays height in MSL values. This means, for example, that if the ground elevation is 1,295 feet MSL, then the 1,800 foot MSL ceiling is 505 feet above ground.)/ the base of the second overcast cloud layer is at 7,200 feet MSL and tops are at 8,900 feet MSL/ and the weather is clear above the upper layer/ weather type: flight visibility is 3 miles in moderate rain/ temperature is -9 degrees Celsius/ the wind is from 080 degrees at 21 knots (pilots can determine wind direction and velocity from the cockpit by using a sophisticated GPS system)/ turbulence is *light* between 5,500 feet and 7,200 feet/ there was light to moderate rime icing between 7,200 feet and 8,900 feet.

Pilot reports are quite useful. They are, however, most meaningful when they are first issued. Conditions can change with time. Be very suspicious of pilot reports more than an hour old.

A TYPICAL PILOT REPORT (PIREP)

KTUL UA /OV KOKC-KTUL /TM 1800 /FL 120
/TP BE90 /SK BKN018-TOP055/OVC072-TOP089 /CLR ABV
/WX FV03SM RA /TA M9 /WV 08021KT /TB LGT 055-072
/IC LGT-MDT RIME 072-089.

Fig.46

KEY FOR ENCODING PILOT REPORTS

1. 3-letter station identifier - nearest weather reporting location to the reported phenomena

2. UA - Routine PIREP, UUA is an urgent PIREP

3. /OV - **Location**: Use 3-letter NAVAID idents only
   a. *Fix:* /OV ABC or OV/ABC090025 (the first three numbers are the radial from the VOR and the last three numbers are the distance. In this example the PIREP concerns the area near the 090 degree radial of the ABC VOR at the 025 or 25 nautical mile position).
   b. *Fix to fix:* /OV ABC-DEF, OV/ABC-DEF120020

4. /TM - **Time:** 4 digits in UTC (Zulu) (e.g. /TM 0915)

5. /FL - **Altitude/Flight Level:** 3 digits for hundreds of feet, if not known use UNKN (e.g. FL085 is 8,500 feet and FL310 is 31,000 feet).

6. /TP - **Type aircraft:** 4 digits maximum, if not known use UNKN (e.g. /TP C150, /TPB747).

7. /SK - **Cloud layers:** Describe as follows:
   a. Cloud amount.
   b. Height of cloud bases in hundreds of feet.
   c. Height of cloud tops in hundreds of feet. If unknown, UNKN is used
   d. (e.g. /SK SCT038-TOP080)- means a scattered layer exists at 3,800 feet MSL and the tops are at 8,000 feet MSL. (Remember this is a pilot report and pilots use their altimeter to measure height above sea level so all reported clouds heights are MSL.) (e.g. /SK BKN-OVC055-TOPUNKN - means a broken to overcast cloud base starts at 5,500 feet MSL and its tops are unknown.

8. /WX - **Weather:** Flight visibility (FV) reported first in METAR format, precipitation, restrictions to visibility, etc. Standard weather symbols are used and intensity reported same as in METAR (e.g. /WX FV02SM -RA HZ means that the flight visibility is 2 miles in light rain and haze).

9. /TA - **Air temperature in Celsius:** If below zero prefix with an "M" (e.g. /TA M08). Temperature shall also be reported if icing is reported.

10. /WV - **Wind:** Direction and speed in 6 digits. Wind direction less than 100 degrees is preceded by a zero. (e.g. /WV 27045KT - means the wind is from 270 degrees at 45 knots.)

11. /TB - **Turbulence:** Use standard contractions for intensity and type (use CAT - Clear Air Turbulence or CHOP when appropriate). Include altitude only if different from FL, (e.g. /TB LGT-MDT BLW 060 - means that the turbulence is light to moderate below 6,000 feet MSL. A report showing /TB EXTRM means extreme turbulence is reported at the altitude identified in position 5 above).

12. /IC - **Icing:** Describe using standard intensity and type contractions. Include altitude if different than FL (e.g. /IC LGT-MDT RIME).

13. /RM - **Remarks:** Use free form to clarify the report. /RM LRG FLOCK OF GOOSEY LOOKING BIRDS HDG GNLY NORTH OF AIRPORT MAY BE SEAGULLS, FORMATION LOUSY AND COURSE ERRATIC....

Fig. 45

Detailed Info on the Graphical Forecasts for Aviation (GFA)

The FAA stated that, as of October 2017, the once venerable Area Forecast will no longer be available for the continental United States (referred to as CONUS). In its place, the FAA is now offering the "Optimus Prime" of weather forecasting tools known as the *GFA* or *Graphical Forecast for Aviation,* as shown in Figure 47.

The purpose of the GFA is to give you a look at the weather across the continental United States from 14 hours into the past (in the form of observational data and warnings) up to 15 hours into the future (as forecasts).

See? I told you it was the Optimus Prime of weather tools. No doubt you won't be time traveling 14 hours into the past, but it's often valuable to see how the weather has evolved over time, which helps you evaluate your confidence level in the newest forecast weather. This is just one of the wonderful things about the Graphical Forecast for Aviation (GFA).

Perhaps the most unique thing about the GFA is that it allows the overlaying of AIRMETs, SIGMETs. and Convective SIGMETs (Figure 48, position A) onto the selected weather product. In the past, you'd have to compare the relevant AIRMETs and SIGMETs to the area forecast (no longer in use) to get an updated and accurate picture of forecast weather. The GFA makes this process a lot easier. You can also zoom in and out on any weather panel for the weather detail needed by using your mouse wheel to scroll.

The GFA's main panel provides two main selections for this tool: *Forecasts* and *Obs/Warn* (observations and warnings) in Figure 49, position A). Selecting the "Forecast" button reveals eight buttons directly above, which provide different forecasting panels (position B). Forecasts are provided for Ceilings and Visibility (CIG/VIS), Clouds, Precipita-tion and Weather (PCPN/WX), Thunderstorms (TS), Winds, Turbulence (TURB) and Ice. Once you've selected

The GFA (Graphical Forecast for Aviation) panel is accessible via the "Tools" drop down menu (Figure 47, position A).

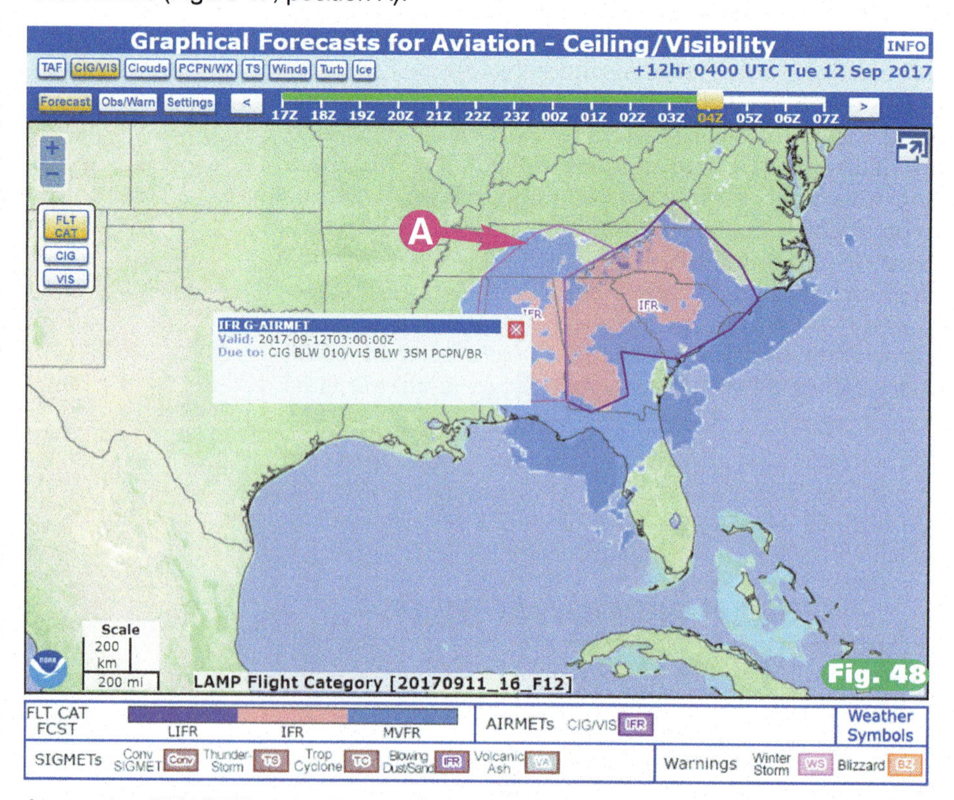

Appropriate SIGMETS and AIRMETS are overlaid on GFA panels (Figure 48, position A).

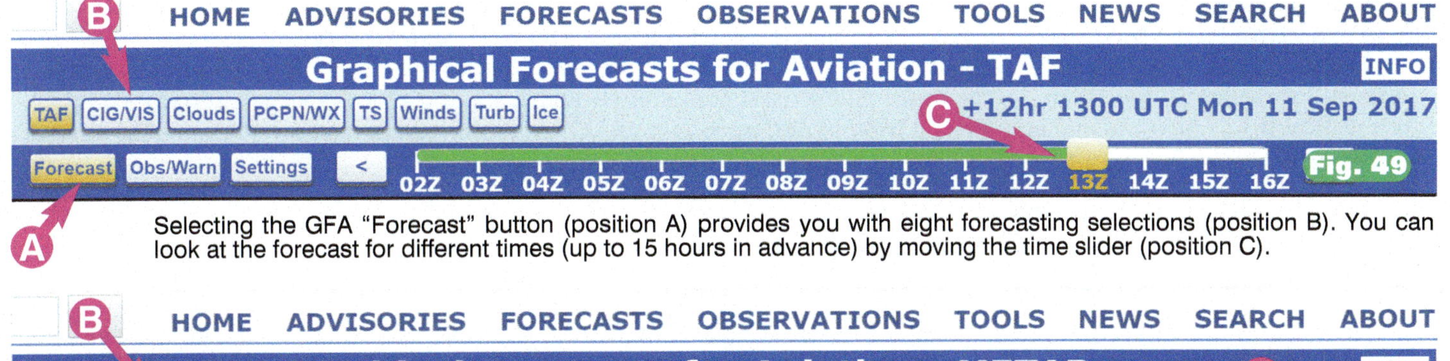

Selecting the GFA "Forecast" button (position A) provides you with eight forecasting selections (position B). You can look at the forecast for different times (up to 15 hours in advance) by moving the time slider (position C).

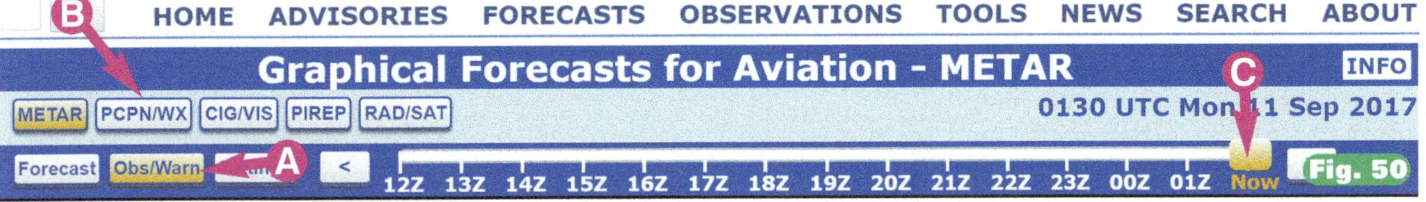

Selecting the GFA "Obs/Warn" button (position A) provides you with five weather observation selections (position B). You can look back in time up to 14 hours by moving the time slider (position C).

the appropriate button and the weather panel opens, you can scale in or out for the detail you need in making a weather assessment.

One of the very unique aspects of the GFA is the ability to look ahead 15 hours at the particular forecast panel chosen. This is done by using the time slider as shown in Figure 49C. When choosing the observation and warnings (Obs/Warn) button (Figure 50, position A), you are provided with five different weather observations (not forecasts), as shown in Figure 50, position B. The time slider (Figure 50, position C) allows you to look at the current weather as well as 14 hours into the past. We'll discuss all these items in detail shortly.

The TAF or Terminal Aerodrome Forecast Button

The first of these forecasting buttons is "TAF" for terminal aerodrome forecasts (Figure 51).

Each TAF reporting station has a station symbol that's color-coded (Figure 51, position A). This allows you to make an immediate weather assessment of that airport. If a station symbol is green, then VFR weather is forecast at that airport based on the time selected by the time slider. Wind barbs (Figure 51, position B) show the direction the wind blows and feathers on the arrows show wind strength. One feather is for 10 knots of wind and one-half feather represents five knots of wind. A red feather represents forecast gust values above the depicted wind speed.

If you'd like a textual forecast for a specific airport then click on the station model and the airport forecast will appear in textual form (Figure 51, position C). Please keep in mind that the graphical TAF provides a 15-hour graphical forecast while the textual TAF typically provides a

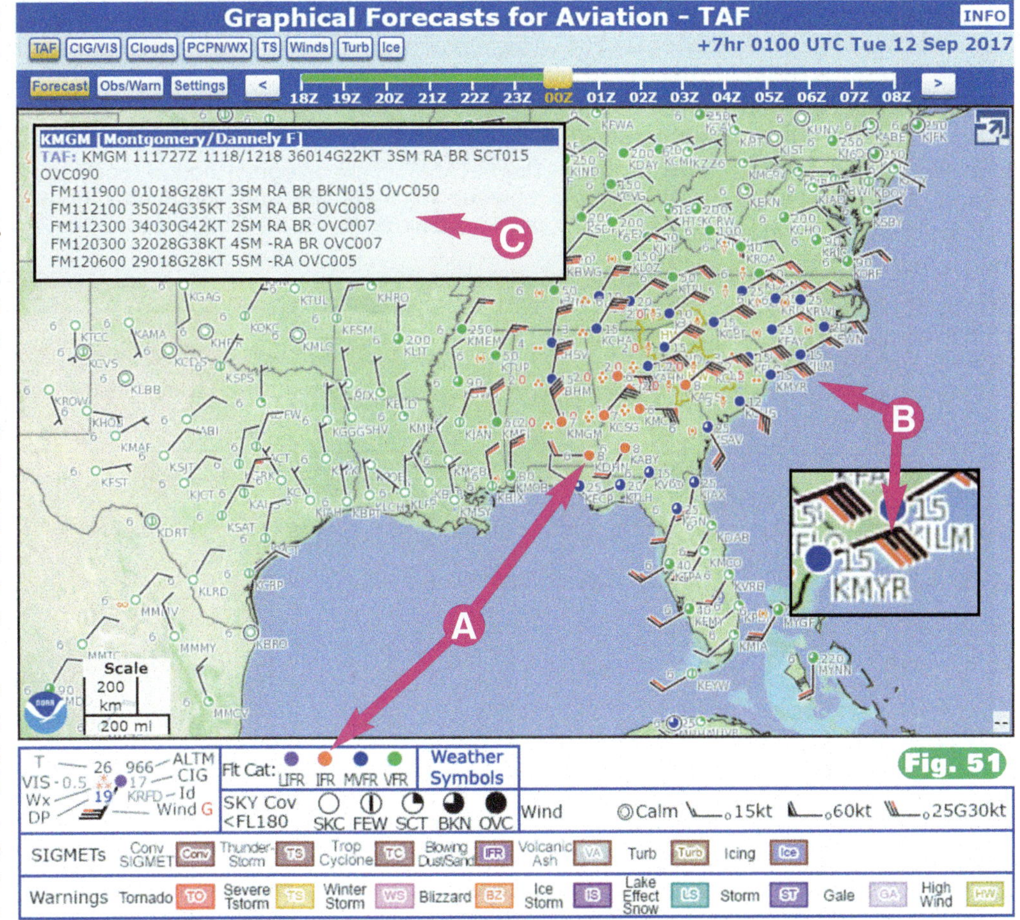

Forecast winds for position B are 25 knots with gusts to 40 knots (position B).

forecast for 24 hours in advance (or 30 hours at some airports). This is one reason why you might want to look carefully at the textual TAF by clicking on the station model. This provides you with an additional nine hours of forecast weather just in case this would be appropriate for your flight. Please don't miss the main concept of this being a "graphical" forecasting tool. For a long time, pilots have complained about having to convert their textual understanding of weather into a visual one. For all intents and purposes, the GFA allows you to easily visualize a 3D view of the atmosphere.

The Ceiling and Visibility Forecast Button

The CIG/VIS button (Figure 52, position A) provides a clouds and visibility forecast, which is easily interpreted by using the visibility color calibration scale at the bottom of the graphic (position B). You have three options to use with this panel by selecting either "FLT CAT" or flight category, "CIG" or ceilings, or "VIS" for visibility on the upper left side of this panel (position C). Flight category is color-coded for MVFR, IFR and LIFR. Areas with VFR ceilings are transparent (position D). Color-coded ceiling grids show ceilings up to 3,000 feet AGL and visibilities up to five statute miles.

AIRMET and SIGMET polygons that affect ceiling and/or visibility (volcanic ash, blowing dust/sand (IFR), convective, tropical cyclone, and international thunderstorm SIGMETs and AIRMET Sierra) are overlaid on this panel (position E). Borders can be clicked on to reveal that AIRMET's textual information. Select NWS (National Weather Service) hazards are also displayed.

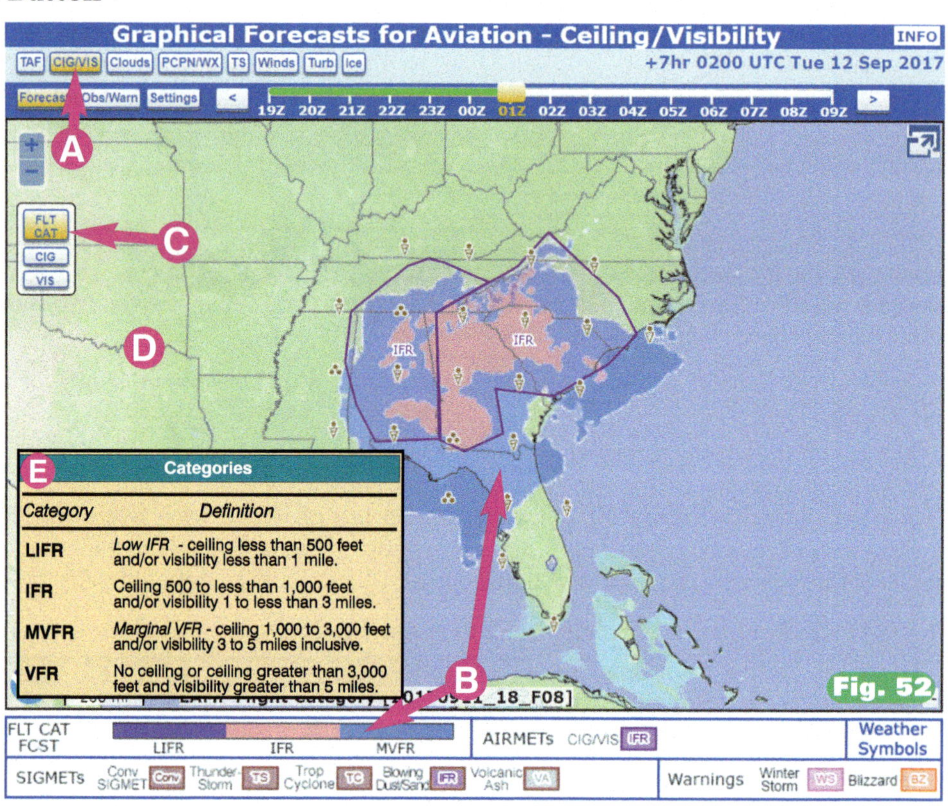

The FLT/CAT (flight category) button (position C) allows you to see color coded areas representing LIFR, IFR and MVFR conditions (position B). The insert in position E provides definitions that all pilots should know.

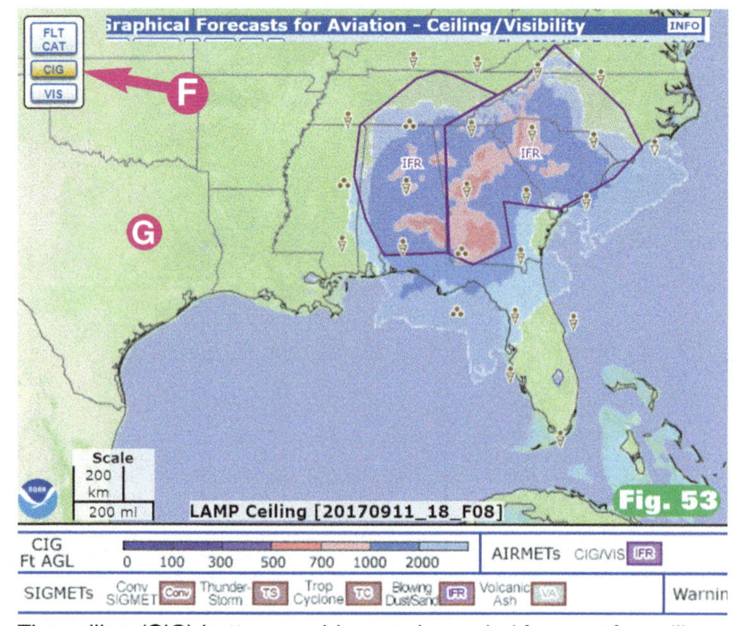

The ceiling (CIG) button provides a color coded forecast for ceilings (Figure 53, position F). Areas not covered by any of the colors in the ceiling-height legend bar are above 3,000 feet AGL (position G).

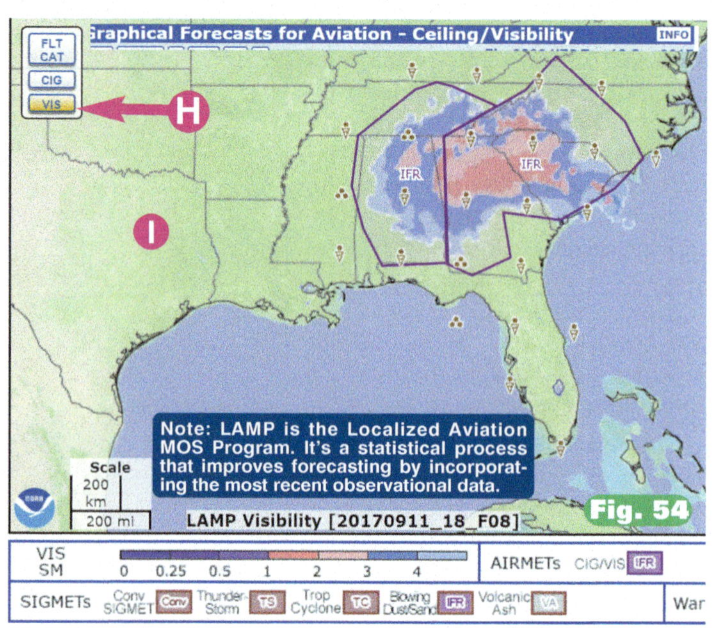

The visibility (VIS) button provides a color coded forecast for visibilities (Figure 54, position H), areas not covered by any legend bar colors have visibilities above five miles (position I).

The Clouds Forecast Button

The Cloud button (Figure 55, position A) allows you to evaluate cloud coverage fractions (i.e., few, scattered, broken, overcast) using the coverage color codes at the bottom of the panel (position B). Cloud tops and cloud bases can also be evaluated by using the three additional buttons to the left of the panel (position C). The density of the grid circles increases as you zoom in on the map (position D). Text data display layers and tops at each grid point. Cirrus (CI) above indicates cirrus type clouds present above FL180.

The GFA is the one tool that allows you to get a very good idea about the weather between reporting stations. After all, it's unlikely that "Bob's Airport" has a TAF specifically dedicated to it. With the GFA, you can get a feel for the weather at Bob's place (and, when the weather is good, you'll make sure you're out of town so as to avoid Bob's barbecue steaks, which are 5% meat, 95% lighter fluid). Keep in mind that the forecast time slider allows you to look through a 15-hour forecasting window. Frankly, weather reporting just doesn't get much better than this. Bases and tops are available by selecting the tab in the upper left corner of the display (position B). Keep in mind that all color-codes and text information provide cloud heights above mean sea level (MSL), not above ground level (AGL) in the clouds panel. Volcanic ash, convective, tropical cyclone, and international thunderstorm SIGMETs and AIRMETs for mountain obscuration are overlaid on the gridded display (position E).

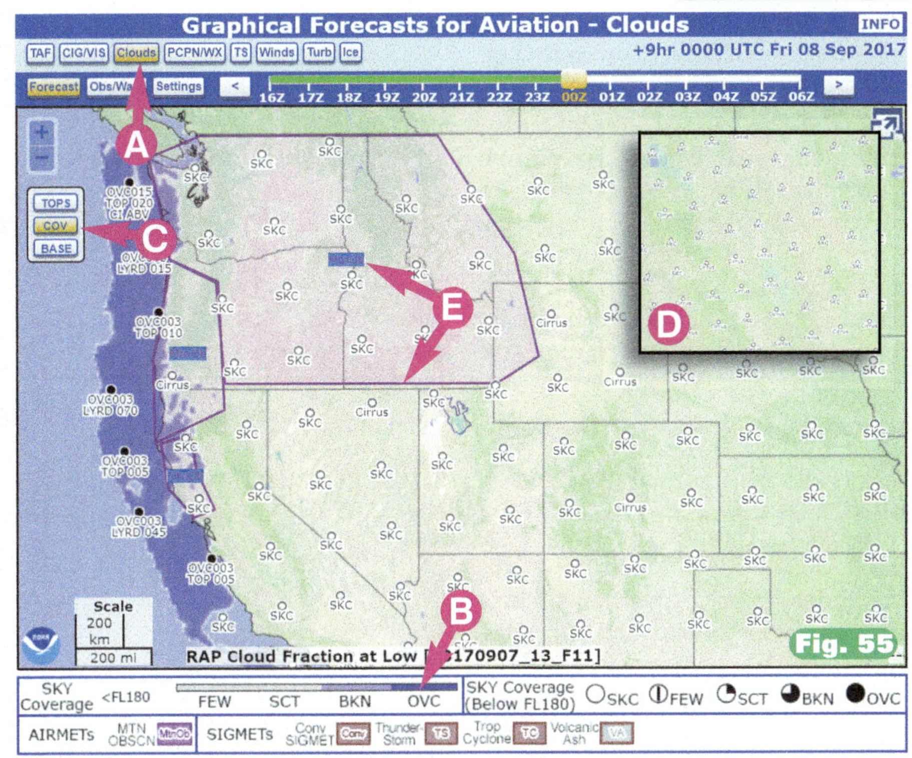

Selecting the Clouds button (position A) under "Forecasts" allows you to choose to view forecast cloud tops, cloud coverage or cloud bases (position C), calibrated according to the color codes shown at the bottom of the chart (position B).

The Precipitation/Weather Forecast Button

The Precipitation/Weather (PCPN/WX) button (Figure 56, position A) forecasts either a chance (25% to less than 55%) of precipitation or that precipitation is likely (55% or higher) as shown in position B. Color codes identify both the type and probability of precipitation. Weather symbols are overlaid on the panel grid. Convective, tropical cyclone, international thunderstorm, and volcanic ash SIGMET polygons are automatically displayed. NWS hazards associated with precipitation including, tornadoes, severe thunderstorms, winter storms, winter weather, ice storms, freezing rain, and lake effect snow are displayed.

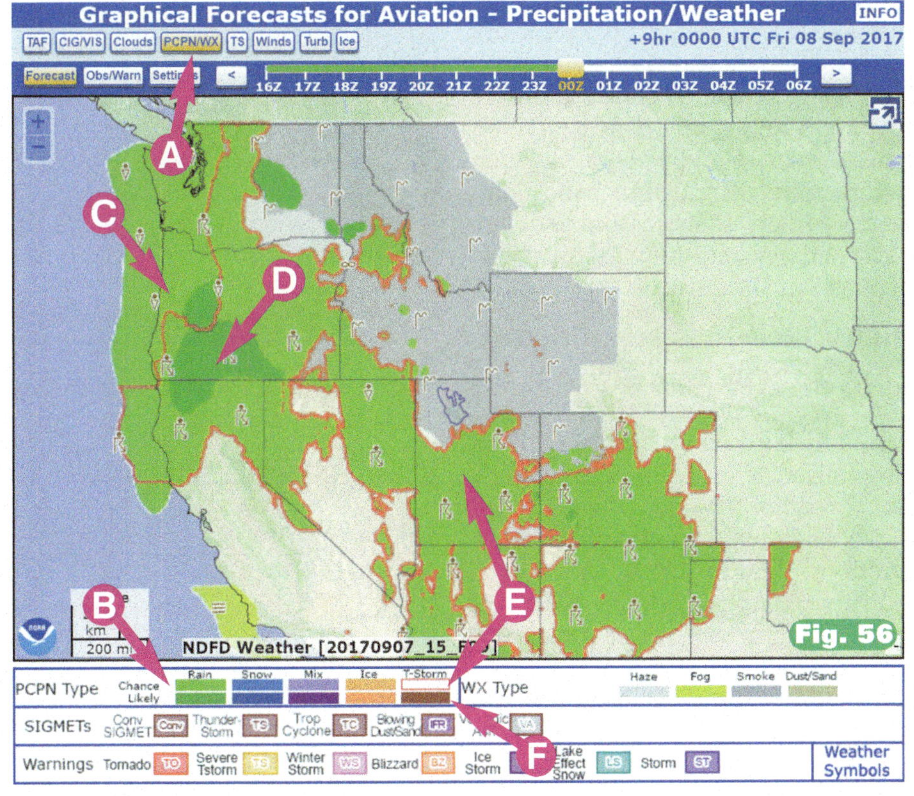

Light green areas indicate that at 00Z (the selected "slider" forecast time), there is a 25% to less than 55% chance of rain on the Oregon coast (position C). Inland, in the dark green area (position D), that probability increases to a 55% or greater chance of rain. All areas surrounded by the red line (position E) indicate that a chance of thunderstorms exist in that area (25% to less than 55%). All areas surrounded by dark red hatching on this panel (none shown) indicate that thunderstorms are likely (55% and above) in the depicted area (position F).

The Thunderstorm Forecast Button

Thunderstorm forecasts (TS) identify three types of coverage (isolated, scattered, or numerous) as color bands along with overlaid type/intensity symbols (Figure 57, position A). Convective, Tropical Cyclone, and International Thunderstorm SIGMET polygons are displayed when active. Only Severe Thunderstorm and Tornado NWS warnings are included (position B).

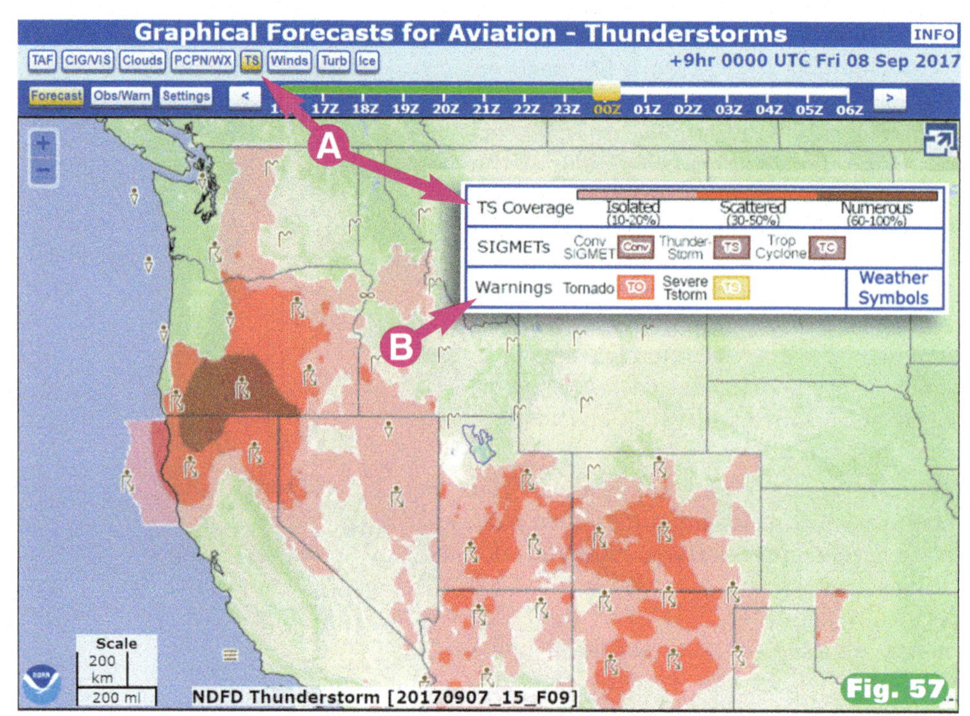

For any VFR or instrument rated pilot the GFA thunderstorm panel is an essential stop during flight planning. What makes this panel so valuable is your ability to obtain a macro perspective on the potential for thunderstorms to affect your cross country flight.

The Winds Forecast Button

Forecast winds (Figure 58, position A) are provided in 3,000-foot increments from the surface to FL300 (30,000 feet). Moving the altitude slider to SFC (position B) provides winds as the surface and moving it to MAX (position C) shows the maximum wind values for all levels.

Color-coded values provide wind speeds and wind barbs showing both wind speeds and directions (position D). Convective, tropical cyclone, and international thunderstorm SIGMET and AIRMET Tango polygons for low-level wind shear and strong surface winds are overlaid on the graphic when appropriate. CNWS wind advisories and warnings, which include gale, wind, high wind, lake wind, winter storm, blizzard, ice storm, storm, and blowing dust are displayed at the surface.

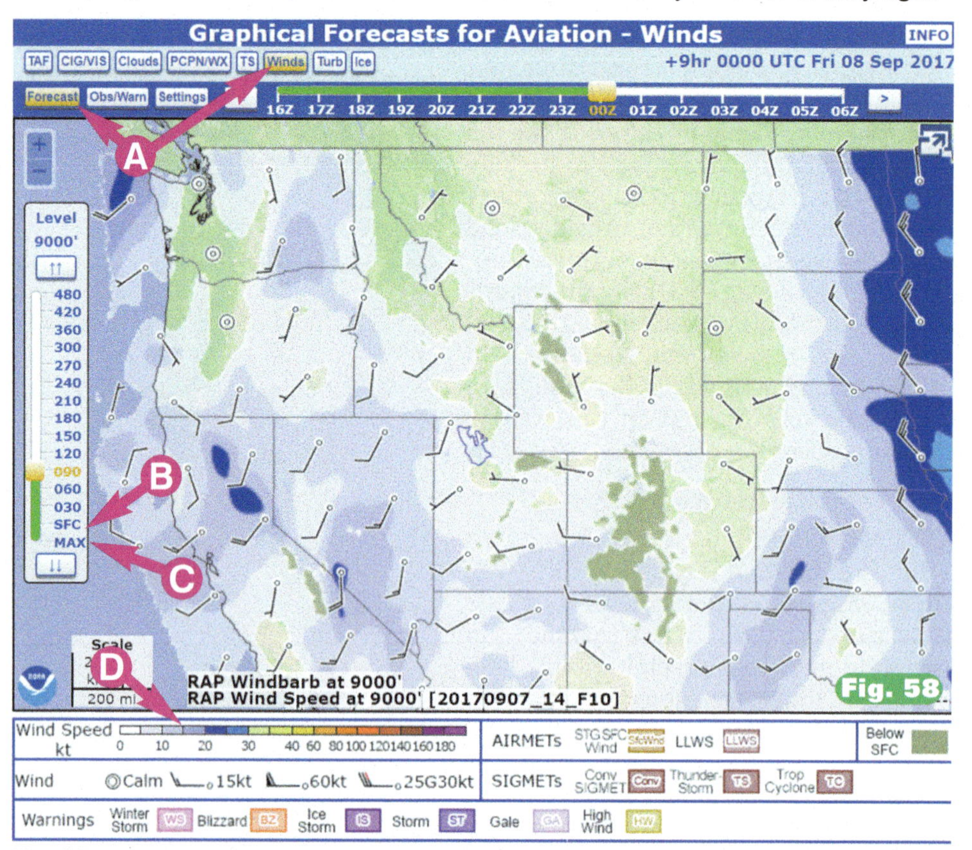

The GFA Wind panel helps you quickly evaluate the best altitude for your cross country flight. Slide the slider for a 3D evaluation of the atmosphere. A valuable aspect of this panel is your ability to estimate the strength of winds over mountain peaks, thus allowing you to more accurately plan crossing (or avoiding) those peaks at a safe altitude.

The Turbulence Forecast Button

Forecast turbulence offered by the GFA (Figure 59) is expressed in terms of something known as the EDR or Eddy Dissipation Rate. They didn't use "Fred" or "Wanda" because the word "eddy" represents circulation motion in fluid or air. In short (or if you're wearing pants), the EDR is a measure of turbulence based on the rate at which the atmosphere dissipates energy. In other words, if the atmosphere dissipates its kinetic energy quickly then that dissipation is more likely to disturb the air. High EDRs mean high energy level dissipation, thus high levels of turbulence.

It turns out that EDRs reflect what the atmosphere does and not necessarily how your airplane responds to them. Therefore, a color code at the bottom of the chart (position B) allows you to convert EDR values into recognizable turbulence levels based on the weight of your airplane (position C). Light (LGT) and moderate (MOD) turbulence are the two

you are most likely to have to deal with (even moderate turbulence is certainly no fun). A light aircraft is one that weighs less than 15,500 pounds. I think that means you, unless you're bringing your flight bag with you again. You definitely want to avoid severe (SEV) turbulence to say nothing about extreme (E) turbulence. AIRMET Tango is displayed for turbulence only. It does not include AIRMET Tango for surface winds or low-level wind shear. Turbulence, convective, tropical cyclone, and international thunderstorm SIGMETs are also overlaid. You can select flight levels in 3,000 foot increments when looking at forecast turbulence.

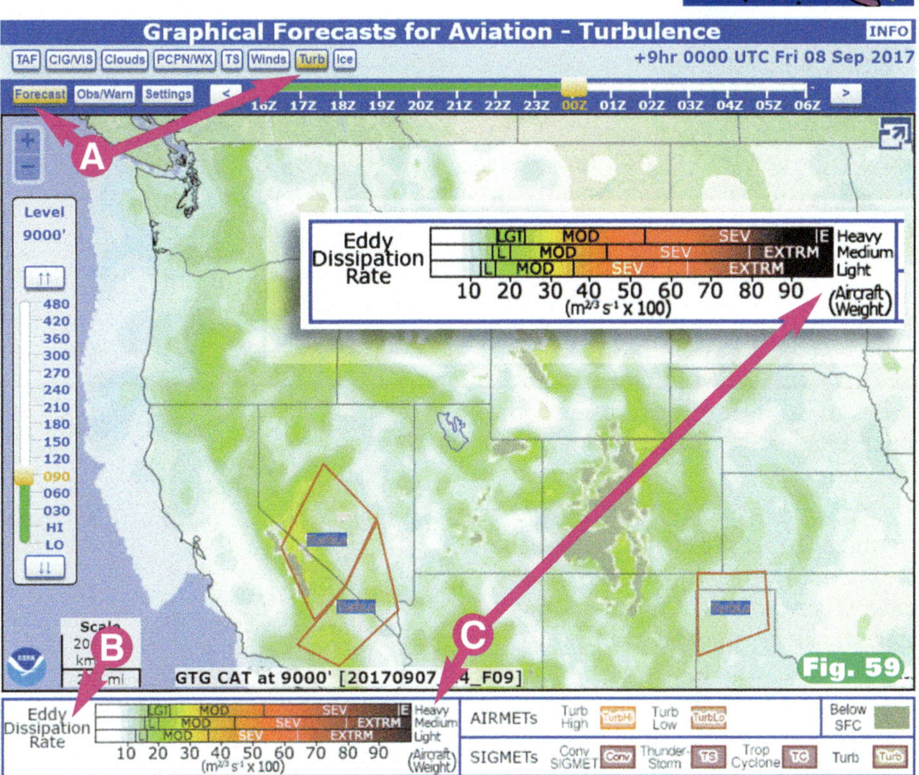

The GFA Turbulence panel calculates turbulence in terms of the EDR or Eddy Dissipation Rate. What matters here is that you can convert the EDR color codes (position B) into the traditional values for evaluating forecast turbulence based on the weight of your aircraft (heavy, medium and light) as shown by the scaled in position B.

The Icing Forecast Button

The forecast icing panel (Figure 60, position A) offers a three-dimensional, color-coded icing severity depiction for various altitudes. Yippie! Finally, another valuable and useful means of portraying the potential for ice during flight (as a VFR pilot you'll be concerned about freezing rain, but not inflight icing, as you won't be flying in the clouds). The icing severity diagnoses areas of expected trace, light, moderate, and heavy icing (position B) at 3,000-foot intervals up to FL300 (position C). Two-dimensional AIRMET Zulu and Icing, convective, tropical cyclone and international thunderstorm SIGMET polygons are overlaid on the graphic valid at the selected level (position D). You may also choose "MAX" to display the maximum icing severity for a location regardless of altitude and all AIRMET Zulu and SIGMET polygons. When "SFC" is selected (position E), the FIP is replaced by a grid showing winter precipitation type and likelihood. Weather symbols denoting the winter precipitation type and intensity are overlaid on the graphic along with the NWS winter storm, blizzard, freezing rain, lake effect snow, winter weather, and freezing fog polygons.

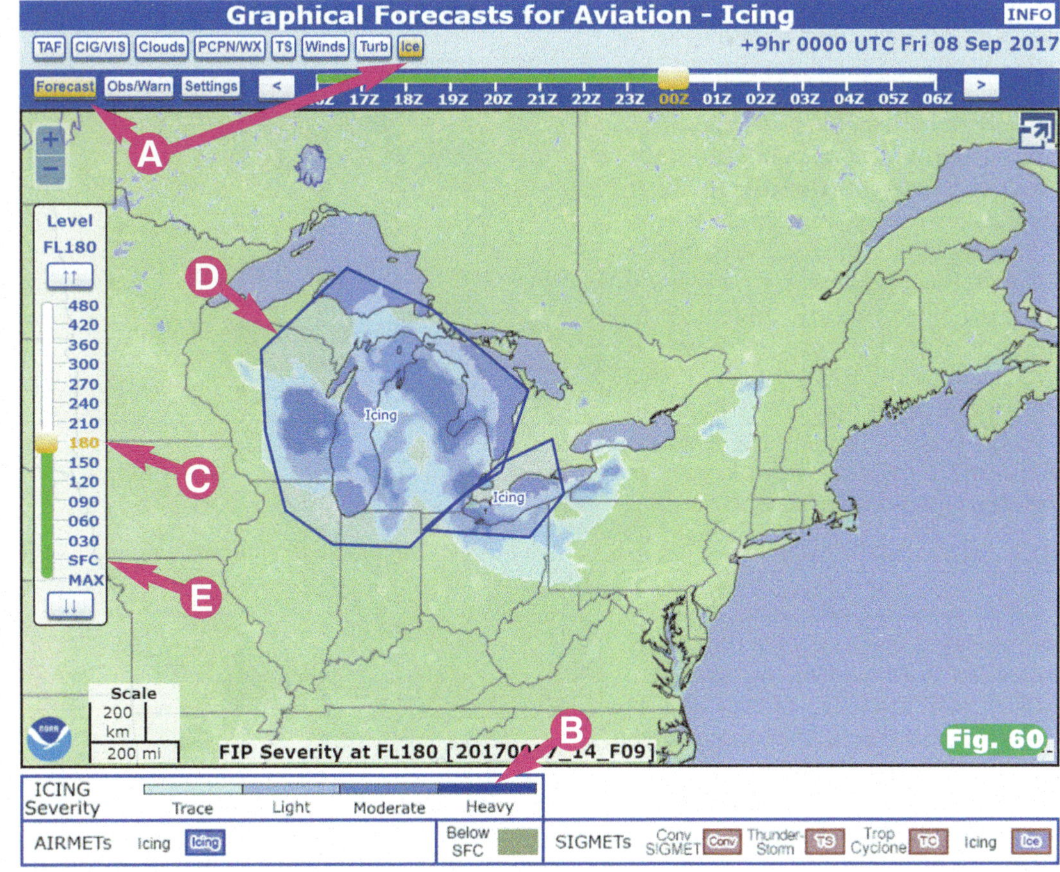

The GFA icing panel is a wonderful tool for providing you with a macro view of the icing potential for your chosen route on a cross country trip.

Observations and Warnings

When you click the Observation and Warnings (Obs/Warn) button on the GFA (Figure 61, position A), you are no longer looking at forecasts. Instead, you're looking at current weather with the ability to move the time slider (position B) and see 14 hours into the past with respect to this weather. Overlaid on all selections of these panels is an infrared satellite image (position C) and a radar loop of the most recent five radar images up to the selected hour (position D).

Aside from providing you with a graphical observation of the weather as it exists now, the ability to look back at the weather from the macro "big picture" perspective is a tool pilots have wanted for a long time (Figure 62, position A). Why? It's all a matter of confidence building.

Suppose you are planning a VFR flight to an airport that presently has IFR conditions. The forecast suggests that the weather should produce VFR conditions at your ETA. However, by looking several hours in the past, you see no rapid improvement toward VFR conditions at your destination airport. In this instance, you might be less likely to depart at your scheduled time. On the other hand, suppose the weather at your destination tended toward VFR conditions quicker than indicated by an earlier forecast. Here is where you'd feel a lot more confident about actually finding VFR conditions when arriving at your destination. There are several ways to use 14 hours of weather history and this is just one of them. Now, let's look at the Obs/Warn panel selections in detail.

METAR

Cloud coverage and flight category are indicated by the colored dots surrounding the observation stations. Using the station model guide (Figure 62, position B) you can identify the weather at the airport during the time the observation was taken.

All METARs, SIGMETs, and National Weather Service (NWS) warnings that impact aviation are

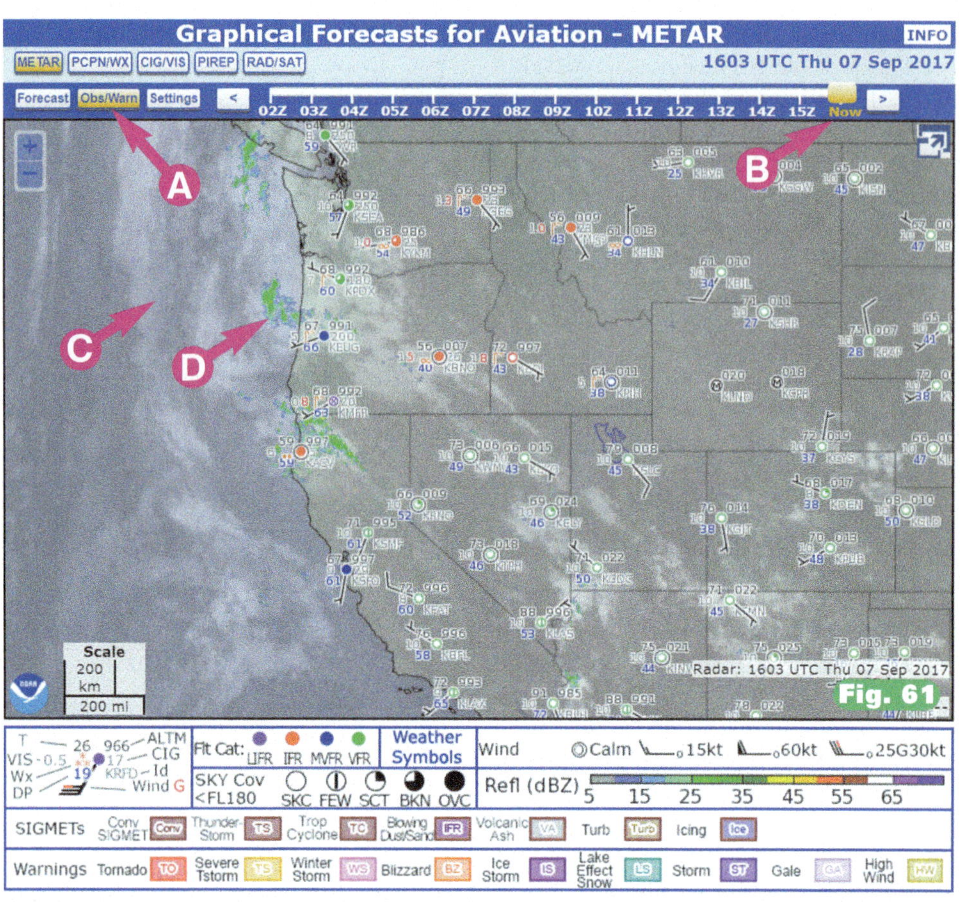

The GFA METAR panel provides the current weather as a station model or text description.

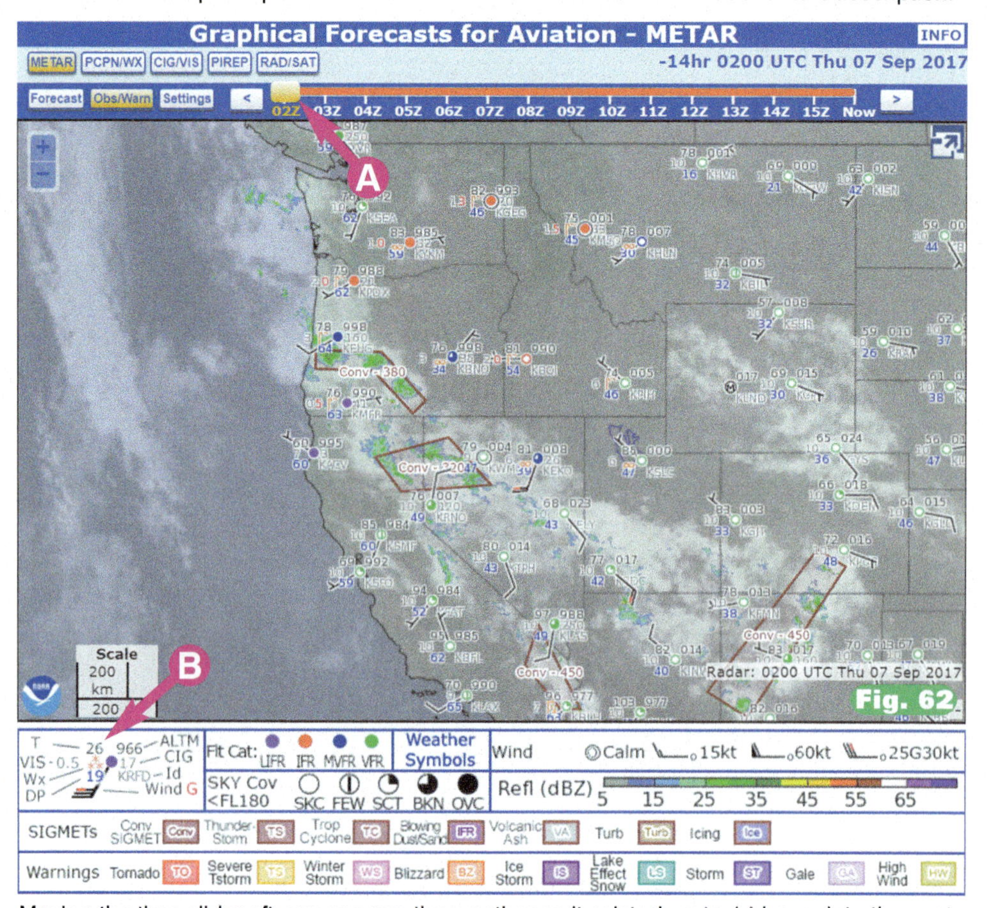

Moving the time slider aft you can see the weather as it existed up to 14 hours into the past.

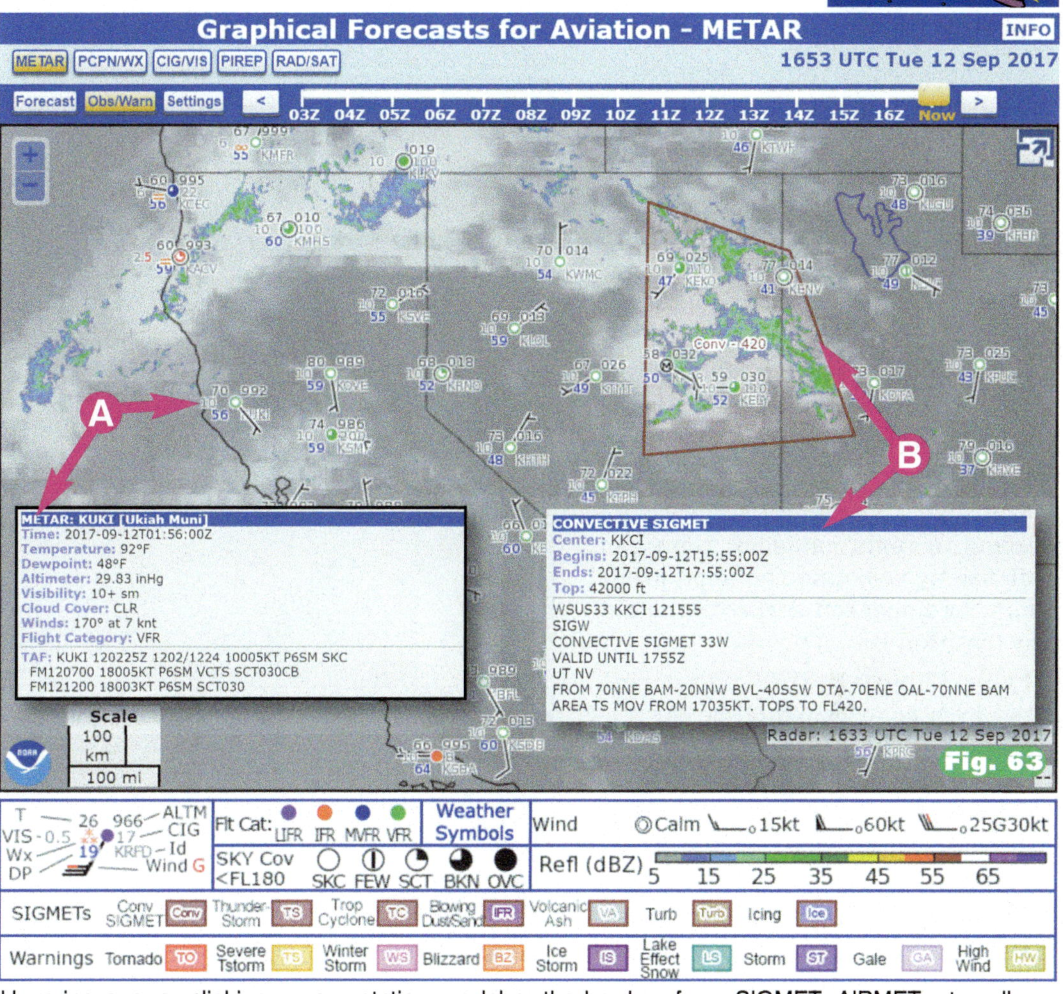

Hovering over or clicking on any station model or the border of any SIGMET, AIRMET, etc., allows you to read a textual description of the observed weather or the specific warning information.

plotted. By clicking (or hovering) any station plot, you can view the METAR in textual form as well as obtain the TAF for that airport (Figure 63, position A). You can also hover or click the border of any warning and obtain additional information about the warning (position B).

Precipitation / Weather (PCPN/WX)

Convective, tropical cyclone and thunderstorm SIGMET polygons (Figure 64, position A) are automatically displayed over the satellite image (position B) and radar loop (position C). Clicking any of the weather symbols shown on this panel provides METAR information from the reporting station nearest the symbol. Hazards associated with precipitation including, tornadoes, severe thunderstorms, winter weather, winter storms, ice storms, freezing rain, and lake effect snow are displayed.

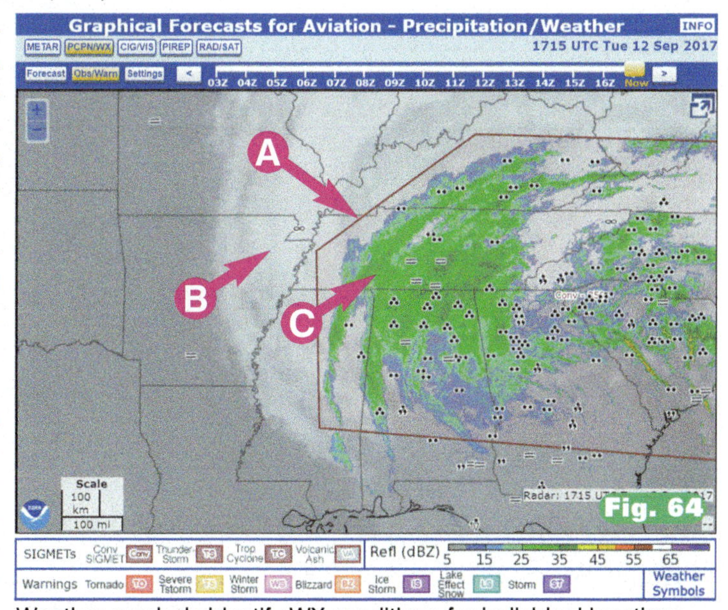

Weather symbols identify WX conditions for individual locations.

The Good, The Bad & The Ugly

OK, there is no ugly, but there is good and bad. So what's the good and the bad of the GFA? First, the old *area forecast* had a human element involved in its development. Here is where the experience of a forecaster can make the difference between an accurate and no-quite-as-accurate forecast. Where this directly applies is in the GFA's Ceiling/Visibility and Clouds weather panels. These two products are generated by computer with little or no human modification based on the experience of a forecaster. In other words, HAL 2000 is predicting ceiling, visibility and clouds over specific areas that do not offer METAR or forecast reports. That means some supercomputer using complex programs described by names such as Model Output Statistics (MOS) take the nearest airports having METAR data and interpolate this information, then correct it for variable topography and estimate the clouds, ceilings and visibilities for that area or specific point. Since the GFA Clouds, CIG/VIS panels are the only means you have of identifying forecast weather between reporting stations, you should use it. And it is getting better all the time. NOAA uses something known as the Rapid Refresh Model (RAP) which takes information from airliners, weather balloons, radar, reporting stations and satellites and incorporates all of this data into its forecast. At present, this information is accurate to a 13 kilometer grid resolution and to altitudes a little above 80,000 feet. The model refreshes itself (no, not with a spritzer, either) every hour and provides an 18-hour forecast (the promise is for 3 kilometer resolution updated hourly.)

Ceiling & Visibility (CIG/VIS)

An infrared satellite image and radar loop is displayed for the selected time. AIRMETs and SIGMETS that affect ceiling and/or visibility (volcanic ash, blowing dust/sand (IFR), convective, tropical cyclone, and thunderstorm SIGMETs and AIRMET Sierra) are overlaid on the graphic (Figure 65, position A).

Select NWS hazards are also displayed, which include winter storm, blizzard, blowing bust, and marine dense fog.

You may also select to view data relating to flight category, ceiling or visibility by selecting the appropriate tab in the upper left corner of the display (position B).

Flight Category (FLT/CAT) is indicated by a color-coded circle for stations with MVFR, IFR, and LIFR conditions (position C). Areas with VFR are not shown.

Ceiling (position D) and visibility (position E) are indicated by a numerical value over each METAR station. The ceiling is in units of feet/100 and visibility is in statute miles. The full text of the METAR can be obtained by clicking on or hovering over the number.

Pilot Reports (PIREP)

PIREPs are overlaid on infrared satellite imagery and a radar loop valid for the time selected (Figure 66, position A). You can choose to display all PIREPs by moving the slider to "All" (position B). Or, you can choose to see PIREPs that are valid within 3,000 feet of a particular flight level, chosen with the vertical slider (position C).

Coded and decoded PIREP text information is available by clicking on the individual report or by using the hover function (position D). All valid SIGMET polygons will also be displayed.

Radar & Satellite (RAD/SAT)

Infrared satellite imagery and a radar loop are displayed. All AWC SIGMET and NWS Hazard polygons are overlaid on the imagery.

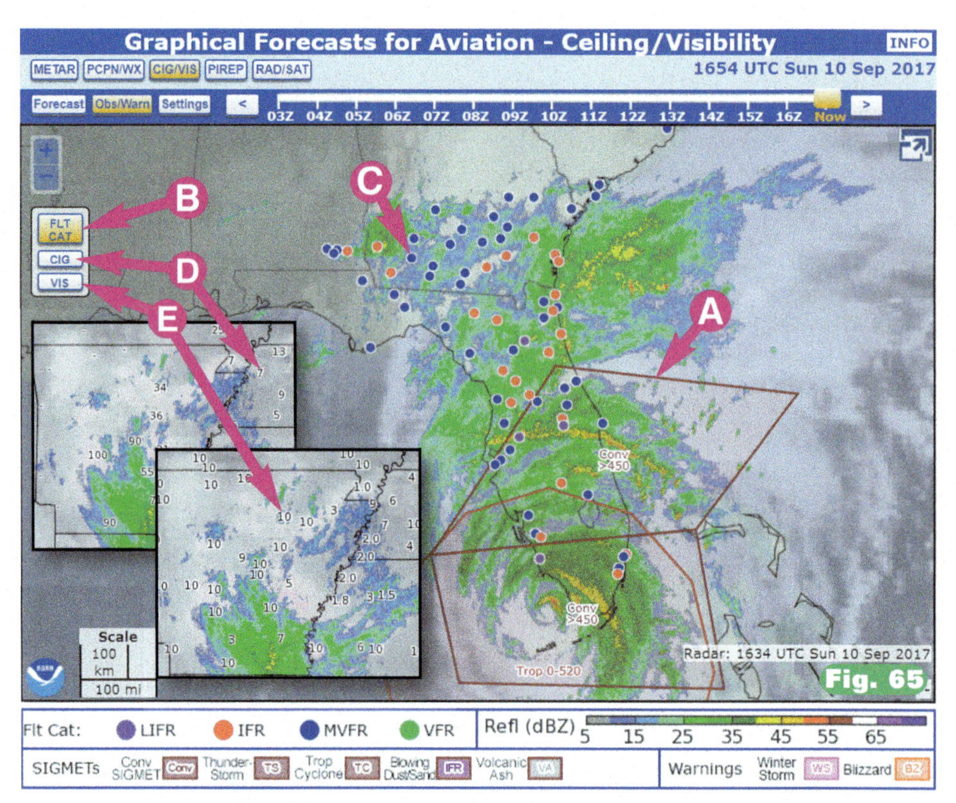

The Ceiling and Visibility observation panel provides you with an immediate assessment of weather conditions when the "FLT CAT" button (position B) is chosen. Using the station model color codes, you can tell if an airport is VFR, IFR, MVFR or LIFR when this observation was taken. You can also look 14 hours into the past to see how the weather has changed. By clicking the "CIG" button (position D) any ceilings will be shown in hundreds of feet. The "VIS" button (position E) provides visibilities in statute miles.

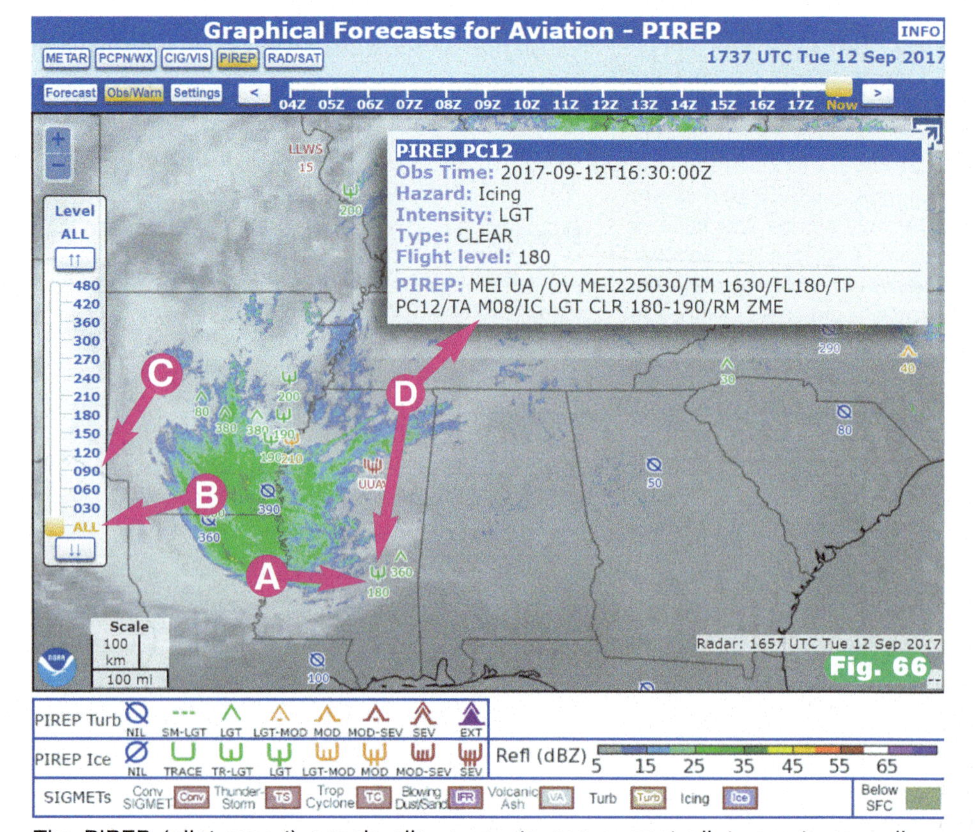

The PIREP (pilot report) panels allows you to see current pilot reports as well as those issued within the past 14 hours by using the time slider above.

Putting It All Together

The secret to successful flight planning is in anticipating the weather's behavior. Comparing one chart or forecast to another greatly enhances this understanding. Here's one way of making these comparisons (there are other ways, too!)

Surface Analysis and ADDS Ceiling and Visibility Chart – Looking at the surface weather map tells you where the fronts and pressure systems are. Comparing this with the ceiling and visibility chart provides you with a picture of what effects these fronts and pressure centers are having on surface weather. Figure 67 shows a typical comparison. (Note: ADDS is the *Aviation Digital Data Service* and it's part of the Aviation Weather Center found at the AFSS.)

Ceiling & Visibility Chart and NEXRAD Chart – With this comparison, shown in Figure 68, you get an idea of the convective activity associated with areas of IFR, MVFR and VFR conditions. If an area of MVFR conditions is associated with large, fast moving echoes (meaning thunderstorms), you might want to reconsider planning a flight in this direction. Thunderstorms mean turbulence and rain showers. Couple this with ceilings of 1,000 to 3,000 feet and visibilities of 3 to 5 miles, and you might be pushing your VFR flying luck. Keep in mind that radar imagery can change quickly so make sure you preflight using the most current radar chart.

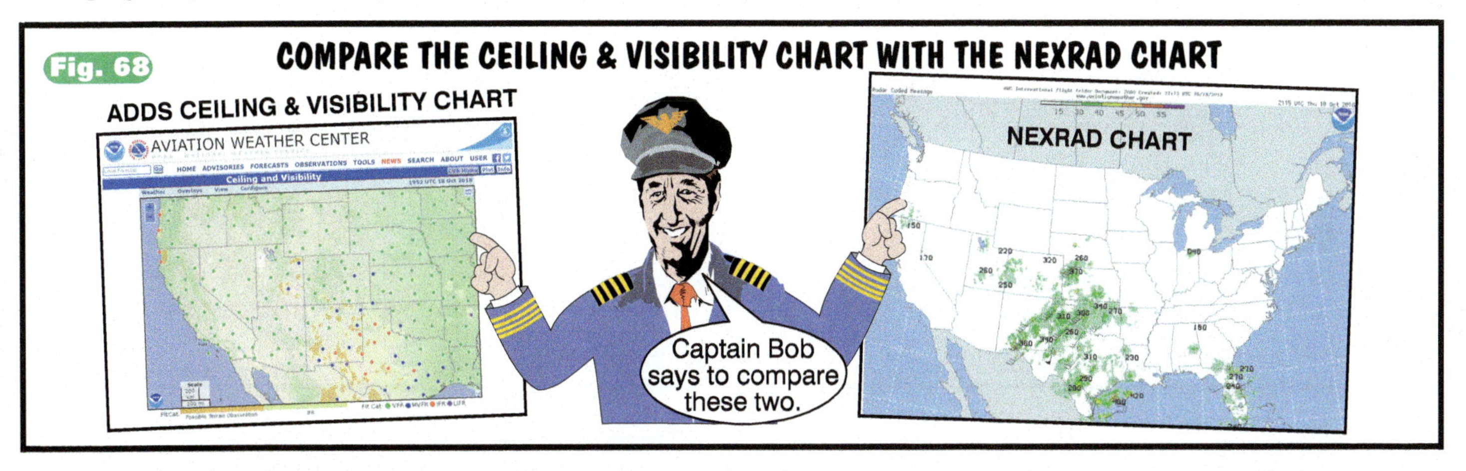

Surface Analysis Chart and Prog Charts – Since the surface analysis chart shows the present location of fronts and pressure systems, you can see which way these systems will move by comparing them against the surface prog chart, as shown in Figure 69. You'll also get an idea about what kind of weather (IFR? MVFR? VFR?) will develop along the front by referring to the prog chart.

METARs and Surface Analysis – Compare individual METARs with the surface weather map, as shown in Figure 70. This provides you with an understanding of surface weather around and between your departure and destination airports. If the surface weather map's reporting stations are all darkened-in along your route, this means you might be flying above a layer of clouds even though the destination airport is reporting clear conditions. Look at the isobars and, using your knowledge about clockwise and counterclockwise airflow around highs and lows, decide on a route that increases the likelihood of a tailwind. Remember, the surface weather map information can be up to three hours old.

Finally, examine the winds aloft forecast for temperatures and the selection of a favorable cruising altitude. Then examine the convective SIGMETs for thunderstorms, SIGMETs for any severe conditions and any AIRMETs for IFR conditions, turbulence or pertinent icing conditions, as shown in Figure 71.

Sunny Side Up

A pilot's skill at handling weather is based on his or her weather sense. In other words, pilots must continually educate themselves about how weather works. Unfortunately, some pilots don't do this. I have a friend who is so weather insensitive he probably couldn't even tell you when it's sunny or rainy. This presents a special problem for him, since he is always forgetting where he left his sunglasses. It's not unusual for him to leave his glasses parked on top his head. One of these days he's going to have 3 or 4 pair up there, walk out into the sun, and start a little fire on his toupee.

Make it a point to check the weather every day, even if you're not flying. Call the FSS, look at the newspaper weather chart, check your personal computer or mobile computing device, or get up off your couch, walk outside and compare what you see in the sky with what happened yesterday. This is how pilots develop a weather sense. It's a sense that allows you to experience many decades of safe flying as indicated by our good friend Captain Bob.

Chapter Fourteen

Flight Planning

Getting There From Here

Despite the navigational ease of certain cross country trips, some pilots still manage to get lost. There are two major islands off the coast of Southern California, Santa Catalina and San Clemente. San Clemente is approximately 57 miles off the coast and Catalina lies about half that distance.

Catalina is a popular fly-in spot for many pilots. San Clemente is a naval base not open to the public. Somehow, about twice a year, a pilot manages to land at San Clemente after mistaking it for Catalina. You might think the pilot would know something was wrong when it takes twice as long as expected to get to Catalina and the runway doesn't have the same numbers. Such details aside, some pilots manage the feat, often while in contact with the Unicom operator on Catalina Island (Catalina is a non-tower airport). The conversation usually goes something like this:

Pilot: "Catalina traffic, this is 2132B, I'm on final to land."

Unicom: "32B, I don't see you, but there's no reported traffic for Runway 24."

Pilot: "Catalina Unicom, this is 32B, a jet just strafed me."

Unicom: "32B, there are no jets in the pattern."

Pilot: "Then someone's flying one heck of a model airplane out here. I'm going to have to talk to somebody about that. It's dangerous."

Unicom: "32B, I don't see anyone flying model airplanes at Catalina."

Pilot: "Well, I just touched down and I bet it belongs to those two kids in Boy Scout uniforms walking over to my airplane with . . .uh, those guns. . .uh oh."

Mistakes happen. Contrary to popular lore, the military doesn't make you enlist for four years. They're pretty nice about it. Often they just talk with the errant pilot, show him all their guns and ammo, then suggest he might want to reread the chapter on flight planning to avoid making the same mistake again.

To avoid having such a misadventure, or worse, let's invest a little time in acquiring some flight planning knowledge.

What is Flight Planning?

Sometimes students get very involved with the details of flight planning. Up to their elbows in calculators and scratch paper, they often lose track of the reason they're crunching numbers. There's a lot more to flight planning than just plotting a course.

The Original Global Positioning System

The original Global Positioning System (GPS) is nothing like its modern day counterpart. It didn't work too well as a navigational device. It did, however, help pilots fly coordinated by conking them in the head during slips in a left turn and skids in a right turn.

Flight planning is information management. Your job is to assemble, interpret, and put to use *all* the information needed to safely make a flight from Point A to Point B.

Here are just *some* of the reasons you flight plan:

- To know how to navigate from departure to destination
- To know if the weather presents any problems
- To know whether there is *any* condition (weather, equipment, runway availability) so adverse that you shouldn't go
- To make certain there is sufficient fuel on board, with an adequate safety margin, to reach your destination given the wind and other conditions enroute
- To enable you to file a flight plan, so that someone will begin looking for you if you don't reach your destination within a reasonable period
- To determine if you, as pilot-in-command, and the equipment (airplane and accessories) meet all the demands of a particular flight
- To identify any areas enroute or at your departure or destination that require special consideration (mountains), preparation (short fields), or equipment (engine preheat in extreme cold, for example)
- To find out if the airplane can safely carry the load of people and fuel you're planning on taking, and whether the weight can be loaded in such a way as to meet certain limitations (more on weight-and-balance a bit later)
- To know whether adequate fueling facilities will be available enroute and/or at your destination
- To calculate how long the flight will take, and to determine whether you, your passengers, or your airplane will need one or more stops enroute and if so, where those will be
- To determine whether the flight can be safely and successfully completed under conditions for which you are licensed and current. If you are not current for carrying passengers at night, will you arrive at your destination before dark, with enough of a time margin to allow for unexpected headwinds? If you don't have an IFR rating, will the flight definitely be in VFR conditions? If conditions are marginal, are you comfortable and capable of handling the airplane in such circumstances?

Properly done, flight planning is like buying an insurance policy for you and your passengers. Done poorly, or not done at all, it exposes everyone involved to unnecessary risks.

Flight planning is not an enormously complex task. It's really just information gathering and some calculation. In fact, planning a flight is often a favorite task of pilots, who get to "fly" the flight once on paper and again in the air. Properly done, flight planning is like buying an insurance policy for you and your passengers. Done poorly, or not done at all, it exposes everyone involved to unnecessary risks.

Measuring Direction

Once upon a time, sailors set out with nothing more than the sun, stars, and their senses to guide them. Today, you're in a more fortunate position. As a pilot, you have a wide variety of means for determining where you are and where you're going.

Everything is somewhere. Keep that in mind next time you're lost. The challenge is in finding out where what you want *is*. Airports are in a fixed location (even in California, despite all the earthquakes). We describe the location of airports (and other things we want to find) by their position on an invisible grid of lines called *latitude* and *longitude,* as shown in Figure 1A. These lines are not actually painted on the earth, of course, but they are drawn on all navigational charts used by pilots. Lines of longitude run from the true north pole to the true south pole as shown in Figure 1B. Think of *longitude* as something running the

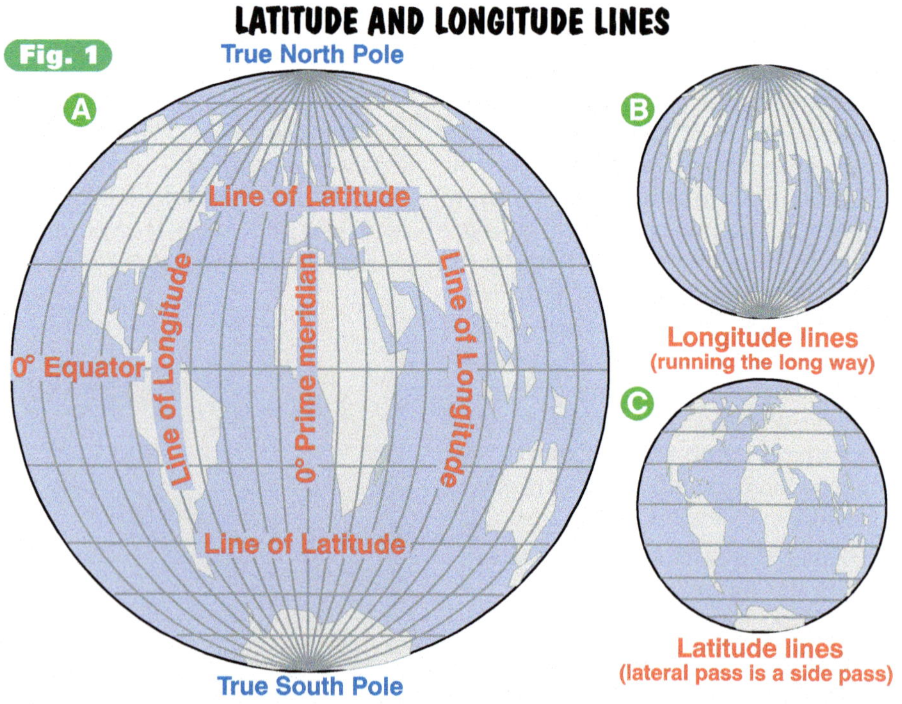

LATITUDE AND LONGITUDE LINES

Fig. 1

True North Pole
A
Line of Latitude
0° Equator
Line of Longitude
0° Prime meridian
Line of Longitude
Line of Latitude
True South Pole
B
Longitude lines
(running the long way)
C
Latitude lines
(lateral pass is a side pass)

Lines of longitude run vertically, from the true north pole to the true south pole. Lines of latitude run horizontally around the globe. By knowing the latitude and longitude coordinates, you can pinpoint any place on earth with great precision. The 0 degree line of longitude, also called the *prime meridian,* runs through the center of Greenwich, England and the 0 degree line of latitude starts at the equator.

long distance from the top to the bottom of the earth. Longitude lines are also known as *meridians*.

Lines of latitude run sideways, like a sideways pass in football—a lateral pass. Lines of latitude are perpendicular to lines of longitude, as shown in Figure 1C. They run in an easterly and westerly direction around the earth and are longest around the equator.

Spaced one degree apart, 360 lines of longitude drop from the north to the south pole, striping the globe. The longitude line running directly through Greenwich, England is known as the *prime meridian* (the 0 degree longitude line). By convention, we start counting lines of longitude east and west from this point, as shown in Figure 2. To the left (west) of the prime meridian are 180 lines of longitude (including the prime meridian). To the right or east of the prime meridian are another 180 lines of longitude (also including the prime meridian)—360 in all. Longitude is stated as being a certain number of degrees *east* or *west* of the prime meridian.

LET'S MAKE A DEAL

Yes, sometimes controllers can talk too fast. In some instances, we are using equipment older than most of today's work force, and it engages a lot slower than our brains. It's hard—very hard—to wait after we key the mike before we speak. With today's hub system there are times when "non-stop" talking isn't enough to keep up.

I'm reminded of the "I Love Lucy" show where Lucy is working in the candy factory. As soon as she "learns" her job the conveyor belt speeds up faster and faster. Well, I can't stuff aircraft in my pockets, or down my shirt, as Lucy did the candy (much less eat them).

Enough can't be said in favor of good radio discipline. It's the only real tool we have to make this system work. So you folks in the air use your full call sign, make sure you hear your call sign, and I'll do my best to make sure that I'm heard and understood.

ASRS Report

MEASURING LATITUDE AND LONGITUDE

Longitude lines to the east and west of the prime meridian are called east and west longitude respectively. These lines meet on the opposite side of the earth at the 180 degree line of longitude. Lines of latitude run north and south of the equator and are called north and south latitude respectively. Lines of latitude start at 0 degrees at the equator and run to 90 degrees at the poles. Their angles are measured based on using the earth's center as an angular reference as shown below.

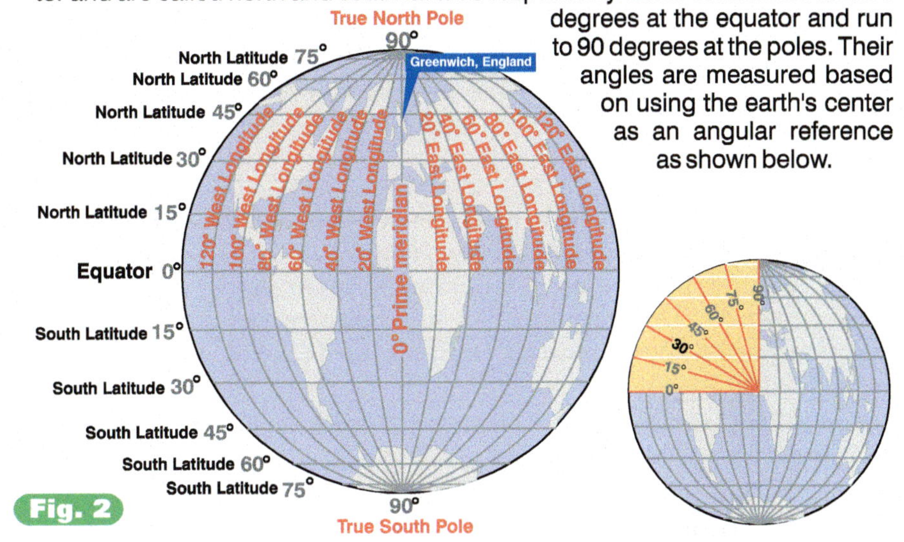

Fig. 2

You can see how the lines of longitude help us locate places on the earth. Africa's west coast, for instance, begins near the 20 degree west longitude line. Central Africa appears to lie on the 20 degree east longitude line. While longitude lines are helpful, they don't quite serve to nail down a position, since 20 degrees west can still be anywhere from up near the north pole to down near the south pole.

With the use of *latitude lines,* we can precisely locate our position. The zero degree line of latitude, otherwise known as the *equator,* is located at the midpoint of the earth. Spaced one degree apart, lines of latitude run parallel to the equator spaced north and south. Latitude lines north of the equator are called *north latitude* and south of the equator are called *south latitude*. They are sometimes called parallels because, unlike lines of longitude, latitude lines are parallel to each other, as shown in Figure 2.

If you were standing at the center of the earth, the angular distance from the equator to either pole would be one-quarter of a circle or 90 degrees. Lines of latitude run from 0 degrees at the equator to 90 degrees at the poles, as shown by the smaller globe insert in Figure 2. The 90 degree north latitude line is a tiny little circle (a dot) sitting at the true north pole. The 90 degree south latitude line is a small circle at the south pole (a point on a polar bear's nose).

The United States is located between 30 degrees and 45 degrees north latitude and 75 degrees and 125 degrees west longitude (see Figure 2). Any specific point on earth can be referenced by lines of latitude and longitude. Washington D.C. for example is located at approximately 39 degrees north latitude and 77 degrees west longitude. Soon we'll discuss how we achieve even more precise measurements with latitude and longitude, making it easy to find individual airports.

Time Measurement

A day is defined as the time it takes for the earth to rotate 360 degrees—one full rotation. With 24 hours in a day, the earth rotates 15 degrees every hour (15 degrees × 24 hours=360 degrees). If the sun were directly over the prime meridian in Greenwich, England, it would be noontime for the English locals.

Flight planning isn't a complex task. It is simply information gathering and some calculation.

But it would be very early morning for everyone on the U.S. west coast. In fact, for everyone on the west coast of California, the difference in longitude between their location and the prime meridian is 120 degrees. This makes the time difference approximately 8 hours (15 degrees per hour × 8 hours = 120 degrees).

It's a standard practice to establish time zones in the United States at 15 degree intervals, as shown in Figure 3. The center of each time zone is located on the 75th, 90th, 105th and 120th meridians. These zones are respectively called the Eastern, Central, Mountain and Pacific time zones. Each zone has one hour time difference (15 degrees/hour) from its neighbor. You would think the borders of different time zones would be straight lines running down the United States. Not so. Time zone borders usually consist of natural landmarks (rivers, canyons, etc.).

Local political reasons often explain why borders of each time zone are irregular rather than neat, straight lines.

When the sun is directly above the 120th, 105th, 90th and 75th longitude line, it's noon in these time zones. For example, when the sun is directly over the 90th meridian, it is noon, Central Standard Time. Under Daylight Saving Time, however, noon occurs when the sun is shifted 15 degrees to the left as an earthling looks up at it while facing south (to your right as you look at Figure 3). In other words, noon in the Central Daylight time zone occurs when the sun is located directly over the 75th longitude line, instead of the 90th. Daylight is *saved* since it's noon before the sun reaches directly overhead. The day appears to last longer because the afternoon is longer. Daylight Saving Time is in effect starting at 2 a.m. on the second Sunday in March and ends at 2 a.m. on the first Sunday in November, except in a few areas such as Arizona, which never goes on Daylight Saving Time (as I said, local politics is a factor).

TO CONVERT FROM:	TO COORDINATED UNIVERSAL TIME
Eastern Standard Time	Add 5 hours
Eastern Daylight Time	Add 4 hours
Central Standard Time	Add 6 hours
Central Daylight Time	Add 5 hours
Mountain Standard Time	Add 7 hours
Mountain Daylight Time	Add 6 hours
Pacific Standard Time	Add 8 hours
Pacific Daylight Time	Add 7 hours
Yukon Standard Time	Add 9 hours
Alaska, Hawaii Standard Time	Add 10 hours
Bering Standard Time	Add 11 hours

Fig. 4

It's important to know about time zones for several reasons. First, the time listed on all weather charts is for Greenwich, England. This time is called Zulu or Universal Coordinated Time (UTC). For any weather chart to be meaningful, you'll need to know how to convert from the time in Greenwich (Universal Coordinated Time—UTC) to local time.

According to the conversion chart in Figure 4, if it's 1:00 p.m. (1300 hours) PST, what time is it UTC? The chart says to add 8 hours (1300 + 800 = 2100 hours). It makes sense to add 8 hours to find the time in Greenwich, England because it's always later there. If you're having trouble seeing how it's always later in England, examine Figure 5. When the sun is directly overhead in Greenwich, England (noon for them), it hasn't

TIME ZONES

Time zones are established at 15 degree intervals of longitude. When the sun is directly above the meridian, the time at points on that meridian is noon. Each time zone is one hour different from its bordering time zone.

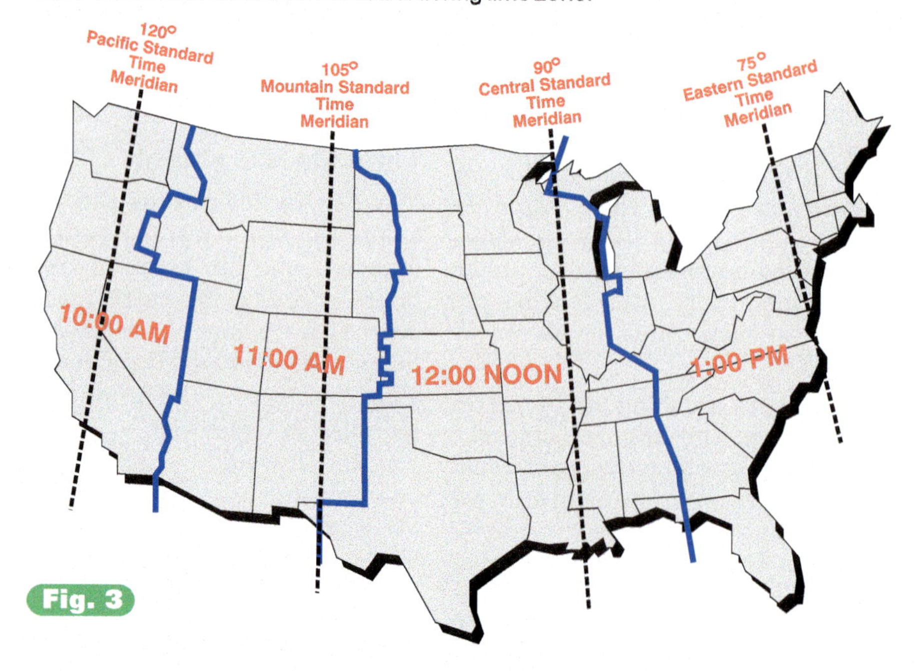

Fig. 3

Pepperoni Minutes

Since Dominos pizza (or another fast food place with similar guarantees) promises to deliver within 30 minutes or it's free, it seems there might be good reason to live near the edge of a time zone. Simply call the Dominos across the street in a different time zone, order a pizza, and wait.

When the delivery person shows up in 20 minutes, grab the pizza and say, "Hey, you're an hour and 20 minutes late," then shut the door. Quickly.

On the other hand, if you do this on the wrong side of the time zone, you can have a pizza delivered 40 minutes before you ordered it. I believe this is called the *Domino Effect*.

IT'S ALWAYS LATER IN ENGLAND

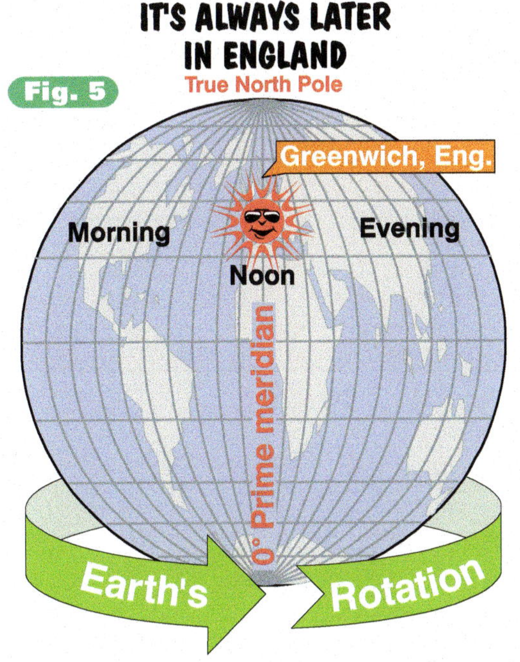

Based on the way the earth rotates the time is always later in Europe. In other words, if it's morning in the United States it's noon in England. And if it's noon in England, then it's morning in the U.S. Thus, when you convert from local time to UTC, you must add hours; from UTC to local, you must subtract hours.

risen in the eastern sky of the U.S. It's still (very early) morning for us. Figure 4 is very useful for converting local time in any time zone to UTC when filing flight plans (all times on a flight plan are given in UTC).

While filing flight plans requires local-to-UTC conversion, interpreting weather charts requires the opposite conversion. For instance, suppose the valid time of a weather report is between 0800 Zulu (UTC) and 1600 Zulu. When would this chart be applicable to you in the Pacific Standard Time zone? To convert 0800Z and 1600Z to PST do the opposite of what the conversion chart in Figure 4 suggests. Simply subtract 8 hours from the Zulu time. This gives us a local chart time of 0000 to 0800 hours, or midnight to 8 a.m. Between the second Sunday in March and the end of first Sunday in November (Daylight Saving Time), you would subtract 7 hours instead of 8 hours.

Most aviation operations are expressed by using the 24 hour clock. Starting at 1:00 a.m. the time is referred to as 0100 hours or *zero one zero zero Zulu,* and 1:00 p.m. is called 1300 hours and spoken as *one three zero zero Zulu.* This count continues to the end of the 24 hour clock with midnight being 2400 hours.

WHO'S IN CHARGE HERE?

I was hired to fly a small airplane to an airport (about an hour away) to pick up the owner of the plane and return to base. The wind at destination was 15, gusting to 25. Being from the full-flap-for-every-landing school, I used 40 degrees and made an acceptable landing. Two men then boarded the airplane. As I taxied out, the one in the back seat asked why I had used full flaps. I asked if he was an instructor and he said yes. Since he was the customer, I remained polite and told him that was my technique. From there the flight went downhill. I filed IFR to get a direct flight back through Class B and Class C airspace in the smoother upper altitudes. As we climbed out, the gentleman in the back seat said there was too much wind at altitude and that I should cancel and go low around Class B and Class C airspace. Since he was the customer, I complied and for the next 1 1/2 hours fought to keep the aircraft on an even keel in moderate turbulence.

The customer then decided he didn't like the way I was navigating (direct) and told me to navigate to a VOR. Once again I bit my tongue and complied. As I got within ten miles of the VOR and now clear of Class B airspace, I set a direct course for home base and the gentleman in the back seat wondered why I wasn't picking up the VOR—four miles from the field (because it was not direct). With the continuous pounding of the turbulence and the continuous badgering from the back seat, all I wanted to do was land. The problem led to my not following my pre-landing checklist —I was too distracted. I had forgotten flaps until I realized that I wasn't as slow as I'd like to be. I was fast and sloppy arriving at the runway, killing power, dropping flaps, and fighting the gusty crosswinds all at the same time, trying to salvage a bad approach. I fishtailed and floated halfway down the runway before touching down. The landing was soft, just embarrassingly sloppy.

I was disgusted with myself for allowing the distraction to get me behind the airplane. The problem was that I was afraid to get the customer mad by exercising my pilot-in-command authority. Pilots in back seats must remember that the pilot flying is PIC and unnecessary distractions can cause problems. I suggest that pilots never fear exercising their PIC authority. Next time I get a back seat pilot I will give one warning as to who is PIC and further distractions will be treated as a violation of FAR 91.3!!! **ASRS Report**

Try: "Sir, I prefer not to talk while flying, so that I may devote my full attention to a safe and comfortable flight. I will be happy to answer any questions after the flight." D.T.

A Matter of Degree: Longitude And Latitude On Sectional Charts

Individual lines of latitude and longitude allow us to precisely pinpoint any spot on a chart (like an airport). Figure 6 shows how we read these positions. Bob's airport lies directly between the 93rd and 94th lines of longitude (running up and down) and the 39th and 40th lines of latitude (running sideways). There's a great deal of real estate within a one degree boundary of longitude or latitude (see sidebar "Miles in a Degree"), so it's necessary to find a more precise means of determining a position.

Every degree of longitude and latitude can be broken down into 60 smaller segments called *minutes,* as shown by scale A and B in Figure 6. We won't think of minutes as a time reference. For our purposes, think of minutes on a sectional chart as being similar to the smaller markings on a ruler. They simply let you physically locate your position between lines of latitude and longitude with greater accuracy.

Imagine 60 smaller lines, each parallel to the 93rd and 94th lines of longitude, running up and down the chart. Were the lines really there, you couldn't locate *anything,* because you wouldn't be able to see the chart. To solve the problem, chartmakers place a small *tick* or line segment to one side, allowing you to see the subdivisions.

DEGREES, MINUTES AND SECONDS ON CHARTS

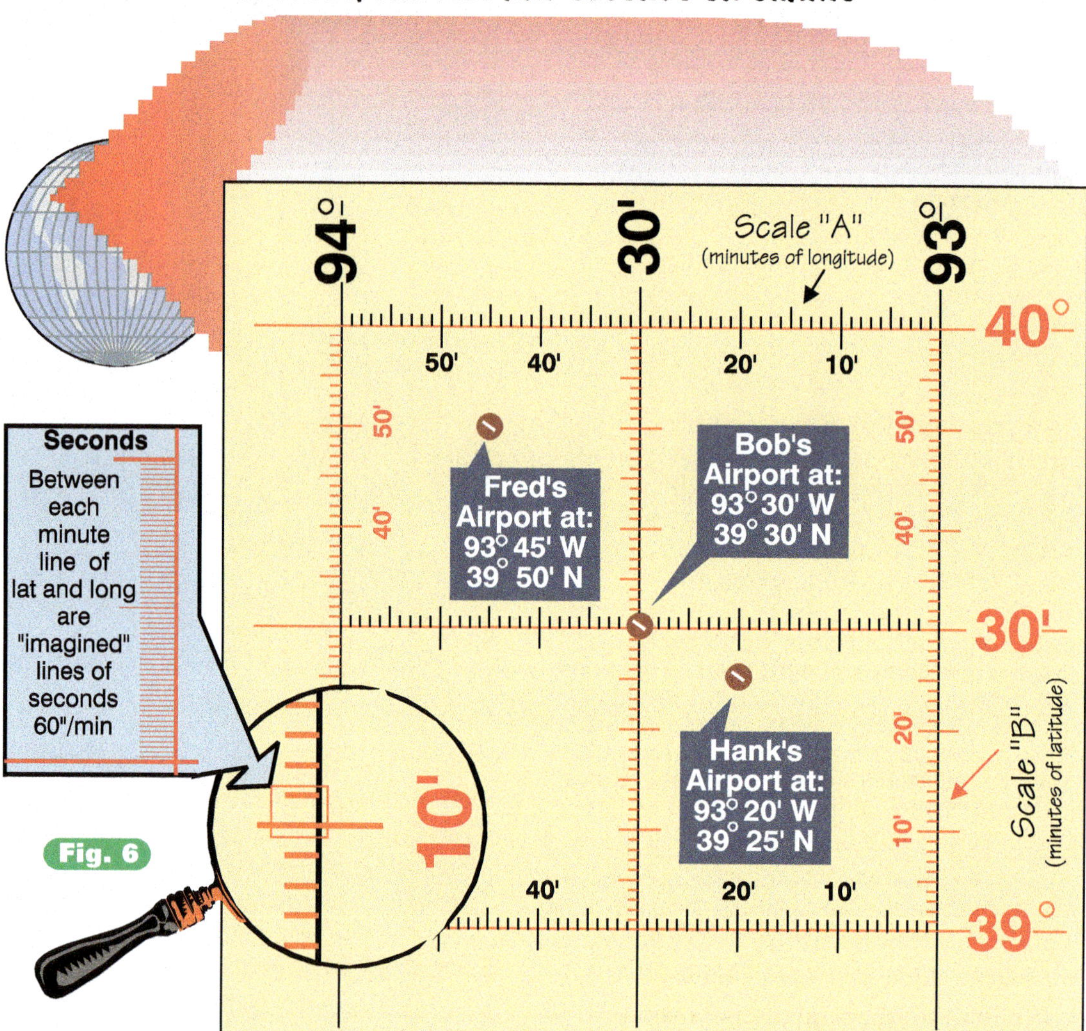

Lines of longitude run vertically up and down the chart. Their scale is identified in minutes by the orientation of the lines on scale A. Lines of latitude run horizontally across the chart. Their scale is identified by the lines on scale B. Between each whole line of latitude and longitude are divisions of minutes. Sixty minutes make up one degree of latitude or longitude and sixty seconds equal one minute (seconds are not depicted on sectional charts).

A BRIEF ON RELIEF

Enroute in a small airplane, the owner was in the right seat and I was in the left. The owner was flying and decided to land on a paved road to relieve himself (no cars in sight for miles, desolate). He landed, exited and returned. During the takeoff roll, at about 40-45 mph, we observed a vehicle appearing on the road in the distance. The pilot seemed startled and abruptly pulled back on the yoke, lifting the plane off. It then mushed back down on to the road's shoulder, hitting a bush with the right main gear, which was separated from the wing. The plane skidded to a stop, with damage to the bottom of the right wing and right landing gear. The pilot shut off the engine and we exited, uninjured. A normal takeoff could have been accomplished had the yoke not been prematurely pulled back because of the vehicle. Although the incident was far from any civilization, we probably shouldn't have landed on the road. A portable relief bottle, available in both women's and men's versions, makes a unique pilot gift and saves expensive airframe modifications, too!

ASRS

The entire 30 minute longitude line, however, is there, helping give a rough division of the degrees of longitude, running up and down the chart. Scale A clearly shows these smaller line segments, which make it easy to identify your position in degrees and minutes. In the same way, each degree of latitude has smaller minute segments as shown by scale B, along with the 30-minute latitude line running across the chart between each degree of latitude.

For even greater accuracy, each minute of distance is broken down into 60 seconds (Figure 6, left side). Although it's not possible for chartmakers to show seconds on the chart, you can simply imagine their presence. The proper symbols for degrees, minutes and seconds are: °, ′, ″, and locations are written as 110° 15′ 10″.

As you can clearly see, Bob's airport lies halfway between the 93rd and 94th longitude lines. It's located at 93° 30′ west longitude and 39° 30′ north latitude. Fred's airport is located at 93° 45′ west longitude and 39° 50′ north latitude. Hank's airport is located at 93° 20′ west longitude and 39° 25′ north latitude.

Miles in a Degree

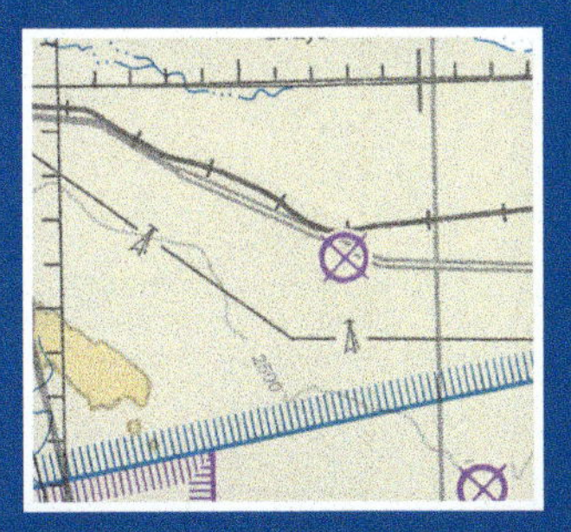

How big is a degree, in statute miles? It depends.

There are degrees of latitude and degrees of longitude and the longitudinal lines converge as you head toward either pole. Measured in an east-west direction, there is more distance in a degree at the equator than higher or lower on the longitude "pole." If the reason for this isn't apparent to you, grab an orange or apple and inscribe (with pen or knife) some longitude lines. You'll readily see what I'm talking about. Then eat the fruit. It's good for you.

At the equator, there are 69.17 statute miles (sm) per degree of longitude. At 40 degrees north (about the midriff of the U.S.), a degree of longitude is 53.06 sm in width. Go to 85 degrees north latitude and it's only 6 sm between one degree of longitude and another. Go a bit farther north, to 89 degrees 30 minutes, and you can walk "around the world"—over all 360 lines of longitude—by going just 218 sm. Say hi to Santa.

Life is easier when measuring degree distance in a north-south direction, because nothing gets squished. Remember that the lines of latitude are sometimes called *parallels* because, yea verily, they are (pretty much) parallel (uniform in distance). That distance is 69.17 sm at the equator, varying by about 1/2 sm from the measurement at the extreme north pole (zero to one degree N, where it's 68.70 sm), and by about 1/4 sm from the measurement at 89-90 degrees south, where it's 69.41 sm. This slight variation reflects the fact that Planet Earth is not perfectly round. Call it 69 sm per degree of latitude and you won't get cited by the parallel police.

There's a good chance all your training as a student pilot will be done within the United States. If your instructor says to plan a cross country to Central America, she probably means somewhere in Kansas. Don't come back with a flight plan to Guatemala (it will make her real suspicious). Knowing that you'll always be flight planning for the U.S. helps, because it means you'll only need to consider west longitude and north latitude coordinates.

Which Way Is Up?

Anywhere in the United States, degrees of west longitude always increases to your left and degrees of north latitude always increases as you move up the chart. If you're looking for the 93° 30′ minute longitude point, and you find the 93° line of longitude, then the 30 minute line is to your left, not to your right. This same bit of wisdom applies to latitude. If you know where the 39° north latitude line is, then you know that 39° 30′ is above this line, not below it.

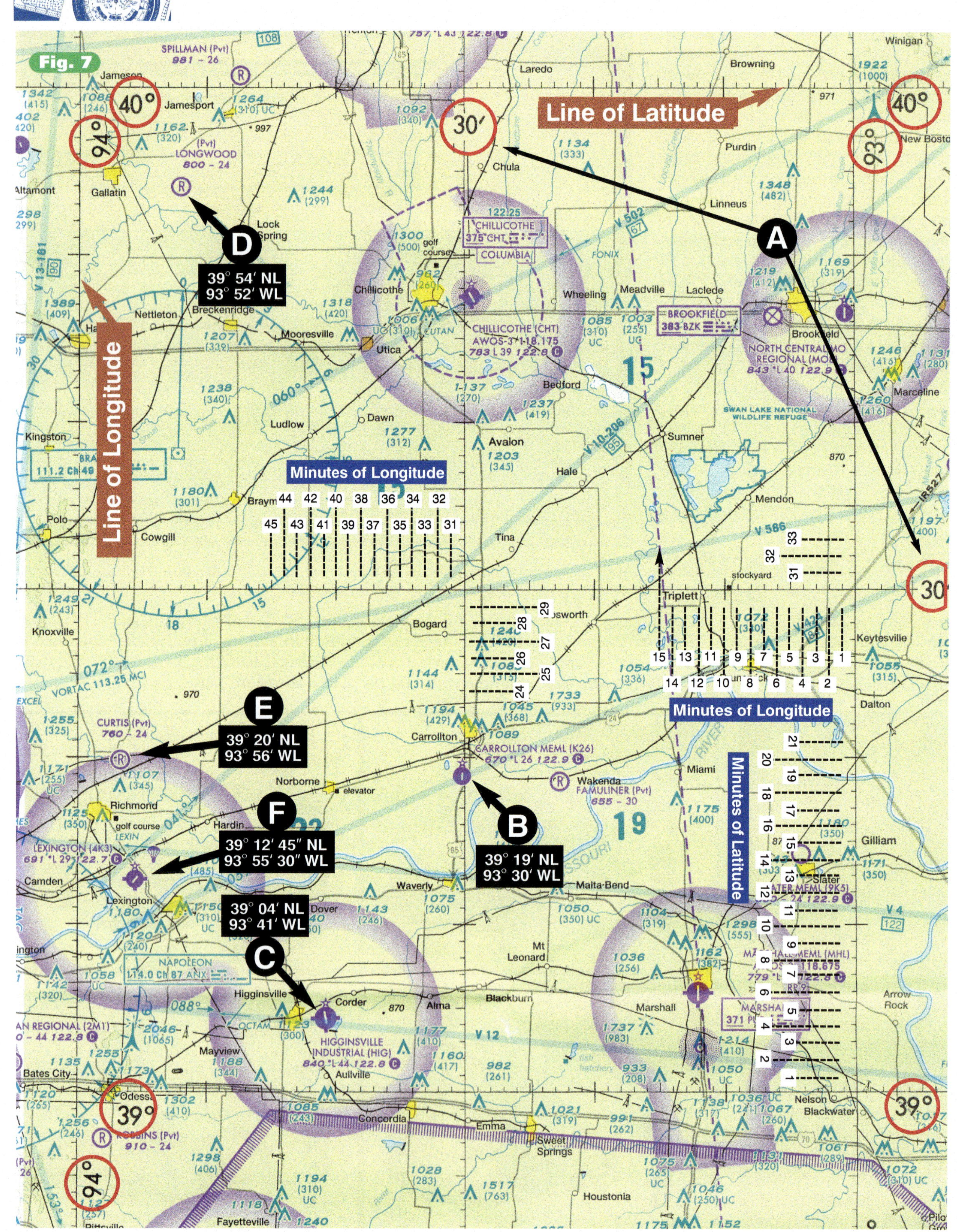
Fig. 7
Line of Latitude
Line of Longitude
Minutes of Longitude
Minutes of Latitude
A
B
39° 19′ NL
93° 30′ WL
C
39° 04′ NL
93° 41′ WL
D
39° 54′ NL
93° 52′ WL
E
39° 20′ NL
93° 56′ WL
F
39° 12′ 45″ NL
93° 55′ 30″ WL
40°
94°
30′
93°
39°

Let's identify specific airports by their latitude and longitude coordinates on a real sectional chart. Figure 7 is a sectional chart excerpt for Kansas. At each corner of the page, the latitude and longitude coordinates are circled. Of course, the 40 degree mark at the top left of the page can only be the 40 degree north latitude line and the 94 degree mark can only be the 94 degree west longitude line (remember, this is in the U.S.). Halfway between whole lines of latitude and longitude are the minute lines. The vertical and horizontal running lines marked on the chart in position A are the 30 minute lines I mentioned before.

The Digital Chart Supplement (dCS) shows the latitude and longitude locations for airports.

RAVENDALE (O39) 0 N UTC–8(–7DT) N40°48.19′ W120°21.98′ **KLAMATH FALLS**
5299 TPA—6099(800)
RWY 17-35: H2920X30 (ASPH)
RWY 35: Thld dsplcd 900′. P–line.
AIRPORT REMARKS: Unattended. Unpaved areas extremely soft when wet.
COMMUNICATIONS: CTAF 122.9
RED BLUFF FSS (RBL) TF 1–800–WX–BRIEF. (1400–0600Z‡). NOTAM FILE RBL.
RANCHO MURIETA FSS (RIU) TF 1–800–WX–BRIEF. (0600–1400Z‡).

RED BLUFF MUNI (RBL) 2 S UTC–8(–7DT) N40°09.06′ W122°15.14′ **KLAMATH FALLS**
349 B S4 **FUEL** 80, 100LL, JET A TPA—See Remarks **H-1A, L-2H**
RWY 15-33: H5984X150 (ASPH) S–30, D–65 MIRL **IAP**
RWY 15: REIL. VASI(V4L)—GA 3.0° TCH 40′. Thld dsplcd 200′. Rgt tfc.
RWY 33: REIL. VASI(V4L)—GA 3.0° TCH 40′.

Fig. 8

Take a look at Carrollton Memorial airport at position B in the bottom, center of the page. Carrollton lies on the 93° 30′ line of longitude. What line of latitude does it lie on? Looking at my drawn-in scale to the right of Carrollton, it look like it lies at 39° 19′ north latitude.

What is the latitude and longitude of Higginsville airport at position C? Higgineville is located at 39° 04′ north latitude and 93° 41′ west longitude.

What airport lies near the point defined by 39° 54′ north latitude and 93° 52′ west longitude? Yes, it's Longwood airport, located at position D.

You're probably thinking, "Oh, come on Rod. Why should I spend time learning about dead reckoning when I'll probably use my GPS or VOR to get me to my destination?" Stick with me for a few minutes, and you will learn to not just navigate but to understand what you're doing and why.

Let's try one more. Identify the latitude and longitude location of Curtis airport, position E. It looks like Curtis is located approximately 3 minutes to the right of the 94 degree line of longitude, running vertically left of the airport. This would locate it at 93° 56′ west longitude. Sometimes you have to just count individual minutes to the right or left from a whole line of latitude or longitude to find the minute value. The 5 and 10 minute marks are often difficult to see.

The latitude of Curtis is best found by counting down from the horizontal 30 minute line just above the airport. It looks like Curtis lies on the 20 minute north latitude line, giving it a coordinate of 39° and 20′ north latitude. Can minutes be subdivided? Yes, they can be divided into an additional 60 small (very small) increments called seconds. They're too hard to see on this chart so the best you can do is estimate them. Lexington airport (position F) is located at 39° 12′ 45″ north latitude and 93° 55′ 30″ west longitude.

You're probably wondering why I'm making such a big fuss about the latitude and longitude coordinates for an airport. Well, it's important since the newer methods of navigation—GPS, in particular—all use latitude and longitude coordinates to determine airport position. You can usually navigate to an airport with your GPS equipment by dialing in the airport's three letter/number code. Figure 8 is an excerpt from the *dCS*. It shows the latitude and longitude coordinates of both airports as well as the airports' three digit codes (shown in parentheses).

Now that you have an idea about how to find airports on a sectional chart, we're ready to jump right into basic cross country navigation. But first, let me tell you about a friend of mine who had a golf ball hit his car's windshield. Surprisingly, he wasn't upset. He said it probably wouldn't have happened if he hadn't been driving on the golf course.

Isn't this like the pilot who got lost and actually said, "It probably wouldn't have happened if the wind hadn't been blowing that day"? You'll never need to worry about getting where you're going once you know the direction to aim the airplane and how to correct for wind. This is the essence of basic navigation.

Cross Country Navigation

As we saw before, there are several ways to get from one airport to the next. The most popular form of navigation is called *electronic navigation.* Devices such as VOR or GPS (and the many forms in which its available today) all allow you to navigate to your destination with relative ease.

You might also recall our discussion of pilotage, in which you read the features (natural and manmade) on the ground and compare them to the map to find your location. This is also used in combination with *dead reckoning,* a term that stands for *deduced reckoning* (and has no reference to what happens to pilots who don't know how to use it). Dead reckoning involves calculating the effects of wind and compass error on a plotted course. It is one of the most important forms of navigation. Why? Because it's the one form of navigation which requires you to understand how the wind affects your airplane. There's no better education for a pilot than to have a mental picture of how wind affects an airplane. That's why I'll be placing the emphasis on dead reckoning and pilotage in this chapter.

You're probably thinking, "Oh, come on Rod. Why should I spend time learning about dead reckoning and pilotage when I'll probably use my GPS or VOR to get me to my destination?" Stick with me for a few minutes, and you will learn to not just navigate but to *understand* what you're doing and why. That will be worth its weight in airplane tires to you some day, no matter how you navigate. Understanding how compass errors and wind affects your flight has a profound effect on your ability to enjoy a lifetime of safe flying.

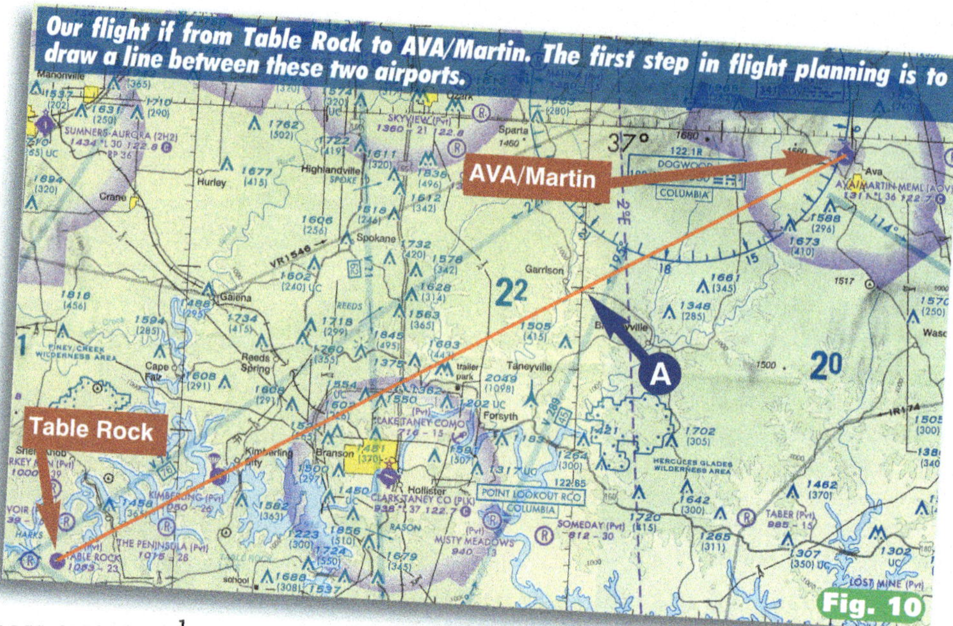

Our flight if from Table Rock to AVA/Martin. The first step in flight planning is to draw a line between these two airports.

Fig. 10

Our Trip

Let's start with the basics of how a course is plotted. The following are the six steps we'll use when planning a cross country flight based on dead reckoning navigation.

Flight Planning Step 1:
Draw a line between airports or checkpoints.

Flight Planning Step 2:
Determine the true course.

Flight Planning Step 3:
Determine the wind correction angle.

Flight Planning Step 4:
Determine the true heading.

Flight Planning Step 5:
Determine the magnetic heading.

Flight Planning Step 6:
Determine the compass heading.

Fig. 9

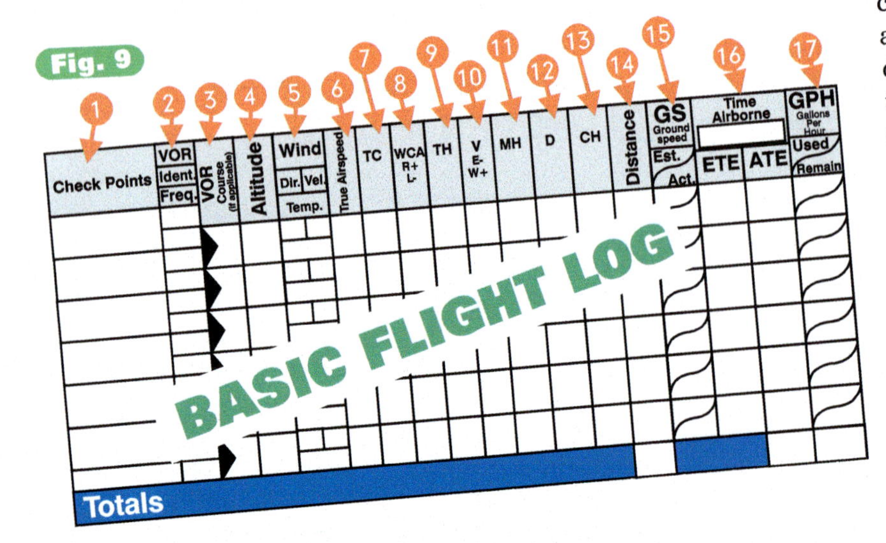

While some if not all of your flights will use advanced forms of navigation (VOR and GPS, for instance), good pilots always keep these basic steps in mind on every flight. As we follow each of these individual steps, we will fill in a flight log (Figure 9). A flight log is a means of keeping track of navigational information, *not* something to use in your airplane's fireplace.

We'll only use a few of the sections in the flight log for this flight. Notice that the log starts with your checkpoints (item 1) and leads you to the TC or true course (item 7). Eventually, it leads to the CH or compass heading (item 13) which is also step 6 of our flight planning sequence. The point here is that the flight log provides you with a visual sequence of the basic steps you need to take to get to your destination airport. Let's fill it out as we proceed with each flight planning step.

Flight Planning Step 1—Draw a line between airports or checkpoints – The first step in cross country flight planning is to draw a line on the chart between our departure and destination airports. For this flight we'll assume we're departing Table Rock airport and our destination is AVA/Martin Memorial airport, as shown in Figure 10. We'll draw a line between the centers of each airport symbol. (If you're not planning a flight as a single, straight course between airports, then draw lines between turning points. Treat each straight segment as an individual course and apply the following steps to each segment.) Let's also insert these two airports as checkpoints in our flight planning form, as shown in Figure 11. (Ideally, we'd pick several checkpoints for every flight. For simplicity, however, we'll only use the departure and destination airport in this example.)

FLIGHT PLAN STEP 1: DRAW LINE BETWEEN CHECKPOINTS

Check Points	VOR Ident. Freq.	VOR Course (if applicable)	Altitude	Wind Dir. Vel. Temp.	True Airspeed	TC	WCA R+ L-	TH	V E- W+	MH	D	CH	Distance	GS Ground speed Est. Act.
Table Rock														
AVA/ Martin														

Fig. 11

MEASURING TRUE COURSES

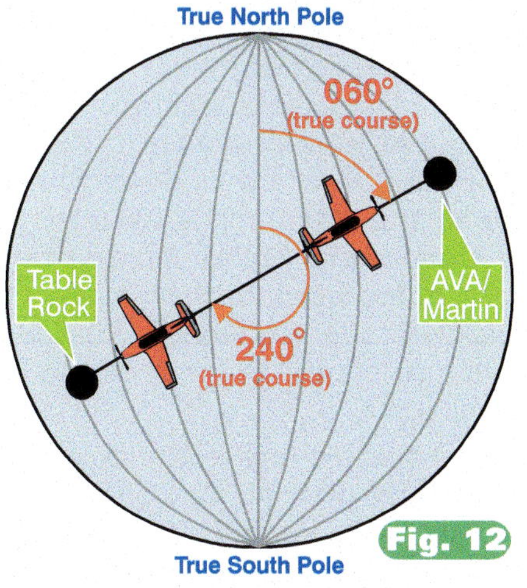

Fig. 12

Your true course is the angle your flight path makes with the true north pole. Since lines of longitude run up and down between the true north and south poles, we can simply measure the angle our flight path makes with the longitude line at the midpoint of our trip.

Flight Planning Step 2—Determine the true course (the angle your flight path makes with the true north pole) – The first thing I like to do is to make a rough eyeball estimate of the course. From Table Rock to AVA, we're flying in a northeasterly direction (Figure 10). What do you think our course should be? Take a guess. I think it's somewhere around 50 degrees or so. These eyeball estimates are important, and should be a prelude to virtually every flight planning calculation. Don't go looking for an answer until you have some idea of what it should be. Believe me when I say that good pilots are always making mental estimates about time, distance, fuel consumption, etc. When one of these estimates doesn't jive with their paper calculation, they recheck their work (or put new batteries in the electronic flight computer). Follow this rule of guesstimating first and I guarantee you will avoid some remarkably embarrassing moments in your aviation activities.

Here's another of those handy rules of thumb—any flight in a right hand (easterly) direction requires a true course of somewhere between 0 degrees and 179 degrees. Any flight in a left hand or westerly direction requires a true course of somewhere between 180 degrees and 359 degrees.

Figure 12 shows that we need to fly an angle of 60 degrees with respect to the true north pole on our flight from Table Rock to AVA. Conversely, for our return flight from AVA to Table Rock, we need to fly an angle of 240 degrees (the reciprocal of our original heading) with respect to the true north pole. An angle is defined as a course. Since this course is relative to the true north pole, we call it a *true course* (unlike some of the courses I had in college). This name allows you to understand the reference the angle is measured against. This is important because, as you'll soon see, there are magnetic courses and compass courses.

To measure the *true course,* find a line of longitude approximately halfway between the airports, as shown by point A in Figure 10. When measuring any true course on a sectional chart, it's best to pick a line of longitude halfway between your departure and destination as shown in Figure 10, point A. We do this because all the lines of longitude converge at the north pole and their angles subtly change as they converge. A halfway measurement point is more than accurate enough for navigation. Remember, we're launching Cessnas, Pipers and Katanas here, not cruise missiles. We only need to be accurate enough to be near the airport, not through the window of some terrorist hideout (Oops! Terrorists now want to be called *hostage administrators).*

Put a dot where the course line intersects this line of longitude. Figure 13, point A shows a closeup view of this intersection point.

Now you're ready to use a simple but effective tool called a *plotter* (see Figure 14). If this looks remarkably like a grade school protractor, that's because it's remarkably like a grade school protractor. The top or curved part of the plotter is for measuring course angles. In the bottom center of the curved section there's a small hole called a *grommet.* The bottom

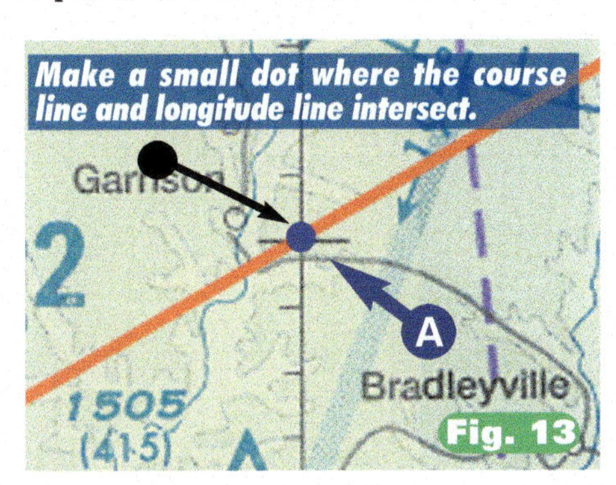

Fig. 13

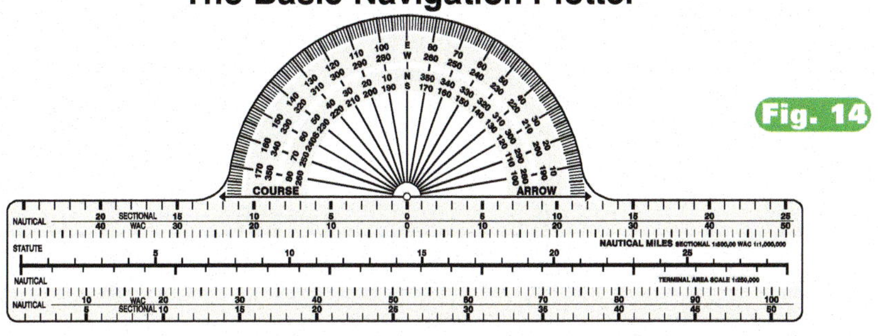

Fig. 14

part of the plotter has several scales used for measuring distances on charts. We will discuss the different parts as we use them.

Use the plotter's angle-measuring device to determine your true course. Place the plotter's straight edge over the course line as shown in Figure 15. Slide the plotter up or down the course line so the grommet is over the small dot we made in Figure 13. You're done! Wait, come back here. I mean you're done with the mechanics. All you have to do now is read the true course on the curved scale.

Your true course is the number that lies directly over the line of longitude at the top of the curved scale. This line is shown, close up, in Figure 16 (point A). It looks like 60 degrees is our true course for a flight from Table Rock to AVA/Martin Memorial. In other words, 60 degrees is the angle your flight path makes with respect to the true north pole. Since this is pretty close to our eyeball estimate of 50 degrees, we know it's an accurate (or at least plausible) measurement. Let's insert the true course of 60 degrees into our flight planning form (Figure 17).

The plotter in Figure 16 has two scales, an outside scale (point B) and an inside scale (point C). The outside scale (the one with the letter *E* next to it), suggests we use this scale if we're going east or from left to right—which we are. The inside scale (the one with the letter *W* next to it), suggests we use this scale if we're going west or from right to left. Using the inside scale you can easily see that the true course on our return flight is 240 degrees—the reciprocal of 60 degrees (180 degrees + 60 degrees = 240 degrees).

One word of caution! The numbers on both scales increase and decrease differently than your intuition might suggest. Moving 3 degrees to the left of the plotter's numerical value of 60 degrees yields 63 degrees, not 57 degrees, violating our notion that things always get smaller to the left and larger to the right. It's printed that way because of the way the plotter is used. Read the scales carefully when measuring courses.

Now you understand how to identify the direction of a course on a sectional chart. Next, we want to determine and correct for the effects of wind that might blow on our course.

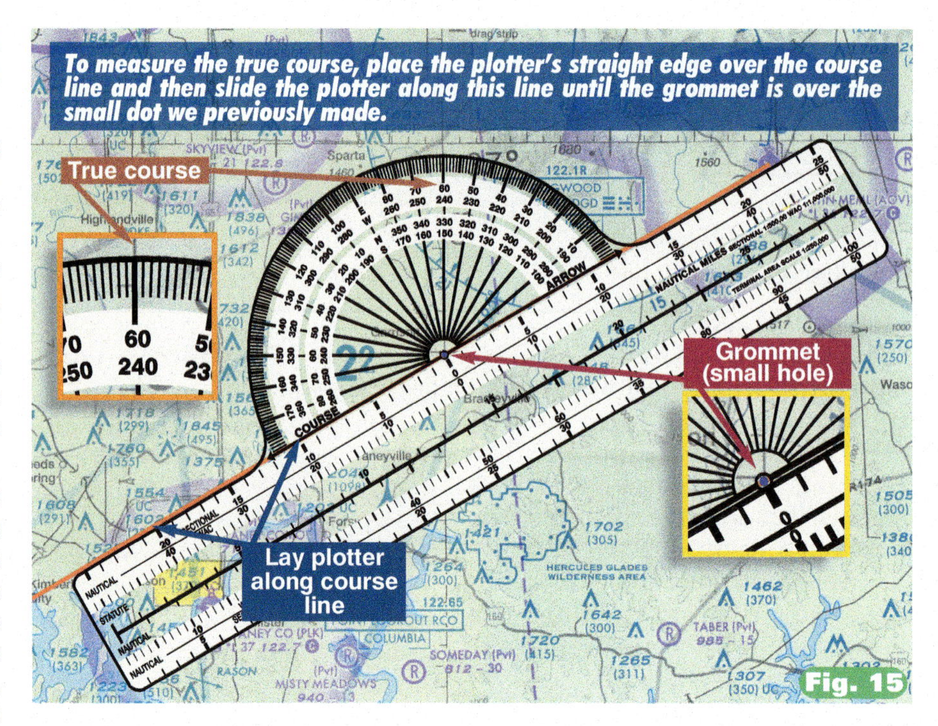

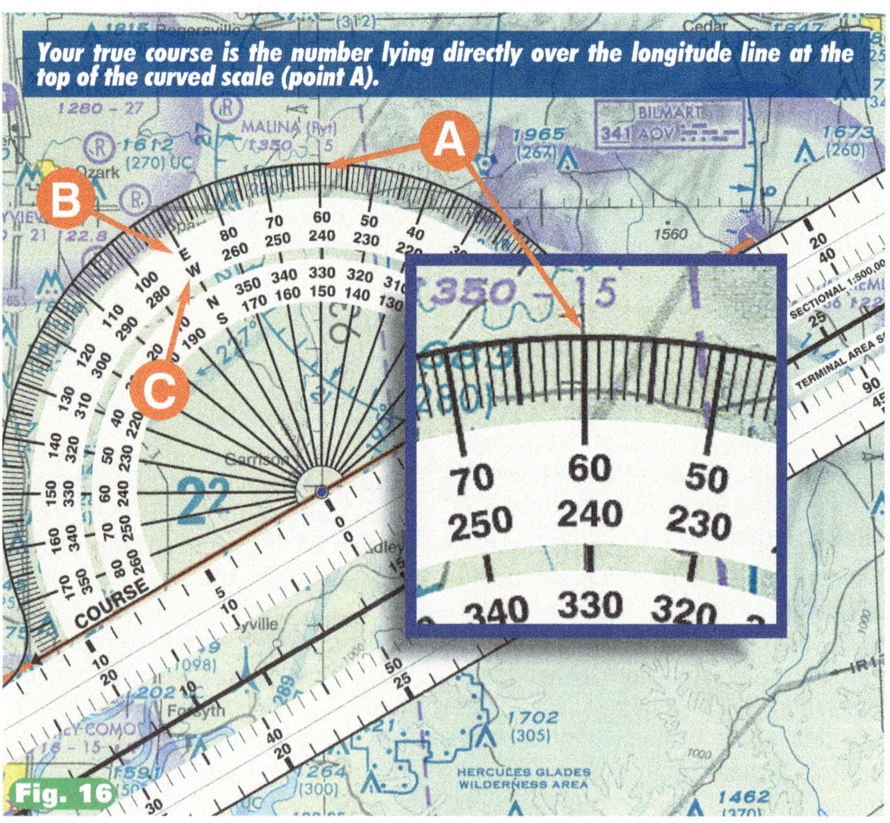

FLIGHT PLAN STEP 2: DETERMINE THE TRUE COURSE

Check Points	VOR Ident. Freq.	VOR Course (if applicable)	Altitude	Wind Dir. Vel. Temp.	True Airspeed	TC	WCA R+ L-	TH	V E- W+	MH	D	CH	Distance	GS Ground speed Est. Act.
Table Rock						60°								66 kts
AVA/ Martin														

Fig. 17

Plotting Your Plotter Practice

For further practice, examine Box 1 below. The plotter shows a true course of 323 degrees when traveling up and to the left (use the W or *west* scale) and 143 degrees when traveling downward and to the right (use the E or *east* scale). If you are not careful, you might mistake 143 degrees for 157 degrees. Box 2 shows a true course indication of 27 degrees up and to the right (E scale), and 207 degrees down and to the left (W scale).

Two additional scales exist inside the plotter's two main outside scales, as shown in Box 3. The smaller, inner scales are useful for plotting courses in a north-south direction when no line of longitude exists near the course centerline. Simply place the base of the plotter along the course line and slide the grommet to a line of latitude, as shown in Box 3. The course number directly over the line of latitude (horizontal line) is your true course. This is shown clearly in Box 4. If traveling in a northerly direction, read the true course on *N* scale; in a southerly direction, use the *S* scale.

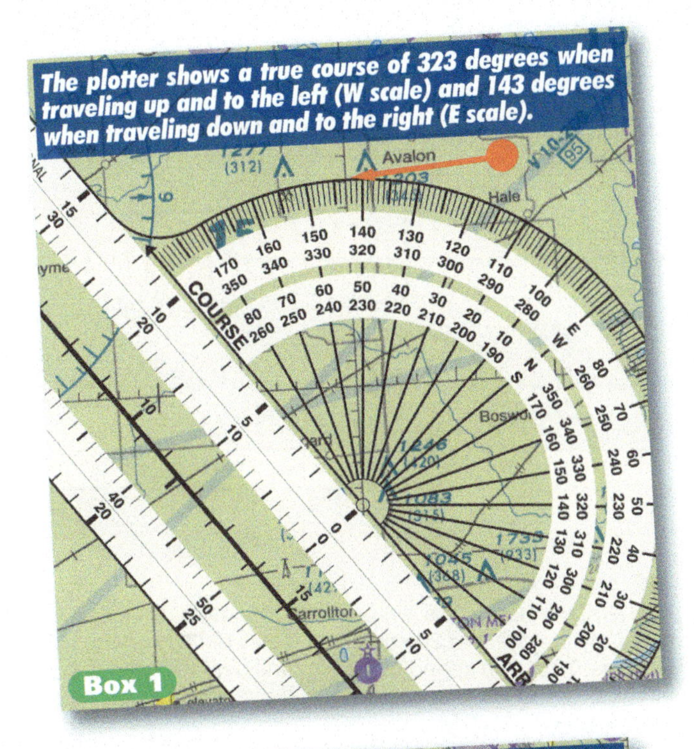

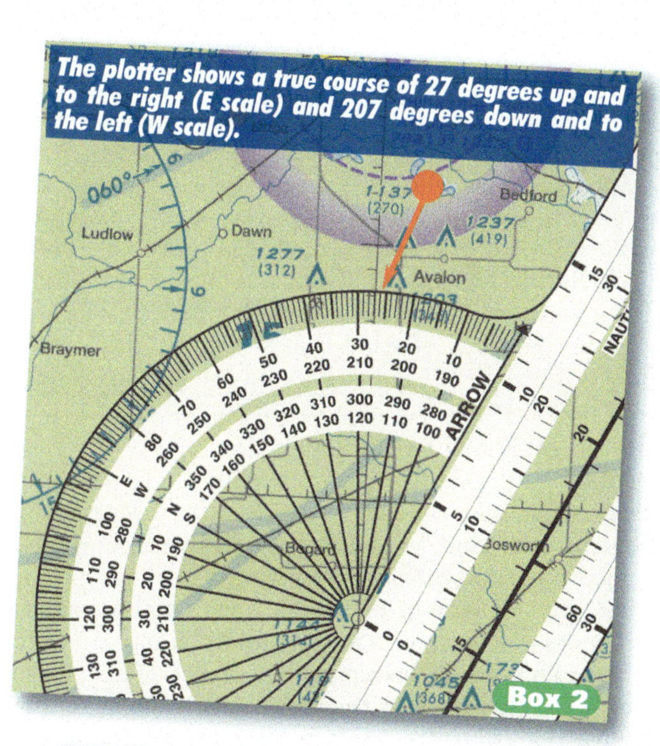

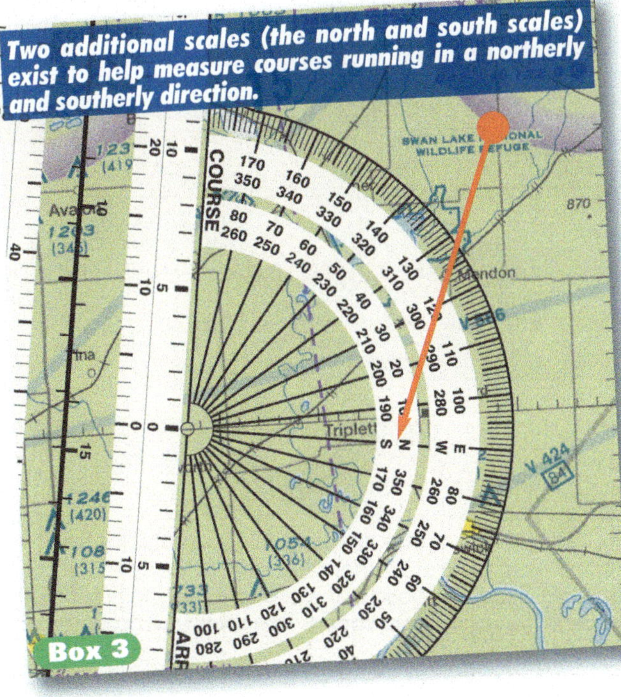

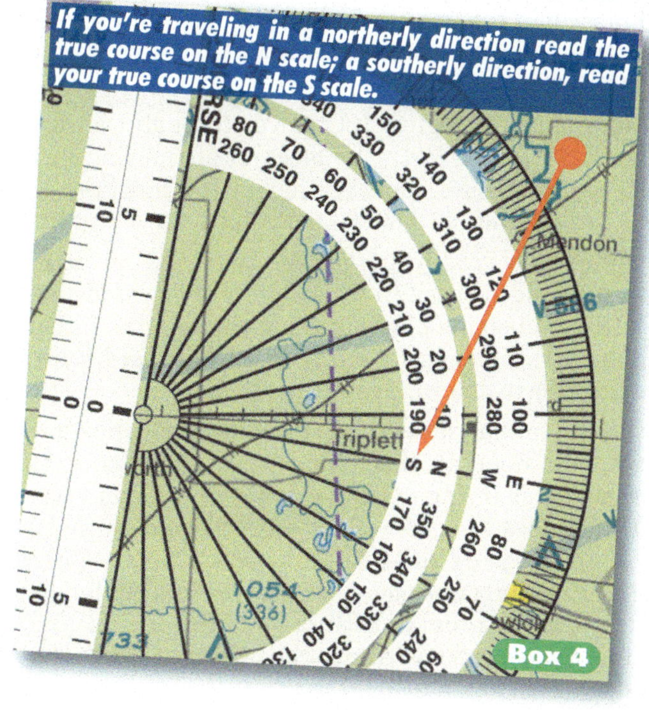

Flight Planning Step 3—Determine the wind correction angle – Before we can discuss how to correct for the effects of wind, let's review some basic principles about how wind affects your airplane in flight.

Without wind, all you'd have to do is fly the compass course and you'd get where you're going. Mother Nature (trickster that she is) is not so accommodating. Wind exists to some degree almost every time you fly. If it blew directly on your nose or tail, it wouldn't blow the airplane off course. Nature, however, is perverse in tooth and law, and most of the time the wind blows at some angle to your flight path. The effect, left uncorrected, is to blow the airplane off its intended course. Your job is to compensate for this drifting tendency.

If the wind is blowing from the north at 20 knots, we're saying the atmosphere is moving across the ground a distance of 20 nautical miles for every hour that passes. If you were in a small hot air balloon and lifted off into this large moving block of wind, you would drift 20 miles in one hour's time, as shown in Figure 18A. Would you feel any wind blowing on you while moving? No, you are stationary within this moving block of wind. It's the block of wind that's moving. Stick your hand over the side of the balloon and the air is perfectly still. In fact, if you didn't look at the ground it's unlikely you'd even know you were moving.

Airplanes also drift with a moving block of wind, which is what inspired the Peter, Paul and Mary song "Blowin' in the Wind." In addition to this drift, however, they also have forward movement generated by their engines. The airplane in Figure 18B has a true airspeed of 100 knots, meaning it is moving at 100 knots through the block of air. It just so happens the block of air is also moving at 20 knots, and they are both moving in the same direction. The airplane's speed over the ground is a combination of the wind and air speeds. Adding our wind speed to our true airspeed gives us a speed over the ground (groundspeed) of 120 knots.

The airplane in Figure 18C moves through the block of air at 100 knots. With the block of air moving at 20 knots in a direction *opposite* that of the airplane, we have a net groundspeed of 80 knots (100 – 20 = 80).

If winds blew exactly on the nose or the tail of the airplane, it would be easy to determine your groundspeed. But the wind usually blows at some angle to the intended flight path, making its effect on groundspeed a little more difficult to determine.

Even worse than its effect on groundspeed, which only represents a delay in reaching your destination, is the fact the wind is trying to push you where you don't want to go. This doesn't bode well for all those pilots who like ending up at the destination they had in mind (remember, it makes the passengers nervous if you keep landing at unknown airports to find out where you are). Fortunately, we can correct for the effects of wind direction and velocity on our flight path.

MOVING WITH A BLOCK OF WIND

The balloon is drifting with a block of wind that's moving over the earth at a speed of 20 knots. Without any mechanical form of propulsion, the balloon has a groundspeed of 20 knots.

MOVING WITHIN A MOVING BLOCK OF WIND

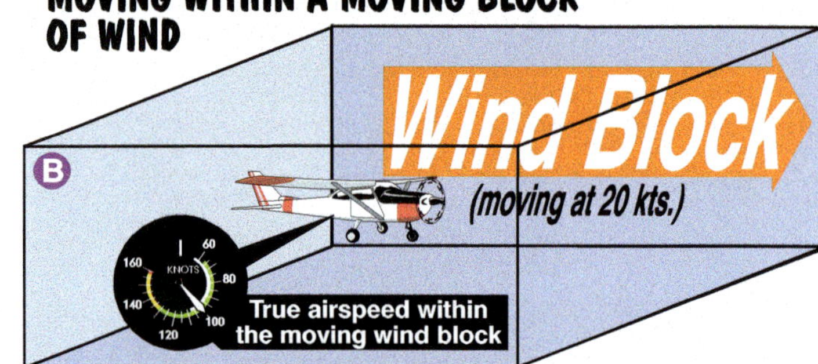

The airplane has a true airspeed of 100 knots. It's flying within a block of air moving at 20 knots that blows directly on the tail of the airplane. Thus, the speed of the airplane over the ground is a combination of the wind speed and true airspeed, which gives us a groundspeed of 120 knots.

MOVING WITHIN A MOVING BLOCK OF WIND

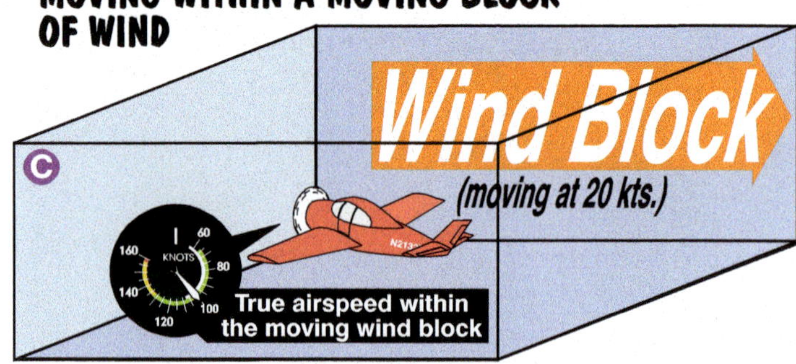

The airplane has a true airspeed of 100 knots. It's flying within a block of air moving at 20 knots that blows directly on the nose of the airplane. Thus, the speed of the airplane over the ground is the true airspeed minus the wind speed. This gives us a groundspeed of 80 knots.

Fig. 18

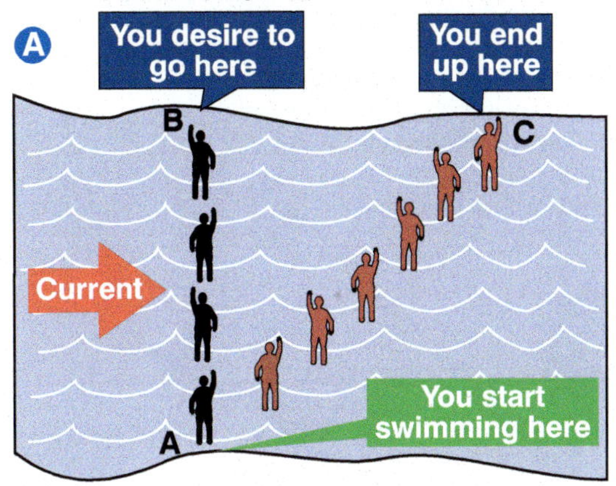

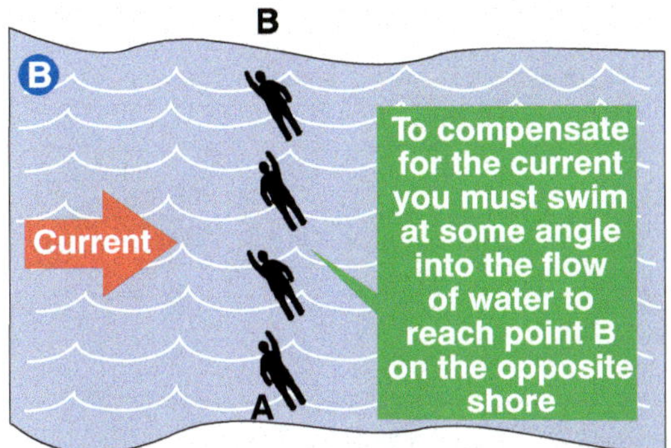

To prevent being carried downstream, a swimmer must swim at some angle into the flow of water. Airplanes must similarly fly (crab) at some angle into the wind to prevent being carried off course.

Fig. 19

The Effect of Water on a Swimmer – Suppose the swimmer in Figure 19A wants to swim across the river from point A to point B. Unless he swims at some angle into the flowing water, he'll be carried downstream to point C (or out to sea!). We'll call this the water correction angle (WCA). Figure 19B shows how angling into the current allows the swimmer to cross the river and arrive where he intended. Despite the fact our swimmer is pointed upstream, he actually travels directly across the river. Lights on? Camera. Action! Airplanes must do something similar when they travel in a stream of moving air.

The Effect of Wind on an Airplane – In Figure 20A, our airplane points in the direction of the desired course while flying with a left crosswind. Its track over the ground is a combination of the motion of the airplane and the motion of the air. The airplane is blown away from the desired course. The angle between the desired course and the actual ground track is called the drift angle. By determining the drift angle and correcting for it, you can fly a ground track exactly along the desired course, as shown in Figure 20B. Like our swimmer, you must head or point the airplane into the wind at enough of an angle to compensate for its effects. Instead of a *water correction angle,* we call this (remarkably) the *wind correction angle (WCA).*

Determining WCAs is where that fancy electronic flight computer you purchased will earn its keep. However, you really can't sense what the wind does to your flight path unless you visualize how it blows on your airplane. This is why I insist you initially use (or at least become familiar with) the venerable and trustworthy E6-B type computer to determine the wind's effect on your drift and groundspeed. (E6-B is an old military designation for the manual, slide type computer.)

Low Blow

In case you don't think it's all *that* important to have a good sense about how the wind affects your airplane, read on.

Several years ago I was returning to California from an Arizona airport on a moonless, pitch black night. I knew the wind was from the north (from my right), yet the VOR showed that a left wind correction angle (indicating a wind from the south) was necessary to remain on the desired course. As time passed, the left wind correction angle I needed to remain on course kept increasing. This shouldn't have been the case with a right (north) wind.

I eventually discovered that FAA maintenance technicians were working on the VOR station and hadn't removed its identification (giving the impression the station was in service). The work they were doing caused the VOR to produce an incorrect and misleading signal. If I hadn't understood the basics of how wind affects an airplane, I might still be looking for my destination.

Believe me, learning about dead reckoning navigation will serve you well in the future.

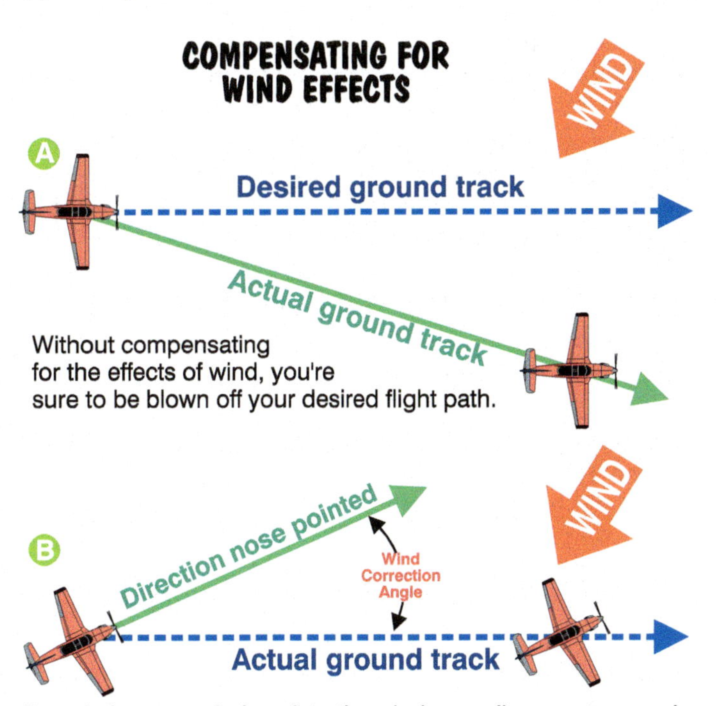

By pointing your airplane into the wind a small amount, your airplane tracks the desired flight path across the ground. The exact amount of angling into the wind is determined by use of your flight computer. This angle is called the WCA or Wind Correction Angle.

Fig. 20

I know I sound a little techno-regressed, but there is a reason I want you to use the manual computer before you start crunching numbers with your Cray Multimegabyte Handheld Captain Kirk Wind Computer. Trust me on this one. Besides, this argument is eternal and probably dates back to Confucius' mom telling him to put down that abacus and use his fingers for counting.

I'll walk you through the steps needed to use the E6-B for calculating a wind correction angle, but that's just the start of the calculations you can perform using this mechanical wonder. For an extended discussion of the workings and capabilities of the E6-B, please take the time to read Postflight Briefing #14-1. You'll need to know something about this to perform basic time, speed and distance computations on the front side of the E6-B.

From now on, we'll refer to the E6-B computer's two sides as the *wind side* and the *front side*.

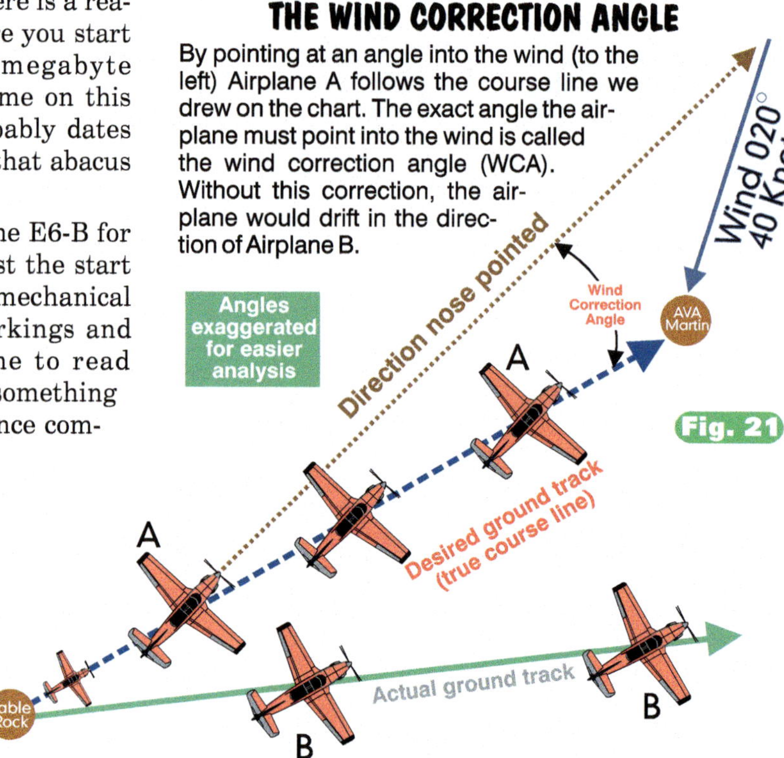

Fig. 21

Using the Wind Side of the Slide Computer – Here's the wind, and the performance information for our trip:

The wind as reported by the FSS for the altitude we'll fly is 020 degrees at 40 knots.

For this flight our performance charts say our true airspeed is 100 knots.

(In Chapter 15 you'll learn about how to use performance charts.)

The true course from Table Rock to AVA is 60 degrees.

Let's take just a second and visualize how the wind is affecting our airplane on this flight (see Figure 21). Notice that the wind is from 020 degrees. Our true course of 060 degrees means we're heading into a left quartering headwind. Common sense (always check for the presence of this when doing computations) indicates we'll need to correct to the left of 060 degrees in order to track the course line. It also indicates our groundspeed will be something less than our true airspeed of 100 knots, since the wind is blowing on the front of the airplane.

Given this, we have enough information to use our flight computer to determine two very important items necessary for all dead reckoning navigation: the wind correction angle (WCA) and our groundspeed. Let's take a look at the wind side of the E6-B type computer.

Figure 22 shows the basic components of the wind side of a typical E6-B computer. A rectangular sliding card fits inside the circular sleeve. The rectangular card has speed arcs with their appropriate values marked vertically along the centerline. It also has diagonal lines running up and down the card. The circular sleeve has a moveable inner scale that rotates about a center point (a small hole) known as the grommet. At the top of the circular scale is a small, white triangular reference point known as the *true index*.

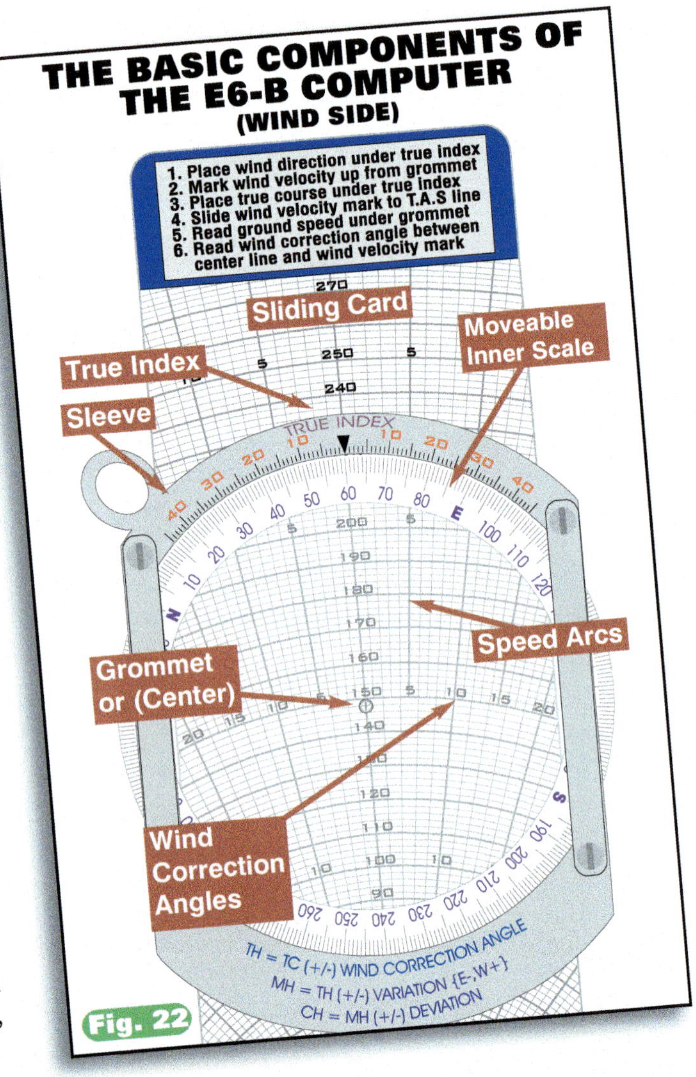

Fig. 22

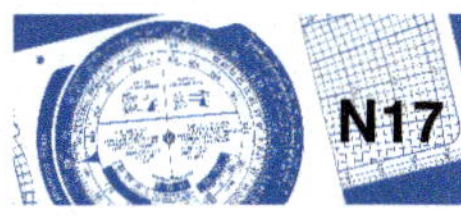

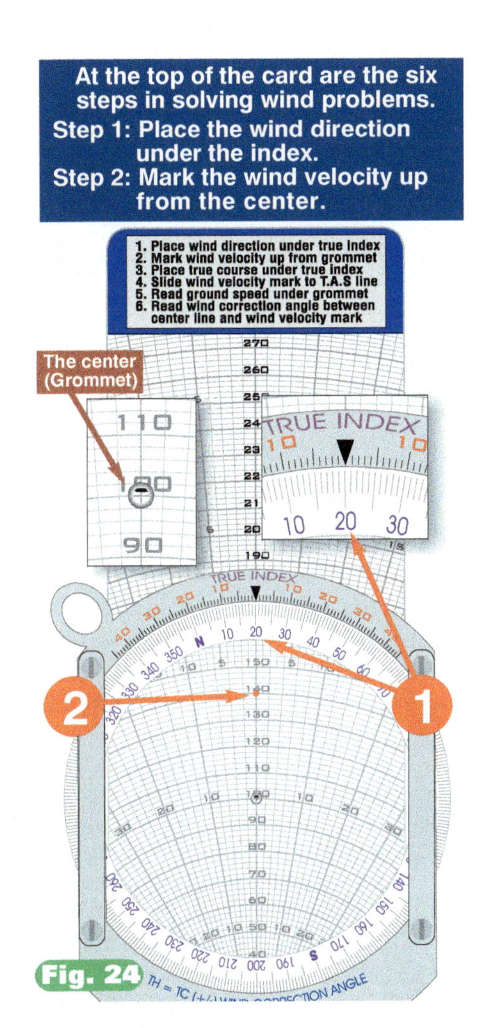

Fig. 24

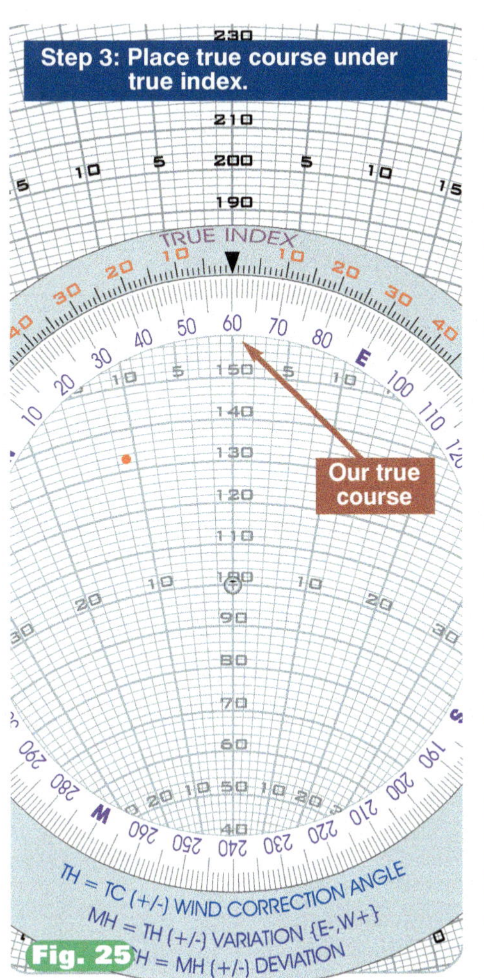

Fig. 25

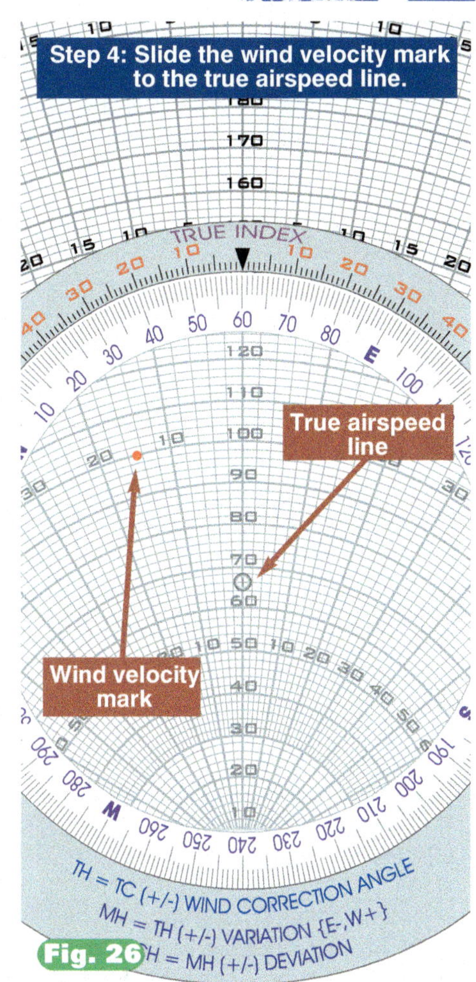

Fig. 26

At the very top of the rectangular card in Figure 22 are a series of 6 steps used in solving a wind problem.

Before starting any problem, it's always best to slide the rectangular card up or down to place the card's 100 arc value under the grommet as shown in Figure 23. This makes it easier to do the measuring required. If your computer has been used before, the rotating circular scale probably has a complexion problem—lots of dots over its plastic face. If there are any pencil marks on this scale, it's best to erase them now or there's no telling what kind of bizarre answers you'll get for your wind problems.

Step one says to place the wind direction under the *true* index. Rotate the inside plastic circle until 020 degrees is under the *true* index (Figure 24, position 1).

Step two says to mark wind velocity up from the center (the center is the grommet). Having placed the 100 arc under the grommet, simply count up the wind velocity along the given scale and make a mark (Figure 24, position 2). In our case the velocity is 40 knots (now do you see why I had you place the 100 arc under the grommet? It simply makes it easier to count up to the specific wind value).

Step three says to place the true course under the *true* index, as shown in Figure 25. Notice that your wind mark is on the left side of the scale.

Step four says to slide the wind velocity mark to the TAS (true airspeed line), as shown in Figure 26. I simply move the cardboard slide upward until the wind mark is on top of the 100 knot true airspeed line (it's actually an arc because it's curved). You're done! Wait, wait, come back here (you've got to stop running to the airplane every time I say "You're done"). All you need do is read the groundspeed and wind correction angle off the computer.

Before starting a wind problem, it's best to slide the wind card until the 100 arc value is under the grommet.

Place grommet (the metal ring) on 100 arc for ease in marking wind velocities up from center.

Fig. 23

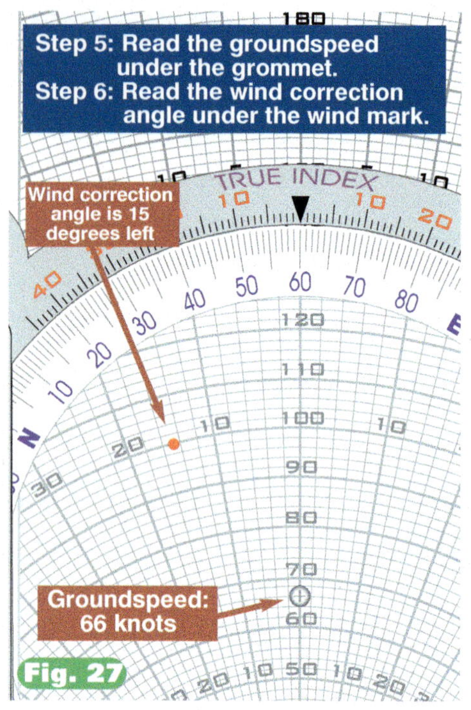

Fig. 27

FLIGHT PLAN STEP 3: DETERMINE THE WCA

Check Points	VOR Ident. Freq.	VOR Course (if applicable)	Altitude	Wind Dir.	Wind Vel.	Temp.	True Airspeed	TC	WCA R+ L-	TH	V E- W+	MH	D	CH	Distance	GS Ground speed Est.	GS Act.
Table Rock				020	40		100 kts.	60°	15L°								66 kts.
AVA/ Martin																	

Fig. 28

Step five says to read groundspeed under center (the grommet). Figure 27 shows a closeup of the center position. The grommet lies directly over a groundspeed of 66 knots.

Step six says to read the wind correction angle between centerline and the wind velocity mark, as shown in Figure 27. Notice the small lines running diagonally down the sliding scale. Our wind mark falls on the 15 degree diagonal line to the left of scale. Our wind correction angle is 15 degrees to the left. This means that a 15 degree angle to the left should compensate for the wind and allow us to track directly along the course line we drew on the chart in Flight Planning Step 1. Let's list the wind correction angle in our flight log as shown in Figure 28. (I'll explain the significance of left and right WCAs in a moment.)

Now look how nicely all this ties together. Figure 29 is a comparison of our previous wind picture (Figure 21) and the computer's wind triangle. They're very similar, aren't they? That's because the computer actually solves wind problems by creating a small wind triangle. Postflight briefing #14-3 shows you how to construct a wind triangle for the flight from Table Rock to AVA/Martin. Please take a good look at this briefing. It's well worth learning how to do a wind triangle (I sound like Confucius' mom, don't I?). The reason we often don't construct wind triangles on charts is because it's easier to do them mechanically on the plastic face of the computer.

The E6-B computer solves a wind problem by constructing a wind triangle (see Postflight Briefing #14-3). A wind triangle is a picture of how the wind affects your airplane. From it you can determine the WCA and airplane's groundspeed. An actual wind triangle is shown below. Notice the similarities.

Flight Planning Step 4—Determine the true heading – The next item in our flight log calls for the TH or *true heading.* A heading is technically a course that's been corrected for wind. In other words, if you correct your true course for the wind correction angle, you obtain a heading that allows you to track directly along the course line you drew on the sectional chart. Given that our WCA is 15 degrees left, we need to subtract this from the true course to obtain the true heading for this flight.

Why subtract? Any time the airplane turns to the left, the numbers of the compass get smaller. A right turn causes the compass numbers to get larger. It seems when most things are turned to the right (including radio dials), their numbers increase. Turning the dial to the left makes things less or smaller. That's why left WCAs are *subtracted* from the true course to obtain the true heading.

Nose points
Wind
Ground track
TH = TC (+/-) WIND CORRECTION ANGLE
Wind 020° 40 knots
Direction nose pointed
Wind Correction Angle
AVA Martin
Desired ground track (true course line)
Angles exaggerated for better analysis
Table Rock

Fig. 29

How True Airspeed Affects Your Wind Correction Angle

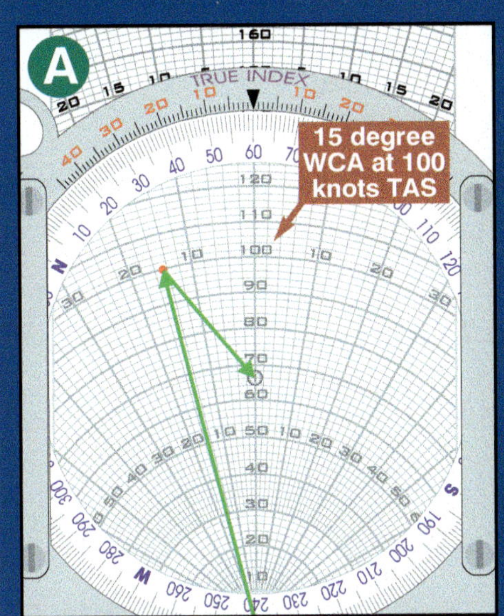

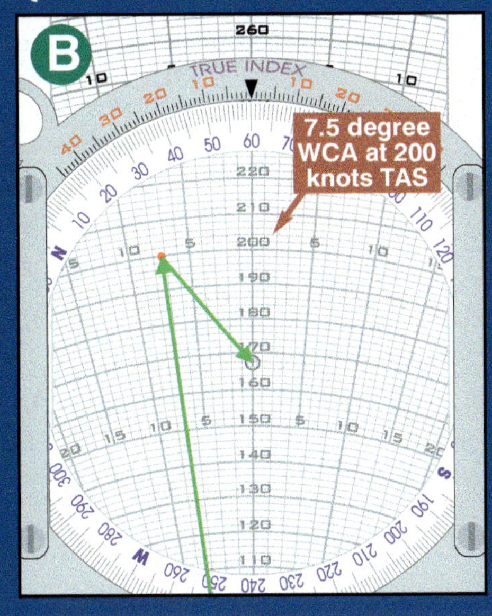

Item A (to the left) is the same problem as our flight from AVA to Table Rock. Item B, however, uses a new true airspeed for the computations. Notice that the wind mark in item B is over the 200 knots TAS arc. This gives us a new wind correction angle of approximately 7.5 degrees instead of 15 degrees for 100 knots TAS.

It's important for you to understand that the faster you fly, the less the wind affects you by blowing you off course. Why? Because you don't spend as much time enroute. There is less time for the wind to blow you off course when you're flying faster. The groundspeed, however, still stays approximately 34 knots below the true airspeed.

Right WCAs are *added* to the true course to obtain the true heading. The flight log reminds you to do this by putting a (-) next to L and a (+) next to R. Our flight log shows that a true course of 060 degrees with a left WCA of 15 degrees gives us a true heading of 045 degrees as shown in Figure 30.

Now that we have a true heading, is this all we need to get to our destination? Not quite. While a true heading corrects a true course for the wind, it's not something you can fly on your compass. In other words, the angles we've measured so far are in relation to the true north pole. Your airplane's compass is called a magnetic compass (not a true compass) because it points to a different pole. In other words, the magnetic compass measures angles with the magnetic north pole, while we have measured angles on the sectional chart with respect to the true north pole. We're mixing kiwi fruit and papayas here (OK, apples and oranges). We need to correct the true heading for the difference (called *variation)* between these two poles. Let's find out how to do that.

Flight Planning Step 5—Determining the magnetic heading – It's been said that women love a man in uniform. I believe this to be a substantiated fact. In fact, my wife fell for me because of the uniform—she couldn't resist the scarf, merit badges, and compass. And no pilot should be without a compass, even if you're out of uniform. As I said before, the compass is our primary means of navigation. But a slight problem exists, because the compass points to a pole that is different from the true north pole.

Recall that lines of longitude converge at the true north pole. In earlier times this was known to you as Santa Claus' house. The true north

FLIGHT PLAN STEP 4: DETERMINE THE TRUE HEADING

Check Points	VOR Ident. Freq.	VOR Course (if applicable)	Altitude	Wind Dir.	Wind Vel.	True Airspeed	TC	WCA R+ L-	TH	V E- W+	MH	D	CH	Distance	GS Ground speed Est. / Act.
				Temp.											
Table Rock				020	40	100 kts.	60°	15L°	45°						
AVA/ Martin															

Fig. 30

Is There an Untrue North Pole?

You might have noticed by now there are two north poles—the *true* north pole, and the *magnetic* north pole.

Once upon a time, just a few million years ago, both of these were in the same place, which is right where they should be, smack dab on top (or bottom, depending on your point of view) of the earth. When a compass needle pointed north (if there had been compass needles back then) it would have pointed to the one and only north pole.

Alas, things change. In the case of the magnetic pole, it began to wander around. Where a compass needle pointed as being north was no longer where the tippy top of the earth was. I won't worry your databank with a deposit on why the magnetic pole moves, but it has and it does and it is and it will.

What you as a pilot need to understand is that while east may be east, and west may be west (and never the twain shall meet), north isn't always north. *Magnetic north* is where the needle on a compass points. *True north* is where it always has been, the place where all the lines of longitude converge at a single point. The difference, at the moment, is a matter of about 1300 miles!

The angular difference between true north and magnetic north is referred to as *magnetic variation.* It varies for every location, and continues to slowly change. The current value can be found on your sectional chart.

Knowing the north pole isn't true should inspire some great country and western songs.

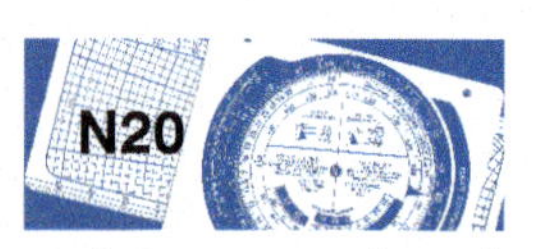

and true south poles represent the spin axis points of the earth. The earth acts like a very large magnet (too big to put on any refrigerator), and has two magnetic poles (Figure 31). As I've previously stated, they are, unfortunately, not located in the same position as the true north pole. Lying just a little north of Hudson Bay, the *magnetic* north pole is separated by a distance of approximately 1300 miles from the *true* north pole.

The variation between these two poles presents a slight challenge in navigation. We measured our course with respect to the *true* north pole, but we must navigate using a compass that points to the *magnetic* north pole. Fortunately, the answer is simple—correct for the angular variation between the true and the magnetic north poles. This is easy to do once you understand that this variation changes depending on your geographic location.

EARTH AS A GIANT MAGNET

Fig. 31

The earth is essentially a very big magnet with north and south poles. Magnetic lines of flux run between the magnetic poles of the earth in the same way they run between the poles of a small magnet. Your compass points to the magnetic north pole while the earth rotates around an axis running between the true north and south poles.

Earth as a Magnet

True North Pole (Santa's house)

Magnetic North Pole

Compass Points To Magnetic North Pole

True South Pole

Figure 32 depicts an airplane in three different locations across the United States. In position B, the airplane is located so the magnetic north pole is directly in front of the true north pole. In this instance, both poles appear in line with one another, so there is no apparent variation in location between poles. Your true heading would be a magnetic heading at this location (a location with zero variation). You could simply fly the number you found with the plotter on the compass (assuming no wind and the compass is free of errors itself).

An airplane in position C views the magnetic north pole to the west (to the left) of the true north pole. We have what is technically known as *westerly variation* between poles. The airplane in position A sees the magnetic pole located to the east (to the right) of the true north pole. Airplane A experiences *easterly variation* between poles.

Clearly, the variation between poles depends on what part of the United States (or the world for that matter) you're in. Fortunately, we can correct for this variation since it's a known quantity dependent on your location. Figure 33 shows the angular variation between the magnetic and true north poles. If you were flying along the western part of Texas (Airplane C), the magnetic north pole would be 10 degrees to the east of the true north pole. Printed lines of

Fig. 32

MAGNETIC VARIATION DEPENDS ON YOUR LOCATION

A

Magnetic North Pole

True North Pole

Compass needle points east of true north pole (easterly variation)

From this position on earth, the magnetic north pole appears to the east of the true north pole. Easterly variation is experienced in this area.

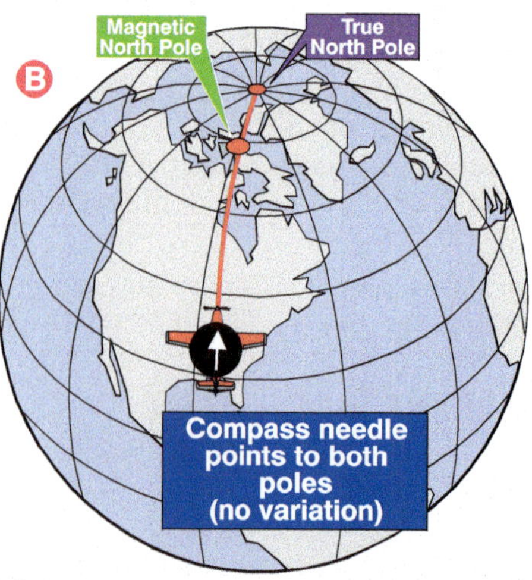

From this position on earth, the magnetic north pole appears to be aligned with the true north pole. No variation is experienced in this area.

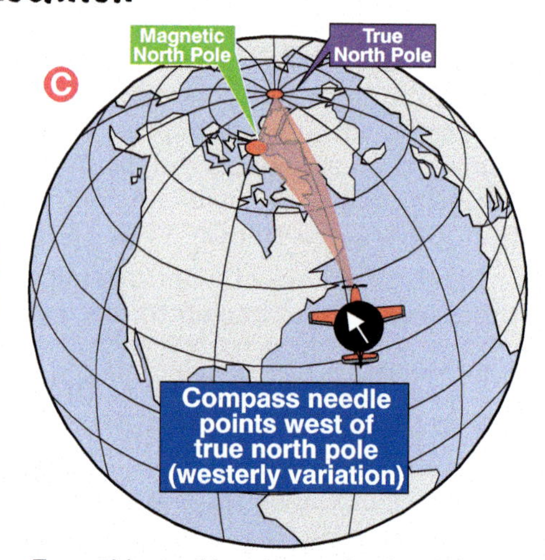

From this position on earth, the magnetic north pole appears to the west of the true north pole. Westerly variation is experienced in this area.

Home Plate

Never leave your flashlight (with its magnetic clip) lying on the dash, next to the compass. Word has it that entire platoons of soldiers went the wrong direction in Vietnam when they held their compasses up next to their steel helmets to take a directional reading. Anything magnetic (and many steels) can affect the compass; keep such items away from wherever the compass is mounted.

A friend had a student who was worried that an anatomical problem might affect his navigation. He had a metal plate in his head (I think he installed it himself). I'm not sure if this would be harmful in terms of navigational accuracy, but it sure would keep him from losing his flashlight!

Another Way Of Looking at It

WHY WE SUBTRACT EASTERLY VARIATION AND ADD WESTERLY VARIATION

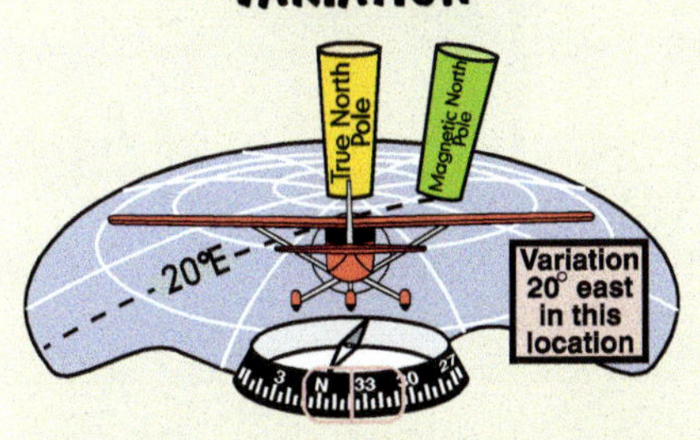

Our airplane is headed directly toward the true north pole. Its true course is 360 degrees. Its magnetic compass, however, says it's flying 340 degrees (it's flying at a 340 degree angle to the magnetic north pole). Thus, when we know our true course and we want to find our magnetic course (or heading), we subtract easterly variation from the true course. Subtracting 20 degrees of easterly variation from a true course of 360 degrees gives us our magnetic course of 340 degrees (the angle our airplane makes with the magnetic north pole).

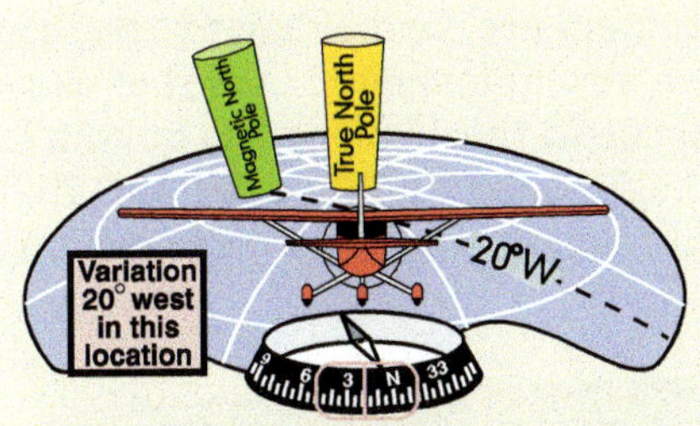

In an area where the westerly variation is 20 degrees, our airplane makes a 0 degree angle (same as 360 degrees) with the true north pole, yet it makes a 20 degree angle with the magnetic north pole. Therefore, to find our magnetic course (or heading) when we are given westerly variation, we need to add this to the true course. Twenty degrees of westerly variation added to a true course of zero degrees give us a magnetic course of 020 degrees.

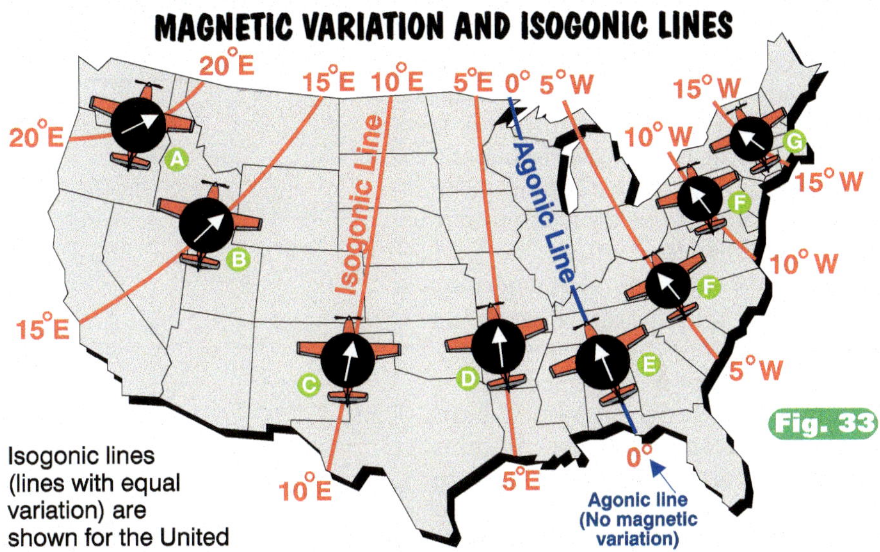

Isogonic lines (lines with equal variation) are shown for the United States. Anywhere along the depicted line, the angular variation between the true north pole and the magnetic north pole is the same (thus the prefix *iso* which means *the same as*). As you can see above, all the airplanes are headed toward the true north pole while their white compass needles are deflected an amount equal to the magnetic variation for that location.

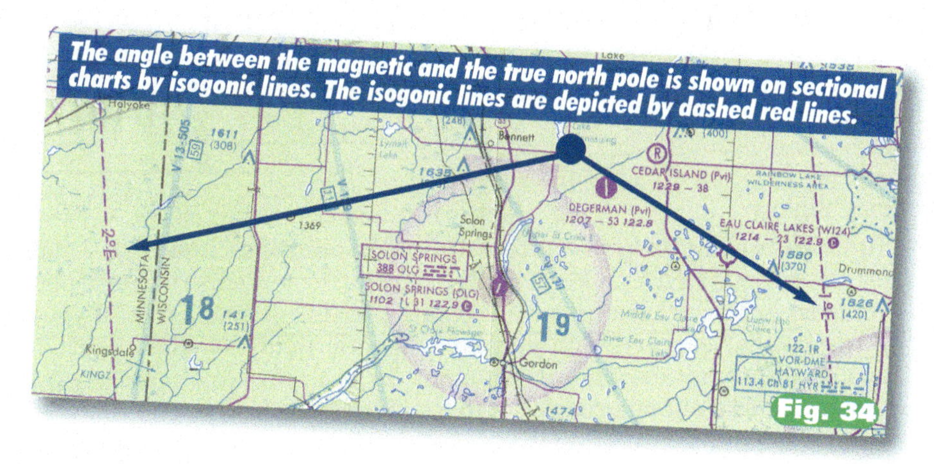

The angle between the magnetic and the true north pole is shown on sectional charts by isogonic lines. The isogonic lines are depicted by dashed red lines.

variation shown on sectional charts are known as *isogonic lines* and are shown in Figure 34. They are spaced at increments of one degree and are marked for either east or west variation with an E or W respectively. *Iso,* like isobar, means *the same as. Gonic* is a Greek derivative meaning *angles.* Anywhere along an isogonic line, the angular variation between the poles is the same.

To the northwest of Florida, Airplane E (Figure 33), is on an *agonic line.* The prefix *a* means *no.* Along the agonic line there is no angular variation between the poles. Standing along this line, the true and magnetic north poles would be aligned with one another and no variation exists in this location. The isogonic lines aren't straight because of the many slight variations in the earth's magnetism (perhaps caused by too many heavy metal rock concerts in one area).

Now you're ready to correct the true heading for the effect of magnetic variation. You can do this by finding the closest whole number (not half degree) isogonic line nearest the center of your course line as shown in Figure 35. The magnetic variation is 2E or 2 degrees east. Our flight log in Figure 36 shows that easterly variation is subtracted from the true heading to obtain the magnetic heading. If we subtract the easterly variation of 2 degrees from our true heading of 45 degrees, this gives us a magnetic heading of 43 degrees.

If we had westerly variation, we would have added this to the true heading to obtain the magnetic heading. An easy way to remember this is to think, East is least, west is best. Least means *subtract,* best implies *add.* After correcting the true heading for variation, you now have an angle with respect to the magnetic north pole or a magnetic heading.

Now we at least have a number we can fly on our compass, right? Almost. There's one more thing to consider. What happens if the compass in our airplane is slightly inaccurate? In other words, what happens if the value it shows deviates slightly from the actual magnetic direction? We need to compensate for this deviation before we can set off on our cross country flight.

Fig. 35

FLIGHT PLAN STEP 5: DETERMINE THE MAGNETIC HEADING

Check Points	VOR Ident. Freq.	VOR Course (if applicable)	Altitude	Wind Dir.	Wind Vel.	True Airspeed	TC	WCA R+ L-	TH	V E- W+	MH	D	CH	Distance	GS Ground speed Est. / Act.
Table Rock				020	40	100 kts.	60°	15L°	45°	-2°	43°				66 kts.
AVA/ Martin															

Fig. 36

Flight Planning Step 6—Determine your compass heading – Many instructors are fond of saying that compasses are devious devices. Occasionally, they lie. Some items in the airplane have a strong magnetic field that causes the compass needle to turn or deviate slightly, resulting in an error. If you think about it, the airplane has quite a few little things that can generate deviant magnetic fields—radios, lights, tools, magnetized metal parts, and flight instructors. Compass deviation is different for each airplane. That's why you will always find a *compass deviation card* mounted near the magnetic compass (Figure 37).

TYPICAL COMPASS DEVIATION CARD

FOR (MAGNETIC)	N	30	60	E	120	150
STEER (COMPASS)	0	28	57	86	117	148
FOR (MAGNETIC)	S	210	240	W	300	330
STEER (COMPASS)	180	212	243	274	303	332

Fig. 37

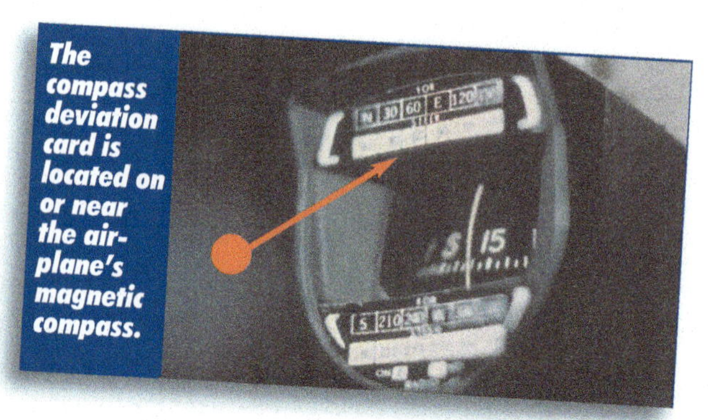
The compass deviation card is located on or near the airplane's magnetic compass.

Have you ever noticed a painted *compass rose* (these are not decorated flowers that point north) around the airport, much like the one shown in Figure 38? This isn't a sacred place where Druids go for a belly button alignment. It's much more practical.

Mechanics place the airplane in the center of this compass rose and point the nose in precise magnetic directions painted around the circle. All the airplane's equipment is turned on to obtain the maximum amount of potential magnetic interference. The actual magnetic direction is measured against the compass' indications. This process is known as *swinging the compass.* To the extent possible, adjustments are made to the compass to eliminate the discrepancies. Any remaining deviation between the actual magnetic direction and what the compass shows is recorded on the compass deviation card (Figure 37). This card will usually be found mounted directly beneath the compass.

The airport's compass rose allows calibration of the airplane's magnetic compass. With the airplane's electrical equipment on, mechanics can compare compass readings with known magnetic directions. Differences are logged on the compass deviation card.

Fig. 38

FLIGHT PLAN STEP 6: DETERMINE THE COMPASS HEADING

Check Points	VOR Ident. Freq.	VOR Course (if applicable)	Altitude	Wind Dir. Vel. Temp.	True Airspeed	TC	WCA R+ L-	TH	V E- W+	MH	D	CH	Distance	GS Ground speed Est. Act.
Table Rock				020 40	100 kts.	60°	15L	45°	-2°	43°	-2°	41°		66 kts
AVA/ Martin														

Fig. 39

Step 6 of cross country flight planning requires you to correct the magnetic heading for the compass deviation, to obtain a heading you can fly on your compass. The compass deviation card in Figure 37 shows that if you wanted to fly a magnetic heading of 060 degrees, you'd need to steer a heading of 057 degrees on your compass. In other words, with a value of 057 degrees showing in the window of your compass, you'd actually be making an angle of 060 degrees with the magnetic north pole. The difference between the magnetic heading you want to fly and what's shown on the compass is the *compass deviation*. In this case, the deviation is -3 degrees.

As you see in Figure 37, the deviation can vary on different headings. What would the deviation be on a magnetic heading of 310 degrees? Since this values isn't listed, use the deviation for the magnetic heading closest to this value—in this case a magnetic heading of 300 degrees (closest to 310 degrees). This deviation is +3 degrees, so we'd fly 313 degrees on our compass. Correcting the magnetic heading for the deviation gives us the correct *compass heading*.

Since we want to fly a magnetic heading of 043 degrees, the closest value on the compass deviation card in Figure 37 is 030 degrees. The deviation on this heading is -2 degrees. So we will steer 041 degrees on the compass, thus making the 2 degree correction which lets us fly the desired 043 degree magnetic heading. Enter this compass heading in the flight log, as shown in Figure 39.

Whew. The flight log shows we have finally arrived at a heading to fly. This compass heading will take us from Table Rock to AVA/Martin, correcting for wind, magnetic variation, and compass deviation.

In these few short pages you've learned the basics of dead reckoning navigation. Of course, we haven't found distances nor used our calculated groundspeeds to estimate fuel consumption and time of arrival. We'll do that in a while. For now, understand that calculating

New Aviation Inventions

Here's a new device that's sure to become a top-of-the-line item for all air traffic controllers. It's a miniature water-cooled radiator that fits over a controller's lips and helps prevent them from catching fire as they deliver those megaspeed clearances.

the compass heading to be flown is an important part of every flight plan. If your flight has two or more legs (places where the course line drawn on the chart changes direction), then you'll need to calculate the compass heading for each leg. On longer flights, you might have several legs, with flight log items 6 through 13 completed for each leg. Once you get a little practice using the computer, you will do these calculations quite quickly.

The basic process of dead reckoning navigation from Table Rock to AVA/Martin involves finding a course, correcting it for wind to obtain a heading then following the steps listed below:

True heading......... 45 degrees

Variation............ -2 degrees east

Magnetic heading... 43 degrees

Deviation.............. -2 degrees

Compass heading.. 41 degrees

Did you notice the first letters of each line? They are TVMDC and they refer to the values of True heading, plus or minus the Variation equals the Magnetic heading, plus or minus the Deviation equals the Compass heading. Don't forget this letter sequence. It will help you remember how to convert a true heading into a compass heading. In fact, here is a great mnemonic to help remember this.

Tele

Vision

Makes

Dull

Company

Simply visualize yourself sitting in front of the TV planning a cross country flight while thinking. Figure 40 shows this process using a flow diagram that we'll use from now on.

You can also use the flow diagram in Figure 40 to obtain something known as the *compass course,* shown in Figure 41. A compass course is essentially a compass heading without the wind correction angle. Sometimes you will want to make a short flight (well within the airplane's fuel range) that doesn't require elaborate navigational calculations. You plan to use VOR or GPS to take you to your destination and neither want nor need detailed flight planning and wind correction. That's fine. There's nothing wrong with this for those short-hop flights. You simply start off toward your destination using the magnetic course backed up with either pilotage or some form of electronic navigation. For longer flights that are sure to consume a lot of fuel, you'll want to do much more detailed flight planning to determine groundspeeds and fuel consumption rates.

Figure 41 also helps you determine your magnetic course. Do you remember FAR 91.159, the VFR cruising altitude regulation? This regulation requires you to fly at even or odd thousand foot levels plus 500 feet, depending on your magnetic course. The magnetic course is easily determined by correcting the true course for the variation, as shown in Figure 41.

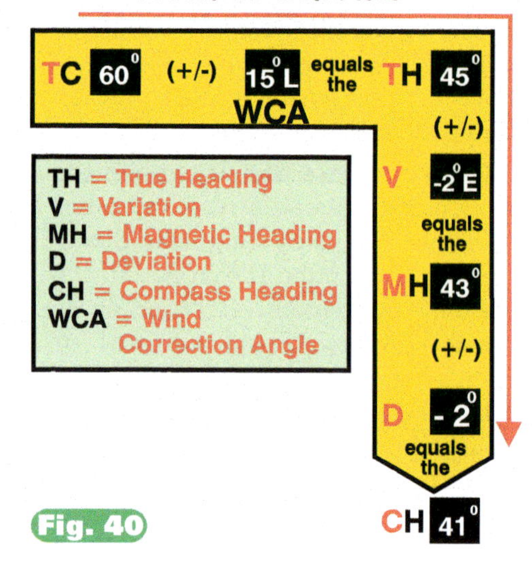

Fig. 40

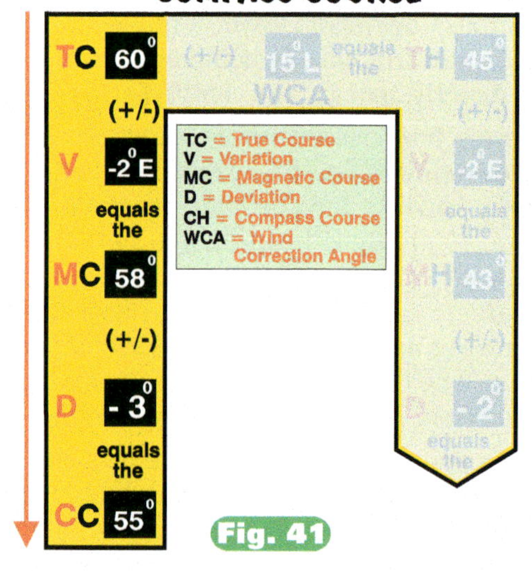

Fig. 41

Return Trip From AVA/Memorial To Table Rock

Let's say we've spent enough money at the pilot supply shop at AVA/Martin airport and have decided to return home (before our airplane becomes too heavy for liftoff because of all the pilot toys—headsets, computers, flight cases—we've purchased). We call the FSS and they tell us the winds are from 350 degrees at 30 knots at all altitudes below 10,000 feet MSL. Let's follow the same six flight planning steps we performed before, and fill out our flight log as we go along. We'll use 120 knots for our true airspeed on the return flight to get home quicker and play with our new pilot toys.

Flight Planning Step 1—Draw a line between checkpoints – We've already done this in Figure 35.

Flight Planning Step 2—Determine the true course – The true course from AVA/Martin to Table Rock is the opposite of

FLIGHT PLAN STEP 2: DETERMINE THE TRUE COURSE

Check Points	VOR Ident. Freq.	VOR Course (if applicable)	Altitude	Wind Dir.	Wind Vel.	True Airspeed	TC	WCA R+ L-	TH	V E- W+	MH	D	CH	Distance	GS Ground speed Est. / Act.
AVA/ Martin															
Table Rock				350	30										

Fig. 42

SELECTING AN ALTITUDE AND TRUE AIRSPEED

Check Points	VOR Ident. Freq.	VOR Course (if applicable)	Altitude	Wind Dir.	Wind Vel.	True Airspeed	TC	WCA R+ L-	TH	V E- W+	MH	D	CH	Distance	GS Ground speed Est. / Act.
AVA/ Martin															
Table Rock			4,500	350	30	120 kts.	240°								

Fig. 43

what it was for the initial trip (which was 060 degrees). We'll put 240 degrees in our flight log form, as shown in Figure 43.

DETERMINING THE WIND CORRECTION ANGLE, STEPS: 1&2

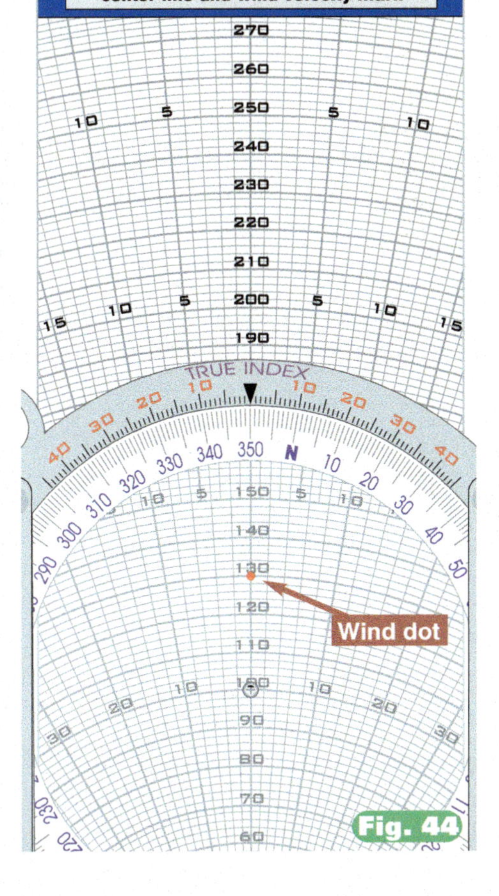

Fig. 44

At this point we can quickly determine the magnetic course to see what altitude (even or odd) to fly. Recall the letter sequence *TVMDC*. Correcting the true course (240 degrees) for the magnetic variation (2 degrees east—it hasn't changed from our first flight) we obtain a magnetic course of 238 degrees (240 degrees – 2 degrees E=238 degrees).

According to FAR 91.159, when flying a magnetic course of 180 degrees through 359 degrees, we need to fly at even thousands plus 500 feet (assuming that we'll be more than 3,000 feet AGL during the flight—we will be). Since AVA/Martin's altitude is 1,311 feet MSL, we can fly at 4,500 feet, 6,500 feet 8,500 feet, and so on. No sense wasting all that fuel in climbing high for such a short flight. For the purposes of this example, let's fly at 4,500 feet MSL, putting us more than 3,000 feet above the surface (realistically, I'd probably fly at 2,500 feet MSL on this flight, meaning that I am not restricted by the hemispherical cruising altitudes). We'll add these values to our flight log, as shown in Figure 43.

Flight Planning Step 3—Determine the wind correction angle – Let's use our flight computer to do this. Using the wind side of the slide computer, set the computer's grommet on the 100 arc before starting a wind problem, as shown in Figure 44. Erase all the other wind marks from previous problems. I hope you used pencil, not indelible ink. Make it a point to use a soft lead pencil. Hard lead pencils require you to take running stabs at your computer to make any type of visible mark (besides, you could accidentally pole vault over your desk).

Step one says to place the wind direction under the true index. Rotate the inside plastic circle until 350 degrees is under the true index, as shown in Figure 44.

Step two says to mark wind velocity up from center (the center is the grommet). Having placed the 100 arc under the grommet, simply count up the wind velocity along the given scale and make a mark. In our case the velocity is 30 knots (Figure 44).

How Rod Determined That TV Makes Dull Company

I know for a fact that TV makes dull company. Television numbs the mind, deactivates dendrites and pickles personalities. In short, watch it long enough and you feel like you have an IQ a grade lower than bean dip.

My friend's grandfather used to watch TV so much he had a hard time distinguishing fantasy from reality. One time, during a football game, he started yelling at the TV quarterback. "Throw it to Winston you fool, throw it to Winston! Geesh! Can you believe that guy?" snapped grandpa. I looked over at him and said, "Ah, sir, calm down, calm down, they can't hear you." He looked at me for a second, then mumbled, "Yeah, I guess you're right. They've got their helmets on."

Step three says to place the true course under the true index as shown in Figure 45. Notice that your wind mark is now on the right side of the scale.

Step four says to slide the wind velocity mark to the TAS (true airspeed line), as shown in Figure 46. Simply move the cardboard slide upward until the wind mark is on top of the 120 knot true airspeed line (arc). You're done! All you need do is read the groundspeed and wind correction angle off the computer (see the next two steps)

Step five says to read groundspeed under center (the grommet). The grommet lies directly over a groundspeed of 127 knots.

Step six says to read the wind correction angle between the centerline and the wind velocity mark. Your wind mark falls on the 14 degree diagonal line to the right of scale. Your wind correction angle is 14 degrees to the right. This makes sense, since the wind is from your right and slightly behind you.

Let's insert our WCA and groundspeed in the flight log form (Figure 47). The rest of the flight planning is a snap.

Flight Planning Step 4: Determine the true heading – When we add the true course of 240 degrees to a right WCA of 14 degrees we obtain a true heading of 254 degrees, as shown in Figure 48.

Flight Planning Step 5: Determine the magnetic heading – Correcting the true heading for variation (TVMDC, remember?) gives us the magnetic heading. The variation of 2 degrees east hasn't changed on this flight. Our magnetic heading is 250 degrees (254 degrees – 2 degrees E=252 degrees). Let's insert this into our flight log as shown in Figure 49. And now for our last step.

Flight Planning Step 6: Determine the compass heading – Correcting the magnetic heading for compass deviation (TVMDC) gives us the compass heading. The compass deviation card shown in Figure 37 shows that for a magnetic heading of 252 degrees (we'll use 240 degrees on the card since it's the closest to our magnetic heading) we should steer 3 degrees more, which gives us a compass heading of 255 degrees (252 degrees+3 degrees=255

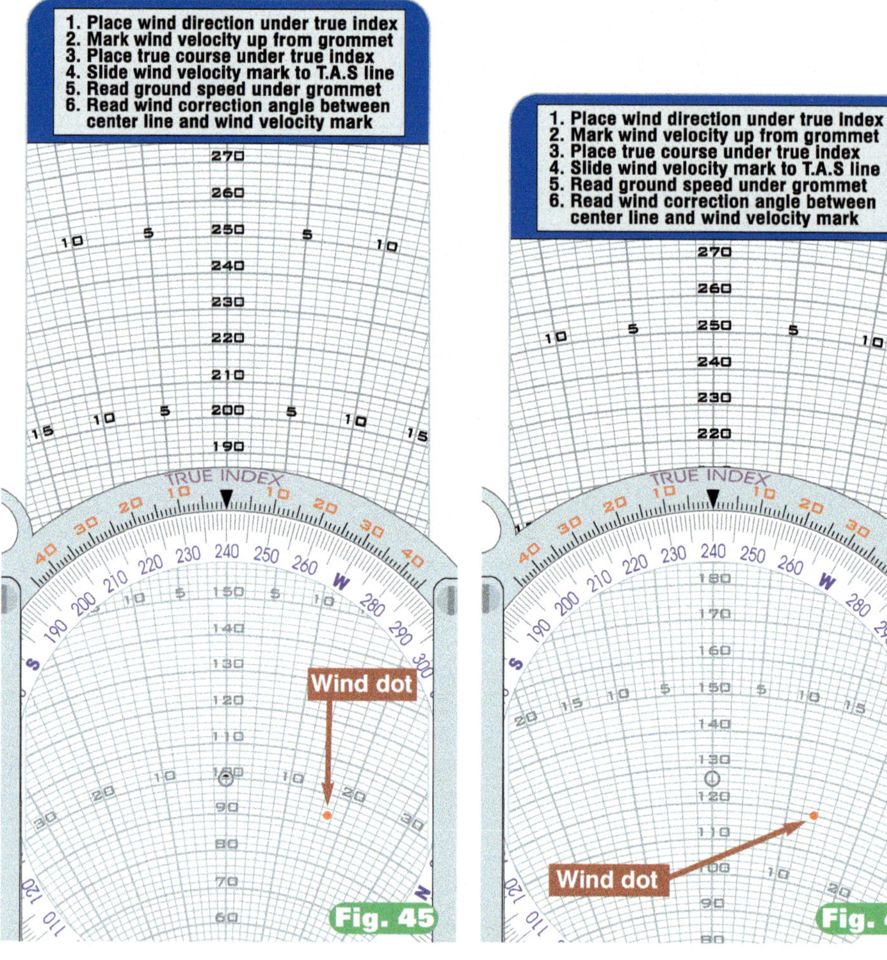

FLIGHT PLAN STEP 3: DETERMINE THE WCA (& GS TOO)

Check Points	VOR Ident. Freq.	VOR Course (if applicable)	Altitude	Wind Dir.	Wind Vel. / Temp.	True Airspeed	TC	WCA R+ L-	TH	V E- W+	MH	D	CH	Distance	GS Ground speed Est. / Act.
AVA/ Martin															
			4,500	350	30	120 kts.	240°	14R							127 kts.
Table Rock															

Fig. 47

FLIGHT PLAN STEP 4: DETERMINE THE TRUE HEADING

Check Points	VOR Ident. Freq.	VOR Course (if applicable)	Altitude	Wind Dir.	Wind Vel. / Temp.	True Airspeed	TC	WCA R+ L-	TH	V E- W+	MH	D	CH	Distance	GS Ground speed Est. / Act.
AVA/ Martin															
			4,500	350	30	120 kts.	240°	14R	254°						127 kts.
Table Rock															

Fig. 48

FLIGHT PLAN STEP 5: DETERMINE THE MAGNETIC HEADING

Check Points	VOR Ident. Freq.	VOR Course (if applicable)	Altitude	Wind Dir.	Wind Vel.	True Airspeed	TC	WCA R+ L-	TH	V E- W+	MH	D	CH	Distance	GS Ground speed Est. / Act.
AVA/ Martin			4,500	350	30	120 kts.	240°	14R	254°	-2°	252°				127 kts.
Table Rock															

Fig. 49

FLIGHT PLAN STEP 6: DETERMINE THE COMPASS HEADING

Check Points	VOR Ident. Freq.	VOR Course (if applicable)	Altitude	Wind Dir.	Wind Vel.	True Airspeed	TC	WCA R+ L-	TH	V E- W+	MH	D	CH	Distance	GS Ground speed Est. / Act.
AVA/ Martin			4,500	350	30	120 kts.	240°	14R	254°	-2°	252°	+3°	255°		127 kts.
Table Rock															

Fig. 50

degrees). Let's insert this value into our flight log form, as shown in Figure 50.

That wasn't too bad, was it? Believe me when I say this becomes real easy with just a little practice. Now that we know how to get to our destination, let's discuss how to obtain our expected time enroute and the amount of fuel we'll use in getting where we're going. We can do this using the groundspeed we've obtained during flight planning step 3 and the front side of our flight computer.

Planning an Actual Flight

Let's put your knowledge to practical use and plan a short cross country flight from Healdsburg to Nut Tree airport, as shown in Figure 51. We'll assume that due to solar flares and vacuum tube shortages all VORs in the area are inoperative, so the flight is to be conducted by dead reckoning and pilotage. This will be a simple, barebones flight plan. The objective is to give you a basic idea of how to make the calculations needed to put you over the destination airport.

Since we're planning on making this flight within the next few hours, we'll place a call to the Flight Service Station to obtain the weather and pertinent NOTAMS. If we were planning this flight for the following day we would call the FSS and obtain an outlook briefing. Before the flight, however, we would call to obtain a standard briefing and current NOTAMS.

Let's say the FSS gave us clear skies, no applicable NOTAMS, and the following winds aloft forecast for the station nearest our area:

3,000 feet—040 degrees at 12 knots

6,000 feet—070 degrees at 24 knots, temperature +1

9,000 feet—080 degrees at 31 knots, temperature –5

Now we're ready to draw the course line. Figure 51 shows a direct line between Healdsburg and Nut Tree airport. Whenever possible, I try and fly direct between airports. After all, that's what makes flying unique, isn't it? Unfortunately, direct flights are not always possible. Restricted

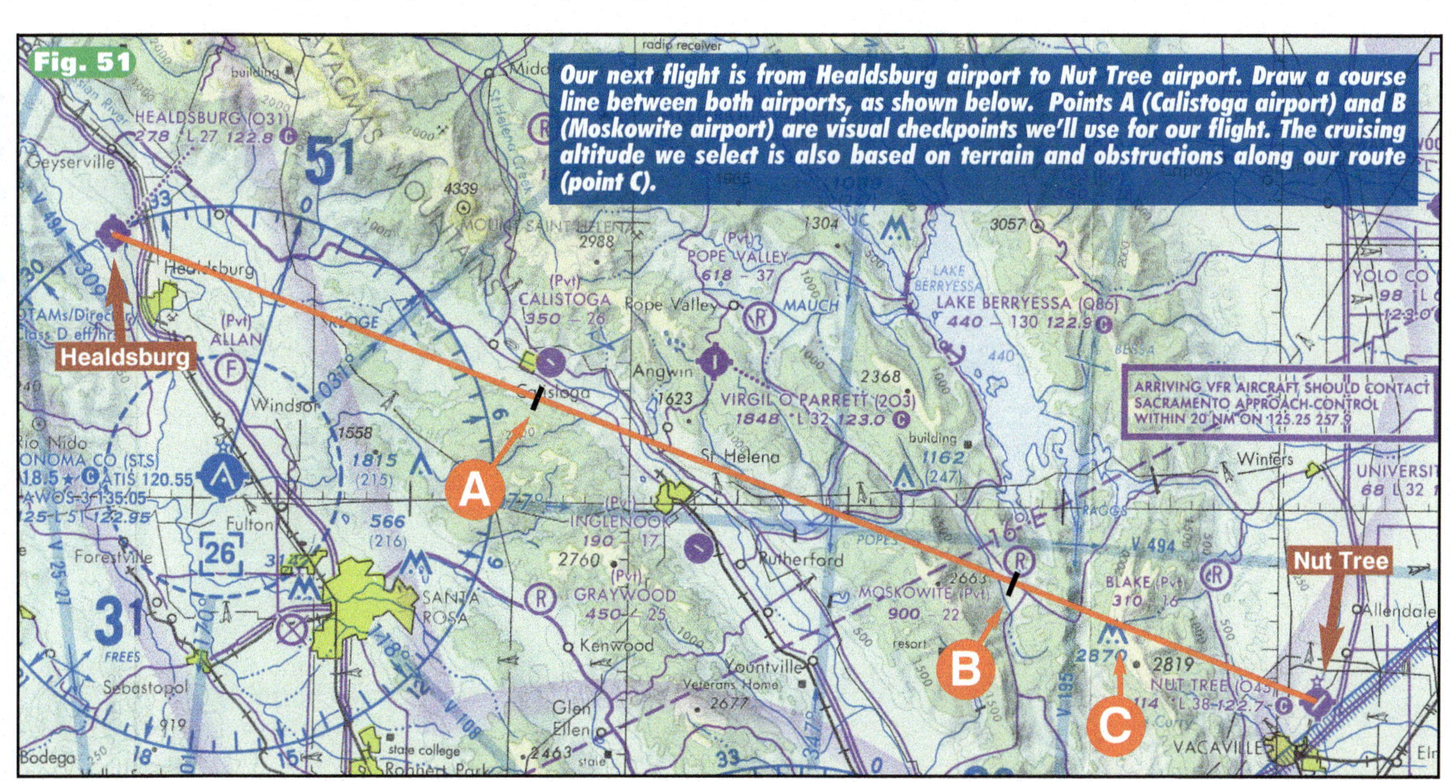

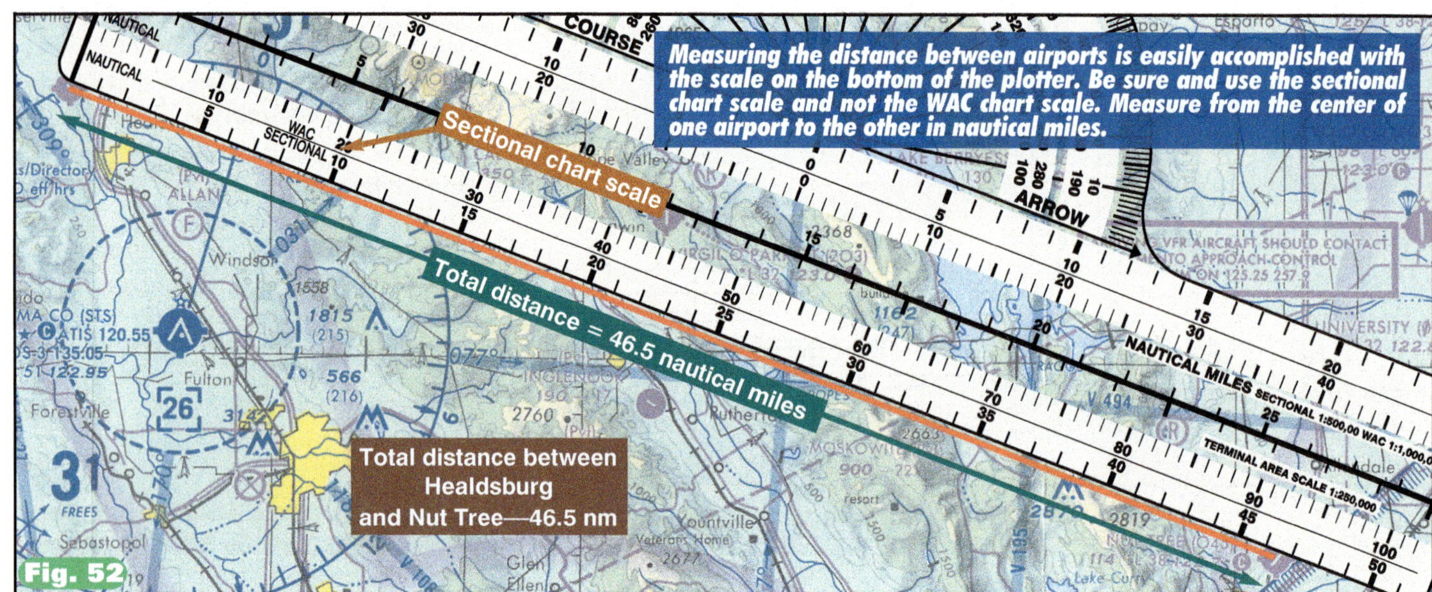

Fig. 52

areas, mountains, AND large bodies of water are just a few of the things that might break up a direct flight into separate segments or *legs,* each having different directions and distances. Look the route over carefully and decide if a direct flight is possible or if the route should be broken down into separate legs having different directions.

Cross Country Planning: Selecting a Route – Since there is no special use airspace and there are no major obstacles on our selected route, we'll fly directly to the destination. This is convenient since it allows us to apply our wind correction to a single route. If you choose several route segments, each having different directions, wind correction must be calculated for and applied to each portion. In other words, you must work separate wind computations for each leg of the flight on your flight computer (this is where an electronic computer comes in handy).

Cross Country Planning: Measuring the Distance – After drawing the route, I like to measure the total distance. I'm concerned about whether the airplane has enough fuel for the flight. Having a general idea of the airplane's range is important here (we'll discuss a performance chart that shows the airplane's range under different power conditions in Chapter 15). Using the nautical mile scale on the bottom of the plotter, we find the total distance between Healdsburg and Nut Tree is 46.5 nautical miles, as shown in Figure 52. Obviously, there is no range problem here. If the total distance were 400.5 nautical miles, range would be a concern—especially if you have strong headwinds (and a small bladder). In that case you might elect to land at an airport(s) along the way to obtain additional fuel. While the FARs require 30 minutes reserve during the day (45 minutes at night), I make it a point never to be airborne with my tanks less than one-quarter full. This may be a bit conservative for some, but I've never had to turn an airplane into a glider because I ran out of fuel.

Cross Country Planning: Selecting Checkpoints – Even though our route is direct, we'll divide it up into segments. Our objective is to select visual checkpoints to aid us in navigation along the route. Yes, dead reckoning will surely point us in the proper direction of Nut Tree, but monitoring checkpoints along the route allows us to make small corrections for variations in winds during the trip (believe me when I say that winds can and do vary). I've chosen two checkpoints along the route, as shown in Figure 51 (points A and B).

BEEP—BEEP

While returning from a pleasure flight, I experienced an engine problem that caused a loss of power. After checking the engine instruments, engine and propeller controls, fuel gauge and selector valve, I decided to land the airplane immediately. A suitable roadway was selected. Upon touching down, I saw a small automobile pull out of a side street and proceed down the road ahead of me. To avoid hitting the car, I veered to the left, where the wing encountered three small mailboxes. At this point, the aircraft passed the small car and the right wing went up and over the full length of the automobile. Both aircraft and automobile stopped. The driver of the car jumped out, chastised me for not using my "horn," looked to see if there was any damage to his car, which there was not, got back in the car and promptly drove away.

ASRS Report

Try and pick checkpoints separated by 10 to 15 miles. You can pick more if you wish, but I don't suggest picking fewer. Select checkpoints you're sure are easily visible from the air. A little flying experience will quickly teach you what can and can't be seen from an altitude of 5,000 or 10,000 feet. You'll find that some shapes and colors stand out much better than others. Narrow things of neutral color, such as power lines, are hard to see. When selecting checkpoints, ask yourself, "Could I see this from a mile away on the ground?" Remembering that 5,000 feet is about a mile high, you'll have some idea of whether a given checkpoint is a sensible choice.

I've chosen Calistoga airport (point A) and Moskowite airport (point B) for our two checkpoints. Given the short distance of this flight, two checkpoints are sufficient. You don't have to chose checkpoints you will fly directly over. In fact, sometimes it's better if they are a little to the side of the flight path (preferably to the left side, since that's where you're typically seated). At night, cities or heavily traveled freeways or highways make great checkpoints, since you can't identify much else in the dark (highways have BLS —Buick Lighting Systems!).

INSERTING TC, VARIATION & DISTANCE INTO THE FLIGHT LOG

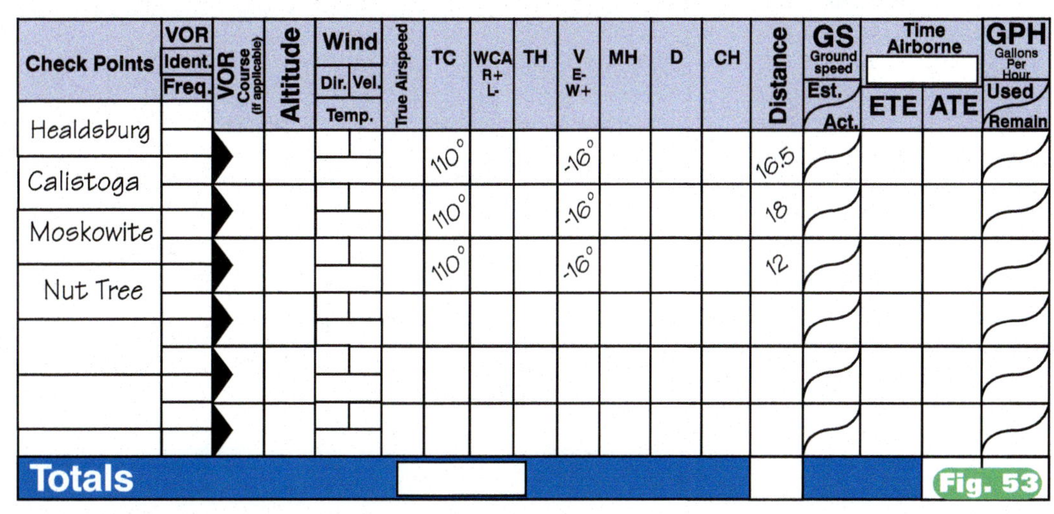

Check Points	VOR Ident. / Freq.	VOR Course (if applicable)	Altitude	Wind Dir. / Vel. / Temp.	True Airspeed	TC	WCA R+ L-	TH	V E- W+	MH	D	CH	Distance	GS Ground speed Est. / Act.	Time Airborne ETE	ATE	GPH Gallons Per Hour Used / Remain
Healdsburg																	
Calistoga						110°			-16°				16.5				
Moskowite						110°			-16°				18				
Nut Tree						110°			-16°				12				
Totals																	

Fig. 53

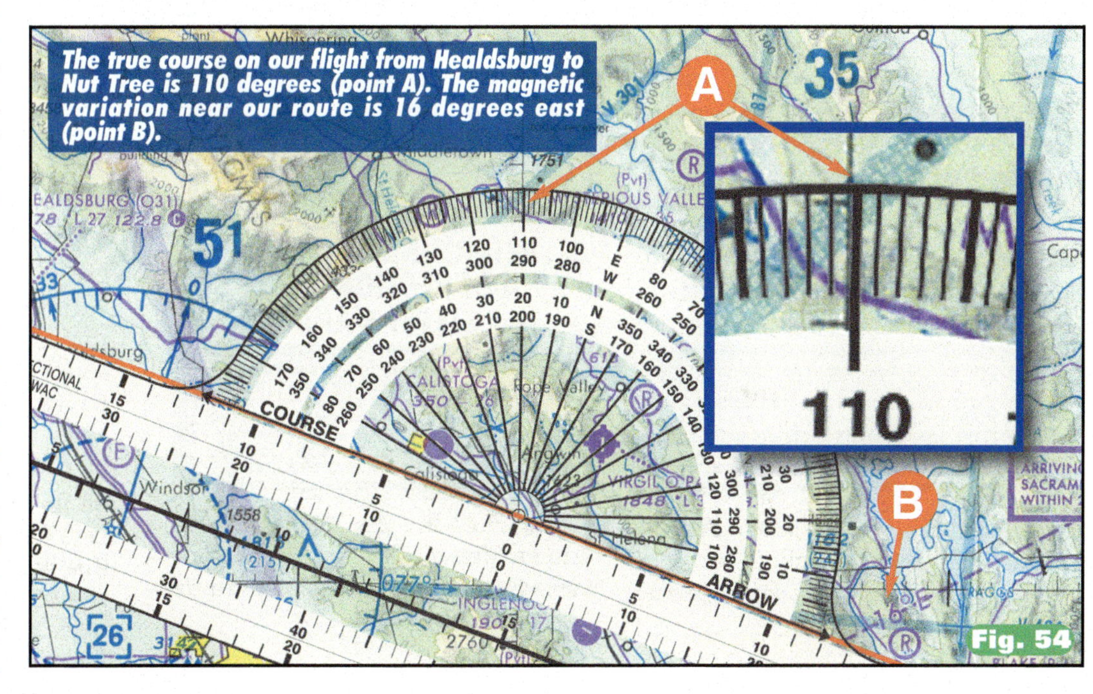

The true course on our flight from Healdsburg to Nut Tree is 110 degrees (point A). The magnetic variation near our route is 16 degrees east (point B).

Fig. 54

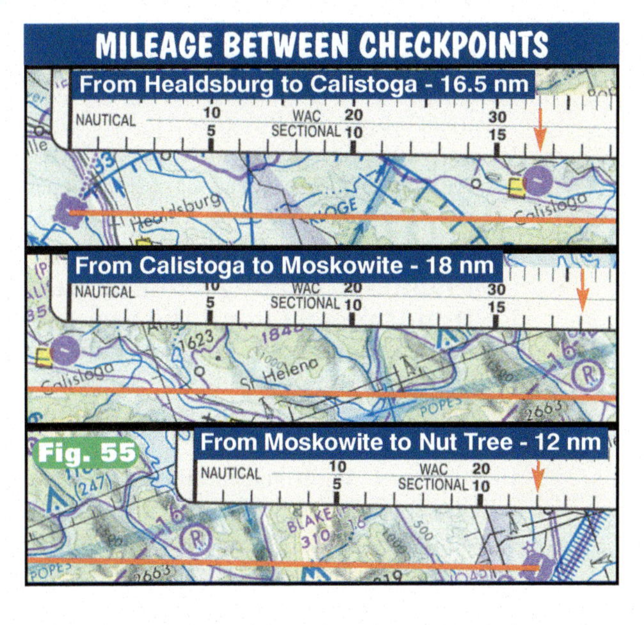

Fig. 55

Cross Country Planning: Input Information – Figure 53 is a typical flight log used for cross country flight planning. I've inserted the three separate legs into the log along with the true course for each leg (it's the same for all legs) and distances between legs. Figure 54 shows how we measured the true course for this flight. Point A shows the line of longitude intersecting the easterly (E) plotter scale at an angle of 110 degrees. This is our true course. Point B shows a variation of 16E for our flight. Figure 55 shows the mileage for each of the three legs. All this information can be placed in our flight log, as shown in Figure 53.

Cross Country Planning: Chose an Altitude for the Flight – What altitude should you choose for this flight? There are several factors to consider when selecting an altitude. First, if your flight takes you over mountainous terrain, plan on flying at least 2,000 feet or more above the ground. Over nonmountainous terrain, a lower altitude AGL is acceptable. If you're planning on receiving a VOR station for navigation, the higher you fly, the better the reception you'll obtain. Don't expect VOR reception for more than 25 miles if you're 1,000 feet AGL or less. Higher altitudes also mean higher true airspeeds and the possibility of favorable winds.

INSERTING CRUISING ALTITUDE INTO THE FLIGHT LOG

Check Points	VOR Ident. Freq.	VOR Course (if applicable)	Altitude	Wind Dir. Vel. Temp.	True Airspeed	TC	WCA R+ L-	TH	V E- W+	MH	D	CH	Distance	GS Ground speed Est. Act.	Time Airborne ETE	ATE	GPH Gallons Per Hour Used Remain
Healdsburg			5,500			110°			-16°				16.5				
Calistoga			5,500			110°			-16°				18				
Moskowite			5,500			110°			-16°				12				
Nut Tree																	
Totals																	

Fig. 56

Figure 51, point C shows obstructions at 2,870 feet MSL. These appear to be the highest obstructions along our route. Another consideration is the hemispherical cruising altitude rule. FAR 91.159 requires that flights conducted at more than 3,000 feet AGL must be flown at odd thousand + 500 foot altitudes while on a magnetic course of 0 degrees through 179 degrees. While on a magnetic course of 180 degrees through 359 degrees, you must fly even thousands + 500 foot altitudes.

DETERMINING THE WIND CORRECTION ANGLE STEPS: 1 AND 2

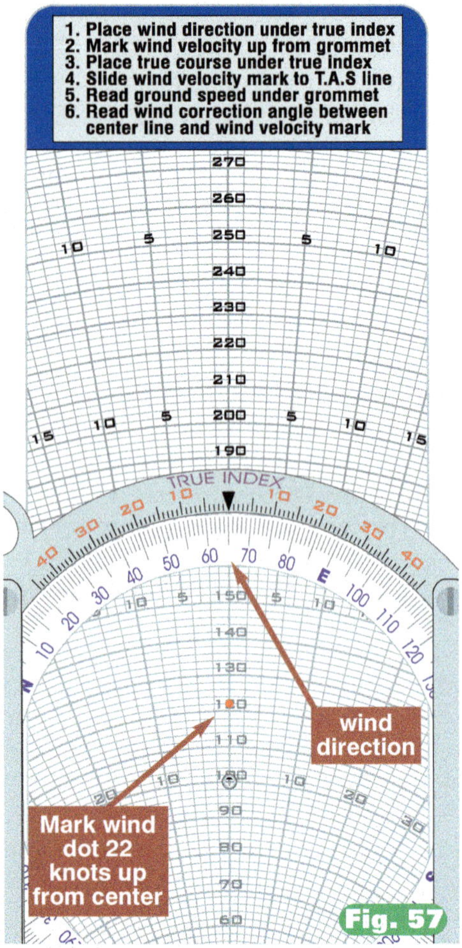

Fig. 57

DETERMINING THE WIND CORRECTION ANGLE STEPS: 3 AND 4

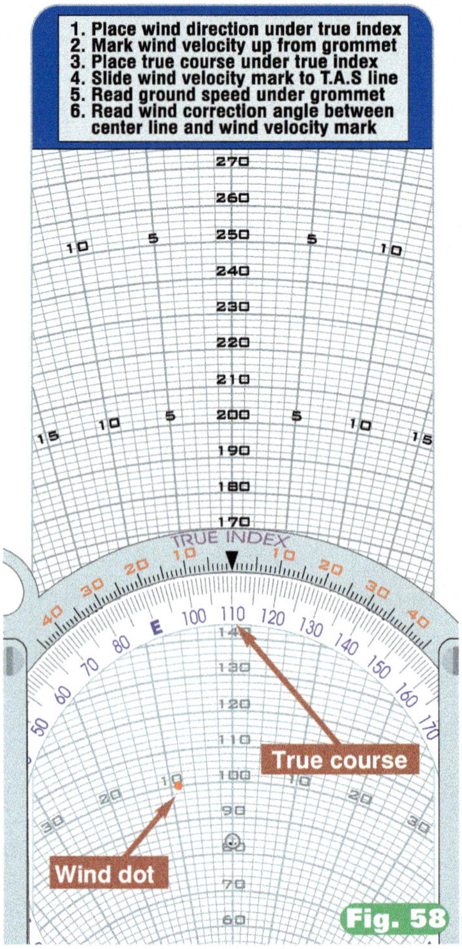

Fig. 58

From our flight log sheet in Figure 53, the magnetic course is easy to find. Simply subtract the variation (it's east so it's least) from the true course to obtain a magnetic course of 94 degrees (don't bother to write the magnetic course down, since we only use the value to decide on cruising altitudes). We need to fly an odd-thousand foot altitude + 500 feet. Our choices are 3,500 feet, 5,500 feet 7,500 feet, etc. Let's choose 5,500 feet. This will be a relatively short flight, and the time needed to climb to 7,500 feet would more than likely wipe out any small gain we might expect from increased true airspeed. Figure 56 shows our log sheet with cruising altitudes inserted (even though we'll be climbing to our cruise altitude from Healdsburg, we'll leave 5,500 feet in the first altitude block).

Cross Country Flight Planning: Finding the Compass Heading – Finding the compass heading requires us to find the wind correction angle on our computer. To do this we need the winds for our altitude as well as the airplane's true airspeed. We'll select 100 knots true airspeed for our flight. Performance charts (to be discussed in Chapter 15) allow us to determine what our

true airspeed will be, based on a selected power setting and atmospheric conditions.

Finding the winds at our altitude requires just a bit of lower math. Referring back to our briefing (page N27), we know we have the wind direction and speed for 3,000 and 6,000 feet. Notice that the difference between the winds at 3,000 and 6,000 feet is 12 knots (nice how that happened eh?). This means the wind velocity increases 4 knots per thousand feet. The winds at 4,000 feet must be 16 knots. At 5,000 feet they must be 20 knots. Between 5,000 and 6,000 feet the winds must be 22 knots. Wind direction also changes, by about 10 degrees per thousand feet. Using the same means of interpolation, you'll find the wind direction at 5,500 feet to be from 065 degrees. At 5,500 feet the winds must be from 065 degrees at 22 knots.

INSERTING COMPASS DEVIATION INTO THE FLIGHT LOG

Check Points	VOR Ident. Freq.	VOR Course (if applicable)	Altitude	Wind Dir. Vel. Temp.	True Airspeed	TC	WCA R+ L-	TH	V E- W+	MH	D	CH	Distance	GS Ground speed Est. Act.	Time Airborne ETE	ATE	GPH Gallons Per Hour Used Remain
Healdsburg																	
Calistoga			5,500'			110°			-16°				16.5	83 kts.			
Moskowite			5,500'			110°			-16°				18	83 kts.			
Nut Tree			5,500'			110°			-16°				12	83 kts.			
Totals																	

Fig. 59

Now we're ready to solve a wind triangle problem on the flight computer.

Figure 57 shows the wind side of the computer with steps 1 and 2 completed. Figure 58 shows steps 3 and 4 completed. Our wind correction angle is approximately 9 degrees to the left and our groundspeed (under the grommet) is approximately 83 knots (differences between computers can easily result in a +/- 1 knot or +/- 1 degree variation). Let's fill in our flight log with the information to obtain our compass heading, as shown in Figure 59 (the compass deviation card in Figure 37 shows a deviation of -4 degrees for a magnetic heading in the vicinity of 90 degrees).

Cross Country Flight Planning: Estimating Time Enroute and Fuel Consumed – The next step in flight planning is to use our groundspeed to estimate the time enroute between checkpoints. If you haven't already done so, now is a good time to study Postflight Briefing #14-1 to learn how to use the front side (time, speed and distance side) of the E6-B flight computer. Given a groundspeed of 83 knots, we can approximate our *estimated time enroute* or *ETE* between checkpoints. Figure 60 shows the front side of the computer with the speed reference (the kitty cat's nose) pointing to 83 knots—our groundspeed. It takes approximately 12 minutes to cover the first 16.5 nautical mile leg. It takes 13 minutes to cover the next 18 nautical mile leg and 8.5 minutes to cover the last leg (we'll round off to the closest 30 second mark). Based on an expected fuel consumption of 8.5 GPH (gallons per hour—obtained from a performance chart you'll learn about in Chapter 15), Figure 61 shows the calculation of our fuel burn based on the time we can expect

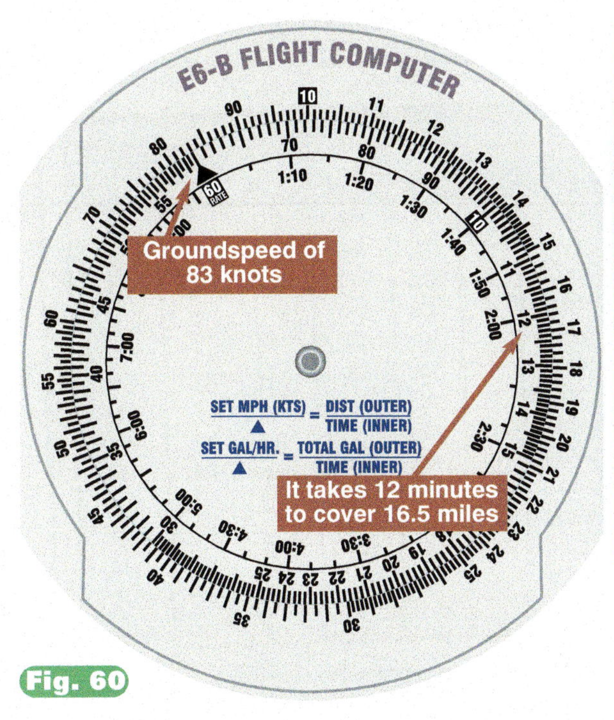

Fig. 60

ESTIMATING TIME ENROUTE AND FUEL CONSUMED (See Postflight Briefing #14-1 to learn how to use this side of the E6-B computer).

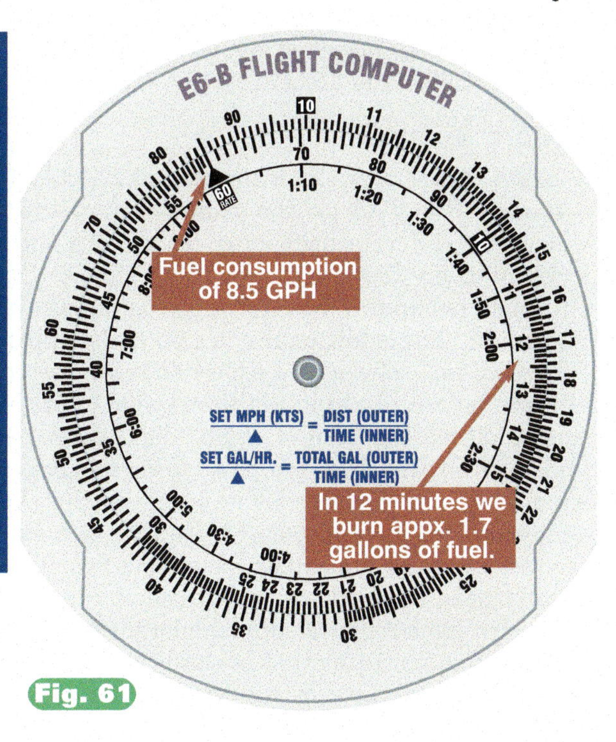

Fig. 61

between checkpoints. We'll insert the rest of this information in our finished flight log as shown in Figure 62.

The total column at the bottom of Figure 62 represents only a *rough estimate* of the fuel used and time required between Healdsburg and Nut Tree. We haven't taken into consideration the extra fuel used in preparation for takeoff, during the climb, or the slower airspeed when climbing. These are important considerations, and are even more significant (as a percentage of the whole) on a short flight. Some pilots have their own formula for determining how much extra fuel they use when climbing. I've heard pilots say just add an extra 1.0 to 1.5 gallons of fuel for the engine start, taxi, takeoff and climb. Frankly, this estimate is only meaningful for specific airplanes and specific conditions you're familiar with. There is a better way to find your true fuel consumption for the flight. It involves a little more work, but it's worth the extra precision you obtain in your flight planning. Let's examine a more precise method of estimating time and fuel consumption.

INSERTING TIME/DISTANCE/FUEL INFO INTO THE FLIGHT LOG

Check Points	VOR Ident. / Freq.	VOR Course (if applicable)	Altitude	Wind Dir. / Vel. / Temp.	True Airspeed	TC	WCA R+ L-	TH	V E- W+	MH	D	CH	Distance	GS Ground speed Est. / Act.	Time Airborne ETE	ATE	GPH Gallons Per Hour Used / Remain
Healdsburg																	
Calistoga			5,500'	065 22	100 kts.	110°	-9°	101°	-16°	85°	-4°	81°	16.5	83 kts.	12 min.		1.7 Gal.
Moskowite			5,500'	065 22	100 kts.	110°	-9°	101°	-16°	85°	-4°	81°	18	83 kts.	13 min.		1.8 Gal.
Nut Tree			5,500'	065 22	100 kts.	110°	-9°	101°	-16°	85°	-4°	81°	12	83 kts.	8.5 min.		1.2 Gal.
Totals													46.5				4.7 Gal.

Fig. 62

Figure 63 is a time, fuel and distance to climb performance chart (you'll see this in the performance chapter but I want to introduce it to you now). Two columns are very important to us: the *time to climb from sea level* column and the *fuel used from sea level* column. At a slower climb speed of 73 knots indicated airspeed (KIAS), it takes approximately 10 minutes to climb from sea level to 5,500 feet (since Healdsburg is at 278 feet MSL, we'll assume a sea level pressure altitude starting point). I interpolated this time by simply observing the times to climb between 5,000 and 6,000 feet. The same process yields an estimate of approximately 2.5 gallons of fuel used during this climb. With this information, you can now complete a more detailed and accurate flight log. Let's do this.

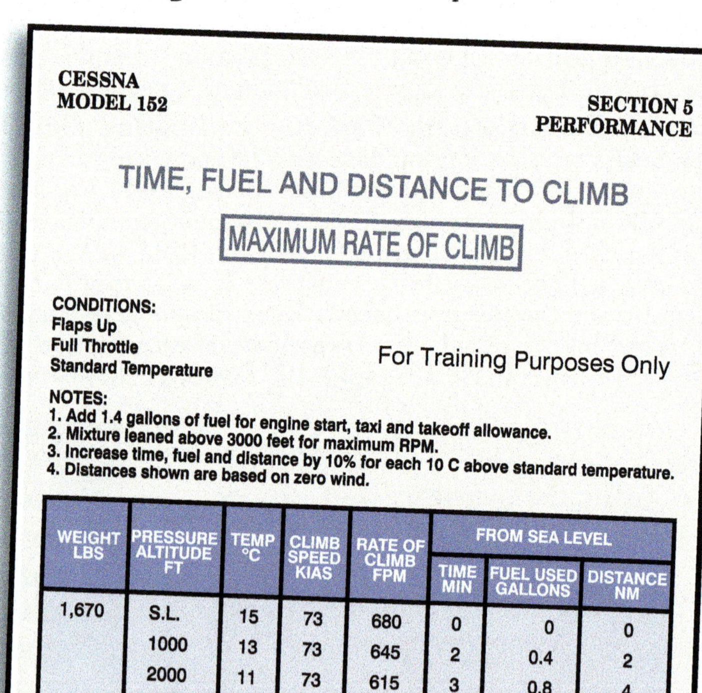

CESSNA
MODEL 152

SECTION 5
PERFORMANCE

TIME, FUEL AND DISTANCE TO CLIMB

MAXIMUM RATE OF CLIMB

CONDITIONS:
Flaps Up
Full Throttle
Standard Temperature

For Training Purposes Only

NOTES:
1. Add 1.4 gallons of fuel for engine start, taxi and takeoff allowance.
2. Mixture leaned above 3000 feet for maximum RPM.
3. Increase time, fuel and distance by 10% for each 10 C above standard temperature.
4. Distances shown are based on zero wind.

WEIGHT LBS	PRESSURE ALTITUDE FT	TEMP °C	CLIMB SPEED KIAS	RATE OF CLIMB FPM	FROM SEA LEVEL		
					TIME MIN	FUEL USED GALLONS	DISTANCE NM
1,670	S.L.	15	73	680	0	0	0
	1000	13	73	645	2	0.4	2
	2000	11	73	615	3	0.8	4
	3000	9	73	580	5	1.3	6
	4000	7	73	545	7	1.7	8
	5000	5	73	510	9	2.2	11
	6000	3	72	475	11	2.7	14
	7000	1	72	[illegible]	13	3.1	17
	8000	[illegible]	72	410	15	3.6	20
	9000	-3	72	37[illegible]	[illegible]	4.2	24
	10,000	-5	72	340	21	4.7	28
	11,000	-7	72	305	24	5.3	32
	12,000	-9	72	270	27	5.9	37

Fig. 63

A More Accurate Flight Plan

Based on a slower climb airspeed of 73 KIAS (we'll assume IAS = TAS for the climb), I know the wind will have a different drift effect on my airplane than it would at my cruise speed of 100 KTAS, so I'll add another checkpoint to my flight log, as shown in Figure 64. The additional checkpoint is called the "top of climb" reference. I expect to reach my cruise altitude before reaching my first visual checkpoint, so I've placed the "top of climb" checkpoint before Calistoga airport. Now we must work an additional wind computer wind problem based on the slower airspeed during climb (see Figure 65). Remember, the winds are the same, only the airspeed varies. Our groundspeed is 55 knots during the climb and the wind correction angle is approximately 12 degrees to the left (this reaffirms that at slower speeds the airplane must crab at a larger angle into the wind).

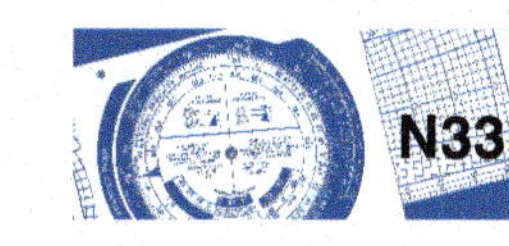

Let's take this new WCA and groundspeed and see how they apply to our flight log (Figure 64).

During the climb from Healdsburg to our cruise altitude, we'll fly a compass heading of 78 degrees, as shown on the first line of Figure 64. What we need to know is how much distance we'll cover in 10 minutes (the time our chart showed was required to climb to 5,500 feet). This is the distance to be placed in position A. We can figure this out by using our computer to determine how much distance we cover in 10 minutes at 55 knots, as shown in Figure 66. It looks like we'll cover approximately 9 miles during the climb. We put this value in position A of our flight log. Since the distance to Calistoga from Healdsburg 16.5 miles, this means that 7.5 miles is left to fly at cruise speed (position B).

The next calculation is how much time it takes to cover 7.5 nautical miles at 83 knots—the rest of the distance to our first visual checkpoint (Calistoga). Figure 67 shows that it takes approximately 5.5 minutes to cover 7.5 miles at 83 knots. We'll put this information in position C of our flight plan.

The last item we must determine is how much fuel we use during the 5.4 minute cruise segment when we're consuming fuel at a previously determined rate of 8.5 GPH. Figure 68 shows that .77 gallons are used for this 5.4 minute segment. We'll put this information in position D of our flight log.

INSERTING TIME/DISTANCE/FUEL INFO INTO THE FLIGHT LOG

Check Points	VOR Ident. Freq.	VOR Course (if applicable)	Altitude	Wind Dir. Vel. Temp.	True Airspeed	TC	WCA R+ L-	TH	V E- W+	MH	D	CH	Distance	GS Ground speed Est. Act.	Time Airborne ETE	ATE	GPH Gallons Per Hour Used Remain
Healdsburg			↑	065 22	73 kts.	110°	-12°	98°	-16°	82°	-4°	78°	A?	55 kts	10 min.		2.5 Gal
Top of climb			5,500'	065 22	100 kts.	110°	-9°	101°	-16°	85°	-4°	81°	B?	83 kts.	C?		D?
Calistoga			5,500'	065 22	100 kts.	110°	-9°	101°	-16°	85°	-4°	81°	18	83 kts	13 min.		1.8 Gal.
Moskowite			5,500'	065 22	100 kts.	110°	-9°	101°	-16°	85°	-4°	81°	12	83 kts	8.5 min.		1.2 Gal.
Nut Tree																	
Totals													46.5				

Fig. 64

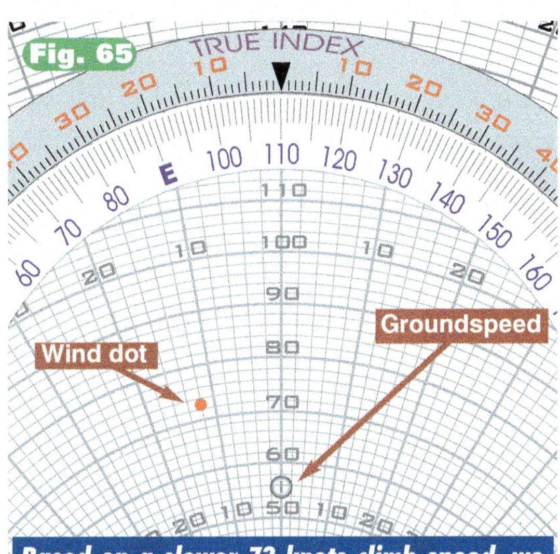

Based on a slower 73 knots climb speed, we have a groundspeed of approximately 55 knots and a wind correction angle of 12 degrees to the left during the climb.

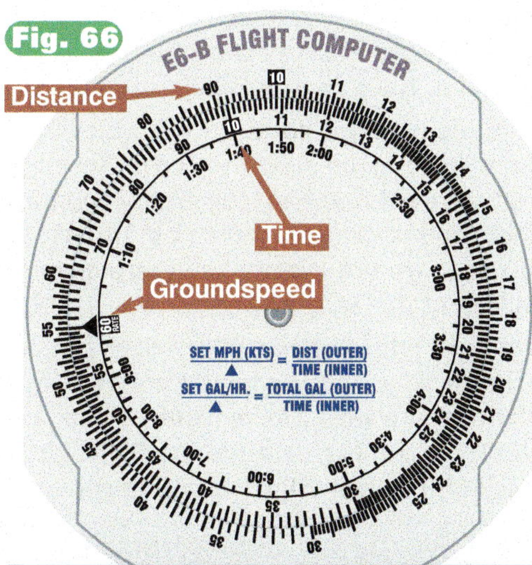

Our computer shows that during the 10 minute climb, we'll cover approximately 9 miles at the climb groundspeed of 55 knots.

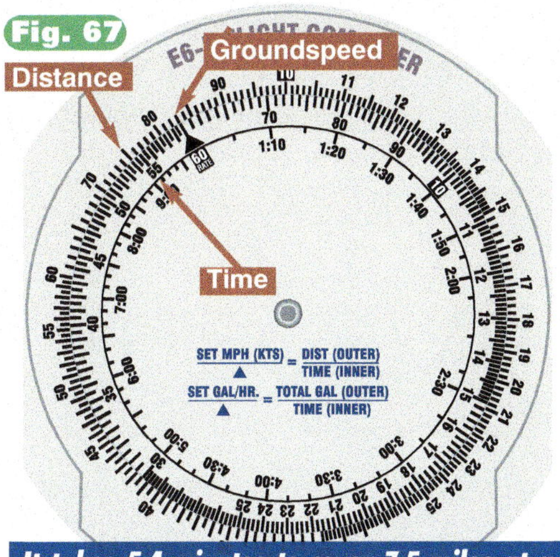

It takes 5.4 minutes to cover 7.5 miles at a cruise groundspeed of 83 knots (7.5 miles is the distance left to our first visual checkpoint after reaching our cruise altitude).

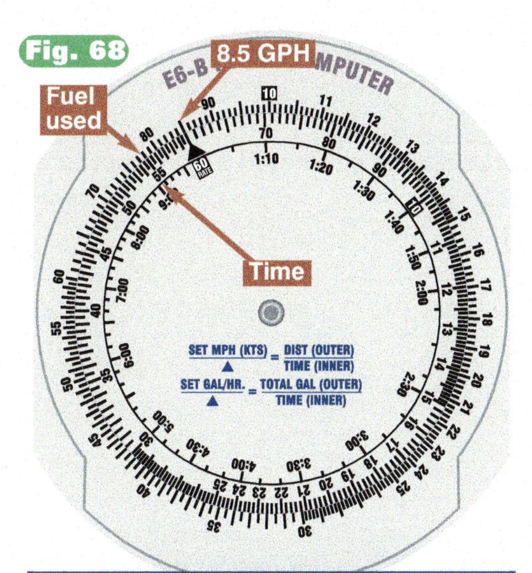

At 8.5 GPH, we'll use .77 gallons of fuel for the 5.5 minute cruise segment.

Our completed flight log is shown in Figure 69. Note the small note I've added at the bottom right of the flight log. It says that note #1 of the performance chart in Figure 63 states we should add 1.4 gallons of fuel for engine start, taxi and takeoff. A total flight time of approximately 37 minutes and fuel consumption of approximately 7.68 gallons is estimated for this flight.

OUR COMPLETED FLIGHT LOG

Check Points	VOR Ident. Freq.	VOR Course (if applicable)	Altitude	Wind Dir.	Wind Vel.	Temp.	True Airspeed	TC	WCA R+ L-	TH	V E- W+	MH	D	CH	Distance	GS Ground speed Est.	GS Act.	Time Airborne ETE	Time Airborne ATE	GPH Gallons Per Hour Used	GPH Remain
Healdsburg																					
Top of climb			↑	065	22		73 kts.	110°	-12°	98°	-16°	82°	-4°	78°	9	55 kts		10 min.		2.5 Gal	
Calistoga			5,500'	065	22		100 kts.	110°	-9°	101°	-16°	85°	-4°	81°	7.5	83 kts		5.4 min.		.77 Gal.	
Moskowite			5,500'	065	22		100 kts.	110°	-9°	101°	-16°	85°	-4°	81°	18	83 kts		13 min.		1.8 Gal.	
Nut Tree			5,500'	065	22		100 kts.	110°	-9°	101°	-16°	85°	-4°	81°	12	83 kts		8.5 min.		1.2 Gal.	
														Performanch chart says add 1.4 gal. for start, taxi and takeoff.						1.4 Gal.	
Totals															46.5					7.67 Gal.	

Fig. 69

It's a good idea to compare the fuel estimate against what really happens in order to see how well the process is working, and whether any of the fixed amounts you're using (such as the rate of fuel burn at cruise, or the amount allowed for startup, taxi, and takeoff) need to be adjusted. Keep in mind that any such numbers are averages, and your number may vary.

While it would be nice to think everything can be measured with great precision, the fact of the matter is your fuel burn will not be accurate to the tenth of a gallon. In fact, there can be several gallons variation in your estimate of fuel onboard based on the size of the fuel tanks and how close to the top the line person (the petroleum-molecule-fluid-allocation person) fills them up. It pays, however, to plan as precisely as possible, while keeping real-world considerations in mind. Do not ever try and stretch your flight based on the fact that by a paper calculation, you "should have" a few gallons of fuel left. Always be aware of the imprecision of these seemingly-precise calculations, and fly conservatively.

Flight planning can be a lot of fun, but I don't want you to think it must be this detailed for short flights. If I'm heading to a local airport 10 miles away that I'm very familiar with, I check the weather and NOTAMS, preflight the plane, make sure I have full fuel and go. It's that simple. It's reasonable to say that the farther away from the airport you fly, the more detailed the flight planning that's necessary. Make no mistake about it, even experienced pilots who slack off on their flight planning get to fly gliders (airplanes with fuel exhausted engines).

Final Words on Electronic Flight Computers

An explanation on the use of the electronic flight computers hasn't been included for a very good reason—they're easy to use. Many of these wonderful little devices are menu driven, making it unbelievably easy to solve wind, time, distance, and fuel problems.

We worked on the mechanical computer so you would know the principles. With that in hand (and in mind) you can feel more confident in the use of an electronic computer, where it's easy to crunch numbers without understanding what they mean. I am all for technology, but only if you understand what it's doing for you.

Quite frankly, I am simply amazed at all the wonderful little devices available for people nowadays. A friend's grandfather purchased a $1200 hearing aid. He claims it has call waiting!

Postflight Briefing #14-1

The Mechanical Flight Computer

Figure 70 shows the most common mechanical flight computer in use today. It's often referred to as the *E6-B computer* and is a device you should become familiar with.

Patented by Lieutenant Phillip Dalton on June 30th, 1936, the E6-B has become one of the most familiar items in all of aviation (E6-B was probably a military designation). You might be wondering why I recommend learning to use a mechanical flight computer when there are so many wonderful electronic computers on the market. There are two reasons. First, it's important that you understand the principles behind the calculations, and the E6-B shows the facts in a way electronic computers can't. Second, you can *always* get a useable calculation from an E6-B. No dead batteries, bad circuit boards, inoperative LCDs, or other electronic maladies.

Putting on a Happy Face

The E6-B does not, at first glance, present a friendly face (Figure 70). Numbers upon numbers, scales upon scales, windows within windows—any of these could cause your blood pressure to rise so fast that if it weren't for your skin, you'd be a fountain. It's even created mental vaporlock in some students, whose heads spin so fast after one look that they feel like a termite in a yo-yo. It would do little good for me to say, "Don't worry, it will all make sense to you soon." So, let me do something better. Figure 71 shows a simplified version of this computer.

THE STANDARD MECHANICAL E6-B TYPE COMPUTER

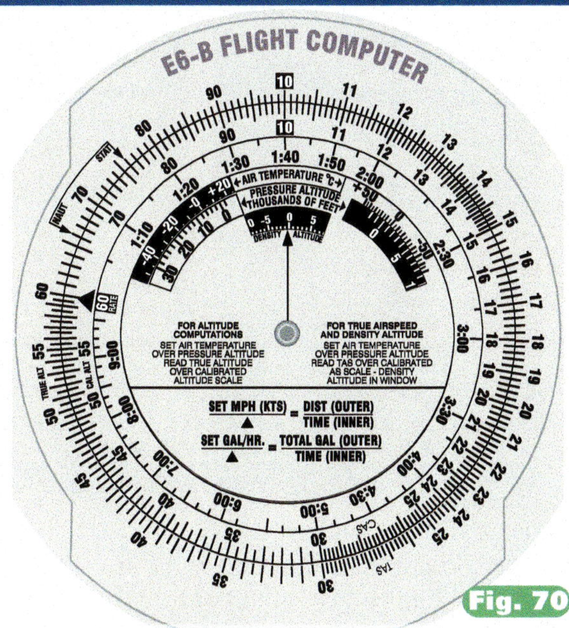

Unlike our simplified version, this is what an actual E6-B computer looks like.

OUR SIMPLIFIED MECHANICAL FLIGHT COMPUTER

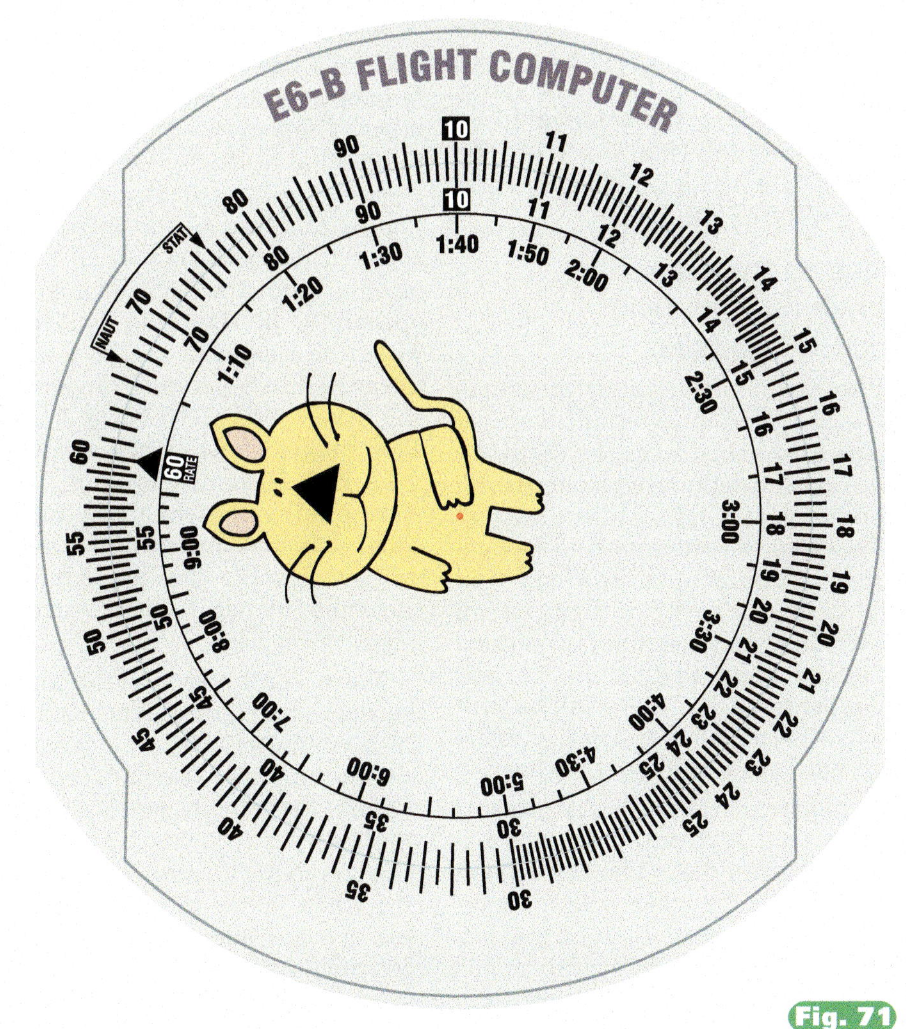

I have taken out all the confusing items on the computer's face, leaving just the basics. You are welcome to photocopy this figure, cut out the white internal ring and paste it (with removable paste) over the internal, moveable ring of your computer (you may have to expand or shrink the photocopy to make it fit). After a short time practicing with this cleaned-up, moveable inner ring, you can pull it off and the original computer's complexity won't be so overwhelming. (Caution: Only use this photocopy to become familiar with the face of the computer. It's not meant for use outside of Postflight Briefing #14-1. Many important items have been removed.)

Another option is to make a photocopy of Figure 71, carefully cut the white inner ring from the black outside ring and construct a temporary,

HOW TO MAKE YOUR OWN PAPER-TYPE MECHANICAL COMPUTER

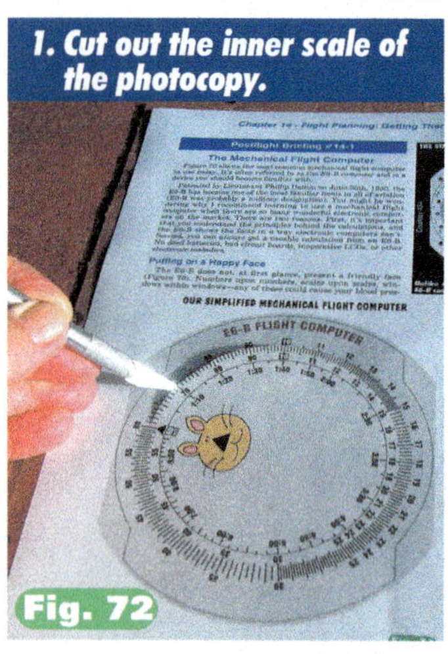

Fig. 72

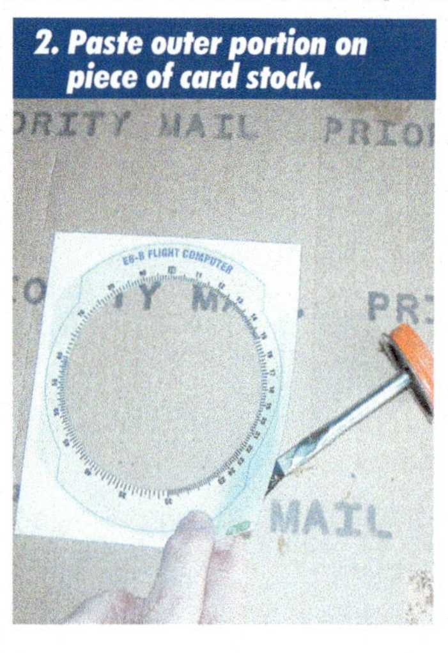

paper computer to practice with, as shown in Figure 72. Either way, this cleaned-up computer is much easier and more enjoyable to use during the learning process.

Dance of the Decimals: The Number Scale

In Figure 71, the inner (white and moveable) ring is matched up against the outer (fixed) ring. The numbers on both scales match one another. Find the number 10 on the very top of the computer's inner or outer ring. Moving clockwise around both scales, the numbers increase in value. To the right of 10 is 11, 12, 13 and so on all the way to a value of 90, which is a full digit left of 10. These numbers can represent any value you want.

These ropes appear to be equal in length. The one with the knot, however, is actually longer when unraveled.

Fig. 73

We could let the number 10 equal 100. Then the digits to the right would be 110, 120, 130 and so on. Or we could let 10 equal the value of 1.0. The number to the right would then be 1.1, 1.2, 1.3 and so on. It's very important that you stay with the same numerical category of values you start with when solving a computer problem (i.e., 1s, 10s or 100s). If you are letting the value of 10 on the scale equal 100, don't let the value of 11 equal 1.1. It should represent a value of 110.

Miles on the Menu: Converting Nautical And Statute Miles

Two forms of distance measurement are used in aviation: nautical miles and statute miles. Statute miles are normally used for measurement of visibility, while nautical miles are more often used in navigational computations. You will find that most airspeed indicators on newer airplanes use knots (nautical miles per hour) instead of (statute) miles per hour, but there will be situations where it's necessary to convert from one type of mile to the other.

A nautical mile is a distance of 6,076.1 feet. A statute mile is a distance of 5,280 feet. The conversion factor is 1.15. In other words, a nautical mile is equal to 1.15 statute miles. Another way of saying this is that one nautical miles is longer than a statute mile. To convert nautical miles to statute miles, simply multiply it by 1.15. For example, 20 nautical miles equals a distance of 23 statute miles (20 x 1.15 = 23). To convert statute miles to nautical miles simply divide the statute mile value by 1.15 (23 statute miles/1.15 = 20 nautical miles).

Here's how to remember the difference between nautical and statute miles. Think of two ropes that appear to be equal in length. One rope, however, has a knot in it, as shown in Figure 73. If we let the length of the rope without the knot equal a value of one, then, the knotted rope also appears to be the same length. But when the rope with the knot in it is unraveled, it's actually longer than the other rope (1.15 times longer). This makes sense, since a nautical mile is 1.15 times longer than a statute mile. So, when you compare equal values of nautical and statute miles, remember that the value with the knot (nautical) in it is actually longer or bigger.

There is an easy way to convert nautical and statute miles using the E6-B computer. On the computer's outside ring, there's a conversion arc (Figure 74). Simply put the mileage value you want to convert under the STAT or NAUT arrow on the inside ring, then follow the arc across and read the equivalent mileage value on the same inside ring. In Figure 74, a value of 6.6 nautical miles is set on the inside ring under the NAUT

The conversion arc is used for converting nautical to statute miles.

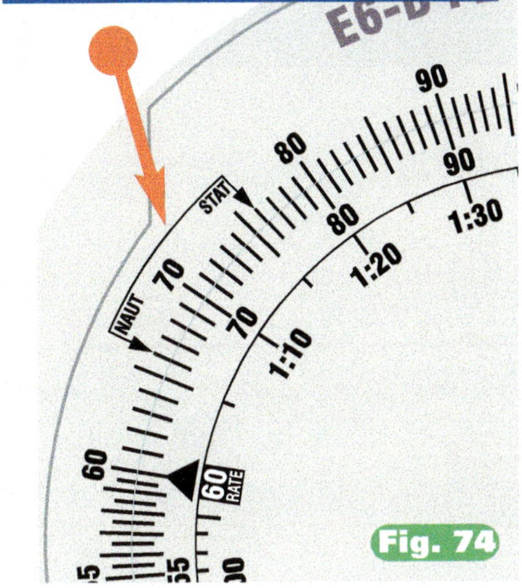

Fig. 74

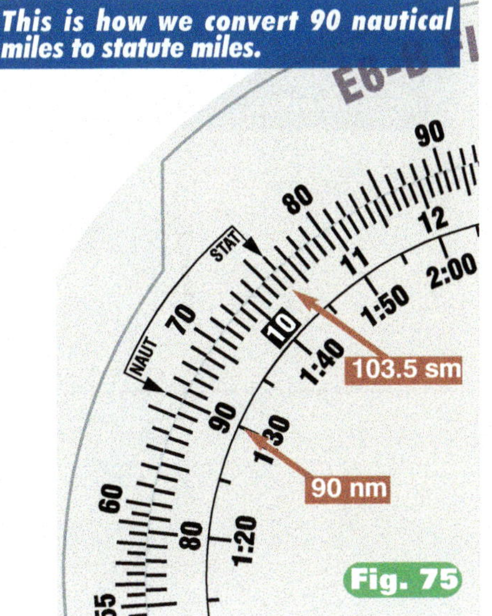

This is how we convert 90 nautical miles to statute miles.

Fig. 75

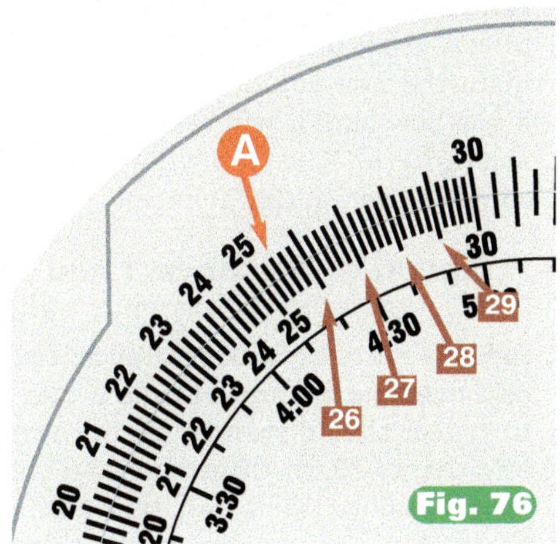

Numbers on the inside or outside scales can represent many values.

Fig. 76

arrow. The STAT arrow points to 7.6 as the statute mile equivalent value.

Let's convert 90 nautical miles to statute miles. Figure 75 shows this conversion. Place 90 under the NAUT arrow on the inside ring and read the statute mile value under the STAT arrow on the same ring. Ninety nautical miles equals 103.5 statute miles. I (or the FAA, on a test) might ask you to convert 103.5 statute miles to nautical miles. You would place 103.5 under the STAT arrow and read the nautical value of 90 miles under the NAUT arrow.

Be careful when reading numerical values on the computer's inside or outside ring when "marks" instead of actual "digits" are used to represent the scale's values. For instance, in Figure 76, between 250 and 300 on the inside ring, there's just not enough space to place whole number values (i.e., 26, 27, 28 and 29). These whole number values are represented by longer slashed lines. Between each longer slashed line are smaller lines representing an increase in value of .2, 2 or 20. As you can see, point A represents either .254, 25.4 or 254 depending on the original value we started with.

Try converting 276 statute miles to nautical miles. Figure 77 shows this process. Placing 276 under the STAT arrow gives you 240 nautical miles. Of course, if the statute mile value was 27.6 then the nautical value would be 24. Remember to keep with the same value of 1s, 10s or 100s. In other words, 27.6 statute miles wouldn't be 240 nautical miles. This is part of the common sense needed when solving these problems.

There is a mileage scale at the bottom of your plotter (Figure 78). Both statute and nautical mileage scales are available for easy use. If you don't have your flight computer with you and can't remember how to convert nautical and statute miles, you can easily do it on the matched scales on the bottom of the plotter. Simply find the statute mile value on the plotter's statute scale and move to the opposite nautical scale to read the nautical mile value. It doesn't get any easier than that.

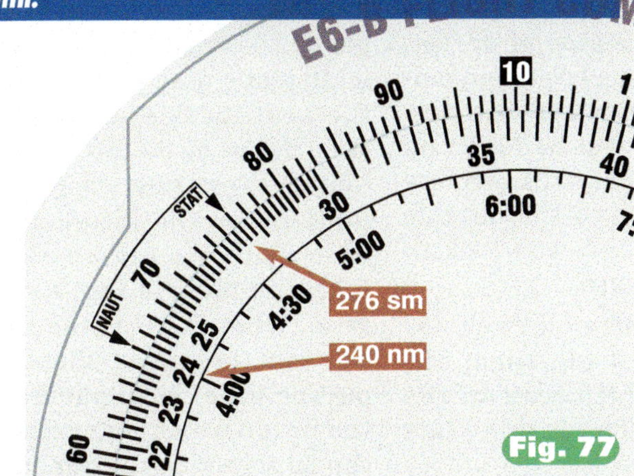

Converting 276 statute miles gives us 240 nautical miles. Remember, 24 can be 2.4, 24, 240 or 2,400. You must stay with the same value in ones, tens or hundreds that you start with.

Fig. 77

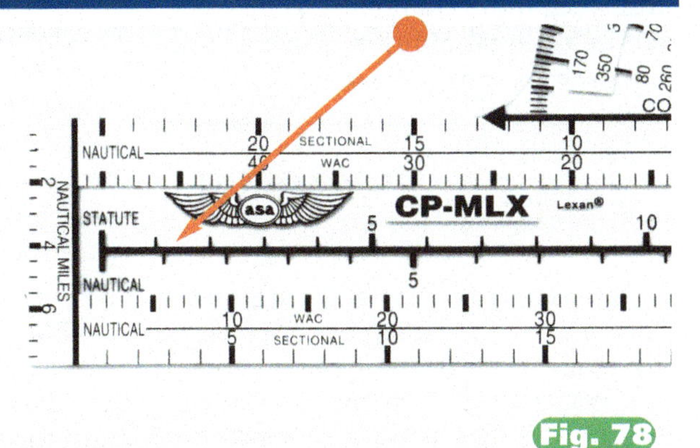

Another way of converting statute and nautical miles is to use your plotter. Simply find the comparative nautical or statute scale (most plotters have them) and read the conversion value on the opposite scale.

Fig. 78

Time, Distance and Speed Computations

Computing time, speed and distance is a necessary skill for all pilots. After all, how can you estimate the fuel you'll use if you don't know how long it will take you to get somewhere? The following formula should be committed to memory:

Speed = Distance/Time

This formula states that your speed is the ratio of the distance traveled over the amount of time it takes to travel that distance. If you have any two of these three items in the formula above (the speed, time or distance), you can determine the third. For instance, if you know how much distance you traveled in a certain amount of time, you can determine your groundspeed. If you know your groundspeed, you can tell how much time it will take to travel a certain distance or you can tell how much distance you'll travel in a certain period of time.

Think about this carefully. We always measure our speed in either miles per hour or knots (which is nautical miles per hour). If you're doing 60 miles per hour, you'll travel 60 miles in one hour. That's one mile per minute, since there are 60 minutes in one hour. At 120 miles per hour you'll travel 2 miles per minute. These are handy numbers to keep in mind.

Whenever the word *per* is used in arithmetic (as in miles per hour or nautical miles per hour), it represents some sort of ratio. If I went 120 miles per hour it means I traveled 120 miles in 60 minutes. Such a ratio is represented as follows:

$$\frac{\text{120 miles}}{\text{60 minutes in an hour}} = \text{120 miles per hour}$$

Your computer is nothing more than a mechanical device for picturing a ratio. You're going to be amazed how easy this little device is once you understand how ratios are shown on the computer's face. For example, setup your computer as shown in Figure 79. From now on we'll refer to the white, moveable ring as the inside scale and the fixed outer ring as the outside scale.

The face of the mechanical flight computer has three areas of concern. The white moveable ring is the inside scale and the fixed portion of the computer is the outside scale. The small black triangle, which we'll call the "kittycat's nose," is the hour index.

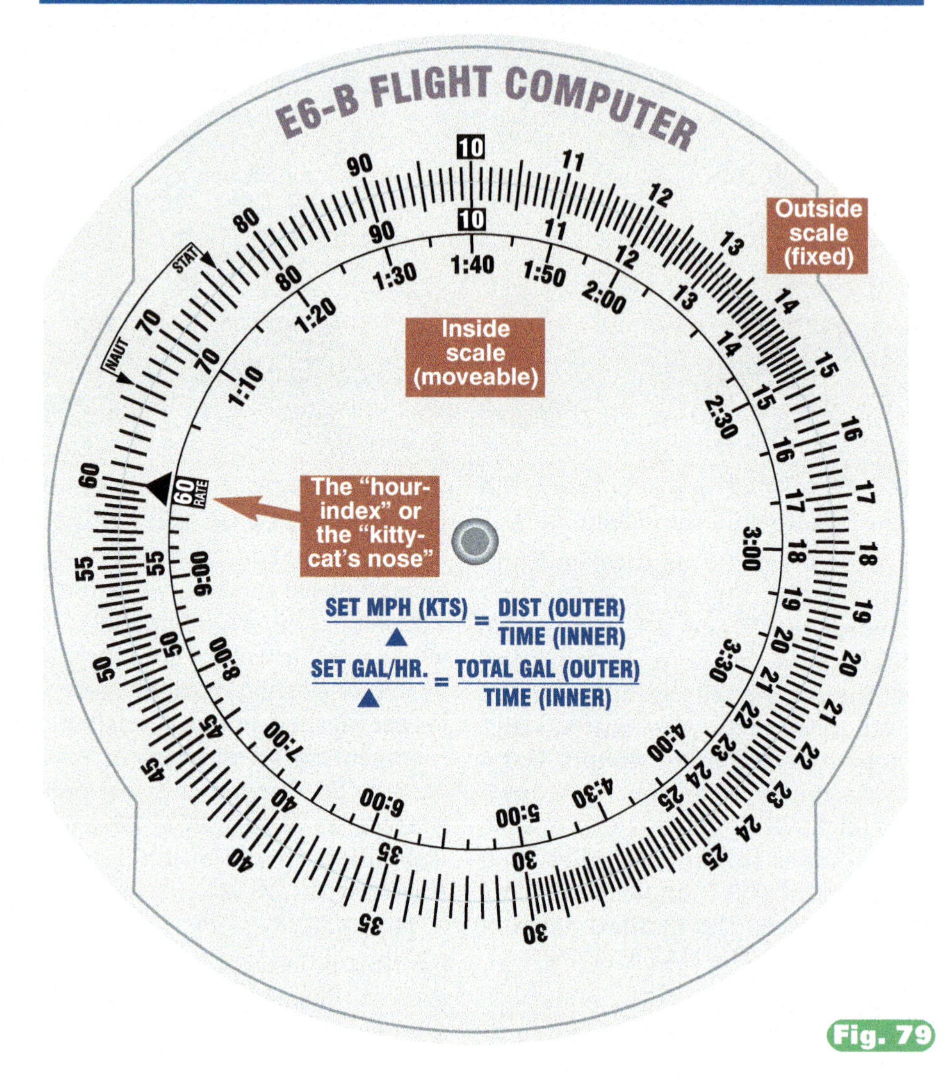

Fig. 79

Which scale of the computer has the greatest distance around it? Yes, the outside scale has a larger circumference, thus the greatest distance. All distance values will be found on the outside scale. That's the memory aid. Distance refers to the outside scale and this is where you look to find any distance values.

What do the hands of a clock do? Yes, of course, they tell time, but they also move. Which scale of the computer moves? The inside scale moves.

As a memory aid, the inside scale of your computer is where you'll find all your time values. Any value other than time (such as distances) will be shown on the outside scale.

Notice there is a blackened triangle on the inside scale that looks like a kittycat's nose in Figure 79. This is the hour-index since it represents a time value of 60 (60 minutes in an hour). From now on we'll call the hour-index the kittycat's or cat's nose. With the cat's nose (the hour index) pointing to 120, we've set up a ratio. What we're saying here is that we went 120 miles (distance on the outside scale) in 60 minutes (time on the inside scale). Many similar ratios can be shown on the computer's face.

By setting the kittycat's nose to the "per" value of 120 miles "per" hour, we see that it takes 30 minutes (position A) to travel 60 miles.

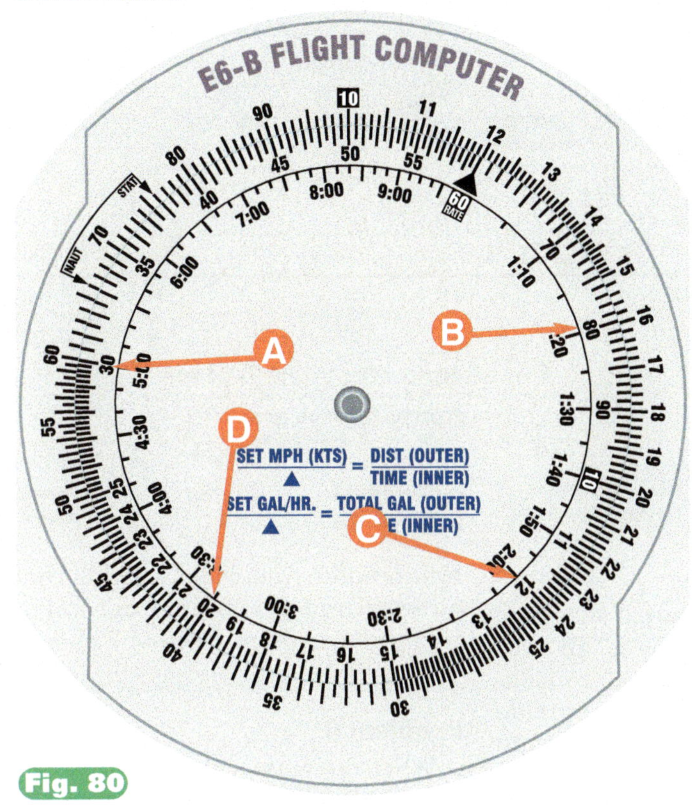

Fig. 80

Problem 1—At 105 MPH (cat's nose) we cover 35 statute miles (outside scale) in 20 minutes (inside scale).

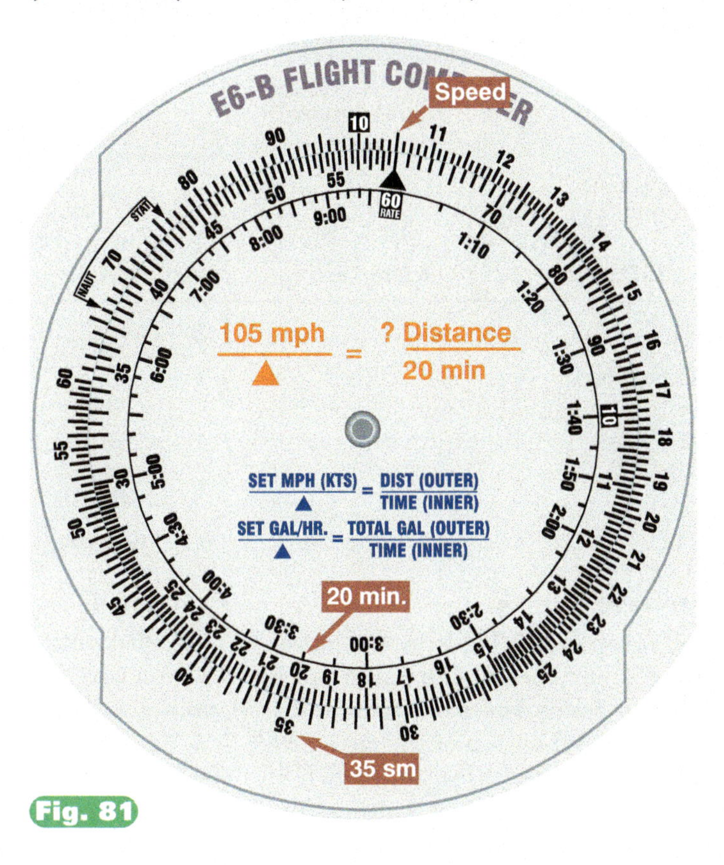

Fig. 81

For instance, we know intuitively that at 120 MPH, we will travel 60 miles in half an hour. Find the 30 minute mark on the inside scale (time) in Figure 80. Opposite the 30 minute mark you'll find 60 miles on the outside scale (distance) as shown by position A. Position B shows a ratio of 16 miles per 8 minutes. Position C shows a ratio of 24 miles per 12 minutes and position D shows a ratio of 40 miles per 20 minutes. All these ratios represent a speed of 120 miles per hour. If you have any two of the three variables of speed, time, or distance you can find the other on the computer's face.

One last thing before we start solving problems. What do kittycats do? I hope you said they PER. No, that's not a typo, I meant PER. Now, this is not the purr we're familiar with, but it sounds the same, doesn't it? As a memory aid, we'll say that the kittycat's nose always points to the PER value you're working with. In other words it points to miles PER hour, nautical miles PER hour or, as you'll soon see, gallons PER hour. Remember, you'll always be working with some PER value when doing speed, time and distance computations.

Now you know where to find speed, time or distance variables. Time is on the inside scale, distance is on the outside scale, and speed (per quantities) is on top of the cat's nose. These ratios are shown in the center of the computer, for your reference (Figure 80).

I like using these types of symbols to solve problems as long as they make sense. Several years ago in a Mexican restaurant, the restroom doors read *matador* and *bull*. Now, those are confusing symbols. I didn't know what to do. Fortunately, the cat's nose is a lot simpler to use. Let's solve a few problems.

Problem 1

If your speed is 105 miles per hour, how much distance will your airplane cover in 20 minutes? To solve this problem ask yourself which of the three variables (speed, time, distance) you have and which one you are looking for. You have speed and the time. What you want is the distance. First, point the cat's nose at the per value of 105 miles per hour as shown in Figure 81. Since time is always found on the inside scale, find 20 minutes on the inside scale. Opposite the time you see a value of 35 on the outside scale. You'll cover 35 statute miles in 20 minutes at 105 MPH. You can also say that at 105 knots you will cover 35 nautical miles in 20 minutes.

Once you find an answer, you must always make certain it makes sense. Since at 120 MPH you travel 2 miles per minute, at 105 MPH (close to 120 MPH for an estimate) you should have a distance/time value somewhere near 2 to 1. A value of 35 miles in 20 minutes is close enough to confirm your numbers are accurate. After all, if you arrived at an answer of 350 miles, you know this wouldn't be correct unless you were captain of the Starship Enterprise.

Problem 2—If we travel 7 miles (outside scale) in 4 minutes (inside scale) our groundspeed 105 MPH (cat's nose).

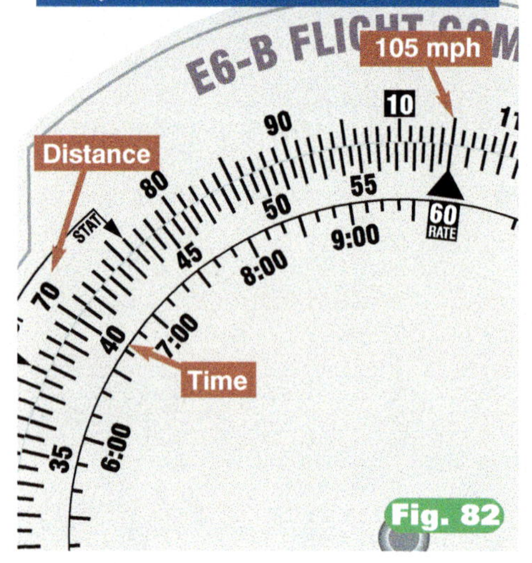

Problem 3—At 138 MPH (cat's nose) it takes about 35 minutes (inside scale) to travel 81 miles (outside scale).

Problem 4—At 90 knots (cat's nose), you'll cover 22.5 nautical miles (outside) in 15 minutes (inside).

Fig. 84

Problem 2

If we travel 7 miles in 4 minutes, what is our speed? The value you're looking for is the *per* value and it will be found on top of the cat's nose (on the outer scale), as shown in Figure 82. Simply set 7 miles (distance) on the outside scale over 4 minutes (time) on the inside scale and read what the cat's nose (per-index) points to. Your speed according to Figure 82 is 105 MPH, which is the same speed as in our previous problem.

Problem 3

At 138 MPH, how long will it take to travel 81 miles? First, what does common sense tell you about the answer? Obviously, it will take you less than one hour or 60 minutes, correct? After all, in one hour at 138 miles per hour, you'd travel 138 miles. The value you're looking for is located on the inside (time) scale. Figure 83 depicts this problem. Set the cat's nose (per index) to 138. On the outer (distance) scale you'll find 81 miles and underneath that value you'll find a time value of 35 minutes. Of course, it's possible to interpret this as either 3.5 minutes or 350 minutes, but neither of these alternatives makes sense.

Problem 4

At 90 knots, how much distance will you cover in 15 minutes? By now you know that the value you're looking for (distance) is on the outside scale. Set the cat's nose (per-index) to 90 and read the distance value on the outside scale over the 15 minute time mark on the inside scale, as shown in Figure 84. You obtain a value of 22.5 miles. This makes sense in that 60 knots is one mile per minute and 120 knots is 2 miles per minute, so 90 knots should be somewhere in between, or 1.5 miles per minute. At 15 minutes, you should travel one and a half times this amount, or 22.5 nautical miles.

Problem 5

What is your groundspeed if you traveled 13 nautical miles in 10 minutes? Figure 85 shows how this answer is derived. Rotating the inside (time) scale so 10 minutes is underneath the distance of 13 miles on the outer (distance) scale leaves you with the cat's nose (per index) pointing to a groundspeed of 78 knots.

I might have also asked what the groundspeed is if you traveled 130 nautical miles in 1 hour and 40 minutes. Directly under the 10 minute mark is the 1:40 mark. Since 1:40 is 100 minutes, you could set this time directly under 130 nautical miles, giving you a groundspeed of 78 knots.

Problem 6

What distance will you cover in 9 minutes at a groundspeed of 172 knots? Figure 86 shows how this answer is derived. Setting the cat's nose (per index) to 172, and locating 9 minutes on the inside (time) scale gives you a value of 26 miles on the outside (distance) scale. Of course, this can't be 2.6 miles, nor can it be 260 miles. Your answers must always make sense.

Problem 5—If we traveled 13 nm (outside) in 10 minutes (inside) our speed is 78 knots (cat's nose).

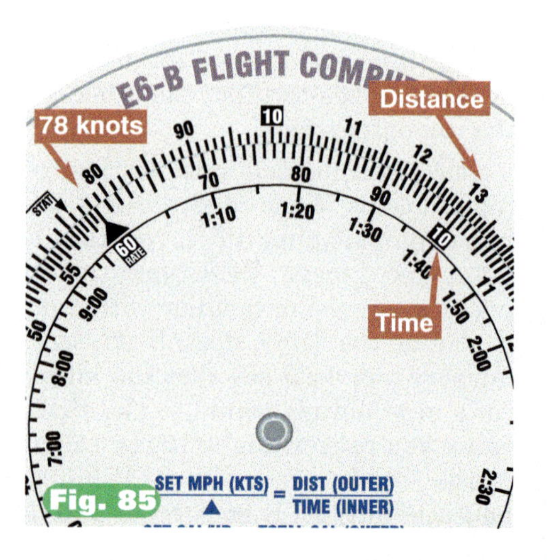

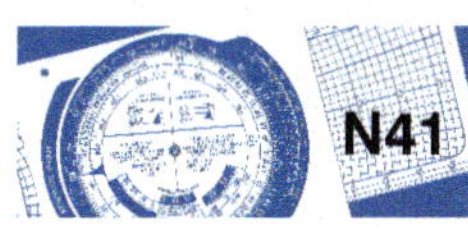

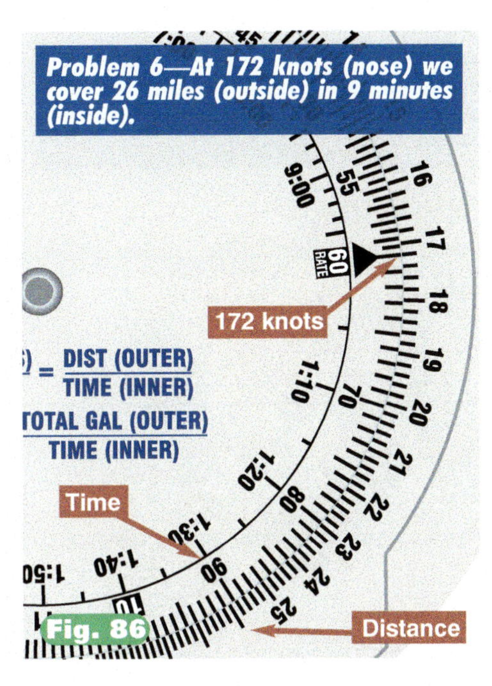

Problem 6—At 172 knots (nose) we cover 26 miles (outside) in 9 minutes (inside).

Problem 7—At 158 knots (nose) it takes 9.5 minutes (inside) to travel 25 nautical miles (outside).

Fig. 87

Problem 7

How much time will it take to travel 25 nautical miles if your groundspeed is 158 knots? Figure 87 shows how this answer is derived. Set the cat's nose (per-index) to 158 and find 25 miles on the outside (distance) scale. Underneath it is a time value of 9.5 minutes.

Fuel Consumption Problems

Finding fuel consumed is very similar to finding speed, time and distance on the computer. The PER value with fuel consumption is gallons PER hour. Instead of distance on the outside scale, you'll find the fuel consumed. Of course, time is always found on the inside scale. Let's work a few problems.

Fuel Problem 1

If your fuel consumption is 9 gallons per hour, how much fuel will the airplane consume in 1:30 (one hour and 30 minutes)? You don't even need a computer for this one, do you? First, set the cat's nose to the *per* quantity, as shown in Figure 88. The amount of fuel burned will be on the outside scale directly above the time value on the inside scale (90 minutes or 1:30). In one hour and 30 minutes you'll use 13.5 gallons of fuel.

Fuel problem 2

If your airplane consumed 21 gallons of fuel in 2 hours and 30 minutes (2:30), what was your rate of fuel consumption? We are looking for the *per* or gallons per hour value, which will be found on top of the cat's nose. Set 21 gallons on the outside (fuel burned) scale over 150 minutes (2:30) on the inside (time) scale as shown in Figure 89. The cat's nose (per index) points to 8.4 gallons per hour fuel consumption rate.

Fuel Problem 3

With a fuel consumption rate of 15.6 gallons per hour, how long can you fly with 90 gallons of fuel on board? Common sense tells you the answer is going to be somewhere around six hours. Set the cat's nose (the per index) to 15.6 as shown in Figure 90. Finding 90 gallons on the outside (fuel burned) scale gives you a time value of approximately 345 minutes (read the time scale carefully). You could divide 345 minutes by 60 to obtain the hours flyable or you could look underneath the minutes scale to find the hours scale. The hours scale is simply easier to use when dealing with large minute values.

Fuel Problem 1—At 9 GPH (nose), for 1 hour and 30 minutes (inside) we use 13.5 gallons (outside).

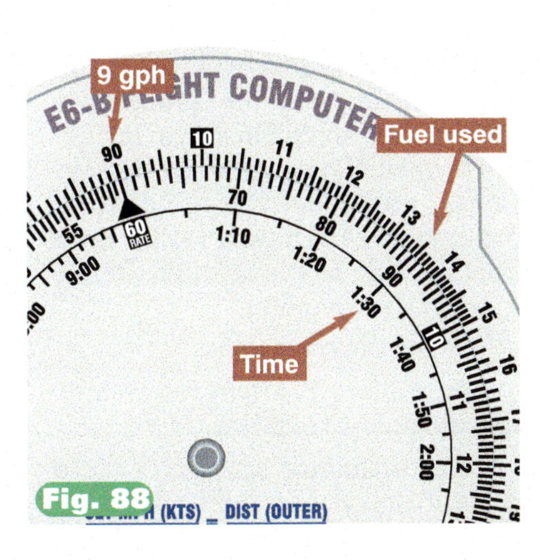

Fuel Problem 2—If we used 21 gallons (outside) in 2:30 (inside), our rate is 8.4 GPH (nose).

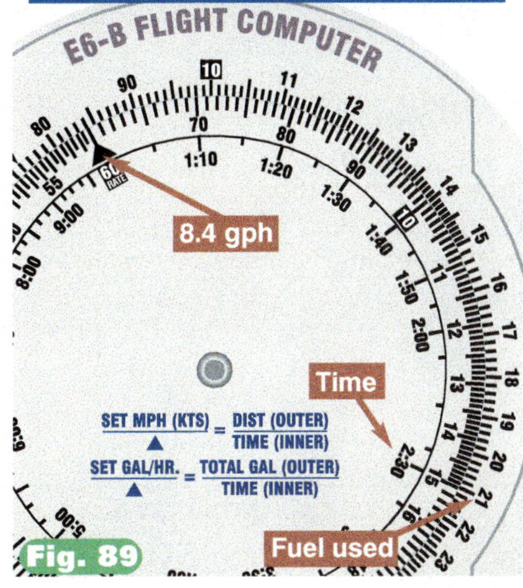

Fuel Problem 3—At 15.6 GPH (nose), with 90 gallons of fuel (outside), we can fly for 345 min or 5:45 (inside).

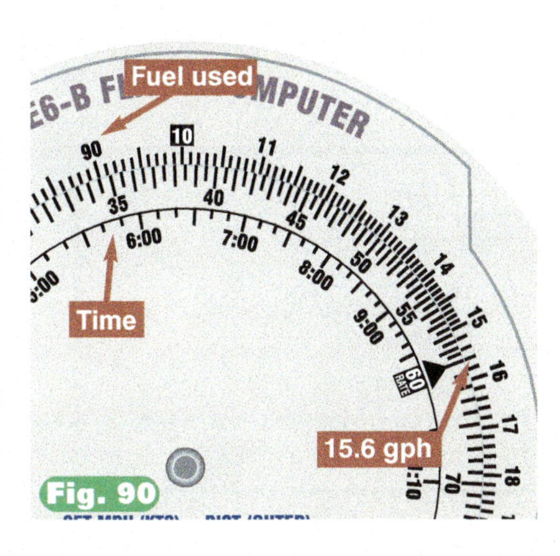

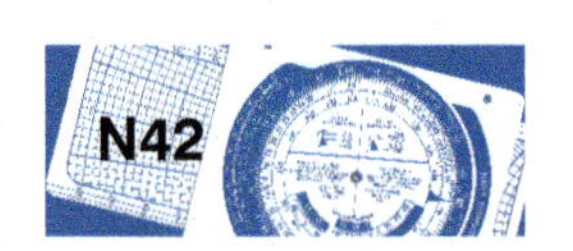

Postflight Briefing #14-2

FINDING DENSITY ALTITUDE, TRUE AIRSPEED AND YOUR TRUE ALTITUDE

Finding Density Altitude

You can use the computer to find density altitude if you have two variables: the pressure altitude and the outside air temperature. Figure 91 shows a density altitude computation scale on a typical flight computer. If you set the outside air temperature on scale A, opposite the pressure altitude on scale B, you can read the density altitude at the window located on scale C. This is a handy way to easily compute density altitude without using a fine-lined graph.

In Figure 91, the outside air temperature at a sea level pressure altitude is 15 degrees Celsius, which is standard temperature at sea level. Under these conditions, pressure altitude is equal to density altitude. A sea level or zero density altitude value is shown at the window located on scale C.

With an outside air temperature of +10 degrees Celsius at a pressure altitude of 10,000 feet, what is the density altitude? Sliding +10 degrees Celsius over a 10,000 foot pressure altitude in Figure 92, you see that your density altitude is 11,700 feet.

To find your density altitude, set the outside air temperature (scale A) over the pressure altitude (scale B). Read the density altitude in the density altitude window (scale C). (Make sure you set the temperature and pressure altitude on the appropriate temp/pressure scale. This is often the scale on the right side of the E6-B and it's usually labeled as the "airspeed correction scale.")

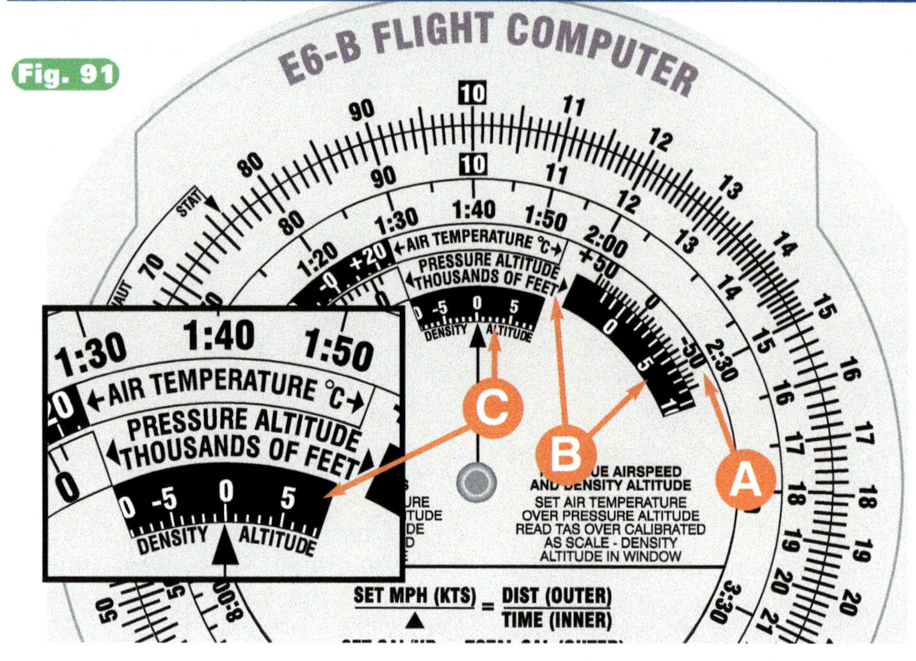

Finding True Airspeed

Using the same procedure for finding density altitude, you can easily find your true airspeed on the face of the flight computer. Figure 93 shows your computer with an outside air temperature of -12 degrees Celsius with a pressure altitude of 5,000 feet (scale A). The true airspeed (TAS) is read on the outside scale opposite the calibrated airspeed (CAS) on the inside scale. We'll use indicated airspeed (IAS) in lieu of calibrated airspeed since they are not that much different at cruise airspeeds. An IAS of 150 knots, produces a TAS of 156 knots as shown by position B. Suppose your IAS is 125 knots. What is your true airspeed under the same condition? Position C shows an IAS (same as CAS for our purposes) of 125 knots on the inside scale, giving you 130 knots TAS on the outside scale.

With an outside air temperature of +10 degrees Celsius and a pressure altitude of 10,000 feet, a density altitude of 11,700 feet exists.

Finding Your True Altitude

In the chapter on flight instruments, we discussed true altitude. Altimeters read our height above sea level when they are corrected for nonstandard pressure and temperature. Typically, however, we don't correct the altimeter for variations in temperature since these variations aren't normally that large. Nevertheless, under certain conditions, temperature can cause a rather large error. Let's do a true altitude computation on the computer.

Here are the conditions:

1. Your aircraft is flying at an indicated altitude 10,500 feet.

2. The altimeter setting is 30.42 inches of Hg.

3. The outside air temperature is -25 degrees Celsius.

What is your true altitude?

Step 1: Find your pressure altitude.

To find the pressure altitude, the altimeter must be set to 29.92 inches of Hg and the face of the altimeter read (i.e., the indicated altitude read). Since we don't have an altimeter knob to twist, we'll use our previous knowledge of how the altimeter works to determine pressure altitude. Moving the numbers down from 30.42 inches to 29.92 inches is a change of .5 inch of Hg. This means the hands move down 500 feet, and the pressure altitude is 10,000 feet.

Step 2: Place the pressure altitude under the temperature in the computer's altitude computation window (the window on left side of the E6-B's face).

Figure 94, position A shows the temperature of -25 degrees Celsius placed over a pressure altitude of 10,000 feet.

Step 3: Read the true altitude over the indicated altitude on the inside scale (we'll assume that *indicated altitude* is the same as *calibrated altitude* for all these examples. See Glossary for definition of CAL. ALT.).

Figure 94, position B, points between the circled abbreviations for true altitude (TRUE ALT.) on the outside scale and calibrated altitude (CAL. ALT.) on the inside scale (we'll use indicated altitude instead of calibrated altitude). Finding 10,500 feet indicated altitude on the inside scale at position C, we see that our true altitude is 9,700 feet as shown directly opposite on the outside scale. Under large differences in pressure and temperature from standard, it's not unusual for indicated altitude to differ substantially from true altitude. Under these extreme conditions you should consider flying a little higher than normal on your cross country flights if you're planning on being close to terrain. This caveat is especially true for night flight.

There are many more things your computer can do for you. They are beyond the scope of this book, but I would recommend that you purchase a mechanical flight computer and study its manual. You're going to be surprised at how versatile this simple little machine really is.

! BUENO !

When traveling south of the border, don't leave your E-6B in the airplane. It can be a useful tool for money conversion. Just place the current peso rate on the outside scale opposite the 10 on the inside scale. Leave the scales in this position. When converting pesos to dollars, find the peso amount on the outside scale, and read the dollar amount on the inside scale. It's great for shopping, dining and bartering. Que bueno! *Jan Peterson, CFI*

To find your true airspeed, use the same procedure for finding density altitude. Match the outside air temperature against the pressure altitude (position A). Read the CAS (calibrated airspeed) on the computer's inside scale (use IAS if you don't have calibrated) and read your TAS opposite this value on the outside scale (position B).

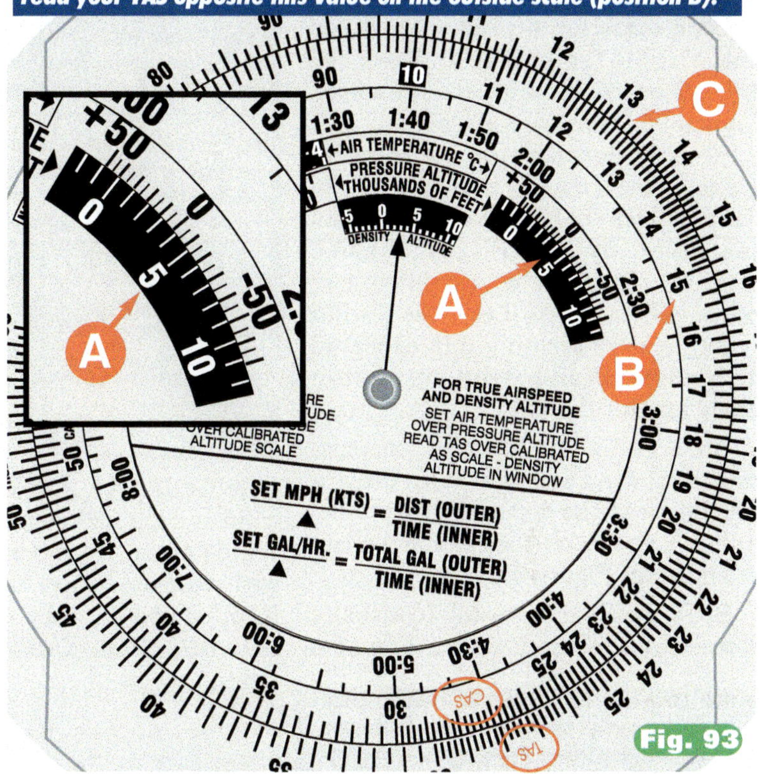

Fig. 93

You can find your true altitude by correcting the indicated altitude for non standard temperature. We'll use the altitude correction window of the E6-B (don't use the density altitude and airspeed correction window). First, place the outside air temperature under the pressure altitude (position A). Second, read true altitude on the computer's outside scale opposite indicated altitude (use CAL. ALT.) on the inside scale (position C).

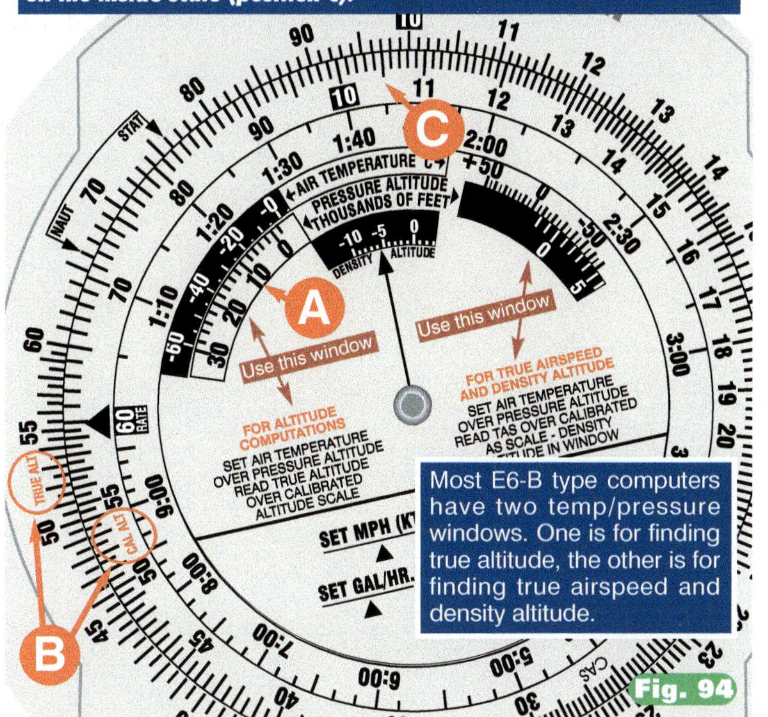

Fig. 94

Postflight Briefing #14-3

CREATING A WIND TRIANGLE

Let's construct a wind triangle for the flight from Table Rock to AVA/Martin Memorial, shown in Figure 95. Our true airspeed is 100 knots (as determined by the airplane's performance charts) and the wind is from 020 degrees at 40 knots (as given by the Flight Service Station). The true course along our route is 60 degrees. Let's use a wind triangle to determine our expected groundspeed and wind correction angle for this flight.

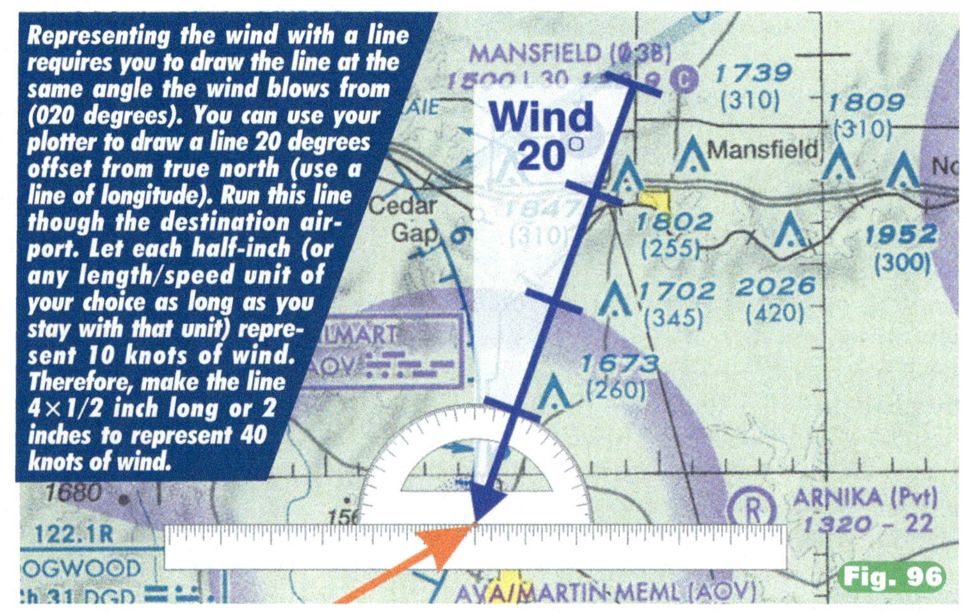

Step 1—The first step in construction of a wind triangle is to draw a line between the departure and destination airports on the sectional chart as shown in Figure 95.

Step 2—Next we want to visually represent the wind with a line of a specific length and direction. The wind is from 020 degrees at 40 knots. Winds given by the FSS are angled with respect to the true north pole. In other words, they are always in a true direction. Simply draw a line angled at 20 degrees to true north, running through the destination airport, as shown in Figure 95, point B. Figure 96 helps you understand how to draw a line at this angle. This line represents the wind direction.

What we need to do now is find some way of representing the wind's velocity with this line. The easiest way is to let the line's length represent the wind's speed. Let's arbitrarily make 1/2 inch equal to 10 knots of wind (we could use any value we want, this is simply a personal choice for this example). Since our wind velocity is 40 knots, make the line 2inches long (4 x 1/2"). I like to mark outward on the line in one-inch intervals, starting at the center of the airport, as shown in Figure 95. From this picture you can easily see the wind is a headwind blowing from your left. This single picture already allows you to visualize that your groundspeed will be slower than your airspeed and you'll have a left wind correction angle.

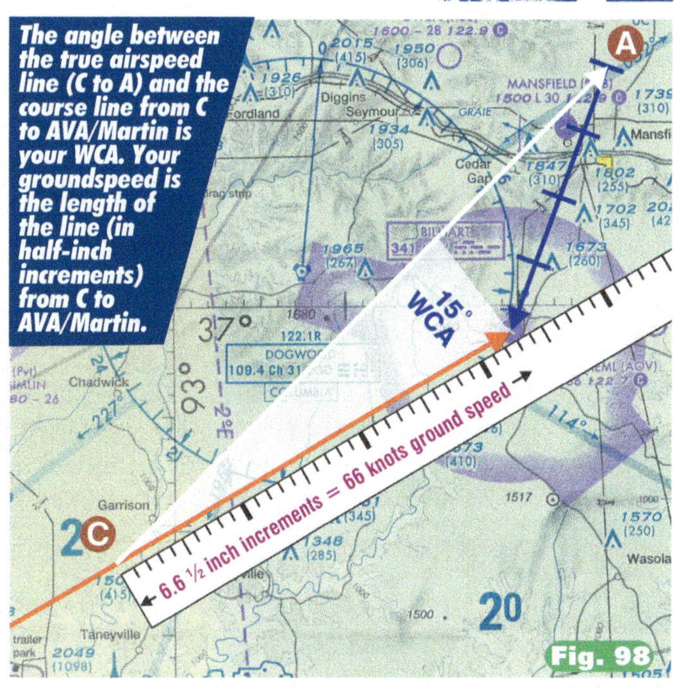

Step 3—Since we've represented the wind's direction and velocity by a line of a specific length pointed in a specific direction, we need to do the same with the airplane's speed and direction. The final step requires you to take the ruler, put one end up against the tail of the wind line, as shown in Figure 97, position A. Next, count outward along the ruler to a value of your true airspeed or 100 knots. Since we've already agreed that 1/2 inch equals 10 knots, measure outward 5 inches (10 x 1/2" = 5") as shown by point B on the ruler. Finally, pivot the ruler about point A until the true airspeed dot (point B on the ruler) is in contact with the course line at position C. Draw a line from C to the tail of the wind arrow at point A. You're done! That's it! You've got yourself a completed wind triangle depicted by points C, A and AVA/Martin airport, as shown in Figure 98.

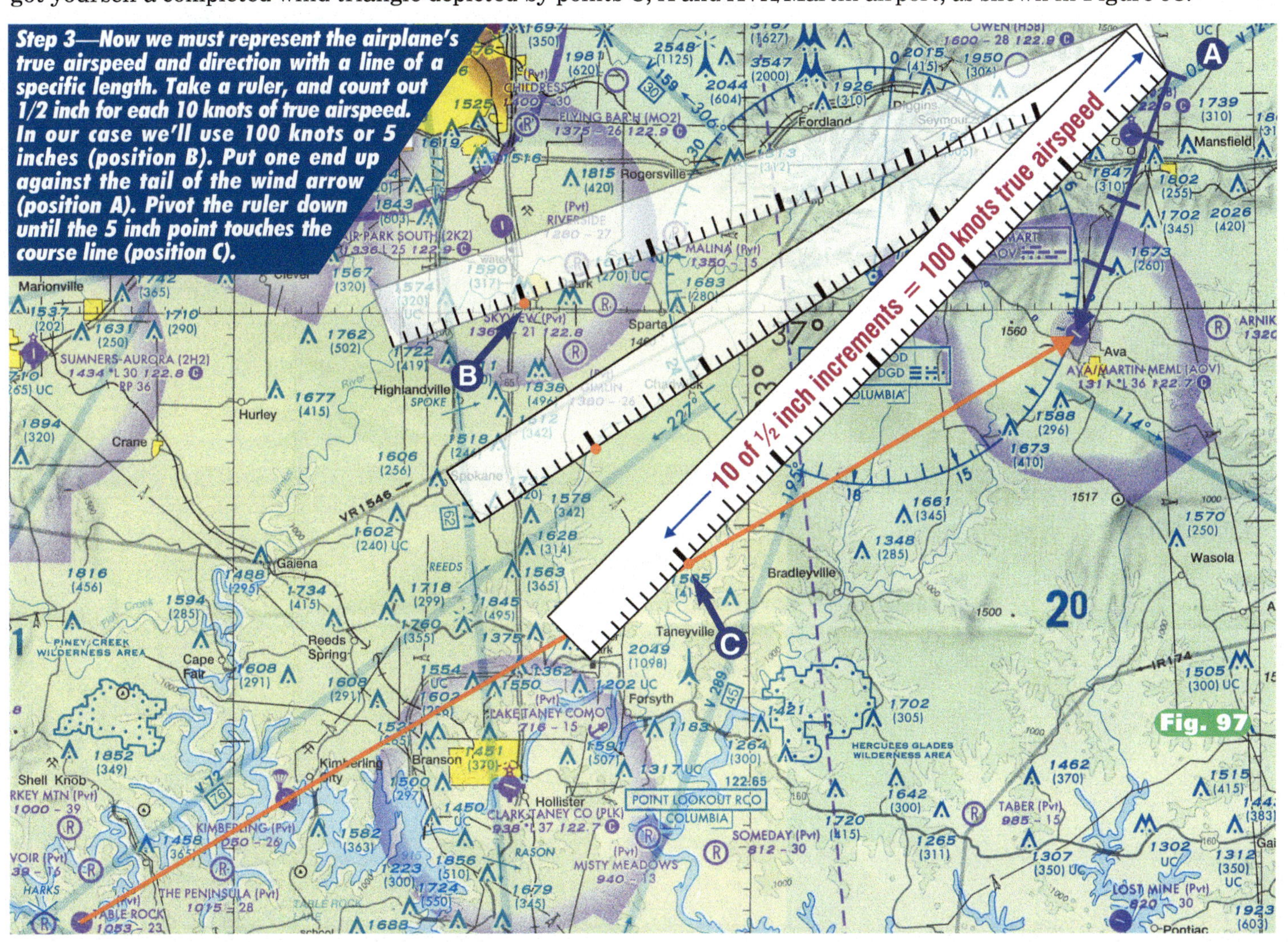

The angle between the true airspeed line (position C to position A) and the course line (position C to AVA/Martin) is our wind correction angle of 15 degrees. This represents how much the nose of the airplane must point to the left of the course to allow you to track directly along the selected course line from Table Rock to AVA/Martin. In other words, the nose must be pointed 15 degrees to the left of a true course of 60 degrees. You must head 45 degrees (60 degrees - 15 degrees=45 degrees) to fly parallel to the line drawn from Table Rock to AVA/Martin airport.

The length of the line, in inches, from position C to AVA/Martin is the groundspeed you can expect. Measuring this distance, as shown in Figure 98 gives you 6.6 inches. At 10 knots per inch increment, this equates to approximately 66 knots groundspeed.

Figure 99 shows the comparison between our completed wind triangle and the wind triangle made by the mechanical flight computer. Notice the similarity. Next time you use the mechanical computer, realize that you're simply creating a wind triangle.

Final Words on Wind Computations

Is it necessary to do hand draw a wind triangle before every flight? Absolutely not. Is it necessary to use a slide type or electronic computer to help determine the effect of wind on your airplane? Yes, I believe it is. You need to know how the wind will affect your fuel consumption and time enroute. This means some sort of wind computation is necessary.

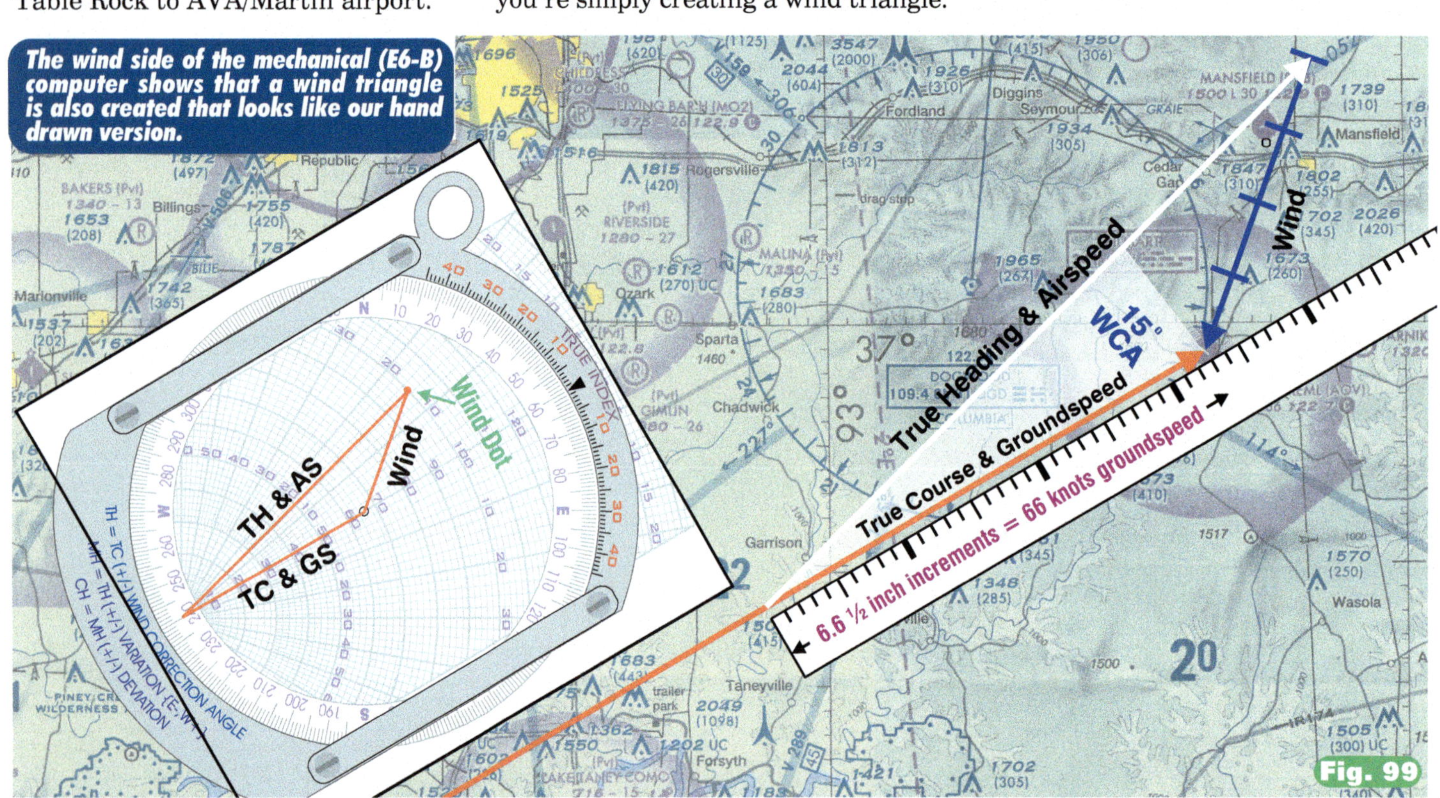

Fig. 99

Postflight Briefing #14-4

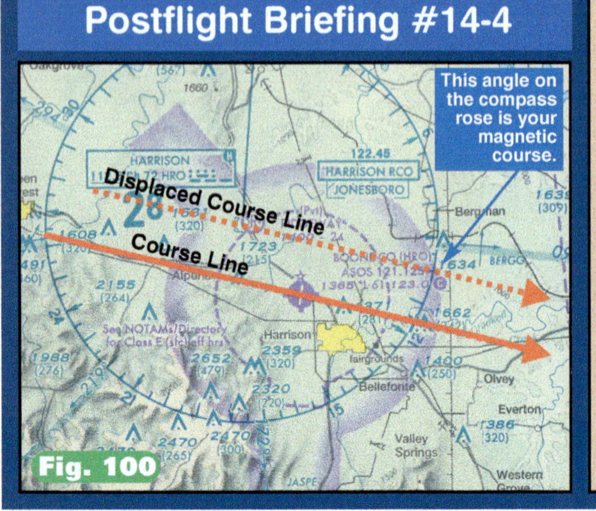

Fig. 100

An Alternate Method of Flight Planning

Another method of flight planning allows you to determine the *magnetic course* directly by displacing the course line through the center of a VOR compass rose. Find the nearest VOR compass rose and run a line parallel to the course line through its center, as shown in Figure 100. Your magnetic course is found on the compass rose. In the case of Figure 100, our magnetic course from Potters eastward is 100 degrees. Simply correct the magnetic course for compass deviation to get the compass course and you're on your way with no further corrections (assuming no wind exists).

If wind does exist, you can correct the winds (which are in true direction) for magnetic variation to obtain winds from a magnetic direction (simply add or subtract the variation from the true winds as appropriate). With your E6-B computer, use winds from the magnetic direction along with the magnetic course (instead of the true course) to find the wind correction angle (WCA). Apply the wind correction angle to your magnetic course, correct this for deviation and you end up with a compass heading for your trip. Why do it this way? If pilots often fly VOR airways (which are magnetic courses) it's sometimes easier to convert the true winds to a magnetic direction, then solve for the WCA and groundspeed.

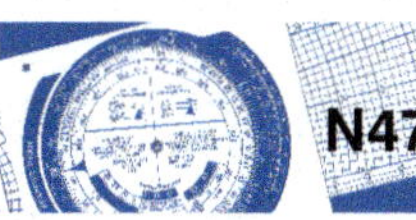

Postflight Briefing #14-5

Flight Planning/Weather Briefings by Computer

We all know someone who's technically challenged. I have a friend like that. He purchased a camera and was happily showing it off when I asked him what kind of "lux" value it had (lux is a measure of the camera's light sensitivity). He replied, "I think it's a Dee-lux." Oh well. If you don't have a fear of things technical, you're in for a treat.

It's the computer age. Knowing how to use one has many benefits. In addition to providing sophisticated means for shooting down Klingons and wasting time, a computer allows you to obtain a complete and legal weather briefing and other essential preflight information, all from the comfort of your home.

You can do things such as file a flight plan, close a flight plan, obtain weather maps and NOTAMS, see temporary flight restrictions, use a flight planner to help select routes, determine mileage and much more. You can also obtain plain language interpretation of things like METAR, TAF and other weather reports. Best of all, the service is free. Whoa! Pick yourself up, and stow that credit card. That's right, for exactly no outlay of money, you get access to highly sophisticated software that provides state-of-the-art flight planning services.

While there are many wonderful flight planning software programs available, I recommend that you begin by using AOPA's real-time FlyQ flight planner (free to all AOPA members—if you're not yet a member, you should join). It can be found on AOPA's web site (www.aopa.org). *Note: This program might disappear as fast as it appeared since AOPA is cutting edge and updates/changes their offerings as technology evolves.*

Before you can begin using most any flight planner, you need to establish an account at the Leidos FSS. Leidos is *not* you and a flight instructor humming a Mariachi tune together. It's your free ticket to flight planning information that's available to you when you register at www.1800wxbrief.com. It's through these service providers that you're able to use AOPA's flight planner to access weather and NOTAM information.

Begin by filling out the appropriate pilot information in the FlyQ intro page, including your new access code and password. Click OK when done. Next, fill out the Aircraft information dialogue box that opens and click "Next" to begin flight planning.

Now you're ready to rock, or flight plan to avoid the rocks, if you will. Let's choose a practice flight from John Wayne airport (KSNA) in Southern California to Reid-Hillview airport (KRHV) in Northern California (Figure 101, position A).

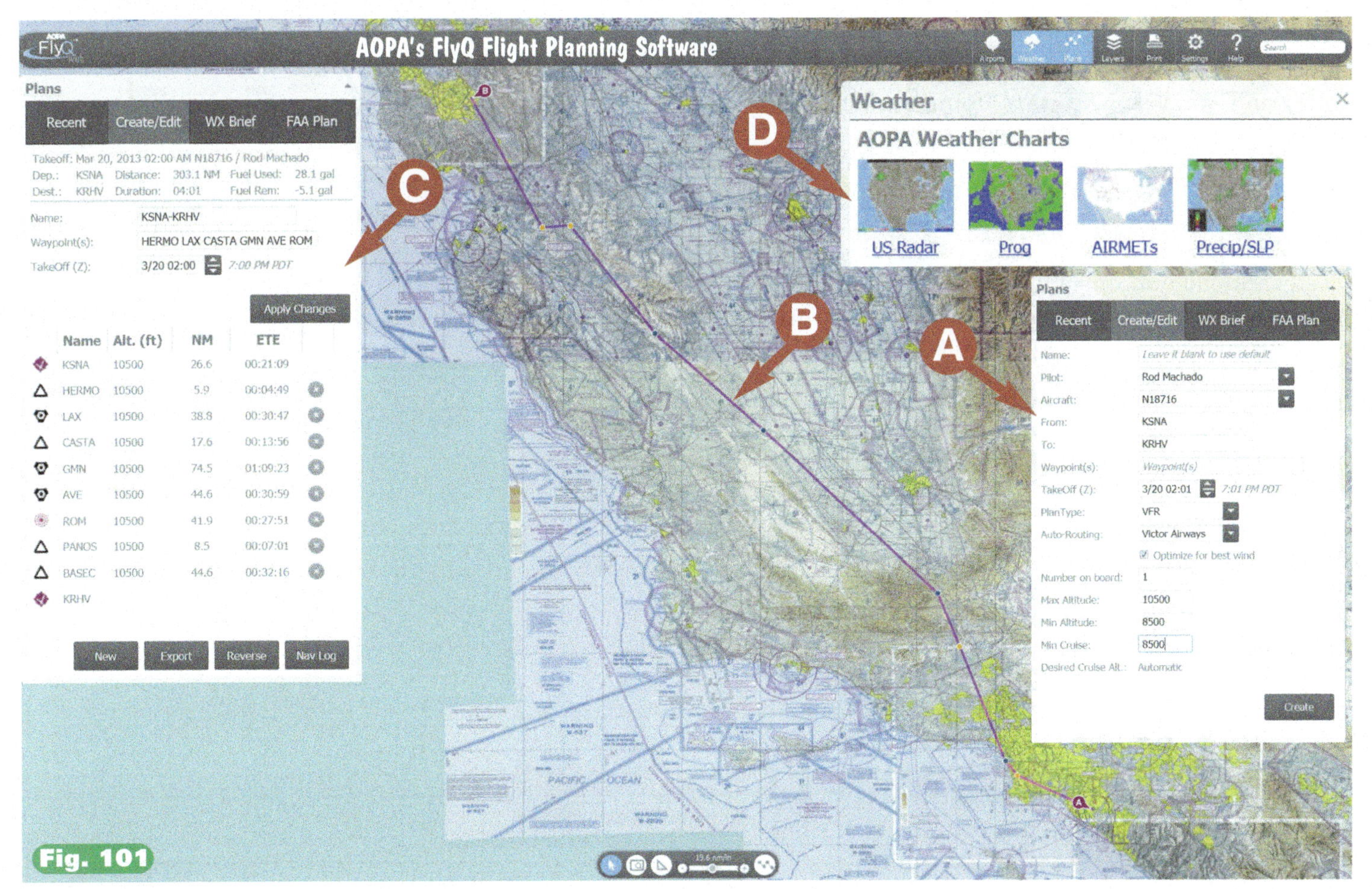

Fig. 101

Begin by clicking the Create/Edit tab in the upper part of the Plans dialogue box (Figure 101, position A). Fill in the departure airport identifier and the destination airport identifier (if either airport has numbers in its identification, then don't place the "K" value in front of the airport identifier). Choose the appropriate date and time for departure, along with the type of route you'd prefer to fly. You can choose either an *airway* routing or a *GPS direct* routing. If you choose the airway option, the flight planner will automatically choose an airway routing for you. We'll also use a cruise altitude of 10,500 feet for this flight. Once done, click OK and the a magenta flight planned route will automatically appear (Figure 101, position B). The Create/Edit dialogue box now shows the individual intersections, VORs or waypoints that make up your routing (Figure 101, position C).

The magenta line represents your airway route from John Wayne to Reid-Hillview. At this point, if you decide that you want to fly an alternate route instead of the one given, click and drag the magenta course line to any intersection, VOR or fix (or waypoint), as necessary, to fly any route desired. See what nice things AOPA does for you here?

The really special part about being able to modify your route is that you can move the route line around any temporary flight restrictions (TFRs) present on the chart,

Now it's time to obtain the weather for this flight. You'll do this by clicking the weather tab at the top of the flight planner (Figure 101, position D). When you do, the Weather Types dialogue box opens as shown in Figure 102. There are several weather types you can choose from here. The winds aloft chart is a good example (Figure 103).

Wonderful as electronic flight planning is, don't let it make you lazy about examining *and understanding* the weather and route information. You always want to keep your head in the game, and have a gut feel for the routes, headings and altitudes you've chosen. There are two reasons for this. First, even computers can hand you the wrong information if there are programming errors, bad data, or other glitches. Catching those things is *your* responsibility. Second, unless you've manually gone over the entire route, you won't have this information at your fingertips and you won't have the extra bit of mental insurance that's so much needed if and when you have to make an important decision about navigation.

While there's quite a bit more to this wonderful software, I'm reluctant to make this book any bigger. At least you understand the salient features of the online flight planning software.

I don't want to give you the impression that flight planning software is your key to rest and relaxation when it comes to creating manual flight logs, as we learned to do in this chapter. That would be a very wrong impression. First, the flight planning you'll initially do is based on dead reckoning and pilotage. This means picking personalized checkpoints off the chart, inserting them in the flight log, then making all the calculations necessary to fly the flight. You can't learn how to do this if you let the flight planning software do the work for you. This is why you should learn all the basics first, then let the flight planning software assist you in making a more complete flight plan with weather overlays and weather chart generation. Remember, you must learn to walk before you run (or taxi before you fly). So please don't skip the basics of flight planning just to spend more time in that lounge chair.

In regard to this book being big, let me just say that it's built that way for safety. In the event you can't clear the trees on the end of a runway during takeoff, let's hope you have my book on board. By opening the window and throwing out the book, you could get an extra 500 feet per minute of climb rate. Now *that's* a safety advantage.

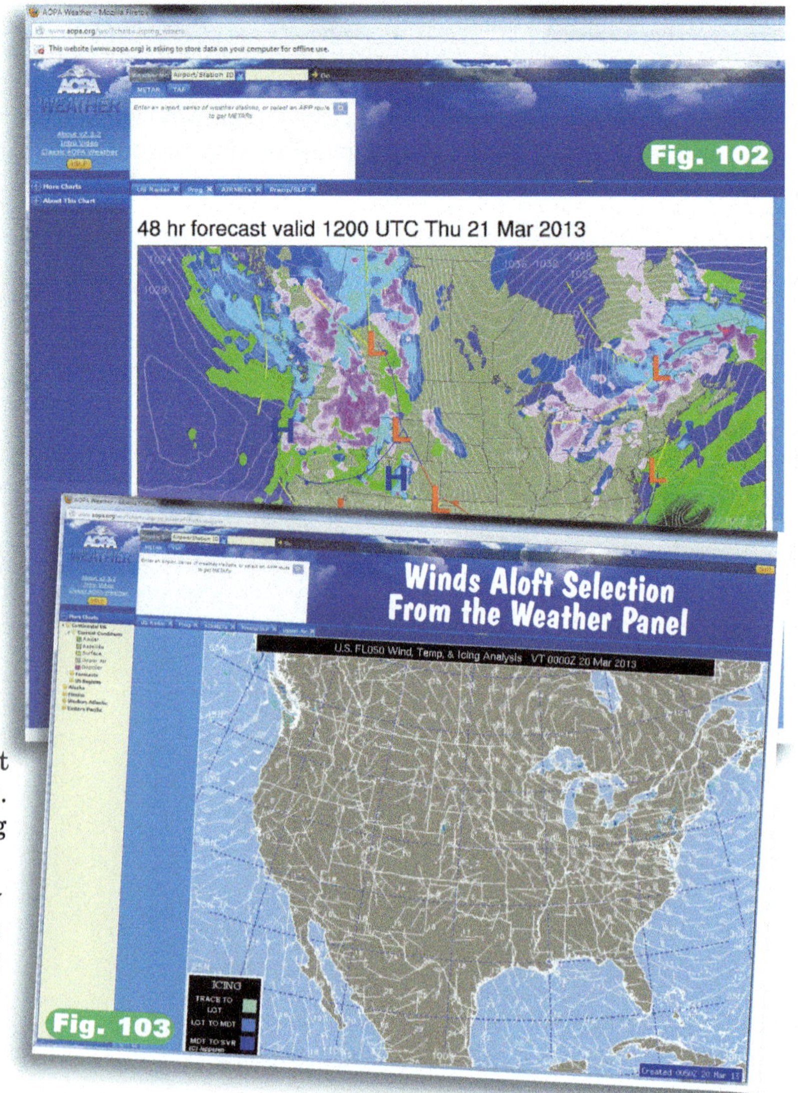

Fig. 102

Fig. 103

Courtesy Cessna

Chapter Fifteen

Airplane Performance

Know Before You Go

"Cessna 2132 Bravo, this is Departure Control, please squawk standby. There's a problem with your transponder," said the controller.

"What's the problem?" asked the pilot of the Cessna 152.

"Well, we show your airplane climbing through 19,500 feet doing 320 knots," replied the controller.

The quick thinking pilot with an excellent sense of humor replied, "Oh no, that's right. We just had our engine overhauled." Now that's real performance! Except, of course, that it was *unreal* performance. The controller could easily predict that no 152 on (or off) Earth was capable of doing 320 knots *or* climbing to 19,500 feet.

Airplane performance *is* predictable. Unlike psychics, pilots don't need crystal balls or Quija boards to make performance estimates that are very close to the mark. An airplane's takeoff, climb, cruise and landing performance is easily estimated from a variety of charts found in the Pilot's Operating Handbook (POH), which is as much a part of the aircraft's equipment as the wings. (If you don't see either the wings or the POH, better ask about it).

Your job is to know how to use the performance charts. As you'll soon see, all airplane performance is based on one very important item—air density. That's because the thickness of the air flowing over the wings or into the engine determines how well the airplane performs (or fails to perform).

Air Density

Airplanes are remarkably similar to people in that both experience decreased performance in less-dense air. Anyone who's ever hiked to the top of a high mountain knows how human performance decreases. One trip up El Capitan at Yosemite and you feel like you're the big, bad wolf, huffing and puffing as though you were trying to blow a house down.

Airplanes, too, are air-breathing machines, and they respond much as you do to lowered air density. The more air molecules flowing over the airplane's wing, the greater the lift developed. Anything that thins the air reduces the wings' ability to generate lift.

Airplane engine performance is affected in the same way. Powerplants require air to run. Anything

reducing the amount of air the engine swallows diminishes its power output. Less power equals less performance. No fancy mathematics here. It's really quite simple. To fly without understanding this important relationship is about as wise as having the three little pigs invite the wolf in for a spot of tea, which would certainly give new meaning to the term "pig out."

Let's take a closer look at the things which affect airplane performance.

Height

As we discussed in an earlier chapter, the higher you go, the less frequently you—or your airplane's wing—will run into air molecules, because they are fewer and farther between with increasing altitude. This is another way of saying that the *air density* is less. Fewer air molecules are available to move past the wing, so lift is reduced and performance is decreased. Expect higher altitudes to provide you with slower acceleration, longer ground runs, and shallower climb profiles, as shown in Figure 1.

Heat

Heat is also notorious for reducing the performance of airplanes. Heated air is much less dense than colder air. Expect slower acceleration, longer takeoff runs, and shallower climb profiles on hot days, as shown in Figure 2.

Humidity

High humidity also reduces airplane performance by thinning the air. Wait a minute, you say! How can adding moisture to air make it thinner? Moist air is lighter (thus less dense) because water molecules are actually lighter than air molecules. Mind you, I said water molecules, not water, which is obviously a lot heavier because of the density. If you've ever tried to carry a bucket of steam (it rises because it's lighter than air), you've had direct proof that moist air is less dense than dry air. By itself, moist air isn't much of a problem. This is why most performance charts make no correction for humidity. Nevertheless, in combination with height and heat it could put your airplane dangerously close to those trees at the end of the runway.

The very best way to think of all this is to remember that you should avoid joining

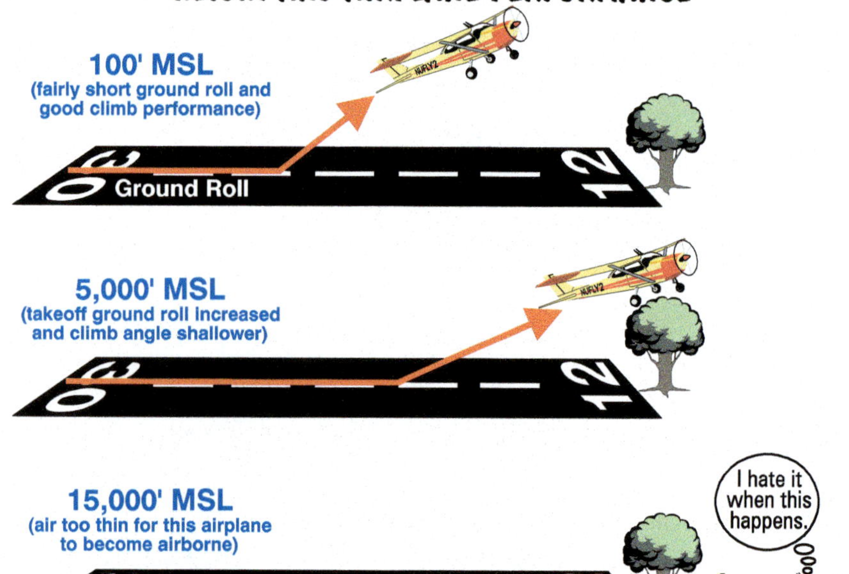

An increase in altitude has an adverse effect on airplane performance. Higher altitude means thinner air, which reduces the wing's ability to develop lift as well as reducing the engine's power output. Higher altitudes are associated with a longer ground run, a reduced rate of climb and a shallower climb angle. The likelihood of climbing over obstacles at the departure end of the runway diminishes at this decreased air density.

Fig. 1

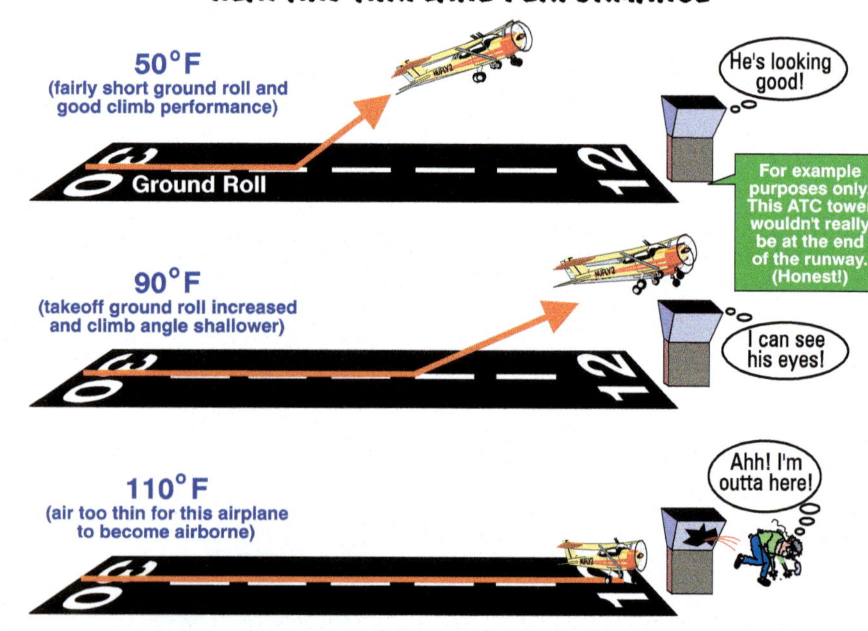

An increase in temperature has an adverse effect on airplane performance. Warmer air means thinner air which reduces the wings' ability to develop lift as well as reduces the engine's power output. Warmer temperatures bring longer ground runs and shallow climb angles.

Fig. 2

Flare when you hear the crickets.

Dave Rossi

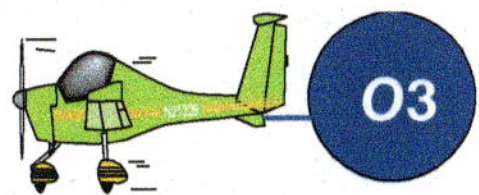

HUMIDITY

An increase in humidity produces an increase in density altitude, but it's not often dramatic. Increasing the relative humidity of standard temperature air from 50% to 100% often doesn't increase the density altitude by more than 100 to 150 feet. Now, if the air is significantly above standard temperature, then the increase in density altitude can be as high as 600 feet.

For example, if the air temperature at 5,000 feet is 80 degrees F with a 0% relative humidity, then the density altitude is approximately 7,445 feet. Increase the humidity in the example above to 100% and the density altitude jumps to 7957 feet. That's an increase in 514 feet due to a 100% increase in relative humidity at these higher temperatures.

If you'd like to see for yourself how humidity affects density altitude take a look at Richard Shelquist's density altitude calculator page at (http://wahiduddin.net/calc/calc_da_rh.htm).

aviation's 4-H club. Because if you have height, heat and humidity, you have heck to pay (ahhh, those 4 H's!). Any one or a combination of these factors can turn an airplane into a car by keeping it from becoming airborne.

If you want to avoid ending up on the Oprah Winfrey show, don't do weird, strange things in your airplane, like taking off with a lot of height, heat and humidity.

"OK, Rod," I hear you saying, "how much is *a lot?*" Good question. The effects of height and heat are all combined into one very important calculation called *density altitude.*

Density Altitude

Taking off at an airport near sea level usually results in good acceleration and climb performance. The elevation has no effect on performance, temperatures are usually moderate, and the humidity is generally not too high. If we take off from an airport situated at 100 feet MSL, the airplane performs quite well.

Suppose, however, that it's an extraordinarily hot day at our 100 foot MSL airport. Will the airplane perform well? No. Because of the high heat, the air might have a density equivalent to an altitude around 3,000 feet. The term *density altitude* describes how dense the air feels to the airplane, regardless of the airplane's present height above sea level. Density altitude is an extremely important term for you to understand.

In the previous example, even though the airplane was physically at 100 feet MSL, in terms of *airplane performance* the airport has a density altitude of 3,000 feet.

In Chapter 5, I mentioned that pressure altitude was the reference to which airplane engineers calibrate their performance charts. Pressure altitude is what the altimeter indicates when 29.92 inches Hg is set in the altimeter's Kollsman window. In addition to the pressure altitude reference, engineers also calibrate many of their performance charts to a standard temperature of 59 degrees F (15 degrees C) at sea level.

Engineers call the conditions of 29.92 inches Hg and 59 degrees F (15 degrees C) at sea level *standard conditions.* Since you must have a starting point or reference when calibrating the performance of airplanes (and their instruments), standard conditions at sea level is a good starting place. For example, when you ask the teacher how your son Bobby is doing in school, he or she normally compares his performance to that of a previous year. The teacher might say, "Well, compared to last year, Bobby is doing better." If the teacher said, "Well, in reference to all forms of animal and plant life on this planet, little Bobby is holding his own against most species of protozoa," then Bobby is in trouble. Standard temperature and pressure conditions are simply a reference point where a baseline of performance is established.

Of course, if standard conditions existed at sea level all the time, we wouldn't have to worry about changes in air density and its effects on airplane performance. Unfortunately, Mother Nature doesn't like constant, standard conditions (that's why a tornado is similar to a divorce or an earthquake—one of them is going to get your house).

Let's assume you're at an airport at 4,000 foot MSL and standard conditions exist at sea level. Let's also assume that temperatures decrease at 3.5 degrees F (2 degrees C) per 1,000 feet (by now you know that while this is the engineer's standard lapse rate and is used for instrument calibration, it is seldom the actual lapse rate found in the environment). Under these conditions, the temperature at 4,000 feet should be 45 degrees F (4x3.5=14 and 59-14=45 degrees F). Suppose it's really hot,

HIGH FRIGHT

I was on a night, scenic VFR flight with a passenger. After one hour my passenger was trying to eat popcorn and talk, but it was all "gibberish." My altimeter was indicating 11,500' and holding steady. However, I noticed a steady rate of climb indication of 120 fpm, and an 11,000' mountain off the wing appeared unusually small. I contacted Approach and asked for Mode C readout. They informed me that Center read me at 19,700' MSL. The controller recommended rapping on the panel. I began a descent for home airport and banged on the panel above the altimeter. It immediately jumped to 16,400 and was moving again. I should have noticed a shallow climb with the other instruments. However, I hadn't had any sleep for 36 hours and thought I was doing a nice job of maintaining my eastbound cruise altitude of 11,500.

ASRS Report

say 100 degrees F (38 degrees C) at 4,000 feet (this is definitely a nonstandard temperature). Is the airplane going to perform like it normally would at 4,000 feet? Definitely not. In fact, the airplane is going to perform more like it's at 7,500 feet (I'll show you in just a moment how I arrived at this value).

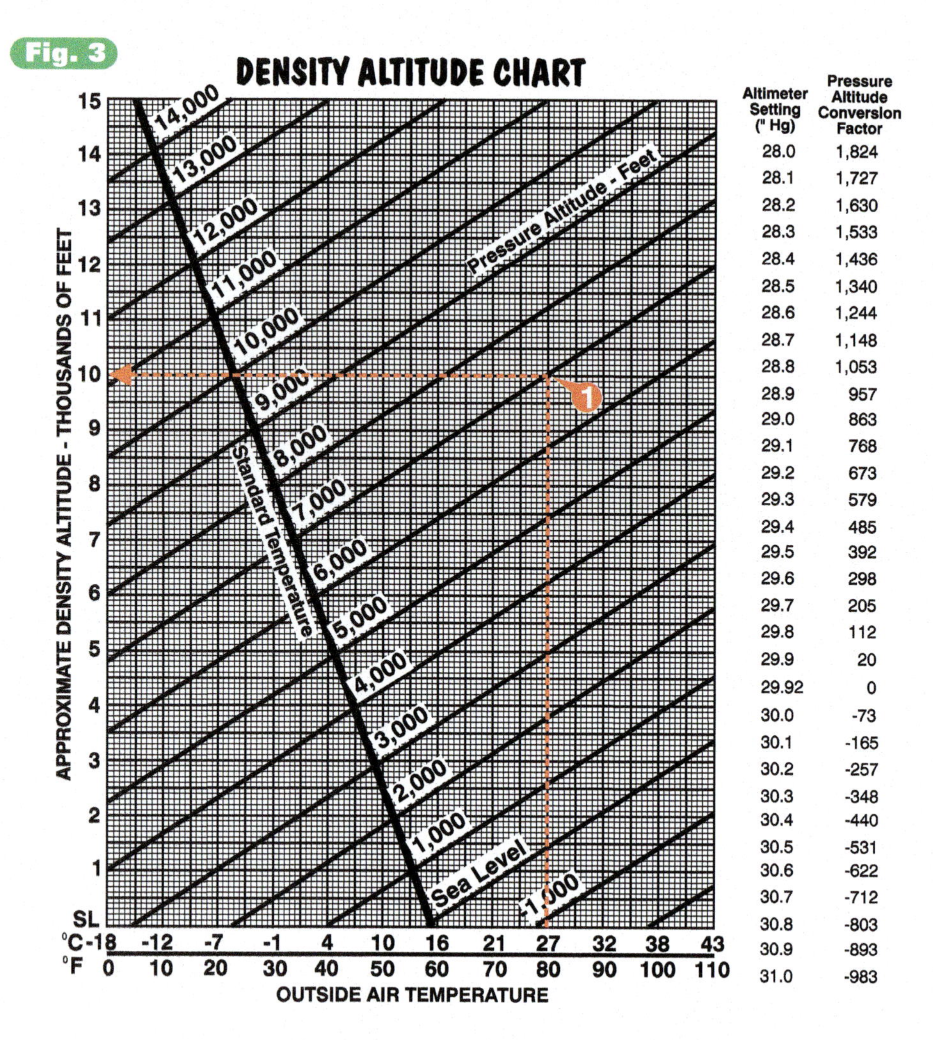

Altimeter Setting (" Hg)	Pressure Altitude Conversion Factor
28.0	1,824
28.1	1,727
28.2	1,630
28.3	1,533
28.4	1,436
28.5	1,340
28.6	1,244
28.7	1,148
28.8	1,053
28.9	957
29.0	863
29.1	768
29.2	673
29.3	579
29.4	485
29.5	392
29.6	298
29.7	205
29.8	112
29.9	20
29.92	0
30.0	-73
30.1	-165
30.2	-257
30.3	-348
30.4	-440
30.5	-531
30.6	-622
30.7	-712
30.8	-803
30.9	-893
31.0	-983

Because of the higher than normal temperature, the air has a density altitude—a performance altitude, if you want to think of it that way—of approximately 7,500 feet. Think of density altitude as you do personal debt. Whenever debt increases, bad things happen; when debt decreases, good things happen. Increasing density altitude decreases airplane performance; decreasing density altitude increases airplane performance.

Density Altitude Example No. 1 – Finding the density altitude is easy with the density altitude chart in Figure 3. Along the bottom (horizontal) axis is a temperature scale with Fahrenheit and Celsius markings. Rising diagonally upward from left to right are pressure altitude lines. On the left side of the chart is the density altitude reading along the vertical scale. If you know the pressure altitude and the air temperature for your location, you can easily find the density altitude. Let's see how this works.

Assume your outside air temperature (OAT) is 80 degrees F (27 degrees C) and the pressure altitude is 7,000 feet. Referring to Figure 3, find 80 degrees F (27 degrees C) on the bottom, horizontal scale and move upwards until reaching the 7,000 foot (diagonal) pressure altitude line. Make a mark at this point (position 1) and move horizontally to the left. The number on the left hand vertical scale is the density altitude. In our example the density altitude is 10,000 feet.

Density Altitude Example No. 2 – What is your density altitude if the pressure altitude is 3,257 feet and the OAT is 75 degrees F (24 degrees C)? First you must locate your pressure altitude between the diagonal lines on the density altitude chart in Figure 4. Locating the pressure altitude value of 3,257 is easy if you draw the intermediate values between the 1,000 foot pressure altitude lines. Simply draw the 3,500 foot pressure altitude value between the 3,000 and 4,000 foot pressure altitude lines, as shown in Figure 4. Now draw an intermediate value between the 3,000 and 3,500 foot pressure altitude line. This will represent the 3,250 foot pressure altitude value. Move up the 75 degree F (24 degree C) line until reaching the pressure altitude line of 3,250, as shown by position 2 (this is very close to the actual pressure altitude value of 3,257 feet). Go across to the left to find a density altitude value of approximately 5,000 feet.

At the end of this chapter in Postflight Briefing #15-1, I've included two different types of density altitude problems that show up on FAA knowledge exams. Unfortunately, one of the problems is more test oriented than it is practical in the real world. Don't ask me why test creators do this. It reminds me of some 8th century monk-scribe inserting words in an ancient text that eventually becomes the foundation of our modern English language. As the monk is writing the official word for sharp instrument with a handle that cuts your steak, he looks around, then mischievously inserts a K in the word knife. No one knows why he did this, but it's a done deed. We've got to live with it. Study Postflight Briefing #15-1 carefully during your final preparation for the knowledge exam.

Let's look at an even more meaningful example of how density altitude relates to airplane performance. Before we can do that we need to understand something known as service ceiling.

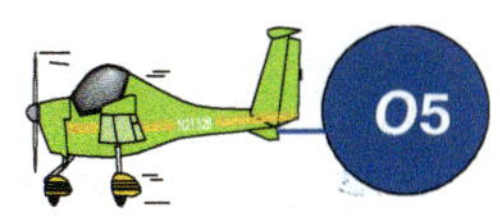

Fig. 4

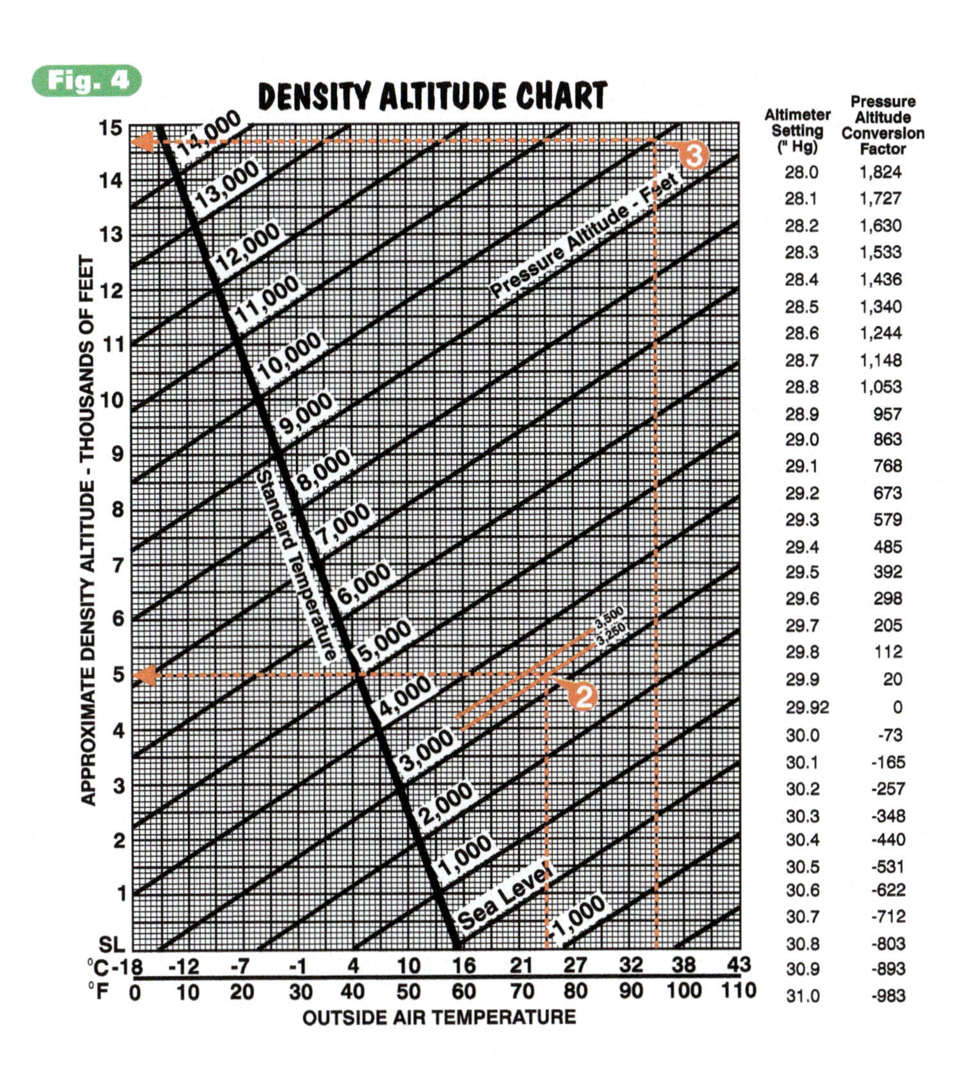

Altimeter Setting (" Hg)	Pressure Altitude Conversion Factor
28.0	1,824
28.1	1,727
28.2	1,630
28.3	1,533
28.4	1,436
28.5	1,340
28.6	1,244
28.7	1,148
28.8	1,053
28.9	957
29.0	863
29.1	768
29.2	673
29.3	579
29.4	485
29.5	392
29.6	298
29.7	205
29.8	112
29.9	20
29.92	0
30.0	-73
30.1	-165
30.2	-257
30.3	-348
30.4	-440
30.5	-531
30.6	-622
30.7	-712
30.8	-803
30.9	-893
31.0	-983

Service Ceiling

Most POHs for individual airplanes inform pilots of the maximum height the airplane can be flown to before it ceases climbing (technically, the altitude at which the climb rate drops to 100 feet per minute). This height is known as the *service ceiling* (Figure 5). The service ceiling applies to a brand new airplane with a new engine. You can expect older airplanes to have service ceilings less than the book value. Figure 6 shows 14,700 feet as the service ceiling of a 1980 Cessna 152. Of course, if the density altitude is close to or equal to that of the 14,700 foot service ceiling, the airplane will only climb at 100 feet per minute or less.

Density Altitude Problem No. 3 – Suppose you're flying a new Cessna 152 from an airport where the pressure altitude is 10,000 feet and the OAT is 95 degrees F (35 degrees C) (that's hot for an airport that high—better be careful!). What is the density altitude at that airport?

Use the density altitude chart (Figure 4) to identify where the 95

THE SERVICE CEILING

14,700' MSL (Service Ceiling)

10,000' MSL

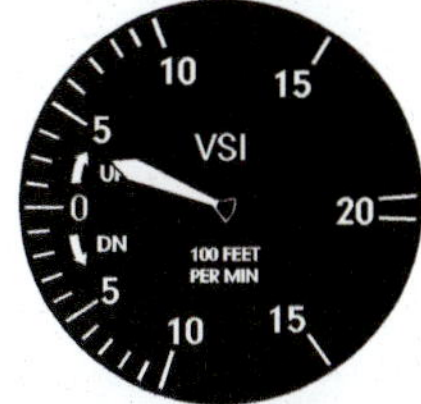

5,000' MSL

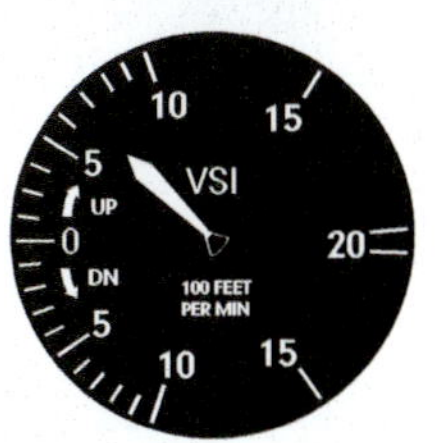

An airplane reaches its service ceiling when its climb rate is reduced to 100 feet per minute or less.

Pilot Operating Handbook Showing Service Ceiling

PERFORMANCE - SPECIFICATIONS

*SPEED:
Maximum at Sea Level . . . . 110 KNOTS
Cruise, 75% Power at 8000 Ft . . . . 107 KNOTS
CRUISE: Recommended lean mixture with fuel allowance for engine start, taxi, takeoff, climb and 45 minutes reserve.
75% Power at 8000 Ft . . . . Range 320 NM
24.5 Gallons Usable Fuel . . . . Time 3.1 HRS
75% Power at 8000 Ft . . . . Range 545 NM
37.5 Gallons Usable Fuel . . . . Time 5.2 HRS
Maximum Range at 10,000 Ft . . . . Range 415 NM
24.5 Gallons Usable Fuel . . . . Time 5.2 HRS
Maximum Range at 10,000 Ft . . . . Range 690 NM
37.5 Gallons Usable Fuel . . . . Time 8.7 HRS
RATE OF CLIMB AT SEA LEVEL . . . . 715 FPM
SERVICE CEILING . . . . 14,700 FT
TAKEOFF PERFORMANCE:
Ground Roll . . . . 725 FT
Total Distance Over 50-Ft Obstacle . . . . 1340 FT
LANDING PERFORMANCE:
Ground Roll . . . . 475 FT
Total Distance Over 50-Ft Obstacle . . . . 1200 FT
STALL SPEED (CAS):
Flaps Up, Power Off . . . . 48 KNOTS
Flaps Down, Power Off . . . . 43 KNOTS
MAXIMUM WEIGHT:
Ramp . . . . 1675 LBS
Takeoff or Landing . . . . 1670 LBS
STANDARD EMPTY WEIGHT:
152 . . . . 1109 LBS
152 II . . . . 1142 LBS
MAXIMUM USEFUL LOAD:
152 . . . . 566 LBS
152 II . . . . 533 LBS
BAGGAGE ALLOWANCE . . . . 120 LBS
WING LOADING: Pounds/Sq Ft 10.5
POWER LOADING: Pounds/HP 15.2
FUEL CAPACITY: Total
Standard Tanks . . . . 26 GAL.
Long Range Tanks . . . . 39 GAL.
OIL CAPACITY . . . . 6 QTS
ENGINE: Av
110 BHP
PROPELLER: Fixed Pitch, Diameter . . . . 69 IN.

For Training Purposes Only!

Fig. 6

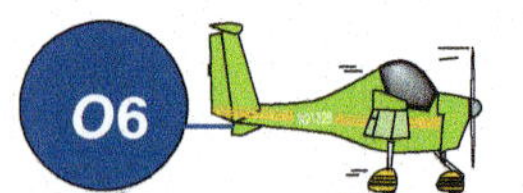

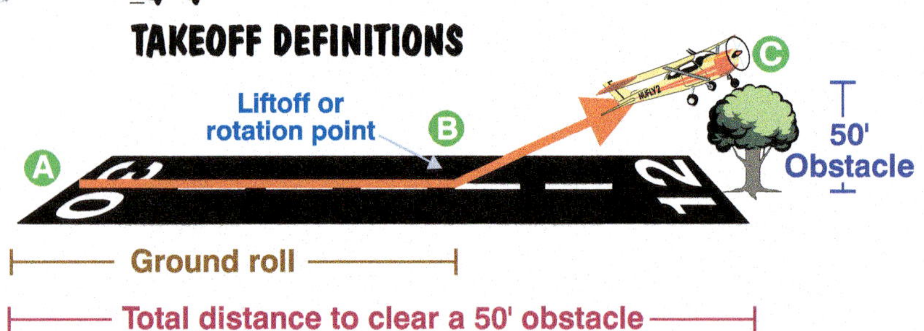

The ground roll is the total distance required for the airplane to become airborne. The point where the airplane reaches 50 feet above the runway is the total distance required for the airplane to clear a 50 foot obstacle (supposedly placed at this precise point).

Fig. 7

degree F (35° C) line intersects the 10,000 foot pressure altitude line (position 3). Moving horizontally to the left you determine the density altitude to be 14,700 feet.

How will our airplane perform? Not well. Better get out your driver's license, since driving is what you'll be doing. The airplane, if it gets off the runway at all, will barely climb 100 feet per minute. You're going to scare quite a few people standing at the end of the runway. Take my word for it, if it's an older airplane, you'll never become airborne under the conditions in this example. And if it's a tired old airplane you'll notice something is wrong because it'll take full power to taxi (that's a joke. But it does emphasize how much the performance decreases).

Here's Machado's Service Ceiling Caveat: Never count on more than 75% of an airplane's posted service ceiling. This is, admittedly, a conservative estimate if the airplane is new, but a wise and realistic one if the airplane is old. By my numbers, I would expect a Cessna 152 to climb no faster than 100 feet per minute at a density altitude of 11,025 feet (75% of 14,700 feet).

Anything that makes the air thinner (lower pressure, high heat, high humidity) increases the density altitude. Anything making the air thicker (increasing pressure, low heat, low humidity) decreases the density altitude.

Machado's Whammo Density Predictor states: For a given pressure altitude, the density altitude increases by 1,000 feet for every 15 degree F (8.5 degree C) temperature increase. Given this, and knowledge of your airplane's service ceiling, you can easily estimate the amount your airplane's performance will decrease.

Performance Charts

As a kid, it was often difficult to predict whether my grandfather was being serious or just joking around. He was a card carrying prankster and proud of it. One time he called me over to his chair and said, "Did you know you were adopted?"

I was crushed and sighed, "You mean I was really adopted? Oh no!"

"That's right," grandpa said, "but they brought you back." Hah!

On another occasion (according to my mom), whenever I cried as a kid my grandfather would threaten to call Tibet and tell the authorities that he suspected I was the new Dalai Lama, knowing that they'd come and take me away. Everybody had a big laugh over that one, except me. To this day, whenever someone knocks at the door, I peep through the hole and yell out, "You aren't from Tibet are you? I was adopted so leave me alone."

Fortunately, while grandpa's antics were hard to predict, airplane performance isn't. That's because airplanes have performance

This type of activity dramatically reduces airplane performance. Nevertheless, credit must be given to the pilot who went out of his way to entertain his passenger on those long flights.

What's A Ground Roll?

Aviation has lots of funny terms. Especially if you think about them.

Ground roll is one of those. Sounds like you fed a dinner roll to a CuisinArt, or maybe something you order along with an egg roll at the local Chinese restaurant.

In fact, *ground roll* is the distance the airplane rolls on the ground during takeoff or landing. On takeoff, it's the distance from the start of the takeoff run until the airplane leaves the ground. On landing, it's the distance from touchdown to where the plane can be brought to a full stop.

Next time you order from that Chinese place, ask for *ground roll* and see what happens.

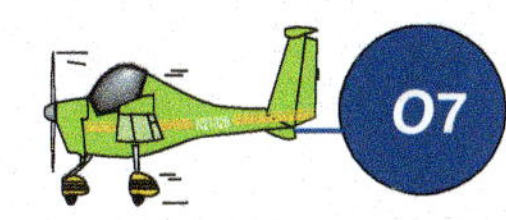

THREE CLIMBING AIRSPEEDS

Climbing at the best rate of climb speed (Vy)

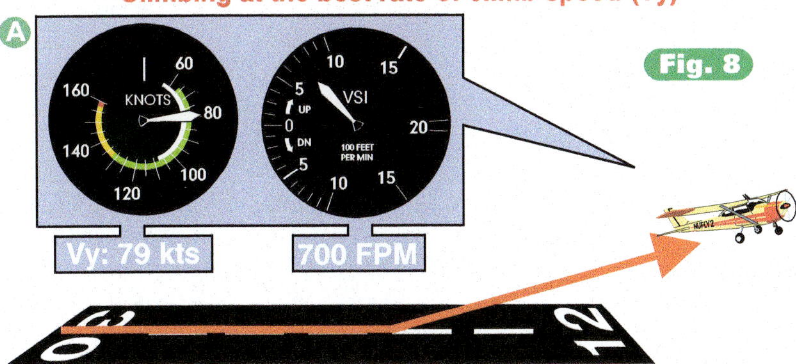

The best rate of climb speed (Vy) gives you the greatest altitude gain for a given amount of time. In other words, it gives you the largest deflection on your vertical speed indicator.

Climbing at the best angle of climb speed (Vx)

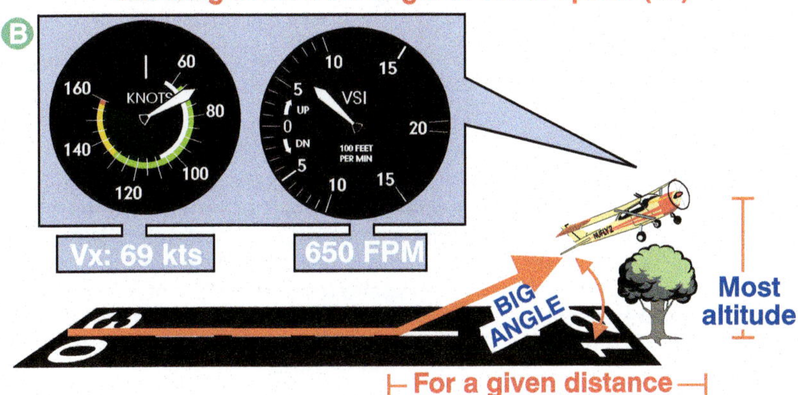

The best angle of climb speed (Vx) gives you the greatest altitude gain for a given distance over the ground. In other words, it gives you the largest climb angle possible.

Climbing at a cruise climb airspeed (pilot's choice)

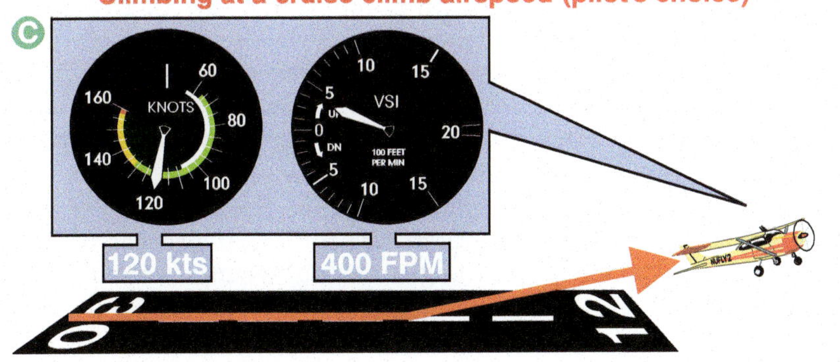

A cruise climb is done with the pilot's choice of airspeed. When no obstacles are present, climbing at a slightly higher speed provides less climb rate yet provides better visibility and good engine cooling.

charts for all facets of their normal activities: takeoff, climb, cruise, landing, etc. Your success at predicting what will happen during these conditions is a matter of your familiarity with these charts. Machado's Ornithological Observation states: All things that fly should use performance charts except birds—since they don't have pockets.

Takeoff Concepts – Takeoffs are second only to landings for their excitement and challenge. While a takeoff may not be as spectacular for some pilots, in my view it requires just as much research and planning to do it well. Figure 7 shows a typical takeoff profile. At position A the airplane applies full power and accelerates down the runway. It eventually reaches liftoff speed at position B and *rotates,* which is a fancy word for *raises the nose to climb.* One time I forgot to tell a student what rotate meant. At the appropriate point during the takeoff, I looked at him and said, "OK Bob, rotate, rotate. He looked really confused. He thought he was supposed to twirl around somehow (perhaps as a bizarre takeoff ritual similar to the secret handshake some flight instructors use). The takeoff ground roll is the distance between A and B.

At position C, the airplane has attained enough height to clear a 50 foot obstacle. The distance between positions A and C is called the *total distance to clear a 50 foot obstacle* (don't you wish all definitions were that easy?). Obviously, the taller the obstacle, the greater the distance required between A and C.

Best Rate and Best Angle Of Climb Speeds

After the liftoff is made, you normally want to climb at a speed that will get you to your selected cruising altitude in the shortest possible time. There is one and only one such speed. It is, as I hope you remember from the discussion in an earlier chapter, called the *best rate of climb speed*—otherwise known as Vy.

Figure 8A shows how a climb at Vy might look. The best rate of climb speed will give you the largest upward deflection on the vertical speed indicator. In other words, you'll be able to gain altitude in the shortest possible time.

Sometimes climb angle instead of time is a concern during takeoff. Altitude gain for a given distance over the ground is a concern when an obstacle looms at the departure end. Watching an obstacle grow in your windshield is exciting in the way it's exciting to be a spotted owl at a lumberjack convention. If you want to gain the most altitude for a given distance over the ground, then climb at the best angle of climb speed, otherwise known as Vx. Figure 8B shows a climb profile at Vx. Notice that if the most altitude is gained by the time the airplane has arrived at the obstacle, this represents a very large angle of climb.

Even though the nose attitude is generally higher at Vx, the airplane won't have as large a rate of climb deflection on the VSI as it would at Vy (it will initially as you rotate, but then returns to a lesser value). The airplane still climbs at a larger angle because Vx is slower than Vy. With a slower forward speed, it gains more altitude per foot of forward distance, making the angle of climb quite large. In many cases, the airplane's POH recommends small flap settings to facilitate a short-field climb over an obstacle.

The easiest way to remember the difference between Vx and Vy is to ask yourself which one, the Y or the X, has more angles? The X has more angles making it the best angle of climb speed (Vx). By default, Y, with fewer angles, becomes the best rate of climb speed.

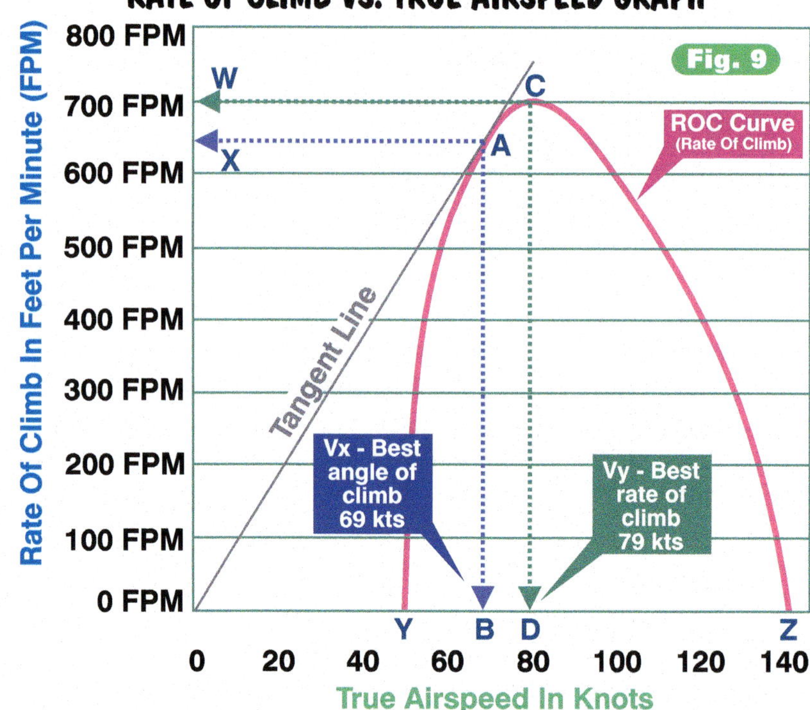

The full throttle rate of climb (ROC) curve depicts a zero rate at point (Z)–the point of maximum level forward speed and point (Y)–the power-on stall speed. Where the tangent line contacts the ROC curve at point A, the airplane attains the maximum altitude gain for a specific forward velocity, otherwise knows as the best angle of climb speed (point B at 69 knots). The maximum rate of climb is achieved at point C. The speed for the maximum rate of climb is found at 79 knots at point D.

Vx and Vy Change With Altitude

The best angle and best rate of climb speeds change slightly with altitude and weight. Since the airplane's ability to climb is predicated on excess thrust (power), changing altitude or changing weight (or both) changes the amount of excess thrust (power) available for a climb. This, in turn, affects the speeds at which Vx and Vy occur.

Figure 9 shows a typical rate of climb (ROC) vs. true airspeed graph under full throttle conditions. The curve identifies the ROC for different airspeeds at a specific altitude. At full throttle (assumed to be maximum power) there is no rate of climb at point Z since all the airplane's power is used to achieve maximum forward speed.

As the airplane slows to point C, parasite drag decreases and the excess thrust (thrust not used to overcome drag) has been converted into a rate of climb. Continued slowing of the airplane further reduces the ROC because of the increasing induced drag. At point Y, the airplane has no ROC since all the airplane's power is used in overcoming an enormous amount of induced drag. (This is *operating behind the power curve,* as described in Chapter 2.)

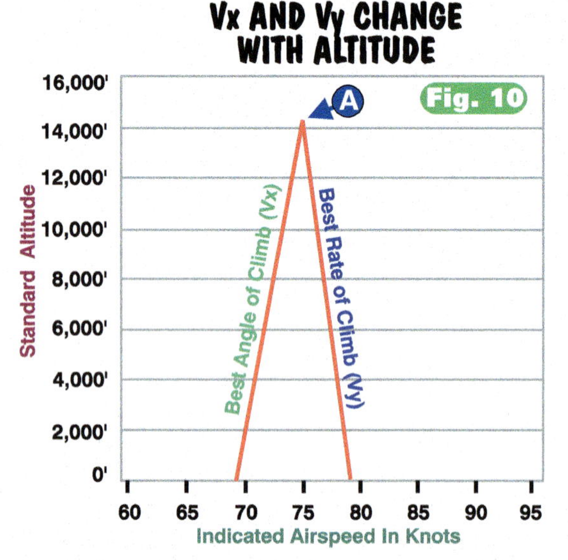

The indicated airspeed for the best angle-of-climb (Vx) increases with an increase in altitude. The indicated airspeed for the best rate-of-climb (Vy) decreases with altitude. The point at which they meet (point A) is the altitude where the airplane can no longer climb. This is known as the *absolute ceiling*.

The sea level, best rate of climb is found at point C. Dropping directly downward to point D identifies the Vy speed for this particular airplane. A tangent line from the bottom left corner of the graph contacts the sea level ROC line at point A. At this point, the airplane experiences its best angle of climb. Dropping downward from point A to point B identifies the airplane's speed for Vx.

Why the tangent line? Mathematically, when the beginning of this line is anchored at the graph's origin (the 0 FPM, 0 airspeed point), it has the steepest slope (largest angle upward) where it contacts the ROC curve at point A.

As you can see, Vx is a little less than Vy. As altitude increases, the indicated airspeed for Vx increases slightly while the indicated airspeed for Vy decreases slightly, as shown in Figure 10. Think about it this way: The smaller one (Vx) gets larger while the larger one (Vy) gets smaller as altitude increases.

Cruise Climb Speed

Most of the time, it's preferable to climb at some speed slightly above Vy. This is often called a cruise-climb speed and it provides you better forward visibility during the climb, as shown in Figure 8C. On hot days it also keeps the engine cooler, preventing overheating and possible detonation. The choice of cruise-climb speeds is a matter of pilot preference.

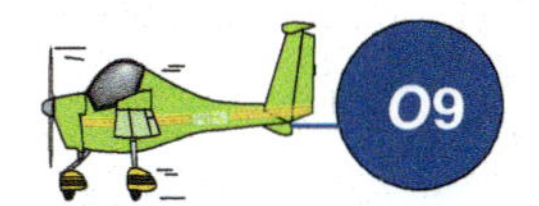

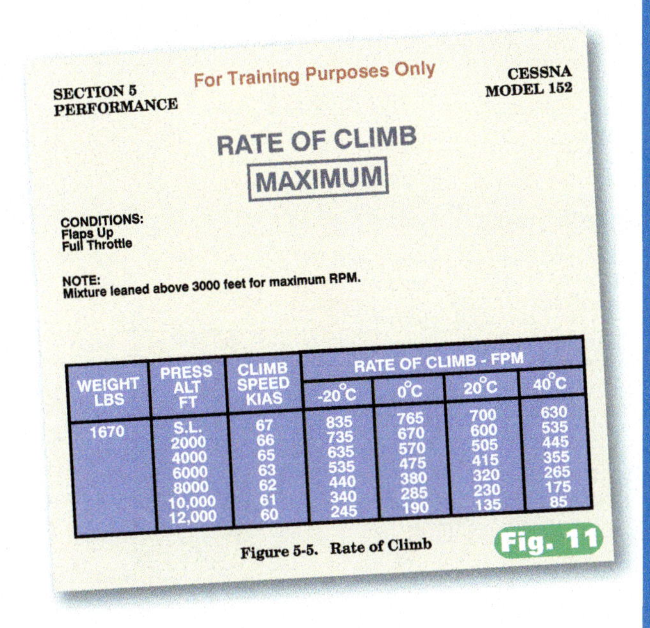

WEIGHT LBS	PRESS ALT FT	CLIMB SPEED KIAS	RATE OF CLIMB - FPM -20°C	0°C	20°C	40°C
1670	S.L.	67	835	765	700	630
	2000	66	735	670	600	535
	4000	65	635	570	505	445
	6000	63	535	475	415	355
	8000	62	440	380	320	265
	10,000	61	340	285	230	175
	12,000	60	245	190	135	85

Figure 5-5. Rate of Climb

Fig. 11

How Do They Figure Out All This Stuff?

Having found out about the stork and babies, you are now perhaps wondering where performance charts come from.

They come from actual flight data gathered by the airplane manufacturers, using experienced test pilots and new airplanes. This is something to keep in mind, because there are few mere mortals who are as adept as a full-time test pilot at coaxing full performance from an airplane, and there are few airplanes that perform as well as they did when they were new or nearly new.

Just so you don't leave here with any illusions, they do *not* test to get the information for every single point on any chart. A certain amount of what's there is by interpolation, the same way you've learned to figure out what the winds are between altitudes where there are published data.

Always keep in mind that performance charts reflect a new airplane, flown by a professional pilot, under optimal conditions. *Your mileage*, as they say on the car stickers, *may vary*. So may your landing roll, rate of climb, and all the other things in the charts. Add a safety margin, especially when you are just getting to know an airplane.

Figure 11 shows the rate of climb chart available for some airplanes. This chart is for a small two-place trainer. Notice that the rate of climb decreases with an increase in pressure altitude and that Vy is found at a slower indicated airspeed (KIAS) at higher altitudes. (KIAS stands for *knots of indicated airspeed*.) Under the rate of climb column are several temperature columns with variable climb rates. Considering how airplane performance varies with air density, it shouldn't come as a synaptic shock that the rate of climb varies with temperature.

Many POHs don't show the slight increase in the indicated airspeed for Vx with an increase in altitude because the increase is usually small. These handbooks do often show the change in Vx with a change in airplane weight. Figure 12A is a short field takeoff distance chart. Section 1 (expanded) shows the variable Vx speeds under the 50 FT column. Notice that these speeds decrease with a decrease in airplane weight (Vy also decreases with a weight decrease).

Remember, at higher altitudes your climb angle at Vx is going to be much less than it would at sea level despite the fact that you're at Vx. So give yourself plenty of extra margin if attempting to climb over an obstacle off the departure end of a high altitude airport.

Also remember that the airplane is going to climb at less of a rate or angle with the gear down. That's why, on retractable gear airplanes, we retract the gear as soon as it's safe after departure (usually when there is no runway left on which to land). Flaps are sometimes used for takeoff when suggested by the POH. The important thing to keep in mind about flaps is that they usually shorten the ground run but reduce the angle or rate of climb (not always, but sometimes. Check your POH to determine if they do). They should be retracted after liftoff when the airplane has accelerated to the recommended climb speed.

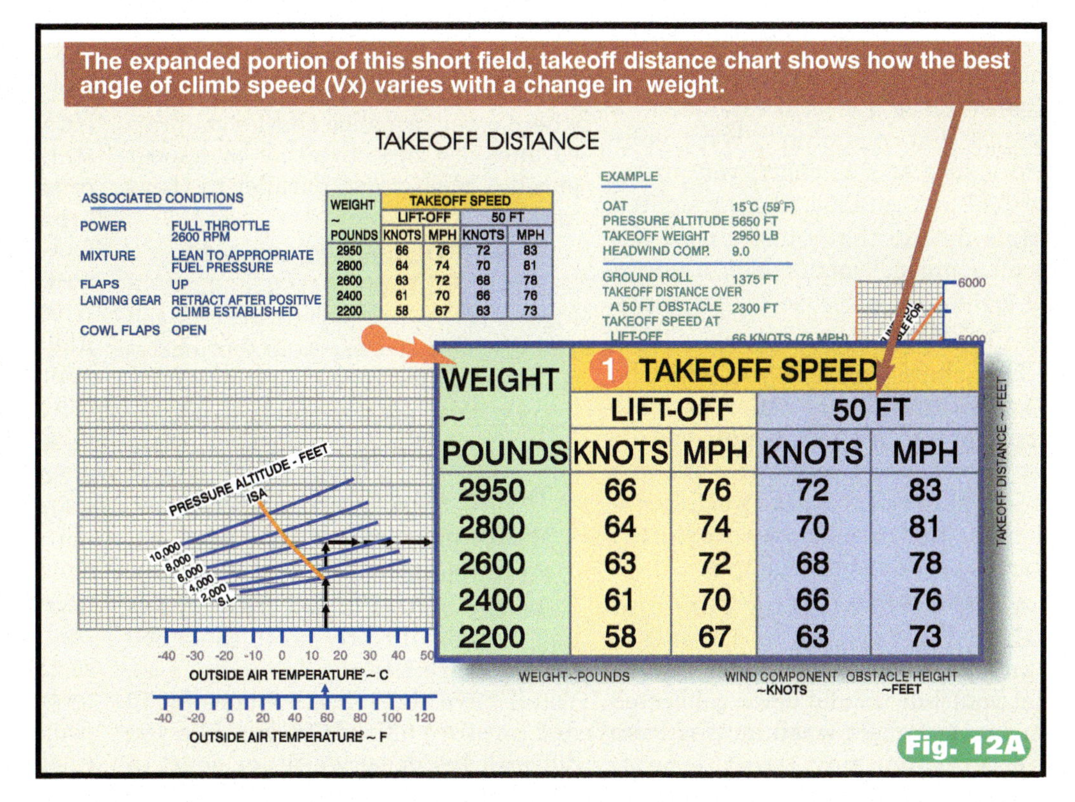

WEIGHT ~ POUNDS	TAKEOFF SPEED LIFT-OFF KNOTS	LIFT-OFF MPH	50 FT KNOTS	50 FT MPH
2950	66	76	72	83
2800	64	74	70	81
2600	63	72	68	78
2400	61	70	66	76
2200	58	67	63	73

Fig. 12A

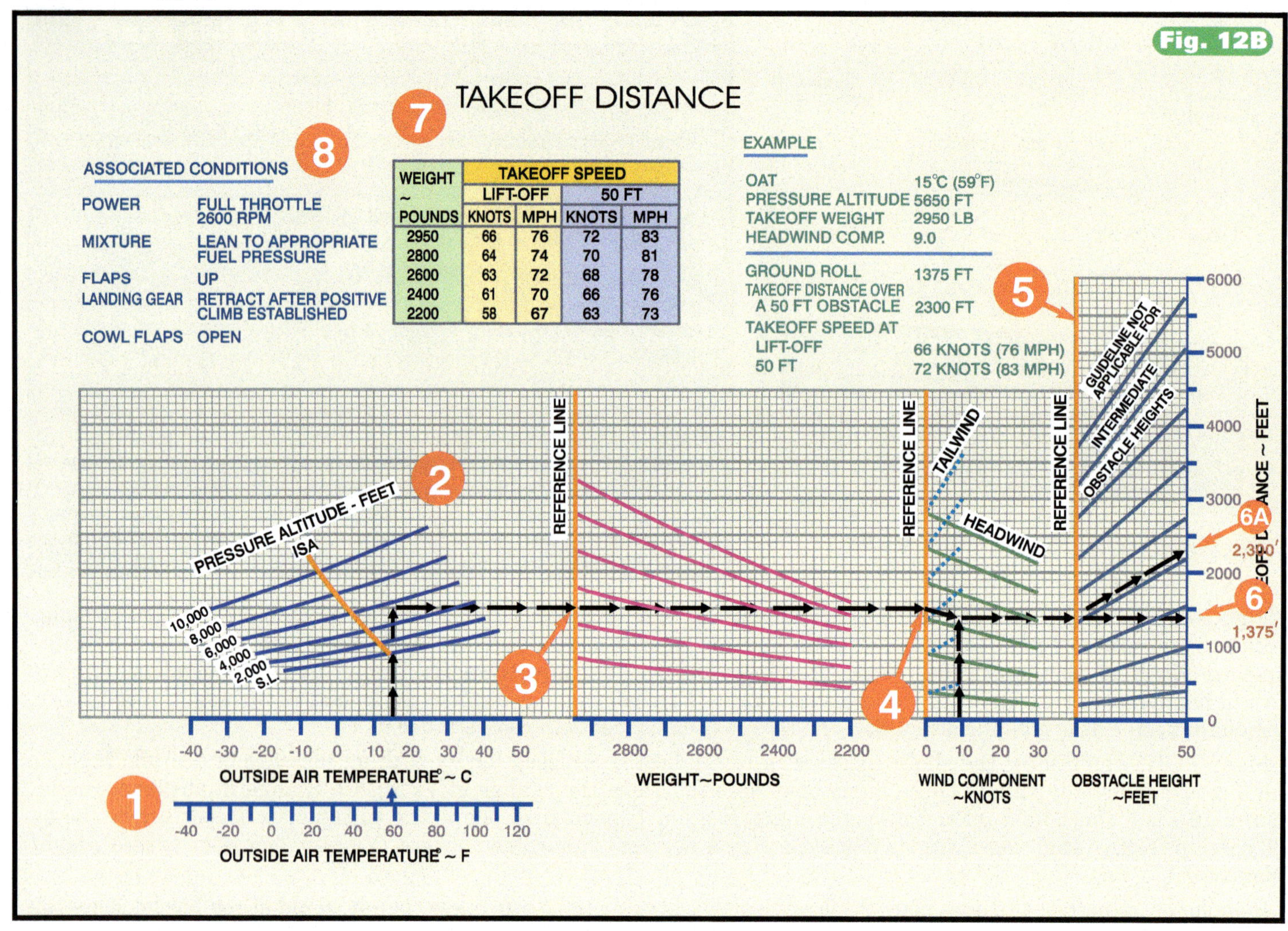

Takeoff Distance Chart

All airplanes have some takeoff and landing performance charts. Figure 12B is a typical example of a takeoff distance chart. With your first glance at this chart, you probably feel as confused as a farsighted Venus flytrap that's just ripped the fly off someone's pants. Not to worry! I'll explain how to use it (the chart, not the flytrap).

This chart provides you with the takeoff ground roll under variable airplane and airport conditions. It also provides the best angle of climb speeds based on various weight conditions. Learning how to use this chart is best done by example.

A Hint When Using This and Other Performance Charts – Many performance charts require that you slide up and down calibrated lines on the chart when moving from one reference point to the next. Movement along these lines should be proportional, not parallel. Figure 13 provides you with a good idea about how to do this. In those cases where a performance chart's calibrated lines are close together or appear parallel, then move parallel to these lines.

Takeoff Distance Example No. 1 – Using the takeoff distance chart in Figure 12B, what is your ground roll and distance to clear a 50 foot obstacle based on the following conditions:

OAT: 59 degrees F (15 degrees C)

Pressure altitude: 5,650 feet

Takeoff weight: 2,950 pounds

Headwind component: 9 knots

First, find 59 degrees F (15 degrees C) on the bottom of the chart in section 1. Move directly up to the 5,650 foot pressure altitude line (section 2). You'll have to estimate where 5,650 feet pressure altitude is, just like you did with the density altitude chart in Figure 3. Use the following method. The 5,000 foot pressure altitude line is halfway between 4,000 and 6,000 feet. Draw a hair-thin proportional line between these altitudes. It stands to reason that the 5,650 foot pressure altitude line is a little above a point halfway between the 5,000 foot line and the 6,000 foot line. Now move horizontally to the right, directly over to the dark, vertical reference line in section 3. As you move horizontally on the chart simply follow the nearest grid line to avoid making mistakes.

In section 3, we'll correct for weight. Since our weight is 2,950 pounds, and this is what the reference line rests on, no correction is necessary. Simply move right, horizontally, to the next reference line in section 4. If we did have a weight different from 2,950 pounds, we'd move proportionally to the diagonal lines until reaching our takeoff weight

MOVING ALONG THE DIAGONAL LINES OF A CHART

When moving along the sloping line of a performance chart, make sure you move proportionally (up or down) the line. In other words, don't parallel the nearest line as you move. Try to remain the same (proportional) distance between lines.

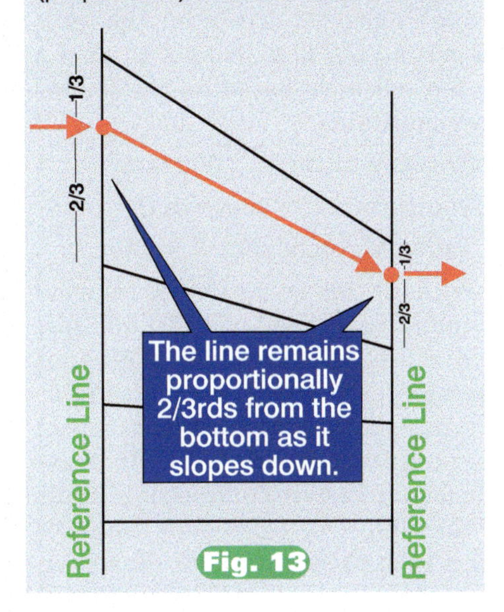

shown on the bottom scale in section 3. Then we'd move right, horizontally, to the reference line in section 4.

Now it's time to correct for a headwind or tailwind component. We have a 9 knot headwind component, so we'll move down, proportionally, to the nearest diagonal line until reaching a 9 knot wind component value, shown on the bottom scale of section 4. From this point we'll move horizontally to the right, toward the next reference line. If we had a tailwind value we'd move up and proportionally to the nearest sloping dashed line until reaching the appropriate wind component value. Then we'd move horizontally to the right toward the reference line.

At the reference line in section 5 we can determine our takeoff ground roll by moving horizontally toward the right. The numerical value of approximately 1,375 feet, listed at section 6, is our takeoff ground roll. This is only our ground roll, not the distance required to clear an obstacle at the end of the runway.

If an obstacle exists at the end of the runway, we can determine how much horizontal distance is required to clear that obstacle. Let's assume we have a 50 foot obstacle at the end of the runway. Move up and proportional to the diagonal line nearest section 5 until reaching the 50 foot height mark on the bottom scale (obstacle heights are calibrated by the scale at the bottom of section 5). When reaching the obstacle height shown horizontally along the bottom of the chart (50 feet in our case), look horizontally to the right to find that 2,300 feet of horizontal distance is required to clear that obstacle (section 6A). Keep in mind that this is just to clear the obstacle. Your tires should just scrape the top of that obstacle, possibly thumping some bird on the head (maybe that's how bald eagles got bald?).

There are several other interesting things you should know about this chart. First, in section 7, there is a list of takeoff speeds for different weights. At 2,950 pounds we want to lift off at 66 knots. If there is an obstacle at the end of the runway then we want to climb at a speed of 72 knots for that weight. Variable weights require different liftoff and obstacle climb speeds.

Second, section 8 lists all the associated conditions this chart is based on. Machado's Inverse Law of Chart Conditions says: The notes on a performance chart will be of value to you only when you forget to read them. Notes at the bottom of performance charts are the fine print of aviation. Always make it a point to read all the conditions listed in this section of a chart. There are many little variables affecting airplane performance listed in this section. Notice that the engine must be leaned to the appropriate fuel flow during takeoff. This assures maximum power is developed. Also, the gear is assumed to be retracted immediately after a positive rate of climb is established. This is done, obviously, if there is an obstacle to clear. Normally, without an obstacle, you wait until there is no more runway on which to land before raising the gear. (Of course if you are attempting to retract your landing gear on an airplane that isn't of the retractable gear type, then I want you to reread those directions on the back of your cold medicine.)

Takeoff Distance Problem No. 2 – Refer to Figure 12B and determine the ground roll and the total distance required for takeoff to clear a 50 foot obstacle based on the following conditions:

OAT: standard conditions

Pressure altitude: 4,000 feet

Takeoff weight: 2,800 pounds

Headwind Component: calm

Figure 14 shows how this problem is solved. ISA stands for *International Standard Atmosphere* and means the same thing as the term *standard conditions* used by U.S. engineers. Just find where the ISA line (standard temperature line) intersects the 4,000 foot pressure altitude line and move right horizontally to the next reference point. Approximately 1,050 feet are required for the takeoff ground roll and 1,750 feet of horizontal distance is required to clear a 50 foot obstacle. Be careful when you are moving horizontally across the chart. Make sure you move parallel to one of the horizontal grid-lines, thus minimizing the chance of error in chart reading.

TAKEOFF DISTANCE COMPUTATION

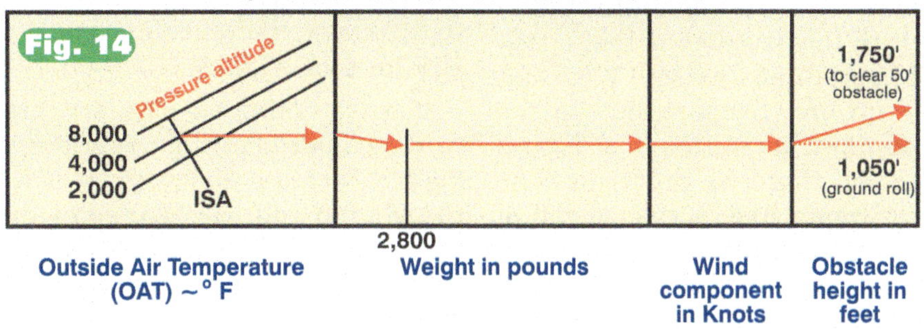

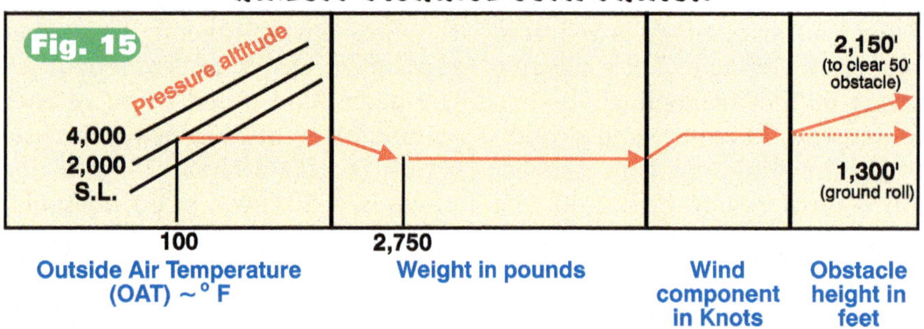

Frankly, there is a time when you might use the standard temperature or ISA line when computing airplane performance. You may want to estimate how the airplane will perform at a given altitude without knowing the actual outside temperature (such as when making rough estimates as to the amount of weight—fuel, payload, etc.—that you can depart with). Simply find where the ISA line intersects the elevation of the departure airport. Since you don't know the temperature and pressure altitude, this gives you a rough way to anticipate airplane performance. Remember, this is only used as an approximation (I still have a feeling that some of those mischievous 8th century monk-scribes got loose from the monastery, became performance chart engineers and inserted these ISA or standard temperature lines in airplane performance charts).

Takeoff Distance Problem No. 3 – Refer to Figure 12B and determine the ground roll and the total distance required for takeoff to clear a 50 foot obstacle based on the following conditions:

OAT: 100°F

Pressure altitude: 2,000 feet

Takeoff weight: 2,750 pounds

Tailwind Component: 5 knots

Figure 15 shows how this problem is solved. The only significant difference with this problem is that a tailwind component exists. We must move upward, proportional to the dashed lines, in section 4 in Figure 12B. From there we proceed to the next reference line. A ground roll of approximately 1,300 feet is required and 2,150 feet of horizontal distance will be used to clear a 50 foot obstacle.

At this point you're probably wondering why the Federal Aviation Administration puts up 50 foot obstacles at all these airports. All these questions make it seem like obstacles are mounted on mobile dollies, towed to different airports (like the old MX missile program) and placed on the departure end of runways to test the skills of a pilot. Well, this isn't true, but it is interesting to consider that most of these obstacles are represented as trees. If that were so, it would seem logical that those obstacles would get smaller whenever pilots, ignorant about takeoff performance charts, depart that runway. In other words, they'd be 50 foot obstacles at first, then, the following week they'd be 46 foot obstacles, then 38 foot obstacles and so on. Eventually, the FAA would have to tow in a new obstacle. Fortunately pilots do a good job in avoiding obstacles.

A Different Takeoff Distance Chart – Figure 16 shows a takeoff distance chart for a small, two-place trainer. As with all performance charts, read the notes before doing any computations. Short field computations are based on 10 degrees of flaps, full throttle then brake release, specific runway conditions, and zero wind. Note #3 states that distances should be decreased 10% for each 9 knots of headwind. For tailwinds up to 10 knots, increase distances by 10% for each 2 knots.

If we're taking off on a dry, grass runway, instead of a hard surface, we need to increase distances by 15% of the ground roll. Grass creates drag and prevents acceleration of the airplane. (If there are groundhogs hiding in the grass, this might also inhibit acceleration. You'll never see a chart that says to add 5% for each suspected groundhog). You'll notice there is no chart variation for different weights. That's because a small two-place trainer doesn't have much variation in its payload compared to a larger, multiseat airplane.

Takeoff Distance Problem No. 4 – Using Figure 16, determine the takeoff ground roll and distance to clear a 50 foot obstacle based on the following conditions:

Pressure altitude: 3,000 feet

Temperature: 20 degrees C

Tailwind component: 4 knots

Without correcting for the tailwind we obtain a ground roll of 1,000 feet and a distance to clear a 50 foot obstacle of 1,870 feet according to Figure 16. Note #3 on the top of Figure 16 states we need to increase our distances by 10% for each 2 knots of tailwind. Our calculated distances need to increase by 20%. Based on the computations in Figure 17 our expected ground roll becomes 1,200 feet and the horizontal distance to clear a 50 foot obstacle becomes 2,244 feet.

Takeoff Distance Problem No. 5 – Using Figure 16, determine the takeoff ground roll and distance to clear a 50 foot obstacle based on the following conditions:

Pressure altitude: 3,500 feet

Temperature: 10 degrees C

Headwind component: 18 knots

Notice that the pressure altitude is halfway between the 3,000 and 4,000 foot values. There are several ways to go about solving this problem and a little interpolation is necessary. Here's one way, as shown in Figure 18.

Determine the ground roll and distance to clear a 50 foot obstacle at 3,500 feet by adding the 3,000 and 4,000 foot values in the 10 degree C column together then dividing by 2. You should get 973 feet (rounded off) for the ground roll and 1,825 feet for the distance over a 50 foot obstacle.

We could stop here if it were not for the 18 knot headwind. Note #3 in

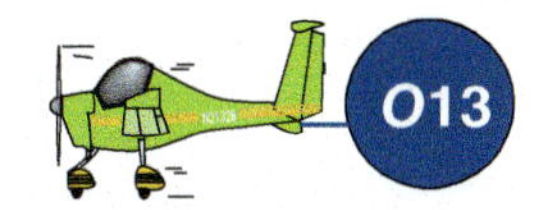

TAKEOFF DISTANCE
SHORT FIELD

Fig. 16

For Training Purposes Only!

CONDITIONS
Flaps 10 degrees
Full Throttle Prior to Brake Release
Paved, Level Dry Runway
Zero Wind

NOTES:
1. Short field technique as specified in Section 4.
2. Prior to takeoff from fields above 3000 feet elevation, the mixture should be leaned to give maximum RPM in a full throttle, static runup.
3. Decrease distances 10% for each 9 knots of headwind. For operations with tailwinds up to 10 knots, increase distances by 10% for each 2 knots.
4. For operations on a dry, grass runway, increase distances by 15% of the "ground roll" figure.

WEIGHT LBS	TAKEOFF SPEED KIAS		PRESS ALT FT	0°C		10°C		20°C		30°C		40°C	
	LIFT OFF	AT 50 FT		GRND ROLL	TOTAL TO CLEAR 50 FT OBS	GRND ROLL	TOTAL TO CLEAR 50 FT OBS	GRND ROLL	TOTAL TO CLEAR 50 FT OBS	GRND ROLL	TOTAL TO CLEAR 50 FT OBS	GRND ROLL	TOTAL TO CLEAR 50 FT OBS
1,670	50	54	S.L.	640	1190	695	1290	755	1390	810	1495	875	1605
			1000	705	1310	765	1420	825	1530	890	1645	960	1770
			2000	775	1445	840	1565	910	1690	980	1820	1055	1960
			3000	855	1600	925	1730	1000	1870	1080	2020	1165	2185
			4000	940	1775	1020	1920	1100	2080	1190	2250	1285	2440
			5000	1040	1970	1125	2140	1215	2320	1315	2525	1420	2750
			6000	1145	2200	1245	2395	1345	2610	1455	2855	1570	3125
			7000	1270	2470	1375	2705	1490	2960	1615	3255	1745	3590
			8000	1405	2800	1525	3080	1655	3395	1795	3765	1940	4195

Takeoff Distance Chart For Training Purposes Only!

Takeoff Distance Problem #4 Answer:
20% of 1,000′ = (.20)x(1,000) = 200′
1,000′+200′ = 1,200′ Ground Roll
20% of 1,870′ = (.2)x(1,870′) = 374′
1,870′+374′ = 2,244′ to clear 50′ obstacle.

WEIGHT LBS	TAKEOFF SPEED KIAS		PRESS ALT FT	0°C		10°C		20°C		30°C		40°C	
	LIFT OFF	AT 50 FT		GRND ROLL	TOTAL TO CLEAR 50 FT OBS	GRND ROLL	TOTAL TO CLEAR 50 FT OBS	GRND ROLL	TOTAL TO CLEAR 50 FT OBS	GRND ROLL	TOTAL TO CLEAR 50 FT OBS	GRND ROLL	TOTAL TO CLEAR 50 FT OBS
1,670	50	54	S.L.	640	1190	695	1290	755	1390	810	1495	875	1605
			1000	705	1310	765	1420	825	1530	890	1645	960	1770
			2000	775	1445	840	1565	910	1690	980	1820	1055	1960
			3000	855	1600	925	1730	1000	1870	1080	2020	1165	2185
			4000	940	1775	1020	1920	1100	2080	1190	2250	1285	2440
			5000	1040	1970	1125	2140	1215	2320	1315	2525	1420	2750
			6000	1145	2200	1245	2395	1345	2610	1455	2855	1570	3125
			7000	1270	2470	1375	2705	1490	2960	1615	3255	1745	3590
			8000	1405	2800	1525	3080	1655	3395	1795	3765	1940	4195

Fig. 17

Takeoff Distance Chart For Training Purposes Only!

Takeoff Distance Problem #5 Answer:
Ground Roll at 3,500′ (925′+1,020′)/2 = 973′
To clear a 50′ obstacle:
973-(20% of 973′) = (973′)-(195′) = 778′ Ground Roll
1,825-(20% of 1,825′) = (1,825′)-(365′) = 1,460′ to clear a 50′ obstacle.

WEIGHT LBS	TAKEOFF SPEED KIAS		PRESS ALT FT	0°C		10°C		20°C		30°C		40°C	
	LIFT OFF	AT 50 FT		GRND ROLL	TOTAL TO CLEAR 50 FT OBS	GRND ROLL	TOTAL TO CLEAR 50 FT OBS	GRND ROLL	TOTAL TO CLEAR 50 FT OBS	GRND ROLL	TOTAL TO CLEAR 50 FT OBS	GRND ROLL	TOTAL TO CLEAR 50 FT OBS
1,670	50	54	S.L.	640	1190	695	1290	755	1390	810	1495	875	1605
			1000	705	1310	765	1420	825	1530	890	1645	960	1770
			2000	775	1445	840	1565	910	1690	980	1820	1055	1960
			3000	855	1600	925	1730	1000	1870	1080	2020	1165	2185
			4000	940	1775	1020	1920	1100	2080	1190	2250	1285	2440
			5000	1040	1970	1125	2140	1215	2320	1315	2525	1420	2750
			6000	1145	2200	1245	2395	1345	2610	1455	2855	1570	3125
			7000	1270	2470	1375	2705	1490	2960	1615	3255	1745	3590
			8000	1405	2800	1525	3080	1655	3395	1795	3765	1940	4195

Fig. 18

Figure 16 says decrease distances 10% for each 9 knots of headwind. This means we must decrease both values by 20%. According to Figure 18 this gives us a 778 foot ground roll and 1,460 feet to clear a 50 foot obstacle.

Be careful when applying corrections for headwinds or tailwinds. You must remember to subtract takeoff distance values for a headwind and add these values for a tailwind. Headwinds decrease takeoff distances and tailwinds increase them.

Sometimes it will be necessary to interpolate for both pressure altitude and temperature when using these charts. If you find yourself close to any whole number value (for temperature or pressure) and feel it's difficult to interpolate, then use the larger, whole number value. This gives you a slightly longer takeoff and obstacle clearance distance but at least it errs on the conservative side.

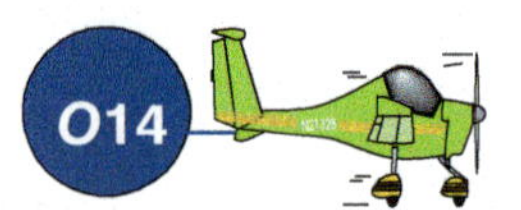

Landing Distance Performance Charts

Remember as a kid watching movies in school (on days when the teacher didn't feel like teaching)? Sometimes the film would jam, and after straightening it out they'd run it backwards a bit so you didn't miss any morsels of knowledge.

We're about to do the same thing. A landing chart is a takeoff chart in reverse. Instead of launching over a 50 foot obstacle, you're assumed to be landing over one. Once again there's the distance over the obstacle to the point of touchdown, and there's a ground roll to account for.

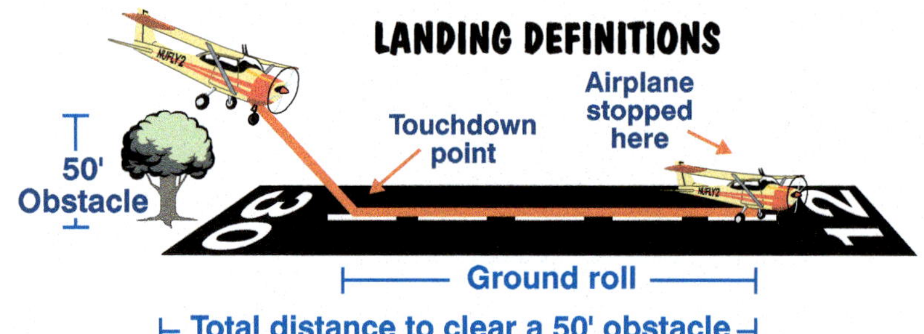

During landing, the ground roll is the distance required to stop the airplane once the wheels have made contact with the runway. The distance to land over a 50' obstacle is the total distance to cross over that obstacle, touchdown and come to a stop. Fig. 20

Figure 19 shows a typical landing distance chart. Notice its similarity to the takeoff chart used in Figure 12B. This chart is used in exactly the same way as Figure 12B. Remember, we're just running the movie backwards.

Keep in mind these distances for landing over a 50 foot obstacle assume that you barely clear the obstacle, as shown in Figure 20. You may assume you will always clear an obstacle by more than just inches, but the chart doesn't assume that. To be practical and safe about this, add a few more feet onto the values shown in the chart. In other words, you shouldn't be landing with branches and twigs protruding from the wheelpants. Let's try the following problems.

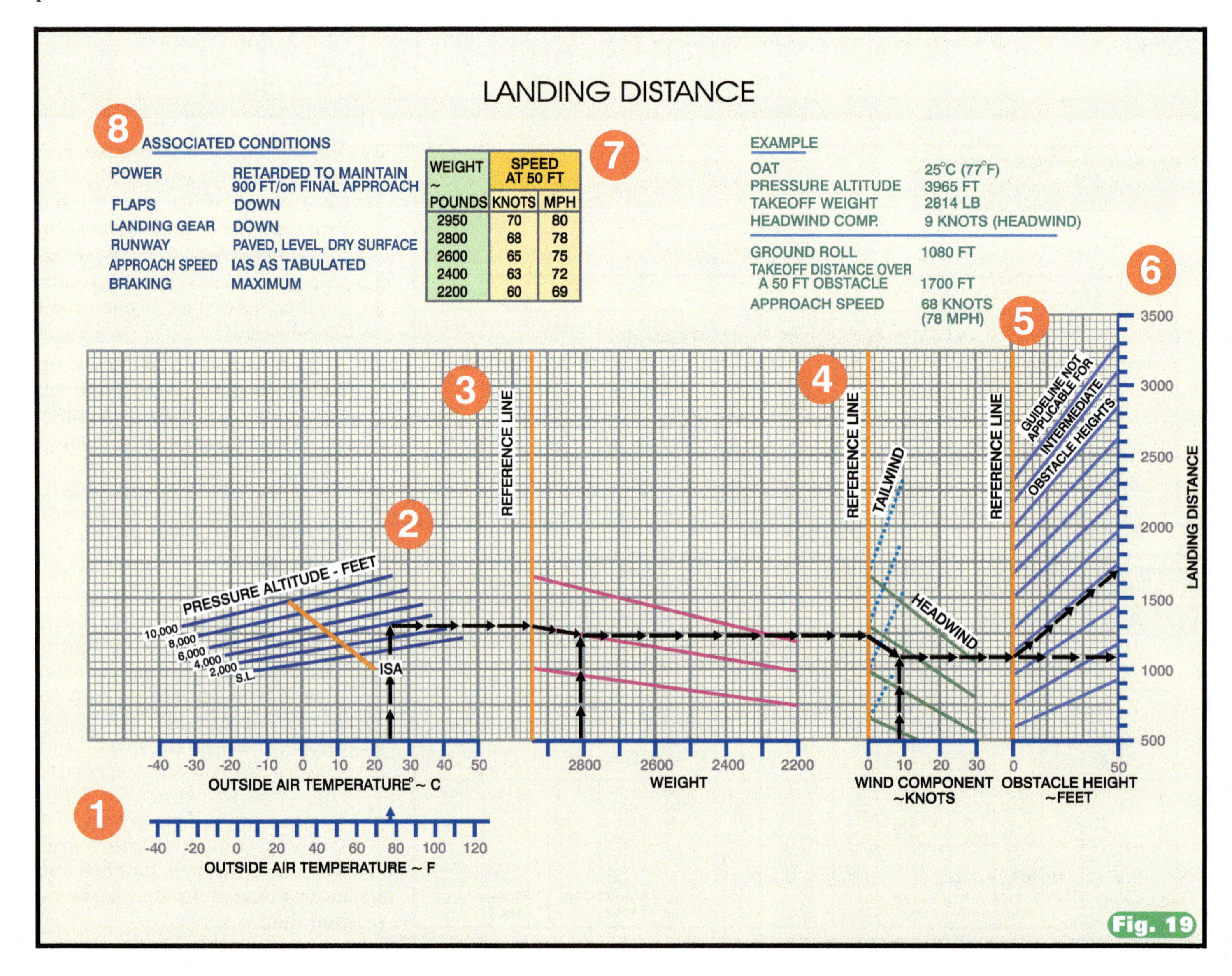

Fig. 19

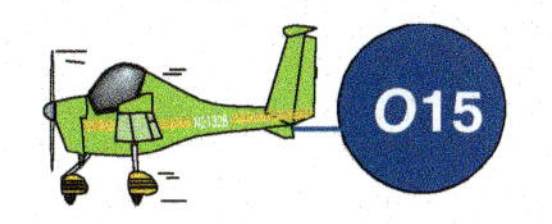

A LEAN MEAN FLYING MACHINE

(Written as an ASRS report by a University flight instructor) *One item that is seldom mentioned in articles on fuel exhaustion and mismanagement deals with student pilots or low-time pilots on cross-country trips. In local area training, the instructors keep the mixture rich because of the varied power settings used and seldom mention or practice proper leaning procedures. So when the solo or low-time pilot is on a trip, under a relatively high workload, they fail to remember to lean the mixture.* (The fuel flow data used in flight planning always assumes a proper leaning of the mixture. Without leaning properly, the actual fuel consumption will be higher than expected and the result is fuel starvation.) *Also, since local area flights are brief, the instructor and the student seldom (and sometimes never) switch fuel tanks. When the training is in an aircraft having a fuel selector with the option of "Both," there is even less incentive for the student pilot to develop the habit of switching fuel tanks.*

ASRS Report

Landing Distance Problem No. 1 – Using the landing distance chart in Figure 19, and based on the following conditions, determine the total distance required to land.

OAT: 32 degrees F

Pressure altitude: 8,000 feet

Weight: 2,600 pounds

Headwind component: 20 knots

Obstacle: 50 feet

Before using any performance chart, always read the conditions listed on that chart. Section 8 in Figure 19 lists the conditions under which the landing is conducted. Section 7 lists the approach speeds you should be using to obtain performance chart values for your landing. I also like how it lists *gear down* as one of the conditions. (Remember, if you forget to put the landing gear down, your landing distance will be cut by approximately 99%, but your maintenance bill will go up considerably!)

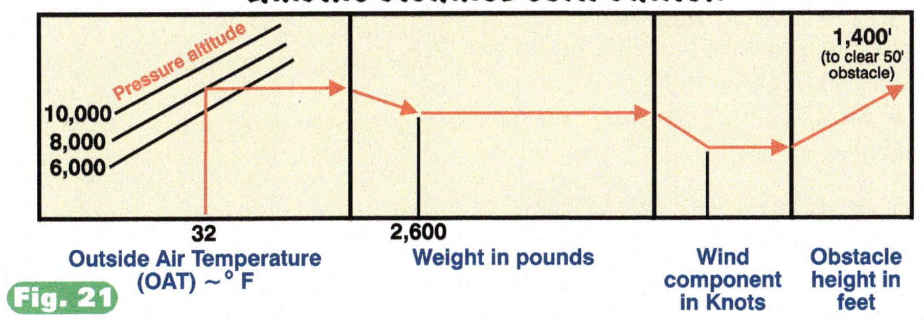

Fig. 21

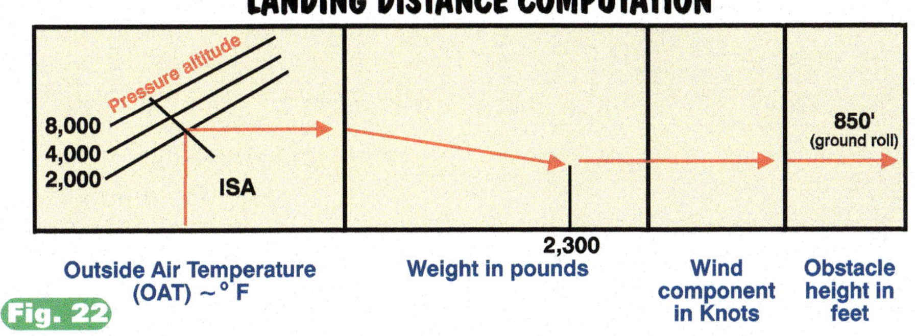

Fig. 22

Figure 21 shows how I computed the answer. Notice the headwind components require that you slide down diagonal lines shown in section 4 of the chart. Sliding downward decreases your final distance value while sliding upward increases any landing value. You need 1,400 feet of horizontal distance to clear a 50 foot obstacle situated on or near the end of the runway. From the instant you cross the obstacle at 50 feet until the time you come to a stop on the runway, you'll need 1,400 feet of distance. Of course this assumes, according to section 7, that at 2,600 pounds of weight, you cross the obstacle at an indicated airspeed of 65 knots. Any faster and the landing distance will increase.

Landing Distance Problem No. 2 – Using the landing distance chart in Figure 19, determine the total distance required to land based on the following conditions:

OAT: standard

Pressure altitude: 2,000 feet

Weight: 2,300 pounds

Headwind component: calm

Obstacle: no obstacle

According to Figure 22, you'll need an 850 foot ground roll under these conditions. This is the distance required to stop from the time the airplane touches down.

LANDING DISTANCE — FLAPS LOWERED TO 40 DEGREES - POWER OFF, HARD SURFACE RUNWAY - ZERO WIND									
		AT SEA LEVEL & 59°F		AT 2500 & 50°F		AT 5000 & 41°F		AT 7500 & 32°F	
GROSS WEIGHT LBS	APPROACH SPEED IAS, MPH	GROUND ROLL	TOTAL TO CLEAR 50 FT OBS	GROUND ROLL	TOTAL TO CLEAR 50 FT OBS	GROUND ROLL	TOTAL TO CLEAR 50 FT OBS	GROUND ROLL	TOTAL TO CLEAR 50 FT OBS
1,600	60	445	1075	470	1135	495	1195	520	1255

NOTES: 1. Decrease the distances shown by 10% for each 4 knots of headwind.
2. Increase the distance by 10% for each 60 degrees F temperature increase above standard.
3. For operations on a dry, grass runway, increase distances (both "ground roll" and "total to clear 50ft obstacle") by 20% of the "total to clear 50 ft obstacle" figure.

Fig. 23

A Different Landing Distance Chart

There are certain things you just never do. For instance, never put the word *yes* on a job application on the line that says *salary expected*. When being interviewed as a police officer candidate and asked why you want the job, you shouldn't say, "The lights man, I love all the lights. Whooo, whooo, whooo." There's one thing you never do when working with a landing distance chart. You should never assume that all landing distance charts are the same. These charts come in several shapes and flavors.

The chart shown in Figure 23 is another version of a landing chart. Once again, before using any chart, look at the notes and conditions listed on the chart.

Notice that note #1 says we must decrease distances by 10% for each 4 knots of headwind. We must increase distances by 10% for every 60 degrees F temperature increases above standard. Standard temperatures are those listed next to the altitudes in each chart column. Sixty degrees is a rather large temperature jump. If temperatures are only 30 degrees F above standard, increase distances by 5%.

Notice that in note 3, landing distances on dry, grass runways increase all calculations by 20%. If dry, grass runways increase our takeoff distance, shouldn't they also decrease our landing distance? Not really. Braking is much less efficient on grass (even if you are conking gophers on the head). Delicate braking is required to slow the airplane, making stopping distances much longer. Read the note carefully! Let's try a few of these problems.

Landing Distance Problem No. 3 – Using the landing distance chart in Figure 23, and based on the following conditions, determine the total distance required to land over a 50 foot obstacle.

OAT: standard

Pressure altitude: 7,500 feet

Headwind component: 8 knots

Runway: dry grass

Based on pressure altitude of 7,500 feet and a standard temperature of 32 degrees F, our landing distance over a 50 foot obstacle is 1,255 feet. With a headwind of 8 knots we need to decrease our distance by 20% according to the chart note #1. This gives us a ground roll of 1,255 - (20% of 1,255)=1,004 feet. Our last correction is for a dry, grass runway. Note 3 states we must increase all distances by 20% of the total to clear a 50 foot obstacle distance. This gives us a final value of 1,004 + (20% of 1,004)= 1,204.8 or 1,205 feet.

Landing Distance Problem No. 4 – Using the landing distance chart in Figure 23, and based on the following conditions, determine the total distance required to land over a 50 foot obstacle.

OAT: 101 degrees F

Pressure altitude: 5,000 feet

Headwind component: calm

According to Figure 23, an altitude of 5,000 feet and 41 degrees F produces a distance over a 50 foot obstacle of 1,195 feet. Our temperature is 60 degrees F more than standard for that altitude. According to note #2, we need to increase our landing distance by 10%. This gives us a 50 foot obstacle clearance value of (10% of 1,195)+1,195=1,315 feet.

Never forget Machado's Calculation Canon: The most important part of the body to use in calculating takeoff and landing distance is the brain, not the wishbone.

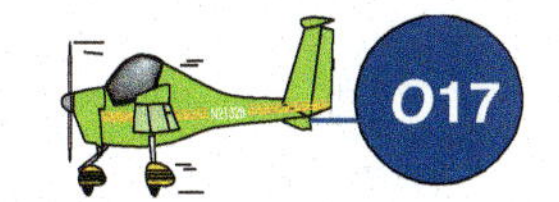

Time, Fuel and Distance To Climb Chart

Another flavor of chart useful in flight planning is the time, fuel and distance to climb chart shown in Figure 24. As always, read all the notes before using the chart. Notice that the columns provide you with a climb speed (the best rate of climb speed, Vy), an expected rate of climb, the time it takes to climb, fuel used in gallons and distance covered (assuming zero wind). The chart shows how Vy decreases with an increase in altitude.

Climb Problem No. 1 – Using Figure 24, estimate the amount of time and fuel consumed to climb from sea level to 5,000 feet pressure altitude under standard temperature conditions.

This is a relatively easy problem to solve. First, look at the fuel used and distance values for the 5,000 foot pressure altitude row. This gives you 8 minutes and 1.2 gallons of fuel used. Adding .8 gallon of fuel per note #1, we find that we consume 2.0 gallons of fuel while taking approximately 8 minutes to climb once airborne. That's easy, so let's make it a little more practical and challenging.

Climb Problem No. 2 – Using Figure 24, estimate the amount of time and fuel used to take off and climb from an airport with a pressure altitude of 2,000 feet to 6,000 feet pressure altitude, when the temperature at the airport is 21 degrees C.

CESSNA MODEL 152 — For Training Purposes Only! — SECTION 5 PERFORMANCE

TIME, FUEL AND DISTANCE TO CLIMB

MAXIMUM RATE OF CLIMB

CONDITIONS:
Flaps Up
Full Throttle
Standard Temperature

NOTES:
1. Add 0.8 of a gallon of fuel for engine start, taxi and takeoff allowance.
2. Mixture leaned above 3000 feet for maximum RPM.
3. Increase time, fuel and distance by 10% for each 10 C above standard temperature.
4. Distances shown are based on zero wind.

Fig. 24

WEIGHT LBS	PRESSURE ALTITUDE FT	TEMP °C	CLIMB SPEED KIAS	RATE OF CLIMB FPM	FROM SEA LEVEL		
					TIME MIN	FUEL USED GALLONS	DISTANCE NM
1,670	S.L.	15.	67	715	0	0	0
	1000	13	66	675	1	0.2	2
	2000	11	66	630	3	0.4	3
	3000	9	65	590	5	0.7	5
	4000	7	65	550	6	0.9	7
	5000	5	64	505	8	1.2	9
	6000	3	63	465	10	1.4	12
	7000	1	63	425	13	1.7	14
	8000	-1	62	380	15	2.0	17
	9000	-3	62	340	18	2.3	21
	10,000	-5	61	300	21	2.6	25
	11,000	-7	61	255	25	3.0	29
	12,000	-9	60	215	29	3.4	34

This problem requires us to subtract the difference in time and fuel consumed from 6,000 feet to 2,000 feet. This gives us a time to climb from 2,000 to 6,000 feet pressure altitude of approximately (10 minutes - 3 minutes = 7 minutes). We also derive a fuel consumption of approximately (1.4 gallons - .4 gallons = 1 gallon).

The last thing we do is make a correction for the nonstandard temperature. Since 21 degrees C at 2,000 feet is 10 degrees C above standard temperature for that altitude, per note #3 we should increase both these values by 10%. Our time to climb value becomes (7 minutes + .7 minutes = 7.7 minutes). Our fuel-used value becomes (1.0 gallon + .1 gallon = 1.1 gallons). We do, however, need to add that .8 gallon according to note #1 for engine start, taxi and takeoff. This gives us a total fuel consumption of 1.9 gallons.

This is a very handy little chart to use. You'll find it very useful for cross country flight planning purposes. Although we didn't compute the distances covered during the climb, this is easily done using the same method described in Chapter 14, page N32, under the section titled: A More Accurate Flight Plan.

To Trust or Not to Trust

The only way to accurately estimate your airplane's actual fuel consumption is to observe what it does over numerous flights. Take note of how much fuel your airplane actually consumes under different conditions and compare this to the chart's estimated fuel consumption. At least you'll know how accurate your charts are.

CRUISE POWER SETTINGS

For Training Purposes Only!

65% MAXIMUM CONTINUOUS POWER (OR FULL THROTTLE)
2800 POUNDS

	Section 1								Section 2								Section 3							
	ISA - 20 °C (-36 °F)								STANDARD DAY (ISA)								ISA + 20 °C (+36 °F)							
PRESS ALT.	IOAT		ENGINE SPEED	MAN. PRESS	FUEL FLOW		TAS		IOAT		ENGINE SPEED	MAN. PRESS	FUEL FLOW		TAS		IOAT		ENGINE SPEED	MAN. PRESS	FUEL FLOW		TAS	
FEET	°F	°C	RPM	IN HG	PSI	GPH	KTS	MPH	°F	°C	RPM	IN HG	PSI	GPH	KTS	MPH	°F	°C	RPM	IN HG	PSI	GPH	KTS	MPH
S.L.	27	-3	2450	20.9	6.6	11.5	147	169	63	17	2450	21.2	6.6	11.5	150	173	99	37	2450	21.8	6.6	11.5	153	176
2000	19	-7	2450	20.4	6.6	11.5	149	171	55	13	2450	21.0	6.6	11.5	153	176	91	33	2450	21.5	6.6	11.5	156	180
4000	12	-11	2450	20.1	6.6	11.5	152	175	48	9	2450	20.7	6.6	11.5	156	180	84	29	2450	21.3	6.6	11.5	159	183
6000	5	-15	2450	19.8	6.6	11.5	155	178	41	5	2450	20.4	6.6	11.5	158	182	79	26	2450	21.0	6.6	11.5	161	185
8000	-2	-19	2450	19.5	6.6	11.5	157	181	36	2	2450	20.2	6.6	11.5	161	185	72	22	2450	20.8	6.6	11.5	164	189
10,000	-8	-22	2450	19.2	6.6	11.5	160	184	28	-2	2450	19.9	6.6	11.5	163	188	64	18	2450	20.3	6.5	11.4	166	191
12,000	-15	-26	2450	18.8	6.4	11.3	162	186	21	-6	2450	18.8	6.1	10.9	163	188	57	14	2450	18.8	5.9	10.6	163	188
14,000	-22	-30	2450	17.4	5.8	10.5	159	183	14	-10	2450	17.4	5.6	10.1	160	184	50	10	2450	17.4	5.4	9.8	160	184
16,000	-29	-34	2450	16.1	5.3	9.7	156	180	7	-14	2450	16.1	5.1	9.4	156	180	43	6	2450	16.1	4.9	9.1	155	178

NOTES: 1. Full throttle manifold pressure settings are approximate.
2. Shaded area represents operation with full throttle.

Fig. 25

Cruise Performance Chart

So far we have charts for predicting takeoff distance, landing distance, and time and fuel to climb. Now let's look at a chart to help compute enroute fuel consumption and expected true airspeed. This chart is the *cruise power setting chart,* shown in Figure 25.

Once again, Machado's Fire and Brimstone Chart Principle No. 666 says, Always read the notes before using the chart lest you be visited by perdition's dark and evil forces. The note at the top of the chart assumes the engine operates at 65% maximum continuous power or full throttle. (Remember, at higher altitudes, even though you have full throttle applied, you might not be able to develop 65% power.) The 65% power figure is based on the RPM and manifold pressure settings provided in the chart. Obviously, this chart is for an airplane with a constant speed propeller since it has both manifold pressure for power and RPM column for prop speed.

Three temperature sections exist on the chart. The middle column is for standard temperature, or ISA. The left and right columns are sections for temperatures below and above standard conditions, respectively. Within each section is an individual temperature column (listed under IOAT—indicated outside air temperature) for variable temperature conditions enroute. When you are given a pressure altitude and temperature, simply find the pressure altitude on the far left column and proceed to the right until you are near a temperature similar to that for your cruise altitude. If it's not exact, that's OK. Just get as close as you can. Immediately to the right will be the RPM and manifold pressure settings required to develop 65% power with the associated fuel flow and true airspeed for those settings .

Cruise Performance Problem No. 1 – Using Figure 25, approximately what fuel consumption and true airspeed should you expect for a flight under the following conditions:

Pressure altitude: 8,000 feet

Temperature: +22 degrees C

Manifold pressure: 20.8 inches of Hg

Wind: calm

Find the 8,000 foot pressure altitude line and follow it horizontally across until reaching a temperature of or near +22 degrees C. This puts you in section #3 of the charts (or in the higher-than-standard temperature section). To produce 65% power an engine RPM of 2450 and a manifold pressure of 20.8 inch of Hg are necessary. Under these conditions you can expect a fuel flow of 11.5 gallons per hour and an estimated true airspeed of 164 knots.

Cruise Performance Problem No. 2 – Using Figure 25, determine the approximate manifold pressure setting with 2,450 RPM to achieve 65% maximum continuous power at 6,500 feet pressure altitude with a temperature of 36 degrees F higher than standard.

A temperature of 36 degrees F higher than standard would put you in section #3 of the chart (the temperature of ISA+20 degrees C is 36 degrees F above standard temperature). Following the 6,000 foot pressure altitude value to the third section we find a manifold pressure value of 21.0 inches. Since 6,500 feet is slightly higher than this, let's interpolate. The 8,000 foot pressure altitude line shows a manifold pressure of 20.8 inches. We can assume that at 7,000 feet the manifold pressure required is 20.9 inches. The value we want is halfway between 6,000 feet and 7,000 feet or halfway between 21.0 and 20.9 inches, so 20.95 inches is the manifold pressure required at 2450 RPM to maintain 65% power. Realistically, you'll use 21.0 inches of manifold pressure since your power gauges (and your eyes) aren't calibrated to read in hundredths. I suppose you could use a small magnifying glass but, under the wrong sunlight conditions, you might burn a little hole in the instrument (just kidding).

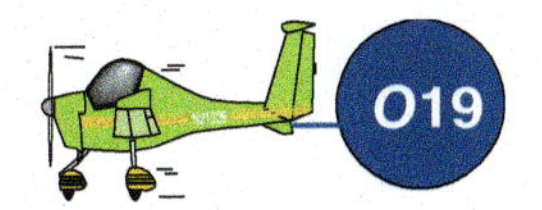

Cruise Performance Problem No. 3 – What fuel flow should a pilot expect at a pressure altitude of 11,000 feet on a standard day with 65% maximum continuous power using Figure 25?

Standard day (ISA) conditions are found in section #2 of the chart. Since there is no value for 11,000 feet, locate fuel flow values for 10,000 feet and 12,000 feet. The fuel flow for 11,000 feet will be halfway between these values.

Simple interpolation:

10,000 foot fuel flow value: 11.5 GPH

12,000 foot fuel flow value: 10.9 GPH

(11.5+10.9)/2 = 11.2 GPH for 11,000 feet

It's hard to believe that people can run out of fuel in airplanes. The fact is, they do. That's why Machado's Above the Ground Fuel Rule says: Pilots coming close to running out of fuel in an airplane can get a $200 advance from an undertaker any time they want.

Another Variety of Cruise Performance Charts

A different variety of cruise performance chart is shown in Figure 26. This chart is for an airplane with a fixed pitch propeller. Pressure altitudes are found on the left side of the chart with variable RPM settings for variable power conditions. Unlike our previous chart, this chart allows us to choose various percentage selections of BHP (brake horsepower) with which to operate. In other words, if the airplane has a 100 horsepower engine, this chart shows what percentage of those 100 horses are being used. Similar to the chart in Figure 25, this chart has three temperature columns. Let's try a few problems.

CRUISE POWER SETTINGS

65% MAXIMUM CONTINUOUS POWER (OR FULL THROTTLE)
2800 POUNDS

SECTION 5
PERFORMANCE

For Training Purposes Only!

CESSNA
MODEL 152

CRUISE PERFORMANCE

CONDITIONS:
1,670 Pounds
Recommended Lean Mixture (See Section 4, Cruise)

Fig. 26

NOTES:
Cruise speeds are shown for an airplane equipped with speed fairings which increase the speeds by approximately two knots

PRESSURE ALTITUDE FT	RPM	20 °C BELOW STANDARD TEMP			STANDARD TEMPERATURE			20 °C ABOVE STANDARD TEMP		
		% BHP	KTAS	GPH	% BHP	KTAS	GPH	% BHP	KTAS	GPH
2000	2400				75	101	6.1	70	101	5.7
	2300	71	97	5.7	66	96	5.4	63	95	5.1
	2200	62	92	5.1	59	91	4.8	56	90	4.6
	2100	55	87	4.5	53	86	4.3	51	85	4.2
	2000	49	81	4.1	47	80	3.9	46	79	3.8
4000	2450				75	103	6.1	70	102	5.7
	2400	76	102	6.1	71	101	5.7	67	100	5.4
	2300	67	96	5.4	63	96	5.1	60	95	4.9
	2200	60	91	4.8	56	90	4.6	54	89	4.4
	2100	53	86	4.4	51	85	4.2	49	84	4.0
	2000	48	81	3.9	46	80	3.8	45	79	3.7
6000	2500				75	105	6.1	71	104	5.7
	2400	72	101	5.8	67	100	5.4	64	99	5.2
	2300	64	96	5.1	60	95	4.9	57	94	4.7
	2200	57	90	4.6	45	89	4.4	52	88	4.3
	2100	51	85	4.2	49	84	4.0	48	83	3.9
	2000	46	80	3.8	45	79	3.7	44	77	3.6
8000	2550				75	107	6.1	71	106	5.7
	2500	76	105	6.2	71	104	5.8	67	013	5.4
	2400	68	100	5.5	64	99	5.2	61	98	4.9
	2300	61	95	5.0	58	94	4.7	55	93	4.5
	2200	55	90	4.5	52	89	4.3	51	87	4.2
	2100	49	84	4.1	48	83	3.9	46	82	3.8
10,000	2500	72	105	5.8	68	103	5.5	64	103	5.2
	2400	65	99	5.3	61	98	5.0	58	97	4,8
	2300	58	94	4.7	65	93	4.5	53	92	4.4
	2200	53	89	4.3	51	88	4.2	49	86	4.0
	2100	48	83	4.0	46	82	3.9	45	81	3.8
12,000	2450	65	101	5.3	62	100	5.0	59	99	4.8
	2400	62	99	5.0	59	97	4.8	56	96	4.6
	2300	56	93	4.6	54	92	4.4	52	91	4.3
	2200	51	88	4.2	49	87	4.1	48	85	4.0
	2100	47	82	3.9	45	81	3.8	44	79	3.7

Cruise Performance Problem No. 4 – Determine the expected fuel consumption and true airspeed for a flight at a pressure altitude of 4,000 feet at 2,300 RPM under standard conditions, using Figure 26.

Find the 4,000 foot pressure altitude column, then move to the 2,300 RPM value. Directly across is our expected true airspeed of 96 knots and fuel consumption of 5.1 gallons per hour at an expected power output of 63%. Are you wondering why we want to know how much power our engine is producing? In many airplanes, leaning of the mixture is recommended when the engine is producing less than 75% power. This chart lets you know when it's reasonable to lean the mixture for more efficient engine operations. It also provides information that might be required in computing values based on other performance charts.

Since this chart doesn't have detailed calibrations for various temperatures, what do you do if the temperature is only slightly different from the values listed in one of the three vertical temperature columns? The answer is to pick the temperature column closest to the actual air temperature.

Cruise Performance Problem No. 5 – Using Figure 26, determine the expected fuel consumption for a flight at a pressure altitude of 5,500 feet at 2,400 RPM under conditions 14 degrees C colder than standard for your flight altitude.

We'll use the first temperature column, since 14 degrees C colder than standard is closest to its -20 degrees C below standard value. Notice that we're using 5,500 feet, which isn't shown on the chart. A little interpolation is necessary here.

Fuel flow for 6,000 feet at 2,400 RPM: 5.8 GPH

Fuel flow for 4,000 feet at 2,400 RPM: 6.1 GPH

From this you can find the fuel flow for 5,000 feet:

(5.8+6.1)/2=5.95 GPH at 5,000 feet at 2,400 RPM

Now, find the fuel flow for 5,500 feet at 2,400 RPM

This is the difference between the 5,000 foot and 6,000 foot values

(5.95 + 5.8)/2=5.87 or approximately 5.9 GPH

Let's be real practical about this. Looking at the numbers, you can usually eyeball the correct value without much difficulty (even without interpolating). This is made much easier when chart values don't vary much between conditions. In other words, at 4,000 feet in this example we had a fuel flow of 6.1 GPH and at 6,000 feet we had 5.8 GPH. It's fairly easy to see that the value for

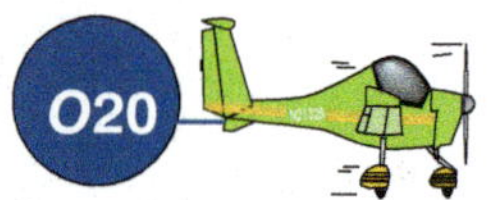

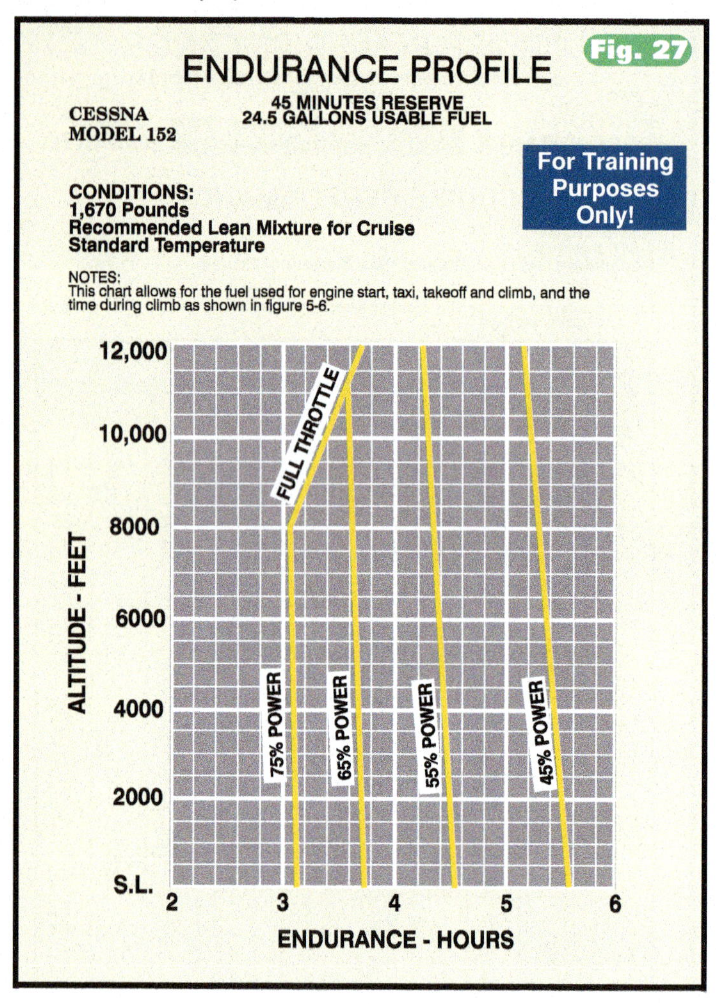

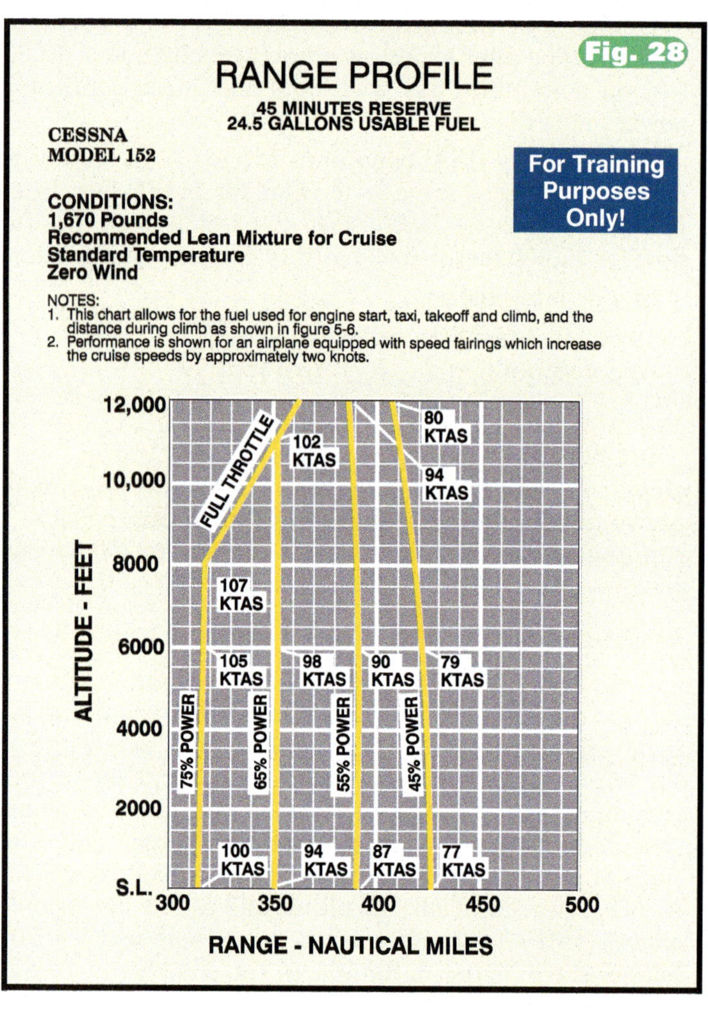

5,500 feet is closest to 5.8 GPH. In the real world this works fine. For FAA testing purposes you want to be as precise as possible. There is nothing wrong with taking liberties at estimating values as long as you know how to be precise when the need arises.

Endurance and Range Profile Charts

Figures 27 and 28 are two additional charts you might see. Figure 27 is a best-endurance chart and Figure 28 is a best-range chart. There are many times when knowing your endurance and range is of immense value. For instance, if I had to remain airborne until the weather cleared for landing, the endurance chart would be of immense value. I'd know how long I could afford to hang around while flying in circles before heading to another airport.

To use either chart, you need to know the percentage of power developed by the engine. Given that information, you can find your endurance and range for various altitudes. Just where will you find the engine's power output in percentages? From the typical cruise performance charts we've already seen in Figures 25 and 26.

If we were using 65% power, what would our endurance be at 8,000 feet? Simply find 8,000 feet in Figure 27 and move across to the 65% power line. Drop straight down and find an endurance of 3 hours and 36 minutes (5 divisions between hour marks=12 minutes per division). At 65% power, according to Figure 28, our range is approximately 354 nautical miles. Of course, assuming you've read all the conditions in both charts you'll know the range is based on no wind, and both charts yield numbers that include a 45 minute fuel reserve.

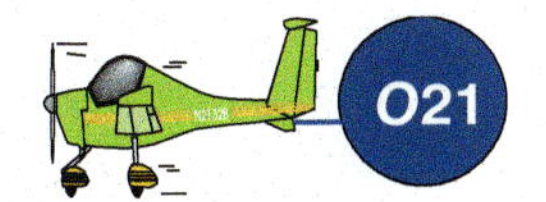

Crosswind Component Chart

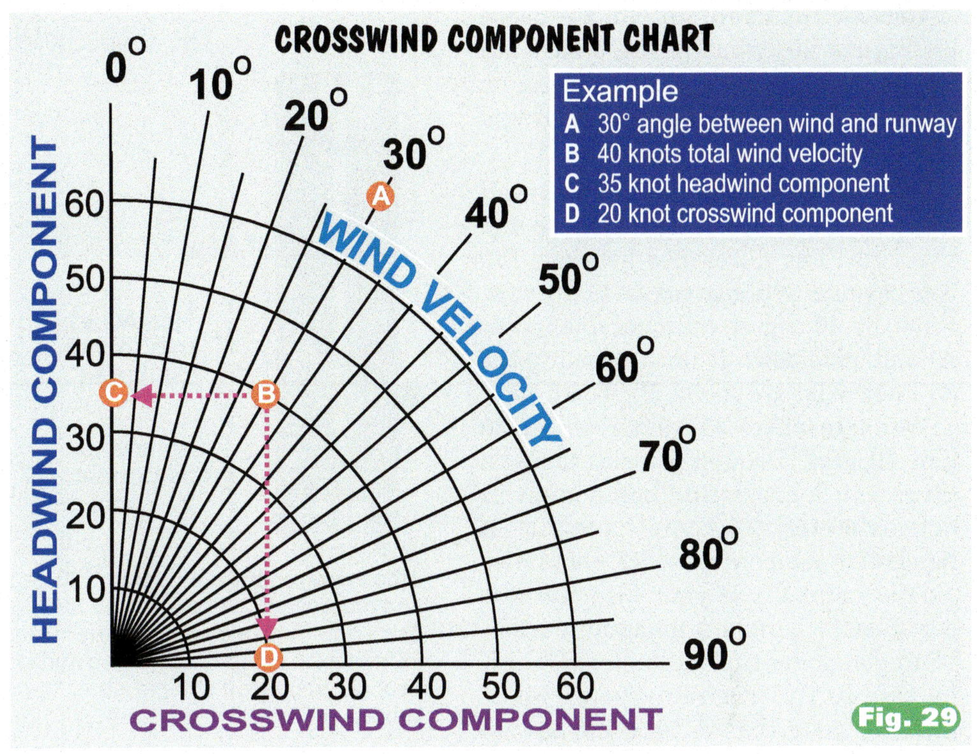

The only pilots who don't have to worry about crosswinds are aircraft carrier pilots. They have a lot more to worry about than crosswinds. Their runway is always moving. How would you like to take off, then return to find your airport has moved to another location? And I bet you never have to worry about rolling off the end of the runway and getting run over by the airport. Compared to such challenges, crosswinds pale. For the rest of us, however, crosswinds are a factor, so we'd better learn how to figure them out.

Several of our performance charts require us to determine the amount of headwind or tailwind component in order to determine our takeoff or landing distance. You will also find in most POHs a value listed for the *maximum crosswind component.* This isn't a maximum crosswind limit for the airplane. Instead, it's the crosswind component that the average pilot should be able to handle without needing exceptional skill.

The chart in Figure 29 allows us to determine the headwind and crosswind components.

Crosswind Problem No. 1 – Assume you're departing on Runway 30, as shown in Figure 30. The tower reports a wind from 330 degrees at 40 knots. What are the headwind and crosswind components associated with this wind?

Runway 30 is aligned in a direction of 300 degrees. A wind from 330 degrees makes a 30 degree angle with the runway. It's reasonable to say that some of this wind imparts a headwind component and some a crosswind component (do you remember Bud and Ed from Chapter 2, the bottom of page B3? It's the same principle). To find exactly how much there is of each, ask yourself what the angle is between the wind and the nose of the airplane.

Obviously the wind is 30 degrees off the right of the nose. The chart in Figure 30 shows degree calibrations in increments of 10, in a right direction. Assume the zero degree mark represents the nose of the airplane. Start the problem there. Find the 30 degree diagonal line (point A). This represents the angle the wind makes with the nose of the airplane. Slide down this 30 degree line until reaching the 40 knot wind velocity arc (point B). Now all you need to do is drop straight down to point D to determine the amount of crosswind blowing on the airplane. We have a right crosswind of 20 knots. To find the amount of headwind blowing on the airplane, simply move left horizontally to point C. This represents the amount of headwind blowing on the airplane. We have a headwind value of 35 knots. This headwind value is what we would use for any takeoff or landing performance computation.

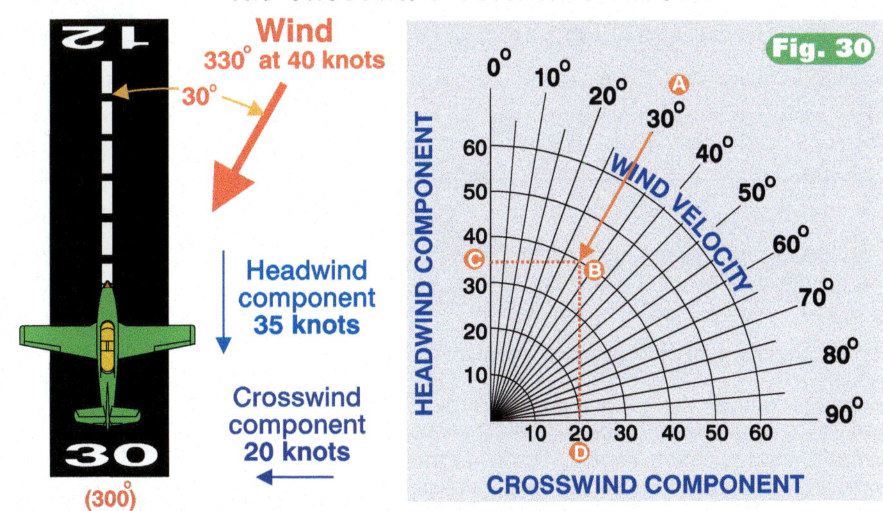

If the tower reports a wind from 330 degrees at 40 knots, you can find your headwind and crosswind components by finding the angle between the wind and the nose. That angle is 30 degrees. Find the 30 degree line (point A) and move downward to the 40 knot wind arc (point B). Move horizontally to point C to find the headwind component (35 knots). Drop straight down to point D to find the crosswind component (20 knots).

Crosswind Problem No. 2 – Based on Figure 29, what is the crosswind component you can expect if landing on Runway 18 with the tower reporting a wind of 220 degrees at 35 knots?

Use Figure 31. First ask yourself what the angle is between the wind and the nose. The difference between 180 degrees and 220 degrees is 40 degrees. Find the 40 degree diagonal line (point A) and slide down it until reaching the 35 knot wind arc (point B). You'll have to estimate where 35 is between the 30 and 40 arcs. Dropping straight down gives you a crosswind component of approximately 23 knots (point D). A headwind component of 27 knots also exists (point C). If your airplane was certified to handle a maximum crosswind component of 20 knots, would it be safe to fly? Probably not. This is another good reason to know how to use this chart.

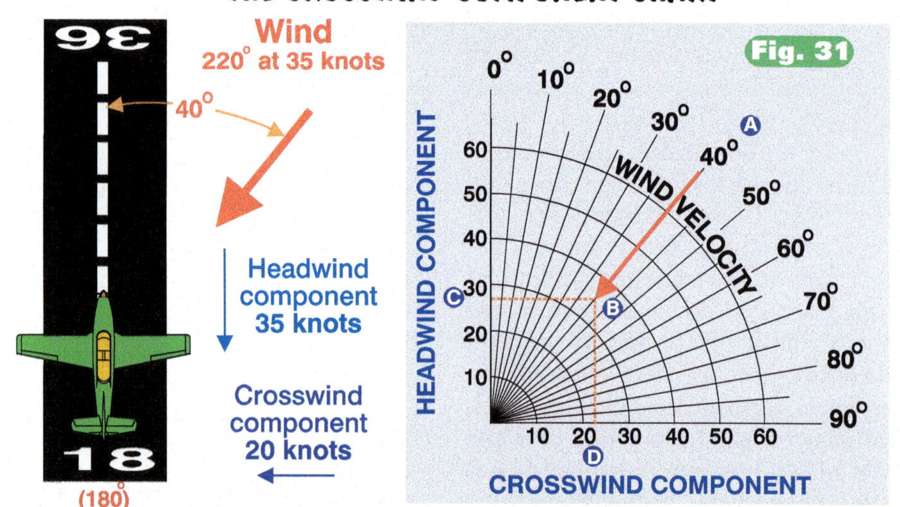

If the tower reports a wind from 220 degrees at 35 knots you can find your headwind and crosswind components by finding the angle between the wind and the nose. That angle is 40 degrees. Find the 40 degree line (point A) and move downward to the 35 knot wind arc (point B). Move horizontally to point C to find the headwind component (27 kts). Drop straight down to point D to find the crosswind component (23 kts.).

Crosswind Problem No. 3. – Using Figure 29, determine the maximum wind velocity for a 30 degree crosswind if the maximum crosswind component for the airplane is 12 knots.

The solution is provided in Figure 32. This problem requires us to work backwards. First, we know our airplane has a maximum crosswind component of 12 knots. Find this position along the bottom of the crosswind chart (point A). Move straight up until reaching the 30 degree diagonal line representing the wind's angle with the nose of the airplane

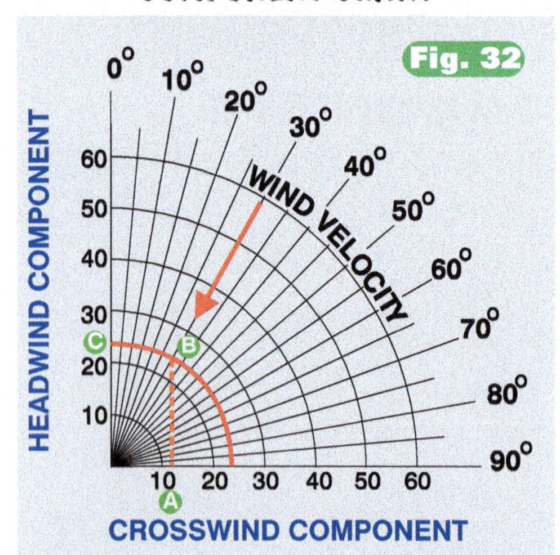

Suppose your airplane has a maximum demonstrated crosswind component of 12 knots. What is the maximum speed of a 30 degree wind that won't exceed this 12 knot limit? We can solve this problem by working backwards. Start with a 12 knot crosswind at point A and move upward till reaching the 30 degree angle line at point B. The 24 knot wind arc runs through this point as seen at the end of the arc (points C).

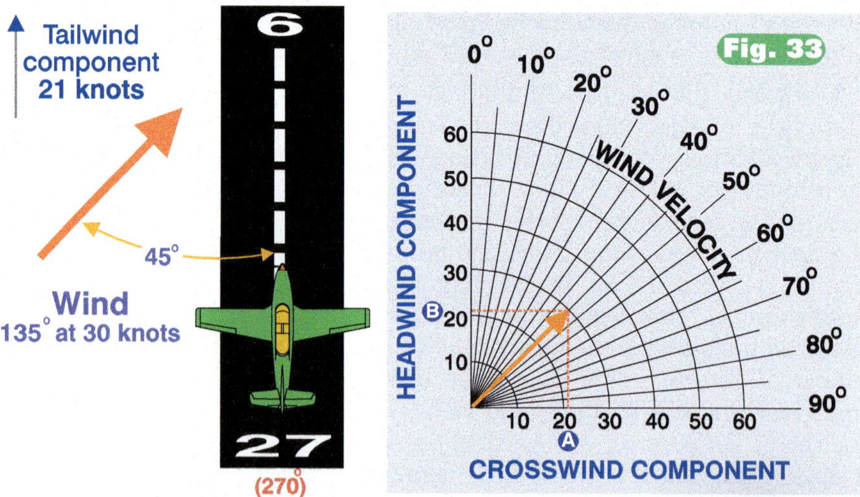

If the winds are from 135 degrees at 30 knots and you're landing on runway 27 (270 degrees), what is the tailwind component during landing? Find the angle between the wind and the runway. The wind makes a 45 degree angle with the runway as shown by the compass rose to the right. Since the wind is blowing from behind the airplane, start at the bottom left hand corner of the crosswind chart and follow the 45 degree line up to the 30 knot arc. Move horizontally to the headwind scale (it tells us tailwind–that should be obvious) and downward to find the tailwind component of 21 knots (point A).

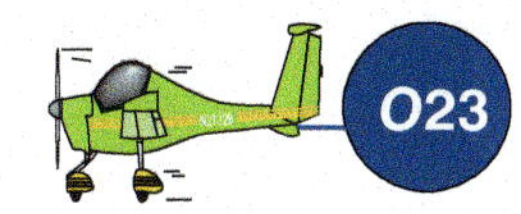

(point B). At this point, ask yourself what wind arc you would be resting on if smaller wind-arc calibrations existed. Parallel this arc around to the end of the scale (either direction). The maximum wind velocity should be 24 knots.

Crosswind Problem No. 4 – Using Figure 29, find the amount of tailwind expected with a 30 knot wind from 135 degrees when landing on Runway 27.

The crosswind chart can also be used to find tailwind and crosswind components quite easily. The same procedure applies, except that we must find the angle between the wind and the tail (since we're talking about tailwinds). Figure 33 shows this problem. If you have trouble finding the angle between the wind and the tail, draw (or find) a circular compass rose with the four major directions (N, E, S, and W) on it as shown in Figure 33.

Aligned with Runway 27 means you are pointed in a direction of 270 degrees. With wind from 135 degrees (remember, wind always blow from somewhere), you have wind that makes a 45 degree angle between itself and the tail. Simply go to the crosswind chart and find the wind components for a 30 knot wind offset at a 45 degree angle. Point A shows a crosswind of 21 knots. Keeping your original picture in mind, you'll recognize this as a left crosswind. Point B shows a headwind component of 21 knots; we know, however, that this is actually a tailwind component. The crosswind chart wasn't necessarily built to find tailwind components, but if you understand the principle involved, it can be done. This is not to encourage you to plan on taking off with a tailwind. Such behavior is rarely prudent unless the tailwind is pretty minor.

Making the Forces Be With You

During my youth, many a school counselor attempted to predict what I might do with my life. One counselor suggested life as a woodworker, then realized it meant handling sharp objects. No go. Another felt I would succeed at hubcap repair, but backtracked once he thought about how distracting all the bright, shiny objects would be.

Fortunately, my counselors didn't predict well. This may be because nobody *ever* predicts someone will grow up to be a flight instructor. That's an inherently unpredictable outcome.

As a pilot, you can't afford to predict poorly when it comes to airplane performance. You need to become very familiar with the performance charts—not only how to crunch numbers, but what those numbers really mean in terms of performance. Additionally, you need to understand the limitations these numbers impose on when and where flight can be safely undertaken.

Remember, performance charts are prediction charts. And good pilots never leave to chance what they can predict.

Postflight Briefing #15-1

Advanced Lessons In Density Altitude

Advanced Density Altitude Problem #1

In the airplane, finding pressure altitude is as easy as being a lifeguard in a car wash. Simply place 29.92 in the altimeter's Kollsman window and read what the hands point to (the indicated altitude). This is your pressure altitude. Take the OAT and the pressure altitude and compute the density altitude by using the chart in Figure 34.

But how do you compute density altitude for an airport if you aren't there to set the altimeter to 29.92 inches of Hg and read the temperature? In other words, if you're reading the METAR for an airport and know the temperature and altimeter setting, can you still find its density altitude? Yes. Here's how. Let's start with a field elevation of 7,257 feet MSL.

To the right of the density altitude chart is a vertical column showing altimeter settings vs. pressure altitude conversion factors. Simply find the airport's current altimeter in the altimeter setting column and see what conversion factor must be applied to the altimeter reading to find pressure altitude. In other words, the altimeter should read the field elevation of 7,257 feet MSL with 30.20 inches of Hg set in the Kollsman window. Moving the window's numbers down to 29.92 would simultaneously move the hands downward (make the indicated altitude read less). The conversion factor specifies how much the hands would move downward.

Figure 34, position 1, shows that the conversion factor for an altimeter setting of 30.20 is -257 feet (you would add this value if it didn't have a "-" sign next to it). Subtracting 257 from 7,257 gives you 7,000 which is the pressure altitude. Take the OAT of 80 degrees F (27 degrees C) and a pressure altitude of 7,000 feet and, as shown by position 2 in Figure 34, the density altitude is 10,000 feet. Even though your airplane is at 7,257 feet MSL, it's going to perform like it's at 10,000 feet MSL.

Advanced Density Altitude Problem #2

Notice the diagonal line labeled "standard temperature" running downward from left to right in Figure 34. Sometimes we want to know the standard temperature for a specific altitude when standard conditions exists at sea level. Find any spot where the standard temperature line intersects a pressure altitude line and drop straight down to the temperature scale. This reading is the standard temperature for that pressure altitude. For example, on Figure 34, find where the standard temperature line intersects the 4,000 foot pressure altitude line (position 3). Drop down to find the standard temperature of 45 degrees F (7°C) for that altitude. The same process works for all other pressure altitude values.

Suppose I ask you to find the density altitude if standard temperature exists at 4,000 feet pressure altitude. Simply find where the standard temperature line intersects the pressure altitude line on Figure 34 and move horizontally left to read a density altitude of 4,000 feet. You'll notice that whenever standard temperature exists at various pressure altitudes, the pressure altitude is always equal to the density altitude. I offer this only as an academic exercise, because standard temperatures seldom exist at various pressure altitudes. I have been flying since 1970 and I have yet to see more than a handful of days having standard temperatures at sea level that stayed that way for any significant amount of time.

Another important reason for offering this to you is because someone decided to put this type of question on the knowledge test (don't ask me why either).

Advanced Density Altitude Problem #3

What is your density altitude if the altimeter setting is 29.96 inches of Hg and the airport elevation is 3,293 feet with an OAT of 75 degrees F (24 degrees C)? First, you must find the pressure altitude. With the altimeter setting in the altimeter window, the altimeter reads the true altitude (a field elevation of 3,293 feet MSL). The pressure altitude conversion for 29.96 inches of Hg is approximately halfway between that for 29.92 and 30.00, as shown in Figure 34, position 4. Since the correction factor for 29.92 is 0 and 30.00 is -73, use a value halfway between them, or approximately -36. Subtracting 36 from 3,293 gives us a pressure altitude of 3,257 feet.

Locating the pressure altitude value of 3,257 is easy if you draw the intermediate values between the 1,000 foot pressure altitude lines. Simply draw the 3,500 foot pressure altitude value between the 3,000 and 4,000 foot pressure altitude lines, as shown by position 5 on Figure 34. Now draw an intermediate value between the 3,000 and 3,500 foot pressure altitude line. This represents the 3,250 foot pressure altitude value. Move up the 75 degree F (24°C) line until reaching the pressure altitude line of 3,250, as shown by position 6 on Figure 34 (this is real close to the actual pressure altitude value of 3,257 feet). Go across to the left to find a density altitude value of approximately 5,000 feet.

Advanced Density Altitude Problem #4

Suppose you're flying a new Cessna 152 from an airport located at 9,702 feet MSL. The altimeter setting is 29.60 and the OAT is 95 degrees F (35 degrees C) (that's hot for an airport that high—better be careful!) What is the density altitude at that airport?

Using the pressure altitude conversion table in Figure 34 you determine that it's necessary to add 298 feet onto the true altitude to obtain a pressure altitude of 10,000 feet (298+9,702=10,000). Using the OAT of 95 degrees F (35°C) and a pressure altitude of 10,000 feet gives you a density altitude of 14,700 feet.

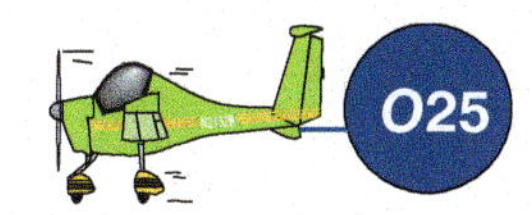

Fig. 34

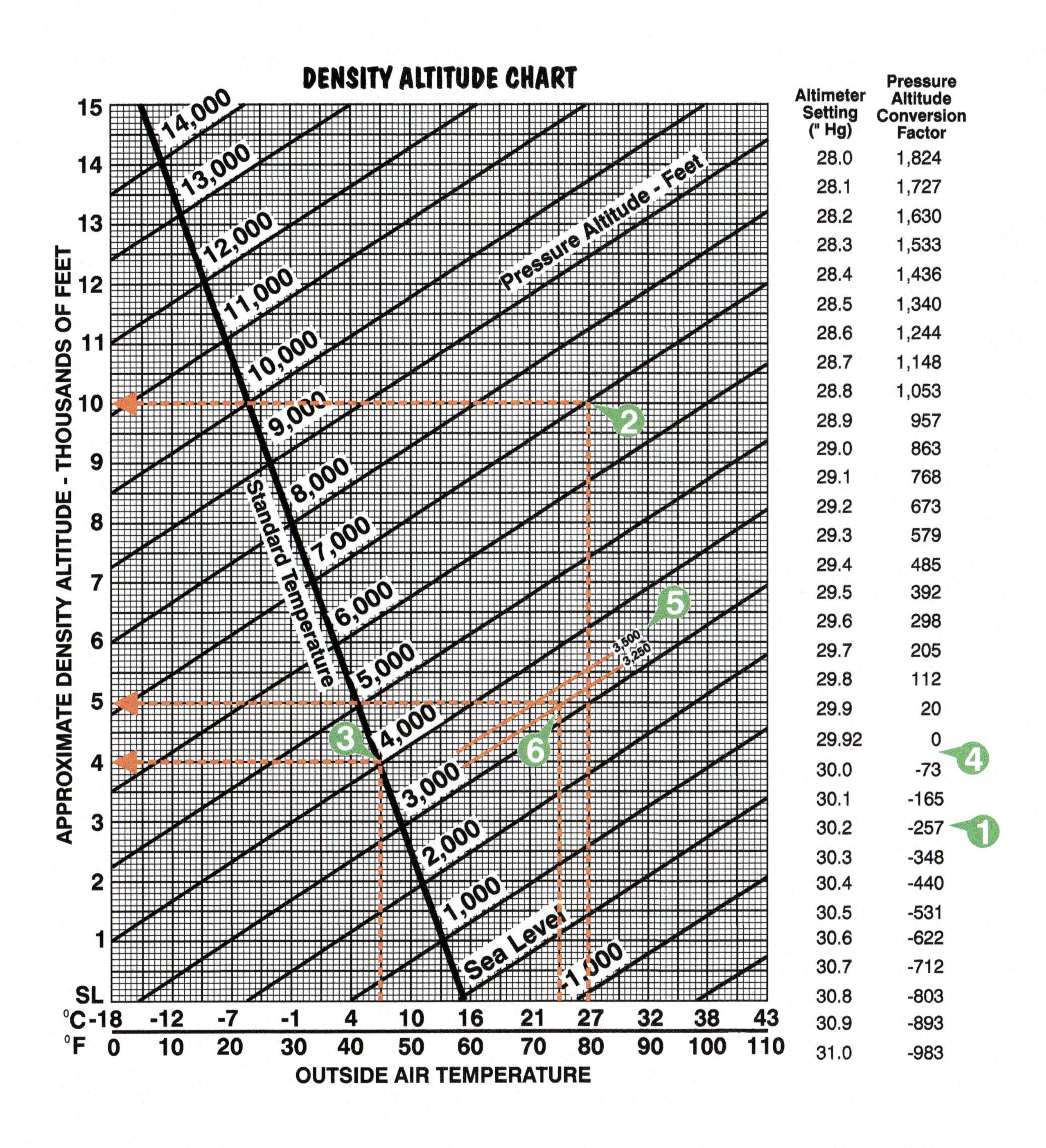

Altimeter Setting (" Hg)	Pressure Altitude Conversion Factor
28.0	1,824
28.1	1,727
28.2	1,630
28.3	1,533
28.4	1,436
28.5	1,340
28.6	1,244
28.7	1,148
28.8	1,053
28.9	957
29.0	863
29.1	768
29.2	673
29.3	579
29.4	485
29.5	392
29.6	298
29.7	205
29.8	112
29.9	20
29.92	0
30.0	-73
30.1	-165
30.2	-257
30.3	-348
30.4	-440
30.5	-531
30.6	-622
30.7	-712
30.8	-803
30.9	-893
31.0	-983

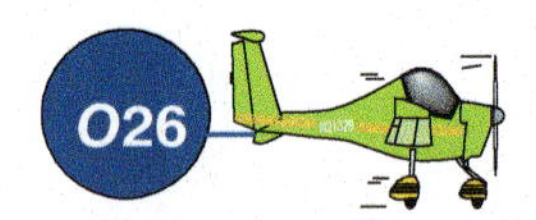

Postflight Briefing #15-2

Higher Knowledge: Cruise Performance (time and fuel planning)

By Steve King

FAA regulations (FAR Part 91) require that you plan your VFR flight to include enough fuel to get to the destination with sufficient reserve to fly for 30 minutes during the day and 45 minutes at night. Realistically, you need to allow substantially more than that to protect against running out of fuel. The following suggestions will help you make safer decisions about how far you can safely go between fuel stops.

1. Assume 5% (x .95) less cruise airspeed than what is shown in the POH charts. Then, calculate actual TAS in flight to compare with your estimate. When you do this comparison, note the aircraft weight, since it will affect the cruise speed a little, especially at higher altitudes/lower power settings.
2. Assume 20% (x 1.2) more fuel consumption (GPH) than what is shown in the POH charts. Then, calculate actual GPH after a flight (using takeoff to landing time) to compare with your estimate.
3. For fairly good conditions, plan on having 1.5 hours of fuel left when you land to refuel. For good to excellent conditions, less than 1.5 hours reserve might be adequate. If flying with a smaller reserve, compare your actual progress (actual elapsed time to checkpoints) with your flight plan. For adverse conditions, you should have at least a 2 hour reserve, possibly more. Consider the following when you make decisions about fuel reserves:

- Day or night? It's wise to add about 1 hour *additional* fuel reserve at night. Why? There are greater consequences associated with running out gas when it's dark. Additionally, the extra fuel reserve helps in case you have difficulty with navigation (pilotage, for instance, is more difficult at night). And, since weather hazards are more difficult to detect at night, you might need the fuel to deviate to another airport. Finally, consider that fewer places sell fuel at night. You might need to travel to find a place that sells it.
- Ease of navigation? Is there any chance of being lost enroute, or of having difficulty in finding the destination?
- How many airports are along the route so you can land if you are low on gas or are behind schedule?
- How many of those airports sell gas? (See #5 below.)
- How good is the weather? If the weather is somewhat marginal, it may become necessary to leave the planned route for things like flying around clusters of thunderstorms. This could add significantly to the planned distance and time. Diverting from a planned route also increases the possibility of becoming lost, especially if the weather is poor. You really want to avoid the possibility that you might be lost (thus not knowing where you could go to land) and be low on fuel and in poor weather *all* at the same time!
- How hazardous is the terrain over which you are flying? For example, how does flying over water, over mountains or over very remote areas compare to following a freeway?

4. To fly with as little as one-half hour fuel reserve (assuming that you have previously assumed 95% TAS and 120% GPH), you should have ideal conditions including:
   - Daytime flight, planned to end well before sunset. (Watch for delays that could affect this.)
   - Very easy navigation, like following a freeway, with careful navigation planning—integrating pilotage, dead reckoning and electronic navigation.
   - Many airports along the latter third of your route, *with fuel available* (you can use these as alternate fuel stops in case you fall behind schedule, or the ideal conditions deteriorate). (See #5 below.)
   - Excellent weather, with essentially no chance of any weather problems. (Make sure you monitor the weather through Flight Watch, etc., during flight.)
   - Non-hazardous terrain that's within easy gliding distance of a freeway, airport, or dry lake at all times during the latter third of the flight.
5. Before planning to depend on an airport or an alternate fuel stop (especially the one during last third of the route), verify that you will actually be able to get fuel at that location, by phoning ahead. Then, before descending from cruise to land at an airport when your fuel level is low, call on Unicom to verify fuel availability. If they don't respond, you might be able to safely fly to a nearby airport to refuel even though you wouldn't have enough fuel to land at the first airport, then take off and fly to the second airport. When you phone, check the following:
   - How late are they open? If you fall behind schedule and arrive late, what are the chances of getting fuel at that airport?
   - Do they have the type of fuel you need? Will they accept your form of payment? Some places only accept cash, traveler's checks (some don't accept these, or only certain brands because of counterfeiting concerns), or their own oil company credit card (often Phillips 66).

Steve King is professor and department head of the Professional Pilot Training Program at Long Beach City College located in Long Beach, California. He has been a pilot since 1965, an A&P since 1966 and is a certificated flight instructor.

Chapter Sixteen

Weight & Balance

Let's Wait and Balance

All airplanes have limits on the maximum weight they can carry and where that weight is placed within the airplane. Within these limits, airplanes perform normally; outside of them, they behave erratically. Structural damage and in-flight stability are the two most important reasons why an airplane's weight is restricted, and why the weight must be distributed in a certain way. Calculating whether the plane is within its stated restrictions is referred to as doing a weight-and-balance calculation. It's a crucial part of your preflight planning.

Some pilots think the term is *wait and balance* and that it refers to time spent in the aviation medical examiner's office before he invites you in and asks you to jump up and down on one foot without having a heart attack.

A friend of mine found out the hard way what weight and balance really meant. Bob was a corporate pilot for a small Orange County firm. One day the boss wanted to take the company's A36 Bonanza on a ski trip. The plane was fully fueled when the boss arrived with enough ski gear to fill a 747.

Taxiing to the runup area, Bob turned the aft-heavy Bonanza into the wind and pressed the brakes. Suddenly the nose started to rise—for no apparent reason. The airplane slowly and deliberately listed aft on the main gear. *Smack.* The nose pointed up, and the tail hit the ground.

Bob was thinking about how he might gain admission to the federal witness protection program. He was embarrassed for not having done a weight and balance computation before the flight. He was even more embarrassed at not having said "No" to the obvious improper loading of an airplane. There was no telling how unsafe the airplane would have been had he taken off in this aft center of gravity condition.

Bob gave the airplane full power, righted it, taxied back to the tiedown area, and unloaded the aircraft. He refused to fly unless the plane was operated within the proper weight and balance limits. This was an embarrassing lesson, but one he would never forget.

No need to worry. The captain of this airliner isn't popping a wheelie to keep the passengers entertained. The airplane was found this way early in the morning after a snow storm. Weight from snow accumulating on the aft portion of the fuselage and stabilizer tilted the airplane on its tail. Perhaps the airline could use this photo in conjunction with a new advertising slogan: "Our airplanes can't wait to get off the ground."

Excessive Weight And Structural Damage

Airplane wings are like bicycle tires in that both are designed to support a certain amount of weight. Too much weight could pop a bicycle's tire. Excessive weight can also damage a wing. Airplanes are designed to be flown up to a specific maximum gross weight. While it's possible to become airborne beyond this maximum certified weight, structural problems can arise when turbulence or high-G maneuvering enters the picture.

Think about it this way. If an airplane is certified in the utility category, it can withstand 4.4 positive Gs without structural damage. If this airplane has a maximum gross weight of 2,000 pounds, its wings are certified to withstand 4.4 times the maximum gross weight of 2,000 pounds or a total of 8,800 pounds. Distributing 8,800 pounds of force over the wings will bend them slightly. However, when the force is removed, the wings will flex back to their original position (this is good!).

Now, suppose you take off in the same airplane with a gross weight of 2,100 pounds. No doubt, the airplane easily becomes airborne when only 100 pounds over gross weight. But what happens if turbulence is encountered? If you experienced 4.4Gs, the airplane's wings must now support 9,240 pounds of weight (4.4 X 2,100). That's 440 pounds beyond the 8,800 pounds the engineers planned for. You're now a test pilot and you are not getting hazardous duty pay. The risk of turbulence-induced damage has increased.

Flying beyond the maximum weight limits presents other problems. For instance, the stall speed increases at heavier weights. More weight requires the wings to move faster through the air before they can develop the minimum lift necessary to sustain flight. It takes more runway to attain this faster speed. The takeoff distance increases. You won't find a performance chart for "How much runway you'll need for takeoff when taking off over the maximum weight limit."

More weight also means less climb performance, higher fuel consumption, reduced range, higher landing speeds, longer landing distances. The list goes on and on. There is just no good reason to fly the airplane beyond its maximum gross weight limits. Pilots who insist on carrying all their friends in one airplane, regardless of their weight, should hang out with skinny people.

A friend of mine owned a small Cessna 150. This situation was unfortunate, since he weighed several hundred pounds (He was 370. That's incredible when you consider that 360 is a full circle). The only way he could fly the airplane and be within proper limits was to drain half the fuel from the tanks. This substantially shortened his range. Fortunately, his bladder was about the size of a BB and shortened range was never really a bother.

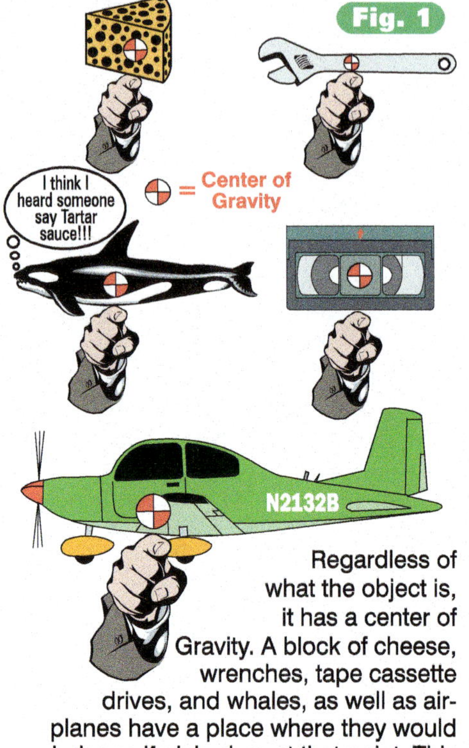

Regardless of what the object is, it has a center of Gravity. A block of cheese, wrenches, tape cassette drives, and whales, as well as airplanes have a place where they would balance if picked up at that point. This point is known as the center of gravity.

Center of Gravity

The *center of gravity (CG)* of any object is the point where, if an imaginary finger lifted it, the object would balance (see Figure 1). For an object whose weight is evenly distributed along its length, such as a Popsicle stick, the CG is precisely at the center. For an object such as an airplane, where weight is *not* distributed evenly along its length, you have to calculate where the CG is.

Moving Moose

Many years ago, two hunters chartered an airplane to fly into the Alaskan wilderness for a hunting expedition. Two weeks later, when the pilot came to fly them out, he noticed the two large moose they shot and said, "I told you fellows that I could only take you and one moose. You'll have to leave the other one behind."

"But we did it last year in a plane this size," protested one hunter, "and the pilot gladly let us take both moose."

"Well, OK, If you did it before, then I suppose we can do it again," said the pilot. So the two moose and the hunters were loaded and the plane departed. Because of the heavy weight, the airplane struggled into the air. Barely climbing, the airplane was unable to clear the obstructing mountain—it crashed. Both men climbed from the wreckage and looked around. One hunter said to the other, "Where are we, anyway?" His companion looked around, and said, "I think we're about a half mile farther than we got last year."

If an airplane will return, unassisted, to level flight after its controls are disturbed, it is said to have *positive dynamic stability,* making it less difficult to control. If the airplane won't return to its original flight configuration, and in fact keeps diverging farther from it in a series of oscillations, it is said to be exhibiting *negative dynamic stability*. Engineers tell us that for an airplane to be positively stable, its weight must not be concentrated too far aft. Weight concentrated too far forward may prevent sufficient pitch control to hold the nose up during landing. These forward and aft weight limits are known as the *center of gravity limits,* as shown in Figure 2.

Engineers know these limits because they have flight tested the airplane (while wearing parachutes) under variable load conditions. The results of this flight test information are provided to you in your airplane's weight and balance papers (always located in the airplane) or in an approved flight manual specifically modified for that airplane.

AN AIRPLANE'S FORWARD & AFT CENTER OF GRAVITY LIMIT

Forward CG limit
Aft CG limit
If the airplane's CG falls beyond its forward or its aft limits, it should be considered unsafe to fly.
CG limit exaggerated
Normal CG range
N2132B
Center of Gravity
UNSAFE SAFE UNSAFE

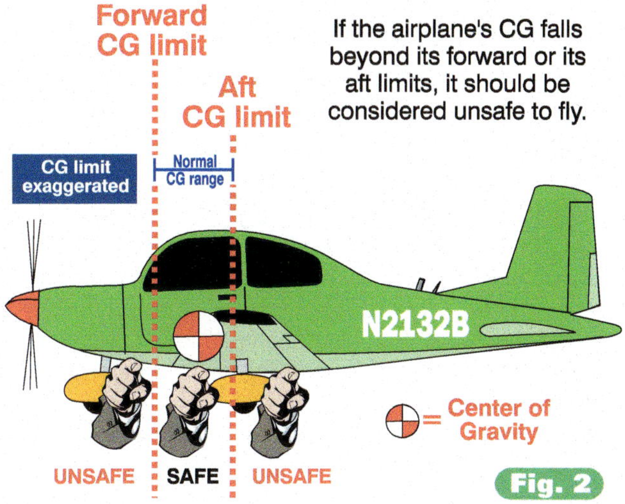

Fig. 2

Beyond the aft CG limit, the airplane demonstrates negative dynamic stability in flight. For example, assume the airplane's weight is loaded within the allowable limits. If the controls are bumped as shown in Figure 3A, the airplane will oscillate up and down and eventually return to its previous level flight position. When the oscillations diminish in amplitude over time, it is a demonstration of positive dynamic stability. Now, assume the airplane is *not* loaded within its allowable limits and the controls are bumped, as shown in Figure 3B. The airplane exhibits negative dynamic stability because it moves farther away from its normal position.

Flying an airplane that is experiencing negative dynamic stability is about as safe as being the fourth crew member to beam down on a Star Trek show (you know something bad is going to happen to this person). Negative dynamic stability means you're always having to fight for control of your airplane. In extreme cases, you may not be able to get the airplane under control. You never want to operate under these conditions. Loading an airplane properly prevents this problem. If the airplane would balance on your finger anywhere between the forward and aft CG limits, it will be positively stable in flight (assuming also that the airplane's weight doesn't exceed its maximum allowable limit).

AIRPLANE STABILITY IN FLIGHT

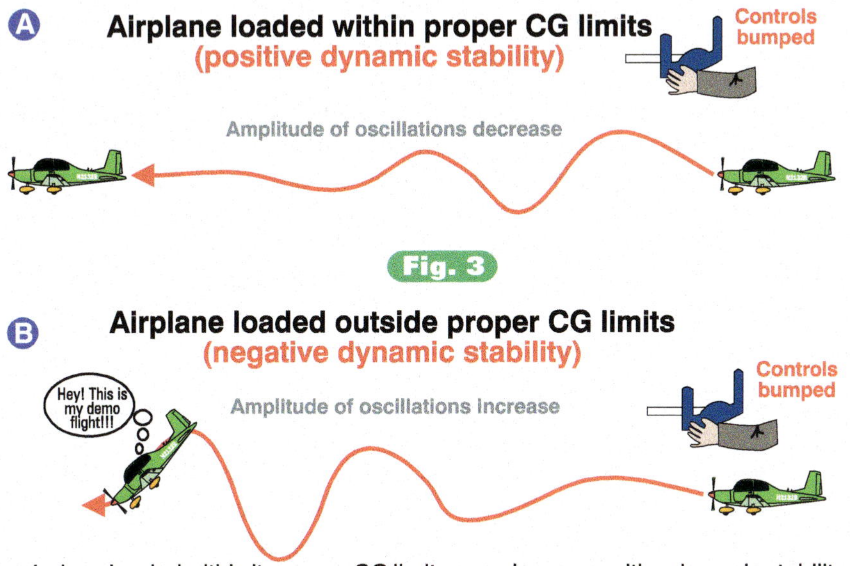

A Airplane loaded within proper CG limits (positive dynamic stability)
Controls bumped
Amplitude of oscillations decrease

Fig. 3

B Airplane loaded outside proper CG limits (negative dynamic stability)
Controls bumped
Amplitude of oscillations increase
Hey! This is my demo flight!!!

An airplane loaded within its proper CG limits experiences positive dynamic stability. When the airplane is disturbed from level flight it pitches up and down with the amplitude of each oscillation decreasing as shown in position A. An airplane loaded beyond its aft CG limit experiences negative dynamic stability when it's disturbed from level flight. The amplitude of each oscillation increases as shown in position B. Airplanes loaded forward of their CG limit may not have sufficient pitch control to raise the nose during landing. Both conditions make the airplane difficult to control and unsafe to fly.

Longitudinal Stability

Longitudinal stability is the term used to describe the airplane's pitching motion. Since the airplane pitches about its lateral (sideways) axis, it's correct to say that *longitudinal stability* describes the airplane's pitching motion about its lateral axis.

Properly loaded airplanes are longitudinally stable. Any pitch away from a trimmed flight condition results in the airplane returning to its original pitch in a series of dampened, decreasing oscillations. The location of the CG with respect to the center of lift (see page P5) determines the airplane's longitudinal stability.

Lateral Stability

Lateral stability is the term used to describe the airplane's rolling motion. Since the airplane rolls about its longitudinal (long) axis, it's correct to say that *lateral stability* describes the airplane's motion about its longitudinal axis.

Airplanes with good lateral stability tend to favor a wings-level flight condition. They resist roll movement. Dihedral, weight placement and keel effect are common means of enhancing lateral stability (see glossary for the definition of *dihedral*).

AFT CG LOADING

In normal flight the center of lift is concentrated behind the CG. Since the airplane always rotates about its CG, the nose wants to pitch down.

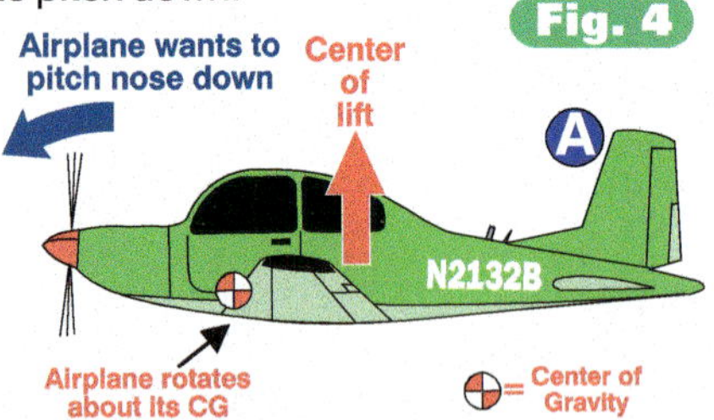

The tails on most airplanes help compensate for this nose down pitching tendency by creating lift in a downward direction.

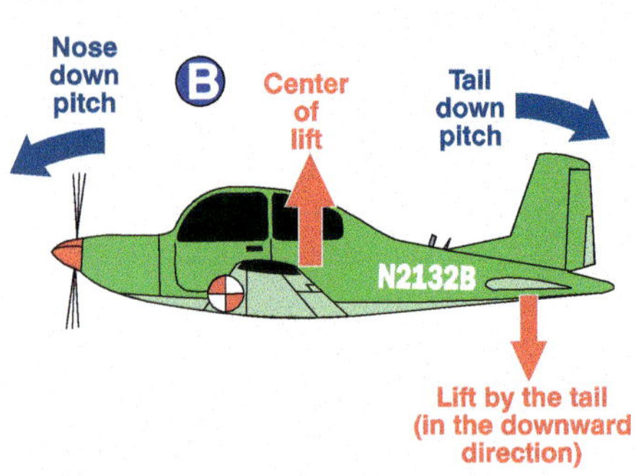

When the airplane increases its angle of attack (as when it slows), the center of lift moves forward along the wing. As long as the center of lift remains behind the CG, the airplane remains positively stable.

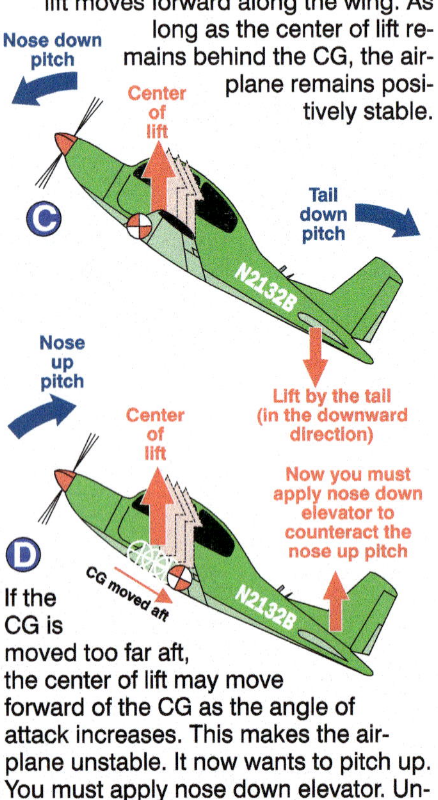

If the CG is moved too far aft, the center of lift may move forward of the CG as the angle of attack increases. This makes the airplane unstable. It now wants to pitch up. You must apply nose down elevator. Under slow airspeed conditions, the nose may not want to go down (bad news!).

Note: All CG positions exaggerated for effect

Other CG Considerations

Negative dynamic stability isn't the only negative outcome of loading a plane outside its CG limits.

The lift an airplane develops is spread over the entire surface of its wings from the leading to the trailing edge. Like weight, lift can be thought of as being focused at one point called the *center of lift* (Figure 4A). (Also see the *Center of Lift* sidebar at the top of opposite page.)

Notice that the center of lift is located behind the CG. Since the airplane rotates about its CG, the wing's lifting force causes a constant nose-down tilting condition. This is why the tails of most airplanes (their horizontal stabilizers) are rigged to provide a downward force as shown in Figure 4B. A downward force on the tail compensates for the downward tilting force of the nose. This allows the airplane to remain controllable in flight (if you lost the tail in flight, you would lose control of the airplane).

As the angle of attack increases, the center of lift moves forward, toward the front of the wing as shown in Figure 4C. As long as the center of lift is behind the CG, the airplane still has a forward-pitching tendency. This is a good thing since this nose-downward pitching tendency acts to automatically reduce the angle of attack. The airplane naturally wants to keep itself away from high angles of attack where stalls occur. It also wants to automatically reduce its angle of attack in the event of a stall.

Moving the CG rearward, beyond the aft CG limit, is very dangerous. If the CG is too far aft, the center of lift, at high angles of attack, might move ahead of the CG, as depicted in Figure 4D. Now the airplane wants to pitch up and increase its angle of attack. You might have to apply a lot of forward elevator control to get the nose to pitch down. Under certain conditions (slow airspeeds and high angles of attack for instance) the airplane may not respond.

An aft CG condition can lead to violent stalls and flat spins. These are not good things. Fly like this and you'll feel like a chicken with the Colonel close behind. When flown within the proper CG limits, however, airplanes are perfectly safe. A pilot's job is to always make sure the CG remains within the limits.

An aft CG tends to give you lower stick forces, meaning that a slight touch on the controls causes a large, and sometimes uncontrollable oscillation of the nose. It's similar to the first time you drove a car with power steering—it's very easy to overcontrol. The airplane can be easily overstressed in this condition.

Airplanes loaded beyond the *forward* CG limit often fare no better. With the CG located ahead of the forward limit (Figure 5A), an excessive tail-down force is required to keep the nose up. During landing, as the airplane slows, there may not be enough airflow over the tail to generate this tail-down force. You might

FORWARD CG LOADING

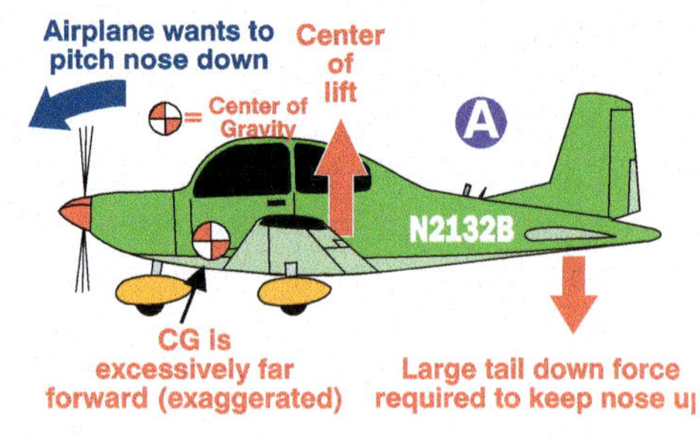

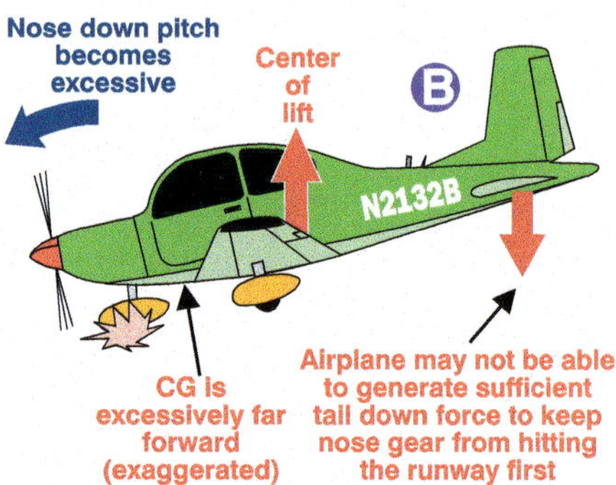

When the CG is too far forward an excessive tail down force is required to keep the nose from pitching forward. While this may not present a problem in cruise flight, it may cause difficulty during landing. At the slower landing speeds, the elevator loses its effectiveness and can't compensate for the excessive nose down pitching. Nose gear damage is possible during the landing flare.

Fig. 5

THE CENTER OF LIFT

The center of lift is the point where the wing's total lifting force is concentrated. Think of it as the sum or the average of all the lifting forces spread across the wing (simulated by all the little black arrows). At low angles of attack the center of lift is found farther back along the wing as shown by wing A. As the angle of attack increases, all the little lifting forces move slightly. They tend to become more concentrated toward the front of the wing as shown by wing B. Therefore, as the angle of attack increases, the center of lift moves forward along the wing.

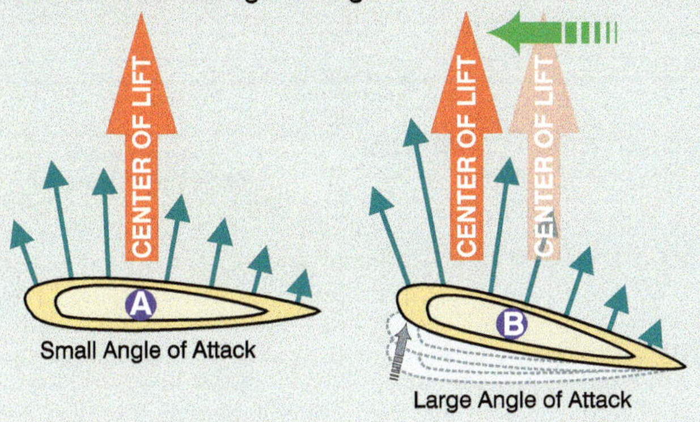

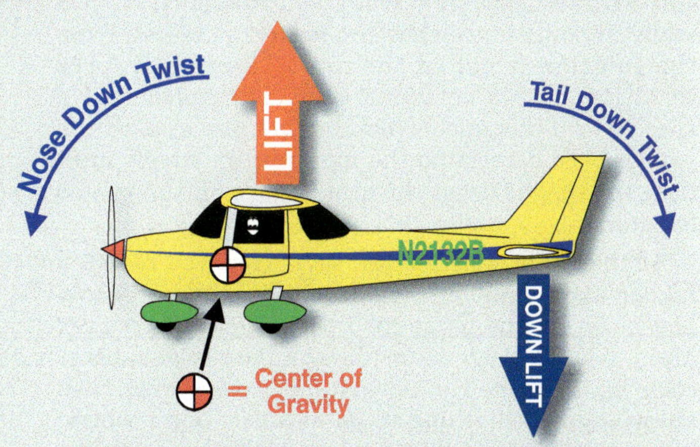

Airplanes are designed so that the center of lift always remains behind the center of gravity (assuming that your airplane is loaded properly). Since all objects rotate about their center of gravity, this causes the airplane to have a nose down pitching tendency. That's why the tail of an airplane must create a slight downward lifting force. This keeps the airplane from nosing end over end.

find yourself needing full, rearward elevator pressure just to keep the nose up during the flare (if it will stay up at all) as shown in Figure 5B. Excessive forward loading causes higher stalling speeds, decreased performance and higher stick forces.

Correct placement of the CG is obviously very important. But how do you measure its location? You can't go sticking your finger under an airplane and lifting it up every time you need to do a weight and balance. You can, however, use that dexterous digit to push calculator buttons or a pencil and find the CG through the magic of mathematics.

Just a Moment

To locate the center of gravity on an airplane you need to understand the concept of *moment* or tilting force. An airplane moment is different than a Kodak moment or a moment of time. A moment, as we're using the term here, is nothing more than a measure of the tilting force that weight imposes on an airplane. Figure 6A shows two 10 pound blocks placed on a plank at equal distances of five feet from the balance point. The plank is perfectly balanced (because of where the weights are placed). The plank's CG or balance point is located at the fulcrum (small triangle).

It's obvious that Block K causes the plank to tilt counterclockwise (to the left). Block R, on the other side of the plank, causes a similar tilt but in the clockwise direction (to the right). It's this tilting force that engineers refer to as the plank's moment. Since the plank balances, it should be obvious that the opposite tilting forces or moments caused by both blocks are opposite yet equal. They cancel out each other and the plank remains balanced at the fulcrum. Seeing is believing, but how do we prove this without actually performing the experiment?

We can prove that the plank is balanced by multiplying the individual weights by their distances from the fulcrum, then comparing these values. Before we

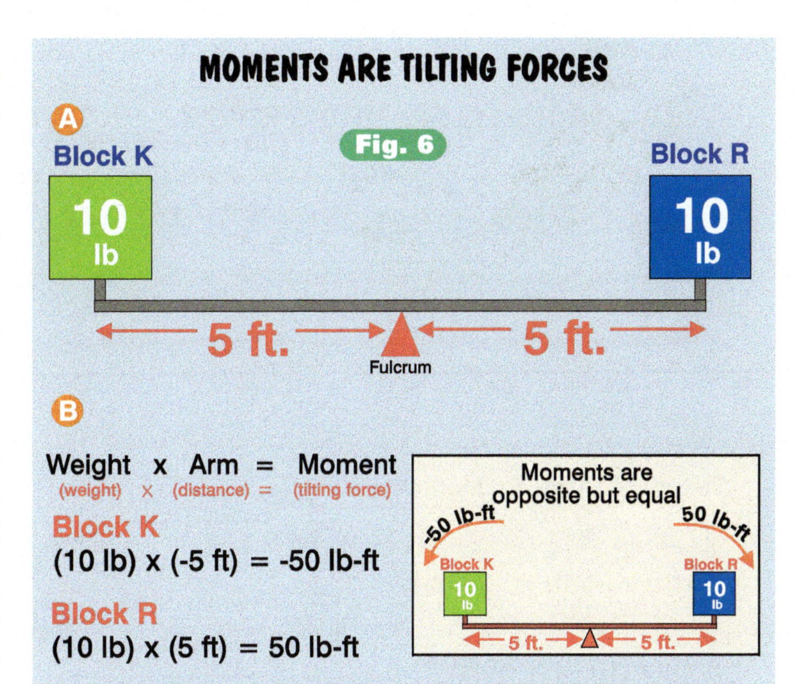

The result of multiplying the weight times its distance from a reference point (the fulcrum in this case) is the moment. A moment is the numerical value of the amount of tilt that an object produces. Block K and Block R both produce the same moment (tilting force) of 50 lb-ft in opposite directions about the fulcrum. Thus, the plank remains balanced.

do this, let's define a few terms. The word *weight* is self explanatory (it's what you measure with a scale). The distance that the weight is placed from the fulcrum is called the *arm*. The tilting force resulting from a certain weight being placed at a specific arm (distance) from the fulcrum is called the *moment*. To determine the moment, we simply multiply the weight times the arm. Figure 6B shows this formula.

At this point most people say, "Hey, you're using higher math, wait just a moment!" That's probably how they got the name for tilting force (not really). Many people treat math like the handle of a bathroom door. In their mind that handle is a Petri dish on a hinge—something to be avoided. Don't worry. The worst math you'll have to do is division (on the private pilot knowledge exam you are welcome to use your calculator).

In Figure 6A, to obtain Block K's moment, simply multiply the weight of Block K times the arm (its distance from the fulcrum). You obtain 10 pounds × 5 ft=50 lb-ft of tilting force in the left or counterclockwise direction (we'll call this the negative direction). Do the same with Block R and you get 10 pounds × 5 ft=50 lb-ft of tilting force in the right or clockwise direction (we'll call this the positive direction), as shown in Figure 6B. It's obvious that both tilting forces or moments are equal and opposite in direction. This is mathematical proof that the plank balances at the fulcrum. (Since the moment is a product of a weight and a distance, the units of foot-pounds or inch-pounds follow its numerical value.)

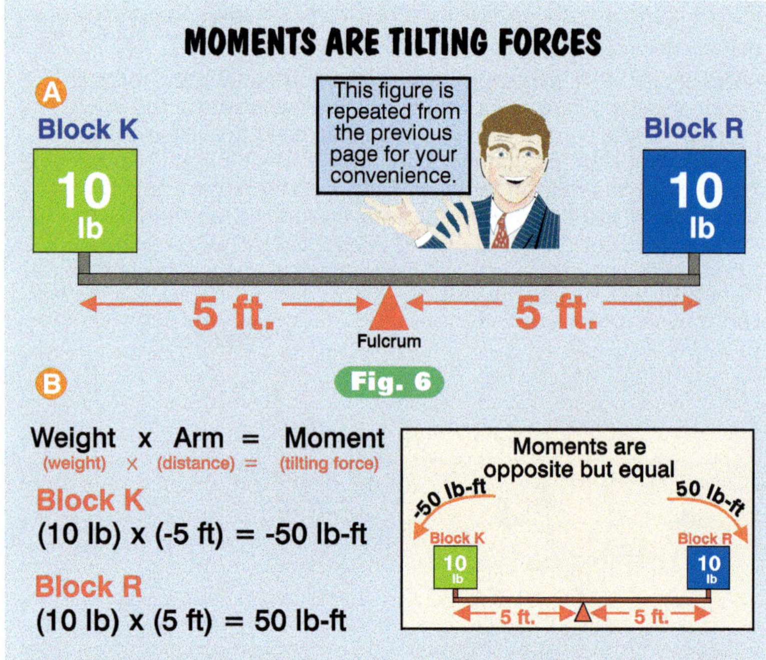

The result of multiplying the weight times its distance from a reference point (the fulcrum in this case) is the moment. A moment is the numerical value of the amount of tilt that an object produces. Block K and Block R both produce the same moment (tilting force) of 50 lb-ft in opposite directions about the fulcrum. Thus, the plank remains balanced.

Now let's make the problem a little more interesting (this is your instructor's way of saying I think you'll be stumped if I don't show this to you). Suppose we have two different weights located at different positions along the plank as shown in Figure 7. Notice that the moments for Block Q are equal and opposite to the moments of Block P. The plank balances at the fulcrum. Despite the differences in weights and their positions along the plank, we can easily (with math) determine whether the plank will balance or tilt.

MOMENTS ARE TILTING FORCES

A

Block Q 10 lb — Fig. 7 — Block P 5 lb

5 ft. — 10 ft.

B

Weight x Arm = Moment
(weight) x (distance) = (tilting force)

Block Q
(10 lb) x (-5 ft) = -50 lb-ft

Block P
(5 lb) x (10 ft) = 50 lb-ft

Moments are opposite but still equal
-50 lb-ft — 50 lb-ft
Block Q 10 lb — Block P 5 lb
5 ft. — 10 ft.

While Blocks P and Q have different weights, they produce the same moment about the reference point (the fulcrum). By multiplying their weights times their arms (distances from the fulcrum) you obtain a moment (tilting force) of 50 lb-ft for both blocks. Since the moments are equal but in opposite directions, the plank remains in balance.

Now that you understand the concept of moments, let's find the center of gravity when the weights and moments are known. Figure 8A shows the same plank without a fulcrum. Our objective is to find where we should place the fulcrum so that the plank will balance. On the left side of Figure 8A is a datum line. This is nothing more than an arbitrary vertical reference line from which we'll measure our distances.

The datum line is easy to understand. For instance, I might ask you what your distance is from the Hawaiian island of Molokai (our datum reference). If you said 4,000 miles east, then I'd have an idea of your position. If you said you were 1,500 miles east of San Francisco (another datum reference) I'd still have an idea of your position, as long as I know which datum (or reference spot) I'm measuring from.

To find the center of gravity of the two weights in Figure 8A, we'll find the moment of Block Z about the datum line. Simply multiply Block Z's weight times its arm (its distance from the datum line—our new measuring reference). Do the same with Block W. These calculations are shown in Figure 8B. Remember, we're trying to find the point past the datum where these weights would balance if a finger or fulcrum were placed under the plank. Now add all the weights and moments up as shown in Figure 8B. These are the total weights and the total moments produced by these weights. Dividing the total moments by the total weights as shown in Figure 8C gives you the arm (distance) at which the plank balances. This distance is 10 feet to the right of the datum line. The arm represents the CG location of these two weights.

Notice how the CG is located in the same place in Figure 8D as it is in Figure 7. The general rule in finding the CG is to add up the individual weights, find the moments of these weights about the datum or reference line, then divide the moments by the total weight. This gives you the arm or the current CG location in inches or feet past the datum line. Finding the CG of an airplane is done in exactly the same way.

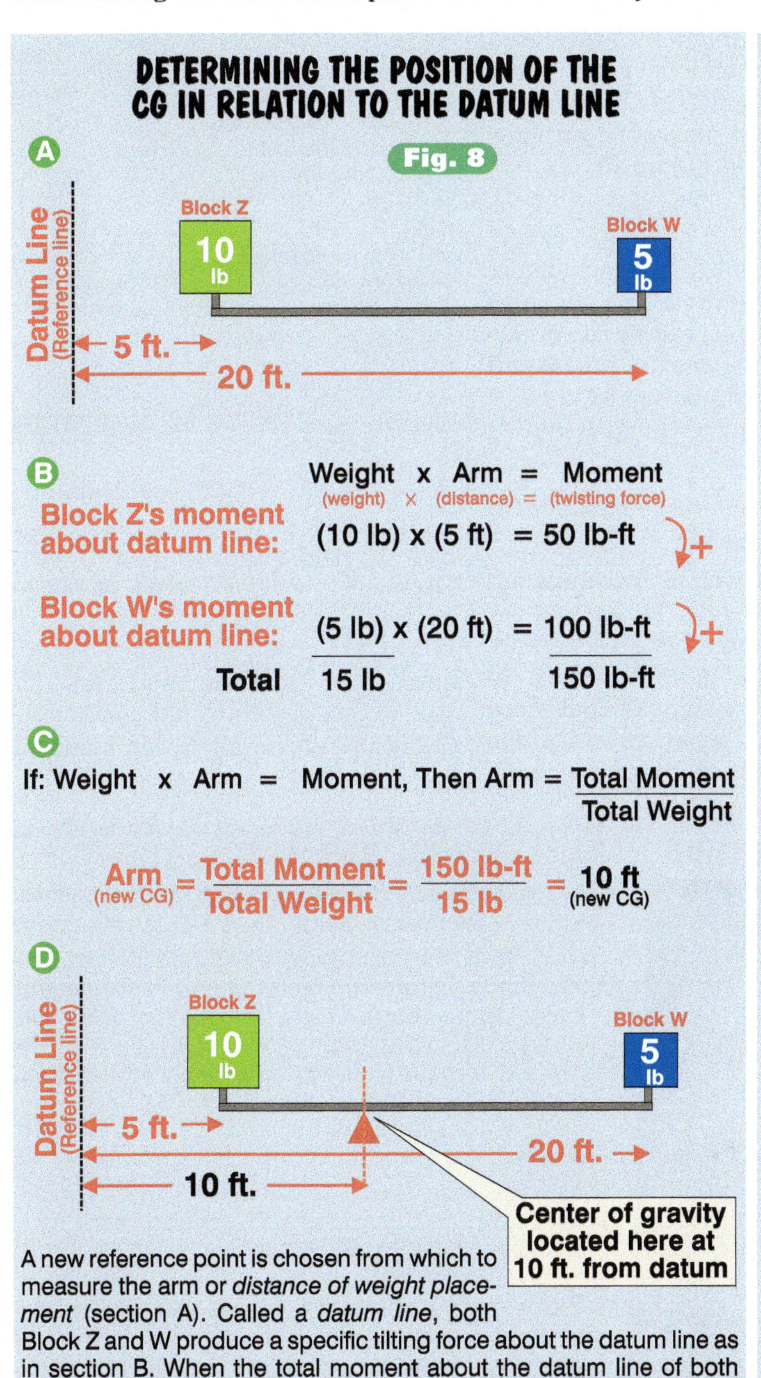

A new reference point is chosen from which to measure the arm or *distance of weight placement* (section A). Called a *datum line*, both Block Z and W produce a specific tilting force about the datum line as in section B. When the total moment about the datum line of both Blocks (Z+W) is divided by the total weight of the blocks, the arm or center of gravity is found (section C). This new CG is located 10 feet past the datum or 5 feet past Block Z (similar to Block Q in Figure 7).

Talking on the Radio is More Frightening Than Doing Weight & Balance Problems

Talking on the radio can be a very uncomfortable experience. All you hear is a disembodied, deep, well modulated, resonant voice coming from overhead. And the last time someone heard that, it convinced him to build a boat (a big boat!).

When we push that mic button, it seems like our brain immediately disconnects from the nerves leading to our mouth and eyes. Our lips seem to flap like a fish on a pier, while nothing comes out. Sometimes our eyes seem to...

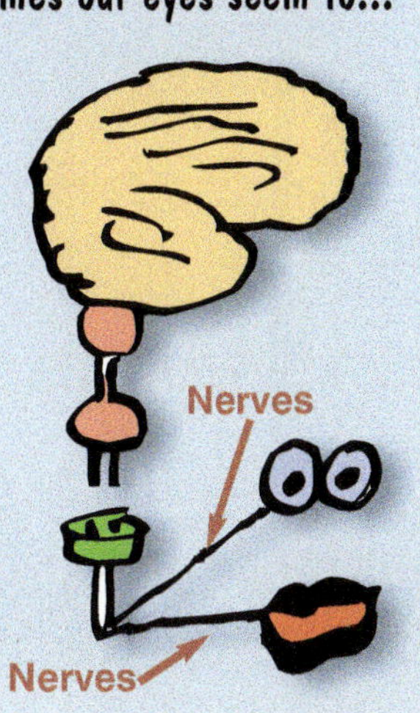

...bug out (their default position), and we can't think of a thing to say to the controller. Welcome to the club. Everyone experiences this at one time or another. Just remember, controllers are just like you and me. Just tell them you're a student and ask them to speak slower.

Some airplanes have datum lines located at the firewall or on the tip of the spinner, as shown in Figure 9. The datum line can be placed wherever the engineer chooses. It's a personal decision, much like how a flight instructor dresses (instructors are not snappy dressers, which explains why they are always asking their spouses, "Honey, does plaid go with a propeller hat?").

When datum lines are located at the firewall, then everything to the left of the datum line produces a negative value; and everything to the right, a positive value. For instance, oil, located to the left of a firewall datum line, produces a moment with a negative value. The negative moment must be subtracted from the total moments before dividing. Don't subtract the weight of the oil, since it is part of the total weight of the airplane.

We're almost ready to work an actual weight and balance problem. But first, we need to add a few more terms to your vocabulary:

1. *Maximum Takeoff Weight* – This is the maximum weight with which you can take off. This is sometimes referred to as the *maximum certificated gross weight* or *maximum gross weight*. The latter term is often shortened to *max gross* by pilots, making it sound like it's someone they know. This weight is based on a structural limitation of the airplane.

2. *Empty Weight* – The weight of a standard airplane, including all nondrainable fluids (this includes unusable fuel, hydraulic fluid and nondrainable oil), all permanently installed equipment (radios, etc.). For some airplanes, the term *basic empty weight* might include engine oil. You should check your airplane's weight and balance information to specifically identify when oil is included in the basic empty weight. This information is always located inside the airplane and can be seen in Figure 10.

3. *Useful load* – The weight of the pilot, passengers, baggage, cargo, usable fuel and oil (if not included in basic empty weight). You can also think of the useful load as the difference between the maximum takeoff weight and the empty weight.

A very important formula to remember is:

The empty weight+the useful load=the gross weight

Aviation fuel weighs 6 pounds per gallon and oil weighs 7.5 pounds per gallon (watch out, that's per gallon, not per quart). It's important to know the exact weight of fuel since there are times when the airplane must be defueled to meet the maximum takeoff weight requirements. Many times airplanes are fueled the day or night before your flight. Deciding to carry an extra passenger or extra baggage the following day might require removing a certain amount of fuel from the tanks. The gas boy or girl (internal combustion liquid petroleum allocation manager) can do this.

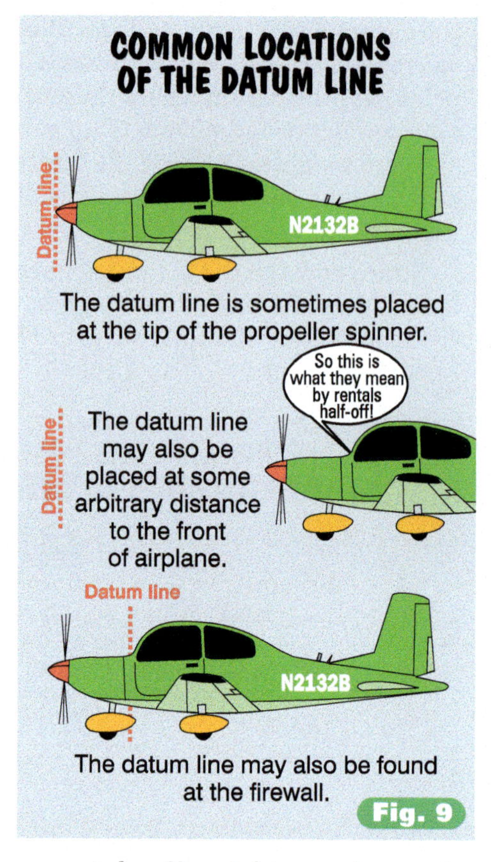

Fig. 9

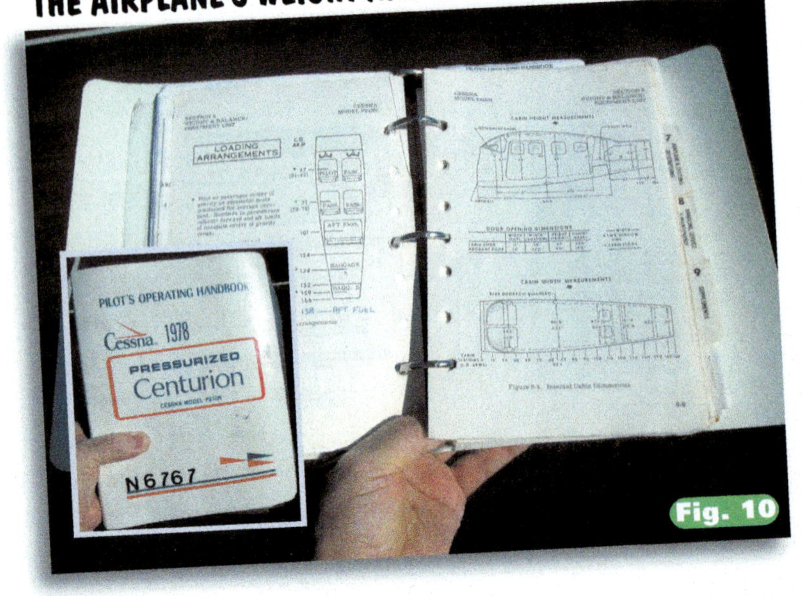

Fig. 10

Some Extra Weights

Two additional definitions may pop up from time to time. Keep them in mind.

A. *Maximum Ramp Weight* – During startup, taxi and runup, a certain amount of fuel is consumed. The maximum ramp weight includes this small fuel allowance with the assumption that, by the time the airplane is ready for takeoff, its weight will be at or below the maximum takeoff weight. This is not normally a consideration for small general aviation planes.

B. *Maximum Landing Weight* – The maximum weight approved for landing. This is also based on a structural limitation of the airplane. In other words, damage to the airframe is possible if a landing is attempted beyond this weight. For most smaller airplanes, the maximum landing weight is the same as the maximum takeoff weight. If an immediate return for landing were necessary after departure, you wouldn't need to concern yourself about possible weight-induced structural damage to the aircraft.

For example, if your airplane is 110 pounds over the maximum takeoff weight, how much fuel must be drained to be within legal weight limits? The answer is approximately 18.3 gallons. Simply divide 110 by 6 pounds/gal of fuel.

Once you know the proper steps to take in solving a weight and balance problem, you'll whip right through the calculations. Believe me when I say it works. It's like using a sunblock with an SPF rating of 2,047. That stuff works! It not only blocks the sun, it makes it rain.

Don't Wait to Balance

Let's apply our new-found knowledge to solve the simple weight and balance problem shown in Figure 11A.

Figure 11A provides the airplane's empty weight along with the arm and moment associated with this weight. Figure 11B shows a visual representation of what the airplane loading might look like. The empty-weight arm is nothing more than the point where the weight of the empty airplane is concentrated (its CG). This arm is used in computing the empty-weight moment. Since the empty-weight moment is given to you in the airplane's weight and balance papers, you need not calculate it.

The pilot and front passenger weigh a combined 380 pounds. They will both sit at an arm (distance) of 64.0 inches aft of the datum. What moment do the pilot and passenger produce? Multiply their weight and arm together. You should get 24,320 lb-in. Fuel is next. We have 30 gallons of usable fuel on this flight. How much does that weigh? Multiply 30 times 6 pounds/gallon=180 pounds. The fuel tanks are located at an arm of 96.0 inches aft of the datum. What moment does the fuel produce? Multiply 180 pounds times 96.0 inches=17,280 lb-in.

To find the CG for the loaded airplane you must divide the total moments by the total weights. Remember, all three arms that are shown in the middle column of Figure 11A are only used in computing the moments. The arms aren't added since this would serve no purpose. The next time that you will use the concept of arm is when you divide the airplane's total moment by its total weight. The arm or distance is now the point where the full airplane would balance (i.e., its center of gravity).

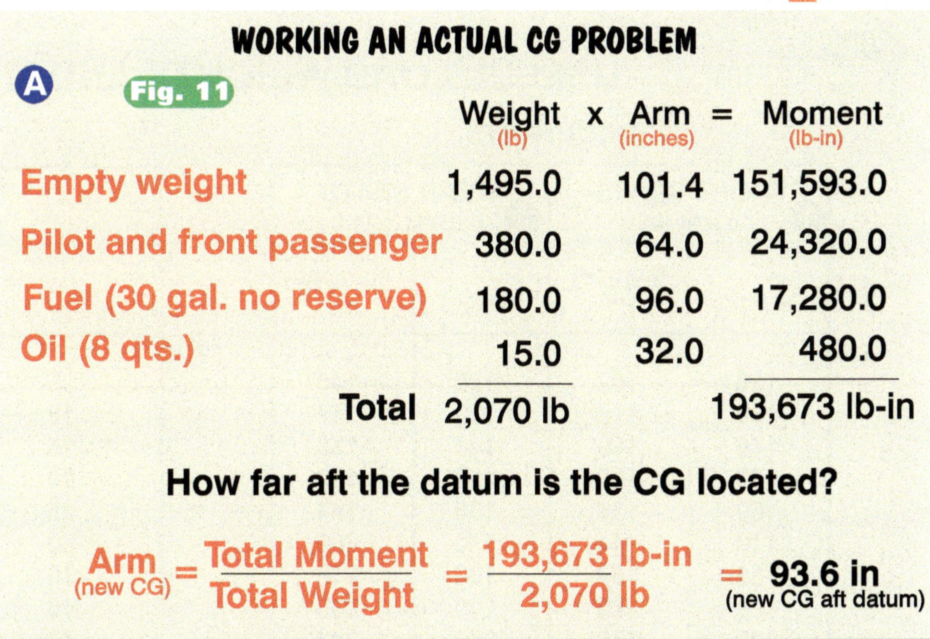
WORKING AN ACTUAL CG PROBLEM

A Fig. 11

	Weight (lb)	x Arm (inches)	= Moment (lb-in)
Empty weight	1,495.0	101.4	151,593.0
Pilot and front passenger	380.0	64.0	24,320.0
Fuel (30 gal. no reserve)	180.0	96.0	17,280.0
Oil (8 qts.)	15.0	32.0	480.0
Total	2,070 lb		193,673 lb-in

How far aft the datum is the CG located?

$$\text{Arm}_{\text{(new CG)}} = \frac{\text{Total Moment}}{\text{Total Weight}} = \frac{193{,}673 \text{ lb-in}}{2{,}070 \text{ lb}} = 93.6 \text{ in}$$

(new CG aft datum)

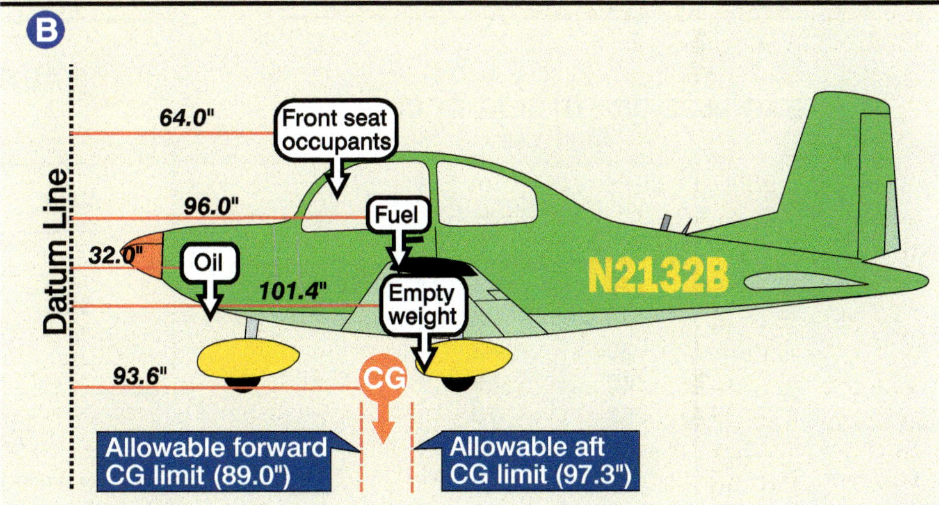

Weight X Arm=Moment

$$\text{Arm (CG)} = \frac{\text{Total Moments}}{\text{Total Weight}}$$

The total weight is 2,070 pounds.
The total moments are 193,673 lb-in.

Divide the total moments by the total weight to get the CG arm (the distance from the datum where the weights balance). Dividing 193,673 by 2070=93.6 inches—the center of gravity as shown in Figure 11B.

Considering that forward and aft CG limits are usually expressed in inches past the datum line, we can easily tell if the CG is within the appropriate limits for safe flight. Suppose the forward CG limit was set at 89.0 inches and the aft limit was 97.3 inches. In this instance, the airplane falls within the proper CG limits.

Fig. 12

USEFUL LOAD WEIGHTS AND MOMENTS

OCCUPANTS

❶ FRONT SEATS ARM 85		❷ REAR SEATS ARM 121	
Weight	Moment/100	Weight	Moment/100
120	102	120	145
130	110	130	157
140	119	140	169
150	128	150	182
160	136	160	194
170	144	170	206
180	153	180	218
190	162	190	230
200	170	200	242

USABLE FUEL

MAIN WING TANKS ARM 75		
Gallons	Weight	Moment/100
5	30	22
10	60	45
15	90	68
20	120	90
25	150	112
30	180	135
35	210	158
40	240	180
44	264	198

BAGGAGE OR 5TH SEAT OCCUPANT ARM 140

Weight	Moment/100
10	14
20	28
30	42
40	56
50	70
60	84
70	98
80	112
90	126
100	140
110	154
120	168
130	182
140	196
150	210
160	224
170	238
180	252
190	266
200	280
210	294
220	308
230	322
240	336
250	350
260	364
270	378

D AUXILIARY WING TANKS ARM 94

Gallons	Weight	Moment/100
5	30	28
10	60	56
15	90	85
19	114	107

E *OIL

Quarts	Weight	Moment/100
10	19	5

*Included in basic Empty Weight

Basic Empty Weight ~ 2015

MOM / 100 ~ 1554

MOMENT LIMITS vs WEIGHT

Moment limits are based on the following weight and center of gravity limit data (landing gear down).

WEIGHT CONDITION	FORWARD CG LIMIT	AFT CG LIMIT
2950 lb (takeoff or landing)	82.1	84.7
2525 lb	77.5	85.7
2475 lb or less	77.0	85.7

MOMENT LIMITS vs WEIGHT (Continued)

Weight	Minimum Moment 100	Maximum Moment 100
2100	1617	1800
2110	1625	1808
2120	1632	1817
2130	1640	1825
2140	1648	1834
2150	1656	1843
2160	1663	1851
2170	1671	1860
2180	1679	1868
2190	1686	1877
2200	1694	1885
2210	1702	1894
2220	1709	1903
2230	1717	1911
2240	1725	1920
2250	1733	1928
2260	1740	1937
2270	1748	1945
2280	1756	1954
2290	1763	1963
2300	1771	1971
2310	1779	1980
2320	1786	1988
2330	1794	1997
2340	1802	2005
2350	1810	2014
2360	1817	2023
2370	1825	2031
2380	1833	2040
2390	1840	2048
2400	1848	2057
2410	1856	2065
2420	1863	2074
2430	1871	2083
2440	1879	2091
2450	1887	2100
2460	1894	2108
2470	1902	2117
2480	1911	2125
2490	1921	2134
2500	1932	2143
B → 2510	1942	2151
2520	1953	2160
2530	1963	2168
2540	1974	2176
2550	1984	2184
2560	1995	2192
2570	2005	2200
2580	2016	2208
2590	2026	2216
2600	2037	2224
2610	2048	2232
2620	2058	2239
2630	2069	2247
2640	2080	2255
2650	2090	2263
2660	2101	2271
2670	2112	2279
C → 2680	2123	2287
2690	2133	2295
2700	2144	2303
2710	2155	2311
2720	2166	2319
2730	2177	2326
2740	2188	2334
2750	2199	2342
2760	2210	2350
2770	2221	2358
2780	2232	2366
D → 2790	2243	2374
2800	2254	2381
2810	2265	2389
2820	2276	2397
2830	2287	2405
2840	2298	2413
2850	2309	2421
2860	2320	2428
2870	2332	2436
2880	2343	2444
E → 2890	2354	2452
2900	2365	2460
2910	2377	2468
2920	2388	2475
2930	2399	2483
2940	2411	2491
A → 2950	2422	2499

Now that we understand how to determine the CG from weights and moments, let's try and work a weight and balance problem from an actual airplane. Figures 12 and 13 (previous page) provide you with information that might come from a typical airplane. As you'll soon see, doing a real weight and balance is easier than it looks.

Figure 12 provides us with the moments for the variable weights of occupants, usable fuel, baggage, auxiliary fuel and oil (oil for this airplane is included in the basic empty weight). The bottom right hand corner (Block G) informs us about the forward and aft CG limits for variable weight conditions. What's nice about this chart is that, in many instances, it's often not necessary to do multiplication to find the moments. For example, assume you wanted to find the moment of the front seat occupants weighing 320 pounds (that's two people, not one big guy!).

Look in the weight column in Block A and find the moments for any weight combinations that add up to 320. For instance, 120 pounds produces a moment of 102 and 200 pounds produces a moment of 170. Adding these together gives you a moment of 272.

Notice that Block A shows that all the moments are divided by 100. Why? This is known as a reduction factor and it makes large moments easier to work with. Since the front seat arm is 85 (you can assume the distance is in inches), multiplying 85 inches × 320 pounds=27,200 lb-in of moment. When divided by a reduction factor of 100 we still arrive at a moment of 272 lb-in (27,200/100 = 272).

Of course, when you're done computing all the moments, you'll want to multiply the total moments by 100 to be able to compute the actual CG. (Or you can move the decimal two places to the right—it's the same thing).

Suppose the weights are between the values shown in the columns, such as 295 pounds. There is no moment value listed for 295 pounds The best way to handle this is do the math and simply multiply the weight times the arm for that location to get the moment (remember the reduction factor of 100).

The same procedure for finding moments is used for rear seats (Block A), usable fuel (Block B), baggage or 5th seat occupant (Block C), auxiliary wing tank fuel (Block D) and oil (Block E). Remember, the weight of the oil and its moment are included in this airplane's basic empty weight. Therefore, don't include oil in this weight and balance problem.

Block F provides you with the basic empty weight and its moment divided by the reduction factor of 100. Block G informs you of the forward and aft CG limits for variable weight conditions.

To avoid becoming complacent during the preflight, try doing your walkaround opposite to the direction in which you normally do it..

OK, let's try it.

Basic Weight and Balance: Problem No. 1 – Using the weight and balance information in Figures 12 and 13, and the loading information given below, determine if the airplane's weight and balance is within safe limits.

Front seat occupants .... 320 pounds

Rear seat occupants .... 295 pounds

Fuel (main wing tanks) ...... 44 gallons

Baggage .... 56 pounds

Before you start, let's remember the big picture here. What you're going to do is find the tilting force produced by all the individual weights to be carried on the airplane by using the Useful Load Weights and Moments chart (Figure 12). Then you'll add all these weights together and add all the moments together. Take these two sums over to the Moment Limits vs. Weight chart (Figure 13). This chart lets you determine if the combination of total weight and total moments allows the airplane to operate within its allowable CG limits.

Now don't worry. I'm going to walk you through this first problem in great detail as shown in Figure 14. Not only will I show you how to proceed, step-by-step, but I'll give you a visual representation of what the loaded airplane would look like in Figure 15. OK, are you ready? Now go to Figure 14 and follow each step in the solution of this problem. Return here when you're done.

Now that wasn't too bad was it? I'm going to show you how to make solving this type of problem even easier. But first, here are a few additional points to remember when doing this type of problem.

To compute the moment of the front seat occupants you need to refer to Figure 12 (Block A, section #1) and find the moments for 200 pounds and 120 pounds, then add these together. You do this because there is no posted moment for 320 pounds. The weight of the baggage isn't listed in Figure 12 (Block C). You can find its moment, however, by multiplying the arm (140) by 56 pounds. When preparing to divide the total moments by the total weights, don't forget to move the decimal of the total moments over two places to the right to compensate for the reduction factor of 100.

The result of Figure 14 (step #9) shows that at a weight of 2,950 pounds we have a CG of 83.4 inches. Figure 12 (Block G) indicates that we are right at the maximum gross weight of the airplane for takeoff or landing. At a weight of 2,950 pounds our CG of 83.4 inches falls within the posted forward and aft limits. We are legal and safe to fly. Figure 15 shows a pictorial representation of how this airplane is loaded.

What if our totaled weights were different than the limits shown in Figure 12 (Block G)? Fortunately, the Pilot's Operating Handbook or the plane's weight and balance papers come with a moment-limit vs. weight chart to help determine if the airplane is within weight and balance limits. Figure 13 shows such a chart. This

Fig. 14

WEIGHT AND BALANCE PROBLEM NO. 1

Determine if the airplane's weight and balance are within safe limits. (Use Figures 12 and 13.)

Pilot & front seat occupants.......	320 lb
Rear seat occupants..................	295 lb
Fuel (6 lb/gal)............................	44 gallons
Baggage...................................	56 lb

These are the numbers you should have computed.

	Weight	X Arm	= Moment/100
E - Empty weight (basic)..................	2,015 lb	..........in	1,554.0
P - Pilot & front seat occupants.......	320 lb	85 in	272.0
R - Rear seat occupants..................	295 lb	121 in	357.0
F - Fuel (6 lb/gal)............................	264 lb	75 in	198.0
B - Baggage....................................	56 lb	140 in	78.4
O - Oil (included in basic empty weight)..	..........lb	..........in	....
Totals	2,950 lb		2,459.4 lb-in / 100

Step 1: See Figure 12(F) to find the basic empty weight and its moment.

Step 2: See Figure 12(A1) to find the moment for 120 lb and 200 lb of front seat occupants.

Step 3: See Figure 12(A2). Since the exact weight of our rear seat occupants doesn't appear in the table, we must multiply their weights times the arm of the rear seat (121"). This gives the moments of the rear seat occupants.

Step 4: See Figure 12(B) to find the moment for 44 gal. of fuel (note: don't forget to use the listed weight of the fuel (264 lb). (i.e., Don't list the gal. in the weight column.)

Step 5: See Figure 12(C) to find the moment for the baggage. Since no moment is listed for 56 lb, multiply this times the arm of 140" & divide by 100 to obtain the moment of the baggage.

Step 6: See Figure 12(E) The note says that oil is included in the basic empty weight, so we don't need to do anything here.

Step 7: Add the total weight and the total moments. You don't need to add the total arms since this is meaningless.

Step 8: Move the decimal place of the total moments two digits to the right to correct for the reduction factor of moment/100.

Divide the total moments by the total weight

$$\text{Arm or CG} = \frac{\text{total moments } 2{,}459.4\ (100)}{\text{total weight}} = \frac{245{,}940 \text{ lb-in}}{2{,}950 \text{ lb}}$$

Arm of CG = 83.4 inches aft of the datum line

Step 9: Compute the CG by dividing the total moments by the total weight.

Step 10: Determine if the CG and weight fall within acceptable limits by looking at Figure 12 (G).

chart makes the computations easier since it allows you to determine proper loading without having to divide the total moments by the total weights. In other words, you compare total weight with the total moment to determine if the airplane is within proper CG limits. In this problem, the total moments was 2,459.4 (moment/100) and the total weights was 2,950 pounds. Compare the weight against the minimum and maximum moment limit (Figure 13, position A) and you'll see that we fall within acceptable limits for flight.

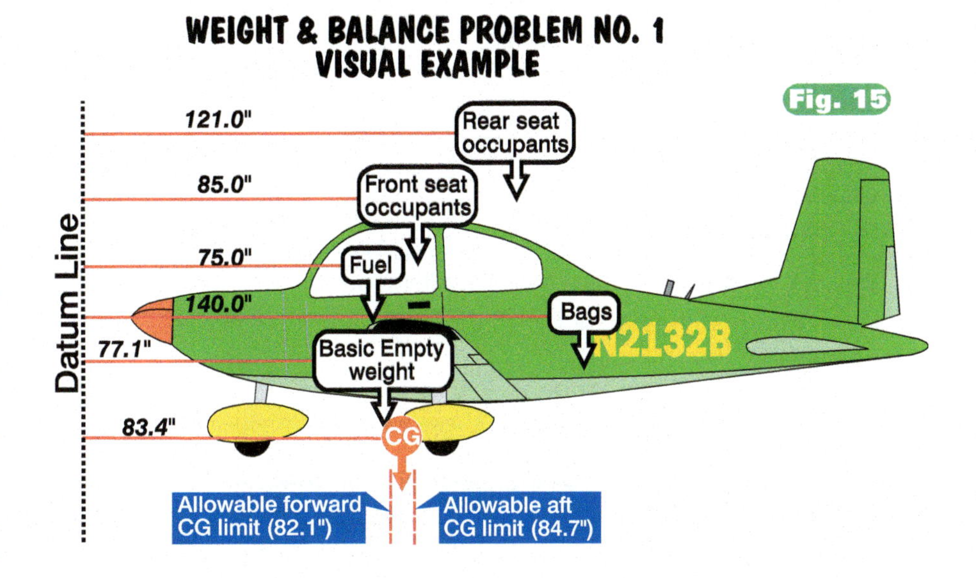

You may be wondering, "How do I know what items to include in the weight and balance calculations?" That's an excellent question. The following letter sequence provides you with an easy way to remember the items to include in a weight and balance calculation: EPRFBO. This stands for Every Pilot Regrets Flying Barely Overweight. (E) is for empty weight, (P) for pilot and front passenger, (R) for rear seat passengers, (F) for fuel, (B) for baggage and (O) for oil (if not included in the basic empty weight). When given a weight and balance problem to solve, simply list these letters

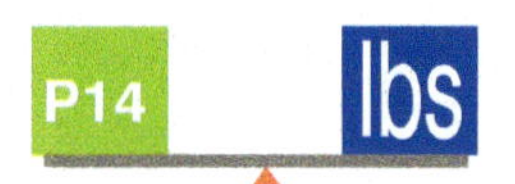

Fig. 16

WEIGHT AND BALANCE FORMAT

	Weight	X Arm	= Moment/100
E - Empty weight (basic).................	lb	in	
P - Pilot & front seat occupants.......	lb	in	
R - Rear seat occupants..................	lb	in	
F - Fuel (6 lb/gal)............................	lb	in	
B - Baggage....................................	lb	in	
O - Oil (7.5 lb/gal)...........................	lb	in	
Totals			lb-in / 100

A wise man says, "A pilot should always stay three mistakes above the ground.

vertically and write W × A=M (Weight × Arm=Moment) equation across the top of the page as shown in Figure 16. Then proceed to fill in the appropriate weights and moments.

Basic Weight and Balance: Problem No. 2 – OK, let's try a problem similar to the previous one. Take a piece of paper and draw the acronym EPRFBO on the left hand side and W × A=M across the top. Use the loading information below and Figures 12 and 13 to determine if the weight and balance is within safe limits:

Front seat occupants .... 415 pounds

Rear seat occupants 110

Fuel, main and aux tanks .... 63 gallons (both tanks full)

Baggage .... 32 pounds

Figure 17 shows the numbers you should have derived.

Consulting Block G in Figure 12 we see that the airplane's weight is within limits but the CG of 81.0 inches is 1.1 inches forward of the allowable limit. We can come to the same conclusion referring to Figure 13, position A. The moments don't fall within the allowable minimum and maximum shown on the chart. For the airplane to be legal for flight we'd need to increase the total moment. In other words, we'd need to move some weight rearward (we can't add more weight because we're already at the airplane's maximum weight limit of 2,950 pounds.) We might solve the problem by rearranging some of the passengers or moving some baggage.

There are formulas for figuring out how much weight to move and what distance to move it. They are, however, beyond the scope of this book. Personally, I would recommend just taking a guess at how much movement or reduction in weight is necessary to put the airplane within allowable CG limits, then working another problem to see if the results are successful. This doesn't take long at all when you are changing only one or two variables.

Hey, you're doing well. Once you understand the basics, the rest of these weight and balance problems should be fairly easy. There is, however, no better way to learn to do these problems than to jump in and give them a try. So, let's move onto something known as a weight change problem.

WEIGHT AND BALANCE PROBLEM NO. 2

Determine if the airplane's weight and balance are within safe limits. (Use Figures 12 and 13.)

Pilot & front seat occupants.......	415 lb
Rear seat occupants.................	110 lb
Fuel (main & aux tanks both full)	63 gallons
Baggage..................................	32 lb

Fig. 17

These are the numbers you should have computed.

	Weight	X Arm	= Moment/100
E - Empty weight (basic).................	2,015 lb	..........in	1,554.0
P - Pilot & front seat occupants.......	415 lb	85 in	352.8
R - Rear seat occupants..................	110 lb	121 in	133.1
F - Fuel (main) (44 gal. x 6 lb/gal)...	264 lb	75 in	198.0
(aux) (19 gal. x 6 lb/gal)...	114 lb	94 in	107.0
B - Baggage..................................	32 lb	140 in	44.8
O - Oil (included in basic empty weight)..	..........lb	..........in	....
Totals	2,950 lb		2,389.7 lb-in / 100

Divide the total moments by the total weights

$$\text{Arm or CG} = \frac{\text{total moments}}{\text{total weights}} \quad 2{,}389.7\,(100) = \frac{238{,}970 \text{ lb-in}}{2{,}950 \text{ lb}}$$

Arm of CG = 81.0 inches aft of the datum line

WEIGHT CHANGE PROBLEM NO. 3

Determine if the airplane's weight and balance are within safe limits. (Use Figures 12 and 13.)

Step 1. What is the weight change?	
Original weight of airplane..................	2,690 lb
Departing passenger..........................	180 lb
New weight.......................................	2,510 lb

Step 2. How does the total moment change?	Weight	X Arm	= Moment/100
Original weight.......................	2,690 lb		2,260.0
Passenger exiting front..........	-180 lb	85 in	-153.0
Passenger exiting rear...........	-204 lb	121 in	-246.8
Passenger into front..............	+204 lb	85 in	+173.4
New weight..........................	2,510 lb		
New moment........................			2,033.6

Step 3. What is the new CG?
Divide the total moments by the total weights to find the new CG.
Total moments x 100 = 203,360 lb-in
Total weights 2,510 lb
New CG = 81" (position B on Figure 13)

Step 4. Answer the original question.
The original question asked what effect does this weight shift and change have on the original CG? To find out you need to know what the original CG was. Since you were given the total moments and weights before shifting, this is easy to compute:
Total original moments..2,260 x 100 = 226,000 lb-in
total original weight..........................= 2,690 lb
Original CG ....= 84"
You can see that the CG moved 3 inches (84-81=3) toward the datum line.

Weight Change: Problem No. 3 – Upon landing, the front seat passenger (180 pounds) departs the airplane (after it comes to a stop, fortunately). A rear passenger (204 pounds) moves to the front passenger position. What effect does this have on the CG if the airplane weighed 2,690 pounds and the moment/100 was 2,260 just prior the passenger transfer?

We'll use the same weight and balance information given in Figure 12 and 13 to solve this problem. Before you proceed, I want you to think about the problem in a step-by-step way as follows:

Step 1. To determine the final CG, you need to know the airplane's total weight and total moment. Ask yourself how much the total weight of the airplane changes.

Step 2. If any weight moves on the airplane (but doesn't exit or enter the airplane), its moment changes. In other words, the weight's moment before moving must be subtracted from the total moment. Then its new moment, based on its new location, must be added to the total moment once again.

Fig. 18

Step 3. Divide the total moment by the total weight to obtain the new CG.

Step 4. Go back to the original problem and make sure you answer the question that was asked.

Figure 18 shows how to proceed with the problem using the steps listed above. Go back and review the other problems to get a good feel for how this one was solved.

I do hope you believe me when I say that once you practice a few more problems, weight and balance is going to be a snap. Problem No. 3 dealt with weight change. Every time you fly you'll need to consider similar problems since the consumption of fuel changes and shifts the airplane's CG. Problem No. 4 deals with a changing CG based on the burning of fuel.

STEP RIGHT UP, GUESS Y'ER WEIGHT

I flew my airplane to an airshow. As in the past, I removed the operating handbook, which included the weight and balance data. I didn't want the book to be damaged by the maneuvers required in the aerobatic flight. Also, I took along a friend who weighed 240 lb. Upon arriving, an inspector immediately approached me wanting to know how much my passenger weighed. He thought I was over gross and out of CG. He asked me to do a weight and balance computation, to which I responded by telling him I didn't have the information in the airplane. Realizing my problem, I immediately grounded the airplane and didn't fly in the airshow. Later, I did a weight and balance computation and found the airplane had been 75 lb. over gross for operations in the normal category, but within CG limits. I believe it would be helpful to clarify the importance of having the proper paperwork in all airplanes.

ASRS Report

Fuel Burn Weight and Balance: Problem No. 4 – What effect does a 35 gallon fuel burn (main tanks) have on the weight and balance if the airplane weighed 2,890 pounds and the moment/100 was 2,452 at takeoff?

Refer to the weight and balance information in Figures 12 and 13 to solve this problem. Keep in mind that the same principles used in problem No. 3 are used in solving this problem. Fuel burn is nothing more than a weight and moment change problem. In this instance, weight (fuel) is leaving the airplane; therefore, the moment is also changing.

Figure 19 (below) shows how to proceed with the problem.

It's important to compute the CG change for fuel consumption. As is evident from this problem, the CG shifted aft as fuel was consumed. It may be necessary to shift weight in flight or prior to takeoff to compensate for this. Expect to have a problem like this when the CG, prior to takeoff, is near the aft or forward limit.

In the following problem, we have an airplane that's out of its safe CG limits and can't take off. The weight is within limits, but the CG is forward of the allowable limit. This doesn't mean you can't fly! All you usually need do is move some of the weight around to place the CG within its acceptable limits. Knowing how to calculate this is a valuable skill to have.

FUEL BURN PROBLEM NO. 4

Fig. 19

Determine if the airplane's weight and balance are within safe limits. (Use Figures 12 and 13.)

Step 1. What is the weight change?
35 gallons of fuel (6 lb/gal) 6 x 35 = 210 lb weight loss.

Step 2. How does the total moment change?
Using Figure 12, block B, 210 lb of fuel located at an arm of 75" equals a moment change of -158 lb-in/100. Remember, the weight is decreasing, therefore its moment is also decreasing.

Step 3. What is the new CG?

	Weight	Moment/100
Original weight	2,890 lb	2,452.0
Final weight loss	-210 lb	-158.0
New weight	2,680 lb	
New moment		2,294.0

New CG equals: Total moments 229,400 lb-in / Total weight 2,680 lb

New CG position = 85.6"

Step 4. Answer the original question.
The original question asked about the effect a 35 gallon fuel burn has on the CG. Using Figure 13, position C, we can see that at a weight of 2,680 lb, our new moment of 2,294.0 lb-in/100 is clearly beyond the limit for this weight. Even though our weight has been reduced by 210 lb, our CG is aft of limits (if the moment is greater than the maximum limit, the CG must also be aft of limits).

WEIGHT SHIFT PROBLEM NO. 5

Fig. 20

With the airplane loaded as follows, what action must be taken to place the airplane within the proper CG limits (Use Figures 12 and 13.)

Front seat occupants	411 lb
Rear seat occupants	100 lb
Main wing tanks	44 gallons

Step 1. Determine the present CG condition.

	Weight	X Arm	= Moment/100
E - Empty weight (basic)	2,015 lb	.....in	1,554.0
P - Pilot & front seat occupants	411 lb	85 in	349.4
R - Rear seat occupants	100 lb	121 in	121.0
F - Fuel (main) (44 gal.x 6 lb-gal)	264 lb	75 in	198.0
B - Baggage	.........lb	.....in	....
O - Oil (included in basic empty weight)	.........lb	.....in	....
Totals	2,790 lb		2,222.4 lb-in/100

Step 2. Shift or add weight to get CG back in limits.
Using the moment limit vs. weight chart in Figure 13 (position D) we can see that the airplane is out of its CG limits. Let's add 100 lb of weight to the baggage compartment to obtain a normal CG condition.

Step 3. Compute the new CG with the added weight.

	Weight	X Arm	= Moment/100
Original weight	2,790 lb		2,222.4
Added weight	+100 lb	140 in	+140.0
New totals	2,890 lb		2,362.4

Step 4. Determine if new CG is within limits.
Using Figure 13 (position E), we see that the CG is within allowable limits.

Weight Shift: Problem No. 5 – With the airplane loaded as follows, what action must be taken to place the airplane within the proper weight and balance limits? Refer to the weight and balance information in Figures 12 and 13 to solve this problem.

Front seat occupants .... 411 pounds
Rear seat occupants .... 100 pounds
Main wing tanks .... 44 gallons

Figure 20 shows how to proceed with this problem.

Using the moment limits vs. weight chart in Figure 13 (see position D), the airplane is determined to be out of CG limits. In other words, our moment is smaller than the minimum moment required for flight. This means there isn't enough weight far enough aft of the datum to get the airplane within CG limits. How can we solve this type of problem?

You might think about transferring some fuel from the main tanks to the auxiliary fuel tanks but that won't help much. Looking closely at the difference in moments produced by the main and aux tanks for similar weights, there isn't much difference. Even if enough fuel was transferred to get the airplane within CG limits prior to takeoff, what's going to happen as fuel is used? Yes, the airplane will lose weight and the resulting moment will still be too small.

The best thing to do when you have a forward CG is to try and move weight aft, like a passenger (of course, only move them aft if there is a seat in back. Otherwise they might be reluctant to go). If that's not possible, and the airplane isn't near gross weight, add some weight to the baggage compartment. Let's try adding 100 pounds of weight to the baggage compartment and see if that brings us within CG limits. Step 3 in Figure 20 shows the results of adding this weight.

Looking at Figure 13, position E, we now see that the CG is within allowable limits. I'd still be cautious and determine what the CG will be as I burn off fuel. That's why I'd do another weight and balance problem based on the amount of fuel I expect to consume during my trip (see previous problem No. 4).

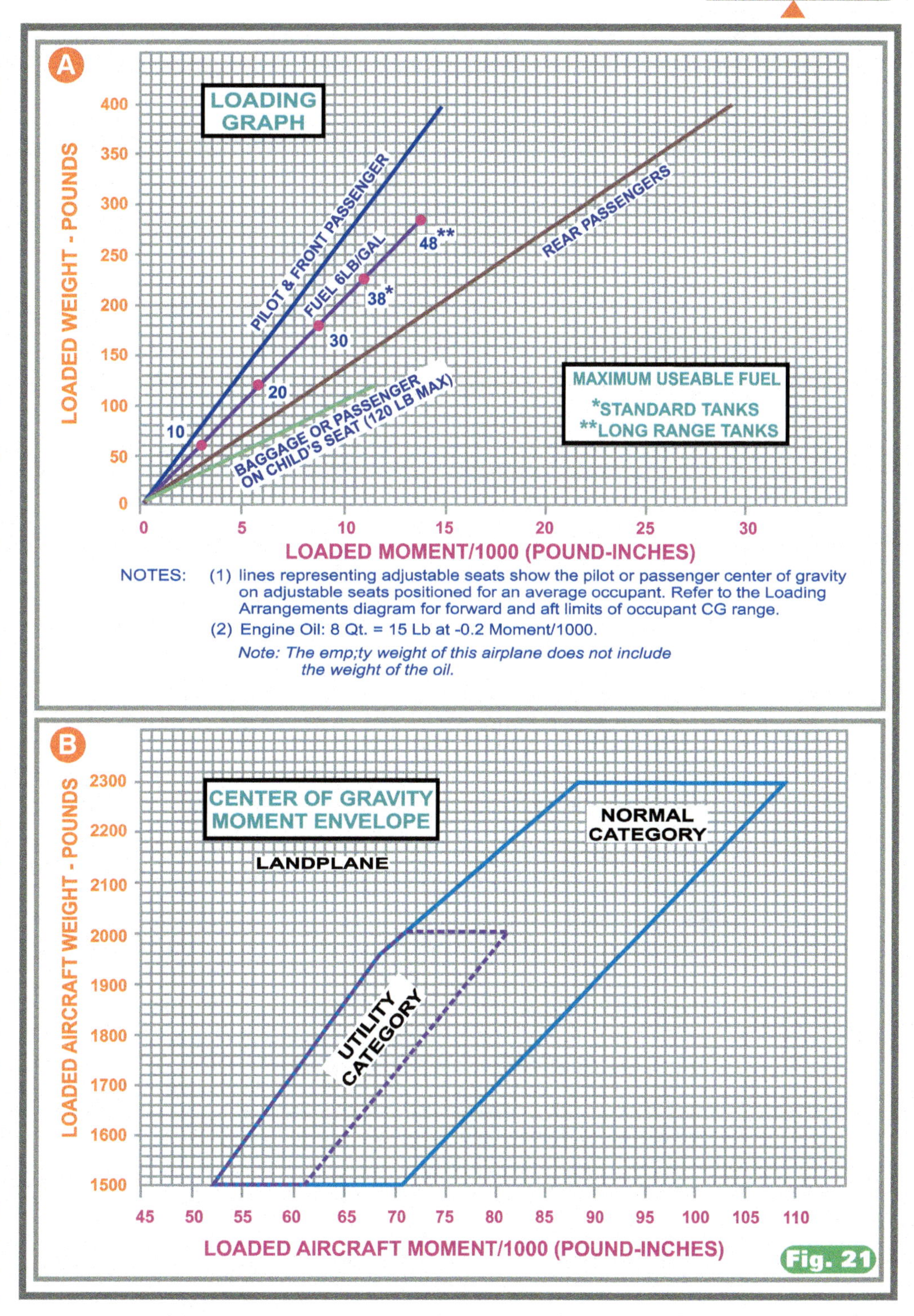

A Different Type Of Weight and Balance Chart

Another type of weight and balance chart exists for airplanes. In fact, for most of the smaller airplanes we fly, this "math-free" type of presentation, shown in Figures 21 A and B, is quite common. What makes this configuration so interesting is that there is no multiplication used in finding moments. The loading graph in Figure 21A has weights along the vertical axis and moments/1000 along the horizontal axis. A reduction factor of 1000 is used for the moments, but, as you'll see, you don't have to worry about using a reduction factor when using this format. To find the moments for specific weights, simply proceed horizontally along the weight lines. When reaching the desired diagonal line (for pilot, passenger, fuel or baggage) drop straight down to find the moments. That's easy!

When the total moments and weights are tallied, simply proceed to the center of gravity/moment envelope shown in Figure 21B. Compare weights and moments to see if they fall within the envelope. Notice that this airplane has both a normal and utility category envelope. Depending on the airplane, the CG must fall within the utility CG envelope for certain flight operations to be performed (such as spins). Using this simple format, you'll be able to do weight and balance problems while using only 50cc's of your turbocharged 1400cc brain.

Weight and Balance: Problem No. 6 – Using the airplane loading information shown in Figure 22A, determine if the airplane is within its proper CG limits. Figure 22B shows the solution for this problem. Figures 23A and 23B show the solution on the loading graph and CG/moment envelope.

This is a relatively straightforward weight and balance problem. Nothing tricky here. You should use caution, however, when calibrating moments from weights in Figure 21A. It's very easy to move up or down a line and end up with an incorrect moment. Watch the calibration for the individual chart lines. In Figure 21A, notice that each line along the weight (vertical) scale is calibrated in tens of pounds. Each line along the moment (horizontal) scale is calibrated in values of one-half.

WEIGHT AND BALANCE PROBLEM NO. 6

Using the loading graph in Figure 21A and the center of gravity envelope in Figure 21B, determine if the airplane is within the proper CG limits based on the information below.

Fig. 22A

	Weight	X Arm	= Moment/1000
E - Empty weight	1,350 lb	..........in	51.5
P - Pilot & front seat occupants	310 lb	..........in	....
R - Rear seat occupants..................	96 lb	..........in	....
F - Fuel (38 gallons)	..........lb	..........in	....
B - Baggage	..........lb	..........in	....
O - Oil (8 quarts)	..........lb	..........in	-0.2

SOLUTION TO PROBLEM NO. 6

Step 1. Using the loading graph in Figure 21A, find the individual moments for the weights listed below. Remember that the oil weighs 7.5 lb/gal. Eight quarts of oil equals two gallons or 15 lb total. The oil moment is negative, indicating that it is ahead of the datum line.

Fig. 22B

	Weight	X Arm	= Moment/1000
E - Empty weight	1,350 lb	..........in	51.5
P - Pilot & front seat occupants	310 lb	..........in	11.5
R - Rear seat occupants	96 lb	..........in	7.0
F - Fuel 38 gal. (6lb x 38 gal = 228 lb)	228 lb	..........in	11.0
B - Baggage	(no bags) lb	..........in	....
O - Oil (8 quarts)	15 lb	..........in	-0.2

Step 2. Add the totals — **Totals** **1,999 lb** — **80.8 lb-in / 1000**

Step 3. Using the center of gravity/moment envelope in Figure 21B, match the total weights on the left vertical axis against the total moments on the bottom horizontal axis. Since both values meet at a point within the envelope, the airplane is within the proper CG limits for safe flight. Figures 23A and 23B show how I calculated the moments and made the CG determination.

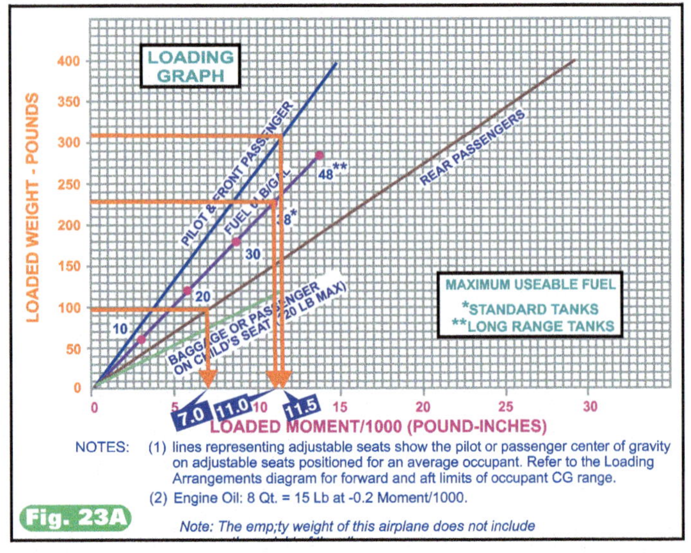

NOTES: (1) lines representing adjustable seats show the pilot or passenger center of gravity on adjustable seats positioned for an average occupant. Refer to the Loading Arrangements diagram for forward and aft limits of occupant CG range.
(2) Engine Oil: 8 Qt. = 15 Lb at -0.2 Moment/1000.

Note: The emp;ty weight of this airplane does not include the weight of the oil.

Fig. 23A

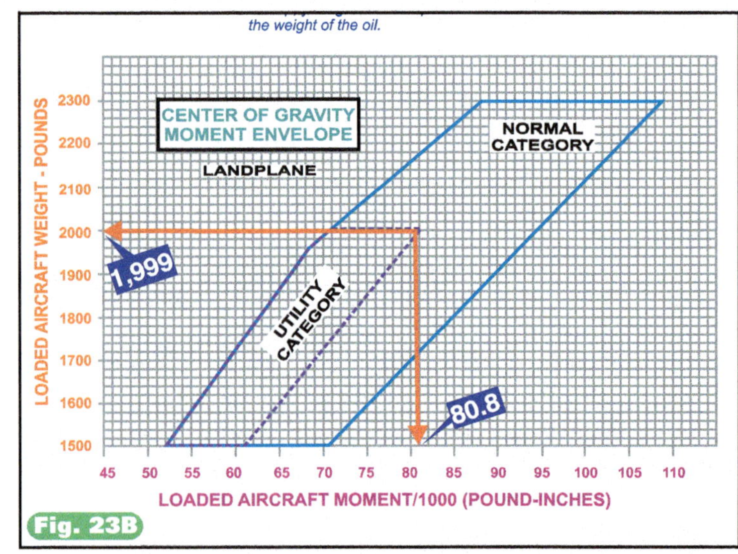

Fig. 23B

Weight and Balance: Problem No. 7 – The next problem, in Figure 24A, requires you to determine the maximum amount of baggage that can be carried in the airplane after all the other items have been loaded. Solving this problem simply requires you to find the current loaded weight of the airplane and subtract that from the maximum allowable weight. The difference is the amount of baggage (or any other item you're interested in) that can be carried onboard. After you determine the allowable weight of baggage, you must make sure that carrying this weight still keeps the airplane within its proper CG limits. Figures 24B, 25A and 25B show the solution to this problem.

WEIGHT AND BALANCE PROBLEM NO. 7

Using the loading graph in Figure 21A and the center of gravity/moment envelope shown in Figure 21B, determine the maximum amount of baggage that can be loaded aboard the airplane for the CG to remain within the center of gravity/moment envelope.

Fig. 24A

	Weight	X Arm =	Moment/1000
E - Empty weight	1,350 lb	..........in	51.5
P - Pilot & front seat occupants	250 lb	..........in	....
R - Rear seat occupants..................	400 lb	..........in	....
F - Fuel (30 gallons)	...........lb	..........in	....
B - Baggage	...........lb	..........in	....
O - Oil (8 quarts)	15 lb	..........in	-0.2

SOLUTION TO PROBLEM NO. 7

Step 1. Using the loading graph in Figure 21A, find the individual moments for the weights listed below. Figure 25A shows how I calculated the following moments.

Fig. 24B

	Weight	X Arm =	Moment/1000
E - Empty weight	1,350 lb	..........in	51.5
P - Pilot & front seat occupants	250 lb	..........in	9.3
R - Rear seat occupants	400 lb	..........in	29.3
F - Fuel 30 gal. (6lb x 30 gal = 180 lb)	180 lb	..........in	8.7
B - Baggage (this is unknown).......	? lb	..........in	?
O - Oil (8 quarts)	15 lb	..........in	-0.2
Step 2. Add the totals — **Totals**	**2,195 lb**		**98.6 lb-in / 1000**

Step 3. The airplane's maximum allowable gross weight is 2,300 lb. I determined this by looking at the upper limit of the normal category CG/moment envelope in Figure 25B. Given this information, you can determine how much baggage can be carried by subtracting the present loaded weight from the maximum allowable gross weight to obtain (2,300 - 2,195 = 105 lb).

Step 4. Add the weight of the baggage and its moment to the totals you found in step 2. (The baggage produces a moment of 10.0 in-lb as determined from Figure 25A. This gives you a total weight of 2,300 lb and a total moment of 108.6 lb-in.)

Step 5. Using the center of gravity/moment envelope in Figure 25B, you determine that the airplane is just barely within its proper CG limits (at the edge of the envelope).

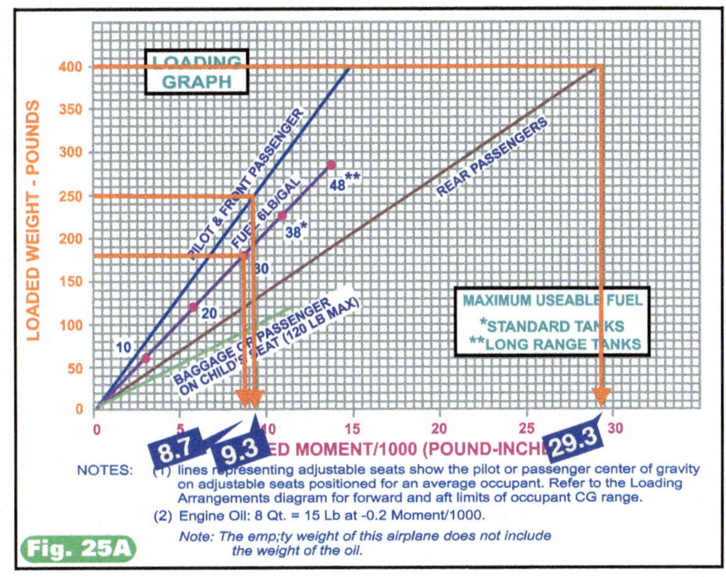

Fig. 25A

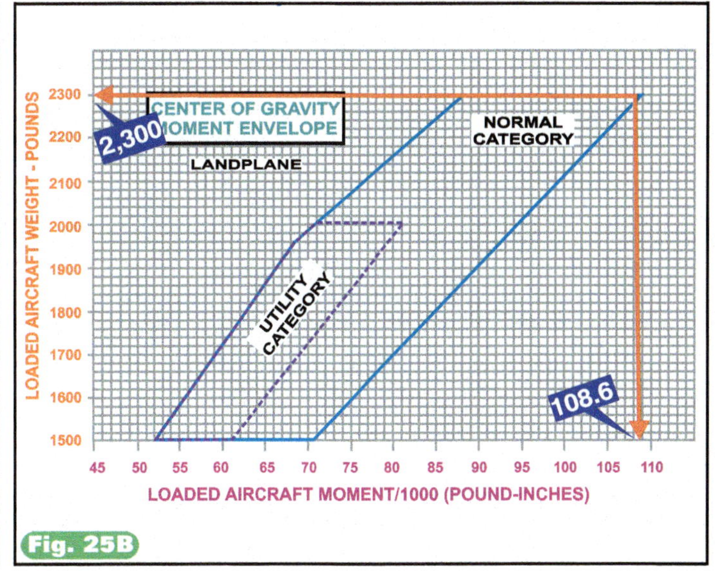

Fig. 25B

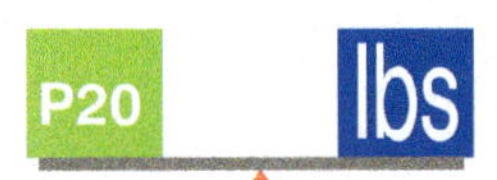

Weight and Balance: Problem No. 8 – Figure 26 is our final problem. This problem is similar to problem No. 7. Instead of finding the maximum amount of baggage that you can carry, this problem asks you to determine the maximum amount of fuel that can be carried aboard the aircraft for takeoff. It's solved in precisely the same way as problem No. 6. Solving this problem simply requires you to find the current loaded weight of the airplane without fuel and subtract that from the maximum weight allowable for that airplane. The difference is the amount of fuel that can be carried on board. After you determine the allowable weight of fuel, you must make sure that carrying this weight still keeps the airplane within its proper CG limits. Figures 26, 27A and 27B show the solution to this problem.

SOLUTION TO PROBLEM NO. 8

Step 1. Using the loading graph in Figures 21A and B, you determine the individual moments for the weights listed to the right (except for the fuel which is our unknown). Figure 27A shows how these moments were derived.

Fig. 26

	Weight	X Arm	= Moment/1000
E - Empty weight	1,350 lb	..........in	51.5
P - Pilot & front seat occupants	340 lb	..........in	12.6
R - Rear seat occupants	310 lb	..........in	22.6
F - Fuel 38 gal. (6lb x 38 gal = 228 lb)	? lb	..........in	?
B - Baggage	45 lb	..........in	4.2
O - Oil (8 quarts)	15 lb	..........in	-0.2
Totals	2,060 lb		90.7 lb-in/1000

Step 2. Add the totals

Step 3. Using the upper limit of the center of gravity/moment envelope in Figure 27B, we determine that our maximum allowable gross weight is 2,300 lb. Subtracting 2,060 lb from 2,300 lb allows us to carry 240 lb of fuel. According to Figure 27A, this produces a moment of 11.5 lb-in.

Step 4. Adding the fuel weight and its moment to the totals in step 2 gives us a new total weight of 2,300 lb and a new total moment of 102.2 lb-in.

Step 5. Using the center of gravity/moment envelope shown in Figure 27B, we determine that the center of gravity is within proper limits for safe flight.

Step 6. Another method of determining if the airplane is within the proper CG limit is to use the *Center of Gravity Limits* chart found in some Airplane Flight Manuals. It's easy to use. First, calculate the airplane's center of gravity by dividing the total moments by the total weights. Multiply 102.2 lb-in x 1000 = 102200 lb-in and divide this by 2,300 lb, which gives a CG of 44.43 inches aft of datum (remember, moments in this example were divided by a reduction factor of 1000 and must be multiplied by that same value to get the actual moment). By matching the total weight to the CG location in Figure 27C, you see that the airplane falls within the allowable CG limits. I show the *Center of Gravity Limits* chart because it's another popular means of computing weight and balance and you're sure to see it in a manual someday.

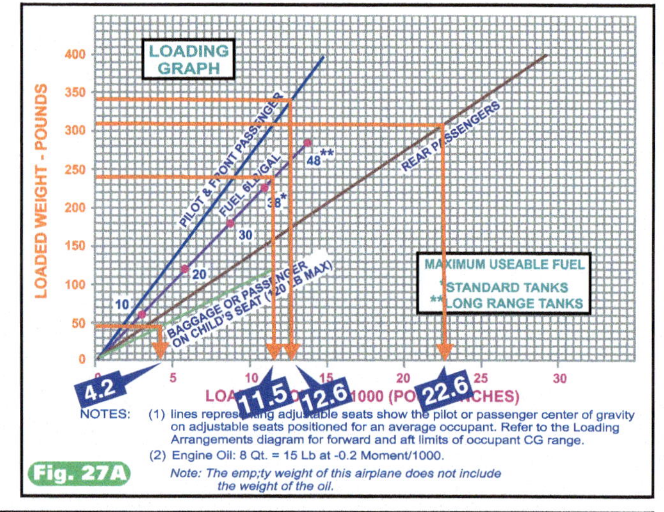

Fig. 27A

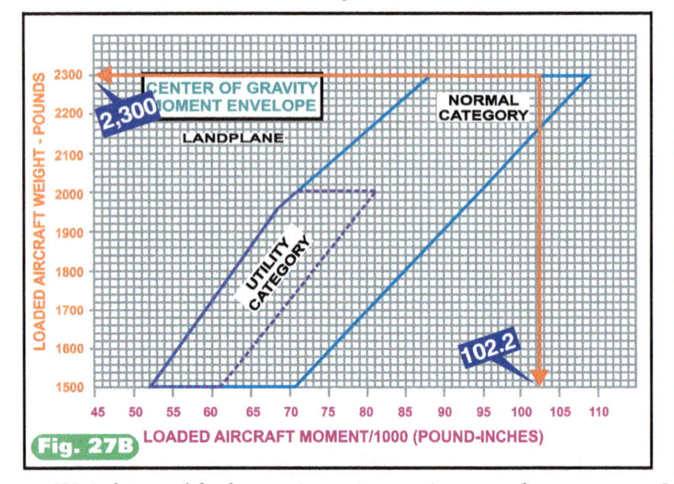

Fig. 27B

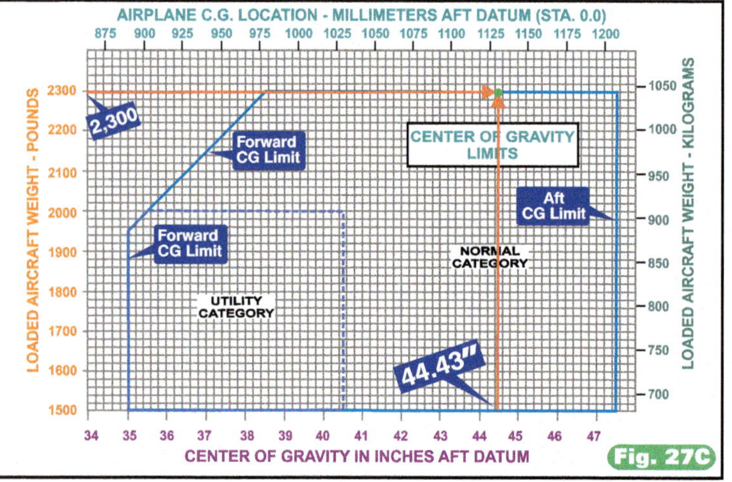

Fig. 27C

Weight and balance is quite serious and necessary for safety. With modern day, handheld calculators, you should be able to do weight and balance problems for your airplane in seconds. Onto our last chapter: Pilot Potpourri.

Empty Weight Data	Empty Weight (pounds)	Empty Weight Moment (/100)
*Oil is included in empty weight		
Certificated Weight	2,110	1,652

Fuel — ARM 75 inches

Gallons	Weight (pounds)	Moment (in-lb)	Gallons	Weight (pounds)	Moment (in-lb)
5	30	23	45	270	203
10	60	45	49	294	221
15	90	68	55	330	248
20	120	90	60	360	270
25	150	113	65	390	293
30	180	135	70	420	315
35	210	158	75	450	338
40	240	180	80	480	360

Occupants

Front seats ARM 85 inches		Rear seats	Fwd Position ARM 111 inches	Alt Position ARM 136 inches
Weight (pounds)	Moment (in-lb)	Weight (pounds)	Moment (in-lb)	Moment (in-lb)
120	102	120	133	163
130	111	130	144	177
140	119	140	155	190
150	128	150	167	204
160	136	160	178	218
170	145	170	189	231
180	153	180	200	245
190	162	190	211	258
200	170	200	222	273

Baggage — ARM 150

Weight (pounds)	Moment (in-lb)
10	15
20	30
30	45
40	60
50	75
60	90
70	105
80	120
90	135
100	150
110	165
120	180
130	195
140	210
150	225
160	240
170	255
180	270
190	285
200	300
210	315
220	330
230	345
240	360
250	375
260	390
270	405

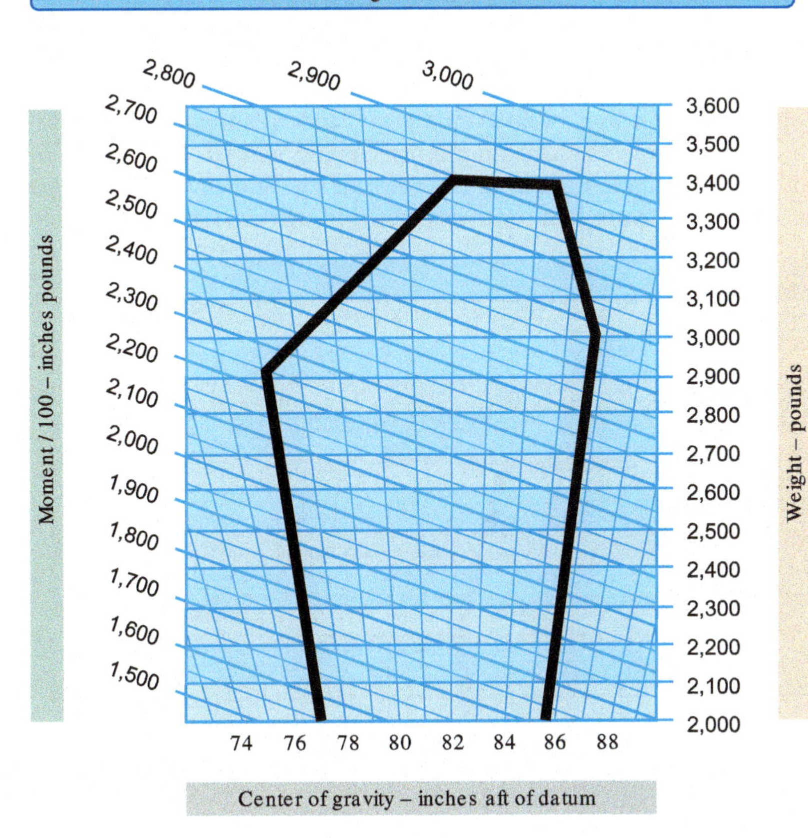

NOTE: All moments are equal to

$$\frac{\text{weight} \times \text{arm}}{100}$$

Fig. 28A

Weight and Balance: Problem No. 9 – Another type of weight and balance envelope allows you to match the airplane's total weights with total moments and easily evaluate the airplane's center of gravity condition (Figure 28A). Assume the airplane is loaded as shown in Figure 28B. Determine the weight and balance condition of this airplane.

PROBLEM NO. 9	Weight	X Arm	= Moment/100
E - Empty weight	2,110 lb	..........in	1,652
P - Pilot & copilot	326 lb	..........in	?
R - Rear seat occupants	.... lb	..........in	?
Fwd position	120 lb	..........in	?
Aft position	137 lb	..........in	?
F - Fuel 70 gal. (6lb x 70 gal = 420 lb)	420 lb	..........in	?
B - Baggage	40 lb	..........in	?
O - Oil included in empty weight	....	..........in	

Fig. 28B

SOLUTION TO PROBLEM NO. 9	Weight	X Arm	= Moment/100
E - Empty weight	2,110 lb	..........in	1,652
P - Pilot & copilot	326 lb	85 in	277.1
R - Rear seat occupants	....	....	....
Fwd position	120 lb	111 in	133
Aft position	137 lb	136 in	186.32
F - Fuel 70 gal. (6lb x 70 gal = 420 lb)	420 lb	75 in	315
B - Baggage	40 lb	150 in	60
O - Oil included in empty weight	....	....	
Totals	3,153 lb		2623.42 lb-in/100

Fig. 29A

You already know how to calculate the moments from the given weight condition. Sometimes individual even-interval weights are paired with their respective moments, making this calculation easier. Some weights, however, must be multiplied times their respective arms to calculate the moments. For instance, the aft-position passenger's weight is 137 pounds which doesn't have a moment-equivalent on the chart. Instead of giving this person three pounds of Hostess Cupcakes to eat before the flight to bring his weight up to 140 pounds, just multiply his weight (137 pounds) times the arm of his seating position (136 inches). This gives you a moment of 186.32 lb-inches/100. Keep in mind that the moments in this graph are in units of 1/100, not 1/1,000.

When you've calculated the total weights (3,153 pounds) and the total moments (2623.42 lb-inches/100), find their point of intersection on the chart (yellow dot, position A in Figure 29B). It's clear that this airplane's c.g. falls within the loading envelope. Since the top of the envelope represents the maximum loaded weight of the airplane (3,400 pounds), you are 247 pounds under the allowable gross weight. Following the vertical c.g. line downward proportionally, it appears that your c.g. is located 83.20 inches aft of the datum line (or divide 262,343 by 3,153 = 83.20 inches).

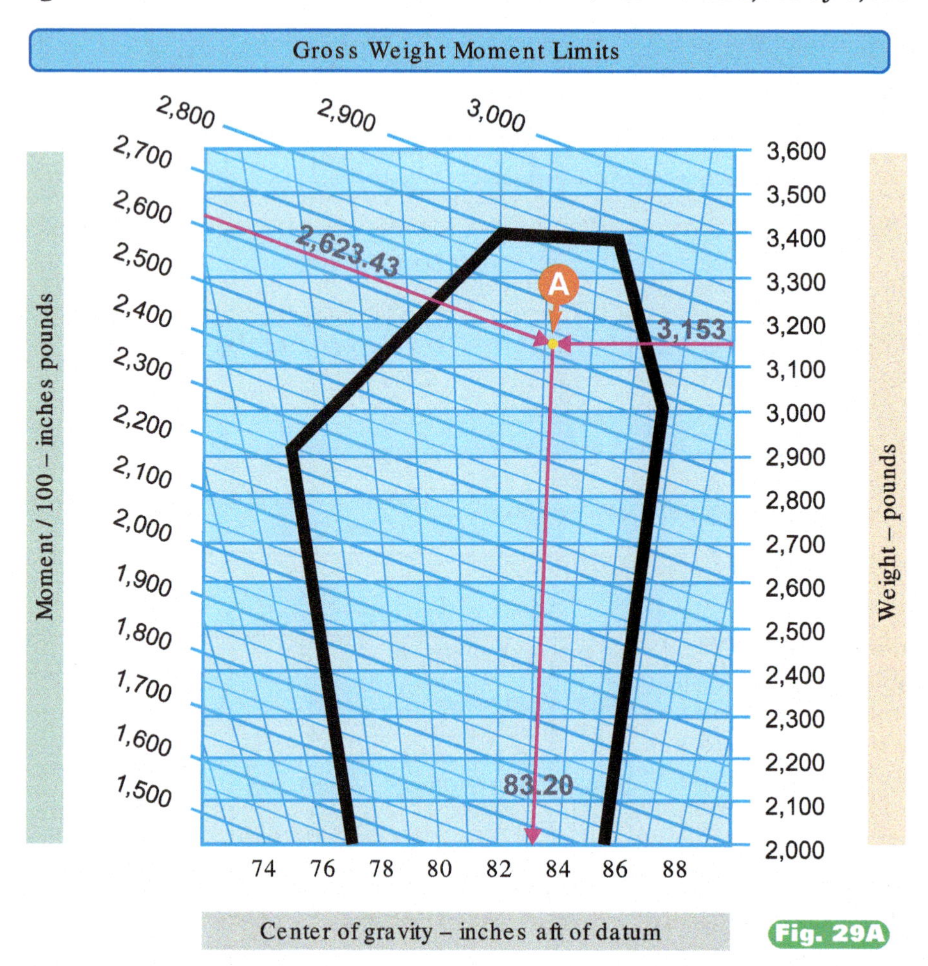

Fig. 29A

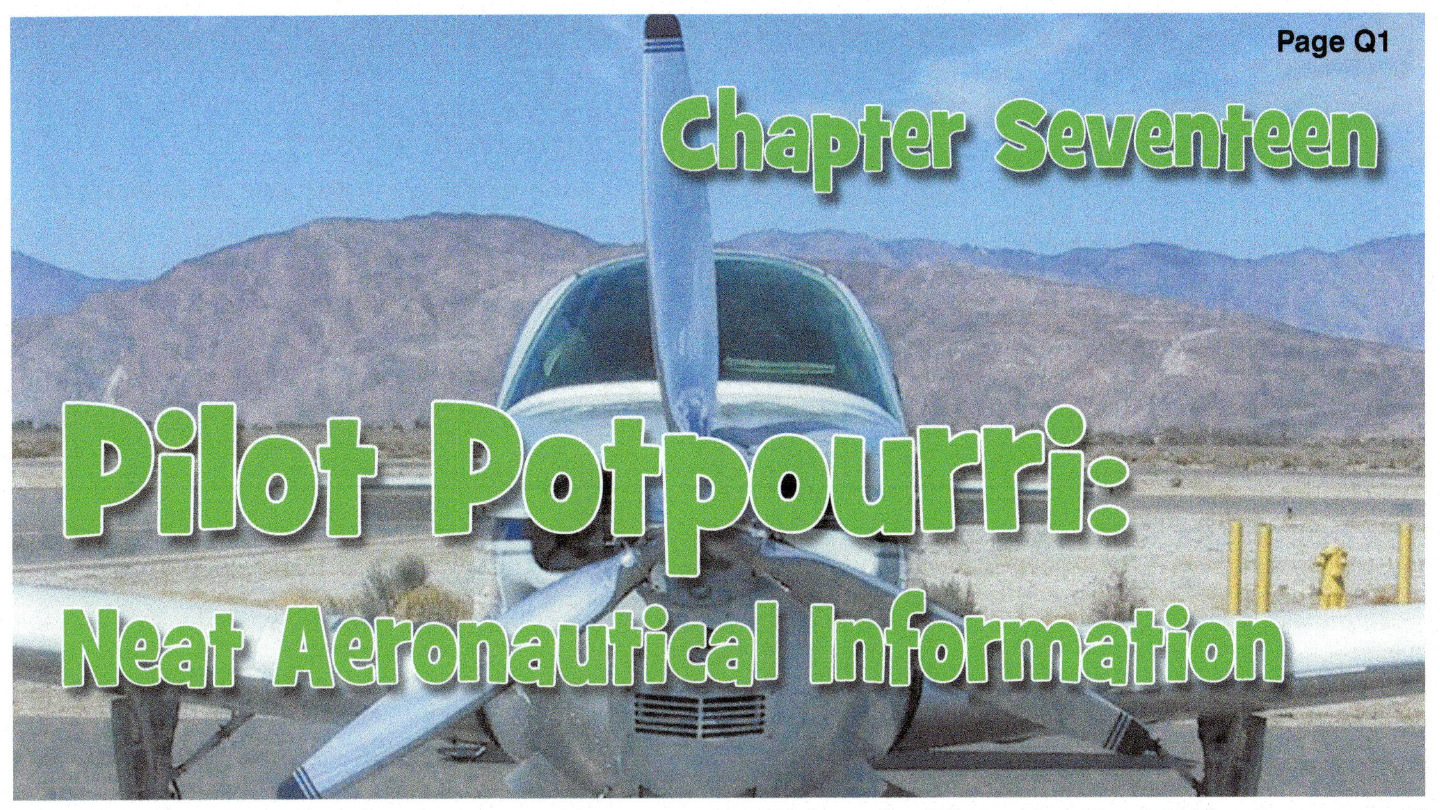

Chapter Seventeen

Pilot Potpourri: Neat Aeronautical Information

"The time has come," the Walrus said,
"To talk of many things:
Of shoes—and ships—and sealing wax
Of cabbages—and kings—
And why the sea is boiling hot—
And whether pigs have wings"

Lewis Carroll
Alice in Wonderland

Pigs do not have wings; airplanes do.

We're almost done, so now the time has come to speak of many things. In this chapter I'll present some information morsels on a variety of topics, all of which I think you will find interesting, useful, and helpful to your flying.

As you read these munchies, keep in mind that part of the fun of aviation is that the learning never stops. New ways of doing old things always emerge, as do new ways of doing new things. We're continually learning new information about human performance and equipment capability. Flight instructors like to say that earning your private pilot license is really getting a license to learn, and I think there's a lot of truth to that.

Taking AIM: The Aeronautical Information Manual

One night my wife awakened me from a sound sleep because she'd heard a noise. "Rod," she said, "I think there's someone outside."

Jostled out of REM sleep I replied, "Honey, that's where they're supposed to be—outside. If they come in here, then *we'll* go outside."

Without the full use of my faculties (brain not warmed up), the answer seemed perfectly reasonable to me. After all, everything has its place, correct? This is especially true with aviation information.

If you're ever looking for the source of aviation's wisdom, common sense and good operating principles, it has its place—in the Aeronautical Information Manual (AIM). Those who've been around aviation awhile knew the AIM under its maiden name, the *Airmen's* Information Manual. In 1995, as part of a government-wide effort to eliminate gender-specific terms wherever possible, the Airmen's Information Manual became the Aeronautical Information Manual. Fortunately, the AIM was the same.

Pilots have been known to behave strangely while under the influence of alcohol.

The AIM is both Bible and Koran for pilots. It is the official source of information on a variety of subjects, all of great importance to aviators, and of late has improved considerably in appearance. It's now replete with color illustrations. I encourage you to subscribe to this publication (now available on the internet at: *http://www.faa.gov/airports_airtraffic*).

Many of the topics and ideas in this chapter are drawn from the AIM, which also contains details about everything from the signal width of an instrument landing system to details on the right way to interact with controllers.

Reno, Nevada, September 17, 1983
RACE PILOT SURVIVES 200 MPH CRASH
By Danny Mortensen

Danny Mortensen

That was the headline on the AP wire. I had walked away from the race plane after scattering parts a thousand feet through the desert at the National Championship Air Races. My miraculous survival though is not as important as the lessons learned.

All pilots have heard of wake turbulence and associate it with large transports, but what many do not realize is that a small aircraft of the same size can put you over on your back and in the dirt. Do not follow another aircraft of any size at or below its altitude.

How would this apply to you? The traffic pattern! If you're following traffic that's close to you, make sure your ground track is offset to the right or left and slightly above its altitude. At the typical 1,000 foot pattern altitude, there is not enough room to recover from an unexpected inverted position for most student pilots.

Additionally, avoid flying while fatigued. I was up the night previous to the race frantically working to repair the airplane. This certainly didn't help my judgement. Fatigue and carelessness are dangerous combinations.

See you at the races.

Danny Mortensen is President of Airline Ground Schools, which specializes in written test preparation for the ATP and FE knowledge exams.

Fitness for Flight

All but sport pilots and those flying gliders and free balloons are required to hold a valid medical certificate (or BasicMed, if appropriate) to act as pilot in command. You do not have to be Joe Weider (a onetime muscle man whose chest looked like an inverted pyramid) to pass the medical. Certain conditions, however, are disqualifying: personality disorders manifested by overt acts (I'm referring to the serious ones, not selfishness or rudeness), alcoholism, drug dependency, epilepsy, an unexplained disturbance of consciousness and heart attack to name a few.

Fortunately, pilots not meeting the medical standards can still be qualified under special issuance provisions of the certification process. This is why it's best for student pilots to visit an Aviation Medical Examiner as soon as possible after starting flight training. If there's going to be a problem getting a medical certificate, it's better to know about it early.

One thing you should be aware of is that the FARs prohibit you from acting as PIC if you have a known medical condition or worsening of a medical condition that would make you unable to meet the standards for a medical certificate. Just because you passed the medical in May does not mean you are legal in June if you had a heart attack in between.

I had a friend who flight instructed for two months with a partial cast on his right leg. I suppose he shouldn't have been flying, but he did it anyway. He rationalized his decision by saying that he could still pass the medical. I suggested that if the doctor made him jump up and down on that leg for 20 seconds he might have jackhammered himself into the floor below. The only good thing about having a heavy cast on his right leg was that he didn't have any trouble using enough right rudder.

Illness

Be cautious if you're thinking about flying when ill. Many day-to-day illnesses will degrade your performance to unsafe levels. Judgment can be impaired, along with memory, the ability to calculate, and alertness. Beyond difficulty in filling out the Hobbs meter sheet, these problems are serious and could impair your ability to safely fly an airplane. You owe it to yourself and your passengers to be as fit as possible when you park yourself in the pilot's seat of any airplane.

Medication

If you don't think your performance can be degraded by over-the-counter medication, then you've probably never taken any. Look on the back of a box on antihistamines. It usually says, "Don't operate heavy equipment after using this drug."

Does that mean you shouldn't take the family bulldozer to the market for some milk? Implied in this statement is a warning of performance degradation. Certainly this applies to airplanes as well as to cars (and bulldozers, too). For instance, some antihistamines can make a pilot more susceptible to hypoxia (oxygen deficiency). You're likely to feel the

Fig. 1 TIME OF USEFUL CONSCIOUSNESS

Altitude	While Sitting Quietly	During Moderate Activity
40,000 Ft.	30 Sec.	18 Sec.
35,000 Ft.	45 Sec.	30 Sec.
30,000 Ft.	1 Min. & 15 Sec.	45 Sec.
25,000 Ft.	3 Min.	2 Min.
22,000 Ft.	10 Min.	5 Min.
20,000 Ft.	12 Min.	5 Min.

Physical exertion noticeably affects your time of useful consciousness when operating at higher altitudes. You may remain conscious beyond the time indicated for several minutes, but you simply won't function in a productive, useful manner.

effects of oxygen deficiency at lower altitudes. And most antihistamines cause some degree of drowsiness.

While antihistamines are an obvious no-no, many drugs have less-obvious effects that can cause a decrement in pilot performance. Quite frankly, if you're taking any medication, call your family physician to determine its side effects. A call to your Aviation Medical Examiner might be an even better idea, because AME's are often familiar with medications' effects that pose a risk to pilots, even though physicians might not think of them as side effects (or even be aware of them).

Don't even think about mixing flying and alcohol.... As little as one ounce of liquor, one bottle of beer or four ounces of wine can impair flying skills.

Alcohol: Don't Fly High

Don't even think about mixing flying and alcohol. Your judgment, behavior and performance are all easily impaired by alcohol consumption. An older mariner who had spent many years on boats decided to take flying lessons. He showed up drunk for a flight, walked over to the airplane, untied all the ropes, threw them in the air and yelled, "Cast off!" A very embarrassing situation.

As little as one ounce of liquor, one bottle of beer or four ounces of wine can impair flying skills. Keep in mind that legally you may not operate an aircraft within 8 hours of having consumed *any* alcohol. Also be aware that the effects of alcohol can linger long after eight hours. Judgment, coordination, and other items you really want to have available as a pilot can be impaired even when you don't have an obvious hangover. It's usually best to wait at least 12 to 24 hours between the bottle and the throttle, depending on the amount of alcohol consumed.

Hypoxia: Low O, Two

Hypoxia is a state of oxygen deficiency in the body sufficient to impair function of the brain and other organs. While the percentage of oxygen in the atmosphere doesn't change with an increase in altitude (it stays about 21%), the amount of pressure that forces oxygen into our body decreases, causing hypoxia. Because of this lower pressure, pilots flying at higher altitudes (50,000 feet and above) often wear pressure suits. (That's pressure suit, not power suit—i.e., double breasted black suit with red tie—which would look pretty dumb at 50,000 feet anyway.)

The effects of hypoxia occur at altitudes as low as 5,000 feet, beginning with a deterioration of night vision. The eyes require a great deal of oxygen to function properly. They are one of the first organs to experience the effects of reduced oxygen within the body. Other significant effects of hypoxia often don't occur in the normal, healthy pilot below 10,000 feet. If you smoke, however, then all bets are off. Smoking reduces the altitude at which the effects of hypoxia are experienced (it also increases the chance of your power suit catching on fire!).

Above 10,000 feet MSL, most individuals begin to experience some decrease in their judgment, memory, alertness and coordination. The ability to calculate also becomes impaired to some degree for most individuals with the increasing effects of hypoxia.

What makes hypoxia such a serious problem is that its effects are usually quite difficult to recognize, especially when they occur gradually. Headache, drowsiness, dizziness and either a sense of well being (otherwise known as euphoria) or belligerence can occur. (You sometimes get a similar feeling when studying the Federal Aviation Regulations—especially the headache and dizziness part.)

The higher the altitude, the less time it takes for hypoxia to start robbing you of your flying faculties. In fact, it's not unusual for pilot performance to seriously deteriorate within 15 minutes at 15,000 feet. Figure 1 identifies the time of useful consciousness at various altitudes without the use of supplemental oxygen.

Preventing hypoxia means avoiding higher altitudes unless you have and use supplemental oxygen. It's recommended that you avoid flying at more than 10,000 feet during the day or more than 5,000 feet at night without the use of oxygen. Understand that this recommendation is lower than those limits required by FAR 91.211. It's best to follow the conservative path.

Pilots using supplemental aviation breathing oxygen need to avoid using greasy or oily rags around oxygen systems. Petroleum-based products and oxygen don't mix. They are a very dangerous combination that could cause a fire, explosion, and def-

Four Different Forms of Hypoxia

Hypoxic hypoxia is a result of insufficient oxygen available to the body as a whole. A blocked airway and drowning are obvious examples of how the lungs can be deprived of oxygen, but the reduction in partial pressure of oxygen at high altitude is an appropriate example for pilots.

Hypemic hypoxia occurs when the blood is not able to take up and transport a sufficient amount of oxygen to the cells in the body. Hypemic means "not enough blood." This type of hypoxia is a result of oxygen deficiency in the blood, rather than a lack of inhaled oxygen. The most common form of hypemic hypoxia is CO poisoning. It can also be caused by the loss of blood due to blood donation (so don't try for your "gallon and a half" pin in one setting).

Stagnant hypoxia. Stagnant means "not flowing," and stagnant hypoxia or ischemia results when the oxygen-rich blood in the lungs is not moving, for one reason or another, to the tissues that need it. Stagnant hypoxia can also occur with excessive acceleration of gravity (Gs). Cold temperatures can also reduce circulation and decrease the blood supplied to extremities.

Histotoxic hypoxia is the inability of the cells to effectively use oxygen. "Histo" refers to tissues or cells, and "toxic" means poisonous. Here, oxygen is being transported to the cells that need it, but they are unable to make use of it. This impairment of cellular respiration can be caused by alcohol or drugs (think: narcotics and poisons).

initely serious injury. In fact, the military recommends that their pilots not use lip balm (Chapstick) when they plan on using oxygen. Why? Because lip balm is petroleum based. Perhaps that's why it sounds like LIP-BOMB. You might have lips heavily coated with lip balm, go on oxygen, hear a boom, then spend the rest of the flight looking around the cockpit for your lips. Can you imagine how difficult it will be to call the tower on the radio without your lips?

Hyperventilation

I once asked a student in class what it means if a pilot starts panting or breathing quickly and shallow-like. This fellow replied, "It means he's been eating Milk Bone dog biscuits." This was the same guy from the airspace chapter who had a Coke machine fall on him.

Hyperventilation is abnormally quick, shallow breathing. It can happen when a person is scared, tense, or otherwise stressed. The rapid breathing has the effect of changing your blood chemistry by expelling a more-than-normal amount of carbon dioxide. The level of carbon dioxide is one of the signals the body uses to regulate breathing. The symptoms resulting from hyperventilation can include lightheadedness, suffocation, drowsiness, tingling in the extremities, and coolness. Incapacitation in the form of a lack of coordination, disorientation, and painful muscle spasms can eventually result, as can unconsciousness.

You can reduce and eliminate the symptoms of hyperventilation by bringing the rate and depth of your breathing under control. In other words, by purposely slowing your breathing rate, you allow the necessary carbon dioxide to rebuild within the body. The symptoms will disappear within a few minutes. Talking loud is one way to overcome the effects of hyperventilation. This forces you to wait longer between breaths and builds up the body's carbon dioxide level (it also causes other people to stare and point at you). Some people recommend breathing into a paper bag to help build up the carbon dioxide. Simply hold it over your nose and mouth until the symptom subside. Don't put the entire bag over your head (even if you poke holes out for the eyes). This is no time to get a little instrument work in. Besides, it scares the passengers!

The early symptoms of hyperventilation and hy-poxia are similar. They can even occur at the same time (you'd definitely be having a bad flying day and M&Ms would probably melt in your hand). If you find yourself using an oxygen system because of hypoxia or hyperventilation, set the oxygen regulator to give you maximum oxygen flow. This may appear contradictory to you. After all, if we are hyperventilating, we need carbon dioxide, not oxygen. The problem is that you may not be sure which it is—hypoxia or hyperventilation. It's best to first attack the problem as hypoxia, by going on oxygen. After doing this you should check to see if the regulator has been functioning properly. Then you should give attention to consciously slowing your breathing rate.

CO Oh Oh

Carbon monoxide (CO) is a colorless, odorless, tasteless gas. It has a much stronger affinity than oxygen for *hemoglobin,* the substance in your blood that transports oxygen. If a hemoglobin molecule is occupied with a CO molecule, oxygen can't get aboard and be transported. Good night, Irene.

CO poisoning is cumulative and dangerous. It can incapacitate quickly, and is rapidly fatal. Because of the already-reduced oxygen supply at higher altitudes, you're even more vulnerable to the effects of CO poisoning as you head upward.

Carbon monoxide is a byproduct of combustion. Every winter, people across the country lose their lives when they burn charcoal or other substances indoors for heat without

The Toynbee Maneuver: Open Eustachian

The *Toynbee maneuver* is a variation of the Valsalva maneuver. Both start by closing off the nostrils (pinch them closed). However, in the Toynbee maneuver, instead of blowing against the closed nostrils you simply swallow.

Swallowing with your nostrils closed off has the effect of decreasing the size of the oropharyngeal (mouth and throat) space, much as if you had stepped on one end of an inflated balloon. This increases the pressure of the air in that space on the eustachian tube, and with any luck at all the e-tube pops right open. If not, keep swallowing slowly, but *do not blow.* You can damage your inner ear, and even when it's successful, the Valsalva maneuver can force unwanted material into the middle ear.

Take a tip and Toynbee.

THE INSIDE OF THE HUMAN EAR

Ear Drum
Otolith Organs
Ear Canal
Middle Ear
Eustachian Tube
To Throat

Fig. 2

It's the eustachian tube that helps keep the pressure in the middle ear equalized with the atmospheric pressure. When the eustachian tube becomes blocked, the ear drum may extend in either direction to equalize the middle ear's pressure with atmospheric pressure.

adequate ventilation. For pilots, the danger arises from exhaust gases leaking into the cockpit. This can occur because of a leak in the exhaust system, or because there is a leak in the heater, which uses exhaust gases to warm air that is sent to the cockpit. Heaters normally work by passing outside air over the heater's manifold, then directing the air into the cabin. If a leak occurs, raw exhaust can be imported directly into the cabin.

If you notice the odor of exhaust or experience symptoms of headache, drowsiness, dizziness or loss of muscular power when the aircraft heater is in use, immediately turn off the heater and open the air vents. Consider opening the windows if that can be done in flight in your aircraft (consult the Pilot's Operating Handbook). The smell of exhaust gas should be considered the prelude to an emergency. You must act immediately.

If your physical symptoms are severe or continue after landing, seek medical treatment.

Ear Ye, Ear Ye

The bane of many pilots is a tiny, flaccid tube connecting the middle ear to the back of the throat. It's normally closed. In an ascent, the eustachian (pronounced: U-STAY-SHUN) tube opens for a second or two, permitting higher pressure air from the middle ear to flow out, equalizing the pressure inside the ear with that of the cabin (see Figure 2). This process, often accompanied by a slight crackling, is rarely a problem.

On the way down, however, things get tougher. Now there is high pressure on the outside, and low pressure trapped in the middle ear. The collapsed eustachian tube is like a hose with a crimp in it, and it doesn't open as readily as it did when you were upward bound. You're now in the position of trying to force water back into the hose. Any nasal congestion will make the problem a lot worse, since it puts additional pressure on the collapsed tube, making it even more difficult to get it open. If you can't get the tube open, you have what's known as an *ear block*. Contrary to the belief of some pilots, this is not a hit in the head from an NFL lineman, though if you ever get an ear block, you may well feel like you've got an entire football in your ear.

If you don't equalize the pressure, the results will be somewhere between excruciating and devastating. As the pressure differential builds, your eardrum bows inward, pressing on sensitive nerves. If the pressure differential is too great, the eardrum ruptures. This is not generally considered to be fun by any but the most bizarre of pilots.

The first line of defense against ear block is to stop descending, and even to climb back up to a higher altitude. The lower you go, the greater the pressure differential, and the less likely you will be successful at springing that trapdoor open.

The second thing to do is to swallow, yawn, or tense the muscles in your throat. What you're trying to do is straighten the eustachian tube out a bit and give it the best chance of opening and equalizing the pressure. When this happens it's generally accompanied by a loud popping sound and an enormous sense of relief.

No go? OK, time for the heavy artillery. What virtually every pilot and flight instructor will tell you to do is perform the *Valsalva maneuver,* in which you close your mouth, pinch your nose, and breathe out in short puffs against the closed nostrils. *I don't recommend you do it.* The Valsalva maneuver is potentially damaging, and it's unfortunate that it has been so blithely handed down as the way to clear a closed eustachian tube. Even airline flight attendants will tell passengers to perform the Valsalva maneuver.

What's the right answer? Though almost nobody has heard of it, the Toynbee maneuver (see box) is a far preferable way of opening the eustachian tube. Tell a friend.

Don't fly with a cold.... The bad news is that I know you will eventually ignore this advice. The good news is that you'll only do it once.

Do NOT fly with a cold or other upper respiratory infection, even a little one. The bad news is that I know you will eventually ignore this advice. The good news is that I know you will probably only ignore it once, because the resulting ear block will be a very memorable experience.

An upper respiratory infection is like standing on the garden hose. The water just doesn't have much chance of getting through. When it comes to your ears, there is no such thing as a "minor" cold. The least bit of fluid and gunk in your head will compress the eustachian tube and make equalizing the pressure on descent almost impossible.

Now that you know better, share the information with your passengers. Don't subject them to the pain and possible injury of an ear block.

If you do land with an ear block, and it doesn't clear shortly after landing, give your doctor a call. On several occasions—one concerning me, another concerning a passenger—I had to climb back up to altitude to reduce the pain of ear block. A more gradual descent eventually helped relieve the pain.

THE INNER EAR

3 Semicircular Canals (each contains fluid)

Fig. 3

PITCH

ROLL

YAW

The three semicircular canals are positioned at right angles to each other to allow the brain to sense motion in three planes: yaw, pitch and roll. Fluid within these canals moves relative to the canal walls. This bends the small hair filaments lining the inside of the canal walls, activating nerves that alert the brain to movement.

Spatial Disorientation

During visual flight, our sense of sight determines the relationship between aircraft attitude and the earth's surface. When flying in the clouds, though, we control the airplane solely be reference to the instruments. Deprived of the normal visual cues, the body can send some very unusual messages to the brain, creating a profound conflict between what the "seat of your pants" is telling you and what the instruments say. Such a conflict is known as *spatial disorientation* or *vertigo*.

You're likely to experience vertigo during instrument training (all private pilot applicants must have some training on flight by instruments), or during day or night flights when the horizon isn't easily defined or identifiable. In such a condition you might find yourself convinced that you're turning, while the instruments are showing straight and level flight. Which do you believe? You must never forget the one most important rule about vertigo—trust your instruments. I can assure you that regardless of how much experience you have, vertigo can affect any pilot. Pilots experiencing vertigo should always believe their instruments instead of their bodily sensations.

Vertigo is caused by problems associated with three of our sensory systems: vestibular, kinesthetic, and visual.

The *visual system* is exactly what is sounds like—information sent to our brain from our eyes. The *kinesthetic system* is the sensory information sent to the brain by the seat of our pants. It's the information transmitted by sensors in our skin and from areas deeper within our body. You don't have to be a rocket scientist to understand how both of these systems work. The *vestibular system*, however, does require a little explanation.

This is what students really see when they first look at the instruments while under the hood.

The vestibular system consists of the semicircular canals located in the inner ear (Figure 3). These canals consists of three circular tubes each containing a fluid whose movement causes the bending of small hair filaments (known as *otolith organs)* located at the base of each canal (Figure 4). Movement of the fluid within the tubes, caused by acceleration (a change in direction or velocity), stimulates the otolith organs, alerting the brain that the body is in motion.

Notice that all three tubes in Figure 3 seem to lie in three planes, corresponding somewhat to the three axes of the airplane. This alignment allows you to sense angular acceleration in any one of these planes. In other words, you can sense yaw, roll and pitch.

ACCELERATION AND THE INNER EAR

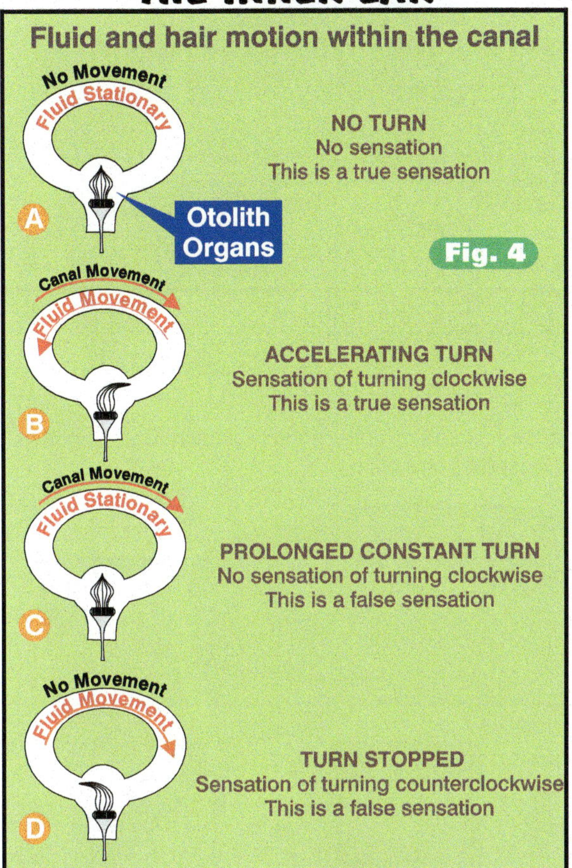

When the head is rotated (accelerated) in any direction, the fluid within one or more of the canals bends small hairs (known as otolith organs) at the base of the canals, as shown in position B. Because of inertia, the fluid lags behind the rotation of the canal, which bends the fine hairs. This stimulates nerve endings, alerting the brain that the body is turning. After acceleration, the fluid eventually catches up with the canal's movement and stimulation stops (position C). This signals the brain that you are no longer turning, even though you're still in a turn. When you stop the turn, the fluid moves in the opposite direction. This gives you a sensation of turning in the opposite direction (position D).

FORCES ACTING ON THE BODY

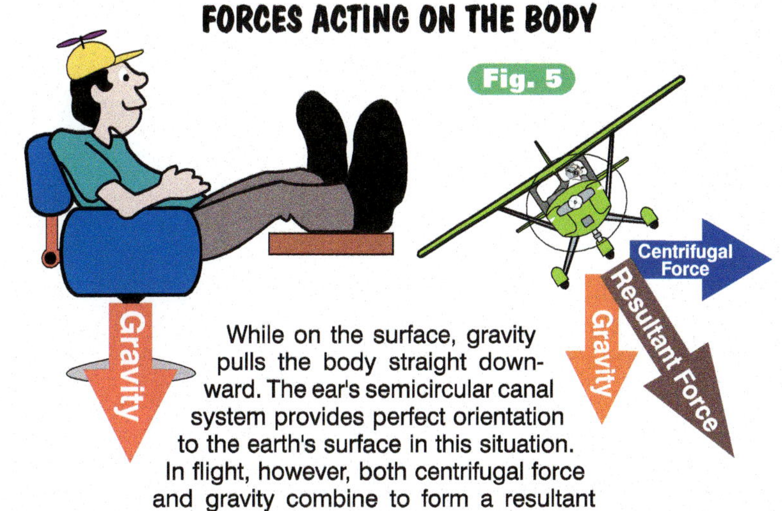

While on the surface, gravity pulls the body straight downward. The ear's semicircular canal system provides perfect orientation to the earth's surface in this situation. In flight, however, both centrifugal force and gravity combine to form a resultant force that makes the seat-of-the-pants sense completely unreliable as a source of attitude information. This false sense is called *vertigo*.

When you move your head or accelerate the airplane (change speed or direction), fluid within these canals move as shown in Figure 4, position B. Since the fluid within the canals has a small amount of inertia (a tendency to resist change of motion), it tends to remain stationary for a short period of time before moving. Thus, the canals can be said to rotate around the fluid within them. Eventually the fluid catches up to the movement of the canal and the feeling of turning stops (position C). Even though you're still turning, you don't feel it. When you stop turning, however, the fluid continues its motion for a short period of time because of its inertia (position D). This signals your mind that you've entered a turn in the opposite direction.

The semicircular canal system was designed as a ground based system where gravity always pulled the body in one direction—straight downward. In flight, however, gravity is not the only force pulling on the body. Centrifugal force as well as gravity tugs on the seat of the pilot's pants as shown in Figure 5.

This explains why your eyes may tell you one thing when looking at the instruments while your brain and your body tell you something entirely different. For instance, when the body is in a prolonged turn, the fluid in the canals eventually comes up to speed with the canal walls (hair no longer stimulated). If the head is then tipped or twisted, the fluid once again moves relative to the canal walls. Now a new sensation of rotation occurs (based on which way the head was turned) even though the airplane didn't change its attitude. Thus, abrupt head movements under instrument or instrument-like conditions can cause you to perceive maneuvers that aren't really happening. This vertigo-type illusion is called the *coriolis illusion*. If you try to correct or turn your airplane in compensation for the sensation, you could be in for a real surprise.

Then there's the *somatogravic illusion* that results from a rapid acceleration (such as you might experience during takeoff) that stimulates your otolith organs the same way as tilting your head backwards. This creates the illusion of being in a nose-up attitude, leading you to believe that you must lower the airplane's nose. A rapid deceleration followed by a quick reduction of the throttle might produce the opposite effect, leading you to believe that the airplane has pitched down. Yikes! Now you know why it's best to believe your instruments. When you start work on your instrument rating

(which I hope you will do this some day), you'll learn all about detecting if and when your instruments are lying to you. Right now, it's best to believe them and avoid instrument or instrument-like conditions.

Visual Illusions

There are situations where, as a VFR pilot, you can encounter instrument-like conditions without being in a cloud. At night, a blending of the earth and sky is often responsible for creating an indiscernible horizon which is an instrument-like condition. This is most prevalent on moonless nights where stars take on the appearance of city lights and city lights appear to be stars (Figure 6A).

Another common visual illusion occurs when you are flying in the direction of a lit shoreline. With dark water underneath, it's easy for shoreline lights to be mistaken for stars as shown in Figure 6B.

Flying above a cloud deck can produce an illusion of a false horizon. If the clouds tops are sloped, you may find yourself attempting to align the aircraft with the horizon made by the clouds.

Flying towards the sun on a hazy day can eliminate the horizon, making it difficult to tell which way is up or down. Situations like these are best handled by climbing above the haze if possible, or getting closer to the surface to establish visual ground contact.

You should be cautious and avoid flying in inclement weather conditions. It's quite easy to lose reference when clouds or other obscuring phenomena are present. Problems with spatial disorientation occur when pilots no longer have sight of the horizon. Until you're instrument rated, avoid flight anywhere at any time where you might lose visual references.

Flight Vision

Make no mistake about it, vision is your most important sense. There is no such thing as a medical wavier for pilots without vision in both eyes. Your vision is important for many reasons. First, you obviously need it to fly the airplane. You also need it to read charts, look for traffic and scan instruments. Let's learn a little about how the eye functions.

FALSE HORIZONS

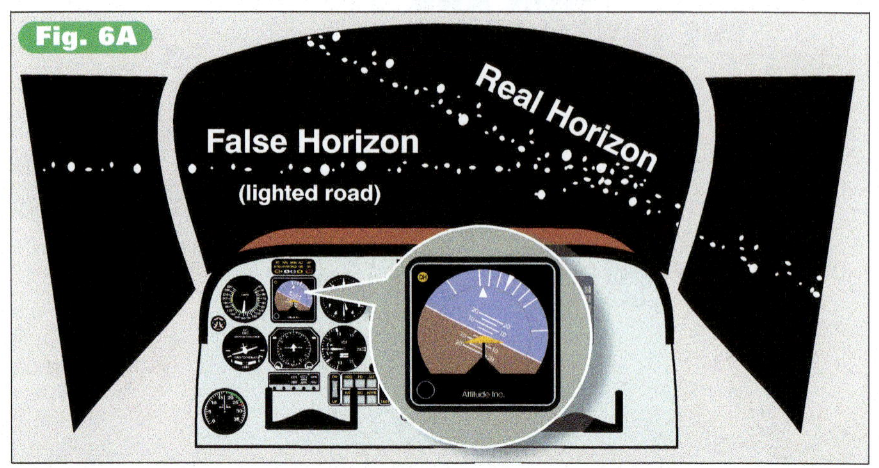

In the example above, a lighted road can be misinterpreted as the actual horizon at night. Such an event is very disconcerting to a pilot.

When the foreground is unlit and the background contains stars, it's relatively easy for a pilot to think he or she has gone inverted.

About Face

One of the most important maneuvers a new VFR pilot can learn to fly is a 180 degree turn, to be executed any time he or she inadvertently enters a cloud.

There should be no hesitancy or delay in executing this. Don't talk yourself into being convinced you can fly "just a little bit" in the clouds. That's like being a little bit pregnant. It's not a possible condition.

Of course, to make a 180 degree turn, you have to know what your heading is to start with. That sounds easy and obvious, but it can be downright terrifying to suddenly find yourself in a cloud, without an instrument rating.

Don't panic. Look at the bottom of the heading indicator and see what number the tail is pointing to. That's where you want to end up. Now begin a gentle turn in the direction of your choice. Be careful not to keep steepening the turn. Make it a nice, gentle, 15 to 20 degree bank, then hold steady until the number that was on the tail is on the nose. Then go straight and level. Faster than you can say *Rod Machado,* you'll be VFR again.

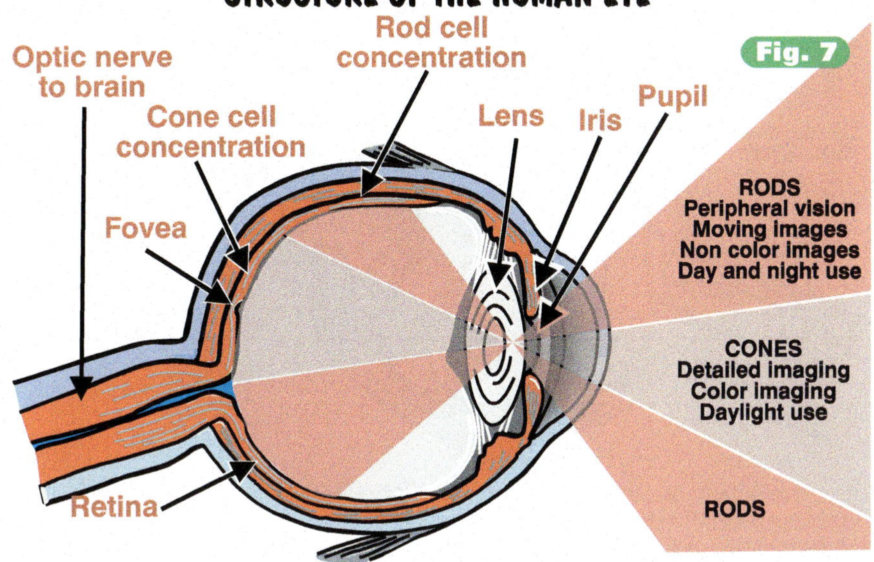

The human eye has separate structures for aiding both night vision and day vision. Cone cells, located within the fovea, are very effective during the day for detailed imagery and color imagery. Rod cells, located outside the fovea, are best used for detection of moving images and noncolor images. They are effective during day and nighttime hours.

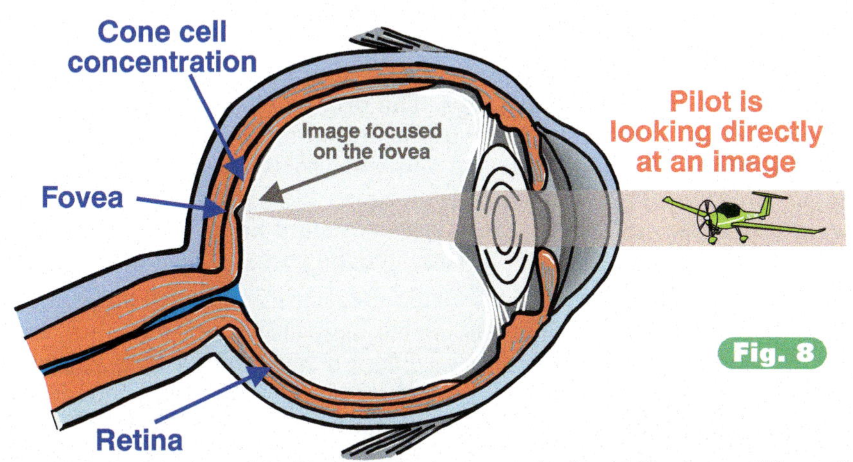

Looking directly at an object focuses the image on the fovea. The image falls on the cone cells that are effective at distinguishing color and image detail. Unfortunately, cone cells are less effective when it's dark. This is why it's difficult to distinguish color and detail at night.

Tips for Passing Your Private Pilot Practical Test

Do you need to know the date of the Wright Brother's first flight to pass your private pilot practical test? No, of course not. You should, however, have a a copy of the FAA's Practical Test Standards (PTS) for the private pilot examination. In it you'll find all the required tasks and areas of knowledge required for private pilot certification.

What is particularly discouraging to me is that many of the applicants who are unable to perform to the published standards fail the test not because they are poor pilots, but because they are simply not prepared for the practical test they are taking. For instance, one applicant told me that the airplane has 10 gyros (not including the one he packed for lunch). He later mentioned the carburetor heat is electric, operating in much the same way that a toaster heats bread.

On the flight portion, applicants seem to fail for any number of reasons. My experience indicates that the most common reason for failure at the private pilot level concerns crosswind landings. The applicants simply have not been trained to land in direct crosswinds of 8 to 12 knots.

When your flight instructor prepares you in accordance with the PTS requirements, there will be no surprises on the practical test.

E. Allan Englehardt,
Airline pilot, Designated Pilot Examiner
National Flight Instructor of the Year

Your Eye – Figure 7 shows a side view of the human eye. Light passes through the pupil and lens, then falls upon the retina at the very back of the eye. Light sensitive cells of the retina are made up of individual cells known as rods and cones.

Cone Cells – Cone cells are concentrated in a small section in the center of the retina known as the fovea. These cells decrease in number with distance from this center point. While the eye can observe an approximate 200 degree arc at a glance, only the light falling on the fovea has the ability to send the brain a sharp, clearly-focused image. All light falling outside the fovea will be of less detail (Figure 8). For example, an airplane at a distance of 7 miles which appears in sharp focus within the foveal center of vision would have to be as close as 7/10 of a mile in order to be recognized if it were outside the foveal field of vision.

Cone cells are responsible for allowing you to perceive color. Looking directly at an object, most of the image is focused on the fovea. Unfortunately, the cones don't work well when it's dark. This explains why it's difficult to perceive color at night compared to the daylight hours.

Rod Cells – No, they didn't name them after me. Rod cells, concentrated on the outside of the fovea, are

dim-light receptors. Since these rods are located outside the fovea, they are responsible for our peripheral vision, as shown in Figure 9. Moving images are more easily detected by rod cells than by cone cells. Catching an object out of the corner of your eye is an example of rod cells at work.

As I've already mentioned, cone cells don't work well in the dark, which explains why it's difficult to see an object at night even though you're looking directly at it. This is why we have a night blind spot in the center of our vision where the light from a dimly lit object falls directly onto the fovea (Figure 9).

ROD CELLS OF THE HUMAN EYE

Fig. 9

Rod cell concentration

Fovea

Good night vision

Area of night blindness

Good night vision

Looking directly at an object at night makes it difficult to see. At night it's best to look 5 to 10 degrees offset from center for better vision. This allows the light from dimly lit objects to fall on the rod cells (surrounding the foveal region) which are better for night vision.

If you want the best view of a dimly lit object you need to expose the rods to the light. You can do this by using your peripheral vision for off-center viewing. Simply look 5 to 10 degrees to the side from the center of the object you want to view. This allows some of the object's reflected light to fall on the rods. You can demonstrate this process at night by looking directly at an airplane's strobe light head on and offset a few degrees. A direct view dims the object while an indirect view increases its brightness. Think of looking at a dim object at night as you might think about looking at a carnival worker. In other words, try not to look directly at their tattoos for fear of finding misspelled words.

Night Vision

How well you see at night is determined by the amount of light passing through the pupil. Pupils close to prevent the eyes from receiving too much light and open when light intensity diminishes. The problem is that it may take at least 30 minutes for your eyes to completely adapt to the dark. You can, however, achieve a moderate degree of dark adaptation within 20 minutes under dim red cockpit lighting. This is one reason you want to avoid very bright lights for at least 30 minutes before the flight if you're planning on flying at night. If you must use a bright white light in the cockpit at night, try closing one eye while the light's in use. This keeps the closed eye night adapted (Be cautious! This looks like a wink and one of the passengers may think you're trying to put the make on them).

Using sunglasses for protection from glare is most helpful in preventing night vision deterioration as well as preventing eye strain and eye damage. Find sunglasses that absorb at least 85% of the visible light (15% transmittance) and have minimal color distortion. Usually, a green or neutral gray is a satisfactory color. I'd recommend that you stay away from sunglass frames like Elton John wears (personally, flaming pink flamingo glasses don't do much for me at all and I can hardly see how they would help you during your private pilot check ride). I make it a point to ensure all my sunglasses have a high degree of impact resistance. Why? They are excellent eye protectors in the event that something penetrates the windshield.

Haze and Collision Avoidance

Keep in mind that all objects (traffic included) appear to be farther away in hazy conditions. The mind equates difficulty in seeing an object with in-creased distance. As a result, you might allow another airplane to get closer to you under hazy conditions before taking corrective action. As an aside, it is rec-

ommended that you turn on your landing light, day or night, in reduced visibility conditions to make it easier for others to see you.

Wearing yellow lens sunglasses is often recommended for hazy, smoggy conditions. Yellow lenses allow for greater definition and contrast of objects. I keep a pair in my flight case for hazy days (I also have a pink-rimmed pair in case I meet Elton John at the airport). Yellow lens sunglasses put a little more strain on my eyes if I wear them for a long time, but the payoff is in easier identification of traffic in smoggy and hazy conditions.

Scanning for Traffic During the Day

Avoiding midairs is predicated upon one important premise: you must look outside the cockpit. Far too often, pilots spend their time with their head inside the cockpit staring at instruments instead of honoring the see and avoid concept. How much time should be spent looking outside and inside the cockpit? Many years ago a military study indicated that on a 17 second cycle, approximately 3 seconds should be spent inside the cockpit with 14 seconds spent looking outside. That's approximately a 1 second inside to 5 second outside ratio. These are good numbers to follow.

THE SECTOR SCANNING METHOD

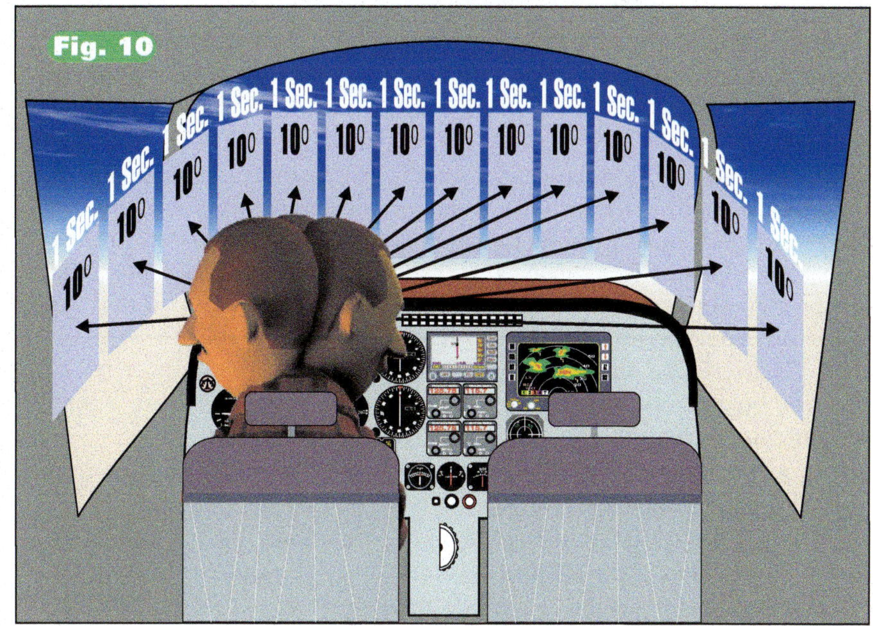

One method of scanning is using the sector scanning method. You simply scan one area 10 degrees in width for one second before moving onto the next sector. By moving your head in a series of short movements, the eye is stationary long enough to focus on an object. This includes scanning the area behind you, too.

Looking outside the cockpit is one thing; knowing how to look, another. Scanning for traffic requires that you understand another peculiarity about the eye: objects are difficult to detect when the eye is in motion. Effective scanning requires the eyes be held still for a very short time to detect objects. Perhaps the best way to scan is to move your eyes in a series of short, regularly spaced movements that bring successive areas of the sky into the central visual field. The FAA suggests that each movement should not exceed 10 degrees with each area being observed for at least 1 second to enable detection, as shown in Figure 10.

SCANNING THROUGH 360 DEGREES

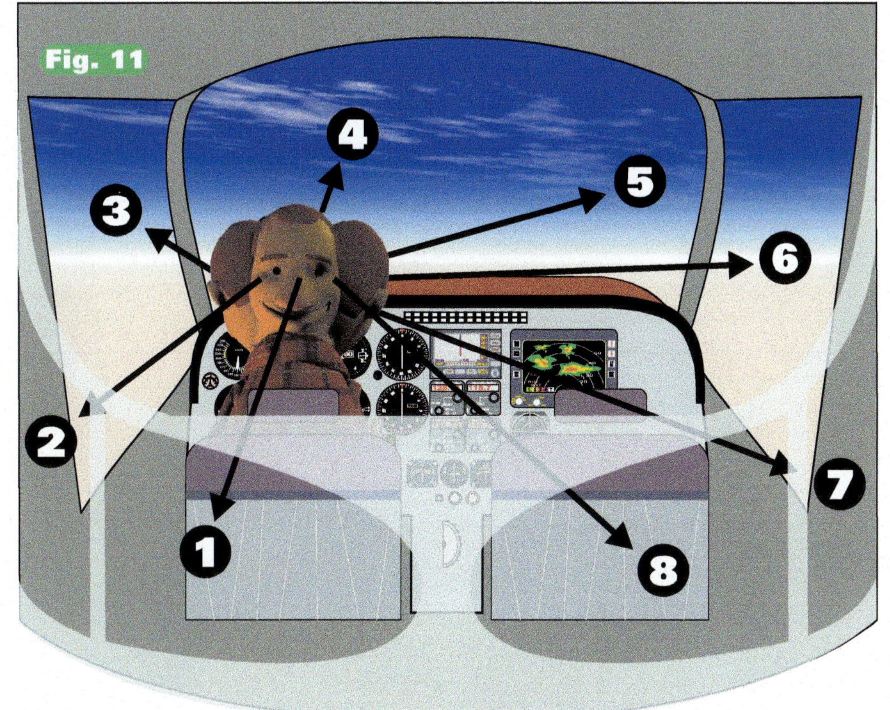

Effective scanning assumes that you'll scan 360 degrees for traffic. Starting at the rearmost window, scan in a clockwise direction until reaching the right rearmost window. Sometimes it may be physically difficult to turn your head in a rearward direction. If so, make right or left turns to effectively scan the rear of the airplane.

Since the brain is already trained to process sight information presented from left to right, you will probably find it easier to start your scan from over your left shoulder proceeding to the right across the windshield, as shown in Figure 11.

Whatever you do, don't forget to scan the area behind you. Many years ago an AOPA (Aircraft Owner's and Pilot's Association) study indicated that the majority of midairs occur with one aircraft overtaking another (one study indicated that 82% of the accidents occurred this way). Obviously this is a faster aircraft overtaking a slower one. This becomes a greater concern when you're operating in an area where fast and slow aircraft mix. Scanning the rear quadrants of the aircraft may take some neck bending or turn-

ing of the aircraft, depending on the aircraft configuration. Granted, unless you've seen the movie *The Exorcist,* you may not realize that such neck twisting is possible. Nevertheless, even if your head can't spin on its axis, make gentle turns in the airplane to take a peek at what's behind you (Figure 12). Making gentle turns is also a good idea when climbing or descending on an airway to check for traffic.

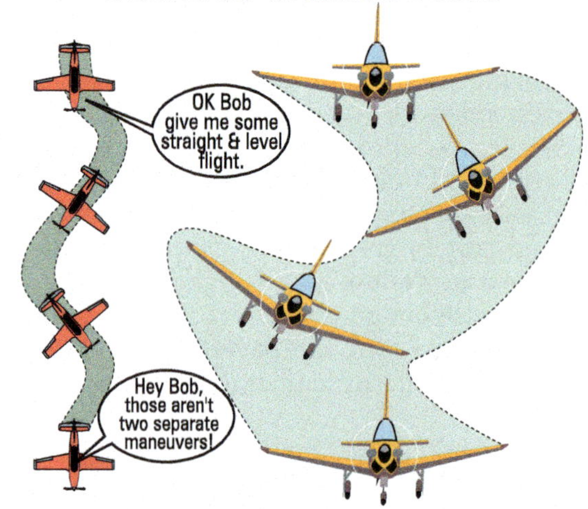

In some airplanes, the only way to see what's behind you is to make clearing turns while looking rearward. Don't be reluctant to make turns as often as necessary to watch for faster traffic approaching from behind.

Fig. 12

Another consideration when scanning is to prevent being a victim of *empty-field myopia.* This condition usually occurs when you're flying above a cloud or haze layer with nothing specific to focus on outside the airplane. This causes the eyes to relax and seek a comfortable focal distance ranging anywhere from 10 to 30 feet. This means you may be looking outside the airplane without actually being able to identify traffic. To overcome this problem you should try to momentarily fix your eyes on a ground object off in the distance (if possible) before commencing your scan.

If you spot a target and it has no apparent motion, then it means one of two things: it's either coming directly at you or moving away from you, or a big bug has smashed into your window. Targets moving directly toward you can close the distance in a very short time. Figure 13 demonstrates how quickly aircraft can converge. Little or no relative movement can also occur when aircraft are converging, as shown in Figure 14. If you detect a target with little or no relative motion in your windshield, it's best to take evasive action immediately. Don't just wait for the target to grow larger—make a turn. Make the target move.

Just remember to scan the *entire area* for collision avoidance prior to starting any maneuver. Also remember to raise the inside wing of a high wing airplane and look before beginning the turn. If you're flying a low wing airplane, don't forget to look in the direction opposite that which you'll turn. Why? The outside wing will often prevent you from seeing any converging traffic. In short, do what your mom told you to do: look both ways, then look up, down, behind and ahead. Keep your head outside the cockpit (no, that will mess up your hair. I mean keep your eyes outside the cockpit).

AIRPLANES CONVERGING HEAD ON

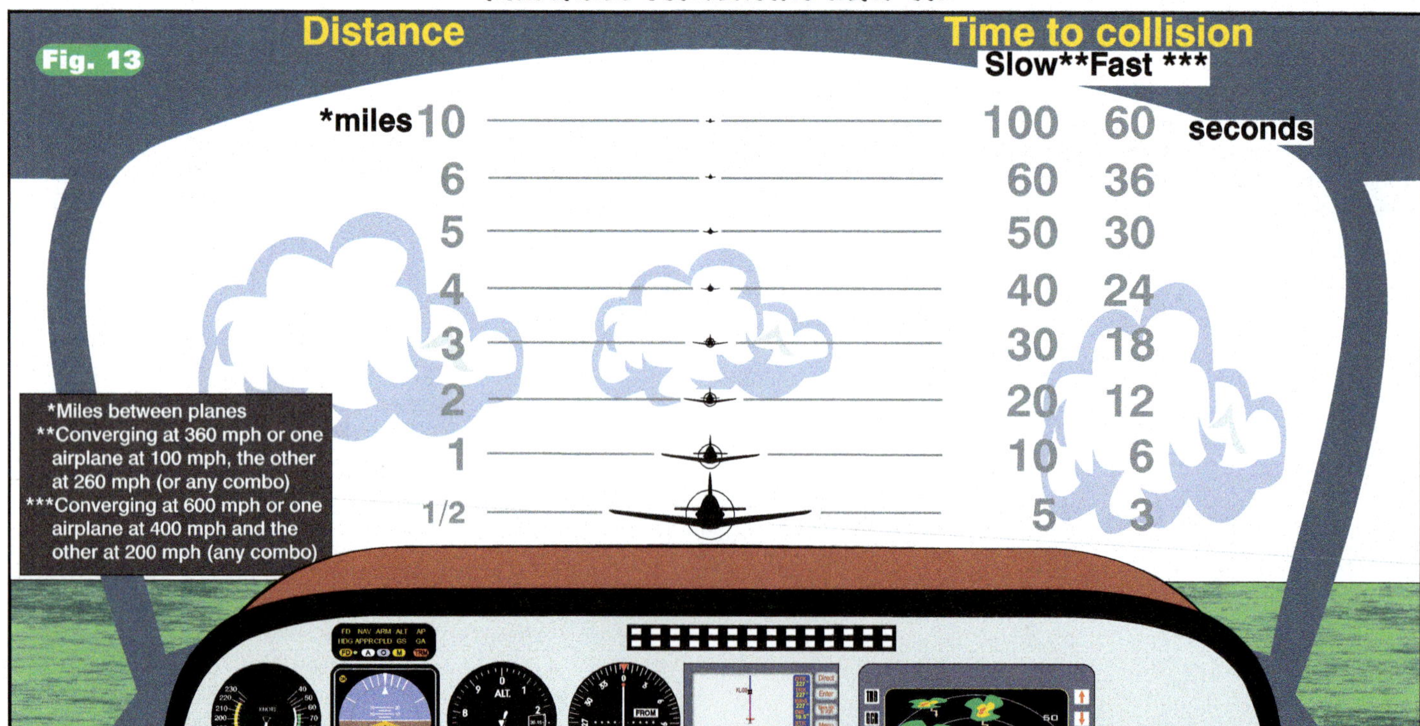

Airplanes converging head-on cover distances quickly. Additionally, there is little or no relative movement between targets making it more difficult to identify a collision threat. For instance, a slower airplane and a faster airplane converging at a rate of 360 mph (or any combination of speeds equaling 360 mph as shown by the "slow" speed column) have 20 seconds before impact when two miles apart. A 500 mph airliner and a 100 mph airplane (600 mph converging speed as shown by the "fast" speed column) have 12 seconds before colliding at a distance of 2 miles.

AIRPLANES ON A CONVERGING COURSE

As two airplanes approach on a converging course, there may be little or no apparent movement of the airplane in your windscreen. This is a sign to take evasive action.

Fig. 14

Night Scanning For Traffic

While it's easier to spot aircraft lights at night, this doesn't necessarily mean it's easier to identify the aircraft's direction of movement, much less its size and shape. That's why airplanes are required to have their position lights on from sunset to sunrise (anticollision lights are to be on when the airplane is in operation). You can determine the direction of airplane travel by noting the position of the airplane's red navigation light (on the left wing), the green navigation light (on the right wing) and the steady white light (on the tail). The red or white anticollision light is often visible from many directions (see Figure 15).

DETERMINING THE DIRECTION OF AN AIRPLANE'S TRAVEL BY USE OF ITS POSITION LIGHTS

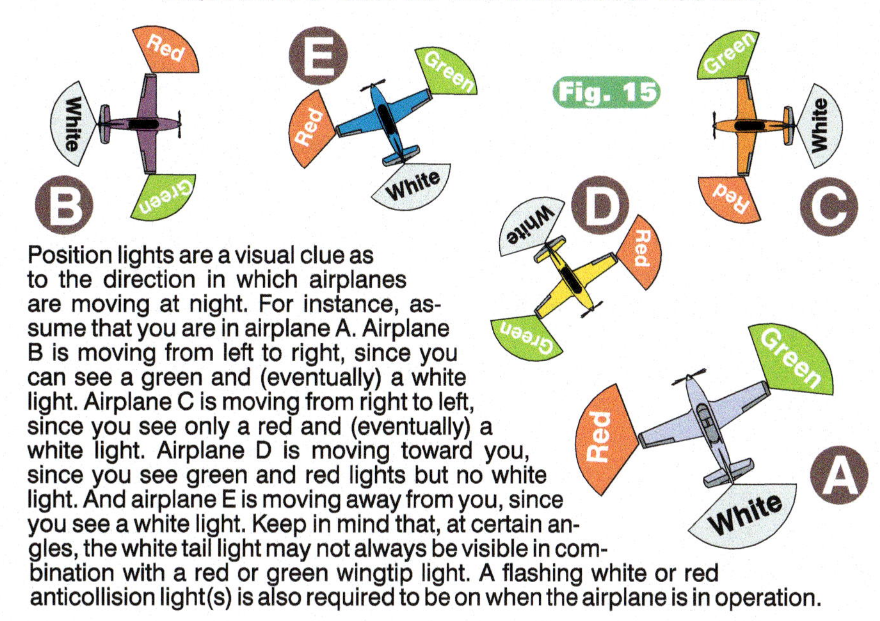

Position lights are a visual clue as to the direction in which airplanes are moving at night. For instance, assume that you are in airplane A. Airplane B is moving from left to right, since you can see a green and (eventually) a white light. Airplane C is moving from right to left, since you see only a red and (eventually) a white light. Airplane D is moving toward you, since you see green and red lights but no white light. And airplane E is moving away from you, since you see a white light. Keep in mind that, at certain angles, the white tail light may not always be visible in combination with a red or green wingtip light. A flashing white or red anticollision light(s) is also required to be on when the airplane is in operation.

One more thing before we leave the topic of night scanning. Something known as autokinesis (meaning self-moving) might occur at night if you don't keep up a regular scan pattern. Staring at a single light source for a few seconds at night can cause that light to appear to move, much like an airplane on a collision course. If you're using the light as an attitude reference, this apparent motion could cause you to lose your spatial orientation. You can prevent autokinesis by scanning in the manner I've previously discussed as well as by observing the flight instruments to affirm the correct attitude.

Airplane Blind Spots

All airplanes have blind spots where traffic is difficult to see. High wing aircraft make seeing above difficult, while low wing aircraft make seeing below difficult (biplane pilots

have both problems). Figure 16 shows how these blind spots look on different aircraft. This doesn't mean that it's impossible to see in the directions of blind spots. You may need to turn the airplane or lift a wing to compensate for those areas blocked by aircraft structure.

This is one reason I recommend that pilots of high wing airplanes lift their wing slightly and look before starting a turn (tell the passengers that you're looking for traffic if you're worried that they may think you don't know which way to turn). This prevents turning into an airplane that is descending from your direction of turn. Pilots of low wing airplanes need to be especially alert to clear the areas below them during descents. If you're flying a low wing airplane, be sure to make the necessary clearing turns during descents to check for traffic below you.

Whatever you do, don't be hesitant to turn that airplane and look when operating in areas of high traffic density. It's possible for a low wing and a high wing airplane to remain within each other's blind spot, as shown in Figure 17 (this isn't how they make biplanes, either). This is good motivation to keep your eyes open and the airplane maneuvering to clear those blind spots.

BLIND AREAS COMMON IN HIGH AND LOW WING AIRPLANES

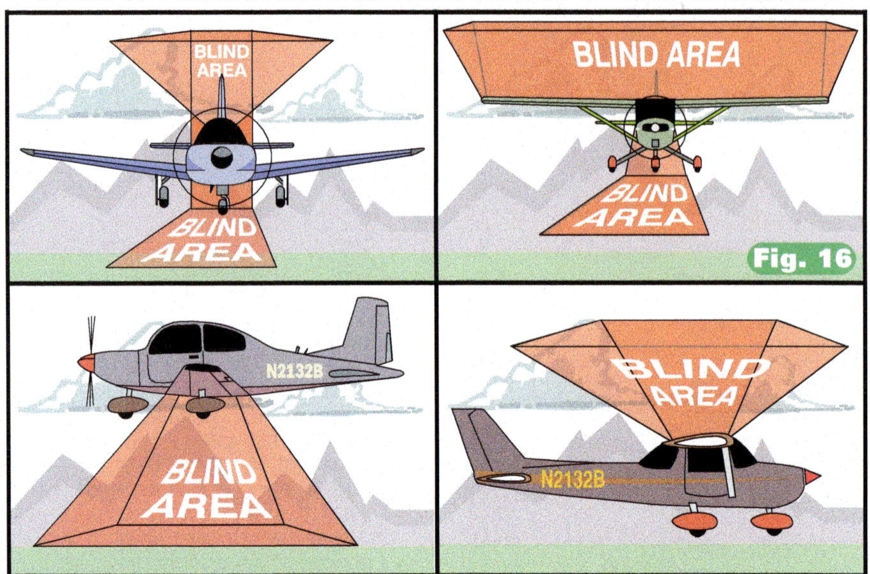

It's not unusual to have a substantial portion of your view blocked by either the fuselage or the wings. Compensating for those areas of blocked view requires that you make turns and gentle pitch changes.

If there is ever a best time to remain vigilant for traffic, it's when you're within 5 miles of an airport below 3,000 feet AGL. One study of midair collisions found that 79% of all midairs occurred within these distances. That same study reported that 49% occurred within 5 miles and 500 feet AGL of the airport. Furthermore, most midair collisions occur on clear days. Hard to believe but it's quite true. So use caution!

Keep in mind that a near midair collision is one in which the possibility of a collision occurred as a result of being less than 500 feet from another aircraft. If you determine that a near midair collision event happened you are required to report this. You can do this by saying to ATC, "I wish to report a near midair collision."

Don't let the presence of a tower controller relax your vigilance. Many

OVERLAPPING BLIND AREAS

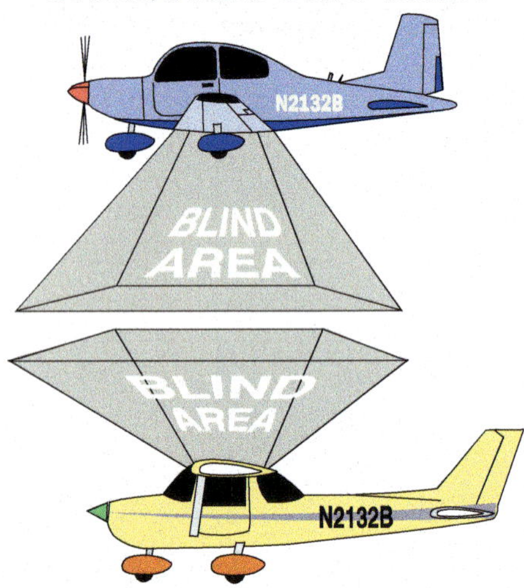

A low wing airplane above a high wing airplane presents a problem since both airplane blind areas overlap. There is a greater chance of a collision occurring when the low wing descends or the high wing climbs.

Fig. 17

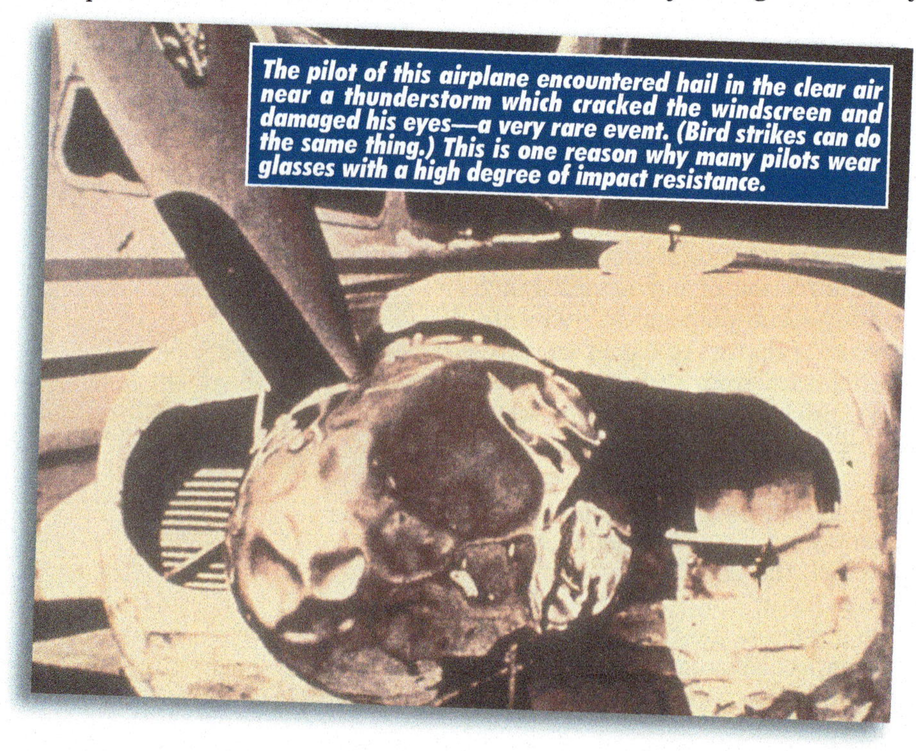

The pilot of this airplane encountered hail in the clear air near a thunderstorm which cracked the windscreen and damaged his eyes—a very rare event. (Bird strikes can do the same thing.) This is one reason why many pilots wear glasses with a high degree of impact resistance.

a midair has occurred in the presence of a tower controlled field. Pilots are still responsible for their own see and avoid traffic separation even when the tower is in operation.

Filing a VFR Flight Plan

Although not required, it's simply good practice to file a VFR flight plan for all your cross country trips. A VFR flight plan, filed with the Flight Service Station, is good insurance in case your airplane is forced down for any number of reasons, including bad weather or engine problems.

Since every flight plan has a departure time and an estimated time enroute (ETE), an FSS specialist will be expecting you to close that flight plan when the ETE has expired. After 30 minutes or so past the ETE time, search and rescue procedures are initiated. This usually starts with a ramp search of the destination airport and can end in a full scale search and rescue operation by local authorities.

Fortunately, most airplanes are found on the ramp at the destination airport when the pilot forgets to close his or her flight plan. You can close it with the FSS by phone or radio or with Easy Close (see Page M39).

Figure 18 shows the ICAO flight plan form. We'll do a quick review of the information to be inserted into this form. You can read more detail about this form in Postflight Briefing #17-2. Keep in mind that some numbered blocks require more than one type of inserted information. You'll normally start by filling out block 7 in Figure 18. So let's begin there.

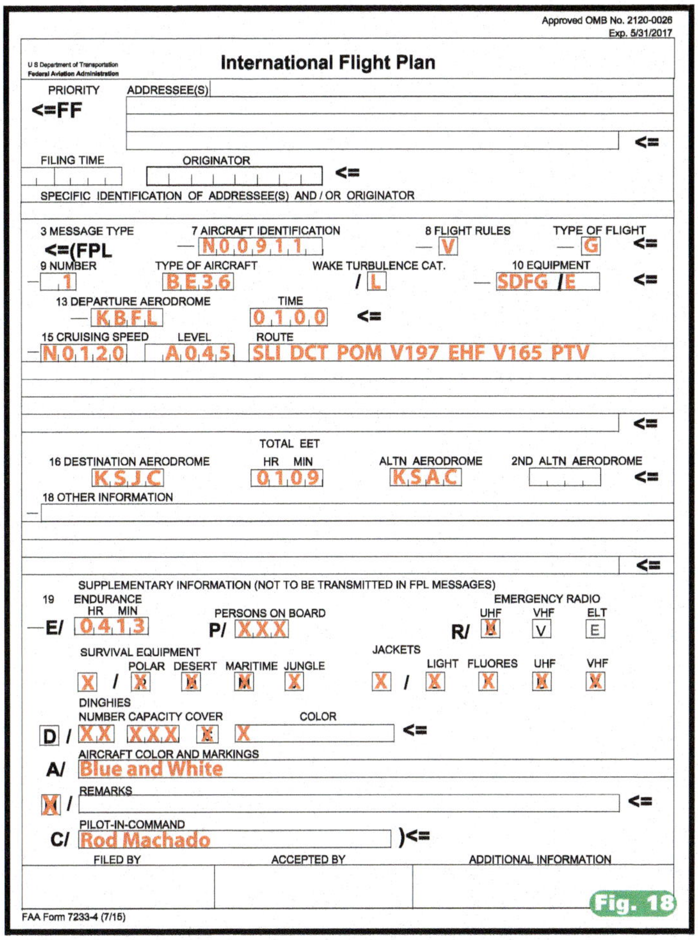

Block-7: Enter your complete aircraft identification including the prefix "N" if applicable.

Block-8: Enter "V" for a VFR flight plan (that's you). Then enter "G" as the designator for general aviation.

Block-9: Unless your flight instructor is following you in another airplane (a formation flight), then enter a value of 1 for one airplane. In *Type of Aircraft* block you'll put your aircraft type (see Document 8643 at www.icao.int for aircraft type info). For this flight we'll use an A36 Bonanza which is designated as BE36. In the Wake Turbulence Category block, after the forward slash, you'll list an "L" to indicate you're in a light aircraft, which is one with a takeoff weight of 15,500 pounds or less. Of course, if your Bonanza weighs that much, then leave your flight bag on the ground which will bring your total weight down to about 3,500 pounds.

Block-10 (left side of /): In the Equipment block you'll identify Your airplane's equipment (no, not engines, flashlights, and landing gear, either) is defined in detail in AIM Table 5-1-4. You should list the letters representing the navigation and surveillance equipment that's on board the airplane. No space is required between items. For example, **SDFG**.

S – VHF (receive and transmit frequencies), VOR and ILS. This is a single letter representing at least three types of equipment.

Approved OMB No. 2120-0026
Exp. 5/31/2017

U S Department of Transportation
Federal Aviation Administration

International Flight Plan

PRIORITY <=FF ADDRESSEE(S) <=

FILING TIME ORIGINATOR <=

SPECIFIC IDENTIFICATION OF ADDRESSEE(S) AND / OR ORIGINATOR

3 MESSAGE TYPE <=(FPL — 7 AIRCRAFT IDENTIFICATION N0091 1 — 8 FLIGHT RULES V TYPE OF FLIGHT — G <=

9 NUMBER — 1 TYPE OF AIRCRAFT BE36 WAKE TURBULENCE CAT. / L — 10 EQUIPMENT SDFG / E <=

13 DEPARTURE AERODROME — KBFL TIME 0100 <=

15 CRUISING SPEED — N0120 LEVEL A045 ROUTE SLI DCT POM V197 EHF V165 PTV

<=

16 DESTINATION AERODROME KSJC TOTAL EET HR MIN 0109 ALTN AERODROME KSAC 2ND ALTN AERODROME <=

18 OTHER INFORMATION —

<=

SUPPLEMENTARY INFORMATION (NOT TO BE TRANSMITTED IN FPL MESSAGES)

19 ENDURANCE HR MIN —E/ 0413 PERSONS ON BOARD P/ XXX EMERGENCY RADIO UHF VHF ELT R/ X V E

SURVIVAL EQUIPMENT X / POLAR X DESERT X MARITIME X JUNGLE X JACKETS X / LIGHT X FLUORES X UHF X VHF X

DINGHIES NUMBER CAPACITY COVER COLOR D / XX XXX X X <=

AIRCRAFT COLOR AND MARKINGS A/ Blue and White

REMARKS X / <=

PILOT-IN-COMMAND C/ Rod Machado)<=

FILED BY ACCEPTED BY ADDITIONAL INFORMATION

FAA Form 7233-4 (7/15)

Fig. 18

Flight plans filed in the United States can now use the ICAO (International Civil Aviation Organization) flight plan format (soon this format will be mandatory).

D – DME

F – ADF (in case you still have one on board because you haven't found something to plug up the hole it will leave once it's removed).

G - GNSS (i.e., GPS that's approved for the type of operation you're conducting. As a non-instrument rated private pilot there is no need to identify the specific type of GPS equipment you're using much less its specific capabilities).

O – VOR

Block-10 (right side of /): In the surveillance equipment section to the right of the forward slash, list the airplane's surveillance equipment. No, I don't mean binoculars, camouflage kit and the fake mustache you use when you're on one of your secret agent missions. Instead, I'm speaking of the equipment your airplane uses to directly send/receive information to ATC. This equipment is covered in detail in Postflight Briefing #17-2 on Page Q39. However, the most common items you'll list here are your airplane's Mode A, Mode C or Mode S transponder (see Page Q36 for Mode S Transponders). Here are the codes you'd use to describe this equipment.

A Transponder - Mode A (4 digits – 4096 codes)

C Transponder - Mode A (4 digits – 4096 codes) & Mode C

WHATEVER WORKS

I had not seen my son in a long time and [at the end of the flight, I] forgot to close flight plan. My Remedy? I purchased a 1/8 inch brazing rod and bent it to go over my head with yellow iridescent lettered tag attached. Causes laughs but accomplishes the correct results.

The following pilot dutifully closed flight plan, only to discover an ATC procedural breakdown didn't get the message through. Even though he wasn't at fault, he learned...*There is one thing I could have done that would have saved a lot of people a lot of unnecessary trouble: I could have provided FSS with a destination phone number. This item is optional on flight plan forms. From now on, I will provide a destination phone* number if at all available because mistakes happen. The more information FSS has to work with the easier it is to correct a problem. **ASRS Report**

SSR Mode S

E – Transponder - Mode S, including aircraft identification, pressure-altitude & extended squitter (ADS-B) capability

H – Transponder - Mode S, including aircraft identification, pressure altitude and enhanced surveillance capability

I – Transponder - Mode S, including aircraft identification, but no pressure-altitude capability

L – Transponder - Mode S, including aircraft identification, pressure-altitude, extended squitter (ADS B) and enhanced surveillance capability

P – Transponder - Mode S, including pressure-altitude, but no aircraft identification capability

S – Transponder - Mode S, including both pressure- altitude and aircraft identification capability

X – Transponder - Mode S with neither aircraft identification nor pressure-altitude capability.

Block-13: Enter the departure airport using its four-letter designator (Figure 19). Airports designated by less than four letters (i.e., O27) or that use numbers (i.e., 39LL) are not official ICAO designations. In this instance, use ZZZZ in this block and specify the non-ICAO identifier in Block 18 following the characters "DEP/" which stands for departure airport (i.e., DEP/O27).

In the time block, insert the estimated departure time using HHMM format.

Block-15: Based on your performance chart calculations, insert your four-digit cruising TAS in knots following the letter "N" for a maximum of five characters. The letter "N" refers to a speed value in knots. If your speed is 120 knots TAS, then you'll enter N0120 in this block.

To the right of your TAS, insert your cruising altitude for the first or the whole portion of the route preceded by an "A" followed by three figures. For example, an altitude of 4,500 feet MSL would be listed as A045. If you're planning on using more than one cruising altitude, list the first one you intend to use.

The airport identifier is found in the airport information block on the sectional chart.

Fig. 19

To the right of your cruising altitude insert the routing desired as you have typically done when filing using the older flight plan format. If you're flying direct (i.e., no airway), then insert the letters DCT (which means "direct") between each fix, navaid or waypoint.

Define your route by navaid identifiers (such as three letter identifiers for VORs or NDBs, or names if you don't know the three letter identifiers), airways, or waypoints (if you're using RNAV). For instance, I could depict my route as:

SLI DCT POM V197 EHF V165 PTV

This tells the FSS specialist that you'll fly from your departure airport (don't need to list the departure airport in the route since it's already listed in block 13) to the SLI VOR direct to the POM VOR then via Victor 197 (an airway) to the EHF VOR then via Victor 165 (airway) to the PTV VOR. You don't need to list your destination airport in the route section since it will be listed in Block-16.

If you plan on stopping at different airports enroute, simply list them in Block-18 (other information). For instance, with the routing listed above and with a final destination of Porterville, I might elect to stop at Brackett field to stock up on pilot supplies and Rosamond for lunch. In Block-18 (other information) I'd say, "Intermediate stops at Brackett and Rosamond." I could, of course, file three separate flight plans but this is more work.

Block-16: Define the destination airport in Block #16 just as you did in the departure airport Block-13.

Use ZZZZ if no official ICAO identifier is listed for the airport, then list

the non-ICAO identifier in Block 18 after the letters "DEST/" (remember, ICAO doesn't recognize airport identifiers having numbers or having less than four letters). For airport O88, you'd list DEST/ (for destination) followed by O88 for DEST/O88 in Block 18.

Keep in mind that you might want to stop at an intermediate airport prior to reaching the destination airport (called a "stopover" flight). If so, then it is recommended that a separate flight plan be filed for each "leg" when the stop is expected to be more than 1 hour duration at an intermediate airport(s).

To the right of Block-16, define the total estimated enroute time to the destination using the HHMM format. To the right of the EET, define the alternate airport the same way you defined the destination and departure airports.

Block-18: if you found that there was no need to list any additional information here in Block 18, then you'd list a "0" in this block and fill out the remaining supplementary information blocks.

Block-19: Enter your airplane's endurance in the HHMM format. Don't enter the time of your last gasping run at the gym, either.

Then enter the number of people on the airplane.

Next, you'll identify the emergency radio information on the airplane. By leaving the boxes in this category empty you are indicating that you have that capability (go figure). If you have VHF with 121.5 MHz capability, then leave the "VHF" box unchecked. Cross out UHF if you don't have this capability on board. The "ELT" is your emergency locator transmitter, which I assume you have onboard, so leave this box unchecked.

Cross out any of the survival equipment items that you don't have onboard. List the number of jackets on board or place an X in this box. Cross out any of the other items to the right that you don't have onboard.

Regarding dinghies, this doesn't reflect the number of goofy people on your airplane, either. Cross out NUMBER and CAPACITY if no dinghies are carried or insert the number of dinghies.

Identify the predominant colors of the aircraft. This information is especially important for search and rescue.

Finally, list the name of the pilot in command.

Congratulations, by the time you've finally completed this flight plan, it's probably time for dinner and a nap. Fortunately, filing a flight plan becomes much easier given the many and varied flight plan services available for your computer, pads and tablet devices (see Page Q42).

The easiest way to file this flight plan is can by calling the Leidos Flight Service Station at 1-800-WX-BRIEF or at www.800wxbrief.com. Internet filing makes this process quick and easy.

When airborne, you can open your flight plan by calling the nearest FSS on the radio. If the departure airport has a tower, and they aren't too busy, you can ask them

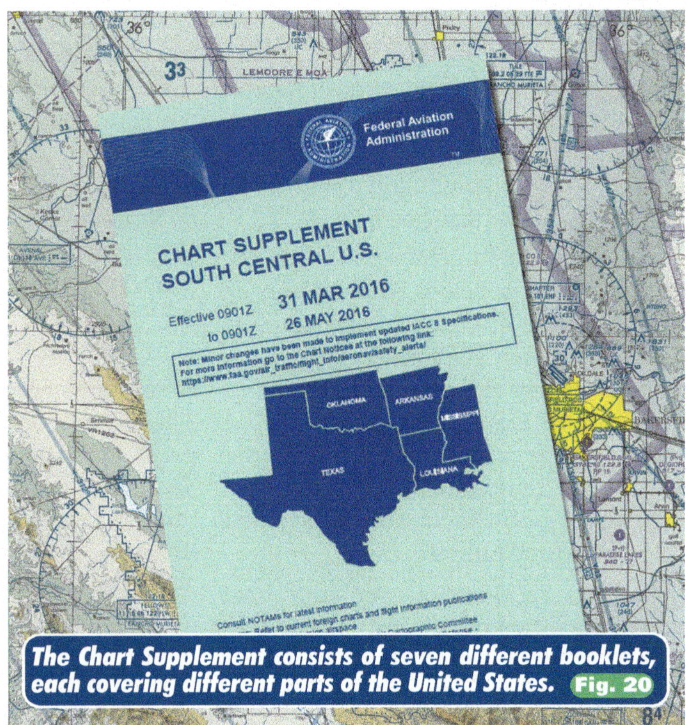

The Chart Supplement consists of seven different booklets, each covering different parts of the United States. Fig. 20

to open your VFR flight plan. They simply make the call to the FSS for you. The moment you open the flight plan, the time starts counting down from your EET. This is why you always want to note this time and, as I've already mentioned, be prepared to extend the time with the nearest FSS if you're running late. Keep in mind that the tower doesn't automatically close your VFR flight plan upon landing (even assuming you land at a tower controlled field). If you ask them to and they agree, then you can assume the flight plan will be closed. (Note: See Postflight Briefing #17-2 for more detailed information on the ICAO Flight Plan Form.)

FAA & Industry Publications

Throughout this book I've mentioned several aviation documents, including the *Digital Chart Supplement* (*d-CS*), the *Aeronautical Information Manual* (AIM), NOTAMS and advisory circulars. These documents are all valuable sources of information that you need to help fly safely. Let's examine them again to ensure your familiarity with these valuable information sources. We'll also look at a few other sources of aviation information you might find useful.

Chart Supplement

The *Chart Supplement* (or its digital version, *d-CS*) consists of several booklets, each covering different parts of the United States (Figure 20). Each directory contains detailed information on all public-use airports including frequencies, runway information, services available and much, much more. Issued once every eight weeks, it's available on a subscription basis or free, via PDF download at http://www.faa.gov/.

Each public airport, heliport and seaplane base has an entry in the *CS* (see Figure 21). Don't worry if you don't

understand all this information. At the beginning of each *CS* a legend explains what each bit of data means. Believe me, there is ample information here to help with almost all questions you might have about the airport and its facilities.

In addition to airport information, the *CS* also provides information on updates and changes to aeronautical charts. Since sectional charts are revised only once every 6 months, while the *CS* is reissued every 8 weeks, any change to a sectional chart can be found in the aeronautical chart bulletin in the rear of the *CS* (Figure 22, box A).

Figure 22 shows all the additional information you'll find in the *CS*: FAA FSDO (Flight Standards District Office) and NWS telephone numbers (box B), and a section for special notices (box C), VOR receiver checkpoints (box D), parachute jump areas (box E), FSS frequencies (box F) and ARTCC frequencies (box G). The *CS* also contains information that's important for the IFR rated pilot.

You can't help but pay attention to the rocket firing area notice east of Reno, at the top of Figure 22 (box C). Of course this area extends vertically up to but not including 1,000 feet AGL, but you don't want to tempt anyone in charge of those rockets by flying a little lower than normal. If you don't think people become tempted, just think back to the time when you were at the driving range as a child. You saw that fellow in a steel caged tractor scooping up fallen golf balls. You probably thought, "Since he is protected, it probably won't hurt much if I do manage to hit the tractor..." It's best to avoid any area with the word rocket in it.

The Aeronautical Information Manual

At the beginning of the chapter I mentioned the Aeronautical Information Manual (AIM), shown in Figure 23, but it's hard to say too much about this encyclopedia of aviation information. It's your best guide to aviation information on the following topics:

Air Navigation Radio Aids

Aeronautical Lighting and Other Airport Visual Aids

Airspace

Air Traffic Control

Air Traffic Procedures

Emergency Procedures

Safety of Flight

Medical Facts For Pilots

Aeronautical Charts and Related Publications

Pilot/Controller Glossary

Revised several times a year, this document is available on a subscription basis. It contains recommendations and procedures involving the safety of flight, and information that exists as regulations in other FAA publications.

High Priests Of Aviation Knowledge

As young flight instructors, we used to challenge each other about topics within the AIM. It was considered important to have knowledge of even the most esoteric data.

One day a fellow CFI and I decided to play a joke on a new instructor. We were going to ask each other questions and pretend we knew the answers by making them up. For instance, I would ask my friend what the candlelight power of an airport's rotating beacon was. He'd say, "11,200 foot-candles." Then he'd ask an even more esoteric question such as, "What is the minimum thickness of the white paint used to paint runway numbers?"

What really got our new CFI friend was when I asked this question. "If you're flying a Boeing 747 loaded with 15,000 live turkeys, and you're 8,516 pounds overweight, how many turkeys would you have to make jump into the air, with a stick, at one time, to get under gross weight?"

I think our friend gave up instructing and went back to being an automobile mechanic.

Rod Machado

PUBLIC AIRPORTS AND THE DIGITAL CHART SUPPLEMENT

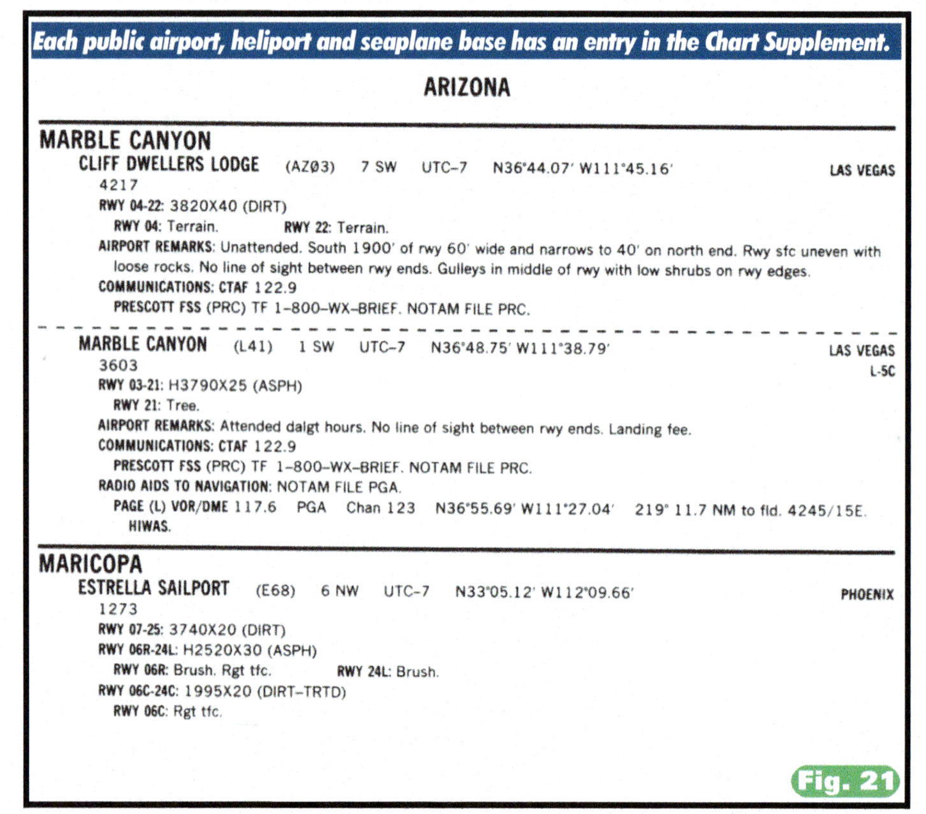

Each public airport, heliport and seaplane base has an entry in the Chart Supplement.

ARIZONA

MARBLE CANYON

CLIFF DWELLERS LODGE (AZØ3) 7 SW UTC–7 N36°44.07′ W111°45.16′ **LAS VEGAS**
4217
RWY 04-22: 3820X40 (DIRT)
RWY 04: Terrain. **RWY 22:** Terrain.
AIRPORT REMARKS: Unattended. South 1900′ of rwy 60′ wide and narrows to 40′ on north end. Rwy sfc uneven with loose rocks. No line of sight between rwy ends. Gulleys in middle of rwy with low shrubs on rwy edges.
COMMUNICATIONS: CTAF 122.9
PRESCOTT FSS (PRC) TF 1-800-WX-BRIEF. NOTAM FILE PRC.

MARBLE CANYON (L41) 1 SW UTC–7 N36°48.75′ W111°38.79′ **LAS VEGAS L-5C**
3603
RWY 03-21: H3790X25 (ASPH)
RWY 21: Tree.
AIRPORT REMARKS: Attended dalgt hours. No line of sight between rwy ends. Landing fee.
COMMUNICATIONS: CTAF 122.9
PRESCOTT FSS (PRC) TF 1-800-WX-BRIEF. NOTAM FILE PRC.
RADIO AIDS TO NAVIGATION: NOTAM FILE PGA.
PAGE (L) VOR/DME 117.6 PGA Chan 123 N36°55.69′ W111°27.04′ 219° 11.7 NM to fld. 4245/15E.
HIWAS.

MARICOPA

ESTRELLA SAILPORT (E68) 6 NW UTC–7 N33°05.12′ W112°09.66′ **PHOENIX**
1273
RWY 07-25: 3740X20 (DIRT)
RWY 06R-24L: H2520X30 (ASPH)
RWY 06R: Brush. Rgt tfc. **RWY 24L:** Brush.
RWY 06C-24C: 1995X20 (DIRT–TRTD)
RWY 06C: Rgt tfc.

Fig. 21

LAS VEGAS SECTIONAL
85th Edition, 10 Mar 2011

OBSTRUCTIONS
10 Mar 2011 – 30 Jun 2011 No Major Changes.

AIRPORTS
10 Mar 2011 – 5 May 2011 No Major Changes.
30 Jun 2011 ST GEORGE arpt abandoned, 37°05'26"N, 113°35'35"W.

NAVAIDs
10 Mar 2011 – 5 May 2011 No Major Changes.
30 Jun 2011 Delete ST GEORGE VOR/DME, 37°05'17"N, 113°35'30"W.

AIRSPACE
10 Mar 2011 – 5 May 2011 No Major Changes.
30 Jun 2011 Revise BRYCE CANYON, UT. Class E: That airspace extending upward from 700 feet above

Fig. 22 Box A

FAA AND NWS

Fig. 22 Box B

FSS
TELEPHONE NUMBERS

Flight Service Station (FSS) facilities provide flight planning and weather briefing services to pilots. FSS services in the contiguous United States, Hawaii and Puerto Rico, are provided by a network of large FSS facilities and a few select remote facilities some of which operate part-time. Because of the interconnectivity between the facilities, all FSS services including radio frequencies are available continuously using published data.

Telephone Information Briefing Service (TIBS) is a FSS service that provides continuous recordings of meteorological and/or aeronautical information. A touch-tone telephone is required to fully utilize this service.

Further information can be found in the Aeronautical Information Manual (AIM).

NATIONAL FSS TELEPHONE NUMBER

Pilot Weather Briefings 1-800-WX-BRIEF (1-800-992-7433)

SPECIAL NOTICES

Fig. 22 Box C

DENVER TERMINAL RADAR APPROACH CONTROL
Denver, Colorado

The Denver Terminal Radar Approach Control has been issued a waiver which enables controllers to assign speed restrictions without obtaining pilot concurrences; e.g., speeds of less than 250 knots below FL280 and speeds of less than 210 knots when the aircraft is greater than 20 flying miles from the threshold of the airport of intended landing.

EXTENSIVE HELICOPTER FLIGHT TRAINING IN THE VICINITY OF ROCKY MOUNTAIN METROPOLITAN AIRPORT (BJC), BROOMFIELD, COLORADO

Frequent usage of Runway 11R–29L, Taxiway D, and the north end of Runway 20 by helicopter flight schools. Pilots are cautioned to listen carefully to ATC for turnoff instructions when landing on Runway 11R–29L. Helicopters flight schools use three primary local procedures: Charlie Two, Ball, and Erie. CHARLIE TWO: Expect departures to the south thence turning to the northwest. Expect arrivals from the northwest. BALL: Expect departures to the south thence turning east. Expect arrivals from the east. ERIE: Expect departures northbound. Expect arrivals from the north.

INTENSE HELICOPTER OPERATIONS
LOS ANGELES BASIN AREA, CALIFORNIA

VOR RECEIVER CHECK
VOR RECEIVER CHECKPOINTS
AND
VOR TEST FACILITIES (VOT)

ARIZONA
VOR RECEIVER CHECKPOINTS

Facility Name (Arpt Name)	Freq/Ident	Type Check Pt. Gnd. AB/ALT	Azimuth from Fac. Mag.	Dist. from Fac. N.M.	Checkpoint Description
Bard	116.8/BZA	A/2000	242	5.9	Over interstate 8 freeway crossing canal.
Drake (Ernest A. Love Fld)..........	114.1/DRK	A/7000	124	5.0	Over apch end Rwy 30.
Flagstaff (Pulliam)............	113.85/FLG	A/8000	033	6.5	Over red and white square twr.
Fort Huachuca (Sierra Vista Muni/Libby AAF)..............	113.6/FHU	G	80		Runup area Twy G at 26 end.
Kingman (Kingman)..............	108.8/IGM	G	220	1.0	Center of runup area apch

Fig. 22 Box D

PARACHUTE JUMPING AREAS

Fig. 22 Box E

LOCATION	DISTANCE AND RADIAL FROM NEAREST VOR/VORTAC	MAXIMUM ALTITUDE	REMARKS
	ARIZONA		
(c) **Buckeye Muni**..................	8 NM; 089° Buckeye	14,000	Daily SR–2 hours after SS. 2 NM radius.
(c) **Bullhead City, Eagle Airpark**..	10 NM; 300° Needles..............	15,000	3 NM Daily 0645–1835
(c) **Casa Grande Muni**...............	9 NM; 041° Stanfield...............	12,000	2 NM Daily 0600–1700.
(c) **Coolidge Muni**	25 NM; 070° Stanfield.............	17,999	15 NM radius, daily. High altitude, full canopy, free fall, and low level combat parachute jumping. Large military transports in vicinity of arpt.
(c) **Cottonwood Arpt**.................	22.1 NM; 072° Drake	14,000	Continuous during dalgt hrs. **Albuquerque Center 124.5**

NATIONAL FSS TELEPHONE NUMBER

Pilot Weather Briefings 1-800-WX-BRIEF (1-800-992-7433)

OTHER FSS TELEPHONE NUMBERS (except in Alaska)

TIBS (see description above) 1-877-4TIBS-WX (1-877-484-2799)

Clearance Delivery Only 1-888-766-8267

Lifeguard Flights Only 1-877-LIF-GRD3 (1-877-543-4733)

Flights within DC SFRA & FRZ * 1-866-225-7410

* District of Columbia Special Flight Rules Area & Flight Restricted Zone

Fig. 22 Box F

348 AIR ROUTE TRAFFIC CONTROL CENTERS

Air Route Traffic Control Center frequencies and their remoted transmitter sites are listed below for the coverage of this volume. Bold face type indicates high altitude frequencies, light face type indicates low altitude frequencies. To insure unrestricted IFR operations within the high altitude enroute sectors, the use of 720 channel communications equipment (25 kHz channel spacing) is required.

Ⓡ**ALBUQUERQUE CENTER – 134.6** 132.8 — **H-4-5-6-7, L-5-6-7-8-10-15-17-19**
Alamogordo – 132.65 132.65
Animas – 134.45 **133.0** — **(KZAB)**
Carlsbad – 135.875
Childs Peak – 135.15 132.45 126.45 125.25
Clines Corner – 133.65 132.8 125.075
Globe Nr 1 – 135.725 132.9 132.9
Globe Nr 2 – 135.15 133.85 **132.35** 132.35 125.4
Mesa Rica – 128.675 125.075
Mount Dora – 133.05 128.225 127.85
Prescott – 135.325 134.325 128.45

Fig. 22 Box G

Fig. 23

Notices To Airmen (NOTAMS)

When there are significant and important changes in aeronautical information, you need to know about them. This becomes especially important when such information might affect the safety of your flight. NOTAMS contain information such as airport or primary runway closures, changes in the status of navigational aids, radar service availability and other information essential to planned enroute, terminal or landing operations. When such information is not known far enough in advance to be included in the *Chart Supplement*, it's likely to be found in the listing of NOTAMS. Your job is to check these NOTAMS before every flight. You can ask the Flight Service Station specialist for all pertinent NOTAM information during your weather briefing or just download them when you obtain your weather briefing from an FAA approved service provider, such as Leidos.

There are two types of NOTAMS you should be familiar with: D NOTAMs and FDC NOTAMS. Let's examine both.

D NOTAMS – D (distant and local) NOTAMS contain information that directly affects your ability to fly an airplane safely. This includes information on airport or primary runway closures, changes in the status of navigational aids, radar service availability, and other information essential to planned enroute, terminal, or landing operations. In addition, these NOTAMS now contain less critical (but still very important) airport information such as taxiway closures, personnel and equipment near or crossing runways, and airport lighting aids such as VASIs.

FDC NOTAMS – Occasionally, it becomes necessary to issue information on changes that are regulatory in nature. A regulatory change might be an amendment to an instrument chart used by IFR pilots or the issuance of a temporary flight restriction (such as prohibition of flight over a natural disaster area, which is important to you as a VFR pilot). When such an action is necessary, the National Flight Data Center (NFDC) will issue an FDC NOTAM. FDC NOTAMS are issued once and kept on file at the FSS until published or canceled.

All this information is kept in a computer in Kansas City and is distributed automatically via several sources, such as the FSS when you obtain a weather briefing. (Note: If you call for a weather briefing, make sure you ask the FSS specialist for any pertinent FDC NOTAM information concerning your flight. They usually give these to you, but it's always best to ask, nevertheless.)

There are three additional NOTAM types to consider. The first is **Pointer NOTAMS**. These are issued by the FSS to highlight or point out another NOTAM which makes it easier for you to cross reference information relevant to your flight. Then there are **SAA NOTAMS** that are issued when *Special Activity Airspace* is scheduled outside the regularly published times. Finally, there are **Military NOTAMS**. These pertain to armed forces airports and navigation aids.

As of February, 2020, the FAA has discontinued its publication of the *Notices to Airmen Publication* (NTAP), as shown in Figure 24. Currently, if you'd like to search the NOTAM database you should visit the following link.

https://notams.aim.faa.gov/notamSearch/

When reading D NOTAMS, they will have one of the following keywords as the first part of the text: RWY, TWY, APRON, AD, OBST, NAV, COM, SVC, AIRSPACE, (U), or (O). Each keyword indicates the category of the

THE NOTICE TO AIRMEN PUBLICATION (NTAP)

Fig. 24

D NOTAM KEYWORDS, EXAMPLES AND EXPLANATIONS

RWY (Runway)

Example: !STL STL RWY 12L/30R CLSD EXC TXG

This NOTAM says that Runway Twelve Left and Runway Thirty Right are closed at St. Louis Lambert Airport, except for taxiing.

TWY (Taxiway)

Example: !LNS LNS TWY A LGTS OTS

NOTAM says that the lights on taxiway A are out of service at Lancaster Airport.

APRON (Apron)

Example: !ATL ATL APRON NORTH TWY L3 APRON CLSD

NOTAM indicates that the north taxiway L3 Apron is closed at Atlanta Hartsfield Airport.

AD (Aerodrome)

Example: !CEW CEW AD CLSD WEF 0802041400-0802041800

Explanation: Bob Sikes Airport is closed from 1400 till 1800 UTC on February 4, 2008.

OBST (Obstructions, including obstruction lighting outages)

Example: !PIE CLW OBST CRANE 195 (125 AGL) .25 NE (2755N08241W) TIL 0803032000

NOTAM indicates there is a crane, 195 feet MSL or 125 feet AGL, ¼ statute mile northeast of the Clearwater Air Park Airport until March 3, 2008 at 2000 UTC. The lat/longs of the crane are 27° 55″ North and 082° 41″ West.

NAV (Navigation Aids)

Example: !DCA DCA NAV GTN NDB OTS

NOTAM indicates that the Georgetown NDB, that services Washington National Airport, is out of service.

COM (Communications)

Example: !DCA PSK COM RCO OTS

NOTAM shows that the remote communications outlet is out of service at New River Valley Airport.

SVC (Services)

Example: !PBF PBF SVC TEMPO TWR 121.0 1400-2100 DLY

NOTAM indicates that at Grider Field, a temporary control tower is available between 1400 and 2100 UTC daily, and frequency 121.0 will be used to control aircraft on all movement areas and traffic patterns.

AIRSPACE (Airspace)

Example: !IPT RAV AIRSPACE R5802 ACT TIL 0802211230

NOTAM indicates that Restricted Area R5802A is active until February 21, 2008 at 1230 UTC

(U) – Unverified Aeronautical Information

Example: !ORT 6K8 (U) RWY ABANDONED VEHICLE

This is an unverified NOTAM indicating that there is an abandoned vehicle on the runway at Tok Junction Airport.

(O) – Other Aeronautical Information

Aeronautical information received from any authorized source that may be beneficial to aircraft operations and does not meet defined NOTAM criteria.

Example: !LOZ LOZ (O) CONTROLLED BURN OF HOUSE 8 NE APCH END RWY 23 WEF 0802271300-0802271700

NOTAM says that there is a controlled burn of a house 8 statute miles northeast of the approach end of Runway 23 at the London-Corbin Airport between 1300 and1700 UTC on February 27, 2008.

Fig. 25

NOTAM. For instance, RWY indicated this NOTAM refers to the *runway*, and so on. Each NOTAM begins with an exclamation mark (they are important, right?), followed by the accountability location (the source generating the NOTAM), followed by the affected airport (or facility). Figure 25 shows all the major D NOTAM categories, along with examples and explanations. Take some time to familiarize yourself with these, since you'll most likely encounter similar type NOTAMS during the preflight briefing. If you have trouble interpreting the NOTAM codes, then see Postflight Briefing #17-3 at the end of this chapter.

FDC NOTAMS are shown in Figure 26. These are NOTAMS that pertain mostly to instrument rated pilots, although you should look them over for anything relevant to your flight.

FDC NOTAM EXAMPLE

FDC 4/0435 SJC FI/T NORMAN Y. MINETA SAN JOSE INTL,
SAN JOSE, CA.
NDB/DME RWY 30L, AMDT 6.
S-30L MDA 780/HAT 723 ALL CATS. VIS CAT C 1 1/2, CAT D 2.
SIDESTEP RWY 29 MDA 780/HAT 728 ALL CATS. VIS CAT C 2,
CAT D 2 1/4.
SIDESTEP RWY 30R MDA 780/HAT 725 ALL CATS. VIS CAT C 2,
CAT D 2 1/4.

Fig. 26

This FDC NOTAM for San Jose airport contains information on instrument approach procedures. Nevertheless, it's always wise to ask the FSS specialist for FDC NOTAMS pertinent to your flight.

FAA ADVISORY CIRCULARS

1. PURPOSE. This advisory circular has been published for the following p

a. To inform pilots of the airworthiness standards for the type certif of small airplanes prescribed in Section 23.221 of the Federal Aviation Reg (FAR) concerning spin maneuvers;

b. To emphasize the importance of observing restrictions which prohibi intentional spinning of certain airplanes;

c. To recommend specific flight operations procedures to reduce the pr of entering an inadvertent spin during the performance of stall entries and recoveries; and

Advisory Circulars

For years the FAA has been providing pilots with useful information in the form of advisory circulars (AC) (Figure 27). Advisory circulars are a means of disseminating nonregulatory information of interest. The subjects covered include procedures, techniques, aircraft, airmen, airspace, ATC, airports and general operating rules. Since these are advisory in nature only, their contents should not be considered legally binding unless they become regulations. You can order advisory circulars from the Superintendent of Documents, U.S. Government Printing Office or just download them for free at http://www.faa.gov/.

You'll find that advisory circulars are numbered according to the Federal Aviation Regulation numbering system. For instance, the advisory circulars in Figure 27 is numbered AC 61-67. AC's marked anywhere in the 60's represent information dealing with FAR Part 61— Certification: Pilots and Flight Instructors. AC's marked anywhere is the 90's represent information on Part 91—Air Traffic and General Operating Flight Rules. ACs marked anywhere is the 20's pertain to Certification and Testing of Aircraft (FAR Part 23) and deal with certification of small airplanes. AC's marked anywhere in the 70's represent information on airspace (FAR Part 71 deal with airspace construction).

Novel Student Pilot Solutions

HUH?

A student of mine showed me that there are BETTER ways to deal with fast-talking controllers and an overabundance of communication on the frequency.

We were doing touch and go landings at NAS Corpus Christi in a T-28B (This is important because it establishes the fact that I was BEHIND the student and couldn't really see what he was doing!) In any event, NAS Corpus has two parallel runways and on that day we had a full bag of left and right traffic, as well as occasional straight in instrument approaches to the instrument runway. On the downwind, I could barely hear my student doing his checklist items among all the chatter. Mercifully, there was a brief pause as we approached the 180 - and then I heard, "Delta 685, Corpus Christi Approach, cleared for the ILS 13, contact the Tower at the marker". I hollered up front, "What did you do?" The student replied, "Sir, there were too many people talking on that other frequency so I picked one that wasn't as busy".

A Fellow Instructor (name unknown)

Aviation Decision Making: Thoughts for Life

The fact is, not everyone on this planet exercises good judgment. For instance, every so often you'll read that someone in a black wetsuit, floating on a surfboard and dangling four limbs over the side, was attacked by a great white shark. Isn't that amazing? What was this person thinking? Doesn't dressing up this way make you look like the shark's favorite food—the seal? Is it the shark's fault he was served breakfast on board? You could say the surfer sealed his own fate in opting to dress as he did. Clearly a bad decision.

Fortunately, exercising good judgment is something we can do on the ground or in the air. With a few simple tools, you can keep yourself from being eaten by some of aviation's well known predators.

It's true, the exercise of good judgment can be taught, despite a once-popular belief that good judgment only came with years of experience. We now know that you can learn to identify and control several of the variables leading to poor decisions. For instance, it's possible to identify attitudes that are hazardous to safe flight as well as learn how to modify our personal behavior. These are just a few of the useful techniques that help you make better decisions. Let's cover a few of the most important features of aviation decision making.

Two Types of Decisions

Decisions usually fall into two categories—those tied to time constraints and those that are not. A time-constrained decision often requires an immediate solution. For example, if you have an engine fire, this requires immediate action. If, on the other hand, your alternator just failed in VFR conditions, you need not rush to solve the problem. You can take your time and collect information before deciding on a course of action.

In fact, most of the aviation decisions you make will not require immediate action. Preflight is a good example. It's rare to hear of someone having an emergency when preflighting the airplane. You can take your time and carefully consider all the information available to you.

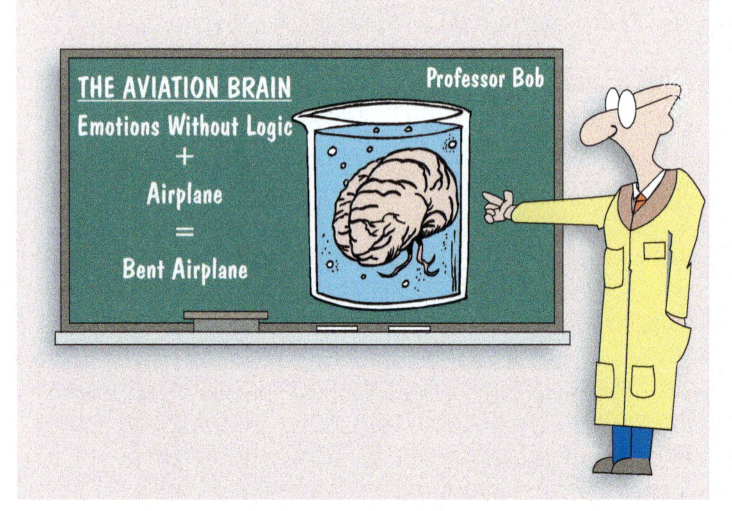

That's what makes the results of a NASA study all the more interesting. The research revealed that 80% of the poor decisions leading to an in-flight incident occurred during the preflight phase, when pilots had all the time in the world to get it right.

Fuel exhaustion is a good example of this type of error. If a pilot had taken more time to carefully think about fuel, he or she wouldn't have crashed short of the destination with bone-dry tanks. In case you're interested, one study found that 70% of fuel exhaustion accidents occurred within 10 miles of the destination airport and 50% occurred within one mile of the airport. Close, so close, and yet so far.

Of course, pilots could handle this problem by planning a flight, then switching the destination to an airport that's 10 miles closer. You're right, that seems ridiculous, doesn't it? I think it's much simpler to do some proper preflighting to begin with. Thoughtful preparation, having sufficient fuel reserves and careful planning are the ways to prevent accidents.

Factors That Influence Our Decisions

Knowledge

There are several factors that influence your ability to make good aviation decisions. First, in order to successfully cope with any aviation situation you need knowledge. This is typically acquired during flight training, where you'll learn things such as how to calculate airplane performance, evaluating weather, and selecting alternatives if the flight can't be completed as planned. These are a just a few of the many practical topics you'll be exposed to during the course of your training (I said practical topics, so don't expect to learn something like how to look good in scarf and goggles, etc.)

Skill

In addition to knowledge, you must develop skill in applying that knowledge. That's why the FAA requires a minimum of 40 hours of flight time for the private pilot license. This also explains why you can't obtain a pilot's license via a home correspondence course (if you could, it would properly be called a crash course). In addition to this, you have to pass both a practical flight test and a written knowledge exam to demonstrate your flight and knowledge skills.

Aids That Help With Decision Making

There are several aids available to help you make decisions properly. A checklist is a good example of one of these aids. Written-type checklists are normally used for repetitive tasks when it's not wise to rely on short- or long-term memory. Checklists are commonly used for the preflight inspection of the airplane, starting the engine,

emergencies, and engine shutdown. Checklists can also be used during the preflight phase, and these don't necessarily need to be of the written variety, either. A simple acronym is often sufficient to cover the essentials.

For instance, before every flight you should take inventory of your psychological and physiological readiness to pilot an airplane. You can use the acronym "I'M SAFE" to do this. Here's what the acronym means.

1. *Illness.* Do I have any symptoms?

2. *Medication.* Have I been taking prescription or over-the-counter drugs?

3. *Stress.* Am I under psychological pressure from work or home situations? Do I have money, health, or family problems?

4. *Alcohol.* Have I been drinking within 8 hours? Within 24 hours?

5. *Fatigue.* Am I tired and not adequately rested?

6. *Eating.* Have I eaten enough of the proper foods to keep adequately nourished during the entire flight?

Pilots using this checklist are less likely to suffer some sort of impairment that can lead or at least contribute to an accident. Statistics show that impairment contributes to many more accidents than mechanical problems. Please commit this checklist to memory and use it before every flight.

Self Awareness and Hazardous Thinking

Common Behavioral Pilot Traps

If there is such a thing as an enemy to a pilot, then it's the pilot himself. It's a pilot's inability to deal with some very common behavioral traps that usually gets him or her into trouble. You don't want to fall into these traps. I'm specifically referring to traps like always trying to complete the flight the way you planned it, trying to please your passengers, trying to meet schedules, as well as trying to demonstrate that you have the right stuff. Well, at hundreds of miles per hour, the fabled right stuff can turn you and your airplane into bent stuff.

Here are 12 common traps of which you should be aware. Most experienced pilots have fallen into one or more of these somewhere along the way. If they were lucky, they escaped unscathed and learned from the experience. Here's your chance to learn before the experience. Avoiding these traps requires recognizing the behaviors or tendencies associated with them.

1. *Peer Pressure.* No, this doesn't have anything to do with flying near the beach. It's simply poor decision making based upon emotional response to peers rather than evaluating a situation objectively.

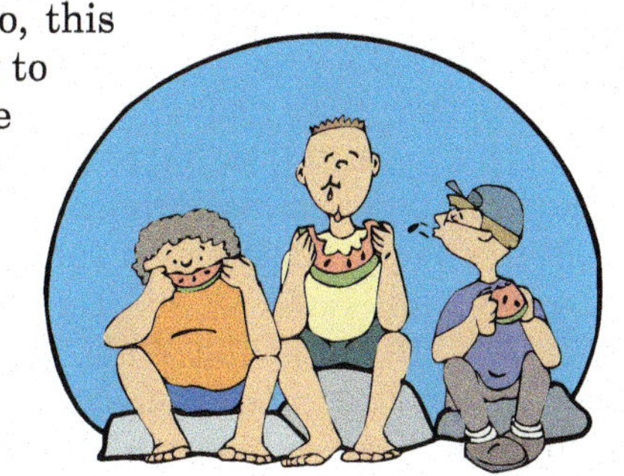

2. *Mindset.* This trap results from a pilot's inability to recognize and cope with situations that differ from those anticipated or planned. In other words, things change. When necessary, pilots should, too.

3. *Get-There-Itis.* This tendency, common among pilots, clouds the vision and impairs judgment. It's caused by a fixation on the original goal or destination combined with a total disregard for any alternative course of action. Get-There-Itis is suspected to be the root cause of another malady that I just made up called Break-and-Crumple-Your-Airplane-Itis.

4. *Duck-Under Syndrome.* This is a tendency instrument rated pilots have to sneak a peek by descending below minimum altitudes during an instrument approach. It's based on a belief that there is always a built-in fudge factor that can be used or on an unwillingness to admit defeat and shoot a missed approach. Pilots from China might call this the Peaking-Duck-Under-Glass-Syndrome.

5. *Scud Running.* Scud running involves pushing the capabilities of the pilot and the aircraft by flying in poor visibility and/or under low clouds while trying to maintain visual contact with the terrain (and trying to avoid physical contact with it as well. Very dangerous business).

6. *Continuing visual flight rules (VFR) into instrument conditions.* This often leads to spatial disorientation or collision with the ground and/or obstacles. It is even more dangerous if the pilot is not instrument qualified (and it's especially dangerous if the pilot isn't wrapped in a big, thick mattress, too).

7. *Getting Behind the Aircraft.* The only time it's good to get behind the aircraft is when you untie the tail before departure. Unfortunately, some pilots allow events or the situation to control their actions rather than the other way around. This condition is characterized by a constant state of surprise at what happens next. Pilots in this condition often look like they drew their eyebrows in at too great an angle during makeup time.

8. *Loss of Positional or Situational Awareness.* Another case of getting behind the aircraft, which results in not knowing where you are, an inability to recognize deteriorating circumstances, and/or misjudging how fast your situation is worsening.

9. *Operating Without Adequate Fuel Reserves.* Ignoring minimum fuel reserve requirements, either VFR or Instrument Flight Rules (IFR), is generally the result of overconfidence, lack of flight planning, or ignoring the regulations. In other words, you can fuel some of the people some of the time but you can't fuel everyone all the time (especially when they need to be fueled).

10. *Descent Below the Minimum Enroute Altitude.* Here, the duck-under syndrome (discussed earlier) manifests itself during the enroute portion of an IFR flight.

11. *Flying Outside the Envelope.* This results from a pilot's unjustified reliance on the (usually mistaken) belief that the aircraft's high performance capability meets the demands imposed by his or her (usually overestimated) flying skills.

12. *Neglect of Flight Planning,* preflight inspections, checklists, etc. This is a problem associated with a pilot's unjustified reliance on his or her short and long term memory, regular flying skills, repetitive and familiar routes, etc.

Hazardous Thought Patterns And Their Antidotes

Another factor affecting the quality and safety of flight is a pilot's attitude. Unlike personality, most psychologists agree that you can change an attitude. Your attitude is a state of mind, a feeling, a disposition. Not all attitudes, unfortunately, are conducive to safe flying. The following are five attitudes that aviation psychologists believe to be particularly hazardous to safe flight:

Anti-authority—This attitude belongs to people who don't like being told what to do. Folks like these often rebel against the rules and regulations on which safe flying are built. This hazardous attitude causes some pilots to rebel against authority by deliberately breaking rules intended for safety. For instance, I knew of a private pilot who removed the right seat from his airplane so there would be no place for an instructor to sit and tell him what to do. It's a good bet that he had the North American distributorship on anti-authority attitudes.

Impulsivity—Some people often feel the need to do something and do it immediately even when it's not the right thing to do. Often these folks will do the first thing that comes to mind, without thinking about what the best alternative might be. This is why I always get a little nervous when a pilot I'm flying with suddenly says, "Hey, watch this." It's likely that he's about to engage in some strange behavior that he probably hasn't thought about very carefully. Having a front row seat at Aviation Impulsive Theater is not my idea of having a good time.

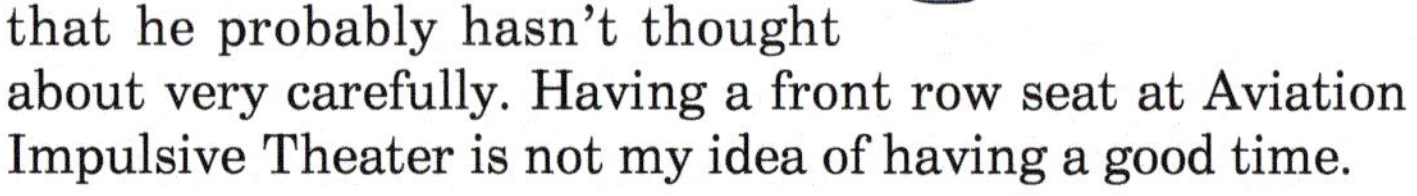

Invulnerability—It's not uncommon for people to feel that accidents only happen to others, not to them. These folks know that accidents can happen, and they know that anyone can be affected, but they never really feel or believe they will be personally involved. A pilot with this attitude is more likely to take chances and increase risk. Pilots like this often think they're Superman, but Superman doesn't really need an airplane, does he?

Macho—A macho pilot is someone with an exaggerated sense of masculinity, stressing attributes such as physical courage, virility, aggressiveness, overt manliness, etc. This can lead a pilot to rely on his "machismo" attributes rather than on rational information. Instead of checking the weather, a pilot with a macho attitude might say, "There's no weather problem I can't handle." Yikes!

Resignation—Pilots who thinks, "What's the use?" are people who don't feel in control of the events in their lives. They often blame bad luck for whatever happens. They tend to not seek information and to not make positive decisions. Instead, they drift along hoping that good things happen while doing little or nothing to ensure that they do. It's as if they fold their hands and sit back passively, doing nothing, like a little pilot-Gandhi. While that behavior may liberate a country from the clutches of foreign domination, it's not likely to make you any safer in the air.

Hazardous Attitude Antidotes Fig. 28

Attitude	Antidote
Anti-authority—Don't tell me.	Follow the rules. They are usually right.
Impulsivity—Do something quickly.	Not so fast. Think first.
Invulnerability—It won't happen to me.	It could happen to me.
Macho—I can do it.	Taking chances is foolish.
Resignation—What's the use?	I'm not helpless. I can make a difference.

These attitudes can contribute to poor judgment. They can compel you to make decisions involving greater risk. Once you've recognized them, however, you've taken the first step in neutralizing their dangerous effects on your decision making process. Remember, most people have these attitudes to some degree. To be frank about it, all of us, at one time or another, have probably acted macho, impulsive or invulnerable. Avoiding problems with judgment means that you should be aware of how these attitudes can negatively influence flying safely.

Hazardous Attitude Antidotes

Recognition of hazardous thoughts is the first step toward neutralizing them. After recognizing a thought as hazardous, the pilot should label it as hazardous, and then state the corresponding antidote. Antidotes should be memorized for each of the hazardous attitudes so they automatically come to mind when needed (Figure 28).

At this point, however, any intelligent person is bound to ask, "If I am acting in a hazardous manner, how is it possible that I'd be self-reflective enough to identify it, much less apply an antidote to stop it?" Great question!

The fact is that hazardous attitudes are *temporary* dispositions, not *permanent* ones. Like the temporary feeling of fear or anxiety, hazardous attitudes stand out from the background of your personality sufficiently for you to recognize them, but only if you know they exist in the first place. That is why we're discussing them here. Now that you know they exist, you're in a better position to do something about them. Do what? How about talking to yourself.

Perhaps, at one time or another, you've found yourself anxious, rushed, or panicky and told yourself to, "Calm down, relax, take your time." The amazing thing is that self-talk actually works in modifying your behavior, especially in high anxiety conditions. That's why it also works well in controlling behavior associated with any of the five hazardous attitudes. The next time you recognize that you're demonstrating any of the five hazardous attitudes, apply the accompanying self-talk antidote.

Do antidotes actually work? You bet they do, and I'm not just saying that so that you'll keep reading this book, either. They work, and they can save your life for one very important reason. You can be the best stick and rudder pilot on the planet (or other planets, too), but this means nothing in terms of safety if you let a bad attitude influence your behavior. That's a fact. So be proactive, tune your personal antenna to recognize and identify these attitudes and, if you catch yourself exhibiting one or more, don't be surprised. It happens to the best of us. The difference is that good pilots use the antidote to prevent bad behavior

Professor Bob

Professor Bob has found proof, via X-ray pictures, that it's a pilot's bad attitude that can cause accidents. The X-ray shown is taken from a pilot who ran out of fuel because he didn't want to waste his valuable time stopping for gas. An X-ray from the other side of the pilot's head also proved he had a bad attitude, but you need a mirror to figure this out.

Bad Attitude

Being Pilot In Command

What would you think if I told you that even if you fly a Cessna 172, you have the same authority as the captain of a Boeing 777? It's true, though you have no say-so over his or her 777. There is only one regulation authorizing PIC authority, and that's FAR 91.3, which applies to anyone who flies anything (Area 51 UFO vehicles are an exception). This means that even if you're operating under FAR Part 121 or 135, this regulation is the one that applies to the PIC. The problem here is that most pilots aren't taught how to be pilot in command. They sort of accept the authority without acknowledging or really understanding the responsibility.

THE PILOT IN COMMAND

TWA Captain Dave Gwinn

The way the FAA looks at it, as PIC you have the final authority and the final say as to the operation of your aircraft. FAR 91.3 is one of the clearest, most succinct and least ambiguous regulations ever written, and for good reason, too. The FAA wants to make sure you know, unambiguously, that you're the one in command and you're the one responsible for making the proper decisions on an airplane. And finally, that you're the one on whom they'll pin the tail if anything goes wrong.

Years ago I met a fellow who ran a medevac helicopter operation. He said that when he hired someone to fly his medical helicopters, he hired them on the basis that these people would tell him "no" when it was appropriate to do so. In other words, he wanted his pilots to have the leadership and strength of character to say that they shouldn't go flying when the risks were too great.

The reality is that many people are just plain scared to say "no" when it's not safe to fly. That's not the type of person this man wanted piloting his machines. Just imagine how difficult a decision it must be to say "no" to a medevac flight to retrieve someone injured on a freeway somewhere when the weather makes it unsafe to fly. Do you have the mental sinew to make this call, based on your level of experience? If not, then you need to reconsider your priorities, because this is precisely what the pilot in command is expected to do.

Sure, you say that telling the boss "no" might mean you get fired. OK, that's possible. You might also say that this is just unfair, even though it's the right thing to do. Yes, that's true. My reply would be that life doesn't have to be fair (check your contract), but it's not as if death gives you some sort of advantage. Being PIC means that you have to be willing to take charge, be in charge and make the necessary decisions willingly, without concern for your personal needs, especially when the needs of others are more important. That's hard language, but it's the way the world works.

A friend who once did the hiring for Flying Tiger airlines told me that they never hired pilots. Instead, they hired captains, even though this person would sit in the flight engineer's seat for many years. Flying Tigers wanted pilots who were captain material, not just pilot material. There *is* a difference.

Sometimes you'll have to make decisions that are unpopular and might upset or disappoint your passengers. The weather might require delaying or even canceling a flight. Sure, the passengers won't like it, but if that's the appropriate thing to do, then it must be done. Do you have the character to behave in the right way? Hopefully you do, since this is part of what being PIC is all about. Of course, there's much more to being PIC of an airplane, too. So let's see what else is involved.

Crew/Cockpit Resource Management

Crew/cockpit resource management (CRM) is all about using the resources that are available to you during your duty as PIC. These resources might be the human resources you have in a copilot, the hardware you have in the cockpit, or the information available to you via that hardware or from ATC. It's a major misconception that only pilots of multi-pilot crews can use CRM or CRM philosophy. Single-pilot operators also need to know how to make better use of all the resources available to them, perhaps even more so than those who've got triple redundancy and a six-planet GPS.

Human Resources

Those resources include all the people with whom you routinely work in preparing and executing a flight—weather briefers, line personnel, mechanics, crewmembers, pilots and air traffic controllers. The real issue here is whether or not you're making good use of these resources. Let's examine how you'd use a copilot (or a capable, non-pilot passenger) if you had one on your flight.

Let's say you're flying for a Part 135 charter operation and the flight requires a copilot. Obviously this flight won't be in a Cessna 152 or there wouldn't be much room for the passengers, would there? What does a copilot do for you? The answer is, anything you want. Within reason, of course. They don't do windows or ironing.

Copilots are wonderful resources if you know how to use them properly. Tuning radios, finding charts, making calls to ATC or the automated flight service station, monitoring your performance and gaining experience are all

Thanks for the Memories

Most folks want a better memory, at least when they can remember that they want it. Memory is an important part of the flying process. A pilot has to remember a lot of small things as well a lot of big things, not to mention many in-between things. Here are a few concepts to consider about how your memory works and how to make it work better for you.

Memory works in a multistage process involving three systems: *the sensory register*, *working* or *short term memory* and *long term memory*. Each functions in a slightly different way.

The sensory register receives input from the environment through your senses based on what you think is important, and discards what's perceived as extraneous. This is why a mother responds immediately to the sound of her crying baby at night, while other family members might not notice it (or pretend not to notice if getting out of bed is involved).

That is also why you will usually respond to certain environmental stimuli such as a panel warning light, regardless of the flying chores you may be involved at the time. The moment you notice the warning light, important information passes into working or short term memory. Here, the information may stay or fade rapidly, depending on your priorities. For instance, when ATC calls your "N" number, this activates the sensory register and places the controller's call in your short term memory queue. Trained pilot that you are (or will be), you know that you'll soon have to respond or the controller will call again (requiring you to dredge up some good excuses from long term memory). If ATC calls and gives you a new transponder code, and this information makes it to your short-term memory (you register it), it won't remain there for long. That's why it's called *short term* memory!

Normally, information only has about a 20 second lifespan in short term memory, varying slightly depending on the nature of your priorities. You can help information stay longer by repeating it out loud. This is one good reason to always read back your clearances. Rehearsing, repetition, sorting, rhyming, associations, mnemonics or categorizing the material into systematic chunks is called *coding,* and it's another way to help information stay in short term memory and move it into long-term memory if you want. Most commercial memory courses just teach various coding techniques.

For instance, if ATC instructs you to fly via Victor 11 and climb to 11,500 feet, you may notice the similarities between the first two numerical values to help remember the information until you can write it down. Saying to yourself, "Fly eleven-five to eleven," should keep the information present until you grab your pencil (or spray can, chunk of charcoal or whatever you copy clearances with). If you want to remember to place your GPS in OBS mode versus Leg mode before crossing FISHY intersection, you could visualize a big FISH (for FISHY intersection), swallowing a BUS (for OBS) out of which runs a lone LEG (for Leg mode). Depending on the amount of information given and your skill, it can take several seconds to properly code information (to make the chunks, rhymes, verbal repetitions, etc.). Interrupt the process and all the short-term information is likely to be lost from short-term memory within 20 seconds.

Short term memory has a capacity limit, in addition to its time limit. It's usually capable of handling about seven bits or chunks of information at a time. A seven digit telephone number is a good example. If your friend has too many digits for a phone number, you might want to get some friends in your area code (or get used to playing with the cat on Saturday night). This is why you shouldn't count on keeping a long clearance in short term memory. Of course, if you're good at coding you can overcome this problem, keeping the material in short-term memory for a much longer period of time.

Actual learning doesn't take place until the information moves into long term memory, where it's stored for future use. By use of the coding concepts listed above as well as by rote memorization, it's possible for information to move from short term to long term memory, where it can remain stored for a lifetime. I'm not speaking of remembering all the transponder codes and clearances you've ever received, either. You're not Rainman. I'm speaking of the information that will have value to you in the long term, like flying skills, foreign languages or, heaven forbid, foreign flying skills. The more extensive the coding process, the easier it is to recall information in the long term.

Keep in mind, however, that it takes effort to move information beyond short term memory. Good students are hip to this point and go out of their way to acquire some basic skill at mnemonics to help them learn more efficiently. A mnemonic is a word whose letters (or the word itself) help trigger your memory. I'M SAFE, for *illness, medication, stress, alcohol, fatigue,* and *eating,* is an example of a mnemonic.

Make a quick trip to the bookstore and ask the book specialist where the self-help section is. If this person says, "If I do that, then you won't be helping yourself," suggest that you're also looking for a book on how to do karate chops. I'm sure the specialist will immediately offer to help you find a book on memory techniques.

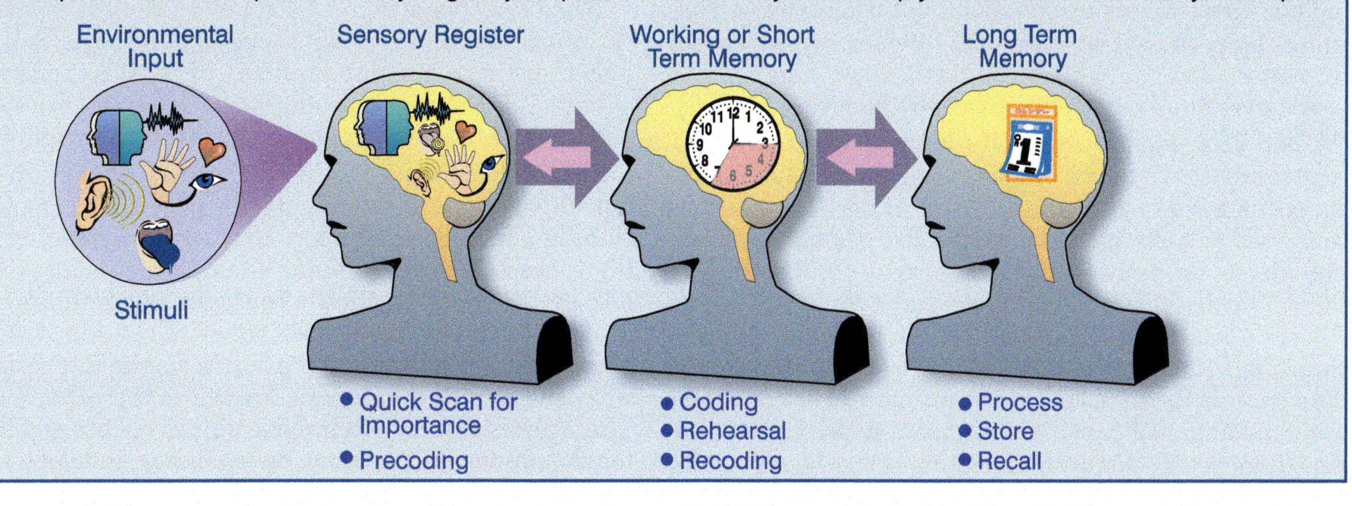

part of what copilots do. My friend, retired TWA Captain Dave Gwinn, once told me that when he was a copilot he looked at his job as one where he always tried to make the captain look good. In other words, he'd remind the captain of the assigned altitude as they approached it, he'd call out localizer or airway intercepts, he'd tune radios and make ATC calls and so on.

The real problem with copilots is pilots. Most pilots are independent people and like to do things themselves. That may be OK as long as the situation isn't demanding. But in some situations it's easy to be overwhelmed by the workload. Even then, some pilots will try doing it all themselves while their copilots sit nearby, actively idle. Improper (or no) use of a copilot is one of the main reasons pilots fail checkrides on airplanes where there's a two pilot crew.

I'll take this a step further and say that even on airplanes where only one pilot is necessary, but a passenger occupies the right seat, this person should be informed that he or she might be asked to do a bit of work. I don't mean fly, but perhaps hold or fold a chart. Of course, the more aviation experience a person has, the more they can do for you.

With an experienced copilot sitting in the right seat, you have a wonderful resource to tap. You can bounce ideas and questions off this person. But don't bounce paper balls off his forehead (copilots hate that). Remember, two heads are better than one, unless you don't know where you're heading or you're paying for everyone's haircuts.

Using your copilot (and other human resources) properly means that you know something about communications, teamwork, task allocation, and decision making. You must be able to communicate your thoughts, needs, and wishes properly to these resources. So how do you know if you're communicating properly? The best way to tell is to ask yourself if you're getting the help you requested. It's simply a matter of feedback. If you ask your copilot for assistance in finding a chart and he's busy wadding up a paper ball to throw at the flight attendant, then you're not communicating properly, are you?

Looked at in a more academic way, the communications aspect of CRM becomes a matter of inquiry, advocacy, and assertion. As PIC, you may have to ask a lot of questions to get the information you need. Once you have these information tidbits, you may need to press ATC, your copilot, and your company to do what you think is safe at the time. For instance, if your copilot is suggesting that you fly to the destination despite one of your two engines running rough, you might need to explain and justify your position to the copilot. This assumes, of course, that you have the time to do this.

Which brings us back to the fact that when all is said and done and communicated, *you* are the pilot in command and the final decision is entirely yours. That's true whether the flight vessel is a 172 or a 757. Your job is to make the best possible use of all resources to gather the information needed to make a wise decision, but making that decision is your job. That's why you are called the *pilot in command.* When it comes to the cockpit, it's one man or woman, one vote.

One of the initial problems with CRM was the failure of crew members to recognize the difference between experience and inexperience. If a copilot said, "Captain, I'm not comfortable with what you're going to do," and the captain replied, "Well, I'm going to do it," then this certainly wasn't what the spirit of CRM intended.

Instead, the captain should reply with something like, "Well, here's why we need to do it this way," followed by an explanation. The intent here is for the captain to educate the copilot based on his or her years of experience. After all, the first officer will eventually replace the captain and he or she would certainly benefit from the captain's experience. In this sense, CRM implies that captains should be educators as well as professional pilots. This shouldn't be too demanding, since most folks fill an educational role in one way or another, especially if they have children. Of course, I'm not suggesting that a captain treat a copilot like a child. After all, he can't restrict a copilot's allowance, since the airline the copilot's working for has probably already done this based on the typical new-hire pay rate.

Hardware

When I say "hardware," I don't mean things like wrenches and screwdrivers. I mean things like the advanced, automated equipment found on many of today's modern airplanes. CRM means knowing how to use this equipment and when to use it (or stop using it, as the case might be).

Take, for instance, the newest primary and multi-function flight displays (see Figure 30, page A10, Chapter 1). This is amazing equipment that can provide you with flight instrumentation when used as the primary flight display (PFD), or location when used as a multi-function display (MFD). It can provide you with checklist information and engine instrumentation readings and help you with situational awareness, among many other things. There are rumors it will provide dinner recipes and advice for the lovelorn if you know certain secret codes.

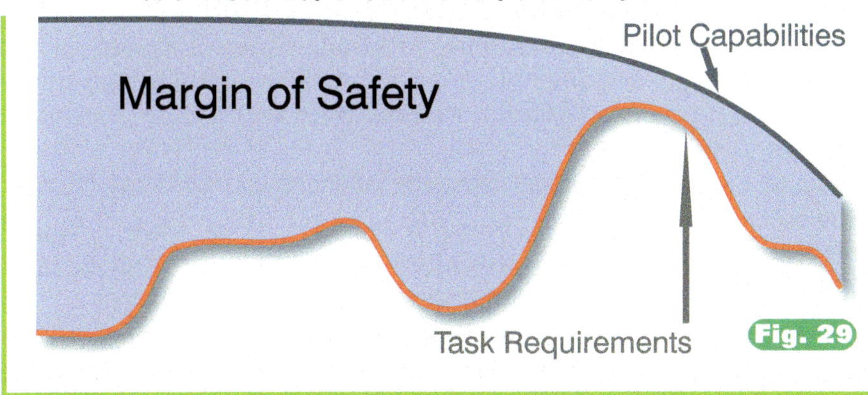

The amount of effort exerted by a pilot for a given period of time varies based on the demands of the task. As this accompanying graph clearly shows, preflight requires very little extended effort compared to approaching and landing an airplane.

The versatility comes at the cost of complexity. Some instructors say that it can take as much as 20 hours of flight and ground training to become sufficiently familiar with some primary flight displays. Twenty hours? Yep. What about those who use this equipment but don't use it often enough to remain proficient in its use? You can bet that more than one pilot has scared himself by hopping into an airplane with advanced avionics equipment for a simple VFR flight only to find out that he can't remember how to set the GPS unit up for basic navigation. If the display flashes "Dear Abby," or has a recipe for Salisbury Steak, you are in over your head, especially if you're a vegetarian. You don't want to go there.

That's why the use of an autopilot is so valuable on airplanes with advanced equipment. The autopilot is the ultimate CRM tool. It's like a copilot except that it doesn't wad up paper balls and throw them back at you (at least the older versions don't).

Many years ago, a NASA study of single-pilot operations suggested that pilots were often best served by autopilots having only a single axis control (i.e., heading hold). Two axis autopilots (those with altitude and heading control) tended to take the pilot out of the performance loop. In other words, the pilot ended up flying the autopilot and not the airplane. That led to the pilot often getting so far behind the airplane that if there were a crash, he wouldn't arrive at the scene for an additional 30 minutes.

Things have changed. Now, if you're using a primary and multifunction flight display, it's just too easy to be overwhelmed by the need to push buttons, checking menus, etc. So, you'll definitely want to put that autopilot to use when operating in airplanes having this equipment. It means you're less likely to drift from your heading, altitude or clearance.

Information Workload

VFR pilots, especially those operating in high density traffic areas, can only do so many things at one time. That's usually one less than the number of things that need doing. Sure, there are some among us who can multitask in the sense that we can fly and talk on the radio at the same time. Copying a clearance while flying, navigating, and working advanced avionics often overloads even the most capable pilot, especially if he's fiddling with the CD changer at the same time. That's why the very best pilots know two secret words that helps reduce cockpit workload to a workable minimum. Would you like to know what they are? *Stand by.* Those are the words to say.

When you're busy and ATC calls, you don't have to immediately honor the controller's request. You can simply say, "Stand by." ATC understands that, don't they? After all, this is exactly what they tell you when you call and *they're* busy? And guess what? They'll respect you in the morning (or afternoon, or whenever you get back to them). Some pilots, in an attempt to maintain their burnished on-the-air image, never turn down an ATC call, even when they've got a one-track mind and four channels of input happening. The result is mistakes, repeats, and other things that compromise the safety of flight. As soon as you're really ready, call ATC and communicate. That's how smart pilots fly.

Sometimes things get busy in the cockpit. That's why the two most important things in aviation are the next two things. By that I mean you should always be asking yourself what the next two things are that you need to accomplish to get the flying job done. Doing your chores ahead of time (like obtaining the ATIS, completing a checklist, etc.) is essential to minimizing your cockpit workload.

In fact, you could become so overwhelmed when preparing to fly into a high density traffic area like the Los Angeles basin or the New York area, that you might accidentally drift into Class D, C or B airspace. That is why it's important to do as much as possible as early as possible in the flight. You never know what will happen later. You can be sitting there eating your tuna sandwich and thinking, "I'll get the ATIS in a few minutes," when suddenly the controller who's providing flight following gives you a heading change that takes you directly toward a cloud (which you should not fly into under any circumstance as a non-instrument rated pilot). Now who's got time to get the ATIS? The graph shown in Figure 29 gives you a good idea of just where the workload increases and pushes the limits of our performance during flight.

Aeronautical Decision Making (ADM)

As a general rule, very few pilots receive formal training in aeronautical decision making (ADM), yet many are effective decision makers. Why? They developed some strategy that lets them to make the right decision at the right time. Perhaps they learned it by watching their instructor, or they acquired the common base of knowledge possessed by most people. Maybe the tooth fairy gave it to them as a bonus. It doesn't matter. They've got it. But even if they and you do have it, there's nothing that says you can't become a better aviation decision maker by using some of the ADM tools presented in this chapter.

ADM is a systematic approach to understanding and modifying the mental process used by pilots to determine the best course of action in any given circumstance. This is a process that builds on the traditional concepts of decision making, as shown in Figure 30, but is modified slightly in consideration of the fact that the person making the decision is probably moving in a metal tube at a hundred miles per hour or more. Thus, ADM helps minimize the probability of pilot error by providing the means to analyze changes that occur in flight and evaluate how these changes could affect the outcome of that flight.

For instance, in the traditional decision making model (Figure 30), the need to make a decision occurs when the pilot notices that something has changed or hasn't changed when it was expected to (Figure 30, position 1). The engine begins to run rough (change) or the throttle is moved forward in cruise flight and the power doesn't increase (no change). The pilot must recognize this change or the lack of it for good decision making to occur (Figure 30, position 2). Failure to notice the change can lead to a mishap. Change indicates an appropriate response is necessary to favorably modify the situation (Figure 30, position 3). Now the pilot must evaluate all the possible responses using skills, procedures, techniques or book knowhow to solve the problem (Figure 30, position 4). Lack of ability in any of these areas can lead to a mishap (Figure 30, position 5).

Traditionally, ADM addresses all aspects of decision making in the cockpit and identifies the steps involved in good decision making. Here they are for your consideration:

1. Identifying any personal hazardous attitudes.
2. Learning behavior modification techniques.
3. Learning how to recognize and cope with stress.
4. Developing risk assessment skills.
5. Using all resources.
6. Evaluating the effectiveness of one's ADM skills.

Let's look at what we've already learned, and examine in some detail the factors we haven't discussed so far.

We've already learned to identify personal attitudes hazardous to safe flight along with the behavior modification techniques that work as antidotes to counter these attitudes. We've learned a bit about stress and how to use CRM. Now it's time to develop some useful risk assessment skills. One of the most useful tools from ADM is the risk assessment checklist in the form of the acronym DECIDE—detect, estimate, choose, identify, do, evaluate.

This is a six-step checklist that provides you with a logical way to approach decision making. The model represents a continuous loop process of decision making that is useful when a pilot is faced with a change in a situation where somebody had better decide something pretty soon. This model focuses on the intellectual component of the decision process, but it can also influence the motivational component of judgment as well.

The secret here is to practice using the DECIDE checklist in all your decision making. Then, when it's needed aloft, the process will be more natural and more likely to positively affect the outcome of important decisions in the air.

I don't want you to think that in the event of an inflight problem, you'll simply pull out a piece of paper,

A Good or Bad Decision?

Yes, people still handprop airplanes. It is, however, risky business. In spite of the risks, I believe you should be taught the basics of handpropping. Why? I know from experience that one day you might find yourself in a situation where you'll be tempted to try this on your own. Doing so without prior training is not very wise. Besides, even if you elect not to handprop your airplane, basic instruction in the correct techniques will enhance your respect for the propeller.

Find a qualified instructor who's experienced in handpropping airplanes (he shouldn't look like the guy to the left). Have that person show you the correct procedures, which include how to grip the propeller, the stance for best leverage and maximum safety, body movement and communication with the person inside the cockpit.

Perhaps the most important rule for handpropping is to have a *competent pilot, who's familiar with the airplane, at the controls.* Why? Once that engine starts, an airplane can move on its own and do a lot of damage. You don't want this to happen to you. There are several recorded cases of airplanes taking off without a pilot on board after being incorrectly handpropped (try explaining that to the owner of the flight school).

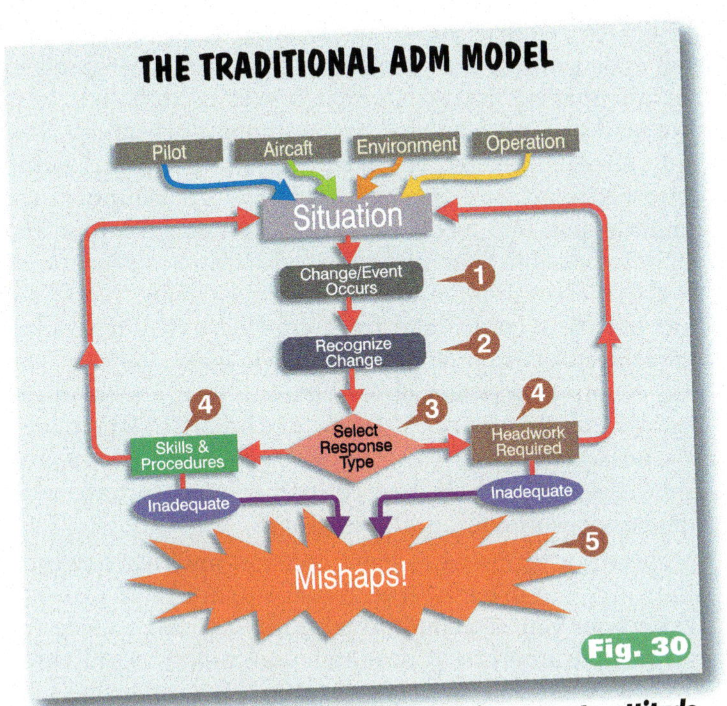

The traditional decision model doesn't incorporate attitude awareness, stress management and CRM as does the non-traditional ADM model (Figure 31).

review the DECIDE checklist, and excellent answers will appear (brought by that same tooth fairy, no doubt). It doesn't work that way. This checklist works best when it is internalized to the point of being intuitive. When you need it most is when you'll have the least time to think about each step.

Detect. The decision maker detects the fact that change has occurred.

Estimate. The decision maker estimates the need to counter or react to the change.

Choose. The decision maker chooses a desirable outcome (in terms of success) for the flight.

Identify. The decision maker identifies actions that could successfully control the change.

Do. The decision maker takes the necessary action.

Evaluate. The decision maker evaluates the effect(s) of his action countering the change.

Let's see how this is applied to a critical in-flight situation by assuming you're climbing to cruise altitude and notice an increase in oil temperature. We'll follow the DECIDE checklist here and refer it to a more comprehensive and effective non-traditional ADM model. This model allows us to incorporate several additional tools of psychology, such as attitude awareness, stress management and CRM.

The first step is to *detect* the problem (Figure 31, position 1). Let's say that our oil temperature is increasing and approaching red line on the gauge. This is easy to detect if you make it a habit to scan your engine instruments during flight. It's a bit more difficult if you never look at the panel or you don't know where the oil temperature gauge is on the panel.

Step two requires you to *estimate* the need to counter or react to this change (Figure 31, position 2). Without experience in this type of problem, you may not be sure of the severity of the problem. It is, after all, normal for the oil temperature to increase somewhat during a climb (along with cylinder head temperatures, too). Nevertheless, because you've read Chapter Three of this book, you know that the oil temperature should never reach or exceed redline without your taking immediate action to reduce the temperature. Fortunately, you also learned in Chapter Three that a decrease in oil pressure is followed by an increase in oil temperature. After checking your oil pressure, you notice that it is reading within normal limits.

You estimate that there is a need to act, but it's not an urgent need to act. In other words, you don't have an emergency—not yet, anyway!

Step three requires you to *choose* a desirable outcome for this situation (Figure 31, position 3). Lowering your oil temperature to a normal level is your objective here.

Step four wants you to *identify* the actions needed to accomplish step three (Figure 31, positions 3 and 4). This is often a decision about which of your skills and procedures to use, plus attitude management, stress management, and CRM necessary to solve the problem. These include, decreasing the airplane's attitude (if you're in a climb), opening the cowl flaps, reducing power (if you're operating at high power settings), and so on.

Since it's a hot day and you are climbing, you decide that it's best to try increasing the airflow through the engine as a solution to the problem. If, at any time, you

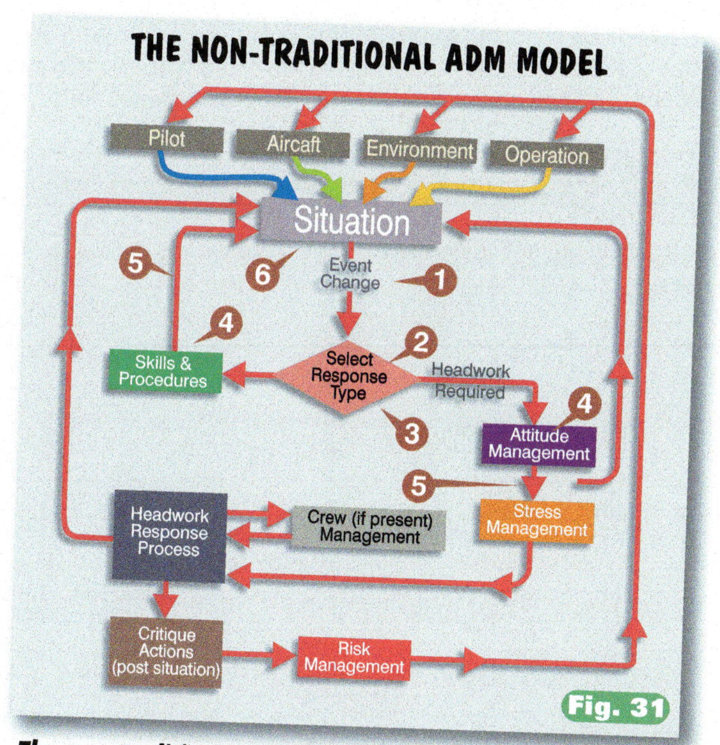

The non-traditional aviation decision making (ADM) model incorporates attitude awareness, stress management and CRM. This provides a pilot with a better chance of making a good decision.

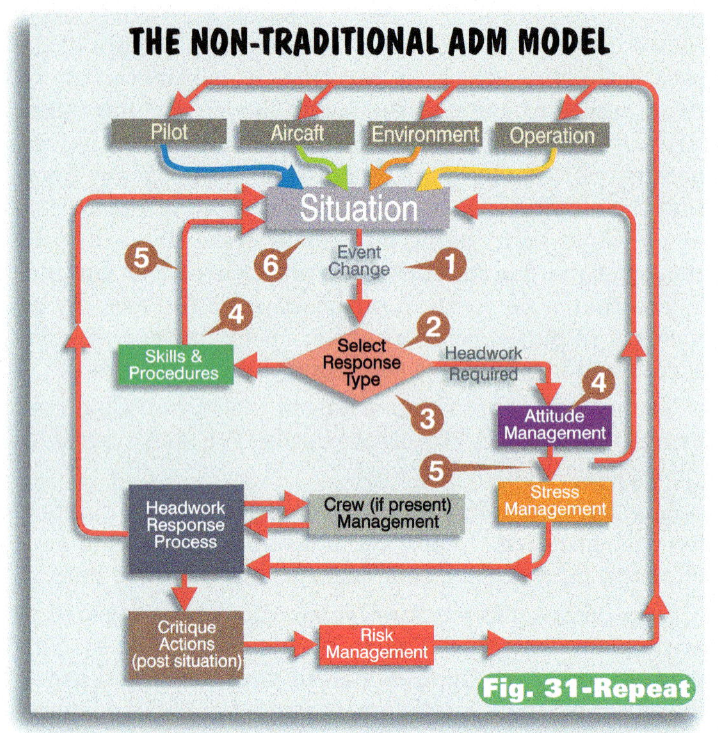

The non-traditional aviation decision making model incorporate attitude awareness, stress management and CRM. This provides a pilot with a better chance of making a good decision.

identify that you're feeling nervous, like you have no control over the situation, you might engage in a little attitude management and invoke the resignation hazardous thought antidote and say to yourself, "I'm not helpless. I can make a difference."

Step five requires you to *do* the action you selected in step four (position 5). So you lower the nose and increase the airspeed. You also make sure the cowl flaps are opened fully.

Step six requires you to *evaluate* the effect of this decision (position 6). Has the oil temperature decreased to within normal limits? It has. It's still high, but it is decreasing. Fine. You're flying and doing so safely. Now you can run through the DECIDE model again, asking yourself what you need to do if the oil temperature remains high and never returns to its normal limits. It's entirely possible that you departed without sufficient oil to provide reasonable engine cooling. Given that it's a hot day, this could lead to engine detonation at high power settings in a climb. That's not good. Perhaps you may need to land and check the oil. That's a potential problem that requires full use of the DECIDE model. It's possible that in running through the model again, you'll decide that it's best to land at an alternate with fuel services and oil up if necessary.

There's a bit more to good decision making, however, than just having a useful model in the ADM process. Sometimes you need additional skills that fall outside the normal parameters of academic psychology. And these are the skills you'll learn as you gain flying experience. So start slowly, then try new things, visit new places and fly new airplanes. Each action will contribute to your continuing education.

In case you think the FAA has run short of useful ways to use acronyms, think again. Here are a two more essential "mental" checklists that have practical value in helping you assess risk during the preflight process as well as during flight. One of these mental checklists is PAVE which stands for *pilot, aircraft, enVironment* and *external pressures*. PAVE represents the four major categories of risk pilot's face. The next mental checklist is IMSAFE which stands for *illness, medication, stress, alcohol, fatigue* and *emotion*.

When Decisions Go Right

The outstanding performance of this student pilot during a solo cross-country emergency was enhanced by helicopter training, and a thorough understanding of flight dynamics.

...During solo cross-country...the engine began to run rough. I put the mixture in full rich with the problem getting worse. I put the carb heat on and trimmed the C-150 to its best glide speed. Within 30 seconds, the engine at full power would only develop 1700-1800 rpm. At that time I turned 180 degrees into the wind while putting a direct to ZZZ1 airport. I was tuned on the ZZZ1 VOR and centered the needle so as to not drift my course. I then checked both magnetos and engine oil pressure/temperature, all of which were normal. I was over rolling hills and knew I wasn't going to make the airport.

The pilot made several Mayday calls on local frequencies, but no one responded.

As I passed through 1,700 feet MSL, I saw a small set of telephone lines in my original landing area. With partial power applied, I was unable to maintain my altitude, but could reduce my rate of descent. I dropped 10 degrees of flaps to gain lift and banked hard at about 300 feet. I crossed a hedgerow of 80-foot trees, knowing I would make my landing area. [I] dropped full flaps to get down, because slipping the aircraft into the field would not have allowed me to line up with the rows in the field made by the owner's tractor. At about 15 feet AGL, I cut the fuel off to the motor, and pulled the engine off. At 5 feet I flared, holding the nose up until I heard the stall horn. I continued to hold the nose off as the mains touched. I applied full brake pressure after the nose settled. The aircraft was landed with about 75 feet of ground run and no damage.

The cause of the failure is believed to be a dropped cylinder or valve. As a student fixed wing pilot, I was able to use my experience as a commercial instrument helicopter pilot to safely land the aircraft without damage. I attribute this to proper emergency procedures, and a thorough understanding of aerodynamics.

Courtesy NASA Callback Report

Q33

The IMSAFE Checklist

This mental checklist is very helpful for determining your physical and mental state prior to initiating a flight. Run though this acronym during the preflight stage of your flight as well as just prior to departure and even during flight if you suspect your physical or mental condition is changing.

1. **Illness**—Am I sick? Illness is an obvious pilot risk. If you have a temperature that's contributing to global warming, then the cockpit is not a place to be (maybe the refrigerator, but not the cockpit). See a doctor if necessary.

2. **Medication**—Am I taking any medicines that might affect my judgment or make me drowsy? If you pop a pill and suddenly feel like going to a Heavy Metal concert while wearing a tie without a shirt, then this medication has definitely affected your judgment. Stay on the ground so you don't become part of it.

3. **Stress**—Am I under psychological pressure? Do I have money, health, or family problems (and who doesn't)? Stress causes concentration and performance problems. While the regulations list medical conditions that require grounding, stress is not among them. Please consider the effects of stress on your performance.

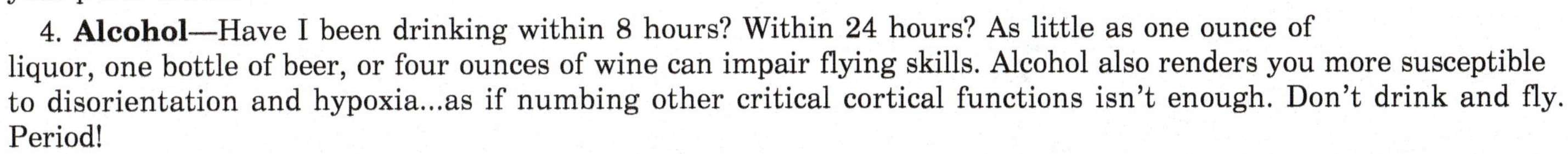

4. **Alcohol**—Have I been drinking within 8 hours? Within 24 hours? As little as one ounce of liquor, one bottle of beer, or four ounces of wine can impair flying skills. Alcohol also renders you more susceptible to disorientation and hypoxia...as if numbing other critical cortical functions isn't enough. Don't drink and fly. Period!

5. **Fatigue**—Am I tired and not adequately rested? Did you fall asleep reading this? Wake up! The fact is that fatigue continues to be one of the most insidious hazards to flight safety since it might not be apparent to a pilot until serious errors are made...and that is the worst time to find out you're fatigued.

6. **Emotion**—Am I emotionally upset? We're assuming that you're not so sensitive that you cry at untied shoelaces, and that you are legitimately upset in such a way that your judgment might be impaired. If so, don't fly.

The PAVE Checklist

Here's another very useful mental checklist that helps you identify four major areas of risk. The word PAVE stands for *Pilot, Aircraft, enVironment,* and *External pressures*. This is actually a very good "big picture" verbal checklist to help you mitigate risk by identifying areas that can be hazardous to you as a pilot. You should run through this checklist during your preflight planning and anytime you feel it's necessary while aloft.

P is for **Pilot** (Pilot in command): Do you feel up to the demands of this flight? The fact is that you, the pilot, are the biggest risk factor on any flight. After all, the NTSB says that over 75% of all aviation accidents are directly attributed to pilot error. Here is where you have a chance of reducing these types of errors.

A is for **Aircraft**: How might your airplane's limitations affect your flight? Think about it. All airplanes have limitations. They have a vertical limit (i.e., *service ceiling*) which is also the density altitude limit for the airplane's climb performance. Airplanes also have a horizontal limit in terms of their range which is based on fuel capacity, wind and a few other variables. They have a weight limit, too. There are quite a few airplane limits and you should become familiar with the ones relevant to your flight.

V is for **enVironment**: OK, just because the FAA's top cerebral specialists couldn't find an English word for "environment" doesn't mean they can't use the letter "v" in "environment" to hint at the word they really wanted to use. The letter V should remind you to examine the risks associated with the environment in which you'll fly. Clearly we're speaking about the weather in which you'll fly and the terrain over which you'll operate. So, what's the ceiling? The visibility? Crosswind component? Winds? Thunderstorms? Clouds? Icing? And so on. You get the point, right? Check the weather and geography for potential hazards and risks during the preflight phase of your flight.

E is for **External Pressures**: Apparently, the FAA folks in charge of the "E" for PAVE had senority and got their first choice of letters when designing this acronym. These are the external pressures we discussed earlier in the *Self Awareness and Hazardous Thinking* section of this chapter.

Final Thoughts on Thoughts

Here's something else I want you to consider. It's possible that the very qualities that make pilots good are the same ones that can injure them. There seems to be a thin line between positive personality traits for aviators and an extension of those same traits that lead to hazardous thinking. For example, wimpy pilots aren't safe pilots; neither are macho pilots. A certain degree of self-confidence and assertiveness is necessary to fly an airplane, so these personality traits are over represented in the pilot population. They are useful, up to a point. There is, however, a very thin line between these traits being productive and counterproductive. Confidence is good, cockiness isn't, and it's not a long distance between the two.

Canine Conniptions (When Decisions Go Bad)

A PA-28 pilot took off with two dogs as passengers. The pilot, who had not filed a flight plan, was talking to Approach, when...

My two large dogs went crazy. [They] jumped on me and with no one in the co-pilot seat, one of my dogs pushed the control yoke and caught his front leg on the yoke, causing an uncontrolled turn to the right. This turn put me in the clouds (IMC). Once I regained control of the plane and the dogs, I realized I had turned toward Class B airspace... ATC did advise me that I was not cleared [into this airspace]. My dog, with headphones hanging from mouth, caused me to enter Class B and descend below 5,000 feet AGL. Shortly thereafter ATC asked me if I was in VFR conditions and if I could I see the ground. I was then in VFR and could see the ground....

The moral of this flight is that I should have secured my dogs with seat belts. This is the main error I committed. My second error was flying VFR into IMC without an IFR clearance. **ASRS Report**

You may be sitting there thinking to yourself silently, "I'm not afraid of anything. You can't scare me off with some clouds or the threat of fuel exhaustion. Heck, if I run out of fuel, I just land that bad boy in a field, light a cigarette, and have a soda from the cooler." That is certainly a macho attitude, but you may not realize it despite having it. You may just think that you're naturally braver that everyone else.

The fact is that we (every one of us) may harbor a hazardous thought attitude and not even recognize it as being hazardous. It is, after all, normal for most people to think that they are pilots capable of handling even the most unusual circumstances. So there is a dividing line between normal confidence and hazardous thinking, but only you can know where that is. That means you have a chance of figuring out where that line is, but only if you monitor the internal dialogue that is constantly going on in your head. Given that pilots may have personality characteristics that can evolve into some forms of hazardous thinking, it makes sense that they should monitor their attitudes for signs of this behavior. The moment an attitude is detected that's a counterproductive extension of a normal, safe mode of thinking, they should apply one or more of the appropriate hazardous-thought antidotes. Said another way, if pilots don't modify their behavior when necessary, Mother Nature will. Finally, be aware that almost all aviation accidents are caused by human error. Pilots can do something to prevent accidents. They are not subject to the vicissitudes of luck or poor maintenance. Safe flying is within the control of every pilot. Fate is not the hunter!

BORN TO FLY

We see the emergence of a new breed of man:

Homoflighticus

The Aviation Super High Way

Books, books and more books, not to mention pamphlets, magazines, videotapes, audio tapes, computer programs, aviation forums, the Internet—it sometimes seems that airplanes are supported by an information jetstream. There is so much to learn and so little time to fly.

Every source of information makes its own unique contribution. You will eventually evolve your own combination of resources that works in terms of keeping up and having fun. On days when the weather doesn't cooperate, or there isn't time to go flying, it can be entertaining to crank up a video or read a pilot publication and share the experiences and knowledge of others.

I'm glad you were able to join me for this tour of the aviation wonderland. May all your skies be blue, and all your flying hours as interesting and exciting as mine have been.

Postflight Briefing #17-1

Traffic Alerting/Avoidance Systems

Not too long ago, it was only a dream that pilots would fly with onboard equipment that alerted them to the location of airborne traffic, then provided the proper resolution for avoiding an unwanted encounter. Things have changed. There are now three common categories of traffic alerting or collision-avoidance systems you're likely to encounter. Before I explain each one, let me provide you with an overview of the three categories of traffic alerting/avoidance system by explaining the service each provides.

Category 1. This system detects a target's distance and altitude, but provides no bearing and target direction information. This system is called a TCAD.

Category 2. These systems detect a target's distance, bearing, direction of flight, altitude and whether that target is climbing or descending. These systems are called either, TAS, TIS, ADS-B, or TIS-B.

Category 3. This system is called TCAS and has three different variations.

A TCAS I system can detect a target's distance, bearing, direction of flight and altitude.

A TCAS II system has TCAS I capabilities and it can tell whether a target is climbing or descending as well as telling you to climb or descend to resolve the conflict, thus providing what is known as "resolution advisories."

A TCAS III system does all that a TCAS II system can do as well as providing resolution advisories in the horizontal direction, too.

Let's examine each system in detail.

TCAS

Most of today's modern airliners are equipped with TCAS or *traffic alert and collision avoidance system*. This is a high tech and very expensive piece of equipment that provides a proximity warning of other aircraft. There are three versions of TCAS.

A "TCAS I" system provides a proximity warning in the form of a target's distance, bearing, direction of flight and altitude. This system doesn't provide a means of resolving the traffic conflict, also known as *resolution advisories*. In other words, it doesn't tell you to climb, descend, turn right or left. You have to figure out how to avoid traffic on your own, but at least you have help in finding it.

A "TCAS II" system provides traffic advisories and single-axis vertical resolution advisories. You are given a recommended maneuver in a vertical direction (climb or descend only) to avoid

How TCAS Presents Traffic Alert And Avoidance Information

The movement behind the development of the modern TCAS system was the result of two airliners colliding over the Grand Canyon on June 30th, 1956. The aviation industry understood that, at the speeds modern airliners fly, pilots needed a system that would help them avoid collisions.

In 1974 the MITRE Corporation's Center for Advanced Aviation System Development (CAASD) proposed using the transponders that were already on modern airplanes in development of an *alerting and collision avoidance* device. This proposal led to the development of an onboard system that sent transponder interrogation signals to nearby aircraft. These interrogated transponders then sent reply signals that were received by the original sending aircraft. Through this exchange, it was possible to determine the location, the speed and the direction of flight for each target and present this data to a pilot for collision avoidance.

In 1981 the FAA elected to pursue MITRE's concept in lieu of a ground based collision avoidance system that was concurrently under consideration. Many other companies were involved in the development of what has become known as TCAS.

Here's what the typical symbols on TCAS indicate. Keep in mind that different TCAS units can be set up to display information in different ways. Target A indicates other traffic in level flight 2,000 feet below. Target B indicates proximate traffic 900 feet above climbing at 500 ft/min or greater. Target C indicates a *Traffic Advisory* or TA with the traffic shown in yellow at 700 feet below climbing at 500 ft/min or greater. A Traffic Advisory is indicated by the accompanying aural warning of "TRAFFIC, TRAFFIC," which sounds once and then is reset until the next TA occurs. Target D indicates a TCAS *Resolution Advisory* (RA) with traffic shown in red and 400 feet below climbing at 500 ft/min or greater. RAs are indicated by one or more aural warnings that offer guidance in avoiding the target aircraft. This may include warnings like, 'Climb-Climb Now, Increase Descent, Descend-Descend Now," etc.

A TA or RA message followed by the traffic's range, altitude and (if applicable) vertical motion arrow appear on the display if TCAS cannot determine the other aircraft's bearing.

Avidyne/Ryan TAS-600

The TAS-600 system is similar to TCAS in that it provides realtime traffic monitoring and advisories and is not dependent on radar coverage ground-based transmitters. As with TCAS, this system independently interrogates the transponders of nearby aircraft up to a range of seven nautical miles with a 3,500 foot vertical separation. The TAS600 provides three levels of alert, so pilots can monitor traffic before it ever becomes a threat. The first level of alert is indicated on the display as an open diamond shape (Figure 34, position A), with the altitude separation indicated between the host and threat aircraft and an arrow indicating if the threat aircraft is climbing, descending, or at the same altitude (as shown in position A). This is referred to as Other Traffic (OT). OT is not an immediate threat but is within the surveillance area and the pilot should be aware of existing traffic.

The second level of alert is Proximity Alert (PA) and is displayed with the same information as OT, with the exception that the diamond shape is now a solid shape on the traffic display (Figure 34, position B and C). The target in Position B is 300 feet above you and descending while the target in position C is 500 feet below you and climbing. Both OT and PA alerts are white on a color display or are not highlighted on a monochromatic display.

Traffic with a calculated intercept course for altitude and direction become a Traffic Alert (TA). When a TA is encountered, the intruder traffic is indicated as an yellow circle (Figure 34, position D). The target is position D is 200 feet above you in level flight. When a traffic conflict is eminent, pilots need the right information in real time. Avidyne's heads-up audible system tells you the target's bearing, range and relative altitude for rapid visual acquisition of traffic.

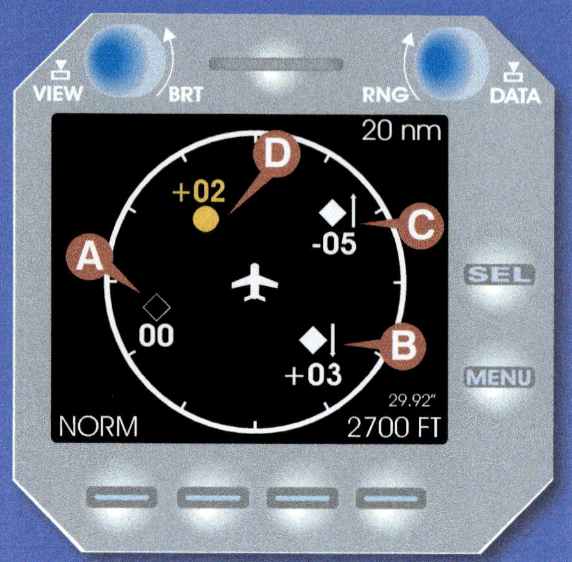

exchanging paint with the other aircraft. TCAS II is usually intended for airliners and larger commuter and business aircraft that carry many passengers. You won't typically find these systems on smaller airplanes, because most private pilots find the cost of $150,000-$200,000 a bit steep for equipping a 172.

TCAS III is similar to TCAS II, but the system also provides resolution advisories in the horizontal direction. You'll be instructed to go right or left as well as up or down, to avoid traffic. These systems are even more expensive, and thus even less likely to be seen on anything that doesn't have "jet" as part of its name.

TCAS works through the magic of an antenna (and fancy circuitry, too) that sends and receives transponder interrogation signals. After an interrogating pulse is sent to another airplane's transponder by the antenna, the target airplane's transponder receives and returns the signal (it has been interrogated, so to speak). The return signal is received by the TCAS antenna in such a way that the target airplane's direction can be identified. While a technical description of how this works is beyond the scope of this book, it's safe to say that an antenna laid out in two dimensions (similar to an ADF loop antenna) will receive different parts of the signal at different times. This is essentially how the TCAS antenna works its magic. Then, through some incredibly sophisticated electronics (about $200,000 worth), calculations are made that determine the target's direction and distance along with the target's altitude from its Mode C/S transponder. The key point here is that a target airplane without an operating transponder won't show up on anyone's TCAS. If the target airplane's pilot is operating in Mode A only (because he doesn't have his transponder set to ALT) then his altitude won't be shown on a TCAS unit.

TAS

TAS or *traffic advisory system* is very similar to TCAS in that it is an active system that interrogates the transponders of other aircraft and provides information on a target's distance, bearing and altitude. But no resolution advisories are provided, making this unit similar to a TCAS I system in its capabilities. The difference between TAS and TCAS is cost. Avidyne's TAS-600 traffic advisory system and the Goodrich SkyWatch HP Traffic Alerting System are good examples of traffic advisory systems (Figure 34). These systems cost around $14,000 and $20,000–$25,000 respectively. Like TCAS, these systems actively interrogate the transponders of other aircraft. They just happen to do so at much less cost to you, the pilot.

TCAD

TCAD or *traffic and collision alerting device* is a phrase that is becoming less common. These systems are often referred to as "passive" or "listening" systems in that they listen for a transponder that's already being interrogated. For systems like this to work, you must be in an area where the transponders on aircraft are being interrogated by ATC radar or by the TCAS/TAS systems on other aircraft (remember, TCAS/TAS interrogate transponders on their own). Leave radar coverage (or be beyond the TCAS/TAS coverage from other airplanes) and your TCAD system stops showing traffic.

Once the TCAD identifies a target airplane's transponder reply to someone else's interrogation, it typically displays the target's altitude and distance from your airplane. It doesn't display target bearing and direction of flight. There is also no "avoidance" information provided as there is with a TCAS II or III system.

Sometimes manufacturers use the term TAS for their TCAD devices. This can be a bit confusing but that's the way aviation is sometimes. TCAD devices are relatively inexpensive and serve a good purpose in aviation. For instance, the Monroy TrafficWatch ATD-300 (Figure 32) unit sells for less than $650. These units are small, fit easily on the top of your panel and provide target distance and altitude information. You shouldn't, however, wear them on top of your headset. If you're like me, you've probably already glued a small, spinning propeller up there.

The ATD-300 Traffic-Watch is a passive receiver capable of detecting transponder replies from nearby aircraft and displaying their range and altitude

TIS

TIS or *traffic information service* provides traffic information in terms of distance, bearing, direction of flight, and altitude. It doesn't provide resolution advisories. TIS requires that your airplane have a Mode S transponder, like Garmin's GTX330 (Figure 33), and some means of presenting target information visually, such as a moving map display. TIS also requires that your aircraft be within range of a ground station (Figure 34). A Mode S transponder does the same thing as a Mode A and C transponder, and a bit more. It has the capability of uplinking the transponder data from other airplanes to your cockpit via the ground station I just mentioned. This is how you get all that traffic information in your cockpit. The Mode S transponder also transmits your airplane's call sign and the transponder's permanent unit code (not the four digit squawk code).

Here's how TIS works. The ground based stations (Figure 35) collect information on all transponder equipped aircraft (operating in Modes A, C or S) and uplink this information to your airplane's Mode S transponder (the GTX330 from Garmin that I just mentioned). This information can then be displayed on certain moving map displays, such as Garmin's 400/500/1000 series GPS units. Not only can you see altitude, direction and distance of the target aircraft, but it's possible on Garmin's unit to see a target aircraft's vector line (its direction of flight). Keep in mind that all this occurs without your airplane having to actively interrogate or even passively identify another aircraft's transponder. That's because the TIS ground station is doing all the work. Your Mode S transponder is providing the means of data uplink and your moving map display is electronically displaying the information received.

Garmin's Mode S Transponder

Garmin's GTX330 is a Mode S transponder (retailing for about $5,000) that allows data uplinking/downlinking from ground based transmitters (GBTs) to your airplane. The Mode S transponder is an essential part of TIS (traffic information service).

What you get with a Mode S transponder and a moving map display is the ability to do what the Avidyne/Ryan TAS-600 or Goodyear's SkyWatch system does, but at a price that might be affordable even if you're not a publicly held company. A Mode S transponder typically sells for less than $5,000 (if you purchase it from the back of a van in a

How Traffic Information Service (TIS) Works

TIS or the Traffic Information Service uses the airplane's Mode S transponder to communicate with ground based stations (GBTs). GBTs send the Mode S information to ATC and ATC sends information on all airplanes with Mode A/C/S transponders in their local area via the GBTs. These aircraft targets are displayed on your cockpit multi-function display. There is no direct airplane-to-airplane exchange of information with TIS. A non-transponder equipped airplane will not show up on your MFD.

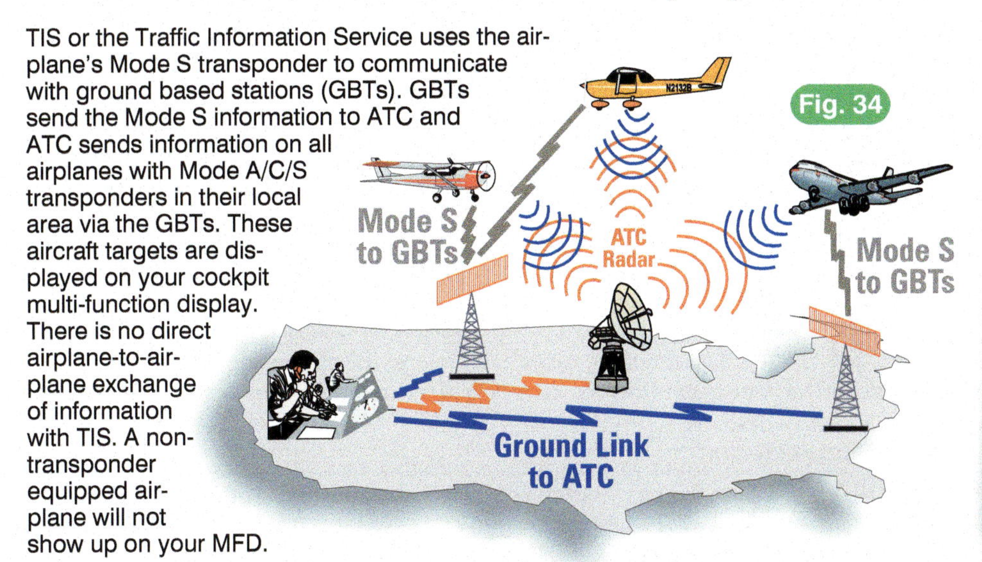

A TIS Ground Based Transmitter (GBT)

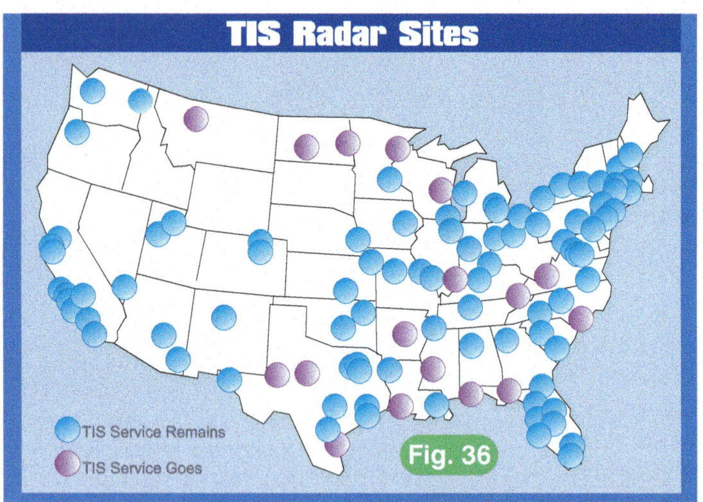

Less than 25% of the continental U.S. has TIS ground based stations (GBTs). GBTs are often associated with approach ASR 7/8/9 radar sites. As these sites are upgraded to ASR 11 status, they are not being given TIS functionality. It's possible that ADS-B will eventually replace TIS as a means of controlling traffic and for traffic awareness and collision avoidance.

parking lot, it probably costs a lot less and probably belonged to someone else, too. So don't do this).

Unfortunately, as of this writing, less than 25% of the continental United States has TIS ground station coverage and this number appears to be decreasing (Figure 36). TIS is currently available from 107 Mode S terminal radars, which were the older ASR7/8/9 units. During facility upgrades to ASR 11 facilities, the FAA failed to require TIS functionality, so these newer ASR 11 facilities don't have TIS capability. Whether or not TIS will be made available at these newer facilities is not clear. It appears, however, that the FAA has become more interested in our next system, known as *ADS-B*.

ADS-B and TIS-B

ADS-B or *automatic dependent surveillance broadcast* is cutting edge technology that is already present in the cockpit of many airplanes. It's a revolutionary new way of identifying and controlling air traffic. The concept is simple. Here's how it works.

Unlike radar, which bounces radio waves from ground-based antennas off airborne targets and then captures the reflected signals for interpretation, ADS-B uses conventional *Global Navigation Satellite System* (GNSS) technology and a relatively simple broadcast communications link as its fundamental components. It does this with a UAT or *universal access transceiver* (Garmin's GDL 90 is a UAT that interfaces with a multi-function cockpit display). This UAT is remotely mounted in your airplane and is designed to transmit, receive, and decode ADS-B messages sent from other airplanes and from ADS-B ground stations (called GBTs). This data link broadcasts your aircraft's position, velocity, projected track (all derived from GPS) and flight identification to other ADS-B equipped aircraft in your area, as well as to GBTs (Figure 37).

It's important to remember that ADS-B allows airplane-to-airplane information exchange. No GBTs are required for ADS-B equipped airplanes to talk (exchange data) with each other. This is what allows ADS-B equipped airplanes to identify each other's position, direction of flight, speed and altitude. Unfortunately, resolution advisories are not provided by ADS-B units at this time.

The interesting thing about the GBTs is that they can uplink to your airplane the traffic information shown on ATC's secondary surveillance radar. This means that, in addition to identifying other ADS-B equipped airplane, you can see the Mode A/C/S targets that the controller sees on his or her radar screen. In fact, there is a special name for this very specific uplink activity. It' called TIS-B or *traffic information service-broadcast.*

So, if you're asked what TIS-B is, you should say that it's nothing more than the reception of GBT uplinked secondary surveillance radar traffic information to your ADS-B equipped airplane. Figure 38 shows how TIS-B information is typically presented on a cockpit multi-function display. You can remember this by thinking of

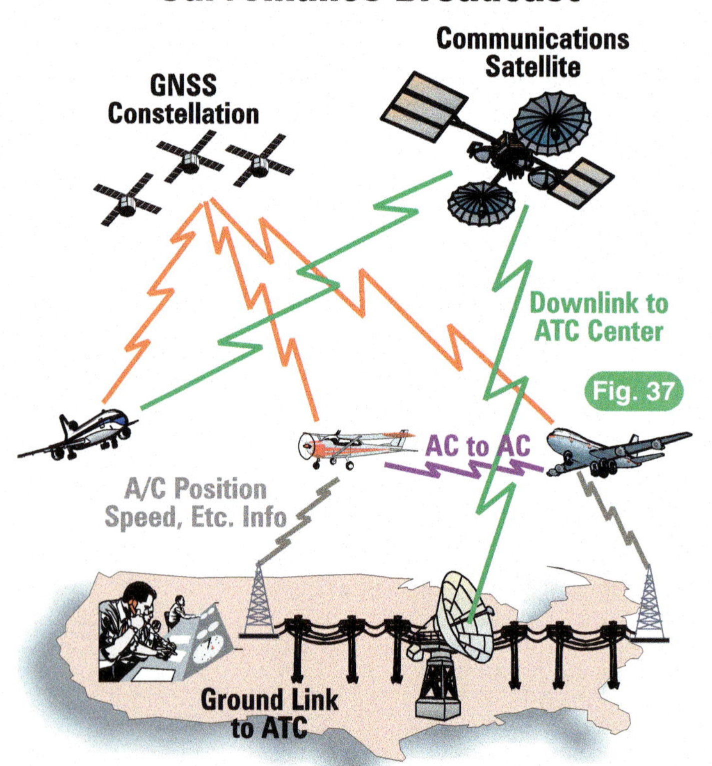

ADS-B or Automatic Dependent Surveillance Broadcast is the latest cutting edge technology for controlling traffic and collision awareness. It uses a UAT or Universal Access Transmitter to send and receive data between other airplanes and ground based stations (GBTs). In this way there is airplane-to-airplane data exchange and airplane to GBTs data exchange (which means airplane-to-airplane data exchange with ATC via the GBTs). Airplanes don't have to be within range of a GBT to have a traffic information exchange.

ADS-B Presentation On Garmin's MX 20 Multi-Function Display

ADS-B displays traffic information using the same convention we've already seen with TCAS and TAS. Target position and direction of flight are identified by blue symbols (position A). Next to each target is an altitude reference (position B) indicating whether the airplane is above (a + sign) or below (a - sign) your airplane and the amount of altitude difference in hundreds of feet. Your airplane is centered in the display (position C). At present, it costs approximately $8,000 to equip an airplane with ADS-B equipment. The cost should dramatically decrease in the next few years.

Fig. 38

the Christmas song that includes the words, "Do you see what I see?"

ADS-B accuracy does not seriously degrade with range, atmospheric conditions, or target altitude. And update intervals do not depend on the rotational speed or reliability of mechanical antennas. It is also a relatively simple, cost effective technology that works well at low altitudes and on the ground. It's completely effective in remote areas or in mountainous terrain where there is either no radar coverage, or where radar coverage is restricted by problems with elevation, or line of sight. In fact, ADS-B proved itself successful during its early tests conducted in Alaska. Now that's mountainous and isolated terrain.

What TCAS/TCAD/TAS/TIS/ADS-B or TIS-B Allows You to Do

Be aware that the information provided by TIS-B or any other traffic system (other than TCAS II and III, as you'll see shortly) is for pilot situational awareness (since they don't provide resolution advisories). These units are not collision avoidance systems, they're traffic alerting or information type systems only. These units most definitely do not relieve you of the responsibility to see and avoid.

Unless there's an imminent conflict requiring immediate action, any deviation from an air traffic control clearance based on an electronically displayed target must be approved by ATC prior to commencing the maneuver. A deviation made on your own without informing ATC could place your airplane in close proximity to another aircraft under ATC control (one that you can't or didn't see on your airborne traffic equipment). This could result in a pilot deviation action, since you're expected to maintain your assigned altitude within +/– 300 feet while flying IFR. It could also result in a crash, which is even worse. Exceeding these limits as a response to an alert without visually identifying a real collision threat is in violation of the regulations.

If you are alerted to the presence of a target you should search for it visually and quickly. Set aside your tuna sandwich for a moment. If you spot the traffic and there's a problem, the ideal strategy is to ask for permission to maneuver. But it's entirely possible that you will see a critical intruder target on your TIS unit before the controller does. You are not expected to swallow a 747 (or your tuna sandwich) while waiting for permission to deviate. Implied in the regulations is your right to do what's necessary to stay alive. If, in your judgment, there's no time to ask, then act. Period.

Avoiding a potential target is an entirely different matter if you're using a TCAS II or III unit. If you're equipped with either of these units, then you're expected to maneuver to avoid a collision based on their *resolution advisories* (see TCAS sidebar, page 17-22). Once that's done, you're expected to notify ATC of that deviation ASAP, and then return to your assigned altitude, heading and/or route. Unless the controller is on a break, it's highly likely he or she will notice if your plane suddenly plummets or climbs a few hundred feet, which should be enough to get the dialog going. TCAS units are sophisticated enough to minimize the chance that a false or erroneous target might generate an avoidance maneuver in the form of a resolution advisory.

Postflight Briefing #17-2

The New Kid on the Block

There's a new kid on the block and it's called the ICAO flight plan form (Figure 39). Your older flight plan form has gone the way of the elevator operator and the manually-tuned channel dial on your television. Flight plans filed in the United States can now use the ICAO flight plan format (soon this format will be mandatory). Don't, however, worry, too much. Many things are the same with the exception of having to input your aircraft's communication, navigation, surveillance and survival equipment when filing. So let's walk through manually filing this new flight plan for a VFR flight. This process is made a lot easier when using some of the high-end flight planning software for tablet and iThingy devices.

Aircraft Identification

Enter your complete aircraft identification including the prefix "N" if applicable.

Flight Rules

Enter "V" for VFR.

Type of Flight

Enter "G" as the designator for general aviation. (I'm assuming you're GA here, otherwise check the AIM for different designators.)

Number (of Aircraft)

Number: Unless your flight instructor is following you in another airplane (a formation flight), then enter a value of 1 for one airplane.

Type of Aircraft

Your aircraft type is found in ICAO Document 8643 at www.icao.int under *publications*. For this flight we'll use an A36 Bonanza which is designated as BE36.

Wake Turbulence Category

Insert a forward slash followed by "L" to indicate you're in a light aircraft, which is one with a takeoff weight of 15,500 pounds or less. Of course, if your Bonanza weighs that much then leave your flight bag on the ground which will bring your total weight down to about 3,500 pounds.

Equipment

Your airplane's equipment (no, not engines, flashlights, and landing gear, either) is defined in detail in AIM Table 5-1-4. You should list the letters representing the navigation and surveillance equipment that's on board the airplane (Figure 40). No space is required between items. For example, **SDF**.

S – VHF (receive and transmit frequencies), VOR and ILS. This is a single letter representing at least three types of equipment.

D – DME

F – ADF (in case you still have one on board because you haven't found something to plug up the hole it will leave once it's removed).

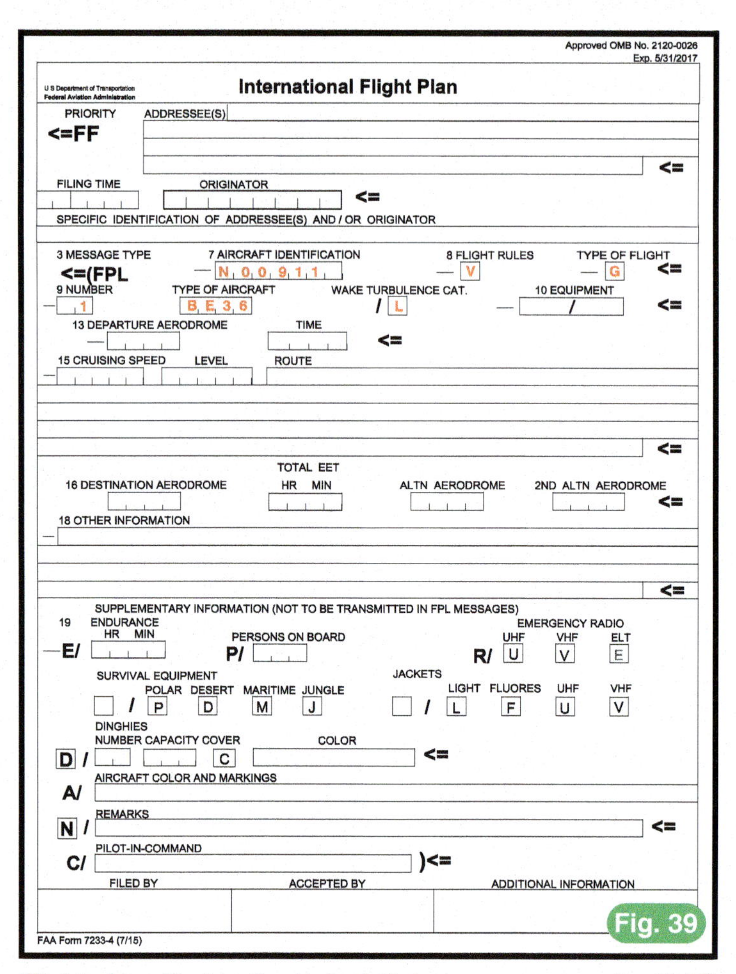

Approved OMB No. 2120-0026
Exp. 5/31/2017

U.S. Department of Transportation
Federal Aviation Administration

International Flight Plan

PRIORITY <=FF — ADDRESSEE(S) <=

FILING TIME — ORIGINATOR <=

SPECIFIC IDENTIFICATION OF ADDRESSEE(S) AND / OR ORIGINATOR

3 MESSAGE TYPE <=(FPL — 7 AIRCRAFT IDENTIFICATION — N009 11 — 8 FLIGHT RULES — V — TYPE OF FLIGHT — G <=

9 NUMBER — 1 — TYPE OF AIRCRAFT — BE36 — WAKE TURBULENCE CAT. / L — 10 EQUIPMENT — / <=

13 DEPARTURE AERODROME — TIME <=

15 CRUISING SPEED — LEVEL — ROUTE <=

16 DESTINATION AERODROME — TOTAL EET HR MIN — ALTN AERODROME — 2ND ALTN AERODROME <=

18 OTHER INFORMATION <=

SUPPLEMENTARY INFORMATION (NOT TO BE TRANSMITTED IN FPL MESSAGES)

19 ENDURANCE HR MIN — E/ — PERSONS ON BOARD P/ — EMERGENCY RADIO R/ UHF U VHF V ELT E

SURVIVAL EQUIPMENT / POLAR P DESERT D MARITIME M JUNGLE J — JACKETS / LIGHT L FLUORES F UHF U VHF V

DINGHIES D / NUMBER CAPACITY COVER C COLOR <=

A/ AIRCRAFT COLOR AND MARKINGS

N / REMARKS <=

C/ PILOT-IN-COMMAND)<=

FILED BY — ACCEPTED BY — ADDITIONAL INFORMATION

FAA Form 7233-4 (7/15)

Fig. 39

Flight plans filed in the United States can now use the ICAO (International Civil Aviation Organization) flight plan format (soon this format will be mandatory).

G - GNSS (i.e., GPS that's approved for the type of operation you're conducting. As a non-instrument rated private pilot there is no need to identify the specific type of GPS equipment you're using much less its specific capabilities).

O – VOR

Z – Other equipment carried on board which should be specified in Block 18.

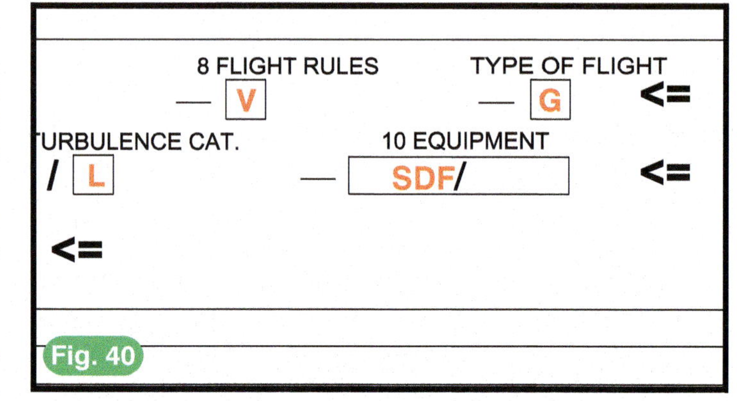

8 FLIGHT RULES — V — TYPE OF FLIGHT — G <=

URBULENCE CAT. / L — 10 EQUIPMENT — SDF/ <=

<=

Fig. 40

List S for VHF capability, D for DME and F for ADF equipment.

Surveillance Equipment

Let's cover how to list the airplane's surveillance equipment to the right of the slashed line in block 10 (Figure 41). (The FAA's Leido FSS site has a flight plan form that uses a separate block/box to list surveillance information—vive la difference). By surveillance equipment, I don't mean binoculars, camouflage kit and the fake mustache you use when you're on one of your secret agent missions. Instead, I'm speaking of the equipment your airplane uses to directly send/receive information to ATC. This equipment is designated as follows:

SSR Modes A and C

SSR is the *secondary surveillance radar* system that ATC uses to detect your airplane on radar as well as identify the additional information sent by your airplane's Mode A, Mode C or Mode S transponder. Here are the codes you'd use to describe this equipment.

A Transponder - Mode A (4 digits – 4096 codes)
C Transponder - Mode A (4 digits – 4096 codes) & Mode C

SSR Mode S

E – Transponder - Mode S, including aircraft identification, pressure-altitude & extended squitter (ADS-B) capability

H – Transponder - Mode S, including aircraft identification, pressure altitude and enhanced surveillance capability

I – Transponder - Mode S, including aircraft identification, but no pressure-altitude capability

L – Transponder - Mode S, including aircraft identification, pressure-altitude, extended squitter (ADS B) and enhanced surveillance capability

P – Transponder - Mode S, including pressure-altitude, but no aircraft identification capability

S – Transponder - Mode S, including both pressure-altitude and aircraft identification capability

X – Transponder - Mode S with neither aircraft identification nor pressure-altitude capability

Followed by one or more of the following codes if the aircraft has ADS-B capability:

B1 – ADS-B with dedicated 1090 MHz ADS-B "out" capability

B2 – ADS-B with dedicated 1090 MHz ADS-B "out" and "in" capability

U1 – ADS-B "out" capability using UAT

U2 – ADS-B "out" and "in" capability using UAT

V1 – ADS-B "out" capability using VDL Mode 4

V2 – ADS-B "out" and "in" capability using VDL Mode 4

NOTE–File no more than one code for each type of capability; for example, file B1 or B2, but not both. Follow this by adding one or more of the following codes if the aircraft has ADS-C capability:

D1 – ADS-C with FANS 1/A capability

G1 – ADS-C with ATN capability

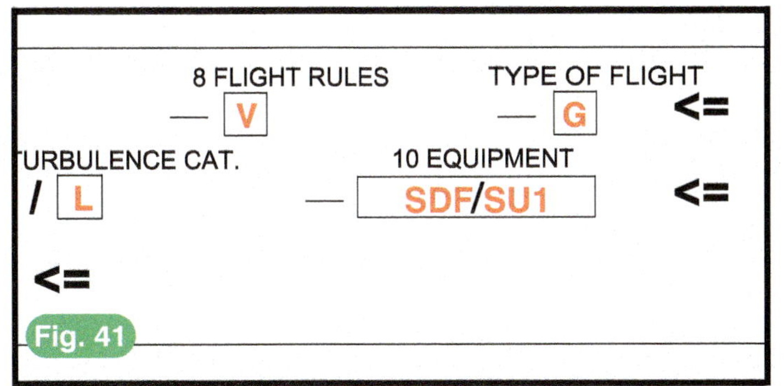

Surveillance equipment: S is for "S" Mode Transponder and U1 is for ADS-B "out" capability using a universal access transceiver.

For instance, suppose your airplane has a Mode S transponder (S) and ADS-B "out" capability using a UAT or universal access transceiver (U1). You'd list that information to the right of the slashed line as shown in Figure 41.

Departure Airport

Enter the departure airport using its four-letter designator (Figure 42).

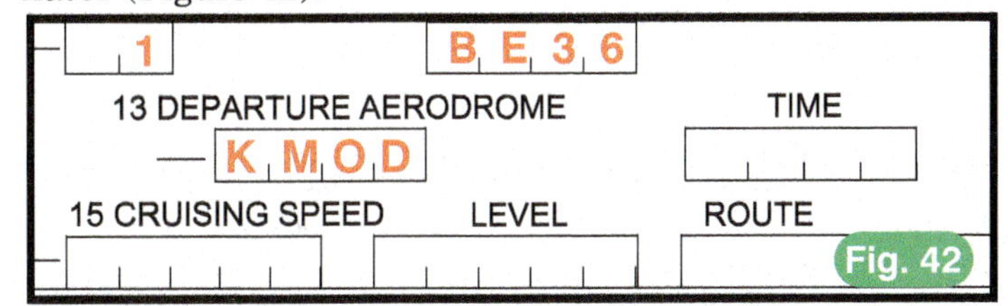

KMOD is the airport identifier for Modesto City Airport.

Airports designated by less than four letters (i.e., O27) or that use numbers (i.e., 39LL) are not official ICAO designations. In this instance, use ZZZZ in this block and specify the non-ICAO identifier in Block 18 following the characters "DEP/" which stands for departure airport (Figure 43).

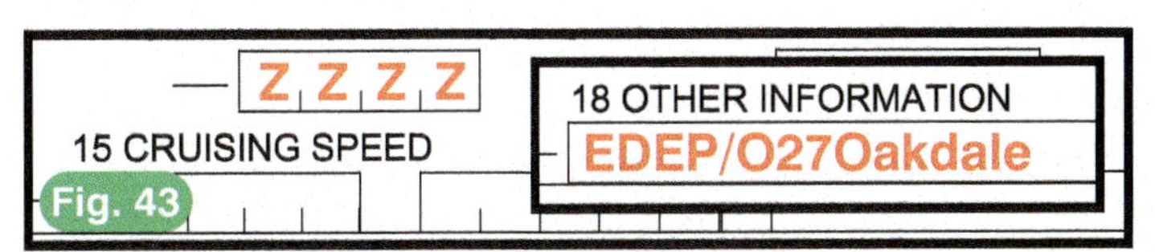

For airports without an official ICAO designation, identify the specific airport after the letters "DEP/" in Block 18 of the flight plan.

Time

In the time block, insert the estimated departure time using HHMM format (Figure 44).

Speed

Insert your four-digit cruising TAS in knots following the letter "N" for a maximum of five characters. The letter "N" refers to a speed value in knots. If your speed is 120 knots TAS, then you'll enter N0120 in this block (Figure 44).

Level

Insert the altitude for the first or the whole portion of the route preceded by "F" for flight levels or "A" for altitudes (followed by three figures). For example, an altitude of 4,500 feet MSL would be listed as A045 (Figure 44).

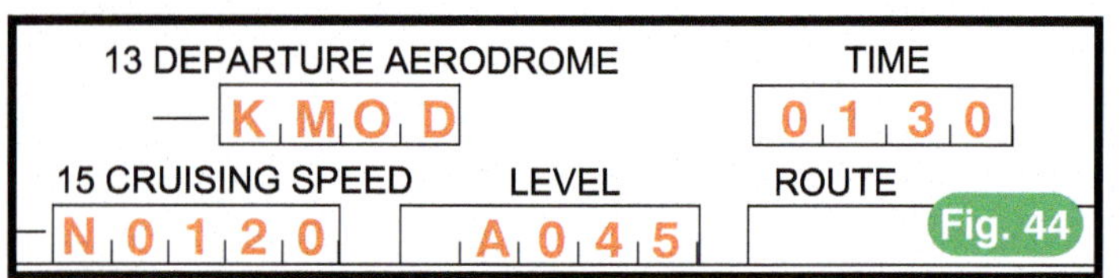

Airspeed in knots is preceded by the letter "N" and the crusing altitude is preceded by the letter "A."

Route

Insert the routing desired as you have typically done when filing using the older flight plan format. If you're flying direct (i.e., no airway, T or Q route) between fixes, navaids and waypoints, then insert the letters DCT (which means "direct") between each fix, navaid or waypoint (Figure 45).

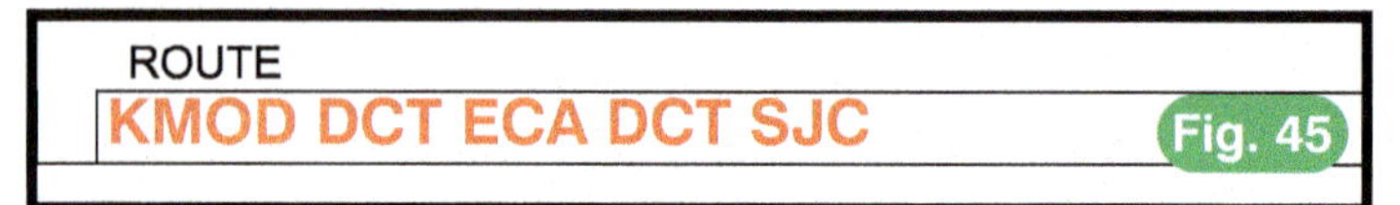

Route is from Modesto airport direct to the Manteca VOR (ECA) direct to San Jose VOR.

Destination

Define the destination airport in Block #16 just as you did in the departure airport Block #13 (Figure 46).

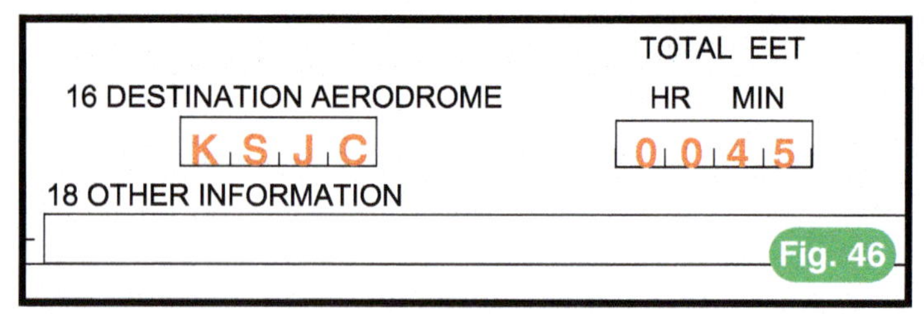

The destination airport for our trip is San Jose International Airport (KSJC).

Use ZZZZ if no official ICAO identifier is listed for the airport, then list the non-ICAO identifier in Block 18 after the letters "DEST/" (remember, ICAO doesn't recognize airport identifiers having numbers or having less than four letters). For airport O88, you'd list DEST/ (for destination) followed by O88 for DEST/O88 in Block 18 (Figure 47). If you're planning a stopover for more than 1 hour at first airport of intended landing, then file separate flight plans for each leg of trip.

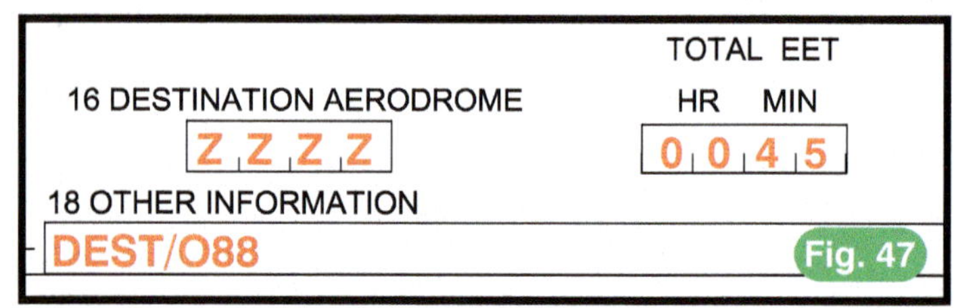

If the destination airport has a three letter or number designation list ZZZZ in Block #16 and the airport code after the letters "DEST/" in Block #18.

Total EET

Define the total estimated enroute time to the destination using the HHMM format (Figure 47).

Alternate Airport

Define the alternate airport the same way you defined the destination and departure airports (Figure 48). If this airport uses a non-ICAO identifier, then use ZZZZ in this block and insert ALT/ followed by the non-ICAO identifier in Block 18. For example, if an airport is defined as O88, you'd list it as ALT/O88 for an alternate airport.

2nd Alternate Airport

This is optional.

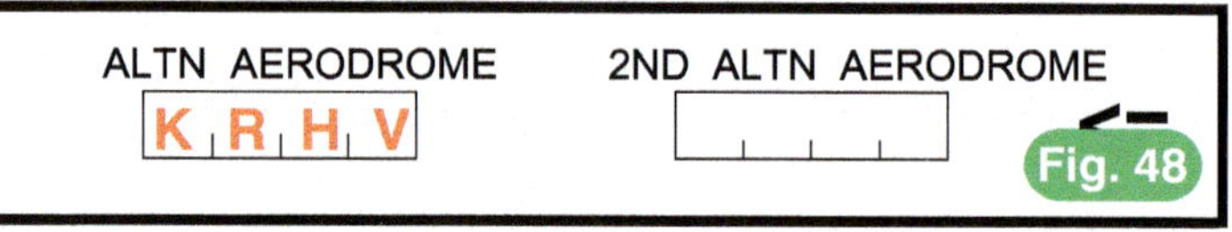

List the alternate airport (if desired) as shown above.

Other Information

If you found that there was no need to list any additional information here in Block 18, then you'd list a "0" in this block and fill out the remaining blocks (Figure 49).

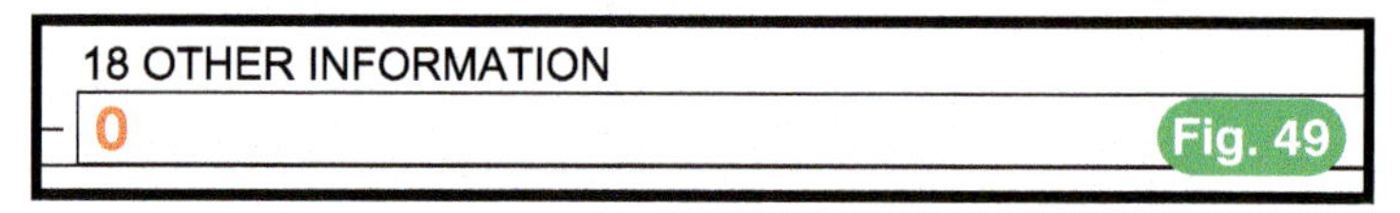

Endurance

Enter your airplane's endurance in the HHMM format. Don't enter the time of your last gasping run at the gym, either (Figure 50).

Persons on Board

Enter the number of people on the airplane (Figure 50).

Enter the aircraft's endurance using the HHMM format.

Emergency Radio

By leaving the boxes in this category empty you are indicating that you have that capability (go figure). If you have VHF with 121.5 MHz capability, then leave the "VHF" box unchecked. Cross out UHF if you don't have this capability on board. The "ELT" is your emergency locator transmitter, which I assume you have onboard, so leave this box unchecked (Figure 51).

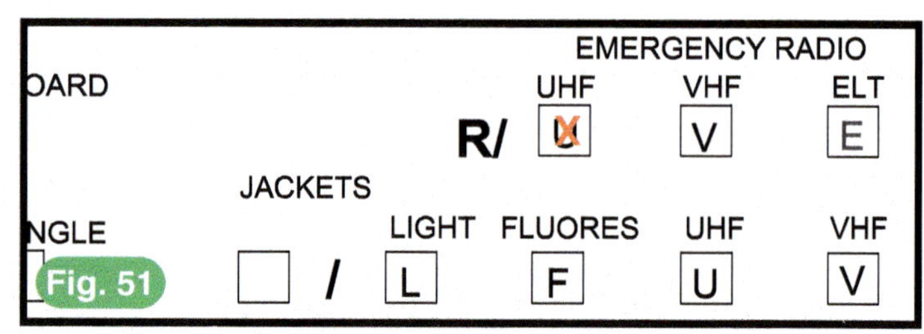

Use an "X" to cross out any emergency equipment that you don't have on board the aircraft.

Survival Equipment

Cross out any of these that you don't have onboard (Figure 52).

Jackets

Cross out any of these that you don't have onboard (Figure 52).

Dinghies

No, this doesn't reflect the number of goofy people on your airplane, either. Cross out NUMBER and CAPACITY if no dinghies are carried or insert the number of dinghies.

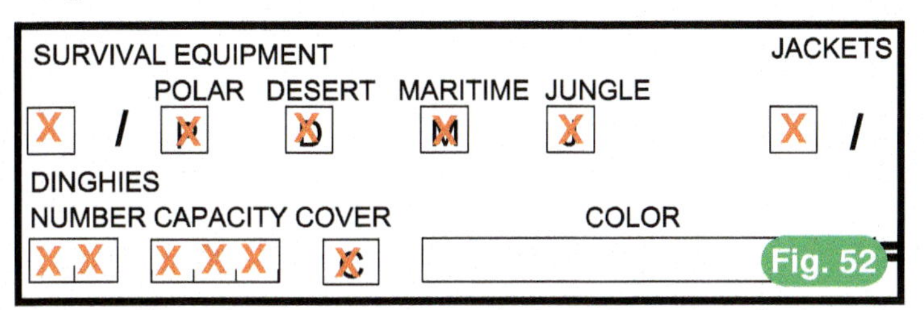

Use an "X" to cross out any survival equipment or jackets or dinghies that you don't have on board the aircraft.

Aircraft Color and Markings

The color(s) of your aircraft separated by a slash.

Remarks

Cross out N if you have no remarks to list.

Pilot in Command

Your name goes here.

Congratulations, by the time you've finally completed this flight plan, it's probably time for dinner and a nap. Fortunately, filing a flight plan becomes much easier given the many and varied flight plan services available for your computer, pads and tablet devices.

The Leidos FSS Presents the ICAO Flight Plan.

Filing your flight plan in the ICAO format is a lot easier when done through the Leidos Flight Service Station (www.1800wxbrief.com). Figure 53 is the ICAO flight plan form used by Leidos. What makes the filing process easier are the "spyglass" help icons found at the end of critical data blocks. For instance, clicking the spyglass icon at the end of the equipment line brings up a list of aircraft equipment and codes (Figure 54). Check the box appropriate to your airplane and that data will be automatically entered in the appropriate data block. The same thing applies to listing your surveillance equipment, too (Figure 55). In terms of emergency radios, survival equipment, jackets and dinghies, you'll check the box only if you have that equipment on board. Of course, if you have an account at Leidos, you can save the basic flight plan data as a "Favorite" flight plan. This allows you to file future flight plans without having to input repetitive data for your airplane.

Flight Planning Software for Your iThingy or Android Tablet

Today's modern and mobile flight planning software makes simple work of creating a flight log and filing an ICAO flight plan. Most pilots today are using some sort of advanced and mobile flight planning software to automate the flight planning process. As you can see below, ForeFlight's makes selecting a route and creating a flight log an easy and simple activity. Filing an ICAO flight plan is also much easier since you only need to click on the screen to add the aircraft equipment and surveillance equipment you have on board the airplane. Now, there are several great software companies producing this software so ask your instructor which one is right for you. Happy flight planning!

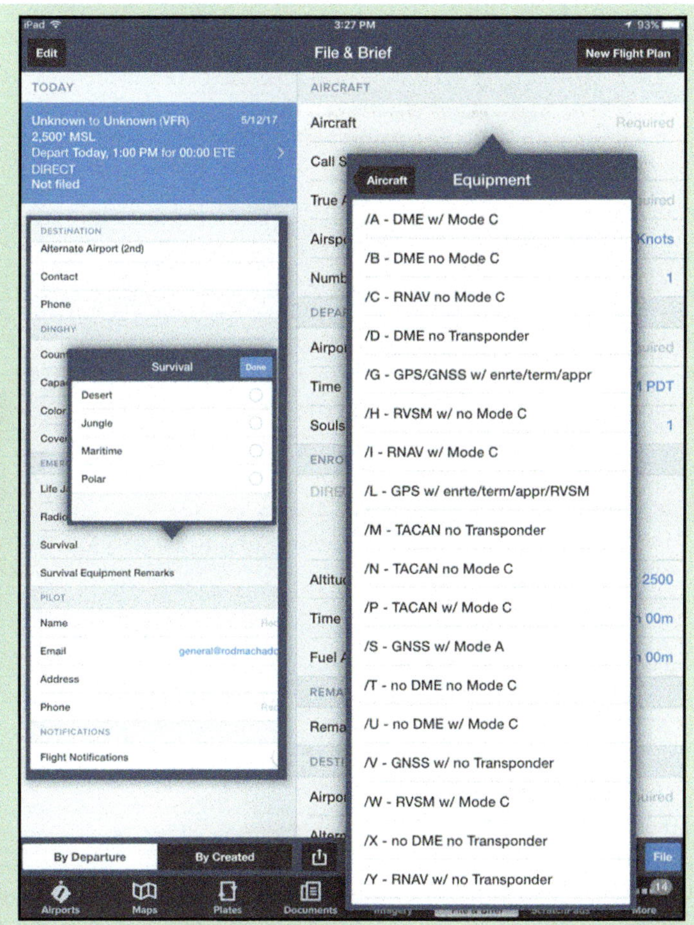

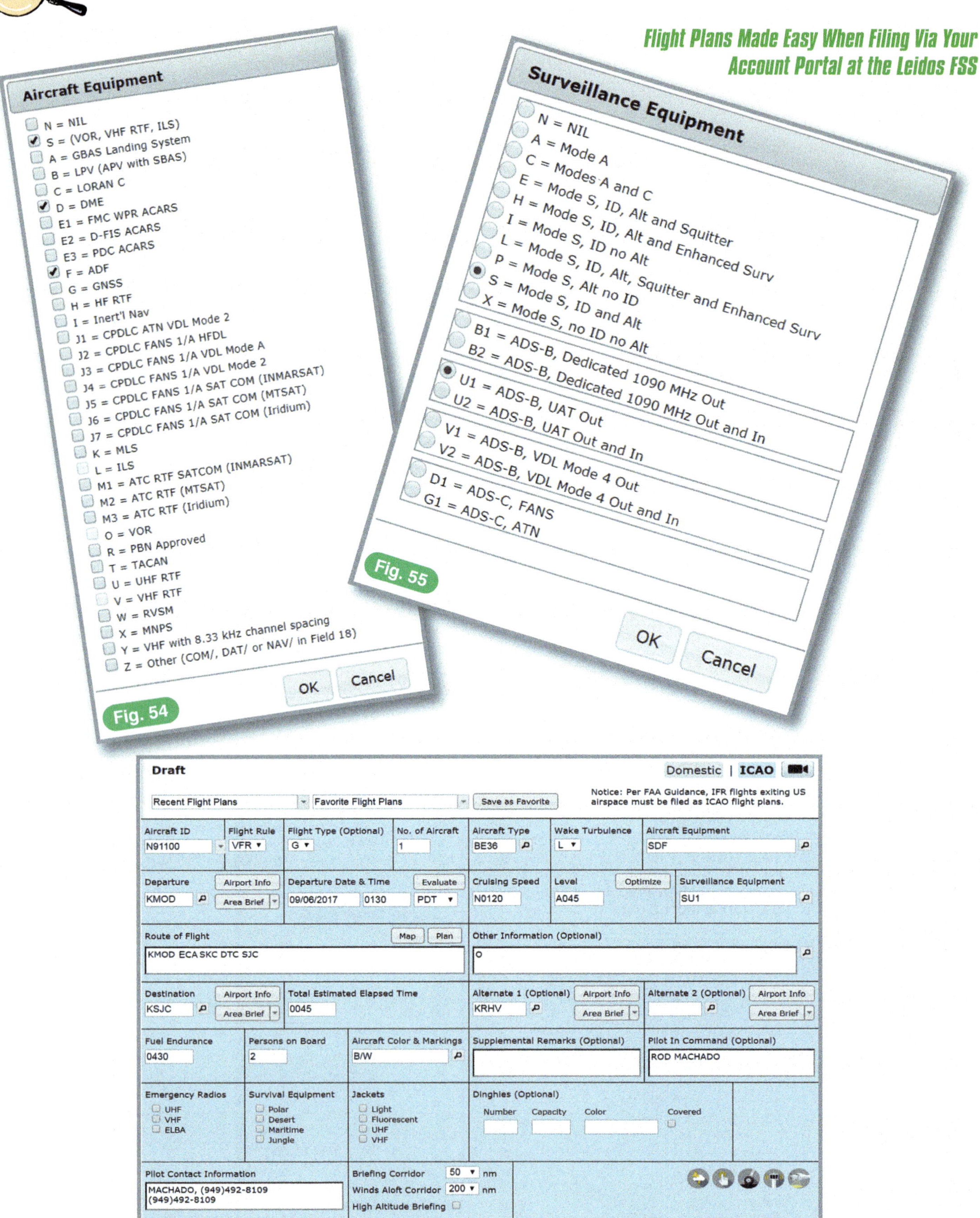

Filing a VFR flight plan is a lot easier when done through your account portal at the Leidos Flight Service Station. You can even save your airplane equipment/performance data for easier flight plan filing on future flights.

Postflight Briefing #17-3

NOTAM Abbreviations

AADC - Approach and Departure Control
ABV - Above
A/C - Approach Control
ACCUM - Accumulate
ACFT - Aircraft
ACR - Air Carrier
ACTV/ACTVT - Active/Activate
ADJ - Adjacent
ADZ/ADZD - Advise/Advised
AFD - Airport/Facility Directory
AFSS - Automated Flight Service Station
ALSA - Approach Light System
ALTM - Altimeter
ALTN - Alternate
ALTNLY - Alternately
ALSTG - Altimeter Setting
AMDT - Amendment
APCH - Approach
APL - Airport Lights
ARPT - Airport
ARSR - Air Route Surveillance Radar
ASDE - Airport Surface Detection Equipment
ASOS - Automated Surface Observing System
ASPH - Asphalt
ASR - Airport Surveillance Radar
ATC - Air Traffic Control
ATCT - Airport Traffic Control Tower
ATIS - Automated Terminal Information Service
AVBL - Available
AZM - Azimuth
BC - Back Course
BCN - Beacon
BERM - Snowbank/s of Earth/Gravel
BLO - Below
BND - Bound
BRAF - Braking Action Fair
BRAG - Braking Action Good
BRAN - Braking Action Nil
BRAP - Braking Action Poor
BYD -Beyond
CAAS - Class A Airspace
CAT - Category
CBAS - Class B Airspace
CBSA - Class B Surface Area
CCAS - Class C Airspace
CCLKWS - Counterclockwise
CCSA - Class C Surface Area
CD - Clearance Delivery
CDAS - Class D Airspace
CDSA - Class D Surface Area
CEAS - Class E Airspace
CESA - Class E Surface Area
CFA - Controlled Firing Area
CGAS - Class G Airspace
CHG - Change
CLKWS - Clockwise
CLNC - Clearance
CLSD - Closed
CMSN - Commission
CMSND - Commissioned
CNCL/CNCLD/CNL - Cancel/Canceled/Cancel
CNTRLN - Centerline
CONC - Concrete
CONT - Continuously
CRS - Course
DALGT - Daylight
DCMS - Decommission
DCMSND - Decommissioned
DCT - Direct
DEP - Depart/Departure
DEPT - Department
DH - Decision Height
DISABLD - Disabled
DLA/DLAD - Delay/Delayed
DLT/DLTD - Delete/Deleted
DLY - Daily
DMSTN - Demonstration
DPCR - Departure Procedure
DRCT - Direct
DRFT - Drift Snowbank/s
DRFTD - Drifted Snowbank/s
DSPLCD - Displaced
DSTC - Distance
DWPNT - Dewpoint
E- East
EBND - Eastbound
EFF - Effective
ELEV - Elevate/Elevation
ENG - Engine
ENTR - Entire
EXCP - Except
FAC - Facility
FAF - Final Approach Fix
FDC - Flight Data Center
FM - Fan Marker
FREQ - Frequency
FRH - Fly Runway Heading
FRZN - Frozen
FRNZ SLR - Frozen Slush on Runway/s
FSS - Flight Service Station
GC - Ground Control
GP - Glide Path
GRVL - Gravel
GS - Glide Slope
HAA - Height Above Airport
HAT - Height Above Touchdown
HAZ - Hazard
HEL - Helicopter
HELI - Heliport
HF - High Frequency
HIRL - High Intensity Rwy Lights
HOL - Holiday
HP - Holding Pattern
IBND - Inbound
ID - Identification
IDENT - Identifier/Identification
IFR - Instrument Flight Rules
ILS - Instrument Landing System
IM - Inner Marker
IN - Inch/Inches
INDEFLY - Indefinitely
INOP - Inoperative
INST - Instrument
INT - Intersection
INTST - Intensity
IR - Ice On Runway/s
L - Left
LAA - Local Airport Advisory
LAT - Latitude
LB - Pound/Pounds
LC - Local Control
LCL - Local
LCTD - Located
LDA - Localizer Type Directional Aid
LDIN - Lead In Lighting System
LGT/LGTD/LGTS- Light/Lighted/Lights
LIRL - Low Intensity Runway Edge Lights
LLWAS - Low Level Wind Shear Alert System
LMM - Compass Locator at ILS Middle Marker
LNDG - Landing
LOC - Localizer
LOM - Compass Locator at ILS Outer Marker
LONG - Longitude
LRN - LORAN
LSR - Loose Snow on Runway/s
LT - Left Turn After Take-off
MAP - Missed Approach Point
MED - Medium
MIN - Minute
MIRL - Medium Intensity Runway Edge Lights
MM - Middle Marker
MNM - Minimum
MOCA - Minimum Obstruction Clearance Altitude
MONTR - Monitor
MSA - Minimum Safe Altitude
MSAW - Minimum Safe altitude Warning
MSL - Mean Sea Level
MU - Designate a Friction Value Representing Runway Surface Conditions
MUD - Mud
MUNI - Municipal
N - North
NA - Not Authorized
NBND - Northbound
NE - Northeast
NGT - Night
NM - Nautical Mile/s
NMR - Nautical Mile Radius
NW - Northwest
OBSC - Obscured
OBSTN - Obstruction
OM - Outer Marker
OPER - Operate
OPN - Operation
ORIG - Original
OTS - Out of Service
OVR - Over
PAEW - Personnel and Equipment Working
PAJA - Parachute Jumping Activities
PAPI - Precision Approach Path Indicator
PAR - Precision Approach Radar
PARL - Parallel
PAT - Pattern
PCL - Pilot Controlled Lighting
PERM - Permanent
PERMLY - Permanently
PLA - Practice Low Approach
PLW - Plow/Plowed
PN - Prior Notice Required
PPR - Prior Permission Required
PREV - Previous
PRIRA - Primary Radar
PROC - Procedure
PROP - Propeller
PSGR - Passenger/s
PSR - Packed Snow on Runway/s
PT/PTN - Procedure Turn
PVT - Private
RAIL - Runway Alignment Indicator Lights
RCAG - Remote Communication Air/Ground Facility
RCL - Runway Centerline
RCLS - Runway Centerline Light System
RCO - Remote Communication Outlet
RCV/RCVR - Receive/Receiver
REF - Reference
REIL - Runway End Identifier Lights
RELCTD - Relocated
RMDR - Remainder
RNAV - Area Navigation
RPRT - Report
RQRD - Required
RRL - Runway Remaining Lights
RSVN - Reservation
RT - Right Turn after Take-off
RTE - Route
RTR - Remote Transmitter Receiver
RTS - Return to Service
RUF - Rough
RVR - Runway Visual Range
RVRM RVR Midpoint
RVRR - RVR Rollout
RVRT - RVR Touchdown
RVV - Runway Visibility Value
RY/RWY - Runway
S - South
SBND - Southbound
SDF - Simplified Directional Facility
SE - Southeast
SECRA - Secondary Radar
SFL - Sequenced Flashing Lights
SI - Straight-In Approach
SIR - Packed or Compacted Snow and Ice on Runway/s
SKED - Scheduled
SLR - Slush on Runway/s
SNBNK- Snowbank/s Caused by Plowing
SND - Sand/Sanded
SNGL - Single
SNW - Snow
SPD - Speed
SR - Sunrise
SS - Sunset
SVC - Service
SW - Southwest
SWEPT - Swept or Broom/Broomed
TACAN - Tactical Air Navigational Aid
TFC - Traffic
TFR - Temporary Flight Restriction
TGL - Touch and Go Landings
THN - Thin
THR - Threshold
THRU - Through
TIL - Until
TKOF - Takeoff
TMPRY - Temporary
TRML - Terminal
TRNG - Training
TRSN - Transition
TSNT - Transient
TWR - Tower
TWY - Taxiway
UNAVBL - Unavailable
UNLGTD - Unlighted
UNMKD - Unmarked
UNMON - Unmonitored
UNRELBL - Unreliable
UNUSBL - Unusable
VASI - Visual Approach Slope Indicator
VDP - Visual Descent Point
VFR - Visual Flight Rules
VIA - By Way Of
VICE - Instead/Versus
VIS/VSBY - Visibility
VMC - Visual Meteorological Conditions
VOL - Volume
VOLMET - Meteorlogical Information for Aircraft in Flight
VOR - VHF Omni-Directional Radio Range
VORTAC - VOR and TACAN
VOT - VOR Test Signal
W - West
WBND - Westbound
WEA/WX - Weather
WI - Within
WKDAYS - Monday through Friday
WKEND - Saturday and Sunday
WND - Wind
WP - Waypoint
WSR - Wet Snow on Runway/s
WTR - Water on Runway/s
- WX Weather
/ - And
+ - In Addition/Also

Postflight Briefing #17-4

General Abbreviations

AAWU Alaskan Aviation Weather Unit
AAS Airport Advisory Service
AC Advisory Circular
ADDS Aviation Digital Data Service
ADF Automatic Direction Finder
ADIZ Air Defense Identification Zone
ADS-B Automatic Dependent Surveillance-Broadcast
A/FD Airport/Facility Directory
AFIS Automatic Flight Information Service
AFSS Automated Flight Service Station
AGL Above Ground Level
AIM Aeronautical Information Manual
AIRMET Airmen's Meteorological Information
ALS Approach Light Systems
AMSL Above Mean Sea Level
APV Approach with Vertical Guidance
ARINC Aeronautical Radio Incorporated
ARSA Airport Radar Service Area
ARSR Air Route Surveillance Radar
ARTCC Air Route Traffic Control Center
ASDE-X Airport Surface Detection Equipment - Model X
ASOS Automated Surface Observing System
ASR Airport Surveillance Radar
ASRS Aviation Safety Reporting System
ATC Air Traffic Control
ATCRBS Air Traffic Control Radar Beacon System
ATCT Airport Traffic Control Tower
ATD Along-Track Distance
ATIS Automatic Terminal Information Service
ATT Attitude Retention System
AWC Aviation Weather Center
AWOS Automated Weather Observing System
AWSS Automated Weather Sensor System
AWW Severe Weather Forecast Alert
CAT Clear Air Turbulence
CDI Course Deviation Indicator
CERAP Combined Center/RAPCON
CFIT Controlled Flight into Terrain
CFR Code of Federal Regulations
CTAF Common Traffic Advisory Frequency
CVRS Computerized Voice Reservation System
CWA Center Weather Advisory
CWSU Center Weather Service Unit
DA Decision Altitude
DF Direction Finder
DH Decision Height
DME Distance Measuring Equipment
DP Instrument Departure Procedure
DUATS Direct User Access Terminal System
DVA Diverse Vector Area
DVFR Defense Visual Flight Rules
EDCT Expect Departure Clearance Time
EFAS En Route Flight Advisory Service
ELT Emergency Locator Transmitter
ETA Estimated Time of Arrival
ETD Estimated Time of Departure
ETE Estimated Time En Route
FA Area Forecast
FAA Federal Aviation Administration
FAF Final Approach Fix
FAROS Final Approach Runway Occupancy Signal
FAWP Final Approach Waypoint
FB Fly-by
FCC Federal Communications Commission
FD Flight Director System
FDC Flight Data Center
FMS Flight Management System
FO Fly-over
FPA Flight Path Angle
FPNM Feet Per Nautical Mile
FSDO Flight Standards District Office
FSS Flight Service Station
GBAS Ground Based Augmentation System
GLS GNSS Landing System
GNSS Global Navigation Satellite System
GNSSP Global Navigation Satellite System Panel
GPS Global Positioning System
HAT Height Above Touchdown
HDTA High Density Traffic Airports
HIRL High Intensity Runway Lights
HIWAS Hazardous Inflight Weather Advisory Service
HUD Head-Up Display
Hz Hertz
IAF Initial Approach Fix
IAP Instrument Approach Procedure
IAS Indicated Air Speed
IAWP Initial Approach Waypoint
ICAO International Civil Aviation Organization
IF Intermediate Fix
IFR Instrument Flight Rules
ILS Instrument Landing System
ILS Instrument Landing System
IM Inner Marker
IMC Instrument Meteorological Conditions
INS Inertial Navigation System
IR IFR Military Training Route
IRU Inertial Reference Unit
kHz Kilohertz
LAA Local Airport Advisory
LAAS Local Area Augmentation System
LAHSO Land and Hold Short Operations
LDA Localizer Type Directional Aid
LDA Localizer Type Directional Aid
LIRL Low Intensity Runway Lights
LLWAS Low Level Wind Shear Alert System
LLWAS Low Level Wind Shear Alert System
LNAV Lateral Navigation
LOC Localizer
LP Localizer Performance
LPV Localizer Performance with Vertical Guidance
LUAW Line Up and Wait
MAHWP Missed Approach Holding Waypoint
MAP Missed Approach Point
MAWP Missed Approach Waypoint
MDA Minimum Descent Altitude
MEA Minimum En Route Altitude
METAR Aviation Routine Weather Report
MHz Megahertz
MIRL Medium Intensity Runway Lights
MM Middle Marker
MOA Military Operations Area
MOCA Minimum Obstruction Clearance Altitude
MRA Minimum Reception Altitude
MRB Magnetic Reference Bearing
MSA Minimum Safe Altitude
MSAW Minimum Safe Altitude Warning
MSL Mean Sea Level
MTI Moving Target Indicator
MTOS Mountain Obscuration
MTR Military Training Route
MVA Minimum Vectoring Altitude
MWA Mountain Wave Activity
MWO Meteorological Watch Office
NACO National Aeronautical Charting Office
NAS National Airspace System
NAVAID Navigational Aid
NCWF National Convective Weather Forecast
NDB Nondirectional Radio Beacon
NEXRAD Next Generation Weather Radar
NM Nautical Mile
NMAC Near Midair Collision
NoPT No Procedure Turn Required
NOTAM Notice to Airmen
NPA Nonprecision Approach
NRS Navigation Reference System
NSA National Security Area
NSW No Significant Weather
NTAP Notices to Airmen Publication
NWS National Weather Service
OAT Outside Air Temperature
OBS Omni-bearing Selector
ODP Obstacle Departure Procedure
OM Outer Marker
PA Precision Approach
PAPI Precision Approach Path Indicator
PAR Precision Approach Radar
PAR Preferred Arrival Route
PDC Pre-departure Clearance
PIREP Pilot Weather Report
POB Persons on Board
POI Principal Operations Inspector
PT Procedure Turn
RAA Remote Advisory Airport
RAIM Receiver Autonomous Integrity Monitoring
RAIS Remote Airport Information Service
RCAG Remote Center Air/Ground
RCLS Runway Centerline Lighting System
RCO Remote Communications Outlet
REIL Runway End Identifier Lights
REL Runway Entrance Lights
RIL Runway Intersection Lights
RMI Radio Magnetic Indicator
RNAV Area Navigation
RNP Required Navigation Performance
ROC Required Obstacle Clearance
RPAT RNP Parallel Approach Runway Transitions
RVR Runway Visual Range
RVSM Reduced Vertical Separation Minimum
RWSL Runway Status Light
SAAAR Special Aircraft/Aircrew Authorization Required
SAR Search and Rescue
SDF Simplified Directional Facility
SFL Sequenced Flashing Lights
SFR Special Flight Rules
SIAP Standard Instrument Approach Procedure
SID Standard Instrument Departure
SIGMET Significant Meteorological Information
SM Statute Mile
SMGCS Surface Movement Guidance Control System
STAR Standard Terminal Arrival
STARS Standard Terminal Automation Replacement
STMP Special Traffic Management Program
TA Traffic Advisory
TAA Terminal Arrival Area
TAC Terminal Area Chart
TACAN Tactical Air Navigation
TAF Aerodrome Forecast
TAS True Air Speed
TCAS Traffic Alert and Collision Avoidance System
TCH Threshold Crossing Height
TD Time Difference
TDLS Tower Data Link System
TDZE Touchdown Zone Elevation
TDZL Touchdown Zone Lights
TEC Tower En Route Control
THL Takeoff Hold Lights
TPP Terminal Procedures Publications
TRSA Terminal Radar Service Area
TSO Technical Standard Order
UA Unmanned Aircraft
UAS Unmanned Aircraft System
UAV Unmanned Aerial Vehicle
UFO Unidentified Flying Object
UHF Ultrahigh Frequency
UTC Coordinated Universal Time
UWS Urgent Weather SIGMET
VAR Volcanic Activity Reporting
VASI Visual Approach Slope Indicator
VDA Vertical Descent Angle
VDP Visual Descent Point
VFR Flight Rules
VGSI Visual Glide Slope Indicator
VHF Very High Frequency
VMC Visual Meteorological Conditions
VNAV Vertical Navigation
VNE Never exceed speed
VOR Very High Frequency Omni-directional Range
VOT VOR Test Facility
VR VFR Military Training Route
VREF The reference landing approach speed
VV Vertical Visibility
VVI Vertical Velocity Indicator
VY Speed for best rate of climb
WA AIRMET
WAAS Wide Area Augmentation System
WAC World Aeronautical Chart
WMS Wide-Area Master Station
WP Waypoint
WRS Wide-Area Ground Reference Station
WS SIGMET
WSO Weather Service Office
WSP Weather System Processor
WST Convective Significant Meteorological Infor
WW Severe Weather Watch Bulletin

The Fellow With the Tough Job

The Senior Editor: Mr. Brian Weiss

Brian Weiss is the owner of WORD'SWORTH, a marketing communications and design company. WORD'SWORTH provides services for all forms and formats of communications materials. Capabilities include the creation of brochures, books, newsletters, direct response letters, advertising, catalog sheets, slide shows and videos.

WORD'SWORTH clients have included Bank of America, Xerox Corporation, the National Childhood Cancer Foundation, Childrens Hospital (Los Angeles), the University of California (Irvine and Los Angeles campuses), Health Valley Foods, McGraw-Hill/CRM Films, Saint Joseph Hospital, *American Health* magazine, *Psychology Today* magazine, *Equity Quarterly*, Saint John's Hospital, *Aviation Safety* magazine, Long Beach and Santa Monica airports, and many others in a wide variety of fields.

In addition to general business expertise, WORD'SWORTH provides specialized background and knowledge in the areas of medicine and health care, science and technology, aviation and fundraising.

WORD'SWORTH also offers consulting on marketing strategies, direct mail campaigns, and fundraising proposals.

A little about Brian Weiss:

Founder (1977) and owner, WORD'SWORTH
Former editor, *Baja Explorer* magazine
Former associate editor, *Psychology Today* magazine
Served on the faculties of UCLA and the University of Michigan teaching introductory courses and advanced seminars in departments of human behavior, geography, and journalism.
Author for six years of a nationally syndicated consumer newspaper column (*FREEBIES*), and creator of a national magazine of the same name
Former medical/science editor, *Aviation Safety* magazine
Member (and former Board of Directors member), of Angel Flight, a not-for-profit community service organization.
Brian has been a pilot since 1980. He packs a private pilot certificate with an instrument rating and is the proud owner of a Cessna 172. He's one of the organizers of Flight Log, a group which provides information for pilots flying in Baja and throughout Mexico.

"Brian is one of the most talented, energetic and intelligent people with whom I've had the pleasure of working. His advice and dedication to this project were simply invaluable!"
Rod Machado

The Gal With Talent and a Lot of Patience

The Aviation Speakers Bureau

Providing Quality Aviation Speakers Since 1986

The Aviation Speakers Bureau features speakers for your banquet, educational seminar, safety standdown, convention, conference, forum, trade show, keynote, corporate training, airshow, safety program or association meeting. We guarantee a perfect match for your needs and objectives, and recommend only the very best in speakers. Our professionals shine and make YOU look good every time!

"We will help you find the perfect speaker for your budget and there is ***never*** *a charge for our service."*

Presentation and Topics

Safety, Weather, Instrument Flying, Inspirational, Cockpit Resource Management, Aviation Humor, Understanding Airspace, Test Pilots, Teamwork, Stress, Fighter Pilots and Aces, Weather Radar, In-flight Emergencies, Multi-engine Procedures, Celebrities and Heroes, Vietnam Pilots, Aviation Management, Interpreting Instrument Charts, Comedy, Air Racers, Policies and Politics of Aviation, Motivational, Industry Specific Training, Maneuvers, Success, Patriotic, Aviation Firsts, Stunt Flying, Air Combat, Aviation Psychology, Survival, Aviation Careers, Jeppesen Charts, Aerobatic Pilots, Wright Brothers, Accident Investigations, Survival and much more.

For information on our speakers call
800-247-1215
For all other calls 949-498-2498

P.O. Box 6030
San Clemente, CA 92674-6030

Read speaker biographies and view video clips:

Charter Member

The Ongoing Editor: Diane Titterington

Diane Titterington

Learning to fly in 1973, Diane holds a commercial certificate with an instrument rating. Her logbook is a Heinz 57 mixture of different makes and models. Flights include ferrying aircraft from the factory, flying fire patrol and a number of air races. Until 1981, she worked as a radar qualified air traffic controller on the high/low sectors at Houston Center. Diane has been a passenger on a carrier landing and takeoff, flown a T-38, rode dozens of airline jumpseats and logged a few blimp flights.

Her father, who worked at WPAFB, told tales of test pilots Bob Hoover, Scott Crossfield and Chuck Yeager when she was young. Diane never dreamed that she would later work with such aviation greats. As the President of The Aviation Speakers Bureau, Diane supplies speakers for hundreds of safety seminars, banquets and conventions. She places aviation speakers, celebrities and specialists at events across the United States, Canada and other countries.

"It is a pure pleasure to work with dozens of brilliant and gifted individuals such as Jim Tucker, Bob Hoover, Col. Joe Kittinger, Brian Udell, Al Haynes, Dave Gwinn, Dr. Jerry Cockrell and Ralph Hood. With their unusual experiences, unique delivery styles, and vast knowledge of aviation, our speakers are the most sought after in the business. By providing inspiring speakers for aviation events, we help motivate and educate. And we help to keep the skies safe too." Visit our web site: www.aviationspeakers.com

Diane has been the ongoing editor of *Rod Machado's Private Pilot Handbook* and *Rod Machado's Instrument Pilot's Survival Manual*. She is the designer, compiler, managing editor and producer of *Speaking of Flying*, a book of stories from 44 aviation speakers.

Rod Machado's Private Pilot Handbook and Audiobook

R3

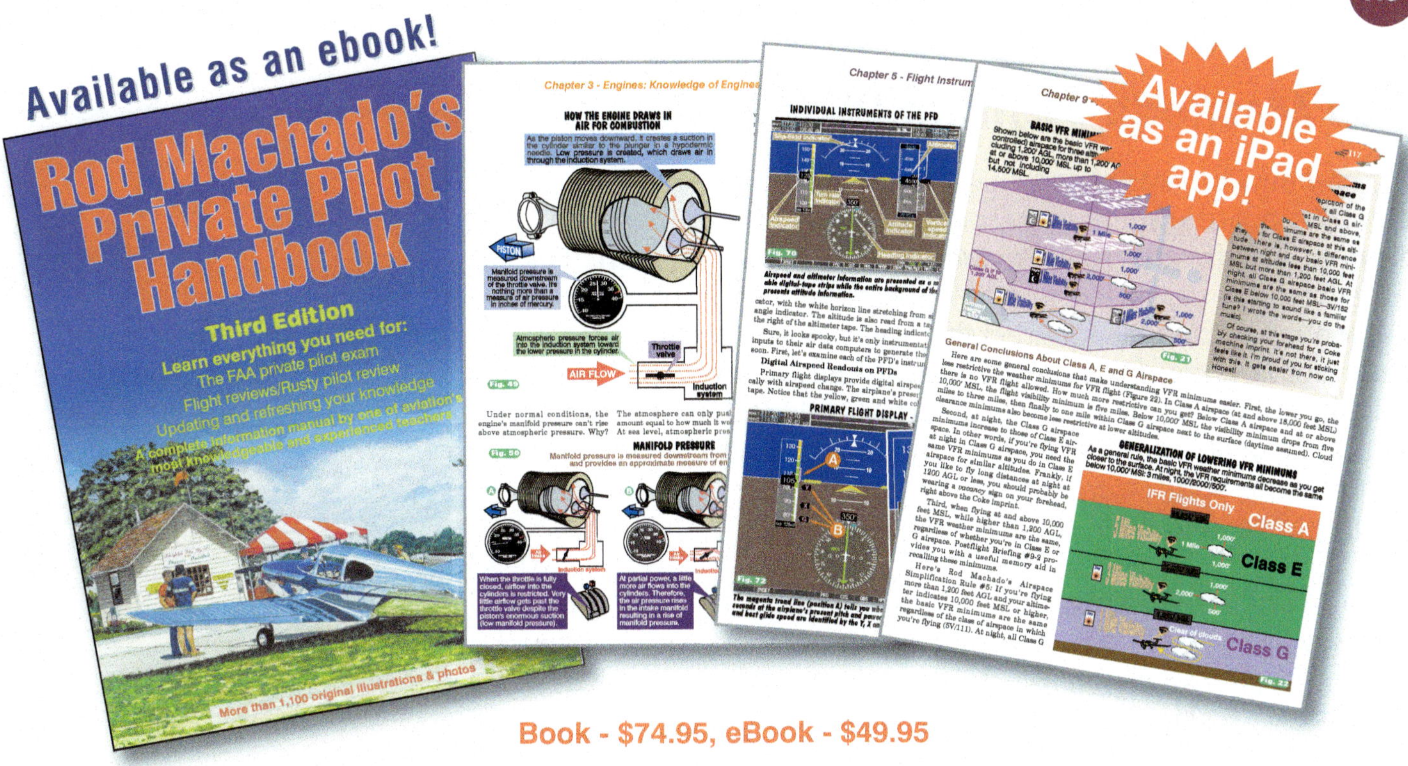

Rod Machado's Private Pilot Handbook 656 pages 8-3/8 x 10-7/8, Softbound

---

Rod Machado's Private Pilot Audiobook - MP3 Files (30 Hours+)

Retention can increase by 70% with auditory learning!
SHOULDN'T YOU BE REVIEWING?

Price: $74.95

Welcome to your instructor in an audiobook. Rod's entire Handbook is presented in a warm, conversational manner. His tried-and-true method of instruction can be enjoyed during your commute, relaxing at home, or almost anywhere. It allows you to learn in a new, novel and often more efficient manner. Turn wasted freeway time into learning time. As one pilot said, "I felt like I had a flight instructor right there in the car with me."

Perfect if you don't have the time or inclination to read, or for "tired" eyes at the end of the day. It's a pleasure to be read to, especially from a lively text spiced with humor. You can listen to the first eight chapters without referring to the book's graphics. For some chapters, you'll want to review pictures, picture text, graphs and charts in the Handbook.

This valuable one-stop audiobook will help you:

Fly as a knowledgeable and competent pilot
Prepare for the Private Pilot FAA Knowledge exam
Prepare for the Private Pilot practical oral exam
Refresh for required currency training
Remain an up-to-date confident pilot

Download MP3 Version $74.95

LISTEN and LEARN while:

- DRIVING
- RELAXING
- GARDENING
- EXERCISING
- EATING LUNCH
- BUILDING A KITPLANE

Narrator: Capt. Philip E. Hewitt Ph.D., CFII, ATP, Pilot Examiner, pro narrator
Guest Narrator: Alec

Visit our web site at: www.rodmachado.com

Rod Machado's Private Pilot Workbook

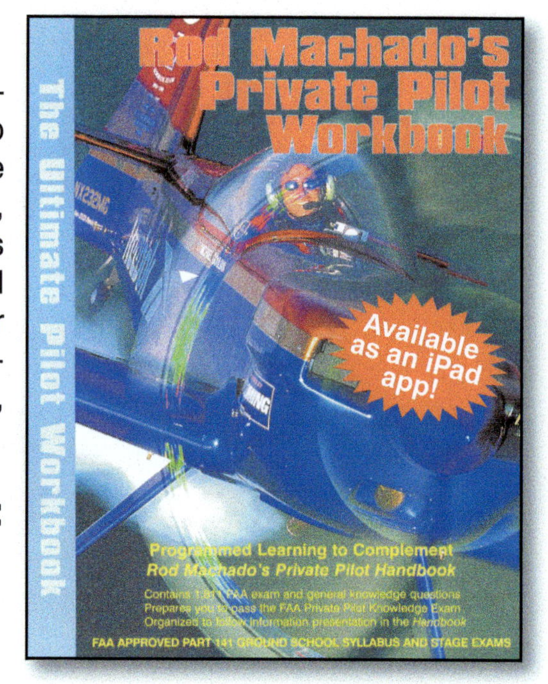

The new *Rod Machado's Private Pilot Workbook* is now available. As a programmed learning guide, this book will help prepare you for the FAA Private Pilot Knowledge Exam. The questions are organized to follow the presentation of material, section for section, as found in the *Handbook*. Not only will this book prepare you for the Private Pilot Knowledge Exam, it will help you understand and absorb the knowledge necessary for you to fly safely. You can test your knowledge and comprehension in each subject area with numerous weight and balance, performance, and flight planning problems.

This valuable one-stop workbook contains:

- An excellent, thorough and complete self-study system when used with *Rod Machado's Private Pilot Handbook*.
- 1,811 FAA Private Pilot Knowledge Exam and general aviation knowledge questions.
- Questions organized to follow the layout of *Rod Machado's Private Pilot Handbook* so you can test your knowledge and comprehension in each subject area.
- Color navigation charts & numerous weight-and-balance, performance, and flight planning problems.
- An FAA approved, Part 141 ground training syllabus for use in an FAA approved Part 141 ground school.

Available as an ebook Only! **$19.95**

Speaking of Flying

This wonderful 438 page hardbound book was written by 44 pilots who are speakers with The Aviation Speakers Bureau. These funny, dramatic, and inspiring stories are some of aviation's finest tales. You would expect nothing less from aviation's celebrities, experts and specialists.

Our flight plan sees us barnstorming in the U.S., flying aerial combat missions in World War II and Vietnam, test piloting new aircraft, performing air rescue, winging to exotic places, and flying to historically important aviation places from Kitty Hawk to the moon. You will go along as history is being made and hear the pilot's perspective on some of these aviation firsts. You will find ACES and true heroes within these pages. *Speaking of Flying* is your ticket to adventure. Step aboard, and be prepared to laugh, cry, and feel the excitement.

$29.95

Available as an ebook!

Rod Machado's IFR Audiobooks &How to Fly an Airplane

Download MP3 Audiobook - $74.95

Rod Machado's Instrument Pilot Audiobook in MP3 Format

Now you can enjoy Rod's popular *Instrument Pilot's Handbook* during your daily commute or at home in the comfort of your own chair. This audiobook is a 30 hour narration of the *Instrument Pilot Handbook* by Rod Machado.

While you can listen to the first ten chapters of the book without referring to the text, you'll still want to use the actual *Instrument Pilot's Handbook* as a reference for reviewing pictures, graphs and many of the incidental ASRS stories scattered throughout the text. This exciting audiobook is the key to learning quickly and efficiently while maximizing use of your scarce time.

Download MP3 Version $74.95

See www.rodmachado.com for download version!

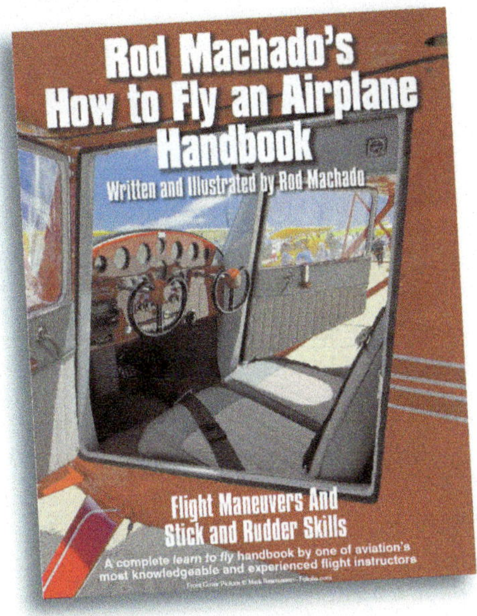

Book-$59.95/eBook-$44.95

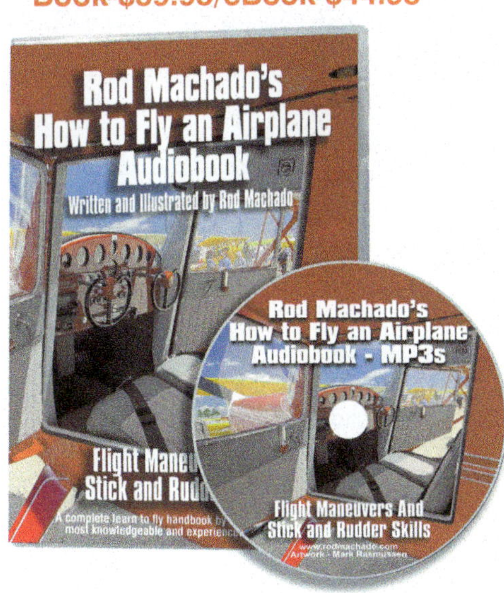

Audiobook MP3 Download Version
$59.95

Rod Machado's How to Fly an Airplane Handbook & Audiobook

Rod Machado's *How to Fly an Airplane Handbook* (or audiobook recorded by Rod Machado) is a full color, 597 page softbound handbook. It contains all the information you need to learn the physical skills associated with flying an airplane. The book was written to help all pilots learn the basic maneuvers for flying an airplane as well as helping already

This handbook contains the information necessary to:

- Learn the basic fundamentals of flying any airplane.
- Make flight training easier, less expensive and more enjoyable.
- Master all the private and commercial checkride maneuvers.
- Learn the "stick and rudder" philosophy of flying an airplane.
- Prevent an airplane from accidentally stalling and spinning.
- Allow you to learn to land an airplane quickly and enjoyably.
- Make you a better instructor by providing unique teaching strategies and explanations for student training.

These pages include:

- Practical flying skills that rely on sights, sounds and touch.
- The theory and practice of attitude flying for pilots of all levels.
- Multiple strategies for evaluating the roundout and flare.
- Multiple methods for controlling the airplane's glidepath.
- Strategies for evaluating the desired landing spot.
- Techniques for flying ground reference maneuvers.
- Handling bounces, floating, porpoising and ballooning.
- Wisdom and insights based on practical flying experience.
- Complex airplane operations, night flying, traffic pattern operations, slow flight, stall and spin recognition and recovery, and much more.

With this book you are ensured an enjoyable learning experience and quality instruction.

See www.rodmachado.com for download version!

Rod Machado's Plane Talk

The Mental Art of Flying an Airplane

You'll Learn, You'll Laugh, You'll Remember!

Welcome to a collection of Rod Machado's most popular aviation articles and stories from the last 15 years. *Rod Machado's Plane Talk* contains nearly 100 flights of fun and knowledge that will stimulate your aviation brain and tickle your funny bone. In addition to the educational topics listed below, you'll read about higher learning, the value of aviation history, aviation literature, aviation art and how an artist's perspective can help you better understand weather. You'll also find more than a few articles written just to make you laugh.

In this book you'll discover...

Available as an ebook!

How to Assess and Manage Aviation Risks
Learn how safe pilots think, how to apply the safety strategy used by General Jimmy Doolittle (known as the master of the calculated risk), how famed gunfighter Wyatt Earp can help you cope with aviation's risks, how misleading aviation statistics can be and why flying isn't as dangerous as some folks say it is.

Several Techniques for Making Better Cockpit Decisions
Discover how to use your inner copilot in the cockpit and the value of one good question asked upside down.

New Ways to Help You Cope With Temptation
Fly safer by developing an aviation code of ethics, understand how human nature can trick you into flying beyond your limits, why good pilots are prejudiced and how a concept like honor will protect you while aloft.

How to Use Your Brain for a Change
You can learn faster by understanding how the learning curve—the brain's performance chart—is affected by the little lies we tell ourselves, the mistakes we need to make, our need to please our instructors, and simulator and memory training.

The Truth About Flying, Anxiety and Fear
Learn why it's often the safest of pilots that make excuses instead of flights, why anxiety should be treated as a normal part of flying, and a three-step process to avoiding panic in the cockpit.

How to Handle First Time Flyers and Anxious Passengers
Discover how to behave around new passengers, how to avoid most common mistakes that scare passengers in airplanes and how to reduce the cockpit stress between pilot and spouse.

Favorite Skills Used By Good Pilots
Learn why good pilots scan behind an airplane as well as ahead of it, are sometimes rough and bully-like on the flight controls, occasionally fly without using any of the airplane's electronic navigation equipment, don't worry about turbulence breaking their airplanes, master airspeed control as a means of making better landings and much more.

eBook - $24.95/Physical Book $29.95

See website for eBook version!

Rod Machado's Instrument Pilot's Handbook Second Edition

Available as an iPad app!

Learn everything you need for:
- The FAA instrument knowledge exam
- Your instrument proficiency check
- Updating and refreshing your knowledge

Rod Machado has taught millions the basics of flying through flight lessons, simulation, and training materials.

ROD MACHADO'S Instrument Pilot's Handbook

656 Full Color Pages - Softbound - $74.95, ebook $49.45

Rod Machado's Instrument Pilot's Handbook is a teaching tour de force that takes pilots through the complex world of instrument flying.

Long known for his unique ability to transform difficult concepts into simple-yet-complete explanations, Machado takes both new and experienced IFR pilots on a guided tour of instrument flying, from the basics through subtleties that even many professional pilots will find useful. He turns complexity into curiosity. Nearly 1,000 illustrations shine further light on the topic at hand.

From how the basic aircraft instruments really work through what's inside a thunderstorm and how a GPS approach works, Machado teaches IFR pilots not just the minimum needed to pass the instrument pilot written exam, but every aspect of IFR flying. This up-to-date text covers the latest information on GPS, glass cockpits, data uplinks, computer-based resources, and other new (and future) technologies and techniques. It is also a rich source of practical information about how real pilots really fly IFR. Readers learn how to gauge the thunderstorm potential of a cumulus cloud by estimating the rainfall rate, scan their instruments in a way that provides maximum performance with minimum effort, and keep the needle centered during an ILS or LPV approach by using the sky pointer on the attitude indicator.

There's flying by the book, and then there's flying by THIS book. *Rod Machado's Instrument Pilot's Handbook* is fun, thorough, and the next best thing to having Rod Machado sit by a pilot's side and talk him through each topic. Once again, Machado proves that you can have fun while learning what you need to know in order to fly safely.

As a comprehensive information source book, these pages include:

- Simplification of the FAA's instrument scan concepts and an easy-to-use, cockpit-practical instrument scan technique
- Latest information on aviation decision making for instrument pilots
- Detailed understanding of analog and glass (PFD) flight instruments
- Detailed procedures for planning an IFR cross-country flight
- Easy to apply navigation methods for VOR, GPS, ADF and for flying approaches to LPV, LNAV, LNAV/VNAV minimums
- Clear, down-to-earth explanations of pertinent FARs, including instrument currency, lost comm, alternate requirements, etc.
- Step-by-step explanation of how instrument approach charts are constructed, including MDAs, DAs, procedure turns, etc.
- Practical understanding of the IFR system, GPS procedures, icing and thunderstorm avoidance, NEXRAD, RADAR. etc.

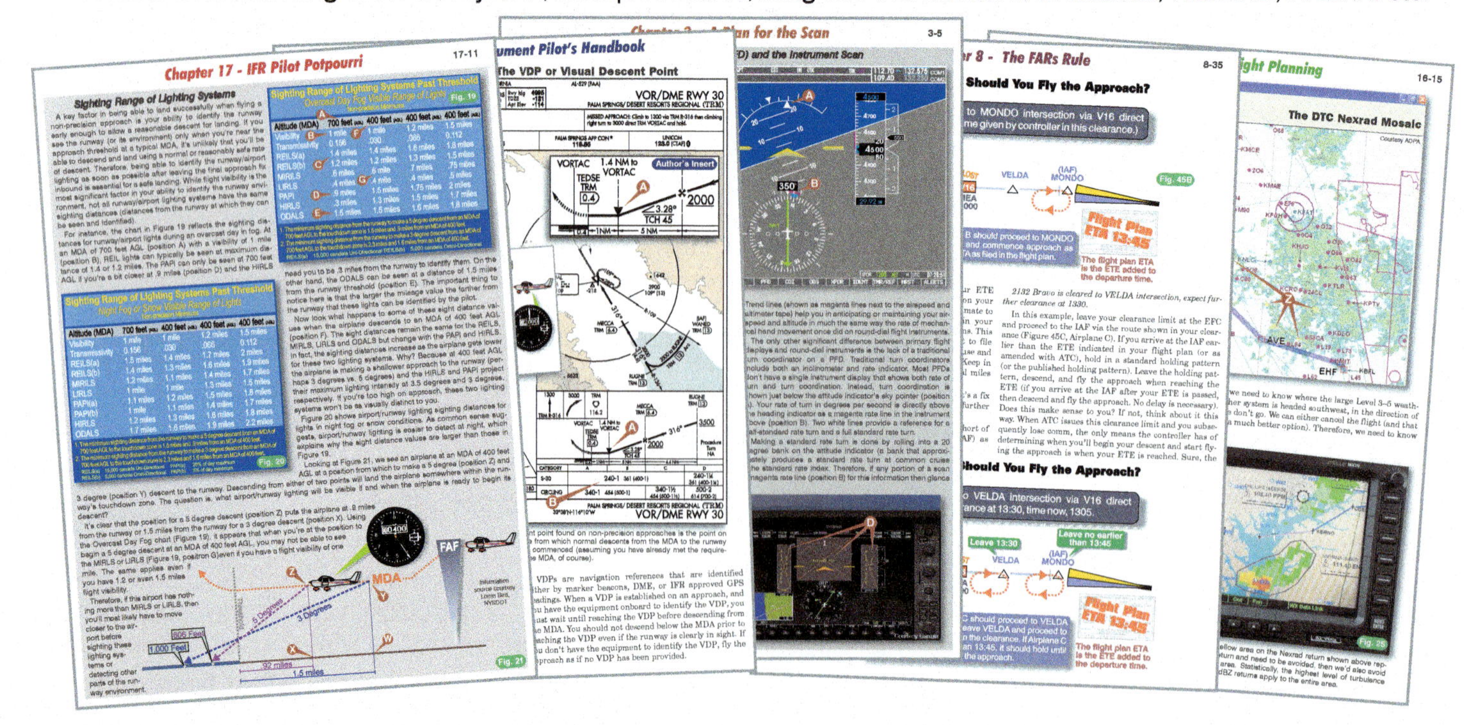

The Best of Rod Machado Live in MP3 Format

Rod combined 10 of his best "live audience" recordings from the original "Laugh and Learn" tape series and added four additional live recordings to produce this exciting 14 program set (12.5 hours of recorded material). Included are Rod's popular *Handling In-flight Emergencies* seminar and his latest programs on defensive flying, the art of flying, the nonpilot's guide to landing an airplane, and three additional live programs containing some of Rod's funniest standup aviation humor. You can laugh and learn while driving, gardening, or building your own plane. DVD contains files in MP3 format that are transferred to your MP3 player via computer for use.

Download MP3 Version $24.95

See website for download version!

CONTENTS

DVD containing MP3 files - Download Version $24.95 (see www.rodmachado.com)

Audio-1 Laugh Your Empennage Off (95/5)*
Audio-2 Samurai Airmanship (30/70)*
Audio-3 Reducing Cockpit Stress Between the Sexes (60/40)*
Audio-4 Cockpit Management (40/60)*
Audio-5 An Aviation Sense of Humor (95/5)*
Audio-6 Creative Solutions to Common Problems (40/60)*
Audio-7 Handling In-flight Emergencies 1 (10/90)*
Audio-8 Handling In-flight Emergencies 2 (10/90)*
Audio-9 Handling In-flight Emergencies 3 (10/90)*
Audio-10 Handling In-flight Emergencies 4 (10/90)*
Audio-11 The Nonpilot's Guide to Landing an Airplane (30/70)*
Audio-12 Aviation Humor: The Light Stuff (95/5)*
Audio-13 Yoke and Pedal: The Art of Flying (10/90)*
Audio-14 More Defensive Flying (10/90)*

*(% Humor content / % Information content)

"Rod has a wonderful sense of humor that will keep you in stitches and when you're done laughing, you'll be amazed at how much you've learned."
John & Martha King, King Video

"Mary Poppins once sang, 'A spoon full of sugar helps the medicine go down.' Rod Machado goes one step further by sugar coating invaluable aeronautical wisdom with entertaining wit and humor."
Barry Schiff, TWA Captain/Noted Author

How to Order

Please Visit:
www.rodmachado.com
To Order.

INDEX

For page letters: → A B C D E F G H I J L M N O P Q R
See chapter: → 1 2 3 4 5 6 7 8 9 10 11 12 13 14 15 16 17

A

B

C

INDEX

For page letters: → A B C D E F G H I J L M N O P Q R
See chapter: → 1 2 3 4 5 6 7 8 9 10 11 12 13 14 15 16 17

W

X-Y-Z

GLOSSARY

A

ABEAM-An aircraft is "abeam" a fix, point, or object when that fix, point, or object is approximately 90 degrees to the right or left of the aircraft track. Abeam indicates a general position rather than a precise point.

ABORT-To terminate a preplanned aircraft maneuver; e.g., an aborted takeoff.

ACKNOWLEDGE-Let me know that you have received my message.

ACROBATIC FLIGHT- An intentional maneuver involving an abrupt change in an aircraft's attitude, an abnormal attitude, or abnormal acceleration not necessary for normal flight.

ADMINISTRATOR- The Federal Aviation Administrator or any person to whom he/she has delegated his/her authority in the matter concerned.

ADVISE INTENTIONS-Tell me what you plan to do.

ADVISORY- Advice and information provided to assist pilots in the safe conduct of flight and aircraft movement.

ADVISORY FREQUENCY- The appropriate frequency to be used for Airport Advisory Service.

ADVISORY SERVICE- Advice and information provided by a facility to assist pilots in the safe conduct of

AERODROME- A defined area on land or water (including any buildings, installations and equipment) intended to be used either wholly or in part for the arrival, departure, and movement of aircraft.

AERONAUTICAL BEACON- A visual NAVAID displaying flashes of white and/or colored light to indicate the location of an airport, a heliport, a landmark, a certain point of a Federal airway in mountainous terrain, or an obstruction.

AERONAUTICAL INFORMATION MANUAL (AIM)- A primary FAA publication whose purpose is to instruct airmen about operating in the National Airspace System of the U.S. It provides basic flight information, ATC Procedures and general instructional information concerning health, medical facts, factors affecting flight safety, accident and hazard reporting, and types of aeronautical charts and their use.

AIR DEFENSE IDENTIFICATION ZONE (ADIZ)- The area of airspace over land or water, extending upward from the surface, within which the ready identification, the location, and the control of aircraft are required in the interest of national security.

a. Domestic Air Defense Identification Zone. An ADIZ within the United States along an international boundary of the United States.

b. Coastal Air Defense Identification Zone. An ADIZ over the coastal waters of the United States.

c. Distant Early Warning Identification Zone (DEWIZ). An ADIZ over the coastal waters of the State of Alaska.

d. Land-Based Air Defense Identification Zone. An ADIZ over U.S. metropolitan areas, which is activated and deactivated as needed, with dimen sions, activation dates and other relevant information disseminated via NOTAM.

AIR ROUTE SURVEILLANCE RADAR- Air route traffic control center (ARTCC) radar used primarily to detect and display an aircraft's position while en route between terminal areas. The ARSR enables controllers to provide radar air traffic control service when aircraft are within the ARSR coverage. In some instances, ARSR may enable an ARTCC to provide terminal radar services similar to but usually more limited than those provided by a radar approach control.

AIR ROUTE TRAFFIC CONTROL CENTER- A facility established to provide air traffic control service to aircraft operating on IFR flight plans within controlled airspace and principally during the en route phase of flight. When equipment capabilities and controller workload permit, certain advisory/assistance services may be provided to VFR aircraft.

AIR TAXI- Used to describe a helicopter/VTOL aircraft movement conducted above the surface but normally not above 100 feet AGL. The aircraft may proceed either via hover taxi or flight at speeds more than 20 knots. The pilot is solely responsible for selecting a safe airspeed/altitude for the operation being conducted.

AIR TRAFFIC- Aircraft operating in the air or on an airport surface, exclusive of loading ramps and parking areas.

AIR TRAFFIC CLEARANCE- An authorization by air traffic control for the purpose of preventing collision between known aircraft, for an aircraft to proceed under specified traffic conditions within controlled airspace. The pilot-in-command of an aircraft may not deviate from the provisions of a visual flight rules (VFR) or instrument flight rules (IFR) air traffic clearance except in an emergency or unless an amended clearance has been obtained. Additionally, the pilot may request a different clearance from that which has been issued by air traffic control (ATC) if information available to the pilot makes another course of action more practicable or if aircraft equipment limitations or company procedures forbid compliance with the clearance issued. Pilots may also request clarification or amendment, as appropriate, any time a clearance is not fully understood, or considered unacceptable because of safety of flight. Controllers should, in such instances and to the extent of operational practicality and safety, honor the pilot's request. 14 CFR Part 91.3(a) states: "The pilot in command of an aircraft is directly responsible for, and is the final authority as to, the operation of that aircraft." THE PILOT IS RESPONSIBLE TO REQUEST AN AMENDED CLEARANCE if ATC issues a clearance that would cause a pilot to deviate from a rule or regulation, or in the pilot's opinion, would place the aircraft in jeopardy.

AIR TRAFFIC CONTROL- A service operated by appropriate authority to promote the safe, orderly and expeditious flow of air traffic.

AIRCRAFT- Device(s) that are used or intended to be used for flight in the air, and when used in air traffic control terminology, may include the flight crew.

AIRCRAFT CLASSES- For the purposes of Wake Turbulence Separation Minima, ATC classifies aircraft as Heavy, Large, and Small as follows:

a. Heavy- Aircraft capable of takeoff weights of 300,000 pounds or more whether or not they are operating at this weight during a particular phase of flight.

b. Large- Aircraft of more than 41,000 pounds, maximum certificated takeoff weight, up to but not including 300,000 pounds.

c. Small- Aircraft of 41,000 pounds or less maximum certificated takeoff weight.

AIRMET-In-flight weather advisories issued only to amend the area forecast concerning weather phenomena which are of operational interest to all aircraft and potentially hazardous to aircraft having limited capability because of lack of equipment, instrumentation, or pilot qualifications. AIRMETs concern weather of less severity than that covered by SIGMETs or Convective SIGMETs. AIRMETs cover moderate icing, moderate turbulence, sustained winds of 30 knots or more at the surface, widespread areas of ceilings less than 1,000 feet and/or visibility less than 3 miles, and extensive mountain obscurement.

AIRPORT- An area on land or water that is used or intended to be used for the landing and take-off of aircraft and includes its buildings and facilities, if any.

AIRPORT ADVISORY AREA- The area within ten miles of an airport without a control tower or where the tower is not in operation, and on which a Flight Service Station is located.

AIRPORT ELEVATION- The highest point of an airport's usable runways measured in feet from mean sea level.

Digital Chart Supplement- A publication designed primarily as a pilot's operational manual containing all airports, seaplane bases, and heliports open to the public including communications data, navigational facilities, and certain special notices and procedures. This publication is issued in seven volumes according to geographical area.

AIRPORT LIGHTING- Various lighting aids that may be installed on an airport. Types of airport lighting include:..

b. Runway Lights/Runway Edge Lights- Lights having a prescribed angle of emission used to define the lateral limits of a runway. Runway lights are uniformly spaced at intervals of approximately 200 feet, and the intensity may be controlled or preset.

c. Touchdown Zone Lighting-Two rows of transverse light bars located symmetrically about the runway centerline normally at 100 foot intervals. The basic system extends 3,000 feet along the runway.

d. Runway Centerline Lighting- Flush centerline lights spaced at 50-foot intervals beginning 75 feet from the landing threshold and extending to within 75 feet of the opposite end of the runway.

e. Threshold Lights- Fixed green lights arranged symmetrically left and right of the runway centerline, identifying the runway threshold.

f. Runway End Identifier Lights (REIL)- Two synchronized flashing lights, one on each side of the runway threshold, which provide rapid and positive identification of the approach end of a particular runway.

g. Visual Approach Slope Indicator (VASI)- An airport lighting facility providing vertical visual approach slope guidance to aircraft during approach to landing by radiating a directional pattern of high intensity red and white focused light beams which indicate to the pilot that he/she is "on path" if he/she sees red/white, "above path" if white/white, and "below path" if red/red. Some airports serving large aircraft have three-bar VASIs which provide two visual glide paths to the same runway.

h. Precision Approach Path Indicator (PAPI)- An airport lighting facility, similar to VASI, providing vertical approach slope guidance to aircraft during approach to landing. PAPIs consist of a single row of either two or four lights, normally installed on the left side of the runway, and have an effective visual range of about 5 miles during the day and up to 20 miles at night. PAPIs radiate a directional pattern of high intensity red and white focused light beams which indicate that the pilot is "on path" if the pilot sees an equal number of white lights and red lights, with white to the left of the red; "above path" if the pilot sees more white than red lights; and "below path" if the pilot sees more red than white lights.

i. Boundary Lights- Lights defining the perimeter of an airport or landing area. (Refer to AIM.)

AIRPORT MARKING AIDS- Markings used on runway and taxiway surfaces to identify a specific runway, a runway threshold, a centerline, a hold line, etc. A runway should be marked in accordance with its present usage such as:

a. Visual.

b. Nonprecision instrument.

c. Precision instrument.

AIRPORT REFERENCE POINT (ARP)-The approximate geometric center of all usable runway surfaces.

AIRPORT ROTATING BEACON- A visual NAVAID operated at many airports. At civil airports, alternating white and green flashes indicate the location of the airport. At military airports, the beacons flash alternately white and green, but are differentiated from civil beacons by dualpeaked (two quick) white flashes between the green flashes.

AIRPORT SURFACE DETECTION EQUIPMENT (ASDE)-Surveillance equipment specifically designed to detect aircraft, vehicular traffic, and other objects, on the surface of an airport, and to present the image on a tower display. Used to augment visual observation by tower personnel of aircraft and/or vehicular movements on runways and taxiways. There are three ASDE systems deployed in the NAS:

a. ASDE-3- a Surface Movement Radar.

b. ASDE-X- a system that uses a X-band Surface Movement Radar and multilateration. Data from these two sources are fused and presented on a digital display.

c. ASDE-3X- an ASDE-X system that uses the ASDE-3 Surface Movement Radar.

AIRPORT SURVEILLANCE RADAR- Approach control radar used to detect and display an aircraft's position in the terminal area. ASR provides range and azimuth information but does not provide elevation data. Coverage of the ASR can extend up to 60 miles.

AIRWAY BEACON- Used to mark airway segments in remote mountain areas. The light flashes Morse Code to identify the beacon site.

ALONG-TRACK DISTANCE (ATD)- The distance measured from a point-in-space by systems using area navigation reference capabilities that are not subject to slant range errors.

ALPHANUMERIC DISPLAY- Letters and numerals used to show identification, altitude, beacon code, and other information concerning a target on a radar display.

ALTERNATE AIRPORT- An airport at which an aircraft may land if a landing at the intended airport becomes inadvisable.

ALTIMETER SETTING- The barometric pressure reading used to adjust a pressure altimeter for variations in existing atmospheric pressure or to the standard altimeter setting (29.92).

ALTITUDE- The height of a level, point, or object measured in feet Above Ground Level (AGL) or from Mean Sea Level (MSL).

a. MSL Altitude-Altitude expressed in feet measured from mean sea level.

b. AGL Altitude-Altitude expressed in feet measured above ground level.

c. Indicated Altitude- The altitude as shown by an altimeter. On a pressure or barometric altimeter it is altitude as shown uncorrected for instrument error and uncompensated for variation from standard atmospheric conditions.

ALTITUDE READOUT-An aircraft's altitude, transmitted via the Mode C transponder feature, that is visually displayed in 100-foot increments on a radar scope having readout capability.

ALTITUDE RESTRICTION- An altitude or altitudes, stated in the order flown, which are to be maintained until reaching a specific point or time. Altitude restrictions may be issued by ATC due to traffic, terrain, or other airspace considerations.

APPROACH CLEARANCE- Authorization by ATC for a pilot to conduct an instrument approach. The type of instrument approach for which a clearance and other pertinent information is provided in the approach clearance when required.

APPROACH CONTROL FACILITY- A terminal ATC facility that provides approach control service in a terminal area.

APRON- A defined area on an airport or heliport intended to accommodate aircraft for purposes of loading or unloading passengers or cargo, refueling, parking, or maintenance. With regard to seaplanes, a ramp is used for access to the apron from the water.

ARC- The track over the ground of an aircraft flying at a constant distance from a navigational aid by reference to distance measuring equipment (DME).

AREA NAVIGATION (RNAV)- A method of navigation which permits aircraft operation on any desired flight path within the coverage of ground- or space-based navigation aids or within the limits of the capability of self-contained aids, or a combination of these.

Note: Area navigation includes performance-based navigation as well as other operations that do not meet the definition of performance-based navigation.

ARRIVAL DELAY- A parameter which specifies a period of time in which no aircraft will be metered for arrival at the specified airport.

ARRIVAL SECTOR- An operational control sector containing one or more meter fixes.

ARRIVAL TIME- The time an aircraft touches down on arrival.

ATC ADVISES- Used to prefix a message of noncontrol information when it is relayed to an aircraft by other than an air traffic controller.

ATC ASSIGNED AIRSPACE- Airspace of defined vertical/lateral limits, assigned by ATC, for the purpose of providing air traffic segregation between the specified activities being conducted within the assigned airspace and other IFR air traffic.

ATC CLEARS- Used to prefix an ATC clearance when it is relayed to an aircraft by other than an air traffic controller.

ATC INSTRUCTIONS- Directives issued by air traffic control for the purpose of requiring a pilot to take specific actions; e.g., "Turn left heading two five zero," "Go around," "Clear the runway."

ATC PREFERRED ROUTE NOTIFICATION- URET notification to the appropriate controller of the need to determine if an ATC preferred route needs to be applied, based on destination airport.

ATC REQUESTS- Used to prefix an ATC request when it is relayed to an aircraft by other than an air traffic controller.

AUTOMATED WEATHER SYSTEM- Any of the automated weather sensor platforms that collect weather data at airports and disseminate the weather information via radio and/or landline. The systems currently consist of the Automated Surface Observing System (ASOS), Automated Weather Sensor System (AWSS) and Automated Weather Observation System (AWOS).

AUTOMATED UNICOM- Provides completely automated weather, radio check capability and airport advisory information on an Automated UNICOM system. These systems offer a variety of features, typically selectable by microphone clicks, on the UNICOM frequency. Availability will be published in the Digital Chart Supplement and approach charts.

AUTOMATIC ALTITUDE REPORTING- That function of a transponder which responds to Mode C interrogations by transmitting the aircraft's altitude in 100-foot increments.

AUTOMATIC DEPENDENT SURVEILLANCE-BROADCAST (ADS-B)- A surveillance system in which an aircraft or vehicle to be detected is fitted with cooperative equipment in the form of a data link transmitter. The aircraft or vehicle periodically broadcasts its GPS-derived position and other information such as velocity over the data link, which is received by a ground-based transmitter/receiver (transceiver) for processing and display at an air traffic control facility.

AUTOMATIC DIRECTION FINDER- An aircraft radio navigation system which senses and indicates the direction to a L/MF nondirectional radio beacon (NDB) ground transmitter. Direction is indicated to the pilot as a magnetic bearing or as a relative bearing to the longitudinal axis of the aircraft depending on the type of indicator installed in the aircraft. In certain applications, such as military, ADF operations may be based on airborne and ground transmitters in the VHF/UHF frequency spectrum.

AUTOMATIC TERMINAL INFORMATION SERVICE- The continuous broadcast of recorded noncontrol information in selected terminal areas. Its purpose is to improve controller effectiveness and to relieve frequency congestion by automating the repetitive transmission of essential but routine information; e.g., "Los Angeles information Alfa. One three zero zero Coordinated Universal Time. Weather, measured ceiling two thousand overcast, visibility three, haze, smoke, temperature seven one, dew point five seven, wind two five zero at five, altimeter two niner niner six. I-L-S Runway Two Five Left approach in use, Runway Two Five Right closed, advise you have Alfa."

AVAILABLE LANDING DISTANCE (ALD)- The portion of a runway available for landing and roll-out for aircraft cleared for LAHSO. This distance is measured from the landing threshold to the hold-short point.

AVIATION WEATHER SERVICE- A service provided by the National Weather Service (NWS) and FAA which collects and disseminates pertinent weather information for pilots, aircraft operators, and ATC. Available aviation weather reports and forecasts are displayed at each NWS office and FAA FSS.

AZIMUTH (MLS)- A magnetic bearing extending from an MLS navigation facility.

B

BACK-TAXI- A term used by air traffic controllers to taxi an aircraft on the runway opposite to the traffic flow. The aircraft may be instructed to back-taxi to the beginning of the runway or at some point before reaching the runway end for the purpose of departure or to exit the runway.

BEARING- The horizontal direction to or from any point, usually measured clockwise from true north, magnetic north, or some other reference point through 360 degrees.

BELOW MINIMUMS- Weather conditions below the minimums prescribed by regulation for the particular action involved; e.g., landing minimums, takeoff minimums.

BLOCKED-Phraseology used to indicate that a radio transmission has been distorted or interrupted due to multiple simultaneous radio transmissions.

BRAKING ACTION (GOOD, FAIR, POOR, OR NIL)-A report of conditions on the airport movement area providing a pilot with a degree/quality of braking that he/she might expect. Braking action is reported in terms of good, fair, poor, or nil.

BRAKING ACTION ADVISORIES- When tower controllers have received runway braking action reports which include the terms "fair," "poor," or "nil," or whenever weather conditions are conducive to deteriorating or rapidly changing runway braking conditions, the tower will include on the ATIS broadcast the statement, "Braking action advisories are in effect" on the ATIS broadcast. During the time braking action advisories are in effect, ATC will issue the latest braking action report for the runway in use to each arriving and departing aircraft. Pilots should be prepared for deteriorating braking conditions and should request current runway condition information if not volunteered by controllers. Pilots should also be prepared to provide a descriptive runway condition report to controllers after landing.

C

CALCULATED LANDING TIME- A term that may be used in place of tentative or actual calculated landing time, whichever applies.

CARDINAL ALTITUDES-"Odd" or "Even" thousand-foot altitudes or flight levels; e.g., 5,000, 6,000, 7,000, FL 250, FL 260, FL 270.

CEILING- The heights above the earth's surface of the lowest layer of clouds or obscuring phenomena that is reported as "broken," "overcast," or "obscuration," and not classified as "thin" or "partial."

CHARTED VFR FLYWAYS- Charted VFR Flyways are flight paths recommended for use to bypass areas heavily traversed by large turbine-powered aircraft. Pilot compliance with recommended flyways and associated altitudes is strictly voluntary. VFR Flyway Planning charts are published on the back of existing VFR Terminal Area charts.

CIRCLE-TO-LAND MANEUVER- A maneuver initiated by the pilot to align the aircraft with a runway for landing when a straight-in landing from an instrument approach is not possible or is not desirable. At tower controlled airports, this maneuver is made only after ATC authorization has been obtained and the pilot has established required visual reference to the airport.

CIRCLE TO RUNWAY (RUNWAY NUMBER)- Used by ATC to inform the pilot that he/she must circle to land because the runway in use is other than the runway aligned with the instrument approach procedure. When the direction of the circling maneuver in relation to the airport/runway is required, the controller will state the direction (eight cardinal compass points) and specify a left or right downwind or base leg as appropriate; e.g., "Cleared VOR Runway Three Six Approach circle to Runway Two Two," or "Circle northwest of the airport for a right downwind to Runway Two Two."

CLASS G AIRSPACE- That airspace not designated as Class A, B, C, D or E.

CLEAR AIR TURBULENCE (CAT)-Turbulence encountered in air where no clouds are present. This term is commonly applied to high-level turbulence associated with wind shear. CAT is often encountered in the vicinity of the jet stream.

CLEAR OF THE RUNWAY-

a. Taxiing aircraft, which is approaching a runway, is clear of the runway when all parts of the aircraft are held short of the applicable runway holding position marking.

b. A pilot or controller may consider an aircraft, which is exiting or crossing a runway, to be clear of the runway when all parts of the aircraft are beyond the runway edge and there are no restrictions to its continued movement beyond the applicable runway holding position marking.

c. Pilots and controllers shall exercise good judgement to ensure that adequate separation exists between all aircraft on runways and taxiways at airports with inadequate runway edge lines or holding position markings.

CLEARANCE LIMIT- The fix, point, or location to which an aircraft is cleared when issued an air traffic clearance.

CLEARANCE VOID IF NOT OFF BY (TIME)- Used by ATC to advise an aircraft that the departure clearance is automatically canceled if takeoff is not made prior to a specified time. The pilot must obtain a new clearance or cancel his/her IFR flight plan if not off by the specified time.

CLEARED APPROACH- ATC authorization for an aircraft to execute any standard or special instrument approach procedure for that airport. Normally, an aircraft will be cleared for a specific instrument approach procedure.

CLEARED (Type of) APPROACH- ATC authorization for an aircraft to execute a specific instrument approach procedure to an airport; e.g., "Cleared ILS Runway Three Six Approach."

CLEARED AS FILED- Means the aircraft is cleared to proceed in accordance with the route of flight filed in the flight plan. This clearance does not include the altitude, DP, or DP Transition.

CLEARED FOR TAKEOFF- ATC authorization for an aircraft to depart. It is predicated on known traffic and known physical airport conditions.

CLEARED FOR THE OPTION- ATC authorization for an aircraft to make a touch-and-go, low approach, missed approach, stop and go, or full stop landing at the discretion of the pilot. It is normally used in training so that an instructor can evaluate a student's performance under changing situations.

CLEARED THROUGH-ATC authorization for an aircraft to make intermediate stops at specified airports without refiling a flight plan while en route to the clearance limit.

CLEARED TO LAND- ATC authorization for an aircraft to land. It is predicated on known traffic and known physical airport conditions.

CLIMB TO VFR- ATC authorization for an aircraft to climb to VFR conditions within Class B, C, D, and E surface areas when the only weather limitation is restricted visibility. The aircraft must remain clear of clouds while climbing to VFR.

CLIMBOUT- That portion of flight operation between takeoff and the initial cruising altitude.

CLOSED RUNWAY- A runway that is unusable for aircraft operations. Only the airport management/military operations office can close a runway.

CLOSED TRAFFIC- Successive operations involving takeoffs and landings or low approaches where the aircraft does not exit the traffic pattern.

CLOUD- A cloud is a visible accumulation of minute water droplets and/or ice particles in the atmosphere above the Earth's surface. Cloud differs from ground fog, fog, or ice fog only in that the latter are, by definition, in contact with the Earth's surface.

COMBINED CENTER-RAPCON- An air traffic facility which combines the functions of an ARTCC and a radar approach control facility.

COMMON TRAFFIC ADVISORY FREQUENCY (CTAF)- A frequency designed for the purpose of carrying out airport advisory practices while operating to or from an airport without an operating control tower. The CTAF may be a UNICOM, Multicom, FSS, or tower frequency and is identified in appropriate aeronautical publications.

COMPASS LOCATOR- A low power, low or medium frequency (L/MF) radio beacon installed at the site of the outer or middle marker of an instrument landing system (ILS). It can be used for navigation at distances of approximately 15 miles or as authorized in the approach procedure.

a. Outer Compass Locator (LOM)- A compass locator installed at the site of the outer marker of an instrument landing system.

b. Middle Compass Locator (LMM)- A compass locator installed at the site of the middle marker of an instrument landing system.

COMPASS ROSE- A circle, graduated in degrees, printed on some charts or marked on the ground at an airport. It is used as a reference to either true or magnetic direction.

CONFIDENCE MANEUVER- A confidence maneuver consists of one or more turns, a climb or descent, or other maneuver to determine if the pilot in command (PIC) is able to receive and comply with ATC instructions.

CONFLICT ALERT- A function of certain air traffic control automated systems designed to alert radar controllers to existing or pending situations between tracked targets (known IFR or VFR aircraft) that require his/her immediate attention/action.

CONFLICT RESOLUTION- The resolution of potential conflictions between aircraft that are radar identified and in communication with ATC by ensuring that radar targets do not touch. Pertinent traffic advisories shall be issued when this procedure is applied.

Note: This procedure shall not be provided utilizing mosaic radar systems.

CONTACT-

a. Establish communication with (followed by the name of the facility and, if appropriate, the frequency to be used).

b. A flight condition wherein the pilot ascertains the attitude of his/her aircraft and navigates by visual reference to the surface.

CONTERMINOUS U.S.- The 48 adjoining States and the District of Columbia.

CONTINENTAL UNITED STATES- The 49 States located on the continent of North America and the District of Columbia.

CONTINUE- When used as a control instruction should be followed by another word or words clarifying what is expected of the pilot. Example: "continue taxi," "continue descent," "continue inbound," etc.

CONVECTIVE SIGMET- A weather advisory concerning convective weather significant to the safety of all aircraft. Convective SIGMETs are issued for tornadoes, lines of thunderstorms, embedded thunderstorms of any intensity level, areas of thunderstorms greater than or equal to VIP level 4 with an area coverage of 4/10 (40%) or more, and hail 3/4 inch or greater.

COORDINATES- The intersection of lines of reference, usually expressed in degrees/minutes/seconds of latitude and longitude, used to determine position or location.

CORRECTION- An error has been made in the transmission and the correct version follows.

COURSE-

a. The intended direction of flight in the horizontal plane measured in degrees from north.

b. The ILS localizer signal pattern usually specified as the front course or the back course.

c. The intended track along a straight, curved, or segmented MLS path.

CROSS (FIX) AT (ALTITUDE)- Used by ATC when a specific altitude restriction at a specified fix is required.

CROSS (FIX) AT OR ABOVE (ALTITUDE)- Used by ATC when an altitude restriction at a specified fix is required. It does not prohibit the aircraft from crossing the fix at a higher altitude than specified; however, the higher altitude may not be one that will violate a succeeding altitude restriction or altitude assignment.

CROSS (FIX) AT OR BELOW (ALTITUDE)- Used by ATC when a maximum crossing altitude at a specific fix is required. It does not prohibit the aircraft from crossing the fix at a lower altitude; however, it must be at or above the minimum IFR altitude.

CROSSWIND-

a. When used concerning the traffic pattern, the word means "crosswind leg."

b. When used concerning wind conditions, the word means a wind not parallel to the runway or the path of an aircraft.

CROSSWIND COMPONENT- The wind component measured in knots at 90 degrees to the longitudinal axis of the runway.

CRUISE CLIMB- A climb technique employed by aircraft, usually at a constant power setting, resulting in an increase of altitude as the aircraft weight decreases.

CRUISING ALTITUDE- An altitude or flight level maintained during en route level flight. This is a constant altitude and should not be confused with a cruise clearance.

D

DEAD RECKONING- Dead reckoning, as applied to flying, is the navigation of an airplane solely by means of computations based on airspeed, course, heading, wind direction, and speed, groundspeed, and elapsed time.

DECISION ALTITUDE/DECISION HEIGHT-A specified altitude or height (A/H) in the precision approach at which a missed approach must be initiated if the required visual reference to continue the approach has not been established.

DECISION HEIGHT- With respect to the operation of aircraft, means the height at which a decision must be made during an ILS, MLS, or PAR instrument approach to either continue the approach or to execute a missed approach.

DEFENSE VISUAL FLIGHT RULES-Rules applicable to flights within an ADIZ conducted under the visual flight rules in 14 CFR Part 91.

DELAY INDEFINITE (REASON IF KNOWN) EXPECT FURTHER CLEARANCE (TIME)- Used by ATC to inform a pilot when an accurate estimate of the delay time and the reason for the delay cannot immediately be determined; e.g., a disabled aircraft on the runway, terminal or center area saturation, weather below landing minimums, etc.

DEPARTURE CONTROL- A function of an approach control facility providing air traffic control service for departing IFR and, under certain conditions, VFR aircraft.

DEPARTURE TIME- The time an aircraft becomes airborne.

DESIRED COURSE-

a. True- A predetermined desired course direction to be followed (measured in degrees from true north).

b. Magnetic- A predetermined desired course direction to be followed (measured in degrees from local magnetic north).

DESIRED TRACK- The planned or intended track between two waypoints. It is measured in degrees from either magnetic or true north. The instantaneous angle may change from point to point along the great circle track between waypoints.

DEVIATIONS-

a. A departure from a current clearance, such as an off course maneuver to avoid weather or turbulence.

b. Where specifically authorized in the CFRs and requested by the pilot, ATC may permit pilots to

DIGITAL-AUTOMATIC TERMINAL INFORMATION SERVICE (D-ATIS)- The service provides text messages to aircraft, airlines, and other users outside the standard reception range of conventional ATIS via landline and data link communications to the cockpit. Also, the service provides a computer-synthesized voice message that can be transmitted to all aircraft within range of existing transmitters. The Terminal Data Link System (TDLS) D-ATIS application uses weather inputs from local automated weather sources or manually entered meteorological data together with preprogrammed menus to provide standard information to users. Airports with D-ATIS capability are listed in the Digital Chart Supplement.

DIRECT-Straight line flight between two navigational aids, fixes, points, or any combination thereof. When used by pilots in describing off-airway routes, points defining direct route segments become compulsory reporting points unless the aircraft is under radar contact.

DISCRETE CODE-As used in the Air Traffic Control Radar Beacon System (ATCRBS), any one of the 4096 selectable Mode 3/A aircraft transponder codes except those ending in zero zero; e.g., discrete codes: 0010, 1201, 2317, 7777; nondiscrete codes: 0100, 1200, 7700. Nondiscrete codes are normally reserved for radar facilities that are not equipped with discrete decoding capability and for other purposes such as emergencies (7700), VFR aircraft (1200), etc.

DISCRETE FREQUENCY- A separate radio frequency for use in direct pilot-controller communications in air traffic control which reduces frequency congestion by controlling the number of aircraft operating on a particular frequency at one time. Discrete frequencies are normally designated for each control sector in en route/terminal ATC facilities. Discrete frequencies are listed in the Digital Chart Supplement and the DOD FLIP IFR En Route Supplement.

DISPLACED THRESHOLD- A threshold that is located at a point on the runway other than the designated beginning of the runway.

DISTANCE MEASURING EQUIPMENT- Equipment (airborne and ground) used to measure, in nautical miles, the slant range distance of an aircraft from the DME navigational aid.

DISTRESS- A condition of being threatened by serious and/or imminent danger and of requiring immediate assistance.

DME FIX- A geographical position determined by reference to a navigational aid which provides distance and azimuth information. It is defined by a specific distance in nautical miles and a radial, azimuth, or course (i.e., localizer) in degrees magnetic from that aid.

DOMESTIC AIRSPACE- Airspace which overlies the continental land mass of the United States plus Hawaii and U.S. possessions. Domestic airspace extends to 12 miles offshore.

DOWNBURST- A strong downdraft which induces an outburst of damaging winds on or near the ground. Damaging winds, either straight or curved, are highly divergent. The sizes of downbursts vary from 1/2 mile or less to more than 10 miles. An intense downburst often causes widespread damage. Damaging winds, lasting 5 to 30 minutes, could reach speeds as high as 120 knots.

DVFR FLIGHT PLAN- A flight plan filed for a VFR aircraft which intends to operate in airspace within which the ready identification, location, and control of aircraft are required in the interest of national security.

E

EMERGENCY-A distress or an urgency condition.

EMERGENCY LOCATOR TRANSMITTER-A radio transmitter attached to the aircraft structure which operates from its own power source on 121.5 MHz and 243.0 MHz. It aids in locating downed aircraft by radiating a downward sweeping audio tone, 2-4 times per second. It is designed to function without human action after an accident.

EN ROUTE AIR TRAFFIC CONTROL SERVICES-Air traffic control service provided aircraft on IFR flight plans, generally by centers, when these aircraft are operating between departure and destination terminal areas. When equipment, capabilities, and controller workload permit, certain advisory/assistance services may be provided to VFR aircraft.

EN ROUTE FLIGHT ADVISORY SERVICE- A service specifically designed to provide, upon pilot request, timely weather information pertinent to his/her type of flight, intended route of flight, and altitude. The FSSs providing this service are listed in the Digital Chart Supplement.

EN ROUTE MINIMUM SAFE ALTITUDE WARNING- A function of the EAS that aids the controller by providing an alert when a tracked aircraft is below or predicted by the computer to go below a predetermined minimum IFR altitude (MIA).

ESTABLISHED-To be stable or fixed on a route, route segment, altitude, heading, etc.

ESTIMATED ELAPSED TIME [ICAO]-The estimated time required to proceed from one significant point to another.

ESTIMATED TIME OF ARRIVAL- The time the flight is estimated to arrive at the gate (scheduled operators) or the actual runway on times for nonscheduled operators.

ESTIMATED TIME EN ROUTE- The estimated flying time from departure point to destination (lift-off to touchdown).

EXPECT DEPARTURE CLEARANCE TIME (EDCT)- The runway release time assigned to an aircraft in a traffic management program and shown on the flight progress strip as an EDCT.

EXPEDITE-Used by ATC when prompt compliance is required to avoid the development of an imminent situation. Expedite climb/descent normally indicates to a pilot that the approximate best rate of climb/descent should be used without requiring an exceptional change in aircraft handling characteristics.

F

FAST FILE- A system whereby a pilot files a flight plan via telephone that is tape recorded and then transcribed for transmission to the appropriate air traffic facility. Locations having a fast file capability are contained in the Digital Chart Supplement.

FINAL-Commonly used to mean that an aircraft is on the final approach course or is aligned with a landing area.

FINAL APPROACH COURSE- A bearing /radial/track of an instrument approach leading to a runway or an extended runway centerline all without regard to distance.

FIX- A geographical position determined by visual reference to the surface, by reference to one or more radio NAVAIDs, by celestial plotting, or by another navigational device.

FLIGHT INFORMATION REGION- An airspace of defined dimensions within which Flight Information

FLIGHT LEVEL-A level of constant atmospheric pressure related to a reference datum of 29.92 inches of mercury. Each is stated in three digits that represent hundreds of feet. For example, flight level (FL) 250 represents a barometric altimeter indication of 25,000 feet; FL 255, an indication of 25,500 feet.

FLIGHT MANAGEMENT SYSTEMS- A computer system that uses a large data base to allow routes to be preprogrammed and fed into the system by means of a data loader. The system is constantly updated with respect to position accuracy by reference to conventional navigation aids. The sophisticated program and its associated data base insures that the most appropriate aids are automatically selected during the information update cycle.

FLIGHT PLAN- Specified information relating to the intended flight of an aircraft that is filed orally or in writing with an FSS or an ATC facility.

FLIGHT SERVICE STATION (FSS) - An air traffic facility which provides pilot briefings, flight plan processing, en route radio communications, search and rescue services, and assistance to lost aircraft and aircraft in emergency situations. FSSs also relay ATC clearances, process Notices to Airmen, broadcast aviation weather and aeronautical information, and notify Customs and Border Protection of transborder flights. In addition, at selected locations, FSSs provide En Route Flight Advisory Service (Flight Watch) and Airport Advisory Service (AAS). In Alaska, designated FSSs also provide TWEB recordings and take weather observations.

FLIGHT STANDARDS DISTRICT OFFICE- An FAA field office serving an assigned geographical area and staffed with Flight Standards personnel who serve the aviation industry and the general public on matters relating to the certification and operation of air carrier and general aviation aircraft. Activities include general surveillance of operational safety, certification of airmen and aircraft, accident prevention, investigation, enforcement, etc.

FLIGHT WATCH- A shortened term for use in air-ground contacts to identify the flight service station providing En Route Flight Advisory Service; e.g., "Oakland Flight Watch."

FLY HEADING (DEGREES)- Informs the pilot of the heading he/she should fly. The pilot may have to turn to, or continue on, a specific compass direction in order to comply with the instructions. The pilot is expected to turn in the shorter direction to the heading unless otherwise instructed by ATC.

FLY-BY WAYPOINT- A fly-by waypoint requires the use of turn anticipation to avoid overshoot of the next flight segment.

FLY-OVER WAYPOINT- A fly-over waypoint precludes any turn until the waypoint is overflown and is followed by an intercept maneuver of the next flight segment.

FORMATION FLIGHT-More than one aircraft which, by prior arrangement between the pilots, operate as a single aircraft with regard to navigation and position reporting. Separation between aircraft within the formation is the responsibility of the flight leader and the pilots of the other aircraft in the flight. This includes transition periods when aircraft within the formation are maneuvering to attain separation from each other to effect individual control and during join-up and breakaway.

FUEL REMAINING- A phrase used by either pilots or controllers when relating to the fuel remaining on board until actual fuel exhaustion. When transmitting such information in response to either a controller question or pilot initiated cautionary advisory to air traffic control, pilots will state the APPROXIMATE NUMBER OF MINUTES the flight can continue with the fuel remaining. All reserve fuel SHOULD BE INCLUDED in the time stated, as should an allowance for established fuel gauge system error.

G

GATE HOLD PROCEDURES-Procedures at selected airports to hold aircraft at the gate or other ground location whenever departure delays exceed or are anticipated to exceed 15 minutes. The sequence for departure will be maintained in accordance with initial call-up unless modified by flow control restrictions. Pilots should monitor the ground control/clearance delivery frequency for engine start/taxi advisories or new proposed start/taxi time if the delay changes.

GENERAL AVIATION- That portion of civil aviation which encompasses all facets of aviation except air carriers holding a certificate of public convenience and necessity from the Civil Aeronautics Board and large aircraft commercial operators.

GLIDESLOPE- Provides vertical guidance for aircraft during approach and landing. The glideslope/glidepath is based on the following:

a. Electronic components emitting signals which provide vertical guidance by reference to airborne instruments during instrument approaches such as ILS/MLS, or

b. Visual ground aids, such as VASI, which provide vertical guidance for a VFR approach or for the visual portion of an instrument approach and landing.

c. PAR. Used by ATC to inform an aircraft making a PAR approach of its vertical position (elevation) relative to the descent profile.

GLOBAL POSITIONING SYSTEM (GPS)-A space-base radio positioning, navigation, and time-transfer system. The system provides highly accurate position and velocity information, and precise time, on a continuous global basis, to an unlimited number of properly equipped users. The system is unaffected by weather, and provides a worldwide common grid reference system. The GPS concept is predicated upon accurate and continuous knowledge of the spatial position of each satellite in the system with respect to time and distance from a transmitting satellite to the user. The GPS receiver automatically selects appropriate signals from the satellites in view and translates these into three-dimensional position, velocity, and time. System accuracy for civil users is normally 100 meters horizontally.

GO AHEAD-Proceed with your message. Not to be used for any other purpose.

GO AROUND-Instructions for a pilot to abandon his/her approach to landing. Additional instructions may follow. Unless otherwise advised by ATC, a VFR aircraft or an aircraft conducting visual approach should overfly the runway while climbing to traffic pattern altitude and enter the traffic pattern via the crosswind leg. A pilot on an IFR flight plan making an instrument approach should execute the published missed approach procedure or proceed as instructed by ATC; e.g., "Go around" (additional instructions if required).

GROUND SPEED- The speed of an aircraft relative to the surface of the earth.

H

HAVE NUMBERS- Used by pilots to inform ATC that they have received runway, wind, and altimeter information only.

HAZARDOUS INFLIGHT WEATHER ADVISORY SERVICE-Continuous recorded hazardous inflight weather forecasts broadcasted to airborne pilots over selected VOR outlets defined as an HIWAS BROADCAST AREA.

HAZARDOUS WEATHER INFORMATION-Summary of significant meteorological information (SIGMET/WS), convective significant meteorological information (convective SIGMET/ WST), urgent pilot weather reports (urgent PIREP/UUA), center weather advisories (CWA), airmen's meteorological information (AIRMET/WA) and any other weather such as isolated thunderstorms that are rapidly developing and increasing in intensity, or low ceilings and visibilities that are becoming widespread which is considered significant and are not included in a current hazardous weather advisory.

HELIPAD- A small, designated area, usually with a prepared surface, on a heliport, airport, landing/takeoff area, apron/ramp, or movement area used for takeoff, landing, or parking of helicopters.

HELIPORT- An area of land, water, or structure used or intended to be used for the landing and takeoff of helicopters and includes its buildings and facilities if any.

HERTZ- The standard radio equivalent of frequency in cycles per second of an electromagnetic wave. Kilohertz (kHz) is a frequency of one thousand cycles per second. Megahertz (MHz) is a frequency of one million cycles per second.

HIGH SPEED TAXIWAY- A long radius taxiway designed and provided with lighting or marking to define the path of aircraft, traveling at high speed (up to 60 knots), from the runway center to a point on the center of a taxiway. Also referred to as long radius exit or turn-off taxiway. The high speed taxiway is designed to expedite aircraft turning off the runway after landing, thus reducing runway occupancy time.

HIWAS BROADCAST AREA- A geographical area of responsibility including one or more HIWAS outlet areas assigned to an AFSS/FSS for hazardous weather advisory broadcasting.

HOLD FOR RELEASE- Used by ATC to delay an aircraft for traffic management reasons; i.e., weather, traffic volume, etc. Hold for release instructions (including departure delay information) are used to inform a pilot or a controller (either directly or through an authorized relay) that an IFR departure clearance is not valid until a release time or additional instructions have been received.

HOLD IN LIEU OF PROCEDURE TURN- A hold in lieu of procedure turn shall be established over a final or intermediate fix when an approach can be made from a properly aligned holding pattern. The hold in lieu of procedure turn permits the pilot to align with the final or intermediate segment of the approach and/or descend in the holding pattern to an altitude that will permit a normal descent to the final approach fix altitude. The hold in lieu of procedure turn is a required maneuver (the same as a procedure turn) unless the aircraft is being radar vectored to the final approach course, when "NoPT" is shown on the approach chart, or when the pilot requests or the controller advises the pilot to make a "straight-in" approach.

HOLD-SHORT POSITION MARKING-The painted runway marking located at the hold-short point on all LAHSO runways.

HOLD-SHORT POSITION SIGNS- Red and white holding position signs located alongside the hold-short point.

HOMING-Flight toward a NAVAID, without correcting for wind, by adjusting the aircraft heading to maintain a relative bearing of zero degrees.

HOW DO YOU HEAR ME?- A question relating to the quality of the transmission or to determine how well the transmission is being received.

I

I SAY AGAIN- The message will be repeated.

ICING- The accumulation of airframe ice.

IDENT-A request for a pilot to activate the aircraft transponder identification feature. This will help the controller to confirm an aircraft identity or to identify an aircraft.

IFR AIRCRAFT- An aircraft conducting flight in accordance with instrument flight rules.

IFR MILITARY TRAINING ROUTES (IR)- Routes used by the Department of Defense and associated Reserve and Air Guard units for the purpose of conducting low-altitude navigation and tactical training in both IFR and VFR weather conditions below 10,000 feet MSL at airspeeds in excess of 250 knots IAS.

IMMEDIATELY- Used by ATC or pilots when such action compliance is required to avoid an imminent situation.

INERTIAL NAVIGATION SYSTEM- An RNAV system which is a form of self-contained navigation.

INSTRUMENT APPROACH PROCEDURE-A series of predetermined maneuvers for the orderly transfer of an aircraft under instrument flight conditions from the beginning of the initial approach to a landing or to a point from which a landing may be made visually. It is prescribed and approved for a specific airport by competent authority.

INSTRUMENT FLIGHT RULES- Rules governing the procedures for conducting instrument flight. Also a term used by pilots and controllers to indicate type of flight plan.

INSTRUMENT METEOROLOGICAL CONDITIONS- Meteorological conditions expressed in terms of visibility, distance from cloud, and ceiling less than the minima specified for visual meteorological conditions.

INSTRUMENT RUNWAY- A runway equipped with electronic and visual navigation aids for which a precision or nonprecision approach procedure having straight-in landing minimums has been approved.

INTERNATIONAL CIVIL AVIATION ORGANIZATION [ICAO]- A specialized agency of the United Nations whose objective is to develop the principles and techniques of international air navigation and to foster planning and development of international civil air transport.

INTERSECTION-

a. A point defined by any combination of courses, radials, or bearings of two or more navigational aids.

b. Used to describe the point where two runways, a runway and a taxiway, or two taxiways cross or meet.

INTERSECTION DEPARTURE- A departure from any runway intersection except the end of the runway.

J

JET STREAM- A migrating stream of high-speed winds present at high altitudes.

JET BLAST-Jet engine exhaust (thrust stream turbulence).

JET ROUTE- A route designed to serve aircraft operations from 18,000 feet MSL up to and including flight level 450. The routes are referred to as "J" routes with numbering to identify the designated route; e.g., J105.

K

KNOWN TRAFFIC- With respect to ATC clearances, means aircraft whose altitude, position, and intentions are known to ATC.

L

LAHSO- An acronym for "Land and Hold Short Operation." These operations include landing and holding short of an intersecting runway, a taxiway, a predetermined point, or an approach/departure flightpath.

LAND AND HOLD SHORT OPERATIONS- Operations which include simultaneous takeoffs and landings and/or simultaneous landings when a landing aircraft is able and is instructed by the controller to hold-short of the intersecting runway/ taxiway or designated hold-short point. Pilots are expected to promptly inform the controller if the hold short clearance cannot be accepted.

LANDING DIRECTION INDICATOR- A device which visually indicates the direction in which landings and takeoffs should be made.

LANDING ROLL- The distance from the point of touchdown to the point where the aircraft can be brought to a stop or exit the runway.

LANDING SEQUENCE- The order in which aircraft are positioned for landing.

LAST ASSIGNED ALTITUDE- The last altitude/flight level assigned by ATC and acknowledged by the pilot.

LATERAL NAVIGATION (LNAV)– A function of area navigation (RNAV) equipment which calculates, displays, and provides lateral guidance to a profile or path.

LATERAL SEPARATION- The lateral spacing of aircraft at the same altitude by requiring operation on different routes or in different geographical locations.

LIGHTED AIRPORT- An airport where runway and obstruction lighting is available.

LIGHT GUN- A handheld directional light signaling device which emits a brilliant narrow beam of white, green, or red light as selected by the tower controller. The color and type of light transmitted can be used to approve or disapprove anticipated pilot actions where radio communication is not available. The light gun is used for controlling traffic operating in the vicinity of the airport and on the airport movement area.

LINE UP AND WAIT (LUAW)- Used by ATC to inform a pilot to taxi onto the departure runway to line up and wait. It is not authorization for takeoff. It is used when takeoff clearance cannot immediately be issued because of traffic or other reasons.

LOCAL AIRPORT ADVISORY (LAA)- A service provided by facilities, which are located on the landing airport, have a discrete ground-to-air communication frequency or the tower frequency when the tower is closed, automated weather reporting with voice broadcasting, and a continuous ASOS/AWSS/AWOS data display, other continuous direct reading instruments, or manual observations available to the specialist.

LOCALIZER- The component of an ILS which provides course guidance to the runway.

LONGITUDINAL SEPARATION- The longitudinal spacing of aircraft at the same altitude by a minimum distance expressed in units of time or miles.

LOST COMMUNICATIONS- Loss of the ability to communicate by radio. Aircraft are sometimes referred to as NORDO (No Radio). Standard pilot procedures are specified in 14 CFR Part 91. Radar controllers issue procedures for pilots to follow in the event of lost communications during a radar approach when weather reports indicate that an aircraft will likely encounter IFR weather conditions during the approach.

LOW ALTITUDE AIRWAY STRUCTURE- The network of airways serving aircraft operations up to but not including 18,000 feet MSL.

LOW ALTITUDE ALERT SYSTEM- An automated function of the TPX-42 that alerts the controller when a Mode C transponder equipped aircraft on an IFR flight plan is below a predetermined minimum safe altitude. If requested by the pilot, Low Altitude Alert System monitoring is also available to VFR Mode C transponder equipped aircraft.

LOW APPROACH- An approach over an airport or runway following an instrument approach or a VFR approach including the go-around maneuver where the pilot intentionally does not make contact with the runway.

LPV- A type of approach with vertical guidance (APV) based on WAAS, published on RNAV (GPS) approach charts. This procedure takes advantage of the precise lateral guidance available from WAAS. The minima is published as a decision altitude (DA).

M

MAINTAIN-

a. Concerning altitude/flight level, the term means to remain at the altitude/flight level specified. The phrase "climb and" or "descend and" normally precedes "maintain" and the altitude assignment; e.g., "descend and maintain 5,000."

b. Concerning other ATC instructions, the term is used in its literal sense; e.g., maintain VFR.

MAKE SHORT APPROACH-Used by ATC to inform a pilot to alter his/her traffic pattern so as to make a short final approach.

MANDATORY ALTITUDE- An altitude depicted on an instrument Approach Procedure Chart requiring the aircraft to maintain altitude at the depicted value.

MARKER BEACON-An electronic navigation facility transmitting a 75 MHz vertical fan or boneshaped radiation pattern. Marker beacons are identified by their modulation frequency and keying code, and when received by compatible airborne equipment, indicate to the pilot, both aurally and visually, that he/she is passing over the facility.

MAYDAY- The international radiotelephony distress signal. When repeated three times, it indicates imminent and grave danger and that immediate assistance is requested.

METEOROLOGICAL IMPACT STATEMENT- An unscheduled planning forecast describing conditions expected to begin within 4 to 12 hours which may impact the flow of air traffic in a specific center's (ARTCC) area.

MICROBURST- A small downburst with outbursts of damaging winds extending 2.5 miles or less. In spite of its small horizontal scale, an intense microburst could induce wind speeds as high as 150 knots

MILES-IN-TRAIL- A specified distance between aircraft, normally, in the same stratum associated with the same destination or route of flight.

MILITARY TRAINING ROUTES-Airspace of defined vertical and lateral dimensions established for the conduct of military flight training at airspeeds in excess of 250 knots IAS.

MINIMUM VECTORING ALTITUDE (MVA) - The lowest MSL altitude at which an IFR aircraft will be vectored by a radar controller, except as otherwise authorized for radar approaches, departures, and missed approaches. The altitude

meets IFR obstacle clearance criteria. It may be lower than the published MEA along an airway or J-route segment. It may be utilized for radar vectoring only upon the controller's determination that an adequate radar return is being received from the aircraft being controlled. Charts depicting minimum vectoring altitudes are normally available only to the controllers and not to pilots.

MINUTES-IN-TRAIL- A specified interval between aircraft expressed in time. This method would more likely be utilized regardless of altitude.

MONITOR- (When used with communication transfer) listen on a specific frequency and stand by for instructions. Under normal circumstances do not establish communications.

MOVING TARGET INDICATOR- An electronic device which will permit radar scope presentation only from targets which are in motion. A partial remedy for ground clutter.

MULTICOM- A mobile service not open to public correspondence used to provide communications essential to conduct the activities being performed by or directed from private aircraft.

N

NATIONAL AIRSPACE SYSTEM- The common network of U.S. airspace; air navigation facilities, equipment and services, airports or landing areas; aeronautical charts, information and services; rules, regulations and procedures, technical information, and manpower and material. Included are system components shared jointly with the military.

NAVAID CLASSES- VOR, VORTAC, and TACAN aids are classed according to their operational use.

The three classes of NAVAIDs are:

a. T- Terminal.

b. L- Low altitude.

c. H- High altitude.

NEGATIVE-"No," or "permission not granted," or "that is not correct."

NEGATIVE CONTACT- Used by pilots to inform ATC that:

a. Previously issued traffic is not in sight. It may be followed by the pilot's request for the controller to provide assistance in avoiding the traffic.

b. They were unable to contact ATC on a particular frequency.

NIGHT- The time between the end of evening civil twilight and the beginning of morning civil twilight, as published in the American Air Almanac, converted to local time.

NONDIRECTIONAL BEACON- An L/MF or UHF radio beacon transmitting nondirectional signals whereby the pilot of an aircraft equipped with direction finding equipment can determine his/her bearing to or from the radio beacon and "home" on or track to or from the station. When the radio beacon is installed in conjunction with the Instrument Landing System marker, it is normally called a Compass Locator.

NONMOVEMENT AREAS- Taxiways and apron (ramp) areas not under the control of air traffic.

NONPRECISION APPROACH PROCEDURE- A standard instrument approach procedure in which no electronic glideslope is provided; e.g., VOR, TACAN, NDB, LOC, ASR, LDA, or SDF approaches.

NORDO (No Radio)- Aircraft that cannot or do not communicate by radio when radio communication is required are referred to as "NORDO."

NOTICE TO AIRMEN- A notice containing information (not known sufficiently in advance to publicize by other means) concerning the establishment, condition, or change in any component (facility, service, or procedure of, or hazard in the National Airspace System) the timely knowledge of which is essential to personnel concerned with flight operations.

a. NOTAM(D)- A NOTAM given (in addition to local dissemination) distant dissemination beyond the area of responsibility of the Flight Service Station. These NOTAMs will be stored and available until canceled.

b. FDC NOTAM- A NOTAM regulatory in nature, transmitted by USNOF and given system wide dissemination.

NOTICES TO AIRMEN PUBLICATION- A publication issued every 28 days, designed primarily for the pilot, which contains current NOTAM information considered essential to the safety of flight as well as supplemental data to other aeronautical publications. The contraction NTAP is used in NOTAM text.

NUMEROUS TARGETS VICINITY (LOCATION)- A traffic advisory issued by ATC to advise pilots that targets on the radar scope are too numerous to issue individually.

O

OBSTACLE- An existing object, object of natural growth, or terrain at a fixed geographical location or which may be expected at a fixed location within a prescribed area with reference to which vertical clearance is or must be provided during flight operation.

OBSTRUCTION- Any object/obstacle exceeding the obstruction standards specified by 14 CFR Part 77, Subpart C.

OBSTRUCTION LIGHT- A light or one of a group of lights, usually red or white, frequently mounted on a surface structure or natural terrain to warn pilots of the presence of an obstruction.

ONE-MINUTE WEATHER- The most recent one minute updated weather broadcast received by a pilot from an uncontrolled airport ASOS/AWSS/AWOS.

OPTION APPROACH- An approach requested and conducted by a pilot which will result in either a touch-and-go, missed approach, low approach, stop-and-go, or full stop landing.

OUT-The conversation is ended and no response is expected.

OUTER AREA (associated with Class C airspace)- Nonregulatory airspace surrounding designated Class C airspace airports wherein ATC provides radar vectoring and sequencing on a full-time basis for all IFR and participating VFR aircraft. The service provided in the outer area is called Class C service which includes: IFR/IFR-standard IFR separation; IFR/VFR-traffic advisories and conflict resolution; and VFR/VFR-traffic advisories and, as appropriate, safety alerts. The normal radius will be 20 nautical miles with some variations based on site-specific requirements. The outer area extends outward from the primary Class C airspace airport and extends from the lower limits of radar/radio coverage up to the ceiling of the approach control's delegated airspace excluding the Class C charted area and other airspace as appropriate.

OVER-My transmission is ended; I expect a response.

P

PAN-PAN- The international radio-telephony urgency signal. When repeated three times, indicates uncertainty or alert followed by the nature of the urgency.

PARALLEL RUNWAYS- Two or more runways at the same airport whose centerlines are parallel. In addition to runway number, parallel runways are designated as L (left) and R (right) or, if three parallel runways exist, L (left), C (center), and R (right).

PILOT'S DISCRETION- When used in conjunction with altitude assignments, means that ATC has offered the pilot the option of starting climb or descent whenever he/she wishes and conducting the climb or descent at any rate he/she wishes. He/she may temporarily level off at any intermediate altitude. However, once he/she has vacated an altitude, he/she may not return to that altitude.

POSITION REPORT- A report over a known location as transmitted by an aircraft to ATC.

POSITIVE CONTROL- The separation of all air traffic within designated airspace by air traffic control.

PRECIPITATION- Any or all forms of water particles (rain, sleet, hail, or snow) that fall from the atmosphere and reach the surface.

PRECIPITATION RADAR WEATHER DESCRIPTIONS - Existing radar systems cannot detect turbulence. However, there is a direct correlation between the degree of turbulence and other weather features associated with thunderstorms and the weather radar precipitation intensity. Controllers will issue (where capable) precipitation intensity as observed by radar when using weather and radar processor (WARP) or NAS ground based digital radars with weather capabilities. When precipitation intensity information is not available, the intensity will be described as UNKNOWN. When intensity levels can be determined, they shall be described as:

a. LIGHT (< 30 dBZ)

b. MODERATE (30 to 40 dBZ)

c. HEAVY (> 40 to 50 dBZ)

d. EXTREME (> 50 dBZ)

PRECISION APPROACH RADAR- Radar equipment in some ATC facilities operated by the FAA and/or the military services at joint-use civil/military locations and separate military installations to detect and display azimuth, elevation, and range of aircraft on the final

approach course to a runway. This equipment may be used to monitor certain nonradar approaches, but is primarily used to conduct a precision instrument approach (PAR) wherein the controller issues guidance instructions to the pilot based on the aircraft's position in relation to the final approach course (azimuth), the glidepath (elevation), and the distance (range) from the touchdown point on the runway as displayed on the radar scope.

PRIMARY RADAR TARGET- An analog or digital target, exclusive of a secondary radar target, presented on a radar display.

PROGRESSIVE TAXI- Precise taxi instructions given to a pilot unfamiliar with the airport or issued in stages as the aircraft proceeds along the taxi route.

PROPOSED DEPARTURE TIME- The time that the aircraft expects to become airborne.

PROTECTED AIRSPACE- The airspace on either side of an oceanic route/track that is equal to one-half the lateral separation minimum except where reduction of protected airspace has been authorized.

Q

QNE- The barometric pressure used for the standard altimeter setting (29.92 inches Hg.).

QNH- The barometric pressure as reported by a particular station.

R

RADAR ADVISORY- The provision of advice and information based on radar observations.

RADAR APPROACH-An instrument approach procedure which utilizes Precision Approach Radar (PAR) or Airport Surveillance Radar (ASR).

RADAR APPROACH CONTROL FACILITY- A terminal ATC facility that uses radar and nonradar capabilities to provide approach control services to aircraft arriving, departing, or transiting airspace controlled by the facility.

RADAR CONTACT-

a. Used by ATC to inform an aircraft that it is identified on the radar display and radar flight following will be provided until radar identification is terminated. Radar service may also be provided within the limits of necessity and capability. When a pilot is informed of "radar contact," he/she automatically discontinues reporting over compulsory reporting points.

b. The term used to inform the controller that the aircraft is identified and approval is granted for the aircraft to enter the receiving controllers airspace.

RADAR CONTACT LOST- Used by ATC to inform a pilot that radar data used to determine the aircraft's position is no longer being received, or is no longer reliable and radar service is no longer being provided. The loss may be attributed to several factors including the aircraft merging with weather or ground clutter, the aircraft operating below radar line of sight coverage, the aircraft entering an area of poor radar return, failure of the aircraft transponder, or failure of the ground radar equipment.

RADAR FLIGHT FOLLOWING- The observation of the progress of radar identified aircraft, whose primary navigation is being provided by the pilot, wherein the controller retains and correlates the aircraft identity with the appropriate target or target symbol displayed on the radar scope.

RADAR IDENTIFIED AIRCRAFT- An aircraft, the position of which has been correlated with an observed target or symbol on the radar display.

RADAR SERVICE TERMINATED-Used by ATC to inform a pilot that he/she will no longer be provided any of the services that could be received while in radar contact. Radar service is automatically terminated, and the pilot is not advised in the following cases:

a. An aircraft cancels its IFR flight plan, except within Class B airspace, Class C airspace, a TRSA, or where Basic Radar service is provided.

b. An aircraft conducting an instrument, visual, or contact approach has landed or has been instructed to change to advisory frequency.

c. An arriving VFR aircraft, receiving radar service to a tower-controlled airport within Class B airspace, Class C airspace, a TRSA, or where sequencing service is provided, has landed; or to all other airports, is instructed to change to tower or advisory frequency.

d. An aircraft completes a radar approach.

RADIAL- A magnetic bearing extending from a VOR/VORTAC/TACAN navigation facility.

RADIO ALTIMETER- Aircraft equipment which makes use of the reflection of radio waves from the ground to determine the height of the aircraft above the surface.

RADIO MAGNETIC INDICATOR-An aircraft navigational instrument coupled with a gyro compass or similar compass that indicates the direction of a selected NAVAID and indicates bearing with respect to the heading of the aircraft.

RECEIVER AUTONOMOUS INTEGRITY MONITORING (RAIM)- A technique whereby a civil GNSS receiver/processor determines the integrity of the GNSS navigation signals without reference to sensors or non-DoD integrity systems other than the receiver itself. This determination is achieved by a consistency check among redundant pseudorange measurements.

RELEASE TIME- A departure time restriction issued to a pilot by ATC (either directly or through an authorized relay) when necessary to separate a departing aircraft from other traffic.

REMOTE AIRPORT ADVISORY (RAA)- A remote service which may be provided by facilities, which are not located on the landing airport, but have a discrete ground-to-air communication frequency or tower frequency when the tower is closed, automated weather reporting with voice available to the pilot at the landing airport, and a continuous ASOS/AWSS/AWOS data display, other direct reading instruments, or manual observation is available to the AFSS specialist.

REMOTE AIRPORT INFORMATION SERVICE (RAIS)- A temporary service provided by facilities, which are not located on the landing airport, but have communication capability and automated weather reporting available to the pilot at the landing airport.

REMOTE COMMUNICATIONS OUTLET-An unmanned communications facility remotely controlled by air traffic personnel. RCOs serve FSSs. RTRs serve terminal ATC facilities. An RCO or RTR may be UHF or VHF and will extend the communication range of the air traffic facility. There are several classes of RCOs and RTRs. The class is determined by the number of transmitters or receivers. Classes A through G are used primarily for air/ground purposes. RCO and RTR class O facilities are nonprotected outlets subject to undetected and prolonged outages. RCO (O's) and RTR (O's) were established for the express purpose of providing ground-to-ground communications between air traffic control specialists and pilots located at a satellite airport for delivering en route clearances, issuing departure authorizations, and acknowledging instrument flight rules cancellations or departure/landing times. As a secondary function, they may be used for advisory purposes whenever the aircraft is below the coverage of the primary air/ground frequency.

REPORTING POINT- A geographical location in relation to which the position of an aircraft is reported.

RESUME OWN NAVIGATION- Used by ATC to advise a pilot to resume his/her own navigational responsibility. It is issued after completion of a radar vector or when radar contact is lost while the aircraft is being radar vectored.

ROGER- I have received all of your last transmission. It should not be used to answer a question requiring a yes or a no answer.

RUNWAY- A defined rectangular area on a land airport prepared for the landing and takeoff run of aircraft along its length. Runways are normally numbered in relation to their magnetic direction rounded off to the nearest 10 degrees; e.g., Runway 1, Runway 25.

RUNWAY GRADIENT- The average slope, measured in percent, between two ends or points on a runway. Runway gradient is depicted on Government aerodrome sketches when total runway gradient exceeds 0.3%.

RUNWAY HEADING- The magnetic direction that corresponds with the runway centerline extended, not the painted runway number. When cleared to "fly or maintain runway heading," pilots are expected to fly or maintain the heading that corresponds with the extended centerline of the departure runway. Drift correction shall not be applied; e.g., Runway 4, actual magnetic heading of the runway centerline 044, fly 044.

RUNWAY IN USE/ACTIVE RUNWAY/DUTY RUNWAY- Any runway or runways currently being used for takeoff or landing. When multiple runways are used, they are all considered active runways. In the metering sense, a selectable adapted item which specifies the landing runway configuration or direction of traffic flow. The adapted optimum flight plan from each transition fix to the vertex is determined by the runway configuration for arrival metering processing purposes.

RUNWAY OVERRUN- In military aviation exclusively, a stabilized or paved area beyond the end of a runway, of the same width as the runway plus shoulders, centered on the extended runway centerline.

S

SAY AGAIN- Used to request a repeat of the last transmission. Usually specifies transmission or portion thereof not understood or received; e.g., "Say again all after ABRAM VOR."

SAY ALTITUDE-Used by ATC to ascertain an aircraft's specific altitude/flight level. When the aircraft is climbing or descending, the pilot should state the indicated altitude rounded to the nearest 100 feet.

SAY HEADING- Used by ATC to request an aircraft heading. The pilot should state the actual heading of the aircraft.

SEARCH AND RESCUE- A service which seeks missing aircraft and assists those found to be in need of assistance. It is a cooperative effort using the facilities and services of available Federal, state and local agencies. The U.S. Coast Guard is responsible for coordination of search and rescue for the Maritime Region, and the U.S. Air Force is responsible for search and rescue for the Inland Region. Information pertinent to search and rescue should be passed through any air traffic facility or be transmitted directly to the Rescue Coordination Center by telephone.

SECONDARY RADAR TARGET- A target derived from a transponder return presented on a radar display.

SEE AND AVOID-When weather conditions permit, pilots operating IFR or VFR are required to observe and maneuver to avoid other aircraft. Right-of-way rules are contained in 14 CFR Part 91.

SEGMENTED CIRCLE- A system of visual indicators designed to provide traffic pattern information at airports without operating control towers.

SEPARATION MINIMA- The minimum longitudinal, lateral, or vertical distances by which aircraft are spaced through the application of air traffic control procedures.

SIGMET-A weather advisory issued concerning weather significant to the safety of all aircraft. SIGMET advisories cover severe and extreme turbulence, severe icing, and widespread dust or sandstorms that reduce visibility to less than 3 miles.

SPEAK SLOWER- Used in verbal communications as a request to reduce speech rate.

SPECIAL USE AIRSPACE- Airspace of defined dimensions identified by an area on the surface of the earth wherein activities must be confined because of their nature and/or wherein limitations may be imposed upon aircraft operations that are not a part of those activities. Types of special use airspace are:

a. Alert Area- Airspace which may contain a high volume of pilot training activities or an unusual type of aerial activity, neither of which is hazardous to aircraft. Alert Areas are depicted on aeronautical charts for the information of nonparticipating pilots. All activities within an Alert Area are conducted in accordance with Federal Aviation Regulations, and pilots of participating aircraft as well as pilots transiting the area are equally responsible for collision avoidance.

b. Controlled Firing Area- Airspace wherein activities are conducted under conditions so controlled as to eliminate hazards to nonparticipating aircraft and to ensure the safety of persons and property on the ground.

c. Military Operations Area (MOA)- A MOA is airspace established outside of Class A airspace area to separate or segregate certain nonhazardous military activities from IFR traffic and to identify for VFR traffic where these activities are conducted.

d. Prohibited Area- Airspace designated under 14 CFR Part 73 within which no person may operate an aircraft without the permission of the using agency.

e. Restricted Area- Airspace designated under 14 CFR Part 73, within which the flight of aircraft, while not wholly prohibited, is subject to restriction. Most restricted areas are designated joint use and IFR/VFR operations in the area may be authorized by the controlling ATC facility when it is not being utilized by the using agency. Restricted areas are depicted on en route charts. Where joint use is authorized, the name of the ATC controlling facility is also shown.

f. Warning Area- A warning area is airspace of defined dimensions extending from 3 nautical miles outward from the coast of the United States, that contains activity that may be hazardous to nonparticipating aircraft. The purpose of such warning area is to warn nonparticipating pilots of the potential danger. A warning area may be located over domestic or international waters or both.

SPECIAL VFR CONDITIONS- Meteorological conditions that are less than those required for basic VFR flight in Class B, C, D, or E surface areas and in which some aircraft are permitted flight under visual flight rules.

SPECIAL VFR OPERATIONS- Aircraft operating in accordance with clearances within Class B, C, D, and E surface areas in weather conditions less than the basic VFR weather minima. Such operations must be requested by the pilot and approved by ATC.

SPEED BRAKES- Moveable aerodynamic devices on aircraft that reduce airspeed during descent and landing.

SQUAWK (Mode, Code, Function)-Activate specific modes/codes/functions on the aircraft transponder; e.g., "Squawk three/alpha, two one zero five, low."

STAND BY-Means the controller or pilot must pause for a few seconds, usually to attend to other duties of a higher priority. Also means to wait as in "stand by for clearance." The caller should reestablish contact if a delay is lengthy. "Stand by" is not an approval or denial.

STANDARD RATE TURN- A turn of three degrees per second.

STEP TURN- A maneuver used to put a float plane in a planing configuration prior to entering an active sea lane for takeoff. The STEP TURN maneuver should only be used upon pilot request.

STOP ALTITUDE SQUAWK-Used by ATC to inform an aircraft to turn-off the automatic altitude reporting feature of its transponder. It is issued when the verbally reported altitude varies 300 feet or more from the automatic altitude report.

STOP AND GO- A procedure wherein an aircraft will land, make a complete stop on the runway, and then commence a takeoff from that point.

STOP SQUAWK (Mode or Code)- Used by ATC to tell the pilot to turn specified functions of the aircraft transponder off.

STOPOVER FLIGHT PLAN- A flight plan format which permits in a single submission the filing of a sequence of flight plans through interim full-stop destinations to a final destination.

STOPWAY- An area beyond the takeoff runway no less wide than the runway and centered upon the extended centerline of the runway, able to support the airplane during an aborted takeoff, without causing structural damage to the airplane, and designated by the airport authorities for use in decelerating the airplane during an aborted takeoff.

STRAIGHT-IN APPROACH VFR- Entry into the traffic pattern by interception of the extended runway centerline (final approach course) without executing any other portion of the traffic pattern.

SUNSET AND SUNRISE- The mean solar times of sunset and sunrise as published in the Nautical Almanac, converted to local standard time for the locality concerned. Within Alaska, the end of evening civil twilight and the beginning of morning civil twilight, as defined for each locality.

SURFACE AREA- The airspace contained by the lateral boundary of the Class B, C, D, or E airspace designated for an airport that begins at the surface and extends upward.

T

TACTICAL AIR NAVIGATION- An ultra-high frequency electronic rho-theta air navigation aid which provides suitably equipped aircraft a continuous indication of bearing and distance to the TACAN station.

TAILWIND- Any wind more than 90 degrees to the longitudinal axis of the runway. The magnetic direction of the runway shall be used as the basis for determining the longitudinal axis.

TARMAC DELAY- The holding of an aircraft on the ground either before departure or after landing with no opportunity for its passengers to deplane.

TAXI- The movement of an airplane under its own power on the surface of an airport (14 CFR Section 135.100 [Note]). Also, it describes the surface movement of helicopters equipped with wheels.

TAXI PATTERNS- Patterns established to illustrate the desired flow of ground traffic for the different runways or airport areas available for use.

TELEPHONE INFORMATION BRIEFING SERVICE- A continuous telephone recording of meteorological and/or aeronautical information.

TERMINAL RADAR SERVICE AREA- Airspace surrounding designated airports wherein ATC provides radar vectoring, sequencing, and separation on a full-time basis for all IFR and participating VFR aircraft. The AIM contains an explanation of TRSA. TRSAs are depicted on VFR aeronautical charts. Pilot participation is urged but is not mandatory.

TERRAIN AWARENESS WARNING SYSTEM (TAWS)- An on-board, terrain proximity alerting system providing the aircrew 'Low Altitude warnings' to allow immediate pilot action.

TETRAHEDRON- A device normally located on uncontrolled airports and used as a landing direction indicator. The small end of a tetrahedron points in the direction of landing. At controlled airports, the tetrahedron, if installed, should be disregarded because tower instructions supersede the indicator.

THAT IS CORRECT- The understanding you have is right.

THRESHOLD- The beginning of that portion of the runway usable for landing.

TOUCH-AND-GO- An operation by an aircraft that lands and departs on a runway without stopping or exiting the runway.

TOWER- A terminal facility that uses air/ground communications, visual signaling, and other devices to provide ATC services to aircraft operating in the vicinity of an airport or on the movement area. Authorizes aircraft to land or takeoff at the airport controlled by the tower or to transit the Class D airspace area regardless of flight plan or weather conditions (IFR or VFR). A tower may also provide approach control services (radar or nonradar).

TRAFFIC ADVISORIES- Advisories issued to alert pilots to other known or observed air traffic which may be in such proximity to the position or intended route of flight of their aircraft to warrant their attention. Such advisories may be based on:

a. Visual observation.

b. Observation of radar identified and non-identified aircraft targets on an ATC radar display, or

c. Verbal reports from pilots or other facilities.

Note 1: The word "traffic" followed by additional information, if known, is used to provide such advisories; e.g., "Traffic, 2 o'clock, one zero miles, southbound, eight thousand."

Note 2: Traffic advisory service will be provided to the extent possible depending on higher priority duties of the controller or other limitations; e.g., radar limitations, volume of traffic, frequency congestion, or controller workload. Radar/nonradar traffic advisories do not relieve the pilot of his/her responsibility to see and avoid other aircraft. Pilots are cautioned that there are many times when the controller is not able to give traffic advisories concerning all traffic in the aircraft's proximity; in other words, when a pilot requests or is receiving traffic advisories, he/she should not assume that all traffic will be issued.

TRAFFIC ALERT (aircraft call sign), TURN (left/right) IMMEDIATELY, (climb/descend) AND MAINTAIN (altitude).

TRAFFIC ALERT AND COLLISION AVOIDANCE SYSTEM- An airborne collision avoidance system based on radar beacon signals which operates independent of ground-based equipment. TCAS-I generates traffic advisories only. TCAS-II generates traffic advisories, and resolution (collision avoidance) advisories in the vertical plane.

TRAFFIC INFORMATION SERVICE- BROADCAST (TIS-B)- The broadcast of ATC derived traffic information to ADS-B equipped (1090ES or UAT) aircraft. The source of this traffic information is derived from ground-based air traffic surveillance sensors, typically from radar targets. TIS-B service will be available throughout the NAS where there are both adequate surveillance coverage (radar) and adequate broadcast coverage from ADS-B ground stations. Loss of TIS-B will occur when an aircraft enters an area not covered by the GBT network. If this occurs in an area with adequate surveillance coverage (radar), nearby aircraft that remain within the adequate broadcast coverage (ADS-B) area will view the first aircraft. TIS-B may continue when an aircraft enters an area with inadequate surveillance coverage (radar); nearby aircraft that remain within the adequate broadcast coverage (ADS-B) area will not view the first aircraft.

TRAFFIC IN SIGHT- Used by pilots to inform a controller that previously issued traffic is in sight.

TRAFFIC NO FACTOR- Indicates that the traffic described in a previously issued traffic advisory is no factor.

TRAFFIC NO LONGER OBSERVED- Indicates that the traffic described in a previously issued traffic advisory is no longer depicted on radar, but may still be a factor.

TRAFFIC PATTERN- The traffic flow that is prescribed for aircraft landing at, taxiing on, or taking off from an airport. The components of a typical traffic pattern are upwind leg, crosswind leg, downwind leg, base leg, and final approach.

a. Upwind Leg- A flight path parallel to the landing runway in the direction of landing.

b. Crosswind Leg- A flight path at right angles to the landing runway off its upwind end.

c. Downwind Leg- A flight path parallel to the landing runway in the direction opposite to landing. The downwind leg normally extends between the crosswind leg and the base leg.

d. Base Leg- A flight path at right angles to the landing runway off its approach end. The base leg normally extends from the downwind leg to the intersection of the extended runway centerline.

e. Final Approach. A flight path in the direction of landing along the extended runway centerline. The final approach normally extends from the base leg to the runway. An aircraft making a straight-in approach VFR is also considered to be on final approach.

TRAFFIC SITUATION DISPLAY (TSD)- TSD is a computer system that receives radar track data from all 20 CONUS ARTCCs, organizes this data into a mosaic display, and presents it on a computer screen. The display allows the traffic management coordinator multiple methods of selection and highlighting of individual aircraft or groups of aircraft. The user has the option of superimposing these aircraft positions over any number of background displays. These background options include ARTCC boundaries, any stratum of en route sector boundaries, fixes, airways, military and other special use airspace, airports, and geopolitical boundaries. By using the TSD, a coordinator can monitor any number of traffic situations or the entire systemwide traffic flows.

TRANSMISSOMETER- An apparatus used to determine visibility by measuring the transmission of light through the atmosphere. It is the measurement source for determining runway visual range (RVR) and runway visibility value (RVV).

TRANSPONDER- The airborne radar beacon receiver/transmitter portion of the Air Traffic Control Radar Beacon System (ATCRBS) which automatically receives radio signals from interrogators on the ground, and selectively replies with a specific reply pulse or pulse group only to those interrogations being received on the mode to which it is set to respond.

TURBOJET AIRCRAFT- An aircraft having a jet engine in which the energy of the jet operates a turbine which in turn operates the air compressor.

TURBOPROP AIRCRAFT- An aircraft having a jet engine in which the energy of the jet operates a turbine which drives the propeller.

TURN ANTICIPATION- (maneuver anticipation).

U

ULTRAHIGH FREQUENCY- The frequency band between 300 and 3,000 MHz. The bank of radio frequencies used for military air/ground voice communications. In some instances this may go as low as 225 MHz and still be referred to as UHF.

ULTRALIGHT VEHICLE- An aeronautical vehicle operated for sport or recreational purposes which does not require FAA registration, an airworthiness certificate, nor pilot certification. They are primarily single occupant vehicles, although some two-place vehicles are authorized for training purposes. Operation of an ultralight vehicle in certain airspace requires authorization from ATC.

UNABLE-Indicates inability to comply with a specific instruction, request, or clearance.

UNDER THE HOOD- Indicates that the pilot is using a hood to restrict visibility outside the cockpit while simulating instrument flight. An appropriately rated pilot is required in the other control seat while this operation is being conducted.

UNICOM- A nongovernment communication facility which may provide airport information at certain airports. Locations and frequencies of UNICOMs are shown on aeronautical charts and publications.

UNPUBLISHED ROUTE- A route for which no minimum altitude is published or charted for pilot use. It may include a direct route between NAVAIDs, a radial, a radar vector, or a final approach course beyond the segments of an instrument approach procedure.

UNRELIABLE (GPS/WAAS)- An advisory to

pilots indicating the expected level of service of the GPS and/or WAAS may not be available. Pilots must then determine the adequacy of the signal for desired use.

V

VECTOR- A heading issued to an aircraft to provide navigational guidance by radar.

VERIFY- Request confirmation of information; e.g., "verify assigned altitude."

VERTICAL TAKEOFF AND LANDING AIRCRAFT- Aircraft capable of vertical climbs and/or descents and of using very short runways or small areas for takeoff and landings. These aircraft include, but are not limited to, helicopters.

VERY HIGH FREQUENCY- The frequency band between 30 and 300 MHz. Portions of this band, 108 to 118 MHz, are used for certain NAVAIDs; 118 to 136 MHz are used for civil air/ground voice communications. Other frequencies in this band are used for purposes not related to air traffic control.

VFR AIRCRAFT- An aircraft conducting flight in accordance with visual flight rules.

VFR CONDITIONS-Weather conditions equal to or better than the minimum for flight under visual flight rules. The term may be used as an ATC clearance/instruction only when:

a. An IFR aircraft requests a climb/descent in VFR conditions.

b. The clearance will result in noise abatement benefits where part of the IFR departure route does not conform to an FAA approved noise abatement route or altitude.

c. A pilot has requested a practice instrument approach and is not on an IFR flight plan.

VFR MILITARY TRAINING ROUTES- Routes used by the Department of Defense and associated Reserve and Air Guard units for the purpose of conducting low-altitude navigation and tactical training under VFR below 10,000 feet MSL at airspeeds in excess of 250 knots IAS.

VFR NOT RECOMMENDED- An advisory provided by a flight service station to a pilot during a preflight or inflight weather briefing that flight under visual flight rules is not recommended. To be given when the current and/or forecast weather conditions are at or below VFR minimums. It does not abrogate the pilot's authority to make his/her own decision.

VFR-ON-TOP- ATC authorization for an IFR aircraft to operate in VFR conditions at any appropriate VFR altitude (as specified in 14 CFR and as restricted by ATC). A pilot receiving this authorization must comply with the VFR visibility, distance from cloud criteria, and the minimum IFR altitudes specified in 14 CFR Part 91. The use of this term does not relieve controllers of their responsibility to separate aircraft in Class B and Class C airspace or TRSAs as required by FAAO JO 7110.65.

VISIBILITY- The ability, as determined by atmospheric conditions and expressed in units of distance, to see and identify prominent unlighted objects by day and prominent lighted objects by night. Visibility is reported as statute miles, hundreds of feet or meters.

VISUAL APPROACH- An approach conducted on an instrument flight rules (IFR) flight plan which authorizes the pilot to proceed visually and clear of clouds to the airport. The pilot must, at all times, have either the airport or the preceding aircraft in sight. This approach must be authorized and under the control of the appropriate air traffic control facility. Reported weather at the airport must be ceiling at or above 1,000 feet and visibility of 3 miles or greater.

VISUAL DESCENT POINT- A defined point on the final approach course of a nonprecision straight-in approach procedure from which normal descent from the MDA to the runway touchdown point may be commenced, provided the approach threshold of that runway, or approach lights, or other markings identifiable with the approach end of that runway are clearly visible to the pilot.

VISUAL FLIGHT RULES- Rules that govern the procedures for conducting flight under visual conditions. The term "VFR" is also used in the United States to indicate weather conditions that are equal to or greater than minimum VFR requirements. In addition, it is used by pilots and controllers to indicate type of flight plan.

VISUAL METEOROLOGICAL CONDITIONS- Meteorological conditions expressed in terms of visibility, distance from cloud, and ceiling equal to or better than specified minima.

VISUAL SEPARATION- A means employed by ATC to separate aircraft in terminal areas and en route airspace in the NAS. There are two ways to effect this separation:

a. The tower controller sees the aircraft involved and issues instructions, as necessary, to ensure that the aircraft avoid each other.

b. A pilot sees the other aircraft involved and upon instructions from the controller provides his/her own separation by maneuvering his/her aircraft as necessary to avoid it. This may involve following another aircraft or keeping it in sight until it is no longer a factor.

VOR- A ground-based electronic navigation aid transmitting very high frequency navigation signals, 360 degrees in azimuth, oriented from magnetic north. Used as the basis for navigation in the National Airspace System. The VOR periodically identifies itself by Morse Code and may have an additional voice identification feature. Voice features may be used by ATC or FSS for transmitting instructions/information to pilots.

VORTAC- A navigation aid providing VOR azimuth, TACAN azimuth, and TACAN distance measuring equipment (DME) at one site.

VORTICES- Circular patterns of air created by the movement of an airfoil through the air when generating lift. As an airfoil moves through the atmosphere in sustained flight, an area of area of low pressure is created above it. The air flowing from the high pressure area to the low pressure area around and about the tips of the airfoil tends to roll up into two rapidly rotating vortices, cylindrical in shape. These vortices are the most predominant parts of aircraft wake turbulence and their rotational force is dependent upon the wing loading, gross weight, and speed of the generating aircraft. The vortices from medium to heavy aircraft can be of extremely high velocity and hazardous to smaller aircraft.

VOT- A ground facility which emits a test signal to check VOR receiver accuracy. Some VOTs are available to the user while airborne, and others are limited to ground use only.

W

WAKE TURBULENCE- Phenomena resulting from the passage of an aircraft through the atmosphere. The term includes vortices, thrust stream turbulence, jet blast, jet wash, propeller wash, and rotor wash both on the ground and in the air.

WAYPOINT- A predetermined geographical position used for route/instrument approach definition, progress reports, published VFR routes, visual reporting points or points for transitioning and/or circumnavigating controlled and/or special use airspace, that is defined relative to a VORTAC station or in terms of latitude/longitude coordinates.

WHEN ABLE- When used in conjunction with ATC instructions, gives the pilot the latitude to delay compliance until a condition or event has been reconciled. Unlike "pilot discretion," when instructions are prefaced "when able," the pilot is expected to seek the first opportunity to comply. Once a maneuver has been initiated, the pilot is expected to continue until the specifications of the instructions have been met. "When able," should not be used when expeditious compliance is required.

WIDE-AREA AUGMENTATION SYSTEM (WAAS)- The WAAS is a satellite navigation system consisting of the equipment and software which augments the GPS Standard Positioning Service (SPS). The WAAS provides enhanced integrity, accuracy, availability, and continuity over and above GPS SPS. The differential correction function provides improved accuracy required for precision approach.

WILCO-I have received your message, understand it, and will comply with it.

WIND SHEAR- A change in wind speed and/or wind direction in a short distance resulting in a tearing or shearing effect. It can exist in a horizontal or vertical direction and occasionally in both.

WORD TWICE -

a. As a request: "Communication is difficult. Please say every phrase twice."

b. As information: "Since communications are difficult, every phrase in this message will be spoken twice."

Z

ZULU TIME - Greenwich Mean Time, or the time in Greenwich, England.